*Encyclopedia of the Supreme Court
of the United States*

Editorial Board

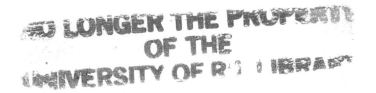

Encyclopedia of the Supreme Court of the United States

VOLUME I
A–C

David S. Tanenhaus
EDITOR IN CHIEF

MACMILLAN REFERENCE USA
A part of Gale, Cengage Learning

Detroit • New York • San Francisco • New Haven, Conn • Waterville, Maine • London

Encyclopedia of the Supreme Court of the United States

David S. Tanenhaus, Editor in Chief

For product information and technology assistance, contact us at
Gale Customer Support, 1-800-877-4253.
For permission to use material from this text or product,
submit all requests online at **www.cengage.com/permissions.**
Further permissions questions can be emailed to
permissionrequest@cengage.com

LIBRARY OF CONGRESS CATALOGING-IN-PUBLICATION DATA

Encyclopedia of the Supreme Court of the United States / David S. Tanenhaus, editor in chief.
    p. cm. --
  Includes bibliographical references and index.
  ISBN 978-0-02-866124-7 (set) -- ISBN 978-0-02-866125-4 (v. 1) -- ISBN 978-0-02-866126-1 (v. 2) -- ISBN 978-0-02-866127-8 (v. 3) -- ISBN 978-0-02-866128-5 (v. 4) -- ISBN 978-0-02-866130-8 (v. 5)
  1. United States. Supreme Court--Encyclopedias. I. Tanenhaus, David Spinoza

KF8742.A35E525 2008
347.73'2603--dc22
    2008025484

Gale
27500 Drake Rd.
Farmington Hills, MI, 48331-3535

ISBN-13 978-0-02-866124-7 (set)   ISBN-10 0-02-866124-9 (set)
ISBN-13 978-0-02-866125-4 (v. 1)   ISBN-10 0-02-866125-7 (v. 1)
ISBN-13 978-0-02-866126-1 (v. 2)   ISBN-10 0-02-866126-5 (v. 2)
ISBN-13 978-0-02-866127-8 (v. 3)   ISBN-10 0-02-866127-3 (v. 3)
ISBN-13 978-0-02-866128-5 (v. 4)   ISBN-10 0-02-866128-1 (v. 4)
ISBN-13 978-0-02-866130-8 (v. 5)   ISBN-10 0-02-866130-3 (v. 5)

This title is also available as an e-book.
ISBN-13: 978-0-02-866129-2 ISBN-10: 0-02-866129-X
Contact your Gale, a part of Cengage Learning sales representative for ordering information.

Printed in the United States of America
1 2 3 4 5 6 7 12 11 10 09 08

Editorial and Production Staff

Contents

Contents

Introduction

Just as historians use the last name of a president to describe an administration (e.g., the Bush Administration, 2001–2009), court-watchers use the last name of the chief justice to describe his or her court. Although more than forty Americans have served as President of the United States, on September 29, 2005, fifty-year-old John G. Roberts, Jr. became only the seventeenth person in the nation's history to serve as Chief Justice of the Supreme Court of the United States. Four months later, Chief Justice Roberts swore in Samuel Anthony Alito, Jr., as an Associate Justice to fill the seat vacated by the resignation of Justice Sandra Day O'Connor, the first woman to serve on the nation's High Court. Like the dramatic conclusion to the first act of a play, on the last day of its first term, the Roberts Court announced its most anticipated decision of the year.

At issue in *Parents Involved in Community Schools v. Seattle School District/Meredith v. Jefferson County Schools*, 551 U.S. ___ (2007) was whether public school systems, without violating the equal protection clause of the Fourteenth Amendment, could create racial balance and reduce racial isolation by assigning students to schools using explicit, race-based classifications. Putting aside for the time being how the justices answered this question, it is important to note how remarkable it was that the nation expected the Supreme Court to settle an issue that had such momentous public policy implications. Although there would be winners and losers in the case, it was clear to all the participants that the Supreme Court was the final arbiter of the meaning of the U.S. Constitution.

The Roberts Court had become the new protagonist in the ongoing national conversation about race in America. Moreover, Chief Justice Roberts and Justice Alito had replaced justices who had offered strikingly different answers to questions about government using racial classifications. Former Chief Justice William H. Rehnquist had, for instance, opposed affirmative action programs, while Justice O'Connor had provided the decisive fifth vote on the Rehnquist Court to sustain their use. The Roberts Court, as it delivered its opinion on June 28, 2007, stood in the national limelight.

The Supreme Court, which held its first session on February 2, 1790, in the Royal Exchange Building in New York City, did not begin its career on center stage. Many of its early justices doubted that the Court had much of a future. John Jay, the first chief justice, resigned to become governor of New York. Several other justices also resigned, and President George Washington had difficulty finding people willing to replace them, both because the court lacked prestige and because they found riding circuit—hearing cases in several of the states—grueling and unrewarding.

The *Encyclopedia of the Supreme Court of the United States*, through its historical essays on all seventeen chief justices and their respective courts, shows how the High Court developed into a commanding presence in American law, politics, and culture. Thematic essays on the major issues of the day, such as Slavery in the Territories, the Civil War, Progressive Era Business Regulation, World War II and the Growth of Individual Rights, Watergate and the Constitution, Violence Against Women, and the Global War on Terror, all provide in-depth analyses of how the Court responded to controversial circumstances.

The Supreme Court, which Alexander Hamilton famously described in *Federalist* No. 78 as possessing the power of neither the sword nor the purse, instead relies on its published decisions to shape the American experience. The court issues written opinions, which explain not only the court's final judgment in the case, but more importantly the legal reasoning used to reach the result. More than five hundred essays in this encyclopedia contextualize specific cases and analyze their legal reasoning and holdings. Building on these case studies are sweeping thematic essays that guide the reader through the evolution of case law on specific issues, such as Bankruptcy and Insolvency, Intimacy, Parental Rights, and Water Pollution and Wetlands.

To make the legal process accessible to lay readers, the encyclopedia includes essays on essential legal concepts and procedures such as Jurisdiction, Case or Controversy, Dicta, Holding, Overrulings, Stare Decisis, and the Writ of Certiorari. Separate essays on theories of law and interpretation, such as Judicial Pragmatism, Originalism, and Sociological Jurisprudence, introduce the reader to different approaches that the Court has used in its work.

The encyclopedia also reveals the Supreme Court's inner workings, including providing entries on its members and Staff, and specific practices, such as the Discuss List, the Rule of Four, and the Conferences of the Justices. Essays on lawyers practicing before the Court as well as articles on famous journalists, such as Anthony Lewis and Linda Greenhouse, provide additional perspectives on the Court's operations, its members, and its relationship to popular culture.

Used properly, the *Encyclopedia of the Supreme Court of the United States*, which presents its 1,100 entries in alphabetical order, can help students and lay readers become sophisticated court-watchers. For example, suppose that a reader wanted to know how the Roberts Court answered the constitutional question presented by *Parents Involved in Community Schools v. Seattle School District/Meredith v. Jefferson County Schools*, 551 U.S. __ (2007). The reader should first read the entry on the case, written by Professor Ashutosh A. Bhagwat of the University of California, Hastings College of Law. Professor Bhagwat explains that this case resulted in a five-to-four decision, in which the Court declared that the school districts' policies violated the Constitution. His clear legal analysis of the separate opinions in the case elucidates why Justice Anthony Kennedy's concurrence, not Chief Justice Roberts's majority opinion, serves as the controlling opinion and guide for schools districts seeking to implement constitutionally acceptable policies to create racial balance or reduce racial isolation.

Professor Bhagwat's brief essay serves as superb introduction to this decision, but the *Encyclopedia of the Supreme Court of the United States* offers much more. The biographical essays on all nine justices of the Roberts Court, coupled with the long entry on the court itself, provide additional insight. Thematic essays on Affirmative Action, Education and the Constitution, Rights of Students, School Desegregation, and Resegregation, for example, further elucidate the history of race, education, and the Supreme Court. And, if the reader wants to learn more about the technical aspects of the decision, he or she should refer to our cogent essays on Plurality Opinions and Strict Scrutiny. In addition, several complete opinions and excerpts from other notable decisions, including this case, are included in the back matter. The reader may also consult the Supreme Court's homepage, http://www.supremecourtus.gov/, to access recent opinions as well as links to past ones. To locate essential, digitized primary sources on the Court's history, the reader should access *U.S. Supreme Court Records and Briefs, 1832–1978* and *Making of Modern American Law: A Mirror on Society*. The first collection contains more than 100,000 cases, including the legal briefs filed; the second is a comprehensive and searchable database of 22,000 British and American legal treatises from 1800 to 1926.

The reader who uses this encyclopedia to research *Parents Involved in Community Schools* will also be directed to *Brown v. Board of Education*, 347 U.S. 483 (1954). In this landmark decision, Chief Justice Earl Warren famously declared, "We conclude that, in the field of public education, the doctrine of 'separate but equal' has no place." Just as the justices of the Roberts Court, in *Parents Involved in Community Schools v. Seattle School District/Meredith v. Jefferson County Schools* debated the meaning and legacy of *Brown*, this encyclopedia provides multiple perspectives on this historic case. For example, Professor Michael Klarman of Harvard Law School provides the comprehensive overview of the road to *Brown*; Professor Alfred Brophy of the University of North Carolina School of Law analyzes African-American understandings of law and justice in the years leading up to *Brown*; Professor Kara Miles Turner, Associate Dean of the College of Liberal Arts, Morgan State writes on the case itself; Professor Lucas A. "Scot" Powe of the University of Texas at Austin School of Law examines the subsequent decision in *Brown v. Board of Education* (*Brown II*), 349 U.S. 294 (1955), which provided the remedy for the constitutional wrong announced in *Brown I*; Emeritus Professor Kenneth L. Karst of the UCLA School of Law analyzes the Court's use of the intentionally vague phrase "all deliberate speed" in *Brown II*; and Professor Kathleen Bergin of South Texas Law School examines critiques of *Brown* that have emerged in recent years. These essays, in turn, introduce the readers to fundamental questions about the proper role of the Court, how justices decide cases, and the impact of judicial decisions, including the public reaction to them. See also references at the end of each entry, plus a detailed Thematic Outline in the front matter, guide readers to related essays in the encyclopedia.

Thus, beginning with one case, the drama unfolds. And, as the Marshal of the Court chants at the beginning of every public session: "The Honorable Chief Justice and the Associate Justices of the Supreme Court of the United States. Oyez! Oyez! Oyez! All persons having business before the Honorable Supreme Court of the United States are admonished to draw near and give their attention, for the Court is now sitting. God save the United States and this Honorable Court!" As you draw near and give this encyclopedia your attention, we hope that it will meet your—and our—expectations.

BIBLIOGRAPHY

Greenburg, Jan Crawford. 2007. *Supreme Conflict: The Inside Story of the Struggle for Control of the United States Supreme Court*. New York: Penguin Books.

Greenhouse, Linda. 2007. "Justices, Voting 5–4, Limit the Use of Race in School Plans for Integration." *New York Times*, June 29: A1.

Estreicher, Samuel. 2006–2007. "Equal Protection: The Non-Preferment Principle and the 'Racial Tiebreaker' Cases." *Cato Supreme Court Review*: 239–250.

Klarman, Michael. 2004. *From Jim Crow to Civil Rights: The Supreme Court and the Struggle for Racial Equality*. New York: Oxford University Press.

McCloskey, Robert G. 2005. *The American Supreme Court*. 4th edition. Revised by Sanford Levinson. Chicago: University of Chicago Press.

Powe, Lucas A. 2000. *The Warren Court and American Politics*. Cambridge, MA: Belknap Press of Harvard University Press, 2000.

Toobin, Jeffrey. 2007. *The Nine: Inside the Secret World of the Supreme Court*. New York: Doubleday.

David S. Tanenhaus

Preface

This encyclopedia, like the Supreme Court of the United States, has a history. In August 2006, William J. Novak, Associate Professor of History at the University of Chicago and Research Professor at the American Bar Foundation, recruited me to serve as an associate editor of an encyclopedia of the nation's high court. Together, Bill explained, we could assemble a dynamic board of editors to create something truly special: a reference work that would present the leading interdisciplinary scholarship on the Supreme Court to a broad audience. I was sold on the project, including the prospect of working with Hélène Potter, director of development at Macmillan Reference. Unexpectedly, Bill had to withdraw from the project in October, and I became editor in chief on Halloween.

Four outstanding associate editors soon joined the project. Professor Felice Batlan of Chicago—Kent College of Law is an expert in corporate law, securities regulation, legal history, and feminist legal theory. Alfred L. Brophy of the University of North Carolina School of Law writes extensively on race and property law. Professor Mark A. Graber of the University of Maryland Department of Government and Politics, who holds a joint appointment in the University of Maryland School of Law, is a political scientist whose research focuses on constitutional law and politics. Kay Kindred, Associate Dean for Academic Affairs and Professor of Law at the William S. Boyd School of Law, University of Nevada, Las Vegas (UNLV), specializes in family law, children's rights, and education law.

In mid December, the editorial board met in Farmington Hills, Michigan, to develop the encyclopedia's overarching themes and construct a table of contents. The associate editors all contributed passion and vision to the project and provided complementary perspectives on how best to introduce our readers, ranging from advanced-placement high school students and undergraduates to professors, lawyers, journalists, and judges, to the Supreme Court's remarkable history, most significant decisions, and issues of rising significance such as climate change, immigration, and the status of people with handicaps in the workplace. We chose to emphasize the Court's involvement in American political and economic development and provide close and contextual examination of case law. We also decided to focus on the Court's relationship to gender and sexuality, the impact of its decisions on struggles to achieve equal justice, and to highlight its critical role in shaping public policy, especially race relations and education.

We recruited five consultants from the American West to enrich our coverage. Professor Vikram Amar of the University of California Davis School of Law, a former law clerk to Justice Harry A. Blackmun, became our criminal law and criminal procedure point person. Similarly, Professor Stuart Banner of the UCLA School of Law, a former law clerk to Justice Sandra Day O'Connor, handled our entries on capital punishment, Native Americans, and territorial expansion. Professor Bret Birdsong of the William S. Boyd School of Law at UNLV, who had worked as a trial attorney for the U.S. Department of Justice, Environment and Natural Resources Division, served as our specialist on administrative and environmental law. Gabriel J. (Jack) Chin, Chester H. Smith Professor of Law, Professor of Public Administration and Policy, & Co-Director, Program in Criminal Law and Policy at the University of Arizona, became our expert on immigration and naturalization. Professor Calvin R. Massey of the University of California, Hastings College of Law, the author of a leading constitutional law casebook, assumed primary responsibility for our coverage of the Rehnquist and Roberts Courts.

Professor Sanford V. Levinson, who holds the W. St. John Garwood and W. St. John Garwood, Jr. Centennial Chair in Law at the University of Texas at Austin School of Law, generously agreed to evaluate our table of contents. After incorporating his insightful suggestions, the board worked tirelessly to write scope descriptions for 1,100 entries, so that we would be ready by April Fools' Day to invite the leading scholars in the United States and abroad to contribute accessible, original, and in-depth essays on the Supreme Court.

The *Encyclopedia of the Supreme Court of the United States* is the final product. It includes 523 entries on specific court cases, 468 thematic essays, and 109 biographies. Collectively, these entries, which vary in length from more than 6,500 words to 250 words, examine the Court's contributions to the American experience from the daunting task of establishing and maintaining the New Republic in the 1790s to grappling with the challenges of the twenty-first century, including global warming and international terrorism. All the entries also include a short bibliography that directs the reader to essential sources for further study.

The 563 authors who contributed are a who's who of scholars of law and society. They include academic and practicing lawyers, historians, political scientists, and sociologists. Some have clerked for justices of the Supreme Court; others have argued cases before the high court; and most are the leading authority on their subject.

The encyclopedia strives to make legal concepts, language, and processes accessible to students and lay persons. Lance D. Muckey and Mary D. Wammack, Ph.D. candidates in the UNLV History Department, Jamie Kulpa-Hauser, a UNLV undergraduate, and Mark Towell, a government teacher at Reed High School in Sparks, Nevada, all helped to design features to enhance the encyclopedia's accessibility. These include illustrative sidebars, a detailed timeline, and a user-friendly glossary. The back matter also contains more than thirty primary sources, including foundational texts, landmark cases, and debates over the proper role of the Supreme Court in American governance.

The *Encyclopedia of the Supreme Court of the United States* is obviously the product of many people working together. The editorial board worked closely with the publisher. Hélène Potter, director of new product development, made sure that this project was launched smoothly and surely, and our project editors at Cengage—Angela Doolin, Andrea Henderson, Kristin Mallegg, Jenai Mynatt, Scot Peacock, Darcy Thompson, and Jennifer Wisinski—all helped us to reach the final shores safely and expeditiously.

On a personal note, I am delighted to thank my wife, Virginia Tanenhaus, who not only spent hours working on the databases for the project, but also convincingly explained to Isaac, our two-year-old son, why his daddy needed to work on an encyclopedia instead of racing cars. Finally, I'm pleased that this encyclopedia makes a contribution to the study of an institution that my father, Joseph Tanenhaus, loved dearly.

David S. Tanenhaus
Las Vegas, Nevada
June 2008

Key to Citations

The *Encyclopedia of the Supreme Court of the United States* includes citations to cases and statutes that contain information for readers wishing to do further research. The citations refer to one or more series, called "reporters," which publish court opinions and related material. Each citation includes a volume number, an abbreviation for the reporter, and the starting page reference. Underscores in a citation indicate that a court opinion has not been officially reported as of the publication of this encyclopedia. Two sample citations, with explanations, are presented below.

1. *Case title.* The title of the case is set in italics and indicates the names of the parties. The suit in this sample citation was between Ernesto A. Miranda and the state of Arizona.

2. *Reporter volume number.* The number preceding the reporter abbreviation indicates the reporter volume containing the case. The volume number appears on the spine of the reporter, along with the reporter abbreviation.

3. *Reporter abbreviation.* The suit in the sample citation is from the reporter, or series of books, called *U.S. Reports*, which contains cases from the U.S. Supreme Court. Numerous reporters publish cases from the federal and state courts.

4. *Reporter page.* The number following the reporter abbreviation indicates the reporter page on which the case begins.

5. *Additional reporter citation.* Many cases may be found in more than one reporter. The suit in the sample citation also appears in volume 86 of the *Supreme Court Reporter*, beginning on page 1602.

6. *Additional reporter citation.* The suit in the sample citation is also reported in volume 16 of the *Lawyer's Edition* second series, beginning on page 694.

7. *Year of decision.* The year the court issued its decision in the case appears in parentheses at the end of the cite.

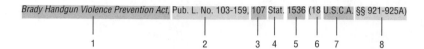

1. *Statute title.*

2. *Public law number.* In the sample citation, the number 103 indicates this law was passed by the 103d Congress, and the number 159 indicates it was the 159th law passed by that Congress.

3. *Reporter volume number.* The number preceding the reporter abbreviation indicates the reporter volume containing the statute.

4. *Reporter abbreviation.* The name of the reporter is abbreviated. The statute in the sample citation is from *Statutes at Large.*

5. *Reporter page.* The number following the reporter abbreviation indicates the reporter page on which the statute begins.

6. *Title number.* Federal laws are divided into major sections with specific titles. The number preceding a reference to the U.S. Code stands for the section called Crimes and Criminal Procedure.

7. *Additional reporter.* The statute in the sample citation may also be found in the *U.S. Code Annotated.*

8. *Section numbers.* The section numbers following a reference to the *U.S. Code Annotated* indicate where the statute appears in that reporter.

List of Articles

Thematic Outline

This outline provides a general overview of topics covered in the encyclopedia, listing the titles of each entry. Because the section headings are not mutually exclusive, certain entries in the encyclopedia may be listed in more than one section.

ADMINISTRATIVE LAW

Administrative Agencies
Administrative Procedure Act
Chevron U.S.A. v. Natural Resources Defense Council, 467 U.S. 837 (1984)
Gonzales v. Oregon, 546 U.S. 243 (2006)
Industrial Union Department, AFL-CIO v. American Petroleum Institute, 448 U.S. 607 (1980)
Interstate Commerce Commission
Judicial Review of Administrative Action
Judicial Review of Statutory Interpretation by Agencies
Motor Vehicles Manufacturers Association v. State Farm Mutual Automobile Insurance Co., 463 U.S. 29 (1983)
New Deal and Workers
New Deal Lawyers
Norton v. Southern Utah Wilderness Alliance, 542 U.S. 55 (2004)
United States v. Mead Corporation, 533 U.S. 218 (2001)
Vermont Yankee Nuclear Power Corp. v. Natural Resources Defense Council, 435 U.S. 519 (1978)

AFRICAN AMERICANS

Amendments, Post-Civil War
Brown v. Board of Education, 347 U.S. 483 (1954)
Brown v. Board of Education (Brown II), 349 U.S. 294 (1955)
Brown v. Board of Education, Critiques
City of Richmond v. J.A. Croson Co., 488 U.S. 469 (1989)
Fifteenth Amendment
Great Constitutional Dream Book
Houston, Charles Hamilton
King, Martin Luther, Jr.
Marshall, Thurgood
McCleskey v. Kemp, 481 U.S. 279 (1987)
Nabrit, James
Plessy v. Ferguson, 163 U.S. 537 (1896)
Thirteenth Amendment
Thomas, Clarence
Washington v. Davis, 426 U.S. 229 (1976)
World War II and the Growth of Civil Rights

CHILDREN

Bellotti v. Baird, 443 U.S. 622 (1979)
Bender v. Williamsport Area School District, 475 U.S. 534 (1986)
Bethel School District No. 403 v. Fraser, 478 U.S. 675 (1986)
Board of Education of Island Trees School District No. 26 v. Pico, 457 U.S. 853 (1982)
Board of Education v. Rowley, 458 U.S. 176 (1982)
Children and the Constitution
Children and the First Amendment
Davis v. Monroe County Board of Education, 526 U.S. 629 (1999)
DeShaney v. Winnebago County Dept. of Social Services, 489 U.S. 189 (1989)
Education for All Handicapped Children Act of 1975 (EAHCA)
Elementary and Secondary Education Act of 1965 (Title I)
Franklin v. Gwinnett County Public Schools, 503 U.S. 60 (1992)
Goss v. Lopez, 419 U.S. 565 (1975)
Hazelwood School District v. Kuhlmeier, 484 U.S. 260 (1988)
Ingraham v. Wright, 430 U.S. 651 (1977)
In re Gault, 387 U.S. 1 (1967)
Juvenile Justice
Lau v. Nichols, 414 U.S. 563 (1974)
Michael M. v. Superior Court of Sonoma, 450 U.S. 464 (1981)
Morse v. Frederick, 551 U.S. ___ (2007)
New Jersey v. T.L.O., 469 U.S. 325 (1985)
Nguyen v. Immigration and Naturalization Service, 533 U.S. 53 (2001)
Quilloin v. Walcott, 434 U.S. 246 (1978)
Rights of Students
Tinker v. Des Moines School District, 393 U.S. 503 (1969)

EDUCATION

Naturalization Power
Nguyen v. Immigration and
  Naturalization Service, 533 U.S.
  53 (2001)
Non-citizens and Civil Liberties
Non-citizens and Equal Protection
  (Federal)
Non-citizens and Equal Protection
  (State)
Plenary Power Doctrine
Progressive Era Immigration and
  Naturalization
Schneiderman v. United States,
  320 U.S. 118 (1943)

JUDICIAL REVIEW

Cohens v. Virginia, 19 U.S. 264
  (1821)
Eakin v. Raub, 12 Sergeant and
  Rawle (Pennsylvania) 330 (1825)
Judicial Review
Judicial Review before Marbury
Judicial Review of Administrative
  Action
Judicial Review of Statutory Inter-
  pretation by Agencies
Judicial Supremacy
Lochner v. New York, 198 U.S. 45
  (1905)
Marbury v. Madison, 5 U.S. 137
  (1803)
Martin v. Hunter's Lessee, 14 U.S.
  304 (1816)
M'Culloch v. Maryland, 17 U.S. 316
  (1819)
United States v. Nixon, 418 U.S.
  683 (1974)

JURISPRUDENCE

Ackerman, Bruce
Anti-slavery Constitutionalism
Aspirationalism
Bickel, Alexander
Black, Charles
Bork, Robert
Brandeis Brief
Cardozo, Benjamin N.
Citations to Foreign Sources
Comparative Constitutional Law
Constitutional Interpretation
Constitutionalism
Constitutional Theory
Constitution and American Civil
  Religion
Cooley, Thomas
Eakin v. Raub, 12 Sergeant and
  Rawle (Pennsylvania) 330 (1825)
Great Constitutional Dream Book
Holmes, Oliver W.
Implied Powers
Incorporation Debate
Intersections of Race and Gender

Judicial Activism
Judicial Pragmatism
Judicial Restraint
Judicial Supremacy
Kent, James
King, Martin Luther, Jr.
Law and Economics
Legal Process
Legal Realism
MacKinnon, Catharine
Marbury v. Madison, 5 U.S. 137
  (1803)
Models of Judicial Decision-making
Murray, Pauli
Natural Rights
Originalism
Pound, Roscoe
Roane, Spencer
Rutledge, John
Sociological Jurisprudence
Structuralism
Substantive Due Process
Taylor, John
Textualism
Thayer, James Bradley
Tiedeman, Christopher
Tribe, Laurence
Tucker, St. George
Unwritten Constitution
Webster, Daniel
Wechsler, Herbert

LABOR

Abood v. Detroit Board of
  Education, 431 U.S. 209 (1977)
American Federation of Labor v.
  Swing, 312 U.S. 321 (1941)
Bishop v. Wood, 426 U.S. 341
  (1976)
Board of Regents of State Colleges v.
  Roth, 408 U.S. 564 (1972)
Cleveland Brd. of Education v.
  Loudermill, 470 U.S. 532 (1985)
Coppage v. Kansas, 236 U.S. 1
  (1915)
Coronado Coal v. United Mine
  Workers, 268 U.S. 295 (1925)
Debs, Eugene
Dothard v. Rawlinson, 433 U.S 321
  (1977)
Elrod v. Burns, 427 U.S. 347 (1976)
Fair Labor Standards Act
Government Employees
In re Debs, 158 U.S. 564 (1895)
Jones v. North Carolina Prisoners'
  Labor Union, 433 U.S. 119
  (1977)
Labor Unions
Massachusetts Board of Retirement
  v. Murgia, 427 U.S. 307 (1976)
Muller v. Oregon, 208 U.S. 412
  (1908)

National League of Cities v. Usery,
  426 U.S. 833 (1976)
New Deal and Workers
Peonage
Perry v. Sindermann, 408 U.S. 593
  (1972)
Police Department of Chicago v.
  Mosley, 408 U.S. 92 (1972)
Pollock v. Williams, 322 U.S. 4
  (1944)
Progressive Era Worker Regulation
Protective Legislation for Women
  Workers
Rutan v. Republican Party of
  Illinois, 497 U.S. 62 (1990)
Taylor v. Georgia, 315 U.S. 25
  (1942)
Thornhill v. Alabama, 310 U.S. 88
  (1940)
UAW v. Johnson Controls, 499 U.S.
  187 (1991)
Wieman v. Updegraff, 344 U.S. 183
  (1952)
Wygant v. Jackson Board of
  Education, 476 U.S. 267 (1986)

NATIONAL SECURITY/WAR

Civil War
Cold War
Confederate Constitution
Dennis v. United States, 341 U.S.
  494 (1951)
Ex parte Endo, 323 U.S. 283 (1944)
Ex parte Milligan, 71 U.S. 2 (1866)
Ex parte Quirin, 317 U.S. 1 (1942)
Free Speech and World War I
Global War on Terror
Hamdan v. Rumsfeld, 548 U.S. 557
  (2006)
Hamdi v. Rumsfeld, 542 U.S. 507
  (2004)
Hirabayashi v. United States, 320
  U.S. 81 (1943)
Japanese American Internment
Kentucky and Virginia Resolutions
Korematsu v. United States, 323
  U.S. 214 (1944)
Lincoln, Abraham
Martial Law
Mexican War
New York Times Co. v. United
  States, 403 U.S. 713 (1971)
Pennsylvania v. Nelson, 350 U.S.
  497 (1956)
Prize Cases
Raising Armies
Rasul v. Bush, 542 U.S. 466 (2004)
Rumsfeld v. Padilla, 542 U.S. 426
  (2004)
Secession
Texas v. White, 74 U.S. 700 (1869)
War of 1812

SOCIAL MOVEMENTS

SOCIAL PROGRAMS/SOCIAL WELFARE

SUPREME COURT JUSTICES

SUPREME COURT PRACTICES AND PROCEDURES

List of Contributors

Kathryn Abrams
Herma Hill Kay Distinguished
Professor of Law
University of California, Berkeley
School of Law (Boalt Hall)
FEMINIST DEBATE OVER
PORNOGRAPHY

Jeffrey Abramson
Stulberg Distinguished Professor of
Law and Politics
Brandeis University
JURIES

Kaisa Adams
William-Mitchell College of Law
JUDICIAL INDEPENDENCE

Danny M. Adkison
Associate Professor of Political Science
Oklahoma State University
TWENTY-FOURTH AMENDMENT

Raquel Aldana
Professor of Law, William S. Boyd
School of Law
University of Nevada, Las Vegas
DENATURALIZATION AND
EXPATRIATION

Dean Alfange
Professor Emeritus of Political Science
University of Massachusetts, Amherst
PER CURIAM

Austin Allen
Associate Professor of History
University of Houston—Downtown

DRED SCOTT V. SANDFORD, 60 U.S.
393 (1857)
POWELL, LEWIS F., JR.
SLAVERY IN THE TERRITORIES
TANEY, ROGER
WIRT, WILLIAM

David Alvis
Assistant Professor
University of West Florida
NATURAL RIGHTS

Diane Marie Amann
Professor of Law
University of California, Davis, School
of Law
GLOBAL WAR ON TERROR

Vikram D. Amar
Associate Dean for Academic Affairs
and Professor of Law
University of California, Davis, School
of Law
ADARAND CONSTRUCTORS, INC. V.
PEÑA, 515 U.S. 200 (1995)
CALIFORNIA DEMOCRATIC PARTY V.
JONES, 530 U.S. 567 (2000)
ROBERTS, JOHN
SEVENTH AMENDMENT
SHAW V. RENO, 509 U.S. 630 (1993)

Angelo N. Ancheta
Assistant Professor of Law
Santa Clara University
CITIZENSHIP BY BIRTH

David A. Anderson
Fred and Emily Wulff Centennial Chair

University of Texas Law School
FREEDOM OF THE PRESS

William L. Andreen
Edgar L. Clarkson Professor of Law
University of Alabama School of Law
WATER POLLUTION AND WETLANDS

Peter A. Appel
Associate Professor
University of Georgia School of Law
HAWAII HOUSING AUTHORITY V.
MIDKIFF, 467 U.S. 229 (1984)
PUBLIC LANDS

Annette Ruth Appell
Professor of Law
University of Nevada, Las Vegas
PALMORE V. SIDOTI, 466 U.S. 429
(1984)
SANTOSKY V. KRAMER, 455 U.S. 745
(1982)

Michael Ariens
Professor of Law
St. Mary's University School of Law
UNITED STATES V. CRUIKSHANK, 92
U.S. 542 (1876)

Hadley Arkes
Ney Professor of Jurisprudence
Amherst College
FLETCHER V. PECK, 10 U.S. 87
(1810)

Frank Askin
Professor of Law and Robert Knowlton
Scholar

Rutgers School of Law
MARSH V. ALABAMA, 326 U.S. 501
(1946)

David N. M. Atkinson
Curators' Teaching Professor of
Political Science and Law
University of Missouri, Kansas City
RESIGNATION AND RETIREMENT

Joaquin G. Avila
Assistant Professor of Law, Seattle
University School of Law
Former President and General Counsel
of MALDEF
MEXICAN AMERICAN LEGAL DEFENSE
AND EDUCATIONAL FUND (MALDEF)

Richard L. Aynes
John F. Seiberling Chair of
Constitutional Law
University of Akron
MISSOURI COMPROMISE
SECESSION
STONE V. MISSISSIPPI, 101 U.S. 814
(1880)
TEST OATH CASES
WAITE, MORRISON
WRITS

Larry Catá Backer
Professor of Law
Pennsylvania State University
ACCOMMODATION OF RELIGION

Paul R. Baier
George M. Armstrong, Jr., Professor of
Law
Paul M. Hebert Law Center, Louisiana
State University
WHITE COURT
WHITE, EDWARD D.

H. Robert Baker
Assistant Professor of History
Georgia State University
ABLEMAN V. BOOTH, 62 U.S. 506
(1858)
ARTICLE IV
PRIGG V. PENNSYLVANIA, 41 U.S. 539
(1842)

Katherine K. Baker
Professor
Chicago–Kent College of Law
CABAN V. MOHAMMED, 441 U.S. 380
(1979)
MICHAEL H. V. GERALD D., 491 U.S.
110 (1989)

Lynn A. Baker
Frederick M. Baron Chair in Law

University of Texas School of Law
SOUTH DAKOTA V. DOLE, 483 U.S.
203 (1987)

Peter Banick
St. John's University
St. Benedict/St. John's University
DEBS, EUGENE

Christopher P. Banks
Associate Professor, Department of
Political Science
Kent State University
LEGISLATIVE INVESTIGATIONS

Carl L. Bankston, III
Professor and Chair, Department of
Sociology; Co-Director, Asian Studies
Program
Tulane University
AFFIRMATIVE ACTION
IMMIGRATION

Lorraine K. Bannai
Legal Writing Professor
Seattle University School of Law
EX PARTE ENDO, 323 U.S. 283
(1944)
HIRABAYASHI V. UNITED STATES, 320
U.S. 81 (1943)
JAPANESE AMERICAN INTERNMENT
KOREMATSU, FRED

David G. Barnum
Professor of Political Science
DePaul University
LOCHNER V. NEW YORK, 198 U.S. 45
(1905)
NEW DEAL: THE SUPREME COURT VS.
PRESIDENT ROOSEVELT

Amy Coney Barrett
Associate Professor
Notre Dame Law School
FEDERAL JURISDICTION

John Q. Barrett
Professor of Law
St. John's University
JACKSON, ROBERT H.

D. Benjamin Barros
Associate Professor of Law
Widener University School of Law
BERMAN V. PARKER, 348 U.S. 26
(1954)
HADACHECK V. SEBASTIAN, 239 U.S.
394 (1915)

Charles L. Barzun
Lecturer on Law

University of Virginia School of Law
CHICAGO V. STURGES, 222 U.S. 313
(1911)

Felice Batlan
Assistant Professor of Law
Chicago–Kent College of Law
ELECTRIC BOND AND SHARE V. SECU-
RITIES AND EXCHANGE COMMIS-
SION, 303 U.S. 419 (1938)

William Baude
Law Clerk
Salt Lake City, Utah
TREATY POWER

Michal Belknap
Earl Warren Professor of Law,
California Western School of Law
Adjunct Professor of History,
University of California, San Diego
VINSON COURT
VINSON, FRED M.
WATERGATE AND THE CONSTITUTION

Michael Les Benedict
Professor Emeritus of History
The Ohio State University
BANK OF AUGUSTA V. EARLE, 38 U.S
519 (1839)
RECONSTRUCTION

Alvin K. Benson
Emeritus Professor of Geophysics,
Brigham Young University
Professor of Physics, Utah Valley
University
BREYER, STEPHEN

Lenni Benson
Professor of Law and Associate Dean
for Professional Development
New York Law School
DEPORTATION PROCEDURE AND DUE
PROCESS

Michael A. Berch
Professor of Law
Sandra Day O'Connor College of Law,
Arizona State University
REMOVAL UNDER THE JUDICIARY ACT
OF 1789
RES JUDICATA

Rebecca White Berch
Vice Chief Justice
Arizona Supreme Court
WISDOM, JOHN MINOR

Thomas C. Berg
St. Ives Professor of Law

University of St. Thomas School of
Law, Minnesota
  CHURCH OF THE LUKUMI BABALU AYE
    V. CITY OF HIALEAH, 508 U.S. 520
    (1993)

Kathleen A. Bergin
Associate Professor of Law
South Texas College of Law
  BROWN V. BOARD OF EDUCATION,
    CRITIQUES
  GINSBERG V. NEW YORK, 390 U.S.
    629 (1968)
  JOHNSON V. TRANSPORTATION
    AGENCY, 480 U.S. 616 (1987)
  LOCKE V. DAVEY, 540 U.S. 712
    (2004)
  REYNOLDS V. SIMS, 377 U.S. 533
    (1964)
  VAN ORDEN V. PERRY, 545 U.S. 677
    (2005)

David E. Bernstein
Professor
George Mason University School of
Law
  ALLGEYER V. LOUISIANA, 165 U.S.
    578 (1897)
  FREEDOM OF CONTRACT
  MUNN V. ILLINOIS, 94 U.S. 113
    (1877)

Robert Berring
Professor of Law
Berkeley Law School, Boalt Hall
  WEST PUBLISHING COMPANY

Ashutosh A. Bhagwat
Professor of Law
University of California, Hastings
College of the Law
  BARTNICKI V. VOPPER, 532 U.S. 514
    (2001)
  MILLER V. CALIFORNIA, 413 U.S. 15
    (1973)
  PARENTS INVOLVED IN COMMUNITY
    SCHOOLS V. SEATTLE SCHOOL DIS-
    TRICT/MEREDITH V. JEFFERSON
    COUNTY SCHOOLS

Jagdeep S. Bhandari
Professor of Law
Florida Coastal School of Law,
Jacksonville
  ALIENS INELIGIBLE FOR CITIZENSHIP

Stephanos Bibas
Professor
University of Pennsylvania Law School
  JUDICIAL FACT-FINDING AT
    SENTENCING

Gayle Binion
Professor, Department of Political
Science
University of California, Santa Barbara
  EQUAL PAY ACT

Bret C. Birdsong
Professor of Law
William S. Boyd School of Law,
University of Nevada, Las Vegas
  JUDICIAL REVIEW OF STATUTORY
    INTERPRETATION BY AGENCIES

J. Michael Bitzer
Professor, Department of History &
Politics
Catawba College
  KATZENBACH V. MORGAN, 384 U.S.
    641 (1966)

Barbara Aronstein Black
George Welwood Murray Professor of
Legal History
Columbia Law School
  HAYBURN'S CASE, 2 U.S. 409 (1792)
  RUTLEDGE, JOHN

Christopher L. Blakesley
The Cobeaga Law Firm Professor of
Law
Boyd School of Law, University of
Nevada, Las Vegas
  DAMES & MOORE V. REGAN, 453 U.S.
    654 (1981)

Marc J. Blitz
Associate Professor
Oklahoma City University School of
Law
  AMENDMENT, OUTSIDE OF ARTICLE V
  HAGUE V. COMMITTEE FOR INDUS-
    TRIAL ORGANIZATION, 307 U.S.
    496 (1939)
  LANE V. WILSON, 307 U.S. 268
    (1939)
  PARIS ADULT THEATRE I V. SLATON,
    413 U.S. 49 (1973)

Robert M. Bloom
Professor of Law
Boston College Law School
  MASSIAH V. UNITED STATES, 377 U.S.
    201 (1964)
  TERRY V. OHIO, 392 U.S. 1 (1968)
  ZURCHER V. STANFORD DAILY, 436
    U.S. 547 (1978)

Richard Blum
Staff Attorney
Legal Aid Society
  MOTLEY, CONSTANCE BAKER

Richard C. Boldt
Professor of Law
University of Maryland School of Law
  DICKERSON V. UNITED STATES, 530
    U.S. 428 (2000)

Caitlin E. Borgmann
Associate Professor of Law
City University of New York School of
Law
  GONZALES V. CARHART, 550 U.S. ___
    (2007)
  STENBERG V. CARHART, 530 U.S. 914
    (2000)

Winston A. Bowman
Independent Researcher
  BISHOP V. WOOD, 426 U.S. 341
    (1976)
  DANIELS V. WILLIAMS, 474 U.S. 327
    (1986)
  FREEMAN V. PITTS, 503 U.S. 467
    (1992)
  GRAY V. SANDERS, 372 U.S. 368
    (1963)
  MASSACHUSETTS BOARD OF RETIRE-
    MENT V. MURGIA, 427 U.S. 307
    (1976)
  PIKE V. BRUCE CHURCH, INC., 397
    U.S. 137 (1970)
  SCHMERBER V. CALIFORNIA, 384 U.S.
    757 (1966)
  UNITED STATES V. LEON, 468 U.S.
    897 (1984)
  VILLAGE OF BELLE TERRE V. BORAAS,
    416 U.S. 1 (1974)

Craig Bradley
Robert Lucas Professor of Law
Indiana University School of Law,
Bloomington
  BATSON V. KENTUCKY, 476 U.S. 79
    (1986)
  MIRANDA WARNINGS

Martha Sonntag Bradley
Professor, College of Architecture and
Planning; Program Director, Honors
College
University of Utah
  LATE CORPORATION OF THE CHURCH
    OF JESUS CHRIST OF LATTER-DAY
    SAINTS V. UNITED STATES, 136 U.S.
    1 (1889)

Deborah Brake
Professor of Law
University of Pittsburgh
  FARAGHER V. CITY OF BOCA RATON,
    524 U.S. 775 (1998)

Mark E. Brandon
Professor of Law and Political Science
Vanderbilt University
PREAMBLE

Pamela Brandwein
Associate Professor, Department of
Political Science
University of Michigan
CIVIL RIGHTS CASES, 109 U.S. 3 (1883)

Andrew Brasher
Associate
Bradley Arant Rose & White
AMENDMENTS, REJECTED

Daan Braveman
President, Nazareth College
Professor Emeritus, Syracuse University
College of Law
KASTIGAR V. UNITED STATES, 406 U.S.
441 (1972)

Candice Bredbenner
Associate Professor, Department of
Language, Cultures, and History
Arizona State University
MACKENZIE V. HARE, 239 U.S. 299
(1915)

David A. Brennen
Professor of Law
University of Georgia, School of Law
BOB JONES UNIVERSITY V. UNITED
STATES, 461 U.S. 574 (1983)

Pamela D. Bridgewater
Professor of Law
American University, Washington
College of Law
BEAL V. DOE, 432 U.S. 438 (1977)
BELLOTTI V. BAIRD, 443 U.S. 622
(1979)
DALTON V. LITTLE ROCK FAMILY
PLANNING SERVICES, 516 U.S. 474
(1996)
MAHER V. ROE, 432 U.S. 464 (1977)

Richard Briffault
Joseph P. Chamberlain Professor of
Legislation
Columbia Law School
REPUBLICAN PARTY OF MINNESOTA V.
WHITE, 536 U.S. 765 (2002)

Richard A. Brisbin, Jr.
Associate Professor, Department of
Political Science
West Virginia University
ARTICLE VII
JUDICIAL ACTIVISM

Alfred L. Brophy
Professor of Law
University of North Carolina School of
Law
GREAT CONSTITUTIONAL DREAM
BOOK
MADISON, JAMES
PLESSY V. FERGUSON, 163 U.S. 537
(1896)

Josie F. Brown
Assistant Professor
University of South Carolina School of
Law
ALEXANDER V. HOLMES COUNTY
BOARD OF EDUCATION, 396 U.S.
19 (1969)
BOARD OF EDUCATION OF OKLAHOMA
CITY PUBLIC SCHOOLS V. DOWELL,
498 U.S. 237 (1991)
GREEN V. SCHOOL BOARD OF NEW
KENT COUNTY, 391 U.S. 430
(1968)
SCHOOL CHOICE

Kevin Brown
Professor of Law and Director of the
Hudson & Holland Scholars Program
Indiana University, Bloomington
MILLIKEN V. BRADLEY (MILLIKEN II),
433 U.S. 267 (1977)
MILLIKEN V. BRADLEY, 418 U.S. 717
(1974)

Alan E. Brownstein
Professor
University of California, Davis, School
of Law
ABORTION PROTESTS
RELIGIOUS EXEMPTIONS

Aaron-Andrew P. Bruhl
Assistant Professor
University of Houston Law Center
ABBOTT LABS V. GARDNER, 387 U.S.
136 (1967)
SUBJECT MATTER JURISDICTION

A. Christopher Bryant
Professor of Law
University of Cincinnati
BIBB V. NAVAJO FREIGHT LINES, INC.,
359 U.S. 520 (1959)
BRANIFF AIRWAYS, INC. V. NEBRASKA
STATE BOARD OF EQUALIZATION,
347 U.S. 590 (1954)
CITY OF CLEBURNE V. CLEBURNE
LIVING CENTER, 473 U.S. 432
(1985)
CITY OF PHILADELPHIA V. NEW JERSEY,
437 U.S. 617 (1978)

DUKE POWER CO. V. CAROLINA
ENVIRONMENTAL STUDY GROUP,
438 U.S. 59 (1978)
GARCIA V. SAN ANTONIO METROPOLI-
TAN TRANSIT AUTHORITY, 469 U.S.
528 (1985)
GRAVEL V. UNITED STATES, 408 U.S.
606 (1972)
HODEL V. VIRGINIA SURFACE MINING
AND RECLAMATION ASSOCIATION,
452 U.S. 264 (1981)
LOUISIANA POWER & LIGHT V. CITY
OF THIBODAUX, 360 U.S. 25
(1959)
MISSOURI V. JENKINS, 495 U.S. 33
(1990)
NIXON V. FITZGERALD, 457 U.S. 731
(1982)
WILLIAMSON V. LEE OPTICAL OF
OKLAHOMA, 348 U.S. 483 (1955)
YOUNGER V. HARRIS, 401 U.S. 37
(1971)

W. Hamilton Bryson
Professor
University of Richmond School of Law
TUCKER, ST. GEORGE

Johnny Rex Buckles
Associate Professor of Law
University of Houston Law Center
CUTTER V. WILKINSON, 544 U.S. 709
(2005)
LAMB'S CHAPEL V. CENTER MORICHES
UNION FREE SCHOOL DISTRICT,
508 U.S. 384 (1993)

Regina F. Burch
Associate Professor of Law
Capital University Law School
POPULISM

Veronica Cruz Burchard
Director of Curriculum Development
The Bill of Rights Institute
PRIVACY

William Bush
Department of History
University of Nevada, Las Vegas
SCOTTSBORO BOYS

Emily Buss
Mark and Barbara Fried Professor of
Law
University of Chicago Law School
CHILDREN AND THE FIRST
AMENDMENT

William G. Buss
O. K. Patton Professor of Law

University of Iowa
NATIONAL LABOR RELATIONS BOARD
V. JONES & LAUGHLIN STEEL, 301
U.S. 1 (1937)

Paul Butler
Carville Dickinson Benson Research
Professor of Law
George Washington University Law
School
JURY NULLIFICATION

David S. Calihan
Associate Professor, Political Science
Longwood College
EAKIN V. RAUB, 12 SERGEANT AND
RAWLE (PENNSYLVANIA) 330
(1825)

Amy Leigh Campbell
CEO
Bloom Consulting and Publishing
ACLU WOMEN'S RIGHTS PROJECT

Christopher Capozzola
Associate Professor of History
Massachusetts Institute of Technology
BRANDENBURG V. OHIO, 395 U.S.
444 (1969)

Mary L. Carver
Department of Political Science
University of Missouri, St. Louis
RELIGIOUS LAND USE AND INSTITU-
TIONALIZED PERSONS ACT

William Casto
Paul Whitfield Horn University
Professor
Texas Tech University
ELLSWORTH, OLIVER
UNITED STATES V. CURTISS-WRIGHT
EXPORT CORP., 299 U.S. 304
(1936)

Jonathan G. Cedarbaum
Partner
Wilmer Cutler Pickering Hale & Dorr
LLP
HAMDAN V. RUMSFELD, 548 U.S. 557
(2006)

Jennifer M. Chacón
Acting Professor of Law
University of California, Davis, School
of Law
MILLER V. ALBRIGHT, 523 U.S. 420
(1998)
NGUYEN V. IMMIGRATION AND NAT-
URALIZATION SERVICE, 533 U.S. 53
(2001)

Martha Chamallas
Robert J. Lynn Chair in Law
Moritz College of Law, The Ohio State
University
STANTON V. STANTON, 421 U.S. 7
(1975)

Henry L. Chambers, Jr.
Professor of Law
University of Richmond School of Law
BAKER V. CARR, 369 U.S. 186 (1962)
CIVIL RIGHTS ACT OF 1964
RANDOM DRUG TESTING
RIGHT TO AN ATTORNEY

April L. Cherry
Associate Professor of Law
Cleveland-Marshall College of Law,
Cleveland State University
HARRIS V. MCRAE, 448 U.S. 297
(1980)

Miriam A. Cherry
Associate Professor
University of the Pacific, McGeorge
School of Law
BROWN V. MARYLAND, 25 U.S. 419
(1827)
MASSACHUSETTS V. MELLON, 262 U.S.
447 (1923)
PRINCIPALITY OF MONACO V. MISSIS-
SIPPI, 292 U.S. 313 (1934)
WEST COAST HOTEL V. PARRISH, 300
U.S. 379 (1937)

Bradley Stewart Chilton
Professor, Department of Political
Science/Criminal Justice
Appalachian State University
BURGER, WARREN E.

Gabriel J. Chin
Chester H. Smith Professor of Law
University of Arizona, James E. Rogers
College of Law
PLENARY POWER DOCTRINE
YICK WO V. HOPKINS, 118 U.S. 356
(1886)

Stephen J. Choi
Murray and Kathleen Bring Professor
of Law
New York University Law School
BASIC INC. V. LEVINSON, 485 U.S.
224 (1988)

Susanna Y. Chung
Adjunct Associate Professor
Fordham University School of Law
CASTLE ROCK V. GONZALES, 545 U.S.
748 (2005)

Suzanne G. Clark
Arkansas Law Review, Editor in Chief
University of Arkansas
LABINE V. VINCENT, 401 U.S. 532
(1971)

Cornell W. Clayton
Professor of Political Science
Washington State University
ATTORNEY GENERAL

Robert N. Clinton
Foundation Professor of Law
Sandra Day O'Connor College of Law,
Arizona State University
MANDATORY JURISDICTION
MARBURY V. MADISON, 5 U.S. 137
(1803)

Douglas Clouatre
Professor of Political Science
Mid-Plains Community College
NEW DEAL AND WORKERS
POLITICAL QUESTION DOCTRINE

Morgan Cloud
Charles Candler Professor of Law
Emory University
FOURTH AMENDMENT

Augustus B. Cochran, III
Loridans Professor of Political Science
Agnes Scott College
FRANKLIN V. GWINNETT COUNTY
PUBLIC SCHOOLS, 503 U.S. 60
(1992)

Dan T. Coenen
University Professor and J. Alton
Hosch Professor of Law
University of Georgia School of Law
HOLDING
IMPLIED POWERS

David S. Cohen
Associate Professor of Law
Drexel University College of Law
THORNBURGH V. AMERICAN COLLEGE
OF OBSTETRICIANS AND GYNECOL-
OGISTS, 476 U.S. 747 (1986)

Morris L. Cohen
Professor Emeritus, School of Law
Yale University
ELECTRONIC RESOURCES
UNITED STATES REPORTS

Sherman L. Cohn
Professor
Georgetown University Law Center
FAHY, CHARLES

Ruth Colker
Heck Faust Memorial Chair in
Constitutional Law
Michael E. Moritz College of Law, The
Ohio State University
ACCESS TO ABORTION CLINICS
PERSONNEL ADMINISTRATOR OF
MASSACHUSETTS V. FEENEY, 442
U.S. 256 (1979)
PLANNED PARENTHOOD V. CASEY,
505 U.S. 833 (1992)
TURNER V. DEPARTMENT OF EMPLOY-
MENT SECURITY, 423 U.S. 44
(1975)

Kristin Collins
Associate Professor of Law
Boston University
HOYT V. FLORIDA, 368 U.S. 57
(1961)
TAYLOR V. LOUISIANA, 419 U.S. 522
(1975)

Charlton C. Copeland
Associate Professor
University of Miami School of Law
RIPENESS

Matthew C. Cordon
Director of Legal Research and
Professor of Law
Baylor University School of Law
ARTICLE I COURTS
ARTICLE III
ARTICLE VI
COMMON LAW
FEDERAL JUDICIAL SYSTEM
PRECEDENT

Jim Cornehls
Professor and Director, Graduate
Certificate Program in Law and Public
Policy
School of Urban and Public Affairs,
University of Texas at Arlington
THIRD AMENDMENT

Christopher A. Cotropia
Associate Professor of Law
University of Richmond School of Law
INTERNET

Michael Coulter
Professor, Department of Political
Science
Grove City College
BUCKLEY V. VALEO, 424 U.S. 1
(1976)
JUDICIARY ACT OF 1789
MUELLER V. ALLEN, 463 U.S. 388
(1983)

Barbara J. Cox
Professor
California Western School of Law
HURLEY V. IRISH-AMERICAN GAY,
LESBIAN, 515 U.S. 557 (1995)

Dennis J. Coyle
Adjunct Scholar
American Enterprise Institute
BREWER, DAVID

Robin Kundis Craig
Attorneys' Title Insurance Fund
Professor of Law
Florida State University College of Law
ENVIRONMENTAL CITIZEN SUITS
PRIVATE ATTORNEY GENERAL
RAPANOS V. UNITED STATES, 126 S.
CT. 2208 (2006)
SOLID WASTE AGENCY OF NORTHERN
COOK COUNTY V. U.S. ARMY CORPS
OF ENGINEERS, 531 U.S. 159
(2001)

Thomas P. Crocker
Assistant Professor of Law
University of South Carolina School of
Law
BOARD OF EDUCATION OF TRUSTEES
OF STATE UNIVERSITY OF NEW
YORK V. FOX, 492 U.S. 469 (1989)
BRENTWOOD ACADEMY V. TENNESSEE
SECONDARY SCHOOL ATHLETIC AS-
SOCIATION, 531 U.S. 288 (2001)
BUSH V. GORE, 531 U.S. 98 (2000)
RUTAN V. REPUBLICAN PARTY OF
ILLINOIS, 497 U.S. 62 (1990)

Mary Crossley
Dean and Professor, School of Law
University of Pittsburgh
RIGHT TO DIE

Margaret A. Crouch
Professor of Philosophy
Eastern Michigan University
MERITOR SAVINGS BANK V. VINSON,
477 U.S. 57 (1986)
SEXUAL HARASSMENT

Michael Kent Curtis
Judge Donald L. Smith Professor of
Constitutional and Public Law
Wake Forest University School of Law
BARRON V. BALTIMORE, 32 U.S. 243
(1833)
SAENZ V. ROE, 526 U.S. 489 (1999)

Judith F. Daar
Clinical Professor of Medicine
University of California–Irvine, College
of Medicine

EISENSTADT V. BAIRD, 405 U.S. 438
(1972)
GRISWOLD V. CONNECTICUT, 381
U.S. 479 (1965)
PLANNED PARENTHOOD V.
DANFORTH, 428 U.S. 52 (1976)

David Dana
Professor of Law and Associate Dean
for Faculty Research
Northwestern University School of
Law
PENNSYLVANIA COAL V. MAHON, 260
U.S. 393 (1922)

Perry Dane
Professor
Rutgers School of Law–Camden
WEST VIRGINIA STATE BOARD OF
EDUCATION V. BARNETTE, 319 U.S.
624 (1943)

Michele Landis Dauber
Bernard D. Bergreen Faculty Scholar
Stanford University
NEW DEAL LAWYERS

Lincoln L. Davies
Associate Professor of Law
S. J. Quinney College of Law,
University of Utah
PACIFIC GAS & ELECTRIC V. STATE
ENERGY RESOURCES CONSERVATION
AND DEVELOPMENT COMMISSION,
461 U.S. 190 (1983)

Martha F. Davis
Professor
Northeastern University School of Law
BODDIE V. CONNECTICUT, 401 U.S.
371 (1971)
CALIFANO V. WEBSTER, 430 U.S. 313
(1977)
DANDRIDGE V. WILLIAMS, 397 U.S.
471 (1970)
KING V. SMITH, 392 U.S. 309 (1968)
NOW LEGAL DEFENSE AND EDUCA-
TION FUND
UNITED STATES V. MORRISON, 529
U.S. 598 (2000)
YOUNGBERG V. ROMEO, 457 U.S. 307
(1982)

Thomas J. Davis
Professor, Department of History
Arizona State University, Tempe
RUNYON V. MCCRARY, 427 U.S. 160
(1976)
SIPUEL V. BOARD OF REGENTS OF
UNIVERSITY OF OKLAHOMA, 332
U.S. 631 (1948)

SWANN V. CHARLOTTE-MECKLENBURG
BOARD OF EDUCATION, 402 U.S. 1
(1971)

Jacob W. Day
Graduate Student (PhD)
Washington State University, Pullman
STANLEY V. GEORGIA, 394 U.S. 557
(1969)

Erin F. Delaney
Academic Fellow
Columbia Law School (2009–2010)
CITIZENSHIP

Kevin R. den Dulk
Associate Professor, Department of
Political Science
Grand Valley State University
SANTA FE INDEPENDENT SCHOOL
DISTRICT V. DOE, 530 U.S. 290
(2000)

Brannon P. Denning
Professor, Cumberland School of Law
Samford University
AMERICAN INSURANCE ASSOCIATION
V. GARAMENDI, 539 U.S. 396
(2003)
C & A CARBONE, INC. V. CLARKS-
TOWN, 511 U.S. 383 (1994)
COOLEY V. BOARD OF WARDENS, 53
U.S. 299 (1851)
CROSBY V. NATIONAL FOREIGN TRADE
COUNCIL, 530 U.S. 363 (2000)
DAVIS V. BANDEMER, 478 U.S. 109
(1986)
KATZENBACH V. MCCLUNG, 379 U.S.
294 (1964)
M.L.B. V. S.L.J., 519 U.S. 102 (1996)
PROGRESSIVE ERA INTERSTATE
COMMERCE
RIGHT TO BEAR ARMS
UNITED STATES V. LOPEZ, 514 U.S.
549 (1995)
VIETH V. JUBELIRER, 541 U.S. 267
(2004)
WEST LYNN CREAMERY V. HEALY, 512
U.S. 186 (1994)

Anuj C. Desai
Assistant Professor of Law
University of Wisconsin
CONDITIONAL FUNDING

Neal Devins
Goodrich Professor of Law, Professor
of Government, and Director, Institute
of Bill of Rights Law
William and Mary School of Law
CONGRESSIONAL RESPONSE TO JUDI-
CIAL DECISIONS

Victoria Diaz
Law Student
University of Arizona, Rogers College
of Law
MALINSKI V. NEW YORK, 324 U.S. 401
(1945)

Bruce J. Dierenfield
Professor of History
Canisius College
ABINGTON TOWNSHIP V. SCHEMPP,
374 U.S. 203 (1963)
ENGEL V. VITALE, 370 U.S. 421
(1962)
EVERSON V. BOARD OF EDUCATION,
330 U.S. 1 (1947)
MCCOLLUM V. BOARD OF EDUCATION,
333 U.S. 203 (1948)
SCHOOL PRAYER
WALLACE V. JAFFREE, 472 U.S. 38
(1985)
ZORACH V. CLAUSON, 343 U.S. 306
(1952)

J. Herbie DiFonzo
Professor of Law
Hofstra University Law School
DIVORCE

John Dinan
Associate Professor, Department of
Political Science
Wake Forest University
STATE CONSTITUTIONAL LAW

Scott Dodson
Assistant Professor of Law
University of Arkansas Law School
ABSTENTION
ADEQUATE AND INDEPENDENT STATE
GROUNDS
APPELLATE JURISDICTION

Holly Doremus
Professor, School of Law
University of California, Davis
TENNESSEE VALLEY AUTHORITY V.
HILL, 437 U.S. 153 (1978)

Candidus K. Dougherty
Adjunct Professor
Rutgers School of Law–Camden
HEFFRON V. INTERNATIONAL SOCIETY
FOR KRISHNA CONSCIOUSNESS, 452
U.S. 640 (1981)
RIGHTS OF STUDENTS
TEXTUALISM

Davison M. Douglas
Hanson Professor of Law
College of William and Mary
JIM CROW AND VOTING RIGHTS

Donald A. Downs
Professor of Political Science, Law, and
Journalism
University of Wisconsin, Madison
HATE SPEECH
OBSCENITY AND PORNOGRAPHY
TEXAS V. JOHNSON, 491 U.S. 397
(1989)

Donald Dripps
Professor of Law
University of San Diego
EXCLUSIONARY RULE
SIXTH AMENDMENT

Danielle A. DuBois
Law Student at the James E. Rogers
College of Law
University of Arizona
WEEKS V. UNITED STATES, 232 U.S.
383 (1914)

Katelyn Dumont
J.D. Candidate
Pace University School of Law
ELEMENTARY AND SECONDARY EDU-
CATION ACT OF 1965 (TITLE I)

Meredith J. Duncan
George Butler Research Professor of
Law
University of Houston Law Center
BATES V. STATE BAR OF ARIZONA, 433
U.S. 350 (1977)

Joshua M. Dunn
Assistant Professor, Department of
Political Science
University of Colorado–Colorado
Springs
CUMMINGS, HOMER

Anne Proffitt Dupre
J. Alton Hosch Professor of Law
University of Georgia School of Law
BOARD OF EDUCATION V. ROWLEY,
458 U.S. 176 (1982)
HONIG V. DOE, 484 U.S. 305 (1988)

Philip A. Dynia
Associate Professor, Political Science
Department
Loyola University, New Orleans
BOWERS V. HARDWICK, 478 U.S. 186
(1986)
NEW YORK V. FERBER, 458 U.S. 747
(1982)
THEORIES OF THE UNION

Keith Rollin Eakins
Associate Professor, Department of
Political Science

University of Central Oklahoma
LEE V. WEISMAN, 505 U.S. 577
(1992)

Peter B. Edelman
Professor of Law
Georgetown University Law Center
KENNEDY, JOHN F.
KENNEDY, ROBERT

J. Shoshanna Ehrlich
Associate Professor, Legal Studies
University of Massachusetts Boston
MAYNARD V. HILL, 125 U.S. 190
(1888)
ROE V. WADE, 410 U.S. 113 (1973)
WEBSTER V. REPRODUCTIVE HEALTH
SERVICES, 492 U.S. 490 (1989)

Ward E. Y. Elliott
Burnet C. Wohlford Professor of
American Political Institutions
Claremont McKenna College
MINOR V. HAPPERSETT, 88 U.S. 162
(1875)

Richard E. Ellis
Professor, Department of History
University at Buffalo, SUNY
MARSHALL, JOHN
PROTECTIVE TARIFFS
WAR OF 1812

Jonathan L. Entin
Professor of Law and Politics
Case Western Reserve University
BROWN V. MISSISSIPPI, 297 U.S. 278
(1936)
COMMERCE CLAUSE
CONCURRING OPINIONS
KELO V. CITY OF NEW LONDON, 545
U.S. 469 (2005)
RATIONAL BASIS
RAYMOND MOTOR TRANSPORTATION
V. RICE, 434 U.S. 429 (1978)

Charles R. Epp
Associate Professor, Department of
Public Administration
University of Kansas
AMICUS CURIAE

Garrett Epps
Orlando John and Marian H. Hollis
Professor
University of Oregon School of Law
FOURTEENTH AMENDMENT

Lee Epstein
Professor of Law
Northwestern University
INTEREST GROUPS

Timothy L. Evans
Independent Researcher
Fayetteville, AR
FLOOD V. KUHN, 407 U.S. 258

Cynthia R. Farina
Professor of Law
Cornell Law School
CHEVRON U.S.A. V. NATURAL RE-
SOURCES DEFENSE COUNCIL, 467
U.S. 837 (1984)

Barry C. Feld
Centennial Professor of Law
University of Minnesota Law School
JUVENILE JUSTICE

Stephen M. Feldman
Jerry W. Housel/Carl F. Arnold
Distinguished Professor of Law and
Adjunct Professor of Political Science
University of Wyoming
FREEDOM OF SPEECH
SOCIOLOGICAL JURISPRUDENCE

Cleveland Ferguson, III
Associate Professor of Law
Florida Coastal School of Law
RATE REGULATION

Martha A. Field
Langdell Professor of Law
Harvard Law School
PARENTAL RIGHTS

Martha Albertson Fineman
Robert W. Woodruff Professor of Law
Emory University
INTIMACY
PREGNANCY

Paul Finkelman
President William McKinley
Distinguished Professor of Law and
Public Policy
Albany Law School, Albany, New York
ABOLITIONISM
CIVIL WAR
SLAVERY

Alan M. Fisher
Professor of Political Science
California State University, Dominguez
Hills
CARDOZO, BENJAMIN N.

Louis Fisher
Specialist in Constitutional Law
Law Library, Library of Congress
EXECUTIVE PRIVILEGE

Martin S. Flaherty
Visiting Professor
Woodrow Wilson School, Princeton
University
ORIGINALISM

Taki Flevaris
Juris Doctor Candidate
Harvard Law School
LEVITT V. COMMITTEE FOR PUBLIC
EDUCATION, 413 U.S. 472 (1973)

John Fliter
Associate Professor, Department of
Political Science
Kansas State University
MOOSE LODGE NO. 107 V. IRVIS, 407
U.S. 163 (1972)
SOUTER, DAVID

Elizabeth Price Foley
Professor, College of Law
Florida International University
ENUMERATED POWERS
UNWRITTEN CONSTITUTION

Damon Freeman
Assistant Professor, School of Social
Policy & Practice
University of Pennsylvania
CLARK, KENNETH
DU BOIS, W. E. B.

Lloyd Freeman
Litigation Associate
Archer & Greiner, P.C., Haddonfield,
NJ
ORAL ARGUMENT

Tony A. Freyer
University Research Professor of
History and Law
University of Alabama
ERIE RAILROAD CO. V. TOMPKINS, 304
U.S. 64 (1938)
WELTON V. MISSOURI, 91 U.S. 275
(1876)

Richard D. Friedman
Ralph W. Aigler Professor of Law
University of Michigan Law School
CRAWFORD V. WASHINGTON, 541
U.S. 36 (2004)

Bruce P. Frohnen
Associate Professor of Law
Ave Maria School of Law
DIRECT TAXES
INDUSTRIAL UNION DEPARTMENT,
AFL-CIO V. AMERICAN PETROLEUM
INSTITUTE, 448 U.S. 607 (1980)

UNITED STATES TRUST CO. V. NEW
JERSEY, 431 U.S. 1 (1977)

José Gabilondo
Associate Professor, College of Law
Florida International University
ROMER V. EVANS, 517 U.S. 620
(1996)

Richard Gambitta
Director, Institute for Law and Public
Affairs; Associate Professor of Political
Science
University of Texas at San Antonio
SWEATT V. PAINTER, 339 U.S. 629
(1950)

Richard W. Garnett
John Cardinal O'Hara, C.S.C.
Associate Professor of Law
University of Notre Dame
EMPLOYMENT DIVISION, DEPARTMENT
OF HUMAN RESOURCES OF OREGON
V. SMITH, 494 U.S. 872 (1990)
MINERSVILLE SCHOOL DISTRICT V.
GOBITIS, 310 U.S. 586 (1940)
VACCO V. QUILL, 521 U.S. 793 (1997)

Elizabeth Garrett
Sydney M. Irmas Professor of Public
Interest Law, Legal Ethics, Political
Science, Policy, Planning, and
Development
University of Southern California
LEGISLATIVE IMMUNITY

Tim Alan Garrison
Director of Native American Studies
and Associate Professor of History
Portland State University
MISSISSIPPI CHOCTAW INDIAN BAND V.
HOLYFIELD, 490 U.S. 30 (1989)

Patrick M. Garry
Associate Professor of Law
University of South Dakota School of
Law
AGOSTINI V. FELTON, 521 U.S. 203
(1997)
AGUILAR V. FELTON, 473 U.S. 402
(1985)
ASHCROFT V. THE FREE SPEECH
COALITION, 535 U.S. 234 (2002)
BOARD OF COMMISSIONERS V. UM-
BEHR, 518 U.S. 668 (1996)
BRANZBURG V. HAYES, 408 U.S. 665
(1972)
COHEN V. CALIFORNIA, 403 U.S. 15
(1971)
FEDERAL COMMUNICATIONS COMMIS-
SION V. PACIFICA FOUNDATION,
438 U.S. 726 (1978)

LEMON V. KURTZMAN, 403 U.S. 602
(1971)
LYNCH V. DONNELLY, 465 U.S. 668
(1984)
MOTOR VEHICLES MANUFACTURERS
ASSOCIATION V. STATE FARM MU-
TUAL AUTOMOBILE INSURANCE CO.,
463 U.S. 29 (1983)
NATIONAL LEAGUE OF CITIES V.
USERY, 426 U.S. 833 (1976)
O'HARE TRUCK SERVICES, INC. V. CITY
OF NORTHLAKE, 518 U.S. 712
(1996)
RENO V. AMERICAN CIVIL LIBERTIES
UNION, 521 U.S. 844 (1997)
ROSENBERGER V. RECTOR AND VISI-
TORS OF THE UNIVERSITY OF
VIRGINIA, 515 U.S. 819 (1995)
UNITED STATES V. PLAYBOY ENTER-
TAINMENT GROUP, INC., 529 U.S.
803 (2000)
WIDMAR V. VINCENT, 454 U.S. 263
(1981)

Scott D. Gerber
College of Law
Ohio Northern University
JAY, JOHN
JUDICIAL REVIEW BEFORE MARBURY
SERIATIM OPINIONS

Michael J. Gerhardt
Samuel Ashe Distinguished Professor
of Constitutional Law
University of North Carolina at Chapel
Hill Law School
BLACK, CHARLES
CASE OR CONTROVERSY
CLINTON V. JONES, 520 U.S. 681
(1997)
IMPEACHMENT

Steven G. Gey
Professor, College of Law
Florida State University
CITY OF ERIE V. PAP'S A.M., 529 U.S.
277 (2000)
LEGAL SERVICES CORPORATION V.
VELAZQUEZ, 531 U.S. 533 (2001)
RUMSFELD V. FORUM FOR ACADEMIC
AND INSTITUTIONAL RIGHTS, INC.,
547 U.S. 47 (2006)
UNITED STATES V. AMERICAN LIBRARY
ASSOCIATION, 539 U.S. 194
(2003)

Robert Don Gifford
Assistant U.S. Attorney and Adjunct
Professor of Criminal Law
U.S. Army JAG School
STONE COURT

David W. Glazier
Associate Professor
Loyola Law School Los Angeles
MARTIAL LAW

Robert L. Glicksman
Robert W. Wagstaff Professor of Law
University of Kansas, Lawrence
COMPREHENSIVE ENVIRONMENTAL
RESPONSE, COMPENSATION, AND
LIABILITY ACT (CERCLA)
ENVIRONMENTAL IMPACT ASSESSMENT
(NATIONAL ENVIRONMENTAL
POLICY ACT)

Rachel D. Godsil
Professor of Law
Seton Hall University School of Law
VILLAGE OF ARLINGTON HEIGHTS V.
METROPOLITAN HOUSING DEVEL-
OPMENT CORP., 429 U.S. 252
(1977)

Carole Goldberg
Professor of Law and Director, Joint
Degree Program in Law & American
Indian Studies
UCLA School of Law
MORTON V. MANCARI, 417 U.S. 535
(1974)
NATIVE AMERICANS

Suzanne B. Goldberg
Clinical Professor of Law
Columbia Law School
BOY SCOUTS OF AMERICA V. DALE,
530 U.S. 640 (2000)

Joel K. Goldstein
Vincent C. Immel Professor of Law
Saint Louis University School of Law
ADMIRALTY JURISDICTION
PRESIDENTIAL IMMUNITY
PRESIDENTIAL RESPONSE TO JUDICIAL
DECISIONS
UNITARY EXECUTIVE

Leslie F. Goldstein
Judge Hugh M. Morris Professor of
Political Science and International
Relations
University of Delaware
EQUAL RIGHTS AMENDMENT (ERA)
NINETEENTH AMENDMENT

Robert D. Goldstein
Professor of Law
UCLA School of Law
HAZELWOOD SCHOOL DISTRICT V.
KUHLMEIER, 484 U.S. 260 (1988)

Risa L. Goluboff
Professor of Law and History
University of Virginia
PEONAGE

Mark A. Graber
Professor of Law and Government
University of Maryland School of Law
BONHAM'S CASE
CLINTON V. CITY OF NEW YORK, 524 U.S. 417 (1998)
HEPBURN V. GRISWOLD, 75 U.S. 603 (1870)
KENTUCKY AND VIRGINIA RESOLUTIONS
LAND GRANTS
MARTIN V. HUNTER'S LESSEE, 14 U.S. 304 (1816)
MAYOR OF THE CITY OF NEW YORK V. MILN, 36 U.S. 102 (1837)
STUART V. LAIRD, 5 U.S. 299 (1803)

Michael Green
Professor of History
College of Southern Nevada
CURTIS, BENJAMIN
FORTAS, ABE
LEWIS, ANTHONY
STEWART, POTTER

Kent Greenfield
Professor of Law
Boston College Law School
ULTRA VIRES DOCTRINE
WORLD WAR II AND THE GROWTH OF INDIVIDUAL RIGHTS

Richard K. Greenstein
Professor, James E. Beasley School of Law
Temple University
MOOTNESS
REMAND

Daniel J.H. Greenwood
Professor
Hofstra University School of Law
FIRST NATIONAL BANK V. BELLOTTI, 435 U.S. 765 (1978)

Douglas B. Grob
Assistant Professor, Department of Government and Politics
University of Maryland, College Park
GIBBONS V. OGDEN, 22 U.S. 1 (1824)
MASSACHUSETTS V. ENVIRONMENTAL PROTECTION AGENCY, 549 U.S. ___ (2007)

Wendy Groce-Smith
Law Student

University of Louisville
INTERSTATE COMMERCE COMMISSION

Jill I. Gross
Associate Professor of Law
Pace University School of Law
RODRIGUEZ DE QUIJAS V. SHEARSON/ AMERICAN EXPRESS, 490 U.S. 477 (1989)

Joanna L. Grossman
Professor
Hofstra University School of Law
FAMILY AND MEDICAL LEAVE ACT

Catherine M. Grosso
Assistant Professor
Michigan State University College of Law
WRIGHT, J. SKELLY

Martin Guggenheim
Fiorello LaGuardia Professor of Clinical Law
New York University School of Law
LASSITER V. DEPARTMENT OF SOCIAL SERVICES, 452 U.S. 18 (1981)
MOORE V. CITY OF EAST CLEVELAND, 431 U.S. 494 (1977)
NEW JERSEY V. T.L.O., 469 U.S. 325 (1985)
STANLEY V. ILLINOIS, 405 U.S. 645 (1972)

Frank Gulino
Assistant Professor of Legal Writing
Hofstra University School of Law
TAFT COURT
TWENTY-THIRD AMENDMENT

Guadalupe Gutierrez
J.D. Candidate 2009
University of Arizona, Rogers College of Law
NATURALIZATION AND THE CONSTITUTION

Louise Halper
Professor of Law
Washington & Lee University School of Law
TIEDEMAN, CHRISTOPHER

Justin Halpern
Professor of Social Sciences
Northeastern State University
BOLLING V. SHARPE, 347 U.S. 497 (1954)

Marci A. Hamilton
Paul R. Verkuil Chair in Public Law

Benjamin N. Cardozo School of Law, Yeshiva University
ESTABLISHMENT CLAUSE
FREE EXERCISE OF RELIGION

Richard F. Hamm
Associate Professor, Department of History
State University of New York at Albany
PROHIBITION
TWENTY-FIRST AMENDMENT

Katy J. Harriger
Professor of Political Science
Wake Forest University
INDEPENDENT COUNSEL
MORRISON V. OLSON, 487 U.S. 654 (1988)
SOLICITOR GENERAL

Leslie Joan Harris
Dorothy Kliks Fones Professor
University of Oregon School of Law
ORR V. ORR, 440 U.S. 268 (1979)

Ron Harris
Professor of Law and Legal History
School of Law, Tel Aviv University
SANTA CLARA V. SOUTHERN PACIFIC RAILROAD, 118 U.S. 394 (1886)

Melissa Hart
Associate Professor
University of Colorado Law School
CORNING GLASS WORKS V. BRENNAN, 417 U.S. 188 (1974)
DOTHARD V. RAWLINSON, 433 U.S 321 (1977)
FRONTIERO V. RICHARDSON, 411 U.S. 677 (1973)
HARRIS V. FORKLIFT SYSTEMS, 510 U.S. 17 (1993)
KAHN V. SHEVIN, 416 U.S. 351 (1974)
PRICE WATERHOUSE V. HOPKINS, 490 U.S. 228 (1989)

James R. Hawkins
Independent Researcher
University of Houston Law School, Houston, TX
FREE SPEECH AND WORLD WAR I
FREE SPEECH BETWEEN THE WORLD WARS

Bradley Hays
Assistant Professor of Political Science
University of Nevada, Las Vegas
SUBSTANTIAL EFFECTS
TAYLOR, JOHN

Thomas Lee Hazen
Cary C. Boshamer Distinguished
Professor
University of North Carolina at Chapel
Hill
PIPER V. CHRIS-CRAFT INDUSTRIES,
430 U.S. 1 (1977)

Eliot M. Held
Student
University of Arizona Rogers College of
Law
COMMITTEE FOR PUBLIC EDUCATION
AND RELIGIOUS LIBERTY V. REGAN,
444 U.S. 646 (1980)

Joan MacLeod Heminway
Associate Professor
University of Tennessee College of Law
JONES V. SECURITIES AND EXCHANGE
COMMISSION, 298 U.S. 1 (1936)

Lynne Henderson
Professor of Law
William S. Boyd School of Law,
University of Las Vegas, Nevada
SINGLE SEX EDUCATION

Timothy J. Henderson
Professor, Department of History
Auburn University at Montgomery
MEXICAN WAR

Jennifer S. Hendricks
Associate Professor, College of Law
University of Tennessee
CALIFANO V. GOLDFARB, 430 U.S.
199 (1977)
WIMBERLY V. LABOR AND INDUSTRIAL
RELATIONS COMMISSION, 479 U.S.
511 (1987)

F. Andrew Hessick
Visiting Associate Professor, Sandra
Day O'Connor College of Law
Arizona State University
ORDERS
SUPREME COURT CALENDAR

Steven J. Heyman
Professor of Law
Chicago-Kent College of Law
COMPELLED SPEECH

B. Jessie Hill
Associate Director, Center for Social
Justice
Case Western Reserve University
School of Law
CAPITOL SQUARE REVIEW AND ADVI-
SORY BOARD V. PINETTE, 515 U.S.
753 (1995)

MCCREARY COUNTY V. AMERICAN
CIVIL LIBERTIES UNION OF KEN-
TUCKY, 545 U.S. 844 (2005)

John Lawrence Hill
Professor of Law
Indiana University School of Law
Indianapolis
MUGLER V. KANSAS, 123 U.S. 623
(1887)

Elizabeth L. Hillman
Professor of Law
University of California, Hastings
College of the Law
EX PARTE QUIRIN, 317 U.S. 1 (1942)
GENDER AND THE MILITARY
WORLD WAR II AND THE PRESIDENT'S
POWER

Bill Ong Hing
Professor of Law
University of California, Davis
ASIAN EXCLUSION LAWS

Ran Hirschl
Professor of Political Science and Law;
Canada Research Chair in
Constitutionalism, Democracy, and
Development
University of Toronto
COMPARATIVE CONSTITUTIONAL LAW

Janet C. Hoeffel
Associate Professor
Tulane Law School
COKER V. GEORGIA, 433 U.S. 584
(1977)
VIOLENCE AGAINST WOMEN

Williamjames Hull Hoffer
Assistant Professor, Department of
History
Seton Hall University
STONE, HARLAN F.

Kurt Hohenstein
Assistant Professor of History
Winona State University
INSIDER TRADING
NEW DEAL: SHIFTING HISTORICAL
INTERPRETATIONS
RULE 10B-5

David Holland
Assistant Professor
University of Nevada, Las Vegas
CONSTITUTION AND AMERICAN CIVIL
RELIGION

Herbert Hovenkamp
Ben V. & Dorothy Willie Professor

University of Iowa College of Law
ANTITRUST

Roman J. Hoyos
Ph.D. Candidate
University of Chicago
CONFEDERATE CONSTITUTION

Wilson R. Huhn
C. Blake McDowell, Jr., Professor of
Law
University of Akron School of Law
BOARD OF REGENTS OF STATE
COLLEGES V. ROTH, 408 U.S. 564
(1972)
PUBLIC PURPOSE
R.A.V. V. CITY OF ST. PAUL, 505 U.S.
377 (1992)

Renée Hutchins
Assistant Professor
University of Maryland School of Law
STOP AND FRISK

Harry G. Hutchison
Professor
George Mason University School of
Law
WITTERS V. WASHINGTON DEPART-
MENT OF SERVICES FOR THE BLIND,
474 U.S. 481 (1986)

Allan Ides
James P. Bradley Professor of
Constitutional Law
Loyola Law School, Los Angeles
FUNDAMENTAL INTERESTS
YOUNGSTOWN SHEET & TUBE V.
SAWYER, 343 U.S. 579 (1952)

Robert M. Ireland
Professor, Department of History
University of Kentucky
POSTAL POWER

Gregg Ivers
Professor of Government
American University
CONSTITUTIONAL THEORY
EMINENT DOMAIN
MODELS OF JUDICIAL DECISION-
MAKING
SCHECHTER POULTRY CORP. V.
UNITED STATES, 295 U.S. 495
(1935)
STRAUDER V. WEST VIRGINIA, 100
U.S. 303 (1880)

Jeffrey D. Jackson
Associate Professor of Law

Washburn University School of Law,
Topeka, Kansas
MCREYNOLDS, JAMES

Charles F. Jacobs
Assistant Professor, Department of
Political Science
St. Norbert College
DAYTON BOARD OF EDUCATION V.
BRINKMAN (DAYTON II), 443 U.S.
526 (1979)
PASADENA CITY BOARD OF EDUCA-
TION V. SPANGLER, 427 U.S. 424
(1976)

Daniel A. Jacobs
Attorney at Law
Gleason, Dunn, Walsh, and
O'Shea–Albany, New York
JUDICIARY ACT OF 1925
UNITED STATES V. E.C. KNIGHT CO.,
156 U.S. 1 (1895)

Robert Jacobs
Professor Emeritus of Political Science
Central Washington University
FIFTEENTH AMENDMENT
FORCE ACT

Gary Jeffrey Jacobsohn
Patterson-Banister Professor of Political
Science and H. Malcolm MacDonald
Professor of Constitutional and
Comparative
University of Texas at Austin
ASPIRATIONALISM

Erik M. Jensen
David L. Brennan Professor of Law
Case Western Reserve University
HYLTON V. UNITED STATES, 3 U.S.
171 (1796)
LIFE TENURE OF JUSTICES
SIXTEENTH AMENDMENT

Richard Jensen
Professor of History Emeritus
University of Illinois
JOHNSON, LYNDON B.
NIXON, RICHARD
WILSON, WOODROW

Elizabeth Joh
Professor of Law
University of California at Davis
KATZ V. UNITED STATES, 389 U.S.
347 (1967)

Calvin H. Johnson
Professor of Law
University of Texas
INCOME TAX CASES

Herbert A. Johnson
Distinguished Professor of Law
Emeritus
University of South Carolina
CHIEF JUSTICE
CIRCUIT RIDING

John W. Johnson
Department of History
University of Northern Iowa
BETHEL SCHOOL DISTRICT NO. 403 V.
FRASER, 478 U.S. 675 (1986)
MORSE V. FREDERICK, 551 U.S. ___
(2007)
TINKER V. DES MOINES SCHOOL
DISTRICT, 393 U.S. 503 (1969)

Scott P. Johnson
Associate Professor of Political Science
Frostburg State University
KING, MARTIN LUTHER, JR.

Steve R. Johnson
E. L. Wiegand Professor, William S.
Boyd School of Law
University of Nevada, Las Vegas
COMPLETE AUTO TRANSIT V. BRADY,
430 U.S. 274 (1977)

Timothy R. Johnson
Assistant Professor of Political Science
University of Minnesota
SUPREME COURT BAR

Bernie D. Jones
Assistant Professor, Department of
Legal Studies
University of Massachusetts, Amherst
AMERICAN FEDERATION OF LABOR V.
SWING, 312 U.S. 321 (1941)
JIM CROW IN THE EARLY TWENTIETH
CENTURY
MYERS V. ANDERSON, 238 U.S. 368
(1915)
PACE V. ALABAMA, 106 U.S. 583
(1883)

John Paul Jones
Professor of Law
University of Richmond
EXPATRIATION
PROCEDURAL DUE PROCESS

Gwen Hoerr Jordan
J. Willard Hurst Legal History Fellow
University of Wisconsin Law School
BRADWELL V. ILLINOIS, 83 U.S. 130
(1873)

David J. Jung
Professor of Law

University of California, Hastings
College of the Law
CONSTITUTIONAL TORTS

Ronald Kahn
James Monroe Professor of Politics and
Law
Oberlin College
DESHANEY V. WINNEBAGO COUNTY
DEPT. OF SOCIAL SERVICES, 489
U.S. 189 (1989)
JUDICIAL SUPREMACY

James L. Kainen
Professor
Fordham University School of Law
HOME BUILDING AND LOAN V. BLAIS-
DELL, 290 U.S. 398 (1934)

Sam Kalen
Visiting Assistant Professor, 2007–
2008
Florida State University College of Law
SOSNA V. IOWA, 419 U.S. 393 (1975)

John P. Kaminski
Director, The Center for the Study of
the American Constitution
University of Wisconsin–Madison
JAY COURT
WASHINGTON, GEORGE

Roberta S. Karmel
Centennial Professor of Law and
Co-Director, Center for the Study of
International Business Law
Brooklyn Law School
CENTRAL BANK V. FIRST INTERSTATE
BANK, 511 U.S. 164 (1994)

Kenneth L. Karst
David G. Price and Dallas P. Price
Professor of Law Emeritus
School of Law, University of
California, Los Angeles
ALL DELIBERATE SPEED
FREEDOM OF ASSOCIATION

Herma Hill Kay
Barbara Nachtrieb Armstrong Professor
of Law
School of Law, University of
California, Berkeley
GINSBURG, RUTH BADER

Ken I. Kersch
Associate Professor of Political Science
and Law
Boston College
BOYD V. UNITED STATES, 116 U.S.
616 (1886)

CITATIONS TO FOREIGN SOURCES
EIGHTEENTH AMENDMENT

Richard B. Kielbowicz
Associate Professor, Department of
Communication
University of Washington
MIAMI HERALD PUBLISHING CO. V.
TORNILLO, 418 U.S. 241 (1974)
NEBRASKA PRESS ASSOCIATION V.
STUART, 427 U.S. 539 (1976)
RED LION BROADCASTING V. FEDERAL
COMMUNICATIONS COMMISSION,
395 U.S. 367 (1969)

Mark R. Killenbeck
Wylie H. Davis Distinguished
Professor of Law
University of Arkansas
FIRST AND SECOND BANKS OF THE
UNITED STATES
INTERNAL IMPROVEMENTS
M'CULLOCH V. MARYLAND, 17 U.S.
316 (1819)
NECESSARY AND PROPER CLAUSE
ROANE, SPENCER
STATE RIGHTS
STORY, JOSEPH

Andrew Kirk
Associate Professor and Program
Director, Department of History
University of Nevada, Las Vegas
PENN CENTRAL TRANSPORTATION
COMPANY V. CITY OF NEW YORK,
438 U.S. 104 (1978)

George Kiser
Associate Professor, Department of
Politics and Government
Illinois State University, Normal
LEHR V. ROBERTSON, 463 U.S. 248
(1983)
MICHAEL M. V. SUPERIOR COURT
OF SONOMA, 450 U.S. 464 (1981)
PEREMPTORY CHALLENGES
UNITED STATES V. KRAS, 409 U.S.
434 (1973)

Michael J. Klarman
Kirkland & Ellis Professor
Harvard Law School
BROWN V. BOARD OF EDUCATION,
ROAD TO
MARSHALL COURT
SCHOOL DESEGREGATION

Douglas W. Kmiec
Chair and Professor of Constitutional
Law

Pepperdine University
NOLLAN V. CALIFORNIA COASTAL
COMMISSION, 483 U.S. 825
(1987)

Helen J. Knowles
Assistant Professor, Department of
Political Science
State University of New York at
Oswego
CITY OF BOERNE V. FLORES, 521 U.S.
507 (1997)
NUMBER OF JUSTICES

Donald P. Kommers
Robbie Professor of Law and Political
Science
University of Notre Dame
STRUCTURALISM

Margery B. Koosed
Aileen McMurray Trusler Professor of
Law
University of Akron School of Law
COUNSELMAN V. HITCHCOCK, 142
U.S. 547 (1892)
ROADSIDE STOPS

Lewis A. Kornhauser
Alfred B. Engelberg Professor of Law
New York University
LAW AND ECONOMICS

Candace Saari Kovacic-Fleischer
Professor, Washington College of Law
American University
GEDULDIG V. AIELLO, 417 U.S. 484
(1974)
GENERAL ELECTRIC CO. V. GILBERT,
429 U.S. 125 (1976)

Harold J. Krent
Dean and Professor
Chicago–Kent College of Law
PARDONING POWER
UNITED STATES V. NIXON, 418 U.S.
683 (1974)

Samuel Krislov
Scholar in Residence
American University
BICKEL, ALEXANDER
NEW DEAL AND THE REGULATION OF
BUSINESS AND COMMERCE

Wen-Hsiang Kung
S.J.D. Candidate; Research Assistant
Indiana University—Bloomington,
School of Law
MITCHELL V. UNITED STATES, 313
U.S. 80 (1941)

Angela Mae Kupenda
Professor of Law
Mississippi College School of Law
NAACP V. CLAIBORNE HARDWARE,
458 U.S. 886 (1982)
PAUL V. DAVIS, 424 U.S. 693 (1976)
SPEECH IN PUBLIC SCHOOLS
WOOD V. STRICKLAND, 420 U.S. 308
(1975)

Alex Kurt
College of St. Benedict/St. John's
University
FEDERAL COMMUNICATIONS COMMIS-
SION V. LEAGUE OF WOMEN VO-
TERS, 468 U.S. 364 (1984)
NORTON V. SOUTHERN UTAH WIL-
DERNESS ALLIANCE, 542 U.S. 55
(2004)

Alison L. LaCroix
Assistant Professor of Law
University of Chicago Law School
DARTMOUTH COLLEGE V. WOOD-
WARD, 17 U.S. 518 (1819)
OGDEN V. SAUNDERS, 25 U.S. 213
(1827)

Josiah Bartlett Lambert
Associate Professor of Political
Science
Saint Bonaventure University
IN RE DEBS, 158 U.S. 564 (1895)
LABOR UNIONS

Brian Landsberg
Professor of Law
University of the Pacific, McGeorge
School of Law
SCREWS V. UNITED STATES, 322 U.S.
718 (1945)

Kurt T. Lash
Professor and W. Joseph Ford
Fellow
Loyola Law School, Los Angeles
NINTH AMENDMENT
UNENUMERATED RIGHTS

Audrey Wolfson Latourette
Professor of Law, School of Business
Richard Stockton College of New
Jersey
PAPISH V. BOARD OF CURATORS OF
UNIVERSITY OF MISSOURI, 410 U.S.
667 (1973)

Robert M. Lawless
Professor, College of Law
University of Illinois at Urbana–
Champaign

BANKRUPTCY AND INSOLVENCY
MARQUETTE NATIONAL BANK V. FIRST
OF OMAHA SERVICE CORP., 439
U.S. 299 (1978)

Richard J. Lazarus
Professor of Law
Georgetown University
ENVIRONMENTAL LAW

Sophia Z. Lee
Graduate Student, Department of
History
Yale University
FLAGG BROTHERS, INC. V. BROOKS,
436 U.S. 149 (1978)

Thomas R. Lee
Professor of Law
Brigham Young University
OVERRULINGS

Arthur G. LeFrancois
Professor
Oklahoma City University School of
Law
JUDICIAL PRAGMATISM
LYONS V. OKLAHOMA, 322 U.S. 596
(1944)
SKINNER V. OKLAHOMA, 316 U.S. 535
(1942)

Ashleigh Leitch
College of St. Benedict/St. John's
University
NORTON V. SOUTHERN UTAH
WILDERNESS ALLIANCE, 542 U.S.
55 (2004)

Vicki Lens
Associate Professor, School of Social
Work
Columbia University
PHILLIPS V. MARTIN MARIETTA CORP.,
400 U.S. 542 (1971)

Paul Lermack
Professor of Political Science
Bradley University
CONSTITUTIONAL INTERPRETATION

Laurie L. Levenson
Professor of Law, William M. Rains
Fellow, and Director for the Center for
Ethical Advocacy
Loyola Law School, Los Angeles
BIVENS V. SIX UNKNOWN FED.
NARCOTICS AGENTS, 403 U.S. 388
(1971)
INEVITABLE DISCOVERY

MIRANDA V. ARIZONA, 384 U.S. 436
(1966)
PAYTON V. NEW YORK, 445 U.S. 573
(1980)

David I. Levine
Professor of Law
University of California, Hastings
College of the Law
BMW OF NORTH AMERICA, INC. V.
GORE, 517 U.S. 559 (1996)
BROWNING-FERRIS INDUSTRIES OF
VERMONT, INC. V. KELCO DIS-
POSAL, INC., 492 U.S. 257 (1989)
HONDA MOTOR COMPANY V. OBERG,
512 U.S. 415 (1994)
PUNITIVE DAMAGES

Sanford Levinson
W. St. John Garwood and W. St. John
Garwood Jr. Centennial Chair in Law
University of Texas Law School
ARTICLE V
CONTINUITY IN GOVERNMENT
GREENHOUSE, LINDA
TWELFTH AMENDMENT
TWENTY-SEVENTH AMENDMENT

Matthew J. Lindstrom
Associate Professor of Political Science
St. Benedict/St. John's University
DEBS, EUGENE
FEDERAL COMMUNICATIONS COMMIS-
SION V. LEAGUE OF WOMEN
VOTERS, 468 U.S. 364 (1984)
JUDICIAL INDEPENDENCE
NORTON V. SOUTHERN UTAH WIL-
DERNESS ALLIANCE, 542 U.S. 55
(2004)

Peter Linzer
Professor of Law
University of Houston Law Center
DISSENTING OPINIONS

Robert Justin Lipkin
Professor
Widener University School of Law
UNCONSTITUTIONAL ON ITS FACE

Christine A. Littleton
Professor of Law and Women's Studies
University of California at Los Angeles
MACKINNON, CATHARINE

Carolyn N. Long
Associate Director, Department of
Political Science
Washington State University
MAPP V. OHIO, 367 U.S. 643 (1961)

Alberto B. Lopez
Associate Professor of Law
Salmon P. Chase College of Law,
Northern Kentucky University
SHELLEY V. KRAEMER, 334 U.S. 1
(1948)

David Luban
University Professor and Professor of
Law and Philosophy
Georgetown University Law Center
HAMDI V. RUMSFELD, 542 U.S. 507
(2004)

Gerard N. Magliocca
Professor
Indiana University School of Law–
Indianapolis
CURRENCY
JACKSON, ANDREW
LEGAL TENDER CASES
VETO POWER
WEBSTER, DANIEL
WEEMS V. UNITED STATES, 217 U.S.
349 (1910)

Paul G. Mahoney
David and Mary Harrison
Distinguished Professor of Law
University of Virginia School of Law
HALL V. GEIGER-JONES CO., 242 U.S.
539 (1917)

Daniel R. Mandelker
Howard A. Stamper Professor of Law
Washington University
ENVIRONMENTAL IMPACT ASSESSMENT
(NATIONAL ENVIRONMENTAL
POLICY ACT)

Mathew Manweller
Assistant Professor of Political Science
Central Washington University
RECALL
REFERENDUM

Nancy S. Marder
Professor of Law
Chicago–Kent College of Law
J.E.B. V. ALABAMA EX REL T.B., 511
U.S. 127 (1994)
JOHNSON V. LOUISIANA, 406 U.S. 356
(1972)
WOMEN ON JURIES

Gregory A. Mark
Professor, School of Law
Rutgers University, Newark
BANK OF UNITED STATES V. DAN-
DRIDGE, 25 U.S. 64 (1827)
CORPORATION AS A PERSON

LOUISVILLE, CINCINNATI & CHARLESTON RAILROAD CO. V. LETSON, 43 U.S. 497 (1844)

OLMSTEAD V. UNITED STATES, 277 U.S. 438 (1928)

Calvin Massey
Professor of Law
University of California, Hastings
College of the Law
PLURALITY OPINIONS
PREEMPTION
ROBERTS COURT

Ann MacLean Massie
Professor of Law
Washington and Lee University School
of Law
CRUZAN V. DIRECTOR, MISSOURI DEPARTMENT OF HEALTH, 497 U.S. 261 (1990)
GOOD NEWS CLUB V. MILFORD CENTRAL SCHOOL, 533 U.S. 98 (2001)

John Austin Matzko
Chair, Division of Social Science
Bob Jones University
CHARLES RIVER BRIDGE V. WARREN BRIDGE, 36 U.S. 420 (1837)

Serena Mayeri
Assistant Professor of Law
University of Pennsylvania Law School
MURRAY, PAULI

Thomas B. McAffee
Professor of Law
University of Nevada, Las Vegas
BOARD OF EDUCATION OF ISLAND TREES SCHOOL DISTRICT NO. 26 V. PICO, 457 U.S. 853 (1982)
BOARD OF EDUCATION OF KIRYAS JOEL VILLAGE SCHOOL DISTRICT V. GRUMET, 512 U.S. 687 (1994)
BOARD OF EDUCATION OF WESTSIDE COMMUNITY SCHOOL DISTRICT V. MERGENS, 496 U.S. 226 (1990)
COMMITTEE FOR PUBLIC EDUCATION V. NYQUIST, 413 U.S. 756 (1973)
EQUAL ACCESS
GRAND RAPIDS V. BALL, 473 U.S. 373 (1985)

Michael W. McConnell
Circuit Judge, U.S. Court of Appeals
for the Tenth Circuit
Presidential Professor, S.J. Quinney
College of Law, University of Utah
MARSH V. CHAMBERS, 463 U.S. 783 (1983)
ZELMAN V. SIMMONS-HARRIS, 536 U.S. 639 (2002)

G. Roger McDonald
Lecturer, Department of Government
John Jay College of Criminal Justice
ADKINS V. CHILDREN'S HOSPITAL, 261 U.S. 525 (1923)
BRIDGES V. CALIFORNIA, 314 U.S. 252 (1941)
MULFORD V. SMITH, 307 U.S. 38 (1939)

Gary L. McDowell
Tyler Haynes Interdisciplinary
Professor of Leadership Studies,
Political Science, and Law
University of Richmond
REAGAN, RONALD

Kevin McElroy
Visiting Assistant Professor of Legal
Research and Writing
Hofstra University School of Law
WOLMAN V. WALTER, 433 U.S. 229 (1977)

Lisa T. McElroy
Associate Professor of Law
Drexel University College of Law
PRESS COVERAGE

Aman McLeod
Assistant Professor of Political Science
Rutgers University
ELROD V. BURNS, 427 U.S. 347 (1976)

Kevin J. McMahon
Associate Professor of Political Science
Trinity College
COURT-PACKING
POLITICAL FOUNDATIONS OF JUDICIAL POWER
ROOSEVELT, FRANKLIN D.

Genna Rae McNeil
HOUSTON, CHARLES HAMILTON

Salil Mehra
Professor
Temple University, Beasley School of
Law
CORONADO COAL V. UNITED MINE WORKERS, 268 U.S. 295 (1925)

Ajay K. Mehrotra
Associate Professor of Law
Indiana University, Bloomington
BANK OF UNITED STATES V. DEVEAUX, 9 U.S. 61 (1809)

Philip L. Merkel
Professor of Law

Western State University College of
Law
FEDERAL SOVEREIGN IMMUNITY
GERTZ V. ROBERT WELCH, INC., 418 U.S. 323 (1974)

William G. Merkel
Associate Professor of Law
Washburn Law School
RAISING ARMIES
SECOND AMENDMENT

Gillian E. Metzger
Professor of Law
Columbia Law School
VERMONT YANKEE NUCLEAR POWER CORP. V. NATURAL RESOURCES DEFENSE COUNCIL, 435 U.S. 519 (1978)

Susan Gluck Mezey
Professor, Department of Political
Science
Loyola University Chicago
REHABILITATION ACT OF 1973
SOUTHEASTERN COMMUNITY COLLEGE V. DAVIS, 442 U.S. 397 (1979)
UAW V. JOHNSON CONTROLS, 499 U.S. 187 (1991)
WASHINGTON V. GLUCKSBERG, 521 U.S. 702 (1997)

Robert A. Mikos
Professor of Law
Vanderbilt University Law School
UNITED STATES V. BUTLER, 297 U.S. 1 (1936)

Martha Minow
Jeremiah Smith Jr. Professor of Law
Harvard University
PIERCE V. SOCIETY OF SISTERS, 268 U.S. 510 (1925)

Reginald Mombrun
Associate Professor of Law
North Carolina Central University
School of Law
SCALIA, ANTONIN

William V. Moore
Distinguished Professor, Political
Science
College of Charleston
VOTING RIGHTS ACT OF 1965 AND ITS AMENDMENTS

Rachel F. Moran
Robert D. and Leslie-Kay Raven
Professor of Law

University of California, Berkeley
(Boalt Hall)
BUSING
EDUCATION AND THE CONSTITUTION

Juliet Moringiello
Professor
Widener University School of Law
MGM STUDIOS, INC. V. GROKSTER,
LTD., 545 U.S. 913 (2005)

Jeffrey E. Morrison
Ph.D. Candidate, History Department
Georgia State University
GARRISON, WILLIAM LLOYD

Lance David Muckey
Doctoral Candidate, Department of
History
University of Nevada, Las Vegas
COHENS V. VIRGINIA, 19 U.S. 264
(1821)
HEALY V. JAMES, 408 U.S. 169 (1972)

Bruce Allen Murphy
Fred Morgan Kirby Professor of Civil
Rights
Lafayette College
EXTRAJUDICIAL ACTIVITIES

Richard W. Murphy
Professor of Law
William Mitchell College of Law
UNITED STATES V. MEAD CORPORA-
TION, 533 U.S. 218 (2001)

Walter F. Murphy
McCormick Professor of Jurisprudence
(Emeritus)
Princeton University
STARE DECISIS

Melissa Murray
Assistant Professor of Law
Boalt Hall School of Law, University of
California, Berkeley
QUILLOIN V. WALCOTT, 434 U.S. 246
(1978)

Carol Nackenoff
Professor, Department of Political
Science
Swarthmore College
U.S. TERM LIMITS, INC. V. THORN-
TON, 514 U.S. 779 (1995)
VIRGINIA V. BLACK, 538 U.S. 343
(2003)

Premilla Nadasen
Associate Professor of History

Queens College, University of New
York
WELFARE AND WOMEN

Robert F. Nagel
Ira C. Rothgerber, Jr., Professor of
Constitutional Law
University of Colorado School of Law
FEDERALISM
PRINTZ V. UNITED STATES, 521 U.S.
898 (1997)

John Copeland Nagle
John N. Matthews Professor of Law
Notre Dame Law School
SEVERABILITY
TWENTIETH AMENDMENT

John B. Nann
Associate Librarian, School of Law
Yale University
ELECTRONIC RESOURCES

Robert G. Natelson
Professor of Law
University of Montana
MAGNA CARTA

Rebecca Nathanson
James E. Rogers Professor of Education
& Law
University of Nevada, Las Vegas
EDUCATION FOR ALL HANDICAPPED
CHILDREN ACT OF 1975 (EAHCA)

John Neiman
Counsel, Bradley Arant Rose & White
LLP.
Adjunct Professor of Law, University of
Alabama
HAND, LEARNED

David L. Nersessian
Executive Director
Harvard Law School Program on the
Legal Profession
APPOINTMENT OF ATTORNEYS
BRIEFS
JUDICIAL BUDGET
JUDICIAL CONFERENCE OF THE
UNITED STATES
PUBLIC UNDERSTANDING OF SUPREME
COURT
STAFF OF THE SUPREME COURT
SUPREME COURT HISTORICAL SOCIETY
SUPREME COURT REPORTER

Roger K. Newman
Professor, Graduate School of
Journalism
Columbia University
BLACK, HUGO

Brent E. Newton
Visiting Professor of Law
University of Houston Law Center
EIGHTH AMENDMENT
PROFESSIONAL BASEBALL CASES
RETROACTIVITY
SUBSTANTIVE DUE PROCESS

Lynnette Noblitt
Associate Professor
Department of Government, Eastern
Kentucky University
GOVERNMENT EMPLOYEES
TERRITORIES
UNCONSTITUTIONAL AS APPLIED

Jill Norgren
Professor Emerita, John Jay College of
Criminal Justice and the Graduate
School and University Center
City University of New York
CHEROKEE NATION V. GEORGIA, 30
U.S. 1 (1831)
WOMEN PRACTICING IN FRONT OF
THE COURT
WORCESTER V. GEORGIA, 31 U.S. 515
(1832)

Sheldon M. Novick
Adjunct Professor of Law and History
Vermont Law School
CONSTITUTION OF THE UNITED
STATES
HOLMES, OLIVER W.
ROOSEVELT, THEODORE
TAFT, WILLIAM H.

Ruth O'Brien
Professor & Executive Officer, Political
Science MA/Ph.D Program
Graduate Center of the City University
of New York
DISABILITY

Johnathan O'Neill
Assistant Professor of History
Georgia Southern University
JUDICIAL RESTRAINT

Timothy J. O'Neill
Tower Hestor Chair in Political
Science
Southwestern University
REGENTS OF UNIVERSITY OF CALIFOR-
NIA V. BAKKE, 438 U.S. 265 (1978)

Michael A. Olivas
William B. Bates Distinguished Chair
of Law; Director, Institute of Higher
Education Law & Governance

University of Houston Law Center
BOARD OF CURATORS OF THE UNIV.
OF MISSOURI V. HOROWITZ, 435
U.S. 78 (1978)
COLLEGES AND UNIVERSITIES
NON-CITIZENS AND FEDERALISM

Nathan B. Oman
Assistant Professor of Law
William & Mary Law School
CHURCH OF JESUS CHRIST OF
LATTER-DAY SAINTS

Angela Onwuachi-Willig
Professor of Law
University of Iowa College of Law
THOMAS, CLARENCE

Craig N. Oren
Professor of Law
Rutgers School of Law
AIR POLLUTION
IMMIGRATION AND NATURALIZATION
SERVICE V. CHADHA, 462 U.S. 919
(1983)

Norman Ornstein
Resident Scholar
American Enterprise Institute for
Public Policy
CAMPAIGN FINANCE

John V. Orth
William Rand Kenan Jr. Professor of
Law
University of North Carolina–Chapel
Hill
ELEVENTH AMENDMENT
FEDERAL COMMON LAW JURISDICTION
GELPCKE V. DUBUQUE, 68 U.S. 175
(1864)
NORTHWEST ORDINANCE
PAPASAN V. ALLAIN, 478 U.S. 265
(1986)
PENNHURST STATE SCHOOL & HOS-
PITAL V. HALDERMAN, 465 U.S. 89
(1984)
PROPERTY RIGHTS

Richard L. Pacelle, Jr.
Professor and Chair, Department of
Political Science
Georgia Southern University
DOCKET
WRIT OF CERTIORARI

Chester Pach
Department of History
Ohio University
EISENHOWER, DWIGHT D.

Kunal M. Parker
James A. Thomas Distinguished
Professor of Law
Cleveland–Marshall College of Law,
Cleveland State University
PROGRESSIVE ERA IMMIGRATION AND
NATURALIZATION

Michael Parrish
Professor of History
University of California, San Diego
BRIDGES V. UNITED STATES, 346 U.S.
209 (1953)
NEW DEAL AND THE ECONOMY
SCHNEIDERMAN V. UNITED STATES,
320 U.S. 118 (1943)

Ellen Frankel Paul
Professor of Political Science; Deputy
Director, Social Philosophy and Policy
Center
Bowling Green State University
ROTARY INTERNATIONAL V. ROTARY
CLUB OF DUARTE, 481 U.S. 537
(1987)

James W. Paulsen
Professor
South Texas College of Law
INTERNATIONAL SHOE CO. V. WA-
SHINGTON, 326 U.S. 310 (1945)
LAWRENCE V. TEXAS, 539 U.S. 558
(2003)

Bruce G. Peabody
Associate Professor, Department of
Social Sciences and History
Fairleigh Dickinson University
TWENTY-FIFTH AMENDMENT
TWENTY-SECOND AMENDMENT

Eric Pearson
Professor of Law
Creighton University School of Law
ILLINOIS CENTRAL RAILROAD V.
ILLINOIS, 146 U.S. 387 (1892)

Robert V. Percival
Robert F. Stanton Professor of Law and
Director, Environmental Law Program
The University of Maryland School of
Law
GEORGIA V. TENNESSEE COPPER CO.,
206 U.S. 230 (1907)

Barbara A. Perry
Carter Glass Professor of Government
Sweet Briar College
SUPREME COURT AND POPULAR
CULTURE

Twila L. Perry
Professor of Law and Judge Alexander
T. Waugh Sr. Scholar
Rutgers University School of Law
KIRCHBERG V. FEENSTRA, 450 U.S.
455 (1981)

Shawn Francis Peters
School of Education
University of Wisconsin, Madison
BOARD OF EDUCATION V. ALLEN, 392
U.S. 236 (1968)
EDWARDS V. AGUILLARD, 482 U.S.
578 (1987)
EPPERSON V. ARKANSAS, 393 U.S. 97
(1968)

Todd E. Pettys
Professor of Law
University of Iowa College of Law
LAISSEZ-FAIRE

James E. Pfander
Professor of Law
Northwestern University School of
Law
JURISDICTION
ORIGINAL JURISDICTION

Huyen Pham
Professor
Texas Wesleyan University School of
Law
NON-CITIZENS AND EQUAL
PROTECTION (STATE)

Stuart Phillips
Author
Clarksdale, Mississippi
HARLAN, JOHN MARSHALL, II
HUGHES COURT

Richard Pierce
Lyle T. Alverson Professor of Law
George Washington University
FOOD AND DRUG ADMINISTRATION V.
BROWN & WILLIAMSON TOBACCO
CORP., 529 U.S. 120 (2000)

Lydie Nadia Cabrera Pierre-Louis
Assistant Professor of Law
St. Thomas University School of Law
CORPORATE LAW

Richard H. Pildes
Sudler Family Professor of
Constitutional Law
New York University School of Law
APPORTIONMENT

Ngai Pindell
Professor of Law
William S. Boyd School of Law
LORETTO V. TELEPROMPTER MAN-
HATTAN CATV CORP., 458 U.S.
419 (1982)

Richard M. Pious
Adolph and Effie Ochs Professor
Barnard College, Columbia University
RASUL V. BUSH, 542 U.S. 466 (2004)

Lucas A. Powe, Jr.
Anne Green Regents Chair in Law and
Professor of Government
The University of Texas
BROWN V. BOARD OF EDUCATION
(BROWN II), 349 U.S. 294 (1955)
DOUGLAS, WILLIAM O.
GOOD BEHAVIOR
NAIM V. NAIM, 350 U.S. 985 (1956)
TWENTY-SIXTH AMENDMENT

Cedric Merlin Powell
Professor of Law, Louis D. Brandeis
School of Law
University of Louisville
MISSOURI V. JENKINS (MISSOURI III),
515 U.S. 70 (1995)
NEW YORK TIMES CO. V. UNITED
STATES, 403 U.S. 713 (1971)

Garrett Power
Professor Emeritus, School of Law
University of Maryland
REGULATORY TAKINGS

Stephen B. Presser
Raoul Berger Professor of Legal History
Northwestern University School of
Law
JEFFERSON, THOMAS
SWIFT V. TYSON, 41 U.S. 1 (1842)

Adam C. Pritchard
Professor of Law
University of Michigan
DEFINITION OF A SECURITY
ERNST & ERNST V. HOCHFELDER,
425 U.S. 185 (1976)
SECURITIES AND EXCHANGE COMMIS-
SION V. RALSTON PURINA, 346 U.S.
119 (1953)

Norman Provizer
Professor of Political Science
Metropolitan State College of Denver
CITY OF MOBILE V. BOLDEN, 446 U.S.
55 (1980)

Paul M. Pruitt, Jr.
Special Collections Librarian

Bounds Law Library, University of
Alabama
BRYCE, JAMES
NAACP V. ALABAMA, 357 U.S. 449
(1958)

Linda Przybyszewski
Associate Professor, Department of
History
University of Notre Dame
CHASE COURT
HARLAN, JOHN MARSHALL

Steve Puro
Professor, Department of Political
Science
St. Louis University
HARPER V. VIRGINIA BOARD OF ELEC-
TIONS, 383 U.S. 663 (1966)

David W. Raack
Professor of Law
Ohio Northern University
KENT, JAMES

Ofer Raban
Assistant Professor of Law
University of Oregon School of Law
GERRYMANDERING

Mitzi Ramos
Doctoral Candidate, Department of
Political Science
University of Illinois at Chicago
O'CONNOR, SANDRA DAY

Gautham Rao
Doctoral Candidate
University of Chicago
FUGITIVE SLAVE CLAUSE

Chris Rasmussen
Associate Professor, School of History,
Political Science, and International
Studies
Fairleigh Dickinson University
WICKARD V. FILBURN, 317 U.S. 111
(1942)

John David Rausch, Jr.
Associate Professor, Department of
Political Science and Criminal Justice
West Texas A&M University
ROBERTS, OWEN J.

Adam Ravitch
Law Clerk
United States District Court, District
of Nevada
LARSON V. VALENTE, 456 U.S. 228
(1982)

Frank S. Ravitch
Professor of Law
Michigan State University College of
Law
CEREMONIAL DEISM
SHERBERT V. VERNER, 374 U.S. 398
(1963)

Ryan A. Ray
Juris Doctor Candidate
University of Arkansas School of Law
DOLAN V. CITY OF TIGARD, 512 U.S.
374 (1994)

William Reynolds
Professor
University of Maryland School of Law
MGM STUDIOS, INC. V. GROKSTER,
LTD., 545 U.S. 913 (2005)

Deborah L. Rhode
Ernest W. McFarland Professor of Law,
and Director, Stanford Center on
Ethics
Stanford Law School
CRAIG V. BOREN, 429 U.S. 190 (1976)

Neil M. Richards
Associate Professor of Law
Washington University School of Law
MISSOURI V. HOLLAND, 252 U.S. 416
(1920)
REHNQUIST, WILLIAM

Sandra L. Rierson
Assistant Professor
Thomas Jefferson School of Law
MEYER V. NEBRASKA, 262 U.S. 390
(1923)
PALKO V. CONNECTICUT, 302 U.S.
319 (1937)

Lori Ringhand
Associate Professor
University of Kentucky College of Law
KENNEDY, ANTHONY

R. Volney Riser
Assistant Professor of History
University of West Alabama
NAACP LEGAL DEFENSE FUND
POWELL V. ALABAMA, 287 U.S. 45
(1932)

Cassandra Burke Robertson
Assistant Professor of Law
Case Western Reserve University
JUDICIAL PAY

David Brian Robertson
Professor, Department of Political
Science

University of Missouri–St. Louis
ANTI-FEDERALIST/FEDERALIST RATIFI-
CATION DEBATE
GREAT COMPROMISE

Lindsay G. Robertson
Orpha and Maurice Merrill Professor
of Law and History
University of Oklahoma
JOHNSON V. M'INTOSH, 21 U.S. 543
(1823)

Donald Roper
Associate Professor, Emeritus
State University of New York at New
Paltz
JOHNSON, WILLIAM
TANEY COURT

Kenneth M. Rosen
Associate Professor
The University of Alabama School of
Law
SECURITIES AND EXCHANGE
COMMISSION

Jason Ross
Doctoral Candidate
Georgetown University
ZOBREST V. CATALINA FOOTHILLS
SCHOOL DIST., 509 U.S. 1
(1993)

William G. Ross
Professor of Law
Cumberland School of Law, Samford
University
CHAMPION V. AMES, 188 U.S. 321
(1903)
COPPAGE V. KANSAS, 236 U.S. 1
(1915)
DAVIS, JOHN W.
HUGHES, CHARLES E.
MOREHEAD V. TIPALDO, 298 U.S. 587
(1936)
PARKER, JOHN
PROGRESSIVE ERA WORKER
REGULATION
SUTHERLAND, GEORGE

Jim Rossi
Professor and Associate Dean for
Research
Florida State University College of Law
NONDELEGATION DOCTRINE

Ralph A. Rossum
Professor
Claremont McKenna College
DUAL FEDERALISM
SEVENTEENTH AMENDMENT

Allen Rostron
Associate Professor, School of Law
University of Missouri–Kansas City
JEHOVAH'S WITNESSES
RIGHT TO LIFE

Kyndra Rotunda
Visiting Assistant Professor of Law
Chapman University School of
Law–Orange, California
SPENDING CLAUSE

Ronald D. Rotunda
University Professor and Professor of
Law
George Mason University School of
Law
DORMANT COMMERCE CLAUSE

Judith Royster
Professor of Law, College of Law
University of Tulsa
LONE WOLF V. HITCHCOCK, 187 U.S.
553 (1903)

Sandra C. Ruffin
Visiting Associate Professor of Law
Saint Thomas University School of
Law, Miami
LEGAL PROCESS

Sharon E. Rush
Irving Cypen Professor of Law
University of Florida, Levin College of
Law
BENDER V. WILLIAMSPORT AREA
SCHOOL DISTRICT, 475 U.S. 534
(1986)
COLUMBUS BOARD OF EDUCATION V.
PENICK, 443 U.S. 449 (1979)
KEYISHIAN V. BOARD OF REGENTS,
385 U.S. 589 (1967)
KRAMER V. UNION FREE SCHOOL
DISTRICT, 395 U.S. 621 (1961)

J. B. Ruth
Matthews & Hawkins Professor of
Property
The Florida State University College of
Law
ENDANGERED SPECIES

Tuan Samahon
Associate Professor
William S. Boyd School of Law,
University of Nevada, Las Vegas
BOWSHER V. SYNAR, 478 U.S. 714
(1986)
MICHIGAN V. LONG, 463 U.S. 1032
(1983)

SUPREME COURT OF NEW HAMPSHIRE
V. PIPER, 470 U.S. 274 (1985)

A. K. Sandoval-Strausz
Associate Professor of History
University of New Mexico
CIVIL RIGHTS ACT OF 1866
HEART OF ATLANTA MOTEL V. UNITED
STATES, 379 U.S. 241 (1964)
RECONSTRUCTION ERA CIVIL RIGHTS
ACTS

Kurt M. Saunders
Associate Professor of Business Law
California State University, Northridge
DIVERSITY JURISDICTION

Logan E. Sawyer, III
Fellow
Georgetown University Law Center
JUDICIAL REVIEW OF ADMINISTRATIVE
ACTION
PROGRESSIVE ERA BUSINESS
REGULATION

John M. Scheb, II
Professor and Interim Head of Political
Science
University of Tennessee, Knoxville
TEN COMMANDMENTS

Reuel E. Schiller
Professor of Law
University of California, Hastings
College of the Law
ABOOD V. DETROIT BOARD OF EDU-
CATION, 431 U.S. 209 (1977)
CLEVELAND BRD. OF EDUCATION V.
LOUDERMILL, 470 U.S. 532 (1985)
FAIR LABOR STANDARDS ACT

Mark G. Schmeller
Assistant Professor of History
Northeastern Illinois University
JUDICIARY ACT OF 1801
REPEAL ACT OF 1802

Christopher W. Schmidt
Visiting Scholar
American Bar Foundation
ADDERLEY V. FLORIDA, 385 U.S. 39
(1966)
ASHWANDER V. TENNESSEE VALLEY
AUTHORITY, 297 U.S. 288 (1936)
CARTER V. CARTER COAL, 298 U.S.
238 (1936)
COLD WAR

Matthew M. Schneider
Assistant Professor, Department of
Political Science

University of Tennessee, Knoxville
FEDERAL TRADE COMMISSION V.
KEPPEL & BROTHERS, INC., 291
U.S. 304 (1934)

Paul M. Schoenhard
Associate
Ropes & Gray LLP
COMMERCIAL SPEECH

Herman Schwartz
Professor
American University–Washington
College of Law
INFLUENCE OF SUPREME COURT
ABROAD

Wendy Scott
Professor, School of Law
North Carolina Central University
INTERSECTIONS OF RACE AND GENDER

Judith A. M. Scully
Professor of Law
West Virginia University
BUCK V. BELL, 274 U.S. 200 (1927)
EUGENICS

Alfreda A. Sellers Diamond
Revius O. Ortique Professor of Law
Southern University Law Center
AID TO PAROCHIAL SCHOOLS

Barry Alan Shain
Associate Professor of Political Science
Colgate University
DECLARATION OF INDEPENDENCE

Peter M. Shane
Jacob E. Davis and Jacob E. Davis II
Chair in Law
Moritz College of Law, The Ohio State
University
ELECTORAL COLLEGE
PENNSYLVANIA V. NELSON, 350 U.S.
497 (1956)
PERRY V. SINDERMANN, 408 U.S. 593
(1972)

Fred R. Shapiro
Associate Librarian for Collections and
Access and Lecturer in Legal Research
Yale Law School
RANKING THE JUSTICES

Jamelle C. Sharpe
Bigelow Teaching Fellow and Lecturer
in Law
University of Chicago Law School
CONTRACTS CLAUSE

Robert E. Shepherd, Jr.
Emeritus Professor of Law
University of Richmond Law School
PERRY EDUCATION ASSOCIATION V.
PERRY LOCAL EDUCATORS' ASSOCI-
ATION, 460 U.S. 37 (1983)
PICKERING V. BOARD OF EDUCATION,
391 U.S. 563 (1968)

Brie D. Sherwin
Attorney
Gardere Wynne Sewell LLP
MORGAN V. UNITED STATES TRILOGY

Robert T. Sherwin
Visiting Associate Professor of Law
Texas Wesleyan University School of
Law
44 LIQUORMART, INC. V. RHODE
ISLAND, 517 U.S. 484 (1996)
GARCETTI V. CEBALLOS, 547 U.S. 410
(2006)
WISCONSIN V. MITCHELL, 508 U.S.
476 (1993)

Rebecca S. Shoemaker
Professor Emeritus of History
Indiana State University
FULLER COURT
FULLER, MELVILLE
WABASH, ST. LOUIS & PACIFIC RAIL-
WAY V. ILLINOIS, 118 U.S. 557
(1886)
WAITE COURT

Christopher Shortell
Assistant Professor of Political Science
California State University, Northridge
STATE SOVEREIGN IMMUNITY

Andrew M. Siegel
Associate Professor of Law
Seattle University School of Law
COMMENTARIES ON THE
CONSTITUTION
IN FORMA PAUPERIS
LAU V. NICHOLS, 414 U.S. 563 (1974)

Stephen A. Siegel
Distinguished Research Professor of
Law
DePaul University College of Law
STRICT SCRUTINY

David J. Siemers
Assistant Professor of Political Science
University of Wisconsin–Oshkosh
ARTICLES OF CONFEDERATION

Katharine B. Silbaugh
Associate Professor

Boston University School of Law
CALIFANO V. WESTCOTT, 443 U.S. 76
(1979)
CLEVELAND BOARD OF EDUCATION V.
LAFLEUR, 414 U.S. 632 (1974)

Gordon Silverstein
Assistant Professor of Political Science
University of California, Berkeley
ARTICLE II

Mark Silverstein
Professor, Political Science Department
Boston University
BORK, ROBERT
CONFIRMATION PROCESS

David M. Skover
Dean's Distinguished Scholar and
Professor of Constitutional Law
Seattle University School of Law
ROTH V. UNITED STATES, 354 U.S.
476 (1957)

Bradley A. Smith
Professor of Law
Capital University Law School
FREEDOM OF PETITION
MCCONNELL V. FEDERAL ELECTION
COMMISSION, 540 U.S. 93 (2003)

Christopher E. Smith
Professor, School of Criminal Justice
Michigan State University
MURPHY, FRANK

Damon Y. Smith
Assistant Professor
Rutgers School of Law–Camden
BUCHANAN V. WARLEY, 245 U.S. 60
(1917)

Robert Samuel Smith
Assistant Professor, Department of
Africana Studies
University of North Carolina at
Charlotte
MORRILL ACT

Rodney A. Smolla
Dean
Washington and Lee University School
of Law
HUSTLER MAGAZINE V. FALWELL, 485
U.S. 46 (1988)
LIBEL
MAJORITY OPINIONS
NEW YORK TIMES V. SULLIVAN, 376
U.S. 254 (1964)
UNITED STATES V. O'BRIEN, 391 U.S.
367 (1968)

Sylvia Snowiss
Professor Emerita, Department of
Political Science
California State University, Northridge
   THAYER, JAMES BRADLEY

Geoff J. Sogi
Class of 2009
William S. Richardson School of Law,
University of Hawaii
   KOREMATSU V. UNITED STATES, 323
   U.S. 214 (1944)

Aviam Soifer
Dean and Professor
William S. Richardson School of Law,
University of Hawai'i
   HILL, OLIVER WHITE

Ilya Somin
Assistant Professor of Law
George Mason University School of
Law
   PUBLIC USE
   YEE V. CITY OF ESCONDIDO, 503 U.S.
   519 (1992)

Bartholomew H. Sparrow
Associate Professor, Department of
Government
The University of Texas at Austin
   ADMISSION OF NEW STATES CLAUSE
   INSULAR CASES

Clyde Spillenger
Professor, School of Law
University of California, Los Angeles
   ACKERMAN, BRUCE

Vasilios Spyridakis
Former Editor in Chief
*Immigration and Nationality Law
Review*
   DETENTION OF NON-CITIZENS IN
      DEPORTATION PROCEEDINGS
   NATURALIZATION POWER
   NON-CITIZENS AND EQUAL PROTEC-
      TION (FEDERAL)

Kevin M. Stack
Professor of Law
Vanderbilt University Law School
   SECURITIES AND EXCHANGE COMMIS-
      SION V. CHENERY, 318 U.S. 80
      (1943)

Maxwell Stearns
Marbury Research Professor of Law
University of Maryland School of Law
   DICTA
   RULE OF FOUR
   STANDING

David L. Stebenne
Associate Professor of History and
Adjunct Professor of Law
Ohio State University
   GOLDBERG, ARTHUR J.

Tracy L. Steffes
Assistant Professor of Education and
History
Brown University
   INGRAHAM V. WRIGHT, 430 U.S. 651
   (1977)

Edward Stein
Professor, Cardozo School of Law
Yeshiva University, New York
   MISCEGENATION

Mark E. Steiner
Professor of Law, South Texas College
of Law
Houston, Texas
   SLAUGHTER-HOUSE CASES, 83 U.S. 36
   (1873)

Marc D. Stern
General Counsel
American Jewish Congress
   RELIGIOUS SPEECH IN PUBLIC
      SCHOOLS

Stephen Stetson
Attorney at Law
Tuscaloosa, Alabama
   AMERICAN CIVIL LIBERTIES UNION
      (ACLU)
   FIFTH AMENDMENT

Lee J. Strang
Visiting Associate Professor of Law
Michigan State University College of
Law
   CHISHOLM V. GEORGIA, 2 U.S. 419
      (1793)
   EX PARTE MCCARDLE, 74 U.S. 506
      (1869)
   MITCHELL V. HELMS, 530 U.S. 793
      (2000)

Peter L. Strauss
Betts Professor of Law
Columbia Law School
   APPOINTMENT AND REMOVAL OF
      EXECUTIVE OFFICERS
   CITIZENS TO PRESERVE OVERTON
      PARK V. VOLPE, 401 U.S. 402
      (1971)
   HUMPHREY'S EXECUTOR V. UNITED
      STATES, 295 U.S. 602 (1935)

Philippa Strum
Director
Woodrow Wilson International Center
for Scholars
   BRANDEIS, LOUIS
   FRANKFURTER, FELIX
   UNITED STATES V. VIRGINIA, 518 U.S.
   515 (1996)

Catherine Struve
Professor
University of Pennsylvania Law School
   JUDICIARY ACT OF 1891

Kathleen S. Sullivan
Professor and Pre-Law Advisor
Ohio University
   INTERMEDIATE SCRUTINY

Scott E. Sundby
Professor of Law
Washington and Lee University
   DUNCAN V. LOUISIANA, 391 U.S. 145
   (1968)

Erwin C. Surrency
Professor of Law and Director of Law
Library, Emeritus
University of Georgia School of Law
   CAMPBELL, JOHN
   ELECTION OF 1876
   PRIZE CASES

Martin J. Sweet
Honors College
Florida Atlantic University
   CITY OF RICHMOND V. J.A. CROSON
      CO., 488 U.S. 469 (1989)

David S. Tanenhaus
James E. Rogers Professor of History
and Law
William S. Boyd School of Law,
University of Nevada, Las Vegas
   BURGER COURT
   DENNIS V. UNITED STATES, 341 U.S.
   494 (1951)
   IN RE GAULT, 387 U.S. 1 (1967)
   SEX DISCRIMINATION

Karen M. Tani
Doctoral Candidate, Department of
History
University of Pennsylvania
   GOLDBERG V. KELLY, 397 U.S. 254
   (1970)
   LALLI V. LALLI, 439 U.S. 259 (1978)
   MATHEWS V. ELDRIDGE, 424 U.S. 319
   (1976)

A. Dan Tarlock
Distinguished Professor of Law
Chicago–Kent College of Law
  EQUITABLE APPORTIONMENT OF
    WATER RESOURCES AMONG STATES

G. Alan Tarr
Professor, Department of Political
Science
Rutgers University–Camden
  JACKSON V. METROPOLITAN EDISON,
    419 U.S. 345 (1974)
  STATE COURTS

Andrew E. Taslitz
Professor
Howard University School of Law
  FERGUSON V. CITY OF CHARLESTON,
    532 U.S. 67 (2001)

Kellye Y. Testy
Dean
Seattle University School of Law
  BRIGGS V. SPAULDING, 141 U.S. 132
    (1891)

Joseph Thai
Presidential Professor
University of Oklahoma College of
Law
  STEVENS, JOHN PAUL

George Thomas
Assistant Professor, Department of
Government
Claremont Mckenna College
  CONSTITUTIONAL CONVENTION,
    FRAMING
  FEDERALIST PAPERS

Tracy A. Thomas
Professor, School of Law
University of Akron
  WOMEN'S SUFFRAGE

Rebecca U. Thorpe
Ph.D. Candidate, Government &
Politics
University of Maryland, College Park
  TOCQUEVILLE, ALEXIS DE

Debora L. Threedy
Professor of Law
S. J. Quinney College of Law,
University of Utah
  NEBBIA V. NEW YORK, 291 U.S. 502
    (1934)

Donald F. Tibbs
Assistant Professor of Law

Southern University Law Center
  JONES V. NORTH CAROLINA PRISON-
    ERS' LABOR UNION, 433 U.S. 119
    (1977)
  POLLOCK V. WILLIAMS, 322 U.S. 4
    (1944)
  TAYLOR V. GEORGIA, 315 U.S. 25
    (1942)

James J. Tomkovicz
Edward F. Howrey Professor of Law
University of Iowa College of Law
  GIDEON V. WAINWRIGHT, 372 U.S.
    335 (1963)

Bernard Trujillo
Professor of Law
Valparaiso University
  NON-CITIZENS AND CIVIL LIBERTIES

Robert L. Tsai
Associate Professor
American University, Washington
College of Law
  CHAMBERS V. FLORIDA, 309 U.S. 227
    (1940)
  FIRST AMENDMENT
  PUBLIC FORUM

Alexander Tsesis
Assistant Professor of Law
Loyola University of Chicago–School
of Law
  ANTI-SLAVERY CONSTITUTIONALISM
  THIRTEENTH AMENDMENT

David L. Tubbs
Assistant Professor of Politics
King's College, New York City
  CONTRACEPTION

Arianna Tunsky-Brashich
Senior Articles Editor 2008–2009
Boston College Third World Law
Journal
  ULTRA VIRES DOCTRINE
  WORLD WAR II AND THE GROWTH OF
    INDIVIDUAL RIGHTS

Kara Miles Turner
Associate Dean, College of Liberal Arts
Morgan State University
  BROWN V. BOARD OF EDUCATION,
    347 U.S. 483 (1954)

Mark V. Tushnet
William Nelson Cromwell Professor of
Law
Harvard Law School
  CONSTITUTIONALISM
  JUDICIAL REVIEW

  MARSHALL, THURGOOD
  REHNQUIST COURT
  WORLD WAR II AND THE GROWTH OF
    CIVIL RIGHTS

Melvin I. Urofsky
Professor of Law and Public Policy
Virginia Commonwealth University
  BRANDEIS BRIEF

Jon M. Van Dyke
Professor of Law, William S.
Richardson School of Law
University of Hawaii at Manoa
  BILL OF RIGHTS
  TRIBE, LAURENCE

Theodore M. Vestal
Professor, Department of Political
Science
Oklahoma State University
  BRENNAN, WILLIAM J., JR.
  WARREN, EARL
  WIEMAN V. UPDEGRAFF, 344 U.S. 183
    (1952)

John R. Vile
Professor and Chair, Department of
Political Science
Middle Tennessee State University
  SEPARATION OF POWERS

Michael Vitiello
Distinguished Professor and Scholar
University of the Pacific, McGeorge
School of Law
  GONZALES V. RAICH, 545 U.S. 1
    (2005)
  MCNABB V. UNITED STATES, 318 U.S.
    332 (1943)
  SCHEIDLER V. NATIONAL ORGANIZA-
    TION FOR WOMEN, 547 U.S. 9
    (2006)
  UNITED STATES V. CAROLENE PRO-
    DUCTS, 304 U.S. 144 (1938)
  WECHSLER, HERBERT

Stephen I. Vladeck
Associate Professor
American University, Washington
College of Law
  RUMSFELD V. PADILLA, 542 U.S. 426
    (2004)

David M. Wagner
Professor
Regent University School of Law
  LICENSING LAWS

Randy Wagner
Independent Researcher

Vancouver, Washington
FLAG BURNING
LEGAL REALISM

Paul J. Wahlbeck
Professor of Political Science
George Washington University
CONFERENCE OF THE JUSTICES
DISCUSS LIST

Peter Wallenstein
Professor, Department of History
Virginia Polytechnic Institute and State
University
LOVING V. VIRGINIA, 388 U.S. 1
(1967)

Camille Walsh
Ph.D. Candidate, Department of
History
University of Oregon
BEREA COLLEGE V. COMMONWEALTH
OF KENTUCKY, 211 U.S. 45 (1908)
DAVIS V. MONROE COUNTY BOARD OF
EDUCATION, 526 U.S. 629 (1999)
EDUCATION AMENDMENTS OF 1972
(TITLE IX)
EDWARDS V. CALIFORNIA, 314 U.S.
160 (1941)
GONZALES V. OREGON, 546 U.S. 243
(2006)
KADRMAS V. DICKINSON PUBLIC
SCHOOLS, 487 U.S. 450 (1988)
MISSISSIPPI UNIVERSITY FOR WOMEN
V. HOGAN, 458 U.S. 718 (1982)
RESEGREGATION
SAN ANTONIO INDEPENDENT SCHOOL
DISTRICT V. RODRIGUEZ, 411 U.S.
1 (1973)
VERNONIA SCHOOL DISTRICT V. AC-
TON, 515 U.S. 646 (1995)
ZABLOCKI V. REDHAIL, 434 U.S. 374
(1978)

Artemus Ward
Associate Professor, Department of
Political Science
Northern Illinois University
BRADLEY, JOSEPH
CLERKS
FEMALE LAW CLERKS
GENERAL WELFARE CLAUSE
WHITE, BYRON

Leland Ware
Louis L. Redding Chair and Professor
of Law and Public Policy
University of Delaware
ACADEMIC FREEDOM
BETTS V. BRADY, 316 U.S. 455
(1942)
GREENBERG, JACK

GRIFFIN V. COUNTY SCHOOL BOARD
OF PRINCE EDWARD COUNTY, 377
U.S. 218 (1964)
GRUTTER V. BOLLINGER, 539 U.S.
306 (2003)/GRATZ V. BOLLINGER,
539 U.S. 244 (2003)
JONES V. ALFRED H. MAYER CO., 392
U.S. 409 (1968)
KEYES V. SCHOOL DISTRICT NO.1,
DENVER, COLORADO, 413 U.S. 189
(1973)
MCLAURIN V. OKLAHOMA STATE
REGENTS, 339 U.S. 637 (1950)
MISSOURI EX REL GAINES V. CANADA,
305 U.S. 337 (1938)
NABRIT, JAMES
UNITED STATES V. FORDICE, 506 U.S.
717 (1992)
WASHINGTON V. DAVIS, 426 U.S. 229
(1976)
WYGANT V. JACKSON BOARD OF
EDUCATION, 476 U.S. 267
(1986)

Stephen L. Wasby
Professor Emeritus, Department of
Political Science
State University of New York, Albany
LITIGATION CAMPAIGNS
TEST CASE

Andrew J. Waskey
Professor, Department of Social
Science
Dalton State College
ALITO, SAMUEL
BLASPHEMY
ELLSWORTH COURT
ENGLISH CONSTITUTIONALISM
EX POST FACTO LAWS
HISS, ALGER
RAILROADS
SUPREME COURT BUILDING

Howard M. Wasserman
Associate Professor of Law
Florida International University
College of Law
SUBSIDIZED SPEECH

Bradley C. S. Watson
Philip M. McKenna Professor of
American and Western Political
Thought
Saint Vincent College
BLACKMUN, HARRY

Russell L. Weaver
Professor of Law & Distinguished
University Scholar

University of Louisville, Louis D.
Brandeis School of Law
ADMINISTRATIVE AGENCIES
ADMINISTRATIVE PROCEDURE ACT
CANTWELL V. CONNECTICUT, 310
U.S. 296 (1940)
MARRIAGE
POLICE POWER
ROBERTS V. UNITED STATES JAYCEES,
468 U.S. 609 (1984)
SEARCH AND SEIZURE
SEDITIOUS LIBEL

Derek Webb
Post-Doctoral Fellow, James Madison
Program in American Ideals and
Institutions
Princeton University
LINCOLN, ABRAHAM

Robert Weisberg
Edwin E. Huddleson Jr. Professor of
Law
Stanford University
CAPITAL PUNISHMENT
FURMAN V. GEORGIA, 408 U.S. 238
(1972)
GREGG V. GEORGIA, 428 U.S. 153
(1976)
MCCLESKEY V. KEMP, 481 U.S. 279
(1987)
STRICKLAND V. WASHINGTON, 466
U.S. 668 (1984)

Carol Weisbrod
Ellen Ash Peters Professor
University of Connecticut School of
Law
WISCONSIN V. YODER, 406 U.S. 205
(1972)

Michael L. Wells
Professor
University of Georgia Law School
FLAST V. COHEN, 392 U.S. 83 (1968)

Mark D. Welton
Professor, Department of Law
U.S. Military Academy, West Point
LEAVITT V. JANE L., 520 U.S. 1274
(1997)

Kaimipono Wenger
Assistant Professor
Thomas Jefferson School of Law
UNITED STATES V. SOCONY-VACUUM
OIL CO., 310 U.S. 150 (1940)

Justin Wert
Assistant Professor

University of Oklahoma
  EX PARTE MILLIGAN, 71 U.S. 2 (1866)
  HABEAS CORPUS ACT OF 1867
  HABEAS CORPUS

Robin L. West
Professor of Law
Georgetown University Law Center
  POSITIVE RIGHTS

Robert Westley
Professor, School of Law
Tulane University
  SEXUAL ORIENTATION

Linda J. Wharton
Associate Professor of Political Science
Richard Stockton College of New
Jersey
  GEBSER V. LAGO VISTA INDEPENDENT
    SCHOOL DISTRICT, 524 U.S. 274
    (1998)
  LOS ANGELES DEPARTMENT OF WATER
    AND POWER V. MANHART, 435 U.S
    702 (1978)

Gloria A. Whittico
Director, External Relations and
Community Affairs
Regent University School of Law
  ARTICLE I
  BLACKSTONE, WILLIAM

Keith E. Whittington
Professor, Department of Politics
Princeton University
  AMERICAN SYSTEM
  CHASE IMPEACHMENT
  DEPARTMENTALISM

Bryan H. Wildenthal
Professor
Thomas Jefferson School of Law
  AMENDMENTS, POST-CIVIL WAR
  INCORPORATION DEBATE
  MILLER, SAMUEL
  SHAPIRO V. THOMPSON, 394 U.S. 618
    (1969)
  STATE ACTION
  TRAVEL

Norman R. Williams
Associate Professor of Law
Willamette University College of Law
  NIXON V. UNITED STATES, 506 U.S.
    224 (1993)

R. Owen Williams
Ph.D. Candidate
Yale University
  CHASE, SALMON

COOLEY, THOMAS
FIELD, STEPHEN
TEXAS V. WHITE, 74 U.S. 700 (1869)

Michael Willrich
Associate Professor of History
Brandeis University
  POUND, ROSCOE

John W. Winkle, III
Professor of Political Science
University of Mississippi
  JUDICIARY ACT OF 1875

Alexander Wohl
Adjunct Professor, Department of
Justice, Law, and Society
American University
  BALLARD V. UNITED STATES, 329 U.S.
    187 (1946)
  WARREN COURT

Michael Allan Wolf
Richard E. Nelson Chair in Local
Government Law
University of Florida, Levin College of
Law
  EUCLID V. AMBLER REALTY, 272 U.S.
    365 (1926)
  LUCAS V. SOUTH CAROLINA COASTAL
    COUNCIL, 505 U.S. 1003 (1992)
  LUJAN V. DEFENDERS OF WILDLIFE,
    504 U.S. 555 (1992)

Nancy Woloch
Adjunct Professor
Barnard College, Columbia University
  MULLER V. OREGON, 208 U.S. 412
    (1908)
  PROTECTIVE LEGISLATION FOR
    WOMEN WORKERS

Barbara Bennett Woodhouse
David H. Levin Chair in Family Law,
Director of Center on Children and
Families
Frederic G. Levin College of Law,
University of Florida
  CHILDREN AND THE CONSTITUTION

Larry Yackle
Professor of Law
Boston University
  ADVISORY OPINIONS
  ALDEN V. MAINE, 527 U.S. 706
    (1999)
  BOARD OF TRUSTEES OF THE UNI-
    VERSITY OF ALABAMA V. GARRETT,
    531 U.S. 356 (2001)
  EX PARTE YOUNG, 209 U.S. 123
    (1908)

JUDICIAL IMMUNITY
NEVADA DEPARTMENT OF HUMAN
  RESOURCES V. HIBBS, 538 U.S. 721
  (2003)
SEMINOLE TRIBE OF FLORIDA V.
  FLORIDA, 517 U.S. 44 (1996)
TENNESSEE V. LANE, 541 U.S. 509
  (2004)

David Yalof
Associate Professor of Political Science
The University of Connecticut
  AMERICAN BAR ASSOCIATION
  NOMINATION PROCESS

Eric K. Yamamoto
Professor of Law
William S. Richardson School of Law,
University of Hawaii
  KOREMATSU V. UNITED STATES, 323
    U.S. 214 (1944)

Ellen Liang Yee
Associate Professor
Drake University School of Law
  OHIO V. ROBERTS, 448 U.S. 56
    (1980)

Kyu Ho Youm
Jonathan Marshall First Amendment
Chair Professor
University of Oregon
  PITTSBURGH PRESS V. PITTSBURGH
    COMMISSION ON HUMAN RELA-
    TIONS, 413 U.S. 376 (1973)
  POLICE DEPARTMENT OF CHICAGO V.
    MOSLEY, 408 U.S. 92
    (1972)
  PRIOR RESTRAINT
  THORNHILL V. ALABAMA, 310 U.S. 88
    (1940)

Ernest A. Young
Professor of Law
Duke University Law School
  TENTH AMENDMENT

Gordon G. Young
Marbury Research Professor of Law
University of Maryland School of Law
  JURISDICTION STRIPPING
  UNITED STATES V. KLEIN, 80 U.S. 128
    (1872)

Rosalie R. Young
Associate Professor
State University of New York at
Oswego
  WELFARE STATE

Deborah Zalesne
Professor of Law
City University of New York School of
Law
   ONCALE V. SUNDOWNER OFFSHORE
     SERVICES, 523 U.S. 75 (1998)

David Zarefsky
Professor, Department of
Communication Studies
Northwestern University
   DOUGLAS, STEPHEN

Sara L. Zeigler
Chair and Professor, Department of
Government
Eastern Kentucky University
   ROSTKER V. GOLDBERG, 453 U.S. 57
    (1981)
   SCHLESINGER V. BALLARD, 419 U.S.
    498 (1975)

Franklin E. Zimring
William G. Simon Professor of Law
and Wolfen Distinguished Scholar

University of California, Berkeley
(Boalt Hall)
   GOSS V. LOPEZ, 419 U.S. 565
    (1975)

Simon Zschirnt
Ph.D. Candidate, Department of
Political Science
Washington State University
   RACIAL DISCRIMINATION,
    VOTING

A

ABBOTT LABS V. GARDNER, 387 U.S. 136 (1967)

Abbott Labs v. Gardner, 387 U.S. 136 (1967) is a leading Supreme Court case dealing with the "ripeness doctrine," which prevents courts from ruling on matters that have not yet developed into a form that is appropriate for judicial resolution. In the federal courts, the ripeness doctrine derives in part from Article III of the Constitution, which gives the federal courts jurisdiction over "cases and controversies" but not over abstract questions or hypothetical disputes. Although ripeness concerns can arise in many contexts, one recurring issue—and the one at the heart of the Abbott Labs litigation—is whether a person can seek a review of an administrative regulation before the administrative agency attempts to enforce it.

The *Abbott Labs* case concerned a new Food and Drug Administration (FDA) regulation implementing a federal statute that required drug labels and advertisements to prominently display the drug's generic name. The main purpose of the statute was to inform doctors and patients that many expensive drugs were identical to cheaper generic products. As the FDA interpreted the statute through this new regulation, the generic name had to appear every time the brand name appeared. Several dozen drug companies and their trade association filed a lawsuit against the FDA, contending that the regulation required more extensive use of the generic name than the authorizing statute contemplated. The government argued that the regulation's validity could not be challenged until the agency enforced it against a violator. That is, the government contended that the suit was not "ripe."

The Supreme Court, in an opinion by Justice John Marshall Harlan II, allowed the drug companies' challenge to proceed. The Court first considered whether the specific statutes governing the FDA barred pre-enforcement review. Statutory provisions expressly allowed pre-enforcement judicial review in certain types of situations, but this did not persuade the Court that Congress meant to preclude pre-enforcement review in cases in which the FDA statutes did not mention such review. Having determined that there was no implicit statutory bar to review, the Court turned to more general principles of the ripeness doctrine. The Court stated that the ripeness inquiry has "a twofold aspect, requiring us to evaluate both the fitness of the issues for judicial decision and the hardship to the parties of withholding court consideration."

By applying these standards, the Court determined that the companies' challenge to the regulation could be decided without waiting for any further factual development, because it presented a purely legal question regarding the agency's statutory authority to issue the regulation. Further, turning to the consideration of hardship, the Court stated that the regulation was harming the companies even before enforcement, because in order to comply they would have to spend a great deal of money to prepare new labels. Yet if they did not comply and waited to be cited for a violation, they faced serious penalties. Given the dilemma facing the companies, the Court decided it would be inappropriate to delay a ruling.

Three justices, led by Justice Abe Fortas, sharply dissented. They argued that the statutory scheme did not allow for pre-enforcement review, and that these FDA regulations had to be challenged in the context of an enforcement action. They also contended that even if review were otherwise available under the governing statutes, this particular case did not present a concrete dispute ripe for review. The dissenters warned that the decision would endanger the public by allowing regulated entities to delay for years the implementation of regulations meant to protect public heath and safety, a harm that far outweighed the hardship on the drug companies.

Abbott Labs v. Gardner was decided at the same time as two other related cases involving FDA regulations. One of those cases, *Toilet Goods Assn. v. Gardner*, 387 U.S. 158 (1967), provides a useful contrast. Here, the Court dismissed the suit on ripeness grounds. The lawsuit involved a challenge to the validity of an FDA regulation that required manufacturers of color additives to provide FDA inspectors with access to their facilities and formulas. The Court determined that a proper resolution of the case required further factual development regarding how and why the FDA would carry out the inspections, which the agency had not yet conducted. Turning to the issue of hardships, the Court stated that the regulation did not require the manufacturers to change any of their present processes in order to comply, and that the risk of hardship was too speculative.

The *Abbott Labs* litigation marked an important turning point. Before the case, pre-enforcement review of agency action was rare. Afterwards, it became a familiar feature of the administrative state. In addition, while Abbott Labs arose in the particular context of administrative law, its two-part ripeness inquiry is commonly cited in other contexts as well.

SEE ALSO *Article III; Case or Controversy; Ripeness*

BIBLIOGRAPHY

Levin, Ronald M. 2006. "The Story of the *Abbott Labs* Trilogy: The Seeds of the Ripeness Doctrine." In *Administrative Law Stories*, ed. Peter L. Strauss, pp. 430–479. New York: Foundation Press.

Pierce, Richard J., Jr. 2002. *Administrative Law Treatise*, Vol. 2, chap. 15. 4th edition. New York: Aspen Law & Business.

Aaron-Andrew P. Bruhl

ABINGTON TOWNSHIP V. SCHEMPP, 374 U.S. 203 (1963)

On a September day in 1956, sixteen-year-old Ellory (later changed to Ellery) Schempp refused to participate in morning Bible reading at Abington High School in suburban Philadelphia, Pennsylvania. State law mandated that public school teachers begin each day by reading aloud ten verses from the Bible without comment; the Lord's Prayer was routinely recited afterward. Four other states also had statutes compelling public school districts to read from the Bible and twenty-five more states allowed Bible reading. Edward Schempp, Ellory's father, sued to stop this practice because Bible reading contradicted their Unitarian beliefs and their freedoms under the First and Fourteenth Amendments of the U.S. Constitution.

When *Abington Township v. Schempp*, 374 U.S. 203 (1963) reached the U.S. Supreme Court, it was consolidated with *Murray v. Curlett*, 374 U.S. 203 (1963). Madalyn Murray (later O'Hair) was an unapologetic atheist whose teenaged son, William, III, attended Woodbourne Junior High School in Baltimore, Maryland, where teachers read a chapter from the Bible or recited the Lord's Prayer. Murray sued the school district because the required devotions preferred religious belief over nonbelief. The difference between *Schempp* and the controversial case of the prior year, *Engel v. Vitale*, 370 U.S. 421 (1962), was that in *Schempp* government officials selected the prayer or scripture reading, both of which appeared in the Bible; in *Engel*, the school prayer had been crafted by clergymen at the behest of the New York State Board of Regents, a government body.

In oral argument before the U.S. Supreme Court, attorneys for the states of Pennsylvania and Maryland argued that required Bible readings and prayers were not intended as religious exercises but contributed in important secular ways to a well-rounded education. The devotions, it was claimed, intrinsically promoted morality, spiritual values, American institutions, and the study of great literature. The states claimed further that if the Court struck down Bible reading and the Lord's Prayer it would establish "a religion of secularism."

On June 17, 1963, the Supreme Court rejected these contentions and reaffirmed its holding in the *Engel* decision. It was Justice Tom C. Clark (1899–1977), a Presbyterian elder from Texas, who wrote the opinion and not Justice Hugo Black, the controversial dean of church-state jurisprudence. Clark observed that the states knew that Bible reading was religious because teachers were forbidden to comment on the passages they read and because a prayer was recited in unison afterwards. Public schools, Clark declared, may not use religious means to achieve secular ends because the Constitution requires government at all levels to remain neutral in matters of religion. For the first time, the Court articulated two tests for a law to pass muster under the First Amendment's establishment clause: (a) it must have a secular purpose; and (b) its primary effect must neither advance nor hinder religion. To demonstrate that the Court was not hostile to religion, Clark went so far as to endorse the teaching, but not the practice, of religion.

Justice Potter Stewart was the lone dissenter, arguing that the majority opinion expressed hostility, not neutrality, toward religion. He argued that the United States had long permitted the free exercise of religious practices, even in the public sphere. Examples of such expression abounded, with the Supreme Court itself opening its sessions with the declaration, "God Save this Honorable Court." Stewart rejected the claim that the religion clauses of the First Amendment established "a single constitutional standard of 'separation of church and state.'" He maintained that the establishment clause was intended to prevent Congress from establishing a national church and from interfering with established state churches.

The *Schempp* decision was highly unpopular among conservative Christians, who wrongly believed it prohibited religious activity in public schools, and there was a groundswell in the body politic to reverse it. Within a year, Congress received 150 resolutions to overturn *Schempp* by a constitutional amendment. No such amendment ever passed and the Supreme Court has never reversed course from *Schempp*, but the controversy over Bible reading and school prayer lingered for decades.

SEE ALSO *Engel v. Vitale, 370 U.S. 421 (1962); Establishment Clause; Free Exercise of Religion; School Prayer*

BIBLIOGRAPHY

Dierenfield, Bruce J. 2007. *The Battle over School Prayer: How Engel v. Vitale Changed America.* Lawrence: University Press of Kansas.

Eastland, Terry, ed. 1993. *Religious Liberty in the Supreme Court: The Cases that Define the Debate over Church and State.* Washington, DC: Ethics and Public Policy Center.

LeBeau, Bryan F. 2003. *The Atheist: Madalyn Murray O'Hair.* New York: New York University Press.

Solomon, Stephen D. 2007. *Ellery's Protest: How One Young Man Defied Tradition and Sparked the Battle over School Prayer.* Ann Arbor: University of Michigan Press.

Bruce J. Dierenfield

ABLEMAN V. BOOTH, 62 U.S. 506 (1858)

In 1854 a fugitive slave named Joshua Glover was discovered in Wisconsin and apprehended by his owner. Under authority of the Fugitive Slave Act of 1850, Glover's owner arrested him and prepared to take him to Missouri. Abolitionists led by Sherman M. Booth sued out a writ of habeas corpus from the county court, with which the federal marshal refused to comply. A crowd of several hundred then liberated Glover by force and spirited him to Canada.

The federal government charged Sherman Booth with rescue. Booth sued out a writ of habeas corpus directed to U.S. marshal Stephen Ableman, and the Wisconsin Supreme Court freed Booth and declared the Fugitive Slave Act of 1850 unconstitutional. The U.S. Supreme Court issued a writ of error in 1856, but the Wisconsin Supreme Court refused to deliver the official record. After obtaining a copy, the Supreme Court issued its ruling in *Ableman v. Booth*, 62 U.S. 506, in 1859.

Writing for the Court, Chief Justice Roger B. Taney ruled that the Wisconsin Supreme Court had erred when it refused to acknowledge the U.S. Supreme Court's jurisdiction. When judicial cases presented constitutional disputes for resolution, argued Taney, the ultimate appeal lay with the Supreme Court. Such was the nature of federal supremacy laid out in the Constitution and in the 1789 Judiciary Act. This did not necessarily mean that federal law would trump the laws of the states, Taney argued, because the Court was bound to test congressional law as well as state law against the Constitution. Despite this pronouncement, Taney declined to review the substance of the Fugitive Slave Act of 1850 in *Ableman*, ignoring the Wisconsin Supreme Court's lengthy analysis and merely declaring it constitutional. Sherman Booth was eventually arrested and imprisoned, and then pardoned by President James Buchanan (1791–1868) in 1861.

Ableman became the iconic statement of federal judicial supremacy. Indeed, when the Supreme Court intervened a century later in the Little Rock, Arkansas, desegregation case of *Cooper v. Aaron*, 358 U.S. 1 (1958), the unanimous opinion signed by all nine justices cited *Ableman* in support of its contention that the Supreme Court was the final expositor of the Constitution. Ever since *Marbury v. Madison*, 5 U.S. 137 (1803), the opinion read that the Court had maintained its preeminent position in constitutional interpretation, and its pronouncements were final and binding on all branches of government. The opinion interpreted *Ableman* to support *Marbury*, and cited it also to vitiate the contention that the states could put forward alternative constitutional interpretations.

The Court's use of *Ableman* in *Cooper v. Aaron* was a telling indication of how much power the Supreme Court had gained by the 1950s. Taney did not cite *Marbury*, most likely because he did not see the case as a precedent for the position that the Court's constitutional interpretation was binding on Congress or the president. *Cooper v. Aaron* asserted that the federal courts could supervise the desegregation of state-run schools. Taney had only claimed in *Ableman* that the states could not interfere with federal process.

SEE ALSO *Slavery; Taney Court*

BIBLIOGRAPHY

Baker, H. Robert. 2006. *The Rescue of Joshua Glover: A Fugitive Slave, the Constitution, and the Coming of the Civil War.* Athens: Ohio University Press.

Parrish, Jenni. 1993. "The *Booth* Cases: Final Step to the Civil War." *Willamette Law Review* 29: 237–278.

H. Robert Baker

Cartoon attacking abolitionists. *In the years preceding the Civil War, abolitionists were generally unsuccessful in the majority of cases they brought before the Supreme Court on behalf of African Americans, both slave and free. Depictions of abolitionists in league with the devil, such as this cartoon which appeared in 1800, demonstrate the fervor with which the proslavery media argued their cause.* © **THE LIBRARY OF CONGRESS/CORBIS**

ABOLITIONISM

Prior to 1864, the Supreme Court was never particularly friendly to the interests of abolitionists and opponents of slavery. Except for a few years in the late 1820s and early 1830s, the Court was dominated by southerners and their proslavery northern "doughface" allies. Until the late 1850s, Congress was usually dominated by coalitions in which slave-state representatives held enormous power. Thus, most legislation favored slavery and rarely harmed it. The Constitution protected slavery in a variety of ways, and the Court implemented these provisions—especially the fugitive slave clause of Article IV—with a strong proslavery bias. Only one justice in this period, John McLean (1785–1861; served 1829–1861) of Ohio, could be characterized as "antislavery" in any important way. Gabriel Duvall (1752–1844; served 1811–1835) of Maryland and Smith Thompson (1768–1843; served 1823–1843) of New York and also sometimes sided with slaves. Joseph Story (served 1811–1845) of Massachusetts personally disliked slavery, and he issued some strong charges to grand juries on the illegal African slave trade, but he also wrote the majority opinion in *Prigg v. Pennsylvania*, 41 U.S. 539 (1842), which, next to *Dred Scott v. Sandford*, 60 U.S. 393 (1857), was the Court's most proslavery decision. Benjamin Curtis (served 1851–1857), also of Massachusetts, made a strong dissent in *Dred Scott*, but he was not committed to the antislavery cause and left the Court after only six years.

On the other hand, a number of justices were rabidly proslavery, including John McKinley (1780–1852; served 1837–1852), Peter V. Daniel (1784–1860; served 1841–1860), John Campbell (served 1853–1861), and Chief Justice Roger Taney (served 1836–1864) of Maryland. Doughfaces (northerners with proslavery leanings), such as Samuel Nelson (1792–1873; served 1845–1872) of New York, Robert Grier (1794–1870; served 1846–1870) of Pennsylvania, and Levi Woodbury (1789–1851; served 1846–1851) of New Hampshire, were reliable allies of the South, as were slaveholding southern moderates, such as

James Wayne (1790–1867; served 1835–1867) of Georgia, John Catron (1786–1865; served 1837–1865) of Tennessee, Bushrod Washington (1762–1829; served 1798–1829) of Virginia, William Johnson of South Carolina, and Chief Justice John Marshall of Virginia.

Before the 1830s the Court heard a number of freedom suits from slaves in the District of Columbia, although none of these involved abolitionists or the abolitionist movement. All were brought by individual slaves who had a prima facie claim to freedom, and the slaves usually lost. These cases involved the claims of individual slaves, and none of them tested the legitimacy of slavery per se. The Court also heard a number of cases involving the illegal Atlantic slave trade after 1808, the year of the American abolition of the trade. These cases involved slavery, and certainly opponents of slavery were pleased when the Court upheld the prosecution of slave traders, but they were federal prosecutions and did not actually involve abolitionists.

THE *AMISTAD*

The first case with an abolitionist connection was *United States v. The Amistad*, 40 U.S. 518 (1841). This case involved a coasting vessel sailing out of Cuba that had been hijacked by Africans who had been illegally brought to Cuba and sold as slaves. After killing the captain and crew, the Amistads, as these Africans were thereafter called, forced the two surviving whites, Pedro Montez and Jose Ruiz, to sail the ship back to Africa. Montez and Ruiz, who had purchased the Amistads in Havana, sailed east during the day, but at night they went northwest, hoping to reach one of the American slave states. Instead, they ended up in Long Island Sound, where a Coast Guard crew boarded the ship and took it to New Haven. The U.S. government initially planned to either return the Amistads to Cuba as slaves or try them for murder on the high seas.

A group of abolitionists, meanwhile, led by Lewis Tappan of New York, organized a defense for the Amistads, with the help of Roger Sherman Baldwin, a Connecticut lawyer; Seth P. Staples and Theodore Sedgwick, antislavery lawyers from New York; and Ellis Gray Loring, the leading antislavery lawyer in Boston. Working with a Yale linguist and two British sailors who were natives of West Africa, the abolitionists were able to prove conclusively that the Amistads were natives of West Africa who only spoke Mende, thus destroying the argument of Ruiz and Montez that they were Cuban-born slaves. Eventually, the U.S. District Court ruled that the Amistads were free and ordered the United States to return them to Africa. Instead of accepting this result, the Van Buren administration appealed to the Supreme Court.

The abolitionist argument was presented to the Court by Baldwin and the former president John Quincy Adams, whose argument ran over 130 printed pages. Speaking for the Court, Justice Story upheld the lower court ruling. Story found that if the Amistads had been Cuban and legally enslaved in Cuba, they could have been returned to Cuba under Pinckney's Treaty of 1795. But Story found it "beyond controversy" that "the negroes never were the lawful slaves of Ruiz and Montez, or of any other Spanish subjects. They are natives of Africa, and were kidnapped there, and were unlawfully transported to Cuba, in violation of the laws and treaties of Spain, and the most solemn edicts and declarations of that

government." Story concluded by stating that "these negroes are not slaves" but had been "kidnapped" and were "entitled to their freedom." After upholding their freedom, Story reversed the order that the Amistads be returned to Africa at government expense. Instead, he ordered them released from confinement in Connecticut. The abolitionists not only raised the money to send them back to West Africa, they also sent them to school before they left in January 1842.

Although legally insignificant, the *Amistad* case served as a powerful example of the horrors of slavery. It also revealed the extent of proslavery complicity on the part of the national government. The case is also one of the few to come to the Court that had a happy ending for opponents of slavery, as well as for the thirty-nine captives.

THE *PRIGG* CASE AND THE FUGITIVE SLAVE LAWS

A year after the *Amistad* the Supreme Court struck down Pennsylvania's personal liberty law in *Prigg v. Pennsylvania*. This case was brought by a Maryland man, Edward Prigg, who had been convicted under a Pennsylvania law of kidnapping a black woman. The state of Pennsylvania defended the law and abolitionists were not involved in the case, although they were surely disappointed by the result, for Justice Story upheld the constitutionality of the Fugitive Slave Law of 1793 and nationalized the law of slavery. Justice McLean offered a bitter and penetrating dissent, arguing for the right of the states to protect their black citizens from kidnapping.

Five years later, in *Jones v. Van Zandt*, 46 U.S. 215 (1847), Justice Levi Woodbury, speaking for a unanimous court, offered a particularly harsh interpretation of the 1793 Fugitive Slave Law and upheld damages against the abolitionist John Van Zandt, who had offered a ride to a group of blacks walking along a road in Ohio. These were fugitive slaves, it turned out, and one of them evaded capture. The owner of this slave, Wharton Jones, sued Van Zandt for his value, and Justice Woodbury ruled that Van Zandt was liable for the loss, even though he had no knowledge that the blacks he encountered walking down a road in the free state of Ohio were slaves. Senator William H. Seward of New York, a committed opponent of slavery, represented Van Zandt. Salmon Chase of Ohio, who was later nicknamed the "Attorney General for Fugitive Slaves," wrote a brief that was over 100 pages that was submitted to the Court. These political abolitionists found, however, that the Supreme Court was unsympathetic to their arguments for freedom.

OTHER SLAVERY-RELATED CASES

In the 1850s the Court heard a number of case involving slavery. In *Strader v. Graham*, 51 U.S. 82 (1850), the Court held that the states were free to determine the status of blacks within their jurisdiction, unless they were limited by the fugitive slave clause of the Constitution. The case involved a suit to recover the value of slaves who escaped on Jacob Strader's steamboat. Strader claimed the blacks were free because their owner, Christopher Graham, had allowed them to visit and work as musicians in free states. The Kentucky court upheld Graham's claim, however, declaring that a mere visit to a free state did not emancipate the slaves. In affirming this result, the Supreme Court effectively declared that the law of slavery could trump the law of freedom. Some abolitionists correctly viewed this as a dangerous precedent for the free states.

Norris v. Crocker, 54 U.S. 429 (1851) was a minor victory for some abolitionists, but it was based entirely on a statutory technicality. Edwin Crocker and a number of others had helped a group of slaves escape in what is known as the South Bend Fugitive Slave Case. The owner, John Norris, successfully sued Crocker and the others for the value of the slaves. However, he improperly filed his suit for the $500 penalty allowed under the Fugitive Slave Law of 1793. By the time he refiled the case, Congress has passed the Fugitive Slave Law of 1850 and repealed the $500 penalty. The Court concluded that Norris could not sue for the penalty because the law under which he could have sued was no longer in force. This was Salmon Chase's only antislavery victory before the high court. The case did not signal a change in the Court's proslavery jurisprudence, however, but was merely a narrow and technical response to a question of statutory interpretation. More importantly, even though the Fugitive Slave Law of 1850 was not directly before the Court, this case signaled that the Court would have no problem accepting the constitutionality of that act.

In *Moore v. Illinois*, 55 U.S. 13 (1852), the Court upheld an Illinois law imposing a fine on an abolitionist, Dr. Richard Eels, who had harbored a fugitive slave. Justice McLean dissented, arguing that this amounted to double jeopardy because Eels was also punished under federal law. Salmon Chase argued the case for Eels.

THE *DRED SCOTT* CASE

Dred Scott v. Sandford (1857) provided the most dramatic victory for slavery in the Supreme Court. The case had developed out of Scott's seemingly strong claim to freedom, based on his residence in the free state of Illinois and the territory made free by the Missouri Compromise. This claim did not challenge the legitimacy of slavery or any proslavery legislation. On the contrary, Scott wanted the Supreme Court to uphold the Missouri Compromise, a federal law, and give him his freedom. A victory for Scott would not have undermined slavery in any of the states or in the nation. Thus, the case did not attract abolitionists lawyers, such as Chase or Seward, who had taken cases involving fugitive slaves.

At the same time, if Scott lost there might not be much fallout. In *Strader v. Graham* the Court had held that the states had the sole power to determine who was a slave and who was not. Initially, the Court planned to follow this precedent, with New York's Samuel Nelson writing the opinion for the Court. After reargument, however, Chief Justice Taney took over, crafting an opinion that struck down the Missouri Compromise, declared that Congress could never ban slavery in the territories, and held that free blacks, even if citizens of the states in which they lived, could never be considered citizens of the United States, and thus had no rights under the Constitution.

The decision shocked much of the North and helped fuel support for the Republican Party. Abolitionists denounced the decision whereas most southerners cheered it. The decision reaffirmed what many opponents of slavery had long believed: The Supreme Court was a bastion of slavery. It also reaffirmed the radical abolitionist view that the Constitution itself was a proslavery conspiracy.

In *Ableman v. Booth*, 62 U.S. 506 (1858), the Court upheld the constitutionality of the Fugitive Slave Law of 1850, setting the stage for the incarceration of Sherman Booth, a Wisconsin newspaper editor who had helped rescue the slave Joshua Glover from federal custody. The state of Wisconsin had tried to prevent Booth's incarceration, and the Wisconsin Supreme Court had issued a writ of habeas corpus to remove Booth from federal custody. Chief Justice Taney denounced the actions of the Wisconsin court as constituting an assault on the Constitution and the nation. Wisconsin had adopted an extreme states' right position, arguing that its courts were superior to both federal law and the federal courts. The Supreme Court denounced these states' rights arguments, and in the process it reaffirmed that the national government had an obligation to protect slavery. Earlier in the decade, the antislavery lawyer Salmon Chase, who would later become chief justice of the Supreme Court, had given a speech entitled "Freedom National." But after *Dred Scott* and *Ableman v. Booth* most abolitionists understood that slavery was not a national institution, and that freedom was local.

KENTUCKY V. DENNISON

The final antebellum case involving abolition and slavery illustrated the strange proslavery jurisprudence of the Taney Court. It also showed that, with the possible exception of *Amistad*, abolitionists could only win in this court when their case dovetailed with a larger victory for slavery, or if there was a technical need to reach a particular outcome. It was on both of these grounds that the Court had supported the Indiana fugitive slave rescuers in *Norris v. Crocker* in 1851. The case of *Kentucky v. Dennison*, 65 U.S. 66 (1861) would have a similar result.

Dennison involved an attempt by Governor Beriah Magoffin of Kentucky to extradite Willis Lago, a free black in Ohio, on charges of theft. The object of Lago's "theft" was a slave woman he had brought to Cincinnati. Kentucky officials knew that Ohio would not cooperate with the recovery of a slave. In addition, they knew that this was really a federal issue under the Fugitive Slave Law of 1850. The 1850 law did not, however, provide any penalties for those who helped slaves escape from the South—the penalties were only for those who rescued fugitives from federal custody or prevented their capture by slave owners or federal officials. Acting under traditional local criminal law, Kentucky officials charged Lago with theft and asked Governor Salmon P. Chase of Ohio to approve his extradition. Chase refused, and Governor Magoffin waited patiently for Ohio's next governor, William Dennison, to take office, hoping that he would comply with the request. Dennison, however, like Chase, concluded that because Ohio did not recognize a property interest in a slave, the state could not recognize that there was a crime of stealing a slave. After a series of communications between the two governors, Magoffin brought the case to the U.S. Supreme Court, under the Court's original jurisdiction to hear cases between two states.

The Court decided the case in February 1861. At that point in time, Abraham Lincoln was president-elect and seven slave states had already declared they were no longer part of the United States. Under these circumstances, Chief Justice Taney did not want to order the governor of a state to obey a mandate of the federal government. Thus, Taney berated Governor Dennison for not complying with the extradition requisition, but in the end the Court held that he could not be forced to do so. In *Ableman v. Booth* the Court had rejected the states' rights arguments of Wisconsin in order to enforce the Fugitive Slave Law. Here, however, the Court accepted Ohio's states' rights claims, because to do otherwise would have handed the incoming Lincoln administration a powerful precedent for fighting secession. Thus, Taney gave the antislavery administration in Ohio a victory in order to secure a larger proslavery principle.

Taney remained chief justice until his death in 1864. The Court never heard any other cases that touched on abolition, although it did uphold some prosecutions for violations of the ban on the African slave trade. But these results were consistent with earlier precedents and did not affect slavery in the United States. Over the course of some sixty years, the opponents of slavery rarely won much in the Supreme Court, for both the Marshall and Taney courts were friends of slavery. This changed in 1864, when the most important antislavery lawyer of the antebellum period, Salmon P. Chase, became chief justice of the United States.

SEE ALSO *Anti-slavery Constitutionalism; Article IV; Fugitive Slave Clause; Garrison, William Lloyd; Prigg v. Pennsylvania, 41 U.S. 539 (1842); Slavery*

BIBLIOGRAPHY

Baker, H. Robert. 2006. *The Rescue of Joshua Glover: A Fugitive Slave, The Constitution, and the Coming of the Civil War.* Athens: Ohio University Press.

Fehrenbacher, Don E. 1978. *The Dred Scott Case: Its Significance in American Law and Politics.* New York: Oxford University Press.

Finkelman, Paul. 1981. *An Imperfect Union: Slavery, Federalism, and Comity.* Chapel Hill: University of North Carolina Press.

Finkelman, Paul. 1985. *Slavery in the Courtroom: An Annotated Bibliography of American Cases.* Washington, DC: Library of Congress.

Finkelman, Paul. 1994. "Story Telling on the Supreme Court: *Prigg v. Pennsylvania* and Justice Joseph Story's Judicial Nationalism." *Supreme Court Review* 1994: 247–294.

Jones, Howard. 1987. *Mutiny on the Amistad: The Saga of a Slave Revolt and Its Impact on American Abolition, Law, and Diplomacy.* New York: Oxford University Press.

Wiecek, William M. 1977. *The Sources of Antislavery Constitutionalism in America, 1760–1848.* Ithaca, NY: Cornell University Press.

Wiecek, William M. 1978. "Slavery and Abolition before the United States Supreme Court." *Journal of American History* 65(1): 34–59.

Paul Finkelman

ABOOD V. DETROIT BOARD OF EDUCATION, 431 U.S. 209 (1977)

Abood v. Detroit Board of Education, 431 U.S. 209 (1977) is one in a series of cases in which the U.S. Supreme Court held that "union security" agreements do not violate the First Amendment, so long as the dues taken from dissenting workers are used solely for activities related to collective bargaining and grievance arbitration (see *Machinists v. Street*, 367 U.S. 740 [1961] and *Communications Workers v. Beck*, 487 U.S. 735 [1988]).

Many collective bargaining agreements contain union security provisions. These provisions require workers to pay dues to the union that has been selected as their exclusive representative by a majority of the employees in the workplace. Even workers who do not wish to be represented by the union are required to pay. The purpose of these provisions is to prevent employees from "free riding" on the benefits of union representation. Under federal and state law, unions are required to represent the interests of all employees in the workplace—the union must bargain on their behalf and represent them if they have a grievance—even if a given worker is opposed to the union and has refused to join it. Thus, without a union security provision, employees have no incentive to pay dues to a union since they will receive the services that unions are statutorily required to provide regardless of whether they pay or not.

Union security provisions raise two First Amendment issues. First, they might be seen as a form of compelled association. Second, to the extent that the union uses the dues to engage in political speech (contributing to a political campaign or publishing materials endorsing a candidate, for example), the union security agreement is compelling workers to engage in speech with which they may disagree.

In *Abood*, as with previous cases on this subject, the Court held that so long as the dues were not used for ideological purposes, the government's interest in promoting industrial stability through collective bargaining outweighed the First Amendment's protections against compelled association and compelled speech. Justice Lewis F. Powell, Jr. wrote a vigorous concurrence—a dissent in all but name. He argued that *Abood* should be distinguished from the Court's previous cases because it involved a public-sector union. Unlike private-sector collective bargaining, in public-sector collective bargaining state actors were actually parties to the contract that restricted freedom of speech and assembly. Additionally, because public-sector collective bargaining agreements impact the fiscal priorities of the government, they have "all the attributes of legislation." Consequently, the Court's previous holdings that dues expenditures in private-sector collective bargaining were not political activity should not apply in the case of public-sector unions.

Justice Potter Stewart's majority opinion rejected this distinction. In terms of the First Amendment's state action requirement, legislation that allowed private parties to place union security provisions in collective bargaining agreements was indistinguishable from the government being a party to the collective bargaining agreement. Furthermore, the fact that the demands of public-sector unions impacted the public treasury was irrelevant to the constitutional inquiry. The proper question was whether union security agreements "muzzle[d] a public employee who ... might wish to express his view about governmental decisions concerning labor relations." Since they did not, the First Amendment was not violated.

Abood has remained good law, though the Court has increasingly narrowed the uses of dues that it considers related to collective bargaining and contract administration.

SEE ALSO *Burger Court; Labor Unions*

BIBLIOGRAPHY

Haggard, Thomas R. 1977. *Compulsory Unionism, the NLRB, and the Courts: A Legal Analysis of Union Security Agreements.* Philadelphia: Industrial Research Unit, Wharton School, University of Pennsylvania.

Rehmus, Charles M., and Benjamin Kerner. 1980. "The Agency Shop after *Abood*: No Free Ride, But What's the Fare?" *Industrial and Labor Relations Review* 434: 90–100.

Reuel E. Schiller

ABORTION

SEE *Abortion Protests; Access to Abortion Clinics; Burger Court; Dalton v. Little Rock Family Planning Services, 516 U.S. 474 (1996); Gonzales v. Carhart, 550 U.S. ___ (2007); Harris v. McRae, 448 U.S. 297 (1980); Planned Parenthood v. Casey, 505 U.S. 833 (1992); Planned Parenthood v. Danforth, 428 U.S. 52 (1976); Rehnquist Court; Roberts Court; Roe v. Wade, 410 U.S. 113 (1973); Stenberg v. Carhart, 530 U.S. 914 (2000); Thornburg v. American College of Obstetricians, 476 U.S. 747 (1986); Webster v. Reproductive Health Services, 492 U.S. 490 (1989).*

ABORTION PROTESTS

Free speech doctrine has developed out of crisis and controversy in American society. Since the U.S. Supreme Court decided *Roe v. Wade*, 410 U.S. 113 (1973), and extended substantive due process protection to a woman's decision to terminate her pregnancy, there has been continued social conflict over the right to have an abortion. Numerous protests were directed at the patients and staff of medical clinics providing abortion services. Some protests involved massive demonstrations, threats and violence, obstruction of entrances, and loud and frightening expressive activity. Others utilized sidewalk counseling to persuade women not to have an abortion. Suits were filed, injunctions issued, and new federal and state laws enacted to limit these protests. The Supreme Court played a critical role in determining how and to what extent restrictions on abortion protests violated the First Amendment, although that doctrinal line proved a difficult one to draw.

CHALLENGING ABORTION PROTESTS UNDER FEDERAL STATUTES

Initially, clinics and abortion rights supporters sought unsuccessfully to enjoin abortion protests under preexisting federal statutes. In *Bray v. Alexandria Women's Health Clinic*, 506 U.S. 263 (1993), the Court denied injunctive relief under the Civil Rights Act of 1871 (42 U.S.C. § 1985 [3]). The Court determined the protestors were not motivated by invidious, class-based animus such as racism, nor did they conspire to threaten rights that are protected against private as well as state impairment, as the act required.

Later, in *Scheidler v. National Organization for Women, Inc.*, 537 U.S. 393 (2003) and *Scheidler v. National Organization for Women, Inc.*, 547 U.S. 9 (2006), the Court rejected suits brought pursuant to the Racketeer Influenced and Corrupt Organizations Act (RICO) (18 U.S.C. § 1964). Petitioners alleged the protestors committed extortion through threats and force in violation of the Hobbs Act (18 U.S.C. § 1951) and state law extortion statutes. The Court ruled that the protestors did not commit extortion under either federal or state law, and, accordingly, their RICO claims must be rejected.

In 1994 Congress enacted the Freedom of Access to Clinic Entrances Act (FACE) (18 U.S.C. § 248). FACE subjected to criminal and civil sanction any person who "by force or threat of force or by physical obstruction, intentionally injures, intimidates or interfere[s] with … any person because that person is or has been … obtaining or providing reproductive health services." Whereas the Supreme Court has never reviewed the constitutionality of FACE, numerous lower courts have upheld the law against free speech challenges and arguments that it exceeded the scope of congressional power.

INJUNCTIONS RESTRICTING ABORTION PROTESTS

In many cases, trial courts have issued injunctions restricting abortion protests. Court orders prohibiting trespass, obstruction, threats, or acts of violence did not raise difficult constitutional questions. The First Amendment does not protect such conduct. The hard questions involved limits on verbal protests directed at patients approaching the entrance to clinics.

Protestors claimed the injunctions constituted prior restraints on speech and were presumptively unconstitutional. Further, their activities took place on public sidewalks, a traditional public forum where expression received maximum constitutional protection. Finally, protestors argued the injunctions were content-discriminatory because they were directed solely at persons expressing antiabortion messages.

Clinics and their supporters responded that the injunctions were constitutional because the protestors' freedom of speech was outweighed by the serious harms they caused by targeting women seeking medical treatment. The trauma of walking through a gauntlet of protestors to approach and enter a clinic increased the medical risks associated with having an abortion. Medical facilities were special locations where free speech rights were necessarily subordinate to the goal of protecting the physical and mental health of patients. Also, patients were followed and continually accosted by protestors despite repeated rejection of the protestors' message. This was harassment, not persuasion. Women wanted to exercise their right to have an abortion without intrusive interference by strangers into their private affairs. The state's interest in maintaining access to health-care facilities, protecting women's health and medical privacy, and preventing harassment justified the injunctions at issue.

In *Madsen v. Women's Health Center*, 512 U.S. 753 (1994), the Court struck down part of an injunction restricting abortion protestors, but upheld a prohibition barring protestors from entering a thirty-six-foot buffer zone around the clinic's entrance. Justice Rehnquist's majority opinion characterized the injunction as content-neutral, a conclusion that distinguished it from presumptively unconstitutional prior restraints on speech. The majority explained that the trial judge's order limited the location where protestors could speak, not the content of their message. Moreover, the injunction was issued because the protestors' prior unlawful activities had made it impossible to protect clinic access through less-restrictive court orders. More problematically, the Court developed an entirely new standard of review for content-neutral injunctions—one that fell somewhere between the relatively lenient standard applied to content-neutral statutes and the strict scrutiny applied to content-discriminatory statutes. In evaluating the constitutionality of a content-neutral injunction, courts must determine "whether the challenged provisions of the injunction burden no more speech than necessary to serve a significant governmental interest."

Justices Scalia, Kennedy, and Thomas, dissenting in part, argued that the injunction should receive strict-scrutiny review. Content-neutral statutes, commonly described as time, place, and manner regulations, received lenient review because they applied to so many different subjects and viewpoints of speech that they seldom served the purpose, or had the effect, of favoring one side or the other in public debate. Injunctions, such as the one before the Court, lacked such generality. Here, it was clear to everyone, including the judge who issued the order, that the injunction restricted only antiabortion speech.

The dissenting justices assigned little weight to the state's interest in protecting women from increased health risks or intrusions into their privacy. To the dissenters, the majority opinion distorted well-settled free speech doctrine out of a misguided commitment to protecting a woman's right to have an abortion.

In *Schenck v. Pro-Choice Network of Western New York*, 519 U.S. 357 (1997), the Court upheld an injunction creating a fixed fifteen-foot buffer zone around a clinic's entrance. While consistent with *Madsen* in its holding, the Court relied almost exclusively on the state's interest in preventing the obstruction of clinic entrances to justify its decision. Concerns about medical privacy and increased risks to the health of patients, acknowledged in *Madsen*, were barely mentioned. More importantly, Justice Rehnquist's majority emphatically rejected the argument that patients approaching a medical clinic had a right "to be left alone" as inconsistent with "our First Amendment jurisprudence in this area."

STATE STATUTES RESTRICTING ABORTION PROTESTS

In *Hill v. Colorado*, 530 U.S. 703 (2000), the Supreme Court reviewed a state statute making it "unlawful [within one hundred feet of the entrance to any health-care facility] for any person 'to knowingly approach' within eight feet of another person, without that person's consent, 'for the purpose of passing a leaflet or handbill to, displaying a sign to, or engaging in oral protest, education or counseling with such other person.'"

The challenged law was a statute, not an injunction. Therefore, the new standard developed in *Madsen* did not apply. After concluding that the law was content-neutral, the Court applied the conventional, relatively lenient standard it employs to review such speech regulations and upheld the law.

Justice Stevens' majority opinion in *Hill* focused explicitly on the state concerns the injunction cases had largely ignored. It emphasized the state's interest in avoiding the "potential trauma to patients associated with confrontational protests" and in assisting persons seeking medical care from being conscripted into intrusive expressive encounters without their consent. The interests implicit in the right to be left alone while approaching the entrance to a medical clinic sufficiently outweighed the burden on speech imposed by the statute to justify upholding the law.

The most difficult issue in this case involved the nature and scope of the law. To avoid restricting speech that did not jeopardize patient privacy or health, the statute prohibited only "oral protest, education or counseling." Justice Kennedy's dissent, with considerable justification, argued that by targeting particular speech, the statute discriminated on the basis of the content of speech and warranted more rigorous review. Further, the statute's language was not adequately tailored to further the state's interest. Education and counseling need not be traumatic or intrusive. If the purpose of this law was to protect women from harassment, it should prohibit harassment, not education.

EVALUATING THE CASES

Neither the majority nor the dissenting opinions in the abortion protest cases seem fully persuasive or adequate. Whereas the majority in *Madsen* and *Schenck* probably understate the risks to freedom of speech created by content-neutral injunctions, the dissenting opinions overstate those concerns. Content-neutral statutes may predictably burden only one side in a public debate as effectively as content-neutral injunctions. Both an ordinance and an injunction prohibiting picketing in front of local factories would be understood to restrict the union side, not management, in a labor dispute. Yet content-neutral statutes that obviously impact some speakers more than others are routinely upheld under relatively lenient review. The risks the dissent recognizes are real, but they do not typically justify rigorous review—as the decision in *Hill* demonstrates.

The more important problem with the injunction cases was the Court's unwillingness to fully acknowledge the reasons why trial courts issued orders restricting abortion protests. These injunctions were sought to protect women entering medical clinics from increased health risks resulting from their exposure to traumatic protests and invasive intrusions by strangers into their medical privacy and decision-making. The dissents trivialized these interests. The majority largely ignored them in its emphasis on obstruction and past unlawful behavior.

In *Hill*, none of the conflicting opinions adequately addresses the issue of exactly how a statute can be drafted to prohibit harassment at medical clinics or other locations. The underlying problem here is that there is no accepted definition of harassment that would give either the police or protestors adequate guidance as to what activities were prohibited by a law. If restricting education and counseling prohibits too much speech, a ban on harassment is too vague to be enforced. In the real world, legislatures must sometimes choose between these alternatives in regulating speech. From a constitutional perspective, it is not always clear which approach is preferable.

SEE ALSO *Access to Abortion Clinics; Right to Life; Roe v. Wade, 410 U.S. 113 (1973)*

BIBLIOGRAPHY

Blanchard, Dallas A. 1994. *The Anti-Abortion Movement and the Rise of the Religious Right: From Polite to Fiery Protest.* New York: Twayne.

Brownstein, Alan E. 1996. "Rules of Engagement for Cultural Wars: Regulating Conduct, Unprotected Speech, and Protected Expression in Anti-Abortion Protests." *U.C. Davis Law Review* 29(3): 553–638.

Brownstein, Alan E. 1996. "Rules of Engagement for Cultural Wars: Regulating Conduct, Unprotected Speech, and

Protected Expression in Anti-Abortion Protests—Section II." *U.C. Davis Law Review* 29(4): 1163–1216.

Chen, Alan K. 2003. "Statutory Speech Bubbles, First Amendment Overbreadth, and Improper Legislative Purpose." *Harvard Civil Rights–Civil Liberties Law Review* 38(1): 31–90.

Jacobs, Leslie Gielow. 1996. "Nonviolent Abortion Clinic Protests: Reevaluating Some Current Assumptions about the Proper Scope of Government Regulations." *Tulane Law Review* 70(5): 1359–1443.

LaMarche, Gara, ed. 1996. *Speech & Equality: Do We Really Have to Choose?* New York: New York University Press.

Wells, Christina E. 2000. "Bringing Structure to the Law of Injunctions against Expression." *Case Western Reserve Law Review* 51(1): 1–67.

Alan E. Brownstein

ABSTENTION

Abstention is the doctrine created by the federal courts that allows a court to decline jurisdiction even though all other rules and requirements of jurisdiction and justiciability (the susceptibility of a case or controversy to judicial decision) are satisfied. Abstention derives from the historical powers of equity of federal courts. The Supreme Court has identified five primary forms of abstention, each named after the case that created it:

- *Pullman Abstention.* A federal court should abstain from deciding a federal constitutional question if that question likely would be obviated by a state court's clarification of an unsettled issue of state law. *Railroad Commission of Texas v. Pullman Co.*, 312 U.S. 496 (1941).

- *Burford Abstention.* A federal court should dismiss a claim for declaratory or equitable relief whose resolution would interfere with a comprehensive state administrative mechanism that exists to ensure uniformity of decision-making. *Burford v. Sun Oil Co.*, 319 U.S. 315 (1943).

- *Thibodaux Abstention.* A federal court hearing a diversity case (a case in which both state and federal courts have jurisdiction) should abstain from deciding an unclear issue of state law that is intimately involved with the state's sovereign prerogative, such as a state's exercise of eminent domain. *Louisiana Power & Light Co. v. City of Thibodaux*, 360 U.S. 25 (1969).

- *Younger Abstention.* A federal court may not enjoin pending state court criminal proceedings, *Younger v. Harris*, 401 U.S. 37 (1971), or state judicial or administrative civil proceedings implicating a

significant state interest, *Pennzoil Co. v. Texaco, Inc.*, 481 U.S. 1 (1987); *Middlesex County Ethics Committee v. Garden State Bar Association*, 457 U.S. 423 (1982). The Younger abstention may also apply when certain declaratory relief is sought if the declaratory relief would result in the same interference and disruption of state proceedings as an injunction, *Samuels v. Mackell*, 401 U.S. 66 (1971). The Younger abstention is subject to exceptions for bad faith prosecution, *Juidice v. Vail*, 430 U.S. 327 (1977), and for patently unconstitutional laws, *Younger*, 401 U.S. at 53–54.

- *Colorado River Abstention.* Although parallel state and federal proceedings generally are no bar to federal jurisdiction, under exceptional circumstances a federal court may abstain out of deference to the state court after considering the following factors:
  1. the problems of concurrent jurisdiction over a single legal matter;
  2. the relative inconvenience of the federal forum;
  3. the need to avoid piecemeal litigation;
  4. the order in which the parallel proceedings were filed. *Colorado River Water Conservation District v. United States*, 424 U.S. 800 (1976).

Abstention rests upon several rationales, including the need to avoid causing tension in federal/state relations, the need to avoid unnecessary federal constitutional rulings, and the need to avoid duplicative litigation. However, abstention often creates high costs and delays for litigants, who must relitigate their disputes in state court. As a way of minimizing delays in abstention cases, the Supreme Court, in *Arizonans for Official English v. Arizona*, 520 U.S. 43, 75–79 (1997), has endorsed the use of certification procedures, in which a federal court certifies a question to a state court for binding resolution.

SEE ALSO *Jurisdiction*

BIBLIOGRAPHY

Chemerinsky, Erwin. 2007. *Federal Jurisdiction*. 5th edition. New York: Aspen Publishers.

Scott Dodson

ACADEMIC FREEDOM

Academic freedom concerns the right of professors to engage in teaching, research, and related activities without undue interference from university administrators or groups outside of the academy. Academic freedom includes the right of colleges and universities to pursue their educational missions without unwarranted interference from outsiders. Academic freedom has two components. The first is *individual* as it relates to the rights of faculty members. The second is *institutional*, which denotes the interests of colleges and universities in their relationships with governmental officials and other groups external to the institution. Academic freedom is premised on the belief that uninhibited inquiry and the free expression of ideas are essential to the educational mission of the academy. When scholars express ideas that are controversial, they can be threatened with job loss or other forms of retaliation. Academic freedom assures that unpopular views can be expressed without fear of retribution.

AAUP STATEMENT ON ACADEMIC FREEDOM AND TENURE

In the case of public institutions, academic freedom is grounded in the U.S. Constitution's protection of speech. Academic freedom has long been viewed by the courts as a "special concern" of the First Amendment, which prohibits the government from interfering with the expression of ideas. In private institutions, academic freedom is a contract right for those institutions that adhere to the American Association of University Professors (AAUP) 1940 Statement on Academic Freedom and Tenure, which provides in pertinent part that:

1. Teachers are entitled to full freedom in research and in the publication of the results, subject to the adequate performance of their other academic duties; but research for pecuniary return should be based upon an understanding with the authorities of the institution.

2. Teachers are entitled to freedom in the classroom in discussing their subject, but they should be careful not to introduce into their teaching controversial matter which has no relation to their subject. Limitations of academic freedom because of religious or other aims of the institution should be clearly stated in writing at the time of the appointment.

3. College and university teachers are citizens, members of a learned profession, and officers of an educational institution. When they speak or write as citizens, they should be free from institutional censorship or discipline, but their special position in the community imposes special obligations. As scholars and educational officers, they should remember that the public may judge their profession and their institution by their utterances. Hence they should at all times be accurate, should exercise appropriate restraint, should show respect for the opinions of others, and should make every effort to indicate that they are not speaking for the institution.

CUSTOM AND USAGE DOCTRINE AND CONTRACT RIGHTS

Most private colleges and universities in the United States adhere to these principles in their official policies and procedures. This makes academic freedom an enforceable contract right for college professors. Academic freedom may also be protected as part of the *customs and usages* of an institution. In *Greene v. Howard University*, 412 F.2d 1128 (D.C. Cir. 1969), the Court of Appeals for the District of Columbia Circuit explained that: "Contracts are written, and are to be read, by reference to the norms of conduct and expectations founded upon them. This is especially true of contracts in and among a community of scholars, which is what a university is. The readings of the market place are not invariably apt in this non-commercial context."

In *Perry v. Sindermann*, 408 U.S. 593 (1972), the Supreme Court found that there may be an "unwritten 'common law' in a particular university" that is binding on the faculty and administration. The custom and usage doctrine is derived from well-established contract law principles derived *from Resolution Trust Corp. v. Urban Redevelopment Authority*, 638 A. 2d. 972, 975 (Pa. 1994), which state that "when a custom or usage is once established, in absence of express provision to the contrary it is considered a part of a contract and binding on the parties though not mentioned therein, the presumption being that they knew of and contracted with reference to it." This means that a customary way of operating can be binding and enforceable even if it is not expressly stated in a written document.

FREEDOM FROM EXTERNAL INTERFERENCE

The first Supreme Court cases involving academic freedom focused on faculty and institutional freedom from external interference. In these cases, faculty members and institutions sought protection from governmental pressures. The cases arose during the McCarthy era of the 1950s, when federal and state governments required employees to sign "loyalty oaths" stating that they were not members of subversive organizations. These practices were challenged, and in *Sweezy v. New Hampshire*, 354 U.S. 234 (1957), the Supreme Court held that a Marxist lecturer could not be compelled to answer the state attorney general's questions about the content of his remarks. Writing for the majority, Chief Justice Earl Warren stated:

The essentiality of freedom in the community of American universities is almost self-evident. No one should underestimate the vital role in a democracy that is played by those who guide and train our youth. To impose any strait jacket upon the intellectual leaders in our colleges and universities would imperil the future of our Nation. No field of education is so thoroughly comprehended by man that new discoveries cannot yet be made. Particularly is that true in the social sciences, where few, if any, principles are accepted as absolutes. Scholarship cannot flourish in an atmosphere of suspicion and distrust. Teachers and students must always remain free to inquire, to study and to evaluate, to gain new maturity and understanding; otherwise our civilization will stagnate and die.

In *Keyishian v. Board of Regents*, 385 U.S. 589 (1967), the Supreme Court relied on the First Amendment and academic freedom to strike down New York laws designed "to prevent the appointment or retention of 'subversive' persons in state employment." The majority stated that "our Nation is deeply committed to safeguarding academic freedom, which is of transcendent value to all of us and not merely to the teachers concerned. That freedom is therefore a special concern of the First Amendment, which does not tolerate laws that cast a pall of orthodoxy over the classroom." In an influential concurring opinion in *Sweezy*, Justice Felix Frankfurter identified "the four essential freedoms" of an academic institution as the right "to determine for itself on academic grounds who may teach, what may be taught, how it shall be taught, and who may be admitted to study."

One year after its broad endorsement of academic freedom in *Keyishian*, the Court began to recognize some limitations. In *Pickering v. Board of Education*, 391 U.S. 563 (1968), a newspaper published a high school teacher's letter to the editor that criticized the board of education's financial plans for high schools. The teacher was later dismissed from employment. When the case reached the Supreme Court, it concluded that the teacher's speech interests had to be balanced against the state's interest in maintaining an efficient educational system. The Court found that teachers must be allowed to speak publicly on matters of "public concern," as long as the speech does not unduly interfere with the efficient operation of the institution.

STUDENT-BODY DIVERSITY

Academic freedom has been invoked to justify efforts to promote student-body diversity. In *Regents of the University of California v. Bakke*, 438 U.S. 265 (1978), Justice Lewis Powell's plurality opinion relied on academic freedom to support his determination that race could be a legitimate factor in selecting a university's student body. Powell stated that one of the "four essential freedoms" identified in Justice Frankfurter's concurring opinion in *Sweezy*—namely, the right to determine "who may be admitted to study"—provided a First Amendment justification for the university's decision to use race as a factor in student admissions. This reasoning was affirmed

in a 2003 decision involving an affirmative action admission program at the University of Michigan. The majority relied on academic freedom principles to affirm the validity of Michigan's program. Citing Justice Powell's opinion in *Bakke*, the majority in *Grutter v. Bollinger*, 539 U.S. 306 (2003) used academic freedom as a basis for according a presumption of validity to the university's claims concerning the value of diversity.

JUDICIAL DEFERENCE TO ACADEMIC DECISION MAKING

Judicial deference to decision making in matters falling within the academic community's special expertise is a well-established principle of higher education law that is grounded in academic freedom. As the Supreme Court explained in *Regents of the University of Michigan v. Ewing*, 474 U.S. 214 (1985):

> When judges are asked to review the substance of a genuinely academic decision ... they should show great respect for the faculty's professional judgment. Plainly, they may not override it unless it is such a substantial departure from accepted academic norms as to demonstrate that the person or committee responsible did not actually exercise professional judgment.

In a 2001 decision, the U.S. Court of Appeals for the Fourth Circuit held in *Urofsky v. Gilmore*, 167 F.3d 191 (4th Cir. 1999) that professors do not have an individual right to academic freedom, stating "any right of academic freedom ... inheres in the University, not in individual professors." However, *Urofsky* is at odds with other rulings and is viewed by legal scholars as an exception to the way in which academic freedom has been interpreted by the courts. In the case of classroom speech, courts have accorded professors broad latitude, but they have upheld terminations when professors persistently used vulgar, profane, or heavily sexualized speech that was unrelated to the subject matter of the courses they were teaching. The AAUP itself has recognized that professors "should be careful not to introduce into their teaching controversial matter which has no relation to their subject." An individual professor's right to academic freedom has been consistently recognized by the Supreme Court.

STUDENTS' RIGHTS

The Supreme Court has also recognized students' rights to academic freedom. This was first recognized in 1969 in *Tinker v. Des Moines Ind. Comm. School Dist.*, 393 U.S. 503. That case involved a group of high school students who decided to protest the Vietnam War (1957–1975) by wearing black armbands to their schools. School officials demanded the removal of the armbands and, when the students refused, they were suspended. The Supreme

Court held that wearing armbands was expression protected by the First Amendment. The school officials had failed to show that the students' conduct would substantially interfere with appropriate school discipline.

The First Amendment rights of high school students are limited. In a 1988 case, *Hazelwood School District v. Kuhlmeier*, 484 U.S. 260, a high school principal withheld two articles that were slated for publication in the student newspaper. A suit was filed, and when the case reached the Supreme Court, it held that school officials did not violate the First Amendment by exercising editorial control over the content of student speech so long as their actions were reasonably related to legitimate pedagogical concerns.

In 1995 the Supreme Court held in *Rosenberger v. Rector*, 515 U.S. 819 that the University of Virginia could not prohibit indirect subsidies to a student publication generated from student fees based solely on the publication's religious perspective. In 2007, however, the Court imposed limitations on the expressive rights of high school students. *Morse v. Frederick*, 127 S. Ct. 2618, began when a student unveiled a fourteen-foot paper sign containing the words "BONG HiTS 4 JESUS" on a public sidewalk outside his Alaska high school. The principal confiscated the sign and suspended the student. When the case reached the Supreme Court, the majority ruled that the student's free speech rights had not been violated. The principal's belief that the banner promoted illegal drug use was reasonable and that "failing to act would send a powerful message to the students in her charge."

The Supreme Court has not defined the precise contours of academic freedom; the decisions have not been entirely consistent. Critics of the academy accuse professors of indoctrinating students, presenting only a single point of view, and being intolerant of different ideological perspectives. Others deny these assertions and state that it is unlikely that professors will have a significant influence on the political views of college students. As these examples suggest, the many issues surrounding academic freedom are likely to remain contested in the law, in academic discourse, and in public dialogue.

SEE ALSO *Colleges and Universities; Education and the Constitution; First Amendment; Keyishian v. Board of Regents, 385 U.S. 589 (1967); Perry v. Sindermann, 408 U.S. 593 (1972); Pickering v. Board of Education, 391 U.S. 563 (1968); Rights of Students*

BIBLIOGRAPHY

American Association of University Professors (AAUP). 1940 Statement of Principles on Academic Freedom and Tenure. Available from http://www.aaup.org/AAUP/pubsres/policy-docs/contents/1940statement.htm.

Kaplin, William A., and Barbara A. Lee. 2006. *The Law of Higher Education: A Comprehensive Guide to Legal Implications of Administrative Decision Making*. 4th edition. San Francisco: Jossey-Bass.

Menand, Louis, ed. 1996. *The Future of Academic Freedom*. Chicago: University of Chicago Press.

Olivas, Michael A. 2006. *The Law and Higher Education: Cases and Materials on Colleges in Court*. 3rd edition. Durham, NC: Carolina Academic Press.

Leland Ware

ACCESS TO ABORTION CLINICS

The constitutional law with respect to abortion clinic access is a combination of First Amendment and commerce clause jurisprudence. There are also important statutory decisions about the meaning and scope of various statutes, such as the racketeering laws that relate to this topic, but those issues are beyond the scope of this entry.

TACTICS AND COUNTERTACTICS

Antiabortion advocates have used many tactics to discourage women from procuring abortions. The most well-known strategy is to use the law to make abortions illegal. That strategy has been limited by the U.S. Supreme Court's decision in *Roe v. Wade*, 410 U.S. 113 (1973), and the Court's reaffirmation of *Roe*'s core holding in *Casey v. Planned Parenthood*, 505 U.S. 833 (1992). Unable to use the law to ban abortion entirely, abortion opponents also began to use other methods to limit access to abortion. Waiting period and "informed consent" laws, among others, have been such mechanisms, and Supreme Court decisions have upheld the validity of some of these measures, notwithstanding *Roe*.

Another tactic has been for antiabortion advocates to hold protests, and even engage in violence, to persuade women not to procure abortions or persuade physicians not to offer them. These tactics have included:

- blocking parking lots to clinic facilities
- shoving clinic employees, escorts, or patients as they seek to enter a facility
- gluing locks or pouring butyric acid on clinic entrances
- threatening violence
- stalking a clinic employee or a reproductive health provider
- arson or bombings

In response to these activities, or threats of these activities, abortion providers have sought legal recourse.

Antiabortion protestors outside a clinic in Buffalo, New York, April, 1992. *In addition to encouraging laws designed to place restrictions on women seeking abortions, some antiabortion protestors also attempt to limit physical access to abortion clinics by blocking entrances, damaging door locks, and even bombing buildings where pregnancies may be terminated.* **AP IMAGES**

They have often sought injunctions from state courts under traditional state law or state law specifically designed to keep abortion protesters off their private property and limit protest activities.

Since 1994, abortion providers have also sought injunctions under federal law. Congress enacted the Freedom of Access to Clinic Entrances Act (FACE) soon after the murder of Dr. David Gunn in March 1993 outside a Pensacola, Florida, clinic and the attempted murder of Dr. George Tiller in August 1993 outside a Wichita, Kansas, clinic. President Bill Clinton signed this bill into law in May 1994.

The Freedom of Access to Clinic Entrances Act provides uniform, national standards when an individual intentionally uses force, the threat of force, or physical obstruction to injure, intimidate, interfere with, or attempt to injure, intimidate, or interfere with someone who provides or is obtaining reproductive health services. FACE provides penalties if anyone intentionally damages or destroys a facility that provides reproductive health

services. The facility is covered even if it does not provide abortion services and even if it provides counseling to persuade women *not* to procure abortions. The statute provides for both civil and criminal penalties. The statute only prohibits acts of force, or threats of force, but allows individuals to seek an injunction if they have reason to believe that a FACE violation is likely. In 1998 the Department of Justice established the National Task Force on Violence against Health Care Providers to provide for more vigorous enforcement of FACE after Dr. Barnett Slepian, an obstetrician who provided abortion services, was shot and killed by an antiabortion activist in Amherst, New York.

Whether abortion providers seek injunctions under state law or under FACE, courts have had to deal with the question of whether the scope of these injunctions violated the First Amendment. Abortion protestors have argued that these injunctions act as a "prior restraint" under First Amendment doctrine, precluding them from conveying their antiabortion message.

SIGNIFICANT SUPREME COURT RULINGS

By 2007, the Supreme Court had decided three major cases in which it considered the argument that state or federal law, or injunctions issued under these laws, violated the First Amendment rights of protestors.

Madsen v. Women's Health Center In *Madsen v. Women's Health Center*, 512 U.S. 753 (1994), the Court considered the constitutionality of an injunction that created a thirty-six-foot buffer zone around the abortion clinic entrances, driveway, and the private property to the north or west of the clinic; restricted excessive noise-making within earshot of the clinic and the displaying of images from the outside that would be observable to patients inside the clinic; prohibited protesters within a three-hundred-foot zone around the clinic from approaching patients and potential patients who did not consent to talk; and created a three-hundred-foot buffer zone around the residences of clinic staff. In a six to three decision, Chief Justice William Rehnquist upheld some of these provisions.

One of the most important aspects of this decision was the issue of what level of scrutiny to apply to the restrictions. Petitioners had sought to persuade the Court to invoke heightened scrutiny under the rationale that the restrictions were content- or viewpoint-based. The Court rejected that claim, concluding that the constitutionality of the restrictions should be assessed under the more lenient, content-neutral framework, under which an injunction's challenged provisions must burden no more speech than necessary to serve a significant government interest. The Court ruled that the content-neutral framework was appropriate because the injunction was in response to the *actions* of the petitioner rather than the *content* of their speech. The fact that the injunction covered people who shared the same viewpoint merely suggested that those in the group whose *conduct* violated the trial court's original order happened to share that viewpoint, but it did not mean that the injunction itself was content or viewpoint based.

Having resolved the constitutional framework, the remainder of the Court's opinion focused on applying that legal theory to the particular facts. The Court affirmed the constitutionality of the thirty-six-foot buffer zone around the clinic entrances and driveway in light of the failure of an earlier injunction to meet its objectives. Its holding also reflected deference to the Florida state court's familiarity with the evidence. Similarly, the Court upheld the noise restrictions.

Nonetheless, the Court found that several of the measures were unduly restrictive:

- the thirty-six-foot buffer zone around private property because patients and staff did not have to cross that private property to enter the clinic

- the ban on observable images because the clinic could simply draw its curtains to protect a patient from a disagreeable placard

- the three-hundred-foot no-approach zone absent evidence that petitioners' language constitutes fighting words or conveys threats

- the three-hundred-foot buffer zone around staff residences because it sweeps too broadly

In sum, the *Madsen* decision was a split decision. The Court used the constitutional framework proposed by the pro-choice community and upheld two aspects of the injunction under that framework. But, despite the evidence that a prior, more limited injunction was ineffective, the Court overturned four aspects of this injunction as overly restrictive while purporting to defer to the expertise of the state trial court.

Schenck v. Pro-Choice Network of Western New York The *Madsen* decision left some confusion about the proper scope of a state court's injunction; the Court offered further clarity in *Schenck v. Pro-Choice Network of Western New York*, 519 U.S. 357 (1997). Once again, Chief Justice Rehnquist authored the opinion for the Court. For the most part, the vote was the same six to three vote found in *Madsen*.

As in *Madsen*, the injunction involved both fixed and floating buffer zones. Under the fixed buffer zones, protestors had to remain fifteen feet from clinic doorways, driveways, and driveway entrances. Under the floating buffer zones, protestors had to stay fifteen feet away from people and vehicles entering and leaving the clinics, and sidewalk counselors could be required to "cease and desist" their activities, upon request of patients, and to retreat and remain outside the fixed buffer zones.

Using a content-neutral framework, the Court concluded that the fixed buffer zones were constitutional but that the floating buffer zones violated the First Amendment. The Court did not object to some kind of "required separation" but, on the facts of this case, concluded that a fifteen-foot floating zone "leads to a substantial risk that much more speech will be burdened than the injunction by its terms prohibits." Because the sidewalk was only seventeen feet in width, the Court was concerned that this rule would prohibit any communication at all.

Hill v. Colorado The last decision in this trilogy was *Hill v. Colorado*, 530 U.S. 703 (2000), in which the Court assessed the constitutionality of a state criminal statute that prohibited any person from knowingly approaching within eight feet of another person who was within one hundred feet of a health-care facility for purposes of displaying a sign, engaging in oral protest, education, or counseling, or passing out leaflets or handbills, without that person's consent. Even though this statute imposed what could be described as a "floating buffer zone," and such zones had been struck down in both *Madsen* and *Schenck*, the Court upheld the eight-foot floating zone established by this state statute. The Court, in an opinion authored by Justice John Paul Stevens, concluded that the eight-foot zone was within a "normal conversational distance" and the "knowing" requirement protected a protestor who inadvertently stepped closer than eight feet. Other states, and some cities, have similar buffer zone laws that have been upheld as constitutional.

Following the Court's decision in *Hill*, lower courts had sufficient guidance as to how they could impose injunctions that might even include floating buffer zones to protect patients and others who sought to enter abortion clinics.

ARGUMENTS REGARDING CONSTITUTIONALITY

Individuals who have been prosecuted under FACE have sought to challenge the statute's constitutionality. They have argued that the statute is invalid under the First Amendment and exceeded Congress's commerce clause authority.

With respect to the First Amendment arguments, most lower court judges have found that injunctions issued under FACE are consistent with *Madsen*. Nonetheless, the Second Circuit concluded in 2001 that Judge Richard Arcara violated the First Amendment with an overly broad injunction under FACE when the district court issued an injunction against Operation Rescue and its members. This Second Circuit case is a product of more than a decade of antiabortion protests in western New York. In 1992 antiabortion protestors had targeted western New York for protest activity and had brought to the area thousands of protestors who engaged in widespread clinic blockades. Abortion providers obtained an injunction to be able to get their clinics open. When a new protest was scheduled for March 22, 1999, abortion providers immediately sought an injunction under FACE, arguing that there was a genuine threat that their rights would be violated absent an injunction. District Court Judge Arcara issued a preliminary injunction that was even broader than the one issued in 1992. It applied a buffer zone to all reproductive health facilities in western New York, not merely those providing abortions. At two clinics, it expanded the buffer zones beyond fifteen feet and eliminated the "sidewalk counselor" exception, which would have allowed two activists to approach individuals to communicate with them. At one clinic, the enlarged buffer zone extended sixty feet to the south and fifty-eight feet to the north. At a second clinic, more than one hundred feet of sidewalk were designated a no-protest

zone, forcing demonstrators to move across the street. The injunction also prohibited the use of sound amplification systems at protests near all covered facilities.

The Second Circuit found that the enlarged buffer zones violated the First Amendment because they effectively prevent "protestors from picketing and communicating from a normal conversational distance along the public sidewalk." In *New York v. Operation Rescue National*, 273 F.3d 184, 204 (2nd Cir. 2001), the Second Circuit concluded that a fifteen-foot buffer zone would have been sufficient with a few slight modifications at both facilities. The court was influenced, in part, by the fact that the protests in 2000 were much smaller than those in 1992, so an expanded buffer zone was not necessary. The Second Circuit also concluded that the ban on sound amplification devices was overbroad and needed to be narrowly tailored to each facility. Nonetheless, the Second Circuit did uphold the elimination of the sidewalk counselor exception, concluding that that exception was often subject to abuse and was not needed to foster appropriate communication.

The Second Circuit case is reflective of the current law with respect to injunctions against antiabortion protestors. Protest activity no longer appears to reach the scope of activities from the 1980s and 1990s. Possibly, the murders of some abortion providers has tempered the strength of this social movement. Even liberal courts, such as the Second Circuit, are therefore cutting back on the kinds of injunctions that are appropriate against such protest activity. *Madsen* continues to be the measure for whether such injunctions are constitutional, but the scope of the protest activity is a factor in whether the injunction is overbroad.

A second argument made by abortion protesters in cases challenging injunctions issued under FACE is that the federal statute exceeds Congress's proper authority under the commerce clause. The circuit courts have concluded that the statute is within Congress's commerce clause authority, although that conclusion did engender a strong dissent from Judge Harold DeMoss in the Fifth Circuit (see *United States v. Bird*, 401 F.3d 633 [5th Cir. 2005]). Judge DeMoss argued, in dissent, that the Supreme Court's decision in *United States v. Morrison*, 529 U.S. 598 (2000), precludes Congress from enacting a federal criminal statute regulating intrastate noncommercial conduct. The Third and Sixth Circuits have agreed with the Fifth Circuit that FACE does not exceed Congress's commerce clause authority, and the Supreme Court has not accepted certiorari of those decisions. They have concluded that FACE is best understood as a regulation of commercial activity because abortion-related violence has an impact on the ability of clinics to conduct their business. They distinguished FACE from the Violence Against Women Act (1994), which was overturned in *Morrison*, because the activity at issue in *Morrison* was not of an obvious commercial character. Hence, it appears that the Supreme Court will probably not consider the constitutionality of FACE under the commerce clause in light of the uniform opinion of lower federal courts that it is constitutional.

EFFECTS OF VIOLENCE

In the 1990s, violence against abortion providers was considered to be a significant problem in the United States. Dr. David Gunn, Dr. John Britton, and Dr. Barnett Slepian were shot and killed by antiabortion activists from 1993 to 1998. Dr. George Tiller was shot in 1993 and Dr. Calvin Johnson was stabbed fifteen times in 1996, losing four pints of blood. Other violence occurred against clinic employees, security guards, clinic escorts, and patients. Although certain organizations, such as the "Army of God," supported such violence, nearly all mainstream antiabortion organizations now reject violence as a form of opposition to abortion. Some antiabortion organizations have even offered rewards for the arrest and conviction of those responsible for abortion-related violence. In the end, opposition to these acts of violence within the antiabortion community, rather than injunctions, has probably had the biggest effect on limiting antiabortion protest activities. As the number of antiabortion protestors has diminished from the thousands to the hundreds, courts have found it less necessary to invoke extensive injunctive relief. Although these injunctions can be important to making it possible for clinics to remain open for business, and for women to feel comfortable obtaining abortion services, they have become less important as the nature of antiabortion protest activity has changed.

SEE ALSO *Abortion Protests; Planned Parenthood v. Casey, 505 U.S. 833 (1992); Rehnquist Court; Right to Life; Roe v. Wade, 410 U.S. 113 (1973)*

BIBLIOGRAPHY

Campbell, Regina R. 1996. "'FACE'ing the Facts: Does the Freedom of Access to Clinic Entrances Act Violate Freedom of Speech?" *University of Cincinnati Law Review* 64: 947.

Jacobs, Leslie Gielow. 1996. "Nonviolent Abortion Clinic Protests: Reevaluating Some Current Assumptions about the Proper Scope of Government Regulations." *Tulane Law Review* 70: 1359.

Reichman, Courtland L. 1995. "Federal Remedies for Abortion Protest: Discordance of First Principles." *Emory Law Journal* 44: 773.

Sule, Steven E. 1994. "Racketeering, Anti-Abortion Protesters, and the First Amendment." *UCLA Women's Law Journal* 4: 365.

Tribe, Laurence H. 1994. "The Constitutionality of the Freedom of Access to Clinic Entrances Act of 1993." *Virginia Journal of Social Policy and Law* 1: 291.

CASES

Hill v. Colorado, 530 U.S. 703 (2000).

Madsen v. Women's Health Center, 512 U.S. 753 (1994).

New York v. Operation Rescue National, 273 F.3d 184, 204 (2nd Cir. 2001).

Schenck v. Pro-Choice Network of Western New York, 519 U.S. 357 (1997).

United States v. Bird, 401 F.3d 633 (5th Cir. 2005).

Ruth Colker

ACCOMMODATION OF RELIGION

The First Amendment to the U.S. Constitution prohibits the establishment of religion by the state, first limited to the federal government and then extended in the twentieth century to the states through the Fourteenth Amendment. A number of interpretative theories have arisen around the meaning and application of this prohibition. At one extreme are those very few cases adhering to or at least describing a theory of strict separation between religion and the state, such as *Everson v. Board of Education*, 330 U.S. 1 (1947). Since the 1980s, however, the Supreme Court has been moving toward more of an "accommodation" approach based on a neutrality/coercion view of the prohibition at the heart of the establishment clause. This movement has shifted the Court away from a jurisprudence deliberately designed to make it difficult for the state to accommodate religion (as in *Lemon v. Kurtzman*, 403 U.S. 602 [1971] and its three-prong balancing test of intent, effects, and entanglement), a point emphasized by Justice John Marshall Harlan in *Sherbert v. Verner*, 374 U.S. 398 (1963), to one in which accommodation is broader and easier to justify.

The new accommodation jurisprudence is more deferential, based on a coercion standard of ambiguous contour (*Lee v. Weisman*, 505 U.S. 577 [1992]) and a neutrality standard that appears poised to privilege religion (in the aggregate) over the secular (*County of Allegheny v. American Civil Liberties Union, Greater Pittsburgh Chapter*, 492 U.S. 573 [1989]; *McCreary County v. American Civil Liberties Union of Ky.*, 545 U.S. 844 [2005]). Adherents to an accommodation theory are more open to the view that the establishment clause privileges religion within society and that accommodation is necessary to avoid using the establishment clause to promote irreligion. At its limit, under these theories of accommodation, the government violates the establishment clause only if it literally establishes a church, discriminates in favor of one religion over others, or coerces religious participation. The key questions under this approach, then, are what constitute nonneutrality and coercion sufficient to trigger the protection of the clause.

What follows is a brief suggestion of the way the Supreme Court is rewriting the analytical bases for approaching interpretive issues touching on the religion clauses. As in previous interpretive eras, the Supreme Court remains deeply divided. At least three conflicting foundations of religion clause jurisprudence continue to dominate the Court. Their advocates are among the ablest jurists of the last several generations.

PRIVILEGING RELIGION OVER IRRELIGION

One foundation of religion clause jurisprudence, led ever more aggressively by Justice Antonin Scalia, is grounded in appeals to tradition (*Marsh v. Chambers*, 463 U.S. 783 [1983])—not jurisprudential tradition, but the cultural understandings and practices of the people in the United States around the time of the adoption of the Bill of Rights. This approach has led Justice Scalia to adopt an aggressively antiseparationist position. Justice Scalia starts from the position that the religion clauses were not meant to force a separation of state from religion, something that would have been at odds with the lived reality of the republic at its founding. Neutrality is defined from the perspective of the benefits or grants offered by the state. Where the government offers any benefit or privilege, it must make it available to religion on an equal basis. Indeed, the religion clauses compel the privileging of religion as against irreligion and may permit the state to accommodate the beliefs of the majority religion over those of all others (as long as there is no formal establishment).

For minority religions, there is the solace of an individually applied free exercise clause. However, where majority religious morals or ethics result in enactment of a statute that is otherwise generally applicable and not purposely intended to target a religion, then even the protections of the free exercise clause would not be available. States are otherwise free to accommodate religion, either through direct funding or through the support of religious activities of citizens (*Mitchell v. Helms*, 530 U.S. 793 [2000]: "So long as the governmental aid is not itself 'unsuitable for use in the public school because of religious content,' . . . and eligibility for aid is determined in a constitutionally permissible manner, any use of that aid to indoctrinate cannot be attributed to the government and is thus not of constitutional concern").

For Scalia, the way to avoid the problem of the establishment of any one religion is to permit the establishment of them all (or at least of most of them). In effect, Scalia would like to see a return to *Reynolds v. United States*, 98 U.S. 145 (1878) ("Congress was deprived of all legislative power over mere opinion but was left free to reach actions which were in violation of social duties or subversive of good order"), and especially *Davis v. Beason*, 133 U.S. 333 (1890) ("It was never intended or supposed that the amendment could be invoked as a protection against legislation for the punishment of acts inimical to the peace, good order, and morals of society. . . . Probably never before in the history of this country has it been seriously contended that the whole punitive power of the government for acts, recognized by the general consent of the Christian world in modern times as proper matters for prohibitory legislation, must be suspended"). Justice Scalia would apply these ideas as a general principle in both free exercise and establishment clause jurisprudence, but in a more modern, neutrality and "original understanding" guise, and without the underlying anti-Catholic and anti-Mormon element.

ACCOMMODATION WITH LIMITS

In its more benign form, expounded in the opinions of Chief Justice William Rehnquist in his final year, there is also an emphasis on neutrality and a willingness to carve a wider ambit for governmental accommodation of religion. But there is also a definitive reluctance to abandon a formal adherence to some measure of separation between organized religion and the state. Thus, for example, Rehnquist found no constitutional infirmity in the provision of governmental vouchers to students to be used to pay the tuition of private religious schools, but only where it is clear that the choice is made by individuals (and not the state) and where it is also clear (at least as a formal matter) that the individual was offered a true and free choice among religious and secular options (*Zelman v. Simmons-Harris*, 536 U.S. 639 [2002]).

This group is less convinced that the religion clauses compel a privileging of religion over irreligion (or secular interests). They view formal separation as important, but based on a sense that the forms of establishment important to the founding generation, rather than official acts of formal establishment, ought to guide the courts in the setting of the limits of accommodation. As a consequence, Chief Justice Rehnquist was unwilling to require the state to provide aid to students when that aid was to be applied to training in theology (*Locke v. Davey*, 540 U.S. 712 [2004]).

At the same time, this group is much more willing to defer to the state, both in matters of generally applicable laws that appear formally neutral with respect to religion (*Employment Div. v. Smith*, 494 U.S. 872 [1990)]) and state rules that accommodate religion, as long as formal neutrality is observed and direct endorsement is avoided (*Lynch v. Donnelly*, 465 U.S. 668 [1984]). This position consolidates the coercion touchstone at the center of *Lee v. Weisman*, in which coercion itself serves as a proxy for issues of privileging religion over secular interests and the contours of neutrality among religions.

STRICT SEPARATION BETWEEN CHURCH AND STATE

The third jurisprudential school, represented on the Supreme Court by Justices David Souter, Ruth Bader Ginsburg, and John Paul Stevens, adheres to the more traditional jurisprudence of the post–World War II (1939–1945) period. At its core, this group privileges principles of separation (*Everson*) and strict neutrality between religion and the secular (*Santa Fe Indep. School Dist. v. Doe*, 530 U.S. 290 [2000]). It views tradition, especially in the form of original understanding, as less useful because of the difficulty of extracting any sort of consensus from the older cases or the writings of the founders.

Justice Souter remains truest to the *Lemon* standard, but even he concedes that it has been substantially reworked in cases after the late 1990s. Neutrality is important in this context, but not dispositive. Moreover, the old "effects" prong in modified form becomes the great battleground for establishment. Mere formal neutrality is rejected in favor of more intensive scrutiny of effects. The greater the resemblance of effects to the forms or indicia of establishment understood in an eighteenth-century sense, the less likely the law would be viewed as neutral (*Rosenberger v. Rector and Visitors of the University of Virginia*, 515 U.S. 819 [1995]). For this group, the mere fact that the accommodation is indirect—for example, religious choices are made by individuals rather than the state—makes no difference in the analysis; any indirect connection between state action and religious benefit is suspect (*Zelman v. Simmons-Harris*, 536 U.S. 639 [2002], Souter dissenting). Ironically, this view (that the character of state involvement as either direct or indirect should have no effect) is shared by Justice Scalia, but for the purpose of expanding the power of the state to directly aid religion, even in its religious endeavors (*Mitchell v. Helms*, 530 U.S. 793 [2000]).

Lastly, the group Justice Souter represents remains true to the idea that a foundational purpose of the religion clauses is to avoid social and political divisiveness by avoiding the injection of religion into the national political discourse (to which the "Scalia camp's" response is that the only way to avoid religious discord is to permit all religions to freely participate in political life).

CONCLUSION

All three camps have substantially abandoned the three-part *Lemon* standard (secular purpose, secular effect, and little entanglement) or have reconstituted it to a greater or lesser extent in a neutrality standard (conservative majorities essentially turning the "effects" prong of *Lemon* into a neutrality and endorsement standard over the strong jurisprudentially based objections of the Souter/ Stevens camp). But the use of a common language belies the gulf that separates the definition of those terms as used

by either camp. Souter starts from a foundation of separation, and the principles (if not even necessarily the holding) of *Everson*. He uses "original understanding" to paint a more complicated picture of the cultural understandings and consensus of the 1790s than does Scalia and his camp (*Lee v. Weisman*). For Souter, neither the discourse nor the practices of the times can fairly lead one to any sense of consensus about the meaning of the religion clauses. For Scalia, while the writings of the times might be conflicting, the practices of the times, in the aggregate, point to a general consensus against separation of government and religion.

Neutrality has also acquired one of three meanings, sprung from an unresolved conflict over the core animating principle of the religion clauses. The most traditional approach, now held by the most liberal camp, posits that neutrality requires neither governmental involvement in, nor support of, religion and is based on the idea that the religion clauses require separation. The middle ground posits neutrality between religion and irreligion, that is, that state action can neither privilege nor burden religion as against secular interests, and tolerates incidental benefits to religion where the benefit is evenhanded (*Everson*). Depending on how one interprets burdening or benefiting, this approach can be, and has been, useful to both separationists and religionists. The most radical approach, now held by the most religiously conservative justices, posits the idea (derived from the nineteenth-century Mormon cases and Justice Potter Stewart's dissent in *Sherbert*) that religion must be privileged over irreligion and that neutrality requires evenhandedness among religions, even those religions previously suppressed (see *Church of the Lukumi Babalu Aye v. Hialeah*, 508 U.S. 520 [1993]).

The Court has moved its jurisprudential moorings to permit it to tolerate greater state accommodation of religion, even accommodations that might incidentally favor religion. That movement has been accomplished by a change in the language of analysis—from purpose, effects, and entanglement, to neutrality, benefit, burden, and choice.

SEE ALSO *Church of the Lukumi Babalu Aye v. City of Hialeah, 508 U.S. 520 (1993); Establishment Clause; First Amendment; Free Exercise of Religion; Lemon v. Kurtzman, 403 U.S. 602 (1971); Rosenberger v. Rector and Visitors of the University of Virginia, 515 U.S. 819 (1995)*

BIBLIOGRAPHY

Berg, Thomas C. 1997. "Religion Clause Anti-Theories." *Notre Dame Law Review* 72(3): 693, 721–724, 737–742.

Gey, Steven G. 2007. "Life after the Establishment Clause." *West Virginia Law Review* 110: 1–50.

Greenawalt, Kent. 2008. *Religion and the Constitution*, Vol. 2: *Nonestablishment and Fairness*. Princeton, NJ: Princeton University Press.

Hamburger, Philip. 2002. *Separation of Church and State*. Cambridge, MA: Harvard University Press.

Harwood, Christopher B. 2006. "Evaluating the Supreme Court's Establishment Clause Jurisprudence in the Wake of *Van Orden v. Perry* and *McCreary County v. ACLU*." *Missouri Law Review* 71: 317–366.

Lupu, Ira C. 1996. "To Control Faction and Protect Liberty: A General Theory of the Religion Clauses." *Journal of Contemporary Legal Issues* 7: 357–384.

McConnell, Michael W. 1992. "Accommodation of Religion: An Update and a Response to the Critics." *George Washington Law Review* 60(3): 685, 695–696.

Tushnet, Mark. 1988. "The Emerging Principle of Accommodation of Religion." *Georgetown Law Journal* 76: 1691, 1695–1699.

Larry Catá Backer

ACKERMAN, BRUCE
1943–

Bruce Arnold Ackerman, Sterling Professor of Law and Political Science at Yale University, is one of the leading constitutional theorists of the past thirty years. His scholarly work transcends disciplinary boundaries, moving comfortably among the fields of law, political science, constitutional history, and public policy.

Ackerman is best known for his theory of American constitutional change, which has become identified with the term *constitutional moment*, used by him in the first two volumes of his projected trilogy, *We the People* (1991, 1998). The traditional view of American constitutionalism assumes that fundamental constitutional change results from the formal amendment process of Article V of the Constitution; that view also associates constitutional politics almost exclusively with the decisions of the U.S. Supreme Court. In *We the People*, by contrast, Ackerman asserts that the United States is a *dualist democracy*. At most times, *normal politics*, based on the polity's tacit and consensual understanding of the Constitution's meaning, prevails. On rare occasions, however, this state of affairs is ruptured by a transformative *constitutional moment*, not necessarily involving a formal amendment, that results in a process of *higher lawmaking*, reflecting a deep and pervasive alteration in Americans' understanding of the constitutional order. This might happen, for example, when a president is elected who can persuasively claim a mandate for fundamental change. In such cases, "the people" have effected a real change in the constitutional order—

Bruce Ackerman testifying on Capitol Hill, December, 1998. *As a professor of law and political science at Yale University, Ackerman suggested in his book* We the People *that particular events he termed* constitutional moments, *such as the Civil War, have altered the way Americans view the Constitution, in effect changing the document without amending a word of it.* LUKE FRAZZA/AFP/GETTY IMAGES

"amended" the Constitution, in a word—without necessarily having invoked the formal amendment process.

Such constitutional moments are far rarer than formal constitutional amendments. Few would disagree with Ackerman's choice of (1) the republic's founding and (2) the Civil War (1861–1865) and Reconstruction as constitutionally transformative events. However, Ackerman's identification of the New Deal as a third instance of extratextual constitutional amendment dramatizes his theory's departure from the traditional conception. The momentous changes wrought by the New Deal were not, after all, embodied in formal amendments to the Constitution. Yet Ackerman regards Franklin D. Roosevelt's reelection in 1936 as a resounding popular affirmation of both the New Deal and the basic changes in the constitutional order that it augured—vastly expanded national powers to regulate the economy; the rise of an administrative state unforeseen by the founding generation; and, ultimately, the withering of a Supreme Court jurisprudence that had resisted these developments.

We the People is a major contribution to the history and theory of American constitutionalism. Its shift of emphasis from the Supreme Court toward other actors in the constitutional regime is widely admired and has been echoed in much recent scholarship on the Constitution. Some critics, however, have found Ackerman's set of criteria for determining when a "constitutional moment" has occurred difficult to apply consistently. Moreover, it is not clear what the theory implies for how judges and other political actors should act in light of a conclusion that a particular political episode in American history, such as the New Deal, counts as "transformative" rather than as "normal" politics. Does Ackerman's theory suggest that congressional legislation departing from the basic premises of the New Deal (for example, the phasing out of Social Security or the repeal of legislation guaranteeing the right of collective bargaining) or a return by the Supreme Court to its conservative pre-1937 jurisprudence would be unconstitutional?

Ackerman's scholarly accomplishments go well beyond *We the People* and constitutional moments, and they have often been addressed to an audience beyond the academy. In *The Stakeholder Society* (1999), he and his coauthor, Anne Alstott, proposed that the government endow every American with a lump sum of $80,000 on his or her twenty-first birthday. *Deliberation Day* (2004), coauthored with James S. Fishkin, proposed that a one-day national holiday be declared during each presidential election year, during which voters would convene in public spaces to debate the issues dividing the presidential candidates. Alongside these inventive if quixotic proposals lies Ackerman's prodigious record of scholarship concerning such diverse issues as the constitutionality of the North American Free Trade Agreement (NAFTA), the inadequacy of the Constitution's provisions for presidential succession, the foundations of political liberalism, and a great deal besides.

SEE ALSO *Amendment, Outside of Article V*

BIBLIOGRAPHY

Ackerman, Bruce. 1991. *We the People: Foundations*. Cambridge, MA: Belknap Press.

Ackerman, Bruce. 1998. *We the People: Transformations*. Cambridge, MA: Belknap Press.

Ackerman, Bruce, and Anne Alstott. 1999. *The Stakeholder Society*. New Haven, CT: Yale University Press.

Ackerman, Bruce, and James S. Fishkin. 2004. *Deliberation Day*. New Haven, CT: Yale University Press.

Ackerman, Bruce. 2007. "The Holmes Lectures: The Living Constitution." *Harvard Law Review* 120: 1738–1812.

Clyde Spillenger

ACLU WOMEN'S RIGHTS PROJECT

The mission of the American Civil Liberties Union (ACLU) extends from the simple premise that if the rights of society's most vulnerable members are denied, the rights of all citizens are imperiled. Guided by this, citizen activists led by Roger Baldwin (1884–1981), Crystal Eastman (1881–1928), and Albert DeSilver (1888–1924) founded the ACLU in 1920. The nonprofit and nonpartisan organization has grown from a roomful of concerned citizens to an organization of more than 500,000 members and supporters with offices in almost every state.

The U.S. Constitution serves to protect citizens from government encroachment on their liberty. Originally applicable only to the federal government, since the Civil War the Bill of Rights's guarantees have extended to infringement by state action as well. In particular, the ACLU concentrates on First Amendment rights, equal protection under the law, and due process and privacy in personal affairs. It is the balance between governmental action and personal liberty that concerns the ACLU and underpins the 6,000 annual legal challenges they mount in the judicial system.

Since entering the twenty-first century, the ACLU has been the leading advocate of the position that civil liberties must be respected, even in times of national emergency. Outside of wartime and throughout much of its history, the ACLU's focus has been to extend rights to segments of the population that have traditionally been denied their rights, including Native Americans and other people of color; lesbians, gay men, bisexuals, and transgender people; women; mental-health patients; prisoners; people with disabilities; and the poor.

THE WRP'S PAST VICTORIES IN COURT

The ACLU Women's Rights Project (WRP) is part of the National ACLU. It was founded in 1972 by then professor and advocate (later Supreme Court Justice), Ruth Bader Ginsburg, and since that time has been a leader in the legal battles to ensure women's full equality in American society. Ginsburg became general counsel for the ACLU Women's Rights Project in 1973. The work of the Women's Rights Project was a natural fit for the ACLU because women's rights are part of the overall human rights agenda of the ACLU. Throughout the second wave of feminism, from the late 1960s through the early 1980s, progress in the advancement of women's rights took place on two fronts. The more visible front involved political advocacy and consciousness-raising. This piece of the movement was led by Betty Friedan (1921–2006), Gloria Steinem (1934–), and others like them, through organizations such as the National Organization for Women (NOW). The less visible, yet arguably more important front, was led by Professor Ginsburg and involved incremental changes in the way the Court interpreted the balance between governmental action and the rights of citizens.

Ginsburg was not the first to take up the cause of fighting for women's rights at the ACLU. As she has said, she stood on the shoulders of many giants, including ACLU cofounders Jane Addams (1860–1935), Emily Greene Balch (1867–1961), Crystal Eastman, and Jeanette Rankin (1880–1973), and later, Dorothy Kenyon (1888–1972) and Pauli Murray. Ginsburg deliberately chose the ACLU as the vehicle for her legal work, rather than an organization with a narrower women's rights agenda, in large part because she believed that the ACLU would enhance the credibility of the women's rights cause. The ACLU was a natural home for what became the Women's Rights Project because of its recognition of, and dedication to, the integral interconnection between civil liberties and civil rights, including women's rights.

The bulk of Ginsburg's litigation strategy was implemented in the 1970s, following closely on the heels of the most active chapter in the fight against segregation and racial discrimination led by Justice Thurgood Marshall and the National Association for the Advancement of Colored People (NAACP). Like the NAACP, the WRP built precedent upon precedent, not advancing too far in any one case but gradually leading the Supreme Court to a series of decisions that combined to impact the law. Unlike the NAACP, which relied on Reconstruction amendments to guarantee the highest level of scrutiny to governmental discrimination based on race, the WRP was without the ultimately failed Equal Rights Amendment (ERA) and had to first raise the level of scrutiny afforded cases involving gender discrimination. The Women's Rights Project's litigation strategy is one of the masterpieces of American cause litigation. It remains the model for multistate, multivenue case coordination on any social justice issue.

Ginsburg's first case on behalf of the ACLU to reach the Supreme Court, *Reed v. Reed*, 404 U.S. 71 (1971), resulted in the Court's holding that a law categorically providing for differential treatment of men and women violates the Fourteenth Amendment's equal protection clause. In the first case that Ginsburg herself argued to the Court, *Frontiero v. Richardson*, 411 U.S. 677 (1973), the Court invalidated an Air Force policy providing automatic dependents's benefits to wives of service members but requiring proof of dependency for husbands seeking benefits. Likewise challenging a policy that assumed men and women's roles in the family, the Court in *Weinberger v. Wiesenfeld*, 420 U.S. 636 (1975), struck down differential treatment for men and women for Social Security survivor's benefits. Finally, in *Craig v. Boren*, 429

U.S. 190 (1976), Ginsburg succeeded in convincing the Court to adopt a heightened standard of review for gender-based classifications, thereby solidifying the intermediate review option that had emerged three years prior in *Frontiero*. This new level of review made it more difficult for a state to justify most differences in its treatment of women and men.

Throughout the later part of the 1970s, Ginsburg successfully tackled law after law that treated women as second-class citizens, either overtly or disguised as protection of "the weaker sex." Laws were rewritten and newly interpreted, so as to establish women's right to full partnership with men at work, in the home, and in every sphere of life. Ginsburg's work, and that of other feminist lawyers during this decade, resulted in extraordinary change in women's legal status in the United States. It is worth noting that the political and legal debate about a woman's right to choose whether to continue or terminate her pregnancy also began during this decade, but traveled a different path. Shortly after its inception in 1974, The ACLU Reproductive Freedom Project formally separated from the Women's Rights Project to pursue legal guarantees of reproductive choice based on the right to privacy. In 2007, the right to privacy is an increasingly faltering foundation for personal liberty, whereas Ginsburg's reliance on the concept of equal protection of the laws has effectively enacted the Equal Rights Amendment.

Pregnancy discrimination cases were a key part of WRP's agenda during this active decade; however, one of the most successful efforts mounted by WRP began with a setback. In *General Electric Co. v. Gilbert*, 429 U.S. 125 (1976), the Court rejected the ACLU's amicus brief proposing that pregnancy discrimination in the workplace was tantamount to sex discrimination. Such discrimination, the Court concluded, did not treat women and men differently; rather, it treated pregnant women differently from nonpregnant persons. After losing that battle, WRP staff attorney Susan Deller Ross helped rally WRP's supporters to form the Coalition to End Discrimination Against Pregnant Workers. Ginsburg and Ross coauthored a column for the *New York Times*, calling for legislators to mend the law post-*Gilbert*, and they continued lobbying, reporting, and testifying in Congress. The result of their efforts was the passage of the Pregnancy Discrimination Act in 1978, an amendment to Title VII that established that pregnancy discrimination in the workplace is indeed unlawful sex discrimination.

THE WRP IN THE TWENTY-FIRST CENTURY

The Women's Rights Project continues to achieve systemic legal reforms through the courts in the area of equality for women nearly forty years after its founding. In 2005, the WRP expanded its work in employment with a particular focus on low-wage immigrant women workers and women in nontraditional occupations. Increasingly integrating a global perspective, the WRP has also infused international human rights frameworks and mechanisms into its advocacy and litigation in each of its four areas of focus: employment, violence against women, criminal justice, and education.

The WRP's employment work focuses on removing barriers to women's economic security in a variety of different spheres. The ACLU's low-wage immigrant women workers program sheds light on labor and sexual exploitation faced by women working in hotels, retail stores, restaurants, and private homes. WRP attorneys have litigated cases on behalf of Latina, Asian, and African immigrant women seeking redress for wage violations, poor working conditions, and sexual harassment. As a counterpart to litigation efforts, the WRP uses international human rights mechanisms to seek reforms. In one notable example, the WRP brought to the United Nations Human Rights Commission in Geneva the problems faced by domestic workers employed by UN diplomats with immunity from suit.

Gender discrimination battles in the United States continue as well. The WRP continues to challenge discrimination against women in nontraditional occupations in cases on behalf of female and minority public school custodians employed by New York City, and female police officers in Suffolk County, New York. By defending the use of affirmative action in hiring practices and the right of women to continue working during their pregnancies, women gain occupational choices that they have historically been denied.

The Women's Rights Project has overall responsibility for implementing ACLU policy in the area of gender discrimination. WRP staff conduct direct litigation, file amicus curiae (friend-of-the-court) briefs, provide support for ACLU affiliate litigation, serve as a resource for ACLU legislative work on women's rights, and seek to advance ACLU policy goals through public education, organizing, and participating in coalitions. The WRP has been an active participant in virtually all of the major gender discrimination litigation in the Supreme Court since Ginsburg's tenure, and in congressional and public education efforts to remedy gender discrimination, plus myriad other endeavors on behalf of women. In the future, the Women's Rights Project will continue to explore novel and creative ways to use litigation, legislative advocacy, international human rights law, and public education to advance women's rights in the systematic model started by Ruth Bader Ginsburg.

SEE ALSO *American Civil Liberties Union (ACLU); Ginsburg, Ruth Bader; Murray, Pauli; Sex Discrimination*

BIBLIOGRAPHY

American Civil Liberties Union. "About the Women's Rights Project." Available from http://www.aclu.org/womensrights/index.html

Amy Leigh Campbell

ADAMS, JOHN

SEE *Marbury v. Madison, 5 U.S. 137 (1803); Marshall Court; Washington, George.*

ADARAND CONSTRUCTORS, INC. V. PEÑA, 515 U.S. 200 (1995)

Adarand Constructors, Inc. v. Peña, 515 U.S. 200 (1995), was a five-to-four ruling by the U.S. Supreme Court concerning the constitutional permissibility of federal race-based affirmative action programs. The case was brought by a white contractor challenging a federal program that set aside federal contracting dollars for minority-owned construction companies in order to remedy past discrimination against minority contractors. The plaintiff, whose bid to install a guardrail on a federally constructed highway was lower than that of the contract-winning, minority-owned company, argued that the set-aside violated his constitutional right to equal protection of the laws under the Fifth Amendment (which in earlier cases had been held to include an "equal protection component"). The Court, with Justice Sandra Day O'Connor writing for the majority, called for strict scrutiny and hinted that the program was unconstitutional. In so doing, the Court overruled its 1990 decision in *Metro Broadcasting v. FCC*, 497 U.S. 547 (1990), which had held that federal, unlike state, racial set-aside programs should receive only intermediate scrutiny from the judiciary.

The *Adarand* ruling had important symbolic and doctrinal significance. It was the first important racial affirmative action case since Justice Clarence Thomas joined the Court, replacing Justice Thurgood Marshall. Justice Thomas had joined with the four dissenters in *Metro Broadcasting* to create a working five-member bloc on the Court that was skeptical of the very concept of race-based government affirmative action. This skepticism was reinforced by a separate concurrence in *Adarand* penned by Justices Antonin Scalia and Thomas in which these Justices amplified a nearly absolute colorblind vision of the Constitution.

As for the elimination of the different standards of review for federal and state programs, the Court's rejection of *Metro Broadcasting* is plausible. The argument in *Metro Broadcasting* that the federal government enjoys a special authority to engage in affirmative action because it was empowered in Section 5 of the Fourteenth Amendment to redress equal protection violations seems flawed. While Section 5 certainly gave Congress powers the federal government did not otherwise enjoy under the American system of limited enumerated federal powers, it did not give the federal government any remedial authority that states did not already have under the residual plenary powers. So Section 5 was not a strong basis for differentiating federal and state authority (although the historical track record and the ease with which smaller local governments can be captured by a racial faction might have been).

But as Justice John Paul Stevens's dissent in *Adarand* pointed out, the resulting "symmetrical" application of strict scrutiny to all laws (federal or state) that make use of race—whether the laws on their face exclude or draw in racial minorities—leads to an anomalous situation in which, say, a law giving African Americans (the primary intended beneficiaries of the equal protection clause) a "plus" in law school admissions would be judged by courts under a more stringent and more skeptical standard (strict scrutiny) than would a law that excluded women from law school altogether (which would be assessed under the so-called intermediate scrutiny applicable to all gender-based classifications.)

Yet *Adarand* is opaque on exactly what strict scrutiny entails in this setting and the degree to which it would be impossible to implement race-based affirmative action at any government level. Read one way, the Court was insisting on "race neutrality" across the board, saying in effect that the government could never take race into account, except in narrowly defined remedial contexts. This reading is plausible in light of the stark-sounding test the Court announced: "All racial classifications, imposed by whatever federal, state, or local governmental actor, must be analyzed by a reviewing court under strict scrutiny." But other language betrays the Court's unwillingness to demand complete race neutrality the way Justice Scalia's separate writing might. As Justice O'Connor insisted in her opinion, "strict scrutiny is not [necessarily] fatal in fact" and "does take 'relevant differences' into account"—a rejection of absolutism. The Court added that affirmative action might be justified by the "unhappy persistence of both the practice and the lingering effects of racial discrimination against minority groups in this country." In a related passage, the Court indicated that in implementing strict scrutiny, judges can still differentiate between a race-conscious "No Trespassing" sign and a race-conscious "welcome mat." In fact, only two Justices, Thomas and Scalia, sounded the note of complete colorblindness.

Adarand's skepticism of race-based affirmative action might also have been limited to the particular context of government public-works contracts. Government contracts are highly susceptible to fraud, since contracts may be awarded to "minority" firms in which minorities are merely figurehead owners in corporate documents, but not in reality. The multimillion-dollar contracts that may be at stake can provide a powerful incentive for corruption.

The *Adarand* Court did not actually apply strict scrutiny to the federal program before it; the Court remanded to the lower courts to apply the test in the first instance. Thus, while *Adarand* made important law, precisely what *strict scrutiny* would mean in practice would have to await further high court rulings.

Since *Adarand*, the Court has not addressed another race-based government contracting program in which the asserted justification for the racial classification was remedying past discrimination, so the meaning of *strict scrutiny* in this setting remains open. In *Grutter v. Bollinger*, 539 U.S. 306 (2003), the Court did uphold (with Justice O'Connor joining the *Adarand* dissenters to make a five-member majority) the University of Michigan Law School's race-based admissions policy, which was ostensibly designed not for remedial purposes but rather to ensure a diverse classroom and campus environment for pedagogical gain. Justice O'Connor's majority opinion in *Grutter* was much more respectful of carefully tailored race-based law school admissions policies than the *Adarand* opinion was toward set-aside programs, leading some observers to conclude that the *Adarand* ruling should be understood as a product of special problems associated with contracting, rather than all, race-based affirmative action programs.

SEE ALSO *Affirmative Action; Rehnquist Court*

BIBLIOGRAPHY

Amar, Akhil Reed, and Neal Kumar Katyal. 1996. "Bakke's Fate—Symposium on Bakke." *UCLA Law Review* 43: 1745.

Chemerinsky, Erwin. 2005. "Racial Classifications Benefitting Minorities." Ch. 5, *Constitutional Law.* New York: Aspen.

Vikram D. Amar

ADDERLEY V. FLORIDA, 385 U.S. 39 (1966)

Adderley v. Florida, 385 U.S. 39 (1966) marked a turning point in the Warren Court's treatment of civil rights protests. Since 1961, when it decided the first case arising out of the lunch-counter sit-in movement, the Court consistently overturned convictions of civil rights demonstrators. The array of laws southern states used against protesters—trespass, disorderly conduct, and breach of peace were the most frequently employed—was matched by a Court that was equally eclectic in its use of the law, drawing on the due process and equal protection clauses and the First Amendment to overturn convictions. But in *Adderley* the steadily weakening majorities in the protester cases broke, and, in a five-to-four decision, the Court upheld the trespass convictions of thirty-two students who had participated in a demonstration outside a jailhouse.

The demonstration, which took place in September 1963, involved approximately two hundred Florida A&M University students who marched to the Tallahassee jail to protest the recent arrest of fellow African-American students for their effort to desegregate local movie theaters. Outside the jail, protesters sang freedom songs, clapped, and danced. When the sheriff ordered them to disperse, they refused, and over one hundred students were arrested.

Justice Hugo Black wrote the opinion of the Court upholding the convictions. Over the previous two years, Black had voiced his concern with civil rights protests in increasingly vitriolic dissents. Most recently, in *Brown v. Louisiana*, 383 U.S. 131 (1966), involving a peaceful library sit-in, he warned "that the crowd moved by noble ideals today can become the mob ruled by hate and passion and greed and violence tomorrow." In *Adderley*, Justice Byron White, who had voted to overturn the convictions in *Brown v. Louisiana*, switched sides, and Black had his majority.

Black distinguished the situation in *Adderley* from two recent decisions, *Edwards v. South Carolina*, 372 U.S. 229 (1963) and *Cox v. Louisiana*, 379 U.S. 536 (1965), in which the Court overturned, on First Amendment grounds, breach-of-peace convictions stemming from civil rights demonstrations. Unlike these cases, Black noted, *Adderley* involved trespass law, which does not have the vagueness problems associated with breach-of-peace charges. He also distinguished *Edwards*, which involved a protest at the South Carolina state capitol, because jails, unlike statehouses, have no tradition of being open to the public. Most controversially, Black extended the rights associated with ownership of private property to government property: "The State, no less than a private owner of property, has power to preserve the property under its control for the use to which it is lawfully dedicated."

Justice William O. Douglas's dissent—which Warren Court scholar Lucas Powe praised as "his best opinion in fifteen years" (2000, p. 279)—accused the majority of allowing Florida to use its trespass law "to bludgeon those who peacefully exercise a First Amendment right to protest to government against one of the most grievous of all modern oppressions which some of our States are inflicting on our citizens." Under the First Amendment, there was no reason to distinguish a jail from "an executive mansion, a legislative chamber, a courthouse, or the statehouse itself"—all are "seats of government." Douglas also highlighted the class element involved with public demonstrations:

Conventional methods of petitioning may be, and often have been, shut off to large groups of our citizens. Those who do not control television and radio, those who cannot afford to advertise in newspapers or circulate elaborate pamphlets may have only a more limited type of access to public officials. Their methods should not be condemned as tactics of obstruction and harassment as long as the assembly and petition are peaceable, as these were.

In summarizing his dissent from the bench, speaking in a "quiet, passionate voice," Douglas described the Court's decision as a "great break with the traditions of the Court" (Graham 1966, p. 1).

Along with *Walker v. City of Birmingham*, 388 U.S. 307 (1967), *Adderley* reflected a growing discomfort within the late Warren Court toward direct-action protest. The justices were far from alone in their concern with the direction of the civil rights struggle, however. By 1966 urban rioting had become a national epidemic, and a new generation of militant black activists were grabbing headlines with demands for "Black Power." At a time of an intensifying anti-Vietnam War (1957–1975) movement and rising crime rates, many Americans were concerned that the country was being overrun by protests and lawlessness, and turned to conservative politicians who promised to restore "law and order" to the country. Just six days before *Adderley* was decided, Republicans gained seats in both houses of Congress in the midterm elections, and Californians elected Ronald Reagan as their governor.

SEE ALSO *First Amendment; Warren Court*

BIBLIOGRAPHY

Graham, Fred P. 1966. "High Court Backs Conviction of 32 in Rights Protest." *New York Times*, November 15: 1, 30.

Horwitz, Morton J. 1998. *The Warren Court and the Pursuit of Justice: A Critical Issue*. New York: Hill and Wang.

Powe, Lucas A., Jr. 2000. *The Warren Court and American Politics*. Cambridge, MA: Harvard University Press.

Schmidt, Christopher W. 2008. "Hugo Black's Civil Rights Movement." In *The Transformation of Legal History: Ideology, Politics, and Law*, eds. Alfred L. Brophy and Daniel W. Hamilton. Cambridge, MA: Harvard University Press.

Christopher W. Schmidt

ADEQUATE AND INDEPENDENT STATE GROUNDS

Although the U.S. Supreme Court can review a state court decision on an issue of federal law, the Court will not do so if the state court resolved the case on an *independent and adequate state ground*. In other words, if the state court resolved the case on a matter of state law that was both independent of the federal question and adequate to resolve the case by itself, the Court will not hear the federal question. To do so would constitute an advisory opinion because the state law resolution—on which the state court's judgment is conclusive—would still be dispositive. As the Court explained, "If the same judgment would be rendered by the state court after we corrected its views of federal laws, our review would amount to nothing more than an advisory opinion" (*Herb v. Pitcairn*, 324 U.S. 117 [1945]).

The doctrine stems from *Fox Film Corp. v. Muller*, 296 U.S. 207 (1935). In that case, Fox Film sued Muller in Minnesota state court for breach of contract. Muller answered and asserted a defense that the arbitration clauses in the contracts were invalid under federal antitrust laws. The state court held the arbitration clauses invalid under the antitrust laws. It also held the arbitration clauses inseparable from the other contractual provisions under state law and therefore held the entire contract invalid. The Minnesota Supreme Court affirmed, and Fox Film appealed to the U.S. Supreme Court. The Court held that the state law issue of severability was an independent ground justifying the decision and stated that "the case is controlled by the settled rule that where the judgment of a state court rests upon two grounds, one of which is federal and the other nonfederal in character, our jurisdiction fails if the nonfederal ground is independent of the federal ground and adequate to support the judgment."

STATE GROUNDS MUST BE ADEQUATE

A state ground is *adequate* if a reversal of the federal issue would not change the decision. There are exceptions. A state ground is not adequate if the state law giving rise to the ground is unconstitutional (*Staub v. City of Baxley*, 355 U.S. 313 [1958]). In addition, a state ground is not adequate if it is not fairly or substantially supported in the record (*Ward v. Board of Commissioners of Love County*, 253 U.S. 17 [1920]).

A state procedural rule can constitute an adequate state ground barring federal review (*Michigan v. Tyler*, 436 U.S. 499 [1978]). However, a state procedural rule will not constitute an adequate state ground if it prevents the vindication of important federal rights while failing to advance significant state interests (*Henry v. Mississippi*, 379 U.S. 443 [1965]). Nor will a state procedural rule constitute an adequate state ground if it is an obvious subterfuge to evade consideration of a federal issue or if it is applied inconsistently by the state courts (*Radio Station WOW, Inc. v. Johnson*, 326 U.S. 120 [1945]; *James v. Kentucky*, 466 U.S. 341 [1984]). Finally, a state rule cannot constitute an adequate state ground if it is

discretionary, rather than mandatory (*Williams v. Georgia*, 349 U.S. 375 [1955]).

STATE GROUNDS MUST BE INDEPENDENT

In addition to being adequate, a state ground must also be *independent* to preclude review. A state ground is independent if it is not reliant upon federal law. Thus, if the state ground incorporates federal law, review is permitted (*South Dakota v. Neville*, 459 U.S. 553 [1983]).

In some cases, whether a state law ground is independent of federal law is unclear. In such cases, the Supreme Court will presume that the state ground is not independent unless the state court clearly and expressly relies on state law for its decision. For example, in *Michigan v. Long*, 463 U.S. 1032 (1983), Long was questioned by police officers after he drove his car into a ditch. The police officers noticed a knife in his car and, on that basis, searched him. Though they found no weapons, they then conducted a protective search of the car. In the car, they found no weapons, but they did find a bag of marijuana. They then searched the truck and found another seventy-five pounds of marijuana. Long was criminally prosecuted in Michigan state court. He moved to suppress the marijuana on the grounds that the search of the car violated the Fourth Amendment to the U.S. Constitution. The Michigan Supreme Court agreed and held that the search violated the Fourth Amendment. The court also held that the search violated the Michigan constitution.

The U.S. Supreme Court reversed. It first held that the state court's ruling that the search violated the state constitution was not an independent state ground precluding federal review. Instead, the Court assumed that the Michigan Supreme Court believed that if the U.S. Constitution prohibited the search, then the Michigan constitution must have prohibited it as well, and that that was the reason why the Michigan Supreme Court held the search violative of the state constitution. The Supreme Court then held that the Michigan Supreme Court erred in concluding that the U.S. Constitution prohibited the search, and therefore it reversed the state court.

Long creates a presumption that state courts decide cases on federal grounds for the purposes of the independent and adequate state ground doctrine. If state courts wish instead to ground their decision on state law, they must "clearly and expressly" so indicate.

VIRTUES AND VICES OF THE DOCTRINE

The independent and adequate state ground doctrine has at least three benefits. First, it enforces Article III's prohibition on advisory opinions. Second, it reduces the need to pass unnecessarily on constitutional questions

(*Ashwander v. TVA*, 297 U.S. 288 [1936]). Third, it reduces friction between state and federal courts by eliminating the need for the Supreme Court to pronounce a state court wrong on an issue of federal law. The doctrine is not without its criticisms. The principal vice is that the doctrine allows erroneous state court interpretations of federal law to stand uncorrected.

SEE ALSO *Article III; Ashwander v. Tennessee Valley Authority, 297 U.S. 288 (1936); Federalism; Federal Jurisdiction; Michigan v. Long, 463 U.S. 1032 (1983)*

BIBLIOGRAPHY

Chemerinsky, Erwin. 2007. *Federal Jurisdiction.* 5th edition. New York: Aspen.

Scott Dodson

ADKINS V. CHILDREN'S HOSPITAL, 261 U.S. 525 (1923)

By 1923, the year of *Adkins v. Children's Hospital*, 261 U.S. 525, the U.S. Supreme Court had for more than two decades used the Fifth and Fourteenth Amendments' due process clauses to protect a personal right to make contracts. The Court had held—most famously in *Lochner v. New York*, 198 U.S. 145 (1905)—that this constitutional "liberty" encompassed employers' and employees' freedom to contract about such matters as wages and hours without undue or unreasonable constraints imposed by government. In *Lochner*, the Court had dismissed a state maximum-hours law as "mere meddlesome interference" in a private matter and an unconvincing means to protect health.

Adkins involved a 1918 federal law mandating a minimum wage for female employees in the District of Columbia. Congress had reason to believe the act would satisfy the Court's freedom of contract standard. Since *Lochner* foreclosed legal intervention to compel economic consequences, Congress framed the statute as a means to protect health and morals. The Court had shown some solicitude for women's physical vulnerabilities in the workplace, sustaining a state maximum-hours law limited to female workers (*Muller v. Oregon*, 208 U.S. 412 [1908]). In a more recent decision, *Bunting v. Oregon,* 243 U.S. 426 (1917), the Court had indicated some leeway on wage legislation by sustaining a maximum-hours law that mandated time-and-a-half overtime pay.

Nonetheless, a five-to-three majority in *Adkins* struck down the federal law. (Justice Louis Brandeis did not participate.) Justice George Sutherland's opinion for the Court rested on the premise that freedom of contract is "the general rule and restraint the exception." Minimum-wage laws compelled some persons to succor others. Free agreements between particular employers and employees were more just than blanket rates set by a federal agency. Government could pass reasonable health or morals laws: The sustaining of legislation in *Muller* and *Bunting* had relied on the reasonable connection between hours of labor and the health of laborers. Sutherland, though, could find no rational thread that might tie a particular wage to a woman's health. The link between wages and morality was equally attenuated: Indeed, in the present case, the government's mandated wage had priced an elevator operator—and likely other women—out of her job. In addition, the recently adopted Nineteenth Amendment, nationalizing women's suffrage, suggested that women's status was now sufficient to obviate the need for most protective legislation.

Chief Justice William Howard Taft and Justice Oliver Wendell Holmes Jr. wrote dissents. Holmes, echoing his famous *Lochner* dissent, forcefully rejected what he termed the liberty of contract "dogma." Valid laws, he pointed out, limit contracts in myriad ways. More surprisingly, the chief justice adopted Holmes's 1905 charge that the majority's opinion was tainted by its disagreement with the legislature's "economic view." Believing that *Bunting* had tacitly discredited *Lochner*, Taft thought that Congress had reason to believe that low wages were as harmful to laborers as long hours. Wages, especially those of exploitable women, were a legitimate matter of public concern, subject to reasonable regulation.

The *Adkins* decision anticipated a spate of what is now labeled *substantive due process* activism by the Court, many state laws in the next decade failing the Court's reasonableness standard. As precedent, though, *Adkins* proved short-lived. Its overruling in *West Coast Hotel v. Parrish*, 300 U.S. 379 in early 1937 signaled the Court's acquiescence to the New Deal and a far more deferential acceptance of economic and commercial legislation. Yet, in their effort to reason through the proper relation between law and freedom, the justices in *Adkins v. Children's Hospital* addressed a constitutional question perpetually arising.

SEE ALSO *Freedom of Contract; Protective Legislation for Women Workers*

BIBLIOGRAPHY

Arkes, Hadley. 1994. *The Return of George Sutherland: Restoring a Jurisprudence of Natural Rights.* Chaps. I and III. Princeton, NJ: Princeton University Press.

G. Roger McDonald

ADMINISTRATIVE AGENCIES

Administrative agencies perform a variety of functions. Some are regulatory agencies that regulate the actions of private individuals, corporations, and associations. For example, the Consumer Products Safety Commissions (CPSC) controls and even prohibits unsafe consumer products to ensure they are safe. A host of other administrative agencies perform similar functions in other areas, including the Federal Aviation Administration (FAA), which controls aircraft and aviation generally; the Securities and Exchange Commission (SEC), which regulates the securities industry; and the Environmental Protection Agency (EPA), which promulgates and enforces regulations designed to protect the environment. Other administrative agencies perform the quite different function of administering governmental entitlements programs. Included in this group is the Social Security Administration (SSA), which is in charge of Social Security and disability payments and determinations, among other things.

Because virtually all administrative agencies are housed in the executive branch of government, and therefore serve under the president, there has been controversy regarding the scope of their authority. Clearly, executive branch agencies can perform "executive" functions, in the sense of administering and enforcing federal statutes or distributing federal funds pursuant to congressional directives. But most modern administrative agencies also perform functions that appear to be non-executive in nature. For example, some administrative agencies promulgate administrative regulations (which seem "legislative" in that the final rule functions much like a statute, in the sense of creating binding rules and obligations). Some also perform judicial functions, in the sense of adjudicating issues related to whether there are violations of regulatory requirements or whether individuals are (or are not) entitled to governmental payments.

Prior to the late 1930s, the number, size, and complexity of U.S. administrative agencies tended to be relatively small. In part, this was due to the fact that the federal courts adopted a relatively narrow view of Congress's authority to delegate power to administrative agencies. But the dynamics changed in the mid-1930s, when the country was mired in the Great Depression. By 1931 more than 2,000 banks had failed. By the winter of 1932–1933, "one-fourth of the nation's work force was unemployed," industrial production had fallen by 60 percent, and the price of wheat had dropped by "nearly 90 percent" (McElvaine 1984, p. 137). When President Franklin D. Roosevelt was elected in 1932, he demanded that elected officials take action, and he managed to push through his New Deal legislative program.

Roosevelt's legislative program was met with hostility by the courts, which restrictively construed the federal commerce power, and ultimately struck down four major pieces of New Deal legislation: the National Industrial Recovery Act, the Bituminous Coal Act, the Agricultural Adjustment Act, and the Railway Pension Act (see, for example, *Carter v. Carter Coal Co.*, 298 U.S. 238 [1936]). In addition, the federal courts issued hundreds of injunctions against New Deal legislation. Although the courts' decisions adopted a restrictive view of the federal commerce power, they also adopted a restrictive view of Congress's authority to delegate legislative and judicial power to administrative agencies (see particularly *Schechter Poultry Corp. v. United States*, 295 U.S. 495 [1935] and *Panama Refining Co. v. Ryan*, 293 U.S. 388 [1935]). In essence, the Court concluded that Congress had transgressed the separation of powers principle by delegating its legislative power to executive branch officials.

In what has come to be regarded as a constitutional crisis, Roosevelt attempted to sway the Court's jurisprudence on the commerce clause and delegation issues. Following his landslide victory in the 1936 elections, Roosevelt pushed his so-called Court Packing Plan, which would have altered the Supreme Court's membership (and, presumably, its decisions) by adding additional members to the Court. The plan provided that when a judge or justice of any federal court reached the age of seventy without retiring, a new justice would be appointed by the president (subject, of course, to confirmation by the United States Senate). Because six Supreme Court justices were seventy years old or older at the time, the plan would have expanded the number of justices to fifteen and allowed Roosevelt to appoint six new justices. Roosevelt hoped that a majority of the reconfigured Court would then be sympathetic to his legislative program.

Although the plan was never enacted, Roosevelt may have influenced the Court to alter its approach to commerce clause and delegation questions, and in *NLRB v. Jones & Laughlin Steel Corp.*, 301 U.S. 1 (1937) the Court effectively overruled *Panama Refining* and *Schechter*. In later cases, the Court sustained increasingly broad delegations of power. As the Court recognized in *Immigration and Naturalization Service v. Chadha*, 462 U.S. 919, 985 (1983), "In practice[,] restrictions on the scope of the power that could be delegated diminished and all but disappeared." Although the Court required that delegations be supported by a so-called "intelligible principle," the Court readily found intelligible principles in such vague formulations as "'just and reasonable,' 'public interest,' 'public convenience, interest, or necessity,' and 'unfair methods of competition.'"

Since the mid-1980s, as the Court has loosened its approach to unlawful delegation and commerce clause issues, Congress has delegated more and more power to administrative agencies. These trends have led to a dramatic growth in both the number and size of administrative agencies. As the D.C. Circuit noted in

Ballerina Pen Co. v. Kunzig, 433 F.2d 1204 (1970), "administrative agencies may well have a more far-reaching effect on the daily lives of all citizens than do the combined actions of the executive, legislative and judicial branches." The growth of agency power is reflected in the size of the Code of Federal Regulations, which now includes 208 volumes (dramatically more than in the 1930s when FDR sparred with the Court).

While the growth of administrative power may have been necessary, and perhaps inevitable, it has not been without costs. In *Federal Trade Commission v. Ruberoid Co.*, 343 U.S. 470 (1952), Justice Robert Jackson stated in his dissent that "[t]he rise of administrative bodies probably has been the most significant legal trend of the last century. . . . They have become a veritable fourth branch of the Government, which has deranged our three-branch legal theories."

SEE ALSO *Administrative Procedure Act; Judicial Review of Administrative Action; Judicial Review of Statutory Interpretation by Agencies; New Deal and the Economy*

BIBLIOGRAPHY

Aman, Alfred C., Jr., and William T. Mayton. 2001. *Administrative Law*. 2nd edition. St. Paul, MN: West Group.

Leuchtenburg, William F. 1966. "The Origins of Franklin Delano Roosevelt's 'Court Packing' Plan." *Supreme Court Review* 1966: 347–394.

McElvaine, Robert S. 1984. *The Great Depression: America, 1929–1941*. New York: Times Books.

Pierce, Richard J., Jr.; Sidney A. Shapiro; and Paul R. Verkuil. 2004. *Administrative Law and Process*. 4th edition. New York: Foundation Press.

Weaver, Russell L., and William D. Araiza. 2006. *Administrative Law*. St. Paul, MN: Thomson/West.

Russell L. Weaver

ADMINISTRATIVE PROCEDURE ACT

The federal Administrative Procedure Act (APA) represented a major advance in the history of administrative law in the United States. Prior to the enactment of the APA, many administrative agencies had broad discretion to structure their processes in the way they saw fit. In many instances, agencies could issue substantive rules and regulations (i.e., rules and regulations designed to govern the conduct of regulated entities) without public participation or input from those who might subsequently be subject to the regulatory requirements. Likewise,

subject to constitutional constraints, agencies had broad discretion to structure their investigative and adjudicative processes in the way they saw fit. However, the constitutional constraints were relatively limited and did not provide a realistic or comprehensive check on administrative authority.

Although the APA dramatically altered and improved administrative processes, passage of the APA was neither simple nor easy. During the 1930s, while the nation was mired in the Great Depression, President Franklin D. Roosevelt took office with an aggressive plan of action that he referred to as his "New Deal." Among other things, the New Deal resulted in the creation of new administrative agencies, as well as a dramatic growth in the authority and impact of administrative agencies. There were many complaints at the time, especially from those in the business community, that administrative agencies had become so powerful as to constitute a "fourth branch" of government. These expressions of concern ultimately led to the passage of the APA, which was designed to limit and control administrative authority. However, because there was a bitter tug of war regarding the content of the APA, as the United States Supreme Court recognized in *Universal Camera Corp. v. NLRB*, 340 U.S. 474 (1951) the final version of the APA necessarily involved compromises between competing factions.

Despite these compromises, the APA revolutionized the way administrative agencies created rules and regulations (hereafter, the terms *rule* or *rules* will be used to refer to either "rules" or "regulations"). With some exceptions, agencies were generally required to use the APA's "legislative" procedures to articulate new rules (see 5 U.S.C. § 553, 556, 557). In some instances, the APA mandated the application of "formal" rulemaking procedures, which involve, essentially, trial-type procedures (see 5 U.S.C. § 556–557). Agencies that are forced to use these procedures must conduct judicial trials to create rules. In other words, they must allow the parties to present witnesses and documents, to cross-examine opposing witnesses, and generally provide the level of protection ordinarily accorded in a formal judicial proceeding. The APA also gave some agencies the option of articulating policy using "informal" rulemaking procedures (also known as "notice and comment" procedures; see 5 U.S.C. § 553). Whereas informal procedures do not require the agency to provide a trial as part of its legislative process, those procedures do require the agency to allow public participation. Absent a congressional directive, the informal process requires the affected agency to provide notice of a proposed rulemaking to interested parties, to give interested parties the opportunity to submit comments, and to consider the comments.

The APA also revolutionized agency judicial processes by providing strict requirements governing the use of those processes (see 5 U.S.C. § 556–557). For example, the APA provided rules regarding who may preside at agency adjudications, as well as the content and form of agency decisions and agency review processes. It also imposed procedural requirements designed to ensure fairness, such as placing restrictions on *ex parte* communications between the parties to proceedings and the person who presides at those proceedings, or limiting the ability of those involved in prosecuting or investigating regulatory offenses to serve as presiding officers or judges in the cases that they prosecuted or investigated. In later statutes, Congress supplemented the APA with additional requirements In some cases, for example, agencies are required to use administrative law judges (who receive various job protections designed to ensure their impartiality), rather than a presiding judge who might be nothing more than an agency employee.

As previously noted, the APA involved compromises between opposing social forces, and these compromises have led to litigation regarding the meaning of the APA. In a number of post-enactment decisions, the courts have fleshed out the APA's meaning and application. For example, in *Universal Camera Corp.*, the Court held that the APA was compromise legislation, as to which opposing legislative forces had reached compromise, and the courts may not, therefore, supplement the APA's notice and comment rulemaking procedures with additional procedures. Likewise, in *Securities and Exchange Commission v. Chenery*, 332 U.S. 194 (1947) (known as *Chenery II*) and *NLRB v. Bell Aerospace Co.*, 416 U.S. 267 (1974), the Court held that agencies had discretion to articulate new "rules" through the adjudicative process, rather than through the APA's legislative processes.

In *Universal Camera Corp.* and *Consolidated Edison v. NLRB*, 305 U.S. 197 (1938), the Court held that the results of formal rulemakings must be reviewed under the "substantial evidence" standard, meaning that there must be substantial evidence to support the agency's conclusions. In addition, the Court ruled that the determination of whether substantial evidence exists should be determined by examining the entire administrative record, not just those parts that are favorable to the agency's position. Last, but far from least, in the Court's landmark decision in *Chevron U.S.A. v. Natural Resources Defense Council*, 467 U.S. 837 (1984), the Court held that federal courts could defer to an agency's interpretation of its governing statute.

SEE ALSO *Administrative Agencies; Chevron U.S.A. v. Natural Resources Defense Council, 467 U.S. 837 (1984); Judicial Review of Administrative Action; Judicial Review of Statutory Interpretation by Agencies; Securities and Exchange Commission v. Chenery, 318 U.S. 80 (1943)*

BIBLIOGRAPHY

Aman, Alfred C., Jr., and William T. Mayton. 2001. *Administrative Law*. 2nd edition. St. Paul, MN: West Group.

Pierce, Richard J.; Jr., Sidney A. Shapiro; and Paul R. Verkuil. 2004. *Administrative Law and Process*. 4th edition. New York: Foundation Press.

Weaver, Russell L., and William D. Araiza. 2006. *Administrative Law*. St. Paul, MN: Thomson/West.

Russell L. Weaver

ADMIRALTY JURISDICTION

Article III of the U.S. Constitution includes admiralty and maritime cases among the nine types of cases or controversies within the subject-matter jurisdiction of the federal courts. This grant has enabled the Supreme Court to play an important role in maritime law. The Court is now less oriented to admiralty cases than it was in the nineteenth century, when admiralty implicated much of the nation's foreign policy and when many justices had extensive maritime experience. Still, the Court continues to play an important role in maritime matters.

Admiralty jurisdiction carries with it important consequences. It affords a litigant a federal forum with trial to a judge rather than a jury and access to some unique admiralty procedures. Admiralty jurisdiction is usually concurrent, not exclusive; those instances where admiralty affords the only forum are generally limited to an esoteric but important group of cases in which the vessel itself, rather than its owner or operator, is essentially the plaintiff or defendant. Even when admiralty jurisdiction is concurrent, two important consequences follow: Federal maritime law, both judge-made and statutory, plays a substantial, though not exclusive, role, and the Supreme Court may have the final say.

Admiralty jurisdiction in the United States initially extended essentially to cases on the high seas or waterways the tide affected. In *The Thomas Jefferson*, 23 U.S. 428 (1825), the Court held admiralty jurisdiction did not extend to a wage claim regarding an interstate voyage on the Missouri River because it occurred hundreds of miles above the ebb and flow of the tide. The Court reached the same conclusion in *The Steamboat Orleans v. Phoebus*, 36 U.S. 175 (1837) because the vessel navigated on the Mississippi, not on the high seas or in tidal waters. The tidewater test, which found its justification in history rather than logic, precluded admiralty jurisdiction from the inland waterways which territorial expansion and the steamboat made increasingly prominent venues of maritime commerce. In *The Propeller Genesee Chief v. Fitzhugh*, 53 U.S. 443 (1851) and *Jackson v. The*

Magnolia, 61 U.S. 296 (1857), the Court abandoned that restrictive test and soon extended admiralty jurisdiction to inland waterways that, alone or in conjunction with other waters, were navigable in interstate or international commerce (*The Daniel Ball,* 77 U.S. 557 [1870]).

In trying to define admiralty jurisdiction, the Court has debated between traditional bright-line tests, which focus on the locality of an incident or harm, and approaches that consider additional factors. If admiralty jurisdiction exists to facilitate maritime commerce, as is often suggested, a traditional bright-line locality test proves both underinclusive and overinclusive.

It is underinclusive because admiralty jurisdiction traditionally did not apply when a vessel on a navigable waterway caused damage or injury on land. Congress closed that gap in 1948 when it passed the Admiralty Extension Act, extending admiralty jurisdiction to include ship-to-shore damage. A strict locality test proved overinclusive when the maritime situs was essentially fortuitous. The Court rejected such a locality test in *Executive Jet Aviation, Inc. v. City of Cleveland,* 409 U.S. 249 (1972), when it held that admiralty jurisdiction did not extend to a tort claim by an airplane owner against the City of Cleveland arising from the crash in Lake Erie of a land-based plane that took off from Cleveland's airport. The maritime situs of the incident was insufficient to establish admiralty jurisdiction.

Following *Executive Jet,* the Court sought to craft "a locality plus" approach. In *Foremost Insurance Co. v. Richardson,* 457 U.S. 668 (1982), the Court held that admiralty jurisdiction did apply to a collision between two pleasure vessels because the negligent operation of a vessel "on navigable waters … ha[d] a significant relationship with maritime commerce." Similarly, in *Sisson v. Ruby,* 497 U.S. 358 (1990), the Court held that admiralty jurisdiction extended to claims arising from a fire that began in the washer-dryer of a pleasure craft while moored at a marina. A "fire on a vessel docked at a marina on navigable waters" could cause "potential disruptions to commercial maritime activity." Moreover, there was a "substantial relationship between the activity giving rise to the incident"—that is, "storage and maintenance of a vessel at a marina on navigable waters"—and "traditional maritime activity."

Finally, in *Jerome B. Grubart, Inc. v. Great Lakes Dredge & Dock Co.,* 513 U.S. 527 (1995), the Court found admiralty jurisdiction applied to claims for damage to the Chicago Loop from negligent work by a crane on a barge several months earlier. The tortfeasor's activity on navigable waters was "so closely related to activity traditionally subject to admiralty law that the reasons for applying special admiralty rules" applied. Similarly, in maritime contract cases, the Court has long applied a multifactor test that is even more conceptual and less spatial than that used in torts.

The use of multifactor tests has created some uncertainty, which results in occasional battles over subject-matter jurisdiction. Justice Antonin Scalia has suggested that the Court would do better to base admiralty jurisdiction simply on whether the incident arose from activity of a vessel on navigable waters.

The existence of admiralty jurisdiction, whether invoked or not, often brings with it the substitution of maritime, for state, law. Judges and scholars have debated the extent to which courts should fashion and apply federal judge-made maritime law. Whereas the Court often used to articulate the view that general maritime law should apply in admiralty in the interests of uniformity, the Court always made some exceptions, and there may be a trend to apply some state law more often in localized incidents on domestic waters where a state has a strong interest in the issues or parties.

Admiralty cases have given the Court opportunity to address a number of important questions that frequently arise in a common law context. For instance, in *Bisso v. Inland Waterways Corp.,* 348 U.S. 310, 349 U.S. 85 (1955), the Court held that a towboat could not contractually exonerate itself from all liability from its own negligence; the Court drew upon tort and contract law to conclude that such a provision violated public policy. In *Kermarec v. Compagnie Generale Transatlantique,* 358 U.S. 625 (1959), the Court rejected the common law distinction between the duty owed a licensee and invitee in favor of a duty of reasonable care. In *United States v. Reliable Transfer Co.,* 421 U.S. 397 (1975), the Court held that comparative fault applied in maritime collision cases. In *East River Steamship Corp v. Transamerica Delaval, Inc.,* 476 U.S. 858 (1986), the Court held that a maritime products liability action did not exist when a defective product causes damage only to itself.

In such cases, the Court not only makes general maritime law for admiralty cases in federal and state courts. Its resolution of these issues in a maritime context also provides examples of Supreme Court reasoning on familiar contracts or torts questions. As such, the Court's work in such maritime cases may, by analogy, influence the work of other courts in fashioning the common law in a land context.

SEE ALSO *Article III; Common Law; Jurisdiction*

BIBLIOGRAPHY

Bederman, David J. 2000. "Admiralty Jurisdiction." *Journal of Maritime Law and Commerce* 31: 189–215.

Edginton, John A., Thomas J. Fennell, Steven F. Friedell, et. al. 2007. *Benedict on Admiralty.* 7th edition. Albany, NY: Matthew Bender.

Gilmore, Grant, and Charles Black, Jr. 1975. *The Law of Admiralty.* 2nd edition. Mineola, NY: Foundation.

Robertson, David W. 1970. *Admiralty and Federalism: History and Analysis of Problems of Federal-State Relations in the Maritime Law of the United States.* Mineola, NY: Foundation.

Robertson, David W. 1998. "Summertime Sailing and the U.S. Supreme Court: The Need for a National Admiralty Court." *Journal of Maritime Law and Commerce* 29: 275–304.

Joel K. Goldstein

ADMISSION OF NEW STATES CLAUSE

Article IV, Section 3, Clause 1 of the U.S. Constitution provides that "New States may be admitted by the Congress into this Union; but no new State shall be formed by the Junction of two or more States, or Parts of States, without the Consent of the Legislatures of the States concerned as well as of Congress."

Under this authority, Congress has admitted thirty-seven new states as members of the United States. These new states, perhaps eleven of which were anticipated by the founders, were nonetheless able to join the Union on an "equal footing" with the existing states. A nine-to-two majority of the Committee of Detail at the Constitutional Convention in Philadelphia in fact voted to strike out proposed text that "If the admission [of new states] be consented to, the new States shall be admitted on the same terms with the original States"; the founders did not want to limit Congress and they were wary of the possible influence of new western states in the government of the United States. Even so, the equal footing doctrine predates the Constitution and stands at the core of the American federal system of government. "[W]hen a new State is admitted into the Union," the U.S. Supreme Court majority wrote in *Coyle v. Oklahoma,* 221 U.S. 559, 573 (1911), "it is so admitted with all of the powers of sovereignty and jurisdiction which pertain to the original states, and ... such powers may not be constitutionally diminished, impaired or shorn away." There are no limits to the numbers of state or the size of new states, for that matter, that Congress may admit as members of the United States.

The equal footing doctrine received its first expression in the Resolution of 1780. Congress, acting under the Articles of Confederation, resolved that states with claims on the U.S. public domain of the former "Crown" lands should cede their lands so that new states with republican governments could be created and then be admitted as full members of the Confederation. The Northwest Ordinance of 1787 directed, too, that the states formed out of the Northwest Territory be admitted on an "equal footing" with the existing states. One of Congress's first acts under the new U.S. Constitution was, on August 7, 1789, to re-pass the Northwest Ordinance.

The Tenth Amendment, adopted in 1791, further upholds the equal footing doctrine with its simple declaration that "powers not delegated to the United States, nor prohibited by it to the States, are reserved to the States, respectively, or to the people." And each of the enabling acts passed by Congress to admit one of the thirty-seven new states specified that the new state be admitted "on an equal footing" with the original states.

The U.S. Supreme Court endorsed the equal footing doctrine in *Pollard's Lessee v. Hagan,* 44 U.S. 212 (1845). The Court ruled that the state of Alabama had the same ownership rights—in this case, of the shores of inland navigable waters and of the submerged lands beneath—as had the state of Georgia and as had the other, original states. "Alabama is ... entitled to the sovereignty and jurisdiction over all the territory within her limits, subject to the common law, to the same extent Georgia possessed it, before she ceded it to the United States," the Court ruled. "To maintain any other doctrine is to deny that Alabama has been admitted into the union on an equal footing with the original states." As the Court later declared in *Coyle v. Oklahoma,* " 'This Union' was and is a union of States, equal in power, dignity, and authority, each competent to exert that residuum of sovereignty not delegated to the United States by the Constitution itself."

In *Spooner v. McConnell,* 22 F 939 (1838), *Scott v. Jones,* 46 U.S. (5 How.) 343 (1847), *Case v. Toftus,* 39 Fed. 730 (C.C.D. Ore. 1889), and other cases, however, federal courts and the U.S. Supreme Court made clear that the admission of states as equals to the original states meant equality with respect to the U.S. Constitution and the new states' powers as states. The equal footing doctrine did not preclude the imposition by Congress of conditions for the admission of states or the preemption of state laws by congressional statutes. Specifically, equal footing did not mean equality of rights in the soil, per the terms of the Northwest Ordinance and all subsequent state enabling acts that reserved to the federal government the disposal of the soil of the territories. "Equal footing" did not mean equality "in all respects," as some of the early resolutions admitting new states phrased it, and it did not necessitate economic equality.

Although Congress has never outright refused to admit a new state (notwithstanding the U.S. Senate's refusal in 1844 to approve the treaty annexing Texas as a new state), Congress has on numerous occasions used its authority to delay the admission of new states; on three occasions U.S. presidents have vetoed acts admitting new states. But once new states have been admitted to the Union, they—like the original states—cannot secede, per the Supreme Court ruling in *Texas v. White,* 74 U.S. 700 (1869).

Although Congress can admit new states, it cannot *create* new states. States, for the purposes of the Constitution, have to arise from the people constituting political communities. They have to have defined territorial boundaries and written constitutions that prescribe and limit governmental power. Twenty-two states had independent governments before becoming part of the Union (the original thirteen states and state governments previously established in the Missouri, Michigan, Oregon, Kansas, Minnesota, and Nebraska territories and in Vermont, Texas, and West Virginia), in fact, whereas the other twenty-eight states acquired their state governments the moment that they were admitted into the Union. The new state governments thereby replaced the existing territorial and other governments (California had military government, and Kentucky and Maine were governed by Virginia and Massachusetts, respectively).

Because the admission of new states clause establishes that states cannot be formed out of preexisting states without the approval of the mother states' legislatures, few states have been formed from existing states: Vermont (from New York), Kentucky, Maine, and West Virginia. West Virginia stands as the exception. Northern Virginians who did not want to secede from the Union formed their own wartime government and in 1863 petitioned the Republican Congress for admission as a separate state. But the Virginia legislature, part of the Confederate States of America, never agreed to the legislation.

SEE ALSO *Article IV; Territories; Texas v. White, 74 U.S. 700 (1869)*

BIBLIOGRAPHY

Grupo de Investigadores Puertorriqueños. 1984. *Breakthrough from Colonialism: An Interdisciplinary Study of Statehood*. 2 vols. Río Piedras: Universidad de Puerto Rico, 1984.

Onuf, Peter S. 1987. *Statehood and Union: A History of the Northwest Ordinance*. Bloomington: Indiana University Press.

Bartholomew H. Sparrow

ADVISORY OPINIONS

American courts are chiefly dispute-resolution institutions and rarely express opinions on legal questions in the abstract. In part, the explanation is historical. English common law courts typically acted in the context of particular quarrels between adversaries. American courts, too, naturally assumed the same primary function of settling actual disputes. The historical account is incomplete, however. English courts offered abstract advice in some circumstances. Moreover, many modern state courts have abandoned any historically rooted doubts about advisory opinions. Some state courts routinely deliver advisory opinions when solicited by authorized officers under local law. Many more state courts answer abstract questions about local law certified to them by federal courts.

Federal courts have no formal authority to issue advisory opinions. The classic illustration came early. In 1793 President George Washington asked his secretary of state, Thomas Jefferson, to seek advice from the Supreme Court regarding the interpretation of treaties with European nations. When Jefferson wrote to the justices, however, they responded in a famous letter to Washington himself, in which they explained that if they were to answer his questions outside the context of a particular case, they would not be acting as judges at all, but would be serving "extrajudicially," as though they were employees of the executive branch.

The ban on advisory opinions by federal courts has roots in the Constitution. The judicial power of the United States, established by Article III of the Constitution, is limited to the adjudication of "cases" and "controversies." The Supreme Court has long understood "cases" and "controversies" to be actual disputes between competing parties. Moreover, purely advisory opinions are thought to be inconsistent with the role of unelected, life-tenured federal judges in the American democracy. Judicial lawmaking is accepted because it is necessarily entailed in the essential function of resolving disputes. Advisory opinions, which by hypothesis cannot be justified on the basis of necessity, are therefore aberrant in a system that hopes generally to leave lawmaking to politically accountable public servants.

The prohibition on federal court advisory opinions is also, in part, methodological. Courts are thought to perform at their best when they examine legal issues illuminated by interested parties arguing for different outcomes in the circumstances of concrete disputes. Judges can use particular factual circumstances both to fashion good solutions to real problems and to avoid announcing unduly expansive rulings they may come to regret. Arguably, then, a solid brand of judicial lawmaking occurs when courts hold their tongues until they have thought issues through in the crucible of actual quarrels.

The ban is related to the general principle that federal court judgments on legal questions must be final. The judgment of an inferior federal court can be reviewed and perhaps reversed by a higher court, and ultimately by the Supreme Court. Yet court judgments cannot be reexamined or revised by the president or Congress. If the courts were to render judgments that are subject to revision in one of the other branches, they, again, would be serving, in effect, as subordinate officers in the branch with genuine final authority.

Doubts about advisory opinions figured in the history of the Declaratory Judgment Act of 1934, which empowers federal courts to set aside ordinary forms of judicial relief (like compensatory damages or injunctions) and to settle disputes by declaring the rights and duties of the parties. Prior to that act, the Supreme Court had expressed concern that declaratory judgments would be advisory and, therefore, unconstitutional. Nevertheless, in *Aetna Life Ins. v. Haworth*, 300 U.S. 227 (1937), the Court sustained the Declaratory Judgment Act on the theory that it does not restrict federal courts to the giving of advice, but merely authorizes them to state the law clearly so that interested parties can act accordingly.

The Supreme Court cites the prohibition on advisory opinions in a variety of contexts to explain, at least in part, the federal courts' inability to determine federal questions. Nevertheless, the ban bears critical examination. There are countless ways in which federal courts express themselves beyond the narrow requirements of particular cases. For example, judges are involved in the drafting of general rules of procedure that apply to all cases in the future and thus cannot be justified as necessary to resolve any particular case. In its own work, the Court itself routinely addresses abstract legal questions when it manipulates the issues presented in appellate cases in order to isolate the matters on which it wishes to rule. The ban on advisory opinions may not be a hard-and-fast rule at all, but a general admonition that it is usually prudent to avoid unnecessary declarations about legal questions.

Federal judges often make *extrajudicial* public statements on legal topics in speeches, books, and law journal articles. In those contexts, too, prudence usually prevails. Judges rarely take controversial positions on issues that might come before them on the bench. Typically, they concentrate on systemic problems regarding the federal judicial system. For example, the chief justice delivers annual addresses about the state of the federal judiciary and, in that context, often suggests changes in federal law that he and other justices think are advisable—again outside the context of any particular case. Judges are known to have given confidential advice to officers of one of the other branches. Yet activities of that kind are conventionally thought to be illegitimate or, at the least, poor form. Abe Fortas served as a key advisor to President Lyndon Johnson after Johnson appointed him to the Supreme Court. That relationship was widely criticized and was almost certainly one of the reasons the Senate failed to confirm Fortas's nomination as chief justice.

SEE ALSO *Article III; Case or Controversy; Jay Court*

BIBLIOGRAPHY

Frankfurter, Felix. 1924. "A Note on Advisory Opinions." *Harvard Law Review* 37: 1002–1009.

Jay, Stewart. 1997. *Most Humble Servants: The Advisory Role of Early Judges.* New Haven, CT: Yale University Press.

Murphy, Bruce A. 1988. *Fortas: The Rise and Ruin of a Supreme Court Justice.* New York: Morrow.

CASES

Aetna Life Ins. v. Haworth, 300 U.S. 227 (1937).

Larry Yackle

AFFIRMATIVE ACTION

The term *affirmative action* refers to a voluntary or involuntary plan adopted by an employer in hiring or promotion decisions, or by an educational institution for admissions decisions, that has the goal of providing a remedy for past discrimination or of diversifying a work force or student body. The Civil Rights Act of 1964 has provided the primary modern legal basis for the affirmative action cases that have come before the Supreme Court, but the equal protection clause of the Fourteenth Amendment, enacted in 1868, has also been a source of reasoning on affirmative action. Both the supporters and the opponents of affirmative action programs have cited the Civil Rights Act and the equal protection clause, with different interpretations.

HISTORICAL BACKGROUND

At the end of the Civil War, governments in the states that had formed the Confederacy attempted to restrict the rights and opportunities of newly freed slaves. In response, the United States adopted the Fourteenth Amendment to the Constitution, intended to define national citizenship to include former slaves and their descendants, to provide due process of law, and to prohibit states from denying equal protection of the law to some of their citizens. This last prohibition was essentially an attempt to abolish discrimination through law. Known as the *equal protection clause*, this part of the amendment mandates that all states provide equal protection to individuals under their jurisdiction.

With the close of the Reconstruction Era in 1877, the United States began a long period of relative inattention to questions of discrimination. The Supreme Court became actively involved with antidiscrimination issues in the early 1950s, with *Brown v. Board of Education*, 347 U.S. 483 (1954); *Bolling v. Sharpe*, 347 U.S. 497 (1954); and *Brown v. Board of Education* (*Brown II*), 349 U.S. 294 (1955). By a unanimous decision, the Warren Court ruled that segregated schools violated the equal protection clause. *Brown II* can be regarded as an early Supreme Court statement prefiguring affirmative action in education, since it did not simply prohibit schools from enrolling students on the basis of race, but required that district courts oversee the active dismantling of separate school systems by school districts. *Bolling v. Sharpe* dealt with segregated schools in Washington D.C., which is not part of any state and therefore is not explicitly covered by the equal protection clause. In this case, the Court unanimously ruled school segregation unconstitutional, arguing that equal protection was implied by the Fifth Amendment's guarantee of due process of law.

President John F. Kennedy was the first to use the term affirmative action in his Executive Order 10925, creating the Committee on Equal Employment Opportunity, in 1961. The order required federally funded projects "take affirmative action" to avoid racial bias in hiring and employment. President Kennedy also initiated the legislation that would later become the legal basis of affirmative action when he sent a civil rights bill to Congress on June 19, 1963. After Kennedy's death, pressure from civil rights groups and the leadership of President Lyndon B. Johnson helped move the bill forward, despite strong opposition led by Senator Richard Russell, Jr. (1897–1971) of Georgia. Finally, the Civil Rights Act of 1964 was passed a year after its introduction, with forty-six Democrats and twenty-seven Republicans voting in favor of it, and twenty-six Democrats and one Republican voting against it.

Title VI of the new legislation carried forward the intentions of Kennedy's executive order. It prohibited discrimination on the basis of race, color, and national origin for all programs receiving federal funding. It provided for the termination of federal assistance or the initiation of legal action by the Department of Justice in cases of discrimination, and it enabled those who believed themselves victims of discrimination to complain to the funding agency or to file suit in federal court. Title VII of the act made it unlawful for any employer with fifteen or more employees to discriminate against any individual on the basis of race, color, national origin, religion, or sex. Title VII contained a section prescribing remedies for cases of discrimination in which judges were given authority to order "such affirmative action as may be appropriate," such as punitive damages or reinstatement of employment for discrimination victims. Further, Title VII defined the mandate of the Equal Employment Opportunity Commission (EEOC), which had been initiated by President Kennedy's Executive Order 10925, as bringing suit on behalf of those believed to have suffered discrimination.

THE COURT AND AFFIRMATIVE ACTION IN THE 1970S AND 1980S

During the second half of the 1970s, cases regarding affirmative action plans in both employment and education began to reach the Supreme Court. The

> *In order to get beyond racism, we must first take account of race. There is no other way. And in order to treat some persons equally, we must treat them differently.*
>
> SOURCE: Harry A. Blackmun, *University of California Regents v. Bakke,* 438 U.S. 265, 407 (1978) (concurring in part and dissenting in part).

essential question in all of these cases concerned the nature of equal protection and discrimination, as defined by the Fourteenth Amendment and the Civil Rights Act of 1964. Did attempting to address historic discrimination, or to produce desirable social ends through promoting opportunities for some categories of people, involve discriminating against other categories of people? In *McDonald v. Santa Fe Trail Transportation Co.,* 427 U.S. 273 (1976), the Court faced the issue of possible discrimination against white citizens. The Santa Fe Trail Transportation Company had discharged two white employees who had misappropriated cargo. However, a black employee who had been charged with the same offense was not discharged. The two discharged employees attempted to address the perceived discrimination through their union and they filed complaints with the EEOC. They sued on the basis of Title VII and of section 1981 of Title 42 of the U.S. Code, which guarantees all persons equal rights.

A District Court had dismissed the suit on the grounds that section 1981 did not cover discrimination against whites and that the facts stated by the petitioners did not constitute a claim under Title VII. Justice Thurgood Marshall wrote the decision for the Supreme Court, holding that Title VII prohibited discrimination against whites, as well as nonwhites, thereby mandating that all employees be treated the same with respect to discipline for the same offense. Chief Justice Warren E. Burger and Justices William J. Brennan, Jr., Potter Stewart, Harry Blackmun, Lewis F. Powell, Jr., and John Paul Stevens joined Marshall in his opinion. Justices Byron White and William Rehnquist joined in the critical parts of the opinion and posted a separate statement.

Regents of University of California v. Bakke, 438 U.S. 265 (1978) was the most critical Supreme Court case regarding affirmative action in education. The case originated in 1973 when Allen Bakke, a white man, applied for admission to the medical school at the University of California, Davis. Under its affirmative action program, the school had reserved sixteen of one hundred seats for minority or socioeconomically disadvantaged applicants, who were judged by a committee

> *The way to stop discrimination on the basis of race is to stop discriminating on the basis of race.*
>
> SOURCE: John G. Roberts, *Parents Involved in Community Schools v. Seattle School District,* 551 U.S. ___ (2007).

separate from the one that judged regular applicants and who could be admitted with lower grade point averages (GPAs) and Medical College Admissions Test (MCAT) scores than regular applicants. After Bakke was denied admission, he wrote to the chairman of the admissions committee complaining because he had not been considered for a reserved seat for the disadvantaged and because no whites received these reserved seats. Bakke applied again in 1974, this time with a substantially higher MCAT score and was again denied admission, although minority applicants with lower scores and GPAs than his own were admitted through the separate special admissions process. Bakke sued in the California Superior Court, maintaining that he had experienced discrimination, in violation of the equal protection clause and Title VI of the Civil Rights Act of 1964, as well as the California constitution. The case went before the California Supreme Court, which decided in Bakke's favor by eight to one. The university then appealed to the Supreme Court.

The University of California maintained that it was justified in using race as a factor in admissions and that its separate admissions program was a legitimate way of doing so. Bakke maintained, again, that reserving places violated his right to equal treatment and subjected him to discrimination. Justices Brennan, White, Marshall, and Blackmun supported the use of race in admissions to educational programs in order to provide a remedy to minorities for the present-day consequences of past discrimination and racial prejudice. Chief Justice Burger and Justices Stewart, Stevens, and Rehnquist opined that the admissions policy at Davis violated Bakke's rights under the equal protection clause and the Civil Rights Act. Justice Powell argued that treating individuals differently on the basis of race requires a compelling state interest, and in this case was met by the interest of achieving a heterogeneous student body.

Justice Powell wrote the opinion of the Court, in which the four justices who favored race conscious admissions joined in part. A special admissions quota, such as the one employed by the University of California, could not be used because it constituted discrimination. Race could be treated as a factor, but was subject to strict

scrutiny. Bakke was ordered admitted and the most important Court decision on educational affirmative action entered history as a split decision in which no other justice agreed entirely with Powell's opinion for the Court. The Bakke decision therefore meant that educational institutions could continue to seek to increase their admissions of members of racial minorities or other underrepresented groups, but only to increase diversity and not to compensate for past discrimination. Moreover, membership in an underrepresented group could be only one of many factors in an admissions decision.

The Court took up the issue of affirmative action in employment again in *United Steelworkers of America, AFL-CIO v. Weber*, 443 U.S. 193 (1979). A 1974 agreement between the United Steelworkers union and Kaiser Aluminum Chemical Corporation reserved half the openings in a craft training program for black employees until the percentage of black craft employees at the plant became similar to the percentage of blacks in the local labor force. Brian Weber, a white employee who was not chosen for the training program after black employees with less seniority were, maintained that this violated Title VII's prohibition of race discrimination. A lower court in Louisiana found in Weber's favor, as did the Court of Appeals of the Fifth Circuit. In a five-to-two decision authored by Justice Brennan and joined by Justices Stewart, White, Marshall, and Blackmun, the Court held that Title VII did not prohibit the private sector from taking steps to eliminate patterns of segregation. Chief Justice Burger and Justice Rehnquist dissented. Burger argued that the Court was making decisions belonging to the legislature by extending Title VII and Rehnquist maintained that the Court was ruling that some forms of discrimination were legitimate. Justices Powell and Stevens did not participate.

Affirmative action in education and in employment came together in the case of *Wygant v. Jackson Board of Education*, 476 U.S. 267 (1986). The Jackson Education Association had an agreement with the board of education of Jackson, Michigan, that teachers with more seniority would not be laid off before teachers with less seniority. In 1972, this agreement was modified to protect minority teachers. Two years later, there was a layoff and Wendy Wygant, a white teacher, lost her job while minority teachers with less seniority did not. She sued, but a district court held that her rights under the equal protection clause had not been violated. The district court held that minority teachers served as role models for students. Therefore, retaining minority teachers as role models— even during layoffs—created a remedy for past discrimination and marginalization.

After an appeals court upheld the decision, the Supreme Court took up the case. Again, the Court reached a split decision. In another five-to-four decision, with the judgment authored by Justice Powell, the Court held that Wygant's layoff did indeed violate the equal protection clause because it stemmed directly from race, the racial classification of teachers did not serve a compelling state interest, and the means of serving a compelling interest were not narrowly tailored. Chief Justice Burger and Justice Rehnquist joined in the decision and Justices O'Connor and White voted with the majority but authored special concurrences. Justices Marshall, Brennan, Blackmun, and Stevens voted not to reverse the decision of the lower court. Justice Marshall and Justice Stevens both wrote dissents. Justice Marshall, joined by Justices Brennan and Blackmun, maintained that the agreement with the board of education had helped address past discrimination by sharing the burden of layoffs between whites and blacks, who did not have seniority because of past discrimination. Justice Stevens argued that the agreement had served the public interest of educating children.

The year after the *Wygant* decision, the Court rendered a decision on affirmative action on the basis of sex that harkened back to *Weber*. *Johnson v. Transportation Agency*, 480 U.S. 616 (1987) involved Paul Johnson and Diane Joyce, who were both qualified employees of the Transportation Agency of California. The two were considered for a promotion to road dispatcher and, with gender taken into consideration, Joyce received the promotion. Johnson sued, maintaining that the agency had engaged in sex discrimination under Title VII. Justice Brennan authored the decision of the Court, arguing that merely taking sex into consideration in a promotion decision, without a quota, was reasonable and did not constitute discrimination. Justices Marshall, Blackmun, Powell, O'Connor, and Stevens joined Brennan's opinion, with Justices O'Connor and Stevens producing separate concurrences. Chief Justice William Rehnquist and Justices Antonin Scalia and White voted in the minority. Scalia and White both wrote dissents. Scalia, joined by Rehnquist and in part by White, argued that sex was the determining factor in the promotion, and that the agency had not been seeking to remedy its own prior discrimination. Further, Scalia pointed out that although the *Weber* ruling had held that Title VII did not prohibit the private sector from taking steps to eliminate patterns of discrimination, the Transportation Agency of California was a public sector employer. According to Scalia, the decision in *Weber* therefore did not apply to the *Johnson* case. Justice White joined Scalia on the first and second points, but argued that the earlier *Weber* decision should also be rejected.

AFFIRMATIVE ACTION IN A CHANGING COURT

By the 1990s, several of the justices who had supported decisions favorable to affirmative action had left the Court. Notably, William J. Brennan, Jr., retired in 1990

> *We expect that 25 years from now, the use of racial preferences will no longer be necessary to further the interest approved today.*
>
> SOURCE: Sandra Day O'Connor, *Grutter v. Bollinger*, 539 U.S. 306, 322–23 (2003).

and Thurgood Marshall in 1991. Harry Blackmun retired in 1994. Some of those who tended not to support affirmative action policies were also gone. Potter Stewart died in 1985 and Warren E. Burger in 1995. By the time of *Adarand Constructors, Inc. v. Peña*, 515 U.S. 200 (1995), the Court consisted of the relatively liberal John Paul Stevens and Ruth Bader Ginsburg; centrists David Souter, Stephen Breyer, Sandra Day O'Connor, and Anthony Kennedy; and conservatives William Rehnquist, Antonin Scalia, and Clarence Thomas. Adarand Constructors was a Colorado contracting company that submitted the lowest bid on a federal contract with the U.S. Department of Transportation. However, the contract went to Gonzalez Contracting Company, which had made a higher bid but was certified as a minority business. Adarand argued that this violated the equal protection portion of the Fifth Amendment's due process clause.

Following the rule of strict scrutiny for permitting racial classifications, the Court decided in an opinion authored by Justice O'Connor that all action based on race or other such categories should be prohibited unless it can be shown that there is a compelling interest for allowing the consideration of racial or other categories. Chief Justice Rehnquist and Justices Kennedy, Scalia, and Thomas voted with O'Connor to constitute a five-to-four majority. In concurrences, Justice Scalia argued that the government can never take a compelling interest in discriminating, even to make up for past discrimination, and Justice Thomas opined that affirmative action programs in government contracts violate the moral basis of equal protection. Justices Stevens, Breyer, Souter, and Ginsburg maintained that the Department of Transportation program did not violate the Fifth Amendment. Justices Ginsburg, Stevens, and Souter authored dissents in which they argued that the program had no discriminatory intent, that it was just trying to make up for past discrimination, and strict scrutiny would interfere with achieving this benign intent.

The outcome of the *Adarand* case was unclear. The Court sent the case back to the Tenth Circuit Court to determine whether the measures applied by the Department of Transportation satisfied the standards of strict scrutiny. However, the case established that federal affirmative action programs would be held to the highest level of scrutiny and that such programs would be more difficult to institute than they had previously been. Moreover, the combination of justices who would permit affirmative action only under strict scrutiny with those who would reject affirmative action under any situation created a less favorable environment for affirmative action than had previously existed.

As the nation entered the twenty-first century, two cases concerning the University of Michigan, both with split decisions, illustrated the continuing, difficult balancing act of the Court on affirmative action. In the case of *Grutter v. Bollinger*, 539 U.S. 306 (2003), Barbara Grutter had been denied admission to the University of Michigan Law School, despite a 3.8 GPA and a score of 161 on the Law School Admissions Test (LSAT). The law school maintained a policy that gave special consideration to members of minority groups. Grutter's attorneys argued that this policy had denied her a place, and therefore constituted discrimination against her under the equal protection clause of the Fourteenth Amendment and Title VI of the Civil Rights Act. At the same time, the Court considered the case of two white applicants to the University of Michigan's undergraduate program in *Gratz v. Bollinger*, 539 U.S. 244 (2003). Jennifer Gratz had been classified as "well-qualified" when she applied in 1995 and Patrick Hamacher as "qualified" when he applied in 1997, but both were rejected. The university maintained an undergraduate admissions policy that automatically gave twenty points to underrepresented racial minorities. Gratz had actually been rejected before the point system had been enacted, raising questions about whether she had standing to bring suit, but the Court ruled that she did.

Ultimately, the Court ruled that the law school's policy was acceptable because it served the compelling national interest of diversity and simply took race into consideration, whereas the undergraduate admissions policy was unacceptable because the point system was too inflexible and was not narrowly tailored to promote diversity. *Grutter v. Bollinger* was narrowly decided by a five-to-four majority, with an opinion written by Justice O'Connor and joined by Justices Stevens, Souter, Ginsburg, and Breyer, with Justice Ginsburg writing a concurrence. Justice O'Connor argued that narrowly tailored race-based decisions for the sake of diversity were constitutional. However, she also suggested that affirmative action could not be permanent in character and suggested that twenty-five years later it would no longer be necessary to consider race. Chief Justice Rehnquist and Justices Scalia, Kennedy, and Thomas all disagreed and wrote dissents, with Thomas strongly suggesting that the Court should not wait twenty-five years to find the practice unconstitutional.

In *Gratz v. Bollinger*, Chief Justice Rehnquist wrote the six-to-three opinion, in which he was joined by Justices O'Connor, Scalia, Kennedy, and Thomas. Justice O'Connor wrote a concurrence in which she was joined by Justice Breyer, who also wrote a concurrence. The majority decided that the automatic point system was unconstitutional because it did not bring race into consideration on a flexible, individual basis. Justices Stevens, Souter, and Ginsburg all wrote dissents. Justice Ginsburg and Souter both said that the university should not be penalized for the openness and honesty of its affirmative action program.

The history of Supreme Court decisions, then, has largely been one of split decisions. Differing interpretations of equal protection and freedom from discrimination have prevented unanimity of views. Majorities have consistently allowed race-based decisions in educational admissions and employment, but have agreed that these decisions must be subject to strict scrutiny. Especially in education cases, the tendency has been to accept affirmative action as a means of pursuing a compelling national interest of diversity, rather than as a means of compensating individuals or groups for past discrimination.

SEE ALSO *Adarand Constructors, Inc. v. Peña, 515 U.S. 200 (1995)*; Burger Court; *Grutter v. Bollinger, 539 U.S. 306 (2003)/Gratz v. Bollinger, 539 U.S. 244 (2003)*; Parents Involved in Community Schools v. Seattle School District/Meredith v. Jefferson County Schools; *Regents of University of California v. Bakke, 438 U.S. 265 (1978)*; Rehnquist Court; Roberts Court; School Desegregation

BIBLIOGRAPHY

Anderson, Terry H. 2004. *The Pursuit of Fairness: A History of Affirmative Action.* New York: Oxford University Press.

Ball, Howard. 2000. *The Bakke Case: Race, Education, and Affirmative Action.* Lawrence: University Press of Kansas.

Bankston, Carl L., III. 2006. "Grutter v. Bollinger: Weak Foundations?" *Ohio State Law Journal* 67(1): 1–13.

Caldas, Stephen J. 2006. "The Plessy and Grutter Decisions: A Study in Contrast and Comparison." *Ohio State Law Journal* 67(1): 67–82.

Caplan, Lincoln. 1997. *Up against the Law: Affirmative Action and the Supreme Court.* New York: Twentieth Century Fund Press.

Dale, Charles V. 2005. "Affirmative Action Revisited: A Legal History and Prospectus." In *Affirmative Action: Federal Laws, Regulations, and Legal History,* ed. James S. Peterson. New York: Novinka Books.

Eisaguirre, Lynne. 1999. *Affirmative Action: A Reference Handbook.* Santa Barbara, CA: ABC-CLIO.

Elliott, Euel W., and Andrew I. E. Ewoh. 2005. "Beyond Gratz and Grutter: Prospects for Affirmative Action in the Aftermath of the Supreme Court's Michigan Decisions." *Review of Policy Research* 22(4): 541–553.

Rubio, Philip F. 2001. *A History of Affirmative Action: 1619–2000.* Jackson: University Press of Mississippi.

Yuill, Kevin L. 2006. *Richard Nixon and the Rise of Affirmative Action: The Pursuit of Racial Equality in an Era of Limits.* Lanham, MD: Rowman and Littlefield.

Carl L. Bankston III

AGOSTINI V. FELTON, 521 U.S. 203 (1997)

In *Agostini v. Felton*, 521 U.S. 203 (1997), the Court, in a five-to-four opinion written by Justice Sandra Day O'Connor, overruled its earlier decision in *Aguilar v. Felton*, 473 U.S. 402 (1985), which held that the establishment clause precluded publicly funded teachers from teaching secular, remedial courses on the premises of religious schools under a federally funded program that supported teaching at nonreligious schools as well. By overruling *Aguilar,* the Court significantly refashioned the *Lemon* test (*Lemon v. Kurtzman*, 403 U.S. 602 [1971]) in a way that became much more accommodating of government interaction with religion.

In *Aguilar,* the Court had struck down a New York City Board of Education policy of sending public school teachers into private religious schools to provide remedial instruction to economically disadvantaged children, pursuant to Title I of the Elementary and Secondary Education Act of 1965. Subsequently, the New York City board incurred great expense in providing remedial instruction to parochial students in ways that would comply with *Aguilar.* For this reason, petitioners in *Agostini* sought reconsideration of *Aguilar,* arguing that *Aguilar* was no longer good law and had been undermined by subsequent establishment clause decisions in *Zobrest v. Catalina Foothills School District*, 509 U.S. 1 (1993) and *Witters v. Washington Department of Services for the Blind*, 474 U.S. 481 (1986).

Writing for the *Agostini* Court, Justice O'Connor applied a refashioned *Lemon* test, transforming it from a three-prong test to a two-prong test. Under this new two-prong test, federal funding programs must have a secular purpose and cannot have the primary effect of advancing or inhibiting religion. The third prong of the traditional *Lemon* test—the prohibition on excessive entanglement—now became a factor within the new second prong. This effects prong, according to *Agostini*, required that: (1) the government aid does not result in religious indoctrination; (2) the aid is distributed according to religiously neutral criteria; and (3) the aid does not result in excessive entanglement between government and religion.

Agostini removed the presumptive hostility toward religion that had crept into the Court's establishment clause jurisprudence by removing various presumptions from the *Lemon* test. For instance, the Court rejected the presumption in *Aguilar* that the placement of public employees on parochial school grounds inevitably results in the impermissible effect of state-sponsored indoctrination. Thus, without any evidence of actual indoctrination resulting from the Title I program, *Agostini* held that the program could not be struck down because of impermissible religious indoctrination. Moreover, absent a presumption that government employees would engage in religious indoctrination when placed in a sectarian institution, pervasive monitoring of those employees was not required. Consequently, contrary to the finding in *Aguilar,* the Court in *Agostini* held that the Title I program did not result in excessive entanglement. Furthermore, in an interpretation that fosters greater religious accommodation, the Court stated that an entanglement will be excessive only if it has the effect of advancing or inhibiting religion.

With respect to the second factor of the second prong (the neutrality factor), the Court reasoned that the Title I program applied to all eligible children, no matter what kind of school they attended. By rejecting the rule that all government programs that directly aid the educational function of religious schools are invalid, the Court incorporated a neutrality principle within the *Lemon* test. According to this neutrality principle, an aid program is unlikely to have the impermissible effect of advancing religion if the aid is allocated on the basis of neutral criteria that neither favor nor disfavor religion, and is made available to both religious and secular beneficiaries on a nondiscriminatory basis.

In dissent, Justice David Souter argued that Title I provided direct and substantial aid to religious schools and that such aid could not be justified on neutrality grounds. Justice Souter also argued that contrary to the majority's assertion that it was not changing the principles underlying the *Lemon* test but only reinterpreting them, *Agostini* had created a whole new test.

SEE ALSO *Aguilar v. Felton, 473 U.S. 402 (1985); Education and the Constitution; Establishment Clause*

BIBLIOGRAPHY

Conkle, Daniel O. 2000. "The Path of American Religious Liberty: From the Original Theology to Formal Neutrality and an Uncertain Future." *Indiana Law Journal* 75(1): 1–36.

Lupu, Ira C., and Robert W. Tuttle. 2005. "The Faith-Based Initiative and the Constitution." *DePaul Law Review* 55(1): 1–118.

Patrick M. Garry

AGUILAR V. FELTON, 473 U.S. 402 (1985)

In *Aguilar v. Felton*, 473 U.S. 402 (1985), the Court struck down parochial school participation in a special education program in the New York City school system. The program was authorized under Title I of the Elementary and Secondary Education Act of 1965 and was enacted as a cornerstone of Lyndon Johnson's Great Society. This program provided remedial English, reading, and mathematics assistance to economically and educationally disadvantaged students in both public and private schools, including religious schools.

The instructional services received by parochial students were provided by public school employees who had volunteered to teach in the parochial schools. In an attempt to avoid any establishment clause problems, the teachers were prohibited from participating in any religious activities conducted within the private schools and from using any religious materials in their classrooms. Public school instructors were assigned separate classrooms in the parochial school, where students were sent for special instruction. Parochial school administrators were also required to remove all religious symbols from any classrooms used by the Title I teachers, and unannounced supervisory visits were conducted monthly to ensure compliance with the Title I requirements.

In a five-to-four opinion for the Court, Justice William J. Brennan, Jr., applied the *Lemon* (*Lemon v. Kurtzman*, 403 U.S. 602 [1971]) test to find New York City's implementation of the Title I program a violation of the establishment clause. This holding principally rested on the Court's analysis under the excessive entanglement prong of the three-part *Lemon* test. Specifically, the Court found that the supervisory system used by the city of New York to try to prevent an establishment clause violation itself resulted in an excessive governmental entanglement with religion.

Justice Brennan's opinion reflected the no-aid separationist approach of *Lemon*, as previously used in *Wolman v. Walter*, 433 U.S. 229 (1977) and *Meek v. Pittenger*, 421 U.S. 349 (1975). Critics accused *Aguilar* of being overly hostile to government interaction with religion, since the Court's decision incorporated a presumption that the placement of public employees on parochial school grounds inevitably results in the impermissible effect of state-sponsored indoctrination and constitutes a symbolic union between government and religion.

Dissenting from the majority decision in *Aguilar* were Chief Justice Warren E. Burger and Justices William Rehnquist, Byron White, and Sandra Day O'Connor. Chief Justice Burger argued that the decision exhibited nothing less than hostility toward religion and the children who attend church-sponsored schools. Justice Rehnquist noted the paradox that the Court had inadvertently created: that in order to avoid entanglement, the aid must be supervised; but then this supervision itself causes an unconstitutional entanglement.

Justice O'Connor pointed out that in the nineteen-year history of the program, not a single instance of unconstitutional involvement by agents of one school system in the other was documented, even after concerted efforts by the program opponents to do so. Justice O'Connor criticized the Court's decision as violating the principle of government neutrality between religion and nonreligion, since the ruling prevented public school teachers from providing on-site educational services to children enrolled at religious schools while permitting such services to continue at private nonreligious schools. Twelve years later, the Court overruled *Aguilar v. Felton* in *Agostini v. Felton*, 521 U.S. 203 (1997).

SEE ALSO *Agostini v. Felton, 521 U.S. 203 (1997); Education and the Constitution; Establishment Clause*

BIBLIOGRAPHY

Conkle, Daniel O. 2000. "The Path of American Religious Liberty: From the Original Theology to Formal Neutrality and an Uncertain Future." *Indiana Law Journal* 75(1): 1–36.

Patrick M. Garry

AID TO PAROCHIAL SCHOOLS

The question of governmental aid to parochial schools involves the constitutional question of whether federal or state governmental actors may provide money or services to religiously affiliated schools in concert with the First Amendment's proscription against the establishment of religion. The establishment clause provides that "Congress shall make no law respecting an establishment of religion." The text of the establishment clause seems to only proscribe congressional action; however, the proscription is made applicable to the states through the Fourteenth Amendment's due process clause. Thus, should a state or local governmental actor violate the establishment clause, the aggrieved person's "liberty interest" in freedom from the establishment of religion has been violated.

Even before the advent of the School Choice Movement, the Court addressed the question of how, and under what circumstances, public money can be used to assist or fund private religious school education. Beginning with its decision in *Everson v. Board of Education*, 330 U.S. 1 (1947), the Court has required that there exist an "impregnable" "wall of separation" between church and state. The metaphor may be helpful as a starting point for analyzing an establishment clause problem, however, generally it has not garnered uniform agreement on the Supreme Court in deciding when the wall has been breached. Additionally, the Court has mandated that the government remain neutral in matters concerning religion and that no public benefits be given in aid to religion. Nonetheless, it is not practical to expect that the "wall of separation" be strictly observed or that no aid be given to religion. For example, if a state or local government did no more than provide police, fire, and emergency services to religious institutions such as parochial schools, churches, synagogues, or mosques, it would—in theory—breach a strict wall of separation in providing these public services (*Widmar v. Vincent*, 454 U.S. 263 [1981]). And the requirement of neutrality must necessarily be balanced with the idea that government should not be an adversary of religion.

LEMON ANALYSIS

Modern establishment clause jurisprudence seeks to accommodate a workable relationship between religion and government through the articulations of *Lemon v. Kurtzman*, 403 U.S. 602 (1971). *Lemon* involved a challenge to Pennsylvania and Rhode Island state laws that reimbursed parents of nonpublic schools students, including religiously affiliated schools, for expenses incurred for teachers' salaries, textbooks, and other instructional aids. The Court's framework for analyzing the constitutional question required an evaluation of the statute's purpose, effect, and involvement with government. Under the *Lemon* analysis a governmental practice, custom, usage, regulation, statute, or ordinance involving a question of whether religion and government are improperly intertwined is constitutional if: 1) it has a secular legislative purpose; 2) it has a principal and primary effect that neither endorses, nor inhibits, religion; and 3) it does not excessively entangle religion and government. The governmental action in question must pass each tier of the *Lemon* analysis in order to pass constitutional muster. The *Lemon* Court determined that the Pennsylvania and Rhode Island state laws in question violated the excessive entanglements tier of analysis because the administrative work required to ensure the maintenance of their secular purposes and the non-advancement of religion required too much governmental administrative involvement with the sectarian schools.

Since the Court decided *Lemon*, the case has provided the primary analysis for aid to parochial schools cases. Generally, the Court has had little difficulty articulating the secular legislative purposes of government-sponsored programs benefiting children attending religiously affiliated schools. In most cases, the Court understands that the state has a legitimate nonreligious purpose in creating a well-educated citizenry. In *Agostini v. Felton*, 403 U.S. 203 (1997), the excessive entanglement tier of the *Lemon* analysis was revised by the Court in scope of importance in aid to parochial schools cases. In these cases, the *Agostini* Court determined that excessive entanglement questions often duplicate the inquiries made under the effects tier of analysis. Therefore, the Court modified the *Lemon* analysis in aid to parochial school cases, inquiring only into the statute's purpose and effects. Whether the principal and primary effect of a particular program serves to advance religion, however, has been the intense focus of most aid to parochial school analyses and has required the Court to engage in extraordinary fact-intensive evaluations.

PRIVATE CHOICE CASES AND THE EFFECTS ANALYSIS

Cases involving government aid to religiously affiliated schools have provided the Court with a welter of factual situations and the *Lemon* effects analysis has been applied to each. For example, *Everson* considered the constitutionality of a local board of education's reimbursement of transportation costs incurred by parents, some of whom attended Catholic parochial schools. In *Everson*, Justice Hugo Black introduced Thomas Jefferson's now famous "wall of separation" metaphor in explaining the nature of establishment clause limitations. He found the reimbursement program constitutional because it represented a "neutral" offering made to all parents. Since *Everson*, cases such as *Mueller v. Allen*, 463 U.S. 388 (1983), wherein all parents were allowed a tax deduction for costs incurred "in providing 'tuition, textbooks and transportation,'" have usually been resolved in favor of the state action. Generally, if the Court finds that a program contains neutral selection criteria, "attenuated financial benefits" to the parochial school resulting from the true "private choice" of the parents, the program will withstand constitutional scrutiny.

Zobrest v. Catalina Foothills School District, 509 U.S. 1 (1993) followed the same rationale. By the time the Court decided *Zobrest*, it was willing to abandon the idea that the use of public school employees in the delivery of services to parochial school students resulted in the advancement of religion simply because of the "appearance that [government] was a 'joint sponsor' of the [religious] school's activities." In this case, the provision of a public school sign-language interpreter to a deaf student enrolled in a parochial school, pursuant to the Individuals with Disabilities Education Act, was simply the result of the parents' private choice to avail themselves of a neutral federal program available to all disabled children. In *Zelman v. Simmons-Harris*, 536 U.S. 639 (2002), the same analysis applied to an Ohio state statute providing for financial vouchers for families residing in any school district that had been "under federal court order requiring supervision and operational management of the district by the state superintendent." It was "neutral with respect to religion," "permit[ting] ... individuals to exercise genuine choice among options public and private, secular and religious." The private choice rationale of the Court has remained a constant since the *Mueller* decision in 1983.

DIRECT VS. INDIRECT AID AND THE EFFECTS ANALYSIS

Some of the most challenging aid to parochial schools problems have been those involving direct or indirect transfer of government funds or services to religiously affiliated schools. Unlike the cases that focus on the private choice rationale, the direct or indirect aid to parochial schools case analysis has changed greatly over time. With these problems, the Court has struggled to achieve a principled analysis assuring that government and religion occupy their appropriate spheres of autonomy.

In the early direct versus indirect aid cases, the Court engaged in formalistic and mechanical evaluations of the effects prong of *Lemon*. In *Wolman v. Walter*, 433 U.S. 229 (1977), for example, the Court's analysis of the principal and primary effect of the provision of instructional materials, equipment loan services, and field trip funding was found to advance religion. This is an excellent example of the Court's historical insistence on distinguishing between the directness versus the indirectness of the aid to religious schools in characterizing the aid's principal or primary effect. According to the Court, field trips were a constituent part of the child's school experience and the Court was troubled by the direct funding of the program to the religious schools. The instructional materials and equipment loan program also failed the neutrality requirement because the materials, once loaned to parents or students, could be easily divertible to religious usages.

In contrast, the *Wolman* Court easily found a textbook loan program, standardized testing and scoring, and diagnostic and therapeutic services provided for children in parochial schools constitutionally devoid of the principal and primary effect of advancing religion. Neutrality was the hallmark of the provision of these services. They were made available to all children irrespective of their public or private school status, measures were taken to insulate the testing from religious school control, and public school employees involved in the provision of diagnostic and therapeutic services were less likely to "transmit ideological views" to students and were therefore distinguishable teachers in this respect.

Two programs under consideration, the Shared Time program and the Community Education program in *Grand Rapids v. Ball*, 473 U.S. 373 (1985) allowed public school teachers to teach core curricular courses at private schools during the regular school day and during after school programs, respectively. Both programs failed the effects prong of *Lemon*. Most of the private schools participating in these programs were religious schools and the Court noted the "symbolic link" between the parochial schools and government would have the effect of advancing religion to small children. Public school teachers physically present in the parochial school classroom and participating in the programs could "intentionally or inadvertently [inculcate] particular religious tenets or beliefs." Lastly, the religious "subsidization" factor was high in both programs because of the directness of the aid to religion through the provision of public school teachers teaching secular subjects.

In *Agostini* a challenge to the New York City School District's plan administering Elementary and Secondary Education Act (ESEA) Title I funds for remedial educational services for at-risk children failed as a result of the Court's abandonment of the "symbolic link" analysis of effects. Additionally, the Court indicated its increasing devaluation of "direct aid" as having a principal and primary effect of advancing religion. According to the Court, directness of aid was not a fatal establishment clause flaw. Overruling its contrary decision in *Aguilar v. Felton*, 473 U.S. 402 (1985) and *Ball*, the *Agostini* Court approved this Title I program because it was "allocated on the basis of neutral, secular criteria that neither favor[ed] nor disfavor[ed] religion, and [it was] made available to both religious and secular beneficiaries on a nondiscriminatory basis."

A similar rationale was used by the Court in *Mitchell v. Helms*, 530 U.S. 793 (2000) in denying a challenge to the use of funds under chapter two of the Education Consolidation and Improvement Act of 1981 to benefit children in parochial schools. The statute provided "assistance" and "instructional and educational materials" to children in elementary and secondary schools, irrespective of the school's public or private status. Thirty percent of the school district's chapter two funds were awarded to private schools and thirty-four out of forty-six of those were parochial. The Court firmly anchored its analysis in the principles of neutrality and private-choice rationale. The *Mitchell* Court specifically abandoned the direct/indirect aid evaluation as a dispositive mark of unconstitutionality. While directness of aid is not wholly irrelevant, a central focus on neutrality of eligibility requirements provided a more coherent analysis for this particular program. The program determined "eligibility for aid neutrally, allocate[d] that aid based on the private choices of the parents of schoolchildren and [did] not provide aid that [had] an impermissible content." Any aid that redounded to the benefit of the parochial school was the mere "consequence of private decision making" of the parents.

SEE ALSO *Agostini v. Felton, 521 U.S. 203 (1997); Education and the Constitution; Establishment Clause; Everson v. Board of Education, 330 U.S. 1 (1947)*

BIBLIOGRAPHY

Berg, Thomas C. 2003. "Vouchers and Religious Schools: The New Constitutional Questions." *University of Cincinnati Law Review* 72(1): 151–221.

Brown, Kevin. 2006. "The Supreme Court's Role in the Growing School Choice Movement." *Ohio State Law Journal* 67(1): 37–65.

Brownstein, Alan E. 1999. "Interpreting the Religion Clauses in Terms of Liberty, Equality, and Free Speech Values—A Critical Analysis of 'Neutrality Theory' and Charitable Choice." *Notre Dame Journal of Law, Ethics, and Public Policy* 13(2): 243–284.

Choper, Jesse H. 1995. *Securing Religious Liberty: Principles for Judicial Interpretation of the Religion Clauses.* Chicago: University of Chicago Press.

Eisgruber, Christopher L., and Lawrence G. Sager. 1996. "Unthinking Religious Freedom." *Texas Law Review* 74(3): 577–614.

Gedicks, Frederick Mark. 1995. *The Rhetoric of Church and State: A Critical Analysis of Religion Clause Jurisprudence.* Durham, NC: Duke University Press.

Hall, Timothy L. 1998. *Separating Church and State: Roger Williams and Religious Liberty.* Urbana: University of Illinois Press.

Howe, Mark De Wolfe. 1965. *The Garden and the Wilderness: Religion and Government in American Constitutional History.* Chicago: University of Chicago Press.

Laycock, Douglas. 1986. "A Survey of Religious Liberty in the United States." *Ohio State Law Journal* 47(2): 409–451.

Leedes, Gary C. 1993. "Rediscovering the Link between the Establishment Clause and the Fourteenth Amendment: The Citizenship Declaration." *Indiana Law Review* 26(3): 469–518.

Levy, Leonard W. 1986. *The Establishment Clause: Religion and the First Amendment.* New York: Macmillan.

Lupu, Ira C. 2001. "Government Messages and Government Money: Santa Fe, *Mitchell v. Helms,* and the Arc of the Establishment Clause." *William and Mary Law Review* 42(3): 771–822.

Lupu, Ira C., and Robert W. Tuttle. 2002. "Sites of Redemption: A Wide-Angle Look at Government Vouchers and Sectarian Service Providers." *Journal of Law and Politics* 18(2): 539–606.

Lupu, Ira C., and Robert W. Tuttle. 2003. "Zelman's Future: Vouchers, Sectarian Providers, and the Next Round of Constitutional Battles." *Notre Dame Law Review* 78(4): 917–994.

McConnell, Michael W. 2001. "State Action and the Supreme Court's Emerging Consensus on the Line between Establishment and Private Religious Expression." *Pepperdine Law Review* 28(3): 681–718.

Patrick, John J., and Gerald P. Long, eds. 1999. *Constitutional Debates on Freedom of Religion: A Documentary History.* Westport, CT: Greenwood Press.

Tushnet, Mark V. 2002. "Vouchers after Zelman." *Supreme Court Review* 2002: 1–39.

Alfreda A. Sellers Diamond

AIR POLLUTION

People often think of the U.S. Supreme Court as the interpreter of the Constitution. But the Court also has other roles. These include the fashioning of law to solve interstate disputes. Another is interpretation of federal statutes in accordance with their language. Both are implicated by the Court's air pollution jurisprudence.

The Supreme Court's involvement in air pollution goes back more than a century to *Georgia v. Tennessee Copper Co.*, 206 US. 230 (1907). There the Court upheld Georgia's complaint that an out-of-state copper smelter was causing a public nuisance. Justice Oliver Wendell Holmes, Jr., speaking for the Court, remarked that it is "fair and reasonable" for a sovereign to wish to protect its natural resources from air pollution, and found that Georgia had carried its burden of proof that the smelter's emissions are transported into the state and cause harm to forest and vegetable life. The economic effects on the pollution source, according to Justice Holmes, were subordinate to Georgia's rights—a statement that foreshadows the beliefs of the drafters of the federal Clean Air Act.

Nuisance law and similar common law doctrines proved inadequate to remedying growing air pollution. Resolving pollution disputes requires more technical expertise than a court is likely to have, and the nuisance plaintiff, who must prove his or her case by a preponderance of the evidence, has a heavy burden because of the many uncertainties regarding the effects of air pollution. States and localities began to pass air pollution control ordinances in the 1940s and 1950s, but Congress increasingly felt that a federal solution was needed both to resolve interstate transport issues and to prevent a "race-to-the-bottom" in which states would use lax standards to attract industry.

THE CLEAN AIR ACT

Congress created the basics of the Clean Air Act in 1970. The act directs the Environmental Protection Agency (EPA) to set national ambient air quality standards—limits on the permissible concentration of air pollutants in the outdoor air—for pollutants that endanger public health. Primary ambient standards must protect health with an adequate margin of safety; secondary standards must protect public welfare.

The Clean Air Act consists largely of mechanisms to ensure that the standards are attained and maintained, and that no significant degradation of clean air occurs. Most importantly, states submit to EPA implementation plans that show how the state will attain and maintain attainment of the air quality standards. The state implementation plan (SIP) must demonstrate that attainment of the primary standards will take place no later than the deadline established by statute. In general, a state may use any mix of measures it likes, so long as it demonstrates that timely attainment will occur. States must include in their plans

Stacks at the Navajo Generating Station coal burning power plant in Arizona, 2006. *After Congress approved a series of regulations intended to curb air pollution, the Supreme Court has generally favored federal enforcement of clean air standards, forcing states to comply with existing anti-pollution legislation.* © **MOMATIUK-EASTCOTT/CORBIS**

new source review provisions that require that new and modified "stationary sources"—factories, refineries, power plants, and the like—use advanced control technology and neither slow progress toward cleaning up dirty air nor degrade clean air. EPA establishes programs to ensure that a state's sources do not contribute to air pollution in downwind states. EPA also sets emission standards for new motor vehicles and for categories of new and modified stationary sources.

THEMES OF THE COURT'S CLEAN AIR ACT JURISPRUDENCE

One theme has been deference to EPA's interpretations of the Clean Air Act. The epitome of this came in *Chevron, U.S.A. v. Natural Resources Defense Council,* 467 U.S. 837 (1984), in which the Court announced that, when a statute is silent or ambiguous concerning an issue, the agency should be allowed to fill the gap in a reasonable way. But the Court does not always defer, as in *Massachusetts v. EPA,* 127 S. Ct. 1438 (2007). There, EPA denied that it had the authority to regulate emissions of greenhouse gases from motor vehicles and asserted that

it would be undesirable to do so even if the agency had the authority. The Court held that EPA's reading of the act was unreasonable, and that the agency had strayed beyond its statutory power in assessing whether to exercise its jurisdiction.

Another theme has been the need to give weight to the federal interest in curbing air pollution. In *Train v. Natural Resources Defense Council,* 421 U.S. 60 (1975), the Court characterized the 1970 Clean Air Act amendments as "taking a stick to the States." Thus the Court has allowed substantial federal supervision of the states. An example is *Alaska Department of Environmental Conservation v. EPA,* 540 U.S. 461 (2004): EPA believed that Alaska had been unreasonably lenient in deciding what controls a new source should have, and so the agency brought an action to bar the source's construction. A sharply divided Court held that the Clean Air Act gave EPA the authority to do so over a heated dissent that stressed preserving the integrity of the states.

Particularly interesting has been the Court's treatment of issues of cost. Early in the Clean Air Act's history, the Court read the statute in *Union Electric v. EPA,* 427

U.S. 246 (1976) as allowing states to require in their plans measures that are not economically or technologically feasible. The Court relied partly on the language of the statute, which did not require EPA to find that a plan was feasible, and partly on legislative history stressing that protecting public health is more important than economic considerations, and that sources should either meet the act's requirements or close down.

The same reliance underlies *Whitman v. American Trucking Associations*, 531 U.S. 457 (2001). Here, industries challenged EPA's choice of air quality standards on the ground, among others, that the agency had failed to consider cost. The Court, speaking through Justice Antonin Scalia, asserted that industry had to show a clear textual commitment of authority to EPA to consider costs in setting ambient air quality standards. The Court found no such commitment, noting that when Congress wanted consideration of costs, it said so expressly.

It may seem odd that economic factors are excluded when cost considerations must play some kind of role in the standard-setting process and in the process of designing SIPs. Congress's intent seems to have been to ban the use of cost and feasibility as factors in order to minimize their use in writing regulations. If EPA decides to be lenient in setting an ambient air quality standard, the agency must justify its decision in terms of public health rather than fall back on cost considerations.

SEE ALSO *Environmental Law; Georgia v. Tennessee Copper Co., 206 U.S. 230 (1907); Massachusetts v. Environmental Protection Agency, 549 U.S. ___ (2007)*

BIBLIOGRAPHY

Belden, Roy S. 2001. *The Clean Air Act*. Chicago: Section of Environment, Energy, and Resources, American Bar Association.

Currie, David. 1981. *Air Pollution, Federal Law, and Analysis*. Wilmette, IL: Callaghan.

Craig N. Oren

ALDEN V. MAINE, 527 U.S. 706 (1999)

Alden v. Maine, 527 U.S. 706 (1999) was among the most aggressive of the U.S. Supreme Court's *new federalism* decisions in the 1990s. In that case and others, the Court restricted the power of Congress to implement federal regulatory programs and fortified the ability of individual states to resist federal regulation. Specifically, the Court held in *Alden* that the Constitution immunizes the states from lawsuits brought by private citizens not only in

federal court, but in state court as well. Moreover, the Court held that Congress ordinarily cannot eliminate the states' immunity. Accordingly, a state may refuse to comply with a federal statute and defeat a private lawsuit brought to enforce compliance. Justice Kennedy wrote the majority opinion. Four justices dissented.

The federal Fair Labor Standards Act (FLSA) of 1938 requires the states to pay their employees an accelerated rate for overtime work. A group of probation officers in Maine alleged that they did not receive that rate. Maine had in fact failed to comply with the FLSA. Nevertheless, the state refused to reimburse the probation officers for overtime payments they had been denied in the past. The officers sued Maine in state court, seeking compensation. The state responded that the U.S. Constitution granted it immunity from such a suit. The Supreme Court recognized that Maine's sovereign immunity argument was novel. The Court nonetheless held that the state was constitutionally immune from a suit brought by its employees in state court and that Congress could not override that immunity by authorizing the suit.

The state's immunity argument in *Alden* plainly was unprecedented. In previous cases, the Supreme Court had recognized that the states are immune from suits by private citizens in federal court. Yet the Court had never suggested that the states are also immune from private suits in state court. In part, the explanation for prior understanding was the link between state immunity and the Eleventh Amendment, added to the Constitution in 1798. That Eleventh Amendment provides that "the Judicial Power of the United States shall not be construed to extend to any suit in law or equity, commenced or prosecuted against one of the United States by Citizens of another State, or by Citizens or Subjects of any Foreign State." By its explicit text, the Eleventh Amendment is concerned only with federal, not state, judicial power, and any sovereign immunity anchored on that amendment is necessarily limited to suits in federal court.

In *Alden*, the Supreme Court acknowledged that previous decisions had described state sovereign immunity as "Eleventh Amendment immunity" and therefore indicated that state immunity exists only in federal court. Yet the Court insisted that the "Eleventh Amendment immunity" label is a "misnomer." Quoting the important precedent three years earlier in *Seminole Tribe of Florida v. Florida*, 517 U.S. 44 (1996), the Court explained in *Alden* that it would not give "blind deference" to the Eleventh Amendment's text. Instead, the Court inferred the existence of state immunity in both federal and state court from history, from the structure of the federal system of government, and from the dignity of individual states as constituent elements of that system.

The Court recognized that numerous provisions of the Constitution empower Congress to enact federal statutes that impose legal obligations on the states. In this instance, the power to regulate interstate commerce provided Congress with sufficient authority for enacting the Fair Labor Standards Act and, accordingly, for requiring Maine to pay its workers the wages specified in that act. There was no doubt, then, that Maine had a legal duty to comply with the federal statute the probation officers claimed the state had violated. The Supreme Court also recognized that the Fair Labor Standards Act explicitly authorizes state workers to sue the state for failure to meet its obligations to them. Yet the Court drew a distinction between congressional power to visit a legal duty on the state, on the one hand, and congressional power to enforce that duty by authorizing private lawsuits, on the other. The Court readily agreed that Congress had the first power, but held that Congress lacked the second. In sum, Maine had a legal duty to pay the compensation the workers were owed, but the workers were unable to force Maine to pay by bringing a lawsuit.

The Court's explanation of state sovereign immunity in *Alden* relied on numerous grounds. Having disclaimed the Eleventh Amendment as a textual basis for state immunity, the Court turned to the Constitution's overarching structure and to the special constitutional position of the states implied by various provisions, including the Tenth Amendment, which states that "the powers not delegated to the United States by the Constitution, nor prohibited by it to the States, are reserved to the States respectively, or to the people." The Court declared that the Constitution recognizes the states as sovereign entities that retain the "dignity" of sovereignty. By inference, then, the states enjoy the immunity to which the sovereign was entitled in England.

Coming to the original understanding of the Constitution, the Court acknowledged that there is no historical evidence indicating that anyone in 1789 proposed that the Constitution would authorize states to assert immunity from suits in their own courts. The Court explained, however, that "silence" in this instance is "instructive." By the Court's account, state immunity from lawsuits in state court was so well entrenched in the eighteenth century that no one conceived it would be affected by the new federal Constitution. By contrast, according to the Court, the Constitution would not have been adopted if it had been understood that states would not continue to enjoy sovereign immunity both in the federal courts to be created under the new system and in their own local courts.

The Court fortified its explanation of state immunity with other, more pragmatic arguments: If Congress could abrogate state immunity, it could "thrust" a state into the "disfavored status" of a debtor. That status, in turn, would deny states the "dignity and respect" to which they are entitled as "members of the federation." It would be more "offensive" for Congress to subject the states to suits in their own courts than to force them to respond to suits in federal court. To press state courts into service would be to turn states' own institutions against them, thus to "commandeer" state "political machinery" in the pursuit of national objectives. By forcing states to respond to suits for monetary relief, Congress would expose state treasuries to the claims of private citizens. That, in turn, might interfere with the states' capacity to allocate scarce resources through the political process. By requiring states to prefer the claimants that Congress authorizes to sue, Congress would substitute its priorities for those the states might choose and thus corrupt ordinary channels of political accountability. By effectively giving state courts the authority to make budgetary judgments, Congress would "blur" the "distinct responsibilities" of state judicial and legislative institutions.

None of these arguments quieted the controversy that the *Alden* decision stirred up. Dissenting justices contended that the majority's analysis rendered the text of the Constitution irrelevant to the immunity question, except to the extent the majority relied on the Tenth and Eleventh Amendments to "confirm" the existence of state immunity. They also found the majority's historical analysis dissatisfying. The dissenters emphasized that the majority identified no evidence that anyone at the time thought that the Constitution would affirmatively incorporate immunity as itself a feature of federal constitutional law.

Controversial as *Alden* was, the decision did not deprive Congress of any way to force states to comply with federal statutes like the Fair Labor Standards Act. The Court explained, for example, that state sovereign immunity does not defeat suits by agents of the federal government. Accordingly, Congress can authorize suits by federal officers and achieve state compliance by that means. The constitutional difficulty with the suits Congress had actually authorized in *Alden* was that they would be brought by private citizens and thus would subject states to the indignity of treatment as common debtors.

Even if the practical effect of *Alden* is only to make Congress select an enforcement mechanism other than private lawsuits, the conceptual significance of the Court's decision is extremely important. By most accounts, *Alden* illustrates a "conservative" agenda that means to decentralize American government, channeling authority away from the central government and toward individual states. This "new federalism" contrasts with the centralization that had previously characterized American politics and jurisprudence since the New Deal. It is the product of creative thinking by "conservative" justices who insist, in other contexts, that the Constitution should be interpreted according to its explicit text and should not be used as an instrument of social reform.

SEE ALSO *Eleventh Amendment; Federalism; Rehnquist Court; Seminole Tribe of Florida v. Florida, 517 U.S. 44 (1996); State Sovereign Immunity*

BIBLIOGRAPHY

Orth, John V. 1987. *The Judicial Power of the United States: The Eleventh Amendment in American History.* New York: Oxford University Press.

Symposium. 2000. *Notre Dame Law Review* 75.

Larry Yackle

ALEXANDER V. HOLMES COUNTY BOARD OF EDUCATION, 396 U.S. 19 (1969)

From the Supreme Court's 1955 announcement in *Brown v. Board of Education (Brown II)*, 349 U.S. 294 that the desegregation of all schools previously segregated by law should proceed with "all deliberate speed" to the 1968 *Green v. School Board of New Kent County*, 391 U.S. 430 decision, which rededicated the federal district courts to the task of exerting all of their constitutional authority to the elimination of the vestiges of school segregation, almost no progress had been made toward the integration of southern schools. For example, at the time of the enactment of the 1964 Civil Rights Act, approximately 99 percent of black children in the South continued to attend one-race schools. The Mississippi public schools were no exception to this pattern of resistance to educational integration.

Refusing to tolerate further delay in the implementation of effective school-desegregation remedies, the unanimous Supreme Court in *Alexander v. Holmes County Board of Education*, 396 U.S. 19 (1969) vacated an order of the U.S. Court of Appeals for the Fifth Circuit allowing Mississippi school districts to have more time to prepare to desegregate. The per curiam opinion acknowledged that proceeding with "all deliberate speed," the standard articulated by the Court in *Brown II* could no longer be considered constitutionally permissible in the face of the recalcitrance of southern school districts when ordered to dismantle their de jure segregated systems.

Since *Brown II*, Mississippi had made negligible integration efforts, resorting to a variety of strategies, including "freedom of choice" school-assignment regimes and "grade-a-year" plans, to maintain racially separate schools. These dilatory tactics had been consistently rebuffed by the Fifth Circuit until late 1969, when President Richard Nixon, departing from the policy of previous administrations, directed the Department of

Health, Education, and Welfare and the Justice Department to ask the Fifth Circuit to postpone implementation of desegregation plans previously approved by the appellate court. When the Fifth Circuit acquiesced, black schoolchildren in affected districts, represented by the Legal Defense Fund of the National Association for the Advancement of Colored People (NAACP), sought review by the Supreme Court and obtained a ruling underscoring "the obligation of every school district to terminate dual school systems at once and to operate now and hereafter only unitary schools." The *Alexander* Court went on to somewhat cryptically describe a unitary school system as one "in which no person would be effectively excluded from any school because of race or color."

SEE ALSO *Burger Court; Education and the Constitution; School Desegregation*

BIBLIOGRAPHY

Tatel, David S. 2004. "Judicial Methodology, Southern School Desegregation, and the Rule of Law." *New York University Law Review* 79: 1071–1133.

Josie F. Brown

ALIENS INELIGIBLE FOR CITIZENSHIP

This article discusses federal racial limits on entry and naturalization in the United States from the late eighteenth century to the mid-twentieth century, as well as state restrictions on citizenship, particularly those imposed through anti-Asian land laws.

THE EARLY PERIOD, 1776–1850

In the early years of the new Republic, Americans (like others in the New World) generally welcomed immigrants, and immigration remained largely unregulated. As late as 1843, President John Tyler (1790–1862) encouraged persons from other countries to settle in the United States.

The first federal legislation concerning naturalization in the United States, passed in 1790, provided that only free white persons could become naturalized citizens. After the Civil War (1861–1865), persons of African descent were also permitted to naturalize. Persons of Asian ancestry, however, were not afforded this privilege until the mid-twentieth century. Congress passed other isolated pieces of restrictive federal immigration legislation (such as the Alien and Sedition Act of 1798) during the early period, but, in general, preferred to let the states regulate immigration.

THE SECOND CENTURY, 1850–1952

The 1850 to 1952 period was an active one for both federal immigration legislation and Supreme Court decisions on immigration, with most of the activity occurring prior to 1925. The acquisition of former Mexican territories, gold discoveries in California, and the building of the transcontinental railroad led to a large influx of unskilled laborers from China and Europe in response to domestic labor needs. Not surprisingly, this fueled native sentiments, leading to federal immigration legislation directed at increasing the cost of transport for Chinese laborers coming to the United States. At the same time, states such as California had already set in motion various restrictive measures, such as special taxes imposed specifically on the Chinese.

In 1882 the prohibition on Chinese immigration was made complete by the Chinese Exclusion Act, which brought about a ban on admission of Chinese laborers to the United States. It was not long before the power of Congress to enact such legislation was challenged in the Court. The two most important cases—never overturned and still good law for their principal pronouncements regarding the plenary power of Congress over immigration matters—are *Chae Chan Ping v. United States (The Chinese Exclusion Case)*, 130 U.S. 581 (1889) and *Fong Yue Ting v. United States,* 149 U.S. 698 (1893). Both upheld the Chinese Exclusion Act and reaffirmed the virtually unreviewable power of Congress in immigration matters. *Chae Chan Ping* dealt with the exclusion of a returning Chinese worker, while *Fong Yue Ting* concerned the deportation of resident Chinese laborers.

While the Chinese were early targets of federal exclusionary action (both legislative and judicial), it was not long before other persons of Asian descent also fell prey. Immigration from Japan was curtailed by the so-called "Gentlemen's Agreement" of 1907 to 1908 between the United States and Japan, whereby the Japanese government agreed to refuse travel or exit documents to Japanese desirous of immigrating to the United States. Asian Indians and other Asians were finally barred from admissibility in the Immigration Act of 1917, which was enacted over four presidential vetoes. The 1917 Act also established an adult literacy requirement (targeted primarily at Eastern and southern Europeans) and created the Asiatic Barred Zone, by virtue of which nearly all Asians from the western reaches of European Asia to the Pacific were barred from admission to the United States. An important loophole that had hitherto been open was also finally closed—the right to be admitted to the United States was now tied to the right to naturalize. Because Asians were not Caucasian, they were deemed incapable of assimilation and could not naturalize; hence, they were considered inadmissible. Asians who had been previously naturalized found their naturalizations canceled retroactively by the Supreme Court and by various

U.S. Courts of Appeals and some persons were rendered stateless. Three important cases in this context were *United States v. Thind*, 261 U.S. 204 (1923) and *United States v. Pandit*, C.C.A. 9 (Cal. 1926), cert. denied 273 U.S. 579 (1927), both involving Asian Indians, and *Ozawa v. United States*, 260 US 178 (1922), concerning a Japanese man.

By 1924 racial-origins quotas for immigration were legislatively cemented in the Johnson-Reed Act. They remained in place until their abolition by the McCarran-Walter Act of 1952 and its 1965 amendments. Racially based exclusions on the entry of Chinese were nominally removed in 1943 (the quota was extremely limited), on Indians and Filipinos in 1946, on Guamanians in 1950, and then universally in 1952. In 1965, with the emergence of the civil rights movement, the national-origins quotas were also revoked, with the eastern and western hemispheric distinctions being abolished in 1968.

A little-known aspect of the exclusionary immigration provisions that operated in the early part of the twentieth century is that the intersection of racial and gender classifications worked to exclude certain women (including American women) from the national community and citizenship. The 1907 Expatriation Act denationalized American women who took foreign husbands. In 1922 the Cable Act ended expatriation of American women, other than those of Asian descent and non-Asian American women who married Asian men. American women such as Mary Das (a *Mayflower* descendant) who married Asian men were unable to reclaim their former U.S. nationalities because of the presumed primacy of racial exclusion over gender equality (see *Chang Chan v. Nagle*, 268 US 346 [1925]; Volpp 2005). Loss of citizenship also meant loss of voting rights and, in most states, the right to acquire land.

ALIEN LAND RESTRICTIONS

Even today, about half the states have restrictions on ownership of land by aliens (Price 1999), although only a few states prohibit aliens outright from land ownership. In most cases the limitations extend to the right to inherit real property and acquire agricultural land.

Such restrictions predate the American Revolution (1775–1783), and following independence many states continued the practice, first by common law and then by statute toward the end of the nineteenth century. The rationale for permitting only citizens to hold land is traceable to the English common law in which the king's subjects, who owed allegiance to the crown, held land in trust for the monarch. Early American common law "received" this system with the modification that "subject" was substituted by "citizen" and the tenure-based system of landholding by allodial land rights.

Most court cases concerning land ownership occurred in the state courts and fall into three main categories: (1) aliens who purchased land might forfeit it during their lifetimes at the pleasure of the state (although this rarely occurred); (2) aliens who did not naturalize during their lifetimes could not transmit land to heirs (even if the latter were U.S. citizens); and (3) because aliens lacked "inheritable blood," they could not inherit real property owned by another by intestate succession. Aliens could purchase and hold land during their lifetimes, but the interest was not secure and amounted only to a defeasible estate. In a rare high court decision in the area, the U.S. Supreme Court upheld in *Orr v. Hudson*, 17 U.S. 453 (1819) the rescission action of a potential purchaser of land from an alien on the grounds that the alien could not convey good title. Even U.S. citizens could find their titles vulnerable if they traced their titles through a remote alien ancestor. Naturalization after conveyance of the land could not cure the latent defect due to alienation in the chain of title.

SEE ALSO *Asian Exclusion Laws; Immigration; Non-citizens and Equal Protection (State); Progressive Era Immigration and Naturalization*

BIBLIOGRAPHY

Price, Polly J. 1999. "Alien Land Restrictions in the American Common Law: Exploring the Relative Autonomy Paradigm." *American Journal of Legal History* 43: 152–208.

Volpp, Leti. 2005. "Divesting Citizenship: On Asian American History and the Loss of Citizenship through Marriage." *UCLA Law Review* 53: 405–483.

Jagdeep S. Bhandari

Supreme Court Justice Samuel Alito. *Alito served more than fifteen years on the federal appellate bench before becoming a Supreme Court Justice in 2006. In his first years on the highest court, Alito has frequently voted with the conservative bloc, often using legislative history to ground his decisions.* PAUL J. RICHARDS/AFP/ GETTY IMAGES

ALITO, SAMUEL
1950–

On February 1, 2006, Samuel Anthony Alito Jr. joined the U.S. Supreme Court, replacing retiring Associate Justice Sandra Day O'Connor. He took his seat on the bench as the 110th justice to serve on the court.

Justice Alito was born in Trenton, New Jersey, on April 1, 1950. His mother was an elementary school teacher and, eventually, elementary school principal. His father had immigrated to America from Italy as a boy.

Alito graduated from Princeton in 1972 with an undergraduate degree and from Yale Law School in 1975. In 1976 Leonard I. Garth (1921–), Judge in the Third Circuit Court of Appeals, hired Alito as a law clerk. Later, the association was to continue when Alito was appointed to the same bench. He impressed Judge Garth with his quiet diligence.

From 1977 to 1981 Alito served as an assistant U.S. attorney for the District of New Jersey. He served in this position until 1985 when he was promoted to deputy assistant to the U.S. attorney general. He eventually argued a dozen cases before the U.S. Supreme Court. In 1987 he returned to New Jersey to serve as a U.S. attorney. He handled cases ranging over a wide variety of criminal activity from child pornography to organized crime.

President George H. W. Bush (1924–) nominated Alito to the Third Circuit Court of Appeals in 1990. The appointment was confirmed by the Senate on April 27, 1990. He served until January 31, 2006, when he was confirmed a justice of the Supreme Court.

The conservative opinions issued by Judge Alito on the Third Circuit at times marked him as a lone dissenter but at times as an independent jurist. In 1988 he wrote that a government-sponsored holiday display that included both secular symbols and religious symbols did not violate the First Amendment to the Constitution. In 1991 he was the lone dissenter against the pro-abortion position in a case arising in Pennsylvania from a statute that required husbands to be informed prior to an abortion being performed upon their wives. In another case adjudicated on the issue of late-term abortion, Alito sided with the majority allowing the abortion because the only reason for the abortion was the health of the mother.

All of Alito's fifteen years of service as a judge on the circuit court, his legal opinions, his activity as a member of society, and other matters were given microscopic examinations when he was nominated to the Supreme Court on October 31, 2005, by President George W. Bush (1946–). Political considerations were intense during the confirmation process for Alito. However, he was confirmed by the Senate on January 31, 2006, by a vote of fifty-eight to forty-two, and was sworn in a short time later.

Alito's February 1st arrival at the Supreme Court, then about halfway through its term, meant that some cases had to be decided without him. None of these ultimately involved a tie vote, so his nonparticipation was not of consequence. Three cases were reargued so that he could join the Court in its decisions: *Garcetti v. Ceballos*, 547 U.S. 410 (2006); *Hudson v. Michigan*, 547 U.S. 586 (2006); and *Kansas v. Marsh*, 548 U.S. ___ (2006).

Alito's first day on the job was February 1, 2006. His first decision was a split with the most conservative member of the court. In a six-to-three decision he refused to allow Missouri to proceed with the execution of Michael Taylor. On May 1, 2006, Justice Alito issued his first Supreme Court opinion in the case of *Holmes v. South Carolina*, 547 U.S. 319 (2006). It was an opinion for a unanimous court because the Rehnquist Court had established a tradition that a new justice's first written opinion should be for a unanimous court.

In the three cases that were reargued, Alito was aligned with the conservatives along the conservative-liberal split in the Court. He also joined with conservatives, Justices Antonin Scalia, Clarence Thomas, Chief Justice John Roberts, and Anthony Kennedy (who is usually a swing vote) to form a majority in *Zedner v. United States*, 547 U.S. 489 (2006); *Woodford v. Ngo*, 548 U.S. ___ (2006); *Arlington Central School District Board of Education v. Murphy*, 548 U.S. ___ (2006); *Sanchez-Llamas v. Oregon*, 548 U.S. ___ (2006); and *Rapanos v. United States*, 126 S. Ct. 2208 (2006). And in the important case involving the rights of accused terrorists, *Hamdan v. Rumsfeld*, 126 S. Ct. 2749 (2006), Alito voted in the minority with Justices Scalia and Thomas. Late-term abortion, so-called partial-birth abortion, was the issue in *Gonzales v. Carhart* (2007), and Alito voted with the new conservative majority without reservation. At issue in *Morse v. Frederick*, 551 U.S. ___ (2007) was whether schools can ban speech that advocates drug use. Alito joined with the conservative majority to ban the speech; however, the decision included a caveat that the ban should not be used to stifle debate on medical marijuana.

Opponents of Justice Alito have given him the nickname *Scalito*, referring to his similarity to Justice Scalia.

However, they differ in a number of areas, particularly in the use of legislative history in deciding a case. Scalia is very opposed to relying on legislative history, whereas Alito is much more inclined to use it.

SEE ALSO *Roberts, John*; *Roberts Court*

BIBLIOGRAPHY

Alito, Samuel A. 1989. "Racketeering Made Simple(r)." In *The RICO Racket*, ed. G. McDowell. Washington, DC: National Legal Center for the Public Interest.

Lewis, Thomas Tandy, ed. 2007. *The U. S. Supreme Court*. 3 vols. Pasadena, CA: Salem Press.

Nemacheck, Christine L. 2007. *Strategic Selection: Presidential Nomination of Supreme Court Justices from Herbert Hoover through George W. Bush*. Charlottesville: University of Virginia Press.

U.S. Congress. Senate. 2006. *Confirmation Hearing on the Nomination of Samuel A. Alito, Jr., to Be an Associate Justice of the Supreme Court of the United States*. 109th Cong., 2nd sess., January 9–13. Washington, DC: U.S. Government Printing Office.

Andrew J. Waskey

ALL DELIBERATE SPEED

In order to produce a unanimous Court in *Brown v. Board of Education* (*Brown I*), 347 U.S. 483 (1954), Chief Justice Earl Warren had to agree that the desegregation of schools by court order would proceed gradually. The first step in this process was to ask the parties to present further argument on the judicial orders that should be granted to the plaintiffs. In *Brown v. Board of Education* (*Brown II*), 349 U.S. 294 (1955), the Court rejected Thurgood Marshall's argument that the courts should follow their usual pattern in ending governmental misbehavior by ordering immediate desegregation. Instead, a unanimous Court delegated the crafting of decrees to the lower courts in the cases at hand, with only this guidance: a school board must make "a prompt and reasonable start" and proceed toward full desegregation with "all deliberate speed."

The latter phrase was vague, and the vagueness was intentional. It was suggested by Justice Felix Frankfurter, who had found it in an old opinion by Justice Oliver Wendell Holmes, Jr. The words seem to have originated in an 1889 poem, "The Hound of Heaven," by the dreamy Victorian poet Francis Thompson (1859–1907). Origins aside, Frankfurter offered the phrase as an instrument of gradualism, a compromise that would avoid defiance of the courts by giving time for the white South to get used to the idea of desegregation. This hope was in vain; the actual response in the South was defiance, as political leaders rushed to allay the fears of many white southerners. Ten

> *The judgments below ... are accordingly reversed and the cases are remanded to the District Courts to take such proceedings and enter such orders and decrees consistent with this opinion as are necessary and proper to admit to public schools on a racially nondiscriminatory basis with all deliberate speed the parties to these cases.*
>
> SOURCE: Earl Warren, *Brown v. Board of Education,* 349 U.S. 294, 301 (1955).

years after *Brown I*, in the states of the old Confederacy just 2 percent of black children were attending school with white children. The Civil Rights Act of 1964 conditioned federal financial aid to state agencies on the avoidance of racial segregation. A year later, the Elementary and Secondary Education Act of 1965 offered massive aid to local schools, and increasing numbers of southern districts decided that they needed the federal money. Soon afterward, the Supreme Court followed Congress's lead; in *Alexander v. Holmes County Board of Education,* 396 U.S. 19 (1969), the Court said that the time for "deliberate speed" had run out, and that from that time forward, lower courts were to order school boards to desegregate "at once."

Whatever the Supreme Court might have ordered in 1954 or 1955, no one thought that the courts could easily end the systematic segregation of the Jim Crow South. Even the more modest goal of court-ordered desegregation of public schools would have taken time, absent help from the other branches of the federal government. In the mid-1950s neither Congress nor the Dwight D. Eisenhower administration showed any inclination to support the Court in such an effort. The problem with "all deliberate speed" is not only that it abandoned a generation of black children to segregated schools for more than a decade, but also that it abandoned principle for political accommodation. The commands of courts have moral authority only if they are seen to be founded on principle. The phrase "all deliberate speed" was widely seen as the political compromise it was intended to be.

SEE ALSO *Brown v. Board of Education, 347 U.S. 483 (1954); Brown v. Board of Education (Brown II), 349 U.S. 294 (1955); Brown v. Board of Education, Critiques; School Desegregation; Warren Court*

BIBLIOGRAPHY

Klarman, Michael J. 2007. Brown v. Board of Education *and the Civil Rights Movement.* New York: Oxford University Press.

Kluger, Richard. 2004. *Simple Justice: The History of* Brown v. Board of Education *and Black America's Struggle for Equality.* Rev. edition. New York: Knopf.

Wilkinson, J. Harvie, III. 1979. *From* Brown *to* Bakke: *The Supreme Court and School Integration, 1954–1978.* New York: Oxford University Press.

Kenneth L. Karst

ALLGEYER V. LOUISIANA, 165 U.S. 578 (1897)

Allgeyer v. Louisiana, 165 U.S. 578 (1897) is often credited with inaugurating the so-called *Lochner* era of Supreme Court jurisprudence, during which the Court used the due process clause to enforce a right to liberty of contract. In *Allgeyer* the Court was faced with a Louisiana statute that prohibited in-state companies from contracting for marine insurance with insurers not licensed in Louisiana. Defendant E. Allgeyer & Co. ran afoul of the statute when it contracted with the Atlantic Mutual Insurance Company of New York for insurance on a shipment of one hundred bales of cotton.

The Supreme Court held that the law was unconstitutional because it deprived the defendants of their liberty without due process of law. Justice Rufus Peckham (1809–1873), writing for a unanimous court, stated that the Fourteenth Amendment's protection of liberty from arbitrary deprivation included "the right of the citizen to be free in the enjoyment of all his faculties; to be free to use them in all lawful ways; to live and work where he will; to earn his livelihood by any lawful calling; to pursue any livelihood or avocation," and to enter into all related contracts. The government could only interfere with this liberty if it was acting within its police power. In other words, the due process clause protected the right to pursue an occupation free from unreasonable government interference.

Peckham's opinion built on prior Supreme Court opinions, including Justice Joseph Bradley's dissent in the *Slaughter-House Cases*, 83 U.S. 36 (1873) and Justice John Marshall Harlan's opinion in *Powell v. Pennsylvania*, 127 U.S. 678 (1888). These precedents, however, were dubious authority for a broad right to occupational liberty. Bradley's *Slaughter-House* opinion, as Peckham acknowledged, dealt only with the question of the ancient right to be free of government-sponsored monopoly. And Harlan, in *Powell*, had articulated a general ban on class legislation, not a right to liberty as such.

Contrary to conventional wisdom, however, *Allgeyer* was not the first Supreme Court opinion to assert the right to pursue an occupation. Three years earlier, Justice Henry

Brown (1836–1913) wrote for the Court that the "legislature may not, under the guise of protecting the public interests, arbitrarily interfere with private business, or impose unusual and unnecessary restrictions upon lawful occupations" in *Lawton v. Steele*, 152 U. S. 133, 137 (1894). The following year, Justice David Brewer stated even more directly that "generally speaking, among the inalienable rights of the citizen is that of the liberty of contract" in *Frisbie v. United States*, 157 U.S. 160, 165 (1895).

Nevertheless, Justice Peckham's *Allgeyer* opinion was especially important because it was the first one not only to articulate a right to liberty of contract that included a right to pursue an occupation, but also to declare that the statute in question was unconstitutional for interfering with that right. It was therefore an important precursor to *Lochner v. New York*, 198 U.S. 45 (1905), which held that a law restricting bakers' hours to sixty per week violated the right to liberty of contract. Peckham's opinion for the majority in *Lochner* cited *Allgeyer* for the proposition that the "general right to make a contract in relation to his business is part of the liberty of the individual protected by the 14th Amendment of the Federal Constitution."

SEE ALSO *Freedom of Contract; Fuller Court*

BIBLIOGRAPHY

Gillman, Howard. 1993. *The Constitution Besieged: The Rise and Demise of* Lochner *Era Police Powers Jurisprudence*. Durham, NC: Duke University Press.

David E. Bernstein

AMENDMENT, OUTSIDE OF ARTICLE V

Article V of the United States Constitution lays out the procedures by which the Constitution may be amended. It sets out two methods by which new amendments may proposed: (1) Congress may propose amendments itself, "whenever two thirds of both Houses shall deem it necessary," or (2) Congress may call a convention for proposing amendments "on the Application of Legislatures of two thirds of the several states." Once proposed, a constitutional amendment will become a part of the Constitution (i.e., ratified) if it is approved in three-fourths of the states, either by the legislatures of those states or by ratifying conventions, "as one or the other mode of ratification may be proposed by Congress."

ALTERNATIVE APPROACHES

Although the Constitution does not expressly describe any other means for adding new provisions to the Constitution, some legal scholars—most notably Professor Bruce Ackerman and Professor Akhil Amar, both from Yale Law School—have argued that constitutional amendment may occur outside of Article V. For both Amar and Ackerman, allowing for constitutional amendment outside Article V is both legally permissible and wise policy. For both of them, the key justification for permitting amendment outside of Article V is that the even when constitutional change is not authorized under Article V by the people's representatives in Congress, state legislatures, or state conventions, such change may be proposed or ratified by the people themselves.

In Amar's view, constitutional amendment by the people can take place only when a majority votes in favor of a specific proposed amendment. In Ackerman's view, by contrast, such constitutional change by the people may occur without such a formal voting process—and even without a specific proposed amendment. This can occur when citizens who are seeking constitutional change (whether embodied in specific proposed constitutional language or not) "succeed in mobilizing their fellow citizens and gaining repeated support in response to their opponents' counterattacks" (1991, p. 6–7). For Ackerman, in other words, the people may act to amend the Constitution not as a voting majority in a particular election or referendum, but as a social movement that earns the right to be called "the people." Unlike the electoral coalitions that triumph in the "normal politics" of a typical legislative or presidential election—the winners of which may create new laws and policies within the existing constitutional framework, the "people" can and do engage in the "higher law-making" that alters the constitutional framework itself.

THE PEOPLE'S RIGHT TO AMEND

To defend their distinctive arguments for the legitimacy of non-Article V amendment, both Amar and Ackerman closely analyze the Constitution's text, structure, and history, but they do so in different ways. Amar focuses his argument on the language and historical background of Article V itself—and of the Constitution (and constitutional debates) of which it was a part. His core argument is that an interpretation of the Constitution that treats Article V as the exclusive means for amending the Constitution would be squarely inconsistent with a belief that was almost universally accepted among the Constitution's framers and ratifiers and acknowledged in other parts of the Constitution: the belief that the people have an "inalienable legal right . . . to alter or abolish their form of government" (Amar 1988, p. 1050). Such an inalienable right to alter their government would be severely undermined if its use could be effectively vetoed by any of the governing institutions whose support is required under Article V: the Senate, House of Representatives, and state legislatures or conventions.

Supporters of the Constitution in the state ratifying conventions, says Amar, made it clear that the people could not be blocked in this way by the representatives who were supposed to be their agents, because the people could always circumvent the officials to whom Article V grants power to initiate and approve constitutional change. For example, Amar quotes James Pendleton, the president of the Virginia Ratifying Convention, assuring other delegates that if the "servants" of the people are led by "motives of self-interest" to thwart popular constitutional reforms, the people can nonetheless enact such reforms—they can "assemble in Convention; wholly recall our delegated powers, or reform them so as to prevent such abuse" (1988, p. 1056).

Moreover, says Amar, one need not ignore or stretch the Constitution's text to find a warrant for such a non-Article V amendment. Article V itself, he writes, "nowhere declare[s] that it [is] the exclusive mode of amendment" (1988, p. 1053). A warrant for direct constitutional amendment by the people itself, says Amar, can be found in other language in the Constitution that clearly acknowledges the people's right to directly alter their government. The Preamble, for example, "begins by declaring that the Constitution is ordained and established by We the People of the United States" (1988, p. 1055). In addition, the First Amendment gives the people a right to petition for change (including constitutional changes), while the Ninth Amendment warns readers of the Constitution not to ignore rights that existed before the Constitution was written, including the people's right to change their form of government at will. The same historical sources lead Amar to believe that "the people" empowered to make this alteration comprise a majority. He therefore argues that such direct constitutional amendment—outside of Article V's boundaries—can take place only when a referendum establishes that a majority does in fact support a particular constitutional provision.

THE "PEOPLE" REDEFINED

For Ackerman, in contrast, "the people" that hold this right to engage in constitution-making are harder to define. They do not comprise a majority of voters in a single referendum. Rather, the definition of "the people" for constitution-making purposes is more contestable—and it is generally contested over a longer period of time. More specifically, Ackerman argues that people empowered to change the constitution directly and outside of the Article V framework do not automatically receive that status by being in the majority. He identifies and examines three key "constitutional moments" where such a claim to engage in higher lawmaking was made successfully—namely, the adoption of the United States Constitution in 1787, the

passage of the Reconstruction Amendments in the mid-nineteenth century, and the New Deal in the 1930s.

Each of these constitutional revolutions, says Ackerman, happened outside the existing formal framework for constitutional alteration. The Constitution of 1787, for example, went into effect when it was ratified by only nine out of the thirteen states, even though Article XIII of the Articles of Confederation barred such constitutional changes unless they were approved unanimously by the thirteen states. The Radical Republican Congress that passed the Reconstruction Amendments in the wake of the Civil War, claimed to be following the provisions of Article V, but according to Ackerman it actually ignored these requirements by treating many southern state governments' approval as unnecessary for the ratification of the Fourteenth Amendment (even after using these same state goverments' approval as a basis for finding that there had been a ratification of the Thirteenth Amendment). Finally, in constructing the New Deal, the Roosevelt administration succeeded in revolutionizing the constitutional system—and making room within it for activist government—without even adopting the pretext of doing so through Article V.

Ackerman identifies an underlying pattern in the amendment process outside of Article V by asking what these constitutional revolutions shared. He identifies in each of them a process whereby a group seeking constitutional change (usually with some representation in Congress, the executive branch, or both) mobilized a majority of voters in its favor and convinced Americans to adhere to this movement in the face of opposing arguments. The challenge of sustaining such a "mobilized majority," says Ackerman, resembles the challenge that Article V requires amendment proponents to meet when it demands that they not only win a majority for a proposed amendment, but that they also win a supermajority in Congress and among the states, in a process that normally extends over a much longer period of time than a single vote. In a sense then, Article V provides a template for non-Article V amendment.

ACKERMAN'S PROCESS

Unlike Article V amendment, amendment by "a mobilized majority" is not constrained by written constitutional rules: on the contrary, those seeking such non–Article V amendments have often improvised new methods for achieving it—methods that fit the particular circumstances and political culture of their time. Thus, in the founding era, when states were more powerful vis-à-vis the federal government, the Federalist proponents of the new constitution had to debate and overcome anti-Federalist opposition in the separate states. Since the founders generally viewed legislative bodies and assemblies as the key representatives of the people's will, the framers went outside the Articles of Confederation by calling for approval of the Constitution through conventions that resembled legislative bodies. By contrast, the constitutional moment after the Civil War arose in an era when national institutions had greater significance, and national popular elections more importance in the democratic process. Thus, the constitutional struggle between the Radical Republican Congress and President Andrew Johnson was resolved not in separate state conventions, but in a national election, the mid-term election of 1866. The New Deal's constitutional transformation was likewise triggered and solidified in national elections. But, in contrast to the higher lawmaking of the reconstruction era, the New Deal was forged not so much in legislative elections as in presidential contests, contests that made the president a key player in the process of mobilizing constitutional change and increased the plebiscitary role played by national elections in resolving competing claims between proponents of constitutional change and their detractors.

The specific form of non–Article V amendment, Ackerman argues, is determined not only by the existing political culture, but also by the (often unpredictable) events that determine whether a president or Congress insisting on constitutional change meets with resistance or acquiesence from the other branches of government; For example, he argues, President Andrew Johnson's opposition to the Republican congress of the Reconstruction era left it little choice but to propose Article V amendment as part of its larger, non–Article V higher lawmaking project, while President Roosevelt had little need to invoke Article V when both Congress, and after some initial resistance, the Supreme Court, supported the constitutional transformation required by the New Deal.

Ackerman also looks at failed attempts to amend the Constitution outside of Article V. (He identifies President Reagan's unsuccessful attempt to appoint Judge Robert Bork to the Supreme Court as one such failed constitutional revolution.) Such failures are explained as mobilizations that dissolved in the face of challenge. Ackerman proposes that in the wake of such major constitutional changes, the courts must confront the challenge of synthesizing the new constitutional provisions with older constitutional elements, which sometimes appear inconsistent. At the same time, the courts must defend this newly altered system of higher law against attempts by legislators and majorities within "normal politics" to trump the higher law system that is designed to constrain them.

OPPOSING VIEWPOINTS

These arguments for the constitutionality of the amendment outside the Article V process have not convinced all legal academics. One prominent challenge to Amar and Ackerman's arguments comes from Professor Laurence Tribe, who has defended the position that Article V

should be read as providing the exclusive means of amending the Constitution, in large part, he says, because the "provisions of the Constitution that are manifestly instrumental and means-oriented and that frame the architecture of the government ought to be given as fixed and determinate a reading as possible" (1995, p. 1247). Other critics have questioned Amar and Ackerman's claims that Article V was meant by the framers to identify only one of multiple permissible methods for altering the Constitution, or (in Ackerman's case) that major instances of constitutional amendment after the founding have taken place outside of Article V's requirements.

Finally, while Amar and Ackerman's arguments overlap, they have also taken issue with each other. Ackerman rejects Amar's formalistic definition of "the people" as simply and invariably consisting of a majority in a referendum on a formal constitutional amendment—although he has proposed that the American people may benefit from formalizing non–Article V amendment process in a process whereby (1) second-term presidents may propose new constitutional amendments and (2) such amendments will then take effect when approved by two-thirds of Congress and by majorities in the next two presidential elections (1998, pp. 414–416). But this process, like the historical constitutional transformations that Ackerman analyzes and the Article V process itself, is slower and more laden with political hurdles than the majority referendum that Amar argues would by itself place a constitutional stamp of approval on a people's alteration of their form of government.

Amar, meanwhile, believes that Ackerman's support for an informal, atextual process for amendment by the people is both too ill-defined and too dependent on the same institutions of ordinary, nonconstitutional politics that some members of the ratifying conventions worried would betray the people's interests and thus require a route around Article V. In Ackerman's model, as in Article V amendment, people rely on their representatives in government—primarily, presidents and members of Congress—to shepherd constitutional alterations through electoral, political, and legal battles. Amar, however, believes that the people may sometimes have to go entirely around such "ordinary branches of government" to enact the extraordinary changes that mark a constitutional transformation, and that it such a constitutional act by the people themselves, unmediated by their elected representatives, that make non–Article V amendment a necessary feature of the U.S. constitutional system.

SEE ALSO *Ackerman, Bruce; Article V*

BIBLIOGRAPHY

Ackerman, Bruce A. 1991. *We the People*, Vol. 1: *Foundations.* Cambridge, MA: Belknap Press.

Ackerman, Bruce A. 1998. *We the People*, Vol.2: *Transformations*. Cambridge, MA: Belknap Press.

Amar, Akhil Reed. 1988. "Philadelphia Revisited: Amending the Constitution Outside Article V." *University of Chicago Law Review* 55(4): 1043–1104.

Amar, Akhil Reed. 1994. "The Consent of the Governed: Constitutional Amendment Outside Article V." *Columbia Law Review* 94(2): 457–508.

Tribe, Laurence H. 1995. "Taking Text and Structure Seriously, Reflections on Free-Form Method in Constitutional Interpretation." *Harvard Law Review* 108(6): 1221–1303.

Marc J. Blitz

AMENDMENTS, POST–CIVIL WAR

The Thirteenth, Fourteenth, and Fifteenth Amendments to the U.S. Constitution together constitute the post–Civil War Reconstruction Amendments. They were, and remain, the centerpiece of Congress's program of national reform following the Union Government's 1865 victory over the rebellious Southern Confederacy of slave states. The amendments also reflect fundamental ideological goals of the Republican Party of that time—the dominant political force in the Union states during the war and in the nation as a whole for decades afterward. The amendments abolished slavery, and granted citizenship and basic legal rights—including voting rights, for men— to the newly freed millions of African Americans. For a brief time in the late 1860s and early 1870s, they dramatically recast the face of American politics and society. But a racist reaction to Reconstruction—the so-called redemption of the South by white supremacists— soon reversed much of that progress. A central and tragic theme of American history and law is the ensuing failure of the nation—until a century after the end of the Civil War—to fulfill much of the promise of the Reconstruction Amendments. Not until the civil rights movement of the 1950s and 1960s—often called the *second Reconstruction*—did the amendments and their original design and vision begin to gain a lasting foothold within American law and society. The reform process they initiated, however, has yet to achieve full fruition.

BACKGROUND AND RATIFICATION OF THE THIRTEENTH AMENDMENT, 1862–1865

It is often emphasized by cynics that President Abraham Lincoln's Emancipation Proclamation—announced in September 1862 and effective in January 1863—did not free a single slave, because it only applied to areas not then under Union control. That unfairly understates its epic importance in reframing the Union's goals in the Civil War. In fact, it soon did bring freedom to many slaves, as Union armies advanced and African Americans, inspired by news of Lincoln's decision, took matters into their own hands. But it is fair to note that only with the ratification of the Thirteenth Amendment, more than two years later, did the goal of full national abolition of slavery reach fruition. First proposed in Congress in December 1863, the amendment achieved the required two-thirds approval in the Senate in April 1864. But then, while winning a majority in the House, it fell short of two-thirds in that chamber in June 1864. Only Lincoln's decisive reelection in 1864, together with major Republican gains in Congress, provided the needed impetus. Even before the new Congress took office, Lincoln's tireless lobbying helped change enough votes to secure its submission to the states in January 1865. Even then, it was not until December 1865—after Union demands that provisional southern state legislatures ratify it—that it won approval by three-fourths of all the states.

This amendment did more than simply abolish "slavery" and "involuntary servitude" as stated in Section 1. As the debates over the amendment made clear, it was also understood to eradicate all badges and incidents of slavery. And it is more than simply a negative restriction, enforceable in the courts. Section 2 granted Congress the "power to enforce" the amendment "by appropriate legislation." Similar provisions were included in the Fourteenth and Fifteenth Amendments. And because slavery was an institution of private property as well as public law, the Thirteenth Amendment's reach is not limited to state action. It does not merely impose duties on the government but also regulates private conduct. This became a crucial distinguishing feature of the Thirteenth Amendment as compared to the Fourteenth and Fifteenth Amendments.

BACKGROUND AND RATIFICATION OF THE FOURTEENTH AMENDMENT, 1865–1868

In December 1865, the same month that the Thirteenth Amendment was ratified, the Thirty-ninth Congress convened. As a result of the landslide 1864 elections and the fact that representatives of the Confederate states were not yet readmitted, Republicans held a huge supermajority in Congress. But because of Lincoln's assassination in April 1865, his 1864 vice-presidential running mate Andrew Johnson (1808–1875)—a white-supremacist Southern Democrat by background—now occupied the White House. President Johnson, though a fervent Unionist, had little interest in protecting the civil rights of the freed slaves, and favored quick and easy readmission of the southern states, including his own native Tennessee. A collision was inevitable, and soon emerged.

Congress, asserting its power to enforce the Thirteenth Amendment, passed the Freedmen's Bureau Bill to

THE FIFTEENTH AMENDMENT AND ITS RESULTS.

Celebration of the Fifteenth Amendment. *After the conclusion of the Civil War, amendments thirteen, fourteen, and fifteen were made to the Constitution, helping guarantee full rights to former slaves. The Fifteenth Amendment in particular helped ensure that political rights could not be denied to a citizen based on his or her race, color, or former status as a slave.* **MPI/HULTON ARCHIVE/GETTY IMAGES**

provide relief to the former slaves. Johnson shocked the Republicans by vetoing the bill in February 1866 and they narrowly failed to muster the two-thirds vote needed to override him. Ironically, Johnson's obstructionism united Republicans, pushing moderate-to-conservative legislators into closer alliance with the impassioned Radical Republican wing of the party. The most famous Radical Republicans were Thaddeus Stevens (1792–1868), in the House, and Charles Sumner (1811–1874), in the Senate. Contrary to many biased accounts, the radicals never controlled Congress and they did not dictate policy. But they did provide an influential cutting edge and they eagerly seized the initiative from Johnson.

Republicans agreed on a bill to guarantee African Americans citizenship and basic civil rights, especially relating to property, contracts, and access to the courts.

This time they succeeded in overriding Johnson's veto and enacted the Civil Rights Act in April 1866. They also finally enacted the Freedmen's Bureau Act in July 1866. Even some Republicans, however—notably a leading House moderate, John Bingham (1815–1900)—feared that the Civil Rights Act exceeded Congress's power under the Thirteenth Amendment. Many Republicans also feared that Democrats would repeal such laws if they recaptured Congress. Thus, in order to entrench and constitutionalize their key reforms, they proposed the Fourteenth Amendment.

As finally passed by Congress in June 1866, the new amendment was something of a cobbled-together compromise dealing with several separate issues. Section 1, mainly drafted by Bingham, guaranteed national citizenship to all persons born under U.S. jurisdiction, and declared them also to be citizens "of the State wherein they reside." It prohibited states from denying such citizens "the privileges and immunities of citizens of the United States" (without defining what those were), and from denying "any person" within state jurisdiction "life, liberty, or property, without due process of law" or "the equal protection of the laws." These three great provisions—the privileges and immunities clause, the due process clause, and the equal protection clause—have been the subject of innumerable Supreme Court decisions and vast legal controversy ever since. But ironically, this was the least controversial section of the amendment at the time it was proposed and ratified, and received less discussion than other provisions and issues.

Section 2 dealt indirectly with the far more explosive issue of black voting rights. It was generally understood that the amendment would not clearly or affirmatively guarantee voting rights. In the parlance of the time, voting, office holding, and serving on juries—not to be confused with the right to be tried by jury—were viewed as political rights separate from more fundamental civil rights. Most Republican leaders were coming to favor equal political as well as civil rights for blacks—if only, in some cases, out of partisan self-interest because they needed black political support, especially in the Deep South where blacks formed a large percentage of the population. But the issue was still very controversial for many whites, North and South. It was thought that pushing too hard or too soon on that front might jeopardize the entire Reconstruction program. At the same time, if the southern states were readmitted with only whites voting but with representation in the House apportioned according to their entire populations, the ironic result would be to strengthen Democrats and white supremacists, and endanger Republican control of Congress. The awkward solution of Section 2 was to provide that a state's apportionment of representatives would be reduced in proportion to whatever percentage of a state's entire adult male population (excluding Indians and criminals) might be denied the right to vote.

Section 3 denied the right to serve in Congress, or hold any other federal or state office, to anyone who had previously taken an oath (as such an officer) to support the U.S. Constitution and who then violated that oath by supporting the Confederate rebellion. But Section 3 also provided that Congress could "remove such disability" by a two-thirds vote. Congress passed a general amnesty doing so in 1872. An alternative version of Section 3—pushed by radicals such as Stevens, and initially approved by the House but then rejected by the Senate—would have denied the right to vote or hold any political office to all Confederate supporters until 1870. That might have effectively disenfranchised most white southerners. Even the mild compromise version of Section 3 aroused bitter debate.

Section 4 forbade payment of the Confederate debt and guaranteed the validity of the Union debt. This too, while perhaps an arcane issue for modern readers, aroused great controversy and discussion. Section 5, finally, granted Congress the power to enforce the amendment.

Whether to ratify the amendment was the dominant issue of the 1866 midterm elections. Johnson and the Democrats bitterly opposed and denounced the amendment. But the Republicans again won a landslide victory at the polls, confirming their dominant grip on Congress. By early 1867 many northern states had ratified the amendment. Yet all the former Confederate states except Tennessee refused. The amendment appeared stymied, well short of approval by three-fourths of all the states.

The emboldened Republicans in Congress then took matters into their own hands. They passed a sweeping Reconstruction Act in March 1867, placing the recalcitrant southern states under federal military control and demanding their ratification of the amendment as the price of readmission to Congress. Congress mandated black voting rights in those states, and also in the District of Columbia and all federal territories. Enough reconstructed southern legislatures then ratified the amendment in time for it to be proclaimed in force in July 1868. With the crucial help of southern black voters the Republicans then won the 1868 elections, including the election of President Ulysses S. Grant (1822–1885). But their victory margin was smaller than in 1864 or 1866. Without southern black support Grant would have lost the national popular vote, and his narrow margins in several states, North and South, brought him perilously close to losing the electoral college vote as well.

BACKGROUND AND RATIFICATION OF THE FIFTEENTH AMENDMENT, 1868–1870

The Republicans learned a clear lesson from 1868: They were increasingly dependent on black voters. Their control of many southern states was fragile and already starting to slip in the face of Ku Klux Klan terrorism. While blacks were a majority of the population in a few southern states, they could be outvoted by die-hard white supremacists in many others. Federal military enforcement of Reconstruction did not appear politically sustainable. In many northern states, by ironic contrast, blacks still could not vote. But Republicans desperately needed their support there as well, as Democrats gained ground. Even though Northern blacks were fewer in number, their votes could be crucial in close elections. At the same time, many Republicans sincerely believed in the justice of securing political rights for black men, many of who had fought and died for the Union. It was a classic merger of principle and pragmatism—a case of enlightened self-interest.

Thus, in order to entrench black political rights in the South and extend them in the North, the Republicans made it their first order of business in 1869 to propose the Fifteenth Amendment. Section 1 prohibited federal or state denial of voting rights "on account of race, color, or previous condition of servitude," with a grant of enforcement power to Congress in Section 2.

The amendment was passed by the lame-duck Fortieth Congress in February 1869, just before President Grant took office along with the new Congress, with its smaller Republican majority. In an ominous portent, Congress rejected alternative proposals that would have guaranteed universal male suffrage with no literacy or property qualifications. By allowing any restrictions on voting not provably based on race, the amendment left the door open for the subterfuges later used to effectively disenfranchise most southern blacks. Congress also rejected proposals to explicitly protect the right to seek public office. Some argued that was already implicit in the right to vote, while others shied away from the added controversy of black office holding. Thus, doubt would remain, even after the ratification of the Fifteenth Amendment, regarding whether blacks could still be denied such political rights as office holding and jury service.

Republicans needed three-fourths of the thirty-seven states to ratify the amendment. By February 1870, thirty had ratified—just two more than the minimum. But one of those, New York, rescinded its earlier ratification at the last minute. Four other states—Georgia, Mississippi, Texas, and Virginia—were required to ratify as the price of readmission to Congress. Ohio and Georgia first rejected the amendment, then later approved it in the nick of time. When the dust cleared, the amendment was proclaimed in force in March 1870.

What made the ratification especially remarkable is that the idea of black suffrage did not command even majority (much less supermajority) support among white Americans at the time. Numerous northern states and territories held popular referenda on the issue between 1865 and 1869. In all but two staunchly Republican states with hardly any black residents—Iowa and Minnesota—voters rejected it. The New England states—apart from Connecticut, which rejected the idea in an 1865 referendum—had long allowed their small number of black citizens to vote. Other states enfranchised blacks by judicial or legislative action.

But support was generally far stronger among the Radical Republican political elite than among white rank-and-file party members. Most Democrats remained bitterly opposed. Republicans brawled furiously among themselves over issues of strategy and principle. Many radicals accurately predicted that the amendment, by failing to outlaw literacy and property tests, would be ineffective. Pacific Coast politicians of both parties pandered to fears about Chinese immigrants voting. Nevada ratified, reluctantly, but California and Oregon

refused. The most heated debates, ironically, were in the North and West. In the South, black suffrage was viewed as a fait accompli to which even many Democrats were, at the time, resigned.

No other constitutional amendment has ever been ratified in the face of such polarized views and limited popular support. Like most amendments, however, the fifteenth was ratified by state legislatures. Republican party discipline, strong-arm political tactics, and the support of President Grant were, in the end, sufficient to secure passage in enough of those legislatures.

THE FIRST HEYDAY OF CONGRESSIONAL AND EXECUTIVE ENFORCEMENT, 1870–1875

With all three Reconstruction Amendments in place, Congress passed a series of Enforcement Acts to implement the new constitutional guarantees. The first, passed in May 1870, dealt mainly with voting rights and also reenacted the Civil Rights Act of 1866. Another, known as the Ku Klux Klan Act, was passed in April 1871. Among other things, it authorized President Grant to suspend the writ of habeas corpus, which he did later that year in cracking down on a violent Klan rebellion in South Carolina. It also provided for a powerful civil cause of action against violations of federal rights carried out "under color of" state laws and customs. Commonly referred to as *section 1983* (codified at 42 U.S.C. § 1983), this remains one of the most frequently used provisions of federal law.

The capstone of this era was the Civil Rights Act of 1875. Proposed versions of this bill would have banned racial segregation in schools, foreshadowing by almost a century the Supreme Court's decision in *Brown v. Board of Education*, 347 U.S. 483 (1954). But while majorities of both houses of Congress endorsed that provision at various times, it was jettisoned as too controversial. The final act—passed by a lame-duck Republican Congress in March 1875, following a sweeping midterm-election victory for the Democrats in 1874—banned racial segregation in transportation, and in public accommodations such as restaurants and theatres. As discussed below, it was struck down by the Supreme Court in 1883.

Armed with the tools provided by the Reconstruction Amendments and these acts of Congress, the Grant administration vigorously enforced African-American civil and voting rights for several years. Grant's second attorney general, Amos T. Akerman (1821–1880), was especially active in this regard, during 1870 and 1871. As a result, the Klan suffered severe setbacks, though it was never completely eliminated. Black men voted in large numbers and won offices throughout much of the former Confederacy, including two U.S. senators, several members of the House of Representatives, and many state legislators and executive officers. After 1872, however, such efforts flagged. Violence and fraud drove many black voters from the polls, and white supremacists began reasserting control of the South.

JUDICIAL DECONSTRUCTION, 1872–1896

The end of Reconstruction is usually dated to 1877, when President Rutherford B. Hayes (1822–1893) took office after a disputed election, as part of a compromise that involved withdrawing the remaining federal troops from the South. But the Supreme Court had already begun chipping away at the scope of the Reconstruction Amendments and Congress's enforcement legislation. Conventional wisdom holds that the Court chose to first construe the amendments in a nonracial context, in the *Slaughter-House Cases*, 83 U.S. 36 (1873). But a year before, the Court issued an important ruling on the scope of the Civil Rights Act of 1866, in *Blyew v. United States*, 80 U.S. 581 (1872), a case that could not have been more racially charged.

Blyew, a white man, was prosecuted in Kentucky federal court for ordinary state-law murder, because Kentucky law barred the testimony (including a dying declaration) of the black victims of his racially motivated attack. The Civil Rights Act allowed for such federal-court jurisdiction in cases "affecting" persons denied equal rights under state law. Rather incredibly—not to mention callously—the five-to-two majority held that black crime victims and witnesses in such cases were not "affected" in any relevant sense, partly because a murder victim, no longer being "in existence," was "beyond being affected by the cause itself." Justice Joseph Bradley, joined by Justice Noah Swayne (1804–1884), protested in dissent that this put "a premium on murder." The Court generally argued that potential witnesses were not sufficiently affected by court cases in which they were barred from testifying on account of race, even though a central purpose of the Civil Rights Act was precisely to guarantee the equal right, without regard to race, to testify and otherwise gain access to courts. While the Court technically avoided constitutional issues, its implausibly cramped statutory interpretation can only be understood as motivated by concerns that a broader reading might expand federal-court jurisdiction beyond permissible constitutional understandings of the federal-state balance.

In *Slaughter-House* itself, a five-to-four majority—with Bradley and Swayne again dissenting, along with Justice Stephen Field and Chief Justice Salmon Chase—rejected a claim by New Orleans butchers that a state law regulating their trade violated their rights under the Fourteenth Amendment. The butchers relied primarily on the privileges and immunities clause. While the Court's holding seems eminently defensible, the needlessly broad reasoning of Justice Samuel Miller's majority opinion has conventionally been read as a virtual judicial repeal of the clause. Some have disputed that reading of *Slaughter-House*, but there is little argument that later decisions, in any event, indicated a sharply restrictive attitude by the Court toward the Reconstruction Amendments.

The Court enforced a state action requirement on the Fourteenth and Fifteenth Amendments in *United States v. Cruikshank*, 92 U.S. 542 (1876) and *United States v. Reese*, 92 U.S. 214 (1876), which threw out prosecutions under the Enforcement Act of 1870. The Court followed up in the *Civil Rights Cases*, 109 U.S. 3 (1883) by striking down the Civil Rights Act of 1875. Justice Bradley's majority opinion, over the solitary and powerful dissent of Justice John Marshall Harlan the elder, held that it exceeded the scope of Congress's enforcement power by regulating discrimination in public accommodations offered by private businesses. Some have suggested that these cases still allowed for a broader concept of state neglect to come within Congress's power, at least as to basic civil rights, which many at the time distinguished from social rights said to be implicated by such matters as public accommodations.

Indeed, the Court did not entirely abandon the legal promise of the amendments during this era. It struck down, seven-to-two, the openly race-based exclusion of blacks from jury service in *Strauder v. West Virginia*, 100 U.S. 303 (1880). In *Ex parte Yarbrough*, 110 U.S. 651 (1884), the Court unanimously upheld, in an opinion by Justice Miller, Congress's power to punish private, racially motivated violence interfering with a federal election.

But the impact of *Strauder* was rendered hollow by the Court's decision the same day, in *Virginia v. Rives*, 100 U.S. 313 (1880), that a systematic pattern of de facto exclusion of blacks from juries did not establish a constitutional violation. Thus, just as with voting, it became clear that as long as blacks were not denied rights openly on the basis of race, subterfuges designed to achieve the same practical result would escape censure.

The capstone of the Court's judicial dismantling of much of the promise of the Reconstruction Amendments was its infamous decision in *Plessy v. Ferguson*, 163 U.S. 537 (1896). Again with only Justice Harlan dissenting—a passionate, prophetic protest that has become almost legendary—the Court upheld the explicit, state-mandated racial segregation of transportation facilities. The majority's offensively weak rationalization was that separate accommodations complied with the Fourteenth Amendment's equal protection clause as long as the material comforts were the same, that the message of racial inferiority was merely the subjective perception of blacks, and that the law could not overcome racial prejudice in any event. Harlan's dissent pointed out that one obvious effect of such a mandatory color line was to deny the liberty of an individual of one race to associate with a business companion of another race—hardly equal treatment of such a pair as compared to an otherwise identical same-race pair.

Plessy legitimized the entire social and legal system of Jim Crow, under which a racial minority still struggling to overcome the legacy of slavery was isolated and cut off from most normal interaction with a privileged white majority—except on terms reinforcing racial subordination. A common and telling exception to segregation laws was that a black domestic employee could travel with a white employer. But in educational facilities, public accommodations, and even courthouses, blacks as a whole were restricted to a subordinate racial enclave. The Court in *Plessy*, by approving the legal entrenchment of race as a social concept, did not simply bow to social realities. It actively promoted and perpetuated racist attitudes, and the use of race as an artificial legal concept. Even the promise of material equality of the separate accommodations, not surprisingly, was abandoned in practice.

MISUSE AND QUIESCENCE, 1897–1936

The very year after *Plessy*, in *Allgeyer v. Louisiana*, 165 U.S. 578 (1897), the Court squarely embraced the doctrine that has become known as *substantive due process*. This doctrine converted the Fourteenth Amendment, for a time, into a weapon for business corporations, and other wealthy and powerful interests, to block state regulation of wages, hours, and working conditions. The most notorious such decision was *Lochner v. New York*, 198 U.S. 45 (1905). The Reconstruction Amendments were rendered largely quiescent during this era when it came to advancing racial justice and overcoming the legacy of slavery.

There were, however, a few reminders of the amendments' true goals. In *Bailey v. Alabama*, 219 U.S. 219 (1911), for example, the Court applied the Thirteenth Amendment, together with *Lochner*-style economic freedom principles, to strike down state laws criminalizing breach of labor contracts. The Court held that such laws supported a system of peonage constituting involuntary servitude banned by the amendment. In *Buchanan v. Warley*, 245 U.S. 60 (1917), the Court—following *Strauder* and distinguishing *Plessy*, and again reflecting the era's dominant concern with property rights—struck down the explicitly race-based exclusion of homeowners from certain neighborhoods. But *Giles v. Harris*, 189 U.S. 475 (1903) found federal courts essentially helpless to remedy massive disenfranchisement of African-American voters and *Berea College v. Kentucky*, 211 U.S. 45 (1908) extended *Plessy* by upholding a state law mandating racial segregation even in private educational institutions. The latter cases were again decided over Harlan's dissent.

Civil liberties cases were also a mixed bag during this era. With regard to the great incorporation debate over whether the Fourteenth Amendment applied Bill of Rights guarantees to the states, the Court generally said no, most notably in *Twining v. New Jersey*, 211 U.S. 78 (1908), which concerned the Fifth Amendment privilege against self-incrimination. The Court did, however, subject the states to the limits of the Fifth Amendment guarantee of just compensation for takings of private property. In *Chicago, Burlington & Quincy Railroad Co. v. Chicago*, 166 U.S. 226 (1897), the Court found that guarantee implicit in the Fourteenth Amendment due process clause.

The Court initially allowed states to restrict the freedoms of speech and press, in cases such as *Patterson v. Colorado*, 205 U.S. 454 (1907) and *Gitlow v. New York*, 268 U.S. 652 (1925)—over the dissents of Justice Harlan, in the former, and Justice Oliver W. Holmes (who wrote the *Patterson* majority opinion) joined by Justice Louis Brandeis, in the latter. But *Gitlow*, very significantly, assumed without deciding that such First Amendment freedoms were incorporated in the Fourteenth Amendment. That assumption was confirmed in *Stromberg v. California*, 283 U.S. 359 (1931), which struck down a restriction on the red flag as a radical political symbol, and in *Near v. Minnesota*, 283 U.S. 697 (1931), which threw out, as an invalid prior restraint, an injunction shutting down a newspaper that had criticized city officials.

JUDICIAL REVIVAL, 1937–1956

The Court, in what has become known as the Judicial Revolution of 1937, ended the *Lochner* era and renounced the use of the Fourteenth Amendment as a barrier to progressive economic regulations, most notably in *West Coast Hotel v. Parrish*, 300 U.S. 379 (1937). At the same time the Court accelerated its protection of civil liberties, confirming and expanding the incorporation of First Amendment rights in the Fourteenth Amendment. Perhaps the most famous of many libertarian speech decisions during the 1930s and 1940s was *West Virginia State Board of Education v. Barnette*, 319 U.S. 624 (1943), which affirmed, in ringing tones at the height of World War II (1939–1945), the right of schoolchildren to refuse to salute the American flag. The Court also expanded criminal procedural rights under the Fourteenth Amendment, albeit more cautiously and without yet embracing the incorporation doctrine in that area.

Most importantly, the Court returned to the issue of racial equality during this era. While continuing at first to adhere to the separate-but-equal doctrine, the Court gave it teeth by striking down state laws that failed to provide material equality in cases such as *Missouri ex rel. Gaines v. Canada*, 305 U.S. 337 (1938) and *Sweatt v. Painter*, 339 U.S. 629 (1950). In *Smith v. Allwright*, 321 U.S. 649 (1944), the Court overruled its decision in *Grovey v. Townsend*, 295 U.S. 45 (1935) and struck down all-white party primary elections as a violation of the Fifteenth Amendment.

The culmination of this trend was the epic decision in *Brown*. The Court unanimously declared, in an opinion by Chief Justice Earl Warren, that the separate-but-equal doctrine had no place in public education. The broader implication of *Brown*, soon confirmed by lower-court rulings and summary Supreme Court affirmations, was that *Plessy* was now overruled in every field of public life. Transportation, parks, courthouses, and similar facilities were desegregated with relative speed over the ensuing years, without much further guidance from the Supreme Court. For example, city buses in Montgomery, Alabama, were desegregated by 1956 following the famous boycott campaign of the Reverend Martin Luther King Jr. and a lower-court ruling (summarily affirmed by the Supreme Court) joined by U.S. District Judge Frank M. Johnson Jr. (1918–1999). Johnson would become perhaps the most famous of the many judges throughout the South who labored in the trenches of implementing the Supreme Court's mandates as the second Reconstruction unfolded.

But the Supreme Court faltered when it came to racially integrating schools, putting off for a year its consideration of the appropriate remedy in *Brown*. The Court's follow-up decision in *Brown v. Board of Education* (*Brown II*), 349 U.S. 294 (1955) has been criticized for inviting stalling and delay with its use of the notorious phrase "all deliberate speed" to describe the required time frame of compliance. Not until 1970 were schools actually desegregated in Mississippi, the last holdout.

JUDICIAL, CONGRESSIONAL, AND EXECUTIVE REVIVAL, 1957–1969

Congress, which had taken the lead during the first Reconstruction of the 1860s and 1870s, at first lagged behind the Supreme Court in the second Reconstruction of the 1950s and 1960s. Congress passed weak Civil Rights Acts in 1957 and 1960. But the grassroots activism of civil rights advocates, the example of *Brown*, the election and assassination of President John F. Kennedy, and the skillful leadership of President Lyndon B. Johnson prodded Congress into bolder action. The Civil Rights Act of 1964, although based on the commerce clause rather than Congress's enforcement powers under the Reconstruction Amendments, effectively restored the protections of the 1875 Act.

The Voting Rights Act of 1965 followed—a notably forceful use of Congress's power to enforce the Fifteenth Amendment. The Civil Rights Act of 1968 banned racial discrimination in the private housing market. Shortly afterward, the Supreme Court, in *Jones v. Alfred H. Mayer Co.*, 392 U.S. 409 (1968) broadly construed the Civil Rights Act of 1866 and Congress's enforcement power under the Thirteenth Amendment to also reach private discrimination in property transactions.

President Kennedy's election in 1960 was important in another respect. His 1962 appointment of Justice Arthur J. Goldberg, who forged his career as an activist lawyer for labor unions, solidified liberal control of the Court. For the next seven years, the Warren Court aggressively applied the Reconstruction Amendments to expand civil liberties and criminal procedural guarantees, incorporating against the states almost all the remaining provisions of the Bill of Rights. The Court also revived the doctrine of substantive due process, but in a new direction—finding in *Griswold v. Connecticut*, 381 U.S. 479 (1965) an implicit right of privacy in the Fourteenth Amendment that protected the use of contraceptives by married couples.

The high point of the second Reconstruction, and of liberal influence on the Court, came in 1967 when President Johnson appointed Thurgood Marshall, who had argued *Brown* as an activist civil rights lawyer, as the first African-American justice. But this high-water mark lasted only until 1969. The Court largely completed its incorporation of the Bill of Rights in the Fourteenth Amendment in *Benton v. Maryland*, 395 U.S. 784 (1969). That same year, President Richard Nixon took office, Chief Justice Warren retired, and Justice Abe Fortas (who had succeeded Goldberg in 1965) resigned. President Nixon eventually appointed four new justices, including Chief Justice Warren E. Burger, all more conservative than their predecessors.

RETRENCHMENT, ADVANCES, AND UNCERTAINTY: DEVELOPMENTS SINCE 1970

The Burger Court, despite its conservatism, generally did not reverse the Warren Court's expansive applications of the Reconstruction Amendments. Indeed, the Court further extended their reach in several ways. In *Roe v. Wade*, 410 U.S. 113 (1973), for example, and in other decisions, the Court expanded the privacy and reproductive rights pioneered in *Griswold* and extended them to unmarried and even underage persons. *Roe* recognized a sweeping Fourteenth Amendment right to choose abortion during the early stages of pregnancy, triggering bitter controversy both on and off the Court that rages up to the present day. The Court did, however, cut back somewhat on the Fourteenth Amendment rights of criminal defendants.

Among the more notable doctrinal innovations of the 1970s was the Court's application of the equal protection clause to ban most forms of sex discrimination, whether directed against women or men, starting with *Reed v. Reed*, 404 U.S. 71 (1971). From the 1970s to the 1990s, the Court also applied the Fourteenth Amendment in other areas outside its historically understood coverage of race discrimination. For example, the Fourteenth Amendment was used to strike down, under varying standards of review, discrimination against legal resident aliens in

Graham v. Richardson, 403 U.S. 365 (1971); against unauthorized immigrant children in *Plyler v. Doe*, 457 U.S. 202 (1982); against mentally handicapped persons in *Cleburne v. Cleburne Living Center*, 473 U.S. 432 (1985); against children born out of wedlock in *Clark v. Jeter*, 486 U.S. 456 (1988); and against gay and lesbian persons in *Romer v. Evans*, 517 U.S. 620 (1996).

The Supreme Court under Chief Justice Burger and his successors, Chief Justices William Rehnquist and John Roberts, has remained divided over several difficult issues at the frontier of the rights and liberties arguably protected by the Reconstruction Amendments. Abortion, noted above, is but one example. Another is sexual privacy. The Burger Court, in a five-to-four decision, upheld state sodomy laws banning gay sex in *Bowers v. Hardwick*, 478 U.S. 186 (1986). The Rehnquist Court, in a six-to-three decision over Rehnquist's own dissent, overruled *Bowers* and struck down such laws in *Lawrence v. Texas*, 539 U.S. 558 (2003).

An especially difficult issue has been how much affirmative action the government can engage in to overcome the legacy of slavery and segregation, without risking so-called reverse discrimination that might itself betray the legacy of the Reconstruction Amendments. The Court, for example, struck down rigid racial quotas in university admissions in *Regents of University of California v. Bakke*, 438 U.S. 265 (1978); upheld universities' consideration of race as one factor to advance diversity in *Grutter v. Bollinger*, 539 U.S. 306 (2003); and struck down race-based assignments of schoolchildren, even when used to maintain integrated schools in districts no longer subject to desegregation decrees, in *Parents Involved in Community Schools v. Seattle School District No. 1*, 551 U.S. ___ (2007).

It seems fair to predict that, even 140 years and counting since the ratification of the post–Civil War Reconstruction Amendments, they will continue to remain central to the most important constitutional issues confronting the Court.

SEE ALSO *Chase Court; Civil Rights Cases, 109 U.S. 3 (1883); Civil War; Fifteenth Amendment; Fourteenth Amendment; Incorporation Debate; Plessy v. Ferguson, 163 U.S. 537 (1896); Reconstruction; Reconstruction Era Civil Rights Acts*

BIBLIOGRAPHY

Bass, Jack. 1993. *Taming the Storm: The Life and Times of Judge Frank M. Johnson, Jr. and the South's Fight over Civil Rights.* New York: Doubleday.

Epps, Garrett. 2006. *Democracy Reborn: The Fourteenth Amendment and the Fight for Equal Rights in Post-Civil War America.* New York: Henry Holt.

Foner, Eric. 1988. *Reconstruction: America's Unfinished Revolution, 1863–1877.* New York: Harper and Row.

Gillette, William. 1965. *The Right to Vote: Politics and the Passage of the Fifteenth Amendment.* Baltimore, MD: Johns Hopkins Press.

Hyman, Harold M., and William M. Wiecek. 1982. *Equal Justice under Law: Constitutional Development, 1835–1875.* New York: Harper and Row.

James, Joseph B. 1956. *The Framing of the Fourteenth Amendment.* Urbana: University of Illinois Press.

James, Joseph B. 1984. *The Ratification of the Fourteenth Amendment.* Macon, GA: Mercer University Press.

Kaczorowski, Robert J. 2005 [1985]. *The Politics of Judicial Interpretation: The Federal Courts, Department of Justice, and Civil Rights, 1866–1876.* New York: Fordham University Press.

Tsesis, Alexander. 2004. *The Thirteenth Amendment and American Freedom: A Legal History.* New York: New York University Press.

Vorenberg, Michael. 2001. *Final Freedom: The Civil War, the Abolition of Slavery, and the Thirteenth Amendment.* New York: Cambridge University Press.

Bryan H. Wildenthal

AMENDMENTS, REJECTED

For a proposed amendment to the U.S. Constitution to be ratified it must first be approved by a two-thirds majority in both houses of Congress, or else it must be put forward by a constitutional convention called by two-thirds of the state legislatures (a route that has never been taken). The proposal must then be approved by three-fourths of the states, either by their legislatures or special conventions. Of the thousands of constitutional amendments proposed in Congress, the great majority have failed to garner the necessary support of two-thirds of both houses. Among the notable failed amendments are the 1875 "Blaine Amendment," an attempt to forbid government aid to educational institutions with religious affiliations; the "Bricker Amendments" of the 1950s, designed to reverse ambiguous Supreme Court decisions that implied international treaties could trump the Constitution, and the 1983 "Hatch-Eagleton Amendment," which would have reversed *Roe v. Wade*, 410 U.S. 113 (1973).

The most well-known amendment to pass in one house but fail in the other is the proposal to give Congress the power to outlaw the "physical desecration" of the United States flag. In *Texas v. Johnson*, 491 U.S. 397 (1989), a five-to-four majority of the Supreme Court held that laws banning flag desecration unconstitutionally abridge the right to free speech. Two-thirds of the House of Representatives has frequently agreed to reverse *Johnson*, but the Senate has killed the proposal every time.

Once an amendment makes it way through Congress, however, the odds are in its favor—the states have failed to ratify only six of the thirty-three amendments Congress has proposed.

The first two failures addressed insignificant and uncontroversial issues. Concurrent with the Bill of Rights, Congress proposed an amendment to set the size of the House according to population, but support for this effort fizzled, and the House's size has been governed by uncontroversial federal statutes ever since. The 1810 Reed Amendment likewise addressed an imagined problem—it forbade citizens from accepting titles of nobility. Despite wide support, this amendment fell one state short of ratification.

The next two failures were mooted by events. On the eve of President Abraham Lincoln's inauguration, Congress proposed to placate the South with an amendment to deny the federal government the power to abolish slavery. Maryland, Illinois, and Ohio hastily ratified this last-ditch effort, but a few months later the South seceded anyway and the proposal became irrelevant. In the early 1900s, Congress twice tried to outlaw child labor by statute, but both times the Supreme Court held the law exceeded Congress's commerce clause power. In 1924 Congress proposed a constitutional amendment banning child labor. The proposal languished on the edge of ratification for twenty years and was eventually mooted after the Supreme Court reversed course and held—in *United States v. Darby Lumber Co.*, 312 U.S. 100 (1941)—that Congress already had the power to regulate employment.

More recent failures are harder to categorize and can only be chalked up to the partisan politics of the 1970s and 1980s. The Equal Rights Amendment would have guaranteed equal legal rights to all people regardless of gender. It passed the Congressional gauntlet in 1972, but despite thirty-five quick ratifications, support for the amendment withered. Its mostly Republican opponents argued that the amendment would have unintended consequences, such as calling into question the legality of the all-male draft.

Similarly, the District of Columbia Voting Rights Amendment, which would have given the District of Columbia full representation in the House and Senate, was proposed by Congress in 1978. State legislatures, however, had little incentive to dilute the influence of the states in Congress and the Electoral College by enacting the amendment. Although a few (mostly Democratic) state legislatures supported the amendment, it expired quietly.

SEE ALSO *Article V*

BIBLIOGRAPHY

Keller, Morton. 2003. "Failed Amendments to the Constitution: A Look at the Various Crusades to Introduce Amendments That Failed." *World and I* 18 (February).

Lynch, Michael J. 2001. "The Other Amendments: Constitutional Amendments That Failed." *Law Library Journal* 93(2): 303, 309.

Andrew Brasher

AMERICAN BAR ASSOCIATION

Founded in 1878, the American Bar Association (ABA) is the leading national membership organization of the American legal profession, boasting a membership of more than 400,000 attorneys nationwide. The ABA's self-described mission is to serve as "the national representative of the legal profession, serving the public and the profession by promoting justice, professional excellence and respect for the law." Given this sweeping mandate, the ABA must be prepared to navigate the various tensions that arise between its influential role as advocate of specific legal positions before tribunals such as the U.S. Supreme Court, and its concurrent obligation to serve as representative of all its members's professional interests. During the past half century, the ABA has also assumed its role as primary vetter of the qualifications of Supreme Court nominees. Certainly at the ABA's founding no one could have predicted the degree to which the ABA would one day influence Supreme Court decision making on a regular basis, whether by direct means (as a party or friend of the court in ongoing litigation), or by indirect means (as a key player in the recruitment process).

AN ADVOCATE IN U.S. SUPREME COURT CASES

As a litigator, the ABA of the late nineteenth century concerned itself primarily with cases addressing federal court procedures, jurisdictional issues, and other subjects related to the administration of justice in criminal or civil courts. Yet despite token efforts in this regard, before 1900, the ABA "never proved to be much more than a gathering of dignified, well-to-do lawyers" voicing mostly conventional sentiments about such law reforms. (Friedman 1973, p. 651). Although the ABA condemned trusts and endorsed food and drug legislation around the turn of the twentieth century, its membership more often opposed progressive reforms. Consistent with this conservative philosophy, the ABA assumed its first controversial public policy position in 1912, when it opposed the ratification of the Sixteenth Amendment allowing for a national income tax.

Far more frequently, the ABA has participated in Supreme Court cases during the past century by filing amicus curiae (friend of the court) briefs, usually at the behest of one or more of its organized sections. To manage the process, the ABA Standing Committee on Amicus Curiae was established in the 1970s at the recommendation of former U.S. solicitor general, Erwin Griswold (1904–1994). As a matter of ABA policy, the organization files amicus curiae briefs only in the highest court in which the issue is "likely to be finally determined," which usually is the U.S. Supreme Court (ABA Internet site). The ABA files amicus curiae briefs in the Circuit Courts of Appeal or at the Supreme Court's certiorari stage less often.

The five-member ABA committee reviews all amicus briefs and makes recommendations to the ABA's Board of Governors, both as to whether a proposed ABA amicus curiae brief fairly represents the official policy of the ABA, and whether it is of sufficiently high professional quality. Given the many issues that come before the Supreme Court, the ABA also limits participation as amicus to cases that address matters of compelling public interest and to cases that are of special significance to lawyers or the legal profession.

Accordingly, the ABA routinely files briefs on issues that are of direct concern to the legal profession as a whole. For example, it has been a consistent advocate of expanding the attorney-client privilege. Thus, in *Swidler & Berlin v. United States*, 524 U.S. 399 (1998), the ABA successfully advocated the survival of the attorney-client privilege after the death of a client. It has also played a vital role as amicus curiae trumpeting the importance of greater access to counsel, advocating expanded access to the writ of habeas corpus for prisoners, and promoting access to counsel in a wide range of civil, criminal, and regulatory proceedings.

Many other issues before the Supreme Court affect the interests of certain categories of lawyers in different ways, such as those that pit attorneys for corporate America against attorneys representing indigent or blue-collar defendants. For example, the ABA participated as amicus curiae in *Pennsylvania v. Delaware Valley Citizens' Council for Clean Air*, 483 U.S. 711 (1987), which addressed the process for calculating attorney's fees chargeable to a losing defendant under the Clean Water Act. In *DVCC* the ABA pressed the losing position that lawyers normally working on contingency fees should be able to enhance their fees to compensate for an attorney's assuming the risk of loss and of nonpayment. In explaining its position in the case, the ABA brief fell back on the somewhat questionable ground that "all of its members have a strong interest in the application of federal fee-shifting statutes and the principle at issue is one as to which members are in substantial accord" (ABA 1986).

More often the ABA finds itself on the other side of this divide in the legal profession. For example, in 1908 the ABA adopted Canon 27, which condemned solicitation through advertising as "unprofessional." Since then the ABA has consistently opposed lawyer advertising, much to the chagrin of the plaintiffs' bar. In *Bates v. State Bar of Arizona*, 343 U.S. 350 (1977), the Supreme Court ruled against the Arizona state bar (and indirectly, the ABA) in holding that the First Amendment protects the advertising of routine legal services. After *Bates*, the ABA was forced to shift course, redrafting its model code to account for the landmark decision.

Beginning in the 1970s the ABA began to adopt official positions in Supreme Court cases whose connection to the particular interests of the legal profession must be considered tenuous at best. Although the Supreme Court may consider the ABA's input less vital in cases concerning sexual and reproductive privacy, artistic freedom, and racial discrimination, internal ABA debates are never so fierce as when it chooses to takes sides on such issues before the Supreme Court. A nonexhaustive list of some of the ABA's more controversial positions include the following:

Opposition to the Death Penalty In recent decades the ABA has established itself as an especially adamant opponent of the death penalty. Frustrated that federal and state governments have been moving in the opposite direction, the ABA in 1997 adopted a resolution calling upon jurisdictions with capital punishment *not* to carry out the death penalty on the ground that its administration "has become so seriously flawed" (ABA 1998). More recently, in 2004, it filed an amicus brief in the U.S. Supreme Court, successfully opposing application of the death penalty to juvenile offenders in *Roper v. Simmons*, 543 U.S. 551 (2005).

Support for Abortion Rights The ABA's activism has proven especially controversial when grappling with the hot-button issue of abortion. Whereas the ABA has long defended abortion rights, its willingness to stake out public positions in high-profile abortion cases before the Supreme Court has varied considerably through the years. The ABA firmly cast its lot as a proponent of abortion rights when it reaffirmed its support for *Roe v. Wade*, 410 U.S. 113 (1973) in *Webster v. Reproductive Health Services*, 492 U.S. 490 (1989).

Affirmative Action The ABA stirred some disagreement within its own ranks when it filed an amicus brief supporting the University of Michigan Law School's affirmative action plan in *Grutter v. Bollinger*, 539 U.S. 306 (2003). Following the Supreme Court ruling upholding the law school's plan, the ABA then revised its own criteria for law school accreditation: It adopted Standard 211, which now requires law schools to "demonstrate by concrete action" a commitment to diversity, even if a constitutional provision or statute purports to prohibit consideration of gender, race, ethnicity or national origin in admissions (ABA 2007).

VETTING SUPREME COURT NOMINEES

The ABA's involvement in the Supreme Court selection process dates back to 1916, when the organization—dominated at that time by a membership that favored conservative judges committed to theories of laissez-faire government—actively opposed the appointment of progressive advocate Louis Brandeis as associate justice of the Supreme Court. ABA officials feared that as a justice, Brandeis would subscribe to a radical judicial philosophy that would recognize few limits on the Court's power. Although ABA leaders opposed Brandeis's political and social views, at the time there existed no formal mechanism for the organization to formally evaluate candidates. Instead, the ABA's opposition took the form of a signed statement of opposition to Brandeis' appointment by former presidents of the ABA to members of the Senate Judiciary Committee. Disturbed by the Senate's rejection of John Parker's Supreme Court nomination in 1930, the ABA in 1932 established a special committee of fifty-two lawyers to advise the Senate Judiciary Committee on such matters.

A more permanent role for the ABA did not come about until the mid-1940s. In 1946 the ABA created the Standing Committee on the Federal Judiciary to assess the professional qualifications of all nominations for the federal bench, including Supreme Court nominees. Since 1948, the Senate has specifically asked the ABA for its objective evaluation of the professional qualifications of all nominees to serve on the federal bench. The ABA also established a formal rating system, with candidates rated as either not qualified, qualified, or well qualified.

In 1952, Harry S. Truman (1884–1972) became the first U.S. president to actively consult the committee during the course of his own decision-making on judicial nominees. Subsequent presidents quickly followed suit, soliciting input from the ABA on Supreme Court nominees as well. Little controversy arose over this form of consultation until 1971, when the Nixon administration submitted a list of six potential Supreme Court nominees to the ABA for review. Immediately after the mostly undistinguished list of names (including Senator Robert Byrd [b. 1917], who had never even practiced law) was leaked to the public, President Richard Nixon elected to discard that list entirely, leaving the ABA in the dark until he publicly announced his intention to nominate Lewis F. Powell, Jr. and William Rehnquist to the Supreme Court. In 1975, President Gerald Ford (1913–2006) resumed the practice of allowing the ABA to prevet nominees for the only Supreme Court vacancy of his tenure.

The controversy over the ABA's ratings of Robert Bork in 1987 (nine out of fourteen committee members rated Bork as "not qualified" on grounds of his lack of judicial temperament) and Clarence Thomas in 1991 (a committee majority rated Thomas as merely "qualified") led to increased complaints from conservative legal organizations such as the Federalist Society that the ABA maintained a liberal bias.

Still, ABA ratings continue to play an important role in the selection process in the early twenty-first century. Both of President George W. Bush's (1946–) Supreme Court nominees, John Roberts and Samuel Alito, received the highest ratings possible from the ABA. At the same time, administrations during the last quarter century have mostly refused to afford the ABA the privilege of vetting Supreme Court nominees prior to their formal nominations (the Bush administration made headlines in 2001 when it announced that it would also cease sending the names of lower court candidates to the ABA for prenomination vetting). Regardless, so long as so many members of the Senate continue to place significance on ABA ratings of Supreme Court nominees, future presidents who ignore such ratings will be forced to do only at their peril.

SEE ALSO *Amicus Curiae; Interest Groups; Nomination Process*

BIBLIOGRAPHY

American Bar Association (ABA). 1986. "Amicus Curiae Brief Filed in *Commonwealth of Pa. V. Delaware Valley Citizens' Council,* U.S. S.CT. NO. 85-5."

American Bar Association (ABA) 1998. "American Bar Association Report No. 107 (Feb. 1997)." Reprinted in *Law and Contemporary Problems* 61(4): 220.

American Bar Association (ABA) 2007. "2007-2008 ABA Standards for Approval of Law Schools." Available from http://www.abanet.org/legaled/standards/20072008StandardsWebContent/Chapter%202.pdf.

American Bar Association (ABA). Undated. "Amicus Curiae Brief Policies, Procedures and Application." Available from http://www.abanet.org/amicus/.

Federalist Society for Law and Policy Studies. 1994. *The ABA in Law and Social Policy: What Role?* Washington, DC: The Federalist Society.

Friedman, Lawrence B. 1973. *A History of American Law.* New York: Simon & Schuster.

Grossman, Joel B. 1965. *Lawyers and Judges: The ABA and the Politics of Judicial Selection.* New York: John Wiley and Sons.

Melone, Albert P. 1977. *Lawyers, Public Policy, and Interest Group Politics.* Washington, DC: University Press of America.

Sunderland, Edson R. 1953. *History of the American Bar Association and Its Work.* Chicago: American Bar Association.

David Yalof

AMERICAN CIVIL LIBERTIES UNION (ACLU)

The American Civil Liberties Union (ACLU) is a nonpartisan public interest organization devoted to protection of constitutional rights. The organization engages in lobbying, as well as litigation, and has appeared before the U.S. Supreme Court more than any other nongovernmental organization. It is the nation's largest and oldest civil liberties organization.

ORIGINS AND EARLY YEARS

Roger Baldwin (1884–1981), a wealthy Bostonian, founded the ACLU in New York following time as a social worker and professor in St. Louis. Although born into privilege in New England, Baldwin went to Missouri on the advice of his father's lawyer, Louis Brandeis. There, he established the School of Social Economy at Washington University in St. Louis and wrote a leading manual on juvenile courts. When the United States entered the First World War in 1917, Baldwin, a fierce critic of the war, moved to New York City and became involved with the American Union Against Militarism (AUAM).

As the head of the AUAM's National Civil Liberties Bureau (NCLB), Baldwin became concerned with the treatment of antiwar protesters, particularly the International Workers of the World (IWW). After imprisonment in 1919 for violating the Selective Service Act, Baldwin and Crystal Eastman (1881–1928), a journalist and executive secretary of the AUAM, transformed the NCLB into the ACLU. The ACLU began in 1920 with Baldwin as director, a post he would hold for forty years.

The organization began to spread, gaining legitimacy as it added members. The group depended not only on the tireless efforts of supporters, but also was fueled by Baldwin's political idealism and philosophies. When marine transport workers went on strike in Los Angeles in 1923, the resulting tumult led Upton Sinclair (1878–1968) and others to found the first permanent ACLU affiliate.

Although founded with radical origins, the ACLU began to garner greater mainstream acceptance when Baldwin made a break with the Communists in 1939. Baldwin was initially quite sympathetic to the Soviet Union, spending two months there in 1927, and communists were frequent clients during the ACLU's early years. However, various Communist Party tactics, including secrecy and perjury, repelled ACLU members. The ACLU began to move into the mainstream and professionalize, moving away from the popular-front approach to social-justice organizing and activism, toward a strategy of litigation. The ACLU charter was revised to exclude members with ties to totalitarian organizations.

In the early years of the ACLU, the group helped litigate numerous high profile and controversial cases including the trial of the Scottsboro Boys in Alabama, the Scopes trial, and the Sacco and Vanzetti trials. The group further rose to prominence confronting issues such as censorship of literature, the internment of Japanese Americans during the Second World War, racial segregation, and McCarthyism.

THE MODERN ACLU

The ACLU also became a lightning rod for conservative criticism of progressive social reforms throughout the twentieth century. Opposition to the cases taken on by the ACLU became ongoing rallying cries for groups of federalists, Christian factions, anti-Communists, and assorted moralists outraged by the organization's unpopular clients in free speech defenses.

Baldwin resigned as executive director of the ACLU in 1960. Nadine Strossen (1950–), a New York law professor, became the president of the ACLU in 1991. She is the first woman to head the organization. She is the author of *Defending Pornography: Free Speech, Sex, and the Fight for Women's Rights*, an influential reflection on critical constitutional and human rights issues.

The ACLU has over 300,000 members and supporters, and the group's financial situation stabilized considerably in the late twentieth century. In 1997 the group launched an endowment campaign designed to give it a permanent financial reserve. The ACLU has an affiliate in every state and Puerto Rico. The affiliates handle requests for legal assistance, lobby the state legislatures, and host public forums throughout the year.

It is difficult to understate the influence of the ACLU in the modern American jurisprudential understanding of constitutional liberties. According to one historian, the ACLU has been "involved in 80 percent of the post-1920 'landmark' cases regularly cited in constitutional law texts" (Walker 1990, p. 371). The ACLU has been successful over a long period of time in defending the rights of individual citizens, particularly those that may be asserted against the government.

SIGNIFICANT ACLU CASES

A combination of drought and economic collapse caused a huge migration to California in the 1920s and 1930s. In 1935 the federal government discontinued aid to the migrants, often derisively called Okies. The next year, the City of Los Angeles dispatched local police to keep migrants out of the city. The ACLU filed a federal lawsuit, causing Police Chief James Davis to back down from enforcing the city's so-called bum blockade. In 1939 police began arresting migrants under a California law making it a crime to knowingly bring an indigent person into the state. One such defendant was Fred Edwards, a preacher arrested for driving his brother-in-law, Frank

Duncan, from Texas to California. After his conviction, the ACLU came to Edwards's defense and filed an appeal eventually heard by the U.S. Supreme Court. In *Edwards v. California*, 314 U.S. 160 (1941), the Court ruled that California's law (and similar laws in twenty-seven other states) was unconstitutional.

The ACLU struck a major blow against racial discrimination in the landmark *Shelley v. Kraemer*, 334 U.S. 1 (1948), a case that concerned the enforceability of restrictive covenants prohibiting a person from owning or occupying property on the basis of race. In 1911 thirty of thirty-nine property owners in a St. Louis neighborhood signed an agreement preventing the residences in the neighborhood from being occupied for the next fifty years by nonwhites. In 1945 the Shelley family, without knowing of the restriction, purchased one of the properties. Neighbors sued to strip title from the Shelleys. Although the Shelleys were occupying the property, the Supreme Court of Missouri held that the covenant was valid and violated no constitutional rights. However, even though race-based restrictive covenants are not invalid under the Fourteenth Amendment, the U.S. Supreme Court held that enforcement of such a covenant would constitute unconstitutional discriminatory state action. The plaintiffs, including those from a separate Michigan case consolidated by the Supreme Court, were represented by legendary attorneys George L. Vaughn, Herman Willer, Thurgood Marshall, and Loren Miller (an ACLU board member). The case was an important victory in the struggle for racial equality and catapulted housing discrimination further into the national consciousness.

Another famous ACLU moment involved Nazis in Skokie, Illinois. In 1977 Frank Collin's (c. 1944–) National Socialist Party of America wanted to have a march in the Chicago suburb, which was heavily populated with Holocaust survivors. The city adopted three municipal ordinances designed to block Nazi demonstrations: a liability insurance requirement, a ban on public demonstrations by members of any political party wearing military-style uniforms, and prohibition of materials or symbols anywhere in the village that promoted hatred against people by reason of their race, national origin, or religion. The ACLU shocked a number of observers when it decided to defend the free speech rights of the Nazis. The U.S. Supreme Court, in *National Socialist Party of America v. Skokie*, 432 U.S. 43 (1977), let stand a decision by the Circuit Court of Cook County to invalidate the local ordinances limiting public demonstrations. It was a costly victory for the ACLU. The Nazis did not march in Skokie because the City of Chicago eventually allowed them to assemble, and an estimated 30,000 members left the ACLU causing serious financial problems for the organization.

The ACLU continued to make national headlines in the early 1990s. *Lee v. Weisman*, 505 U.S. 577 (1992) was the first major Rehnquist Court school prayer case. In a case about whether graduation ceremonies at a public school can contain an invocation to God, the Supreme Court heard strong ACLU opposition to the content of a Rhode Island middle-school commencement proceeding. The Court held that the establishment clause forbids the inclusion of clergy offering prayers as part of an official public school graduation ceremony.

At the behest of the ACLU and others, the Supreme Court declared portions of the Communications Decency Act to be unconstitutional in *Reno v. American Civil Liberties Union*, 521 U.S. 844 (1997). According to the Court, the provisions of the act prohibiting "indecent transmission" through cyberspace and forbidding "patently offensive display" on the Internet abridged speech protected by the First Amendment.

The ACLU was also on the front lines of opposing the erosion of rights in the post-2001 era, as exemplified by the so-called war on terror and the USA PATRIOT Act. In particular the ACLU has led opposition to Sections 206 and 215 of the USA PATRIOT Act, as well as to the so-called lone wolf provision of the 2004 intelligence bill, which applies the Foreign Intelligence Surveillance Act's secret surveillance powers to noncitizens in the United States. The ACLU has also filed Freedom of Information Act requests and litigated to defend Internet service providers, librarians, and others against the use of secret National Security Letters by federal law enforcement agencies.

The ACLU regularly finds itself on the cutting-edge frontiers of emerging areas of litigation. As DNA and genetic collections have proliferated in recent years, ACLU attorneys have been on the front lines of questioning whether uses by law enforcement of DNA databanks of presumed or actually innocent people are justified, given privacy and civil liberties concerns. The ACLU has also been active in protecting consumer, workplace, and medical privacy.

SEE ALSO *Amicus Curiae*; *Edwards v. California, 314 U.S. 160 (1941)*; *First Amendment*; *Freedom of Speech*; *Free Speech and World War I*; *Interest Groups*; *Lee v. Weisman, 505 U.S. 577 (1992)*; *Shelley v. Kraemer, 334 U.S. 1 (1948)*

BIBLIOGRAPHY

Cottrell, Robert C. 2000. *Roger Nash Baldwin and the American Civil Liberties Union*. New York: Columbia University Press.

Kutulas, Judy. 2006. *The American Civil Liberties Union and the Making of Modern Liberalism, 1930–1960*. Chapel Hill: University of North Carolina Press.

Strum, Philippa. 1999. *When the Nazis Came to Skokie: Freedom for Speech We Hate*. Lawrence: University Press of Kansas.

Walker, Samuel. 1999. *In Defense of American Liberties: A History of the ACLU.* Carbondale: Southern Illinois University Press

Stephen Stetson

AMERICAN FEDERATION OF LABOR V. SWING, 312 U.S. 321 (1941)

American Federation of Labor v. Swing, 312 U.S. 321 (1941) addressed the question of limitations upon a state's common law regulation of First Amendment free-speech rights in the context of picketing. Local members of the American Federation of Labor (AFL) sought to unionize a Chicago beauty parlor owned by Swing. There was no employer-employee labor dispute at stake; instead, outsiders were doing outreach work among Swing's employees. Were the union members fulfilling a legitimate purpose in addressing the needs and issues of workers, or were they harassing Swing, his workers, and their clients?

Alleging that the union organizers used false placards and forcible behavior toward customers, Swing objected, joining with his employees in seeking an injunction that would bar union activity. The injunction was granted in order to prevent interference with Swing's business interests and to protect the employees' freedom not to join a union. At trial, the union motion to strike Swing's complaint against the union was granted, and the preliminary injunction dissolved. Thereafter, the Illinois appellate court reversed the trial court, and the state supreme court affirmed this reversal on the basis that: "(1) there was no dispute between the employer and his immediate employees; (2) the placards were libelous; [and] (3) there were acts of violence." The U.S. Supreme Court reversed the opinion of the Illinois Supreme Court, thus upholding the union organizers' efforts.

Justice Felix Frankfurter, writing for the Court, noted that "the case clearly presents a substantial claim of the right to free discussion . . . to be guarded with a jealous eye." Frankfurter perceived the union organizing as "an instance of 'peaceful persuasion' disentangled from violence and free from 'picketing en masse or otherwise conducted' so as to occasion 'imminent and aggravated danger.'" He stated that limiting free-speech rights to employers and employees in disputes was "inconsistent with the guarantee of freedom of speech." Granted, states have powers to preserve the peace while regulating the problems of modern industry, "but not even these essential powers are unfettered by the requirements of the Bill of Rights."

In the Court's view, states could not prevent workers "from peacefully exercising the right of free communication by drawing the circle of economic competition between employers and workers so small as to contain only an employer and those directly employed by him." Moreover,

> interdependence of economic interest of all engaged in the same industry has become a commonplace. . . . The right of free communication cannot therefore be mutilated by denying it to workers in a dispute with an employer, even though they are not in his employ. Communication by such employees of the facts of a dispute, deemed by them to be relevant to their interests, can [not] . . . be barred because of concern for the economic interests against which they are seeking to enlist public opinion.

Justice Owen Roberts, writing a dissenting opinion in which Chief Justice Charles Evans Hughes joined, argued that deference to the state was appropriate, particularly in light of the greater social concerns that were implicit. The Illinois Supreme Court found evidence of no disputes between the employer and the employees; instead, a dispute was being fomented by outsiders who engaged in libel, threats, and violence. Under those circumstances, an injunction was appropriate as a matter of protecting the public peace from groups bent upon unlawful behavior.

The decision can be understood in light of the Court's developing jurisprudence of First Amendment rights and labor rights within a regulatory regime. Under the common law, labor organizing was illegal as a matter of criminal conspiracy. Employer-employee relations were private contractual matters. Organizing to strike was defined as criminal interference with the contractual relationships of employees and unreasonable interference with an employer's business dealings. Thus, throughout the nineteenth century and into the early twentieth century, American courts were hostile to labor union organizing, particularly when it became linked in the minds of many elites to anarchists and communists threatening social unrest.

Illinois had its own share of problems arising out of labor unrest in the previous century; this contributed to support for the common law rule raised in *AFL v. Swing.* Chicago was a large manufacturing city; this lay the groundwork for battles between workers and management. Worker protest over working conditions and compensation could spill over into the community at large, in the form of demonstrations and protests that threatened the public peace. Thus, the common law rule was important: Limiting organizers to do outreach within their own workspaces meant that large-scale social unrest and riots could be prevented.

Nonetheless, by the middle of the twentieth century, various political and legal elites began to see labor organizing not as a detriment, but as an important tool to

Transport Workers Union member picketing at a bus stop, New York City, 1941. *Union organizers scored an important victory with the decision of American Federation of Labor v.* Swing, *which secured the right of union activists to peacefully picket private businesses.* **AP IMAGES**

balance worker demands and employer interests in the workplace, particularly in the face of the nationwide economic crisis of the Great Depression. Led by President Franklin D. Roosevelt, the New Deal laid a foundation for government to become more actively involved in developing regulatory schemes. Through statutes like the National Labor Relations Act (also known as the Wagner Act) passed in 1935, labor organizing would become controlled by administrative agencies like the National Labor Relations Board. A radical movement thus became blunted through mainstream acceptance. American industry would be made secure from the threat of labor crisis. Workers, in turn, would become secure in their employment and be protected from abuse in the workplace.

For workers' rights to be protected, workers needed First Amendment rights to communicate with each other and organize. Thus, according to the decision in *AFL v. Swing*, workers' rights could not be limited to whether or not a dispute existed within a particular business between employer and employees. The old common law rule made no sense in an economy that was built upon complexity: numerous employers and numerous employees, all of whom faced issues of how to negotiate the needs of labor and capital in the workplace. Instead, community and industry-wide labor issues could be hashed out in individual workplaces as employees organized with workers elsewhere to improve the conditions for everyone.

SEE ALSO *Labor Unions; New Deal and Workers*

BIBLIOGRAPHY

Berman, Geoffrey D. 1994. "A New Deal for Free Speech: Free Speech and the Labor Movement in the 1930s." *Virginia Law Review* 80: 291–322.

Haggard, Thomas R. 1983. "Private Injunctive Relief against Labor Union Violence." *Kentucky Law Journal* 71: 509–568.

Summers, Clyde W. 1998. "Taft-Hartley Symposium: The First Fifty Years: Questioning the Unquestioned in Collective Labor Law." *Catholic University Law Review* 47: 791–823.

Bernie D. Jones

AMERICAN INDIANS

SEE *Native Americans.*

AMERICAN INSURANCE ASSOCIATION V. GARAMENDI, 539 U.S. 396 (2003)

In response to mounting frustration over the inability of Holocaust survivors to get information about, let alone settle claims made on, insurance policies issued to Jews in the Holocaust era, California passed the Holocaust Victim Insurance Relief Act (HVIRA) in 1999. The law required companies doing business in the state to disclose information about policies issued in Europe from 1920 to 1945. Failure to disclose would result in California's suspension of a company's license to do business. In *American Insurance Association v. Garamendi*, 539 U.S. 396 (2003), the U.S. Supreme Court invalidated the HVIRA, finding that it interfered with the ability of the executive branch to make foreign policy.

HOLOCAUST LITIGATION AND THE U.S. GOVERNMENT

The question of reparations had been a difficult one for the Allies following World War II (1939–1945). As quoted from *Garamendi*, once it became clear that the Soviet Union was the new adversary, the remaining Allies "moved to end their occupation and reestablish a sovereign Germany as a buffer against Soviet expansion." These countries were disinclined to saddle the new state of West Germany with payments that could wreck its economy, and "placed the obligation to provide restitution to victims of Nazi persecution on the new West German Government." This situation changed once Germany was reunified in 1990 and a German High Court lifted a postwar debt moratorium; as a result, "class-action lawsuits for restitution poured into United States courts against companies doing business in Germany during the Nazi era."

At this point, the U.S. government began a series of negotiations with the German government to settle these claims without litigation. Germany established a compensation fund, but, as a precondition, desired assurances that its citizens would receive "legal peace" in U.S. courts. In addition, both countries agreed to work with a voluntary body, the International Commission on Holocaust Era Insurance Claims (ICHEIC), established in 1998 to gather information and settle claims resulting from policies bought by Jews who perished in the Holocaust. In many cases, heirs had been unable to collect because they lacked death certificates, documentation that the policy was purchased, and the like.

In the executive agreement between the United States and Germany creating the compensation fund, the United States agreed that it would file a document with any court hearing a suit against a German company on a Holocaust-era claim stating that it was the position of the United States that the fund ought to be the exclusive forum for the settlement of such claims. But the understanding specifically disclaimed that such a statement of U.S. foreign policy interests would, in and of itself, provide a basis for dismissing such claims.

Frustrated at the slow pace with which claims were settled, California acted independently, passing the HVIRA. In addition, the state passed a statute opening up its courts to such claims until 2010. While that cause of action was also challenged, a lower court ruling that plaintiffs lacked standing to challenge it was not appealed and was not before the Supreme Court.

THE *GARAMENDI* OPINION

Writing for the Court, Justice David Souter began with the observation that "at some point an exercise of state power that touches on foreign relations must yield to the National Government's policy." Moreover, he argued, it was well established that "there is executive authority to decide what that policy should be." Further, the president may express that policy in an executive agreement that, the Court has held, can preempt contrary state law, as the Court held in prior cases like *United States v. Pink*, 315 U.S. 796 (1942) and *United States v. Belmont*, 301 U.S. 324 (1937).

That the U.S.-German agreement at issue not only did not expressly preempt contrary state law (as had those in *Pink* and *Belmont*) but, in fact, disclaimed an intent to do so, did not deter Justice Souter from concluding that the HVIRA was, in fact, preempted. *Zschernig v. Miller*, 389 U.S. 429 (1968), he argued, supported his conclusion. In *Zschernig*, the Court held that state laws that directly impacted foreign policy were impliedly preempted by the U.S. Constitution, since that document placed the federal government in charge of foreign policy.

Because "resolving Holocaust-era insurance claims that may be held by residents of this country is a matter well within the Executive's responsibility for foreign affairs," because the issue "has in fact been addressed in Executive Branch diplomacy and formalized in treaties and executive agreements" going back fifty years, and because "there is evidence of clear conflict" between state and federal approaches here, state law must give way. According to Justice Souter, the conflict was similar to that between Massachusetts and the U.S. statutes sanctioning the government of Myanmar that the Court addressed in *Crosby v. National Foreign Trade Council*, 530 U.S. 363 (2000), in which the Court also invalidated a state law. Further, Justice Souter argued that, in any event, the state's interest in the resolution of Holocaust insurance claims was "weak" when weighed against the federal government's foreign policy interests. He also rejected claims that Congress had approved of the HVIRA by statute.

In a dissent, Justice Ruth Bader Ginsburg, joined by three other justices, claimed that the majority stretched some precedents and ignored some others in reaching its decision. Justice Ginsburg emphasized that *disclosure* was all that was required by the HVIRA, and that the executive agreement disclaimed all preemptive intent. Thus, cases like *Pink* and *Belmont* were clearly distinguishable—as was *Crosby*, where Congress had delegated power to the president to undertake certain actions vis-à-vis Myanmar. Thus the issue really was whether mere executive branch statements of policy were sufficient to preempt a state law. According to *Barclay's Bank, PLC v. Franchise Tax Board*, 512 U.S. 298 (1994), such statements lack the force of law and cannot, alone, preempt state law. Thus, the Court's opinion rests on *Zschernig*'s assertion that the Constitution embodies a broad foreign affairs preemption—a notion that *Barclay's Bank* rejected. "We have not relied on *Zschernig* since it was decided," Justice Ginsburg wrote, "and I would not resurrect that decision here."

SEE ALSO *Rehnquist Court*

BIBLIOGRAPHY

Denning, Brannon P. 2003. "International Decisions: *American Insurance Ass'n v. Garamendi*, and *Deutsch v. Turner Corp.*" *American Journal of International Law* 97(4): 950–961.

Denning, Brannon P., and Michael D. Ramsey. 2004. "*American Insurance Association v. Garamendi* and Executive Preemption in Foreign Affairs." *William and Mary Law Review* 46(3): 825–950.

Van Alstine, Michael P. 2006. "Executive Aggrandizement in Foreign Affairs Lawmaking." *UCLA Law Review* 54(2): 309–371.

Brannon P. Denning

AMERICAN SYSTEM

The American System was the national economic policy championed by the Kentucky politician Henry Clay (1777–1852) from the 1810s through the 1840s. It was embraced by the Whig political party when it formed during the Andrew Jackson (1767–1845) presidency. Although few components of the American System were tested in court, they were constitutionally controversial. The American System was consistent with the Marshall Court's broad reading of congressional powers, but it likely would not have survived a challenge before the Taney Court.

The American System had three integrated components. The first was the Second Bank of the United States, a large and politically powerful bank with branches across the United States that operated under federal charter. The bank received a twenty-year charter in 1816, but a new charter was vetoed by President Andrew Jackson in 1832. The bank was to provide a safe place to store federal funds, to encourage the accumulation of private capital and large-scale loans, and to create a national currency through the circulation of bank notes.

The second component was the protective tariff, a system of high import duties designed to protect domestic manufacturers and some agricultural products from foreign competition. Alexander Hamilton (c. 1755–1804) had earlier argued for protecting "infant industries" from foreign competition until they were well established, but the American System envisioned permanent subsidies to sustain manufacturers deemed to be in the economic or security interests of the United States. The Democratic Party under Andrew Jackson committed itself to a position of free trade, or a "revenue only" tariff. The Compromise Tariff of 1833 effectively ended the protective tariff until the rise of the Republican Party.

The third component was federally subsidized "internal improvements"—the construction of roads, canals, bridges, and the like—which would, it was argued, tie the country together socially and economically. In response to persistent constitutional and political objections to direct congressional appropriations for internal improvements, Clay later proposed as an alternative the distribution of surplus federal land to the states. The states could then sell the distributed land to subsidize their own internal improvement projects. Internal improvement bills with clear national objectives were generally found acceptable, but both Jeffersonian and Jacksonian presidents repeatedly vetoed appropriation bills for projects that they found to be of only local significance.

The American System was at the center of the constitutional debates over congressional powers in the early nineteenth century, and yet the U.S. Supreme Court mostly watched those debates from the sidelines. The most important decisions were political decisions. First were the congressional decisions adopting planks of Clay's program in the 1810s, and second were the congressional and presidential decisions rejecting his program, particularly in the 1830s.

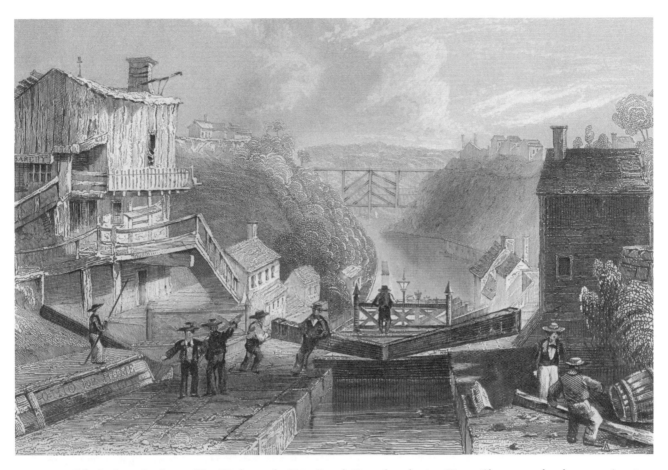

Drawing of the locks at Lockport, New York, on the Erie Canal. *Kentucky politician Henry Clay proposed a three-part American System to aid the United States during the early nineteenth century. Clay's plan of a national bank, high tariffs on imported goods, and government investment in public works projects, like the Erie Canal, generally found acceptance by the Marshall Court but not always by the executive and legislative branches of government.* © **CORBIS-BETTMANN**

When the Supreme Court was asked to rule on these issues, it favored Clay and upheld the powers of government. Most famously and significantly, the Court heard a challenge to the constitutionality of the Bank of the United States in *M'Culloch v. Maryland*, 17 U.S. 316 in 1819. In a sweeping opinion by Chief Justice John Marshall (1755–1835), the Supreme Court upheld the power of Congress to create a bank as "necessary and proper" to the exercise of other federal powers, including the power to borrow money. Although national Jeffersonian leaders such as James Madison (1751–1836) objected to how broadly Marshall interpreted the necessary and proper clause, they supported the bottom line in the case since they, too, had become convinced by the experience of the War of 1812 that the bank was essential to government finances.

But those cases came generally early in this period, and there is reason to believe that the justices who sat on the Court by the 1840s would have adopted a different view had any of the American System survived to generate

an appropriate case to test their beliefs. Andrew Jackson had specifically rejected the substance and authority of *M'Culloch* in vetoing the bank bill in 1832. The Democratic justices appointed to the Court were known opponents of *M'Culloch*, and by the 1840s, informed observers anticipated that a majority would overrule that precedent and strike down nationalist legislation if it were to be passed by Congress and signed by the president. No such case arose in the antebellum era because no such legislation was passed.

SEE ALSO *M'Culloch v. Maryland, 17 U.S. 316 (1819); Taney Court*

BIBLIOGRAPHY

Graber, Mark A. 1998. "Federalist or Friends of Adams: The Marshall Court and Party Politics." *Studies in American Political Development* 12(2): 229–266.

Graber, Mark A. 2000. "The Jacksonian Origins of Chase Court Activism." *Journal of Supreme Court History* 25(1): 17–39.

Whittington, Keith E. 1999. *Constitutional Construction: Divided Powers and Constitutional Meaning.* Cambridge, MA: Harvard University Press.

Keith E. Whittington

AMICUS CURIAE

Amicus curiae, or "friend of the court," briefs are filed in court cases by individuals or groups that are not directly a party to the case in order to supplement the arguments of the primary parties with additional legal analysis, scientific data or observations, historical information, or simply by adding what amounts to a vote in favor of one or another outcome. Although such briefs have been accepted by the Supreme Court since 1821, historically their status was controversial because their very presence acknowledged the Court's political and policymaking role. Nonetheless, amicus briefs have emerged as an accepted and valued element of the decision process, as the vast majority of cases have come to be accompanied by such briefs and as the Court has increasingly referred to particular briefs in its decisions.

The filing of amicus briefs is governed by the Supreme Court's formal rules, which, with limited exceptions, have remained unchanged in their basic requirements for such briefs since adoption in 1938. Nongovernmental parties may file an amicus brief in any case if they have the consent of all of the parties to the case or, in the event consent is denied, if the Court grants permission to do so. Governmental representatives, particularly the solicitor general or the chief attorneys for each state and municipality, may file an amicus brief in any case. Unlike the direct parties to the case, each amici is limited to one brief and may not file replies to the arguments advanced by others.

The most important changes in the Court's accessibility to amici have been found not in formal rule changes but in the Court's willingness to grant leave when consent is denied by a party to a case. In 1949 the Court, apparently believing that too many amicus briefs had become "propagandistic," revised its formal rules principally by adding a formal procedure for obtaining the Court's leave in the absence of parties' consent, and by declaring that such a petition for leave was "not favored." Although neither amounted to a significant change in the formal requirements for amici, at the same time the Court began declining leave to file such briefs in cases in which a primary party had declined consent, resulting in a reduction in the number of amicus briefs in the 1950s. In the 1960s, however, the Court began to reverse this practice, granting leave in an increasing number of cases to the point that most requests were granted, a practice sometimes called the "open-door policy" toward amicus briefs.

The number of amicus briefs filed per term and per case, and the number of participating groups in those briefs, have risen dramatically since the 1950s. As Joseph Kearney and Thomas Merrill (2000) observe, the percentage of cases with such briefs grew steadily from 23 percent in the 1946–1955 decade to 85 percent in the 1986–1995 decade. The overall number of briefs and participants in them, as Paul Collins (2004) observed, has grown as well: By the 1980s, it was not uncommon for the Court to receive nearly 800 amicus briefs each term, and the number of participating groups virtually exploded after the early 1970s from fewer than 800 per year to more than 2,500 per year by the mid-1980s. Some cases draw very high numbers of amici. For example, in *Webster v. Reproductive Health Services*, 492 U.S. 490 (1989), among the most important abortion cases, forty-seven briefs signed by eighty-five different organizations were filed on behalf of the petitioners seeking to restrict access to abortion, whereas thirty-one briefs signed by 335 organizations were filed for the respondents.

Amicus briefs appear to exert a significant impact on Supreme Court decisions. As Gregory Caldeira and John Wright (1988) showed, the Court is more likely to grant petitions for writs of certiorari—that is, to accept cases for full review—when accompanied by amicus briefs. Additionally, there is growing evidence that amicus briefs affect Supreme Court decisions in cases accepted for review: as research by Paul Collins (2007) reveals, the more amicus briefs supporting a particular litigant and decision direction (liberal versus conservative), the greater is the likelihood that the Court will side with that litigant and ideological outcome. The solicitor general's amicus participation appears to be especially influential.

How amicus briefs influence judicial decisions is a matter of debate. Under one view, Supreme Court justices gauge the relative importance of cases and their likely policy impact by the number of amicus briefs and the level of group participation, and the Court thus pays more attention and greater respect to widely supported claims. Under another view, amicus briefs contain substantive information or analysis that is used by justices in reaching their decision and crafting their opinions. Scholarly research provides some support for both views. Interviews with former Supreme Court clerks serving from the 1960s through the 1990s conducted by Kelly Lynch (2004) revealed that many found amicus briefs to be most helpful when they supplement the primary parties' legal arguments with scientific or technical analyses, or when they provide sophisticated legal analyses that supplement the legal briefs of a poorly represented litigant. In exceptional cases, decisions undoubtedly have been significantly affected by the arguments contained in amicus briefs. In *Mapp v. Ohio,*

367 U.S. 643 (1961), for instance, the Supreme Court created the famous exclusionary rule, a requirement that evidence illegally obtained by the police may not be used in court, after being urged to do so by the American Civil Liberties Union's amicus brief—even though neither of the direct parties to the case had addressed the issue of exclusion of evidence. Nonetheless, as James Spriggs and Paul Wahlbeck (1997) observe, the Court rarely accepts an urging by amici to place an issue at the center of its decision if the issue was not raised by the primary parties to the case and, on the whole, amicus briefs probably influence judicial decisions only at the margins.

SEE ALSO *Interest Groups*

BIBLIOGRAPHY

Caldeira, Gregory A., and John R. Wright. 1988. "Organized Interests and Agenda Setting in the U.S. Supreme Court." *American Political Science Review* 82(4): 1109–1127.

Collins, Paul M., Jr. 2004. "Friends of the Court: Examining the Influence of Amicus Curiae Participation in U.S. Supreme Court Litigation." *Law & Society Review* 38(4): 807–832.

Collins, Paul M., Jr. 2007. "Lobbyists before the U.S. Supreme Court: Investigating the Influence of Amicus Curiae Briefs." *Political Research Quarterly* 60(1): 55–70.

Kearney, Joseph D., and Thomas W. Merrill. 2000. "The Influence of Amicus Curiae Briefs on the Supreme Court." *University of Pennsylvania Law Review* 148: 743–855.

Lynch, Kelly J. 2004. "Best Friends? Supreme Court Law Clerks on Effective Amicus Curiae Briefs." *Journal of Law & Politics* 20: 33–75.

Spriggs, James F., II, and Paul J. Wahlbeck. 1997. "Amicus Curiae and the Role of Information at the Supreme Court." *Political Research Quarterly* 50(2): 365–386.

Charles R. Epp

ANTEBELLUM ERA

SEE *Slavery; Slavery in the Territories; Taney Court.*

ANTI-FEDERALIST/FEDERALIST RATIFICATION DEBATE

Leading Americans in 1787 agreed on the need for the kind of independent national judiciary proposed in the Constitution. Even "The Federal Farmer," an anti-Federalist author who opposed the ratification of the Constitution, wrote that "[t]here ought in every government to be one court, in which all great questions in law

shall finally meet and be determined" (Storing 1981, vol. 2, p. 317). Alexander Hamilton (c. 1755–1804), a Federalist supporter of ratification, asserted that "the propriety of the institution in the abstract is not disputed" (Cooke 1961, p. 521). But when the states debated the ratification of the proposed Constitution, its critics argued that it gave the Supreme Court too much power, and the average citizen too little influence in court decisions. The Federalists who defended the Constitution responded that the federal judiciary's power was appropriate and argued that the criticisms of federal judicial power were overblown.

The authors of the Constitution had fueled this debate by providing the federal courts ambiguous but potentially far-reaching powers. First, the Constitution gave Congress the power to create an extensive judicial system with regional and specialized courts. Second, the Constitution authorized the federal courts to exercise broad jurisdiction over politically sensitive issues such as interstate land disputes. Third, the "supremacy" clause encouraged the courts to invalidate state legislation when judged inconsistent with the national laws and Constitution. The Constitution's authors knew that judicial review of *national* legislation was possible under the Constitution and they knew it was a controversial power, but they never considered a proposal to prohibit it. The convention, then, allowed judicial review eventually to "blossom" (Robertson 2005). But the Constitution's framers undoubtedly viewed these judicial provisions as much narrower in scope than they appear two hundred years later. Custom had shaped Americans' expectations of the Constitution and custom had established a much more limited role for courts. Shared views about the nature of that fundamental law, deference to elites, and the modest number of written statutes resulted in few conflicts between laws and the "customary" Constitution. When there were challenges based on fundamental law, they played out in elections, petitions to legislatures, and protests; in the courts, these conflicts were the responsibility of juries, the vehicle for public influence in the judicial system. A small minority of American leaders were developing ideas about strengthening the courts' ability to protect constitutions against legislatures, but even these cautious first steps toward judicial review met with considerable resistance. The modern concept of judicial review was far different from the concept debated in 1787–1788 (Kramer 2004).

THE ANTI-FEDERALISTS' CASE AGAINST THE CONSTITUTION'S JUDICIAL PROVISIONS

Two of the delegates who attended the Constitutional Convention but refused to sign the Constitution raised strong objections to its provisions for judicial power. George Mason of Virginia wrote on a copy of the nearly final draft of the Constitution that "[t]he Judiciary of the

United States is so constructed and extended, as to absorb and destroy the judiciaries of the several States; thereby rendering law as tedious, intricate and expensive, and justice as unattainable, by a great part of the community, as in England, and enabling the rich to oppress and ruin the poor" (Farrand 1911, vol. 2, p. 638). Elbridge Gerry of Massachusetts protested that the plan established "a tribunal without juries" and that the Supreme Court would become "a Star-chamber as to Civil cases" (Farrand 1911, vol. 2, p. 633).

The *Massachusetts Centinel* published Mason's complaints two months after the end of the Convention (Kaminski et al. 1979, vol. 14, pp. 149–152). Another dissatisfied delegate, Luther Martin of Maryland, soon produced "Genuine Information," a tract that fleshed out complaints about the new federal "courts of Congress." Martin charged that the Constitution amputated state courts' power to interpret the powers of the new national government and unjustly placed the power to settle disputes about national authority in the hands of judges it appointed. The provision for lower federal courts "would eventually absorb and swallow up the State judiciaries, by drawing all business from them to the courts of the general government." (Farrand 1911, vol. 3, p. 206). Worse, the federal courts did not provide for juries in civil cases. Because appellate federal courts could review both the facts and the law of criminal convictions, the Constitution "absolutely takes away" the "inestimable privilege" of a jury trial in both civil and criminal cases (Farrand 1911, vol. 3, p. 221). Anti-Federalists especially criticized the lack of these jury guarantees consistently through the ratification debates.

Anti-Federalists amplified these criticisms of the Constitution in newspaper essays written under pseudonyms. The widely circulated "Centinel" essays, published in Philadelphia, argued that the new federal judiciary, including inferior courts, would enjoy a jurisdiction so extensive that "it is more than probable" that the new federal courts would "wholly" supersede the state courts. "Centinel" believed that the supremacy clause, stating that the Constitution was "the supreme law of the land," ensured federal dominance (Storing 1981, vol. 2, p. 140). "The Federal Farmer" believed that "if the jurisdiction of the jury be not final, as to facts, it is of little or no importance" and warned that "we are more in danger of sowing the seeds of arbitrary government in this department than in any other" (Storing 1981, vol. 2, pp. 316, 322).

The most extensive critique of the Constitution's judicial provisions came from the pen of "Brutus," who published a series of anti-Federalist essays in New York. "Brutus," often believed to be an influential New York jurist, argued that it was the federal judiciary that would really make Americans aware of the oppressive scope of the Constitution's federal powers. He drove home the complaint that "there is no security that a trial by jury shall be had in these courts" and that travel required by a centralized judicial system would force "the poorer and midling class of citizens" to submit "to the demands of the rich and the lordly" (Storing 1981, vol. 2, pp. 434, 437).

But "Brutus" went further than other anti-Federalists, arguing that its power to review the validity of *national* laws—"judicial review"—actually would make the judiciary the dominant branch of the federal government. The federal judges would not only uphold the expressed powers of the national government, he reasoned, "but [also] where these are wanting or ambiguously expressed, to supply what is wanting by their own decisions," which would silently result in the total "subversion of the legislative, executive, and judicial powers of the individual states." The Supreme Court "will give the sense of every article of the constitution," wrote "Brutus," and these judges could not be trusted to "confine themselves to any fixed or established rules, but will determine, according to what appears to them, the reason and spirit of the constitution." As ambitious proponents of their own institution's power, the judges will tend "to give such a meaning to the constitution in all cases where it can possibly be done, as will enlarge the sphere of their own authority." The court's decisions then "will become the rule to guide the legislature in their construction of their powers." The Supreme Court's opinions will have "the force of law" because "[f]rom this court there is no appeal" (Storing 1981, vol. 2, pp. 418, 420–421, 424).

Federal judges therefore "under this constitution will controul the legislature" by determining Congress's power, giving federal courts a power that "transcends any power before given to a judicial by any free government under heaven." No power above them can correct their errors, and judges cannot be removed from office "for any error in judgement or want of capacity" (Storing 1981, vol. 2, pp. 438–439).

THE FEDERALISTS' DEFENSE OF THE CONSTITUTION'S JUDICIAL PROVISIONS

The Federalists defended the Constitution by emphasizing the limited power of the federal courts and the continued importance of state courts and juries. Writing under the pseudonym of "the Landholder," Oliver Ellsworth, a Connecticut delegate to the Constitutional Convention, assured readers that national judicial power would extend only to cases in which "the national peace or rights, or the harmony of the states is concerned, and not to controversies between citizens of the same state (except where they claim under grants of different states)" (Kaminski et al. 1979, vol. 14, p. 401). "The Landholder" argued that Congress could require juries in federal civil cases (as it did), the Constitution's judicial provisions could be amended (as they were), and the Supreme Court could meet in other locations (its justices at first participated in federal circuit courts).

Federalists tried to reassure citizens that the proposed federal judiciary would do much more good than harm. "The Landholder" bluntly reminded readers that "[t]he right of the judge to inflict punishment, gives him both power and opportunity to oppress the innocent; yet none but crazy men will from thence determine that it is best to have neither a legislature nor judges" (Kaminski et al. 1979, vol. 14, p. 140). As for oppression, "The Landholder" argued "that we must have" some national legislature and courts with real power, "or soon be hewers of wood and drawers of water for all other people" (Kaminski et al. 1979, vol. 14, p. 338). In the closely contested ratifying convention in Virginia, Governor Edmund Randolph assured doubters that "Congress can regulate" appellate jurisdiction, "and I have no doubt they will." Future Supreme Court Chief Justice John Marshall reminded them that the person who wants to oppress another by filing in a federal court also has to incur great expenses if justice becomes centralized (Elliot 1836–1859, vol. 3, pp. 562–563, 573).

Alexander Hamilton countered "Brutus" with an extensive analysis of the federal judiciary written under the pseudonym "Publius" in the *Federalist*. Far from being the dominant branch, Hamilton argued, the judiciary "will always be the least dangerous to the political rights of the Constitution." Federal courts could never endanger the "general liberty of the people" because the judiciary would always lack the keys to power: control of "the purse" (taxation, controlled by Congress) or "the sword" (the military, controlled by the president). The courts would keep Congress "within the limits assigned to their authority." Because the Constitution flowed from the will of the people, judges have an obligation to uphold the Constitution against any statute enacted by their agents in Congress (Cooke 1961, p. 522). Hamilton admitted that courts sometimes could misconstrue the law, or even contravene "the will of the legislature," but these problems "can never be so extensive as to amount to an inconvenience, or in any sensible degree to affect the order of the political system." The judiciary's inherent weakness, as well as judges' vulnerability to impeachment, guarantee it (Cooke 1961, p. 545). Because judges had to be independent, Hamilton argued, they had to serve without fear of removal for anything but "mal-conduct." A looser standard of judicial removal, such as the criterion of "inability" advocated by "Brutus," would threaten judicial independence. (Cooke 1961, pp. 532–534).

Hamilton, then, did not deny that the court would exercise judicial review, but rather argued that it was wise and safe for the court to do so. Courts should exercise judicial review, not because of anything specified in the Constitution, but because they had that role in any government founded on a limited Constitution, including the governments of the states. Hamilton observed that nothing in the Constitution "*directly* empowers the national courts to construe the laws according to the spirit of the Constitution, or which gives them any greater latitude in this respect than may be claimed by the courts of every State." It could not be safe for Congress to determine the constitutional validity of their own laws; to insist otherwise would violate the fundamental republican principle of the separation of powers (Cooke 1961, p. 543).

Hamilton conceded that "the threat to trial by jury had been one of the most effective arguments against ratification in New York." He tried to reassure readers that nothing precludes the use of juries in these trials "as may be judged advisable," and there was good reason to believe that the Supreme Court would accept juries' findings of fact. Congress "would certainly have full power to provide, that in appeals to the Supreme Court there should be no reexamination of facts where they had been tried in the original causes by juries" (Cooke 1961, p. 550).

RATIFICATION AND CONSTITUTIONAL AMENDMENTS TO THE FEDERAL JUDICIARY

Except for Maryland, all of the final eight states that ratified the Constitution recommended constitutional amendments. Most of these states recommended changes in the Constitution's judicial provisions in particular, proposing amendments limiting national judicial power, protecting state courts, and ensuring jury trials. Both sides in the ratification debate, then, acknowledged the extraordinary power of the courts in the new system. The state ratifications condoned this power, albeit with reservations, because Americans agreed that an independent national judiciary was a valuable addition to national government. The ratification battle, then, chiefly affected the federal judicial system through the Bill of Rights' Sixth, Seventh, and Tenth Amendments. These amendments guarantee the right to a jury trial in a person's locality, protect jury findings of fact during the appeals process, and guard the states' residual powers.

Both sides anticipated that federal courts would review the constitutionality of law, but only New York, the home of "Brutus," proposed a constitutional amendment that addressed the issue of judicial review. New York recommended that anyone "aggrieved" by a decision of the U.S. Supreme Court could apply to the president to nominate (with Senate confirmation) a commission of seven or more "Men learned in the Law" to "correct the Errors in such Judgment or to review such Sentence and Decree, as the case may be, and to do Justice to the parties" (Elliot 1836–1859, vol. 1, pp. 329–331). The Bill of Rights included no provision for a final arbiter of constitutionality after the Supreme Court, allowing the doctrine of judicial review to unfold in future Court rulings. But in 1789, Americans had only a very hazy notion of the possible consequences of this power.

SEE ALSO *Article III; Articles of Confederation; Commentaries on the Constitution; Constitutional Convention, Framing; Constitution of the United States; Federalism; Federalist Papers*

BIBLIOGRAPHY

Cooke, Jacob E., ed. 1961. *The Federalist.* Middletown, CT: Wesleyan University Press.

Elliot, Jonathan, ed. 1836–1859. *The Debates in the Several State Conventions on the Adoption of the Federal Constitution, as Recommended by the General Convention at Philadelphia, in 1787.* 5 vols. Philadelphia: J.B. Lippincott; Washington, DC: Taylor and Maury. Available at http://memory.loc.gov/ammem/amlaw/lwed.html.

Farrand, Max, ed. 1911. *The Records of the Federal Convention of 1787.* 3 vols. New Haven: Yale University Press. Available at http://memory.loc.gov/ammem/amlaw/lwfr.html.

Kaminski, John P., et al., eds. 1976–. *Documentary History of the Ratification of the Constitution.* Madison: Wisconsin Historical Society.

Kramer, Larry D. 2004. *The People Themselves: Popular Constitutionalism and Judicial Review.* New York: Oxford University Press.

Rakove, Jack N. 1996. *Original Meanings: Politics and Ideas in the Making of the Constitution.* New York: Alfred A. Knopf.

Robertson, David Brian. 2005. *The Constitution and America's Destiny.* New York: Cambridge University Press.

Siemers, David J. 2003. *The Antifederalists: Men of Great Faith and Forbearance.* Lanham, MD: Rowman and Littlefield.

Storing, Herbert, ed. 1981. *The Complete Anti-Federalist.* 3 vols. Chicago: University of Chicago Press.

Wood, Gordon S. 1969. *The Creation of the American Republic, 1776–1787.* New York: W. W. Norton.

David Brian Robertson

ANTI-SLAVERY CONSTITUTIONALISM

Prior to the American Civil War (1861–1865), several groups advocated the abolition of slavery but held differing opinions about whether they could rely on the original U.S. Constitution to accomplish that end. Several prominent theorists argued that the Constitution and the Bill of Rights provided sufficient legal basis for ending slavery. While their arguments were ingenious, they ultimately did not sway enough politicians, judges, and voters to end slavery, which required the ratification of the Thirteenth Amendment in 1865. The most prominent members of the antislavery constitutional school of thought were Lysander Spooner (1808–1887), Gerrit Smith (1797–1874), George W. F. Mellen (1804–1875), Joel Tiffany (1811–1893), Lewis Tappan (1788–1873), and William Goodell (1792–1878). They thought the framers of the original Constitution and Bill of Rights provided Congress with the power to protect natural rights, which all people share irrespective of their race.

In its early form, during the 1830s, antislavery arguments against slave power asserted a First Amendment right to disseminate pamphlets and consider congressional petitions against slavery. These efforts were met with violent popular opposition and a political gag rule meant to silence congressional debates on ending slavery.

A group of *radical political abolitionists*, who had been writing actively since the early 1840s, claimed that the institution of slavery violated numerous provisions of the Constitution. They regarded the Constitution as a safeguard of self-evident, universal rights that are rooted in the Declaration of Independence. Any executive regulation, statute, court decision, or municipal code that violated the nation's founding principles, as they were set out by the Declaration, were superseded by core national obligations to equality. The "basis of any consistent and thorough agitation for the . . . removal of slavery" lay in the "self-evident truths of the Declaration of Independence" (Goodell 1852, p. 126). Political abolitionists believed that the founding generation of Americans overwhelmingly believed that with the promulgation of the Declaration, "slavery had received its death blow" (Tiffany 1849, p.19).

Their views were a radical departure from conventional constitutional theory on slavery. The advocates of political constitutional abolitionism persistently argued that the Constitution of the United States contained numerous provisions that prohibited the perpetuation of slavery. This claim was extraordinarily controversial particularly because it ran counter to Supreme Court precedents, such as *Prigg v. Pennsylvania*, 41 U.S. 539 (1842), which upheld the constitutionality of the 1793 Fugitive Slave Act.

The Radical Political Abolitionist Convention, held in Syracuse, New York, in 1855, expressed its support for maintaining the Union and either ratifying a constitutional amendment or passing a statute abolishing slavery. The Constitution, radicals concluded, provided "amply for liberation" but not for national dissolution (*Proceedings of the Convention of Radical Political Abolitionists* 1855, p. 43). From their perspective, "the general structure of the Federal Constitution, as well as its particular provisions, preclude the legal existence of slavery, forbid the States to maintain it, provide for the liberation of the enslaved, and authorize and require, at the hand of the Federal Government, its suppression"

(p. 7). The Supreme Court, in *Dred Scott v. Sandford*, 60 U.S. 393 (1857) squarely rejected this interpretation of the Constitution, finding, to the contrary, that Congress lacked the authority to interfere with slave owners' property rights.

Political radicals like George Mellen (1841) considered the due process clause of the Fifth Amendment to be one constitutional prohibition against slavery. According to this argument, slaves were persons covered under the guarantee that "no person shall be deprived of life, liberty, or property, without due process of law." Slavery was illegitimate because slaves were deprived of their liberty without being indicted or convicted for crimes by a jury of their peers. How, Alvan Stewart (1845) asked rhetorically, could "separation by sale of husband from wife, and wife from husband, and children from both, to suit the convenience of the master ... be due process of law?" Neither could any reasonable understanding of due process of law include the "pursuing of fugitives with blood-hounds," he continued (p. 35). Those who enslaved Africans had infringed on their liberty interests without the due process of law.

Lewis Tappan (1843) claimed that slavery created an aristocratic hierarchy that violated the prohibition against granting titles of nobility. Slaveholders were members of a "powerful landed aristocracy" that "banded together for the preservation of their own privileges" (p. 4).

The Constitution granted the federal government both the power and duty to abolish slavery. If it were to do so, Congress would, as stated in the Preamble to the Constitution, "provide for the common defense, promote the general welfare, and *secure the blessings of liberty*." One source of that power was the commerce clause that Congress could use to prohibit the interstate trade in slaves. An underdeveloped strand of argument for federal intervention claimed that Congress, the president, and the courts could administer remedies against slavery since it violated the Constitution. If the slave states refused to put an end to the "peculiar institution," then secession was the most likely political course.

Since Congress could use the Preamble to the Constitution to authorize the purchase of Louisiana, Florida, and California and the annexation of Texas, argued Spooner (1848), it could also rely on it to end slavery (p. 287). Others asserted that the Preamble, whose express object was "to secure the blessings of liberty" was a temple of freedom, "not a den of Slavery." That guarantee was for the "people," which were not distinguished by race, to "establish justice," while slavery was a great injustice ("Letter of Gerrit Smith to S. P. Chase" 1847, p. 3). Similarly, Lysander Spooner (1845) relied on no precedent, but rather used a plain language construction of the Preamble: "The mass of the people of that day could claim citizenship under the constitution, on no other ground

than as being a part of 'the people of the United States'; and such claim necessarily admits that all other 'people of the United States' were equally citizens" (p. 91).

Frederick Douglass (1818–1895), whose views over the years changed from a criticism of the Constitution to a later antislavery interpretation of it, held an even more inclusive interpretation of the Preamble. According to his *Unconstitutionality of Slavery* lecture of 1860, the Preamble's guarantees of union, defense, welfare, tranquility, justice, and liberty applied to everyone in the Union: "'We the people'; not we the white people, not we the citizens, not we the privileged class, not we the high, not we the low, not we of English extraction, not we of French or of Scotch extraction, but 'we the people'" (p. 15).

Congress could provide for the general welfare of the people through its Article I, Section 8 taxing power. Slavery was opposed to the general welfare for "the necessary evils slavery must and does bring in its course, such as ignorance, dissipation, vice, immorality.... [Further,] the arts, sciences, manufactures, even agriculture, declines under its withering influences" (Mellen 1841, p. 61). The federal legislature could use its taxing power to end these harms against the general welfare.

Whether free or slave, political radicals thought that blacks, like any other persons born in the United States, were citizens. No state could take away their national citizenship rights, and the federal government retained power to protect its citizens' natural rights. The federal government, for instance, could secure the rights to personal liberty and property ownership because they were privileges and immunities of national citizenship. Even those blacks who could not vote in the state of their residency, so the argument went, were made national citizens under the Constitution. After all, white women and children were citizens despite the fact that they had been unable to vote on the ratification of the Constitution.

As citizens, blacks were eligible for every public office, including the presidency of the United States, since the Constitution contained no racial eligibility. The national polity, in accordance with Article IV, guaranteed to each state a republican government, which was defined to protect the equal rights of everyone to freedom and property. Protection of the people's rights was the basis of republican government, since it was not the states that were parties to the Constitution but the people. States, therefore, could not maintain slaves against federal statutes because states lacked any authority to violate the "inalienable rights for the protection of which both the State and National Governments were organized." Each individual was entitled to a republican form of government. Blacks were denied a republican government because they, like women and Native Americans, were politically unrepresented. This, Stewart (1845) and others argued, meant the United States could end slavery in all states. Without federal protections, these groups were also denied any of the rights secured under the Bill of Rights, including the right to jury trials in fugitive slave cases.

The most difficult clauses for radical political abolitionists to explain were those that Garrisonian abolitionists considered to be proslavery. Radical arguments on these points were the most strained. According to Gerrit Smith's perspective in his letter to S. P. Chase (1847), the importation clause did not perpetuate the slave trade; instead, it was the means by which Congress could end it. On the three-fifths clause, Smith dismissed the notion that, since they could not vote, slaves should not be counted in apportioning representatives. He pointed out that other groups who were counted for apportionment, including women and white men without property, were also disenfranchised. He thus thought that not counting slaves at all would be a greater injustice than only counting them partly. The fugitive slave clause, he argued, was not about slavery but about the right of parents to pursue their children, and masters their apprentices. Given southern use of these clauses to strengthen slavery, Smith's arguments were a stretch.

The Garrisonians were the most vocal group of abolitionists who were opposed to the antislavery reading of the Constitution. This most controversial camp of abolitionists was under William Lloyd Garrison's (1805–1879) leadership. With its even more polished spokesman, attorney Wendell Phillips (1811–1884), this group denounced the Constitution's compromises with slave interests. They eschewed politics, refusing to dull their demands for elective reward. Theirs was a moral and religious crusade to restore blacks' and women's equal rights. Sarah Moore Grimké (1792–1873) and Sojourner Truth (c. 1797–1883) added their voices to this group's decision to avoid public office until civil rights, among which they counted the right to vote, received universal protection. Seeing no hope of achieving the necessary reform within the existing federal system, they demanded that the North separate from the South.

Their aversion for the Constitution was best reflected by Garrison's July 4, 1854, speech, when he burned a copy of the Constitution, calling it "a covenant with death and an agreement with hell" (quoted in Potter 1973, p. 48). The proslavery clauses of the Constitution, as Phillips (1847) pointed out in response to political abolitionist Lysander Spooner, could only be disarmed by an amendment. With no change to the Constitution, Garrisonians, like physician and abolitionist Henry I. Bowditch (1808–1892), clung to John Quincy Adams's (1767–1848) statement that calling the United States a democracy was insulting to humankind because its slave-protecting clauses made "the preservation, propagation, and perpetuation of slavery, the vital and animating spirit of the nation government" (quoted in Bowditch 1855, p. 12).

Before Frederick Douglass accepted the antislavery constitutional view, he too was firmly in the Garrisonian camp. In a March 16, 1849, article in his newspaper, *North Star*, he systematically analyzed clauses in the Constitution to show how they protected slavery. His analysis was not only about the most obvious three—the three-fifths, fugitive slave, and importation clauses. Douglass also believed that a variety of other constitutional provisions made the fundamental law of the United States a proslavery document. For instance, the insurrection clause gave Congress the power to call up the militia to suppress revolts, including slave rebellions, such as the 1831 Nat Turner rebellion in Virginia. Another constitutional provision that Douglass denounced made "the whole land one vast hunting ground for men," making felons out of persons who broke the fetters of slavery (Douglass 1847). The fugitive slave clause, which passed without any dissenting votes at the Constitutional Convention in 1787, required fugitives to be returned on demand and prohibited free states from liberating them

A third group, which gained the support of politicians like James G. Birney (1792–1857) and Salmon Chase, is better characterized as antislavery than abolitionist. This political movement sought to prevent the spread of slavery, but it was deferential to the existing order in slave states. Theirs was not a campaign for the immediate end of all slavery, wherever it existed, but against the continued spread of slavery to U.S. territories. They claimed Congress could prevent the spread of slavery into the territories through its exclusive power over those lands under the U.S. Constitution (Article IV, Section 3, clause 2). This faction, along with some radical abolitionists, morphed from the Liberty Party (1840) into the Free Soil Party (1848), finally ending up the Republican Party (1854), under whose banner Abraham Lincoln helped capture the presidency.

SEE ALSO *Ableman v. Booth, 62 U.S. 506 (1858); Article IV; Dred Scott v. Sandford, 60 U.S. 393 (1857); Garrison, William Lloyd; Prigg v. Pennsylvania, 41 U.S. 539 (1842); Slavery; Slavery in the Territories; Taney Court*

BIBLIOGRAPHY

Bowditch, William I. 1855. *United States Constitution.* New York: American Anti-Slavery Society.

Douglass, Frederick. 1847. *Farewell Speech of Mr. Frederick Douglass, Previously to Embarking on Board the Cambria, Upon His Return to America, Delivered at the Valedictory Soiree Given to Him at the London Tavern, on March 30, 1847.* Available from http://www.yale.edu/glc/archive/1086.htm.

Douglass, Frederick. "The Constitution & Slavery" (first published in *The North Star*, Mar. 16, 1849), in vol. 1 *Frederick Douglass, The Life and Writings of Frederick Douglass* (Philip S. Foner ed.). New York: International Publishers 1950.

Goodell, William. 1852. *Slavery and Anti-Slavery: A History of the Great Struggle in Both Hemispheres.* New York: William Harned.

Goodell, William. 1855. *The Constitutional Duty of the Federal Government to Abolish American Slavery.* New York: Abolition Society of New York City.

"Letter of Gerrit Smith to S. P. Chase, on the Unconstitutionality of Every Part of American Slavery." (1847). Available from the Northwestern Library Special Collection: Gerrit Smith S648let.

Mellen, George W. F. 1841. *An Argument on the Unconstitutionality of Slavery.* Boston: Saxton & Peirce.

Phillips, Wendell. 1847. *Review of Lysander Spooner's* Essay on the Unconstitutionality of Slavery. Boston: Andrews & Prentiss.

Potter, David M. 1973. *The Impending Crisis, 1848–1861.* New York: Harper & Row.

Proceedings of the Convention of Radical Political Abolitionists, Held at Syracuse, N.Y., June 26th, 27th, and 28th, 1855. 1855. New York: The Central Abolition Board.

Spooner, Lysander. 1845. *The Unconstitutionality of Slavery.* Boston: Marsh.

Spooner, Lysander. 1848. "Has Slavery in the United States a Legal Basis?" *Massachusetts Quarterly Review* 1: 273–293.

Stewart, Alvan. 1845. *A Legal Argument Before the Supreme Court of the State of New Jersey at the May Term, 1845.* New York: Finch & Weed.

Tappan, Lewis. 1843. *Address to the Non-slaveholders of the South: On the Social and Political Evils of Slavery.* New York: S. W. Benedict.

Tiffany, Joel. 1849. *A Treatise on the Unconstitutionality of American Slavery.* Cleveland, OH: Calyer.

Wiecek, William M. 1977. *The Sources of Antislavery Constitutionalism in America, 1760–1848.* Ithaca, NY: Cornell University Press.

Alexander Tsesis

ANTITRUST

In the United States, the term *antitrust* refers to the Sherman Act and the Clayton Act. The Sherman Act, passed in 1890, prohibits anticompetitive agreements such as price fixing, market division, and some boycotts and mergers. The second section of the statute prohibits "monopolization" by single dominant firms. The interest groups mainly responsible for passage of the statute were small businesses fearful that large corporations such as the Standard Oil Company would ruin them. In 1914, the Sherman Act was supplemented by the Clayton Act, which mainly prohibited anticompetitive tying and exclusive dealing and strengthened the antimerger rule.

The Supreme Court became involved in interpretation of the Sherman Act almost immediately. Historically, the Court has had a large role in making U.S. antitrust policy. For many years, the Expediting Act required direct Supreme Court review of district court antitrust judgments. In 2007, the Expediting Act was largely repealed, and over the past two decades the Supreme Court has ceded more of the final say in technical antitrust matters to the circuit courts.

In 1895 the Supreme Court held in *United States v. E. C. Knight Co.*, 156 U.S. 1 (1895) that under that period's narrow construction of the federal commerce power, the Sherman Act did not apply to an anticompetitive restraint in interstate manufacturing. As a result of the *E. C. Knight* decision, populists for a time largely regarded the Sherman Act as a dead letter. After that unpromising beginning the Court became more aggressive in condemning cartels that involved interstate shipping, developing what is known as the per se rule, under which conduct can be condemned merely upon proof that it occurred, with no analysis of market power or anticompetitive effects. Then in *Standard Oil v. United States*, 221 U.S. 1 (1911), the Supreme Court first developed a "rule of reason" for dealing with single-firm conduct that excludes rivals. Under that rule as applied in the early twenty-first century, the plaintiff must show that the defendant or defendants have substantial market power, which is the power to obtain higher prices and profit by reducing market output. In addition, anticompetitive effects must be assessed in each individual case.

During the fifteen years following the *Standard Oil* decision, there was some confusion about the way the Court would analyze antitrust cases. However, in *United States v. Trenton Potteries Co.*, 273 U.S. 392 (1927), the Court clarified that two modes of analysis would govern antitrust claims. Practices whose economic effects were somewhat ambiguous at first glance were to be governed by *Standard Oil*'s rule of reason, which often requires a complex and costly analysis of overall competitive effects. By contrast, price-fixing, market division, and many boycotts were to be governed by the per se rule, which meant that the conduct could be condemned simply upon proof that it occurred. Anticompetitive effects would be presumed. Problematically, the Supreme Court also extended this per se rule to some practices that were anticompetitive only a small portion of the time. These included tying arrangements and so-called vertical price fixing. Tying arrangements are seller requirements that a buyer can obtain one product only by taking a second product as well. They have remained illegal per se to this day, although the Supreme Court has tried to add some rigor to the law with an expanded market-power requirement (see, e.g., *Jefferson Parish Hosp. Dist. No. 2 v. Hyde*, 466 U.S. 2 [1984]).

In 1997 the Supreme Court overturned the per se rule against maximum vertical price fixing, which is supplier setting of the maximum price a distributor or dealer can charge (*State Oil Co. v. Khan*, 522 U.S. 3 [1997]). Then, in *Leegin Creative Leather Prods., Inc. v. PSKS*, 551 U.S. ___ (2007), a narrowly divided Court overturned the century-old decision in *Dr. Miles Medical Co. v. John D. Park & Sons Co.*, 220 U.S. 373 (1911) and held that henceforth resale price maintenance should be governed by the rule of reason. Nevertheless, the notion that the rule of reason and the per se rule create two different methodologies of antitrust analysis for different types of conduct remains.

ANTITRUST EXPANSIONISM

The period from the 1940s through the Warren Court era (1953–1969) was one of antitrust expansionism. Not only was the scope of the per se rule enlarged, but the Supreme Court also adopted a very aggressive merger policy following congressional amendments (1950) to the merger statute. Decisions such as *Brown Shoe Co. v. United States*, 370 U.S. 294 (1962) seemed to condemn mergers because they produced efficiencies, while *United States v. Von's Grocery Co.*, 384 U.S. 277 (1966) condemned an innocuous merger in a competitively structured market. These cases expressed little concern for the idea that mergers were bad if they facilitated higher prices injuring consumers. Rather, the fear appears to have been *lower* prices, which would benefit consumers but injure the merging firms' rivals.

The Court of that era also condemned many joint ventures and other arrangements among firms that were unlikely to pose a competitive threat, given their small size, and that contained significant efficiency-enhancing potential (e.g., *United States v. Topco Associates*, 405 U.S. 596 [1972]). This period also witnessed considerable expansion in enforcement of the antitrust laws by private parties rather than the government enforcement agencies, to the point that some ninety percent of filed claims are privately brought. Another thing that characterized this period was broad hostility toward intellectual property rights, including exaggerated notions about their anticompetitive potential. In *International Salt Co. v. United States*, 332 U.S. 392 (1947), the Supreme Court created a presumption for tying arrangements that market power in a patented tying product would be presumed, and need not be separately proven. Finally, in numerous cases the Court gave broad application to the Robinson–Patman Act, a badly designed statute forbidding suppliers from charging different wholesale prices to competing dealers. The effect of these decisions was to limit the ability of many manufacturers to make their dealership networks more efficient.

SUPREME COURT LIMITS ANTITRUST

Since the 1970s the Supreme Court has generally been stepping back from many of the broader decisions of this earlier period, although the record is not consistent. In *United States v. General Dynamics Corp.*, 415 U.S. 486 (1974), it reined the government in on merger policy. In *Broadcast Music v. Columbia Broadcasting System*, 441 U.S. 1 (1979), it approved a broad joint venture in the copyrighted recorded music industry. In *Jefferson Parish*, it tightened up the requirements for proof of unlawful tying. In *Monsanto Co. v. Spray–Rite Service. Corp.*, 465 U.S. 752 (1984) and *Business Electronics Corp. v. Sharp Electronics Corp.*, 485 U.S. 717 (1988), the Supreme Court made unlawful resale price maintenance more difficult to prove. In *Brooke Group Limited v. Brown & Williamson Tobacco Co.*, 509 U.S. 209 (1993), the Supreme Court adopted a very stringent test for predatory pricing, which is the offense of driving rivals out of business by charging very low prices and subsequently recouping by charging monopoly prices. A plaintiff must show both that the defendant charged prices below its short-term costs and that it had a reasonable prospect of recouping the costs of a predation strategy through post-predation monopoly pricing. In 2007 the Supreme Court extended these requirements to claims of predatory purchasing in *Weyerhaeuser Co. v. Ross-Simmons Hardwood Lumber Co., Inc.*, 127 U.S. 1069 (2007). These tests have proven very harsh, and very few plaintiffs have been able to succeed under them. Finally, in *Illinois Tool Works Inc. v. Independent Ink, Inc.*, 547 U.S. 28 (2006), the Supreme Court overruled the *International Salt* presumption, discussed above, that patent rights in a tying product automatically conferred market power.

During this period, the Court also severely limited the antitrust enforcement powers of private plaintiffs. Although Congress provided that in the Clayton Act "any person" who is "injured in his business or property" by an antitrust violation can bring a suit, this provision has come to mean much less. *Illinois Brick Co. v. Illinois*, 431 U.S. 720 (1977) limited antitrust damages actions to "direct" purchasers from an unlawful cartel or monopolist. In *Brunswick Corp. v. Pueblo Bowl–O–Mat, Inc.*, 429 U.S. 477 (1977), the Court developed the "antitrust injury" concept, which required a private plaintiff to show not merely injury but also injury that was caused by the adverse impact of the violation on competition. In *Associated General Contractors of California, Inc. v. California State Council of Carpenters*, 459 U.S. 519 (1983), the court limited the scope of private plaintiff standing to sue. In *Verizon Communications, Inc. v. Law Offices of Curtis V. Trinko, LLP*, 540 U.S. 398 (2004), it severely limited the right of private firms or consumers to sue a monopolist for refusing to share scarce inputs with rivals. In *Empagran S.A. v. F. Hoffman-LaRoche, Ltd.*, 542 U.S. 155 (2004), it restricted the protection of the antitrust laws to essentially American interests, holding that foreign plaintiffs could not sue for injuries suffered abroad.

Finally, two important 2007 decisions severely limited enforcement power. *Bell Atlantic Corp. v. Twombly*,

550 U.S. ___ (2007) severely raised the standard governing the amount that an antitrust plaintiff must allege in a complaint in order to avoid dismissal. And in *Credit Suisse Securities, LLC v. Billing*, 551 U.S. ___ (2007), the Court cut back on reach of the antitrust laws into markets that are heavily regulated by federal agencies, provided that the regulator is doing its job adequately and taking concerns for competition into account.

During the Rehnquist era (1986–2005) the Supreme Court issued far fewer antitrust decisions than it had previously, often going several years at a time without reviewing any cases. The result was a less important role for the Supreme Court in antitrust matters and an increasing number of conflicts among the circuit courts of appeal. A firm prediction about the Roberts Court would be premature, but in its first full year of operation, ending in the summer of 2007, the Court reviewed four antitrust cases, which is more than in any single year of the Rehnquist Court. Chief Justice John Roberts's background suggests that he is more interested in antitrust than the late Chief Justice William Rehnquist had been. So one may see increased Supreme Court involvement in antitrust disputes.

SEE ALSO *New Deal and the Regulation of Business and Commerce; Progressive Era Business Regulation; United States v. E.C. Knight Co., 156 U.S. 1 (1895)*

BIBLIOGRAPHY

Areeda, Phillip E., and Herbert Hovenkamp. 2001–2007. *Antitrust Law*. New York: Aspen.

Hovenkamp, Herbert. 2005. *The Antitrust Enterprise: Principle and Execution*. Cambridge, MA: Harvard University Press.

Posner, Richard A. 2001. *Antitrust Law*. 2nd edition. Chicago: University of Chicago Press.

CASES

Associated General Contractors of California, Inc. v. California State Council of Carpenters, 459 U.S. 519 (1983).

Bell Atlantic Corp. v. Twombly, 550 U.S. ___ (2007).

Broadcast Music v. Columbia Broadcasting System, 441 U.S. 1 (1979).

Brooke Group Limited v. Brown & Williamson Tobacco Co., 509 U.S. 209 (1993).

Brown Shoe Co. v. United States, 370 U.S. 294 (1962).

Brunswick Corp. v. Pueblo Bowl–O–Mat, Inc., 429 U.S. 477 (1977).

Business Electronics Corp. v. Sharp Electronics Corp., 485 U.S. 717 (1988).

Credit Suisse Securities, LLC v. Billing, 551 U.S. ___ (2007).

Dr. Miles Medical Co. v. John D. Park & Sons Co., 220 U.S. 373 (1911).

Empagran S.A. v. F. Hoffman-LaRoche, Ltd., 542 U.S. 155 (2004).

Illinois Brick Co. v. Illinois, 431 U.S. 720 (1977).

Illinois Tool Works Inc. v. Independent Ink, Inc., 547 U.S. 28 (2006).

International Salt Co. v. United States, 332 U.S. 392 (1947).

Jefferson Parish Hosp. Dist. No. 2 v. Hyde, 466 U.S. 2 (1984).

Leegin Creative Leather Prods., Inc. v. PSKS, Inc., 551 U.S. ___ (2007).

Monsanto Co. v. Spray–Rite Service. Corp., 465 U.S. 752 (1984).

Standard Oil Co. (N.J.) v. United States, 221 U.S. 1 (1911).

State Oil Co. v. Khan, 522 U.S. 3 (1997).

United States v. E.C. Knight Co., 156 U.S. 1 (1895).

United States v. General Dynamics Corp., 415 U.S. 486 (1974).

United States v. Topco Associates, 405 U.S. 596 (1972).

United States v. Trenton Potteries Co., 273 U.S. 392 (1927).

United States v. Von's Grocery Co., 384 U.S. 277 (1966).

Verizon Communications, Inc. v. Law Offices of Curtis V. Trinko, LLP, 540 U.S. 398 (2004).

Weyerhaeuser Co. v. Ross-Simmons Hardwood Lumber Co., Inc., 127 U.S. 1069 (2007).

Herbert Hovenkamp

APPELLATE JURISDICTION

Both Article III of the U.S. Constitution and federal statutes govern the appellate jurisdiction of the Supreme Court to hear cases from lower federal courts and from state courts. The Constitution gives the Supreme Court appellate jurisdiction in all other cases enumerated in Article III, including appeals from state courts in which the appellee is a state, notwithstanding the Eleventh Amendment. Importantly, Congress can limit the Supreme Court's appellate jurisdiction under the exceptions clause. Thus, Article III's grant of appellate jurisdiction to the Supreme Court is qualified by any exceptions, and under any regulations, that Congress provides.

THE DEVELOPMENT OF THE SCOPE OF APPELLATE JURISDICTION

The first major case interpreting the Supreme Court's appellate jurisdiction was *Marbury v. Madison*, 5 U.S. (1 Cranch) 137 (1803). There, President Adams appointed William Marbury as a Justice of the Peace and ordered the Secretary of State, then John Marshall, to deliver the commission. The commission was not delivered before incoming president Thomas Jefferson took office, and President Jefferson instructed his new Secretary of State, James Madison, to withhold the commission. Marbury sued Madison in an original action in the Supreme Court for a mandamus (a writ requiring a specific action) ordering Madison to give him the commission.

The Supreme Court, in an opinion written by then Chief Justice John Marshall, ruled against Marbury, holding that Article III did not authorize the Supreme Court to exercise original jurisdiction over such a mandamus action. Instead, the Court held, such an action could come to the Supreme Court only through its appellate jurisdiction. Because Marbury filed the action as an original matter, the Supreme Court lacked jurisdiction to hear his claim.

Marbury's statement that the Supreme Court's original jurisdiction and appellate jurisdiction are mutually exclusive has not withstood the test of time. In *Ames v. Kansas ex rel. Johnston,* 111 U.S. 449 (1884), the Court subsequently held that the Court can hear appeals in cases designated by Article III as within its original jurisdiction. Thus, the Court can exercise appellate jurisdiction under Article III over any case within either its original jurisdiction or its appellate jurisdiction.

TYPES OF APPELLATE JURISDICTION

The Supreme Court can review cases either by appeal (which is mandatory) or by writ of certiorari (which is discretionary). Until 1891, the Court had only mandatory appellate jurisdiction. In 1891, Congress gave the Supreme Court the power to review certain cases by writ of certiorari. In 1925, out of concern for the swelling docket of the Supreme Court, Congress granted the Supreme Court the power to hear most appeals by certiorari and eliminated mandatory appellate jurisdiction in most cases. In 1988, Congress eliminated mandatory appellate jurisdiction in all cases except where specifically authorized or in appeals from three-judge courts. Thus, most appeals to the Supreme Court are taken only at the discretion of the Court, which grants certiorari only where there are important and specific reasons to do so. Sup. Ct. R. 17.

THE FINAL JUDGMENT RULE

Although it has given the Court discretion to hear appeals, Congress also has imposed general limits on the Court's appellate jurisdiction. In Section 1257 of Title 28 of the United States Code Congress extended appellate review of state judgments only when the judgment was "final" and "rendered by the highest court of [the] State." By contrast, in Section 1254 Congress extended appellate review of judgments rendered by federal Courts of Appeals to petitions for review made "before or after rendition of judgment or decree." The Supreme Court has itself limited the broad jurisdiction granted by Section 1254 over appeals before final judgment to those cases "of such imperative public importance as to justify the deviation from normal appellate practice and to require immediate settlement in this Court."

Circumvention of the "final judgment rule" has been allowed in extraordinary cases, such as *United States v. Nixon,* 418 U.S. 683 (1974), in which the Court resolved a Watergate issue of critical importance to the impeaching proceedings against President Richard Nixon; *Youngstown Sheet & Tube Co. v. Sawyer,* 343 U.S. 579 (1952), in which the Court held President Truman's attempt to seize steel mills during a labor strike to be unlawful; and *Dames & Moore v. Regan,* 453 U.S. 654 (1981), in which the Court upheld President Carter's executive order unfreezing Iranian assets to secure the release of American hostages.

CONGRESS'S POWER TO STRIP THE SUPREME COURT OF APPELLATE JURISDICTION

The scope of Congress's power to limit the Court's appellate jurisdiction under the Exceptions Clause in specific cases is unsettled and controversial. Proponents, including Martin H. Redish (1982) and Michael Perry (1982), argue that the Exceptions Clause is explicit and plenary and that it serves as a valuable democratic check on judicial power.

Opponents, including Larry Sager (1981), argue that Congress's power to limit the appellate jurisdiction is constrained by other aspects of the Constitution. They argue that Congress could not, for example, eliminate appellate jurisdiction only in cases in which the appeal is brought by African Americans, for such a restriction would violate the Due Process Clause of the Fifth Amendment. Some opponents, such as Raoul Berger (1969), also argue that Congress's power to create exceptions is limited to issues of fact rather than of law (pp. 285–296). Erwin Chemerinsky (2007), an opponent of broad jurisdiction-stripping power, believes that proponents of jurisdiction-stripping act from a desire to change the law substantively and do not trust the federal courts to reach their desired result (pp. 177-178).

The first significant Court pronouncement on jurisdiction-stripping was *Ex parte McCardle,* 74 U.S. (7 Wall.) 506 (1869). There, McCardle was arrested by federal officers for criticizing Reconstruction. McCardle filed a petition for habeas corpus challenging the legality of his detention in federal prison. While the case was pending on appeal in the Supreme Court, Congress passed an act depriving the Supreme Court of appellate jurisdiction over certain federal habeas corpus petitions. The Supreme Court held the act deprived it of jurisdiction to hear McCardle's appeal. The Court was careful, however, to state that the act did not withdraw all appellate jurisdiction in cases such as McCardle's. Thus, some have interpreted McCardle narrowly as allowing exceptions to appellate jurisdiction when opportunities for Supreme Court review nevertheless still remain.

More recently, the Court has upheld Congress's ability to strip its appellate jurisdiction. In Title I of the

Antiterrorism and Effective Death Penalty Act of 1996, Congress eliminated Supreme Court review of any decision by a circuit court granting or denying authorization for a state prisoner to file a second or successive habeas corpus petition. The Supreme Court upheld this restriction on its own appellate jurisdiction in *Felker v. Turpin*, 518 U.S. 651 (1996), though its reasoning hinged on the recognition that the Supreme Court could still hear such a case under its original jurisdiction and therefore that the statute did not withdraw all Supreme Court jurisdiction over the issue.

Congress's ability to limit the Court's appellate jurisdiction, coupled with Congress's power to limit the jurisdiction of the lower federal courts, has raised the possibility that Congress might strip the federal courts of all jurisdiction in certain circumstances. In other words, Congress might deprive the federal courts of both original jurisdiction and appellate jurisdiction to hear a particular case. Although Congress has never attempted such a restriction, doing so would raise significant due process and separation-of-powers concerns (Eisenberg 1974, pp. 504–512).

Another argument against Congress' ability to strip jurisdiction completely is that doing so would amount to a suspension of the writ of habeas corpus in violation of Article I, Section 9 of the U.S. Constitution. In 2006, Congress passed the Military Commissions Act of 2006, which states: "No court, justice or judge shall have jurisdiction to hear or consider an application for a writ of habeas corpus filed by or on behalf of an alien detailed by the United States who has been determined by the United States to have been properly detained as an enemy combatant or is awaiting such determination" (Pub. L. No. 109–366 § 7, 120 Stat. 2600 [2006]). The U.S. Court of Appeals for the District of Columbia has upheld this provision as constitutional in *Boumediene v. Bush*, 476 F.3d 981 (D.C. Cir. 2007), and review was sought in the Supreme Court.

SEE ALSO *Article III; Case or Controversy; Jurisdiction; Writ of Certiorari*

BIBLIOGRAPHY

Berger, Raoul. 1969. *Congress v. the Supreme Court.* Cambridge, MA: Harvard University Press.

Chemerinsky, Erwin. 2007. *Federal Jurisdiction.* 5th edition. Aspen Publishers.

Eisenberg, Theodore. 1974. "Congressional Authority to Restrict Lower Federal Court Jurisdiction." *Yale Law Journal* 83: 498–533.

Perry, Michael. 1982. *The Constitution, the Courts, and Human Rights: An Inquiry into the Legitimacy of Constitutional Policymaking by the Judiciary.* New Haven, CT: Yale University Press.

Redish, Martin. 1982. "Constitutional Limitations on Congressional Power to Control Federal Jurisdiction: A Reaction to Professor Sager." *Northwestern University Law Review* 77: 143–167.

Sager, Larry. 1981. "Forward: Constitutional Limitations on Congress' Authority to Regulate the Jurisdiction of the Federal Courts." *Harvard Law Review* 95: 17–89.

Scott Dodson

APPOINTMENT AND REMOVAL OF EXECUTIVE OFFICERS

Article II of the U.S. Constitution explicitly provides for the distribution of appointive power for executive and judicial positions, but says little about the removal of executive branch officials from office once they are appointed. (Article III covers federal judges, who, once confirmed by the Senate, are removable only by the clumsy impeachment process.) Removal, more than appointment, has been a source of constitutional controversy.

APPOINTMENT

Article II, Section 2, clause 2 provides that the president

shall nominate, and by and with the advice and consent of the Senate, shall appoint ambassadors, other public ministers and consuls, judges of the Supreme Court, and all other officers of the United States, whose appointments are not herein otherwise provided for, and which shall be established by law: but the Congress may by law vest the appointment of such inferior officers, as they think proper, in the President alone, in the courts of law, or in the heads of departments.

Congress exercised this authority from the very start of American government, in conjunction with its general power to legislate as is "necessary and proper" to effectuate the Constitution's terms, to create a wide variety of government posts in varying political relationship with the White House. Three sorts of questions about appointments issues have recently been prominent:

Who is an "inferior officer"? This question has two aspects: whether there are limits on Congress's authority to take appointments authority away from the president; and whether there are any kinds of government officials whose appointment can be put in hands *other* than "the President alone, in the Courts of Law, or in the Heads of Departments"—a civil service commission, for example. Debate on the first of these aspects was most heated respecting the independent counsel, a prosecuting officer able to investigate even claims of presidential misconduct, yet appointed by a special panel of federal judges—"the Courts of Law" *Morrison v. Olson*, 487 U.S. 654 (1988) controversially found that limited-control relationships exercised by the attorney general, including the possibility of his or her removal "for cause," rendered the independent counsel an "inferior officer" and so made the scheme constitutional. A later decision, *Edmond v. United States*, 520 U.S. 651 (1997), appears to require a more direct hierarchical relationship with a supervisor, imperiling any future revival of the Independent Counsel Act legally (if memories of Kenneth Starr's [1946–] investigation of President Bill Clinton [1946–], that seemed chapter and verse to bear out Justice Antonin Scalia's vigorous dissent in *Morrison*, are not in themselves sufficient to achieve that politically). Although *Freytag v. Commissioner*, 501 U.S. 868 (1991) might seem to require appointment by one of Article II's three named authorities of *anyone* exercising significant authority in government, the creation of a civil service system controlling appointments on a merits basis even to quite significant positions was readily approved by the Court in *United States v. Perkins*, 116 U.S. 483 (1886).

Whom can Congress authorize to make appointments? This did not seem to be an important question until Justice Harry Blackmun's surprising opinion for the Court in *Freytag v. Commissioner*. Employing a strongly originalist understanding of the appointments clause, he wrote that the founders understood the power to appoint as "the most insidious and powerful weapon of eighteenth century despotism," and addressed that concern by "carefully husbanding the appointment power to limit its diffusion." "Heads of Departments" must therefore be understood to refer *only* to cabinet-level departments, "limited in number and easily identified," and directly responsible to the president. Blackmun escaped applying his reasoning to the case before him by discovering that the Tax Court official whose appointment had been questioned was in the courts of law. In a conclusory footnote he then observed, in considerable tension with the reasoning of his opinion, "we do not address here any question involving appointment of an inferior officer by the head of one of the principal agencies, such as the Federal Trade Commission, ... the Central Intelligence Agency, and the Federal Reserve Bank of St. Louis" (p. 887, note 4). None of these are cabinet departments, or parts of cabinet departments, as Justice Scalia acidly noted in his concurrence for himself and three others. The confusions thus created have not yet been quieted.

For persons whom the president nominates for Senate confirmation, can Congress restrict qualifications for office? Of course it frequently does. Appointments to independent regulatory commissions are often constrained by statutory provisions that no more than a bare majority may be members of the same political party. The solicitor general must be a person "learned in the law"; the surgeon general, a medical doctor. But at least since the administration of Bill Clinton, presidents have asserted plenary nomination authority, and chafed at such restrictions as that the head of the Federal Emergency Management Administration (FEMA) or the U.S. Postal Service have a record of experience with the problems with which he or she may be expected to have to deal. It is not likely that this issue will wind up in the courts; should the president nominate and the Senate confirm a political hack for the head of FEMA, people in a hurricane's path will have none but political recourse.

REMOVAL

Where Congress properly provides for appointment outside the advice and consent process, it can also set the terms and authority for removal. But what about those officials to whose appointment the Senate must consent? May Congress reserve for the Senate a right also to consent to their removal? May it give the officer protected tenure, so that he or she may be removed only "for cause," and not simply as a matter of the president's political discretion? A seemingly simple set of issues, yet they armed a constitutional crisis, are the source of continuing fundamental debate about the nature of the presidency, and have yet to be fully resolved.

The issue first arose as the first Congress created the first structures of executive government. The drafters had left that task to Congress, after rejecting an initial proposal to define the government's departments in the Constitution itself. Serious debate over the propriety of Senate participation in removal ensued, with James Madison (1751–1836) changing positions in the House, and Vice President Aaron Burr (1756–1836) having to cast a tiebreaking vote in the Senate. The "decision of 1789," as Chief Justice (and former president) William Howard Taft would later characterize it in *Myers v. United States,* 272 U.S. 52 (1926), was to have department heads serve for unspecified terms, at the pleasure of the president, and without Senate participation in their removal. Chief Justice John Marshall's description of the usual function of such officials in *Marbury v. Madison*, 5 U.S. 137 (1803) makes the reason for this decision obvious; they served, he would say, as the mere organ through whom the president's will was made known. If the president were to lose confidence in such officers, obviously the president must be able instantly to remove them, and no judicial control of such functions would be proper.

But officers exercising high political discretion were not the only ones the first Congress created. If Chief Justice Taft had taken the occasion to look harder, as later scholars have revealed, he would have found the first Congress also creating officers (particularly in the Department of the Treasury) who exercised more law-constrained functions. These officials, who were to exercise more bureaucratic and less political functions, were given terms of office with the expectation that they would serve their terms out, absent some cause for removal. Indeed, the plaintiff in *Marbury*, a minor judicial official, would have had such a term. Unlike the question about removing cabinet secretaries, Congress's right to assign subordinate officials a fixed term of office, even ones with significant functions, does not seem to have been a controversial matter. And the kind of discretion *they* would exercise is conventionally subject to quite intrusive judicial oversight.

The removal issue was at the core of the near-impeachment of President Andrew Johnson (1808–1875) in the wake of the Civil War (1861–1865) and Abraham Lincoln's assassination in 1865. Distrusting Johnson, Congress had passed a Tenure of Office Act (1867), requiring senatorial consent to the removal of any member of Lincoln's cabinet. Johnson's efforts to remove Lincoln's secretary of war, Edwin M. Stanton (1814–1869), underlay the principal charge in articles of impeachment that came within a single vote of passage.

The years following saw a more successful exercise of congressional control over executive-branch employee tenure in the passage of the Pendleton Civil Service Act (1883), whose constitutionality was sustained in *United States v. Perkins*, 116 U.S. 483 (1886). For inferior officers—and this act and its protections reach bureau chiefs and others exercising significant policy and administrative responsibilities—Congress had authority to create tenure protected from simply political controls, ending the spoils system with its invitations to incompetence and corruption.

The next major "removals" issue arose in *Myers v. United States* and then again, not many years later, in *Humphrey's Executor v. United States*, 295 U.S. 602 (1935). In *Myers,* the Supreme Court took two years of argument to decide, by the narrowest of margins and in an unusually long and complex opinion, that Congress could not validly require senatorial participation in the removal from office of the postmaster of Portland, Oregon, who had been appointed by the president with the Senate's advice and consent. Chief Justice Taft's opinion reasoned in sweeping terms that as a matter of separation of powers, and as established by congressional practice from the very outset of American constitutional government, the president's control over those who served in executive government could not be impeded. This was about a postmaster's appointment—a political plum perhaps, but hardly an important policy position. In *Humphrey's Executor*, in contrast, it took just a few weeks for the Court to conclude unanimously that the president could *not* remove Federal Trade Commissioner William E. Humphrey (1862–1934) from office simply for reasons of

political expediency when a statute gave Humphrey a fixed term of office from which he could be removed only for "cause." President Franklin D. Roosevelt was stuck with a holdover Republican in a position that actually did have a fair measure of policymaking and policy-applying importance. The Court explained the difference in terms that even at the time were intellectually unsatisfying—that the Federal Trade Commission (FTC) performed no executive functions and was not "in" the executive branch. Just what branch it *was* in, the Court had no occasion to say.

Subsequent cases, building on remarks in the *Myers* case, easily found and upheld "for cause" removal restrictions in settings involving agency adjudication—"quasi-judicial" action. People acting as judges, surely, could properly be protected from political oversight and reprisal. But the difficulties *Humphrey's Executor* presented came to a head in 1988 in *Morrison v. Olson*. In *Morrison,* the Court was required to deal with "for cause" removal restrictions for the independent counsel, a person inescapably performing an executive function. Now *Myers* and *Humphrey's Executor* were re-rationalized. The problem in *Myers*, the Court now explained, was that Congress had tried to *reserve senatorial participation* in the removal decision—*that* was the impermissible element that the Congress had decided against in the "decision of 1789," and that element was missing from *Humphrey's Executor*. As long as it did not claim removal authority for itself, Congress could place reasonable restrictions on the president's exercise of it; absent such self-aggrandizement, the issue would be whether the restriction encroached upon necessary presidential authority. "For cause" removal authority (with some other features discussed in connection with the *Morrison* case) left the president with sufficient authority to preserve the president's constitutional status.

Just what "cause" might be has yet to be defined, and the Court has varied considerably in its assessment of the importance of the restriction. In *Bowsher v. Synar*, 478 U.S. 714 (1986), Congress's control over removal of the head of the General Accounting Office, essentially a congressional agency, was enough to invalidate an important statute on separation-of-powers grounds. Yet in *Mistretta v. United States*, 488 U.S. 361 (1989), the threat that judges might be removed from the Sentencing Commission "for cause" was deemed too trivial to raise a threat to their independence. A mere political preference—Roosevelt's reason respecting Commissioner Humphrey—clearly is not enough to constitute "cause." This way of seeing the case, as most scholars and the courts do today, has the virtue of restoring the FTC to the constitutional framework. No longer outside that framework, the FTC is seen as an element of the executive branch that Congress has "reasonably" removed *somewhat* from the immediate political controls that presidents are able to exercise over officers they can remove from office without legal constraint. The laws Congress implements are still laws that presidents, pursuing their oath of office, must "take care" to see "faithfully executed." But in the interest of limiting the realm of politics and of increasing the domain of law, Congress can protect commissioners from removal, save "for cause."

This issue is intimately tied to general questions about the nature and extent of presidential authority. Some scholars see the Constitution's choice of a single chief executive as so emphatic as to require that the president have unfettered discretion to remove anyone exercising significant governmental authority subject to presidential oversight. Very likely their view would prevail as to those officers, such as the secretary of state, who predominantly act, as Chief Justice Marshall put it in *Marbury*, as the mere organ through whom presidential will is expressed. But the situation is different for those officials, like commissioners of the FTC, who act within a framework of law, and whose acts are regularly subject to oversight and correction by the courts.

Although the more conservative justices, notably Justices Scalia and Clarence Thomas, have expressed continuing skepticism about the constitutional place of the independent regulatory commissions, they have accepted them as an element of contemporary government too firmly established by precedent and practice to be overcome. The present constitutional "settlement" of the removal issue is reasonably clear. Congress cannot reserve participation in the removal of executive officials for itself. But it *can* restrict the president's authority to remove even executive officials exercising significant policymaking or administrative authority under the constraints of law, so long as its doing so does not deprive presidents of the ability to carry out their constitutional function of assuring that they faithfully execute those laws.

SEE ALSO *Article II; Hughes Court; Humphrey's Executor v. United States, 295 U.S. 602 (1935); Marbury v. Madison, 5 U.S. 137 (1803); Morrison v. Olson, 487 U.S. 654 (1988); Taft Court*

BIBLIOGRAPHY

Bruff, Harold H. 2006. *Balance of Forces: Separation of Powers Law in the Administrative State*. Durham, NC: Carolina Academic Press.

Calabresi, Steven G., and Saikrishna B. Prakash. 1994. "The President's Power to Execute the Laws." *Yale Law Journal* 104: 541.

Krent, Harold J. 2005. *Presidential Powers*. New York: New York University Press.

Lessig, Laurence, and Cass Sunstein. 1994. "The President and the Administration." *Columbia Law Review* 94: 1–123.

Strauss, Peter L. 1984. "The Place of Agencies in Government: Separation of Powers and the Fourth Branch." *Columbia Law Review* 84(3): 573–669.

Peter L. Strauss

APPOINTMENT OF ATTORNEYS

Lawyers appointed to represent litigants in the Supreme Court typically are admitted to practice law before the Court as members of the Supreme Court's bar. The basic requirements for admission are experience and character. Applicants must have practiced law in a state or territory of the United States for the three most recent years preceding their application, with no disciplinary action against them during that time period. They also must possess "good moral and professional character," as certified by the member of the Supreme Court Bar that nominates them for admission (Rule 5).

In rare cases, nonmembers of the Supreme Court Bar will be appointed to argue a case before the Court, generally to enable an indigent litigant to continue with the same lawyer that represented them in lower trial or appellate proceedings under the Criminal Justice Act of 1964. The Criminal Justice Act guarantees that all defendants, regardless of their financial circumstances, have adequate legal defense in criminal cases. The Act was a direct outgrowth of the Supreme Court case that established the right to counsel in all criminal trials, which itself was argued by a Court-appointed lawyer.

In *Gideon v. Wainwright*, 372 U.S. 335 (1963), the Supreme Court ruled that legal representation in criminal cases was a fundamental right guaranteed by the Constitution of the United States. In both state and federal courts, criminal defendants are entitled to have counsel appointed at government expense if they cannot afford to hire their own lawyer.

The initial petition for certiorari in *Gideon* was handwritten and filed pro se by the incarcerated Clarence Earl Gideon, who was serving a five-year sentence in the Florida state penitentiary following a conviction on burglary charges. Gideon had defended himself unsuccessfully at trial after his request for a court-appointed lawyer was denied. When the Supreme Court granted certiorari in *Gideon*, it also appointed prominent Washington, DC, lawyer Abe Fortas to brief and argue the case. Fortas later was nominated to the Supreme Court and served as an associate justice from 1965 to 1969. For his part, Gideon was retried on the burglary charges and acquitted, no doubt benefitting from the skills of the trial lawyer that was appointed to defend him.

The Supreme Court's appointment power is not limited to criminal cases, however. Rather, the Court's inherent authority to control its own docket allows it to appoint counsel in any proceeding where the justices deem it necessary. In *Mathews v. Weber*, 423 U.S. 261 (1976), for example, when the respondent failed to participate in the case, the Court appointed a local attorney to appear as *amicus curiae* ("friend of the Court") to brief and argue the matter in support of the lower court's judgment.

SEE ALSO *Fortas, Abe; Gideon v. Wainwright, 372 U.S. 335 (1963)*

BIBLIOGRAPHY

Lewis, Anthony. 1964. *Gideon's Trumpet*. New York: Random House.

Savage, David. 2004. *Guide to the U.S. Supreme Court*. 4th edition. Washington, DC: CQ Press.

Supreme Court of the United States. "Rules of the Supreme Court of the United States." Available from http://www.supremecourtus.gov.

CASES

Gideon v. Wainwright, 372 U.S. 335 (1963).

David L. Nersessian

APPORTIONMENT

The Supreme Court's apportionment cases are among the most important and revolutionary decisions in the Court's history. These decisions culminated in the famous *one-person, one-vote* principle, which has come to be viewed as part of the bedrock of American democracy. The reapportionment decisions had immediate and dramatic effects, which included the restructuring of the institutions of representative government throughout the United States: Congress, state legislatures, city councils, and many other institutions of local and state government. These decisions continue to require that election districts be redrawn every decade, in the wake of a new census, to ensure those districts remain consistent with the one-person, one-vote requirement. As consequential as these immediate practical effects were, the significance of the decisions extends even more broadly, for they also initiated a transformation of the role of courts in overseeing the basic structures of American democracy more generally.

Apportionment is used somewhat differently in different contexts, but for purposes of this entry, apportionment will refer to the process by which various political institutions, such as state legislatures, decide how to design the individual election districts that are used to elect members of the U.S. House and state legislatures. When local governments use individual election districts

to elect members of local government, to a city council for example, those local governments must similarly decide how to design these election districts. These actions are often called the process of apportioning representatives, though they are frequently called *redistricting* as well.

The process of redistricting or apportionment can have enormous political consequence. Even if citizens face no barriers to casting a vote, the way election districts are designed can determine who wins elections and which forces control government. For example, consider a town of 100 people, divided between sixty people who support Blue policies and forty who support Red policies, that elects five representatives to govern it. If the town designs its election districts so that one district includes all sixty Blues and the other four districts all contain ten Reds each, the town council will vote four-to-one for Red policies, even though a clear majority of the town's citizens prefer Blue policies. Thus, democracy requires not just that all citizens be able to vote, but that election districts be designed to aggregate those votes in such a way as to ensure fair and responsive representation.

THE SHIFTING DEMOGRAPHICS OF THE UNITED STATES IN THE TWENTIETH CENTURY

The Supreme Court's foray into apportionment must be understood in relation to the twentieth-century transformation of the United States from a rural nation to an urban one. In 1790 four percent of the population lived in urban or suburban areas. By 1962 the urban sector was 70 percent (Schattschneider 1962, p. 7). But political representation was typically based not on population, but on geographic units, such as counties and towns; thus, each county in a state might be entitled to the same number of legislators, regardless of population or of population shifts over time. As mass urban migration proceeded over the twentieth century, the population disparities between rural and urban counties grew. For example, the typical ratio in 1910 between the county with the most representation in a state legislature and the county with the least was six to one; by 1960, that ratio had exploded to thirty-five to one (Ansolabehere and Snyder 2008, p. 44).

State legislators elected under apportionment schemes that allocated power to once-populous rural areas did nothing to reapportion in response to these demographic changes, sometimes even in violation of state law. By the 1950s, forty states required reapportionment as often as every decade; even so, nearly half of the states had not done so (Lewis 1958, p. 1061). An increasingly urban country was governed by a Congress and state legislatures elected predominantly by a rural minority. One study estimates that in 1947 urban voters comprised 59 percent of the population but elected only 20 percent of state legislators (p. 1064).

Political cartoon of a gerrymandered map by Gilbert Stuart, 1812. Based on the federal census, election districts must change every ten years, reflecting shifts in the population. Supreme Court decisions, such as Reynolds v. Sims *and* Karcher v. Daggett, *have demanded that districts must have equal populations to preserve the equal protection clause of the Fourteenth Amendment.* © CORBIS-BETTMANN

THE SUPREME COURT'S FIRST LOOK AT APPORTIONMENT

In *Colegrove v. Green*, 328 U.S. 549 (1946), the Supreme Court was first asked to hold that the Constitution was violated when counties with radically different numbers of citizens had the same amount of political representation. The case arose from Illinois, which had not successfully reapportioned its congressional seats since 1901, leading to districts that varied in population by as much as 900 percent. The Court declined to intervene, holding that malapportionment was a nonjusticiable political question not appropriate for courts to address. Writing for the majority, Justice Felix Frankfurter argued that courts should not enter into what he called the "political thicket" of deciding what system of election districts was most "fair." In his view, to hold that the Constitution addressed this issue would require courts to

begin to make substantive judgments about proper democratic institutional design. To do so would enmesh courts in partisan democratic politics, causing judges to inevitably determine the outcome of elections. This risked that courts would come to be seen as partisan, which would undermine the authority of judicial institutions. Instead, Justice Frankfurter concluded, the recourse for citizens who thought the current system unfair was not to appeal to the courts, but to bring political pressure to bear on state governments to apportion more fairly or to persuade Congress to use its powers to oversee the design of election districts.

THE SUPREME COURT CHANGES DIRECTION

In the years after *Colegrove*, little changed. The country continued to urbanize, and both state and congressional districts remained grossly malapportioned. State legislators continued not to update the design of election districts and Congress continued not to act. In *Baker v. Carr*, 369 U.S. 186 (1962), voters once again asked the Court to intervene. Tennessee had not reapportioned its state legislature in more than sixty years and urban voters sued, alleging a violation of their right to equal protection. This time around, the Court effectively cast *Colegrove* aside and held that questions about what constituted a fair design of election districts did indeed present constitutional issues the courts could address. Though *Baker* opened the door to the Court addressing the malapportionment problem, it was clear that different justices had different views about how the Court ought to define an unconstitutional malapportionment scheme, and *Baker* did not require the Court to define a particular standard for a constitutionally fair scheme. Justice William J. Brennan Jr. wrote the Court's pathbreaking decision holding that the Court would now judge, under the equal protection clause, whether dramatically different populations of voters across election districts violated the Constitution.

At least some of the justices in *Baker* suggested that the Court might intervene in this arena only in a modest way. Thus, Justice Potter Stewart, who concurred, suggested that the Constitution did not require mathematical equality among electoral districts, as long as the courts assured there was some minimum rationality to a districting plan. Justice Tom C. Clark (1899–1977) concurred as well, offering a process-based explanation for the court's "intervention...into so delicate a field." Justice Clark concluded that the Court had to intervene because there was no realistic alternative institution to which voters could turn; as he saw it, the people of Tennessee were caught in a "legislative straight jacket" because the legislators responsible for reapportioning benefited from existing rules. In addition, Tennessee did not allow for referenda. Given this frozen political process, Justice Clark concluded, judicial intervention was warranted, but noted it may not be in a context where voters did have some political avenue through which they could pursue claims of unfair apportionment.

Justices Frankfurter and John Marshall Harlan II dissented, arguing vehemently that judicial entanglement in these issues would compromise the appearance of judicial impartiality. They argued that legitimate reasons existed to prefer apportionment schemes protecting rural voters from the sheer weight in numbers of an urban population and it was for legislatures, regardless of motive, to make that choice.

Baker was a profoundly destabilizing opinion. Within months of the decision, voters had challenged apportionment schemes in thirty-four states. *Baker* also left many questions unanswered, including the constitutional standard for apportionment and how it would apply to various levels of government.

THE CONSTITUTIONAL STANDARD FOR APPORTIONMENT

Following *Baker*, courts were left to define the constitutional rules of apportionment. Despite the strong presumption in the *Baker* concurrences to the contrary, the eventual answer, at least for congressional districts, was strict mathematical equality. In *Reynolds v. Sims*, 377 U.S. 533 (1964), the Supreme Court established the principle of one-person, one-vote, holding that the equal protection clause requires that each citizen have an "equally effective voice" in the election of state legislatures. The Court explained that the right to select legislators is a personal one: "Legislatures represent people, not trees or acres." In *Wesberry v. Sanders*, 376 U.S. 1 (1964), the Court relied on Article I, Section 2, rather than the equal protection clause, to find a seemingly similar rule for congressional apportionment.

In *Karcher v. Daggett*, 462 U.S. 725 (1983), the Court addressed the degree of flexibility of this equality rule, holding that congressional districts must have precisely the same population. The Court reaffirmed this strict requirement in *Vieth v. Jubelirer*, 541 U.S. 267 (2004), holding that variation between congressional districts of 19 percent was unconstitutional.

APPORTIONING STATE LEGISLATURES

In contrast to *Karcher* and *Vieth*, the Supreme Court has permitted a more flexible substantive standard for apportioning state legislatures. In *Mahan v. Howell*, 410 U.S. 315 (1973), the Court upheld a state-districting plan that deviated within a range of 16.4 percent. The Court reasoned that because judicial review of congressional apportionment could be based on Article I, Section 2, which explicitly describes the right of people to elect Congress, the stronger textual warrant justifies a stronger rule. The Court also gave a functional reason: Congressional districts are larger than state districts, and therefore it is both less feasible and less sensible to design congressional districts consistently with existing political boundaries.

It is generally presumed that for state apportionment, population deviations of 10 percent are permissible. In *Mahan* the Court upheld an apportionment with a variation of 16.4 percent though noted that this "approach[es] tolerable limits." However, deviations do require some neutral reason. In *Cox v. Larios*, 542 U.S. 947 (2004), the Supreme Court summarily affirmed a district-court judgment that population deviations within the traditionally safe 10 percent range were not permissible when justified only by partisan manipulation of districts.

Following *Baker*, several states defended their apportionment schemes as rational democratic choices analogous to the creation of the U.S. Senate. However, the Supreme Court rejected these arguments, holding that the bicameral model of the U.S. Senate was a unique constitutional comprise to federalism. Over the course of the 1960s, the Supreme Court held unconstitutional the design of state senates in virtually every state. In short order, it became clear that the Court would not adopt any of the more modest possibilities some justices had endorsed at the time of *Baker*.

APPORTIONMENT AND LOCAL GOVERNMENTS

Following *Baker* and *Reynolds*, it was necessary to determine how to apply the apportionment doctrine to local governments, including bodies bearing little resemblance to state legislatures. In a series of decisions, the Court held that local governmental bodies were subject to the principle of one-person, one-vote when those bodies exercised general governmental powers, but were not subject to this principle when they performed only more narrowly limited, specialized functions. For example, in *Hadley v. Junior College District*, 397 U.S. 50 (1970), the Court struck down a plan for electing school trustees from districts apportioned according to the population of school-aged children. Because the elective body in *Hadley* performed "important governmental functions" such as levying taxes, issuing bonds, making contracts, and hiring, the Court concluded the body had to be elected consistent with one-person, one-vote. Similar reasoning led the Court to hold unconstitutional the longstanding governance structure for New York City, because that structure was based not on equal population, but on guaranteeing a certain amount of representation to each of the five boroughs that make up the city (*Board of Estimate of City of New York v. Morris*, 489 U.S. 688 [1989]). But the Court has held that more specialized elective bodies, such as water reclamation districts, do not have to comply with one-person, one-vote (*Ball v. James*, 451 U.S. 355 [1981]).

EVALUATING THE APPORTIONMENT DECISIONS

The Supreme Court's apportionment decisions have been widely celebrated and accepted. It is widely recognized in the early twenty-first century that the gross malapportionments that endured until the time of *Baker* were deeply unfair, skewed American democracy, and would not likely have been changed absent Court action. But certain features of the Court's decisions remain problematic.

Most importantly, the decisions have not put an end to the kind of self-interested manipulation that was one of the motivations for the Court's involvement in the first place. In *Reynolds* the Court expressed concern that constitutional standards for apportionment had to be developed because otherwise, self-interested political actors could manipulate the design of districts for narrowly partisan or incumbent-protecting reasons. Yet

the one-vote, one-person principle, standing alone, has not proven to be a particularly strong bulwark against partisan gerrymandering. Even equally populous districts can be shaped to minimize the influence of opposing parties by concentrating supporters of one party in select districts (packing) and breaking effective blocks of voters into numerous ineffective minorities (cracking). The increase in available demographic and voting data and sophisticated computer software facilitates complex and effective partisan gerrymandering. In addition, the problem of sweetheart gerrymanders has become of increasing importance but is not blocked by the one-person, one-vote doctrine; these are gerrymanders in which incumbents of both parties agree to design districts to give each safe, noncompetitive seats. The practice of sweetheart gerrymandering contributed to congressional elections in 2002—right after the first apportionment of the new century—being the least competitive in U.S. history (Pildes 2004, p. 62).

The Supreme Court has been internally divided as it has struggled to decide whether and how to extend *Baker* to address partisan gerrymandering. In *Davis v. Bandemer*, 478 U.S. 109 (1986), the Court held that partisan vote dilution was justiciable and could amount to a constitutional violation. But the Court struggled in *Davis*, and has struggled ever since, to decide what the standard ought to be for identifying an unconstitutional partisan gerrymander. In the years since *Davis*, only one federal court, in an unusual context, found any gerrymander to be unconstitutional under *Davis*.

The Court confronted this issue again in *Vieth v. Jubelirer*, 541 U.S. 267 (2004). But again, the Court was too divided to generate a clear decision or set of standards. Four justices would have overruled *Davis* and held that partisan gerrymandering claims are not justiciable. Writing for these justices, Justice Antonin Scalia argued there is no reasonable way to adjudicate such matters. Justice Anthony Kennedy concurred in judgment, refusing to hold partisan gerrymandering nonjusticiable altogether but observing that no administrable test had yet been found. The remaining four justices would have adopted substantive standards more demanding than the essentially meaningless *Davis* standard for judging when partisan gerrymandering becomes unconstitutional.

THE BROADER SIGNIFICANCE OF THE SUPREME COURT'S APPORTIONMENT DECISIONS

Aside from the direct effects of the Supreme Court's apportionment decisions, these cases have a broader significance: They initiated a transformation of the role of the Supreme Court in overseeing the basic structures of American democracy. The apportionment decisions reflected a new judicial philosophy that the Supreme

Court had a unique role to play in ensuring that the institutions of democracy remained open to change and that the ground rules of democracy were legitimate. Once the malapportionment context compelled the Court to adopt this philosophy, the same vision led the Court to apply the Constitution more aggressively across other areas involving the basic ground rules and institutions of democracy.

One example is the right to vote. Following the Court's entry into the political thicket of apportionment, the Court also concluded it had to treat the right to vote as a fundamental constitutional right and provide aggressive protection of it. Thus two years after *Reynolds,* the Court in *Harper v. Virginia Board of Elections*, 383 U.S. 663 (1966), held that poll taxes violated the Fourteenth Amendment. *Harper* and similar cases during the 1960s redefined the equal right to vote in the United States.

A similar understanding of the Court's role was evident in the Supreme Court's decisions about vote dilution, a line of cases in which the Court accepted the argument that the voting power of a minority group could be unconstitutionally diluted when those voters were placed in legislative districts in which they would be an ineffective minority. These cases particularly drew upon the functional argument from *Reynolds* that "the right of suffrage can be denied by...dilution of the weight of a citizen's vote just as effectively as by wholly prohibiting the free exercise of the franchise." Thus, in cases in the 1970s that built upon *Baker* and *Reynolds,* such as the decision in *White v. Regester*, 412 U.S. 755 (1973), the Court found situations in which the voting power of black or Hispanic voters had been diluted unconstitutionally because of the way election structures had been designed.

The impact of the Court's involvement in apportionment was even visible in the Court's controversial decision in *Bush v. Gore*, 531 U.S. 98 (2000). In holding that a recount of Florida ballots violated the right to equal protection, the Court reasoned that because no recount could be conducted consistently, it would necessarily treat votes cast in different places differently. Citing *Reynolds* and *Harper,* the Court explained that "the right of suffrage can be denied by a debasement or dilution of the weight of a citizen's vote just as effectively as by wholly prohibiting the free exercise of the franchise" and that a state may therefore not by "arbitrary and disparate treatment, value one person's vote over that of another." Thus, the road from *Baker* led eventually to the Court's entanglement in the resolution of a disputed presidential election, which has in turn led some to ask whether the Court's 2000 election decision is Justice Frankfurter's revenge for the Court having entered the political thicket.

SEE ALSO *Baker v. Carr, 369 U.S. 186 (1962); Davis v. Bandemer, 478 U.S. 109 (1986); Gerrymandering;* *Harper v. Virginia Board of Elections, 383 U.S. 663 (1966); Political Question Doctrine; Reynolds v. Sims, 377 U.S. 533 (1964); Vieth v. Jubelirer, 541 U.S. 267 (2004)*

BIBLIOGRAPHY

Ansolabehere, Stephen, and James Snyder, Jr. 2008. *The End of Inequality: One Person, One Vote, and the Transformation of American Politics*. New York: Norton.

Briffault, Richard. 1993. "Who Rules at Home? One Person/One Vote and Local Governments." *University of Chicago Law Review* 60(2): 339–424.

Charles, Guy-Uriel E. 2002. "Constitutional Pluralism and Democratic Politics: Reflections on the Interpretive Approach of *Baker v. Carr*." *North Carolina Law Review* 80(4): 1103–1163.

Dixon, Robert G., Jr. 1968. *Democratic Representation: Reapportionment in Law and Politics*. New York: Oxford University Press.

Ely, John Hart. 1980. *Democracy and Distrust: A Theory of Judicial Review*. Cambridge: Harvard University Press.

Issacharoff, Samuel; Pamela S. Karlan; and Richard H. Pildes. 2007. *The Law of Democracy: Legal Structure of the Political Process*. 3rd edition. New York: Foundation Press.

Jacobson, Gary C. 2003. "Terror, Terrain, and Turnout: Explaining the 2002 Midterm Elections." *Political Science Quarterly* 118(1): 1–22.

Lewis, Anthony. 1958. "Legislative Apportionment and the Federal Courts." *Harvard Law Review* 71(6): 1057–1098.

McConnell, Michael W. 2000. "The Redistricting Cases: Original Mistakes and Current Consequences." *Harvard Journal of Law and Public Policy*. 24(1): 103–117.

Persily, Nathaniel; Thad Kousser; and Patrick Egan. 2002. "The Complicated Impact of One Person, One Vote on Political Competition and Representation." *North Carolina Law Review* 80(4): 1299–1352.

Pildes, Richard H. 2004. "The Constitutionalization of Democratic Politics." *Harvard Law Review* 118(1): 28–154.

Schattschneider, E. E. 1962. "Urbanization and Reapportionment." *Yale Law Journal* 72(1): 7–12.

Richard H. Pildes

ARTICLE I

"In republican government, the legislative authority necessarily predominates." With this assertion in *Federalist* No. 51 of the *Federalist Papers*, James Madison (1751–1836) describes the conceptual foundation of Article I of the U.S. Constitution. Although the powers of the federal government were envisioned to be "separate and distinct" in their instantiation, the delicate balancing of these powers must, of necessity, respect the notion that the power to make law is of extreme importance. The Court, in the words of Alexander Hamilton (c. 1755–1804) in *Federalist* No. 78 of the *Federalist Papers*, was envisioned to be the "least dangerous branch" of the federal government. In many Supreme Court cases, it has been called upon to review congressional actions to ensure that constitutional muster was passed.

THE TEN SECTIONS

The legislative power of the federal government is vested in the Congress of the United States of America. Article I, Section 1 of the Constitution provides that "all legislative power herein granted shall be vested in a Congress of the United States, which shall consist of a Senate and House of Representatives." Article I, Section 2 outlines the qualifications for members of the House of Representatives. This Article describes the method by which representatives and direct taxes were to be calculated, including a provision that excludes "Indians not taxed" and includes only "three fifths of all other persons" in reference to slaves. It continues with a provision by which the governor of a state is empowered to issue writs of election in the event of a vacancy in the House of Representatives. In addition, the House must select "their Speaker and other Officers," and the Article assigns to the House the "sole Power of Impeachment."

Section 3 outlines the qualification for members of the Senate, and specifies that each state legislature is to select two senators for terms of six years each. Senators, once elected, were to be divided into three classes, with the terms of each class expiring in a manner designed to permit the election of one-third of the total number every second year. This section specifies that the vice president of the United States is to serve as the president of the Senate, but would not vote unless required to do so in order to break a tie. In addition, the Senate will choose a president pro tempore and other officers. The "sole Power to try all Impeachments" is conferred upon the Senate and procedures for such trials are specified, as are punishments in the event of conviction.

Section 4 delegates to the legislature of each state the authority to set the "Times, Places and Manner" for the election of members of Congress. Section 5 requires that Congress meet at least once per year and contains provisions governing the conduct of its daily affairs. Further, Congress is required to "keep a Journal of its Proceedings" (the *Congressional Record*) and concludes with requirements concerning adjournment.

Section 6 requires that members of Congress be compensated for their service. It also conveys upon these members immunity from arrest while traveling to and from session, except in cases of treason, felony, or breach of the peace. Similarly, immunity will apply to "any Speech or Debate in either House" and to protect members from liability (known as the speech and debate clause.) This section concludes with a prohibition against a member of Congress serving simultaneously as a civil servant.

Section 7 sets forth the process by which a bill becomes a law. This section specifies the procedures Congress must employ as both the House and Senate contemplate a piece of legislation. It stipulates, among other terms and conditions, that before a bill can become a law it must be "presented to the President of the United States" (the presentment clause).

Section 8 outlines the exclusive legislative powers of the federal government. Subsections 1 through 17 confer to Congress the affirmative powers to, among others: "borrow money on the credit of the United States," "establish an uniform Rule of Naturalization, and uniform Laws on the Subject of Bankruptcies," "establish Post Offices and Post Roads," "promote the Progress of Science and useful arts, by securing for limited Times to Authors and Inventors the exclusive Right to their respective Writings and Discoveries" (copyright and patent protection), and "provide and maintain a navy." In Section 18 Congress is authorized to "make all Laws which shall be necessary and proper for carrying into Execution the foregoing powers" (necessary and proper [or elastic] clause).

Section 9 contains specific limitations on the power of Congress. Subsection 1 is a prohibition of congressional action against the slave trade and provides for a safe harbor for slavery, insulating it from federal action prior to 1808. The section also contains, among other provisions, prohibitions against suspension of the writ of habeas corpus, bills of attainder and ex post facto laws, and the granting of titles of nobility.

Section 10 contains a number of provisions restricting the authority of the states, and includes a number of prohibited actions, including—but not limited to—entering into treaties, coining money, and passing laws impairing the "Obligation of Contracts" (the contract clause).

ARTICLE I LITIGATION

The legislatives powers of the federal government have been categorized as fourfold: enumerated and implied, amendment-enforcing, inherent, and treaty (Ducat 2004, pp. 105–127). Although the Court has been called upon many times to interpret Article I, the subject matter of the litigation has evolved over time. In early cases, such as *M'Culloch v. Maryland*, 17 U.S. 316 (1819), the Court held that Congress had the power to incorporate a bank. While conceding that this power was not enumerated in the Constitution, the court concluded that authority to do so was based upon the necessary and proper clause of

Article I. Some provisions of Article I, such as the presentment clause and speech and debate clause, have been the subject matter of Supreme Court review. The sections that follow offer a discussion of the highlights of some of the key areas of Article I that have been more frequently reviewed by the Court.

The Contract Clause The contract clause and its prohibition against a state passing "any . . . law impairing the obligation of contracts," was the source of several early cases. In *Fletcher v. Peck*, 10 U.S. 87 (1810), the Court reviewed the invalidation of a land grant scheme by the legislature of Georgia. Two private citizens were involved in litigation to determine their relative rights and obligations as parties to a land transfer prior to the invalidation of the scheme. The Court held:

> It is then, the unanimous opinion of the court, that, in this case, the estate having passed into the hands of a purchaser for a valuable consideration, without notice, the state of Georgia was restrained, either by general principles which are common to our free institution, or by the particular provisions of the constitution of the United States, from passing a law whereby the estate of the plaintiff in the premises so purchased could be constitutionally and legally impaired and rendered null and void.

The Commerce Clause Generally The commerce clause and questions of its proper interpretation have provided the basis for much litigation and interpretation by the Court. During the politically chaotic years of the New Deal, the Supreme Court tended to interpret the provisions of the commerce clause in a rather circumspect manner. For example, in *Schechter Poultry Corp. v. United States*, 295 U.S. 495 (1935) and *Carter v. Carter Coal*, 298 U.S. 238 (1936), the Court held that sections of both the National Industrial Recovery Act of 1933 and of the Bituminous Coal Conservation Act of 1935 were unconstitutional in that they exceeded the grant of congressional authority contained in the commerce clause.

The Commerce Clause and Civil Rights In the years after the Civil War (1861–1865), the Court ruled in the *Civil Rights Cases*, 109 U.S. 3 (1883) that the Thirteenth and Fourteenth Amendments did not provide recourse to plaintiffs who complained of private, racial discrimination. However, in *Heart of Atlanta Motel v. United States*, 379 U.S. 241 (1964) and *Katzenbach v. McClung*, 379 U.S. 294 (1964), the Court upheld federal civil rights legislation by asserting that the commerce clause allowed Congress to prohibit racial discrimination by hotels and restaurants as impermissible burdens on interstate commerce. The Court's "expanding definition of the term

'interstate commerce' has . . . become one of the most important and frequently used of the national government's enumerated powers" (Ducat 2004, p. 364). After describing congressional hearings in which African Americans testified about discriminatory treatment they received while traveling in interstate commerce, Justice Tom C. Clark (1899–1977) wrote for the Court in *Katzenbach*:

> Here . . . Congress has determined for itself that refusals of service to Negroes have imposed burdens both upon the interstate flow of food and upon the movement of products generally. Of course, the mere fact that Congress has said when particular activity shall be deemed to affect commerce does not preclude further examination by this Court. But where we find that the legislators, in light of the facts and testimony before them, have a rational basis for finding a chosen regulatory scheme necessary to the protection of commerce, our investigation is at an end. The only remaining question—one answered in the affirmative by the court below—is whether the particular restaurant either serves or offers to serve interstate travelers or serves food a substantial portion of which has moved in interstate commerce.

Habeas Corpus Provision In *Harris v. Nelson*, 394 U.S. 286 (1969), the Supreme Court describes the writ of habeas corpus as follows:

> The writ of habeas corpus is the fundamental instrument for safeguarding individual freedom against arbitrary and lawless state action. Its preeminent role is recognized by the admonition in the Constitution that: "The Privilege of the Writ of Habeas Corpus shall not be suspended. . . ." (U.S. Const., Art. I, § 9, cl. 2). The scope and flexibility of the writ—its capacity to reach all manner of illegal detention—its ability to cut through barriers of form and procedural mazes— have always been emphasized and jealously guarded by court and lawmakers. The very nature of the writ demands that it be administered with the initiative and flexibility essential to insure that miscarriages of justice within its reach are surfaced and corrected.

In the wake of the September 11, 2001, terrorist attacks on the United States, the Supreme Court has been called upon to review the constitutionality of several federal statutes designed to safeguard the country against future attacks. One question is whether congressional legislation promulgated in the wake of the terrorist attacks violates the habeas corpus provisions of Article 1, Section 9, clause 2. In one such case, *Hamdan v. Rumsfeld*, 126 S. Ct. 2749 (2006), the Court held that the statute in question did not deprive the court of jurisdiction to review the petitioner's application for a writ. There are a number of so-called enemy combatant and related cases that will present the Court with additional opportunities to exercise judicial review of this and other constitutional provisions.

SEE ALSO *Article I Courts; Civil Rights Cases, 109 U.S. 3 (1883); Commerce Clause; Constitution of the United States; Fletcher v. Peck, 10 U.S. 87 (1810); Habeas Corpus; M'Culloch v. Maryland, 17 U.S. 316 (1819)*

BIBLIOGRAPHY

Authorization for Use of Military Force in Response to the 9/11 Attacks, Pub. L. No. 107-40, § 2 (a), 115 Stat. 224.

Detainee Treatment Act of 2005, Pub. L. No. 109-148, Div. A. Tit. X, 119 Stat. 2739.

Ducat, Craig R. 2004. *Constitutional Interpretation*. 8th edition. Belmont, CA: Thomson/West.

Gloria A. Whittico

ARTICLE I COURTS

Throughout its history, the Supreme Court has been called upon to review the constitutionality of courts that are established outside of the judiciary created by Article III of the Constitution. Known synonymously as *Article I courts* or *legislative courts*, these bodies can hear disputes that are outside of the scope of Article III, which limits the federal judicial power to cases and controversies arising under the Constitution, laws, and treatises of the United States, among other cases. The Court developed a legislative court doctrine in a series of cases in the nineteenth and twentieth centuries, though few cases since 1982 have further refined the rules governing Article I courts.

Article III vests the judicial power of the United States "in one Supreme Court, and in such inferior Courts as the Congress may from time to time ordain and establish." The Constitution further provides that federal judges enjoy life tenure during good behavior. Moreover, salaries of federal judges may not be diminished during their terms in office. Under these provisions, federal judges are not subjected to the sort of political pressure that legislators face, and the framers believed that these protections were necessary to ensure an independent judiciary. Courts created under Article III are known as *constitutional courts* and may only hear cases as permitted by Article III. Thus, for instance, these courts cannot issue advisory opinions on behalf of the executive branch officer or the legislature.

Article I, section eight, clause nine of the Constitution empowers Congress "to constitution Tribunals inferior to the supreme Court." Courts created under Article I are more similar to administrative agencies because they are created through a delegation of legislative authority rather than empowered with the authority of the federal judiciary. Judges on these courts do not enjoy life tenure or protection against salary diminution, and statutes creating these tribunals usually specify a fixed duration for the judges' terms. Moreover, many of these courts issue advisory opinions that cannot be issued by a constitutional court. Examples of Article I courts include the U.S. Tax Court, federal bankruptcy courts, courts martial, and courts of the various U.S. territories.

The United States has created legislative courts throughout its history. Courts established in the territories led to the first significant Supreme Court cases regarding these tribunals. In *American Insurance Co. v. 356 Bales of Cotton*, 26 U.S. 511 (1828) (also referred to as *American Insurance Co. v. Canter*), the Court reviewed a dispute that arose from a salvage (wreckers) court in the territory of Florida. This tribunal was a court inferior to superior courts established by Congress, and judges in the wreckers court were appointed on a temporary basis and were paid a fee based the value of the salvage awarded at judicial sales held by the court. David Canter bought 356 bales of cotton at this sale and shipped the cotton to Charleston, South Carolina. American Insurance Company, which had insured the owners of the cargo, brought suit in Charleston, arguing that Canter did not have good title to the cotton. According to the insurance company, the sale of cargo was an admiralty matter that should have been heard by a court created by Congress.

In an opinion by Chief Justice John Marshall, the Court disagreed and first employed use of the term legislative court:

> These courts . . . are not Constitutional courts, in which the judicial power conferred by the Constitution on the general government can be deposited. They are incapable of receiving it. They are legislative courts, created in virtue of that clause which enables Congress to make all needful rules and regulations, respecting the territory belonging to the United States. The jurisdiction with which they are invested, is not a part of that judicial power which is defined in the 3d article of the Constitution, bus is conferred by Congress, in the execution of those general powers which that body possesses over the territories of the United States.

A practical result of this decision was that it allowed Congress to create territorial courts outside of the purview of Article III, meaning that these judges could be removed or have their salaries reduced during their terms in office.

For nearly a century, the legislative court doctrine articulated by Chief Justice Marshall was limited mostly to territorial courts. The Court began to expand the concept of this type of court in 1923, when it refused to hear an appeal from the Court of Appeals for the District of Columbia. In *Keller v. Potomac Electric Power Co.*, 261 U.S. 428 (1923), the Court ruled that it could not review a case involving a dispute over utility rates because it was a matter that was not judicial in nature. According to the Court, the D.C. Court of Appeals was created pursuant to Congress's power under Article I, section eight (instead of Article III) and was thus able to assume legislative or administrative duties, such as the determination regarding these rates. Six years later, in *Ex parte Bakelite Corporation*, 279 U.S. 438 (1929), the Court determined that the Court of Customs Appeals was an Article I court. This tribunal had been given power to review findings from the Tariff Commission on matters that were ultimately decided by the president. The party that brought an action before the Tariff Commission argued that the Court of Custom Appeals lacked the power to review this decision because the enabling statute authorized the court to prepare what effectively amounted to an advisory opinion, which Article III courts cannot issue. The Supreme Court rejected this argument, holding that Congress may give judicial or nonjudicial power to this type of legislative court.

In the years that followed, the Court struggled with the issue of what constituted a legislative court, with many of these cases featuring highly splintered opinions. In *Glidden Co. v. Zdanok*, 370 U.S. 530 (1962), the Court reviewed two cases where judges from one court could be assigned to sit on another court. In these two cases, judges from the Court of Customs and Patent Appeals and the Court of Claims were assigned, respectively, to sit on the District Court for the District of Columbia and the U.S. Court of Appeals for the Second Circuit. The Court ruled that each of the courts involved was a constitutional court and that the assignment of these judges to the different courts was constitutional under Article III. The opinions, however, were sharply divided about why the decision was reached, and no single test emerged that could be used to answer it.

The last of the most significant cases involving legislative courts was likewise fractured. The Court in *Northern Pipeline Construction Co. v. Marathon Pipe Line Co.*, 458 U.S. 50 (1982) ruled that bankruptcy courts created under the Bankruptcy Act of 1978 did not have the power to hear a state law claim based on breach of contract and breach of warranty. Bankruptcy courts under the act were clearly Article I courts, for the bankruptcy judges were limited to fourteen-year terms and they were not protected from a reduction in salary. A plurality opinion by Justice William J. Brennan Jr. identified three narrow categories where a legislative court could be created: (1) as tribunals in U.S. territories and possessions; (2) as military courts; and (3) as a means for resolving disputes between the United States and a private citizen, referred to as public rights matters. Brennan concluded that the bankruptcy courts did not fall within any of these exceptions and so the power of these courts was too broad. Other opinions rejected this rationale, with a concurrence by Justice William Rehnquist noting that this area of law was fraught "with its frequently arcane distinctions and confusing precedents." No case since *Northern Pipeline* has resolved the questions surrounding Article I and Article III courts.

SEE ALSO *Article I; Constitution of the United States*

BIBLIOGRAPHY

Chemerinsky, Erwin. 2007. *Federal Jurisdiction*. 5th edition. New York, NY: Aspen Publishers.

Rotunda, Ronald D., and John E. Nowak. 1999. *Treatise on Constitutional Law: Substance and Procedure*. 3rd edition. St. Paul, MN: West Group.

Wright, Charles Alan, and Mary Kay Kane. 2002. *Law of Federal Courts*. 6th edition. St. Paul, MN: West Group.

Matthew C. Cordon

ARTICLE II

Article II of the U.S. Constitution vests "the executive power ... in a President of the United States of America," sets out the manner of election, and assigns to the president relatively few specific powers, each of which has been the subject of both litigation and political struggle. While the Court has been reluctant to explicitly define the boundaries of the executive power, Court rulings have played a decisive role in everything from the appointment and removal power to the war and treaty powers, and, perhaps most dramatically, even in determining the outcome of presidential elections.

THE POWER TO APPOINT AND REMOVE

Article II explicitly grants the president the power to appoint "officers of the United States," subject to the advice and consent of the Senate, but says nothing about their removal, an issue that became increasingly contentious as Congress and the president struggled for power to control the growing administrative state.

Proponents of a strong executive champion the Court's interpretation in *Myers v. United States*, 272 U.S. 52 (1926), in which Chief Justice William Howard Taft (1857–1930) argued that the assignment of "the executive power" to the president, combined with the requirement that he or she "take care that the Laws be faithfully executed" (Art. II, Sec. 3), give the president the power to remove any executive official of any rank, with or without cause. To require congressional approval for removals, Taft noted, "would make it impossible for the President, in case of political or other differences with the Senate or Congress, to take care that the laws be faithfully executed."

Taft's opinion was met by an equally strong dissent from Justice Louis Brandeis (1856–1941). Noting that Congress alone creates inferior statutory offices, Brandeis argued that the power to remove these officers, "like the power of appointment to them, comes immediately from Congress."

While the *Myers* case involved the removal of a postmaster, the growing administrative state increasingly included independent regulatory agencies as well. The Court would revisit *Myers* nine years later when President Franklin Roosevelt (1882–1945) tried to fire a recalcitrant official in the Federal Trade Commission who had been placed there by Roosevelt's predecessor. In *Humphrey's Executor v. United States*, 295 US 602 (1935), the Court insisted that there was a distinction between officers whose functions were of a legislative or judicial quality, and those whose functions were largely or exclusively executive in character. Unlike the postmaster in *Myers*, here the Federal Trade Commissioner played a direct role in carrying out legislative policy in accord with standards set by Congress. Removal in these cases would require explicit statutory authority; any other result would essentially place these "independent" agencies under executive control.

The emphasis on function was challenged when the post-Watergate Congress created the Office of the Independent Counsel as part of the Ethics in Government Act in 1978. Criminal prosecution is unquestionably an executive function, and yet Watergate taught the dangers of leaving the prosecution of executive malfeasance in the hands of someone who could be fired by the president. Thus Congress established an office that would perform an executive function, but would not answer to the executive—nor would they answer to either of the other branches. In upholding this novel arrangement in *Morrison v. Olson*, 487 U.S. 654 (1988), Chief Justice William Rehnquist (1924–2005) ruled that the president's power to remove an official cannot be made to turn on whether or not that official is a "purely executive" one. The key question was whether another branch was seeking to control or impede "the President's ability to perform his constitutional duty," namely, to faithfully execute the laws. The president's removal power, then, remains a work in progress.

EXECUTIVE PRIVILEGE AND IMMUNITY

Although Article II says nothing of executive privilege or immunity, as early as 1803, Chief Justice John Marshall (1755–1835) noted that the president "is invested with certain important political powers, in the exercise of which he is to use his own discretion, and is accountable only to his country in his political character, and to his own conscience" in *Marbury v. Madison*, 5 U.S. 137. But when executive discretion collides with the rights of criminal defendants and litigants in legitimate civil suits, a problem arises—a problem that flared in the wake of the Watergate scandal, catalyzed the impeachment case against President Bill Clinton, and reached new prominence in the last years of the George W. Bush administration.

As Louis Fisher (2003) comprehensively charts, in the early years of the Republic, the question of executive privilege was primarily resolved in struggles between Congress and the president, with the courts playing no significant role, as was the case when George Washington (1732–1799) refused to provide the House with documents concerning the Jay Treaty (1794) (pp. 33–39). Presidents Andrew Jackson (1767–1845) and Ulysses S. Grant (1822–1885) also resisted cooperation with congressional investigations that were seen as a prelude to impeachment efforts, and the Court did nothing to compel their assistance. This changed, dramatically, in the wake of Watergate.

In *United States v. Nixon*, 418 U.S. 683 (1974), a unanimous Supreme Court ordered President Richard Nixon (1913–1994) to produce documents and tape recordings that had been subpoenaed as part of a criminal prosecution by Watergate special prosecutor, Archibald Cox (1912–2004). Echoing *Marbury*, the Court acknowledged that the nature of the American system of separated powers and the need for "the protection of the confidentiality of Presidential communications" both call for "great deference from the courts." There is, the Court ruled, "a presumptive privilege for Presidential communications." However, the Court added, "neither the doctrine of separation of powers, nor the need for confidentiality of high-level communications, without more, can sustain an absolute, unqualified Presidential privilege of immunity from judicial process under all circumstances." The legitimate needs of the judicial process, the Court ruled in this case, outweigh presidential privilege. Nixon delivered the tapes and resigned less than three weeks later.

Other Nixon-era litigation forced the Court to consider claims of presidential immunity from civil suit. In *Nixon v. Fitzgerald*, 457 U.S. 731 (1982), a divided Court held five-to-four that a president "is entitled to absolute immunity from damages liability predicated on his official acts." The majority opinion of Justice Lewis F. Powell, Jr. (1907–1998) declared that the president must make "the most sensitive and far-reaching decisions entrusted to any official under our constitutional system" and could not be open to the distraction of civil litigation as long as the contested actions were within the "outer perimeter" of his official duties.

President Bill Clinton contended that Powell's logic should extend to shield a president from civil suits concerning unofficial conduct, at least during the president's time in office. But in *Clinton v. Jones*, 520 U.S. 681 (1997), a unanimous Court allowed Paula Jones's suit against President Clinton to continue, rejecting Clinton's argument that exposure to civil suits could hamper the performance of his official duties.

The George W. Bush administration will long be remembered for its aggressive claims and defense of executive privilege, executive immunity, and even executive prerogative. Vice President Richard Cheney chaired a series of meetings on energy policy in the early weeks of the new Bush administration in 2001. Rebuffed in its efforts to obtain information about the private parties with whom the task force met, the General Accounting Office (GAO) took the extraordinary step of filing suit. Although a federal district court dismissed the suit, the judge indicated that the result might have been different if Congress had actually issued a formal subpoena for the information. Although the GAO declined to appeal, a separate action was filed by the Sierra Club and the conservative Judicial Watch organization, alleging that the task force was a federal advisory committee and therefore required to open its files to the public. In *Cheney v. U.S. District Court*, 542 U.S. 367 (2004), the Supreme Court in a seven-to-two decision refused to rule on the administration's claims that privacy was implicitly required by Article II, instead sending the case back to the lower courts.

This turned out to be but the opening salvo in the Bush administration's attempt to expand the scope of executive power. Among other significant efforts, the Bush administration dramatically increased the frequency and reach of "signing statements"—statements issued in tandem with the president's signature on congressionally authorized statutes. While certainly not the first to issue such statements, Bush issued them in unprecedented number. By his sixth year in office, the president had attached signing statements to more than 750 laws, asserting the authority to set aside laws passed by Congress if they were to conflict with his interpretation of the powers and responsibilities of the executive branch.

In a statement attached to the renewal of the Patriot Act in 2006, for example, Bush wrote that the executive branch would construe the provisions of the law "in a manner consistent with the President's constitutional authority" and would "withhold information the disclosure of which could impair foreign relations, national security, the deliberative processes of the Executive or the performance of the Executive's constitutional duties." In another signing statement concerning the Detainee Treatment Act of 2005, which limits the use of torture, President Bush wrote that he would interpret the act in a manner "consistent with the constitutional limitations on the judicial power"—suggesting the possibility that he might reject a Supreme Court order if, in his view, it conflicted with his interpretation of the president's constitutional authority, leaving open the distinct possibility of a direct clash not only with Congress, but with the judiciary as well.

WAR, EMERGENCIES, AND THE TREATY POWER

Political scientist Aaron Wildavsky (1930–1993) famously argued that there are "two presidencies," one for domestic affairs and one for foreign and defense policy (1966, pp. 7–14). The claim was that Congress and the Courts were far more deferential to executive claims for power in foreign affairs. More deferential, perhaps, but the Supreme Court has played a significant role in defining and shaping executive power in the context of foreign affairs, treaty negotiations, wars, and national emergencies as well.

Article II assigns the president the power to serve as "Commander-in-Chief of the Army and Navy" and to "take care that the laws be faithfully executed." It provides as well that the president has the power "by and with the Advice and Consent of the Senate, to make Treaties, provided two thirds of the Senators present concur." This does not, of course, assign the president unlimited authority in foreign affairs. There are political and institutional reasons why Congress and the courts tend to be more deferential in this arena, but over the past two centuries, the Court has frequently intervened not only to police the separation of powers, but to protect individual liberties against infringement even in war and emergencies.

In a 1918 ruling (*Oetjen v. Central Leather Co.*, 246 U.S. 297), the Court offered a standing invitation to future jurists to leave any and all foreign policy questions to the political branches. Writing for the majority, Justice John Clarke (1857–1945) held that: "The conduct of the foreign relations of our government is committed by the Constitution to the Executive and Legislative— 'the political'—Departments of the Government, and the propriety of what may be done in the exercise of this political power is not subject to judicial inquiry or decision." But this attempt to remove the courts from foreign policy was short-lived. In his famous opinion in the 1936 case of *United States v. Curtiss-Wright Export Corp.*, 299 U.S. 304, Justice George Sutherland (1862– 1942) insisted that the Constitution does define enforceable limits even in the arena of foreign affairs. But this is an often-misunderstood case: At issue was the limits of the power of the national government—Congress and the president, acting together—in time of war. And the answer was that the only fundamental limits were those explicitly identified in the Constitution. What could the president do independently? And what might the president be able to do even in the face of congressional resistance?

These questions were not directly addressed until 1952 when President Harry S. Truman (1884–1972) ordered the government to seize and operate the nation's steel mills in the midst of the Korean War (1950–1953) to avoid a shutdown of military production in the event of a threatened labor strike. There was no doubt among those in the Court's majority in *Youngstown Sheet and Tube v. Sawyer*, 343 U.S. 579 (1952) that the national government was constitutionally able to seize the nation's steel mills. But this was in no way the same as saying that the president could do it: The "fact that power exists in Government," Felix Frankfurter (1882–1965) wrote, "does not vest it in the President." Whether or not Congress had chosen wisely or well, it had acted and it had authorized the president to deal with industrial conflict without the power to seize property. Where Congress "has laid down specific procedures to deal with the type of crisis confronting the president," Justice Clark wrote, "he must follow those procedures in meeting the crisis."

Justice Robert Jackson (1892–1954), in a concurrence, argued that this was a case where the president acted against the explicit or implied will of Congress, and therefore the president could prevail in Court only if he could demonstrate that the power he had exercised belonged solely to the executive—a claim the Court did not find convincing in this case. Jackson's concurrence asserted that there were three categories of presidential action: cases where the president acts in concert with Congress; those where the president acts against the express will of Congress; and those that exist in what he called a "zone of twilight" where constitutional ambiguity left it unclear which branch might prevail. In 1952, the Court indicated that in this zone of twilight the benefit of the doubt would lean toward Congress: for the president to prevail would require some indication of congressional acquiescence or approval. Since the early years of the Reagan administration, however, this default assumption has shifted in the executive's direction.

By 1981, the Court seemed prepared to tolerate broad presidential discretion in areas where Congress had not explicitly foreclosed executive action. Asked to rule on the executive agreements reached with Iran over the hostage release in 1981, Justice William Rehnquist's majority opinion in *Dames & Moore v. Regan*, 453 U.S. 654 held that though the president was not acting under any authority explicitly and directly granted by an act of Congress, there was no explicit congressional barrier in his way. To demand congressional approval from existing statutes, Rehnquist argued, was unrealistic: The courts could not expect Congress to "anticipate and legislate with regard to every possible action the president may find it necessary to take or every possible situation in which he might act."

Although *Dames & Moore* signaled a Court more inclined to give the executive the benefit of the doubt, the justices remain willing to confront presidential power, particularly where fundamental individual liberties are involved. In three cases stemming from military action following the destruction of the World Trade Center in New York on September 11, 2001, the Court renewed its traditional commitment to enforcing rights even in matters concerning foreign affairs and war. In 2004, the Court decided that foreign nationals being held at Guantánamo Bay, Cuba, were entitled to challenge their detentions in court. The same year, in *Hamdi v. Rumsfeld*, 542 U.S. 507, eight of the nine justices agreed that the executive does not have the authority to detain an American citizen indefinitely, and must afford the detainee some measure of due process before an impartial court. The existence of a congressional authorization for the use of military force was not, the Court's plurality agreed, sufficient to override due process guarantees.

In addition in 2006, the Court rejected a system of military commissions established by the George W. Bush administration to try the Guantánamo detainees (*Hamdan v. Rumsfeld*, 126 S. Ct. 2749). The president had claimed that executive power was at its apex because Congress had authorized the use of military force in Afghanistan and Iraq. But the Court disagreed, with Justice Stephen Breyer arguing that Congress "has not issued the Executive a 'blank check'" and that, in fact, Congress had "denied the President the legislative authority to create military commissions of the kind at issue here." Justice Anthony Kennedy, who provided the crucial fifth vote for the majority, argued that procedural violations in the operation of the commissions made this "a case of conflict between Presidential and congressional action—a case within Justice Jackson's third category, not the second or first."

In response, the administration pressed Congress for new legislation that would strip the Court's jurisdiction to hear similar cases in the future and formally authorize military commissions for Guantánamo detainees. The result was the Military Commissions Act of 2006. New challenges to this act were expected, particularly in light of Justice Sandra Day O'Connor's retirement in 2006 and her replacement by Samuel Alito.

The Court remains reluctant, but not unwilling, to intervene in other disputes involving Article II. Its most dramatic intervention may have come in the confusing aftermath of the 2000 presidential election when, in a bitterly divided set of rulings, the justices put an end to the contested vote-count in Florida in *Bush v. Gore*, 531

U.S. 98. Arguing that the Court was obliged to step in where a continuing standoff and struggle for power posed a dire threat to the authority and legitimacy of the national political system, the Court's ruling effectively assured that George W. Bush would become the forty-third president of the United States.

Thus the Court will intervene where the justices believe they must, particularly in cases involving individual rights and in questions involving interbranch struggles. In the separation-of-powers area, however, the Court continues to be wary of involvement unless there is an explicit confrontation that can be resolved only by the Court. This position was well articulated in a 1979 dispute over whether the president could terminate the provisions of a defense treaty with the Republic of Taiwan without consulting the Senate, which had given its advice and consent to the original treaty. In *Goldwater v. Carter*, 444 U.S. 996 (1979), Justice Powell insisted that "a dispute between Congress and the President is not ready for judicial review unless and until each branch has taken action asserting its constitutional authority." As Powell concluded, "if the Congress chooses not to confront the President, it is not our task to do so."

SEE ALSO *Bush v. Gore, 531 U.S. 98 (2000); Clinton v. Jones, 520 U.S. 681 (1997); Constitution of the United States; Dames & Moore v. Regan, 453 U.S. 654 (1981); Hamdan v. Rumsfeld, 548 U.S. 557 (2006); Hamdi v. Rumsfeld, 542 U.S. 507 (2004); Humphrey's Executor v. United States, 295 U.S. 602 (1935); Marbury v. Madison, 5 U.S. 137 (1803); Morrison v. Olson, 487 U.S. 654 (1988)*

BIBLIOGRAPHY

Fisher, Louis. 2003. *The Politics of Executive Privilege.* Durham, NC: Carolina Academic Press.

Fisher, Louis. 2007. *Constitutional Conflicts Between Congress and the President.* 5th edition. Lawrence: University Press of Kansas.

Silverstein, Gordon. 1997. *Imbalance of Powers: Constitutional Interpretation and the Making of American Foreign Policy.* New York: Oxford University Press.

Wildavsky, Aaron. 1966. "The Two Presidencies." *Trans-Action* (4): 7–14.

Gordon Silverstein

ARTICLE III

Article III of the Constitution establishes the judicial power of the United States. The adoption of Article III allowed the United States to create one of the most unique and powerful judiciaries in history, though the Article's meaning has sparked controversy since the time that it was first ratified. Article III establishes the central tenets of the federal judicial system, including lifetime tenure for judges, and the extension of judicial power to cases and controversies as provided in the text. However, most scholars and other commentators agree that the text cannot be interpreted literally. Robert N. Clinton (1984) stated that the "meaning of the judicial article has perplexed practitioners, judges, and scholars since its inception and has spawned a significant debate concerning the scope of congressional control over federal court jurisdiction" (p. 742). In addition to provisions related to judicial power, Article III also requires that criminal trials be heard by juries and prescribes rules regarding treason against the United States.

HISTORICAL BACKGROUND OF ARTICLE III

The Articles of Confederation contained nothing similar to what became Article III of the Constitution. The only court established in the Articles of Confederation was an admiralty prize court called the Court of Appeals in Cases of Capture in Article IX, a predecessor of which existed prior to the approval of the Articles. Article IX also provided that "the United States in Congress assembled, shall have the sole and exclusive right and power of ... appointing courts for the trial of piracies and felonies committed on the high seas; and establishing courts for receiving and determining finally appeals in all cases of captures." Article IX, moreover, provided that the Confederation Congress served as the "last resort on appeal" for certain controversies, including disputes related to the boundaries or jurisdiction of two or more states.

After six years of experience with the Articles of Confederation, the general consensus of the founders of the Constitution was that a national judiciary must be established. Those involved with drafting the Constitution agreed generally that an independent judiciary was necessary for a number of reasons, especially for instances where state courts would be incapable of protecting interests due to the potential for bias. Numerous proposals emerged for this new judiciary, though the specific plans were debated only periodically. The Virginia Plan introduced by Edmund Randolph (1753–1813) at the Philadelphia Convention in May 1787 specified that the federal judiciary would consist of "one or more supreme tribunals," which suggests that the proposal contemplated dividing the judicial power by subject matter rather than by territory (Claus 2007, p. 68). The plan also established the jurisdiction of the federal courts and did not include a provision that allowed Congress to determine the jurisdiction of the federal judiciary.

Numerous other plans also emerged during the Philadelphia Convention. According to Clinton (1984),

"All of the plans for new national government called for the establishment of an independent national judiciary consisting of at least one supreme court with constitutionally established jurisdiction and, in some plans, inferior federal courts" (p. 761). The specific language in Article III that was eventually adopted vested the judicial power of the United States "in one supreme Court, and in such inferior Courts as the Congress may from time to time ordain and establish." The creation of lower federal courts gave rise to considerable debate by those who thought that these courts were unnecessary. Some critics argued that state courts were sufficient to protect national interests and that federal courts would intrude upon state sovereignty. Other arguments noted that these federal courts would be unnecessarily costly. Some proposals were introduced that would simply allow a national supreme court to hear appeals from the state courts. Proponents of the federal system countered that a supreme court would have limited capacity to hear these appeals, thus rendering protection of federal interest by state courts to be inadequate. As argued by James Madison (1751–1836), "Confidence cannot be put in the State Tribunals as guardians of the National authority and interests" (Chemerinsky 2007, p. 3).

The new constitution established matters over which the courts could exercise jurisdiction, but also allowed Congress to make exceptions. Some provisions of Article III were not the subject of extensive debate at the time of the Constitution's ratification but have since been the focus of controversy. For instance, scholars have long debated the need to extend the jurisdiction of federal courts to cases involving parties of different states, known as diversity jurisdiction. Other clauses of Article III were considered to be important due to specific controversies that existed at the time of the Constitution's ratification. For example, the king of England appointed the judges of the American colonies, and these judges were loyal to the king instead of the colonies in which they served. The framers addressed the concern of direct control over judges by granting life tenure to federal judges and ensuring that the salaries of these judges cannot be decreased.

Two years after the Constitution was ratified, the first Congress approved the Judiciary Act of 1789. The Act established the basic framework of the federal judicial system, much of which still exists today.

JUDICIAL REVIEW

One of the earliest issues that surrounded the application of Article III was whether the Supreme Court could exercise judicial review, meaning that it could declare legislative enactments to be unconstitutional. Alexander Hamilton (c. 1755–1804), in the seventy-eighth of the *Federalist Papers*, addressed this specific question. According to Hamilton,

The complete independence of the courts of justice is peculiarly essential in a limited Constitution. By a limited Constitution, I understand one which contains certain specified exceptions to the legislative authority; such, for instance, as that it shall pass no bills of attainder, no ex-post-facto laws, and the like. Limitations of this kind can be preserved in practice no other way than through the medium of the courts of justice, whose duty it must be to declare all acts contrary to the manifest tenor of the Constitution void. Without this, all the reservations of particular rights or privileges would amount to nothing.

The Court addressed judicial review in both *Hylton v. United States*, 3 U.S. 171 (1796) and *Calder v. Bull*, 3 U.S. 386 (1798). In neither case did the Court make an authoritative decision regarding whether the Court indeed possessed this power.

Judicial review was the focus of the Court's landmark decision in *Marbury v. Madison*, 5 U.S. 137 (1803). William Marbury, brought an original action against Secretary of State James Madison, regarding his undelivered commission to the judiciary made under the previous Adams administration, asserting that section thirteen of the Judiciary Act authorized this type of action. Article III played a significant role in the decision. Section two, clause two establishes that the Court has the original jurisdiction "in all cases affecting Ambassadors, other public Ministers and Consuls, and those in which a state shall be Party." In cases that are addressed in section two, clause one, the Constitution specifies that the Court has appellate jurisdiction, which is subject to exceptions made by Congress. Chief Justice John Marshall opened his opinion by concluding that Marbury indeed had a "vested legal right" to his commission. The problem in the case, though, was a conflict between the Judiciary Act and Article III. Marshall interpreted section thirteen of the Judiciary Act to authorize parties to request writs of mandamus to federal officers through original actions, a power that was not included in Article III. According to Marshall, the founders had intended to limit original jurisdiction to the types of actions specified in section two of Article III, and the Constitution did not allow Congress to expand this authority.

The importance of the case rested on Marshall's opinion that the Court had the power to declare that legislative and executive act unconstitutional and invalid. Marshall stressed in his opinion that "it is emphatically the province and duty of the judicial department to say what the law is." In the case, the Court refused to order the executive to deliver the commission because the action was not authorized by Article III. The lasting principle of the case is that the judiciary serves as the final authority in the interpretation of the Constitution. The debate over whether the judiciary should have this power has continued for more than two hundred years, with scholars emphasizing that the founders rejected a proposal that would have included this power specifically in Article III.

RELATIONSHIP BETWEEN THE SUPREME COURT AND THE LOWER FEDERAL COURTS

Article III delegates the power to establish lower Federal Courts to Congress. The Constitution distributes judicial power so that the Supreme Court has appellate jurisdiction, both as to law and to fact, over cases in which it does not have original jurisdiction. The Court has recognized that in some instances, the Supreme Court may have concurrent original jurisdiction over a matter, such as a dispute about property between two states (*California v. Arizona*, 440 U.S. 59 [1979]). However, coastal boundary disputes should be brought as original actions in the Supreme Court (*United States v. Alaska*, 422 U.S. 184 [1975]).

JUSTICIABILITY AND STANDING

One important principle about the federal judiciary is that it consists of courts of limited, rather than general, jurisdiction. This limited power stands in sharp contrast to most state courts, which are presumed to have the power to hear certain disputes unless it is proven otherwise. A party that wishes to bring a case in a federal court bears the burden of proving that the court has the jurisdiction to hear the dispute. The Supreme Court has interpreted Article III to have limited the power of the federal courts to hear the categories of cases specified in that article. These categories are contained in section two, clause one and include:

1. cases that arise under the Constitution, the laws of the United States, and treaties.
2. cases affecting ambassadors, other public ministers, and consuls.
3. cases of admiralty and maritime jurisdiction.
4. controversies over which the United States is a party.
5. controversies between two or more states.
6. controversies between citizens of different states.
7. controversies between citizens of the same state who claim lands under grants of different states.

Two other provisions that extended the federal judicial power to cases involving a state and citizens of another state or foreign state were changed by the ratification of the Eleventh Amendment.

The specific reference to "cases" and "controversies" in Article III serves as one of the bases for what is known as *justiciability*, meaning that the federal courts are both

permitted and willing to hear the dispute (some justiciability doctrines are based on concerns of prudent judicial administration rather than the text of the Constitution). One of the earliest applications of the principle of justiciability is that the Court has long refused to issue advisory opinions. During President George Washington's administration, then-Secretary of State Thomas Jefferson wrote to the Supreme Court asking for advice regarding the interpretation of several U.S. treaties and laws in the context of America's neutrality during a war between France and England. The justices of the Court responded by refusing to provide this advice, stressing that the concept of separation of powers demanded that the Court decline to become involved extra-judicially in resolving the questions that were presented. The modern application of this principle is that parties that bring cases to the federal courts must have genuine disputes. Thus, for example, the Court has refused to hear a case where the defendant had encouraged the plaintiff to bring the action and actually financed the litigation (*United States v. Johnson*, 319 U.S. 302 [1943]).

One Court-imposed requirement that is grounded in Article III is that the parties must have proper standing to bring a certain action in federal court. To have standing in a federal court, a party must have suffered a legally recognizable injury, though the Court itself has stated that "the concept [of standing] cannot be reduced to a one-sentence or one-paragraph definition" (*Valley Forge Christian College v. Americans United for Separation of Church and State, Inc.*, 454 U.S. 464 [1982]). The issue of standing has often arisen when taxpayers have brought suit to challenge the constitutionality of a legislative or executive action. The Court has frequently reiterated the statement in *Baker v. Carr*, 369 U.S. 186 (1962) that the "gist" of whether a party has standing to bring suit depends on whether the party has "such a personal stake in the outcome of the controversy as to assure that concrete adverseness which sharpens the presentation of issues upon which the court so largely depends for illumination of difficult constitutional questions." Commentators, such as Charles Alan Wright and Mary Kay Kane (2002), have noted that the Court will review three elements in determining whether a party has standing to hear a dispute: (1) whether the plaintiff has suffered a distinct and concrete injury; (2) whether the injury was caused by the activity being challenged; and (3) whether the court's remedy will redress the injury claimed by the party (p. 80).

Two other requirements—ripeness and mootness—also relate to the "case" or "controversy" requirement of Article III. Unlike standing, which determines whether a certain party may bring an action to federal court, the ripeness and mootness doctrines are concerned with the timing of the action. The issue of ripeness focuses on whether the alleged injury has yet occurred. In *Abbott Labs v. Gardner*, 387 U.S. 136 (1967), the Court stated that the purpose of the ripeness requirement is "to prevent the courts, through avoidance of premature adjudication, from entangling themselves in abstract disagreements." The doctrine of mootness requires that the parties retain personal interest in the case throughout its existence. Thus, for example, if a criminal defendant dies before an appeal is complete, then the case must be dismissed as moot. Similarly, if the parties to a civil case settle their dispute before it is adjudicated, then the case is moot and no longer justiciable.

CRIMINAL TRIAL BY JURY

Clause three of section two of Article III provides, "The Trial of all Crimes, except in Cases of Impeachment, shall be by Jury; and such Trial shall be held in the State where the said Crimes shall be been committed; but when not committed within any State, the Trial shall be at such Place or Places as the Congress may by Law have directed." The Court has stated that the purpose of the clause was to preserve the right to trial by jury as it existed at common law (*Ex parte Quirin*, 317 U.S. 1 [1942]). Thus, the Court has held that trials for petty offenses, which were triable at common law without a jury, could be conducted without a jury under the third clause of section two. The Sixth and Seventh Amendments were adopted to guarantee jury trials in situations not mentioned by this clause. However, the Court has long established that these amendments did not enlarge the right to trial by jury that is found in Article III (*Ex parte Quirin*).

TREASON

Section three of Article III contains two clauses pertaining to treason. Under the first clause, "treason against the United States, shall consist only in levying War against them, or in adhering to their Enemies, giving them Aid and Comfort." The significance of this provision is that the founders chose to recognize only two of five types of treason that existed under English law, including the levying of war and adherence to the enemy. Article III likewise provides, "No person shall be convicted of Treason unless on the Testimony of two Witnesses to the same overt Act, or on Confession in open Court." Thus, in *Haupt v. United States*, 330 U.S. 631 (1947), the Court determined that two witnesses must testify to the same act, though the Court also ruled that the testimony does not need to be identical.

The final clause of Article III states that "Congress shall have the Power to declare the Punishment of Treason, but no Attainder of Treason shall work Corruption of Blood, or Forfeiture except during the Life of the Person attained." The purpose of this clause

was to avoid the English practice of disinheriting heirs-to-be of those convicted of treason (*Wallach v. Van Riswick*, 92 U.S. 202 [1876]).

SEE ALSO *Advisory Opinions; Case or Controversy; Constitution of the United States; Hylton v. United States, 3 U.S. 171 (1796); Judicial Review; Judiciary Act of 1789; Marbury v. Madison, 5 U.S. 137 (1803)*

BIBLIOGRAPHY

Chemerinsky, Erwin. 2007. *Federal Jurisdiction.* 5th edition. New York, NY: Aspen Publishers.

Claus, Laurence N. 2007. "The One Court That Congress Cannot Take Away: Singularity, Supremacy, and Article III." *Georgetown Law Journal* 96(1): 59–121.

Clinton, Robert N. 1984. "A Mandatory View of Federal Court Jurisdiction: A Guided Quest for the Original Understanding of Article III." *University of Pennsylvania Law Review* 132(4): 741–866.

Wright, Charles Alan, and Mary Kay Kane. 2002. *Law of Federal Courts.* 6th edition. St. Paul, MN: West Group.

Matthew C. Cordon

ARTICLE IV

Article IV of the U.S. Constitution, which lays down several basic rules for federal and interstate relations, has occasioned numerous constitutional contentions. These have not remained static over time, nor have all sections of Article IV received equal attention before the U.S. Supreme Court. Slavery informed the earliest controversies, a problem ameliorated only by slavery's extirpation from the United States by war and constitutional amendment. The dominant issues thenceforth were connected with commerce and travel, and the results indicated a more general willingness on the part of the Supreme Court to assert federal power vis-à-vis the states.

FUGITIVE SLAVES

Of Article IV problems before the Civil War (1861–1865), none was more pressing than fugitive slaves. Section 2 of Article IV commanded that "no person held to service or labor in one state" would, upon fleeing to a free state, be emancipated by its laws, but rather should "be delivered up on claim of the party to whom such service or labor may be due." To execute this clause, Congress passed the Fugitive Slave Act in 1793, giving federal courts jurisdiction over fugitive slave cases. States also passed personal liberty laws to protect both free blacks and fugitive slaves, and this led to conflicts. In 1842 the Supreme Court ruled in *Prigg v. Pennsylvania*, 41 U.S.

539, that Article IV empowered Congress to pass fugitive slave laws and that this in turn made the free states' personal liberty laws unconstitutional. After Congress passed amendments to the Fugitive Slave Act in 1850, Chief Justice Roger B. Taney confirmed congressional power in *Ableman v. Booth*, 62 U.S. 506 (1859).

Despite Taney's reaffirmation of federal power over the rendition of fugitive slaves, he proved more willing to restrict federal power in other areas where Article IV intersected slavery. In *Dred Scott v. Sandford*, 60 U.S. 393 (1857), Taney wrote that Congress could not prohibit slavery in the territories because this violated the takings clause of the Fifth Amendment. Taney sidestepped Article IV, Section 3's provision that Congress could make "all needful rules and regulations respecting the territories" by claiming that the clause did not apply to territory acquired after ratification of the Constitution. In *Kentucky v. Dennison*, 65 U.S. 66 (1861), Taney held that the United States could not compel state governors to deliver fugitives from justice, another command of Section 2. Written after the Republican victory in the election of 1860 and in the midst of the secession crisis, Taney's ruling was judicial assurance to the slaveholding states that the federal government lacked the coercive authority to meddle with the states' internal affairs. The Court had made such assurances before. In *Luther v. Borden*, 48 U.S. 1 (1849), the Supreme Court refused to intervene in the constitutional troubles of Rhode Island stemming from the Dorr Rebellion of 1842. Despite Article IV, Section 4's promise that the United States would "guarantee to every state in this union a republican form of government," the Court held that whether Rhode Island's was a republican form of government was a political question and thus nonjusticiable.

The Thirteenth and Fourteenth Amendments ended the Constitution's connection with slavery, forever changing the nature of Article IV controversies. New challenges concerning federalism and interstate relations became prevalent in the rapidly industrializing nation.

FEDERALISM AND INTERSTATE RELATIONS

Among these was the question of the right of citizens to travel. Article IV, Section 2's privileges and immunities clause guaranteed to citizens of the states "all privileges and immunities of citizens in the several states." This did not create a general U.S. citizenship, but rather guaranteed that citizens of one state traveling into another would receive the benefit of that state's laws. Traditionally, such privileges were determined by demarcations of status fixed by race, class, and gender. The Supreme Court had affirmed in *New York v. Miln*, 36 U.S. 102 (1837) the power of the states to forbid entry of indigents and other undesirables, whether from abroad or from other states. These restrictions continued to exist side-by-side with the declaration in

Ward v. Maryland, 79 U.S. 418 (1870) that the privileges and immunities grant was "comprehensive," and "plainly and unmistakably" secured the right of citizens to pass from one state to another for reasons of commerce.

The connection between Article IV's privileges and immunities clause and commerce persists today. Even when the Supreme Court held that the states could not abridge U.S. citizens general right of travel from state to state in *Edwards v. California*, 314 U.S. 160 (1941), it relied not upon Article IV, but on the commerce clause of Article I and the equal protection clause of the Fourteenth Amendment. The Court did strike down on Article IV grounds state legislation discriminating against out-of-state workers in *Toomer v. Witsell*, 334 U.S. 385 (1948) and *Hicklin v. Orbeck*, 437 U.S. 518 (1978); state laws denying medical services to nonresidents in *Doe v. Bolton*, 410 U.S. 179 (1973); and residency requirements for membership in state bar associations in *Supreme Court of New Hampshire v. Piper*, 470 U.S. 274 (1985). Nevertheless, the Court has found that nonresidents can be treated differently when a substantial state interest is at stake, for instance in charging more for tuition at state universities (*Vlandis v. Kline*, 412 U.S. 441 [1973]).

Section 1 of Article IV has received the most exposition by the Supreme Court. In one sense this is understandable, as the clause requires that states give "full faith and credit to the public acts, records and judicial proceedings" of other states, which touches the courts directly. Traditionally, this has been interpreted to mean that issues litigated in one state cannot be relitigated in another, as the Court held in *Mills v. Duryee*, 11 U.S. 481 (1813). The definitiveness of the rule has led to some strange results, as in *Fauntleroy v. Lum*, 210 U.S. 230 (1908), where the Supreme Court held that an arbitration award from Mississippi based on an erroneous interpretation of Mississippi law had to be enforced by a Missouri court despite clear knowledge of the error.

The full faith and credit clause has had its biggest impact in the area of family law. In *Williams v. State of North Carolina*, 317 U.S. 287 (1942), the Supreme Court held that the domicile of a deserting spouse could grant a divorce, and that this deserved full faith and credit in other jurisdictions. This overturned the doctrine that had held that a marriage could only be dissolved within the jurisdiction that granted it, thus making divorce easier to obtain.

It also signaled the degree to which state sovereignty had been subordinated to a broader federal power, a general theme in Article IV cases brought since the 1940s. For instance, the Supreme Court held in *Puerto Rico v. Branstad*, 483 U.S. 219 (1987) that federal courts could compel state governors to render fugitives from justice, thus overturning *Kentucky v. Dennison*. The Court also took a bite out of the political questions doctrine of *Luther v. Borden* in *Baker v. Carr*, 369 U.S. 186 (1962), which held that federal courts did have jurisdiction over cases that tested voting apportionment in the states. As in privileges and immunities claims, the Supreme Court rested its authority on the Fourteenth Amendment rather than on the guarantee clause of Article IV. Still, *Baker v. Carr* overruled *Luther v. Borden* by restricting the political questions doctrine to the Supreme Court's relationship with Congress and the president rather than with the states.

SEE ALSO *Admission of New States Clause; Anti-slavery Constitutionalism; Constitution of the United States; Fugitive Slave Clause; Slavery; Territories*

BIBLIOGRAPHY

Bogen, David S. 2003. *Privileges and Immunities: A Reference Guide to the United States Constitution.* Westport, CT: Praeger.

Metzger, Gillian E. 2007. "Congress, Article IV, and Interstate Relations." *Harvard Law Review* 120 (April): 1468–1542.

Reynolds, William L. 1994. "The Iron Law of Full Faith and Credit." *Maryland Law Review* 53(2): 412–449.

Wiecek, William M. 1972. *The Guarantee Clause of the U.S. Constitution.* Ithaca: Cornell University Press.

H. Robert Baker

ARTICLE V

Article V of the U.S. Constitution reads:

> The Congress, whenever two thirds of both Houses shall deem it necessary, shall propose Amendments to this Constitution, or, on the Application of the Legislatures of two thirds of the several States, shall call a Convention for proposing Amendments, which in either Case, shall be valid to all Intents and Purposes, as Part of this Constitution, when ratified by the Legislatures of three fourths of the several States or by Conventions in three fourths thereof, as the one or the other Mode of Ratification may be proposed by the Congress; Provided that no Amendment which may be made prior to the Year One thousand eight hundred and eight shall in any Manner affect the first and fourth Clauses in the Ninth Section of the first Article; and that no State, without its Consent, shall be deprived of its equal Suffrage in the Senate.

This provision sets out the procedures for formally changing the text of the Constitution. A key word here is *formally*, for many contemporary constitutional theorists, the most prominent being Yale Law School professor

Bruce Ackerman (1991, 1998), emphasize the reality of "informal" constitutional amendment as a pervasive part of American constitutional development. Thus, for example, Ackerman argues that the New Deal's remarkable expansion of national power, including the rise of the modern administrative state and its plethora of "independent" agencies, is best understood as just such an amendment of the preexisting Constitution, even though no language was formally added to the canonical text of the Constitution.

SIGNIFICANCE OF ARTICLE V

Even if one accepts the importance of "informal" constitutional amendment in American constitutional history and practice, however, this does not significantly lessen the importance of Article V, for at least three quite different reasons.

The first involves the symbolic importance of recognizing the very possibility of constitutional amendment. As historian Gordon Wood (1969) has written, the very notion of amendment serves to "institutionalize and legitimate revolution," though of a decidedly nonviolent character (p. 614). It not only suggests that the existing constitution may be defective—as George Washington wrote his nephew shortly after the conclusion of the Philadelphia convention: "The warmest friends and the best supporters the Constitution has do not contend that it is free from imperfection" (quoted in Levinson 1995, p. 3)—but it also provides a mechanism whereby "we the people" can respond to those imperfections and, by changing the text, presumably change the contours of the political system as well.

Second, in an American culture that views the *written* Constitution as an almost sacred text, it is of at least rhetorical importance that people can point to the solid language on the printed page rather than refer only to precedents of the U.S. Supreme Court (which can always be overruled, after all) or other nontextual sources. Although, for example, modern lawyers can easily derive full-scale protection of women's rights from the Fourteenth Amendment's guarantee of "equal protection of the laws," much energy during the 1970s was put into ultimately unsuccessful efforts to add an explicit amendment specifying that "equality of rights under the law shall not be denied or abridged by the United States or by any state on account of sex." Supporters of the equal rights amendment (ERA) believed that such rights would be more strongly protected if the specific language were available, to be pointed to, than if one had to rely only on what Justice Robert Jackson once called the "majestic generalities" of the Fourteenth Amendment.

Finally, even if one accepts the reality of "informal" amendment or the practical irrelevance of the ERA, there has been remarkably little change in most of the truly "hardwired" structures of American government established by the 1787 Constitution, and anyone seeking change would undoubtedly have to undertake formal amendment. Interpretive "creativity" is unavailing if one is concerned about such issues as, for example, the allocation of voting power in the Senate, where Wyoming and California have equal power even though California has approximately seventy times the population of Wyoming; the election of American presidents through the mechanism of the Electoral College; or the ability of the president, through the use of the veto power, to stymie legislation that may well be supported by substantial majorities in the House and the Senate (though not the two-thirds in both houses that are necessary to override a presidential veto).

FORMAL AMENDMENTS

Article V is itself such a "hardwired" provision inasmuch as it makes formal amendment difficult, if not functionally impossible, at least with regard to issues of fundamental importance where public opinion might be divided. If one views constitutional amendment as a "game," those playing "offense," seeking to change the Constitution, must gain the support of two-thirds of each house of Congress and then the assent of a minimum of seventy-five legislative houses (given that Nebraska, uniquely, has a unicameral legislature) in thirty-eight states. Those playing "defense," seeking to prevent the proffered change, need only win one-third plus one or either house of Congress, or at least one legislative house in thirteen separate states. Political scientist Donald Lutz has determined that the U.S. Constitution is the most difficult to amend among all currently operating constitutions in the entire world. Indeed, the allocation of voting power in the Senate appears protected even against "ordinary" amendment inasmuch as it seemingly requires unanimous consent of all of the states for any change.

Existing Amendments The very difficulty of amendment helps to account for the fact that the United States has added only seventeen amendments since the original ratification and the immediate addition of the first ten amendments, usually termed the "Bill of Rights," in 1791. And Bruce Ackerman has argued that the Fourteenth Amendment, surely the most important addition since the founding, cannot be regarded as a genuine "Article V amendment" inasmuch as it was proposed by a "rump Congress" that had refused to seat the elected representatives and senators from the yet-unreconstructed former members of the Confederacy—the constitutionally required two-thirds could never have been attained had they been seated, as was the wish of President Andrew Johnson—and was ratified by southern legislatures that did so only after military reconstruction

induced transformation of the existing political systems in those states by, among other things, requiring black suffrage (the Fifteenth Amendment had not yet been added to the Constitution).

Following the ratification of the Fifteenth Amendment in 1870, it took another forty-three years before the Constitution was again amended in 1913—the Sixteenth Amendment, the "income-tax amendment," overturned an 1895 decision of the Supreme Court (*Pollock v. Farmers' Loan & Trust Co.*, 158 U.S. 601 [1895]). That amendment was followed by a spate of other important changes during the decade: The Seventeenth Amendment (1913) requires the popular election of senators, and the Nineteenth Amendment (1920) guaranteed women the right to vote. The Twentieth Amendment (1933) changed not only the date for inaugurating presidents (from March 4 to January 20), but also the date at which a newly elected Congress would meet. Eighteen years later the Twenty-second Amendment limited presidents to serving only two terms. Since then, however, the ensuing five amendments have been of no real significance with regard to the overall structure or operation of American politics.

Interestingly enough, the last amendment to have been formally added, the Twenty-seventh, was actually one of the original twelve amendments submitted by the First Congress in 1789, of which only ten were ratified at the time. Involving the process by which congressional salaries can be raised, the Twenty-seventh Amendment received insufficient support at the time. It was, however, declared to have been ratified in 1992, when Michigan became the thirty-eighth state (of the now fifty states) to ratify it. The 1789 Congress had not indicated a time limit for ratification. The Supreme Court, in *Dillon v. Gloss*, 256 U.S. 368 (1921), had suggested that ratification by the states must be "sufficiently contemporaneous . . . to reflect the will of the people in all sections at relatively the same period." Nevertheless, the archivist of the United States, who by statute is given authority to declare when new amendments have been added to the Constitution, relied on an opinion prepared within the Department of Justice in declaring that the 203-year-long period of ratification was legitimate. Only a few disgruntled academics registered any objection.

As a matter of fact, Congress has invariably placed time limits on amendment since the submission of the Eighteenth Amendment, establishing national prohibition, in 1918. The usual term is seven years, though Congress controversially extended the initial seven-year term for three more years in the case of the equal rights amendment (ERA) in 1979. Some suggested at the time that the extension was an unconstitutional change of the rules in the middle of the amendment game, but the controversy was mooted by the inability to gain more than thirty-five state ratifications.

Constitutional Problems with Amendments The ERA, though ultimately unsuccessful, offered a treasure trove of problems for analysts of Article V, including the already-mentioned congressional extension of the period for ratification. Another problem concerns the ability of states to rescind ratifications, that is, for state legislatures in effect to say that they have changed their minds and wish to transform former acceptance into opposition. Three states in fact attempted such rescissions. Because, under any method of counting, the ERA never achieved the support of the constitutionally necessary three-fourths of the states, the question of the status of rescinding states became moot, though the issue certainly remains with regard to any future proposals and changes of opinion by state legislatures prior to ratification by the thirty-eighth state. (No one believes that a state can rescind ratification after an amendment is declared part of the Constitution.)

Yet a further issue embedded within Article V was suggested by some opponents to an earlier (and successful) amendment involving women's rights, the Nineteenth Amendment guaranteeing a woman's right to vote. They suggested that the amendment itself was unconstitutional because it so fundamentally changed the nature of state polities. Such an argument sounds both frivolous and offensive today. However, whether there could be such a thing as an "unconstitutional constitutional amendment" has been a much-debated issue by constitutional theorists. Princeton professor Walter Murphy (2006), for example, has suggested that there are implicit limits on amendment under Article V, generated by the mission of the Constitution announced in the Preamble.

AMENDMENT PROCESS

Every amendment to the Constitution has begun as a proposal by Congress, followed by ratification by the states. And all but the Twenty-first Amendment (1933), repealing the Eighteenth Amendment, were ratified by state legislatures rather than by state conventions. Although the Supreme Court has declared unconstitutional an attempt by Ohio to delegate ratification to a popular referendum (*Hawke v. Smith*, 253 U.S. 221 [1920]), it is permissible to hold such a referendum, so long as the legislature treats it only as "advisory" before the legislature casts the determinative vote. More important, perhaps, is the fact that states are allowed leeway in what counts as the legislative process. Thus the Illinois constitution requires that three-fifths of each of Illinois's two houses must vote in favor of a proposed amendment, so that the majority support the ERA, in fact, received in repeated votes between 1972 and 1982 was insufficient. Generally speaking, the Supreme Court has held that most questions involving the process of constitutional amendment are "nonjusticiable"; *Hawke* is one of the rare exceptions. The most extensive discussion of the Court's role in such controversies has occurred in the various opinions issued in *Coleman v. Miller*, 307 U.S. 433 (1939).

Article V, however, speaks of a second track for proposing amendments: a new constitutional convention. Although there is reason to believe that at least some of the framers expected such conventions to take place—they have frequently occurred at the state level throughout American history—there has obviously been no successor to the Philadelphia convention. One might explain this as indicating general satisfaction with the first-track, congressionally-based, model of constitutional amendment. Another explanation, though, is the failure of the Constitution to offer the slightest hint of how a new convention would be structured: How, and by whom, would delegates be appointed, and would the ensuing convention operate on the same one-state/one-vote principle as the Philadelphia convention, or would larger states get more votes? Much concern has been expressed about whether Congress could limit the convention as to the range of issues it could consider. The Philadelphia convention itself could easily be regarded as a "runaway" event given its relative disdain for the limited mandate given it by the existing Congress and, even more importantly, the requirement of unanimous state approval for amendments set out in Article XIII of the Articles of Confederation. Might a new constitutional convention emulate its original model and even attempt an end-run around the ratification rules set out by Article V inasmuch as they function quite similarly to Article XIII in making significant amendment close to impossible? Thus, much anxiety has been expressed at the prospect of jumping into basically uncharted waters.

Perhaps a fourth reason for the importance of Article V is that, by making constitutional amendment extremely difficult, Article V serves to discourage any political efforts devoted to constitutional reform, especially of the Constitution's "hardwired" political structures, given the extreme unlikelihood that they will be successful. As cognitive psychologists would predict, this might well lead to people's professing a greater satisfaction with the Constitution than might otherwise be the case if they believed that change was genuinely possible.

SEE ALSO *Ackerman, Bruce; Amendment, Outside of Article V; Amendments, Rejected; Constitution of the United States*

BIBLIOGRAPHY

Ackerman, Bruce A. 1991. *We the People*. Vol. 1: *Foundations*. Cambridge, MA: Harvard University Press.

Ackerman, Bruce A. 1998. *We the People*. Vol. 2: *Transformations*. Cambridge, MA: Harvard University Press.

Bernstein, Richard B., with Jerome Agel. 1993. *Amending America: If We Love the Constitution So Much, Why Do We Keep Trying to Change It?* New York: Times Books.

Levinson, Sanford, ed. 1995. *Responding to Imperfection: The Theory and Practice of Constitutional Amendment.* Princeton, NJ: Princeton University Press.

Lutz, Donald. 2006. *Principles of Constitutional Design.* New York: Cambridge University Press.

Murphy, Walter. 2006. *Constitutional Democracy: Creating and Maintaining a Just Political Order.* Baltimore, MD: Johns Hopkins University Press.

Wood, Gordon. 1969. *The Creation of the American Republic: 1776–1787.* Chapel Hill: University of North Carolina Press.

Sanford Levinson

ARTICLE VI

Article VI of the U.S. Constitution consists of three sections. The most significant of these is the supremacy clause contained in the second section, which provides that the "Constitution, and the Law of the United States which shall be made in Pursuance thereof; and all Treaties made, or which shall be made, under the Authority of the United States, shall be the supreme Law of the Land." The clause was included as an alternative to the proposed council of revision, which would have consisted of the executive and members of the national judiciary and which would have had the power to veto state and national legislation. The supremacy clause has been cited as evidence that the framers of the Constitution intended for the judiciary to have the power to review the constitutionality of legislation, thus eliminating the need for a council of revision. The Supreme Court has addressed Article VI in two distinct areas, including federal preemption of state laws and the relationship of treaties to other laws.

One of the first landmark Supreme Court cases involved the interpretation of the supremacy clause of Article VI. In *Marbury v. Madison*, 5 U.S. 137 (1803), Chief Justice John Marshall issued his famous opinion holding, among other things, that the Court had the power to review the constitutionality of the actions of the executive and legislative branches. The case focused on the interpretation of the Judiciary Act of 1789, which purported to authorize parties to bring original actions in the Supreme Court for writs of mandamus to compel executive officers to take certain actions. The controversy surrounded the appointment of forty-two Federalist judges to justice of the peace positions on the eve of a Republican takeover of Congress in 1801. One of these judges, William Marbury (1762–1835), sought to compel Secretary of State James Madison (1751–1836) to deliver Marbury's commission by bringing an original

action in the Supreme Court. Although much of the opinion focused on the power of the judiciary under Article III, Marshall also concluded that the supremacy clause only authorized the Court to follow laws made in pursuance of Constitution. Because the Judiciary Act conflicted with Article III, Marshall concluded that the Court did not have the power to entertain the original mandamus action.

Supremacy clause cases later focused on federal preemption of state laws. Preemption generally occurs in one of two types of situations: first, a state law may authorize an act that is prohibited by federal law; and second, a federal statute may specifically disallow state legislation in an area covered by federal legislation. In *Pennsylvania vs. Nelson*, 350 U.S. 497 (1956), the Court articulated a three-part test to determine whether Congress has preempted state law through federal legislation. Under this test, the Court considers: (1) whether the federal law is so pervasive that the Court may infer that Congress left no room for states to supplement it; (2) whether the federal law touches on a field where federal interest is so dominant that the Court can assume that state laws on the same subject cannot be enforced; and (3) whether enforcement of the state law would create a danger of conflict with the administration of the federal law.

Although the Court has invalidated state law based on the preemption doctrine, the Court in recent cases has not presumed or inferred that Congress intended to preempt a state law in question. For example, in *California Division of Labor Standards Enforcement vs. Dillingham Construction, N.A., Inc.*, 519 U.S. 316 (1997), the Court determined that the preemption provision of the Employee Retirement Income Security Act (ERISA) did not apply to California's prevailing wage law. The Court determined that the state law had insufficient connection with the ERISA plan for ERISA to preempt the wage law.

With regard to the treaty power, the prevailing view of the Court has been that treaties are subject to constitutional limitations, just as federal statutes are. Treaties are also considered to be the supreme law of the land and will preempt any conflicting state laws (*American Insurance Association v. Garamendi*, 539 U.S. 396 [2003]).

SEE ALSO *Constitution of the United States; Marbury v. Madison, 5 U.S. 137 (1803); Marshall Court*

BIBLIOGRAPHY

Nowak, John E., and Ronald D. Rotunda. 2004. *Constitutional Law.* 7th edition. St. Paul, MN: Thompson West.

Pace, Christopher R. J. 2006. "Supremacy Clause Limitations on Federal Regulatory Preemption." *Texas Review of Law and Politics* 11(1): 157–173.

Waxman, Seth P., and Trevor W. Morrison. 2003. "What Kind of Immunity? Federal Officers, State Criminal Law, and the Supremacy Clause." *Yale Law Journal* 112(8): 2195–2259.

Matthew C. Cordon

ARTICLE VII

Article VII of the U.S. Constitution begins with the statement that "the Ratification of the Conventions of nine States, shall be sufficient for the Establishment of this Constitution between the States so ratifying the same." It then indicates the consent of the delegates to the Philadelphia Constitutional Convention of 1787 to the Constitution, as attested by its president, George Washington.

The procedure for ratification requires the approval of the Constitution by the people "out-of doors" or in conventions constituted to represent the will of the people. The framers regarded this procedure as superior to legislative approval, and it removed state governments from the ratification process. This meant that the Constitution was not a compact among the states but the distinct will of the assembled representatives of a sovereign American people.

During 1787 and 1788, twelve state legislatures called conventions to consider the ratification of the Constitution. By June 21, 1788, nine states had ratified the Constitution, enough to ensure its adoption, and within a month the Virginia and New York conventions also ratified the document. In 1788 the North Carolina convention refused to ratify the Constitution until it was amended. The next year its legislature called a second convention that ratified the document. Rhode Island called a statewide referendum, but the voters overwhelmingly rejected the Constitution. In early 1790 the Rhode Island legislature called a convention, but it did not ratify the Constitution. The U.S. Senate then considered a bill to sever Rhode Island from the Union. The Rhode Island convention soon reconvened and narrowly ratified the Constitution. Meanwhile, fearing that the call for amendments by several of the ratifying conventions might result in a second constitutional convention, in 1789 the Congress considered and approved ten amendments. Three-fourths of the state legislatures ratified the ten amendments, the Bill of Rights, by 1791.

Unlike the Article V provisions for the ratification of constitutional amendments, Article VII ratification has spawned little further judicial interpretation. The most important Supreme Court decision to address Article VII is *Texas v. White,* 74 U.S. 700 (1869), which does so only indirectly. In this case, the Court considered the validity of the acts of the Texas government after it had seceded and joined the Confederacy. Chief Justice Salmon P. Chase, writing for the Court, argued that the Union created by the people, which Texas joined under provisions of Article VI, Section 3, "was something more than a compact; it was the incorporation of a new member into the political body. And it was final. The union between Texas and the other States was as complete, as perpetual, and as indissoluble as the union between the original States. There was no place for reconsideration, or revocation, except through revolution, or through consent of the States." Therefore, the Article VII ratification of the document by the people of the original thirteen states implies that "the Constitution, in all its provisions, looks to an indestructible Union, composed of indestructible States."

SEE ALSO *Constitutional Convention, Framing; Constitution of the United States; Texas v. White, 74 U.S. 700 (1869)*

BIBLIOGRAPHY

Farrand, Max, ed. 1966. *The Records of the Federal Convention of 1787.* Rev. edition. 4 vols. New Haven, CT: Yale University Press.

Jensen, Merrill; John P. Kaminski; and Gaspare J. Saladino, eds. 1976–2005. *The Documentary History of the Ratification of the Constitution.* 21 vols. Madison: State Historical Society of Wisconsin.

Smith, Craig R. 1993. *To Form a More Perfect Union: The Ratification of the Constitution and the Bill of Rights, 1787–1791.* Lanham, MD: University Press of America.

Wood, Gordon S. 1969. *The Creation of the American Republic, 1776–1787.* Chapel Hill: University of North Carolina Press.

Richard A. Brisbin Jr.

ARTICLES OF CONFEDERATION

The Articles of Confederation bound the thirteen original states together in a "firm league of friendship" from 1781 until the U.S. Constitution was implemented in 1789. Its language is no longer legally binding, yet some of its clauses were copied into the Constitution. The document is considered relevant to current American jurisprudence by some because of these clauses. Others emphasize that the adoption of the Constitution marked a departure so fundamental that understandings and practices under the Articles no longer have constitutional relevance.

Individual states exercised almost all judicial powers while the Articles were in force. Nevertheless, Article IX did give the confederation judicial responsibilities.

Disputes between states could be submitted to the Confederation Congress, which would facilitate an arbitration hearing. If arbitration did not settle a dispute, Congress would empower an ad hoc judicial board to hear the case of each state involved and authoritatively rule on the dispute. These procedures were used to settle a notable land dispute between Connecticut and Pennsylvania, the outcome of which was not well received by residents of the Wyoming Valley, many of whose land claims were voided by the decision. The Confederation Congress was also empowered to set up courts that dealt with maritime and international law.

The courts set up by the Confederation Congress had little ability to enforce their decisions. Alexander Hamilton (c. 1755–1804), writing as Publius in *Federalist* No. 7 (1787), suggested that these courts could not solve interstate disputes effectively, citing the Wyoming Valley controversy and a later border dispute involving New York and Massachusetts as evidence. Nevertheless, the determinations of the courts convened under the Articles were considered valid even after the Constitution was adopted.

Several of the Constitution's clauses were adapted from the Articles of Confederation. The most important of them address how citizens of any state are to be treated by all state governments. Article IV guaranteed that citizens of any state would be entitled to all the "privileges and immunities of free citizens of the several states," just as the Constitution does. The "full faith and credit clause," which requires each state to respect the records, acts, and judicial proceedings of other states, was originally part of Article IV as well.

The Articles have occasionally been cited in Supreme Court decisions. In *Woodruff v. Parham*, 75 U.S. 123 (1869), the court determined that the Articles used the words *imports* and *imposts* "with exclusive reference to articles imported from foreign countries." Since this language was also employed in the Constitution, the court concluded that a state could tax goods brought in from other states (but not foreign countries), as long as they are taxed at the same rate as local goods. In *Camps Newfound/Owatonna, Inc. v. Town of Harrison et al.*, 520 U.S. 564 (1997), Justice Clarence Thomas took issue with that ruling. Thomas's dissent charged the court with misconstruing the Articles, inaugurating an extraconstitutional line of jurisprudence that has needlessly struck down many state tax laws.

An alternative use of the Articles is exemplified by Justice John Paul Stevens's dissent in *Printz v. United States*, 521 U.S. 898 (1997). Stevens noted that the Constitution fundamentally differs from the Articles of Confederation, as the former allows the national government to act authoritatively on individuals. Thus Stevens thought that county law officers were obligated to

perform federally mandated background checks on gun purchasers.

As originalist arguments and their counterarguments become more sophisticated, the Articles of Confederation are likely to be increasingly referenced. Ironically, in certain cases, original intent may become a dispute over the original intent of those who wrote and ratified the Articles of Confederation.

SEE ALSO *Anti-Federalist/Federalist Ratification Debate; Constitution of the United States*

BIBLIOGRAPHY

Bourguignon, Henry J. 1977. *The First Federal Court: The Federal Appellate Prize Court of the American Revolution, 1775–1787.* Philadelphia: American Philosophical Society.

Goebel, Julius, Jr. 1971. *History of the Supreme Court of the United States: Antecedents and Beginnings to 1801.* New York: Macmillan.

David J. Siemers

ASHCROFT V. THE FREE SPEECH COALITION, 535 U.S. 234 (2002)

In *Ashcroft v. The Free Speech Coalition* 535. U.S. 234 (2002), the Supreme Court overturned the Child Pornography Prevention Act of 1996 (CPPA). Through the CPPA, Congress attempted to amend the definition of child pornography to include computer-generated images of children engaging in sexual acts, otherwise known as virtual child pornography. The CPPA prohibited the possession, advertisement, and distribution of any visual depiction that "is or appears to be" of a minor engaging in sexually explicit conduct, or that "conveys the impression" of minors engaging in such conduct. Finding that these prohibitions were overbroad, insofar as they infringed on fully protected speech, the Court held in a six-to-three decision authorized by Justice Kennedy that the CPPA violated the First Amendment.

Ashcroft presented the question of whether virtual child pornography would be subject to regulation under the framework established by the Court's decisions in *Miller, Ferber,* and *Osborne. Miller v. California*, 413 U.S. 15 (1973) established the constitutional test for obscenity—a category of speech unprotected by the First Amendment; *New York v. Ferber*, 458 U.S. 747 (1982) held that child pornography, even if not obscene, was also not protected by the First Amendment; and *Osborne v. Ohio*, 495 U.S. 103 (1990) upheld a statute criminalizing the mere possession of child pornography. Both *Ferber* and *Osborne* relied on the finding that states have a compelling interest in protecting children from the sexual abuse and exploitation caused by the production of child pornography, recognizing that such abuse could only be controlled by banning the distribution of pornographic materials produced using children. In *Osborne*, the Court reasoned that outlawing the production and distribution of child pornography solved only a portion of the problem; forbidding possession was also necessary, because the market for child pornography had become so clandestine and its producers so elusive. Despite these precedents, however, the *Ashcroft* Court refused to extend the *Ferber* and *Osborne* approach to the CPPA's ban on virtual child pornography and affirmed the Ninth Circuit's ruling that the CPPA was unconstitutionally overbroad.

In its ruling, the Court declared that the CPPA could not be upheld in reference to *Miller*, because the 1996 act's prohibitions applied to speech that did not qualify as obscenity. Then, distinguishing the CPPA from the law at issue in *Ferber*, the Court stated that the *Ferber* ban only governed pornographic materials when the production of which actually employed children. The CPPA's ban on virtual images of children, however, ran afoul of *Ferber*, which related only to how the pornographic material was produced, not its content. Similarly, in distinguishing the CPPA from the law in *Osborne*, the Court stated that the *Osborne* rule stemmed from a state's compelling interest in protecting children from any abuse inherent in the actual production of child pornography. But since the CPPA's ban on virtual child pornography affected material produced without involving real children and, hence, did not require the sexual exploitation of real children, the Court held that the act could not be supported by *Osborne*.

After distinguishing the relevant precedents, the Court stated that to uphold the CPPA the Court would have to carve out a new type of speech—for example, virtual child pornography—that would be unprotected by the First Amendment. The Court, however, refused to do so.

SEE ALSO *Miller v. California, 413 U.S. 15 (1973); Obscenity and Pornography*

BIBLIOGRAPHY

Koppelman, Andrew. 2005. "Does Obscenity Cause Moral Harm?" *Columbia Law Review* 105(5): 1635–1679.

Volokh, Eugene. 2004. "Pragmatism vs. Ideology in Free Speech Cases." *Northwestern University Law Review* 99(1): 33–46.

CASES

Miller v. California, 413 U.S. 15 (1973).

New York v. Ferber, 458 U.S. 747 (1982).

Osborne v. Ohio, 495 U.S. 103 (1990).

Patrick M. Garry

ASHWANDER V. TENNESSEE VALLEY AUTHORITY, 297 U.S. 288 (1936)

In *Ashwander v. Tennessee Valley Authority*, 297 U.S. 288 (1936), the U.S. Supreme Court upheld key provisions of one of the most ambitious programs of the New Deal, the Tennessee Valley Authority (TVA). The eight-to-one ruling surprised most observers. The TVA, a special favorite of President Franklin D. Roosevelt, who saw it as a model for comprehensive, government-led development of the most impoverished regions of the struggling nation, seemed destined to follow in the footsteps of the National Recovery Administration (NRA) and the Agricultural Adjustment Administration (AAA), two other major early New Deal programs that fell in the face of constitutional challenges brought to the Supreme Court. But the TVA survived unscathed. Although the Court would quickly return to striking down New Deal programs, *Ashwander* reveals a pre-1937 Court that was less predictably antagonistic toward the New Deal than contemporaries (and historians) generally assumed. The decision also retains lasting significance for Justice Louis Brandeis's often-cited concurrence, in which he articulated the principle that the Court should, when possible, avoid deciding cases on constitutional grounds.

At issue in *Ashwander* was the Wilson Dam hydroelectric plant at Muscle Shoals, Alabama. The federal government began construction on the dam during World War I (1914–1918), with the intention of using the plant to support the war effort. After the war, the fate of Wilson Dam became a point of political dispute: Liberals wanted the government to take over power production for the region; conservatives wanted to privatize the facilities. Roosevelt's election gave the upper hand to the liberals. In 1933 Congress created the TVA, a program that New Dealers hoped—and their opponents feared—would demonstrate the radical possibilities of public leadership for the purpose of regional development. The TVA was to be a public corporation that would oversee the construction of a series of dams to control flooding throughout the length of the Tennessee River (nine hundred miles long, with a basin that drained forty thousand square miles in seven different states) and to provide energy to the surrounding area. Roosevelt took a particular interest in the TVA, envisioning it as the basis for the revitalization of an impoverished area that had been struggling since long before the Depression hit the nation, and a model for future development programs. Not only would the public projects provide desperately needed employment, they would encourage investment, leading to new private-sector jobs throughout the area.

The constitutional challenge to the TVA was not long in coming. In September 1934, a group of preferred stockholders of the Alabama Power Company, led by one George Ashwander, sued the TVA, with the intention of blocking a deal company leaders had negotiated with the TVA. Under the terms of the disputed contract, the company would sell power lines and various properties to the TVA and, in exchange, would distribute power produced at the Wilson Dam plant—all part of the TVA's plan to get into the energy business. When Ashwander's case made it to the Supreme Court in late 1935, most assumed, in light of the recent Court decisions in *Schechter Poultry Corp. v. United States*, 295 U.S. 495 (1935) and *United States v. Butler*, 297 U.S. 1 (1936) (striking down, respectively, the NRA and the AAA), the TVA would also fall. As David Lilienthal, the director of the TVA, recalled, "I had completely resigned myself to a bad decision, only holding out hope that we would not be swept completely out to sea, bag and baggage" (Leuchtenburg 1995, p. 104).

On February 17, 1936, the Court issued its opinion. Writing for the Court, Chief Justice Charles E. Hughes refused to consider the "abstract questions" regarding the TVA's constitutionality that had been pushed by the plaintiffs and limited his evaluation to the constitutional authority for the construction of the Wilson Dam and the plan to distribute power produced there. Construction of the dam was justified, Hughes concluded, under the power of Congress to support national defense and interstate navigation. Electric energy produced was "an inevitable incident" to the dam's construction and was therefore public property, which Congress had authority to dispose of as it deemed appropriate.

In his concurrence, Justice Brandeis agreed with Hughes on the constitutional questions, but argued that the Court should never have become involved in what he viewed as an internal dispute of the Alabama Power Company.

The sole dissenter was Justice James McReynolds, who offered a sweeping critique of the constitutional shortcomings of the TVA. He attacked the program as a "pretentious scheme" intended to put private companies out of business. It was simply "artifice" to treat the power produced as nothing more than a byproduct of a legitimate government purpose.

Ashwander brought mixed reactions. In Norris, Tennessee, a town populated by workers responsible for building a new TVA hydroelectric dam, it sparked celebrations among families thankful for continued employment. In sharp contrast, those who saw impending socialism in Roosevelt's policies particularly feared the TVA, a program that generated utopian visions among fervent New Dealers, and were predictably disappointed with the Court, which they had come to rely on as a brake on the excesses of the New Deal. Roosevelt was pleased to see his beloved TVA dodge a bullet, but he also recognized that the decision complicated his plans in the upcoming

presidential election to rally support for his planned offensive against the Court's power. The *New York Times* declared the ruling a "death sentence of any movement to limit the court's power" ("TVA Test," February 23, 1936). Such predictions were short-lived, however. Before the term ended, the Court was back to voiding New Deal programs. Criticism of the Court steadily grew, culminating in the failed 1937 Court-packing bill.

Since, beginning in 1937, Supreme Court decisions upholding congressional economic policy would become commonplace, the most lasting contribution of *Ashwander*, in terms of constitutional law, lies in Brandeis's concurrence and its defense of the idea that the Court should generally avoid deciding cases on constitutional grounds when alternative grounds are available.

Brandeis offered a list of seven "rules" that allow the Court to avoid "passing upon a large part of all the constitutional questions pressed upon it for decision": (1) the parties to a suit lack an adversarial relationship; (2) the constitutional issue is not necessary to the decision; (3) the facts of the case allow for a narrower decision that would avoid the constitutional question; (4) there are nonconstitutional grounds that can decide the case; (5) the plaintiff is unable to demonstrate an injury due to the challenged law; (6) the complainant has "availed himself of [the] benefits" of the statute at issue; and (7) the statute can be construed to avoid the constitutional question.

Brandeis's description of the principle of "constitutional avoidance" proved extremely influential. A half century later, Justice John Paul Stevens, in his dissenting opinion in *Delaware v. Van Arsdall*, 475 U.S. 673 (1986), described it "one of the most respected opinions ever written by a Member of this Court." Exactly what lessons are to be drawn from Brandeis's rules, however, have been less than clear. Legal scholar Alexander Bickel, for example, identified *Ashwander* as a seminal articulation of what he famously termed the Court's "passive virtues"—the idea that the Court can often best serve its role in the political system by not deciding certain controversial issues. Critics such as Gerald Gunther argued that Bickel misread *Ashwander*, and that Brandeis was concerned with encouraging narrow holdings and statutory over constitutional interpretation, rather than avoiding difficult decisions altogether. In today's debates over the meaning and merits of "judicial minimalism," Brandeis's concurrence continues to resonate.

SEE ALSO *Brandeis, Louis; New Deal and the Economy; Roosevelt, Franklin D.*

BIBLIOGRAPHY

Bickel, Alexander M. 1962. *The Least Dangerous Branch: The Supreme Court at the Bar of Politics.* Cleveland, OH: Bobbs-Merrill.

Gunther, Gerald. 1964. "The Subtle Vices of the 'Passive Virtues'—A Comment on Principle and Expediency in Judicial Review." *Columbia Law Review* 64: 1–25.

Kloppenberg, Lisa A. 1994. "Avoiding Constitutional Questions." *Boston College Law Review* 35: 1003–1066.

Leuchtenburg, William E. 1995. *The Supreme Court Reborn: The Constitutional Revolution in the Age of Roosevelt*. New York: Oxford.

McCraw, Thomas K. 1971. *TVA and the Power Fight, 1933–1939*. Philadelphia: Lippincott.

Pritchett, C. Herman. 1943. *The Tennessee Valley Authority: A Study in Public Administration*. Chapel Hill: University of North Carolina Press.

"TVA Test." 1936. *New York Times*. February 23.

Christopher W. Schmidt

ASIAN EXCLUSION LAWS

The discovery of gold, a rice shortage, and the recruitment of Asian labor led to the initiation of noticeable Asian migration in the nineteenth century, triggering a backlash of exclusion laws. Examining the impetus and development of exclusion laws directed first at Chinese immigrants, and eventually at all Asian immigrants, reveals a sordid tale of racism and xenophobia demonstrating the extremes to which the United States would go to keep out groups that did not fit into the prevailing image of being American. These exclusion laws were based on race, rather than citizenship or nativity, as was the case in the national origins quota system of the 1920s.

RESISTANCE TO CHINESE LABORERS

Early on, the Chinese were officially welcomed into the United States. The simultaneous opening of both China and the American West, along with the discovery of gold in 1848, led to a growing demand for and a ready supply of Chinese labor. Chinese were actively recruited to fill needs in railroad construction, laundries, and domestic service. By 1882, about 100,000 Chinese had entered the United States and were working on the West Coast (Hing 1993, pp. 47–48). However, nativistic sentiment eventually took hold, spurred by racial prejudice and economic competition. By 1853, anti-Chinese local ordinances and editorials were common throughout the West Coast.

Eventually, the Sinophobic sentiment prevailed, and any favorable views about the Chinese were overrun by a series of laws that first limited, and then entirely excluded, Chinese from the United States. By the end of the Civil War, Chinese immigrants were judged unworthy of citizenship. While the amended Nationality Act of 1790 limited citizenship through naturalization to "free white persons" (specifically excluding African Americans and Native Americans), in 1870, Congress extended the naturalization rights to aliens of African descent. The Chinese, however, were deliberately denied that right because of their "undesirable qualities" (Hutchinson 1981, pp. 5–6).

The 1870 denial of the opportunity to naturalize was the first congressional step toward excluding Chinese, and the first limitation based on national origin beyond the subordination of African Americans. Five years later, in 1875, responding to law-enforcement claims that Chinese women were being imported for prostitution, Congress passed legislation prohibiting their entry for immoral purposes. The overzealous enforcement of the statute, commonly referred to as the *Page Law*, effectively barred Chinese women from entry into the United States and further worsened an already imbalanced sex ratio among Chinese immigrants.

Responding to continued anti-Chinese clamor, the Chinese Exclusion Act was enacted in 1882. The law excluded Chinese laborers for ten years, and effectively ended Chinese immigration except for a quota permitting entry to a small number of teachers, students, and merchants. Legislation in 1904 extended Chinese exclusion indefinitely, marking the culmination of thirty-five years of laws that, beginning with the Naturalization Act of 1870 (specifically barring Chinese), limited and then excluded Chinese immigrants.

THE GENTLEMEN'S AGREEMENT WITH JAPAN

The early history of Japanese immigration differs considerably from that of the Chinese, mainly because of the strength of the restored Meiji government. Unlike the decaying Chinese Qing dynasty (which fell in 1911), the Japanese government was able to negotiate mutually beneficial emigration treaties with the United States and to enforce its own emigration laws.

The Japanese opening to the West commenced with the arrival of Commodore Matthew Perry's U.S. naval ships in Tokyo Bay in 1854. Perry forced the Japanese to sign the Treaty of Peace and Amity, in which Japan agreed to open its doors to foreign trade. Not coincidentally, the first appreciable numbers of Japanese entered at the height of the Chinese exclusion movement. Agricultural labor demands, particularly in Hawaii and California, led to increased efforts to attract Japanese workers after the exclusion of the Chinese. In 1884, two years after the Chinese Exclusion Act, the Japanese government yielded to pressures to permit laborers to emigrate to work on Hawaiian sugar plantations.

Like the initial wave of Chinese immigrants, Japanese laborers were at first warmly received by employers. By 1894, Japan and the United States reaffirmed their commitment to open travel, each ensuring the other's citizens liberty to enter, travel, and reside in the receiving country.

At the turn of the century, unfavorable sentiment toward the Japanese laborers grew as they began to migrate to the western United States. After Hawaii was annexed in 1898, the Japanese were able to use it as a stepping stone to the mainland, where the majority engaged in agricultural work. Economic competition with white farm workers soon erupted.

After Japan's crushing victories over China in 1895 and Russia in 1905, policymakers contemplated exclusion as a means of controlling a potential enemy. Many Americans regarded Japan as an eager student at the knee of the United States. But when the Japanese Navy defeated its Russian counterpart, American observers realized how powerful the "yellow" nation had become (Thomson et. al. 1981, p. 145). America was so concerned about geopolitical change that President Theodore Roosevelt (1858–1919) helped negotiate the treaty that ended the Russo-Japanese War and ceded Korea to Japan as a protectorate.

Japanese laborers were eventually restricted, but not in conventional legislative fashion. Japan's emergence as a major world power meant that the United States could not restrict Japanese immigration in the heavy-handed, self-serving fashion it had curtailed Chinese immigration. To do so would have offended an increasingly assertive Japan at a time when the United States was concerned about keeping an open door to Japanese markets. To minimize potential disharmony between the two nations while retaining the initiative to control immigration, President Roosevelt negotiated an informal agreement with Japan. Under the terms of the so called *Gentlemen's Agreement*, during 1907 and 1908, the Japanese government refrained from issuing travel documents to laborers destined for the United States. In exchange for this severe, voluntary limitation, Japanese wives and children could be reunited with their husbands and fathers in the United States, and San Francisco would be pressured into rescinding a school segregation order.

Japanese immigrants, like Chinese immigrants, were unsuccessful in seeking citizenship through naturalization. In *Takao Ozawa v. United States* (1922), a Japanese immigrant's request that he be regarded a "free white person" under the naturalization laws was denied.

THE ENTRY OF FILIPINOS AND ASIAN INDIANS

At the turn of the century, the United States was beginning its relationship with the Philippines, as it was changing its view toward Japan. After the U.S. victory over Spain in the 1898 Spanish-American War, President McKinley (1843–1901) concluded that the people of the Philippines, then a Spanish colony, were "unfit for self-government" and that "there was nothing left for [the

United States] to do but to take them all, and to educate the Filipinos, and uplift and civilize and Christianize them" (Patterson 1983, p. 94).

Ironically, the fact that the Philippines became a U.S. colony meant that Filipinos automatically became noncitizen nationals of the United States. They could travel in and out of the United States without regard to immigration laws and were not subject to exclusion or deportation. When appreciable numbers migrated after World War I (when Chinese and Japanese workers could no longer be recruited), exclusionary efforts against them began.

The advent of the twentieth century witnessed the entry of other Asians, such as Asian Indians, but in small numbers. Even though those seeking trade were among some of the earliest migrants to the United States, Indians had insignificant contacts with this country during the nineteenth century. Eventually, more migrated, primarily to California and primarily for agricultural jobs.

Like the Chinese and Japanese before them, many Asian Indians fought for acceptance. Lower federal courts granted them the right to naturalize on the grounds that they were Caucasians and, thus, eligible "white persons" under the citizenship laws. But in *United States v. Bhagat Singh Thind*, 261 U.S. 204 (1923), the Supreme Court reversed this racial stance deciding that Indians, like Japanese, could not be considered white persons and were ineligible to become naturalized citizens.

Congress responded to continued anti-Asian clamor by passing the Immigration Act of 1917, which, including provisions aimed at southern and eastern Europeans, created the "Asiatic barred zone" by extending the Chinese exclusion laws to all other Asians. The zone covered South Asia from Arabia to Indochina; including India, Burma, Thailand, the Malay States, the East Indian Islands, Asiatic Russia, the Polynesian Islands, and parts of Arabia and Afghanistan. Only Filipinos and Guamanians, under U.S. jurisdiction at the time, were not included.

THE 1924 EXCLUSION OF ASIANS INELIGIBLE FOR CITIZENSHIP

The reactionary, isolationist political climate that followed World War I, manifested in the Red Scare of 1919 and 1920, leading to even greater exclusionist demands. The landmark Immigration Act of 1924 again took direct aim at southern and eastern Europeans, while simultaneously eliminating the few remaining categories for Asians, such as those for Chinese students and merchants, and Japanese spouses. The act provided for the permanent exclusion of any "alien ineligible to citizenship." Because Asians were barred from naturalization under the 1790 and 1870 laws, the possibility of their entry was cut off indefinitely. The primary target was the Japanese, who, while subject to the Gentlemen's Agreement, had never been totally barred by federal immigration law until then. Now the message of exclusion to Japanese was reinforced in no uncertain terms.

As if to ensure that Asian-American families would not proliferate, the 1922 Cable Act provided that if a female U.S. citizen married an alien who was ineligible for citizenship, she would be stripped of her U.S. citizenship. The law complemented anti-miscegenation laws in many states.

BARRING FILIPINOS

The only Asians not affected by the 1924 Act were Filipinos, who remained exempt as nationals and who, by then, had settled into a familiar pattern of immigration. Before 1920, few resided in the United States—mostly in Hawaii. They became a convenient source of cheap labor after Japanese immigration was restricted in 1908. Just as the Chinese exclusion law had encouraged employers to look to Japan, the limitations on Japanese immigrants led to an intense recruitment of Filipino laborers, especially by Hawaiian sugar plantations, because of their open travel status as noncitizen nationals.

By the late 1920s, Filipino laborers began to look beyond Hawaii to the mainland where the need for cheap labor, especially in agriculture, was growing. Most Filipinos who had come to the mainland previously were students. But in the late 1920s, Filipinos came to California predominantly to work on citrus and vegetable farms.

Most white racism directed at Filipino laborers sprang from the immigrants' success at acculturation. They were resented largely for their ability to get jobs and even for their contact with white women. In many respects they were perceived as a greater threat to white laborers than their Chinese and Japanese predecessors had been. To white workers in California, the privileged immigration status of Filipinos did not change the fact that they were an economic threat and had the physical characteristics of Asiatics.

Calls for the exclusion of Filipino workers were warmly received in Congress, which welcomed any seemingly uncomplicated proposal that promised relief for the high unemployment of the depression. For policymakers, however, dealing with anti-Filipino agitation was not as simple as responding to earlier anti-Chinese, anti-Asian Indian, and even anti-Japanese campaigns. Because Filipinos could travel in and out of the country without constraint, until the Philippines was granted independence Congress could not exclude Filipinos.

An unlikely coalition of exclusionists, anti-colonialists, and Filipino nationalists managed to band together to promote the passage of the Philippine Independence Act (Tydings-McDuffie Act) in 1934. The law was everything exclusionists could hope for. When the Philippines gained independence on July 4, 1946, Filipinos would lose their status as nationals of the United States, regardless of where they lived. Those already in the United States would be deported unless they became immigrants. Between 1934 and 1946, however, any Filipino who desired to immigrate became subject to the 1924 quota law, and the Philippines was considered a separate country with an annual quota of only fifty visas!

SUMMATION

World War II finally helped to usher in reforms to the Asian exclusion laws. In response to Japanese ridicule of China for supporting the United States—when the Chinese exclusion provisions were still in effect—Congress repealed the Chinese Exclusion Act in 1943. Similarly, in 1946, naturalization rights were extended to nationals of the Philippines and India—countries that were also U.S. allies. In 1952, all racial restrictions on naturalization were repealed. However, the national origins quota system that continued to severely restrict the number of immigrant visas available to Asians was not repealed until 1965, when President Lyndon B. Johnson (1908–1973) followed through on President John F. Kennedy's (1917–1963) push for a more egalitarian immigration system.

SEE ALSO *Aliens Ineligible for Citizenship; Immigration; Non-citizens and Equal Protection (Federal); Plenary Power Doctrine; Progressive Era Immigration and Naturalization*

BIBLIOGRAPHY

Chin, Gabriel J. 1996. "The Civil Rights Revolution Comes to Immigration Law: A New Look at the Immigration and Nationality Act of 1965." *North Carolina Law Review* 75: 273–345.

Hing, Bill Ong. 1993. *Making and Remaking Asian America through Immigration Policy, 1850–1990*. Palo Alto, CA: Stanford University Press.

Hutchinson, Edward P. 1981. *Legislative History of American Immigration Policy, 1798–1965*. Philadelphia: University of Pennsylvania Press.

Patterson, James T. 1983. *America in the Twentieth Century*. New York: Knopf.

Thomson, James C., Jr.; Peter W. Stanley; and John Curtis Perry. 1981. *Sentimental Imperialists: The American Experience in East Asia*. New York: Harper & Row.

Bill Ong Hing

ASPIRATIONALISM

If one believes that a constitution is more than a set of rules establishing limits on the exercise of power, then aspirationalism presents attractive interpretive possibilities. The idea, traceable to Aristotle (384–322 B.C.E.), that a constitution defines the principles of justice toward which a people aspire, is the basis for claiming that aspirational considerations should weigh heavily in determining constitutional policies and meanings. But there are important differences in the way constitutional aspiration has been conceptualized, and these differences in turn point to alternative understandings of the appropriate role of the Supreme Court.

The Constitution's Preamble affirms that the document is about several things, among them establishing justice for ourselves and our posterity. One way to understand this commitment is to see it in aspirational terms; thus, constitutional fulfillment can be measured and assessed in accordance with the progressive achievement of goals identified by the Constitution's interpreters. For some, these goals are the ones inscribed in the Declaration of Independence, which Dr. Martin Luther King Jr. (1929–1968) described as "a promissory note to which every American was to fall heir" (quoted in Jacobsohn 1986, p. 1). In his account, which recalls similar sentiments by Frederick Douglass (1877–1895) a century earlier, "We the People" were unable (and in many cases unwilling) contemporaneously to extend the justice of the Constitution to all those who fell under its sway, but the posterity of the excluded would, in due course, see their promised constitutional entitlement fulfilled. The Constitution is both a legal code and a codification of certain ideals that, according to this view, are historically tethered to moments of constitutional framing and subsequent revision.

A different aspirational perspective, as suggested by Soterios Barber (1984), relies on posterity's determination of its "best current conception of an ideal state of affairs" (p. 156). Or as Justice William Brennan (2004) affirmed in an essay on contemporary ratification, "[W]e are an aspiring people with faith in progress" (p. 183). For Brennan, "contemporary ratification" was the correct response to what he saw as an inescapable reality, namely that "[w]e current Justices read the Constitution in the only way that we can: as twentieth-century Americans" (p. 187). Brennan's "ultimate question"—"[W]hat do the words of the text mean in our time?" (p. 187)— indicates that we have, as Robin West (1994) put it, "a Constitution of present aspirations" (p. 312). But acceptance of Brennan's aspirational constitutionalism comes with the knowledge that justices are quite capable of reading the Constitution in antiquarian ways. And so analysis of the Court's history has led some to a perception of Congress as a more reliable source of progressive aspirationalism and, with it, an insistence on legislative participation in the interpretive enterprise through which constitutional meanings are obtained.

Historically, the first account is most famously associated with the position Abraham Lincoln adopted in connection with the slavery issue. Commenting on the Declaration of Independence, Lincoln said, "The assertion that 'all men are created equal' was of no practical use in effecting our separation from Great Britain; and it was placed in the Declaration, not for that, but for future use" (quoted in Jacobsohn 1986, p. 102). In Lincoln's critique of the *Dred Scott* decision (1857), he articulated a theory of aspiration in which eighteenth-century principles of natural right were at the core of constitutional meaning and, therewith, a standard for evaluating the work of the Court. Chief Justice Roger Brooke Taney had, in Lincoln's estimation, denuded the Declaration of any constitutive significance by transforming it into a positivist document of no moral consequence. But for its signers, "They meant simply to declare the *right* [to human equality], so that the *enforcement* of it might follow as fast as circumstances should permit" (quoted in Jacobsohn 1986, p. 108). In affirming that people of African descent should not expect enforcement of a right to which they were ascriptively not entitled, Taney had failed to understand how the aspirations of the Constitution defined Americans as a people, and thus his ruling obligated other actors—principally Congress—to mount a political challenge to it. Thus for Lincoln, too, a Constitution of aspirations was incompatible with the idea that the Supreme Court exercised an interpretive monopoly over the document.

POST–CIVIL WAR DEVELOPMENTS

Lincoln's position was an elaboration of the *Dred Scott* dissent of Justice John McLean, in which the often lightly regarded justice had referred to the expectations of constitutional framers who believed that slavery had been set on a course of ultimate extinction. It was a much more highly regarded justice, John Marshall Harlan, who later in his two great dissents, in the *Civil Rights Cases*, 109 U.S. 3 (1883) and *Plessy v. Ferguson*, 163 U.S. 537 (1896), continued what Hendrik Hartog (1987) called "the Great Tradition of emancipatory aspiration" (p. 1017). The adoption of the post–Civil War amendments had represented a substantial fulfillment of the Constitution's original promise embodied in the self-evident proposition Lincoln invoked at Gettysburg. Harlan's interpretation of their quickly contested clauses was intended to show that American citizenship embodied an antidiscrimination principle enforceable against both public and private challenges. And consistent with aspirationalism's multilateral institutional commitment, Harlan understood the enforcement provisions of these amendments as directly conferring upon the legislative branch the authority to pursue the goals of this newly won inclusive citizenship.

The jurisprudence of constitutional aspiration is not without its detractors. One criticism is empirically based; others are driven by more normative concerns. For every justice and statesman with a constitutional understanding incorporating aspirations for human equality, one can find counterparts who see very different aspirations in play. For example, as Mark Graber (2006) has pointed out, McLean's version of aspiration finds its opposite in the white-supremacist constitutional interpretations of southern Jacksonian judges (p. 76). These contradictory aspirations only highlight how the founding compromises behind a document that included the taint of slavery surely complicate—perhaps even destroy—anyone's depiction of a Constitution's clear and coherent aspirational content.

This empirical objection also inspires normative worries about the role of the Supreme Court. If there is a choice of constitutional aspirations from which an interpreter is free to select, then justices exercising such jurisprudential options cannot avoid arousing the suspicion that they are engaged in politics, not law. Justice Oliver Wendell Holmes's famous dissent in *Lochner v. New York*, 198 U.S. 45 (1905), which presented a picture of a Constitution essentially devoid of substantive philosophic or economic commitments, is perhaps the most explicitly anti-aspirational opinion in the constitutional canon. While written to challenge the earlier version of aspirationalism, its critique can be used with equal force against the second, in which current conceptions of desirable states of affairs are to be given strong judicial consideration in constitutional cases. Thus, in the older account, what the Constitution aspires to—the right to be considered an equal within a civic community responsible for its own governance—left considerable space for the political pursuit of additional aspirations concerning which the document was essentially agnostic. But under the more recent model of contemporary ratification, the aspirational reach of constitutional provisions limits the policy discretion of the more popular branches, the latter being constrained by the presumed moral obligations contained within the folds of those provisions.

As for the work of the modern Court, *United States v. Carolene Products*, 304 U.S. 144 (1938) is the critical case in the debate over aspirationalism. That 1938 case's famous footnote cast doubt upon the traditional presumption of constitutionality attaching to legislation touching upon fundamental rights and affecting "discrete and insular minorities." It established a constitutional jurisprudence that promoted the Court as the guardian of a coherent set of aspirations, the goal of which was to ensure a more equitable enjoyment of the democratic political experience. If, by drawing upon the resources of contemporary moral theory, Justice Brennan has been the justice most closely associated with the effort to realize these aspirations, Justice Antonin Scalia has been its most persistent critic. With the Fourteenth Amendment as the main constitutional backdrop to broad-ranging issues of moral and political contestation, Scalia has insisted that a judiciary determined to advance its own aspirational agenda not short-circuit the majoritarian political process.

THE CROSS-NATIONAL TURN

Justice Scalia has also been the most outspoken detractor of another trend in contemporary Supreme Court jurisprudence: the use of foreign legal materials in domestic constitutional cases. Cross-national citations have existed for most of the Court's history, but the controversy surrounding the practice has increased steadily with the accelerating pace of judicial globalization in the late twentieth century and early twenty-first. Often, American justices' use of foreign judgments has been generated by aspirational concerns. These judgments have, of course, not been binding on American courts, but they may have had persuasive authority in supporting the kind of change that a judge believed would move American law to a greater approximation of the ideal toward which the Constitution aspires. If America's specific aspirations have included the progressive realization of principles of justice that are expressive of certain universal ideals, then the migration of external legal ideas into the American constitutional domain should be welcomed for its potential to enhance the quality of justice at home.

Indeed, citizens of most countries, it is sometimes argued, have common aspirations with regard to the basics of justice; hence the increasing permeability of constitutional boundaries should be viewed as a positive development. To this it is frequently pointed out that constitutional interpretation must be grounded in the legal and political culture within which it operates; that the infusion of foreign sources into the process of domestic adjudication undermines the Constitution's role in sustaining a viable sense of national and constitutional identity. As Justice Scalia has said in *Thompson v. Oklahoma*, 487 U.S. 815 (1988), "We must never forget that it is a Constitution for the United States of America that we are expounding" (p. 868). So even if aspirations are relevant to constitutional adjudication, they must be the aspirations of the local culture rather than those of places with very different histories and traditions.

Not surprisingly, the most heated exchanges over "judicial borrowing" occur in the context of cases involving hot-button constitutional issues. For example, Justice Anthony Kennedy, who along with Justices Stephen Breyer and Ruth Bader Ginsburg is the most ardent advocate of this type of aspirationalism, cited court rulings in European jurisdictions to support his opinion in *Lawrence v. Texas*, 539 U.S. 558 (2003), that laws criminalizing consensual same-sex conduct were unconstitutional. For the majority in this case, such enactments undermined both spatial and transcendent dimensions of liberty; thus the constitutional aspiration for a society that respects the autonomy of self was effectively negated by these laws' adoption and enforcement. References to foreign law point to an "emerging awareness" that this particular aspiration is consistent with a universal aspiration to liberty. This alone justifies such judicial invocations. But to Justice Scalia, who wrote a passionate dissent in *Lawrence*, the approach taken by the majority only compounded the worst tendencies of aspirationalism. By appealing to extraterritorial aspirations to validate the homegrown variety, the Court improperly expanded the ambit of judicial subjectivity at the expense of its institutional legitimacy.

Justice Scalia, however, has not been averse to citing foreign materials that could illuminate the English common-law origins of American constitutionalism. This practice underscores how aspirationalism is in principle compatible with competing theories of constitutional interpretation, including originalism. As Walter Murphy (2006) has argued, "If a civil society is to have a charter, it must not only lay down rules for a government but also articulate many of the basic principles, values and aspirations that will reconstitute people from a collection of humans sharing a common geography into citizens sharing a common creed" (p. 198). How and whether these aspirations come to be affirmed and enforced are the questions that have driven much of the contemporary debate in constitutional theory.

SEE ALSO *Brennan, William J., Jr.; Constitutional Interpretation; Constitutional Theory; Declaration of Independence; Preamble*

BIBLIOGRAPHY

Barber, Soterios A. 1984. *On What the Constitution Means.* Baltimore: Johns Hopkins University Press.

Brennan, William J. 2004. "The Constitution of the United States: Contemporary Ratification." In *Judges on Judging: Views from the Bench.* Washington, DC: CQ Press.

Graber, Mark A. 2006. *Dred Scott and the Problem of Constitutional Evil.* Cambridge, UK: Cambridge University Press.

Hartog, Hendrik. 1987. "The Constitution of Aspiration and 'The Rights That Belong to Us All.'" *Journal of American History* 74: 1013–1034.

Jacobsohn, Gary J. 1986. *The Supreme Court and the Decline of Constitutional Aspiration.* Totowa, NJ: Rowman & Littlefield.

Murphy, Walter. 2006. *Constitutional Democracy: Creating and Maintaining a Just Political Order.* Baltimore: Johns Hopkins University Press.

West, Robin. 1994. *Progressive Constitutionalism: Reconstructing the Fourteenth Amendment.* Durham, NC: Duke University Press.

CASES

Dred Scott v. Sandford, 19 How. (60 U.S.) 393 (1857).

Civil Rights Cases, 109 U.S. 3 (1883).

Plessy v. Ferguson, 163 U.S. 537 (1896).

Lochner v. New York, 198 U.S. 45 (1905).

Thompson v. Oklahoma, 487 U.S. 518 1988).

United States v. Carolene Products, 304 U.S. 144 (1938).

Gary Jeffrey Jacobsohn

ATTORNEY GENERAL

The attorney general is the chief law enforcement officer in the United States. The office serves as the head of the Department of Justice and a member of the president's cabinet. The attorney general is seventh in the presidential line of succession.

The title of attorney general dates back to fourteenth-century England, and the American office was a part of the colonial heritage. Each state has its own attorney general. In most states, the office is established by the state constitution, and the attorney general is directly elected by the citizens of the state. The federal attorney general's office was established under the Judiciary Act of 1789, the act that also established the lower federal courts. The U.S. attorney general is nominated by the president and confirmed by the Senate. Originally, the office operated as a part-time, quasi-judicial institution with no department to administer. Attorneys general provided legal advice to the president and to Congress and represented the federal government in cases that reached the Supreme Court. Early federal budgets and other documents referred to the post as part of the judicial branch, and early occupants of the office lived in the capital city only when the Court was in session.

Presidents have traditionally selected friends or confidants to serve as attorney general. The first attorney general, Edmund Randolph (1753–1813), was George Washington's aide-de-camp during the Revolutionary War (1775–1783) and a close friend of the president. Washington invited Randolph to attend cabinet meetings and sought his advice on a broad range of policy matters. William Wirt (1772–1834), appointed by President James Monroe (1758–1831) in 1817, served in the office twelve years, longer than any attorney general in history. Wirt was the first to reside year-round in the capital, and he began the process of institutionalizing the office by keeping record books and collecting the office's official legal opinions. In an influential opinion about the office itself, Wirt concluded that the attorney general was responsible for giving legal advice to the president but not Congress, and he stopped the practice of advising Congress.

In 1831 President Andrew Jackson created a precedent by firing Attorney General John Berrien (1781–1856) for refusing to write a legal opinion that supported Jackson's position on the national bank. The action was controversial and served as part of the basis of Congress's censure of Jackson, but the transformation of the office from a quasi-judicial to an executive-branch institution continued. President Franklin Pierce's (1804–1869) attorney general, Caleb Cushing (1800–1879), transformed the office into a full-time position, ending the tradition of keeping a private practice alongside his official duties. New legal advising responsibilities were transferred to the attorney general's office from other agencies and departments under Cushing, increasing the office's political power and linking it firmly to the president's political administration.

The effort of early attorneys general to coordinate the federal government's legal work was frustrated by the lack of statutory control over other government lawyers. U.S. district attorneys had independent authority to represent federal interests in lower courts, and lawyers in other agencies, such as the solicitor of the treasury were given independent authority to litigate on behalf of the government. The upsurge in federal legal work following the Civil War (1861–1865) prompted Congress to centralize government litigation. In 1870 Congress established the Department of Justice (DOJ) and made the attorney general its head. District attorneys were transferred to the department. Agency legal counsel retained authority to advise their agencies on legal matters, but most litigation functions were transferred to the DOJ.

The establishment of the DOJ and its growth into a large bureaucracy transformed the attorney general's office. While early attorneys general were among the most prominent litigators of their day, by the twentieth century attorneys general were increasingly selected for their political acumen and administrative skills. The practice of attorneys general personally arguing cases before the Supreme Court diminished and is now relatively rare, although every attorney general is expected to argue at least one case during his or her tenure.

The 1870 act also created the office of solicitor general. The solicitor general originally served as a general administrative deputy with wide-ranging responsibilities. As the DOJ grew and new divisions and officers were added, the work of the solicitor general grew more specialized. By the 1920s the office had evolved into an elite barrister's office responsible for supervising the government's appellate litigation and representing the government in the Supreme Court. Contemporary solicitors general are selected for their skills as appellate advocates. The office enjoys a unique relationship to the Court: It is the most frequent litigant before the Court, has special leave to intervene in cases as an amicus, and enjoys unparalleled rates of success before the Court. As the fourth-ranking officer in the DOJ, the solicitor general is under the supervision of the attorney general, but in practice the office normally operates with broad independence. The tradition of independence, however, is limited; in cases important to the president's policy agenda, presidents and attorneys general have directed the legal positions of the solicitor general.

The attorney general's conflicting responsibilities as the chief federal law enforcement officer and as a partisan member of the president's administration complicate his or her role during periods of inter-branch conflict or political scandal. No attorney general has been impeached, but several have been forced to resign during scandals. In 1924 Attorney General Harry Daugherty (1860–1941) was indicted as a result of his involvement in the Teapot Dome scandal that engulfed the Warren G. Harding administration. President Harry Truman's (1884–1972) attorney general, James McGrath (1903–1966), was forced to resign as a result of a tax scandal that rocked the administration. Between 1972 and 1975, four separate attorneys general either resigned in protest or were forced out of office as a result of the DOJ's embroilment in the Watergate scandal that brought down the presidency of Richard Nixon. George W. Bush's (1946–) attorney general, Alberto Gonzales (1955–), resigned in 2007 under a cloud of suspicion involving the firing of U.S. district attorneys for partisan reasons and for his role in authorizing controversial antiterrorist policies.

Through 2007 there have been eighty-one individuals to hold the office. Janet Reno (1938–), appointed by Bill Clinton (1946–) in 1992, was the first woman attorney general. Eleven attorneys general were subsequently appointed and served on the Supreme Court (Levi Lincoln [1749–1820], Roger Taney, Nathan Clifford [1803–1881], Edwin Stanton [1814–1869], Joseph McKenna [1843–1926], William Henry Moody [1853–1917], James McReynolds, Harlan Fiske Stone, Frank Murphy, Robert H. Jackson, and Tom Clark [1899–1977]).

SEE ALSO *Cummings, Homer; Fahy, Charles; Judiciary Act of 1789; Kennedy, Robert; Watergate and the Constitution; Wirt, William*

BIBLIOGRAPHY

Baker, Nancy V. 1992. *Conflicting Loyalties: Law and Politics in the Attorney General's Office, 1789–1990.* Lawrence: University Press of Kansas.

Clayton, Cornell W. 1992. *The Politics of Justice: The Attorney General and the Making of Legal Policy.* Armonk, NY: Sharpe.

Clayton, Cornell W., ed. 1995. *Government Lawyers: The Federal Legal Bureaucracy and Presidential Politics.* Lawrence: University Press of Kansas.

United States Department of Justice. Available from http://www.usdoj.gov.

Cornell W. Clayton

B

BAKER V. CARR, 369 U.S. 186 (1962)

Baker v. Carr, 369 U.S. 186 (1962) marked the U.S. Supreme Court's entry into the "political thicket" of apportionment and electoral politics that Justice Felix Frankfurter, in his opinion in *Colegroe v. Green*, 328 U.S. 549 (1946), warned the Court that it should avoid.

The plaintiffs in *Baker* filed suit alleging the violation of their voting rights pursuant to the equal protection clause of the Fourteenth Amendment. The alleged violation stemmed from Tennessee's continued use of a 1901 apportionment statute that, because of population shifts in Tennessee from 1901 to 1961, rendered state legislative districts malapportioned. The result of the malapportionment was the dilution the plaintiffs' votes in state legislative elections.

In response to a ruling by a three-judge panel from the U.S. District Court for the Middle District of Tennessee that the district court did not have subject-matter jurisdiction and that the plaintiffs had failed to state a claim for which relief could be granted, the Supreme Court held that the district court did have jurisdiction, that the plaintiffs had standing to challenge the Tennessee statute, and that the case was justiciable. The district court had subject-matter jurisdiction because the action nonfrivolously sought the vindication of substantial rights under the Constitution. The plaintiffs had standing because their claim focused directly on the dilution of their vote rather than on a more general claim that the Tennessee government had unconstitutionally failed to redistrict. The case presented a justiciable issue, rather than a nonjusticiable *political question*, because even though the case related to the political issue of reapportionment, it stated a standard equal protection claim subject to reasonable adjudication. After suggesting that political questions tend to relate to federal separation-of-powers issues rather than federalism issues, the Court stated a new standard for nonjusticiable political questions, limiting them to questions involving at least one of several conditions relating to the commitment of the issue to other political branches, the need for courts to make political decisions outside of their expertise or authority, and the lack of clear judicial standards for resolving the dispute. The Court explicitly declined to suggest an appropriate remedy for whatever violation might be proved at trial. Justices William O. Douglas, Tom Clark (1899–1977), and Potter Stewart also concurred separately.

Justices Frankfurter and John Harlan dissented. They distinguished voting-rights claims based on population imbalances, which they deemed nonjusticiable political questions, from voting-rights claims based on racial discrimination (and other characteristics), which had been deemed justiciable and remediable in *Gomillion v. Lightfoot*, 364 U.S. 339 (1960). The dissenters were concerned that the Supreme Court improperly inserted the federal judiciary into a political situation that afforded no standards for proper adjudication. They argued that given that the majority suggested that votes did not have to be weighted equally and that equipopulous districts were not constitutionally required, it was unclear how a court could find an equal protection violation based on vote dilution without impermissibly making political judgments.

Though the explicit holding of *Baker v. Carr* was narrow, the case ushered in a new era of direct judicial oversight over legislative apportionment. The *Baker* Court did not hold that votes had to have equal value or that state legislative districts had to have equal populations. However, once the Court made clear that malapportionment could form the basis of a voting-rights claim, the one-person, one-vote requirement was arguably sure to follow. Indeed, in the wake of *Baker*, the Court decided *Gray v. Sanders*, 372 U.S. 368 (1963), *Wesberry v. Sanders*, 376 U.S. 1 (1964), and *Reynolds v. Sims*, 377 U.S. 533 (1964), all of which enshrined the one-person, one-vote principle in equal protection law and triggered the reapportionment battles that have raged since the 1960s.

SEE ALSO *Case or Controversy; Political Question Doctrine; Reynolds v. Sims, 377 U.S. 533 (1964); Warren Court*

BIBLIOGRAPHY

Ansolabehere, Stephen, and Samuel Issacharoff. 2004. "The Story of *Baker v. Carr*." In *Constitutional Law Stories*, ed. Michael C. Dorf. New York: Foundation Press.

Graham, Gene. 1972. *One Man, One Vote:* Baker v. Carr *and the American Levellers*. Boston: Little, Brown.

Symposium. 2002. *Baker v. Carr:* A Commemorative Symposium. *North Carolina Law Review* 80: 1103–1516.

Henry L. Chambers Jr.

BALLARD V. UNITED STATES, 329 U.S. 187 (1946)

Throughout the early years of the twentieth century, many of the constitutional guarantees of equal participation in society that U.S. citizens now take for granted were just beginning to take shape. For women, however, the realization of many of these rights would take decades. This lag in achieving equality resulted in part from the vestiges of historical discriminatory policies established by the nation's male founders, leaders, and law writers. Much of the discriminatory bias derived from the conceptual relic known today as *romantic paternalism*, the notion that "the weaker sex" needed protection from life's many vicissitudes. As a result, women had been barred from making contracts, owning property, voting, and participating in many other basic and integral social functions, including jury service. Allowing them to engage in such activities, the logic went, would take them away from essential duties and obligations in the home.

It was not until 1946, in *Ballard v. United States*, 329 U.S. 187, that the right of jury service was guaranteed to American women, long after it had been granted to other groups, including former male slaves. As far back as 1880, the Court ruled in *Strauder v. West Virginia*, 100 U.S. 303

that a state law preventing African-American men from serving on juries violated the recently enacted Fourteenth Amendment to the U.S. Constitution.

The factual scenario leading to *Ballard* was benign enough—the indictment and conviction of individuals who conspired to use the federal mail system for fraud. Specifically, it involved the distribution of materials promoting an allegedly fraudulent religious movement. The case had already been to the Supreme Court two years earlier. But it took a second go-round for the Court to consider the alleged illegitimacy of the indictment and conviction of the defendants resulting from the "intentional and systematic exclusion of women from the jury panels."

There was no dispute on the factual question. Women *had* been barred from inclusion on both the grand jury, which indicted the defendants, and the petit jury, which tried the case and convicted them. The question for the Supreme Court in *Ballard* was whether that barring of women from jury service violated the principle that juries are intended to reflect "a cross section of the community," as the Court had noted four years earlier in *Glasser v. United States*, 315 U.S. 60 (1942). Such an infringement would not merely insult the women denied the opportunity to serve, it would skew the jury makeup enough to undermine the indictment and verdict.

By the time it heard oral arguments in *Ballard*, the Supreme Court had decided a number of cases involving the jury issue as it related to other groups in society. Earlier that term, in *Thiel v. Southern Pacific*, 328 U.S. 217 (1946), the Court held unconstitutional the exclusion of individuals from a jury for income-based reasons. In that case, the justices explained that while the American tradition of trial by impartial jury does not require representatives from every economic, social, religious, racial, political, and geographical group, "it does mean that prospective jurors shall be selected by court officials without systematic and intentional exclusion of any of these groups.... To disregard [this principle] is to open the door to class distinctions and discriminations which are abhorrent to the democratic ideals of trial by jury."

Justice William O. Douglas refined this further in writing for the Court in *Ballard*: "The systematic and intentional exclusion of women, like the exclusion of a racial group ... or an economic or social class, deprives the jury system of the broad base it was designed by Congress to have in our democratic society." Indeed, he continued, "the injury is not limited to the defendant—there is injury to the jury system, the law as an institution, to the community at large, and to the democratic ideal reflected in the processes of our courts." The Court reasoned further that differences between men and women made it especially important to prohibit systematic exclusion of women from a jury, noting that neither men nor women act as a class but that "a flavor, a distinct quality is lost if either sex is excluded."

In subsequent decisions over the next half century (several of which would be argued by the future Supreme Court justice Ruth Bader Ginsburg), the Court applied this principle of equal participation on juries to state courts as well as federal courts (e.g., *Taylor v. Louisiana,* 419 U.S. 522 [1975]) and to other areas of society. Even as it did so, however, the Court would continue to struggle with defining the role and rights of women in a changing world and workforce.

SEE ALSO *Juries; Women on Juries*

BIBLIOGRAPHY

Cushman, Clare, ed. 2001. "Romantic Paternalism" and "Jury Duty." In *Supreme Court Decisions and Women's Rights: Milestones to Equality*, 1–36. Washington, DC: CQ Press.

Kerber, Linda K. 1998. *No Constitutional Right to Be Ladies: Women and the Obligations of Citizenship*. New York: Hill and Wang.

Alexander Wohl

BANK OF AUGUSTA V. EARLE, 38 U.S. 519 (1839)

In this case, one of three decided together, the U.S. Supreme Court considered whether a corporation chartered in one state was authorized to conduct business in another. The Bank of Augusta's agent in Mobile purchased bills of exchange at discounts. Bills of exchange were promissory notes from one person or business to another, often endorsed by others who passed them along as payment for debts, goods, or services. The endorsees accepted responsibility to pay if the original maker did not. Before the Civil War (1861–1865) such notes, circulated widely, were an essential augmentation to the limited amount of specie and banknotes available. Among the bills the Bank of Augusta acquired was a note Earle had endorsed. When the original maker failed to pay, Earle refused to honor the note, arguing that the bank had no right to operate in Alabama. It brought suit in the federal circuit court. The court found for Earle, and the bank appealed.

Before the Supreme Court, Earle's lawyers argued that a corporation could not engage in business outside the boundaries of the jurisdiction that chartered it. Even if it could, Alabama's constitution and laws precluded it from doing so there. Carrying out the mandate of the state's constitution to establish a single state bank, the legislature had barred other banks.

The lawyers for the banks insisted that according to the international law of comity, by which sovereign states recognized each other's acts, nations permitted foreign corporations to sue and make contracts within their borders. Daniel Webster, representing the bank, went further, arguing that corporations were entitled to the benefits of the Privileges and Immunities Clause of the U.S. Constitution, which gave citizens of one state the privileges of citizens in other states. A law denying corporations the right to do business in Alabama would violate that provision.

Earle's lawyers responded that sustaining the bank's position would permit any state to force its laws and businesses upon all the others, despite state policy to the contrary. In particular, it would permit states that favored corporate interests to foist them upon states that viewed corporations, and banks especially, to be unrepublican instruments of associated wealth.

Speaking for the Court, which voted eight-to-one, Chief Justice Roger Brooke Taney held that corporations could act outside the boundaries of their states, if their charters permitted. But he rejected Webster's argument that the Privileges and Immunities Clause precluded Alabama from banning foreign banks if it wished. While both foreign nations and American states customarily permitted foreign corporations to engage in business activities as a matter of comity, the law allowed them to withdraw this privilege when public policy dictated. While Alabama clearly wanted to limit banking, Justice Taney wrote, its laws did not make clear whether that meant banning foreign banks from doing any business in the state at all. It was up to the state, and not the courts, to make such determinations. Until it did, the courts must enforce the note against endorsees.

The Court's decision was a compromise between states' rights and a developing national market. It allowed states to limit the operations of foreign corporations if they wished but sustained commercialization across state lines until they did so.

SEE ALSO *Corporate Law; Taney Court*

BIBLIOGRAPHY

Currie, David P. 1983. "The Constitution in the Supreme Court: Article IV and Federal Powers, 1836–1864." *Duke Law Journal* 4 (September): 695–747.

Henderson, Gerard Carl. 1918. "The Rule of Comity." In *The Position of Foreign Corporations in American Constitutional Law: A Contribution to the History and Theory of Juristic Persons in Anglo-American Law*, 36–49. Cambridge, MA: Harvard University Press.

Huebner, Timothy S. 2003. *The Taney Court: Justices, Rulings, and Legacy*. Santa Barbara, CA: ABC-CLIO.

Michael Les Benedict

BANK OF UNITED STATES V. DANDRIDGE, 25 U.S. 64 (1827)

What powers to act flow naturally from a corporation's existence and what powers to act must be spelled out were questions that confronted American courts regularly as corporations became common in the early nineteenth century. Legal culture, following a political culture suspicious of rights granted to a corporation that hinted of monopoly or privilege, tended to construe early corporate charters strictly, greatly limiting the implicit powers of a corporation to act. Just as no agreement can anticipate every twist and turn in the relationship of the parties involved, however, so no charter can anticipate every contingency a corporation might face during its existence. The more dynamic the environment, especially the economic environment, the harder it is to anticipate and enumerate every power necessary to act. The economy of the nineteenth century was quite dynamic, especially when compared to the immediately preceding decades.

In *Bank of United States v. Dandridge*, 25 U.S. 64 (1827), the Court faced a simple question. The Bank of the United States sued the officer-signer and sureties of a bond guaranteeing the performance of the bank officer. The bank had not accepted the bond in any formal manner or in writing, but had simply allowed the officer to perform his duties as cashier once the bond had been created. Having failed to reduce the acceptance to writing, could the bank sue, and, if so, what evidence could the court adduce to confirm acceptance? Was the Court limited only to a formal acceptance or could the Court analogize the bank's acquiescence to that of a human being's acceptance by acts?

The Court, in an opinion by Justice Joseph Story, loosened the formal constraints and allowed the inference from acts. Story's opinion, after reviewing some examples under which courts allowed legal relationships to arise even when not evidenced by a writing, and even when a writing was prescribed, asked "upon what ground it can be maintained that the approval of the bond must be in writing? It is not required by the terms of the charter, or the bylaws. In each of them the language points to the fact of approval, and not to the evidence by which it is to be established." Story neatly turned the formalisms required to verify corporate acts from substantive restrictions on corporate capacity to evidentiary presumptions, clearing the way for greater freedom to act, as was common in the everyday life of business conducted between and among individual human beings. The analogy was explicit and had actually introduced the argument. "In short, we think, that the acts of artificial persons afford the same presumptions as the acts of natural persons. Each affords presumptions, from acts done, of what must have preceded them, as matters of right, or matters of duty."

Story's innovation drew a rare dissent from Chief Justice John Marshall who, while hardly an enemy of legal innovation, bespoke a caution grounded in the protection of the bank itself, as well as the public. Admitting that corporate charters were devices that enabled groups of human beings to act in concert, still their capacity was limited to the substance and forms set out in the charter. Noting that the charter of the Bank of the United States made the directors of the bank personally liable on certain practices and bad loans, the better to secure the capital of the shareholders, notably including the United States, Marshall was reluctant to allow the bank to act informally. Bonds protected the bank's officers, and thereby the directors, from loss and liability. That protection should be immediately evident to anyone, Congress included, who might worry about the protections covering so important an institution as the Bank of the United States. Thus, the shareholders were protected by the requirements that many other records be formal, including many of lesser significance. In Marshall's view, a protection as significant as the bond required the formalism that was the presupposition of the ancient rule.

The Court in *Dandridge* took a step in the direction of modern corporate law. Even the chief justice's dissent used ancient arguments to protect an instrument of the emerging modern economy. The disagreements evident in this opinion were hardly ones that arose from two eras of jurisprudence, but rather distinctly different strategies in the service of the nascent political economy.

SEE ALSO *Corporate Law; Marshall Court*

BIBLIOGRAPHY

Hurst, James Willard. 1956. *Law and the Conditions of Freedom in the Nineteenth-Century United States*. Madison: University of Wisconsin Press.

Hurst, James Willard. 1970. *The Legitimacy of the Business Corporation in the Law of the United States, 1780–1970*. Charlottesville: University Press of Virginia.

Gregory A. Mark

BANK OF UNITED STATES V. DEVEAUX, 9 U.S. 61 (1809)

The Constitution, under the principle of diversity jurisdiction, grants federal courts the authority to rule in cases between citizens of different states. In the early nineteenth century, the citizenship of corporations, for the purposes of diversity jurisdiction, seemed to be in doubt. Although corporations had been parties to federal suits in the past, *Bank of United States v. Deveaux*, 9 U.S. 61 (1809) raised the particular question of whether corporations satisfied the diversity jurisdiction requirements. The Court unanimously held that while corporations were not citizens per se, they were entities composed essentially of individual citizens, and thus the citizenship of corporations was determined by the citizenship of their members.

Deveaux was one of the early rulings on the state taxation of the United States Bank. The Bank, a corporation, was suing Deveaux, a Georgia tax collector, in federal court to recover property seized by Deveaux after the Bank refused to pay a Georgia tax. The lower court dismissed the case for lack of jurisdiction, and the U.S. Supreme Court reversed. Writing for the Court, Chief Justice John Marshall ruled that for the purposes of diversity jurisdiction "the term citizen ought to be understood as it is used in the constitution, and as it is used in other laws. That is, to describe the real persons who come into court, in this case, under their corporate name." In effect, *Deveaux* required each of the owners of a corporation that was a party to a federal suit to be diverse from the other party.

The Court relied on the rationale behind diversity jurisdiction to rule in favor of the Bank. Diversity jurisdiction for national tribunals, Marshall explained, was necessary to allay the concern that state courts might not "administer justice as impartially as those of the nation" to parties from outside the state. Outsiders "are not less susceptible of these apprehensions, nor can they be supposed to be less the objects of constitutional provision, because they are allowed to sue by a corporate name."

The case exemplified how the Court at the time viewed corporations mainly as mere aggregates of individuals, rather than as separate legal entities. When the number and activity of corporations increased over the course of the nineteenth century, however, the Court ultimately reversed its position, supporting the growing proposition that a corporation was an entity separate from the individuals who composed it.

Deveaux specifically limited the reach of federal judicial power and the ability of corporations to litigate in federal courts. As interstate corporate activity increased, this jurisdictional restriction became more cumbersome. And in 1844, the Taney Court overruled *Deveaux* in *Louisville Railroad Co. v. Letson*, 43 U.S. 497 to hold that a corporation, for the purposes of diversity jurisdiction, was a citizen of the state in which it was incorporated. In the end, *Deveaux* is best remembered as reflecting the early-nineteenth-century conception of the corporation as a collection of individuals—a conception that was overturned by the end of the century.

SEE ALSO *Corporate Law; Diversity Jurisdiction*

BIBLIOGRAPHY

David P. Currie. 1992. *The Constitution in the Supreme Court: The First Hundred Years, 1789–1888.* Chicago: University of Chicago Press.

Ajay K. Mehrotra

BANKRUPTCY AND INSOLVENCY

Article I of the U.S. Constitution gives Congress the power to pass "uniform Laws on the subject of Bankruptcies throughout the United States." For the first 111 years after the Constitution's adoption in 1787, Congress exercised its bankruptcy power only sparingly. A permanent bankruptcy law was not enacted until 1898, and before that date a series of bankruptcy laws had been in effect for a total of only fourteen years. The first bankruptcy cases to reach the Supreme Court required the Court to find the limits of state authority over debtor-creditor law. It was not until later that the Supreme Court would play a role in defining the scope of the congressional bankruptcy power or in interpreting the bankruptcy laws that Congress enacted.

CREATION OF THE FEDERAL BANKRUPTCY POWER

It is not an exaggeration to say that conflicts over debtor-creditor law contributed to the creation of the U.S.

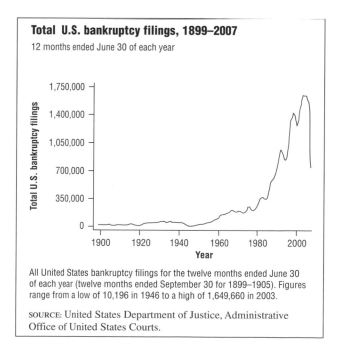

Total U.S. bankruptcy filings, 1899–2007

12 months ended June 30 of each year

All United States bankruptcy filings for the twelve months ended June 30 of each year (twelve months ended September 30 for 1899–1905). Figures range from a low of 10,196 in 1946 to a high of 1,649,660 in 2003.

SOURCE: United States Department of Justice, Administrative Office of United States Courts.

Figure 1

Constitution. In 1786 and 1787 farmers in western Massachusetts rose up against what they saw as favoritism toward merchant interests. The uprising, which became known as Shays's Rebellion, shut down the local courts to prevent enforcement of debts owed to merchants by agrarian interests. Farmers had relied on the easy credit made available by the paper money laws of the revolutionary era. When the war ended and the laws were repealed, the farmers found themselves without specie to repay their creditors. The ineffectiveness of the central government during Shays's Rebellion helped motivate some political leaders to call for a constitutional convention to give the central government more effective powers.

In addition to the class interests typified by Shays's Rebellion, there also was interstate conflict in the area of debtor-creditor relations. During the colonial period and while the Articles of the Confederation were in effect, different state laws and state court favoritism of local debtors thwarted many creditors in their collection efforts across state boundaries. For example, a state court might refuse to enforce a judgment against a local debtor that a creditor had obtained in another state. It was not just creditors who faced inconsistent laws. In one state, a legislature might pass a special act generously discharging a particular debtor from his obligations, but the debtor might find the discharge ineffective in another state. Thus, when the framers met in Philadelphia during the summer of 1787, bringing some order to debtor-creditor law across state laws was an important goal.

The concerns of creditors trying to collect across state boundaries were largely satisfied with the full faith and credit clause, which has developed its own history outside the scope of debtor-creditor relations. More significantly for the development of U.S. bankruptcy law, the framers inserted two other clauses into the Constitution. First and most obviously, they gave Congress the power to enact uniform laws of bankruptcy in the bankruptcy clause. Second, in the contract clause, the framers prohibited the states from impairing the obligation of contract. Both the records of the Constitutional Convention and the ratification debates include very little mention of the reasons for and the scope of the congressional bankruptcy power. In finding the boundaries of both state and federal power over bankrupt debtors, the judiciary would have to act without a clear history to guide it.

DEFINING THE BOUNDARIES OF STATE POWER

For the first fifty years after the Constitution's adoption, the scope of the congressional bankruptcy power was hotly debated, with literalists contending that the bankruptcy clause gave Congress the power only to enact a collection-oriented, merchant "bankruptcy" law as opposed to a more general "insolvency" law providing for debtor relief. This distinction was supported by the common usages of the terms at the time of the Constitution's drafting. For example, in *Federalist* No. 42 (1788), James Madison (1751–1836) stated that the subject of bankruptcy is "so intimately connected with the regulation of commerce" that the expediency of a congressional bankruptcy power "seems not likely to be drawn into question." Madison's conjunction of the word *bankruptcy* with the eighteenth-century speaker's narrow concept of *commerce* suggests that he had perhaps understood congressional power to be narrowly circumscribed to merchants and traders. The Bankruptcy Act of 1800 was the first congressionally enacted bankruptcy law, and its application was limited only to merchants, although widespread dissatisfaction with the 1800 law led to its repeal in 1803.

After repeal, the constitutional question over the scope of congressional power and political battles between agrarian and mercantile interests meant several decades would pass before Congress would enact another bankruptcy law. The states stepped into the void. In 1811, for example, New York passed a law that would eventually give the Supreme Court its first opportunity to define the limits of state authority in bankruptcy. The New York statute granted a discharge to a debtor who had turned over all his property for distribution to creditors in accordance with the provisions of the law. When a debtor pleaded the New York law as a defense to collection of debts created before enactment, his creditor objected that New York could not constitutionally enact such a retroactive law. In *Sturges v. Crowninshield*, 17 U.S. 122 (1819), the Supreme Court first considered whether the New York statute was a law of bankruptcy and, if so, whether the power to pass bankruptcy laws resided exclusively in Congress. Writing for the court, Chief Justice John Marshall found substantial overlap between the subject matters of bankruptcy and insolvency law. Ultimately, the Court held it was not necessary to define the boundary between bankruptcy and insolvency laws, for it found that states retained the power to enact bankruptcy laws when Congress had not exercised its power. Because no federal bankruptcy law was in effect, New York had the power to enact its own bankruptcy law.

The "great question," as Marshall characterized it, was whether the New York law violated the constitutional prohibition against the states from impairing the obligation of contract. The Court ruled that New York's law did impair the obligation of contract, but it rested on an important distinction. New York's law applied to all debts, whether created before or after its enactment and in that sense, the law impaired an obligation of contract. Thus, the Court distinguished between laws that voided a contract from its creation and laws that later voided contracts already made.

The question remained whether a state could pass a general law allowing a discharge that could apply to contracts made after the law's enactment. In *Ogden v. Saunders*, 25 U.S. 213 (1827), a divided Court appeared to uphold the states' power to enact laws providing for the discharge of future obligations, but the facts of the case involved a New York debtor using New York law to shield himself from a lawsuit by a Louisiana creditor in a Louisiana court. The Supreme Court noted that the creditor had done nothing to subject himself to New York law. Thus, the core holding of *Ogden* was only that a state's bankruptcy law could not give a discharge that would bind citizens of other states. The portion of the Court's decision about future obligations was not necessary to its decision and thus arguably not binding precedent.

The Supreme Court decisions in *Sturges* and *Ogden* left a doctrinal legacy that continues to this day. In both decisions, the states' power to enact some sort of bankruptcy law was clearly validated, but the Marshall Court was not about to let the states traffic in bankruptcy discharges in a way that would threaten to bring about the local debtor favoritism seen in the period before the Constitution. In *International Shoe Co. v. Pinkus*, 278 U.S. 261 (1929), the Court would eventually rule that the congressional bankruptcy power, once exercised, preempted even a prospective state law that provided for a discharge of an insolvent debtor. Although state insolvency laws remain today, their principal design is to aid in the liquidation of a debtor's assets so as to maximize creditor recoveries. The Supreme Court decisions made debt collection a matter of state law but put debtor relief within the province of the federal law. Ultimately, the economic climate, the nation's expanding frontier, and the passage of a permanent federal bankruptcy law would largely render irrelevant the scope of the states' authority over debtor relief.

NINETEENTH-CENTURY ECONOMIC CRISES AND THE BANKRUPTCY LAW

Constitutional objections and economic self-interest prevented reenactment of a federal bankruptcy law until the Panic of 1837 led to a national economic crisis that begged for legislative action. Even then, there was substantial opposition from financial interests, and it was not until the Bankruptcy Act of 1841 that a new federal law was in place. The 1841 law was a watershed moment in the development of U.S. bankruptcy law. Gone was any thought of a distinction between a "bankruptcy" or "insolvency" law. For the first time, debtors could voluntarily initiate their own bankruptcy case—the Bankruptcy Act of 1800 and earlier English legal antecedents required creditors to initiate a bankruptcy proceeding. Also, the 1841 act did not limit its relief to merchants. Anyone was eligible to file a bankruptcy petition under the 1841 act and receive a discharge for his or her indebtedness after turning over his or her assets to creditors. The 1841 law also gave the debtor a certain number of exemptions—a minimal amount of assets the debtor could use to build a fresh start after bankruptcy. Although widespread dissatisfaction with the low creditor recoveries under the Bankruptcy Act of 1841 led Congress to repeal the statute in 1843, its effects remain with us today. The voluntary petition, discharge, and exemptions remain central features in U.S. bankruptcy law.

It was not until the economic crisis precipitated by the end of the Civil War (1861–1865) that Congress was again motivated to pass a federal bankruptcy law. The Bankruptcy Act of 1867 introduced several innovations that remain with the bankruptcy system. The federal district courts were to appoint *registers of bankruptcy* to assist with the bankruptcy proceedings. The registers of bankruptcy were the forerunners of today's specialized bankruptcy courts. For the first time, the 1867 law also allowed corporations to be debtors. In 1874 Congress amended the law to allow debtors to propose a plan that would pay creditors over time. These plans, known as *composition agreements*, were the forerunners of modern bankruptcy reorganizations and individual chapter 13 plans. Like its predecessors, Congress eventually repealed the Bankruptcy Act of 1867, although not until 1878.

After its decision in *Ogden*, the Supreme Court did not play a significant role in the further development of nineteenth-century bankruptcy law. One exception was its support for proceedings that would develop into modern corporate reorganizations as discussed below. Although the state of debtor-creditor relations had been one of the reasons for the Constitutional Convention and although the Court initially had decided important questions about state powers of bankruptcy, these topics faded into the background as weightier constitutional questions came to the fore.

Part of the reason the Supreme Court's role faded was that formal, legal debtor-relief mechanisms had become less important while the frontier offered an informal debtor-relief mechanism. Insolvent debtors could escape their obligations simply by moving west. For example, in the 1820s and 1830s, the phrase "G.T.T." or "Gone to Texas" scribbled on a farmhouse door provided many a debtor a discharge beyond the reach of their local creditors. It is not coincidental that the U.S. bankruptcy law became permanent in 1898, as the closing of the frontier also closed an opportunity for insolvent debtors to get a fresh start. The nineteenth-century experience with bankruptcy law is partially the story about the interaction of formal legal institutions with informal institutions that serve similar functions.

Changing economic conditions, however, would eventually lead to demand for another bankruptcy law. As the nation's economy became more integrated, it became increasingly likely that creditors would deal with out-of-state debtors. In the early nineteenth century, cases like *Sturges* and *Ogden* illustrated how moneyed interests looked to the judiciary to protect them from local favoritism. By the end of the nineteenth century, these same interests now turned to Congress for relief. In *Debt's Dominion* (2001), Professor David Skeel traced the nineteenth-century rise of professionalized groups specializing in debt collection. The professional groups lowered the cost of collective action for the interests they represented, and gaining favorable legal change through the legislature became an effective strategy for the financial interests these groups represented.

BANKRUPTCY LAW BECOMES PERMANENT

Although financial interests could more effectively lobby for legislative change, it did not necessarily come easily. Western and agrarian interests were suspicious of the eastern merchants who wanted another bankruptcy law. Roughly the same coalitions that squared off over the gold standard in the 1890s also contested enactment of a new bankruptcy law. The mercantile interests wanted a bankruptcy law that would aid in the collection of debts from far-flung debtors, while populists wanted a bankruptcy law that gave effective debtor relief. The resulting Bankruptcy Reform Act of 1898 set up the federal district courts as courts of bankruptcy, giving them the power to appoint bankruptcy referees who could hear bankruptcy cases. Debtors again could file voluntarily and bankruptcy relief was open to all, including corporations. The 1898 law aimed for a comprehensive resolution of all the claims against a bankrupt debtor, an efficient distribution of assets, and a discharge. Thus, the 1898 act set the stage for the modern bankruptcy system, including relatively generous debtor-relief provisions.

To satisfy the populists that some local control would remain over debtor-creditor law, the promoters of the 1898 law agreed that state law would determine the amount of the exemptions each debtor would be allowed to retain. Five years later, the Supreme Court heard *Hanover National Bank v. Moyses*, 186 U.S. 181 (1902), which challenged the scheme as being outside the congressional power to enact uniform laws of bankruptcy. The Court ruled that the bankruptcy law was uniform in that creditors in each state got what they would have received had no bankruptcy law been enacted. The *Moyses* decision rendered the uniformity requirement an extremely weak check on congressional power to enact bankruptcy laws. The current bankruptcy law still allows states to opt out of the federal exemption law and specify the exemptions that a debtor filing bankruptcy in their state may keep.

The most noteworthy feature of the 1898 law was its endurance. The law would remain in effect until 1979

when it would be replaced by another bankruptcy law. From 1898 forward, the United States would not be without a federal bankruptcy law. With *Moyses* eliminating any remaining limits on congressional power to enact bankruptcy laws, the old arguments over the division of state versus federal power became much less important.

FINDING LIMITS TO CONGRESSIONAL BANKRUPTCY POWER

Not surprisingly, the economic crisis of the Great Depression produced much pressure on Congress to react with changes to the bankruptcy law to help financially distressed citizens. In 1934 Congress passed the Frazier-Lemke Act to help farmers, allowing them to keep their farms for up to five years by paying a fixed amount of rent to their mortgagee. Because the Frazier-Lemke Act expressly applied to mortgages created before its effective date, financial interests challenged the statute as a taking of their property rights in a mortgage in violation of the Fifth Amendment.

The Supreme Court took up the matter in *Louisville Joint Stock Land Bank v. Radford*, 295 U.S. 555 (1935) and held the Frazier-Lemke Act unconstitutional. In an important passage for the later development of U.S. bankruptcy law, Justice Louis Brandeis would write that the congressional bankruptcy power was subject to the Fifth Amendment's prohibition against the taking of property without just compensation. Although the Court's precise reason for striking down the statute was not clear, the retroactive nature of Frazier-Lemke seemed to concern the Court. Congress immediately reacted to the *Radford* decision by amending the Frazier-Lemke Act, but these amendments were relatively minor and did not change the retroactive nature of the statute. Two years later, the Court held in *Wright v. Vinton Branch of Mountain Trust Bank*, 300 U.S. 440 (1937) that these minor amendments saved the Frazier-Lemke Act. In *Wright v. Union Central Life Insurance Co.*, 304 U.S. 502 (1938), the Court again ruled against a creditor's Fifth Amendment claim versus the Frazier-Lemke Act and its amendments.

Radford, *Vinton Branch*, and *Union Central* would come to be known as the Frazier-Lemke cases. Their ambiguity and inconsistency has given these cases a lasting legacy. For example, in *United States v. Security Industrial Bank*, 459 U.S. 70 (1982), the Court would again affirm that there were Fifth Amendment limits on congressional bankruptcy power, although the Court ultimately construed the law to avoid any constitutional problems. After the Frazier-Lemke cases, all subsequent proposals for bankruptcy reform would have to deal with the possibility of a judicial declaration that the reform went too far in adjusting debtor-creditor relations and hence violated the Constitution. The lack of precise boundary lines makes the threat more effective, as reform-minded interest groups and legislators need to steer well clear of the boundary if they want to ensure that a piece of legislation will remain in effect. Because *Radford* strongly hinted but did not clearly hold that retroactivity was the Court's core concern about congressional overreaching, proposals for retroactive debt-relief legislation aiding debtors are often met with statements by financial interests that the legislation will be declared unconstitutional.

CREATION OF THE MODERN BUSINESS REORGANIZATION

Beginning in 1931, government and private reports began to appear that described widespread corruption and conflicts of interest in the bankruptcy system. Many observers believed that legislative reform was needed, especially procedural changes in how the bankruptcy process was administered. As usual, the path through Congress was not unimpeded. The merchant and creditor professional groups that had arisen in the late nineteenth century had continued to gain influence through the first part of the twentieth century. The members of these groups had a self-interest in the status quo, but many also would benefit financially from a better bankruptcy system. The final legislative result, the Chandler Act of 1938, represented a number of compromises to accommodate the competing interests.

The Chandler Act made changes to consumer bankruptcy law, such as the creation of a wage earners' plan that allowed individuals to pay their creditors over time. More significantly for the Supreme Court's role in bankruptcy law, the Chandler Act codified business reorganization practices the Court had helped create. Corporations had not been allowed to file bankruptcy until the 1867 bankruptcy law, and even under the 1898 statute, a corporation could not file bankruptcy voluntarily. Bankruptcy relief was not a practical option for financially distressed corporations.

To aid financially distressed corporations, late nineteenth-century legal professionals had created the fiction of an equity receivership. Financially distressed railroads, whose inherently interstate character made state law a poor place to look for help, often used the federal courts to invoke an equity receivership. The court then would appoint a receiver who would sell the company's assets, usually as a going concern, and distribute the proceeds to creditors. Often the sale was not at arms length, and the entire proceeding resulted in existing management retaining control over the company's assets. The Supreme Court issued a number of opinions that had curbed some of the worst abuses in equity receiverships, and the Court's institutional capital thereby contributed to the receivership's legitimacy. None of these opinions were probably more important than the decision in

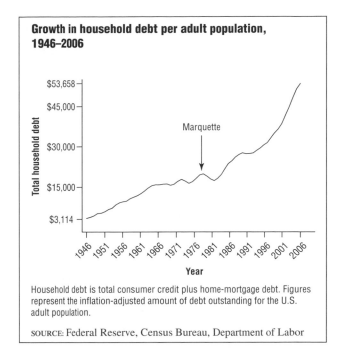

Growth in household debt per adult population, 1946–2006

Household debt is total consumer credit plus home-mortgage debt. Figures represent the inflation-adjusted amount of debt outstanding for the U.S. adult population.

SOURCE: Federal Reserve, Census Bureau, Department of Labor

Figure 2

Northern Pacific Railway v. Boyd, 228 U.S. 482 (1913), where the Court ruled that a senior class of investors, such as bondholders, had to be paid in full before a junior class, such as shareholders, could receive any distribution. This idea, which came to be known as the *absolute priority rule*, remains the core principle of chapter 11 corporate reorganizations to this day.

Congressional enactments from the early days of the Franklin Roosevelt administration in 1933 and 1934 ended the era of equity receiverships by authorizing federal composition agreements and reorganizations. The Chandler Act reworked this patchwork of statutes into a comprehensive federal law for corporate reorganizations. Many of today's corporate-reorganization practices find their antecedents in the Chandler Act, which in turn relied heavily on the equity receivership practices the Supreme Court helped create.

After the Chandler Act's passage in 1938, both Congress and the Supreme Court would intervene only on discrete matters of relatively minor importance to the federal bankruptcy system. In 1946 Congress put bankruptcy referees onto a salaried basis, and in 1964 Congress authorized the Supreme Court to begin promulgating specialized rules for bankruptcy procedure. Both of these developments contributed to the further professionalization of the bankruptcy bench and bar. Overall, however, the forty years after 1938 were a period of relatively little change in U.S. bankruptcy law, which meant that professionals could again reassert their power over the bankruptcy process.

BANKRUPTCY REFORM ACT OF 1978

The increasing professionalization of bankruptcy court helped to contribute to what many persons would call the "bankruptcy ring"—a small, tight-knit group of professionals who controlled the bankruptcy process in their communities. An influential 1971 report from the Brookings Institution documented many shortcomings in how the bankruptcy system worked, focusing especially on the professionals' conflicts of interest that affected the bankruptcy process. A government commission made similar findings in the 1973 *Report of the Commission on the Bankruptcy Laws of the United States*. Both reports recommended a procedural overhaul of the bankruptcy process, placing responsibility for consumer bankruptcies in an administrative agency.

These proposals threatened the status and income of bankruptcy lawyers and judges. (A 1973 change finally gave the title of *judge* to the court officials who heard bankruptcy matters.) These groups strongly resisted any change that would give an administrative agency the power to handle consumer bankruptcy cases, but the need to make some changes to an antiquated eighty-year-old statute was obvious. Thus, Congress passed the Bankruptcy Reform Act of 1978 to replace the 1898 law entirely, but the influence of the professional groups was evident in the system of bankruptcy courts that the new law created.

During the debates that led to the 1978 law, proposals to create an administrative agency to handle bankruptcy fell away. In their place were proposals championed by professional groups to elevate the bankruptcy courts to full Article III status. These new proposals would have cost the federal judiciary its role appointing bankruptcy judges. The existing federal judiciary also felt that the introduction of so many new Article III judges, especially judges who were addressed as mere "referees" only a few years before, would damage the status and prestige of the Article III judiciary. Consequently, the federal judiciary fought hard against any changes to the status of bankruptcy judges, with Chief Justice Warren Burger personally intervening with key legislators. As a result, although it created new bankruptcy courts, the 1978 law left these courts as Article I courts staffed by judges with fourteen-year terms who were appointed by the circuit courts, rather than lifetime appointees nominated by the president and confirmed by the Senate.

AN UNCONSTITUTIONAL SYSTEM AND A FIX

Despite the federal judiciary and Chief Justice Burger's influence over the organization of the new bankruptcy courts, the Supreme Court declared the new system unconstitutional in *Northern Pipeline Construction Co. v. Marathon Pipe Line Co.*, 458 U.S. 50 (1982). The debtor in that case had invoked the jurisdiction of the bankruptcy court to resolve a state law breach of contract claim with another company. The Supreme Court held that Congress had given the bankruptcy courts judicial powers that had to be vested in Article III courts.

The Court stayed its decision for six months so that Congress would have time to pass legislation reconstituting the bankruptcy courts. After the expiration of the Court's stay, the Judicial Conference of the United States adopted an emergency rule of dubious constitutionality that nevertheless allowed the bankruptcy courts to operate. Congress would not act until 1984 and even then was motivated into action only after a different Supreme Court decision. Where the lack of a constitutional system of bankruptcy courts had failed to stir Congress, the furor of organized labor to the Court's decision in *National Labor Relations Board v. Bildisco & Bildisco*, 465 U.S. 513 (1984) was more successful. Congress reacted to *Bildisco* by putting restrictions on the power of bankrupt companies to reject collective bargaining agreements, and at the same time Congress recast the bankruptcy court jurisdictional scheme to satisfy the Court's concerns as expressed in *Northern Pipeline*.

Despite some initial challenges where the Court held that certain bankruptcy matters had to be decided by a jury (*Granfinanciera, S.A. v. Nordberg*, 492 U.S. 33 [1989]) but left open the question of whether bankruptcy judges could supervise a jury trial, the 1984 amendments appear to have settled the jurisdictional structure of the U.S. bankruptcy courts. Serious challenges to the basic structure of the bankruptcy court system have not been raised since 1989.

THE CHAPTERS OF THE BANKRUPTCY CODE

In addition to the major procedural reform just discussed, the 1978 law was a codification of many judicial doctrines that had arisen under the previous law. The resulting Bankruptcy Code, with its different chapters of bankruptcy relief, would become the province of highly specialized lawyers. In the Bankruptcy Code's early years, the Supreme Court had to decipher its meaning on fundamental issues that would greatly affect the relative power of debtors and creditors in the bankruptcy process. For example, the Court decided in *United Savings Association v. Timbers of Inwood Forest Associates*, 484 U.S. 365 (1988) that a creditor holding collateral was not entitled to interest as compensation for any delay the bankruptcy proceeding would cause in allowing the creditor to foreclose and recognize the value of the collateral. Because a debtor has a lot of control over how quickly a bankruptcy case might proceed, the *Timbers* decision gave creditors a reason to be accommodating in out-of-court negotiations lest they suffer the uncompensated effects of delay.

The Bankruptcy Code remains in effect. Chapter 7 bankruptcy requires debtors to turn over all of their assets, except those assets that state or federal law exempts from the bankruptcy process. Chapter 9 allows local governmental entities to seek bankruptcy relief, although only a handful of small governmental bodies invoke chapter 9 each year. Chapter 11 bankruptcy is principally used by insolvent corporations to restructure their business affairs and pay their creditors over time, but individuals who are not eligible under one of the other chapters also use chapter 11. Chapter 13 relief is reserved only for individuals and, like chapter 11, contemplates the payment of creditors over time. In the wake of a farm-debt crisis, Congress added chapter 12 in 1986, giving farmers a procedure very similar to chapter 13. All of these chapters give the debtor a discharge, allow voluntary bankruptcy filings, and do not confine their relief to specific occupations (with some minor exceptions). In 2005 Congress added chapter 15 to give bankruptcy courts the authority to deal with thorny jurisdictional problems in transnational bankruptcies.

With bankruptcy no longer at the forefront of federalism issues and with the major interpretive questions about the 1978 law having been settled, most bankruptcy cases that reach the Supreme Court today require the justices to resolve a narrow interpretative question of the federal Bankruptcy Code on which the lower courts have split. Because the justices have not come to the Supreme Court with strong ideological predispositions on substantive bankruptcy issues, they sometimes have used bankruptcy cases to play out their battles on philosophies of statutory interpretation, such as textualism.

BANKRUPTCY BECOMES PART OF THE MIDDLE-CLASS EXPERIENCE

Immediately after the 1978 law, bankruptcy filings leaped. In the year before the law went into effect, 225,000 bankruptcy cases had been filed. By 1984 that figure had grown over 50 percent to 365,000. Financial interests blamed the generosity of the 1978 law, and in 1984 were successful in persuading Congress to pass changes cutting back on the debtor relief in the 1978 law, including a provision giving the bankruptcy courts the power to dismiss a bankruptcy case the court found to be a "substantial abuse" of the bankruptcy law. These changes—as well as other amendments in 1986, 1988, and 1994—did nothing to stem the growing number of bankruptcy cases. By 1996 more than one million bankruptcy cases were being filed each year. By 2004 there would be 1,600,000 bankruptcy cases filed. There would come to be more bankruptcy cases filed in a year than college degrees conferred or cases of cancer diagnosed, and statistically children would have a greater probability of living through their parents' bankruptcy than living through their parents' divorce. Far from being at the periphery, bankruptcy would become a part of the middle-class experience.

Although some critics maintained that the increasing use of bankruptcy showed a declining moral attitude

toward keeping commitments and a concomitant exploitation of a generous bankruptcy law, the evidence showed that bankruptcy filings had grown hand-in-hand with the growth in outstanding household debt. The 1978 law had coincided with the Supreme Court's decision in *Marquette National Bank v. First of Omaha Service Corp.*, 439 U.S. 299 (1978), which had deregulated the interest rates that consumer lenders could charge. In 1943 the first year the U.S. government tracked consumer credit, there was $2,800 in household debt outstanding (defined as consumer credit plus home mortgages, in inflation-adjusted 2006 dollars) for every adult person in the United States. By 1978 that figure had grown to $20,800, and by 2006 it was $55,400. By 2004 total U.S. household debt had surpassed yearly personal income. With more debt had come more bankruptcy filings.

Like the professional groups in the late nineteenth century, the consumer credit industry turned to Congress. After seven years of lobbying efforts that came with media reports describing huge industry campaign contributions to key congressional allies, the consumer-credit industry succeeded in getting Congress to pass the Bankruptcy Abuse Prevention and Consumer Protection Act of 2005. Professional groups that had played a large role in drafting previous bankruptcy legislation were locked out of the drafting process, and roundly criticized the new law as technically deficient. With the rise of industry influence, the year 2005 may mark the decline of professional influence over the content of debtor-creditor law.

The 2005 law imposed much harsher rules on business and consumer debtors, increased the amount of scrutiny these debtors would face once they got to court, increased the amount of paperwork debtors would have to produce in bankruptcy court, and caused attorneys' fees to increase by 50 percent because of all the new work (and potential liabilities) for bankruptcy attorneys. Not surprisingly, debtors rushed to file bankruptcy before the law took effect. At a time when the bankruptcy filing rate was 1.6 million per year, over 650,000 debtors filed bankruptcy in the last quarter of 2005 alone. Statistics for the end of 2007 and the beginning of 2008 showed that bankruptcy filings had begun a steady climb upward. After the 2007 home-mortgage crisis, experts forecasted that annual U.S. bankruptcy filings would again rise over the one million mark.

In one way, U.S. bankruptcy law has circled back to where it started. In the earliest days of the republic, debtor-creditor law raised momentous constitutional issues and hence was at the center of legal debate, although few persons were touched by the bankruptcy system. Today, debtor-creditor law raises few momentous legal issues—only narrow questions of technical legal doctrine tend to arise—but debtor-creditor law has come back to the center of the legal debate because it touches the lives of so many.

SEE ALSO *Article I; Marquette National Bank v. First of Omaha Service Corp., 439 U.S. 299 (1978); Ogden v. Saunders, 25 U.S. 213 (1827)*

BIBLIOGRAPHY

Balleisen, Edward J. 2001. *Navigating Failure: Bankruptcy and Commercial Society in Antebellum America.* Chapel Hill: University of North Carolina Press.

Coleman, Peter J. 1974. *Debtors and Creditors in America: Insolvency, Imprisonment for Debt, and Bankruptcy, 1607–1900.* Madison: State Historical Society of Wisconsin.

Madison, James. 1788. *Federalist* No. 42: "The Powers Conferred by the Constitution Further Considered." Available from http://thomas.loc.gov/home/histdox/fed_42.html.

Mann, Bruce H. 2002. *Republic of Debtors: Bankruptcy in the Age of American Independence.* Cambridge, MA: Harvard University Press.

Posner, Eric A. 1997. "The Political Economy of the Bankruptcy Reform Act of 1978." *Michigan Law Review* 96(1): 47–126.

Report of the Commission on the Bankruptcy Laws of the United States. 1973. H.R. Doc. No. 93-137.

Sandage, Scott A. 2005. *Born Losers: A History of Failure in America.* Cambridge, MA: Harvard University Press.

Skeel, David A., Jr. 2001. *Debt's Dominion: A History of Bankruptcy Law in America.* Princeton, NJ: Princeton University Press.

Stanley, David T., and Marjorie Girth. 1971. *Bankruptcy: Problem, Process, Reform.* Washington, DC: Brookings Institution.

Sullivan, Teresa A.; Elizabeth Warren; and Jay Lawrence Westbrook. 1989. *As We Forgive Our Debtors: Bankruptcy and Consumer Credit in America.* New York: Oxford University Press.

Sullivan, Teresa A.; Elizabeth Warren; and Jay Lawrence Westbrook. 2000. *The Fragile Middle Class: Americans in Debt.* New Haven, CT: Yale University Press.

Tabb, Charles Jordan. 1995. "The History of the Bankruptcy Laws in the United States." *American Bankruptcy Institute Law Review* 3(1): 5–51.

Warren, Charles. 1935. *Bankruptcy in United States History.* Cambridge, MA: Harvard University Press.

Robert M. Lawless

BARRON V. BALTIMORE, 32 U.S. 243 (1833)

In *Barron v. Baltimore*, 32 U.S. 243 (1833), the U.S. Supreme Court held that the Fifth Amendment prohibition on taking private property for public use without compensation was a limit only on the federal government, not on the state governments. Barron owned a wharf in Baltimore that had become unprofitable after the city dumped sand and gravel from road construction into the water near the wharf. The result was that ships could no longer reach the wharf, and Barron sued the city "to recover damages for injuries to the wharf property."

Chief Justice John Marshall wrote the decision. He explained that the guarantees of the Bill of Rights were designed only to limit the federal government. Except for the First Amendment, which provides that "Congress shall make no law abridging" its freedoms, the rights in the Bill of Rights were written in general terms (for example, "private property shall not be taken for public use without just compensation"). Marshall noted that Article I, Section 9 of the Constitution also contained general statements that limited government power: "No Bill of Attainder or ex post facto Law shall be passed." Article I, Section 10 contained the same restrictions, but was prefaced by the words "No state shall." From this Marshall concluded that had the framers intended the Bill of Rights to limit the states, they would have imitated the framers of the original Constitution and prefaced the guarantees with the words "No state shall."

In addition to this contextual (or intertextual) argument, Marshall appealed to history: The Bill of Rights was a response to a fear about unlimited power in the new federal government. State constitutions typically had their own bills of rights. If people in a state wanted additional guarantees of liberty, they could amend their state constitution. Marshall insisted that "the unwieldy and cumbrous machinery" of obtaining a constitutional amendment to limit states as to Bill of Rights liberties "could never have occurred to any human being." In fact, just such an idea had occurred to James Madison (1751–1836), the principal author of the Bill of Rights. In his proposals, Madison had included the following: "No state shall violate the equal rights of conscience, or the freedom of the press, or trial by jury in criminal cases." Madison thought the amendment was necessary because "state governments are as likely to attack the invaluable privileges as the General Government" (*Annals of Congress 1789*, vol. 1, pp. 452, 458). Madison further suggested that the danger of abuse of governmental power by the states was greater than the danger of abuse by the federal government. The House of Representatives passed Madison's proposal, and it added freedom of speech to his list of limits on the states. The proposal was defeated in the Senate.

The concern Madison and members of the House of Representatives raised about state violations of the "invaluable privileges" of free speech, free press, and the rights of conscience was prophetic. In the years before the Civil War (1861–1865), southern states passed laws that were used to suppress abolitionist speech and antislavery religious and political speech, eventually including speech by supporters of Abraham Lincoln's Republican Party. Because of the decision in *Barron,* these laws were not subject to federal judicial review.

Immediately after the Civil War, in 1866, Congress proposed and the states later ratified the Fourteenth Amendment. It provides that "no state shall make or enforce any law which shall abridge the privileges or immunities of citizens of the United States; nor shall any state deprive any person of life, liberty, or property, without due process of law." By prefacing the guarantee with the phrase "no state shall" and by making reference to "privileges or immunities of citizens of the United States," John Bingham (1815–1900), the author of the amendment, and some of its leading supporters intended to overrule *Barron* and require the states to respect the rights in the Bill of Rights. These Republicans and longtime critics of slavery were strongly influenced by the history of suppression of free speech and other civil liberties in the South.

In the early years after the adoption of the Fourteenth Amendment, the Supreme Court read the amendment narrowly, relied on *Barron,* and rejected the claim that it required states to respect the liberties set out in the Bill of Rights. Only gradually, reaching a high point in the 1960s, did the Court require the states to respect most of the rights in the Bill of Rights. Still, scholarly debate about whether the Fourteenth Amendment should be read to incorporate by reference the privileges and immunities set out in the Bill of Rights continues to this day.

SEE ALSO *Bill of Rights; Incorporation Debate; Marshall Court*

BIBLIOGRAPHY

Amar, Akhil Reed. 1998. *The Bill of Rights: Creation and Reconstruction.* New Haven, CT: Yale University Press.

Annals of Congress 1789, vol. 1. Washington DC: Gales and Seaton.

Berger, Raoul. 1997. *Government by Judiciary: The Transformation of the Fourteenth Amendment.* 2nd edition. Indianapolis, IN: Liberty Fund.

Crosskey, William Winslow. 1954. "Charles Fairman, 'Legislative History,' and the Constitutional Limits on State Authority." *University of Chicago Law Review* 22: 1–143.

Curtis, Michael Kent. 1986. *No State Shall Abridge: The Fourteenth Amendment and the Bill of Rights.* Durham, NC: Duke University Press.

Curtis, Michael Kent. 2000. *Free Speech, "The People's Darling Privilege": Struggles for Freedom of Expression in American History.* Durham, NC: Duke University Press.

Curtis, Michael Kent. 2000. "Historical Linguistics, Inkblots, and Life after Death: The Privileges or Immunities of Citizens of the United States." *North Carolina Law Review* 78: 1071–1151.

Fairman, Charles. 1949. "Does the Fourteenth Amendment Incorporate the Bill of Rights: The Original Understanding." *Stanford Law Review* 2: 5–139.

Michael Kent Curtis

BARTNICKI V. VOPPER, 532 U.S. 514 (2001)

In *Bartnicki v. Vopper*, 532 U.S. 514 (2001), the U.S. Supreme Court addressed the important question, raised but not decided in the famous 1971 Pentagon Papers decision, of whether the First Amendment permits the state to punish the media for disclosing information regarding a matter of public concern if the information was originally obtained illegally. The *Bartnicki* case was brought by two union officials seeking damages against members of the media for disclosing to the public the contents of a cellular telephone conversation between the defendants that had been intercepted and recorded by an unknown person, in apparent violation of federal wiretapping laws.

The Court held that imposing liability on the media in this case would violate the First Amendment. The Court acknowledged that the law in question was "content-neutral," in that it regulated speech based on its source, not the message conveyed, and that the government's interest in protecting the privacy of citizens in their personal communications was a powerful one. Nonetheless, the Court held that when the disclosed information is truthful and of public concern, free speech interests outweigh privacy concerns. As such, the case appears to create a sweeping rule preventing the application of privacy laws to punish media defendants for the disclosure of information of public concern, even when that information was obtained illegally in violation of the privacy rights of citizens, so long as the media were not involved in the original illegality. The case would also seem to affirm the stringency of the "intermediate scrutiny" level of analysis applicable to content-neutral regulations of speech.

In fact, however, the exact scope and doctrinal significance of *Bartnicki* is unclear. Regarding doctrine, the majority was studiously ambiguous regarding precisely which standard of review it was applying. After agreeing that the law challenged in this case was content-neutral, the Court did not apply the standard four-part test for content-neutrality. Instead, the Court cited a series of cases that hold that the media may not be punished for publishing truthful information regarding a matter of public significance "absent a need ... of the highest order," even though in all of them the laws struck down had been content-based, not content-neutral. To further confuse matters, the dissent accused the majority of inappropriately applying strict scrutiny to a content-neutral law, while a two-justice concurring opinion by Stephen Breyer, joined by Sandra Day O'Connor, explicitly disclaimed the application of strict scrutiny.

Breyer's concurring opinion also interjects doubt about the scope of the holding. Breyer (who along with O'Connor provided the crucial fifth and sixth votes for the majority) explicitly states that this case does not "create a 'public interest' exception" to privacy laws. Instead, he says that the result turned on particular, narrow circumstances, including the innocence of the media defendants, the fact that the information disclosed included a threat of violence and so had a lower expectation of privacy, and that the plaintiffs were "limited public figures." Breyer strongly suggests that, generally, legislatures may protect individual privacy, even at the cost of free speech rights.

SEE ALSO *First Amendment*

BIBLIOGRAPHY

Gewirtz, Paul. 2001. "Privacy and Speech." *Supreme Court Review* 2001: 139–199.

Ashutosh A. Bhagwat

BASIC INC. V. LEVINSON, 485 U.S. 224 (1988)

Beginning in late 1976, Combustion Engineering Inc. commenced discussions with Basic Inc.'s management concerning a potential merger. Despite the discussions, Basic Inc. issued three public statements in 1977 and 1978 denying that it was involved in any merger negotiations. Finally, in December of 1978, Basic Inc. announced its pending merger with Combustion Engineering Inc. Investors who had sold Basic Inc. stock from the date of Basic Inc.'s first public denial of any merger up to the announcement of the Combustion Engineering Inc. merger brought a class action suit against Basic Inc. and its board of directors, alleging a material misstatement in violation of Rule 10b-5 and section 10(b) of the Securities Exchange Act of 1934. The investors claimed that Basic Inc.'s public denials depressed the share price, resulting in a lower sale price when the investors sold their Basic Inc. shares during the class period.

Writing for a plurality of the Supreme Court, Justice Harry Blackmun addressed two key issues concerning the application of Rule 10b-5: materiality and reliance. First, Blackmun dealt with the definition of materiality regarding contingent events. Blackmun followed the Second Circuit's lead in assessing contingent events based on the probability multiplied by the magnitude of such events. Because of the large magnitude of a merger, particularly for a target company, information on the merger even at early stages, when the probability is relatively low, may still be material.

While the probability multiplied by the magnitude approach provides a framework to assess the materiality of contingent events, several questions remain after *Basic*. Merely invoking the probability multiplied by the magnitude formulation leaves open the question of the threshold above which the formulation is material. Is it $1 million, $10 million, or more (or less)? Moreover, how is a jury (or judge) to decide the probability of an event at a time in the distant past? Juries may suffer from hindsight bias in assessing the ex ante probability of known events after they actually occurred.

The second major issue in *Basic* involved reliance. For the plurality, Blackmun ruled on whether the Basic Inc. class action plaintiffs had to demonstrate reliance on the part of each class member or, instead, whether a presumption of reliance would apply. The plurality in *Basic* established the "fraud on the market" presumption. Under the presumption, plaintiffs in a securities fraud action under Rule 10b-5 do not individually need to establish reliance on publicly disclosed affirmative misstatements. Instead, if plaintiffs demonstrate that the traded company's securities trade in a relatively liquid, efficient market, a presumption of reliance is applied.

Blackmun justified the fraud on the market presumption in part based on the presence of a growing empirical economic literature in support of the Efficient Capital Markets Hypothesis (ECMH). While debate exists as to the validity of the ECMH, Blackmun justified applying the fraud on the market presumption as follows: "Presumptions typically serve to assist courts in managing circumstances in which direct proof, for one reason or another, is rendered difficult." Several variants of the ECMH exist. For purposes of the fraud on the market presumption, the most important (and empirically defensible) variant is the semi-strong version of the ECMH that holds that securities prices incorporate all publicly available information on the traded company.

Under the fraud on the market reliance presumption, investors are presumed to rely on the "integrity" of the market price when trading in securities. When materially misleading information is released to the public, the information, according to the ECMH, becomes incorporated into the share price. Investors who rely on the integrity of the market price then may purchase (or sell) the securities at the inaccurate market price.

Blackmun noted several different ways defendants may rebut the presumption of reliance on the integrity of the market price. Defendants may, for example, put forth evidence that a particular plaintiff knew of the truth despite the presence of fraud in the marketplace. Alternatively, the defendants could establish that a particular plaintiff would have traded regardless of the presence (or absence) of fraud in the market. An investor, for example, may have to sell its shares due to a government antitrust decree. Alternatively, an investor may not believe that the price is an accurate assessment of value; short sellers trade with the belief that the securities prices are overvalued.

The key effect of the fraud on the market presumption relates to the burdens that the presumption places on litigating parties. Without the presumption, plaintiffs in a class action face the onerous task of demonstrating reliance on the alleged affirmative misstatement for every single class member. Individual issues would swamp collective issues and the class action device would likely disappear from Rule 10b-5 actions. With the presumption, plaintiffs only need to show initially that the company in question's securities trade in a relatively liquid market—perhaps with a focus on the market capitalization of the company, the trading volume, and the number of analysts who cover the company—common issues to all investors in the class. Defendants then bear the burden of rebutting the fraud on the market presumption.

Justice Byron White dissented, calling the ECMH theory a "mere babe." White questioned the ability of judges to determine correctly when to apply the fraud on the market presumption. White argued that even if the "new realities of financial markets" supported the ECMH, the decision to alter the securities laws rested with Congress and not the courts. In contrast, Blackmun for the majority wrote: "Congress expressly relied on the premise that securities markets are affected by information, and enacted legislation to facilitate an investor's reliance on the integrity of those markets." White, in dissent, also took special issue with the notion that investors rely on the integrity of the market price, questioning whether investors rely on the stock market price as an accurate reflection of value.

Investors, of course, do invest in markets around the world where the accuracy (and perhaps integrity as a result) of the stock market price is not guaranteed. How do investors cope with the lack of integrity? Investors discount the price they are willing to pay. Nonetheless, if fraud were rampant and undeterred in the secondary market, investors would have a difficult time knowing the precise amount with which to discount prices. The market price for all companies would then face a *Lemon* problem as good companies exited the market to avoid the investors' discount. Even if investors do not always believe in the accuracy of prices, one could argue that developing Rule 10b-5 doctrine with an assumption that they do, under the fraud on the market theory, helps avoid this *Lemon* problem.

Lower courts have extended the rationale behind the fraud on the market doctrine in *Basic* to develop a "truth on the market" variant. For companies whose shares trade in a relatively efficient market, the truth on the market doctrine assesses the materiality of information based on all the information incorporated into a company's share price. Even if a company discloses information that would be materially misleading standing alone, if correcting information is publicly available, under the truth on the market doctrine investors have the benefit of this correcting information when they trade in the company's stock and, thus, the misleading information is not material. (See *Wielgos v. Commonwealth Edison Co.*, 892 F.2d 509, [7th Cir. 1989] pp. 514–516).

SEE ALSO *Rule 10b-5; Securities and Exchange Commission*

BIBLIOGRAPHY

Choi, Stephen J. and Adam C. Pritchard. 2008. *Securities Regulation: The Essentials*. New York: Aspen Publishers.

Choi, Stephen J. and Adam C. Pritchard. 2008. *Securities Regulation: Cases and Analysis*. 2nd Edition. Radnor, PA: Foundation Press.

Stephen J. Choi

BATES V. STATE BAR OF ARIZONA, 433 U.S. 350 (1977)

Arizona lawyers advertised routine legal services at "very reasonable fees" in a daily newspaper of general circulation. The State Bar of Arizona initiated a disciplinary action against the lawyers for violating Arizona Disciplinary Rule 2-101(b), prohibiting lawyers from publicizing legal services. A divided Arizona Supreme Court ultimately censured the lawyers, and the lawyers appealed, claiming imposition of the Arizona disciplinary rule both (1) violated the Sherman Antitrust Act (a statute prohibiting interference with competitive distribution or production of goods) because of its tendency to limit competition for legal services, and (2) violated their First Amendment right to free speech. The U.S. Supreme Court held, five to four, that Arizona's ban violated the First Amendment.

In an opinion authored by Justice Harry Blackmun, the Court first held that the Sherman Act did not apply against certain state actions such as the one at issue here. The Court explained although the action was brought by the Arizona State Bar, the real party at interest was the Arizona Supreme Court. As such, the disciplinary rules reflected a clear articulation of the state's policy with regard to the professional behavior of its lawyers. The Court concluded that Arizona's rule governing the advertisement of lawyers fit within an exemption to the Sherman Act first recognized in *Parker v. Brown,* 317 U.S. 341 (1943), allowing for a state to impose a restriction as an act of government.

The Court next held that a flat state ban on lawyer advertising violated the First Amendment, at least in the case of advertising routine legal services describing the price and nature of services offered. Relying on *Virginia State Board of Pharmacy v. Virginia Citizens Consumer Council, Inc.,* 425 U.S. 748 (1976), the Court explained that the commercial speech at issue was entitled to First Amendment protection. The Court explained the lawyers there could constitutionally advertise the prices of certain routine services:

- the advertising did not have an adverse effect on legal professionalism;
- was not inherently misleading;
- did not have an adverse effect on the administration of justice;
- did not present undesirable economic effects on the cost of legal services;
- and did not adversely affect the quality of those legal services.

However, the Court emphasized that in appropriate cases, lawyer advertising may be regulated if it were false, deceptive, or misleading.

Writing separately, dissenting in part, Chief Justice Warren Burger explained that legal services varied from case to case. Accordingly, advertising legal services could "never give the public an accurate picture upon which to base its selection of an attorney" and therefore should not necessarily be subject to First Amendment protection. Justice Lewis F. Powell, Jr., joined by Justice Potter Stewart, also dissented in part, explaining that despite the majority's pronouncement, legal services could not easily be classified as "routine" or "unique" and therefore could still be subject to regulation consistent with the First Amendment. Justice William Rehnquist wrote separately as well, cautioning that legal advertising should not be constitutionally protected, regardless of its veracity or reasonableness. Justice Rehnquist described the *Virginia State Board of Pharmacy* decision as misguided, because it led commercial speech into an undesirable case-by-case analysis of its constitutionality.

SEE ALSO *Commercial Speech; First Amendment*

BIBLIOGRAPHY

Hornsby, William. 2005. "Clashes of Class and Cash: Battles from the 150 Years War to Govern Client Development." *Arizona State Law Journal* 37(2): 255.

O'Steen, Van. 2005. "*Bates v. Bar of Arizona*: The Personal Account of a Party and the Consumer Benefits of Lawyer Advertising." *Arizona State Law Journal* 37(2): 245.

Reamey, Gerald S. 2006. "Life in the Early Days of Lawyer Advertising: Personal Recollections of a *Bates* Baby." *St. Mary's Law Journal* 37(4): 887–900.

CASES

Parker v. Brown, 317 U.S. 341 (1943).

Virginia State Board of Pharmacy v. Virginia Citizens Consumer Council Inc., 425 U.S. 748 (1976).

Meredith J. Duncan

BATSON V. KENTUCKY, 476 U.S. 79 (1986)

In *Batson v. Kentucky,* 476 U.S. 79 (1986), the U.S. Supreme Court held, in an opinion by Justice Lewis F. Powell, Jr. that the equal protection clause of the Fourteenth Amendment forbids prosecutors from using peremptory challenges of prospective black jurors "on the assumption that they will be biased in a particular case simply because the defendant is black." The Court established a three-step test for determining whether peremptory challenges were being used in a racially discriminatory fashion. The test was later summarized in *Miller-El v. Cockrell,* 537 U.S. 322 (2003) as follows:

> First, a defendant must make a prima facie showing that a peremptory challenge has been exercised on the basis of race.... Second, if that showing has been made, the prosecution must offer a race-neutral basis for striking the juror in question.... Third, in light of the parties' submissions, the trial court must determine whether the defendant has shown purposeful discrimination.

Justice Thurgood Marshall, concurring, would have gone further because, as he argued, "merely allowing defendants the opportunity to challenge the racially discriminatory use of peremptory challenges in individual cases will not end the illegitimate use of the peremptory challenge." He pointed out that it would be extremely difficult for defendants to establish purposeful discrimination and urged that "only by banning peremptories entirely can such discrimination be ended."

Chief Justice Warren Burger, joined by Justice William Rehnquist, wrote the principal dissent. He argued that peremptory challenges, based as they are on the attorneys' hunches and intuition, cannot be meaningfully subjected to the test envisioned by the Court.

Since *Batson*, the Supreme Court has substantially extended its reach. In *Georgia v. McCollum*, 505 U.S. 42 (1992), the Court held that *defendants* should also be barred from striking prospective jurors on the basis of race. In *J.E.B. v. Alabama ex rel. T.B.*, 511 U.S. 127 (1994), *Batson* was extended to a claim of gender discrimination in a civil case.

The prediction of Marshall and the dissenters in *Batson* that such claims would be difficult to prove and would lead to much litigation has been borne out, as illustrated by the 2005 case of *Miller-El v. Dretke*, 545 U.S. 231. In that case, the defendant raised a *Batson* challenge to the prosecutor's striking ten of the eleven potential black jurors. As Justice Stephen Breyer noted in his concurring opinion:

> This case illustrates the practical problems of proof that Justice Marshall described. . . . Miller-El marshaled extensive evidence of racial bias. But despite the strength of his claim, Miller-El's challenge has resulted in 17 years of largely unsuccessful and protracted litigation—including 8 different judicial proceedings and 8 different judicial opinions, and involving 23 judges, of whom 6 found the *Batson* standard violated and 16 the contrary.

Thus Breyer agreed with Marshall that the only way to eliminate racial bias in peremptory challenges is to abandon peremptory challenges altogether.

SEE ALSO *Juries; Peremptory Challenges*

BIBLIOGRAPHY

Cavise, Leonard L. 1999. "The *Batson* Doctrine: The Supreme Court's Utter Failure to Meet the Challenge of Discrimination in Jury Selection." *Wisconsin Law Review* 1999: 500–552.

Raphael, Michael J., and Edward Ungvarsky. 1993. "Excuses, Excuses: Neutral Explanations under *Batson v. Kentucky*." *University of Michigan Journal of Law Reform* 27: 229–275.

Craig Bradley

BEAL V. DOE, 432 U.S. 438 (1977)

Roe v. Wade, 410 U.S. 113 (1973), the groundbreaking case decriminalizing abortions, did little to quiet the abortion debate in America's courts and legislatures. As few as four years after *Roe*, the issue of abortion funding for women who qualified for financial assistance under Title XIX of the Social Security Act came before the U.S. Supreme Court in *Beal v. Doe*, 432 U.S. 438 (1977). In *Beal*, the plaintiffs (a group of Pennsylvania women who were qualified for financial assistance under the state Medicaid plan) had been denied financial assistance for desired nontherapeutic abortions pursuant to state regulations limiting such assistance to abortions certified by physicians as "medically necessary." The women believed that a state's decision to restrict funding to only those abortions that could be certified as medically necessary, rather than provide financial assistance for women who may desire abortions over childbirth, was unconstitutional under the Fourteenth Amendment's equal protection clause.

Justice Lewis F. Powell, Jr., writing for the Court, held that the Department of Health, Education, and Welfare, the agency that administers Title XIX, allows but does not mandate funding for nontherapeutic abortions as a condition of participation in the Medicaid program. The Court's rationale for denying the women's claim was that Pennsylvania's, indeed any state's, refusal to fund nontherapeutic abortions is not inconsistent with the federal statute; however, the statute allows states the freedom to decide if they wish to provide such coverage. The Court rejected the women's argument that refusing coverage for nontherapeutic abortions was unreasonable on economic and health grounds. They had explained that abortions were less expensive than childbirth; therefore, a state that chose to fund childbirths over abortions would incur greater costs in the long run. Regarding health grounds, the women argued that abortion was a safer procedure for a woman than childbirth. In rejecting both arguments, the Court held that it is not unreasonable or inconsistent with the statute's objective for a state to refuse to fund unnecessary, although perhaps desirable, medical services. The Court further held that the exclusion of nontherapeutic abortions from Medicaid is not unreasonable based on the states' valid, strong, and legitimate interests.

The Court found unpersuasive the dissenting opinion by Justice William Brennan and joined by Justices Thurgood Marshall and Harry Blackmun. In their dissent, the justices pointed out that upholding the medically necessary requirement would have a profoundly negative impact on poor women who preferred abortion over pregnancy. They listed several pragmatic implications of forcing a poor woman to carry an unwanted pregnancy to term, including the near impossibility of the woman to break the cycle of poverty. The Court noted this argument and stated that such policy concerns should be resolved by the people, not the Court.

The Court did find one feature of Pennsylvania's Medicaid program that possibly conflicted with Title XIX: the requirement for two doctors to concur with the attending physician that an abortion was medically necessary. However, the Court was unable to determine if the role of the additional doctors interfered with the attending physician's judgment in a way not contemplated by Congress and remanded the issue back for further consideration.

This case is considered a companion case to *Maher v. Roe*, 432 U.S. 464 (1977) and *Harris v. McRae*, 448 U.S 297 (1980), which also upheld limitations on public funding of abortions.

SEE ALSO *Fourteenth Amendment; Privacy; Roe v. Wade, 410 U.S. 113 (1973)*

BIBLIOGRAPHY

Goldstein, Leslie Friedman. 1994. *Contemporary Cases in Women's Rights.* Madison: University of Wisconsin Press.

Pamela D. Bridgewater

BELLOTTI V. BAIRD, 443 U.S. 622 (1979)

In the years following *Roe v. Wade*, 410 U.S. 113 (1973), opponents and proponents of *Roe* seized the moment as an opportunity to influence state legislatures' efforts to define the parameters and contours of the newly recognized right to decriminalized abortion. As a result, the Supreme Court was often asked to revisit the abortion question in cases challenging the legislative responses to the lobbying efforts arising after *Roe. Bellotti v. Baird*, 443 U.S. 622 (1979) involved one such challenge. The statute at issue was from Massachusetts and required unmarried women under the age of eighteen to get their parents' consent for an abortion. The statute contained a provision that allowed pregnant minors to obtain judicial approval for the procedure if one or both parents refused to consent. Judicial approval under such circumstances has commonly been referred to as *judicial bypass.*

The issue in *Bellotti* was whether the statute requiring parental notice and consent unduly burdened a young woman's right to obtain an otherwise legal abortion. The Supreme Court held that the statute was unconstitutional because a state court could withhold authorization, notwithstanding that court's finding that the young woman was mature and competent. Also, the Supreme Court rejected the statute because in all cases young women seeking an abortion were required to notify their parents first prior to seeking a judicial bypass. Essentially, the statute required pregnant minors to notify their parents even if doing so would subject the minor to violence or other harm. Only if, upon receiving notice, one or both parents refused to grant permission to the minor could the pregnant minor invoke judicial proceedings. After these proceedings, the state court could refuse permission as well.

According to the Court, the Massachusetts statute fell short of passing constitutional muster for two reasons.

First, the statute allowed a court to withhold authorization for an abortion even where the young woman was found to be mature and competent. Second, the statute required parental notification in all situations, including a young woman's intent to obtain a judicial bypass. This requirement could potentially have prevented a young woman's right to go to court altogether and would additionally violate the confidentiality requirement of judicial bypass proceedings.

The Court held that in order to ensure that no one third party had an absolute veto over a minor's decision to obtain an abortion, the state had to provide an expeditious and confidential judicial bypass alternative to parental consent. Further, if a pregnant minor was able to show first, that she was mature and well informed to make her own decision, independent of her parents' wishes; or second, that even though she was not able to make the decision independently, an abortion would be in her best interest, she would be granted judicial authorization to abort, over her parents' objections.

There was considerable lack of cohesion in the Court's opinion in *Bellotti*. The first indication was the fact that holding was written in separate opinions by Justices Lewis F. Powell, Jr., and John Paul Stevens. Justices Warren Burger, Potter Stewart, and William Rehnquist joined Justice Powell's opinion. Justices Harry Blackmun, Thurgood Marshall, and William Brennan joined Justice Stevens' opinion concurring in the judgment. Justice Rehnquist filed a separate concurring opinion and Justice Byron White filed a dissenting opinion wherein he stated that he would not strike down the Massachusetts statute. Justice Stevens (joined by Justices Brennan, Marshall, and Blackmun) agreed with the ultimate outcome of *Bellotti;* however, he disagreed with the majority's finding that the judicial bypass was constitutional. Justice Stevens argued that in the judicial-bypass proceeding, a judge had absolute veto power over the young woman's decision based on his judgment of her best interests, regardless of her maturity and competence. "Thus," according to Justice Stevens, "no minor in Massachusetts, no matter how mature and capable of informed decision making, may receive an abortion without the consent of either both her parents or a superior court judge. In every instance, the minor's decision to secure an abortion is subject to an absolute third-party veto." This check on a minor's decision-making power, even if not granted to the minor's parents, satisfied Stevens' concerns over the statute's constitutionality.

Although subsequent courts have narrowed, clarified, or distinguished *Bellotti*, it has not been overturned. One interesting example is found in *H. L. v. Matheson*, 450 U.S. 398 (1981). In *Matheson*, the only case to date where the Supreme Court took an opportunity to narrow its holding in *Bellotti*, the Court upheld a parental notification requirement in a statute which contained no judicial bypass based on two grounds. First, notification did not give parents veto power. Second, whereas the plaintiffs in *Bellotti* were acknowledged as mature, unmarried, pregnant minors, the plaintiff in *Matheson* did not allege or prove that she was mature or emancipated. In fact, she still lived with and was dependent upon her parents. This difference proved meaningful in the *Matheson* court's decision to uphold a parental notification requirement.

SEE ALSO *Children and the Constitution; Privacy; Roe v. Wade, 410 U.S. 113 (1973)*

BIBLIOGRAPHY

Ehrlich, J. Shoshanna. 2006. *Who Decides?: The Abortion Rights of Teens.* Westport, CT: Praeger.

Fried, Marlene Gerber. 1990. *From Abortion to Reproductive Freedom: Transforming a Movement.* Boston: South End Press.

Rubin, Eva R., ed. 1994. *The Abortion Controversy: A Documentary History.* Westport, CT: Greenwood.

CASES

Roe v. Wade, 410 U.S. 113 (1973).

H. L. v. Matheson, 450 U.S. 398 (1981).

Pamela D. Bridgewater

BENDER V. WILLIAMSPORT AREA SCHOOL DISTRICT, 475 U.S. 534 (1986)

A student-initiated nondenominational prayer club known as Petros sued the Williamsport, Pennsylvania School District, the superintendent, the principal, and the members of the school board, alleging that the denial of Petros's request to meet during regularly scheduled activity periods violated the students' First Amendment religious freedom and free speech. Petros was formed to promote "spiritual growth and positive attitudes in the lives of its members." The superintendent, acting on advice of the school district solicitor and with the school board's support, prohibited Petros from meeting based on the establishment clause. The district court entered judgment in favor of Petros, holding that the denial violated the free speech of its members, and the school district complied with the order. However, one board member, Youngman, appealed in his official and individual capacity. The Third Circuit ruled in his favor, reasoning that the

"constitutional balance" tilted in favor of prohibiting Petros from meeting. Petros appealed.

Justice John Paul Stevens's majority opinion held that Youngman lacked standing, both in his official and individual capacity, and also as a parent. School boards are legal entities as a whole and individual members have no authority to represent the board. Petros's suit therefore was against the board members in their official capacities. Moreover, because no judgment was entered against any board members in their individual capacities, Youngman lacked standing to appeal in that capacity. He also lacked standing as a parent because he failed to assert this from the beginning. It was his responsibility to demonstrate the basis for jurisdiction, as a matter of the Article III "case-or-controversy" requirement or as a prudential matter, and the record was devoid of any argument that he was suing as a parent. Even if he had sued on that basis, the Court noted that his interests as a parent differed from his interests as a board member and the Federal Rules of Civil Procedure required him to make "timely application" to intervene as a parent.

Justice Stevens emphasized that Article III subject-matter jurisdiction must be met at all stages of litigation. Citing to precedent, the Court ruled that Youngman lacked a personal stake in the suit because he could not show that he "personally ha[d] suffered some actual or threatened injury as a result of the putatively illegal conduct of the defendant[s]." The standing requirement ensures that a case is concrete and redressable and it reduces future "lawsuits that have some, but not all, of the facts of the case actually decided." Justice Thurgood Marshall concurred, emphasizing that a litigant cannot invoke the Court's jurisdiction "through a belated nontestimonial statement" that he is suing in a different capacity on appeal.

Chief Justice Warren E. Burger, joined by Justices Byron White and William Rehnquist, dissented, upholding Youngman's standing as a parent. An original party's standing to appeal does not have to be established unless it is challenged. The dissent ruled for Petros, reasoning that the First Amendment "mandates state neutrality, not hostility, toward religion." Justice Lewis F. Powell, Jr., agreed that Youngman had standing as a parent, and ruled in favor of the students on free speech and freedom of association grounds.

SEE ALSO *Standing*

BIBLIOGRAPHY

Zirkel, Perry Alan, Steven S. Goldberg, and Sharon Nalbone Richardson. 2001. *A Digest of Supreme Court Decisions Affecting Education.* 4th edition. Bloomington, IN: Phi Delta Kappa International, Inc.

Sharon E. Rush

BEREA COLLEGE V. COMMON-WEALTH OF KENTUCKY, 211 U.S. 45 (1908)

Berea College v. Commonwealth of Kentucky, 211 U.S. 45 (1908) was an important U.S. Supreme Court decision limiting the due process rights of corporations. The case was significant in its time for limiting rather than expanding corporate rights, and for further affirming the Court's support for state segregation laws announced in *Plessy v. Ferguson*, 136 U.S. 537 (1896).

The school of Berea was founded in 1855 by prominent abolitionist John G. Fee (1816–1901) to provide an education to anyone who was in need. Though not originally specifying any particular group, the school became known over the years for educating both white and black students, male and female. In 1904 Kentucky passed the Day Law, aimed directly at ending Berea's integrated educational approach. The Day Law forbade individuals, unincorporated groups, and corporations from teaching at or attending an integrated school. Kentucky's public schools were already segregated by law, but Berea was the state's only integrated college. Kentucky's court of appeals upheld the Day Law in 1906, and Berea appealed.

Attorneys for the state argued that, because laws requiring segregation of common carriers had been constitutionally upheld, the Day Law was both a valid exercise of the police power and within the general public interest and settled policy of the state to "preserve racial identity." The state also argued that because the statute equally penalized black and white students or teachers involved in integrated education, equal protection was not violated.

Berea's lawyers relied on Fourteenth Amendment jurisprudence from the preceding decades protecting the property rights of individuals and corporations, particularly asserting corporate personhood as a basis for due process rights. In arguing that Berea had been deprived of due process, the college's lawyers also cited the protective attitude toward private business contracts taken by the Court three years earlier in *Lochner v. New York*, 198 U.S. 45 (1905).

Justice David Brewer wrote the majority opinion upholding the state court decision and holding that the law did not violate the corporation's constitutional rights. Because the state could grant or deny a corporation's charter, the majority held, the state could also impose limitations on the exercise of that charter. Unlike individual rights, corporate rights could be limited by the legislature and the state was "under no obligation to treat both alike." The opinion concluded that the portion of the Day Law prohibiting corporations from engaging in interracial teaching was similar to an amendment to a corporate charter, a power reserved by the state when granting charters.

Justice John Harlan wrote a dissent arguing that the right to teach was both a property right and a liberty right. In addition, Harlan argued that the clauses of the Day Law prohibiting individuals or unincorporated associations from teaching white and black students at the same time were not separable from the clause prohibiting corporations from doing so. Given the interdependence of these clauses, Harlan reasoned, the entire law was unconstitutional on the grounds that the prohibition of individual action was a violation of constitutional rights and the law would lose force and intention without all the clauses.

SEE ALSO *Jim Crow in the Early Twentieth Century*

BIBLIOGRAPHY

Peck, Elizabeth S. 1982. *Berea's First 125 Years: 1855–1980.* Lexington: University Press of Kentucky.

Sears, Richard. 1996. *A Utopian Experiment in Kentucky: Integration and Social Equality at Berea, 1866–1904.* Westport, CT: Greenwood.

Camille Walsh

BERMAN V. PARKER, 348 U.S. 26 (1954)

Berman v. Parker, 348 U.S. 26 (1954) is one of three leading U.S. Supreme Court cases on the meaning of "public use" in the Fifth Amendment's just compensation clause. The Court's broad interpretation of "public use" in *Berman* laid the intellectual foundation for the Court's other leading public-use cases, *Hawaii Housing Authority v. Midkiff*, 467 U.S. 229 (1984), and *Kelo v. City of New London*, 545 U.S. 469 (2005). Indeed, the broad language used by the Court in *Berman* has been prominently cited in the Court's opinions in *Midkiff* and *Kelo*, and many scholars view the Court's controversial holding in *Kelo* as following directly from its reasoning in *Berman*.

THE "PUBLIC-USE" PUZZLE

The just compensation clause of the Fifth Amendment reads, "nor shall private property be taken for public use without just compensation." This clause places two limits on the government's inherent power to take private property through eminent domain. First, the government must pay just compensation when it takes private property. Second, the words *public use* suggest that eminent domain may only be used to take private property for public, as opposed to a private, use.

Like other constitutional provisions, the "public-use" requirement is subject to conflicting interpretations. The most narrow way of reading "public use" would require that the property be owned or controlled by the government after the taking is complete. An intermediate interpretation would permit the taken property to be owned by a private party but would require that the property be open to use by the public—for example, the taken property could be transferred to a private entity such as a railroad so long as the railroad was open to use by members of the public. The broadest interpretation would require only that the taking of property serve some public purpose, and would not require public ownership or access to the property. Courts vacillated between these broad and narrow readings of "public use" throughout the nineteenth and early twentieth centuries.

BERMAN AND THE CONSTITUTIONALITY OF URBAN RENEWAL

Berman involved challenges to takings made under the District of Columbia Redevelopment Act of 1945. Like other urban-renewal laws passed in the same era, the act was designed to redevelop blighted areas of cities. Property that was designated for redevelopment was taken using eminent domain and transferred to a private developer. In other words, the act used eminent domain to transfer private property from the original owner to a private entity to serve the public purpose of redevelopment. The case therefore squarely presented the public-use issue to the Supreme Court.

The taking of a building that was blighted in the sense of being decrepit and unfit for human habitation was not controversial—municipalities had long had the power to abate nuisances, and property blighted in this sense fell within traditional definitions of nuisance. Urban-renewal laws, however, were broadly aimed at addressing not only blight itself but also the root conditions of blight. The District of Columbia Redevelopment Act therefore contemplated taking property "that owing to technological and sociological changes, obsolete lay-out, and other factors" would lead to the development of blight. Urban renewal, in other words, was concerned not just with clearing slums but also with modernizing the urban environment. In many instances of urban renewal, the people displaced predominantly came from minority groups. The District of Columbia Act was no exception. Justice Clarence Thomas observed in his dissent in *Kelo* that urban renewal was widely known as "negro removal" and that "[o]ver 97 percent of the individuals forcibly removed from their homes by the 'slum-clearance' project upheld by this Court in *Berman* were black."

The broad scope of urban renewal is reflected in the facts of the *Berman* case. Berman and his coappellants owned a department store that was not itself blighted. The store, however, was located in an area that contained a large amount of blighted property. The District of Columbia wanted to redevelop the entire area, and the department store was taken along with the surrounding property.

Berman challenged the constitutionality of the taking, noting that the property was commercial, was not blighted, and would be transferred after the taking to a private entity for redevelopment. The case was heard by a special three-member district court headed by E. Barrett Prettyman, a respected member of the U.S. Court of Appeals for the District of Columbia Circuit. Judge Prettyman construed the Redevelopment Act narrowly and rejected Berman's challenge. His nuanced and careful opinion, however, expressed serious concerns about the broader constitutionality of urban-renewal laws.

Judge Prettyman had no difficulty with the government's power to clear blighted property as abatement of a public nuisance, but he asked a series of hard questions about blight clearance takings. Prettyman was willing to give the government some latitude to take nonblighted property to prevent the spread of blight, but he was highly critical of the apparent "claim on the part of the authorities for an unreviewable power to seize and sell whole sections of the city" that was reflected in the Redevelopment Act.

The case thus came to the Supreme Court on a lower-court opinion that had given a technical victory to the government but that had raised serious questions about the broader constitutionality of the Redevelopment Act and similar urban-renewal laws. A memorandum filed by the solicitor general specifically asked the Court to consider these broader issues, and highlighted the national importance of the case by noting that laws similar to the Redevelopment Act had been passed in thirty-two states.

The Supreme Court clearly and emphatically rejected Judge Prettyman's concerns about the constitutionality of urban-renewal laws. Justice William O. Douglas's opinion for a unanimous Court equated the permissible scope of eminent domain with the extremely broad scope of the police power. Under this approach, an exercise of eminent domain would be valid if it furthered a public purpose, with public purpose being broadly defined as promoting the public welfare. This "broad and inclusive" concept, the Court noted, represents values that "are spiritual as well as physical, aesthetic as well as monetary." The Court therefore held that it "is within the power of the legislature to determine that the community should be beautiful as well as healthy, spacious as well as clean, well-balanced as well as carefully patrolled."

The opinion of the Court was also highly deferential to the legislature's determinations about the permissible scope of eminent domain. Judge Prettyman had taken the view that the constitutional scope of the eminent domain power was an issue for the courts to decide. The Court, in contrast, held that "the role of the judiciary in determining whether [the power of eminent domain] is being exercised for a public purpose is an extremely narrow one."

The broad interpretation of "public use" and the deference to the legislature reflected in *Berman* featured prominently in the Court's later decisions in *Midkiff* and *Kelo*. Indeed, the holding in *Berman* arguably mandated the outcome in both of those cases, in which the Court rejected "public-use" challenges to takings that transferred property from one private party to another. Commentators have observed that *Berman* virtually wrote the words *public use* out of the constitution, and it is clear from the Court's opinion that it intended to get the courts out of the business of reviewing legislative exercises of eminent domain.

SEE ALSO *Eminent Domain; Fifth Amendment; Kelo v. City of New London, 545 U.S. 469 (2005); Public Use*

BIBLIOGRAPHY

Barros, D. Benjamin. 2008. "Nothing 'Errant' about It: The *Berman* and *Midkiff* Conference Notes and How the Supreme Court Got to *Kelo* with Its Eyes Wide Open." In *Private Property, Community Development, & Eminent Domain*, ed. Robin Paul Malloy, pp. 57–74. London: Ashgate.

Cohen, Charles E. 2006. "Eminent Domain after *Kelo v. City of New London*: An Argument for Banning Economic Development Takings." *Harvard Journal of Law and Public Policy* 29: 491–568.

Pritchett, Wendell E. 2003. "The 'Public Menace' of Blight: Urban Renewal and the Private Uses of Eminent Domain." *Yale Law and Policy Review* 21: 1–52.

D. Benjamin Barros

BETHEL SCHOOL DISTRICT NO. 403 V. FRASER, 478 U.S. 675 (1986)

The U.S. Supreme Court's leading student rights decision, *Tinker v. Des Moines School District*, 393 U.S. 503 (1969), established the principle that "students . . . [do not] shed their constitutional rights to freedom of . . . expression at the schoolhouse gate." Almost four decades since *Tinker*, however, the nation's highest court has inexorably whittled away at that landmark precedent.

One example of this trend is the high court's 1986 decision in *Bethel School District No. 403 v. Fraser*, 478 U.S. 675 (1986). This case was sparked by a nominating speech that Matthew Fraser delivered on behalf of a friend running for a position in student government at a Pierce

County, Washington, high school. Throughout the speech, which was delivered at an assembly attended by about 600 students, some as young as fourteen, Mr. Fraser employed sexual innuendos. For example, he suggested that the candidate he was endorsing "doesn't attack things in spurts—he drives hard, pushing and pushing until finally—he succeeds. [He] . . . will go to the very end— even the climax, for each and every one of you." The speech drew what the district court described as "boisterous" hooting from the student audience. In addition, the lower court record disclosed that teachers observed a few students "simulating the speech through gestures" but that other students appeared "bewildered and embarrassed."

The school's administration felt compelled to suspend Fraser for his "disruptive comments." Fraser, through his father as guardian, challenged the discipline in federal court. The U.S. District Court for the Western District of Washington ruled against the Pierce County schools, holding that the disruption, if any, was minimal and did not warrant Fraser's suspension. The Ninth Circuit Court of Appeals affirmed the district court ruling. The U.S. Supreme Court granted certiorari and, in an opinion written by Chief Justice Warren Burger, reversed the two lower courts, finding in favor of the school district. Burger concluded, "The First Amendment does not prevent . . . school officials from determining that to permit a vulgar and lewd speech . . . would undermine the school's basic educational mission." The Court distinguished the fact situation in the Washington case from that of *Tinker*. In the 1969 Iowa case, the Court recalled, the wearing of black armbands constituted "a nondisruptive, passive expression of a political viewpoint," whereas in *Bethel* "a sexually explicit monologue [was] directed towards an unsuspecting audience of teenage students." In *Tinker*, the whole school campus was considered a "public forum for student expression." In *Bethel*, by contrast, the Burger Court held that school officials had a responsibility for ensuring that expression at a voluntary in-school assembly was not indecent.

The ruling in *Bethel* was seven to two. Dissenting opinions were filed by Associate Justices Thurgood Marshall and John Paul Stevens. Both bemoaned the Court's departure from the spirit of *Tinker*. Marshall saw no evidence in the record that Fraser's nominating speech was in any way disruptive, and Stevens was willing to trust the judgment of the two lower courts on the question of whether Fraser crossed the line in transgressing "contemporary community standards . . . [concerning] expression with sexual connotations."

The tendency to migrate away from *Tinker* was also evident in *Hazelwood School District v. Kuhlmeier*, 484 U.S. 260 (1988), when the Court vindicated a principal's decision to censor a student newspaper because certain articles might offend students and other readers, and, most recently, in *Morse v. Frederick*, 551 U.S. ___ (2007) when it upheld the right of a principal to rip down a student-made banner purportedly advocating drug usage.

SEE ALSO *Children and the Constitution; Rights of Students*

BIBLIOGRAPHY

Geimer, William S. 1988. "Juvenileness: A Single-Edged Constitutional Sword." *Georgia Law Review* 22(4): 949–973.

Johnson, John W. 1997. *The Struggle for Student Rights: Tinker v. Des Moines and the 1960s.* Lawrence: University Press of Kansas.

John M. Johnson

BETTS V. BRADY, 316 U.S. 455 (1942)

In *Betts v. Brady*, 316 U.S. 455 (1942), the U.S. Supreme Court rejected the right to counsel in a criminal prosecution when the defendant lacks the resources to pay for representation. The Sixth Amendment to the U.S. Constitution states: "In all criminal prosecutions, the accused shall enjoy the right . . . to have the Assistance of Counsel for his defence." *Betts* came a decade after the 1932 decision in *Powell v. Alabama*, 287 U.S. 45, which required states to provide attorneys for defendants in cases in which the death penalty could be imposed.

Powell involved a group of African-American youths who were charged by the state of Alabama with raping a white woman. *Powell* was known as the "Scottsboro" case because that was the Alabama town where the defendants were tried. The events transpired in the Deep South during the height of the segregation era, when African-American men were regularly lynched for raping white women. As the Supreme Court explained, the trial "took place in an atmosphere of tense, hostile and excited public sentiment." A lawyer was appointed on the day of the trial to represent the defendants, but "during perhaps the most critical period of the proceedings against these defendants, that is to say, from the time of their arraignment until the beginning of their trial, when consultation, thorough-going investigation and preparation were vitally important, the defendants did not have the aid of counsel in any real sense." When the case reached the Supreme Court, it ruled "in a capital case, where the defendant is unable to employ counsel, and is incapable adequately of making his own defense because of ignorance, feeble mindedness, illiteracy, or the like, it is the duty of the court, whether

requested or not, to assign counsel for him as a necessary requisite of due process of law."

A decade later, in *Betts v. Brady,* the Supreme Court was not yet ready to expand *Powell.* The defendant in *Betts* was an unemployed farmhand who was indicted for robbery in Maryland. The defendant, who lacked the resources to hire counsel, asked the trial judge to appoint an attorney to represent him. The request was denied because the Maryland county in which Betts was tried appointed counsel for indigent defendants only in prosecutions involving murder and rape. The issue in *Betts* was whether the due process clause of the Fourteenth Amendment obligated states to provide counsel for indigent defendants in criminal cases not involving the death penalty. The Fourteenth Amendment prohibits states from depriving "any person of life, liberty, or property, without due process of law." In a criminal case, the defendant can be deprived of his "liberty" if he is found guilty and incarcerated. The "process" that the Fourteenth Amendment requires includes notification that criminal charges have been asserted by the state, and a hearing before a neutral decision maker at which the individual is allowed to present evidence to support any defense that might be mounted.

The issue was whether the state was obligated to appoint an attorney and to pay the cost of the defense. The majority concluded that it was "unable to say that the concept of due process incorporated in the Fourteenth Amendment obligates the states . . . to furnish counsel in every [criminal] case." The Court distinguished *Powell* because the defendants in that case were illiterate youths who were tried in a hostile, racially charged environment and represented by an attorney appointed on the day of the trial. Distinguishing *Powell*, the Supreme Court noted that Betts "was not helpless, but was a man forty-three years old, of ordinary intelligence and ability to take care of his own interests. . . . He had once before been in a criminal court, pleaded guilty to larceny and served a sentence and was not wholly unfamiliar with criminal procedure." The majority was concerned that a ruling for the defendant in *Betts* could lead to a requirement for state-financed representation in all criminal cases, including minor traffic offenses.

Associate Justice Hugo Black dissented. He believed that refusing to appoint an attorney for indigent defendants was the functional equivalent to denying representation for an individual who had the financial resources to retain an attorney. Justice Black contended that a "practice cannot be reconciled with 'common and fundamental ideas of fairness and right,' which subjects innocent men to increased dangers of conviction merely because of their poverty. Whether a man is innocent cannot be determined from a trial in which . . . denial of counsel has made it impossible to conclude, with any satisfactory degree of certainty, that the defendant's case was adequately presented."

In 1963 *Betts* was reversed by *Gideon v. Wainwright,* 372 U.S. 335. Gideon was charged with breaking and entering a poolroom in Florida with intent to commit a misdemeanor, which was a felony in that state. Gideon asked the trial judge to appoint an attorney to represent him. The judge declined, stating that Florida laws authorized the appointment of counsel only when a defendant was charged with a capital offense. Gideon represented himself at his trial. At the conclusion of the proceeding the jury returned a guilty verdict. Gideon was sentenced to serve five years in prison.

When *Gideon v. Wainwright* reached the Supreme Court it ruled, in a unanimous decision, that defendants charged with criminal offenses in state proceedings had a constitutional right to court-appointed counsel. The Court held that the due process clause of the Fourteenth Amendment obligated states to provide indigent defendants with counsel. Justice Black, who had dissented in *Betts*, authored the *Gideon* opinion. He observed that states devoted considerable financial and other resources to the prosecution of criminal cases, and defendants who were not represented by counsel were placed at a severe disadvantage. The opinion noted that laypersons are not usually knowledgeable about the complexities of the law. They are not familiar with the intricate rules of evidence, and they tend not to have the knowledge and skills required to mount an adequate defense. Quoting *Powell v. Alabama*, Black concluded that "the right to be heard would be, in many cases, of little avail if it did not comprehend the right to be heard by counsel."

SEE ALSO *Gideon v. Wainwright, 372 U.S. 335 (1963); Powell v. Alabama, 287 U.S. 45 (1932); Right to an Attorney*

BIBLIOGRAPHY

Carter, Dan T. 1979. *Scottsboro: A Tragedy of the American South.* Rev. edition. Baton Rouge: Louisiana State University Press.

Lewis, Anthony. 1964. *Gideon's Trumpet.* New York: Random House.

Rhode, Deborah L. 2004. *Access to Justice.* New York: Oxford University Press.

Leland Ware

BIBB V. NAVAJO FREIGHT LINES, INC., 359 U.S. 520 (1959)

In *Bibb v. Navajo Freight Lines, Inc.*, 359 U.S. 520 (1959), applying the so-called dormant commerce clause doctrine, the Court invalidated an Illinois statute, which required trucks and trailers operating on the state's highways to use "contour" rear-wheel mudguards.

By its terms, the Constitution's commerce clause (Art. I, § 8) empowers Congress "to regulate Commerce . . . among the several States," and under the supremacy clause, federal statutes sweep aside any conflicting state laws. The Court, however, has long construed the commerce clause as a general commitment to a policy of free trade across state boundaries. Accordingly, the Court implied therefrom a judicial power to strike down state laws impeding interstate commerce even in the absence of a conflict with a federal statute. Prior to *Bibb*, the Court's dormant commerce clause decisions had suggested that state regulations that did not discriminate against out-of-state commercial interests, but applied equally to intrastate and interstate commerce, would ordinarily be upheld. The Illinois statute was just this kind of uniformly applicable regulation. Nevertheless, a unanimous Supreme Court affirmed the ruling of a three-judge district court declaring the Illinois law unconstitutional and enjoining its enforcement.

In his opinion for the Court, Justice William Douglas explained that the statute presented the rare case where a non-discriminatory state law so heavily burdened interstate commerce for so dubious a public benefit as to run afoul of the federal constitution. Douglas highlighted the district court's findings to the effect that the required mudguards were expensive, provided no net safety benefits (indeed, they arguably created additional danger by "causing an accumulation of heat in the brake drum, thus decreasing the effectiveness of the brakes"), were not required by any other state, and were in fact forbidden by Arkansas state law. Moreover, the trucking industry was so structured that it would be extremely difficult for a firm to avoid Illinois highways. As well-established interline practices often led to companies hauling one another's trailers, the owner of any particular trailer did not always have practical control over the exact route it traveled.

In the light cast by these peculiar circumstances, the Illinois law could not stand. Though all nine Justices concurred, Justice John Marshall Harlan appended a separate opinion, in which Justice Potter Stewart joined. Harlan's opinion stressed the "heavy burden" the Illinois statute imposed on interstate commerce and the State's failure to justify the burden by any gain in safety, thereby further underscoring the narrowness of the Court's holding.

Bibb has over the decades produced significant progeny (e.g., *Kassel v. Consol. Freightways Corp.*, 450 U.S. 662 [1981], invalidating Iowa statutes restricting truck length) and remains a reminder of the Court's asserted authority to set aside state laws that, even though nondiscriminatory, severely burden interstate commerce for little or no discernable public benefit.

SEE ALSO *Dormant Commerce Clause*

BIBLIOGRAPHY

Redish, Martin H., and Shane V. Nugent. 1987. "The Dormant Commerce Clause and the Constitutional Balance of Federalism." *Duke Law Journal* 1987(4): 569–617.

Stearns, Maxwell L. 2003. "A Beautiful Mend: A Game Theoretical Analysis of the Dormant Commerce Clause Doctrine." *William & Mary Law Review* 45: 1–155.

A. Christopher Bryant

BICKEL, ALEXANDER
1924–1974

Alexander Mordecai Bickel, constitutional scholar and jurist, was born in Bucharest, Romania, on December 17, 1924, and came with his parents to the United States in 1938. His intellectual gifts won him honors as an undergraduate at City College of New York and at Harvard Law School. He served as a clerk for Judge Calvert Magruder (1893–1968) before becoming law clerk for U.S. Supreme Court Justice Felix Frankfurter from 1952 to 1953. Bickel served briefly in the State Department and joined the faculty at Yale University in 1956, where he taught until his untimely death from cancer in 1974.

Perhaps because of the similarity of their backgrounds, the relationship between Frankfurter and Bickel was unusually close, even for the justice who was famed for father-son relations with his protégés. Besides the regular duties of clerking, Frankfurter assigned Bickel the task of reviewing the historical background of the Fourteenth Amendment with regard to the meaning of the equal protection clause and its consequences for the landmark school segregation case of *Brown v. Board of Education*, 347 U.S. 483 (1954). Bickel's work contributed to the Court's final decision in two significant ways.

First, he wrote a memo for Justice Frankfurter concluding that the drafters and enactors of the amendment did not regard "separate-but-equal" education as a violation. Bickel argued that the framers deliberately chose to use broad and open-ended language that left some issues open for later legal decisions. Frankfurter was impressed enough to have a revision distributed to the other justices, and the final opinion in *Brown* follows that path. (Bickel later published an augmented version of his memo in the *Harvard Law Review*.)

Second, Bickel aided Frankfurter in drafting a memo for the Court setting out five complex questions for rearguing *Brown* in the 1953 term. This helped Frankfurter (in his finest hour) keep the Court from issuing a badly splintered decision in the case. That

postponement and fate—the death of Chief Justice Frederick Vinson in 1953 and his replacement by Earl Warren—resulted in a unanimous decision, which facilitated eventual acceptance of the Court's intervention.

With the publication of his most important book, *The Least Dangerous Branch*, in 1962, Bickel became the preeminent academic spokesman for the *judicial restraint* point of view, felicitously calling for "the passive virtues" of circumscribing judicial intervention, which he saw as necessary, given the Court's "countermajoritarian" place in the American system. Rooting himself in the tradition of James B. Thayer and Justices Oliver Wendell Holmes Jr. and Frankfurter, Bickel suggested that Thayer's classic argument that parsimonious intervention by the justices only in cases of "clear mistake" is needed for a sense of civic responsibility by the average American.

The authority of the Court cannot rest on any text in the Constitution, though Bickel had no doubt that "some form" of judicial review was intended. Although Chief Justice John Marshall's opinion in *Marbury v. Madison*, 5 U.S. 137 (1803), is generally regarded as unconvincing, Bickel, in a virtuoso performance of legal analysis, showed that it not only begs the question "but begs the wrong question" (Bickel 1962, p. 2). *Marbury* deals primarily with the dominance of the Constitution, but the real issue is which branch has ultimate power to interpret it. Court authority ultimately rests on two centuries of functional performance and popular acceptance.

Bickel embraced his colleague Charles Black's notion that the Court legitimates the actions of other branches, but this implies a power to invalidate other measures. Bickel suggested that there is a wide intermediate area, where the Court should neither validate nor nullify, but use legal techniques and rules, especially to avoid ad hoc policy-making where it cannot formulate "neutral principles." By coupling Herbert Wechsler's call for such general legal formulae with Thayer and Black's "legitimating" notions, Bickel gave more texture to the notion of the "passive virtues" of inaction. Still, the judgment he made of Frankfurter could apply equally to Bickel: he failed to provide tests or borderlines for a judge trying to decide between action and inaction (Bickel 1970, p. 34).

None of Bickel's other works have the truly classic quality of *The Least Dangerous Branch*, but they are all scholarly and beautifully written. Foremost among them is *The Supreme Court and the Idea of Progress* (1970), a scorching attack on an entire era of jurisprudence. Bickel suggested that the Warren Court justices thought with their hearts not their brains, were excessively preoccupied with equality, were careless craftsmen, and neglected the need to formulate "neutral principles" that are the essence of law. He accused them of the smug view that careless writing would be cured by history and social progress. But Bickel suggested that their faith in their vision of the future led them to create barriers to what he thought were developments already in the making. Their chief achievements—including desegregation, reapportionment, and the wall of separation between religion and state—were heading toward irrelevance or, worse, dysfunction. Bickel envisioned a society built upon more communitarian principles, for which these lines of decision would serve as obstacles. Bickel's vision of a community-governed society that segmented power has so far proven less applicable than that of the Warren justices.

Bickel functioned as a public intellectual of great erudition and style, publishing in law reviews and more general media such as *The New Republic* and *Commentary*. Some of these writings are incorporated into his books. He was the attorney for *The New York Times* in the Pentagon Papers case (*New York Times Co. v. United States*, 403 U.S. 713 [1971]), involving the publication of Vietnam War (1957–1975) policy documents that were classified as secret, but had no military revelations. Characteristically, he insisted on arguing the narrow grounds that "prior restraint" might be justified, for example, as a military necessity, but not to avoid foreign policy embarrassment. (The six-to-three decision was in favor of *The New York Times*, with three of the six-justice majority based on narrower grounds, as argued by Bickel.) Bickel also served as a political advisor to Robert Kennedy, pursuing his views of legally empowered black communities and of religious education to supplant the nineteenth-century ideal of public schools as a social homogenizer.

At the time of his death, Bickel had completed seven chapters of the ninth volume of the History of the Supreme Court series, drawing in part on papers and reminiscences of Louis Brandeis made available to him by Frankfurter, some of which he utilized in his early work, *The Unpublished Opinions of Mr. Justice Brandeis* (1957). Benno Schmidt added additional chapters to complete coverage on the 1910–1921 period and the work was issued posthumously in 1984 under the title *The Judiciary and Responsible Government*.

SEE ALSO *Brown v. Board of Education, 347 U.S. 483 (1954); Constitutional Theory; Frankfurter, Felix; Judicial Restraint*

BIBLIOGRAPHY

Bickel, Alexander. 1955. "The Original Understanding and the Segregation Decision." *Harvard Law Review* 69: 1–65.

Bickel, Alexander. 1957. *The Unpublished Opinions of Mr. Justice Brandeis: The Supreme Court at Work*. Cambridge, MA: Harvard University Press.

Bickel, Alexander. 1962. *The Least Dangerous Branch: The Supreme Court at the Bar of Politics*. Indianapolis, IN: Bobbs Merill.

Bickel, Alexander. 1970. *The Supreme Court and the Idea of Progress*. New York: Harper.

Bickel, Alexander, and Benno C. Schmidt. 1984. *The Judiciary and Responsible Government, 1910–1921*. New York: Macmillan.

Gunther, Gerald, 1964. "The Subtle Vices of the 'Passive Virtues': A Comment on Principle and Expediency in Judicial Review." *Columbus Law Review* 64: 3–25.

Moeller, John. 1985. "Alexander Bickel: Toward a Theory of Politics." *Journal of Politics* 47: 113–139.

Wright, J. Skelly. 1971. "Professor Bickel, the Scholarly Tradition and the Supreme Court." *Harvard Law Review* 84: 769–786.

Samuel Krislov

BILL OF RIGHTS

The original U.S. Constitution did not have a bill of rights. Indeed, the drafters did not think one was necessary, because they believed they were creating a government with limited powers that would not have the capacity to violate the liberties of its citizens. During the ratification process, however, the citizens debating the document were dubious that this new government would never abuse its powers, and they insisted that a bill of rights be put together. James Madison promised to draft such a document, and he did so in 1789.

The original draft had twelve proposed amendments, but the first two, having to do with the size and structure of the House of Representatives and compensation for members of Congress, did not receive the required approval of three-fourths of the states and thus failed as amendments. (In 1992 the second proposed amendment was later declared to have been ratified by subsequent state action, and it is now the Twenty-seventh Amendment.) The final ten of the proposed amendments were adopted in 1791 and are known as the Bill of Rights. Since then, these amendments have grown from provisions designed only to limit the federal government to provisions that (with only a couple of exceptions) limit the state governments as well. At the same time, the Supreme Court has drawn from the specific provisions in the Bill of Rights to develop the framework to find implicit unstated fundamental rights.

EARLY VIEWS ON THE BILL OF RIGHTS AND THE STATES

The original text of the Constitution, adopted in 1787 and ratified in 1789, gave the federal government detailed powers but contained few limitations—it prevented the federal government only from passing bills of attainder, enforcing ex post facto laws, and granting titles of nobility. The first eight amendments in the Bill of Rights list many

> *The very purpose of a Bill of Rights was to withdraw certain subjects from the vicissitudes of political controversy, to place them beyond the reach of majorities and officials and to establish them as legal principles to be applied by the courts. One's right to life, liberty, and property, to free speech, a free press, freedom of worship and assembly, and other fundamental rights may be submitted to no vote; they depend on the outcome of no elections.*
>
> SOURCE: Robert H. Jackson, *West Virginia State Board of Education v. Barnette*, 319 U.S. 624, 638 (1943).

more limitations, but these restrictions were designed only to limit the federal government; they did not at first apply to the state governments. The First Amendment's text ("Congress shall make no law . . . ") makes it clear that this was the understanding and intent of the framers, at least for this amendment.

In *Barron v. Baltimore*, 32 U.S. 243 (1833), Chief Justice John Marshall explicitly rejected the idea that a state government could be found to have violated a provision of the Bill of Rights. This case involved a claim by John Barron that his rights under the Fifth Amendment's takings clause had been violated by the City of Baltimore. Marshall explained that even though the text of the takings clause did nor refer explicitly to the federal government, "limitations on power, if expressed in general terms, are naturally, and, we think, necessarily applicable to the government created by the instrument," namely the federal government.

The adoption of the Fourteenth Amendment in 1868 gave the Congress a new source of power, for Section 5 of the amendment gave Congress the power of enforcement through legislation. In addition, the broad language of Section 1—prohibiting states from denying life, liberty, or property without due process of law—invited the courts to accept cases alleging that actions by states interfered with liberty interests, but it would many more decades before the courts undertook the challenge of determining what interests should be protected under the broad concept of "liberty." In *The Slaughter-House Cases*, 83 U.S. 36 (1873), the Court considered the contention that the provisions of the Fourteenth Amendment broadly expanded the power of federal courts to review state enactments. The Court rejected this view by a five-to-four vote, however, with the majority expressing concern about a major readjustment in the relationship between the federal government and the states. The majority explained that if it were to accept the views of the butchers in the case—who had argued that a Louisiana law establishing a monopoly in the slaughterhouse industry in New Orleans violated their federal constitutional rights—it "would constitute this court a perpetual censor upon all legislation of the States, on the civil rights of their own citizens, with authority to nullify such as it did not approve as consistent with those rights."

EARLY TWENTIETH-CENTURY VIEWS

The Supreme Court examined the content and extent of the Bill of Rights (and the Constitution as a whole) in some detail at the beginning of the twentieth century, when the Court examined the applicability of their provisions to the island territories acquired by the United States in its spasm of expansion in 1898. These acquisitions (Puerto Rico, Guam, the Philippines, and Hawaii) had populations and historical traditions distinct from those in the continental United States, and the Supreme Court had to determine whether all or parts of the Constitution applied to them. One of the early attempts to define the category of rights that apply wherever the U.S. flag is flown is found in dicta from *Downes v. Bidwell*, 182 U.S. 244, 282 (1901). The opinion in this case, written by Justice Henry Billings Brown (1836–1913), drew upon the concept of "natural rights" to define the constitutional rights that are "fundamental" and thus applicable in all U.S. territories:

> We suggest, without intending to decide, that there may be a distinction between *certain natural rights,* enforced in the Constitution by prohibitions against interference with them, and what may be termed *artificial or remedial rights,* which are peculiar to our own system of jurisprudence. Of the former class are the rights to one's own religious opinion and to a public expression of them, or, as sometimes said, to worship God according to the dictates of one's own conscience; the right to personal liberty and individual property; to freedom of speech and of the press; to free access to courts of justice, to due process of law, and to an equal protection of the laws; to immunities from unreasonable searches and seizures, as well as cruel and unusual punishments; and to such other immunities as are indispensable to a free government. Of the latter class are the rights to citizenship, to suffrage . . . and to the particular methods of procedure pointed out in the Constitution, which are peculiar to Anglo-Saxon jurisprudence, and some of which have already been held by the States to be unnecessary to the proper protection of individuals. (Emphasis added)

Many of the subsequent cases that have grappled with this issue concerned whether jury trials must be granted to accused persons in the territories, and these decisions concluded that a jury trial is not necessarily "fundamental" for this purpose. In a 1902 case involving the newly acquired territory of Hawaii—*Territory of Hawaii v. Mankichi*, 190 U.S. 197—the Court found that the manslaughter conviction of a defendant who had not been indicted by a grand jury and was convicted by a vote of only nine out of twelve jurors (in accordance with the law of the previous "Republic of Hawaii") was valid, even though it was not in compliance with the requirements of the Fifth and Sixth Amendments.

The Court ruled that until Congress enacted laws for the new territory, the existing laws of the previous government would apply, so long as they did not violate "fundamental" rights:

> We would even go farther and say that most, if not all, the privileges and immunities contained in the bill of rights of the Constitution were intended to apply from the moment of annexation; but we place our decision of this case upon the ground that the two rights alleged to be violated in this case [grand jury indictment and unanimous jury verdict] are not fundamental in their nature, but concern merely a method of procedure which sixty years of practice had shown to be suited to the conditions of the islands, and well calculated to conserve the rights of their citizens to their lives, their property, and their well-being.

This ruling that the Sixth Amendment right to a jury trial did not apply to territorial residents was echoed in a subsequent Puerto Rico case—*Balzac v. Porto Rico*, 258 U.S. 298 (1921)—in which the Court stated: "It is well settled that these provisions for jury trial in criminal and civil cases apply to the Territories of the United States. . . . But it is just as clearly settled that they do not apply to territory belonging to the United States that has not been incorporated into the union." The Supreme Court and lower federal courts confronted these issues throughout much of the twentieth century. Similar cases include *Dorr v. United States*, 195 U.S. 138 (1904), in which the Court refused to require an indictment by a grand jury in a criminal libel case in the Philippines; *Ocampo v. United States*, 234 U.S. 91 (1914), in which the Court held that a jury trial was not required in a misdemeanor criminal libel case in Puerto Rico; and *Government of Virgin Islands v. Rijos*, 285 F. Supp. 126 (1968), where the District Court of the Virgin Islands made its position plain: "It is settled that the right to trial by jury and Grand jury presentments are not among those fundamental rights and therefore do not apply to the Virgin Islands without Congressional approval."

In *Meyer v. Nebraska*, 262 U.S. 390 (1923), the Supreme Court struck down a Nebraska law prohibiting any public or private school from teaching young students in any language other than English. In the course of declaring this statute to be unconstitutional, Justice James McReynolds offered a list of those "liberties" that are protected under the due process clause:

> While this court has not attempted to define with exactness the liberty thus guaranteed, the term has received much consideration and some of the included things have been definitely stated. Without doubt, it denotes not merely freedom from bodily restraint but also the right of the individual to contract, to engage in any of the common occupations of life, to acquire useful knowledge, to marry, establish a home and bring up children, to worship God according to the dictates of his own conscience, and generally to enjoy those privileges long recognized at common law as essential to the orderly pursuit of happiness by free men.

Justice Oliver Wendell Holmes was one of the two dissenters from this decision. He stated that that he viewed Nebraska's law as sufficiently "rational" to pass constitutional scrutiny.

FURTHER CONSIDERATION OF "LIBERTY" AND THE BILL OF RIGHTS

The Supreme Court addressed the question of the applicability of the provisions of the Bill of Rights to the states more directly in the decades that followed. In *Gitlow v. New York*, 268 U.S. 652 (1925), the Court held that the guarantees of the First Amendment applied to the states as an element of the "liberty" protected by the due process clause of the Fourteenth Amendment. In *Palko v. Connecticut*, 302 U.S. 319 (1937), the Court rejected a claim that Connecticut's practice of allowing prosecutors to appeal acquittals violated the federal Constitution. Justice Benjamin Cardozo assumed that such a practice in a federal proceeding would violate the Fifth Amendment privilege against double jeopardy, but he said that the provisions of the Bill of Rights do not automatically apply to the states. Writing for the Court's majority, Cardozo ruled that only those procedural protections that "are of the very essence of a scheme of ordered liberty," such that "a fair and enlightened system of justice would be impossible without them," must be provided by the states to their criminal defendants. He explained that a trial by jury and a recognition of the privilege against self-incrimination were not obligatory, but that a real hearing "not a sham or pretense" was required, that defendants could not be tortured during interrogation, and that indigent defendants facing the death penalty must be provided counsel at government expense.

Ten years later, this issue was addressed again in *Adamson v. California*, 332 U.S. 46 (1947) with the justices offering a spectrum of views. The case involved the constitutionality of a California provision that allowed a judge and prosecutor to comment upon a defendant's failure to take the stand and respond to the evidence presented by the prosecution. Justice Stanley Reed (1884–1980), writing for the majority, concluded that this procedure did not violate "the concept of ordered liberty" or compel a finding of guilt, and thus did not violate the due process clause. Justice Hugo Black wrote a strong dissent, arguing that, to the framers, "the language of the first section of the Fourteenth Amendment, taken as a whole, was thought . . . sufficiently explicit to guarantee that . . . no state could deprive its citizens of the privileges and protections of the Bill of Rights." Black did not want to give judges free range to identify rights according to some nebulous standard, and he argued that "the 'natural law' formula which the Court uses to reach its conclusion in this case should be abandoned as an incongruous excrescence on our Constitution." Justice Frank Murphy, also dissenting, supported the idea of full incorporation of the Bill of Rights through the due process clause, but he expressed the view that other unnamed rights may also be implicit in the word "liberty" in the due process clause: "I agree that the specific guarantees of the Bill of Rights should be carried over intact into the first section of the Fourteenth Amendment. But I am not prepared to say that the latter is entirely and necessarily limited by the Bill of Rights."

Justice Felix Frankfurter responded to these dissenters by writing a concurring opinion that an approach of "selective incorporation" of the Bill of Rights should be utilized, rather than the "full incorporation" advocated by Justice Black and the "full incorporation plus" proposed by Justice Murphy. Frankfurter said that the decision regarding which provisions should be made binding on the states should be determined by reference to precedent, notions of federalism, and an examination of the plain language of the amendments. He argued that the ultimate test should be whether a state's use of a procedural device in a trial would "offend those canons of decency and fairness which express the notions of justice of English-speaking peoples." Frankfurter thus departed from Cardozo's approach in one significant way—Cardozo had favored an approach that would determine whether a procedural device was essential to every orderly system of justice, while Frankfurter favored examining this question in the context of the Anglo-American legal system, where the jury plays a prominent role.

The question whether the Constitution implicitly protects unstated fundamental rights was also examined by the Court in *Skinner v. Oklahoma*, 316 U.S. 535 (1942), a case involving an Oklahoma statute requiring sterilization of those individuals convicted of two or more "felonies involving moral turpitude." The Court struck down this law, focusing on the discriminatory distinctions made in the statute between types of crimes, but Justice William O. Douglas's opinion for the Court also noted that "[m]arriage and procreation are fundamental to the very existence and survival of the race," and that a statute creating classifications regarding such fundamental matters must be subjected to "strict scrutiny of the classification."

THE RIGHT TO PRIVACY

In 1965 Justice Douglas again wrote for the Court in *Griswold v. Connecticut*, 381 U.S. 479, in which the Court struck down Connecticut's ban on the use of contraceptives for preventing conception. He found an implicit right to privacy in the penumbras of the First, Third, Fourth, Fifth, and Ninth Amendments, and held that allowing "the police to search the sacred precincts of the marital bedrooms for telltale signs of the use of contraceptives . . . is repulsive to the notions of privacy surrounding the marriage relationship." Justice Arthur J. Goldberg wrote a concurring opinion stressing the Ninth Amendment, which recognizes that unenumerated rights are retained by the people, and explaining that judges must find implicit unenumerated rights by examining the traditions of the nation and balancing burdens on individual choices against valid governmental interests.

Since the *Griswold* ruling, the Court has found that the right to privacy protects a woman's right to have an abortion in *Roe v. Wade*, 410 U.S. 113 (1973); the right to marry in *Zablocki v. Redhail*, 434 U.S. 374 (1978); and the right to engage in same-sex intimate physical relations in *Lawrence v. Texas*, 539 U.S. 558 (2003). The Court has also found that the right to travel and the right to vote are fundamental rights based on the structure and vision of the Constitution, even though they are not explicitly given that status in the text (see *Shapiro v. Thompson*, 394 U.S. 618 [1969]; *Saenz v. Roe*, 526 U.S. 489 [1999]; and *Reynolds v. Sims*, 377 U.S. 533 [1964]).

With regard to the continuing debate over the incorporation of the provisions of the Bill of Rights through the due process clause and their application to the states, the Court ruled in *Duncan v. Louisiana*, 391 U.S. 145 (1968) that the Sixth Amendment requires the states to grant jury trials to all persons facing a possible penalty of six months or more in jail. Justice Byron White wrote for the Court that the right to trial by jury is among those "fundamental principles of liberty and justice which lie at the base of all our civil and political institutions."

Since the *Duncan* decision, most commentators have agreed that all parts of the Bill of Rights have been made obligatory to the states except the Seventh Amendment's guarantee of a jury trial in civil cases involving disputes of more than twenty dollars, the Fifth Amendment's requirement of a grand jury indictment, and the Second Amendment's language regarding "the right of the people to keep and bear Arms." The situation regarding the Second Amendment has been actively discussed in recent years, however, and it was the central issue presented to the Supreme Court in *District of Columbia v. Heller*, which was argued before the Court in March 2008.

The Bill of Rights thus continues to play a central role in U.S. jurisprudence. The specific protections articulated in these amendments laid out a vision of individual dignity that has served to protect Americans from government abuses and to guide the Court in identifying other implicit rights that are fundamental to free people.

SEE ALSO *Anti-Federalist/Federalist Ratification Debate; Barron v. Baltimore, 32 U.S. 243 (1833); Fourteenth Amendment; Incorporation Debate; Slaughter-House Cases, 83 U.S. 36 (1873); Warren Court*

BIBLIOGRAPHY

Amar, Akhil Reed. 1998. *The Bill of Rights: Creation and Reconstruction*. New Haven, CT: Yale University Press.

Brant, Irving. 1965. *The Bill of Rights: Its Origin and Meaning*. Indianapolis: Bobbs-Merrill.

Conley, Patrick T., and John P. Kaminski, eds. 1992. *The Bill of Rights and the States*. Madison, WI: Madison House.

Cornell, Saul. 1999. *The Other Founders: Anti-Federalism and the Dissenting Tradition in America, 1788–1828*. Chapel Hill, NC: University of North Carolina Press.

Labunski, Richard E. 2006. *James Madison and the Struggle for the Bill of Rights*. Oxford: Oxford University Press.

Levy, Leonard W. 2001. *Origins of the Bill of Rights*. New Haven, CT: Yale University Press.

Lieberman, Jethro K. 1987. *The Enduring Constitution: A Bicentennial Perspective*. Saint Paul, MN: West Publishing.

Rutland, Robert Allen. 1955. *The Birth of the Bill of Rights, 1776–1791*. Chapel Hill, NC: University of North Carolina Press.

Van Dyke, Jon M. 1992. "The Evolving Legal Relationships Between the United States and Its Affiliated U.S.-Flag Islands." *University of Hawaii Law Review* 14: 445–517.

Wood, Gordon S. 1998. *The Creation of the American Republic, 1776–1987*. Chapel Hill, NC: University of North Carolina Press.

Jon M. Van Dyke

BISHOP V. WOOD, 426 U.S. 341 (1976)

Bishop v. Wood, 426 U.S. 341 (1976) was one of a series of cases grappling with the meaning of *property* for the purposes of the due process clause, as well as the procedures states must implement when revoking a statutory right or privilege. Although *Bishop* was neither the first nor the last case to examine these issues, it reflects an ideological current that proved persistent in later years, though it frequently failed to command a majority.

Under a North Carolina law, certain public employees were classified as *permanent* employees. Permanent employees could only be dismissed from their positions for specified reasons. The city of Marion, North Carolina terminated Bishop (a policeman classified as permanent employee) claiming he had failed to follow orders, had poor attendance at police training sessions, and had engaged in conduct unbecoming a police officer. Challenging his dismissal and the reasons given therefore, Bishop argued he had a protected property interest in his continued employment under the Fourteenth Amendment's due process clause. Bishop also claimed his termination made it more difficult for him to find new work and thus deprived him of liberty without due process.

The Court looked to state law to determine whether Bishop had a protected property right. Unable to find conclusive North Carolina case law interpreting the permanent employee statute, the Court deferred to the District Court's holding that the statute merely delineated the grounds for an employee's removal and did not create an enforceable guarantee of continued employment. Moving to the second issue, the Court held the potential stigma created by allegations of Bishop's misconduct did constitute an illegitimate deprivation of liberty under the due process clause. The Court pointed out that the reasons for Bishop's dismissal were communicated to him in private, and thus were unlikely to affect his job prospects. As such, even assuming the justifications for his termination were apocryphal, Bishop had not been deprived of liberty without due process.

Justices William J. Brennan Jr. and Thurgood Marshall dissented, claiming Bishop's reputation had been tarnished, notwithstanding the initially private criticisms of his performance. Justices Byron White and Harry Blackmun, meanwhile, criticized the Court's reliance on what they considered a strained reading of the North Carolina statute. All four dissenters joined a third dissent arguing the majority had improperly abandoned the more exacting due process analysis advanced in *Arnett v. Kennedy*, 416 U.S. 134 (1976) by implying the North Carolina statute creating Bishop's employment status should also govern the procedures through which he could be deprived of that status.

In subsequent years, the *Bishop* dissenters generally gained the upper hand in this critique of the majority's analysis. In *Vitek v. Jones*, 445 U.S. 480 (1980) and *Cleveland Board of Education v. Loudermill*, 470 U.S. 532 (1985), the Court determined that the procedures required before a state could deprive an individual of some right were to be determined by federal, rather than state, law. Nevertheless, the actual scope of the procedural rights furnished by federal law has continued to preoccupy the federal dockets even in the aftermath of these cases.

SEE ALSO *Procedural Due Process*

BIBLIOGRAPHY

Rabin, Robert L. 1976. "Job Security and Due Process: Monitoring Administrative Discretion through a Reasons Requirement." *University of Chicago Law Review* 44(1): 60–93.

Winston A. Bowman

BIVENS V. SIX UNKNOWN FED. NARCOTICS AGENTS, 403 U.S. 388 (1971)

In *Bivens v. Six Unknown Fed. Narcotics Agents*, 403 U.S. 388 (1971), the Supreme Court held that a citizen may sue a federal agent for damages for unreasonable searches and seizures. Webster Bivens was at home with his wife and children when federal agents unlawfully entered and searched his apartment. The agents arrested Bivens and took him to the courthouse for further interrogation. Although all charges against Bivens were eventually dropped, Bivens sued the federal agents for damages to receive compensation for his humiliation and mental suffering. Writing for the Court, Justice William J. Brennan Jr. held that Bivens could sue the federal agents for damages for violations of the Fourth Amendment, even though Congress had not established a statutory right to sue. The Court explained that damages were needed because the government had dropped the charges against Bivens, and the exclusionary rule and the disincentive for government misconduct it generated would therefore not be triggered. Justice John Marshall Harlan II, concurring in the judgment, agreed with the decision to award money damages for the agents' unreasonable search and seizure. For people in Bivens's situation, it was "damages or nothing."

The dissenters, Chief Justice Warren E. Burger, Justice Hugo Black, and Justice Harry Blackmun, opposed the Court's efforts to establish a legal remedy for the violation of Bivens's constitutional rights. Burger and Black asserted that Congress was the appropriate branch to create causes of action for constitutional violations. Additionally, Blackmun opined that creating a cause of action against federal agents for Fourth Amendment violations would subject the courts to an "avalanche of new federal cases." If a solution were really needed, it would be for Congress to create.

Bivens is a landmark decision because it created a right to sue directly under the Fourth Amendment. It also opened the door for other civil lawsuits against federal officers. Plaintiffs have brought *Bivens* claims in a wide variety of civil rights suits, ranging from Fourth Amendment to First Amendment violations. So far, the Supreme Court has extended the right to sue for damages to violations of the Fifth Amendment's due process clause and the Eighth Amendment's cruel and unusual punishments clause. However, the Supreme Court has also held back the tide of Bivens claims by refusing to recognize suits for damages for First Amendment violations by federal employers (*Bush v. Lucas*, 463 U.S. 367 [1983]). Notable *Bivens* claims against federal agencies and private prisons are *FDIC v. Meyer*, 510 U.S. 471 (1994) and *Correctional Services Corp. v. Malesko*, 534 U.S. 61 (2001), respectively.

In general, the decision whether to recognize a *Bivens* remedy is a judgment about the best way to implement a constitutional guarantee. The determination requires two steps: (1) whether any alternative process for protecting special interests exists; and (2) whether there are "special factors counseling hesitation before authorizing a new kind of federal legislation" (see *Wilkie v. Robbins*, 551 U.S. [2007] and *Carlson v. Green*, 446 U.S. 14 [1980]). Such special factors include the difficulty the Court would have in defining a workable cause of action.

Bivens will forever be remembered as a groundbreaking decision in the area of civil rights because it recognized an inherent right to sue for damages resulting from constitutional violations. However, the limitations on the doctrine still pose significant hurdles to filing such actions. As of May 1985, more than 12,000 *Bivens* suits had been filed, but only thirty of these have resulted in judgments on behalf of plaintiffs.

SEE ALSO *Fourth Amendment; Search and Seizure*

BIBLIOGRAPHY

Newman, Ryan D. 2006. "From Bivens to Malesko and Beyond: Implied Constitutional Remedies and the Separation of Powers." *Texas Law Review* 85(2): 471–515.

Robeda, Andrea. 2003. "The Death of Implied Causes of Action: The Supreme Court's Recent Bivens Jurisprudence and the Effect on State Constitutional Tort Jurisprudence: Correctional Services Corp. v. Malesko." *New Mexico Law Review* 33(3): 401–429.

Laurie L. Levenson

BLACK, CHARLES
1915–2001

Charles Lund Black, Jr., was one of the twentieth century's most eminent constitutional scholars. Four years after graduating from Yale Law School, he began teaching at Columbia Law School. He remained there for nine years, then moved at Yale Law School, where he taught for thirty years, followed by another thirteen years at Columbia Law School. As a law professor, he taught hundreds of students who went on to become leaders in government, business, and academia, and he wrote more than twenty books and hundreds of articles, many of which became the leading texts on their subjects. Black was a Renaissance man, who taught himself Icelandic, studied Old and Middle English in graduate school, wrote poetry, played the trumpet, loved classics, painted landscapes in oil, and, with his colleague Grant Gilmore (1910–1982), wrote for many years what was widely regarded as the definitive casebook and text on admiralty law. Black began a lifelong love affair with jazz after he attended, as a college freshman, a live performance by Louis Armstrong (1901–1971).

Black may be best remembered for the clarity, power, and elegance of his writing, particularly on civil rights, constitutional theory, and presidential impeachment. While teaching at Columbia Law School, he volunteered to assist the plaintiffs in *Brown v. Board of Education*, 347 U.S. 483 (1954). His contributions so impressed the plaintiffs' lead counsel, Thurgood Marshall (1908–1993), that Marshall later told Black, "You are a Negro." Not long after *Brown*, Black's then-colleague, Herbert Wechsler (1909–2000), questioned *Brown* on the ground that there was no "neutral principle" to allow the plaintiffs' interest in freedom of association to prevail over the white majority's associational interests. In 1960 Black responded in a seminal article, maintaining that the principled basis for *Brown* was its dismantlement of state-mandated segregation as but one feature of a general regime of invidious discrimination aimed at subjugating African Americans. In 1969 Black produced a short book, *Structure and Relationship in Constitutional Law*, arguing that the design or structure of the U.S. Constitution was among the most significant sources of constitutional meaning. The book became a classic.

Black was a liberal Democrat who intensely disliked Richard Nixon's (1913–1994) politics. Yet, in letters to newspapers published as the movement to impeach Nixon was gathering steam, Black argued against forcing Nixon to surrender tapes of conversations in the Oval Office that incriminated him, contending that the balance of federal power required that presidents, including Nixon, be entitled to an absolute executive privilege not to disclose to the other branches, including the Supreme Court, information that they believed should be kept confidential. Black expanded on these arguments in a short book on impeachment published in 1974, not long before Nixon's resignation. In the book, he defended Nixon's entitlement to an absolute executive privilege to maintain equal footing with the other branches and to avoid being subjugated by them. The book became an instant classic, and was reissued in 1998 during impeachment proceedings against President Bill Clinton, who had been Black's student.

The *Yale Law Journal* published two retrospectives on Black's work. It published the first in 1986 when he retired from teaching at Yale Law School. The second was published jointly with the *Columbia Law Review* a few months after Black died in May 2001.

SEE ALSO *Brown v. Board of Education, 347 U.S. 483 (1954); School Desegregation*

BIBLIOGRAPHY

Black, Charles L., Jr. 1960. "The Lawfulness of the Segregation Decisions." *Yale Law Journal* 69: 421–430.

Black, Charles L., Jr. 1967. "Foreword: 'State Action,' Equal Protection, and California's Proposition 14." *Harvard Law Review* 81: 69–109.

Black, Charles L., Jr. 1969. *Structure and Relationship in Constitutional Law*. Baton Rouge: Louisiana State University Press.

Black, Charles L., Jr. 1974. *Capital Punishment: The Inevitability of Caprice and Mistake*. New York: Norton.

Black, Charles L., Jr. 1974. *Impeachment: A Handbook*. New Haven, CT: Yale University Press.

Black, Charles L., Jr. 1981. *Decision According to Law*. New York: Norton.

Michael J. Gerhardt

BLACK, HUGO
1886–1971

Trial lawyer, prosecutor, U.S. senator, and U.S. Supreme Court justice Hugo L. Black had a very unusual background for a Supreme Court justice. Born in Clay County in the eastern Alabama hill country, he grew up in the heyday of populism and imbibed its belief that government had a role in improving the lives of citizens. He dropped out of high school, attended medical school for a year and, without going to college, graduated from the University of Alabama Law School with highest honors in 1906. The class roll noted that he "will use the devil himself with courtesy" (Newman 1997).

BLACK'S BACKGROUND

In 1907, Black moved to Birmingham and almost exclusively practiced accident and negligence law. He taught Sunday school and joined almost every organization in town, from 1910 to 1911 serving as a part-time police judge. Elected district attorney in 1914, Black exposed the use of third-degree to extract confessions in a local jail and eliminated the fee system under which law enforcement personnel were paid based on the number of arrests made. In 1917, he resigned to join the army. Back in private practice after stateside service in World War I, Black routinely won over 90 percent of his cases. He

Supreme Court Justice Hugo Black. *A district attorney, U.S. senator, and Supreme Court Justice, Black fought to preserve the rights of the individual against the power of the government.*
© OSCAR WHITE/CORBIS

lost no more than a few dozen cases out of about 2,000 during his nearly thirty-year legal career. Black was a master at cross-examination—his mild voice and manner masking tough questions—and so good at ingratiating himself with jurors that the saying among Birmingham lawyers was, "if you don't watch out, Hugo will get in the jury box with you every time" (Newman 1997).

In 1923, Black joined the Ku Klux Klan. He was an officer, the Kladd of his local Klavern, whose duty was to swear in new members; but otherwise he did not partake in its activities. Nearly one half of all white men in the greater Birmingham area were members. This gave Black a ready-made base of supporters when he ran for the U.S. Senate in 1926. He was elected as the Klan served as his unofficial campaign organization, and in 1932 he was reelected in a walk.

Black was the most feared congressional investigator of the day. His investigation into lobbying irregularities by public utilities was instrumental in the passage of the Public Utilities Holding Company Act of 1935, and his inquiry into airline and shipping subsidies led to the Merchant

Marine Act of 1936 and ultimately to the establishment of the Civil Aeronautics Board. Black cross-examined witnesses as if he were back in court. "You have me on the hip, senator," protested one witness (Newman 1997). The federal minimum wage law was Black's pet project in the Senate. He introduced it three times before it became law in 1938. No senator more strongly supported Franklin D. Roosevelt's plan to pack the Supreme Court.

ON THE COURT

In August 1937, on the heels of the ill-fated Court-packing plan, Roosevelt appointed a surprised Black (who aspired to the presidency) to the Court. "A kick in the face [with] our own foot," one senator called it (Newman 1997). After he was easily confirmed, Black's former Klan membership was revealed to an unsuspecting nation. He admitted it in a low-key radio address while pointing to his humanitarian record, and the uproar soon died.

On the Supreme Court, Justice Black spearheaded a constitutional revolution. He led the redirection of American law toward the protection of the individual. At the same time, he sought clear standards in order to limit judicial discretion while giving government room to operate. Black presented his views in clear, simple language that admitted of no doubts. His dissents rang with passion. Language and history are the crucial factors in interpreting the Constitution, he wrote.

By 1950, Black came to feel that the clear and present danger rule in First Amendment cases, with inherent balancing of disparate interests, did not sufficiently protect freedom of expression. The advent of McCarthyism led him to adopt the view that all speech about public matters is constitutionally protected. This position remains unprecedented in Supreme Court annals. To Black it meant, for example, that all obscenity laws and—so he suggested off the Court—all libel and slander laws were unconstitutional. "It is my belief," he said in 1960, "that there *are* 'absolutes' in our Bill of Rights, and that they were put there by men who knew what words meant, and meant their prohibitions to be 'absolute'" (Newman 1997).

Black believed that the framers of the Fourteenth Amendment intended to make the specific guarantees of the Bill of Rights applicable to the states in the same way they apply to the federal government. He presented this argument at length in *Adamson v. California*, 332 U.S. 46 (1947), which he considered his most important opinion. The Court followed his lead in many fields, including the right against self-incrimination, the right against coerced confessions, and (perhaps most famously) the right to counsel established in *Gideon v. Wainwright*, 372 U.S. 335 (1963). Similarly, the Court's reapportionment decisions built upon Black's dissent in *Colegrove v. Green*, 328 U.S. 549 (1946). No other justice has been as strong a proponent of jury trial. Black saw no textual basis, however, for a constitutional right of privacy and his record in Fourth Amendment cases might be the most restrictive of any justice in history. Noting that "hardships are part of war," he wrote the Court's opinion in *Korematsu v. United States*, 323 U.S. 214 (1944), upholding the internment of all American citizens of Japanese ancestry during World War II.

Starting in 1950, Black searched for a case to overturn the separate but equal standard under the Fourteenth Amendment. He tried in different ways to persuade any new justice and, after Earl Warren was appointed chief justice in 1953, forged a friendship with Chief Justice Warren built as much on their swapping of political war stories over steaks at Black's house as it was built on their shared legal views. According to Justice Tom C. Clark (1899–1977), Warren wanted Black to write the opinion in *Brown v. Board of Education*, 347 U.S. 483 (1954), but Black dissuaded Warren, who wrote it instead.

Black played a key role in the development of the First Amendment's religious guarantees. He wrote the Court's opinions in *Everson v. Board of Education*, 330 U.S. 1 (1947), the first case to apply the establishment clause to the states; and in his most controversial opinion, *Engel v. Vitale*, 370 U.S. 421 (1962), which outlawed state written and mandated prayers in public schools. Commentators called it the *Warren Court*, after Chief Justice Warren, but as *Time* magazine noted, it was "more accurately called the 'Black Court,' after its chief philosopher" (Newman 1997). More recently, critics have condemned Black's religious opinions as an outgrowth of anti-Catholicism and the result of his Ku Klux Klan membership, but this is a grossly profound misreading of history and the constitutional record.

The direct action cases of the 1960s tested Black's philosophy. They involved peaceful marches and sit-ins (which he called sit downs). And, as his robust health started to deteriorate, Black's philosophy changed. He felt that civil disobedience could result in anarchy and he consistently favored the need for preservation of public order over the First Amendment right to assemble. "Marches lead to violence," Black said, insisting that government had the authority to take over an area if necessary (Newman 1997). His later opinions lacked their former expansiveness and optimism, and his interpretations were often cramped and confining—his categories restricted.

Black's main pursuits off the Court were tennis—which he played regularly and passionately on a court behind his Federal-style home in Alexandria, Virginia—and reading. He read voluminously—largely in history, philosophy and the classics—marking his books and making his own indexes inside their rear covers. A reporter, hearing Black's Senate speeches, said that he sounded like "a talking encyclopedia with a southern accent"; and his opinions on the Court made history come alive as he related

analogous situations and showed continuities in human nature. Black also inspired deep loyalty among friends and associates. Situations, not personalities, animated him. "Strike for the jugular," he exhorted and even though he fought for his views with what he called his "usual tenacity *ad nauseam*," his fiercest adversaries were among his best friends (Newman 1997). During McCarthyism, Black stood as a nearly solitary beacon of hope and his opinions conveyed the forcefulness of his personality, and to the end he retained his naturalness and sense of outrage.

The Supreme Court that rewrote the Constitution in the 1960s was basically Hugo Black writ large, as more of his dissents than those of any other justice became the law of the land. His last opinion came in the so-called Pentagon Papers Case, *New York Times Co. v. United States*, 403 U.S. 713 (1971). The press must be free "to publish news whatever the source, without censorship, injunctions, or prior restraints," Black wrote. "Only a free and unrestrained press can effectively expose deception in government" (Newman 1997). He died three months later, universally recognized as one of the handful of great judges in American history.

SEE ALSO *First Amendment; Incorporation Debate; Korematsu v. United States, 323 U.S. 214 (1944); Roosevelt, Franklin D.*

BIBLIOGRAPHY

Dilliard, Irving, ed. 1963. *One Man's Stand for Freedom: Mr. Justice Black and the Bill of Rights*. New York: Knopf.

Frank, John P. 2000. *Inside Justice Hugo L. Black: The Letters*. Austin, TX: Jamail Center for Legal Research.

Newman, Roger K. 1997. *Hugo Black: A Biography*. 2nd edition. New York: Fordham University Press.

Reich, Charles A. 1963. "Mr. Justice Black and the Living Constitution." *Harvard Law Review* 76(4): 673–754.

Roger K. Newman

BLACKMUN, HARRY
1908–1999

Harry Andrew Blackmun served as an associate justice of the Supreme Court of the United States from June 9, 1970, to June 30, 1994. He was born in Nashville, Illinois, on November 12, 1908, and died in Arlington, Virginia, on March 4, 1999. Blackmun is best remembered for writing the seven-to-two majority decision in the enduringly controversial abortion case of *Roe v. Wade*, 410 U.S. 113 (1973). However, he left his mark in many other areas of the law over his twenty-four-year career on the Court. He played a key role in constitutional jurisprudence in areas as diverse as commercial speech, criminal law, federalism, and the rights of aliens. Blackmun's judicial opinions were often charged with emotion, and his constitutional reasoning varied greatly with circumstances.

Blackmun was raised in St. Paul, Minnesota, and earned his undergraduate and law degrees at Harvard University in 1929 and 1932, respectively. He returned to Minnesota upon graduation, where he was admitted to the bar in 1932. He also served there as a law clerk for the U.S. Court of Appeals for the Eighth Circuit. From 1934 to 1950, Blackmun practiced with a Minneapolis law firm, largely in the areas of taxation and estate planning. In the 1930s and 1940s, he taught law as an adjunct instructor, including stints at what is now the William Mitchell College of Law and at the University of Minnesota Law School. From 1950 to 1959, he served as general counsel to the Mayo Clinic and Mayo Association in Rochester, Minnesota. He went to the bench in 1959, when President Dwight D. Eisenhower appointed him to the Eighth Circuit, succeeding the judge for whom he had clerked. Blackmun, a lifelong Republican and personal friend of Chief Justice Warren Burger, was appointed to the U.S. Supreme Court in 1970 by President Richard Nixon. He was Nixon's third choice for the position, nominated after the U.S. Senate rejected two of Nixon's previous nominees. After his elevation to the Court, Blackmun continued to lecture in a variety of legal educational forums. By the time of his death in 1999, he had been honored with dozens of honorary degrees and other awards.

TENURE ON THE COURT

Many Court observers thought Blackmun would help move the Court in the more conservative direction desired by Nixon. At first, this proved to be the case, with Blackmun voting to support the exercise of state power in criminal justice and free speech matters. For example, he voted to uphold the death penalty in *Furman v. Georgia*, 408 U.S. 238 (1972) and again in *Gregg v. Georgia*, 428 U.S. 153 (1976), despite personal reservations over the practice. Late in his career, these reservations would translate into firm jurisprudential opposition to capital punishment in all circumstances.

In the case of *New York Times v. United States*, 403 U.S. 713 (1971), he dissented, joining with Burger in supporting the Nixon administration's efforts to prevent publication of the Pentagon Papers. He also dissented in *Cohen v. California*, 403 U.S. 15 (1971), siding with the state in its effort to curb offensive conduct. However, in *Bates v. State Bar of Arizona*, 433 U.S. 350 (1977), Blackmun wrote the majority decision to strike down a state bar association's guidelines that prevented members from advertising their legal services. This case restricted the ability of the legal profession to be self-governing when First Amendment issues were at stake.

Blackmun's early concern for individual rights was also made clear in his majority opinion in *Graham v. Richardson*, 403 U.S. 365 (1971), which held alien status to be a suspect classification under the Fourteenth Amendment. This made governmental classifications based on alien status subject to the highest level of judicial scrutiny. In subsequent cases, Blackmun generally supported the rights of aliens against state discrimination.

Blackmun authored the majority opinion in *Roe v. Wade*, one of the most controversial decisions in the Court's history. In embracing the right to privacy adumbrated in *Griswold v. Connecticut*, 381 U.S. 479 (1965), Blackmun evinced a decisive willingness to read the Constitution broadly—and some would say loosely—in order to put into question the police power of the state. Blackmun relied on the Fourteenth Amendment's due process clause, which he claimed established a right to privacy that in turn protected a woman's right to abortion in certain circumstances.

Blackmun became a reliable defender of the right to abortion, viewing it as an essential component of the emancipation of women. Blackmun passionately dissented in the case of *Webster v. Reproductive Health Services*, 492 U.S. 490 (1989), in which he viewed the majority decision that allowed some restrictions on the use of state funds for abortion as in effect giving the state unconstitutional power to interfere with women's rights to control their bodies. In *Planned Parenthood v. Casey*, 505 U.S. 833 (1992), Blackmun used extraordinarily emotional language in speculating openly on the effects of his retirement on the right to abortion. He characterized the opinions of four members of the Court who appeared willing to roll back *Roe* as casting into "darkness the hopes and visions of every woman in this country." He noted that the coming of this "darkness" required only one more vote on the narrowly divided Court.

Blackmun showed himself to be on the cutting edge of social change in a number of other ways. In *Bowers v. Hardwick*, 478 U.S. 186 (1986), Blackmun wrote a stinging dissent in response to the majority's upholding of a Georgia sodomy law. Blackmun saw the Court's refusal to extend privacy protections to homosexual sodomy as an assault on the fundamental "right to be let alone" and argued for constitutional protection for new understandings of sexual intimacy. Almost a decade after Blackmun's retirement, the Court overturned *Bowers* in *Lawrence v. Texas*, 539 U.S. 558 (2003).

In *Regents of the University of California v. Bakke*, 438 U.S. 265 (1978), Blackmun in effect voted to support governmentally sponsored affirmative action programs, as long as the racial classifications used were not stigmatizing and were designed to help people in classes deemed to have suffered past discrimination. He famously claimed that "in order to get beyond racism, we must first take account of race. . . . And in order to treat some persons equally, we must treat them differently."

Throughout the 1980s, Blackmun strengthened his liberal credentials in a number of areas. In *Garcia v. San Antonio Metropolitan Transit Authority*, 469 U.S. 528 (1985), he wrote the majority opinion that supported much of the Court's twentieth-century commerce clause jurisprudence by declining to place any judicial limitations on Congress's economic regulatory power exercised in the name of interstate commerce. Many observers thought this decision—later overturned in *United States v. Lopez*, 514 U.S. 549 (1995)—struck a major blow against a reinvigorated federalism in which states might claim exclusive regulatory domains. Blackmun also interpreted the establishment clause in such a way as to make unconstitutional many forms of prayer in public schools, for example in *Lee v. Weisman*, 505 U.S. 577 (1992).

LEGACY

Blackmun will go down in history as one of the Court's great liberal justices, both procedurally and substantively. By the end of his career, he had placed himself squarely among the Court's liberal wing, often joining with fellow liberals William J. Brennan, Jr. and Thurgood Marshall. He consistently showed a willingness to grant certiorari in order to allow for full hearings on the merits of various rights claims. He also showed great personal interest in the facts of the cases he adjudicated, as well as compassion for the people directly involved. He knew he would be largely defined in the public mind by his decision in *Roe*, though he understood his legacy of vindicating rights to be far broader than this. His passion for certain causes and individuals shined through many of his decisions. It cannot, however, be said that Blackmun's judicial philosophy was consistently liberal. He is therefore difficult to place on a conventional political spectrum.

On many issues, Blackmun drifted to the left over the course of his long term on the Court. At the same time, he seemed to adopt a pragmatic approach to judicial reasoning. He refused to allow rigid formulas or canons of constitutional interpretation to stand in the way of attaining results that he viewed as essential to vindicating the rights of those to whom he believed compassion was due.

SEE ALSO *Burger Court; Greenhouse, Linda; Roe v. Wade, 410 U.S. 113 (1973)*

BIBLIOGRAPHY

Brennan, William J., et. al. 1994. "A Tribute to Justice Harry A. Blackmun." *Harvard Law Review* 108(1): viii–22.

Greenhouse, Linda. 2005. *Becoming Justice Blackmun: Harry Blackmun's Supreme Court Journey.* New York: Holt.

Hair, Penda D. 1994. "Justice Blackmun and Racial Justice." *Yale Law Journal* 104(1): 23–31.

Reuben, Richard C. 1994. "Justice Defined: It Takes More Than a Single Opinion to Understand How Legal Reasoning and Personal Experience Shape a 24-Year Career." *ABA Journal* 80: 46–51.

Rosen, Jeffrey. 1994. "Sentimental Journey: The Emotional Jurisprudence of Harry Blackmun." *New Republic* 210(18): 13–18.

Yarbrough, Tinsley. 2008. *Harry A. Blackmun: The Outsider Justice.* New York: Oxford University Press.

Bradley C. S. Watson

BLACKSTONE, WILLIAM
1723–1780

William Blackstone's *Commentaries on the Laws of England* (1765–1769) has provided a guide to the common law for two centuries of American lawyers and judges. The strength of this influence has varied over time.

Educated at Oxford, Blackstone later became a barrister. Blackstone practiced law for some time before beginning to focus on the study of law from an academic perspective. In 1793 he started lecturing on the subject of the laws of England. These lectures, referred to as his *Commentaries*, were the first of their kind to be offered in a university. The goal of these lectures was to present English law in a systematic fashion. Known for his adherence to the legal tradition of natural law, Blackstone asserted that there

> are . . . eternal immutable laws of good and evil, to which the Creator himself, in all of his dispensations, conforms; and which he has enabled human reason to discover, so far as they are necessary for the conduct of human action. Such, among others, are these principles: that we should live honestly, should hurt nobody, and should render to every one his due; to which these three general precepts Justinian has reduced the whole of the doctrine of law. (1766, 2:40)

A discussion of Blackstone's influence on the early U.S. Supreme Court can be traced to one of its most influential justices, Chief Justice John Marshall. He received a copy of the *Commentaries* as a birthday present from his parents, who wanted to instill in him the desire to become an attorney. He was very impressed with the work, and wrote that "this legal classic is the poetry of the law, just as Pope is logic in poetry" (Miles, Dagley, and Yau 2000, p. 56). Blackstone's influence can be seen in the case of *Marbury v. Madison*, 5 U.S. 137 (1803). In this case "Marshall cited the *Commentaries* several times in support of the proposition that the law must furnish a remedy for violation of a vested legal right and in discussing the nature of the writ of mandamus" (Nolan 1976, p. 755).

Another early justice, Joseph Story, appointed by President James Madison, served on the Court from 1811 to 1845. Justice Story shared Chief Justice Marshall's sentiments concerning the work of Blackstone, especially regarding the jurisprudence of criminal law (Hogan 1956, p. 107). After carefully comparing Justice Story's writings with the *Commentaries* passages discussing public wrongs, John C. Hogan concludes that the justice's work is "essentially a restatement and interpretation of Blackstone's discussion of the subject in the fourth volume of the Commentaries" (1956, p. 107).

The influence of Blackstone on the early Court has been described as follows:

Many of our important early Justices and judges—Wilson, Iredell, Marshall, Story and Kent, to name a few—at some point acknowledged their indebtedness to the Commentator. Justice James Wilson studied the *Commentaries* soon after their publication while reading law ... in the 1760s and throughout his life honored Blackstone by taking scholarly issue with him on a number of points. In a 1774 pamphlet, Wilson took issue with Blackstone's notions of Parliamentary supremacy, and his 1790 law lectures were in large part an attempt to refute Blackstone's definition of municipal law. ... Similarly, James Iredell was favorably impressed by the *Commentaries* while studying law in 1771. Later as a Supreme Court Justice writing in *Chisholm v. Georgia*, the same case in which Wilson rejected Blackstone's definition of sovereignty, Iredell used the *Commentaries* in support of Georgia's claim of sovereign immunity. (Nolan 1976, p. 757) (citations omitted)

In light of the large number of important constitutional law cases decided in the early years of the Court's history, it is certainly the case that Blackstone's work is at the foundation of American jurisprudence.

In modern times, it appears that Blackstone's jurisprudential influence on the Court is not as vigorous as it was during its early history. It has been noted that "the United States Supreme Court still cites the *Commentaries* approximately ten times each year" (Alschuler 1996, p.16). The article states, "The Supreme Court, lower courts and scholars invoke the *Commentaries* today mostly as a source of history. The esteem in which Blackstone's jurisprudence was once held has apparently vanished. Scholars view the *Commentaries* as an illustration of the formal vision of law that Oliver Wendell Holmes and the legal realists condemned" (1996, p. 17). An example of the use of Blackstone as an historical reference is found in the concurring opinion of Justice Clarence Thomas in *Morse v. Frederick*, 551 U.S. ___ (2007). Justice Thomas writes, "Through the legal doctrine of *in loco parentis*, courts upheld the right of schools to discipline students, to enforce

rules, and to maintain order. Rooted in the English common law, *in loco parentis* originally governed the legal rights and obligations of tutors and private schools" (footnote omitted). Justice Thomas then quotes from Blackstone's text describing the delegation of parental rights to a tutor or school official. In conclusion, Blackstone's influence on the decision making process of the Court has ranged from strong and deferential during the Court's formative years, to a weaker form of influence that takes the form of mere historical reference.

SEE ALSO *Common Law; English Constitutionalism*

BIBLIOGRAPHY

Alschuler, Albert W. 1996. "Rediscovering Blackstone." *University of Pennsylvania Law Review* 145(1): 1–55.

Blackstone, William. 1765–1769. *Commentaries on the Laws of England*. 4 vols. Oxford: Clarendon Press.

Hogan, John C. 1956. "Blackstone and Joseph Story: Their Influence on the Development of Criminal Law in America." *Minnesota Law Review* 40(1): 107–124.

Miles, Albert S.; David L. Dagley; and Christina H. Yau. 2000. "Blackstone and His American Legacy." *Australia and New Zealand Journal of Law and Education* 5(2): 46–59.

Nolan, Dennis R. 1976. "Sir William Blackstone and the New American Republic: A Study of Intellectual Impact." *New York University Law Review* 51: 731–768.

Gloria A. Whittico

BLASPHEMY

Blasphemy is evil speech against God, gods, religion, sacred beliefs, or other defamations of divine matters. The words expressing scorn, ridicule, or even vilification may be oral or printed. English laws against blasphemy were adopted in 1610 in Virginia. Massachusetts adopted a blasphemy law in 1641 with Connecticut following suit in 1642; other colonies followed with similar statutes.

In 1811 a New York case, *People v. Ruggles*, 8 Johns 290 (Sup. Ct. N.Y., 1811), upheld the conviction of a blasphemer who claimed that Jesus Christ was a bastard and that his mother was a whore. Chancellor James Kent ruled that freedom of speech did not protect speech that was licentious or likely to evoke breaking the public peace.

The case of *Commonwealth of Massachusetts v. Kneeland*, 37 Mass. 206 (1838) upheld the conviction of a pantheist who denied belief in God, Christ, miracles, and other related beliefs. The chief justice of the Massachusetts Supreme Court, Lemuel Shaw (1781–1861), rejected arguments that blasphemy was protected by either freedom of the press or by theories of religious liberty.

Historically, American courts subscribed to the view that blasphemy was criminal when it was intended as malicious or defaming. In both *Updegraph v. Common-wealth*, 11 Serg. & R. 394 (Pa. 1824) and *State v. Chandler*, 2 Del. 553 (Ct. Gen. Sess. 1837), the ruling was that mere differences of opinion were not sufficient to sustain a charge of blasphemy.

In the 1890s the federal government conducted prosecutions for polygamy against Mormons. The Supreme Court upheld convictions ruling that teaching polygamy was a threat to public peace, even if done with religious motives. The Court did not specifically used the word *blasphemy* in the cases but clearly found the practice to be odious and criminal in a tone in all the Mormon cases that made it clear that the practice was an offense against the Christian religion practiced in all Western countries and thus sacrilegious at best. In *Davis v. Beason*, 133 U.S. 33 (1890) and *Mormon Church v. United States*, 136 U.S. 1 (1890) it treated the teaching and advocacy of polygamy as overt acts against peace and good order motivated by religious opinion. In this way it avoided issues of freedom of speech and theology. While not specially called blasphemy, the issues in the cases were similar to those that would have been raised by charges of blasphemy, specifically what are offenses against the will or law of God that should be proscribed by law.

Michael X. Mockus was prosecuted for blasphemy in Connecticut in 1916 and in Illinois in 1917. A free-thought lecturer, Mockus's cases were either never completed (Connecticut) or dismissed (Illinois) on the grounds that the common law of blasphemy had been ended by constitutional guarantees of freedom of thought. This case began a movement away from prosecuting blasphemy to allowing any form of blasphemous speech whether in the form of words, musical lyrics, alleged art works, or other forms. The justification has been on the grounds that protection of freedom of speech is a fundamental right protected by the Constitution.

The U.S. Supreme Court has never ruled directly on blasphemy. *Burstyn v. Wilson*, 343 U.S. 495 (1952) came close. It involved charges that an English-subtitled movie from Italy, *The Miracle* (1948), was sacrilegious. The Supreme Court ruled that the film was protected by freedom of speech. In 1968 the First Amendment was again used by a Maryland appeals court to overturn a prosecution for blasphemy. It held that the prosecution violated the establishment clause, which protects freedom of religion. In a concurring opinion Associate Justice Felix Frankfurter offered an extensive word study in the history of the English language to show that the word *sacrilegious* and associated words *blasphemy* and *profane* had histories that were unclear. So unclear that there was not a definition available that could justify constraining the creative spirit that was evident in *The Miracle*.

Since the *Burstyn* case there have not been any blasphemy prosecutions. Blasphemy represents a tension between religious speech and political speech. While other works such as the film *The Last Temptation of Christ* (1988) have been denounced as blasphemous to date no cases have appeared before the Supreme Court. It has, however, rejected a protest from the Council on American-Islamic Relations (CAIR) that the bas-relief sculpture depicting Mohammed as one of the law-givers on the North Frieze on the Supreme Court building in Washington, D.C. be sandblasted off because it is blasphemous. Mass demonstrations in Muslim countries have been organized to denounce the depiction. Chief Justice Rehnquist's description of the carving as an honor did not calm Muslim outrage.

Some legal scholars have speculated that any blasphemy prosecution is unlikely to survive review by the Supreme Court because it would be ruled an unconstitutional restriction of freedom of speech. However, more recent adoption of hate crime laws have led to the prosecution of individuals for alleged selected acts, such as putting a Koran into a toilet. The similarity of hate crime laws to blasphemy laws is strong and may produce future cases especially if collegiate or other hate speech codes are enforced against criticism of Islam or other non-Christian religions.

SEE ALSO *First Amendment*

BIBLIOGRAPHY

Levy, Leonard W. 1995. *Blasphemy: Verbal Offense against the Sacred, from Moses to Salman Rushdie*. Chapel Hill: University of North Carolina Press.

Schroedet, Theodore Albert. 1970. *Constitutional Free Speech Defined and Defended in an Unfinished Argument in a Case of Blasphemy*. New York: Da Capo Press.

Andrew J. Waskey

BMW OF NORTH AMERICA, INC. V. GORE, 517 U.S. 559 (1996)

Dr. Ira Gore Jr. purchased a $40,000 car from an authorized BMW dealer in Birmingham, Alabama. After discovering that the car had been repainted before purchase, Gore sued. He alleged that not disclosing the repainting constituted fraud under Alabama law because the car was worth less than an otherwise identical car that had never been repainted. The jury found BMW liable for compensatory damages of $4,000 plus $4 million in punitive damages. The Alabama Supreme Court reduced the punitive award to $2 million because the jury had improperly considered similar transactions in states where the sales might have been legal.

The United States Supreme Court held, for the first time ever, that a punitive damages award was grossly excessive in violation of the due process clause of the Fourteenth Amendment of the Constitution. The Court supported its conclusion by examining three guideposts, each of which indicated that BMW had not received adequate notice of the magnitude of the sanction that Alabama might impose upon it.

The first guidepost was the degree of reprehensibility of the defendant's conduct. However, the harm of presale repainting was purely economic; there was no risk to anyone's health or safety. The Court rejected Gore's contention that BMW's nondisclosure was particularly reprehensible because it was part of a nationwide policy. But BMW could reasonably have interpreted the relevant statutes in other states as establishing a clear line for legal nondisclosure of minor repairs. BMW did not make deliberate false statements or conceal an improper motive.

The second guidepost was the ratio between the plaintiff's compensatory damages and the amount of the punitive damages awarded. The Court found that this guidepost also weighed against the award, which was 500 times the amount of Gore's actual harm. Neither Gore nor any other BMW purchaser in Alabama risked any additional potential harm by the nondisclosure policy. Although the Court recognized that it was not possible to draw a precise line between the constitutionally acceptable and unacceptable for every case, it found this ratio clearly outside the acceptable range.

The third guidepost, the difference between a punitive damages award and the civil or criminal sanctions that could be imposed for comparable misconduct in the state, did not support the award either. The $2 million award was substantially greater than Alabama's applicable $2,000 fine and the penalties imposed in other states for similar conduct.

The Court concluded that BMW's conduct was not sufficiently egregious under the three guideposts to justify the severe punitive sanction. The Alabama Supreme Court subsequently held that a new trial was required unless Gore agreed to a reduction of damages to $50,000 (*BMW of North America, Inc. v. Gore*, 701 So.2d 507 [Ala., 1997]).

A later case confirmed that the jury could consider the defendant's in-state conduct only and also refined the second guidepost to create a presumption that few awards exceeding a single-digit ratio between punitive and compensatory damages will satisfy due process (*State Farm Mutual Automobile Insurance Co. v. Campbell*, 538 U.S. 408 [2003]). A more recent case narrowed the reprehensibility guidepost to allow the jury to hear evidence of actual harm to nonparties to show that the conduct that harmed the plaintiff also posed a substantial

risk of harm to the general public. However, the jury may not punish a defendant directly in its punitive damages verdict for harms it is alleged to have visited on nonparties (*Philip Morris USA v. Williams*, 549 U.S. ___ [2007]).

SEE ALSO *Punitive Damages*

BIBLIOGRAPHY

Harvard Law Review on Leading Cases. 2007. "Punitive Damages." *Harvard Law Review* 121 275–285 (2007).

Sebok, Anthony J. 2007. "Punitive Damages: From Myth to Theory." *Iowa Law Review* 92(3): 957–1036.

David I. Levine

BOARD OF COMMISSIONERS V. UMBEHR, 518 U.S. 668 (1996)

In the 1968 case of *Pickering v. Board of Education*, 391 U.S. 563 (1968), the Court granted First Amendment speech protections to public employees. However, not until twenty-eight years later, in *Board of Commissioners v. Umbehr*, 518 U.S. 668 (1996), did the Court grant similar protections to independent contractors working for the government. Never before had the Court considered whether and to what extent the First Amendment protects the speech of public contractors.

Umbehr involved an independent contractor whose trash-hauling contract with the county was terminated after he repeatedly and boisterously criticized the county commissioners. In his subsequent lawsuit, the independent contractor claimed that he had been punished for speaking out against the county board. Granting certiorari, the Court sought to settle a dispute among the circuits on the issue of whether independent contractors are entitled to First Amendment protections.

In addressing this issue, Justice Sandra Day O'Connor first looked to the doctrines governing public-employee speech. Up until the 1960s, the judicial doctrines covering public-employee speech were deferential to employers, with employee speech given practically no constitutional protection from employer disciplinary action. But during an era of heightened attention to individual rights, this approach to public-employee speech protections was changed in *Pickering v. Board of Education*, which involved the termination of a public-school teacher who had published a letter to the editor criticizing the board of education's handling of a proposed tax increase. Ruling that public employees do not relinquish their First Amendment rights when they assume their government jobs, the Court laid out a new balancing test to determine whether a public employee's speech is constitutionally protected. This test looked to balance the interests of the public employee in commenting upon matters of public concern and the interest of the state employer in promoting the efficiency of the public services it performs through its employees.

In *Umbehr*, finding that government contractors are similar enough to public employees to warrant equal treatment on this issue, the Court granted essentially the same First Amendment protections to government contractors as it had previously granted to government employees. Furthermore, the Court held that the *Pickering* balancing test likewise determined the extent of the independent contractor's speech rights. In dissent, however, Justice Antonin Scalia disagreed with the Court's equation of public employees and independent contractors. To Justice Scalia, a public employee's loss of a job probably meant a denial of a livelihood, whereas an independent contractor, usually a corporation, could normally survive the loss of a contract.

The Court's holding in *Umbehr* not only proved consistent with the Court's ruling in public-employee speech cases, but it was also consistent with the Court's "unconstitutional conditions" doctrine. Under this doctrine, the government may not deprive citizens of a valuable public benefit when such a deprivation restricts their constitutional rights, such as free speech. The rationale for this doctrine is that the government should not be able to do indirectly what it could not do directly, for example, restrict a person's free-speech rights.

SEE ALSO *First Amendment*

BIBLIOGRAPHY

Garfield, Alan. 1998. "Promises of Silence: Contract Law and Freedom of Speech." *Cornell Law Review* 83(2): 261–364.

Secunda, Paul M. 2006. "The (Neglected) Importance of Being *Lawrence*: The Consitutionalization of Public Employee Rights to Decisional Non-Interference in Private Affairs." *U.C. Davis Law Review* 40(1): 85–136.

CASES

Pickering v. Board of Education, 391 U.S. 563 (1968).

Patrick M. Garry

BOARD OF CURATORS OF THE UNIV. OF MISSOURI V. HOROWITZ, 435 U.S. 78 (1978)

Linda Horowitz was a medical student at the University of Missouri, Kansas City, where she encountered difficulties in her studies, failing a number of supervised clinical skills courses, during which medical students would make hospital rounds under the supervision of medical faculty. After failing several classes, Horowitz was required to take additional coursework in an even more supervised setting over the course of an entire year. The faculty also awarded her failing grades, and after invoking internal appeals, she was ultimately dismissed from medical school in what would have been her final year. *Board of Curators of the University of Missouri v. Horowitz*, 435 U.S. 78 (1978) is among the leading U.S. Supreme Court decisions concerning the amount of process due a student who is academically dismissed from a public college, and is widely cited for its distinction between an academic dismissal and a disciplinary dismissal. In addition, the case clearly sets out the rules for academic decision-making governing the levels of deference to be accorded colleges.

Horowitz alleged that her liberty interests had been denied—that is, that she was deprived of opportunities to continue her studies or obtain medical employment. The Court did not bite at this theory, holding instead that whatever process she had received was what she had been due:

> We need not decide ... whether respondent's dismissal deprived her of a liberty interest in pursuing a medical career. Nor need we decide whether respondent's dismissal infringed any other interest constitutionally protected against deprivation without procedural due process. Assuming the existence of a liberty or property interest, respondent has been awarded at least as much due process as the Fourteenth Amendment requires. The school fully informed respondent of the faculty's dissatisfaction with her clinical progress and the danger that this posed to timely graduation and continued enrollment. The ultimate decision to dismiss respondent was careful and deliberate. These procedures were sufficient under the Due Process Clause of the Fourteenth Amendment.

Horowitz was decided in several opinions, which spelled out exactly how much process she had been due, and even Justice Thurgood Marshall, who dissented on the issue of whether or not the dismissal had been an academic judgment or a disciplinary decision, agreed that however the constitutional issue was framed, Horowitz had received a full opportunity to appeal before the faculty:

> I agree with the Court that, "[a]ssuming the existence of a liberty or property interest, respondent has been awarded at least as much due process as the Fourteenth Amendment requires." I cannot join the Court's opinion, however, because it contains dictum suggesting that respondent was entitled to even less procedural protection than she received. I also differ from the Court in its assumption that characterization of the reasons

for a dismissal as "academic" or "disciplinary" is relevant to resolution of the question of what procedures are required by the Due Process Clause. Finally, I disagree with the Court's decision not to remand to the Court of Appeals for consideration of respondent's substantive due process claim.

The Court also set out a test that distinguished between *Goss v. Lopez,* 419 U.S. 565 (1975) settings, where an informal hearing before a disciplinary expulsion was required, and deferred to educational decision makers, particularly in the college and professional school context:

In *Goss,* this Court concluded that the value of some form of hearing in a disciplinary context outweighs any resulting harm to the academic environment. Influencing this conclusion was clearly the belief that disciplinary proceedings, in which the teacher must decide whether to punish a student for disruptive or insubordinate behavior, may automatically bring an adversary flavor to the normal student-teacher relationship. The same conclusion does not follow in the academic context. We decline to further enlarge the judicial presence in the academic community and thereby risk deterioration of many beneficial aspects of the faculty-student relationship.

Very few students who are dismissed prevail in their claims, and most decisions since 1978 cite *Horowitz* as the leading case for these issues.

SEE ALSO *Procedural Due Process*

BIBLIOGRAPHY

Buss, William G. 1979. "Easy Cases Make Bad Law: Academic Expulsion and the Uncertain Law of Procedural Due Process." *Iowa Law Review* 65: 1–101.

Kaplin, William A., and Barbara A. Lee. 2006. *The Law of Higher Education: A Comprehensive Guide to Legal Implications of Administrative Decision Making.* 4th edition. San Francisco: Jossey-Bass.

Michael A. Olivas

BOARD OF EDUCATION OF ISLAND TREES SCHOOL DISTRICT NO. 26 V. PICO, 457 U.S. 853 (1982)

In 1982 the Supreme Court held in *Board of Education of Island Trees School District No. 26 v. Pico,* 457 U.S. 853 that the removal of books from public school libraries violates the First Amendment if the school officials intended to deny students access to ideas with which the authorities disagreed. The First Amendment protects the right to receive information. Nine justices filed seven opinions, with Justice William Brennan writing for a plurality that included justices Thurgood Marshall and John Paul Stevens. Whereas the federal district court had found an adequate educational rationale for excluding the books, the U.S. Supreme Court upheld the decision of the Second Circuit Court of Appeals that reversed that decision. The procedural posture required the Court only to answer affirmatively two basic questions: (1) "Does the First Amendment impose *any* limitations on the discretion to remove library books?" and (2) is there a "genuine issue of fact whether petitioners might have exceeded those limitations?" Despite finding that there is a right to receive information, the Court acknowledged that "nothing in our decision today affects in any way the discretion of a local school board to choose books to *add* to the libraries of their schools." Justices Harry Blackmun and Byron White wrote separate concurring opinions.

Four justices dissented, with three of them setting out dissenting opinions. Chief Justice Warren Burger's dissent contended that "there is not a hint in the First Amendment . . . of a right to have the government provide continuing access to certain books." Moreover, "schools may legitimately be used as vehicles for inculcating fundamental values necessary to the maintenance of a democratic political system," and "school authorities must have a broad discretion to fulfill that obligation."

In the other major dissent, Justice William Rehnquist also emphasized that "when [government] acts as an educator, at least at the elementary and secondary school level, the government is engaged in inculcating social values and knowledge in relatively impressionable young people." Justice Rehnquist also objected to the plurality's use of motive analysis, given Justice Brennan's view that "intent matters because the First Amendment does not tolerate an officially prescribed orthodoxy." But combining the right to receive information with freedom from prescribed orthodoxy "mixes First Amendment apples and oranges," especially because "not every educational denial of access to information casts a pall of orthodoxy over the classroom." Rehnquist objected, lastly, that the distinction between "not selecting" for purchase versus "removing" books from a school library makes no sense, such that "the pall of orthodoxy cast by a carefully executed book acquisition program apparently would not violate the First Amendment under Justice Brennan's view."

Mark Yudof has suggested that, just as many advocate for academic freedom for teachers, there is much to be said for recognizing the power of teachers and librarians in a system of government expression to select books to stock. This approach could help avoid the "ideological indoctrination" that seems "more likely" if elected officials make decisions about the removal of books from school libraries. If this approach were adopted, it would "apply to both removal and acquisition of library books" (1984, p. 557).

SEE ALSO *Education and the Constitution; First Amendment*

BIBLIOGRAPHY

Bitensky, Susan H. 1995. "A Contemporary Proposal for Reconciling the Free Speech Clause with Curricular Values Inculcation in the Public Schools." *Notre Dame Law Review* 70: 769–843.

Yudof, Mark G. 1984. "Library Book Selection and the Public Schools: The Quest for the Archimedean Point." *Indiana Law Journal* 59(4): 527–564.

Thomas B. McAffee

BOARD OF EDUCATION OF KIRYAS JOEL VILLAGE SCHOOL DISTRICT V. GRUMET, 512 U.S. 687 (1994)

In *Board of Education of Kiryas Joel Village School District v. Grumet*, 512 U.S. 687 (1994), the U.S. Supreme Court affirmed a holding that a New York law creating a school district from an enclave of practitioners of a strict form of Judaism had the effect of advancing religion, contrary to the establishment clause. The state had gone beyond valid religious accommodation, granting a preference for a particular religion and departing from denominational neutrality. State religious liberty provisions had all required denominational equality.

The Court concluded that the law making the village of Kiryas Joel a school district delegated "the State's discretionary authority over public schools" to a religious group, and "gives no assurance that governmental power has been or will be exercised neutrally." The statute delegated "'important, discretionary governmental powers' to religious bodies, thus impermissibly entangling government and religion." Justice John Paul Stevens, joined by Justices Harry Blackmun and Ruth Bader Ginsburg, concurred, concluding that a law creating "segregation of this character is unlike the ... decision to grant an exemption from a burdensome general rule." It thus *establishes*, "rather than merely accommodating, religion."

Justice Sandra Day O'Connor, concurring in the judgment, wrote to emphasize that the problem of establishment is better addressed by not holding to the single test set forth in *Lemon v. Kurtzman*, 403 U.S. 602 (1971). The Court's opinion in her view showed that "the slide away from *Lemon*'s unitary approach is well under way." Justice Anthony Kennedy, concurring, thought it clear that the Court should *not* hold that "a legislative accommodation ... is invalid because of the risk that the legislature will not grant the same accommodation to another religious group suffering some similar burden.... The real vice of the school district ... is that New York created it by drawing political boundaries on the basis of religion." Kennedy thus agreed with the Court *only* "insofar as it invalidates the school district for being drawn along religious lines."

Justice Antonin Scalia, joined by Chief Justice William Rehnquist and Justice Clarence Thomas, dissented, concluding that the establishment clause was being "employed to prohibit ... admirably American accommodation of the religious practices (or more precisely, cultural peculiarities) of a tiny minority sect." The justices clarified that "once this Court has abandoned text and history as guides, nothing prevents it from calling religious toleration the establishment of religion." When a legislature acts to accommodate religion, particularly a minority sect, "it follows the best of our traditions."

SEE ALSO *First Amendment*

BIBLIOGRAPHY

Berg, Thomas C. 1995. "Slouching Towards Secularism: A Comment on *Kiryas Joel School District v. Grumet*." *Emory Law Journal* 44: 433–499.

Greene, Abner. 1996. "*Kiryas Joel* and Two Mistakes about Equality." *Columbia Law Review* 96: 1–86.

Thomas B. McAffee

BOARD OF EDUCATION OF OKLAHOMA CITY PUBLIC SCHOOLS V. DOWELL, 498 U.S. 237 (1991)

In 1961 black parents filed suit in federal court seeking to desegregate Oklahoma City schools. Since the decision in *Brown v. Board of Education*, 347 U.S. 483 (1954), the school board had maintained segregation by manipulating transfer policies and designing attendance zones to capitalize on residential segregation traceable to discriminatory city ordinances and the enforcement of restrictive covenants. Progress in dismantling school segregation came only after the federal district court's 1972 order required implementation of an independent expert's desegregation plan. In 1977 the court ended its supervision of school operations, confident that local officials would not abandon the desegregation plan. However, in 1985 the board adopted a new student-assignment policy, citing population shifts that would otherwise require burdensome longer bus trips for many black elementary students. A black parents group then sought to reopen the case, fearing the return to one-race schools in many parts of the city.

In *Board of Education of Oklahoma City Public Schools v. Dowell*, 498 U.S. 237 (1991), the U.S. Supreme Court issued a five-to-three ruling that instructed the trial court to determine if adherence to the original injunction's terms was still necessary by examining the district's past good-faith compliance and its success in eliminating, to the extent practicable, the vestiges of de jure segregation in school operations. The majority opinion, given by Chief Justice William Rehnquist, admonished that desegregation decrees should not "operate in perpetuity" given the importance of local control over schools. In a dissent joined by Justices Harry Blackmun and John Paul Stevens, Justice Thurgood Marshall, who had represented the *Brown* plaintiffs, insisted that, in a district once segregated by law, the Constitution required greater effort to maintain integration so that black students could be spared the stigma of separation and the risk of a return to inferior educational conditions.

SEE ALSO *Education and the Constitution; School Desegregation*

BIBLIOGRAPHY

Parker, Wendy. 2000. "The Future of School Desegregation." *Northwestern University Law Review* 94: 1157–1227.

Josie F. Brown

BOARD OF EDUCATION OF TRUSTEES OF STATE UNIVERSITY OF NEW YORK V. FOX, 492 U.S. 469 (1989)

In *Board of Education of Trustees of State University of New York v. Fox*, 492 U.S. 469 (1989), the Supreme Court held that government restrictions on commercial speech need not be the least restrictive means available, but must be narrowly tailored to achieve a desired government objective. Writing for the majority, Justice Antonin Scalia reversed a Second Circuit decision, which held that restrictions on commercial speech imposed by the State University of New York (SUNY), Cortland must withstand the more demanding First Amendment least-restrictive-means standard. Moreover, the majority held that the lower court must first determine whether the SUNY resolution prohibiting all private, commercial enterprises from operating in university dormitories was valid as applied in this case before it could consider the further claim that the restriction was overbroad in applying to noncommercial speech as well.

This case arose after SUNY applied its resolution limiting commercial speech in dormitories to a representative of American Future Systems, Inc. (AFS), a company that sells housewares to students by hosting "Tupperware parties" in dormitories for groups of ten or more students. The university police arrested the AFS employee, and in response several students, including Todd Fox, filed suit against the university, seeking a declaratory judgment that the university's action violated the First Amendment. The students argued that the resolution infringed their right to free expression in their dorm rooms and that the restriction on commercial speech was overbroad in that it also restricted fully protected noncommercial speech. SUNY argued that it had a substantial interest in promoting an educational, not a commercial, atmosphere, and in maintaining residential tranquility, safety, and security.

In *Central Hudson Gas & Elec. Corp. v. Public Service Comm'n of New York*, 447 U.S. 557 (1980), the Court explained that when considering government restrictions on commercial speech, courts must determine whether the speech concerns lawful activity, whether the government interest is substantial, whether the regulation advances the government interest, and "whether it is not more extensive than is necessary to serve that interest." Applying these factors, the district court in *Fox* held that the restrictions on commercial speech were a reasonable means to achieve the university's objectives. Under the "more extensive than is necessary" element of *Central Hudson*, the Second Circuit reversed and remanded the decision to determine whether the resolution was the least restrictive means to justify the government's interests. In response, the Supreme Court reasoned that this characterization was inconsistent with the less-protected status of commercial speech in the realm of free speech. Clarifying *Central Hudson*, the Supreme Court explained that the government was not required to use the least restrictive means possible when limiting commercial speech, but rather must narrowly tailor its restrictions to fit within the legislature's purpose. Fit must be reasonable and need not be perfect.

Fox also brought an overbreadth challenge, arguing that the resolution prohibits students from meeting with anyone who receives payment for speech in a dormitory room, including doctors, tutors, lawyers, counselors, and music teachers. In response, and over Justice Harry Blackmun's dissent on this point, the Court held that the students' as-applied challenge should be decided first for reasons of judicial efficiency. Accordingly, the Court remanded the case to determine whether the resolution was valid as applied to the students.

SEE ALSO *First Amendment*

BIBLIOGRAPHY

Conrad, Mark A. 1990. "*Board of Trustees of the State University of New York v. Fox—The Dawn of a New Age of Commercial*

Speech Regulation of Tobacco and Alcohol." *Cardozo Arts & Entertainment Law Journal* 9(1): 61.

Post, Robert. 2000. "The Constitutional Status of Commercial Speech." *UCLA Law Review* 48: 1–57.

Thomas P. Crocker

BOARD OF EDUCATION OF WESTSIDE COMMUNITY SCHOOL DISTRICT V. MERGENS, 496 U.S. 226 (1990)

In 1981 the Supreme Court held that the First Amendment right of "equal access" to First Amendment public forums prohibited a state university from denying access to religious student groups who wanted to express their religious views in public meetings held in the university's student union building (*Widmar v. Vincent*, 454 U.S. 263 [1981]). Despite the Court's holding in *Widmar*, a number of commentators as well as lower federal courts continued to take the view that granting First Amendment access to public secondary schools, in light of the likely impact on impressionable secondary school youth, would amount to a violation of the establishment clause requirement that the state act neutrally toward the religious views of its citizens. A result was Congress's enactment of the Equal Access Act, which required public secondary schools to give equal access to student religious groups if they had created at least a limited open forum. When a school district in Nebraska denied access to a student religious group, contending that its policy did not create a limited public forum, the student group brought an action for declaratory and injunctive relief. In *Board of Education of Westside Community School District v. Mergens*, 496 U.S. 226 (1990), the Supreme Court affirmed a ruling of the court of appeals that the federal statute required giving the group access and that such a statutory requirement did not violate the establishment clause.

Justice Anthony Kennedy, joined by Justice Antonin Scalia, concurred in the judgment, contending that Justice Sandra Day O'Connor's opinion found a lack of an establishment clause violation by concluding that the federal law sufficiently prevented the school policy from being an "endorsement" of religion. Justice Kennedy, by contrast, would have focused on whether "the government imposes pressure upon a student to participate in a religious activity." Justice Thurgood Marshall, joined by Justice William J. Brennan Jr., concurred in the judgment, writing separately to underscore "the steps Westside must take to avoid appearing to endorse the Christian Club's goals."

Justice John Paul Stevens dissented, contending that the Act "violates the Establishment Clause by authorizing religious organizations to meet on high school grounds even when the high school's teachers and administrators deem it unwise to admit controversial or partisan organizations of any kind." Stevens contended that Westside had not truly adopted an "open forum" and, moreover, that "nothing in *Widmar* implies that the existence of a French club ... would create a constitutional obligation to allow student members of the Ku Klux Klan or the Communist Party to have access to school facilities."

Mergens supplies a prominent example of the Court's tendency in the post-*Widmar* era, "to see more and more cases through the lens of 'equal access' rather than the lens of 'no aid'" (McConnell, Garvey, and Berg 2006, p. 626). The First Amendment expression theme of equal access eventually prompted the Court to reconsider the general problem of aid to religious education facilities as it expanded the concept of equal access to a general neutrality principle.

SEE ALSO *Establishment Clause*

BIBLIOGRAPHY

Laycock, Douglas. 1986. "Equal Access and Moments of Silence: The Equal Status of Religious Speech by Private Speakers." *Northwestern University Law Review* 81(1): 1–67.

McConnell, Michael W.; John H. Garvey; and Thomas C. Berg. 2006. *Religion and the Constitution*. 2nd edition. New York: Aspen Publishers.

Teitel, Ruti G. 1985. "The Unconstitutionality of Equal Access Policies and Legislation Allowing Organized Student-Initiated Religious Activities in the Public High Schools: A Proposal for a Unitary First Amendment Forum Analysis." *Hastings Constitutional Law Quarterly* 12(4): 529–595.

Thomas B. McAffee

BOARD OF EDUCATION V. ALLEN, 392 U.S. 236 (1968)

As the U.S. Supreme Court began to flesh out its establishment clause jurisprudence in the last half of the twentieth century, it handed down a succession of controversial opinions that attempted to define the limits of state involvement in religious education. In its opinions in such cases as *Everson v. Board of Education*, 330 U.S. 1 (1947) and *Abington Township v. Schempp*, 374 U.S. 203 (1963), the Court focused on the purposes and effects of legislative enactments relating to matters such as the provision of bus transportation for students attending religious schools and compulsory prayer exercises in public schools. Part of the ostensible baseline for these rulings was the Court's holding in *Schempp* that, to be constitutionally valid, a law must have "a secular legislative purpose and a primary effect that neither advances nor inhibits religion." In 1968 the Court endeavored to apply this line of reasoning to *Board of Education v. Allen*, 392 U.S. 236.

At issue in *Allen* was a New York law providing for the lending of textbooks to all children enrolled in grades seven through twelve, even if they attended religious schools. Only secular textbooks approved by the state could be lent under the program; religious books were excluded. The measure violated the establishment clause, a group of school boards argued in challenging the measure's constitutionality, because even the provision of secular textbooks would contribute to the overall promotion of religious education. (Religious schools, for instance, would improve their financial condition by saving money on textbooks.) This stance was supported by the American Jewish Committee, as well as Protestants and Other Americans United for the Separation of Church and State, an advocacy group that often has been involved in church-state litigation.

When the case reached the U.S. Supreme Court in 1968, the parties' arguments—which were opposed by New York's attorney general—failed to persuade a majority of the justices. In a six-to-three ruling, the Court found the New York textbook law constitutional, with Justice Byron White writing for the majority that the measure indeed had a secular purpose (the promotion of education in general) and did not in fact promote religion. For White, two facts were crucial: The books were only lent, not given, to the students, thereby allowing the state to maintain ownership; and none of the books involved were explicitly religious in character. (He also pointed out the difficulties posed by the meager factual record presented by both parties before the Court.) Justices William O. Douglas and Hugo Black penned vigorous dissents in *Allen*. Black—who had written the majority opinion for the Court in *Everson*, the earlier establishment clause case—decried the New York textbook law as "a flat, flagrant, open violation" of the Constitution and insisted that the Constitution required the nation "to keep the wall of separation between church and state high and impregnable." In subsequent cases involving public aid to religious schools and their pupils, the Court attempted to further refine its establishment clause jurisprudence, in part by developing a standard barring excessive entanglement between church and state.

SEE ALSO *Establishment Clause*

BIBLIOGRAPHY

Flowers, Ronald B. 2005. *That Godless Court?: Supreme Court Decisions on Church-State Relationships*. 2nd edition. Louisville, KY: Westminster John Knox Press.

Levy, Leonard W. 1994. *The Establishment Clause: Religion and the First Amendment*. 2nd edition. Chapel Hill: University of North Carolina Press.

Shawn Francis Peters

BOARD OF EDUCATION V. ROWLEY, 458 U.S. 176 (1982)

The federal statute known as the Individuals with Disabilities Education Act (IDEA), first enacted in 1975 as the Education for All Handicapped Children Act (the name was changed in 1990), requires that every state must have a policy that assures that children who are disabled have the right to a "free appropriate public education." The child must have an individualized educational program (IEP) tailored to meet his or her unique needs. In *Board of Education v. Rowley*, 458 U.S. 176 (1982), the U.S. Supreme Court explained what schools must do to satisfy the requirements of the statute.

The case arose when the parents of Amy Rowley objected to her IEP. Amy, a first-grader who was deaf, had minimal hearing, but she was an excellent lip-reader. According to her IEP, Amy was placed in a general classroom, and she was provided with a special hearing aid to amplify words spoken into a wireless receiver. Amy completed her kindergarten year successfully under this program, but her parents, who also were deaf, challenged her first-grade IEP. The proposed IEP would provide Amy with the hearing aid, as well as instruction from a tutor for the deaf for one hour a day and from a speech therapist for three hours a week. Amy's parents insisted that the school also provide a sign-language interpreter. (An interpreter had been provided for part of Amy's kindergarten year, but the interpreter reported that Amy did not need his services.)

Pursuant to the statute's provisions, Amy's parents demanded and received two administrative hearings, where the school's decision was affirmed because "Amy was achieving educationally, academically, and socially." Amy's parents sought judicial review. Both the federal district court and the court of appeals determined that Amy was not receiving an "appropriate education" as required by the statute. The district court defined appropriate education as the "opportunity to achieve [her] full potential commensurate with the opportunity provided to other children."

The Supreme Court, in an opinion authored by Chief Justice William Rehnquist, reversed. The Court construed "appropriate education" as a "basic floor of opportunity." The education of the disabled child must be "sufficient to confer some educational benefit."

The Court also addressed the extent of court authority to review a school's compliance with the statute. A court's inquiry has two parts. First, did the school comply with the procedures set forth in the statute (that is, has the school created an IEP that conforms to the statute's requirements)? Second, is the IEP "reasonably calculated to enable the child to receive educational benefits"? The Court cautioned that "courts must be careful to avoid imposing their view of preferable educational methods on the states."

Because Amy was receiving personalized instruction and related services, and she was performing better than the average student in her class—advancing easily from grade to grade—the statute did not require the school to provide her with a sign-language interpreter.

Justice Harry Blackmun wrote a separate opinion. Justice Byron White wrote a dissenting opinion, joined by Justices William Brennan and Thurgood Marshall.

SEE ALSO *Education and the Constitution*

BIBLIOGRAPHY

Blau, Andrea. 2007. "The IDEIA and the Right to an 'Appropriate' Education." *Brigham Young University Education and Law Journal* 2007 (1): 1.

Kickertz, Allan. 2007. "Holistic Learning: Amending the Rowley Test to Clarify the Inclusion Debate." *Western New England Law Review* 29: 733.

Anne Proffitt Dupre

BOARD OF REGENTS OF STATE COLLEGES V. ROTH, 408 U.S. 564 (1972)

The principle of procedural due process is essentially the right to fair hearing, and under the Fifth and the Fourteenth Amendments this right applies whenever the government deprives a person of "life, liberty, or property." The case of *Board of Regents of State Colleges v. Roth*, 408 U.S. 564 (1972) is significant in that it helps to identify the kinds of situations to which the due process clause applies.

Roth was hired to serve as an assistant professor at Wisconsin State University, Oshkosh, for one academic year, from September 1, 1968, to June 30, 1969. When the academic year was over the University did not rehire him. Roth sued the University on the ground that he was not afforded a hearing at which he would have challenged the decision of the University not to renew his employment. Even though the University is a state institution, and even though the University did not give Roth a hearing when his employment was terminated, the Supreme Court ruled in favor of the University, finding that the due process clause did not apply to this situation because Roth had not been deprived of "life, liberty, or property."

The Court stated, in a majority opinion written by Justice Potter Stewart, "Property interests, of course, are not created by the Constitution." Instead, property interests are created by the common law, by statutes, or by contracts. A civil service statute or a contract of tenure are common ways in which an employee at a state institution can acquire a property interest in continued employment. Both civil service laws and tenure contracts state that employees may be terminated only "for cause" (that is, on account of misconduct by the employee). In addition, a de facto system of tenure may be created, as in the companion case of *Perry v. Sindermann*, 408 U.S. 593 (1972), where a faculty manual issued by the college assured members of the faculty that they should consider themselves to have "permanent tenure" so long as they displayed a "cooperative attitude" and they were "happy" in their work.

In this case, however, Roth was not a civil service employee, he did not have tenure, and there was no faculty manual or other document creating a system of de facto tenure at the University. Instead, he was employed for a specified length of time, and when that period of time expired, so did his employment. The most famous passage from this case is: "To have a property interest in a benefit, a person clearly must have more than an abstract need or desire for it. He must have more than a unilateral expectation of it. He must, instead, have a legitimate claim of entitlement to it." Roth had no statutory or contractual "entitlement" to continued employment with the University, and therefore he had no "property interest" in continued employment. Accordingly, the due process clause of the Fourteenth Amendment did not apply, and Roth was not entitled to a hearing upon the termination of his employment.

Justice Thurgood Marshall dissented in *Roth*. In his view, "every citizen who applies for a government job is entitled to it unless the government can establish some reason for denying the employment." The Supreme Court has not adopted Justice Marshall's position that every citizen has a constitutional right to government employment.

SEE ALSO *Perry v. Sindermann, 408 U.S. 593 (1972); Procedural Due Process*

BIBLIOGRAPHY

Reich, Charles A. 1964. "The New Property." *Yale Law Journal* 73(5): 733–787.

Reich, Charles A. 1990. "Beyond the New Property: An Ecological View of Due Process." *Brooklyn Law Review* 56(3): 731–745.

Wilson R. Huhn

BOARD OF TRUSTEES OF THE UNIVERSITY OF ALABAMA V. GARRETT, 531 U.S. 356 (2001)

In *Board of Trustees of the University of Alabama v. Garrett*, 531 U.S. 356 (2001), the U.S. Supreme Court limited the ability of Congress to enact and implement federal civil rights laws. Under Section 5 of the Fourteenth Amendment, Congress has power to "enforce" provisions of that amendment (such as the due process clause and the equal protection clause) by "appropriate" legislation. Section 5 thus authorizes Congress to adopt national antidiscrimination legislation applicable both to private industry and to the states. Yet *Garrett* interpreted Section 5 to give Congress only limited power to ensure that the states comply with civil rights statutes. Chief Justice Rehnquist wrote the majority opinion. Four justices dissented.

Patricia Garrett was employed as the director of nursing in a hospital operated by the State of Alabama. When she was diagnosed with breast cancer, she took substantial periods of leave in order to undergo treatment. On her return, she was told that she must give up her administrative position. Garrett sued Alabama, alleging that the change in her assignment violated Title I of the federal Americans with Disabilities Act (ADA) of 1990 and seeking compensatory damages. Title I of the ADA bars employers (including the states) from engaging in employment discrimination on the basis of worker disabilities and,

to that end, requires the states to make "reasonable accommodations" to the physical and mental limitations of their employees. In *Garrett*, the Supreme Court acknowledged that Title I was constitutionally valid as a regulation of commerce. Yet the Court concluded that Title I could not be justified as "appropriate" enforcement legislation under Section 5. For that reason, Congress could not authorize an individual like Garrett to sue Alabama to force the state to comply with its legal obligations.

The Supreme Court has long held that Congress has no general power to legislate as it pleases, but only the powers enumerated in the Constitution. Section 5 of the Fourteenth Amendment establishes one of those powers, but there are others. Before the 1990s, it was not typically important to determine which of its many powers Congress relied on for the enactment of any particular statute; as long as one power was adequate to justify a statute, it did not matter whether others were also equal to the task. For this reason, the precise scope of Section 5 power was unsettled. Another enumerated power, the power to regulate interstate commerce, almost always authorized the legislation Congress enacted, and the Supreme Court had no occasion to consider whether the same statutes might have been warranted by Section 5. In *Heart of Atlanta Motel v. United States*, 379 U.S. 241 (1964), for example, the Court sustained the Civil Rights Act of 1964 (which bans racial discrimination in many contexts) as a regulation of commerce and declined to

Patricia Garrett, right, at a news conference with fellow Alabama state employee Milton Ash. After losing her position at a state hospital for taking time off to battle cancer, Garrett sued the state of Alabama for violating the Americans with Disabilities Act (ADA). The Supreme Court ruled, however, that Congress overstepped its authority in allowing private citizens to sue states in federal court for perceived violations of the ADA. AP IMAGES

reach the question whether the Civil Rights Act could also rest on Section 5.

In decisions in the 1990s, however, the Supreme Court held that while the power to regulate commerce lets Congress impose legal duties on the states, that power does not extend to authorizing private citizens to sue the states to enforce those duties. The Court held in *Seminole Tribe of Florida v. Florida*, 517 U.S. 44 (1996) and *Alden v. Maine*, 527 U.S. 706 (1999) that the Constitution immunizes the states from private lawsuits, and that the commerce power does not entail congressional authority to eliminate that immunity. By contrast, the Court explained in *Fitzpatrick v. Bitzer*, 427 U.S. 445 (1976) that Section 5 power does include the ability to abrogate state immunity. The primary explanation is that the Fourteenth Amendment is explicitly addressed to the states, and the power conferred on Congress by Section 5 of that amendment thus can fairly be understood to authorize legislation that affects the states in ways that statutes resting on other enumerated powers do not.

By the time of these decisions, Congress had enacted numerous federal civil rights laws governing the activities of the states. Those statutes were justified under Congress's power to regulate commerce, but only insofar as they imposed legal duties on states—for example, the duty to refrain from racial discrimination. The power to regulate commerce did not warrant provisions in statutes that authorized the victims of discrimination to sue the states over violations. Congress was able to choose that traditional means of enforcement only if the statute in question could also rest on Section 5. It then became essential to specify the scope of Section 5 power, in order to determine the validity of private-suit enforcement provisions in various federal statutes.

The Supreme Court provided guidance in *City of Boerne v. Flores*, 521 U.S. 507, a 1997 case involving the federal Religious Freedom Restoration Act (RFRA) of 1993. Among other things, that act prohibited a state from substantially burdening religious practices, unless the state had a "compelling governmental interest" in doing so. RFRA was plainly adopted in response to an earlier Supreme Court decision holding that the free exercise clause of the First Amendment did not bar states from adopting statutes of general applicability having an incidental, but unintentional, effect on religion. The free exercise clause, in turn, had long been understood to be incorporated into the Fourteenth Amendment. The purpose of the RFRA, according to Congress, was to use Section 5 power to "enforce" the Fourteenth Amendment (and with it the free exercise clause) by means of a federal statute condemning state statutes that the Court had held not to violate the Fourteenth Amendment (or the free exercise clause) itself. The Court balked at that idea, insisting that "appropriate" Section 5

legislation to "enforce" the Fourteenth Amendment could only address state activities that the Court regarded as constitutional violations. Congress could not substitute its own interpretation of the Fourteenth Amendment and enact a federal statute barring state statutes inconsistent with its own view of the Constitution's meaning.

In passing, the Court acknowledged in *City of Boerne* that Congress's power under Section 5 is not limited to banning, by statute, state activities that are already prohibited constitutionally by the Fourteenth Amendment itself. Congress can enact prophylactic legislation, which bars state activities that are not always unconstitutional but include activities that are. For example, Congress can adopt a statute that condemns state conduct that has a disproportionate negative impact on members of minority racial groups. The Fourteenth Amendment itself bars only deliberate racial discrimination. Yet it is often difficult to determine whether a state has acted with a purpose to harm racial minorities, and Congress can ensure that state attempts to do that are caught by condemning a larger circle of activities that are easier to detect. Necessarily, a federal statute that bars all state activities with a disproportionate impact on minorities condemns some activities that are not unconstitutional (because they do not intentionally mistreat members of minority groups), but Congress can be overinclusive in order to be effective in reaching state behavior that does violate the Constitution.

The Court explained, however, that there are limits on Congress's Section 5 power to reach state activities that are not themselves violations of the Fourteenth Amendment. According to the Court, if Congress prohibits many more state activities than are likely to be unconstitutional, the inference is that Congress is not attempting to deal with actions the Court has identified as unconstitutional, but is simply condemning activities that Congress (but not the Court) thinks are constitutionally troubling. That, of course, is precisely what Section 5 does not authorize. Accordingly, the Court said in *City of Boerne* that if a statute is to be sustained as valid Section 5 enforcement legislation, it must satisfy two tests: "congruence" and "proportionality." The prophylactic statute must genuinely be aimed at actual Fourteenth Amendment violations, and while it necessarily may be overinclusive, it cannot be out of proportion to the constitutional problems it is meant to address. If a federal statute does not meet these two criteria, the Court explained, it is not a genuine remedial effort to discourage state activities that the Court regards as unconstitutional, but must be understood as, instead, an attempt to second-guess the Court on what the Fourteenth Amendment means.

In *Garrett*, the Court concluded that Title I of the ADA failed both tests. Congress had gathered evidence indicating that states had not made "reasonable accommodations" to employees with disabilities, but, according to the Court, that evidence did not demonstrate a pattern of deliberate discrimination on the basis of disability. Since only purposeful discrimination could constitute a violation of the Fourteenth Amendment, Title I was not congruent with the actual constitutional violations it was supposed to discourage. Moreover, inasmuch as Title I reached far more state activities than the Fourteenth Amendment itself condemned, it was out of proportion to the constitutional evils it was meant to address.

The *Garrett* decision was controversial. Critics insisted that the Court applied the criteria announced in *City of Boerne* too strictly and, in particular, that the Court improperly discounted Congress's judgment about what was needed to ensure that the states did not violate Fourteenth Amendment rights. Moreover, by denying Congress power to authorize private citizens to sue the states for damages, the Court eliminated a traditional and effective means of policing state compliance.

In later decisions—*Nevada Department of Human Resources v. Hibbs,* 538 U.S. 721 (2003) and *Tennessee v. Lane,* 541 U.S. 509 (2004)—the Supreme Court appeared to be more sympathetic to Congress's attempts to enact prophylactic legislation under Section 5. By some accounts, the criticisms that *Garrett* aroused may have persuaded the Court to apply the *City of Boerne* criteria less stringently and thus to allow Congress more flexibility to enact and implement civil rights statutes.

SEE ALSO *Eleventh Amendment; Federalism; Rehnquist Court; State Sovereign Immunity*

BIBLIOGRAPHY

Buzbee, William W., and Robert A. Schapiro. 2001. "Legislative Record Review." *Stanford Law Review* 54: 87–161.

Colker, Ruth, and James J. Brudney. 2001. "Dissing Congress." *Michigan Law Review* 100: 80–144.

Post, Robert C., and Reva B. Siegel. 2000. "Equal Protection by Law: Federal Antidiscrimination Legislation After Morrison and Kimel." *Yale Law Journal* 110: 441–526.

Larry Yackle

BOB JONES UNIVERSITY V. UNITED STATES, 461 U.S. 574 (1983)

Bob Jones University v. United States, 461 U.S. 574 (1983) is a critically important Supreme Court case—more so for what it says about the scope of the Section 501(c)(3) tax exemption than for what it says about the religion clause of the First Amendment. However, both aspects of the case are interesting. In fact, the statutory issue remains unresolved. The narrow issue in *Bob Jones University* is whether nonprofit religious schools with religious-based racially discriminatory admissions policies qualify for federal income-tax exemption under Section 501(c)(3) of the U.S. Internal Revenue Code. Though the Court held that religious schools cannot discriminate against African Americans and still be exempt, the rule announced by the Court to reach this holding raises broader concerns about the overarching scope of this tax exemption.

The two schools involved in *Bob Jones University* claimed they were entitled to Section 501(c)(3) exemption as "educational" institutions despite their respective discriminatory policies. The schools, Bob Jones University in Greenville, South Carolina, and Goldsboro Christian Schools in Goldsboro, North Carolina, adopted admissions policies that were discriminatory against African Americans. One admissions policy disadvantaged students involved in interracial relationships and the other favored white students. Both schools claimed a genuinely held religious basis for their discriminatory policies. The Internal Revenue Service (IRS) announced in 1970 that it would deny Section 501(c)(3) exemption to organizations engaged in invidious racial discrimination and applied this rule to Bob Jones University and Goldsboro Christian Schools. Both schools challenged the IRS's denial of tax exemption, claiming that the statute does not permit the denial and the First Amendment prohibits it.

The schools based their statutory claim on the plain meaning of the statute. Section 501(a) provides that organizations described in subsection (c) "shall be exempt" from federal income taxation. Section 501(c) describes organizations entitled to tax exemption, including: "Corporations . . . organized and operated exclusively for religious, charitable, scientific, testing for public safety, literary, or educational purposes." The schools argued that the statute only requires that they be "educational" and the IRS's claim that they also be "charitable" (hence, nondiscriminatory) is not supported by the statute's use of the disjunctive "or" to delineate categories of exemption.

The Court responded to the schools' plain-meaning statutory claim with a legislative-purpose argument by stating that courts "should go beyond the literal language" and consider the underlying purpose of a statute, "if reliance on that language would defeat the plain purpose." In this case, the underlying purpose of Section 501(c)(3) is to grant exemption to organizations "meeting certain common law standards of charity," that "serve a public purpose," and that do not act "contrary to established public policy." In reaching this conclusion, the Court did a joint legislative-history construction of two statutes— Section 501(c)(3) and Section 170. Sections 501(c)(3) and 170 are related in that Section 170 permits donors to organizations having Section 501(c)(3) exemption to take an income-tax deduction when computing their separate income-tax liability. Relying on this joint construction, the Court concludes that the Section 501(c)(3) exemption is intended "to encourage the development of private institutions that serve a useful public purpose" or that "supplement ... public institutions."

Based on this legislative-history analysis, the Court concluded that organizations that violate "established public policy" are not "charitable" and thus not entitled to Section 501(c)(3) exemption—even if the specific type of organization is otherwise described in the statute. In looking at the various government policies against racial discrimination, the Court determined that there is no doubt that racial discrimination against African Americans violates established public policy. In reaching this determination, the Court considered the line of judicial rulings since *Brown v. Board of Education*, 347 U.S. 483 (1954), a series of congressional acts since the Civil Rights Act of 1964, and a series of presidential orders enforcing school-desegregation orders. The Court also emphasized how Congress acquiesced in the IRS's 1970 interpretation. Indeed, Congress knew of the IRS interpretation, but enacted no legislation to overrule it. To the contrary, according to the Court, Congress acted consistent with the IRS's interpretation when it enacted, in 1976, Section 501(i) to deny tax exemption to Section 501(C)(7) social clubs that discriminate based on "race, color, or religion."

In addition to claiming that the IRS does not have statutory authority to deny them Section 501(c)(3) exemption, the schools claimed that the First Amendment prevents the IRS from doing so. The religion clause of the First Amendment provides that Congress shall make no law "respecting an establishment of religion, or prohibiting the free exercise thereof" (U.S. Constitution, amendment 1). However, the Court has interpreted this clause to mean that government can regulate religion if such regulation is necessary to accomplish a compelling government interest. Thus, the Court explained, certain government interests (e.g., laws intended to protect children) are so compelling that regulations prohibiting religious conduct are constitutional. Because the government's interest in eradicating racial discrimination is compelling, that interest outweighs any burden that denial of tax benefits places on the schools' exercise of their religious beliefs (presumably because denial of tax benefits is not a prohibition of religious conduct). Interestingly, the Court majority implies in footnote twenty-nine that its decision might have been different if the claimant were a church, or other purely religious institution, instead of a school.

One of the most critical aspects of *Bob Jones University* is the concurring opinion by Justice Lewis F. Powell Jr. Although Powell agreed with the Court's judgment, he did not agree with the broad nature of the majority opinion. As Powell explained: "I am unconvinced that the critical question in determining tax-exempt status is whether an

... organization provides a clear 'public benefit' as defined by the Court." Powell continued that the Court majority seems to suggest an element of "conformity" with government interest that is inconsistent with the role of "tax exemptions in encouraging diverse ... activities and viewpoints" and "a vigorous, pluralistic society." Powell's view is that the exemption serves to limit the influence of government on important aspects of community life. Thus, whereas Powell recognized that Congress could decide otherwise, he expressed reluctance to endorse the idea that the IRS is authorized to determine when a public policy (besides racial discrimination) is sufficiently established for Section 501(c)(3) purposes. Despite Powell's explicit call for congressional action in this area, as of 2008 Congress had not enacted legislation that would codify the holding in *Bob Jones University*.

Although the IRS has relied on the specific ruling in *Bob Jones University* to deny Section 501(c)(3) exemption to other educational institutions that discriminate against African Americans based on race or that fail to adopt racial nondiscrimination policies, it has not ventured much beyond these parameters. Thus, in apparent adherence to Powell's notions of "diversity" and "plurality," the IRS has not relied on the broad principle of "established public policy" to delve into such policy-laden areas as same-sex marriage, medicinal use of marijuana, or other aspects of community life that might diverge from popular or government policies. This is not to say that *Bob Jones University* is a narrow case with no broad application beyond educational institutions that discriminate based on race. Indeed, the case began a conversation in tax law about questions that remain unanswered. What about educational institutions that discriminate on other bases besides race—such as gender or sexual preference, for instance? What about educational institutions that do not discriminate against, but instead engage in benign preferences for, African Americans such as affirmative action? What about Section 501(c)(3) exempt institutions other than educational ones that perform these acts—racial discrimination, gender discrimination, affirmative action, and so forth? Should Congress enact legislation in any of these areas, or should it continue to merely acquiesce to IRS interpretation?

SEE ALSO *Education and the Constitution; First Amendment*

BIBLIOGRAPHY

Brennen, David A. 2000. "The Power of the Treasury: Racial Discrimination, Public Policy, and 'Charity' in Contemporary Society." *University of California Davis Law Review* 33: 389–447.

Brennen, David A. 2002. "Charities and the Constitution: Evaluating the Role of Constitutional Principles in Determining the Scope of Tax Law's Public Policy Limitation for Charities." *Florida Tax Review* 5: 779–849.

Brennen, David A. 2006. "A Diversity Theory of Charitable Tax Exemption: Beyond Efficiency, Through Critical Race Theory, Toward Diversity." *Pittsburgh Tax Review* 4: 1–54.

Colombo, John D. 1993. "Why Is Harvard Tax-Exempt? (And Other Mysteries of Tax Exemption for Private Educational Institutions)." *Arizona Law Review* 35: 841–903.

Drennan, William A. 1985. "Note: *Bob Jones University v. United States*: For Whom Will the Bell Toll?" *St. Louis University Law Journal* 29: 561–596.

Galston, Miriam. 1984. "Public Policy Constraints on Charitable Organizations." *Virginia Tax Review* 3: 291–322.

Galvin, Charles O., and Neal E. Devins. 1983. "A Tax Policy Analysis of *Bob Jones University v. United States*." *Vanderbilt Law Review* 36: 1353–1382.

Gustafsson, Lars G. 1996. "The Definition of 'Charitable' for Federal Income Tax Purposes: Defrocking the Old and Suggesting Some New Fundamental Assumptions." *Houston Law Review* 33: 587–649.

Jones, Darryll K., et al. 2007. *The Tax Law of Charities and Other Exempt Organizations: Cases, Materials, Questions, and Activities.* 2nd edition. St. Paul, MN: Thomson/West.

Kurtz, Jerome. 1978. "Difficult Definitional Problems in Tax Administration: Religion and Race." *Catholic Lawyer* 23: 301, 304ff.

David A. Brennen

BODDIE V. CONNECTICUT, 401 U.S. 371 (1971)

Boddie v. Connecticut, 401 U.S. 371 (1971) held that a state denies due process to indigent persons when it requires that they pay court fees and costs that they cannot afford in order to initiate divorce actions. The case was decided during a period of considerable disagreement on the Court concerning the scope of the due process clause, both in its substantive and procedural aspects. *Boddie's* continued significance rests on the majority opinion's powerful language on access to the courts and its statements regarding the fundamental nature of marriage.

The proceeding was initiated by Connecticut welfare recipients who challenged a state law requiring the payment of fees and costs to bring a divorce action, with an average cost of sixty dollars per divorce. The plaintiff class consisted of all female welfare recipients residing in Connecticut and wishing to file for divorce. They sought a declaration that the state law was invalid as applied to the class and an injunction permitting class members to obtain a divorce without payment.

Connecticut defended the law, arguing that the plaintiffs were simply asking the court to substitute its own judgment for that of the legislature. The plaintiffs countered that Connecticut's law violated both the equal protection and due process principles of the Fourteenth Amendment to the U.S. Constitution. They conceded that the right to divorce is not constitutionally guaranteed, but emphasized that their constitutional claim arose from their right to access the courts. The plaintiffs further argued that they were denied such access simply because they were poor, and that this wealth-based classification could be justified only by a compelling state interest, which was absent here.

The federal district court ruled for the state, holding that Connecticut could constitutionally impose fees even if that effectively barred the plaintiffs from obtaining divorces. On direct appeal, the U.S. Supreme Court reversed.

The majority opinion, authored by Justice John M. Harlan, emphasized the unique status of marriage and the "state monopolization of the means for legally dissolving this relationship." Harlan analogized divorce to a criminal proceeding, noting that in both instances the dispute can only be resolved in court, and he concluded that the denial of access to the court in such a circumstance violated due process requirements.

In concurrence, Justice William Douglas stated that the case should have been decided based on the equal protection clause. Also concurring, Justice William Brennan agreed, observing that "where money determines not merely 'the kind of trial a man gets,' but whether he gets into court at all, the great principle of equal protection becomes a mockery."

In dissent, Justice Hugo Black argued that marriage and divorce have always been under state control, and therefore, states have particular interests in the laws regulating marriages. Further, he opined that the procedural protections afforded under the due process clause should be reserved for criminal proceedings.

Despite some initial predictions about *Boddie's* significance, the majority's opinion was distinguished in subsequent cases because of the state's unique and complete control of marriage. Thus, the decision did not open the floodgates to a free civil court system for indigents. However, its language on access to the courts is cited frequently and its statements on the importance of marriage have played a supportive role in litigation on same-sex relationships.

SEE ALSO *Welfare State*

BIBLIOGRAPHY

Michelman, Frank. 1974. "The Supreme Court and Litigation Access Fees: The Right to Protect One's Rights—Part I." *Duke Law Journal* 1973(6): 1153–1215.

Yarbrough, Tinsley. 1992. *John Marshall Harlan: Great Dissenter of the Warren Court.* New York: Oxford University Press.

Martha F. Davis

BOLLING V. SHARPE, 347 U.S. 497 (1954)

Bolling v. Sharpe, 347 U.S. 497 (1954) was argued before the U.S. Supreme Court the same day as *Brown v. Board of Education*, 347 U.S. 483 (1954). Like *Brown*, this case addressed the question of whether segregation in the public schools violated the U.S. Constitution. However, it could not be consolidated with *Brown* and its companion cases from South Carolina, Virginia, and Delaware because *Bolling* dealt with segregation in the public schools of the District of Columbia. Challenges to segregated state schools were based on the equal protection clause of the Fourteenth Amendment. Because the equal protection clause applies only to the states, the constitutional challenge to segregation in the District of Columbia was based on the due process clause of the Fifth Amendment. In its finding that the broad contours of the due process clause embraced the Constitution's fundamental commitment to equality, the *Bolling* decision helped develop the foundation for equal protection standards on the federal level.

In an opinion delivered by Chief Justice Earl Warren, the Court recognized that issues presented by the District of Columbia case were "somewhat different," because the Fifth Amendment contains no equal protection clause. However, although the Court acknowledged that guarantees of due process of law and equal protection are not "interchangeable," it also argued that "discrimination may be so unjustifiable as to be violative of due process." Moreover, the Court held that racial classifications were to be "scrutinized with particular care, since they are contrary to our traditions and hence constitutionally suspect."

Thus, the determination of whether segregation in the District of Columbia's schools was justifiable was predicated on the position that racial classifications are constitutionally suspect and must be subjected to strict scrutiny. Under this doctrine, racial classifications are presumptively unconstitutional, and can be upheld only if they are necessary to a compelling governmental objective. The Court determined that segregation in the public schools did not serve any "proper governmental objective," and held that segregation in the District of Columbia's schools was "a denial of due process of law."

The District of Columbia moved swiftly to comply with the decision, and *Bolling* did not attract as much attention as *Brown*. However, it was important in developing federal equal protection standards. The significance of the *Bolling* precedent was evident some forty years later, in a case involving a federal program that provided financial incentives for the use of minority contractors. The Court attributed pivotal importance to *Bolling*'s holding that whereas the due process clause's prohibition of racial classifications is less explicit than that of the Fourteenth Amendment, the standards for evaluating racial classifications on the federal level are equally strict. In *Adarand Constructors Inc. v. Peña*, 515 U.S. 200 (1995), the Court articulated a clear standard to be applied to federal affirmative action programs: "Federal racial classifications, like those of a State, must serve a compelling governmental interest, and must be narrowly tailored to further that interest." Hence, despite the absence of an explicit federal equal protection requirement, the *Bolling* decision has helped ensure that the same constitutional requirements apply to state and federal laws involving racial classifications.

SEE ALSO *Brown v. Board of Education, 347 U.S. 483 (1954); Education and the Constitution; School Desegregation*

BIBLIOGRAPHY

Epstein, Lee, and Thomas G. Walker. 2004. *Constitutional Law for a Changing America: Rights, Liberties, and Justice*. 5th edition. Washington, DC: Congressional Quarterly Press.

O'Brien, David M. 1997. *Constitutional Law and Politics*. Vol. 2: *Civil Rights and Civil Liberties*. 3rd edition. New York: Norton.

Justin Halpern

BONHAM'S CASE

Many constitutional commentators trace the judicial power to declare a law unconstitutional to *Bonham's Case*, 8 Coke Reports 651–652 (1610). The most famous passage in that case seemingly asserts a judicial power to declare higher-law limits on legislative power. "The common law will control Acts of Parliament, and sometimes adjudge them to be utterly void," Lord Chief Justice Edward Coke (1552–1634) wrote, "for when an Act of Parliament is against common right and reason, or repugnant, or impossible to be performed, the common law will control it, and adjudge such Act to be void." Although this passage appears to suggest that Parliament could not pass laws inconsistent with certain common-law principles, some commentators insist that the court in *Bonham* was asserting only that judges should interpret statutes as being consistent with common-law principles whenever possible.

The context in which Lord Coke made his famous assertion provides some support for the more restrained interpretation of his opinion. Thomas Bonham had been fined for practicing medicine in London without obtaining a license from the Royal College of Physicians. English law at the time empowered the Royal College to determine who was competent to practice medicine in England and to collect fines from those persons who practiced without a license. Bonham challenged his fine on two grounds. First, he insisted that the law applied only to London residents. As

Portrait of English Lord Chief Justice Edward Coke.
Bonham's Case stems from a 1610 decision in England explaining the check of the judiciary on the legislative branch. Lord Coke suggested that any law Parliament passed must also be in accordance with English common law lest it be ruled void, inspiring Founding Father James Otis to incorporate this feature in the early American government. **POPPERFOTO/GETTY IMAGES**

a graduate of Cambridge University, he was entitled to practice in London during a short stay in the city without obtaining a license. Lord Coke agreed. Most of Coke's opinion in *Bonham* maintained as a matter of statutory interpretation that persons who received medical degrees from other universities could legally practice temporarily in London without a license from the Royal College. Having resolved the statutory question, Lord Coke had no legal reason to explore whether Parliament could vest the same persons with the power to determine whether an applicant was qualified to practice medicine and to collect the fine if they determined the applicant unqualified. As was the case with *Marbury v. Madison*, 5 U.S. (1 Cranch) 137 (1803), much of the most important language in *Bonham* was, thus, unnecessary to resolving the actual issue before the justices.

Whatever *Bonham* may have held as a matter of English law in 1610, Lord Coke's decision had a substantial influence on American revolutionary and constitutional practice. Such American revolutionaries as James Otis (1725–1783) cited *Bonham* for the proposition that parliamentary edicts inconsistent with certain common-law principles were void. "Should an act of parliament be

against any of [God's] natural laws, which are *immutably* true," he wrote, "*their* declaration would be contrary to eternal truth, equity and justice, and consequently void" (Otis 1967, p. 32). Otis then added that English judges had recognized this principle when refusing to enforce certain parliamentary edicts. As transmitted by Otis and other revolutionaries, *Bonham* came to stand for the principle that a higher constitutional law, written or unwritten, limited the power of constitutional legislatures, and that courts were the institution responsible for enforcing that higher law. Whether this was a correct interpretation of *Bonham* remains controversial.

SEE ALSO *English Constitutionalism; Judicial Review*

BIBLIOGRAPHY

Corwin, Edward S. 1955. *The "Higher Law" Background of American Constitutional Law.* Ithaca, NY: Cornell University Press.

Otis, James. 1967. "The Right of the British Colonies Asserted and Proved." In *Tracts of the American Revolution 1763-1776*, ed. Merrill Jensen. Indianapolis: Bobbs-Merrill.

Plucknett, Theodore F. T. 1926. "*Bonham's Case* and Judicial Review." *Harvard Law Review* 40: 30–70.

Mark A. Graber

BORK, ROBERT
1927–

The Senate's failure in 1987 to confirm Robert Heron Bork to succeed Lewis Powell (1907–1998) as associate justice of the Supreme Court stands as the high-water mark of the politics of confrontation that has dominated the judicial confirmation process since the late 1960s. Although he was arguably the most professionally qualified candidate for a seat on the Court since Felix Frankfurter (1882–1965) in 1938, Robert Bork's nomination energized an extraordinary array of interest groups from all points across the political spectrum and produced a dramatic political confrontation that thrust the confirmation process into the vortex of American politics. More than two decades later, the battle over Bork remains a defining moment in modern American political and legal history.

Following graduation in 1953 from the University of Chicago Law School and a period in private practice, Robert Bork joined the Yale Law School faculty to teach antitrust law and to become, in effect, the resident libertarian on a predominately liberal, activist faculty. The political and cultural turmoil of the 1960s, however, pushed Bork to the right, and by the end of the decade, the libertarian had evolved into a social and political

U.S. Supreme Court nominee Robert H. Bork. A former Yale Law School professor and federal circuit court of appeals judge, Bork faced a highly politicized confirmation proceeding, primarily over his conservative interpretation of the Constitution. Despite being considered one of the most qualified nominees for the Supreme Court, the Senate voted fifty-eight to forty-two against Bork. © REUTERS/CORBIS-BETTMANN

conservative. Bork's initial scholarly efforts had been as an advocate of the Chicago school of antitrust interpretation, but by the late 1960s his focus had shifted to constitutional law and the perceived abuses of the Warren Court era. His most widely read scholarly piece, "Neutral Principles and Some First Amendment Problems," published in 1971, remains one of the most challenging and often-cited critiques of Warren Court jurisprudence.

By the early 1970s, Bork had become one of the intellectual stars of the New Right, and in 1972 he was tapped by the Richard Nixon (1913–1994) administration to become solicitor general. In this capacity, he was thrust into the maelstrom of corruption and illegality that marked the Nixon presidency. He played a prominent role in pressuring Vice President Spiro Agnew (1918–1996) to resign after investigations revealed that the vice president had been receiving kickbacks from contractors since his days as the governor of Maryland. In 1973

officials in the Nixon White House unsuccessfully sought to have Bork leave his position as solicitor general to head the Nixon defense team during the investigation of the Watergate scandal. In the summer of that year, when Nixon demanded that Archibald Cox (1912–2004), the special prosecutor in charge of the Watergate investigation, be fired, both the attorney general, Elliot Richardson (1920–1999), and the deputy attorney general, William Ruckelshaus, chose to resign rather than issue the order. The task then fell to Bork as the third-ranking officer in the Justice Department. In the years following Watergate, Bork steadfastly maintained that he only agreed to fire Cox rather than resign to provide leadership and direction to the Justice Department during a period of domestic and constitutional crisis.

With the election of Democrat Jimmy Carter in 1976, Bork returned to Yale for several years before joining the firm of Kirkland and Ellis as the senior partner in the Washington, D.C., office. He continued in the life of a conservative public intellectual, frequently appearing in the popular press and the lecture circuit with his unsparing critique of modern liberalism. When a vacancy appeared on the D.C. Circuit Court of Appeals in 1982, President Ronald Reagan (1911–2004) announced that Robert Bork would be his choice to fill the slot, and Bork, no doubt considering this position a steppingstone to a possible Supreme Court appointment, accepted. Throughout his years on the D.C. Circuit, both on and off the bench, Bork continued to be a highly visible advocate for his ideological agenda.

When Lewis Powell announced his resignation from the Court in 1987, Bork was the choice of President Reagan. Within hours of the announcement, Senator Ted Kennedy took to the floor of the Senate to denounce the nomination in an impassioned speech describing "Robert Bork's America" as a land of racial segregation, illegal abortions, religious curriculum in public schools, and unrestrained police behavior. Administration officials had anticipated a battle over Bork but believed that in the end his outstanding resume would overcome all opposition. In retrospect, this was an extraordinarily naive belief. The battle over the Bork nomination made clear to all concerned that, in the modern era, the confirmation of Supreme Court justices was first and foremost a political undertaking, and the Kennedy speech proved to be politically far more effective than any dry testimony regarding legal competence and academic accomplishment.

During the course of the confirmation proceedings, more than three hundred groups ranging across the spectrum from the United Mine Workers to the National Gay and Lesbian Task Force opposed the nomination. The Bork confirmation process became a case study in interest-group mobilization, and the tactics of those opposing Bork included not only lobbying efforts but the sophisticated use of polling data and focus-group studies to generate highly effective advertising campaigns to mobilize mass public participation. For much of the twentieth century, the appointment of Supreme Court justices had been essentially an insider game, where deals and agreements between key players eased confirmation to the high court. The Bork proceedings signaled the necessity of the promotion of judicial nominees in a manner similar to that of a candidate in a national electoral campaign, and the confirmation process quickly reflected the best and worst of modern mass democracy.

In the end, Bork was also undone by the long paper trail of his writings and public statements and his willingness to engage the members of the Senate judiciary committee in extended discussion of his understanding of the Court and the Constitution. The final legacy of the Bork defeat can be found in the fact that subsequent Supreme Court nominees inevitably were competent jurists, but unknown to the public and unwilling to respond in any meaningful manner to queries regarding their constitutional or judicial thinking.

On October 23, 1987, the Senate rejected the Bork nomination by a fifty-eight-to-forty-two vote. Following his defeat, an embittered Bork found a home as resident scholar in conservative think tanks, and through bestselling books and numerous public appearances, he continued his crusade against the vices of modern liberalism.

SEE ALSO *Interest Groups; Nomination Process; Originalism; Reagan, Ronald*

BIBLIOGRAPHY

Bork, Robert H. 1971. "Neutral Principles and Some First Amendment Problems." *Indiana Law Review* 47: 1–35.

Bork, Robert H. 1990. *The Tempting of America: The Political Seduction of the Law.* New York: Simon and Schuster.

Bronner, Ethan. 1989. *Battle for Justice: How the Bork Nomination Shook America.* New York: Norton.

Pertschuk, Michael, and Wendy Schaetzel. 1989. *The People Rising: The Campaign Against the Bork Nomination.* New York: Thunder's Mouth.

Mark Silverstein

BOWERS V. HARDWICK, 478 U.S. 186 (1986)

Bowers v. Hardwick, 478 U.S. 186 (1986) was the first case in which the U.S. Supreme Court addressed the question whether state laws criminalizing sodomy—here applied solely to homosexual relations in private between consenting adults—violate the U.S. Constitution. The case arose in the context of a gay/lesbian protest movement that had come relatively late to American politics, compared to the struggle (whose origins could be traced to the pre–Civil War era) for the rights of people of color and women. Additionally, the developing Acquired Immune Deficiency Syndrome (AIDS) crisis, which, by the mid-1980s was taking a heavy toll within the gay community, gave a peculiar urgency to challenging homophobia and ending legal discrimination against gays and lesbians.

Many European nations had decriminalized gay and lesbian sex long before—France and the Netherlands as early as 1810, Belgium in 1867, Italy in 1889, Spain in 1932, and the Scandinavian countries between 1930 and 1970. Britain joined Europe in this respect in 1967. Germany finally did so in 1968 to 1969. In 1981, the European Court of Human Rights held invalid under the European Convention on Human Rights laws proscribing gay/lesbian sex acts, a decision authoritative in all member countries of the Council of Europe (twenty-one at the time, forty-five by 2003).

Against this background, the *Bowers* opinion might, with utmost charity, be described as "facetious." The Court offered flawed arguments that sparked widespread outcry, indignation, and severe scholarly criticism both when it was handed down and throughout the seventeen years it survived as precedent until overruled by *Lawrence v. Texas*, 539 U.S. 558 (2003).

MICHAEL HARDWICK'S ROAD TO THE SUPREME COURT

On August 3, 1982, Atlanta police officer Keith Torrick entered the home of Michael Hardwick, a gay man, with an arrest warrant. Possibly admitted by a friend staying at Hardwick's house, and without Hardwick's knowledge, the officer began searching the house. Upon reaching the back bedroom door the officer pushed it open and entered the room, where he found Hardwick and a male guest engaging in oral sex. Hardwick was placed under arrest. He was charged with violating Georgia's sodomy statute, which provided that "any sexual act involving the sex organs of one person and the mouth or anus of another" was a felony punishable by up to twenty years imprisonment. But, after a preliminary hearing, the district attorney decided not to present the matter to the grand jury unless further evidence developed.

Hardwick subsequently brought suit in the federal district court. He asserted that the statute placed him in imminent danger of arrest for conduct inherent in his lifestyle, and that it violated the U.S. Constitution. The district court dismissed for failure to state a claim. A divided panel of the Court of Appeals for the Eleventh Circuit reversed. The appeals court relied on a series of Supreme Court privacy decisions between 1965 and 1973 and held that the Georgia statute violated Hardwick's fundamental right to private, intimate association, protected by the Ninth Amendment and the due process clause of the Fourteenth Amendment. The case was remanded for trial. But other courts of appeals had arrived at contrary decisions in similar cases, and the U.S. Supreme Court granted the Georgia attorney general's petition for certiorari.

In its brief to the Supreme Court, the state of Georgia argued that the appeals court had misunderstood and consequently did not follow an earlier Supreme Court case affirming a lower court finding that Virginia's sodomy statute was constitutional. The state also argued that the Constitution did not grant a fundamental right for homosexuals to engage in sodomy, and that the right of privacy did not encompass acts of sodomy because permitting those acts was inconsistent with history and tradition.

Hardwick's brief (prepared by Harvard constitutional law expert Laurence Tribe [1941–], who also presented the oral argument) argued that the conduct was intimate in nature and took place in the home between consenting adults. Therefore, Georgia's law had to be subjected to heightened scrutiny, and the state would have to show some compelling interest served by the law—a level of scrutiny, the brief added, not necessary for laws against prostitution and public indecency. Finally, Hardwick's brief argued that the state's asserted goal of preserving morality was not substantial enough to outweigh the privacy interest involved in this case.

An amicus curiae brief filed on Hardwick's behalf by the American Psychological Association and American Public Health Association sought to update the Court on the sexual practices of Americans. The brief cited studies indicating that up to 90 percent of heterosexual couples had had oral sex—both fellatio and cunnilingus—and that at least 25 percent of married couples under age thirty-five had engaged in anal sex. The brief also stressed that homosexuality was not a mental disorder and not a matter of choice, and that sodomy laws are in fact psychologically damaging by stigmatizing homosexuals as criminally deviant, fueling heterosexual prejudice and producing self-destructive self-hatred among homosexuals. Moreover, such laws harm the fight against AIDS, in effect driving the disease underground.

Hardwick's case was argued on March 31, 1986. It is evident from transcripts that Professor Tribe was aiming significant portions of his argument at Justice Lewis F. Powell Jr., perceived by Tribe as the possible swing vote. The Court handed down its opinion on June 30, 1986.

OPINION OF THE COURT

Justice Byron White (joined by Chief Justice Warren Burger and Justices William Rehnquist, Powell, and Sandra Day O'Connor) wrote the opinion of the Court reversing the court of appeals decision. White defined the issue as whether the Constitution confers on homosexuals a fundamental right to engage in sodomy. He also argued

---

AMICUS CURIAE IN SUPPORT OF HARDWICK

■

Amicus curiae (Latin for "a friend of the court") briefs are filed by individuals or organizations other than the parties to the case. Often those who file have a political or ideological interest in the court's final decision. In *Bowers v. Hardwick,* such a brief was filed jointly by the American Psychological Association and the American Public Health Association. They emphasized the public health implications (physical and psychological) of the case, including showing that mental health professionals had found that the sexual conduct prohibited by Georgia was not harmful to health or social functioning, whether engaged in by same-sex or opposite-sex couples. Moreover, they cited clinical research studies indicating such conduct was important to psychological health and healthy intimate relationships. They also argued, again based on scientific and clinical studies, that the Georgia statute disserves rather than furthers individual mental health or the public health. For instance, threat of prosecution, they noted, endangered the public health by driving diseases such as AIDS underground, which makes it more difficult to study and prevent. Significantly, they also explained to the Court that health experts no longer considered either homosexuality or sodomy "pathological," but the threat of criminal punishment "actually has harmful psychological consequences for people who wish to engage in the proscribed conduct." Thus, the *amici* urged the Supreme Court to affirm the Eleventh Circuit's decision overturning the Georgia statute.

Philip A. Dynia

---

that the case required the Court to think about its proper role and the nature of its constitutional responsibilities.

White disagreed with the appeals court's reading of the line of due process and privacy cases from *Meyer v. Nebraska*, 262 U.S. (1923) to *Carey v. Population Services International*, 431 U.S. 678 (1977). For White, the rights announced in those cases in no way resembled the right asserted in this case. "No connection between family, marriage, or procreation . . . and homosexual activity . . . has been demonstrated." He also rejected the claim that those cases meant that any kind of private sexual conduct between consenting adults was constitutionally protected.

White conceded that the due process clause of the Fourteenth Amendment had been interpreted as protecting substantive rights. But to assure that the justices did not impose their own values on legislative decisions, the Court required that only rights "implicit in the concept of ordered liberty" or "deeply rooted in this Nation's history and tradition" be included within the Fourteenth Amendment.

A fundamental right of homosexuals to engage in acts of consensual sodomy fit neither of these tests. White noted that proscriptions on sodomy have ancient roots. Sodomy is a criminal offense at common law. Moreover, all of the original states forbade sodomy when the Bill of Rights was ratified. In 1868, when the Fourteenth Amendment was ratified, all but five of the thirty-seven states had criminal sodomy laws. Until 1961, all fifty states outlawed sodomy, and in 1986, twenty-four states and the District of Columbia continued criminal penalties for private, consensual sodomy between adults. "Against this background, to claim that a right to engage in such conduct is 'deeply rooted in the Nation's history and tradition' or 'implicit in the concept of ordered liberty' is, at best, facetious." White was reluctant to discover new fundamental rights in the due process clause. "The Court is most vulnerable and comes nearest to illegitimacy when it deals with judge-made constitutional law having little or no cognizable roots in the language or design of the Constitution."

Further, White rejected Hardwick's argument that homosexual conduct in the privacy of the home should be treated differently. Hardwick's reliance on *Stanley v. Georgia*, 394 U.S. 557 (1969) was inappropriate because that was a First Amendment case. Crimes, even when committed in the privacy of the home, were still crimes. And if Hardwick was claiming that the protection was limited to the voluntary sexual conduct between consenting adults, "it would be difficult, except by fiat, to limit the claimed right to homosexual conduct while leaving exposed to prosecution adultery, incest, and other sexual crimes even though they are committed in the home. We are unwilling to start down that road."

Finally, Hardwick's claim that there was no rational basis for the law—except majority sentiment that homosexual sodomy was immoral and unacceptable—was also rejected. "The law ... is constantly based on notions of morality, and if all laws representing essentially moral choices are to be invalidated under the Due Process Clause, the courts will be very busy indeed."

CONCURRING AND DISSENTING OPINIONS

Chief Justice Burger wrote a brief concurring opinion in which he cites numerous condemnations of homosexual conduct in Western civilization, including Roman law's treatment of sodomy as a capital crime. (There is no suggestion such a sentence would be inappropriate in the twentieth century). "To hold that the act of homosexual sodomy is somehow protected as a fundamental right would be to cast aside millennia of moral teaching."

Justice Powell's concurrence noted that the Georgia statute provided a maximum penalty of twenty years imprisonment for a conviction. If the respondent had been tried, convicted, and given the maximum sentence, Powell argued, that would "create a serious Eighth Amendment issue." But Powell concluded that constitutional question was not raised; thus the Court did not have to address it.

Justice Harry A. Blackmun (joined by justices William Brennan, Thurgood Marshall, and John Paul Stevens) wrote the main dissent. He denied the majority's claim that this case was about "a fundamental right to engage in homosexual sodomy." Quoting Justice Louis D. Brandeis's famous dissent in *Olmstead v. United States*, 277 U.S. 438 (1928), he argued it "is about 'the most comprehensive of rights and the right most valued by civilized men,' namely, 'the right to be let alone.'" He also rejected the majority's notion that the length of time the statute was in effect determined whether or not it is constitutional, quoting Justice Oliver Wendell Holmes Jr.: "It is revolting to have no better reason for a rule of law than that so it was laid down in the time of Henry IV. It is still more revolting if the grounds upon which it was laid down have vanished long since, and the rule simply persists from blind imitation of the past." Rather, Hardwick's claims must be analyzed in the light of the values that underlie the constitutional right to privacy.

Blackmun accused the majority of distorting the question presented by this case in two respects: (1) Despite the Court's "almost obsessive focus on homosexual activity," the Georgia statute was aimed at both homosexual and heterosexual sodomy. Even though Georgia only enforced the statute against homosexuals, Hardwick's claim of an unconstitutional intrusion into his privacy and right of intimate association did not depend in any way on his sexual orientation. (2) The Court should also have addressed the questions of whether the statute violated the Eighth or Ninth Amendments or the equal protection clause of the Fourteenth Amendment. The procedural posture of the case, Blackmun argued, required affirmance of the Eleventh Circuit's judgment "if there is *any* [Blackmun's italics] ground on which respondent may be entitled to relief." Blackmun did not, however, reach those claims because he accepted Hardwick's assertion that his interests in privacy and freedom of intimate association had been violated. "The Court's cramped reading of the issue before it makes for a short opinion, but it does little to make for a persuasive one."

Blackmun summarized the two distinct but complementary lines of the Court's privacy decisions: (1) a privacy interest with reference to certain decisions that are properly for the individual to make; and (2) a privacy interest with reference to certain places without regard for the particular activities in which the individuals who occupy them are engaged. Hardwick's case implicated both aspects of the right to privacy.

Regarding the first aspect, Blackmun argued that the cases were not merely about protection of the family. Rather, they implicated rights protected because they formed a central part of an individual's life. The ability independently to define one's identity is critical to any concept of liberty and cannot be exercised in a vacuum—everyone depends on the emotional satisfaction of close ties with others, most notably sexual intimacy.

> The fact that individuals define themselves in a significant way through their intimate sexual relationships with others suggests, in a Nation as diverse as ours, that there may be many 'right' ways of conducting these relationships, and that much of the richness of a relationship will come from the freedom an individual has to choose the form and nature of these intensely personal bonds.

That interest the majority opinion ignored.

The spatial aspect was implicated by the fact that Hardwick faced prosecution for behavior occurring in his own home. Here too the Court refused to consider the broader principles derived from specific cases. Blackmun found the Court's interpretation of *Stanley v. Georgia* entirely unconvincing in that it failed to stress the Fourth Amendment roots of that decision. The Fourth Amendment provided a clear textual basis for this component of the right to privacy. "Indeed, the right of an individual to conduct intimate relationships in the intimacy of his or her own home seems to me to be the heart of the Constitution's protection of privacy."

Blackmun rejected both of the state's general justifications of the law as grounds for the majority's dismissing Hardwick's challenge for failure to state a claim. Georgia argued that the acts criminalized by this statute had serious adverse consequences for the general public health and welfare. But there was nothing in the record, Blackmun stressed, that provided any justification for finding Hardwick's activity to be physically dangerous, either to the persons engaged in it or to others. (In a footnote at this point, Blackmun identified the specific harms caused by adultery and incest that justified state regulation. He concluded: "Notably, the Court makes no effort to explain why it has chosen to group private, consensual homosexual activity with adultery and incest, rather than with private, consensual heterosexual activity by unmarried persons or, indeed, with oral or anal sex within marriage.")

Equally problematic was the state's claim of a right to maintain a decent society, including its stress on the fact that the acts described in the statute had for centuries been condemned as immoral. Blackmun responded: "I cannot agree that either the length of time a majority has held its convictions or the passions with which it defends them can withdraw legislation from this Court's scrutiny." Blackmun cited the history of segregation laws, antimiscegenation laws, and laws forbidding abortion—all of which were overturned in major Supreme Court decisions. He quoted Justice Robert H. Jackson's opinion in *West Virginia Board of Education v. Barnette*, 319 U.S. 624 (1943): "Freedom to differ is not limited to things that do not matter much. That would be a mere shadow of freedom. The test of its substance is the right to differ as to things that touch the heart of the existing order."

Despite Christianity's condemnation (on again, off again, as John Boswell [1981] has shown), other religious groups, Blackmun noted, had not condemned the behavior at issue. But ultimately religious views were irrelevant, because "the legitimacy of secular legislation depends, instead, on whether the State can advance some justification for its law beyond its conformity to religious doctrine. . . . A state can no more punish private behavior because of religious intolerance than it can punish such behavior because of racial animus."

Blackmun accused the petitioner and the majority of failing to see the difference between laws that protect public sensibilities and those that enforce private morality. Bans on public sexual activity are legitimate. But that fact cannot dictate how states can regulate intimate behavior that occurs in private places.

Blackmun concluded by noting that within three years the Court overturned its decision upholding compulsory flag salutes in public schools in the face of religious objections, and expressed the hope that here too the Court would someday reconsider its analysis. Depriving individuals "of the right to choose for themselves how to conduct their intimate relationships poses a far greater threat to the values most deeply rooted in our Nation's history than tolerance of nonconformity could ever do. Because I think the Court today betrays those values, I dissent."

Justice Stevens (joined by justices Brennan and Marshall) also dissented. His starting point was an understanding of the principle undergirding the Court's privacy cases. He argued that two questions must be answered: (1) May a state prohibit all nonprocreational sex acts, regardless of the gender of the parties? (2) If not, may a state enforce the ban only against same-sex partners?

For Stevens, the principle of the Court's previous privacy cases involved protection of intimate sexual life of both married and unmarried persons. The right was protected when the parties were isolated from others. And it was protected even if the nonreproductive sexual conduct was considered offensive or immoral by a majority. Thus, Georgia could not make criminal all nonprocreational sex acts as the statute at issue on its face (though not as enforced) did. The second question required the state to defend its selective application of the statute against homosexuals but not heterosexuals by putting forward a neutral and legitimate state interest more substantial than dislike for or ignorance about the disfavored group. Stevens argued that the state of Georgia itself did not believe there was such an interest because the state by the very terms of the statute did not choose to ban only gay and lesbian sex; moreover, Georgia prosecutors were not bringing criminal actions against gay and lesbian violators of the statute.

FROM *HARDWICK* TO *LAWRENCE*

The outcry in the gay community over the Court's decision is not difficult to imagine. The gay rights movement described *Hardwick* as its *Dred Scott* case. David A. J. Richards (in *The Case for Gay Rights* [2005]) describes a personal reaction undoubtedly shared by many gays:

> My first response to *Bowers* was an almost physical sense of personal assault not only on myself, as a gay person, but on the subject, constitutional law, that I had, as a teacher and scholar, attempted to impart to my students and readers as one of great human integrity. I grieved that the Supreme Court could so shamelessly betray its trust. (p. 84)

The Court's opinion was seen as callous and insensitive in its dismissal of the fundamental interest at stake as "facetious," as well as in its casual and thoughtless grouping of gay sex with adultery and incest.

But criticism and outrage was not limited to the gay community. *The Washington Post* raised the specter of police in every bedroom; A *New York Times* editorial on July 2, 1986, described White's opinion as "a gratuitous and petty ruling." Further fueling discontent were reports, confirmed a few years later by Justice Powell himself, that he had at first voted to overturn the Georgia statute, but then had second thoughts, prompted possibly by an ignorance of gay life, culture, and sexual practices.

On the other hand, the Reverend Jerry Falwell (1933–2007) praised the decision as an attack on "perverted" behavior. Attorney General Edwin Meese (1931–) pronounced the case a great victory for the Ronald Reagan administration. A week after the ruling, Professor Paul Gewirtz (1986) of Yale University Law School published an op-ed piece in *The New York Times* that captured the essential criticisms. Gewirtz accused the majority of an intellectual failing by refusing to treat, or even respond to, the questions raised in Justice Blackmun's dissent. But worse, Gewirtz charged, the majority failed to acknowledge the human dimension of the issue, adding that "it is one thing to lose; it is even worse to lose believing one's claim has not even received respectful consideration. Fair judicial decision-making requires that consideration. The Court's insensitivity and offhandedness in this case represent more

than a human deficiency; they represent a serious deficiency in the art of judging."

Justice White's opinion came at a time of serious criticism, to which his opinion alludes, aimed at federal judges writing their own values into constitutional law, as allegedly had been done (most egregiously in *Roe v. Wade*, 410 U.S. 113 [1973]) by finding a right to privacy in the due process clause of the Fourteenth Amendment. Certainly White himself was never a strong proponent of this line of cases. In a sense, then, *Hardwick* may be seen as one of the wages of decrying *Roe*. However, with the Court's decision in *Planned Parenthood of Southeastern Pennsylvania v. Casey*, 505 U.S. 833 (1992), both *Roe* and privacy seemed on firmer ground—at least in principle. And when the Court in *Romer v. Evans*, 517 U.S. 620 (1996) declared unconstitutional a Colorado initiative that repealed laws prohibiting discrimination against gays, lesbians, and bisexuals and prevented future laws to protect such individuals, the *Hardwick* decision seemed on shaky grounds (as Justice Antonin Scalia bemoaned in his dissent in *Romer*). From there, it was not a large step to *Lawrence*, simply a long overdue one.

Michael Hardwick did not live to see this ultimate vindication of his rights. He died of AIDS on June 13, 1991, at the age of thirty-seven.

SEE ALSO *Lawrence v. Texas, 539 U.S. 558 (2003); Powell, Lewis F., Jr.; Romer v. Evans, 517 U.S. 620 (1996); Sexual Orientation; White, Byron*

BIBLIOGRAPHY

Arnault, E. Lauren. 2003. "Status, Conduct, and Forced Disclosure: What Does *Bowers v. Hardwick* Really Say?" *UC Davis Law Review* 36: 757–785.

Boswell, John. 1981. *Christianity, Social Tolerance, and Homosexuality: Gay People in Western Europe from the Beginning of the Christian Era to the Fourteenth Century*. Chicago: University of Chicago Press.

Coleman, Andrea Celina. 2004. "Cognitive Dissonance Theory: A Study of *Loving v. Virginia, Bowers v. Hardwick*, and *Lawrence v. Texas*." *Washington and Lee Race and Ethnic Ancestry Law Journal* 10: 75–88.

DeCew, Judith Wagner. 1997. *In Pursuit of Privacy: Law, Ethics, and the Rise of Technology*. Ithaca, NY: Cornell University Press.

D'Emilio, John. 1998. *Sexual Politics, Sexual Communities: The Making of a Homosexual Minority in the United States, 1940–1970*. 2nd edition. Chicago: University of Chicago Press.

Duberman, Martin B.; Martha Vicinus; and George Chauncey, Jr., eds. 1989. *Hidden from History: Reclaiming the Gay and Lesbian Past*. New York: New American Library.

Duong, Phong. 2004. "A Survey of Gay Rights Culminating in *Lawrence v. Texas*." *Gonzaga Law Review* 39: 539–573.

Eskridge, William N. 1999. *Gaylaw: Challenging the Apartheid of the Closet*. Cambridge, MA: Harvard University Press.

Gewirtz, Paul. 1986. "The Court was 'Superficial' in the Homosexuality Case." *New York Times,* July 8. Late city final edition.

Glenn, Richard A. 2003. *The Right to Privacy: Rights and Liberties Under the Law.* Santa Barbara, CA: ABC-CLIO.

Hermann, Donald H. J. 2005. "Pulling the Fig Leaf off the Right of Privacy: Sex and the Constitution." *DePaul Law Review* 54: 909–968.

Irons, Peter. 1988. *The Courage of Their Convictions.* New York: Free Press.

Jeffries, John C., Jr. 2001. *Justice Lewis F. Powell, Jr.: A Biography.* New York: Fordham University Press.

Johnson, Scott Patrick. 2001. "An Analysis of the U.S. Supreme Court's Decision Making in Gay Right Cases (1985–2000)." *Ohio Northern University Law Review* 27: 197–228.

Keynes, Edward. 1996. *Liberty, Property, and Privacy: Toward a Jurisprudence of Substantive Due Process.* University Park: Pennsylvania State University Press.

Knowles, Helen J. 2007. "From a Value to a Right: The Supreme Court's Oh-So-Conscious Move from 'Privacy' to 'Liberty.'" *Ohio Northern University Law Review* 33: 595–620.

McCourt, James. 2003. *Queer Street: Rise and Fall of an American Culture, 1947–1984.* New York: Norton.

Merin, Yuval. 2002. *Equality for Same-Sex Couples: The Legal Recognition of Gay Partnerships in Europe and the United States.* Chicago: University of Chicago Press.

Michaelson, Jay. 2000. "On Listening to the Kulturkampf, Or, How America Overruled *Bowers v. Hardwick,* Even though *Romer v. Evans* Didn't." *Duke Law Journal* 49: 1559–1618.

Mohr, Richard D. 1988. *Gays/Justice: A Study of Ethics, Society, and Law.* New York: Columbia University Press.

Murdoch, Joyce, and Deb Price. 2001. *Courting Justice: Gay Men and Lesbians v. the Supreme Court.* New York: Basic Books.

New York Times. 1986. "Crime in the Bedroom." July 2: A30.

Richards, David A. J. 1998. *Women, Gays, and the Constitution: The Grounds for Feminism and Gay Rights in Culture and Law.* Chicago: University of Chicago Press.

Richards, David A. J. 2005. *The Case for Gay Rights: From* Bowers *to* Lawrence *and Beyond.* Lawrence, Kansas: University Press of Kansas.

Samar, Vincent J. 1991. *The Right to Privacy: Gays, Lesbians, and the Constitution.* Philadelphia: Temple University Press.

Samar, Vincent J. 2005. "Sexual Orientation, the Judicial Response: *Bowers, Lawrence,* and Same-Sex Marriage: A Meeting of Hard and Very Hard Cases." *Saint Louis University Public Law Review* 24: 89–110.

Samuels, Suzanne U. 2004. *First Among Friends: Interest Groups, the U.S. Supreme Court, and the Right to Privacy.* Westport, CT: Praeger.

Spindelman, Marc S. 2001. "Reorienting *Bowers v. Hardwick.*" *North Carolina Law Review* 79: 359–491.

Philip A. Dynia

BOWSHER V. SYNAR, 478 U.S. 714 (1986)

Faced with then-record budget deficits, President Ronald Reagan signed into law the Balanced Budget and Emergency Deficit Control Act of 1985, popularly known as the Gramm-Rudman-Hollings Act. Congressman Michael Synar (1950–1996) immediately challenged its "reporting provisions" as a violation of the separation of powers. These provisions generally required across-the-board budget cuts to reach a target deficit, progressively reducing the budget deficit to zero by the end of five years. The directors of the Congressional Budget Office and the Office of Management and Budget were to estimate the deficit each upcoming fiscal year. If it exceeded a maximum deficit by a specified amount, the directors calculated program-by-program budget cuts and jointly reported their estimates and calculations to the comptroller general. In turn, the comptroller general reported his own estimates and reduction calculations. The act then required the president to comply with the comptroller general's report and order a "sequestration" of the specified budget reductions, which would become effective automatically after a waiting period.

Synar argued that these provisions violated the separation of powers as an impermissible delegation of legislative power and, alternatively, as an impermissible vesting of the executive power in the comptroller general, Charles Bowsher, a legislative officer subject to congressional removal and control. In a parallel action, the National Treasury Employees Union, whose members would lose a cost-of-living adjustment under the act, brought a similar challenge. Bowsher, the U.S. Senate, and the Speaker and Bipartisan Leadership Group of the U.S. House of Representatives intervened to defend the act's constitutionality. Several members of Congress, however, joined Synar's challenge. Both the president and Congress had anticipated the challenges: The president's signing statement expressed reservations about the act, and Congress provided for expedited review and a fallback arrangement in the event of a successful challenge.

Writing for the Court, Chief Justice Warren Burger decided the consolidated appeals on the grounds that the reporting provisions violated the separation of powers. The majority relied heavily on the lower court's reasoning, likely written by then-D.C. Circuit judge Antonin Scalia. Congress vested the comptroller general with executive power. The comptroller general, however, was a legislative officer, removable by a congressional joint resolution. This removal power created a "here-and-now subservience" of the comptroller general to Congress. Congress had created an office subject to itself that could exercise executive power. The Court declared the act unconstitutional and left the removal provision in place but invoked the act's fallback provisions that eliminated the comptroller general's new powers.

Justices John Paul Stevens and Thurgood Marshall concurred in the judgment, but found no difficulty with the congressional removal power. Instead, relying on *INS v. Chadha*, 462 U.S. 919 (1983), they concluded that the act failed to comply with the Constitution's bicameralism and presentment requirements. Congress cannot delegate its lawmaking power to any subset of itself or an agent, such as the comptroller general. The concurrence concluded that the act did precisely that by vesting the comptroller general with important policymaking powers that carry the force of law.

Justice Byron White dissented and offered a functionalist defense of the act. According to White, the act neither constituted an encroachment nor an aggrandizement of congressional power. The act's removal provision did not make the comptroller general subservient to Congress. Congress had never used its power to remove a comptroller general. Moreover, the power did not provide for removal at will and, in the absence of executive consent, was more onerous than impeachment and conviction. White questioned whether the Court ought to police the separation of powers in the case as the legislative process "afford[ed] each branch ample opportunity to defend its interests."

Justice Harry Blackmun's dissent noted that even if the removal provision raised a separation-of-powers question, the plaintiffs lacked standing to challenge it. They had sought only to nullify the automatic budget-reduction provisions, not any actual or threatened use of the removal power. Blackmun thought it would be better to strike the removal provision, as the defendants suggested, rather than strike down the reporting provisions.

Curiously, the central separation-of-powers question raised by the act and noted by the president's signing statement was never addressed: whether Congress can compel the president to follow the comptroller general's rulings regarding amounts to be cut from the budget.

SEE ALSO *Separation of Powers*

BIBLIOGRAPHY

Elliott, E. Donald. 1987. "Regulating the Deficit After *Bowsher v. Synar*." *Yale Journal on Regulation* 4: 317–362.

Tuan Samahon

BOYD V. UNITED STATES, 116 U.S. 616 (1886)

In the late nineteenth and early twentieth centuries, the federal government's regulatory and revenue-collection powers were radically augmented to enable it to manage the effects of the era's revolutionary economic and social transformations. To strengthen the government, it was necessary to enhance its powers to extract an unprecedented amount of information from businesses and individuals. Beginning in 1880s, businesses and individuals resisted these new information-gathering initiatives by challenging them in federal court as invasions of constitutional privacy.

In *Boyd v. United States*, 116 U.S. 616 (1886), a tax case involving resistance to the government's efforts to subpoena business records, the Supreme Court, citing privacy concerns, dealt what might have been a crippling blow to the entire process of building a powerful centralized modern administrative state. In 1882 the supervising architect in charge of constructing new federal buildings in Philadelphia began accepting bids for glass to be used in the new structures. Those bidding were permitted to assume that any imported glass would enter the country duty-free. E. A. Boyd and Sons won the contract. Because the project was rushed, the architect asked that Boyd supply him with glass that was already on hand, and on which a duty had already been paid, with the promise that Boyd could import an equivalent amount of glass later, duty-free.

Problems developed when, first, to cut the glass on hand to the relevant size, Boyd had to destroy more glass than it had permission to import duty-free, and, second, a significant amount of the subsequently imported glass was shattered in transit. Soon Boyd was charged with making false statements to the government concerning the imported glass. The U.S. government seized thirty-five of the cases Boyd was trying to import, and, by court order, insisted that Boyd produce the business's internal records concerning twenty-nine cases that had been imported earlier. Boyd was told that if the company refused to hand over these records, a judgment would be entered against it, and the thirty-five cases would be forfeited. The company resisted, arguing that the compulsory production of business records violated its Fourth Amendment right against unreasonable searches and seizures and its Fifth Amendment right against self-incrimination.

Courts had traditionally held that the Fifth Amendment's privilege against self-incrimination could be invoked only by criminal defendants called upon to testify at their own trials. Writing for a unanimous Court in *Boyd*, though, Justice Joseph Bradley held for the first time that the privilege could be invoked by a nondefendant in a civil proceeding, and, moreover, he newly fused that privilege with the Fourth Amendment's protection against unreasonable searches and seizures. "The principles laid down in this opinion," Bradley thundered, "affect the very essence of constitutional liberty and security.... It is not the breaking of his doors, and the rummaging of his drawers, that constitutes the essence of the offence; but it is the invasion of the indefensible right of personal security, personal liberty, and private property."

In subsequent years, in a series of cases involving novel efforts at railroad regulation and antitrust, the Supreme Court gradually worked through the question of whether *Boyd*'s staunchly pro-privacy ruling would be interpreted strictly—which would have placed perhaps formidable legal barriers in the face of the newly developing modern administrative state—or more flexibly. The Court ultimately arrived at a modus vivendi relatively friendly to the claims of the modern state: While deeming privacy important, and the Fourth and Fifth Amendments relevant, the Court bowed to perceived necessity, holding repeatedly that if the government followed proper procedures in advancing legitimate ends, it would be given the power necessary to collect all of the formerly private information necessary to regulate in the broader public interest. In time, in part relying on the *Boyd* precedent, the Court carved out new forms of privacy protections that, while leaving the new administrative state's powers largely intact, set up an elaborate skein of rules governing searches and seizures by the police and limiting the government's powers to regulate reproductive and sexual autonomy.

SEE ALSO *Fifth Amendment; Fourth Amendment*

BIBLIOGRAPHY

Kersch, Ken I. 2004. *Constructing Civil Liberties: Discontinuities in the Development of American Constitutional Law.* New York: Cambridge University Press.

Kersch, Ken I. 2008. "The Right to Privacy." In *The Bill of Rights in Modern America,* ed. David Bodenhamer and James W. Ely Jr. 2nd edition, pp. 215–240. Indianapolis: Indiana University Press.

Ken I. Kersch

BOY SCOUTS OF AMERICA V. DALE, 530 U.S. 640 (2000)

Boy Scouts of America v. Dale, 530 U.S. 640 (2000) considered whether the Boy Scouts of America could be barred by state law from discriminating against an openly gay scoutmaster. The U.S. Supreme Court held that application of New Jersey's law forbidding sexual-orientation discrimination by public accommodations violated the Boy Scouts' First Amendment right of expressive association.

The case began when the Boy Scouts revoked the adult membership of James Dale, an assistant scoutmaster and exemplary former Boy Scout, on the ground that the Boy Scouts "specifically forbid membership to homosexuals." Dale had never disclosed his sexual orientation to his troop membership or the Boy Scouts leadership; instead, the leadership had acted in response to a newspaper article identifying Dale as copresident of the Rutgers University Lesbian/Gay Alliance. Dale filed suit in the New Jersey Chancery Court seeking reinstatement and damages. The trial court held for the Boy Scouts, but the state appellate and supreme court found in Dale's favor.

At the U.S. Supreme Court, the Boy Scouts argued that application of the New Jersey law against discrimination violated its First Amendment freedoms of speech, expressive association, and intimate association. In its opening brief, the organization wrote that the case involved "the freedom of a private, voluntary, noncommercial organization to create and interpret its own moral code, and to choose leaders and define membership criteria accordingly." More specifically, the Boy Scouts described the question presented as "whether a state law requiring a Boy Scout Troop to appoint an avowed homosexual and gay rights activist as an Assistant Scoutmaster responsible for communicating Boy Scouting's moral values to youth members abridges First Amendment rights of Freedom of Speech and Expression."

James Dale presented a significantly different picture of both the facts and the law at issue. He presented the question as: "Whether a large, unselective membership organization can invoke the First Amendment to defeat application of an anti-discrimination law and expel a long-standing exemplary member, when none of the expressive purposes that bring its members together are significantly altered or burdened by application of that law." As a factual matter, he contested the Boy Scouts' claim that excluding gay people was central to the organization's expressive purposes, showing that the organization discouraged its leaders from discussing sexuality at all. He argued that the Boy Scouts programs and materials did not communicate any message about homosexuality or gay people, that an openly gay scoutmaster would not affect the Boy Scouts expressive aims, and that any burden that might exist could be justified by New Jersey's compelling interest in eradicating sexual-orientation discrimination. Dale also argued that the Boy Scouts' close involvement with government, including through sponsorship of individual troops, precluded treatment of the organization as a highly private association.

A wide array of amici curiae presented related arguments to the Court from the perspective of cities, states, civil rights advocates, civic organizations, and religious bodies. Among many others, the American Bar Association, the American Psychological Association, and the National Education Association filed briefs in support of Dale, and the National Club Association, the U.S.

Former Boy Scoutmaster James Dale, seated with his attorney, New York, 1998. In a five-to-four decision, the Supreme Court ruled that the Boy Scouts of America, as a private organization, held the right to exclude homosexuals from serving as scoutmasters. The court reasoned that forcing inclusion of a member who holds beliefs contrary to the organization violated the group's right of expressive association guaranteed in the First Amendment. **PHOTOGRAPH BY ELIZABETH LIPPMAN. GAMMA LIAISON NETWORK.**

Catholic Conference, and Concerned Women for America supported the Boy Scouts.

On June 28, 2000, the Court issued its five-to-four ruling in the Boy Scouts' favor. The majority opinion, authored by Chief Justice Rehnquist, focused on the expressive association claim, explaining that "forced inclusion of an unwanted person in a group" infringes the right "if the presence of that person affects in a significant way the group's ability to advocate public or private viewpoints." The Court determined that the Boy Scouts engages in expressive activity and deferred to the Boy Scouts' assertion that the antigay position was related to that expression, sincerely held, and important to the organization.

Building on this point, the Court determined that "Dale's presence in the Boy Scouts would, at the very least, force the organization to send a message, both to the youth members and to the world, that the Boy Scouts accepts homosexual conduct as a legitimate form of behavior." In response to Dale's observation that the Boy Scouts permitted heterosexual leaders who oppose the antigay policy to remain in scouting, the Court added that those leaders send a different message than a gay

scoutmaster would and that the organization has a First Amendment right to send one message but not the other.

Two dissenting opinions contested the majority's analysis of both the facts and the law. Justice John Paul Stevens, joined by Justices David Souter, Ruth Bader Ginsburg, and Stephen Breyer, wrote that the New Jersey antidiscrimination law did not impose a serious burden on the Boy Scouts. Reviewing the Boy Scouts' public and private statements, he disagreed with the majority's deferential approach and found "no evidence" that the organization made "any collective effort to foster beliefs about homosexuality." He observed that the Court had never before found a claimed associational right to trump a state antidiscrimination law, and maintained that the Boy Scouts' position was far too equivocal to justify the majority's ruling in this case.

Justice Souter filed an additional, brief concurrence, joined by justices Ginsburg and Breyer. He observed that the Boy Scouts' expressive association claim should have failed, not because the organization's views contrast with the "laudable decline in stereotypical thinking about homosexuality," but rather because the Boy Scouts had not advocated its views about homosexuality clearly, over time, and in an unequivocal way. Without that clarity, Justice Souter argued, antidiscrimination laws could be easily and unduly trumped.

The case is central to First Amendment expressive association jurisprudence in the early twenty-first century. Important questions remain, however, because the majority failed to explain why New Jersey's antidiscrimination commitment was not sufficiently compelling to justify barring the Boy Scouts from discriminating. It is also too soon to tell whether the decision will be read broadly to undermine antidiscrimination protections, as the dissents and some advocates have predicted, or narrowly and cabined largely to its facts.

The Boy Scouts has maintained the exclusionary policy, leaving it as the only major, national, nonreligious youth organization to discriminate in membership based on sexual orientation. This has resulted in serious costs. Some local governments and other troop sponsors have ended the free or low-cost leases or other special benefits they previously granted to the organization. Post-decision litigation has concentrated largely on challenging government funding to the Boy Scouts because of the discriminatory policy. Political pressure has also mounted, both to change and to retain the policy, suggesting that the legal and political questions raised by the case will remain important for years to come.

SEE ALSO *First Amendment; Freedom of Association; Sexual Orientation*

BIBLIOGRAPHY

Carpenter, Dale. 2001. "Expressive Association and Anti-discrimination Law after *Dale*: A Tripartite Approach." *Minnesota Law Review* 85: 1515–1589.

Epstein, Richard A. 2000. "The Constitutional Perils of Moderation: The Case of the Boy Scouts." *Southern California Law Review* 74: 119–143.

Hunter, Nan D. 2001. "Accommodating the Public Sphere: Beyond the Market Model." *Minnesota Law Review* 85: 1591–1637.

Sunder, Madhavi. 2001. "Cultural Dissent." *Stanford Law Review* 54: 495–567.

Suzanne B. Goldberg

BRADLEY, JOSEPH
1813–1892

Joseph P. Bradley was an associate justice of the U.S. Supreme Court from 1870 to 1892. A former railroad attorney, Bradley generally supported conservative business interests and most Republican positions, with the

Supreme Court Justice Joseph Bradley. *Part of the fifteen-member electoral commission to settle the contested presidential election of 1876, Bradley cast the deciding vote, awarding the disputed electoral college votes of Louisiana, South Carolina, Florida, and Oregon to Republican candidate Rutherford B. Hayes.* THE LIBRARY OF CONGRESS

exception of civil rights enforcement, during his tenure on the Court. Scholarly and thoughtful, he was widely regarded by his contemporaries and for many years after as the finest lawyer among those he served with.

Born in Berne, New York, in 1813, Bradley graduated from Rutgers College in 1836, and gained national prominence as one of the top railroad attorneys in the nation. Though he had no prior judicial experience, he was nominated to the Court by President Ulysses Grant (1822–1885) and won confirmation in the Senate by a vote of forty-six to nine. Bradley immediately weighed in on the controversial Legal Tender Act of 1862, which compelled creditors to accept U.S. paper money for debt payment. In *Knox v. Lee*, 79 U.S. 457 (1871), Bradley cast one of the five votes to uphold the act. Though there is no evidence that Grant used the legal tender dispute as a litmus test in selecting Bradley, Republicans were pleased with the outcome.

Bradley again aligned with the GOP when he cast the deciding vote on the fifteen-member electoral commission set up to decide the disputed presidential election of 1876. Divided evenly among Democrats and Republicans, originally Justice David Davis (1815–1886) was to be the decisive final member of the group. But when Davis left the Court, and therefore the commission, to become an Illinois senator, Bradley took his place on the commission and ultimately sided with his fellow Republicans to swing the election to Rutherford B. Hayes (1822–1893).

Though Bradley dissented in the *Slaughter-House Cases*, 83 U.S. 36 (1873), arguing that the privileges and immunities clause protects businesses from state regulation, he sided with the states in other areas. In the *Granger Cases* (1877), Bradley voted with the majority and had considerable influence on Chief Justice Morrison Waite's majority opinion. In *Munn v. Illinois*, 94 U.S. 113 (1877), Waite articulated Bradley's idea that states could use their police power to regulate businesses affecting the public interest. In another case involving states, Bradley wrote the opinion of the Court in *Hans v. Louisiana*, 134 U.S. 1 (1890), holding that the Eleventh Amendment reaffirmed the constitutional principle that states are immune from suits in federal court brought by their own citizens.

Despite his general agreement with Republican positions, he differed with them on the issue of civil rights. He voted against the Enforcement Acts of 1870 to 1871 and the Civil Rights Acts of 1871 and 1875. His majority opinion in the *Civil Rights Cases*, 109 U.S. 3 (1883) stuck down the Civil Rights Act of 1875, holding that Congress could not use the enforcement provision of the Fourteenth Amendment to ban private discrimination, even in public accommodations such as restaurants and hotels. He disparaged the legislation as making African Americans "the special favorite of the laws." Similarly, in *Bradwell v. State of Illinois*, 83 U.S. 130 (1873), he voted with the majority to allow states to bar women from practicing law. In his separate concurrence, Bradley wrote: "The paramount destiny and mission of woman are to fulfill the noble and benign offices of wife and mother. This is the law of the creator."

SEE ALSO *Bradwell v. Illinois, 83 U.S. 130 (1873); Civil Rights Cases, 109 U.S. 3 (1883); Election of 1876*

BIBLIOGRAPHY

Fairman, Charles. 1941. "Mr. Justice Bradley's Appointment to the Supreme Court and the Legal Tender Cases." *Harvard Law Review* 54: 977–1034.

Fairman, Charles. 1964. "Mr. Justice Bradley." In *Mr. Justice*, ed. Allison Dunham and Philip B. Kurland. Rev. edition, pp. 65–91. Chicago: University of Chicago Press.

Fairman, Charles. 1988. *Five Justices and the Electoral Commission of 1877*. New York: Macmillan.

Artemus Ward

BRADWELL V. ILLINOIS, 83 U.S. 130 (1873)

In an eight-to-one decision in *Bradwell v. State of Illinois*, 83 U.S. 130 (1873), the U.S. Supreme Court upheld an Illinois Supreme Court ruling denying Myra Bradwell a license to practice law on the grounds that she was a woman. The effect of the decision was twofold. It severely limited the scope of the privileges and immunities clause of the Fourteenth Amendment to the U.S. Constitution, and it shifted the primary locus of the fight for women's full citizenship status, rights, and privileges from the U.S. Supreme Court to state legislatures. After *Bradwell*, women who wanted to become lawyers continued to apply for state law licenses, but turned to state legislatures to eliminate prohibitions based on sex after state courts rejected their applications on gender grounds. The *Bradwell* decision left unsettled the issue of whether the equal protection and due process clause of the Fourteenth Amendment applied to women.

BACKGROUND

Myra Bradwell, like the other mid-nineteenth-century women who wanted to be lawyers, was a woman's rights activist, and her law license application was part of that movement. Through her effort, Bradwell hoped to establish women's right to work in any profession or occupation, to practice law as a career, and to use her position as a lawyer to advance and enforce the social, civil, and political rights of women. In the summer of 1869 Bradwell was one of seven women who publicly sought entry into the legal profession: Five women (four white and one African American) enrolled in law schools, while Bradwell and Arabella Mansfield of Iowa each applied for a state license to practice law. They acted on the notion that the Fourteenth Amendment, ratified in 1868 granted women full citizenship rights, including the right to practice law. Bradwell was the only one of this group whose application was denied.

The legal profession to which Bradwell sought entry was in the midst of a transformation. The new, and increasingly dominant, view was that the law was a science and should only be interpreted and administered by professional experts. Law schools began replacing apprenticeships as the preferred method of legal study, and state legislatures began to revive the use of law licensing and certification requirements for admission. Despite objections from elite lawyers, the proliferation of law schools resulted in a number of institutions that admitted women and minority men, and the new licensing statutes served to standardized admissions, lessening the opportunities for nepotism and overt discrimination. Bradwell had studied law in her husband's law office and did not attend law school, but she did comply with her state's new licensing requirements and used them to support her application.

AT THE ILLINOIS SUPREME COURT

The Illinois Supreme Court initially denied Bradwell's application on the ground of coverture. Under this common-law principle, when a woman married, her legal identity merged with her husband's, and the husband became the sole embodiment of the union. Thus a wife could neither enter into contracts, sue or be sued, nor execute a will, and all of her personal property, including her wages, the control of her real property, and all the proceeds from her land, became the property of her husband. In a letter to Bradwell, the court explained that because she was a married woman and therefore could not enter into contracts, she would not be bound as an attorney must be in obligation to her clients, and therefore could not practice law. Bradwell responded to the court's letter with a motion to reconsider.

Bradwell submitted two additional briefs to support her position and to establish legal grounds to take her case beyond the state court should it rule against her. The first argued that the common-law notions of coverture no longer applied, and therefore her married status was not a prohibition. The second brief incorporated an argument called the *new departure* that was being employed by suffragist Virginia Minor in her suit against Reese Happersett, a state registrar in Missouri, for refusing to allow her to register to vote. Minor asserted that the right to vote was one of the privileges and immunities protected by the Fourteenth Amendment. Bradwell adapted the argument to her case, asserting that the Fourteenth Amendment and the 1866 Civil Rights Act supported women's right to practice law. Bradwell claimed that the denial of her application based on her status as a married woman violated her U.S. citizenship rights as established by the equal protection clause of the Fourteenth Amendment and the Civil Rights Act. Bradwell also claimed that Illinois had violated the privileges and immunities of her *state* citizenship under Article IV of the Constitution, reasoning that since she was born in Vermont and thus was a citizen of that state, when she moved to Illinois she was guaranteed the full privileges and immunities that were granted to every other citizen of Illinois.

The Illinois Supreme Court denied Bradwell's appeal, ruling definitively that, married or not, no woman could be admitted to the Illinois bar. Chief Justice Charles B. Lawrence wrote the opinion and rested the decision on a mixture of natural and positive law, rather than coverture. He first explained that because the legislature had not intended women be admitted when it passed the law regulating the profession, the court could not grant Bradwell's application, even though women were not expressly excluded. Chief Justice Lawrence further opined

that God's design of separate spheres for men and women prohibited women from being lawyers. Bradwell appealed the Illinois decision to the U.S. Supreme Court.

AT THE U.S. SUPREME COURT

Though Bradwell desired to frame her appeal in the broadest terms, casting the case as a woman's rights issue, her attorney, Matthew Carpenter, narrowed the issues. Carpenter, a U.S. senator, veteran of the Supreme Court bar, leading expert on constitutional issues, and a woman's rights supporter, based the appeal on the privileges and immunities clause of the Fourteenth Amendment. He did assert that women were citizens, but he did not present Bradwell's argument that the court's denial of her law license violated the equal protection clause of the Fourteenth Amendment. Carpenter only argued that the right to work in an occupation was a right of citizenship that the privileges and immunities clause protected from state interference. Further, because the majority of the justices on the Court were opposed to women's suffrage, Carpenter distinguished suffrage as a political right and asserted that allowing women the civil right to practice law would not be grounds to give women the political right to vote.

The Supreme Court considered Bradwell's case in concert with several cases from New Orleans involving the right of the state to control the slaughterhouse industry in that city. At the heart of both cases was how to reconcile an individual's civil right to work and a state's right to regulate occupations within its borders. At issue in the *Slaughter-House Cases*, 83 U.S. 36 (1873) was a new law that prohibited all slaughtering in New Orleans except at two regulated facilities. Numerous slaughterhouses were closed as a result of this law, resulting in the displacement of countless workers. These male workers argued, like Bradwell, that the state law was an infringement on their constitutionally protected right to work. In both *Bradwell* and the *Slaughter-House Cases,* the Court considered the larger implications of its decisions: A favorable ruling would make the right of laboring men and women to work in their chosen field superior to a state's right to control who works in what occupation or profession within its borders.

Matthew Carpenter also represented the Slaughter-House Company in the Louisiana cases. He remained consistent in his argument that the Fourteenth Amendment did protect an individual's right to work, but distinguished factually between the two cases. Carpenter contended in Bradwell's case that the right to work in one's chosen occupation was a privilege protected by the Fourteenth Amendment and that there was no overriding state interest sufficient to interfere with that privilege. In the *Slaughter-House Cases,* in contrast, Carpenter argued that the Louisiana law limiting the right to work was necessary as a health measure and therefore constitutional

MYRA BRADWELL'S RESPONSE TO THE U.S. SUPREME COURT DECISION

∎

We applied at the September Term, 1869, of the Supreme Court of Illinois for admission to the bar ... and were refused admission on the sole ground that we were a woman. Believing that liberty of pursuit was guaranteed to every citizen by the fourteenth amendment, under laws which should operate equally upon all, we applied for and obtained a writ of error. ... We had hoped in taking this case to the Supreme Court of the United States to have demonstrated that women have some rights and privileges as citizens of the United States, which are guaranteed by the 14th amendment. ... Although we have not succeeded in obtaining an opinion as we hoped, which should affect the rights of women throughout the nation, we are more than compensated for all our trouble in seeing, as the result of the agitation, statutes passed in several of the States, including our own, admitting women [to practice law] upon the same terms as men.

SOURCE: Myra Bradwell, "The XIV Amendment and Our Case." 5 *Chicago Legal News* 354 (April 19, 1873).

Gwen Hoerr Jordan

under the police power of the state. The Supreme Court announced the Louisiana case first. Upholding the Louisiana law, it based its decision on its interpretation of the privileges and immunities clause, ruling that the state laws in question did not violate the Fourteenth Amendment because they were a legitimate use of the state's power. This ruling set up its decision in the *Bradwell* case, which it announced one day later, upholding the denial of Bradwell's application to practice law.

The majority decision in Bradwell's case, supported by five of the nine justices, based its ruling on constitutional grounds and abstained from any comment of the issue of women's rights. Relying on the Fourteenth Amendment, it ruled that the right to practice law was not a right protected under its privileges and immunities clause. The decision left the regulation of attorney licensing up to each state. The Court chose not to comment on the lower court's rationale, which was based on a patriarchal interpretation of natural law. The majority also avoided a ruling on the state's relationship to women, though its decision effectively upheld limitations imposed by state governments on

women's rights, including women's suffrage and their right to work in their chosen occupation.

Justice Joseph Bradley, joined by Justices Stephen Field and Noah Swayne (all three of whom dissented in the *Slaughter-House Cases*) concurred in the decision but rejected the majority reasoning in an attempt to use the case to explicitly define the relationship between women and the state. They argued, consistent with their position in the *Slaughter-House Cases*, that the Fourteenth Amendment created a new general rule making positive the natural right of male citizens to pursue their chosen occupation. Therefore, Bradley asserted, a state could not interfere with that right without due process. Through Bradwell's case, Bradley sought to establish that women were exempt from this rule. Bradley rested his opinion on the principle that men and women had different spheres. Women had no right to practice law, he reasoned, as the law fell completely within man's sphere.

AFTERMATH

Throughout the nineteenth century, one by one, state courts and legislatures admitted women to the practice of law in their states. While the U.S. Supreme Court was deliberating Bradwell's appeal, Bradwell joined with a small group of women's rights activists in Illinois and drafted a bill titled, "An act to secure to all persons freedom in the selection of occupation, profession or employment." The bill proposed "that no person shall be precluded or debarred from any occupation, profession or employment on account of sex." State legislators added three exceptions to the bill: Women could not use the law to secure entrance to the military, engage in road construction, or secure the right to serve on juries. After several votes and much debate, the legislature passed the bill and the governor signed it into law in March 1872, before the Supreme Court rendered its decision in *Bradwell*. Bradwell chose to not reapply for her law license and to wait for the Court's decision.

In 1873 Alta Hulett became the first licensed woman lawyer in Illinois. Hulett, who helped draft and advocate the enabling statute, had been denied her license in 1871 after studying law for a year and passing the Illinois bar exam. She had to delay her reapplication because, in addition to the enabling law, the Illinois legislature had increased the number of years of required legal study from one to two. In 1873 Hulett completed an additional year of study and passed a second bar examination, receiving the highest score of all twenty-eight applicants. For her part, Bradwell continued to refuse to reapply for admission under the new law, maintaining her position that the Illinois Supreme Court had erred in its decision and that it should admit her to the bar based on her original application.

Over the next twenty years, Bradwell advocated for women's rights and law reforms primarily as editor of the weekly *Chicago Legal News*, a nationally respected newspaper. Bradwell had established the *Chicago Legal News* in 1868 and, together with her husband, lawyer James Bradwell, founded a company that printed and published the paper. Bradwell used the *News* to advance a wide range of reforms, including railroad regulation, higher standards in the legal profession, improved legal procedures, and the advancement of the social, civil, and political rights of African Americans and women. In 1890 the Illinois Supreme Court, persuaded by James Bradwell, reconsidered Myra Bradwell's 1869 application and granted her a law license. Two years later, Bradwell was also admitted to the practice of law before the U.S. Supreme Court. She died in 1894 at the age of sixty-two.

SEE ALSO *Civil Rights Act of 1866; Fourteenth Amendment; Minor v. Happersett, 88 U.S. 162 (1875)*

BIBLIOGRAPHY

Babcock, Barbara. 1998. "Feminist Lawyers." *Stanford Law Review* 50: 1689–1708.

Drachman, Virginia. 1998. *Sisters in Law: Women Lawyers in Modern American History.* Cambridge, MA: Harvard University Press.

DuBois, Ellen Carol. 1993. "Taking the Law into Our Own Hands: Bradwell, Minor, and Suffrage Militance in the 1870s." In *Visible Women: New Essays on American Activism*, ed. Nancy A. Hewitt and Suzanne Lebsock, 19–40. Urbana: University of Illinois Press.

Friedman, Jane M. 1993. *America's First Woman Lawyer: The Biography of Myra Bradwell.* Buffalo, NY: Prometheus.

Gilliam, Nancy T. 1987. "A Professional Pioneer: Myra Bradwell's Fight to Practice Law." *Law and History Review* 5: 105–133.

Goddard, Caroline K. 2001. "Bradwell, Myra Colby." In *Women Building Chicago 1790–1990*, ed. Rima Lunin Schultz and Adele Hast, 112–114. Bloomington: Indiana University Press.

Hoff, Joan. 1991. *Law, Gender, and Injustice: A Legal History of U. S. Women.* New York: New York University Press.

Morello, Karen Berger. 1986. *The Invisible Bar.* Boston: Beacon.

Olsen, Frances. 1986. "From False Paternalism to False Equality; Judicial Assaults on Feminist Community, Illinois 1869–1895." *Michigan Law Review* 84: 1518–1541.

Gwen Hoerr Jordan

BRANDEIS, LOUIS
1856–1941

Louis Dembitz Brandeis, who sat on the U.S. Supreme Court from 1916 to 1939, was an innovator in the law. He played a major role in creating the basis for the nation's protection of privacy and speech, helped

Supreme Court Justice Louis Brandeis. *As a young attorney, Brandeis shifted the focus of his briefs from relying on previous legal decisions to supplying as much factual information as possible to explain why his position was consistent with current societal norms, setting a new standard in Constitutional court cases. While serving on the nation's highest court, he continued to transform the American legal system with his decisions on the rights of the individual, particularly in the areas of privacy and speech.* © **CORBIS-BETTMANN**

revolutionize its jurisprudence by emphasizing social facts rather than legal doctrines, and articulated its philosophy of judicial restraint.

BRANDEIS AS AN ATTORNEY

Born in Louisville, Kentucky, Brandeis received his education in the Louisville public schools; Dresden, Germany's Annen-Realschule; and Harvard Law School. Shortly after he left Harvard in 1878, he and classmate Samuel Warren (1852–1910) opened a law partnership in Boston. Responding to his new role as an attorney for small businessmen, Brandeis developed an innovative conception of the roles of both the lawyer and the law.

Brandeis came to believe that to assess and respond to his clients' needs, he had to understand not only their immediate problems but the economic context in which they arose, and to familiarize himself not only with legal

> *Experience should teach us to be most on our guard to protect liberty when the Government's purposes are beneficent. Men born to freedom are naturally alert to repel invasion of their liberty by evil-minded rulers. The greatest dangers to liberty lurk in insidious encroachment by men of zeal, well-meaning but without understanding.*
>
> SOURCE: Louis Brandeis, *Olmstead v. United States,* 277 U.S. 438, 479 (1928) (dissenting).

precepts but with the situations to which such rules would be applied. That realization illuminated his emerging legal philosophy, which held that law had to be consistent with societal needs and that societal needs could be assessed only through an accumulation of facts. Law, he decided, was and should be based on history rather than abstract logic or traditional legal doctrines.

When Brandeis was asked to defend Oregon's maximum-hours law for women before a skeptical U.S. Supreme Court, he submitted a brief that contained only two pages of legal precedents but over one hundred pages of factual support for his argument that society would benefit from limiting the number of hours of work that employers could demand from women laborers. His strategy worked; the Court upheld the law (*Muller v. Oregon*, 208 U.S. 412 [1908]). The fact-filled "Brandeis brief" became the model for American constitutional litigation. It has proven particularly important in major civil liberties and civil rights cases such as *Brown v. Board of Education*, 347 U.S. 483 (1954), in which fact-based briefs about the impact of segregated education on young African-American children helped persuade the Supreme Court to strike down the "separate but equal" standard.

Brandeis also believed that law had to be moral in order to be legitimate and that attorneys had an obligation to work on behalf of the people rather than only as employees for wealthy corporations. This conviction led him to involve himself in public causes, beginning in 1893 with a nine-year fight against Boston Elevated Railway's attempt to acquire a monopoly over Boston's transportation system. He also redesigned Massachusetts's utilities laws, invented Savings Bank Life Insurance so that workers could provide for their families, designed much of President Woodrow Wilson's antitrust policy, and advised President Franklin Roosevelt to enact unemployment insurance.

Brandeis advocated legalization of unions, minimum-wage and maximum-hours laws, public ownership of Alaska's natural resources, and, during the Great Depression of the 1930s, public works projects. His articles, collected as *Business: A Profession* (1914), expressed his belief that overly large companies were inefficient and that businesses had an obligation to be socially responsible. He declined to accept fees for his efforts on behalf of the public and, in fact, reimbursed his firm for the hours he spent in such efforts. That practice helped create the American *pro bono* ("for the public good") tradition, and led to the media's dubbing Brandeis the "People's Attorney."

In the early days of their partnership, Brandeis and Warren had been incensed at the way journalists violated socialite Warren's privacy. In reaction, they wrote an article arguing that the law had to protect individual privacy and the right "to be let alone." "The Right to Privacy," which appeared in the 1890–1891 *Harvard Law Review*, is generally credited with being one of the most influential law review articles ever published, and it is still cited today in cases involving issues from abortion and gay rights to wiretapping and the right against unreasonable searches and seizures.

Brandeis's ideas about law and society developed as a result of his professional experiences. In the mid-1880s, for example, he opposed women's suffrage. He participated in social reform efforts during the 1890s with activist women such as Jane Addams (1860–1935), however, and that led him to believe that women were as able as men to function as thoughtful voters. Initially dubious about unions, he become a firm supporter of them after being impressed by the union leaders with whom he negotiated on behalf of clients. Such changes in his own thinking reinforced his beliefs that education was a lifelong process, that experience was the great teacher, and that law had to change as people experimented with new phenomena and new ideas.

BRANDEIS THE JUSTICE

Brandeis carried his fact-based jurisprudence to the U.S. Supreme Court when Woodrow Wilson appointed him to that tribunal in 1916. There he repeatedly voted against "bigness" in government (*Myers v. United States*, 272 U.S. 52 [1926]; *Louisville v. Radford*, 295 U.S. 555 [1935]) and business (*Bedford v. Journeymen*, 274 U.S. 37 [1927]; *Quaker City Cab v. Pennsylvania*, 277 U.S. 389 [1928]), while maintaining that state governments needed the freedom to experiment with solutions to contemporary societal problems (*Liggett v. Lee*, 288 U.S. 517 [1933]). He favored judicial restraint, and, in *Ashwander v. TVA*, 297 U.S. 288 (1936), established tightly self-limiting criteria for Supreme Court involvement in constitutional litigation. These included the Court's rendering decisions about the constitutionality of a statute only when a decision on lesser grounds was impossible and, even then, handing down decisions that were as narrow as possible.

Brandeis also continued to emphasize privacy. When the Court upheld what it saw as the government's constitutional power to wiretap a suspected criminal at will, he dissented, writing that the founding fathers had included the "right to be let alone" in the Constitution, even though the word *privacy* does not appear in that document (*Olmstead v. United States*, 277 U.S. 438 [1929]). The right to privacy, he insisted, had to be interpreted broadly. "Beliefs," "thoughts," "emotions," and "sensations" had to be protected from government intrusion because the free flow of ideas was crucial to a democratic nation. It did not matter if the government's motive for violating privacy was law enforcement. "Experience," Brandeis wrote in his dissent in *Olmstead*, "should teach us to be most on our guard to protect liberty when the Government's purposes are beneficent," because "the greatest dangers to liberty lurk in insidious encroachment by men of zeal, well-meaning but without understanding."

Brandeis's approach to privacy reflected his democratic ideals. One of his colleagues described him as an "implacable democrat" (quoted in Bickel 1957, p. 163); and another commented that to Brandeis, "democracy is not a political program. It is a religion" (quoted in Richberg 1932, p. 137). His formulation of democracy emphasized the rights of the individual, particularly as they affected human dignity and the ability to participate in the democratic process. He believed that democracy could not work unless all citizens had access to as many ideas about public policy issues as possible, so that they could make intelligent choices among them and the politicians who espoused them. He therefore dissented in a number of 1920 speech cases and argued that unpopular and even potentially dangerous views had to be permitted in order to preserve democracy (*Schaefer v. U.S.*, 251 U.S. 466; *Pierce v. U.S.*, 252 U.S. 239; and *Gilbert v. Minnesota*, 254 U.S. 325). The culmination of his writing about speech came in his concurring opinion in *Whitney v. California*, 274 U.S. 357 (1927).

WHITNEY V. CALIFORNIA

In *Whitney*, Brandeis summarized what he thought the writers of the Constitution believed about democracy and speech:

> They believed that freedom to think as you will and to speak as you think are means indispensable to the discovery and spread of political truth; that without free speech and assembly discussion would be futile; that with them, discussion affords ordinarily adequate protection against the dissemination of noxious doctrine; that the greatest menace to freedom is an inert people; that public discussion is a political duty; and that this should be a fundamental principle of the American government.

Criminalizing speech, he thought, would merely drive it underground and make it all the more dangerous:

> But they knew that order cannot be secured merely through fear of punishment for its infraction; that it is hazardous to discourage thought, hope and imagination ... that repression breeds hate; that hate menaces stable government; that the path of safety lies in the opportunity to discuss freely supposed grievances and proposed remedies; and that the fitting remedy for evil counsels is good ones.

Justice Oliver Wendell Holmes had written that speech could be punished if it constituted a "clear and present danger" to society. In *Whitney*, Brandeis responded that the expression of obnoxious ideas did not constitute such a "clear and present danger" unless it included a call to immediate illegal action. If it was simply advocacy of an idea, there was no danger, and the answer was speech by those who opposed the idea. The Court did not adopt his reasoning until 1969 (*Brandenburg v. Ohio*, 395 U.S. 444), but the Brandeis approach then became the philosophical basis for today's uniquely permissive American speech jurisprudence.

When Brandeis resigned from the Court in 1939, he left behind a tradition of lawyers contributing their efforts to public service, a jurisprudence based on interpreting the Constitution in light of societal facts, views of privacy and free speech that gradually became the law of the land, an emphasis on individual dignity, and a certainty that given the efforts of active democrats, liberty would indeed prevail. His signal contributions to American law and public life have been recognized in the naming of Brandeis University and of the Brandeis Law School of the University of Louisville.

SEE ALSO *Ashwander v. Tennessee Valley Authority, 297 U.S. 288 (1936); Brandeis Brief; Muller v. Oregon, 208 U.S. 412 (1908); Privacy; Sociological Jurisprudence; Wilson, Woodrow*

BIBLIOGRAPHY

Baskerville, Stephen W. 1994. *Of Laws and Limitations: An Intellectual Portrait of Louis Dembitz Brandeis*. Rutherford, NJ: Fairleigh Dickinson University Press.

Bickel, Alexander M. 1957. *The Unpublished Opinions of Mr. Justice Brandeis: The Supreme Court at Work*. Cambridge, MA: Belknap.

Blasi, Vincent. 1988. "The First Amendment and the Ideal of Civic Courage: The Brandeis Opinion in *Whitney v. California*." *William & Mary Law Review* 29: 653–697.

Brandeis, Louis D. 1914. *Business: A Profession*. Boston: Small, Maynard.

Mason, Alpheus T. 1946. *Brandeis: A Free Man's Life*. New York: Viking.

Paper, Lewis J. 1983. *Brandeis*. Englewood Cliffs, NJ: Prentice-Hall.

Purcell, Edward A. 2000. *Brandeis and the Progressive Constitution: Erie, the Judicial Power, and the Politics of the Federal Courts in Twentieth-Century America*. New Haven, CT: Yale University Press.

Richberg, Donald. 1932. "The Industrial Liberalism of Mr. Justice Brandeis." In *Mr. Justice Brandeis*, ed. Felix Frankfurter, 130–140. New Haven, CT: Yale University Press.

Strum, Philippa. 1984. *Louis D. Brandeis: Justice for the People*. Cambridge, MA: Harvard University Press.

Philippa Strum

BRANDEIS BRIEF

In 1908, the United States Supreme Court handed down its decision in *Muller v. Oregon*, 208 U.S. 412, upholding a state law that set ten as the maximum number of hours that women in factories, mills, and laundries could work in a day. Justice David Brewer spoke for a unanimous Court in holding that Oregon's law fell within the scope of the state's police powers, and did not contravene the due process clause of the Fourteenth Amendment. The case might not have been considered very noteworthy—after all, the Court had previously upheld other forms of protective legislation—except for the fact that only three years earlier, in *Lochner v. New York*, 198 U.S. 45 (1905), a five-to-four Court had struck down a New York law limiting the number of hours that bakers could work; in arguing the case, Louis D. Brandeis had introduced a totally new style of appellate brief, one that consisted of less than three pages of legal citation and more than one hundred pages of reports from factory commissions, medical texts, and even foreign agencies.

In *Lochner*, Justice Rufus Peckham (1809–1873) brushed away the state's claims about health and safety, and condemned the statute as nothing more than an effort "to regulate the hours of labor between the master and his employees (all being men, sui juris), in a private business, not dangerous to morals or in any real or substantive degree, to the health of the employees." Peckham conceded that a state could enact legislation to protect the health of workers, even bakers, but to do so it had to show that either the occupation itself or the standard working conditions related to it posed a real danger to worker health. This the state had failed to do. Peckham posed the question: "Is this a fair, reasonable and appropriate exercise of the police power of the State, or is it an unreasonable, unnecessary and arbitrary interference with the rights of the individual?" Even more worrisome to reformers than the question itself was the tacit assumption that it would be the courts, and not the legislatures, who would answer that question. Progressives worried that *Lochner,* with its clarion call for freedom of contract, would serve to nullify laws already on the books and operate as a barrier to future protective legislation.

BRANDEIS'S BRIEF ON INDUSTRIAL FEMALE LABOR

The following is from the Brandeis Brief for the State of Oregon in *Muller v. Oregon*, 208 U.S. 412 (1908), quoting from *Hygiene of Occupation in Reference Handbook of the Medical Sciences*. The original quote is from George M. Price, M.D., Medical Sanitary Inspector, Health Department of the City of New York, vol. VI. It is typical of the type of material Brandeis put together in this new style, fact-laden brief.

In many industries . . . female labor is very largely employed; and the effect of work on them is very detrimental to health. The injurious influences of female labor are due to the following factors: (1) The comparative physical weakness of the female organism; (2) The greater predisposition to harmful and poisonous elements in the trades; (3) The periodical semi-pathological state of health of women; (4) The effect of labor on the reproductive organs; and (5) The effects on the offspring. As the muscular organism of women is less developed than that of man, it is evident that those industrial occupations which require intense, constant, and prolonged muscular efforts must become highly detrimental to their health. This is shown in the general debility, anemia, chlorosis, and lack of tone in most women who are compelled to work in factories and in shops for long periods. . . .

The female organism, especially when young, offers very little resistance to the inroads of disease and to the various dangerous elements of certain trades.

Melvin I. Urofsky

When a Portland, Oregon, laundry owner named Curt Muller challenged the state's ten-hour law, the National Consumers' League, which had helped sponsor the legislation, came to Boston attorney Louis D. Brandeis and asked him to defend the law before the Supreme Court. He agreed to do so on two conditions: first, Oregon had to give him complete control of the case; and second, the League would have to provide him with enormous amounts of data on the effects of long hours on women workers. Oregon quickly agreed, and the League set about gathering data.

Brandeis had spotted a loophole in Peckham's opinion, and realized that he did not have to get the Court to reverse *Lochner*. Peckham had said that the New York law bore no relation to the health or safety of the workers. What he intended to do was to show, in full detail, just how the Oregon law did in fact relate to health and safety; but to do so he needed to introduce materials that had never been seen in a Supreme Court brief. Brandeis had earlier written that "a judge is presumed to know the elements of the law, but there is no presumption that he knows the facts" (Mason 1946, pp. 248–249). In the *Muller* brief he set out to make sure that the members of the nation's highest court would, at the least, have the facts before them.

The brief in *Muller* ran 113 pages, with only two pages devoted to the law. The validity of the Oregon statute, which the State claimed did have a legitimate purpose to protect women workers, had to be grounded in fact, and to that end, "the facts of common knowledge will be considered."

The next hundred-some pages set out lists of laws, factory reports, and medical testimony; all revolved around simple facts that even the justices of the nation's highest court must have known—that women are physically different from men and that they, not men, bear children. The excerpts came from sources as varied as British House of Commons reports on a bill to close shops early (1895, 1901); the Maine Bureau of Industrial and Labor Statistics report in which a doctor concluded that "woman is badly constructed for the purpose of standing eight or ten hours upon her feet" (1888); *Journal of the Royal Sanitary Institute* (1904); medical textbooks such as *The Hygiene, Diseases, and Mortality of Occupations* (1892); a report of French district inspectors on the question of night work (1900); reports from various state bureaus charged with gathering industrial statistics; report of German Imperial Factory Inspectors (1895); and *La Réglémentation Légale du Travail des Femmes et des Enfants dans L'Industrie Italienne* (1905).

Brandeis concluded, "in view of the facts above set forth and of legislative action extending over a period of more than sixty years in the leading countries of Europe, and in twenty of our States, it cannot be said that the Legislature of Oregon had no reasonable ground for believing that the public health, safety, or welfare did not require a legal limitation on women's work in manufacturing and mechanical establishments and laundries to ten hours a day."

It was a calculated gamble, but it worked. Moreover, Brewer took the unusual step of noting the "expressions of opinions from other than judicial sources . . . in the brief filed by Mr. Louis D. Brandeis," a highly unusual step for the Court to have taken.

Known immediately as the "Brandeis Brief," it altered the way that lawyers approached defense of public

matters. There is always a tension between private rights, such as property and liberty to contract, and public authority in the form of police power. For the last hundred years, when dealing with laws of economic regulation, the Court has adopted a "rational basis" test: If the legislature had found a rational reason to enact the law and if no constitutional prohibition existed, then the courts would defer, as Justice Holmes had demanded in his *Lochner* dissent, to the wisdom of the legislature and not attempt to impose its own judgment. But when the issue is not clear or when matters of individual rights rather than those of property are involved, lawyers have the responsibility to show the courts what the facts are surrounding the controversy and why they are important to the legal decision. The brief filed by the National Association for the Advancement of Colored People (N.A.A.C.P.) in the original segregation case, *Brown v. Board of Education*, 347 U.S. 483 (1954), is very short on legal precedent—because very little existed—but replete with materials relating to the harm done by segregation to the minds and hearts of little black children.

SEE ALSO *Brandeis, Louis; Briefs; Muller v. Oregon, 208 U.S. 412 (1908); Protective Legislation for Women Workers; Sociological Jurisprudence*

BIBLIOGRAPHY

Brandeis, Louis D. 1916. "The Living Law." *Illinois Law Review* 10: 461–471.

Brandeis, Louis D., and Josephine Goldmark. 1908. *Women in Industry*. New York: National Consumers' League.

Kens, Paul. 1990. *Judicial Power and Reform Politics: The Anatomy of Lochner v. New York*. Lawrence: University Press of Kansas.

Mason, Alpheus T. 1946. *Brandeis, A Free Man's Life*. New York: Viking.

Woloch, Nancy. 1996. *Muller v. Oregon: A Brief History with Documents*. Boston: Bedford/St. Martins.

Melvin I. Urofsky

BRANDENBURG V. OHIO, 395 U.S. 444 (1969)

Brandenburg v. Ohio, 395 U.S. 444 (1969) reversed the conviction of a Ku Klux Klan member who had been prosecuted under an Ohio statute forbidding the advocacy of violence. Coming in the midst of the social upheaval of the 1960s, the ruling moved the U.S. Supreme Court firmly away from its "clear and present danger" test for free speech and established instead the principle that only speech calling for "imminent lawless action" that is in fact "likely" to ensue from a speaker's words may be regulated.

In June 1964, Clarence Brandenburg, a 48-year-old television repairman and Klan member, invited Cincinnati reporters to attend and film a Klan rally outside the city. News broadcasts depicted several armed and hooded Klan members shouting racist diatribes and showed Brandenburg warning that "there might have to be some revengeance [sic] taken" against federal authorities. State officials, alarmed by the Ohio Klan's rapid growth in reaction to civil rights activism, prosecuted Brandenburg under the Ohio Criminal Syndicalism Act, a 1919 statute forbidding "advocat[ing] . . . the duty . . . of crime, sabotage, violence, or unlawful methods of terrorism as a means of accomplishing industrial or political reform." Brandenburg was found guilty, fined $1000, and sentenced to one to ten years in prison. Ohio courts dismissed his appeals, but a further petition on free speech grounds brought Brandenburg, along with attorneys from the American Civil Liberties Union (ACLU), before the Supreme Court in February 1969.

The Justices sided unanimously with Brandenburg, ruling on June 9, 1969, that advocacy of the use of criminal force can be protected speech. The state may not punish "mere advocacy" except when such speech aims at producing "imminent lawless action" and is "likely to incite or produce such action." For decades the Court had been revising the "clear and present danger" test, first articulated by Justice Oliver Wendell Holmes in *Schenck v. United States*, 249 U.S. 47 (1919); most Justices felt the test overly regulated the content of speakers' words rather than listeners' actions. But in drafting *Brandenburg*, they disagreed. An initial opinion authored by Justice Abe Fortas, which included reference to "present danger," prompted anger from Justice Hugo Black, a longtime opponent of any restrictions on speech (and, ironically, a former member of the Ku Klux Klan). After Fortas's resignation from the Court in May 1969, Justice William Brennan crafted the final opinion without any reference to Holmes's test, and the entire Court joined in a rare unanimous per curiam ruling.

Brandenburg featured two additional concurring opinions. Justice William Douglas offered a lengthy account of the history of impositions on free speech, admonishing that Cold War–era jurisprudence had allowed authorities to roam "at will through all of the beliefs of the witness, ransacking his conscience and his innermost thoughts." Justice Black briefly insisted that "the 'clear and present danger' doctrine should have no place in the interpretation of the First Amendment."

In *Brandenburg*, the Court also explicitly overruled *Whitney v. California*, 274 U.S. 357 (1927), thereby doing away with state criminal syndicalism statutes. Such laws, on the books in twenty-two states, dated to the post–World War I Red Scare and had targeted anarchists and communists, but had rarely been invoked until the

1960s; in the five years between Brandenburg's arrest and the Supreme Court's ruling, dormant criminal syndicalism laws had been dusted off and used against members of the militant wing of civil rights movements. After *Brandenburg*, almost no such prosecutions ensued.

The Court's decision in *Brandenburg* to widen the protection of free speech was unsurprising in the wake of the civil rights and antiwar movements of the 1960s, and brought to an end decades of debate over limits on inflammatory political speech. *Brandenburg's* two-part test measuring the imminence and likelihood of criminal violence remains a baseline for interpretation of limits on radical speech, and the decision has rarely been challenged.

SEE ALSO *First Amendment; Freedom of Speech*

BIBLIOGRAPHY

Parker, Richard A. 2003. "Brandenburg v. Ohio." In *Free Speech on Trial: Communication Perspectives on Landmark Supreme Court Decisions*, ed. Richard A. Parker. Tuscaloosa: University of Alabama Press.

Schwartz, Bernard. 1995. "Justice Brennan and the Brandenburg Decision—A Lawgiver in Action." *Judicature* 79(1): 24–29.

Christopher Capozzola

BRANIFF AIRWAYS, INC. V. NEBRASKA STATE BOARD OF EQUALIZATION, 347 U.S. 590 (1954)

In 1945 the federal Civil Aeronautics Board urged Congress to enact legislation that would protect the emerging commercial air-carrier industry from multiple, and potentially ruinous, state taxation. Congress, however, deferred action on the request, and the Court's decision in *Braniff Airways v. Nebraska State Board of Equalization*, 347 U.S. 590 (1954) concerned the outer limits of state authority in the meantime.

Nebraska had adopted an allocation formula to apportion for tax purposes the interstate business of commercial air carriers among the states they served. When Nebraska assessed taxes against Mid-Continent Airlines, the carrier challenged the tax in state court, arguing that existing federal statutes preempted the tax and in the alternative that it violated the commerce clause of the U.S. Constitution (Art. I, Sec. 8). The Supreme Court of Nebraska rejected these claims, and Braniff Airways, Mid-Continent's successor in interest, appealed to the U.S. Supreme Court.

By its terms, the commerce clause empowers Congress "to regulate Commerce . . . among the several States," and under the supremacy clause (Art. VI, Sec. 2), federal statutes sweep aside any conflicting state laws. Justice

Stanley Reed's (1884–1980) opinion for the Court first dismissed Braniff's preemption claims, concluding that no federal statutes "exclude[d] the sovereign powers of the states." That was not, however, the end of the matter, for the Court had long construed the commerce clause as a commitment to a policy of free trade across state boundaries and had accordingly implied therefrom a judicial power to strike down state laws impeding interstate commerce even in the absence of a conflict with a federal statute. Turning to Braniff's constitutional claim, Justice Reed observed that the Court had "frequently reiterated that the Commerce Clause does not immunize interstate instrumentalities from all state taxation, but that such commerce may be required to pay a nondiscriminatory share of the tax burden." Braniff failed even to allege that the Nebraska tax discriminated against it.

Rather, the crux of Braniff's constitutional argument was that it simply did not have sufficient connection to Nebraska to be subject to the tax. The air carrier's routine, fourteen-state circuit included brief stops at Nebraska airports to load and off-load passengers, mail, and freight. But Braniff maintained no ground facilities in Nebraska, instead renting depot space and purchasing other services as required. Braniff insisted that the commerce clause precluded Nebraska from taxing it based on these minimal contacts. Reed answered that this claim was really an invocation of the Fourteenth Amendment's due process clause dressed in commerce clause garb. So characterized, the claim was easily rebuffed. The due process inquiry was a minimal and deferential one: "so far as due process is concerned the only question is whether the tax in practical operation has relation to opportunities, benefits, or protection conferred or afforded by the taxing State." Airlines were, in Reed's estimation, sufficiently analogous to interstate railroads and boats plying inland waters to be subject to the type of state taxation long held permissible as to these older forms of transport.

But there was the rub for Justice Felix Frankfurter, who in dissent stressed the "treacherous tendencies" inherent in the transfer of legal principles between "situations seemingly analogous, yet essentially very different." Where Reed saw similarities, Frankfurter stressed "the drastic differences between slow-moving trains and the bird-like flight of airplanes." In his view, until Congress acted, the Court was obligated to protect "an industry of vital national import" from an onerous multiplicity of state-law burdens.

SEE ALSO *Federalism; Preemption*

BIBLIOGRAPHY

Choper, Jesse H., and Tung Yin. 1998. "State Taxation and the Dormant Commerce Clause: The Object-measure Approach." *Supreme Court Review* 1998: 193–245.

Crowther, Philip E. 2002. "Taxation of Fractional Programs: 'Flying over Uncharted Waters.'" *Journal of Air Law and Commerce* 67: 241–319.

A. Christopher Bryant

BRANZBURG V. HAYES, 408 U.S. 665 (1972)

In *Branzburg v. Hayes*, 408 U.S. 665 (1972), the U.S. Supreme Court declined to grant journalists an absolute First Amendment privilege to refuse to disclose the identity of confidential sources to a grand jury investigating criminal behavior. The Court's decision in *Branzburg* stemmed from a consolidation of four cases, all of which involved journalists who, after being subpoenaed by grand juries, had claimed a constitutional immunity from having to disclose their confidential sources. The cases involved reporters who had acquired knowledge of criminal activity, such as illegal drug manufacture, after promising confidentiality to a source involved in the activity.

In a single opinion governing all four cases, the Court denied granting such constitutional privilege to the press. Even though the Court recognized for the first time that newsgathering possesses some undefined constitutional protection, it concluded that no such protection existed in *Branzburg*. The confidential sources seeking to be protected in *Branzburg* were either members of an allegedly violent, politically dissident group, or involved in the use of illegal drugs. The Court concluded that because the sources' desire for anonymity stemmed from a wish to escape criminal prosecution, it did not deserve constitutional protection.

In his opinion for the Court, Justice Byron White could not find that requiring reporters to reveal their confidential sources to grand juries would impose significant newsgathering burdens. Justice White also could not find that informers were actually deterred from furnishing information when reporters are forced to testify. In his concurring opinion, however, Justice Lewis F. Powell Jr. emphasized the limited nature of the Court's ruling, stating that claims to newsgathering privileges should be judged on a case-by-case basis by balancing freedom of the press and the obligation of all citizens to testify regarding criminal conduct.

Since *Branzburg*, the Supreme Court has not ruled further on the nature of a reporter's constitutional privilege to keep sources confidential. Consequently, *Branzburg* has been the guiding beacon for lower courts, which in turn have adopted various interpretations of its recognition of newsgathering rights. Those courts have generally used *Branzburg* to support some kind of qualified privilege against compelled disclosure of anonymous sources. This support stems from Justice Powell's concurring opinion, in which he stated that journalists were not completely without constitutional rights regarding their newsgathering activities.

The qualified privilege that has arisen in the case law generally employs the three-part test articulated in the *Branzburg* dissent. This test requires that before ordering the disclosure of confidential information, a court must find: (1) that the information sought is clearly relevant; (2) that it cannot be obtained by alternative means; and (3) that there is a compelling need for the information. The outcomes of this test can vary from one jurisdiction to another, because courts apply the test on a case-by-case basis, balancing the need for the testimony against the newsgathering freedoms of the press.

SEE ALSO *First Amendment; Freedom of the Press*

BIBLIOGRAPHY

Berger, Linda L. 2003. "Shielding the Unmedia: Using the Process of Journalism to Protect the Journalist's Privilege in an Infinite Universe of Publication." *Houston Law Review* 39: 1371–1416.

Marcus, Paul. 1984. "The Reporter's Privilege: An Analysis of the Common Law, *Branzburg v. Hayes*, and Recent Statutory Developments." *Arizona Law Review* 25: 815–867.

Patrick M. Garry

BRENNAN, WILLIAM J., JR.
1906–1997

William J. Brennan, Jr. was associate justice from October 16, 1956, through July 20, 1990. An intellectual and social leader of the Court, Brennan had a significant impact on constitutional jurisprudence, and his opinions profoundly changed the way Americans viewed politics, equality, and the protection of individual rights.

PRE-COURT BACKGROUND

Brennan was born on April 25, 1906, in Newark, New Jersey. His parents were Irish-Catholic immigrants who came to the United States in the 1890s. His father, a former coal stoker, later became a labor leader and municipal officer. Brennan grew up in a working-class neighborhood and attended a parochial elementary school and public high school. He was an honors graduate of the Wharton School of the University of Pennsylvania. Following graduation, Brennan married Marjorie Leonard and entered Harvard Law School. A scholarship student, Brennan worked his way through law school and served as president of the Legal Aid Society. He received his law degree in 1931, graduating in the top 10 percent of his class.

After graduation Brennan joined a prominent firm in Newark where he specialized in labor law on the side of management. During World War II (1939–1945) he served

Supreme Court Justice William J. Brennan, Jr. *As a Supreme Court Justice, Brennan frequently argued for the rights of the individual, in particular the rights of the poor, minorities, and women. He is noted for his efforts to ensure that federal rights outlined in the Bill of Rights apply to citizens at the state level as well.* **THE LIBRARY OF CONGRESS**

as an officer in the army, primarily as a procurement and labor troubleshooter in the office of Undersecretary of War Robert Porter Patterson (1891–1952). He was awarded the Legion of Merit and held the rank of colonel when he was discharged in 1945. Brennan returned to private practice after the war and became a partner in his firm in 1949. He was a leader in the New Jersey court reform movement under a new state constitution. Republican Governor Alfred E. Driscoll (1902–1975) appointed Brennan, a Democrat, a judge of the state superior court, a statewide tribunal of original jurisdiction. Upon the recommendation of New Jersey Supreme Court Chief Justice Arthur T. Vanderbilt (1888–1957), who was impressed by Brennan's success in relieving congestion in the courts, Driscoll elevated Judge Brennan to the state appeals court in 1950, and two years later, to the New Jersey Supreme Court.

Brennan's work in the state courts brought him to the attention of U.S. Attorney General Herbert Brownell

(1904–1996), who recommended him to President Dwight D. Eisenhower as a possible replacement for retiring Supreme Court Justice Sherman Minton (1890–1965). During his 1956 reelection campaign, Eisenhower, a Republican, made a recess appointment of Brennan to the Court to demonstrate to the public that partisan politics was not the major consideration in his judicial appointments. In reality, two groups probably influenced Eisenhower in his choice of Brennan: the Conference of Chief Justices of the state courts, who pointed out that there were no sitting justices who had experience on a state court; and the Conference of Catholic Bishops led by Francis Cardinal Spellman (1889–1967), archbishop of New York, who noted that there was no Catholic on the Court although traditionally there had been (Frank Murphy being the last in 1949). Brennan was the first Court nominee to be rated "imminently highly qualified" by the American Bar Association. On March 19, 1957, the U.S. Senate confirmed Brennan's nomination. Only Senator Joseph McCarthy (1908–1957) opposed Brennan's appointment to the bench because of some public criticisms the judge had made of investigating committees indulging in witch-hunting.

THE WARREN COURT YEARS

Brennan served on the Court for thirty-four years, retiring for health reasons on July 20, 1990. He was considered to be among the Court's most influential members and was a consummate coalition builder. Described as always in need of a fifth vote, Brennan would not sacrifice his integrity, but he was willing to revise drafts of his opinions to accommodate colleague's concerns and thereby reach a majority consensus. He was a libertarian judicial activist who espoused the philosophy of a living constitution and viewed the role of the Court as creator of opportunities to ensure liberty, equality, and human dignity. Brennan served during the chief justiceships of Earl Warren, Warren E. Burger, and William Rehnquist; he wrote 1,360 opinions, second only to William O. Douglas in number of opinions written while a Supreme Court justice.

Brennan played a leading role in the Warren Court's dramatic expansion of individual rights in cases dealing with civil rights and civil liberties, due process, equal protection, First Amendment freedoms, and privacy. His first majority opinion on the Court in *Roth v. United States*, 354 U.S. 476 (1957) (and its companion case *Alberts v. California*), upheld federal and state criminal obscenity laws while opening the door to free expression by liberalizing standards to be applied in obscenity cases. Brennan's opinions demonstrated a strong respect for First Amendment freedoms of speech and press, although he rejected the preferred position doctrine of justices Hugo Black and Douglas. He wrote the opinion of the Court in *New York Times v. Sullivan*, 376 U.S. 254 (1964), which transformed libel law by establishing the actual malice test. He also

introduced the concept of "chilling effects" that focused attention on the wider consequences of laws that suppressed speech. During an era of strong anti-communist public opinion, Brennan was a staunch defender of the right of alleged subversives to procedural regularity. As for religion clause cases, Brennan held in *Sherbert v. Verner*, 374 U.S. 398 (1963) that government conditions on public benefits cannot be sustained if they so operate, whatever their purpose, to inhibit or deter the exercise of the free exercise clause; and in his concurring opinion in *Abington Township v. Schempp*, 374 U.S. 203 (1963), striking down compulsory Bible readings and recitation of the Lord's Prayer in public schools, Brennan concluded that government may neither foster nor promote religion under the establishment clause.

Brennan is credited with writing the per curiam opinion in *Cooper v. Aaron*, 358 U.S. 1 (1958), the Little Rock school desegregation case that declared the Court's supreme authority when its civil rights opinions were challenged by state officials. In *Green v. School Board of New Kent County*, 391 U.S. 430 (1968), Brennan's opinion redefining the substantive right instituted by *Brown v. Board of Education*, 347 U.S. 483 (1954), insisted upon a unitary, nonracial system of public education with the elimination, root and branch, of historic and pervasive effects of racial discrimination.

For Warren, Brennan's most important opinion was in *Baker v. Carr*, 369 U.S. 186 (1962), which ruled legislative malapportionment cases justifiable under the equal protection clause. This decision was a precursor to subsequent Court decisions that established the rule of one person, one vote in legislative districting.

Brennan also played a pivotal role in the due process revolution that incorporated almost all of the guarantees of the Bill of Rights to be applied against the states through the Fourteenth Amendment's due process clause. In Brennan's dissent in *Cohen v. Hurley*, 366 U.S. 117 (1961), he advocated "selective incorporation" as a middle position between the Court's traditional fundamental fairness doctrine and total incorporation. In subsequent terms, the Court's use of the selective incorporation doctrine on a case-by-case basis dramatically transformed American criminal justice and fundamentally altered the nature of the federal system. In *Malloy v. Hogan*, 378 U.S. 1 (1964), Brennan's opinion applied the self-incrimination protection to the states, and made clear that the rights and prohibitions nationalized in the past were to be applied to the states with full force as in federal cases. Brennan viewed the incorporation decisions as the most important of the Warren era.

Shortly after joining the Court, Brennan established a close working relationship with Warren, whom he referred to as "Super Chief". The two justices frequently conferred on strategies on Thursdays, the day before the Court's Friday conferences. In his voting patterns Brennan was closely allied with the libertarian-activists Warren, Black, and Douglas (joined later by justices appointed by presidents John F. Kennedy and Lyndon B. Johnson), especially in civil liberty decisions.

SERVICE ON THE BURGER AND REHNQUIST COURTS

On the Burger and Rehnquist Courts, Brennan continued to play a leadership role. He was a staunch opponent of the death penalty and gender discrimination, and a supporter of rights to privacy and abortion. For Brennan, capital punishment was per se a cruel and unusual punishment prohibited by the Eighth and Fourteenth Amendments, and he protested the arbitrariness by which it was administered and its use against minorities, youth, and the mentally retarded.

In *Eisenstadt v. Baird*, 405 U.S. 438 (1972), Brennan maintained that privacy rights protect the individual in deciding whether to bear or beget a child, and that government could not intrude into such matters. He was the Court's strongest advocate of gender equality, and after failing to muster a majority of the Court to apply strict scrutiny in such cases as *Frontiero v. Richardson*, 411 U.S. 677 (1973), Brennan wrote the majority opinion in *Craig v. Boren*, 429 U.S. 190 (1976), providing heightened scrutiny of gender-based classifications. He also consistently sustained the constitutionality of affirmative action against racial and ethnic discrimination.

In new equal protection cases, Brennan's opinions broadened the rights of the poor, mentally handicapped, or imprisoned to battle the government in court and attempted to protect the rights of prison inmates, welfare recipients, and the mentally handicapped. In the mid-1970s, as he increasingly dissented from the Court's decisions, Brennan called upon state courts to interpret their own state constitutions more expansively than the federal Constitution was currently being construed. In his last major opinions for the Court in *Texas v. Johnson*, 491 U.S. 397 (1989) and *United States v. Eichman*, 496 U.S. 310 (1990), Brennan protected the rights of political protest while invalidating laws making it a crime to desecrate the U.S. flag.

Upon the death of his wife Marjorie in 1982, Brennan married Mary Fowler, his longtime secretary, in 1983. He died in 1997 at the age of ninety-one in Arlington, Virginia, and is buried in Arlington National Cemetery. As a champion of individual rights, Brennan is ranked as one of the greatest justices in the Court's history.

SEE ALSO *Aspirationalism; Cold War; Eisenhower, Dwight D.; Sex Discrimination; State Constitutional Law; Warren Court*

BIBLIOGRAPHY

Bigel, Alan I. 1997. *Justices William J. Brennan, Jr. and Thurgood Marshall on Capital Punishment.* Lanham, MD: University Press of America.

Brennan, William J., Jr. 1967. *An Affair with Freedom: A Collection of His Opinions and Speeches Drawn from His First Decade as a United States Supreme Court Justice*, ed. Stephen J. Freidman. New York: Atheneum.

Eisler, Kim Isaac. 2003. *The Last Liberal: Justice William J. Brennan, Jr. and the Decisions That Transformed America.* Hopkins, MN: Beard Books.

Goldman, Roger, David Gallen, and William J. Brennan. 1994. *Justice William J. Brennan, Jr: Freedom First.* New York: Carroll and Graf Publishers.

Marion, David E. 1997. *The Jurisprudence of Justice William J. Brennan, Jr.: The Law and Politics of "Libertarian Dignity."* Lanham, MD: Rowman and Littlefield.

Michelman, Frank I. 1999. *Brennan and Democracy.* Princeton, NJ: Princeton University Press.

Rosenkranz, E. Joshua, and Bernard Schwartz, eds. 1997. *Reason and Passion: Justice Brennan's Enduring Influence.* New York: W.W. Norton.

Theodore M. Vestal

BRENTWOOD ACADEMY V. TENNESSEE SECONDARY SCHOOL ATHLETIC ASSOCIATION, 531 U.S. 288 (2001)

In *Brentwood Academy v. Tennessee Secondary School Athletic Association*, 531 U.S. 288 (2001), the U.S. Supreme Court introduced the *entwinement* theory as a basis for applying the Constitution to private conduct. The Tennessee Secondary School Athletic Association is a not-for-profit membership organization that regulates interscholastic sport within the state of Tennessee and includes both public and private school members. When a private school challenged an association rule forbidding recruiting correspondence for violating free speech, the Court held that "the association's regulatory activity may and should be treated as state action owing to the pervasive entwinement of state school officials in the structure of the association."

Recognizing that private action may be characterized as state action when there is a "close nexus between the State and the challenged action," the Court examined the association's relationship to the state and its connection to the state school officials. Eighty-four percent of the association's members were public schools, the association's staff members were eligible for the state's retirement system, and the association's committee was composed of state employees who often attended meetings during normal school hours. Additionally, the Tennessee State Board of Education continuously acknowledged the association as the organization designated to regulate interscholastic sport throughout the state and abstained from regulating sports for the public schools. Although participation in the association was voluntary, most public schools joined the association because nonmembers could not compete against member schools.

Responding to Brentwood Academy's claim that the association is a state actor, the Supreme Court extended its state action doctrine to include not only financial entanglement but also entwinement between private actors and the state. "The nominally private character of the Association is overborne by the pervasive entwinement of public institutions and public officials in its composition and workings, and there is no substantial reason to claim unfairness in applying constitutional standards to it." The association's decisions were essentially made by public officials in a quasi-public body for the benefit of public institutions. The inclusion of private schools in the association could not overcome the overwhelming representation of public schools and public officials to characterize the association's actions as private. In a five-to-four decision, Justice David Souter, writing for the majority, concluded that the association's rules are open to constitutional challenge. Justice Clarence Thomas wrote the dissenting opinion.

By employing the concept of entwinement, the Court departed from its analytic approach in *Burton v. Wilmington Parking Authority*, 365 U.S. 715 (1961), which focused on the existence of a public function and a close nexus between the state and the challenged action. Considering whether a private restaurant operating within a public parking garage under a long-term leasing contract was a state actor, the Court in *Burton* found that the state's contractual and financial relationship facilitating the construction of the restaurant entangled the operations of both to make them indistinguishable for the purposes of a constitutional challenge under equal protection. Although the Court in *Brentwood* termed the relationship between the association and the state as entwinement over the objections of Justice Thomas writing in dissent, the analytic departure may be reconcilable. The *Brentwood* Court expanded the entanglement doctrine to include interdependence and connectedness based on operational, and not simply financial, relationships.

SEE ALSO *State Action*

BIBLIOGRAPHY

Madry, Alan. 2001. "Statewide School Athletic Associations and Constitutional Liability; Brentwood Academy v. Tennessee Secondary School Athletic Association." *Marquette University Sports Law Review* 12(1): 365–396.

Metzger, Gillian E. 2003. "Privatization as Delegation." *Columbia Law Review* 103: 1367, 1370–1371.

Wells, Michael L. 2004. "Identifying State Actors in Constitutional Litigation: Reviving the Role of Substantive Context." *Cardozo Law Review* 26: 99–125.

Thomas P. Crocker

BREWER, DAVID
1837–1910

David Josiah Brewer is one of the most influential, though least remembered, justices to have served on the Supreme Court. He was a dominant legal intellect and justice in his era, helping to lay the groundwork for much of the character of modern law, including the prominent role of the federal courts, the aggressive use of equitable powers, and the expansive interpretation of constitutional text. Yet the judges and scholars who might seem most indebted to

Supreme Court Justice David Brewer. *Though his decisions issued as a Supreme Court justice were seen as too reactionary at the time, many of Brewer's opinions eventually came into being after his term on the bench ended. For instance, while siding with the federal government's power to stop union strikes in* In re Debs, *Brewer was criticized for supporting federal injunctions, a practice which became commonplace years later.* © **CORBIS**

his contributions—those who forged a central role for the Supreme Court in enlarging and protecting rights and liberties during the mid-twentieth century—dismissed Brewer because of his association with doctrines seen as reactionary. The conservative commentators and scholars who might be closer to Brewer on substantive grounds, meanwhile, have distanced themselves from the activist judiciary that he symbolized.

Justice Brewer was born on January 20, 1837, in what would later become Turkey, where his father was a missionary. He was raised and educated in Connecticut and graduated from Yale University. After graduating from Albany Law School in 1858, he headed to Kansas to establish his practice. He served in several judicial posts, including a seat on the Kansas Supreme Court and, subsequently, the federal Eighth Circuit Court. He took his seat on the Supreme Court in 1890 and served until his death on March 28, 1910. He was a nephew of Justice Stephen J. Field, with whom he served until 1897.

Brewer was a prolific writer and speaker who did not hesitate to write expansively, both in his Court opinions and in other venues. He is most associated with two opinions: *In re Debs*, 158 U.S. 564 (1895), which upheld the use of federal injunctions against labor strikes, and *Muller v. Oregon*, 208 U.S. 412 (1908), which upheld a state law limiting the working hours of women. *Debs* has often been criticized as a blow to the development of organized labor, yet generations later the federal injunction would become an important tool in reforming prisons, schools, and other institutions. *Muller* carved out a major exception to the liberty of contract doctrine, with which Brewer was closely associated. It also helped pave the way for the demise of this doctrine by establishing that labor regulations could indeed be reasonable. Brewer's reliance on the Brandeis brief anticipated a more modern turn by the Court to a jurisprudence that looked to social science for guidance.

The Court on which Brewer was a leading figure was never hesitant to judge the reasonableness of regulation, a position that would be repudiated by the Court in 1937 and 1938 (see *West Coast Hotel Co. v. Parrish*, 300 U.S. 379 [1937], *National Labor Relations Board. v. Jones & Laughlin Steel Corp.*, 301 U.S. 1 [1937], and *United States v. Carolene Products Co.*, 304 U.S. 144 [1938]). But his mode of reasoning would sound very well-known to anyone familiar with the Court's inclination a century later to independently evaluate the rationality or substantial effects of legislation, rather than defer to legislative judgments, in areas from privacy to commerce.

Brewer famously declared that the United States was a Christian nation, and his jurisprudence reflected a Congregationalist understanding that God had made each person distinct and given each person free will. For Brewer, it naturally followed that rights that secured the accomplishments of individuals, most fundamentally private property and contract, must be secured by the courts. But his religion also moderated his conservatism and fueled a reformist tendency, as seen in his advocacy for the rights of women and Chinese residents, and in his criticism of American imperialism.

SEE ALSO *Fuller Court; In re Debs, 158 U.S. 564 (1895)*

BIBLIOGRAPHY

Brodhead, Michael J. 1994. *David J. Brewer: The Life of a Supreme Court Justice, 1837–1910.* Carbondale: Southern Illinois University Press.

Przybyszewski, Linda. 2000. "The Religion of a Jurist: Justice David J. Brewer and the Christian Nation." *Journal of Supreme Court History* 25(3): 228–242.

Dennis J. Coyle

BREYER, STEPHEN
1938–

Stephen Gerald Breyer was born to Irving G. and Anne R. Breyer in San Francisco, California, on August 15, 1938. His interest in law was encouraged by his father, who served as a lawyer and legal counsel for the San Francisco Board of Education. In 1955 Breyer graduated from Lowell High School, where he excelled in debate.

Breyer earned a bachelor's degree in philosophy from Stanford University in 1959 and a bachelor of arts degree from Magdalen College of Oxford University in 1961. In 1964 he was awarded his law degree from Harvard Law School, graduating magna cum laude. While there, he became interested in economics and distinguished himself as an editor of the law review.

From 1964 to 1965, Breyer served as a law clerk for Arthur J. Goldberg, an associate justice of the U.S. Supreme Court. During the following two years he was a special assistant to the U.S. assistant attorney general for antitrust. In 1967 Breyer married Joanna Hare, the daughter of Lord John Blakenham of England. Breyer and his wife reared two daughters, Chloe and Nell, and a son, Michael.

That same year Breyer accepted a position as an assistant professor of law in the Kennedy School of Government at Harvard University, where he was recognized as an expert in administrative law. He was promoted to a professor of law in 1970 and continued teaching at Harvard until 1980. In 1973 he served as an assistant special prosecutor in the Watergate investigation. On December 10, 1980, he took a seat on the U.S. First Circuit Court of Appeals, and served as its chief judge from 1990 to 1994. Breyer has published three important books on deregulation: *Regulation and Its Reform* (1982); *Administrative Law and Regulatory Policy* (with Richard

Supreme Court Justice Stephen Breyer. *A former professor of law at Harvard University and judge on the U.S. First Circuit Court of Appeals, Breyer was nominated to the Supreme Court in 1994 by President Bill Clinton.* **AP IMAGES**

Stewart, 2nd edition, 1985); and *Breaking the Vicious Circle: Toward Effective Risk Regulation* (1993).

On March 13, 1994, Breyer was nominated by President Bill Clinton to fill the vacated seat of Harry Blackmun on the U.S. Supreme Court. After being confirmed by the U.S. Senate by a vote of eighty-seven to nine, he began serving on the Supreme Court during the opening session in 1994.

Although Breyer was inexperienced in issues dealing with the U.S. Constitution, he made contributions to Supreme Court decisions that involved his expertise in the legal aspects of economic regulation, administrative law, and environmental issues. A pragmatist and empiricist, Breyer is generally considered moderate, espousing neither a strong liberal nor a strong conservative philosophy. He has repeatedly joined his more liberal colleagues on the Court in important constitutional cases, including those favoring abortion rights and defending the use of international law as persuasive authority in Supreme Court decisions. Since 1994 he has voted to overturn congressional legislation less often than any other Supreme Court justice. Breyer tends to

take a conservative stance in voting against government regulation of business and supporting strong antitrust laws. He strongly believes that judicial restraint promotes democracy and that complex societal issues are best resolved by citizen participation in the democratic process instead of by governmental solutions forced on society.

Breyer supports civil liberties with balance and proportionality. In the *Board of Education v. Earls*, 536 U.S. 822 (2002), his opinion supported mandatory drug testing of students involved in extracurricular activities. He pointed out that it was a reasonable effort by schools to help curtail the drug epidemic among teenagers. In cases involving the Fourth Amendment, he has typically written dissenting opinions that reject civil libertarian arguments. However, in *Gray v. Maryland*, 523 U.S. 185 (1998), a case involving the Sixth Amendment, his written opinion supported the right of defendants to confront their accusers. Similarly, in *United States v. Booker*, 543 U.S. 220 (2005), Breyer's opinion stated that the Sixth Amendment requires a jury to determine beyond a reasonable doubt any evidence that increases the sentencing time of a defendant in a federal criminal case beyond the limit provided by the Federal Sentencing Guidelines.

In *Kyllo v. United States*, 533 U.S. 27 (2001), Breyer concurred with the Court decision that police cannot use a thermal-imaging device to scan a house without first obtaining a warrant. In contrast, in *Bond v. United States*, 529 U.S. 334 (2000), he opposed a Court decision that prohibited law enforcement officials from exploring the contents of soft-sided carry-on luggage on buses. Soft bags could be examined for weapons or illegal substances by feeling/squeezing them. Breyer argued that such investigation was no more invasive than when the soft bags were physically disturbed/felt by other passengers as they placed their belongings into shared luggage compartments on a bus. In *Easley v. Cromartie*, 532 U.S. 234 (2001), Breyer argued that race cannot serve as the primary factor in establishing the geographical boundaries for voting districts.

Breyer demonstrated his liberal philosophy in *United States v. Lopez*, 514 U.S. 549 (1995), by arguing that Congress has the power to regulate the possession of guns in school zones nationwide. In *Rasul v. Bush*, 542 U.S. 466 (2004), Breyer's opinion supported the verdict that the U.S. court system has the authority to determine whether or not non-U.S. citizens held at Guantánamo Bay were rightfully imprisoned. Breyer also concurred with his liberal colleagues in *Hamdan v. Rumsfeld*, 126 S. Ct. 2749 (2006), which held that the Supreme Court, not the federal government, has the authority to set up military commissions to try Guantánamo detainees.

Breyer's critics believe that he is overly concerned with minor details and lacks a consistent, overall vision of the Constitution. They also accuse him of lacking commitment to matters involving the First Amendment,

ACTIVE LIBERTY: INTERPRETING OUR DEMOCRATIC CONSTITUTION

In this concise treatise on constitutional interpretation, Justice Stephen Breyer argues that the intention of the U.S. Constitution is to establish a democratic government in which the citizens are involved by exercising maximum liberty in governing themselves and in participating in political functions and decisions. Breyer terms this type of citizen involvement "active liberty."

The concept of active liberty—as I said at the outset—refers to a sharing of a nation's sovereign authority among its people. Sovereignty involves the legitimacy of a governmental action. And a sharing of sovereign authority suggests several kinds of connection between that legitimacy and the people.

For one thing, it should be possible to trace without much difficulty a line of authority for the making of governmental decisions back to the people themselves—either directly, or indirectly through those whom the people have chosen, perhaps instructed, to make certain kinds of decisions in certain ways. ...

For another, the people themselves should participate in government—though their participation may vary in degree. Participation is most forceful when it is direct, involving, for example, voting, town meetings, political party membership, or issue- or interest-related activities. It is weak, but still minimally exists ... in the understanding that each individual belongs to the political community with the right to participate should he or she choose to do so.

SOURCE: Stephen Breyer, *Active Liberty: Interpreting Our Democratic Constitution.* New York: Vintage Books, 2005, pp. 15–16.

Alvin K. Benson

civil rights, and privacy. Proponents admire his determination to follow his own path, as well as his wit, energy, and intelligence, and his promotion of regulations that protect health, safety, and the environment.

SEE ALSO *Judicial Pragmatism; Rehnquist Court; Roberts Court*

BIBLIOGRAPHY

Annenberg Foundation Trust at Sunnylands. 2005. *Our Constitution: A Conversation*, with Sandra Day O'Conner and Stephen Breyer (video recording). Philadelphia: Author.

Breyer, Stephen G. 2004. *Economic Reasoning and Judicial Review.* Washington, DC: AEI-Brookings Joint Center for Regulatory Studies.

Breyer, Stephen G. 2005. *Active Liberty: Interpreting Our Democratic Constitution.* New York: Knopf.

U.S. Supreme Court, Judicial Conduct and Disability Act Study Committee. 2006. *Implementation of the Judicial Conduct and Disability Act of 1980: A Report to the Chief Justice.* Washington, DC: U.S. Government Printing Office.

Alvin K. Benson

BRIDGES V. CALIFORNIA, 314 U.S. 252 (1941)

The American constitutional order depends upon the administration of justice by impartial judges. It also depends upon an informed, knowledgeable public. The clash between these two fundamentals—and between two titans of the U.S. Supreme Court—constitutes *Bridges v. California*, 314 U.S. 252 (1941).

Bridges opportunely combined two California cases that lay on both sides of the politically charged labor question. State judges had fined Harry Bridges (1901–1990), a famous labor leader, and the *Los Angeles Times*, then an antiunion newspaper, for contempt of court. Bridges and the *Times* had published biting commentary on pending court decisions in labor-organizing disputes that the judges construed as attempts to intimidate them. The California courts had sustained these summary convictions against the claim that such use of the contempt power infringed the freedom of speech and press.

The Supreme Court initially voted to sustain the State's position but Justice James McReynolds retired and Justice Frank Murphy announced that he had changed his mind. The case was reargued the following term; now, a five-to-four majority supported Bridges and the newspaper. Justice Hugo Black wrote for the Court, opposed—in their first of many important exchanges—by Justice Felix Frankfurter.

Justice Black used *Bridges* as the first vehicle to espouse one of his core beliefs: the vital importance of speech and press freedoms. The American founders intended to give these liberties "the broadest scope that could be countenanced in an orderly society." The First

Amendment, applicable since 1925 to the states, contains "unqualified prohibitions" intended "as commands the breach of which cannot be tolerated." Black expanded the famous clear and present danger test with an adverb, insisting that government needs to show "extremely" imminent and serious evil in order to suppress expression. No harm could be demonstrated from the comments in these cases. Judicial attempts to stifle criticism, even if well-intentioned, operate precisely at the moment when the public mind is engaged by an ongoing controversy. Black also scoffed at California's claim that judges need broad contempt power to maintain respect for the courts: Contempt and suspicion, not respect, arise from "enforced silence."

A "doctrinaire" jurisprudence pervades the Court's opinion, according to Justice Frankfurter's long, comprehensive dissent. The importance of freedom of speech and press must be weighed against other values such as federalism and an independent judiciary. The public's interest here can not be reduced simply to the reception of another viewpoint on labor disputes; rather, the public good more vitally depends upon the ability of courts to render judgments free from outside pressure. Bridges and the *Times* tried to bully judges and sway the outcome of live controversies. Such tactics are not part of any search for truth in the marketplace of ideas, but do threaten the judge's role as the dispassionate voice of law, a task that demands insulation from the pressures of public opinion. The timeliness of publication, contrary to Black's reasoning, perversely occurs "when the need for impartiality and fair proceeding is greatest."

Black and Frankfurter would lock horns on the First Amendment and the proper approach to constitutional interpretation, among other issues, for two more decades. Gradually, Justice Black's assertive judicial protection for civil liberties—if not his disdain for Frankfurter's "balancing" approach—prevailed, as it had in 1941. Perhaps for that reason, the great constitutional historian Robert G. McCloskey began his last book, *The Modern Supreme Court* (1972), with an account of *Bridges v. California*.

SEE ALSO *First Amendment; Freedom of the Press*

BIBLIOGRAPHY

McCloskey, Robert G. 1972. *The Modern Supreme Court.* Cambridge, MA: Harvard University Press.

Silverstein, Mark. 1984. *Constitutional Faiths: Felix Frankfurter, Hugo Black, and the Process of Judicial Decision Making.* Ithaca, NY: Cornell University Press.

Simon, James F. 1989. *The Antagonists: Hugo Black, Felix Frankfurter, and Civil Liberties in Modern America.* New York: Simon and Schuster.

G. Roger McDonald

BRIDGES V. UNITED STATES, 346 U.S. 209 (1953)

With the possible exception of individual members of the Jehovah's Witnesses, no single litigant did more to dramatize the cause of civil liberties in the United States during the 1940s and 1950s than Harry Bridges (1901–1990), the Australian-born leader of the International Longshoreman's and Warehousemen's Union (ILWU), who made three notable trips to the U.S. Supreme Court in those decades. And not even the Jehovah's Witnesses suffered more sustained legal harassment and persecution by agencies of the state and federal government than this fiery West Coast labor leader.

EARLY AGITATION

Bridges's troubles with the U.S. government and powerful California economic interests began in the late 1920s

International Longshoreman's and Warehousemen's Union leader, Harry Bridges. *An influential labor leader, Bridges earned the attention of the Immigration and Naturalization Service after anti-labor business owners and opposing union organizations claimed the Australian-born Bridges should be deported for his lack of U.S. citizenship and his communist sympathies. Bridges survived three deportation attempts, with the Supreme Court ruling in his favor twice.* © **CORBIS-BETTMANN**

when he carelessly missed an initial opportunity to become an American citizen, and then in 1934 when he and his longshoremen played a major role in the San Francisco general strike that at one point involved 150,000 workers. Although the general strike collapsed, Bridges secured recognition for the union, a six-hour workday, and other reforms. But his efforts earned him the enmity of the shipping industry and an initial investigation by the Immigration and Naturalization Service (INS) after accusations surfaced that communists played an important role in the longshoremen's union and that its leader himself was a member of the Communist Party. Bridges never denied the former charge and praised his communist members as strong union men, but he consistently denied his own membership in the party.

Initial INS investigations into these charges against Bridges proved them baseless. High officials in the administration of President Franklin Roosevelt, including Secretary of Labor Frances Perkins (1880–1965), therefore remained reluctant to act against Bridges until 1938, when, under pressure from antilabor members of Congress, West Coast business groups, and conservative trade union leaders, the United States finally charged the longshoremen's leader with violating the 1918 statute that provided for the deportation of aliens who belonged to any organization that believed, taught, or advocated the violent overthrow of the government. The administration delayed Bridges's deportation proceedings until the Supreme Court interpreted the statute in the case of Joseph George Strecker, an alien from the Austro-Hungarian Empire who admitted membership in the Communist Party (*Kessler v. Strecker*, 307 U.S. 22 [1939]). The delay provoked the wrath of congressional conservatives led by members of the House Special Committee on Un-American Activities, who called for an impeachment inquiry into the conduct of Perkins and top INS officials.

THE FIRST DEPORTATION HEARING

Although the Supreme Court's holding in *Strecker* only clarified the law to the extent of barring its application to aliens whose membership in the Communist Party had terminated, the deportation hearing against Bridges commenced a month before World War II began in the summer of 1939, with James Landis (1899–1964), the dean of the Harvard Law School and former chairman of the Securities and Exchange Commission, serving as the INS hearing examiner. After listening to fifty-nine witnesses who filled eight thousand pages of testimony, Landis filed a 150-page report with Secretary Perkins that vindicated Bridges by finding no credible evidence linking him to the Communist Party, a conclusion that made it unnecessary for this leading authority on administrative law to reach the question of the party's ideology or purposes. The Landis report passed a harsh judgment on

the government and its witnesses, accusing them of bureaucratic overreaching, coercion, and perjury.

THE SECOND DEPORTATION HEARING AND APPEAL

In the wake of the Soviet-Nazi Pact of 1940 and strikes in the defense industry attributed to Communist influence, a furious President Roosevelt urged Attorney General Robert Jackson (1892–1954) to commence a fresh round of deportation proceedings against Bridges, with a new hearing examiner, retired federal judge Charles B. Sears (1870–1950). Based on new testimony from former allies of Bridges who claimed he had joined the Communist Party in 1935 or 1937, Sears ruled that the evidence now proved a consistent pattern of affiliation with the party. When the Board of Immigration Appeals rejected Sears's findings, the new attorney general, Francis Biddle (1886–1968), overruled it and ordered Bridges deported in 1942. By then, Roosevelt's attitude had softened considerably, once Germany invaded the Soviet Union and Japan bombed Pearl Harbor. "I'll bet the Supreme Court will never let him be deported," the president remarked to Biddle (Kutler 1982, p. 139).

Bridges lost his appeal of Biddle's deportation order in the federal district court and before the Ninth Circuit Court of Appeals in 1944, but a stinging dissent by Judge William Healy (1881–1962) on the Ninth Circuit became the basis for the Supreme Court's majority opinion in 1945 that overturned Biddle's deportation order. Writing for himself and four others (Justices Hugo Black, Frank Murphy, Stanley Reed, and Wiley Rutledge), Justice William O. Douglas found the Sears report and Biddle's reliance upon it gravely flawed on grounds of admitting hearsay evidence and adopting a defective standard with respect to Bridges's affiliation with the Communist Party.

Deportation might not be a criminal proceeding, Douglas wrote, but "it visits a great hardship on the individual and deprives him of a right to stay and live and work in this land of freedom." When it used the uncorroborated testimony of a former Bridges associate, not under oath, Douglas continued, the government hearing examiner violated due process. The dissenters (Chief Justice Harlan Stone and Justices Felix Frankfurter and Owen Roberts) stressed the Court's traditional deference to the findings of administrative tribunals, such as those conducted by Sears and affirmed by Biddle.

IMPRISONMENT AND RELEASE

Following the Supreme Court decision, Bridges did not hesitate to petition for citizenship, which, despite his estranged wife's contentions about his ties to the Communist Party, the United States finally granted after twenty-five years. His troubles were not over, however; in

1949 the new administration of President Harry Truman (1884–1972), anxious about its anti-Communist credentials, indicted the now notorious union leader for perjury on the grounds that he had lied about his party membership during his citizenship hearing four years earlier. Convicted during the height of anti-Communist hysteria in 1950, Bridges received concurrent sentences of two and five years.

In 1953 the Supreme Court reversed Bridges's perjury conviction on the grounds that the Wartime Suspension of Limitations Act (1942) did not apply to nonpecuniary offenses. In 1955, finally, Judge Louis Goodman (1892–1961) rejected a final civil action to cancel Bridges's naturalization on grounds of fraud; he found, as Landis had done earlier, that the testimony of government witnesses had been riddled with "discrepancies, animosities, vituperations … [and] hates." Bridges was at last free of the government's vendetta to deport him, but not before the Internal Revenue Service collected $11,000 in back taxes owed for his legal defense.

Bridges escaped the worst of the postwar Red Scare, supported by a strong union, key government personnel, and what was for a time the most liberal Supreme Court of the twentieth century. Others, especially aliens who had not become citizens, were not so fortunate. In 1952 the Supreme Court majority sustained provisions of the Alien Registration Act (1940) providing for the deportation of aliens who had been at any time a member of the Communist Party (*Harisiades v. Shaughnessy*, 342 U.S. 580 [1952]). The majority also ruled that aliens could be held without bail pending a determination of their deportability (*Carlson v. Landon*, 342 U.S. 524 [1952]), and as late as 1960, the Court upheld the denial of Social Security benefits to an alien deported for membership in the Communist Party (*Flemming v. Nestor*, 363 U.S. 603 [1960]).

SEE ALSO *Cold War; Naturalization and the Constitution*

BIBLIOGRAPHY

Kutler, Stanley I. 1982. *The American Inquisition: Justice and Injustice in the Cold War*. New York: Hill & Wang.

Larrowe, Charles P. 1972. *Harry Bridges: The Rise and Fall of Radical Labor in the United States*. New York: L. Hill.

Michael Parrish

BRIEFS

The U.S. Supreme Court is principally an appellate court. Except in a narrow category of cases where it has original jurisdiction (such as disputes between states over geographic boundaries), the Supreme Court does not conduct evidentiary trial proceedings. The vast majority of its cases involve the review of decisions made by lower state and federal courts and the resolution of important questions of federal and constitutional law. The Court's appellate docket is discretionary, meaning that the justices can decide for themselves which cases they will hear and decide.

The key written pleadings in an appellate case are called *briefs*. Briefs, which become public records upon filing, are concise documents that detail the dispute's factual background, offer points of authority and precedent, and make legal arguments about how the case should be decided. The Supreme Court made such filings mandatory in 1821, requiring parties to submit "a printed brief or abstract of the cause containing the substance of all the material pleadings, facts, and documents, on which the parties rely, and the points of law and fact intended to be presented at the argument". The three main categories of briefs submitted in the Supreme Court are petitions for a writ of certiorari, merits briefs, and amicus briefs.

PETITIONS FOR CERTIORARI

A party seeking appellate review in the Supreme Court begins the process by filing a petition for a writ of certiorari. The cert petition (which typically is opposed by the party that prevailed in the lower court) is a written request for a further appeal, together with an explanation of why the case justifies the Supreme Court's attention. Only a minute fraction of such requests are granted. During the October 2005 Term, for example, over 8,500 cert petitions were filed, out of which only eighty-seven cases were accepted and argued (Supreme Court of the United States, December 29, 2006).

There is no oral advocacy in the cert process; petitions are granted or denied based solely upon the written briefs. Successful cert petitions typically demonstrate that the case presents either one of two fundamental considerations. First, the case may involve an issue of national importance, such as the 2000 presidential election at issue in *Bush v. Gore,* 531 U.S. 98 (2000). Grants of certiorari in such cases are far less common than those premised on the second factor: that the case will enable the Court to resolve a dispute among lower courts over the meaning of a federal law or constitutional provision.

MERITS BRIEFS

If the justices grant the cert petition, the case is placed on the Court's docket and the clock begins to run on the merits briefing process. Briefs must be submitted in strict compliance with numerous filing deadlines, which ensure the justices sufficient time to study the written materials prior to oral argument. The competing legal arguments are presented largely in the petitioner's merits brief, the respondent's opposition, and the petitioner's reply to the opposition brief.

A high quality brief is critical to success in the Supreme Court. In the American legal system, almost all appellate work involves written legal analysis, with only a comparatively limited part of the process devoted to oral argument. Even the case of *Bush v. Gore*, which involved a disputed presidential election, received a scant thirty additional minutes for oral argument. The advocacy of the parties in the written briefs submitted long before oral argument thus is by far the most important factor in the Court's consideration of the case.

The contents of successful briefs have changed over time. Until the early twentieth century, briefs consisted of pure legal analysis. In 1908, however, Louis Brandeis, who later became an associate Justice on the Supreme Court (1916–1939), pioneered a new form of written advocacy in the case of *Muller v. Oregon,* 208 U.S. 412 (1908). In what subsequently became known as the *Brandeis Brief,* Brandeis supported his client's legal position with empirical data documenting the detrimental effects of long working hours on the health of women. This innovative use of social science later became common practice in many types of cases. It played a particularly important role in cases addressing the legal classification of groups of individuals. In *Brown v. Board of Education,* 347 U.S. 483 (1954), for example, the constitutional equal protection claims were buttressed by factual data on the psychological harm that segregation caused to African American children.

AMICUS BRIEFS

Apart from the litigants, other individuals, organizations, and groups that are potentially impacted by the outcome of a particular case also may wish to make their views known. Such interested parties are known as amicus curiae (friends of the court), who formally state their positions through so-called *amicus briefs*. Amicus briefs appear at both the petition and merits stages. At the petition stage, they suggest additional reasons for the Court to accept the case (or not). At the merits stage, amicus briefs bolster the arguments of one party to the case and offer additional perspectives on the broader implications of the Court's decision.

Cases that attract significant public attention, or which present important or novel questions, often attract the involvement of numerous friends of the court as well. A good example is *Hamdan v. Rumsfeld,* 548 U.S. 507 (2006), where nine amicus briefs were filed in support of Hamdan's cert petition. Once cert was granted, forty-four additional amicus briefs were filed. Extensive amicus practice also occurs in key business disputes. The Court's decision in the patent case of *KSR International Co. v.*

Teleflex Inc., 550 U.S. __ (2007), for example, was informed by amicus briefs filed by some thirty-eight industry and technical organizations.

The U.S. government plays a unique and important role in amicus practice at the Supreme Court. In cases where the federal government is not a party, the solicitor general's office (which represents the United States in all Supreme Court cases) often participates on an amicus basis. Many times at the invitation of the Court itself, the solicitor general will submit a brief detailing the position and policies of the executive branch and offering its views on how the Court should decide the case in question.

CONTENTS OF BRIEFS

Every aspect of the form and content of a Supreme Court brief is detailed in the Court's rules of practice. These specify the minutiae of format, font size, margins, citations to legal authority and the factual record, how briefs must be bound or stapled, the number of copies, and the date, time, and manner in which they must be filed and served (both electronically and in hard copy). The length depends on whether the brief is a cert petition or opposition (9,000 words), a merits brief or opposition (15,000 words), a reply (7,500 words), or an amicus brief (9,000 words). Even color is specified: white and orange covers at the petition stage; blue, red, and yellow covers for merits briefs; and gray (solicitor general briefs) and green covers for amicus briefs.

There is a strong practical basis for such uniformity. Per the late Chief Justice William Rehnquist: "All of this may seem highly ritualistic until it is remembered that the bundle of briefs that a justice pulls out in a particular case may well include eight or ten separate briefs, and it is very handy to be able to identify them by color without first having to read the legends on the cover" (2001, p. 239). The failure to adhere to the numerous technical requirements can lead to a brief being rejected by the clerk's office, although strict compliance is relaxed when fairness requires. For example, pleadings filed in forma pauperis, by indigent litigants without access to a lawyer, need not follow the stringent requirements applied to briefs filed by legal counsel.

As the term suggests, the contents of a brief should be concise, focused, and relevant. The subject matter of merits briefs is limited strictly to the questions presented by the case (meaning, the Court's basis for granting the cert petition in the first place). The Court's rules of practice require briefs to "be concise, logically arranged with proper headings, and free of irrelevant, immaterial, or scandalous matter[. . .]." But something more than technical competence is required to prevail in the Supreme Court. A winning brief not only makes clear and convincing legal arguments but also captures the justices' attention through compelling style and prose.

Justice Wiley Rutledge (1894–1949) offered the following advice to appellate lawyers in 1942, which is equally valid today: "Make your briefs clear, concise, honest, balanced, buttressed, convincing and interesting. The last is not the least. A dull brief may be good law. An interesting one will make the judge aware of this" (Hall, Ely, and Grossman 2005, p. 109).

SEE ALSO *Amicus Curiae; Brandeis Brief; In Forma Pauperis; Interest Groups*

BIBLIOGRAPHY

Hall, Kermit L.; James W. Ely, Jr.; and Joel B. Grossman, eds. 2005. *The Oxford Companion to the Supreme Court of the United States.* 2nd edition. Oxford: Oxford University Press.

Rehnquist, William. 2001. *The Supreme Court.* New York: Alfred A. Knopf.

Supreme Court of the United States. December 29, 2006. "2006 Year-End Report on the Federal Judiciary." Available from http://www.supremecourtus.gov.

Supreme Court of the United States. July 18, 2007. "Rules of the Supreme Court of the United States." Available from http://www.supremecourtus.gov.

CASES

George W. Bush v. Palm Beach County Canvassing Board, Case No. 00-836, U.S. Supreme Court Docket Sheet, available at http://www.supremecourtus.gov/docket/00-836.htm (accessed Nov. 21, 2007).

KSR International Co. v. Teleflex Inc., Case No. 04-1350, U.S. Supreme Court Docket Sheet, available at http://www.supremecourtus.gov/docket/04-1350.htm (accessed Nov. 21, 2007).

Case No. 05-184, U.S. Supreme Court Docket Sheet, available at http://www.supremecourtus.gov/docket/05-184.htm (accessed Nov. 21, 2007).

David L. Nersessian

BRIGGS V. SPAULDING, 141 U.S. 132 (1891)

Briggs v. Spaulding, 141 U.S. 132 (1891), a classic case from 1891 that arose in the context of the failure of a national bank, is often cited on the supervisory duties of directors. Chief Justice Melville Fuller wrote the majority opinion, holding that although the directors had a duty of reasonable oversight, none breached that duty. Justice John Marshall Harlan wrote a dissent, which also recognized the duty but asserted that it had been breached.

The bank became bankrupt around ninety days after the directors were elected, and in that time, they had paid no attention to the business of the bank other than to inquire from time to time how it was doing. The manager and principal stockholder of the bank, who was responsible for making loans that led to the bank's downfall, had induced several of the directors to their posts. He was generally respected and the bank's reputation was sound. It was asserted that the directors should have actively examined the bank's affairs, and had they done so, would have discovered its difficulties and been able to prevent the subsequent losses. The Court examined the actions of each director, and for various reasons (including one being on a leave, another being physically infirm, and another being asked to serve in a merely advisory capacity) held that none was negligent and, therefore, none was liable for the losses.

In finding the directors not liable for losses, the *Briggs* court stated a standard of care that is frequently cited in law review articles. The standard of care articulated in the opinion is as follows:

> Without reviewing the various decisions on the subject, we hold that directors must exercise ordinary care and prudence in the administration of the affairs of a bank, and that this includes something more than officiating as figure-heads. They are entitled under the law to commit the banking business, as defined, to their duly-authorized officers, but this does not absolve them from the duty of reasonable supervision, nor ought they to be permitted to be shielded from liability because of want of knowledge of wrong-doing, if that ignorance is the result of gross inattention....

Justice Harlan's dissent would have found the directors liable:

> Their eyes were as completely closed to what he did, from day to day, in directing the affairs of the bank, as if they had deliberately determined not to see and not to know how he controlled its business.... [T]he proof is clear and convincing that a considerable part of the amount lost to the bank, and therefore to its stockholders and depositors, could have been saved, if they had exercised such care in the supervision and management of the bank's business as men of ordinary diligence exercise in respect to their own business.

In law review articles and other secondary sources, *Briggs* is often cited for the principle that corporate directors are required to act on behalf of the corporation as would be expected of an ordinarily prudent person in the conduct of her own affairs. *Briggs* has been characterized as establishing a corporate governance standard in federal common law. However, in *Erie Railroad Co. v. Tomkins*, 304 U.S. 64 (1938), the Supreme Court held that there is no federal general common law. In *Atherton v. Federal*

Deposit Insurance Corporation, 519 U.S, 213 (1997), the Supreme Court addressed whether *Briggs* survived *Erie*, and concluded that it did not. The *Atherton* opinion states: "We conclude that the federal common law standards enunciated in cases such as *Briggs* did not survive this Court's later decision in *Erie*. There is no federal common law that would create a general standard of care applicable to this case."

Since *Atherton*, most opinions that cite *Briggs* state that *Atherton* overruled *Briggs*, and reiterate the Court's analysis in *Atherton* (e.g., *Motorcity of Jacksonville, LTD. v. Southeast Bank* 120 F.3d 1140, 1142 [11th Cir. 1997] and *F.D.I.C. v. Healey*, 991 F.Supp. 53, 56 [D.Conn., 1998]). *Briggs*, though overruled, is a good, early example of the ongoing controversy in corporate governance over the nature of directors' duties of care in stewarding the corporate enterprise. While courts and commentators often agree that directors have a duty of reasonable care, controversy remains as to how affirmative that duty is and what kinds of factors should put directors on notice that a more hands-on approach is required. For a modern example of a more searching standard similar to what Justice Harlan applied in dissent, see *Caremark International Inc. Derivative Litigation*, 698 A.2d 959 (Del. Ch. 1996), where former Delaware Chancellor William T. Allen held that the fiduciary duty of care of corporate directors included an obligation for directors to take some affirmative law compliance measures. Specifically, the board has a "responsibility to assure that appropriate information and reporting systems are established by management" to ensure that the company complies with the key regulatory regimes under which it operates. In *Stone v. Ritter,* 911 A.2d 362 (Del 2006), the Delaware Supreme court confirmed that the *Caremark* standard is now the law of Delaware, holding that Caremark articulates the necessary conditions for assessing director oversight liability.

SEE ALSO *Corporate Law*

BIBLIOGRAPHY

Bienenstock, Martin J. 2006. "Recent Developments Affecting Chapter 11 Cases." In *Current Developments in Bankruptcy and Reorganization (28th Annual)*. New York: Practising Law Institute.

Narayanan, M.P.; Cindy A. Schipani; and H. Nejat Seyhan. 2007. "The Economic Impact of Backdating of Executive Stock Options." *Michigan Law Review* 105(8): 1597–1642.

Taylor, Celia R. 2006. "The Inadequacy of Fiduciary Duty Doctrine: Why Corporate Managers Have Little to Fear and What Might Be Done about It." *Oregon Law Review* 85(4): 993–1026.

Kellye Y. Testy

BROWNING-FERRIS INDUSTRIES OF VERMONT, INC. V. KELCO DISPOSAL, INC., 492 U.S. 257 (1989)

Joseph Kelley and Kelco Disposal, Inc. filed suit against Browning-Ferris Industries (BFI) in federal court, alleging that BFI used extremely low predatory pricing to try to drive Kelco out of the commercial waste collection business in Burlington, Vermont. A jury found BFI liable for antitrust violations under federal law and for interfering with Kelco's contractual relations in violation of Vermont tort law. The jury awarded Kelco $51,146 in compensatory damages and $6 million in punitive damages on the state-law claim. BFI contended that the excessive fines clause of the Eighth Amendment protected it from such a disproportionate punitive damages award. The Supreme Court of the United States rejected this claim. It held that, in light of the history and purposes of the excessive fines clause, the clause did not constrain an award of money damages in a civil suit when the government neither had prosecuted the action nor had any right to receive a share of the damages awarded.

The Court concluded that the framers of the Eighth Amendment were concerned in 1791 with the potential abuse of the government's prosecutorial power; they expressed no concern with the extent or purposes of civil damages. Nothing in English history indicated to the Court that the excessive fines clause of the English Bill of Rights of 1689, the direct ancestor of the Eighth Amendment, was intended to apply to damages awarded in disputes between private parties. The Court specifically rejected the contention that the history of the use and abuse in England of amercements was a reason to conclude that the excessive fines clause limited a civil jury's ability to award punitive damages. Although the Magna Carta (1215) placed limits on the Crown's use of excessive amercements, ancient limitations placed on excesses of royal power were not applicable to a case where a private party received punitive damages from another party and the government had no share in the recovery. Because the State of Vermont had not taken any steps to punish BFI, nor used the civil courts to extract large payments or forfeiture from the company, the clause did not apply to the case.

The Court refused to consider the possible application of the due process clause of the Fourteenth Amendment to the award because BFI had failed to raise the issue before the lower courts in the case. In later cases, the Court has found the due process clause to be a check on excessive punitive damages awarded in both state and federal courts.

SEE ALSO *Antitrust; Punitive Damages*

BIBLIOGRAPHY

Massey, Calvin. 1987. "The Excessive Fines Clause and Punitive Damages: Some Lessons from History." *Vanderbilt Law Review* 40: 1233, 1240–1269.

Zipursky, Benjamin C. 2005. "A Theory of Punitive Damages." *Texas Law Review* 84: 105–172.

David I. Levine

BROWN V. BOARD OF EDUCATION, 347 U.S. 483 (1954)

On May 17, 1954, the U.S. Supreme Court issued one of its most controversial, yet momentous, rulings in *Brown v. Board of Education of Topeka,* 347 U.S. 483 (1954). The Court, under Chief Justice Earl Warren, unanimously ruled that "in the field of public education, the doctrine of 'separate but equal' has no place. Separate educational facilities are inherently unequal." *Brown* overturned the Court's decision in *Plessy v. Ferguson,* 163 U.S. 537 (1896), which held that de jure racial segregation was constitutional as long as the separate conditions were equal. In ruling that legally sanctioned racial segregation violated the Fourteenth Amendment rights of black children to equal protection under the law, *Brown* firmly established the legal basis and fortified the social mandate for the destruction of racial segregation in all facets of American life. Led by future Supreme Court Justice Thurgood Marshall, *Brown* was the most famous in a long series of lawsuits initiated by the National Association for the Advancement of Colored People (NAACP) Legal Defense and Educational Fund to break down racial segregation in the field of education and beyond.

HISTORICAL CONTEXT

The Thirteenth, Fourteenth, and Fifteenth Amendments passed after the Civil War (1861–1865) had brought some hope for black equality by abolishing slavery, guaranteeing blacks citizenship, and guaranteeing voting rights (for males), respectively. By 1877, however, the former Confederate states had each been "redeemed" by white conservatives determined to push blacks as close back to their former, wholly inferior status as possible. The Court's decision in *Plessy* that racial segregation (also known as "Jim Crow") was acceptable as long as the conditions were equal merely upheld the legality of what had become common practice across the South.

There were numerous pre-NAACP challenges to school desegregation, the earliest being *Roberts v. City of Boston,* 59 Mass. 198 (1849). The road to *Brown,* however, was paved largely by Charles Hamilton Houston. As special counsel of the NAACP from 1934 to 1940, the former Howard University law professor and vice dean focused on the educational system as the most critical battleground in the struggle for black equality.

Houston's strategy, followed also by his successor, Thurgood Marshall, was to file lawsuits forcing states to comply with the "equal" part of the separate-but-equal doctrine from *Plessy.* The thinking was that states would eventually find maintaining two truly equal systems too draining on resources to continue. At the same time, the organization would take every opportunity to argue to the courts that the segregated system should be dismantled rather than mended.

Throughout the 1940s, the NAACP frequently won school equalization cases in state courts. However, the cases had to be argued district by district, which was time-consuming and expensive. The strategy was also limited by the localities' evasion tactics. King George County, Virginia, for example, chose to equalize its curriculum by dropping several advanced courses from its white high school rather than add them at the black school. Additionally, as Virginia NAACP lawyer Spottswood W. Robinson, III (1916–1998) noted, if school systems actually equalized black schools in all measurable factors, courts would have little reason to ever accept the argument that segregation itself violated blacks' right to equal protection under the law.

A series of victories desegregating graduate and professional schools eventually emboldened the NAACP to push for public school desegregation. Blacks were ordered admitted into white law schools in Maryland (*Murray v. Pearson,* 169 Md. 478 [1936]) and Missouri (*Missouri ex rel. Gaines v. Canada,* 305 U.S. 337 [1938]), and into the University of Oklahoma's law and graduate schools (*Sipuel v. Board of Regents of University of Oklahoma,* 332 U.S. 631 [1948] and *McLaurin v. Oklahoma State Regents,* 339 U.S. 637 [1950]). The defining victory came in June 1950 with *Sweatt v. Painter,* 339 U.S. 629 (1950). In affirming Heman Sweatt's (1912–1982) right to attend the University of Texas Law School, the Court noted that there were not only tangible inequalities (such as the 65,000 volumes in the white law library versus 16,500 in the recently opened black one), but also intangible factors like "reputation of the faculty, experience of the administration, position and influence of the alumni, standing in the community, traditions and prestige" that made the education at the white law school superior. In *Sweatt,* the Court essentially acknowledged that, at least in the realm of legal education, separate could not be equal. The NAACP decided it was time to seek the desegregation of public schools.

THE *BROWN* CASES IN THE LOWER COURTS

The desegregation cases that came to be consolidated in the Supreme Court under the heading *Brown v. Board of Education* came out of four states. A fifth case, involving

Students and parents of the* Brown v. Board of Education *Supreme Court case. *In 1954, the Supreme Court issued the Brown v. Board of Education decision, ordering the desegregation of public schools throughout the United States. However, as the Supreme Court charged the lower federal courts with insuring the states integrate their school systems "with all deliberate speed," some southern states used this vague timeframe to delay complying with the ruling.* CARL IWASAKI/TIME LIFE PICTURES/GETTY IMAGES

the District of Columbia, was heard simultaneously, but was ruled upon separately.

Briggs v. Elliott, 342 U.S. 350 (1952) started as a request to the Clarendon County, South Carolina, school board to provide bus transportation for black children as it did for whites. Unsuccessful in this request, a group of twenty parents, including the case's namesake, Harry Briggs, agreed to challenge school segregation. Thurgood Marshall and state NAACP lawyer Harold Boulware (1913–1983) filed the case in December 1950. In district court, the county admitted that the schools were indeed unequal but argued that the state had recently begun preparing to equalize them. It was in *Briggs* that psychologist Kenneth Clark's (1914–2005) famous doll tests were first used to argue segregation's detrimental effect on black children. Clark's argument fell on deaf ears, however. The district court ordered the school board to begin equalizing the separate schools. The Supreme Court agreed to hear the NAACP's appeal, but remanded it back

to the lower court for rehearing after the county filed an equalization progress report. In March 1952, the district court ruled that the county was making substantial progress toward equalization. Marshall argued that the schools would always be unequal as long as they remained separated by race. He reappealed to the Supreme Court that May.

Oliver Brown and twelve other black parents were recruited by the local NAACP chapter to sue for an end to segregated elementary schools in Topeka, Kansas (*Brown v. Board of Education*). Though there was a white school seven blocks from her home, Brown's daughter, Linda, had to walk through a dangerous railroad switching yard to reach her bus stop for a thirty minute ride to school. NAACP lawyer Robert L. Carter (1917–) argued the case in federal district court in June 1951. While agreeing that school segregation was detrimental to black children, the district court refused to order desegregation because the schools were essentially equal in all measurable respects, such as buildings, transportation, and curriculum.

Moton High School in Prince Edward County, Virginia, was grossly overcrowded and did not have a cafeteria, a gym, locker rooms, or a nurse's office. In April 1951, sixteen-year-old Barbara Johns and other student leaders organized a protest walkout by the school's 450 students. The striking students asked Virginia NAACP lawyers Spottswood Robinson, Oliver Hill (1907–2007), and Martin A. Martin to assist them in getting a new, equal school. The NAACP agreed to take the case if their parents consented to seek desegregation instead. In May 1952, the district court ruled in *Davis v. County School Board*, 103 F.Supp. 337 (1952) that there had been "no hurt or harm to either race" as a result of school segregation but did order the school board to equalize the black facilities. The NAACP appealed to the Supreme Court, arguing that equalization of facilities would still not provide the equal education guaranteed black children by the Fourteenth Amendment.

Belton v. Gebhart and *Bulah v. Gebhart,* 32 Del.Ch. 343 (1952) were filed concurrently in Delaware's Court of Chancery by Louis L. Redding (1901–1998), the state's first black attorney, and white NAACP lawyer Jack Greenberg. The first case was brought on behalf of Ethel Belton and seven other parents who lived in Claymont but could not send their children to the town's high school. The students instead had to travel nearly an hour to the state's lone black college-preparatory high school in Wilmington, which was inferior in curricular and extracurricular offerings, size of classes, teacher qualifications, and physical facilities. The second case was brought on behalf of Sarah Bulah, who had sought Redding's help in getting transportation provided for her daughter to the one-room Hockessin School No. 107 for blacks located two miles away from her house. Redding had agreed to assist Mrs. Bulah if she would instead seek admission for her daughter to the well-appointed Hockessin School No. 29. Chancellor Collins J. Seitz (1914–1998) believed that *Plessy* should be overturned, but that it was the Supreme Court's role to do so. He did, however, order the plaintiffs admitted into the white schools, given the clear inequality of the black ones. Claymont High School and Hockessin School No. 29 were integrated in the fall of 1952, without incident.

In September 1950, Howard University law professor James Nabrit filed suit in U.S. district court on behalf of twelve-year-old Spottswood T. Bolling and four other students denied admission to all-white Sousa Junior High. Unlike the other four cases, *Bolling v. Sharpe,* 347 U.S. 497 (1954), did not mention the clearly unequal facilities, as Nabrit was determined to make the courts finally address the issue of the unconstitutionality of segregation itself. The district court dismissed the case, ruling that the District of Columbia Court of Appeals' recent decision in *Carr v. Corning,* 182 F.2d 14 (D.C. Cir. 1950) had clearly stated that segregation was constitutional and that, since he had not complained about the inequality of the schools, there was no basis for the case. Nabrit successfully appealed to the Supreme Court for a writ of certiorari.

BROWN IN THE SUPREME COURT

On June 9, 1952, the Supreme Court agreed to hear *Briggs* and *Brown* in the fall term, but pushed the date into December in order to add *Davis*, the *Gebhart* cases, and *Bolling*. The NAACP's top lawyers and affiliates spent long months crafting their briefs arguing that segregated schools violated black children's Fourteenth Amendment right to equal protection under the law. Important to their case was an appendix prepared by Kenneth Clark outlining the ways segregation produced in black children "feelings of inferiority" and "a lowering of personal ambitions." The report, endorsed by thirty-five prominent scholars, went further to stress the negative effects on white youth as they tried to make sense of a world that preached democracy, morality, and religiosity, yet discriminated so blatantly against the minority race. The *Bolling* brief, prepared separately, argued that blacks' Fifth Amendment right to due process was violated by denying them the right to attend nonsegregated schools because there was no defensible reasonable rationale for the denial.

The federal government filed an amicus brief supporting school desegregation. Written by Assistant Solicitor General Philip Elman (1918–1999), it was an influential brief for the justices, arguing strongly for the rightness of ending school segregation, yet advising the Court that it could avoid chaos in the South by ordering gradual rather than immediate desegregation.

Oral argument in the consolidated *Brown* cases took place from December 9 to 11, 1952. Carter argued for *Brown,* Marshall for *Briggs,* Robinson for *Davis* and Nabrit and George Edward Chalmers Hayes (1894–1968) for *Bolling*. In the *Gebhart v. Belton* case, Redding and Greenberg argued for the defense, since the State had lost the original case. Arguing the case for continued school segregation were Assistant Attorney General of Kansas, Paul Wilson, for Topeka, renowned New York attorney John W. Davis for Clarendon County, Richmond lawyer Justin Moore for Prince Edward County, D.C., Chief Counsel Milton Korman for the District of Columbia, and State Attorney General Albert Young for Delaware. Among their arguments was that the Fourteenth Amendment did not deny states the right to classify students by race; that the black schools were now either equal or on their way to equality as a result of the orders of the lower courts; and that the social science data arguing that segregation was harmful to black children was flimsy and irrelevant to the constitutional issue at hand.

In the justices' initial deliberations after oral argument, only five justices had firmly decided which way they planned to vote. Justices Hugo Black, William O.

Douglas, Harold Burton (1888–1964), and Sherman Minton (1890–1965) were ready to strike down school segregation, whereas Justice Stanley Reed (1884–1980) was ready to affirm the practice. Two others, Chief Justice Fred M. Vinson and Justice Tom C. Clark (1899–1977), were also leaning strongly toward affirmation. Justice Robert H. Jackson was possibly willing to reverse *Plessy* as long as the Court made clear that it was making new law in response to changed times and circumstances, and did not condemn the South as having acting unconstitutionally by operating under *Plessy.* Justice Felix Frankfurter was strongly in favor of ending segregation, but was concerned that the framers of the Fourteenth Amendment had not meant to disallow racial segregation and that forcing the South to comply with a ruling outlawing school segregation would be extremely difficult.

The justices agreed that their decision was too important for a split vote. To give themselves more time to unite around an opinion, they scheduled the cases for reargument in October 1953. The litigants were asked to address issues concerning the Fourteenth Amendment's original intent regarding school segregation. The power of the judiciary to end school segregation if the Fourteenth Amendment's original intent proved to be unclear, as did the question of how the decision might be implemented, assuming that the Court overturned *Plessy.*

Some 200 people worked feverishly throughout the summer and fall on the NAACP's answers to these questions, including noted historians C. Vann Woodward (1908–1999) and John Hope Franklin (1915–). The final 235-page brief argued that the historical evidence demonstrated that the Fourteenth Amendment's intention was to prohibit racial discrimination by the states. However, even if this were not the case, the brief added, justice in modern-day Cold War America necessitated segregation's end: "Twentieth century America, fighting racism at home and abroad, has rejected the race views of *Plessy v. Ferguson* because we have come to the realization that such views obviously tend to preserve not the strength but the weakness of our heritage." *Plessy* had to be struck down because "segregation was designed to insure inequality. . . . There never was and never will be any separate equality." On the other side, the briefs basically all agreed with John W. Davis's assessment that there was not a "scintilla of evidence to the effect that the framers intended the amendment to outlaw segregated schools."

Given Chief Justice Vinson's inclination to affirm *Plessy* and his general lack of leadership in uniting the justices in decisions, the *Brown* decision might well have turned out differently had Vinson not died of a heart attack on September 8, 1953. Of Vinson's passing so close to the start of the *Brown* reargument, Justice Frankfurter remarked, "This is the first indication I have ever had that there is a God" (Kluger 1976, p. 656).

> *To separate them [black children] from others of similar age and qualifications solely because of their race generates a feeling of inferiority as to their status in the community that may affect their hearts and minds in a way unlikely ever to be undone. . . . We conclude that in the field of public education the doctrine of "separate but equal" has no place. Separate educational facilities are inherently unequal.*
>
> SOURCE: Earl Warren, *Brown v. Board of Education,* 347 U.S. 483, 494–495 (1954).

President Dwight D. Eisenhower chose two-term California governor Earl Warren as Vinson's successor. Warren immediately set about building relationships with each Justice, which paid off when it was time to take the final vote on *Brown.* From December 7 to 10, 1953, the reargument took place. From the first deliberations, Warren was convinced *Plessy* should be overturned. The critical issue in his mind was formulating a decision around which all nine justices could unite and that would not unduly agitate the white South. The Court did not take a vote that day, but continued to talk about the case weekly, in an attempt to generate a consensus. The final vote was likely eight for striking down *Plessy* and one against (Reed). Warren wrote the opinions for both the state and D.C. cases, crafting them to be "short, readable by the lay public, non-rhetorical, unemotional and, above all, non-accusatory" (Kluger 1976, p. 696). Ultimately, Reed heeded Warren's pleas about the importance of a united front and decided not to write a dissent.

In now famous words, Warren read the Court's opinion on May 17, 1954. The opinion discussed the Court's inability to truly know the intent of the Fourteenth Amendment's framers on the matter of school segregation, especially given the infant state of public education at that time. Therefore, in approaching the question of whether separate schools could be truly equal, the Court had to consider the importance of education in modern times. Noting how critical education was to the functioning of individuals and society, it "must be made available to all on equal terms." On the question, therefore, of whether separate black and white schools—which in all measurable ways were equal—still denied blacks equal educational opportunities, Warren answered, "We believe that it does." In the document's most famous lines, the decision concluded that "in the field of public education the doctrine of 'separate but equal' has no place. Separate educational facilities are inherently unequal." The decision ended with the Court stating that it would hear arguments regarding implementation in the fall 1955 term. Warren then read the opinion in *Bolling v. Sharpe*, which stated that "in view of our decision that the Constitution prohibits the states from maintaining racially segregated public schools, it would be unthinkable that the same Constitution would impose a lesser duty on the Federal Government."

IMMEDIATE RESPONSE TO THE RULING

There was both enthusiastic praise and fervent denunciation of the *Brown* ruling. Kluger writes that Thurgood Marshall recalled being "so happy I was numb," while Senator James Eastland (1904–1986) of Mississippi indignantly asserted that the South "will not abide by or obey this legislative decision by a political court" (Kluger 1976, pp. 710, 714). The Chicago-based black newspaper, the *Defender*, proclaimed the ruling the "beginning of the end of the dual society in American life," while Jackson, Mississippi's *Daily News* predicted that "human blood may stain Southern soil in many places" (Martin 1998, pp. 203–204).

Many blacks, but not all, were ecstatic over the *Brown* decision. In Prince Edward County, Joan Johns Cobbs, sister of 1951 student strike leader Barbara Johns (1935–1991), felt "jubilant…it meant a lot to us" (Turner 2001, p. 238). However, many students at the new Moton High School, which had opened in 1953, were happy in their brand-new school: "We had the better school by that time. I don't think we wanted it [desegregation] at that time," recalled one (quoted in Turner 2001, p. 239). Educators, too, were often critical of the move toward desegregation, not just out of fear for their jobs, but because of the implications inherent in the argument that separate could never be truly equal, that black children could not conceivably get a good education under an all-black teaching staff (Turner 2001, pp. 228–229, 240–243). Taylor Branch notes in *Parting the Waters* that Barbara Johns, then attending all-black Spelman College, sensed "muted apprehension among her fellow students. They seemed to worry that the great vindication might mean the extinction of schools like Spelman" (Branch 1988, pp. 112–113).

For the most part, both sides took a wait-and-see attitude. Blacks knew better than to think this ruling was going to magically change the racial realities of America overnight. Though in some places—including Baltimore, Maryland, and Wilmington, Delaware—desegregation efforts began in the 1954–1955 school year, most whites did not yet know how the decision would affect them because of the Court's purposeful one-year delay of the implementation phase.

BROWN II

In dealing with what came to be known as *Brown II* (*Brown v. Board of Education*, 349 U.S. 294 [1955]), the Court had to grapple with how to balance black children's constitutional rights with the realities of southern race relations. Peaceful and immediate desegregation might well occur in places like Topeka, where the process would put a small group of black children in a class that was mainly white; but it was highly unlikely in places like Clarendon, South Carolina, where desegregation would entail putting a small group of white children in a class that was overwhelmingly black and where legacies of plantation slavery had left ideas of white superiority deeply ingrained. The NAACP nonetheless pushed aggressively for implementation to be required immediately across the board. The organization believed that black children simply should not have their rights denied any longer and a gradual approach would give the opposition time to organize.

The white southern attorneys argued on behalf of their states that the integration of black and white students would require such a huge shift in southern mores and that an immeasurably long period of time would be needed to effect this change. The U.S. government's brief advised that the Court should insist that all locales start the process immediately, but give the district courts the flexibility to manage the process and timetable based on local conditions.

Oral argument in *Brown II* took place in April 1955, delayed from the fall by the death of Justice Jackson and the need to confirm a new Justice, John Marshall Harlan II (grandson of the sole justice to dissent against the majority opinion in *Plessy*). On behalf of the black students in each of the districts involved, the NAACP lawyers pleaded for the Court to act decisively and order that desegregation begin in the coming school year. Foreshadowing the various methods states would use to delay desegregation, South Carolina's lawyer S. Emory Rogers boldly told the Court that the state had no intention of even making an honest attempt to integrate the schools. For Virginia, attorney Archibald Robertson noted that there were more subtle ways than outright disobedience to forestall desegregation of the schools, such as refusing to fund the schools and repealing compulsory attendance laws.

Very clear on the need for a gradual approach, the Court settled on the phrase "with all deliberate speed" as the timeframe. The oxymoronic phrase had been used in several previous Court opinions, beginning with Oliver Wendell Holmes's usage in *Virginia v. West Virginia*, 246 U.S. 565 (1918). *Brown II* was handed down May 31, 1955, in another unanimous opinion. The decision remanded the cases back to the district courts, which were ordered to "require that the defendants make a prompt and reasonable start toward full compliance with our May 17, 1954 ruling." Additional time might then be granted to fully carry out the order, provided the defendant demonstrated both the necessity of the delay to the public good and good faith efforts to comply "at the earliest practicable date."

Despite the fact that the Court did not order immediate desegregation, Marshall was optimistic. He boasted to Baltimore *Afro* newspaper publisher Carl Murphy, that "those white crackers are going to get tired of having Negro lawyers beating 'em every day in court" as the NAACP went district by district suing for implementation (Kluger 1976, p. 747).

MASSIVE AND PASSIVE RESISTANCE TO *BROWN*

In some ways Marshall's optimism was born out. While *Brown* purposely spoke only to segregation in schools, it became the legal basis for outlawing segregation in the full spectrum of public places across the South, though the actual desegregation of such facilities often involved nonviolent black protest and violent white resistance. Whether *Brown* was a critical source of inspiration for the Civil Rights Movement that began in earnest in December 1955 with the Montgomery bus boycott is debatable. As Michael Klarman (2004) argues, this decision may have been instrumental in causing a violent backlash among southern whites, which then led to the passage of Civil Rights legislation, but it remains a source of debate among scholars.

Progress in the explicit subject of *Brown*, the schools, frequently proved much harder to realize. As the NAACP lawyers had feared, the Court's refusal to order immediate desegregation, coupled with President Eisenhower's refusal to endorse *Brown*, encouraged massive resistance in the South. In Arkansas, Governor Orval Faubus (1910–1994) used National Guard troops to block the entrance of nine black children who were slated to integrate Little Rock's Central High School in the fall of 1957. Ordered to remove the troops by a federal court, he did so, but the white public, emboldened by the governor's resistance, remained rebellious. President Eisenhower reluctantly federalized the National Guard and sent paratroopers from the army's 101st Airborne Division to escort the nine children into the school on September 25, 1957. The National Guard stayed the entire year, enforcing the black students' right to attend the school, though the students continued to face verbal and physical harassment throughout the year. The following year, Little Rock closed all of its public high schools rather than see them integrated. By court order, they opened back in the 1959–1960 school year on a desegregated basis.

Similarly, Virginia closed several white schools in Warren County, Charlottesville, and Norfolk in the fall of 1958 to keep them from being integrated, resulting in some 12,000 children being locked out of their schools. In January 1959, the massive resistance laws that had mandated the closures were struck down. By the fall, in all three localities the public schools had reopened and a

small group of black children had begun attending previously all-white schools, without incident. Statewide massive resistance in Virginia was dead and replaced by token desegregation.

Prince Edward County, meanwhile, continued with its massive resistance program. The courts had ruled only that the state could not close certain schools in an effort to defeat desegregation while it operated others; they had said nothing about the ability of individual counties to close all their schools to skirt desegregation. When ordered to desegregate in the fall of 1959, the board of supervisors simply withdrew funding for the public schools. Schools remained closed for five years (1959–1964), until the U.S. Supreme Court finally ordered them reopened in May 1964, declaring in *Griffin v. County School Board of Prince Edward County*, 377 U.S. 218 (1964) that "the time for mere 'deliberate speed' has run out." The county reopened the public schools as ordered, but most whites remained in the county's private school, which had opened when the public schools closed, through the 1970s.

By 1960, 802 of the 2,909 segregated school districts across the country had started at least token desegregation (Segall 1998, p. 97). However, in 1964, only 1.17 percent of black children in the eleven states of the former Confederacy were attending desegregated schools (Bell 2004, p. 96).

SCHOOL DESEGREGATION AFTER 1964

Southern desegregation efforts picked up significantly in the late 1960s and early 1970s. *Time* magazine reported on November 15, 1971 in the article "The Agony of Busing Moves North" that 39 percent of black children were attending desegregated schools in the South compared to 28 percent in the North and West. The Civil Rights Act of 1964, which authorized the withholding of federal funds from discriminatory school districts, together with the Elementary and Secondary Education Act (1965), which allocated substantial federal funding to local school districts, led southern districts to begin submitting acceptable desegregation plans. The Court signaled its impatience with districts' continued dilatory tactics, stating in rulings such as *Green v. School Board of New Kent County*, 391 U.S. 430 (1968), that it was not enough for districts to remove the barriers to school integration, but rather they had to "fashion steps which promise realistically" to actually achieve integrated schools. In *Swann v. Charlotte-Mecklenburg Board of Education*, 402 U.S. 1 (1971), the Court ruled that one such step could be busing students out of their neighborhoods, even in areas where the lack of integration was not caused by discriminatory pupil placement policies but rather by housing patterns.

Communities in the North and West proved just as massively resistant to school desegregation as southern ones when it became clear in the early 1970s that *Brown* applied to all school districts, not just to those whose inequalities had been caused by de jure segregation. White riots and school boycotts occurred in many cities over busing, most famously in the south section of Boston, Massachusetts. Unable to end the desegregation efforts through disruption, whites began doing so with their feet (so-called *white flight*). They were encouraged in this method of escape by the Court's denial in *Milliken v. Bradley*, 418 U.S. 717 (1974) of Detroit's attempt to achieve integration by busing not just in the city proper but across the entire metropolitan area. *Milliken* signaled the end of an era. In case after case in the 1980s and 1990s, the Court backed further and further away from the active pursuit of substantive integration (*Board of Education of Oklahoma City Public Schools v. Dowell*, 498 U.S. 237 [1991]; *Freeman v. Pitts*, 503 U.S. 467 [1992]; and *Missouri v. Jenkins* (*Missouri II*), 515 U.S. 70 [1995]). More recently, in a five-to-four decision, the Supreme Court sided with parents in Louisville, Kentucky, and Seattle, Washington, who argued that their districts' school integration plans—both adopted voluntarily by the local school boards in order to promote racial integration—violated the equal protection clause of the Fourteenth Amendment by using race as a factor in school assignment (*Parents Involved in Community Schools v. Seattle School District No. 1* and *Meredith v. Jefferson County Schools*, 551 U.S. __ [2007]).

The combination of judicial conservatism and white flight has meant that *Brown*'s promise of an equal education in a nonsegregated setting has still not been achieved in many areas. Many areas have, in fact, experienced resegregation. According to the U.S. Department of Education's National Center for Education Statistics, in 1988, 24 percent of black children in the South attended schools that were 90 percent or more minority. That number had increased by 2001 to 31 percent. In the Northeast, the numbers rose from 48 percent to 51.2 percent during the same time period and in the Midwest from 41.8 percent to 46.8 percent (Orfield and Lee 2004, p. 20).

CRITICISM OF *BROWN*

Brown has faced criticism from many quarters. Much criticism has been leveled at the Court's seeming reliance on social science data, rather than legal precedent, in formulating the decision. Those who believe in strict adherence to original intent argue that the framers of the Fourteenth Amendment did not mean it to ban segregated schools and, therefore, the Court in *Brown* was wrong to do so. Some argue that the Court overstepped its boundaries by interfering in a matter that should have been addressed in the legislative realm. While perhaps used for good in *Brown*, these critics argue that such abuse of judicial authority could just as easily be used against the public good.

Others argue that *Brown*, while the right decision, was issued using the wrong rationale. African-American Supreme Court Justice Clarence Thomas wrote in his concurrence in *Missouri II* that *Brown* "did not need to rely upon any psychological or social-science research in order to announce the simple, yet fundamental truth that the Government cannot discriminate among its citizens on the basis of race.... Psychological injury or benefit is irrelevant."

While the NAACP had always been convinced that the only way to achieve educational equality was through integrating the schools, a significant number of blacks agreed more with the great black intellectual W. E. B. DuBois, who wrote that "The Negro needs neither segregated schools nor mixed schools. What he needs is Education" (DuBois 1935, p. 335). Many blacks who attended separate schools strongly contend that their schools were unequal in resources only; in terms of the quality of teaching and levels of student achievement they were far superior to what most black students get today in either integrated suburban and rural classrooms, or in the majority black, overwhelmingly poor, inner-city schools that are themselves an unintended consequence of *Brown*.

The continuing tragically separate and unequal conditions of inner-city schools have been documented by scholars such as Jonathan Kozol (1991, 2005). With the white (and later black) middle-class flight from major cities, the tax base disappeared too. Inner-city schools often fail miserably to adequately educate their overwhelmingly black and Latino students, having to deal as they do with the massive social problems generally found in areas of highly concentrated poverty, with significantly less funding than their affluent suburban neighbors. In such settings, the NAACP's rationale in *Brown* still seems pertinent. Civil rights leader Julian Bond (2004) explained in a brief essay, *The Unfinished Agenda of Brown*, that it was not the presence of white students per se that made white schools superior to segregated black schools, it was that "whiteness meant access to superior resources. The only way we were going to get equality was to get in that building with those children" (pp. 130–131). But even in those areas where blacks now sit in class with whites and have access to the same resources, they do not necessarily get the same education. In desegregated schools across the country, blacks score less well than whites on standardized tests, are overrepresented in special education classes, and are underrepresented in gifted programs and college preparatory classes. Black children, especially boys, are disciplined more often—and frequently more harshly—than white students, and are more likely to drop out of school. That these problems are often not due to overt racism is only slightly comforting. In fact, if that were the main obstacle, addressing the problems would be easier. Instead, the reasons why black children on the whole do not seem to achieve as highly as whites are more complex and elusive.

Though not wanting to return to a Jim Crow society, many blacks agree with a black school administrator in Prince Edward County, who, in the late 1990s opined, "Without a doubt, if we could get everything that we have in the integrated system as far as facilities, all the resources, in a segregated, all-black school with all-black teachers I'll take it and I'll guarantee you I'll have more productive black students" (Turner 2001, p. 441).

Brown was immensely important for its acknowledgement of black equality and as a precedent for knocking down other legal barriers for both blacks and other groups. But perhaps it is too much to ask of one court ruling to undo centuries of unequal treatment. Where one stands in their beliefs about the rightness of the *Brown* decision and the continued relevance of seeking integrated schools may vary greatly based on race, class, political leaning, and many other variables. What is unquestionable is that it was one of the most significant rulings ever decided by the U.S. Supreme Court.

SEE ALSO *All Deliberate Speed; Bolling v. Sharpe, 347 U.S.497 (1954); Brown v. Board of Education (Brown II), 349 U.S. 294 (1955); Children and the Constitution; Clark, Kenneth; Education and the Constitution; Fourteenth Amendment; Marshall, Thurgood; McLaurin v. Oklahoma State Regents, 339 U.S. 637 (1950); Missouri ex rel Gaines v. Canada, 305 U.S. 337 (1938); NAACP Legal Defense Fund; Plessy v. Ferguson, 163 U.S. 537 (1896); School Desegregation; Sipuel v. Board of Regents of University of Oklahoma, 332 U.S. 631 (1948); Sweatt v. Painter, 339 U.S. 629 (1950); Test Case; Warren, Earl; Warren Court*

BIBLIOGRAPHY

"The Agony of Busing Moves North." November 15, 1971. *Time.* Available from http://www.time.com/time/magazine/article/0,9171,903245-2,00.html.

Bartley, Numan V. 1969. *The Rise of Massive Resistance: Race and Politics in the South during the 1950s.* Baton Rouge: Louisiana State University Press.

Bell, Derrick. 2004. *Silent Covenants: Brown v. Board of Education and the Unfulfilled Hopes for Racial Reform.* New York: Oxford University Press.

Bond, Julian. 2004. "Multicultural Impact II: Voices of the Era." In *The Unfinished Agenda of Brown v. Board of Education,* eds. Editors of *Black Issues in Higher Education.* Hoboken, NJ: Wiley and Sons.

Branch, Taylor. 1988. *Parting the Waters: America in the King Years 1954–63.* New York: Simon and Schuster.

DuBois, W. E. Burghardt. 1935. "Does the Negro Need Separate Schools?" *Journal of Negro Education* 4(3): 328–335.

Dudziak, Mary L. 2000. *Cold War Civil Rights: Race and the Image of American Democracy.* Princeton, NJ: Princeton University Press.

Editors of *Black Issues in Higher Education,* eds. 2004. *The Unfinished Agenda of Brown v. Board of Education.* Hoboken, NJ: Wiley and Sons.

Klarman, Michael J. 2004. *From Jim Crow to Civil Rights: The Supreme Court and the Struggle for Racial Equality.* New York: Oxford University Press.

Kluger, Richard. 1976. *Simple Justice: The History of Brown v. Board of Education and Black America's Struggle for Equality.* New York: Knopf.

Kozol, Jonathan. 1991. *Savage Inequalities: Children in America's Schools.* New York: Crown Publishers.

Kozol, Jonathan. 2005. *The Shame of the Nation: The Restoration of Apartheid Schooling in America.* New York: Crown Publishers.

Martin, Waldo E., Jr., ed. 1998. *Brown v. Board of Education: A Brief History with Documents.* Boston: Bedford Press.

McNeil, Genna Rae. 1983. *Groundwork: Charles Hamilton Houston and the Struggle for Civil Rights.* Philadelphia: University of Pennsylvania Press.

Muse, Benjamin. 1961. *Virginia's Massive Resistance.* Bloomington: Indiana University Press.

Orfield, Gary, and Chungmei Lee. 2004. "Brown at 50: King's Dream or Plessy's Nightmare?" In *Report of the Civil Rights Project.* Cambridge, MA: Harvard University.

Patterson, James T. 2001. *Brown v. Board of Education: A Civil Rights Milestone and Its Troubled Legacy.* New York: Oxford University Press.

Roach, Ronald. 2004. "The Scholar-Activist of Brown: Scholars Reflect on the Intellectual Contributions to the Historic Desegregation Case." *Black Issues in Higher Education* 21(7): 26–31.

Ruff, Jamie C. 1999. "All Is Still Not Well In . . . Prince Edward." *Richmond Times-Dispatch,* April 24: B1.

Segall, William E., and Anna V. Wilson. 1998. *Introduction to Education: Teaching in a Diverse Society.* Upper Saddle River, NJ: Merrill.

Siddle Walker, Vanessa. 1996. *Their Highest Potential: An African American School Community in the Segregated South.* Chapel Hill: University of North Carolina Press.

Turner, Kara Miles. 2001. "'It Is Not at Present a Very Successful School': Prince Edward County and the Black Educational Struggle, 1865–1995." Ph.D. diss. Durham, NC: Duke University.

Tushnet, Mark V. 1987. *The NAACP's Legal Strategy against Segregated Education, 1925–1950.* Chapel Hill: University of North Carolina Press.

Wilkerson, Doxey A. 1960. "The Negro School Movement in Virginia: From 'Equalization' to 'Integration.'" *Journal of Negro Education* 29(1): 17–29.

Wolters, Raymond. 1984. *The Burden of Brown: Thirty Years of School Desegregation.* Knoxville: University of Tennessee Press.

Kara Miles Turner

BROWN V. BOARD OF EDUCATION (BROWN II), 349 U.S. 294 (1955)

When the Supreme Court declared that "separate but equal" in public education was unconstitutional in *Brown v. Board of Education (Brown I),* 347 U.S. 483 (1954), it ordered a further reargument on remedy. The following year, *Brown v. Board of Education (Brown II)*, 349 U.S. 294 (1955) announced that school boards had the primary responsibility to implement desegregation and that they must do so "with all deliberate speed." Everyone understood that "with all deliberate speed" meant significant delay. The Florida legislature was in session when *Brown II* came down, and when it was read aloud, both chambers greeted it with loud cheers.

There were a number of questions implicit in the arguments over remedy. What did *desegregation* mean—to void the offending laws or to affirmatively racially mix the schools? The Court never answered (although subsequently in private the justices agreed it was to require racially mixed public schools). Who were the people entitled to the remedy—the named plaintiffs or the class of plaintiffs or some others? The decree was limited to "the parties to this case." Which institutions would be involved in the process? Local school boards and federal courts. Would there be detailed guidelines? No: The Court decided that ambiguity was the key. When would desegregation commence and when would it be completed? Sometime, but no one knew when it would end (although Chief Justice Earl Warren expected everything to be implemented by 1968, the hundredth anniversary of the Fourteenth Amendment).

The justices had been talking about the remedy for over a year because one of Warren's endeavors in *Brown I* had been to guide discussion to the remedy so that the outcome on the merits—that separate but equal was unconstitutional—would appear inevitable. The justices did not focus on what the right answers to the various questions were; rather, they focused on what had the promise to work. For a majority, the fear was that they would issue a decree and have it treated as a worthless piece of paper. Implicitly, they believed that they had ample leeway to do what would work best, and that in turn would be what was right as a matter of law. One justice, Hugo Black, stood out in the discussions because he told the others that no matter what the Court did, the South was going to ignore it. As an Alabaman, Black was prescient, but the other justices (as well as the NAACP Legal Defense Fund counsel, Thurgood Marshall) were more optimistic.

Marshall's job at argument was to present his clients' case and simultaneously assuage the justices' fears. He tried to make the Court's task look easy: "This Court is not dealing with complexities, this Court is dealing with whether or not race can be used." He claimed that the named plaintiffs had to be granted relief and grade-a-year desegregation was unsatisfactory. Indeed, Marshall dismissed any administrative problems as trivial, justifying, at most, a delay of a year (until September 1956).

There was one other argument that was important. Philip Elman (1918–1999), a former law clerk for Felix Frankfurter, then in the solicitor general's office, argued that the Court should declare segregation unconstitutional and then delay doing anything about it. The argument, which Elman understood was "totally unprincipled," looked better in the spring of 1955, by which time it was clear that neither President Dwight Eisenhower nor the Congress were going to assist the Court. Frankfurter was immediately taken by the gradualism argument, which he thought was statesmanship of the highest order, exactly the type that he believed he represented.

Warren, who had written *Brown I*, took *Brown II* for himself, and unanimity was deemed as essential as it had been in *Brown I*. In his initial draft of the opinion, he required desegregation (which was never defined) to commence "at the earliest practicable date." This was a modification of the standard in the Court's earlier higher-education desegregation cases, where the Court had recognized a "personal and present" right to be admitted to the relevant program. Frankfurter, nevertheless, prevailed on Warren to substitute instead the now-famous formulation "with all deliberate speed." The Court was thereby adopting gradualism, as the Florida legislature immediately understood.

The Court enlisted the only institution it could control, the local federal district courts, staffed by whites, to supervise the decisions of the local school boards, also staffed by whites. Thus local whites would evaluate local conditions. Louisiana senator Allen Ellender (1890–1972) expressed a common theme among segregationists when he noted that he was "delighted that they have left it to the local judges" (quoted in Powe 2000, p. 57). The Court had placed a lot of faith in the southern establishment because there was nowhere else to turn.

Fearing noncompliance, the Court warned that "it should go without saying that the vitality of these constitutional principles cannot be allowed to yield simply from disagreement with them." Unfortunately, that is what *Brown II* was about—delay for an undetermined time because the justices feared southern disagreement with *Brown I*. Thus the Court offered a number of reasons why delay might be acceptable, beginning with the flexibility that equity displays in adjusting public and private needs. The private needs were clear enough, the constitutional rights of the plaintiffs not to be segregated in schools because of their race. The Court claimed that the public needs were "problems related to administration, arising from the physical condition of the school plant, the school transportation system, personnel, revision of school districts and attendance areas." Thurgood Marshall had addressed all these except the physical condition with his apt assertion that a year's delay at most was sufficient to surmount any problems. The Court's conclusion that equity authorized delay until the "variety of obstacles" could be eliminated was disingenuous if delay extended beyond September 1956—as the Court knew it would.

The problem of the condition of the schools, left unmentioned, was that the separate schools were hardly equal. Schools for whites had more of everything except leaky roofs. Waiting for the physical plant to be upgraded would take years, even assuming the South was willing to act in good faith. What the Court was really saying was that the rickety old schoolhouses might be good enough for African-American kids, but you could not expect whites to put up with that. Nevertheless, the reaction to the Court's short opinion was universally favorable. The *Los Angeles Times* editorialized that the decision would "not suit the extremists, but we think most reasonable people will agree with it" (quoted in Powe 2000, p. 58).

Within a year, the South answered the Court. For most of the South—Virginia, South Carolina, Georgia, Florida, Alabama, Mississippi, and Louisiana—the answer was what Hugo Black had predicted: total rejection of the idea of desegregating a single pupil. These states engaged in "massive resistance," and passed a variety of laws declaring *Brown* null and void and seeking to make that declaration real. All passed pupil-placement laws requiring individualized treatment of each pupil. This meant that whites would be placed in white schools, and African Americans in black schools. Some offered free tuition for private schools that sprung up to accept whites who fled the potential of attending a school with an African American. Some allowed a free transfer from any desegregated school. Others proposed closing schools (and Prince Edward County, Virginia, and Little Rock, Arkansas, did shut down their public schools). Mississippi and Louisiana made it a criminal offense to attend a desegregated school.

In the border states of Texas, Arkansas, and Tennessee, there was some token desegregation by 1957. But the emphasis must be on token. Thus a grade-a-year plan for Nashville, approved by both a district judge and a court of appeals, had only 115 of 1,400 African-American children within a white attendance zone and 55 of 2,000 whites within a black attendance zone (Powe 2000, p. 65). All of the whites and about one hundred of the African Americans took a voluntary transfer to attend one-race schools. But that was huge progress compared to the Deep South, where prior to 1964 there was no desegregation. Even in North Carolina, thought by many to be a "good" southern state (because it did not implement massive resistance), 99.44 percent of the state's African-American children were still in all-black schools in 1964 (Powe 2000, p. 165).

Only after passage of the Civil Rights Act of 1964, with its authorization to the Department of Justice to initiate school desegregation lawsuits, did any serious desegregation commence. The justices' worries that the

South would make the Court look impotent and foolish had proven true. Even with the accommodation to the South offered by *Brown II*, the ultimate mandate of *Brown I* was more than the white establishment was willing to swallow. Hence the Court's disingenuousness in *Brown II* was for naught. We will never be able to answer the question of whether an alternative approach might have produced better results.

SEE ALSO *All Deliberate Speed; Brown v. Board of Education, 347 U.S. 483 (1954); Children and the Constitution; Education and the Constitution; Fourteenth Amendment; Marshall, Thurgood; School Desegregation; Warren, Earl; Warren Court*

BIBLIOGRAPHY

Klarman, Michael. 2004. *From Jim Crow to Civil Rights: The Supreme Court and the Struggle for Racial Equality*. New York: Oxford University Press.

Kluger, Richard. 2004. *Simple Justice: The History of* Brown v. Board of Education *and Black America's Struggle for Equality*. Rev. edition. New York: Knopf.

Powe, Lucas A., Jr. 2000. *The Warren Court and American Politics*. Cambridge. MA: Harvard University Press.

Wilkinson, J. Harvie. 1979. *From* Brown *to* Bakke: *The Supreme Court and School Integration, 1954–1978*. New York: Oxford University Press.

Lucas A. Powe Jr.

BROWN V. BOARD OF EDUCATION, CRITIQUES

Brown v. Board of Education, 347 U.S. 483 (1954) has been hailed as a "landmark" decision (Bell 2004, p.4), a "celebrated" civil rights case (Dudziak 1988, p. 62), and "the single most honored opinion in the Supreme Court's corpus" (Balkin 2001, pp. 3–4). The decision to strike down segregated schools crowned a decades-long litigation campaign orchestrated by the National Association for the Advancement of Colored People (NAACP). Thurgood Marshall, the lead counsel for the NAACP, was positively giddy when he heard the news, and he predicted it would take no more than five years to dismantle segregation throughout the South. But Marshall was wrong.

Ten years after *Brown*, less than one percent of black children in the South attended school with whites. Progress realized in the years that followed all but evaporated by the turn of the millennium when school segregation reached a thirty-year high. By 2003 an ever-increasing number of minority students were attending what researchers characterize as "apartheid" schools, where unprecedented rates of student poverty added to the setback.

Confronted with such grim statistics, Harvard law professor Charles Ogletree conceded in 2004 that "fifty years after *Brown* there is little left to celebrate" (p. xv). This assessment is part of an emerging scholarly discourse that challenges the conventional understanding of *Brown's* influence on American law and culture. Professor Derrick Bell's theory of "racial fortuity" and professor Michael Klarman's "backlash theory" reflect this new school of thought, and provide two of the most provocative contemporary critiques of *Brown*.

BELL'S THEORY OF RACIAL FORTUITY

Derrick Bell pioneered the critical race theory movement as a former professor at Harvard Law School. He worked with the NAACP's legal defense fund early in his career, supervising nearly 300 desegregation cases in states across the south. There he witnessed the emotional and physical toll desegregation took on black children, and he himself became the target of death threats, harassment, and racial intimidation.

Once a committed integration advocate, Bell now insists that the nation would have been better off with a decision that upheld, and required actual compliance with, the "separate but equal" standard articulated by the Court in *Plessy v. Ferguson*, 163 U.S. 537 (1896). Had lawmakers been required to allocate additional funds and resources to black schools, he says, the quality of education available to black children would have improved dramatically. "Massive resistance" would not have occurred, and black children would not have been forced into dangerous encounters with hostile white students in schools many of them did not want to attend. Over time, however, whites would have abandoned desegregation on their own in order to avoid the expense of maintaining two truly equal school systems.

Bell's conclusion draws on the theory that policymakers will support racial reforms that advance the needs of white elites, but will sacrifice those reforms when they threaten the economic security or superior status of whites. This pattern of interest-convergence followed by racial-sacrifice, or "racial fortuity" as Bell describes it, explains why prejudice and inequality remained so entrenched following such transformative events as the end of slavery and the Civil War (1861–1865). Racial fortuity also explains the failures of *Brown*. Rather than require a change in racial practices, Bell says, *Brown* settled for symbolic equality under law, and even then, only because it was necessary to advance underlying political objectives—most notably, those related to the Cold War.

In *Silent Covenants* (2004), Bell explains how racial segregation at home interfered with President Truman's strategy to promote democracy abroad as a means of peaceful communist containment. President Truman himself authorized the Department of Justice to submit a brief in *Brown* arguing that the United States could not portray democracy as the "most civilized and most secure form of government" while millions of its own citizens lived under apartheid conditions. Other scholars share Bell's view. In a 1988 article, Professor Mary Dudziak of the University of Southern California Law School showed how desegregation created a "Cold War imperative" the Court could not ignore. Professor Kathleen Bergin of South Texas College of Law further advanced this theory in a 2006 article that examined the justices' personal communications and internal deliberations in the case.

Though *Brown* tempered international criticism against the United States, the decision was virtually meaningless for blacks, Bell maintains. The "all deliberate speed" standard jettisoned any hope for compliance, and over the next ten years the Court itself declined to overturn remedial proposals that were intended to maintain segregated schools. More recently, the Court has invalidated proven integration strategies and has even made it difficult for federal judges to encourage voluntary integration. From Bell's perspective, the events surrounding *Brown* demonstrate how racial fortuity limits the pace and progress of civil rights reform.

KLARMAN'S BACKLASH THEORY

Michael Klarman, the James Monroe Distinguished Professor of Law at the University of Virginia, offers an equally challenging assessment of *Brown*. In *From Jim Crow to Civil Rights* (2004), he argues that *Brown* actually derailed postwar racial progress because of the backlash it inspired from whites. During World War II, Klarman explains, black and white soldiers served together for the first time in integrated units. The victory over fascism abroad made it difficult to defend Jim Crow at home or to justify the second-class treatment of black veterans. Moreover, industrialization gave rise to an economically stable and politically formidable black middle class, especially in the north and midwest, which reoriented the political priorities of the Democratic Party. It was also during this time that many white business owners began to reconsider the economic costs of segregation and open their doors to black customers. In Klarman's view, these events set a course that predetermined the end of Jim Crow, even without *Brown*.

It was one thing to recognize the contributions of black soldiers or abandon profit draining segregation practices, however. It was another to force racial equality by judicial fiat, which is what southerners feared most from *Brown*. More than one hundred members of Congress signed the Southern Manifesto in 1956, condemning the exercise of "naked judicial power" against "rights reserved to the states and to the people." Lawmakers threatened to impeach chief justice Earl Warren and considered amending the constitution to control judicial independence. The decision also changed the trajectory of southern politics, turning racial moderates such as Arkansas governor Orval Faubus into hardline demagogues who incited violence against blacks in order to win white votes. Racial violence indeed intensified, as did economic reprisals, political repression, voter intimidation and harassment. The Ku Klux Klan experienced a new awakening, and white citizens councils, dubbed by one contemporary as "the uptown Klan," increased in prominence and influence across the south.

Extreme as it was, much of the violence that engulfed the South remained under the national radar until the 1960s, when television began to broadcast images of riot police releasing tear gas, fire hoses, and attack dogs on peaceful demonstrators. The breaking point came in 1963 when a church bombing in Birmingham, Alabama, killed four black Sunday school children. The tide had turned, and coalitions of every race and faith cried out for change. The following year, at the urging of president Lyndon B. Johnson, Congress passed the Civil Rights Act of 1964. The statute prohibited discrimination in public accommodations and exacted stiff penalties from non-compliant school districts. Federal authorities finally had the leverage they needed to arrest the firestorm of hate that erupted in the wake of *Brown*.

Klarman views these events as evidence that *Brown* was not indispensable to the civil rights movement, but influenced it only indirectly. The backlash to *Brown* inspired a nation-wide call for action, but change was on its way, though perhaps incrementally, long before the court played its hand.

Bell and Klarman have their own critics, however. University of Iowa law professor Angela Onwuachi-Willig says that *Brown* affirmed a "fundamental moral basis of democracy" and doubts that desegregation could have occurred under *Plessy* as Bell suggests. Paul Finkelman, President William McKinley Distinguished Professor of Law and Public Policy at Albany Law School, also defends *Brown,* a decision he says is directly responsible for the end of Jim Crow. Unlike Klarman, Finkelman does not interpret postwar events as evidence of racial progress and therefore says it would have taken much longer to defeat segregation had it not been for *Brown*.

Brown was surely no panacea, a point on which Bell, Klarman, and their critics would agree. The debate continues, however, on whether the nation is better off with the decision than would have been the case without it.

SEE ALSO *All Deliberate Speed; Brown v. Board of Education, 347 U.S. 483 (1954); Brown v. Board of Education (Brown II), 349 U.S. 294 (1955); Cold War; Plessy v. Ferguson, 163 U.S. 537 (1896); Resegregation; School Desegregation*

BIBLIOGRAPHY

Balkin, Jack M., ed. 2001. "*Brown v. Board of Education*: A Critical Introduction." In *What* Brown v. Board of Education *Should Have Said: The Nation's Top Legal Experts Rewrite America's Landmark Civil Rights Decision*. New York: New York University Press.

Bell, Derrick. 1980. "*Brown v. Board of Education* and the Interest-Convergence Dilemma." *Harvard Law Review* 93: 518–533.

Bell, Derrick. 2004. *Silent Covenants: Brown v. Board of Education and the Unfulfilled Hopes for Racial Reform*. Oxford: Oxford University Press.

Bergin, Kathleen A. 2006. "Authenticating American Democracy." *Pace Law Review* 26: 397–443.

Dudziak, Mary L. 1988. "Desegregation as a Cold War Imperative." *Stanford Law Review* 41: 61–120.

Finkelman, Paul. 2005. "Civil Rights in Historical Context: In Defense of *Brown*." *Harvard Law Review* 118(3): 973–1030.

Klarman, Michael J. 2004. *From Jim Crow to Civil Rights*. Oxford: Oxford University Press.

Ogletree, Charles J., Jr. 2004. *All Deliberate Speed: Reflections on the First Half Century of* Brown v. Board of Education. New York: W. W. Norton & Company.

Onwuachi-Willig, Angela. 2005. "Bell: Silent Covenants: *Brown v. Board of Education* and the Unfulfilled Hopes for Racial Reform." *Michigan Law Review* 103(6): 1507–1538.

Kathleen A. Bergin

BROWN V. BOARD OF EDUCATION, ROAD TO

In the 1920s, the constitutionality of racial segregation in public schools was well established. The equal protection clause of the Fourteenth Amendment to the U.S. Constitution does not plainly bar "separate-but-equal" schools. On the few occasions when Republican framers of that amendment discussed the issue, they consistently denied charges by white-supremacist Democrats that school segregation was forbidden. The vast majority of states ratifying the amendment continued to segregate their schools. Several dozen rulings by lower courts had uniformly sustained the constitutionality of public school segregation—an assessment with which the justices of the U.S. Supreme Court unanimously concurred in *Gong Lum v. Rice*, 275 U.S. 78 (1927).

School segregation was entrenched politically as well as legally. The explosion in black migration to the North beginning with World War I (1914–1918) exacerbated racial prejudice and housing segregation in northern cities, which led to an increase in school segregation. Northern blacks were deeply divided over whether to challenge such segregation, which had the advantages of securing decent jobs for black teachers and of offering a more nurturing environment for black students, who often faced hostility and stereotyping in integrated schools.

Southern blacks knew better than to challenge an aspect of Jim Crow so dear to whites. The policy of the National Association for the Advancement of Colored People (NAACP) was to contest the spread of school segregation in the North, but not in the South where public opinion rendered integration impossible. The NAACP only brought suits it expected to win, and challenges to southern school segregation were not among them.

HIGHER EDUCATION

Before World War I, few southern counties provided blacks with even a high school education. Because so few blacks attended college, southern states saw no need to provide graduate or professional education for blacks. In 1921 Missouri became the first former slave state to do so, establishing Lincoln University and authorizing its board of curators to provide blacks with tuition grants to attend integrated universities in neighboring states for courses not offered at Lincoln. Maryland enacted a similar scheme in 1933, and several other states in the peripheral South, fearing litigation, quickly followed suit.

Most out-of-state grant programs were patently inadequate, failing to cover travel and other living expenses, and providing limited funding on a first-come, first-served basis. Challenging such schemes was appealing to the NAACP because the racial inequalities were so stark and because advanced education was critical to black progress. The initial goal of such litigation was to pressure southern states to spend so much money to equalize black educational opportunities that they would eventually find it cheaper to integrate.

In 1933 a black man sued for admission to the University of North Carolina's School of Pharmacy, but his suit was dismissed on procedural grounds. In 1936 a black man seeking admission to the University of Maryland School of Law convinced the state high court to invalidate the out-of-state scholarship law and order his admission. Lloyd Gaines sued next, seeking admission to the University of Missouri Law School.

None of this litigation directly challenged segregation, only the obvious inequality inherent in denying blacks equal educational opportunities within a state. By the 1930s it was well established that separate had to be equal to be constitutional. In 1914 the Supreme Court, in dicta, had rejected the argument that lower average demand among blacks for a particular service could justify overt racial inequality. In *Missouri ex rel. Gaines v. Canada,* 305 U.S. 337 (1938), the Court ruled that shipping blacks out of state for professional education was unconstitutional.

A contrary ruling would have been surprising. By 1938 black lawyers and economists played unprecedented roles in New Deal administrative agencies. *Gaines* was argued in the Supreme Court by a black man, Charles Hamilton Houston (1895–1950), whose Harvard legal pedigree and impressive forensic skills demonstrated what blacks could achieve if afforded equal educational opportunities. Southern newspaper reaction to *Gaines* was compliant and sometimes even approving; many educated southern whites no longer believed that sending blacks out of state for education was morally acceptable. Because *Gaines* said nothing to indicate that blacks could not be segregated *within* state boundaries, white southerners had no cause for alarm.

CONSEQUENCES OF *GAINES*

Gaines left southern states with only two apparent choices: provide equal but separate facilities for blacks within the state or integrate. Maryland integrated its law school and West Virginia integrated some of its higher-education programs, but no other southern state took similar action. Missouri established a separate but obviously inferior law school for blacks, and a few other states in the peripheral South likewise began providing rudimentary graduate and professional education for blacks in segregated institutions.

Ironically, most southern states responded to *Gaines* by adopting the very out-of-state scholarship laws that the Court had invalidated. Five states had such laws before *Gaines,* but eleven did by 1943, with six more following suit by 1948. These laws were an improvement over what had been offered to blacks by way of advanced education previously—nothing—but they were a rather odd response to *Gaines.* Many southern white educators and politicians also discussed creating regional universities for blacks, which would have saved each state the expense of opening its own black graduate and professional schools. But this solution, too, seemed plainly unconstitutional under *Gaines.*

Gaines did not necessarily portend the abolition of segregation in higher education. The ruling only barred states from transporting black students out of state while educating whites within; even the NAACP interpreted the ruling to require only equalization. Nor did *Gaines* indirectly undermine segregation by raising its costs. The Supreme Court had expressed no opinion on the "substantial equality" doctrine, under which lower courts had sustained schemes in which black schools were denied certain facilities enjoyed by white ones. To be sure, in 1950 the Court would interpret the equality requirement so stringently as to doom segregation in higher education. But American race relations underwent enormous change between 1938 and 1950. There is no way of knowing how inferior a black law school Missouri could have gotten away with after *Gaines*.

WORLD WAR II AND ITS AFTERMATH

Lloyd Gaines mysteriously disappeared after his litigation triumph, and no more higher-education cases reached the Court for the next decade. The NAACP had serious financial difficulties in the late 1930s, plaintiffs proved difficult to locate, and prospective suits were held in abeyance during World War II (1939–1945).

That war proved to be a watershed in the history of American race relations. Its ideology was antifascist and prodemocratic. President Franklin D. Roosevelt urged Americans to "refut[e] at home the very theories which we are fighting abroad." (Klarman 2004, p. 175) Readily perceiving the bitter irony in America's fighting against world fascism with a racially segregated army, blacks demanded their citizenship rights. Roughly 400,000 blacks joined the NAACP during the war, and southern blacks registered to vote in record numbers.

Seizing advantage of the GI Bill of Rights, black veterans filed a slew of postwar lawsuits seeking admission to white universities. In response, southern state legislatures finally appropriated funds to establish black graduate and professional schools. The NAACP called these new institutions "Jim Crow dumps" (Klarman 2004, p. 205), but state judges generally found them adequate to survive constitutional challenges.

In 1946 a black woman, Ada Lois Sipuel, sued for admission to the University of Oklahoma School of Law. Oklahoma offered legal education to whites but not blacks—an obvious violation of *Gaines*. In *Sipuel v. Board of Regents of the University of Oklahoma*, 332 U.S. 631 (1948), the Supreme Court ordered Oklahoma to provide Sipuel with legal instruction "as soon as it does for applicants of any other group."

Yet the Court stopped short of ordering Sipuel's admission to the university, implicitly preserving the possibility that Oklahoma could satisfy the Constitution without desegregating. When Oklahoma responded by almost instantly opening a separate black law school, Sipuel challenged this action as an evasion of the Court's mandate. Yet the justices denied relief, with only two of them dissenting, thus confirming that the Court had yet to overturn the separate-but-equal doctrine.

SWEATT V. PAINTER, 339 U.S. 629 (1950)

Also in 1946, a black man, Heman Sweatt, applied to the all-white University of Texas School of Law. During the litigation, Texas established a separate black law school. The NAACP challenged its adequacy and, more broadly, the constitutionality of segregation in higher education.

The inferiority of Texas's black law school was not so obvious as to be conceded by the state. The admissions requirements and curriculum of the black and white schools were the same, and the three instructors at the black law school also taught at the University of Texas. A former president of the American Bar Association testified that the schools offered equal educational opportunities.

The Court thought otherwise. In addition to noting tangible features of the black school that *were* obviously inferior, such as the absence of opportunities for law review and moot court, Chief Justice Fred Vinson's (1890–1953) unanimous opinion emphasized differences in intangible qualities, such as institutional prestige and alumni stature. Vinson also observed that Sweatt could not possibly receive an equal legal education when denied the opportunity to interact with whites, who accounted for most of the state's lawyers, witnesses, and judges. Unwilling to countenance any delay in the vindication of constitutional rights, the Court ordered the University of Texas immediately to admit Sweatt.

That same day, June 5, 1950, the Court ordered the graduate education school of the University of Oklahoma to cease segregating—in classrooms, the library, and the cafeteria—the black man it had admitted pursuant to a federal court order (*McLaurin v. Oklahoma State Regents*, 339 U.S. 637). The justices declared that segregation restrictions impaired George McLaurin's ability to study, exchange views with classmates, and learn his profession. As he was receiving a tangibly equal education, the justices were apparently no longer prepared to accept segregation *within* an institution of higher education. *Sweatt* had proscribed segregation in *separate* institutions. That seemed to leave nowhere for segregation to remain.

The stringent interpretations of equality offered in *Sweatt* and *McLaurin* were clear departures from *Gaines*, which had simply insisted that blacks receive *something*. These rulings were not as easy for the justices as the unanimous outcomes might suggest. At conference, both Chief Justice Vinson and Justice Stanley Reed (1884–1980) observed that neither the original understanding of the Fourteenth Amendment nor judicial precedent barred school segregation. In correspondence, Justice Robert Jackson (1892–1954) expressed concern that the Court was being asked not merely to "fill gaps or construe the amendment to include matters which were unconsidered" but "to include what was deliberately and intentionally excluded."

Changing political and social mores regarding race account for these rulings. Major league baseball was desegregated in 1947 and in 1948 President Harry S. Truman (1884–1972) ordered the desegregation of the military and the federal civil service. That same year the first black law clerk in the Court's history, William T. Coleman, wrote a memo urging that *Plessy* be overruled. Coleman's very presence at the Court demonstrated that segregated legal education could no longer be defended on the basis of black inferiority. The Truman administration warned the justices that "unless segregation is ended, a serious blow will be struck at our democracy before the world" (Klarman 2004, p. 210). Nearly two hundred legal academics signed a brief denying that separate black law schools could possibly be equal.

The justices were also aware that white southerners were no longer universally opposed to integrated higher education. Two thousand white students and faculty members at the University of Texas rallied behind Sweatt's lawsuit. Shifting white opinion in the South led Justice Jackson to conclude that segregation in higher education was "breaking down of its own weight" (Klarman 2004, p. 209). The justices could be confident that desegregating higher education was unlikely to produce violence and school closures, as southern whites were predicting.

Sweatt doomed racial segregation in higher education but not necessarily in grade schools. In a 1950 memo, Justice Tom Clark (1899–1977) deemed it "entirely possible that Negroes in segregated grammar schools being taught arithmetic, spelling, geography, etc., would receive skills ... equivalent to those of segregated white students" (Klarman 2004, p. 211). The justices had strong practical reasons not to extend the 1950 rulings to grade schools. Desegregation of higher education involved very few blacks, and the whites most directly affected were overwhelmingly adult males with relatively progressive racial attitudes. By contrast, grade school desegregation would involve huge numbers of blacks and whites, including the youngest, and would cut across lines of sex and class. However placid the reaction to their 1950 rulings, the justices understood that grade school desegregation would involve a social revolution.

Internal deliberations confirm that in 1950 the justices had yet to resolve the grade school issue. Justice Hugo Black (1886–1971) proclaimed that segregation in higher education was "wholly unreasonable," but he left open the door to "reasonable segregation." Expressing doubt on the issue of grade school segregation, Justice Clark opposed extending *Sweatt* "at that time." Justice Sherman Minton (1890–1965) also preferred to defer the grade school issue until "whenever we get to it" (Klarman 2004, p. 212).

CONSEQUENCES OF *SWEATT*

Sweatt was instrumental to desegregating higher education in the border states and the peripheral South. Within six months of the decision, roughly a thousand blacks were attending formerly white colleges and universities in those regions. In the Deep South, by contrast, *Sweatt* was almost completely nullified for a decade.

In 1951 the University of Georgia School of Law rejected Horace Ward's application on account of his race. The state legislature threatened to terminate public funding for any university that desegregated, and the state board of regents required law school applicants to submit recommendations from two alumni and a superior-court judge—a virtually impossible requirement for black applicants to satisfy. Ward's lawsuit against the university dragged on for years before being dismissed on procedural grounds. In 1959 a federal court invalidated the recommendation requirements as racially discriminatory, but it refused to deprive university officials of the primary responsibility for admitting students. Higher education in Georgia remained entirely segregated until 1961.

In 1949 Virgil Hawkins commenced a nine-year odyssey to gain admission to the University of Florida School of Law. After several years of legal delay, during which the Florida Supreme Court acted as if *Sweatt* had never been decided, that court finally rejected Hawkins's lawsuit. The U.S. Supreme Court ordered reconsideration in light of *Brown v. Board of Education*, 347 U.S. 483 (1954).

On remand, the Florida jurists postponed further proceedings until the U.S. Supreme Court had resolved the remedial issue that it deferred in *Brown*. After *Brown II*, 349 U.S. 294 (1955), required desegregation "with all deliberate speed," the Florida court rejected Hawkins's demand for immediate admission, instead appointing a commissioner to take evidence on the likely consequences of desegregating the university. In an extraordinary concurring opinion, one Florida justice criticized *Brown* on the grounds that segregation had been "the unvarying law of the animal kingdom" and that "closing cultural gaps is a long and tedious process and is not one for court decrees" (*Hawkins v. Board of Control*, 83 So. 2d 20 [Fla. 1955] [Terrell, J., concurring], rev'd 350 U.S. 413 [1956]). The Supreme Court again vacated the state court judgment, clarifying that "all deliberate speed" only applied to grade schools and observing that Hawkins was entitled to prompt admission.

Incredibly, the Florida supreme court, refusing to surrender, again denied Hawkins's request for a writ of mandamus to compel his admission. The court insisted that its prior refusal to order Hawkins admitted was based not only on its erroneous interpretation of *Brown II* but also on traditional equitable principles governing the discretionary issuance of writs of mandamus. Although the U.S. Supreme Court had now clarified the meaning of *Brown II*, the Florida court refused to assume that the justices had intended to deprive state judges of their traditional discretion over such writs. Because Hawkins's present admission to the university was likely to cause great public harm, the Florida jurists exercised their discretion to deny him relief.

The U.S. Supreme Court now invited Hawkins to seek relief in federal court, but by the time he did, the state board of control had raised the test-score requirements for law school admission. Hawkins was disqualified under the new standards and he finally capitulated, pursuing his further education in the friendlier environment of Boston University. Another black man desegregated the University of Florida in 1958.

In Alabama and Mississippi, violence and intimidation were the preferred methods of circumventing *Sweatt.* In 1950 Autherine Lucy sued the University of Alabama for denying her admission based on her race. After several years of procedural delay, a federal district judge ordered her admitted, and the university complied early in 1956. A race riot ensued, with more than one thousand raucous, rock-throwing demonstrators protesting Lucy's presence on campus and threatening to lynch her. The board of trustees promptly suspended Lucy, ostensibly for her own safety. She then initiated contempt proceedings against university officials, alleging that they had acted in bad faith in suspending her. The court dismissed the contempt motion but ordered Lucy reinstated. University officials then expelled her for filing "shocking and baseless" charges against them in the contempt proceedings (Klarman 2004, p. 258). The federal judge upheld the university. Lucy abandoned her quest, and the University of Alabama remained segregated until 1963.

Mississippi followed a characteristically unique path in nullifying *Sweatt.* When a black man applied to the University of Mississippi Law School in 1954, the board of trustees added a requirement that all applicants secure endorsements from five local alumni. Four years later, when another black man tried to desegregate Ole Miss, state police officers ejected him from the campus and swore out a lunacy warrant against him in court (apparently on the theory that any black man thinking he could attend Ole Miss must be crazy). When a third black man tried to desegregate Mississippi Southern College in 1959, he was prosecuted and convicted of reckless driving and illegal possession of whiskey (even though he did not drink). In 1962 James Meredith finally desegregated Mississippi higher education, but only after a race riot that killed two, injured hundreds, and required fifteen thousand federal troops to quell.

After *Brown* raised the specter of grade school desegregation, whites in the Deep South could no longer abide the prospect of integrated universities. Louisiana had desegregated several public universities after *Sweatt,* and there were predictions that other Deep South states would quickly follow suit. But *Brown* changed everything. Florida did not desegregate its public universities until 1958, Georgia until 1961, Mississippi until 1962, and South Carolina and Alabama until 1963. *Sweatt,* much like *Brown,* was nullified in the Deep South for nearly a decade.

SEE ALSO *Brown v. Board of Education, 347 U.S. 483 (1954); Brown v. Board of Education (Brown II), 349 U.S. 294 (1955); Brown v. Board of Education, Critiques; Du Bois, W. E. B.; Great Constitutional Dream Book; Jim Crow and Voting Rights; Jim Crow in the Early Twentieth Century; Marshall, Thurgood; Missouri ex rel Gaines v. Canada, 305 U.S. 337 (1938); Sipuel v. Board of Regents of University of Oklahoma, 332 U.S. 631 (1948); Sweatt v. Painter, 339 U.S. 629 (1950); Warren Court; World War II and the Growth of Civil Rights; World War II and the Growth of Individual Rights*

BIBLIOGRAPHY

Hutchinson, Dennis J. 1979. "Unanimity and Desegregation: Decision Making in the Supreme Court, 1948-1958." *Georgetown Law Journal* 68(Oct.): 1–87.

Klarman, Michael J. 2004. *From Jim Crow to Civil Rights: The Supreme Court and the Struggle for Racial Equality.* Oxford and New York: Oxford University Press.

Kluger, Richard. 2004 (1976). *Simple Justice: The History of* Brown v. Board of Education *and Black America's Struggle for Equality.* Rev. and expanded ed. New York: Knopf.

Tushnet, Mark V. 1987. *The NAACP's Legal Strategy against Segregated Education, 1925–1950.* Chapel Hill: University of North Carolina Press.

Tushnet, Mark V. 1994. *Making Civil Rights Law: Thurgood Marshall and the Supreme Court, 1936–1961.* New York: Oxford University Press.

U.S. Commission on Civil Rights. 1961 *Equal Protection of the Laws in Public Higher Education, 1960.* Washington, D.C.: Author.

Michael J. Klarman

BROWN V. MARYLAND, 25 U.S. 419 (1827)

Brown v. Maryland, 25 U.S. 419 (1827) helped to define the scope and power of the commerce clause, and was also the first case to deal with the scope of the import-export clause. Coupled with the landmark decision in *Gibbons v. Ogden*, 22 U.S. 1 (1824), *Brown* is perhaps best known for establishing the primacy of the U.S. Congress over commerce.

In *Brown*, the State of Maryland had enacted a statute that required importers of foreign goods in their original packaging to obtain a license at the cost of fifty dollars. The plaintiffs imported and then sold a package of foreign goods without having obtained the proper licensure. When they were indicted, the plaintiffs challenged the validity of the statute. The plaintiffs argued that the licensing requirement imposed a state regulation that conflicted with both the import-export and commerce clauses of the U.S. Constitution.

The Court's opinion, authored by Chief Justice John Marshall (1755–1835), struck down the Maryland statute as "repugnant" to the Constitution. Relying on the plain meaning of the commerce clause, the Court reasoned that the imposition of duties by the states had been preempted. Referring to the framers' intent and the history of the country under the Articles of Confederation, Chief Justice Marshall noted the "necessity of giving the control over this important subject [that is, commerce] to a single government." The Court stated that allowing the states to regulate in this area would be intrusive, and that the states "cannot reach and restrain the action of the national government within its proper sphere." The Court went on to discuss the dangers of letting this statute stand, specifically, that such a measure would "derange the measures of Congress to regulate commerce." Finally, the Court ended by applying its principals "equally to importations from a sister State." The opinion was written over a dissent by Justice Smith Thompson (1768–1843), who expressed his reluctance to dissent, yet felt that he needed to because the statute at issue only governed affairs that were internal to the State of Maryland, and had little to do with interstate commerce.

Ultimately, *Brown v. Maryland* posed the question of whether the states could intrude upon the national government's prerogative vis-à-vis commerce, and answered that question in the negative. In other words, the focus in *Brown* was on state legislation that arguably intruded upon Congress's power, even when Congress had been silent. Later commerce clause cases would focus on the outer limits of congressional power that came along with larger-scale national efforts to regulate the growing national economy. At the end of the nineteenth century, especially with the rise of industrialization, there was a growing consensus that the national economy did need national regulation. The early cases, including *Brown* and *Gibbons v. Ogden*, were instrumental in setting the stage for these later developments.

SEE ALSO *Commerce Clause; Gibbons v. Ogden, 22 U.S. 1 (1824)*

BIBLIOGRAPHY

Collins, Richard B. 1988. "Economic Union as a Constitutional Value." *New York University Law Review* 63: 43–129.

Denning, Brannon P. 2005. "Confederation-Era Discrimination Against Interstate Commerce and the Legitimacy of the Dormant Commerce Clause Doctrine." *Kentucky Law Journal* 94 (1): 37–100.

Miriam A. Cherry

BROWN V. MISSISSIPPI, 297 U.S. 278 (1936)

During the 1930s the U.S. Supreme Court decided several significant cases relating to criminal justice. Perhaps the most highly publicized of those decisions were *Powell v. Alabama*, 287 U.S. 45 (1932) and *Norris v. Alabama*, 294 U.S. 587 (1935), both of which grew out of the Scottsboro affair (see Carter 1969). Those rulings dealt with the conduct of criminal trials: the right to counsel in capital cases and racial discrimination in jury selection. The less prominent 1936 decision in *Brown v. Mississippi*, 297 U.S. 278 addressed the conduct of law enforcement officials and outlawed the use of coerced confessions.

Brown arose from the March 1934 murder of a prominent white planter in Kemper County in east central Mississippi. Lynchings were so common that the area was called "Bloody Kemper." Three black tenant farmers—Ed Brown, Henry Shields, and Arthur (Yank) Ellington—were quickly arrested and confessed after being repeatedly whipped and beaten. To prevent a lynch mob from seizing the defendants, District Attorney John C. Stennis (who went on to serve more than forty years in the U.S. Senate) brought them to trial six days after the murder. The only evidence linking the men to the crime was their confessions. It took the jury half an hour to return guilty verdicts; the judge immediately imposed death sentences.

John A. Clark, one of four local lawyers appointed to represent Brown, Shields, and Ellington, quickly regretted the perfunctory defense that he and his colleagues mounted at trial. With modest financial support from the National Association for the Advancement of Colored People (NAACP) and the Atlanta-based Commission on Interracial Cooperation, Clark pursued a zealous but unsuccessful appeal in the state courts. When serious health problems forced Clark to withdraw, former governor Earl L. Brewer was persuaded to continue the appeal. By a four-to-two vote, the state supreme court affirmed the convictions. The majority refused to reconsider the validity of the confessions because Clark and the other defense lawyers had not properly objected to them at trial.

The U.S. Supreme Court unanimously reversed. Chief Justice Charles E. Hughes devoted almost five pages to quoting the description of the defendants' abuse given in the dissenting opinion in the state court. Finding that the case involved "a wrong so fundamental that it made the whole proceeding a mere pretense of a trial," Hughes brushed aside the state's waiver argument by observing: "The rack and torture chamber may not substituted for the witness stand." Finding it "difficult to conceive of methods more revolting to the sense of justice than those taken to procure the confessions of these petitioners," the Court overturned the convictions. Because District Attorney Stennis insisted on a second trial that could have resulted in renewed death sentences, Brown, Shields, and Ellington accepted a plea bargain and served relatively short sentences. Because the defendants pleaded guilty, there was no further appeal.

Brown v. Mississippi was the first of dozens of cases in which the Supreme Court focused on the voluntariness of confessions (e.g., *Chambers v. Florida*, 309 U.S. 227 [1940]; *McNabb v. United States*, 318 U.S. 332 [1943]; *Mallory v. United States*, 354 U.S. 449 [1957]; *Townsend v. Sain*, 372 U.S. 293 [1963]). Meanwhile, the Court also expanded the right to counsel for criminal suspects (e.g., *Escobedo v. Illinois*, 378 U.S. 478 [1964]). These two lines of cases came together in *Miranda v. Arizona*, 384 U.S. 436 (1966), where the Court established the now-familiar rule that the police may not question persons in their custody without warning them of the rights of silence and counsel.

SEE ALSO *Fourteenth Amendment; Procedural Due Process*

BIBLIOGRAPHY

Carter, Dan T. 1969. *Scottsboro: A Tragedy of the American South.* Baton Rouge: Louisiana State University Press. Rev. ed., 2007.

Cortner, Richard C. 1986. *A "Scottsboro" Case in Mississippi: The Supreme Court and* Brown v. Mississippi. Jackson: University Press of Mississippi.

CASES

Brown v. Mississippi, 297 U.S. 278 (1936).

Chambers v. Florida, 309 U.S. 227 (1940).

Escobedo v. Illinois, 378 U.S. 478 (1964).

Mallory v. United States, 354 U.S. 449 (1957).

McNabb v. United States, 318 U.S. 332 (1943).

Miranda v. Arizona, 384 U.S. 436 (1966).

Norris v. Alabama, 294 U.S. 587 (1935).

Powell v. Alabama, 287 U.S. 45 (1932).

Townsend v. Sain, 372 U.S. 293 (1963).

Jonathan L. Entin

BRYCE, JAMES
1838–1922

Born in Belfast on May 10, 1838, James Bryce was raised in Glasgow from the age of eight. An 1857 graduate of Glasgow University, he won a scholarship to Trinity College of Oxford, which waived its requirement that he (a Presbyterian) should subscribe to the Church of

British historian James Bryce, c. 1910. *A distinguished professor at the University of Oxford, British-born James Bryce enjoyed friendships with educators, presidents, and literary figures. He is perhaps best remembered for his 1888 work,* The American Commonwealth, *which offers readers an in-depth look at the government of the United States from a non-native's perspective.*
GEORGE C. BERESFORD/HULTON ARCHIVE/GETTY IMAGES

England's Thirty-Nine Articles. At Trinity, Bryce won honors in history and law. In 1862 he was awarded the Vinerian Law Scholarship and was made a fellow of Oriel College. In 1864 his prizewinning study of the Holy Roman Empire was published.

Though flourishing at Oxford, Bryce read law at Lincoln's Inn and was called to the bar in 1867. For the rest of his long life (he died on January 22, 1922) he would combine legal interests with public service, politics, authorship, and an impressive propensity for travel. In 1870 Bryce accepted William Gladstone's (1809–1898) offer of the Regius Chair of Civil Law at University of Oxford. He would occupy this post for more than two decades, during which time he was twice (1880 and 1885) elected to Parliament, and served as undersecretary for foreign affairs (1886) and chancellor of the Duchy of Lancaster (1892). Over these years he made four trips to the United States, crisscrossing from Atlantic to Pacific in a love affair with the young republic. An affable companion, Bryce accumulated a list of American friends that began with famous New Englanders (poet Henry Wadsworth Longfellow [1807–1882], essayist and poet Ralph Waldo Emerson [1803–1882], poet, essayist, and medical professor Oliver Wendell Holmes Sr. [1809–1894], and lawyer and future Supreme Court Justice Oliver Wendell Holmes Jr.) and expanded to take in future presidents Theodore Roosevelt and Woodrow Wilson, as well as a host of notables including educator Charles Eliot (1834–1926), Thomas Cooley, educator and politician Seth Lowe (1850–1916), historian and politician George Bancroft (1800–1891), and educator Booker T. Washington (c. 1856–1915).

Bryce was a prolific writer, and by the mid-1880s he was assembling material for *The American Commonwealth* (1888), his greatest work. A follower of Gladstone, Bryce was inclined to favor present-minded reformism, and it is true that the Americans who influenced his work opposed the so-called spoils system and boss-ridden politics. Bryce's style has been criticized as topical and overly detailed; if so, it was because he distrusted generalizations and preconceived ideas. His work thus reflected a preference for the inductive method. In this regard he was a polar opposite of Alexis de Tocqueville, the great antebellum commentator who had interpreted American life according to certain philosophic concepts of freedom and democracy. Intellectually, Bryce was a historicist more akin to such contemporary British legal historians as Edward A. Freeman (1823–1892), Henry Sumner Maine (1822–1888), Sir Frederick Pollock (1845–1937), and F. W. Maitland (1850–1906).

In studying the U.S. Constitution Bryce found consistent patterns of development. Conceptually, he recognized, it had been shaped by the Baron de Montesquieu's (1869–1755) *Spirit of the Laws* and by Blackstone's interpretation of England's unwritten constitution. Practically it was the product of long experience of colonial government. Beyond these influences Bryce detected in American thought a thoroughgoing distrust of government—based, he wrote, on a view of human nature that combined the "theology of Calvin and the philosophy of Hobbes" (Bryce 1995, p. 271). The culmination of these influences was the famous system of checks and balances, designed to resist any power (ideological, economic, or demographic) that might seek dominance. Such notions of balanced government may fairly be described as English; but Bryce found another, persistent theme that set Americans apart: their insistence upon the people's sovereignty. The British view of Parliament as a sovereign body, a counterpart of the Teutonic "folk moot," was foreign to theory and practice in the United States (p. 31). To preserve their freedom Americans insisted on a written instrument, amendable only by their collective will.

Not surprisingly, *The American Commonwealth* devoted much space to the evolving powers of each branch of federal government. Presidents, he observed, have the prestige of representing the whole people—despite their election by an undemocratic electoral college. Bryce saw, too, that presidents have quasi-monarchical powers of foreign policy and military command. Shrewdly he warned that a determined president might, at a time of national emergency, undermine the constitution by diminishing liberty in the name of public safety (Bryce 1995, p. 60). In a famous chapter, "Why Great Men Are Not Chosen President," Bryce reflected that presidents emerge from among the operatives of political parties that did not attract America's best talent (pp. 69–75).

He made a partial exception on behalf of the Senate, whose members had impressed him in part because he regarded them as the leading politicians of their states. The heart of Bryce's congressional analysis, however, is his discussion of the committee system, so different from anything parliamentary. Rule by committee chairmen was, he perceived, subject to many abuses—especially those associated with lobbyists. Yet he correctly stated that the system served as a filter for the vast numbers of bills proposed; and he perceived that it was a natural mechanism for a people who prized "stability above activity" in government (Bryce 1995, p. 103).

Bryce was fascinated with American law courts, whose state and federal complexity often bewildered Europeans. For their benefit he explained the rule of law that "whenever federal law is applicable, federal law must prevail" (Bryce 1995, p. 213). American courts had adapted the English tradition of lawmaking by interpretation; and necessarily so, for they stood at the intersection of state and federal relations, and presided over collisions between popular rights and government prerogatives. The Supreme Court had established its preeminence during the chief justiceship (1801–1835) of John Marshall, a godlike figure in Bryce's eyes. Decades later, despite its involvement in the disputed presidential election of 1876, the Court was still widely regarded as apolitical, at best an oracle of the people's written will.

The American Commonwealth contains—in its various editions—sections on state and municipal governments, political parties and reform proposals, universities, sectional resources, immigration, race relations, woman suffrage, and even more. In writing this massive work, Bryce performed several small miracles. He could be critical (of America's penchant for monotonous cultural uniformity, for instance), but with goodwill and fair-handedness. He contradicted other writers (such as Tocqueville, on the so-called tyranny of the majority), but without denying their merits. Above all his prose is accessible, precise, analytical, and persuasive. For these qualities Bryce is still read, and his interpretations live on in modern classrooms.

SEE ALSO *Commentaries on the Constitution; Constitution of the United States*

BIBLIOGRAPHY

Bryce, James. 1995. *The American Commonwealth*. 2 volumes. Indianapolis, IN: Liberty Fund.

Fisher, H. A. L. 1927. *James Bryce (Viscount Bryce of Dechmont, O.M.)*. 2 volumes. New York: Macmillan.

Ions, Edmund. 1968. *James Bryce and American Democracy 1870–1922*. London: Macmillan.

Tulloch, Hugh. 1988. *James Bryce's American Commonwealth: The Anglo-American Background*. Wolfeboro, NH: Boydell Press.

Paul M. Pruitt Jr.

BUCHANAN V. WARLEY, 245 U.S. 60 (1917)

Buchanan v. Warley, 245 U.S. 60 (1917) was a seminal Supreme Court case that struck down a segregationist municipal ordinance that prevented African Americans from buying property in majority white neighborhoods and white residents from purchasing property in majority African-American neighborhoods. In a unanimous decision predating *Brown v. Board of Education of Topeka*, 347 U.S. 483 (1954) by almost four decades, the Court held that states and localities could not prevent individuals from conveying property solely due to the race of the purchaser without violating the Fourteenth Amendment's due process clause protections of an individuals' right to sell, purchase, and enjoy property. The Court's rejection of an explicit attempt to racially segregate housing has led contemporary scholars to highlight the decision's role at the center of both property rights and civil rights protections for racial minorities.

This controversy arose as a test case created by the National Association for the Advancement of Colored People (NACCP) in its campaign to overturn laws that enforced racial segregation. Charles Buchanan, the plaintiff in the case, was a white property owner in a majority white neighborhood in Louisville, Kentucky. Buchanan sold his property to William Warley, an African American, pursuant to a contract that stated Warley would not have to accept the deed or pay for the property if state or local law made it unlawful for him to occupy it as his residence.

At the time of the sale, Louisville had in force a residential segregation ordinance that prohibited the sale of property located in a majority white residential area to a "colored person." The ordinance also prohibited the sale of the property in a majority "colored" area to a white person. Local authorities argued that separation of

residence by race was a valid exercise of Louisville's police powers and a necessary means for protecting the health, safety, and general welfare of residents by maintaining peaceful race relations and preventing a diminution of white property values. Municipal officials also argued that the ordinance should be upheld under the "separate but equal" doctrine of *Plessy v. Ferguson*, 163 U.S. 537 (1896) because it applied to both white and African-American property purchasers in neighborhoods where either would become a racial minority.

For purposes of the lawsuit, Warley argued that the law absolved him of fulfilling his contractual obligation, and Buchanan sued for specific performance of the contract, claiming that the ordinance was a violation of the Fourteenth Amendment's due process and equal protection clauses. Two Kentucky courts found in favor of Warley, holding that the Louisville ordinance was a constitutional exercise of the state's police powers. The U.S. Supreme Court overturned the lower courts, holding that the ordinance violated Buchanan's property rights, which were protected by the Fourteenth Amendment and related Reconstruction-era civil rights statutes.

The *Buchanan* decision is noteworthy, in part, because the Court acknowledged that although the Fourteenth Amendment was passed initially as a protection for freed slaves of African descent, its language proscribes state actions that impermissibly abridge the property rights of any person based solely on race, including a white plaintiff's right to enforce his purchase contract with an African American.

The Court acknowledged that states and their subdivisions had broad authority to regulate local land use by invoking their police powers, but it also held that they "cannot justify a law or ordinance which runs counter to the limitations of the federal Constitution." The Court rejected the argument that limiting the right of African-American buyers in white neighborhoods would necessarily prevent potential harm resulting from a diminution of property values. The Court did not attempt to refute the point, but it noted that the law was both over- and under-inclusive in regard to this objective because it would not have prevented undesirable white purchasers who would have the same negative impact.

The Court's rhetoric in *Buchanan* was ahead of its time in its explication of the purposes and effects of the due process and equal protection clauses and the civil rights statutes passed by Congress in 1866 and 1870 (now codified as 42 U.S.C. §§ 1982 and 1981, respectively) pursuant to its authority to enforce the Fourteenth Amendment. The Court determined that the text of the amendment and the statutes indicated that all U.S. citizens must enjoy the same right to sell, purchase, and convey property as white citizens enjoyed prior to the

Civil War (1861–1865). The Court quoted precedent from *Strauder v. West Virginia*, 100 U. S. 303 (1880) for the proposition that "the law in the states shall be the same for the black as for the white," and the prohibitory language of the Fourteenth Amendment "implies the existence of rights and immunities . . . for life, liberty, or property." (Strauder held that state laws excluding African Americans from juries without due process were unconstitutional denials of rights protected by the Fourteenth Amendment.)

Despite the rhetoric, the Court overturned the segregation law based on its specific impact upon property rights and distinguished the case from Supreme Court precedents that upheld laws mandating racial segregation in railroad transport (*Plessy v. Ferguson*, 163 U.S. 537 [1896]) and education (*Berea College v. Commonwealth of Kentucky*, 211 U.S. 45 [1908]). In distinguishing *Plessy* and *Berea College*, the Court embraced a vision of the separate-but-equal laws at issue in those cases as ultimately giving the plaintiffs access to their immediate desire (an opportunity to ride a train or get an education), with the racial segregation component merely requiring conformity with reasonable rules and restrictions. In *Buchanan* the Court contrasted this view with the more fundamental "right which the [Louisville] ordinance annulled . . . the civil right of a white man to dispose of his property if he saw fit to do so to a person of color and of a colored person to make such disposition to a white person."

The U.S. Supreme Court and state supreme courts reaffirmed the holding in *Buchanan* in the face of concerted attempts by municipalities to claim alternative rationales to achieve racially restrictive zoning (see, e.g., *City of Richmond v. Deans*, 281 U.S. 704 [1930], upholding a lower court decision that held zoning restrictions based on inability to intermarry were unconstitutional and stating that the issue was controlled by *Buchanan*; *Allen v. Oklahoma City*, 52 P.2d. 1054, [1935], holding that an Oklahoma City ordinance nearly identical to the Louisville ordinance at issue in *Buchanan* was unconstitutional notwithstanding the assertion that it was passed as the only legislative alternative for achieving racial harmony in the face of a declaration of martial law by the governor).

Ultimately, cities circumvented the *Buchanan* decision by encouraging the use of private restrictive covenants to accomplish the same racial restrictions on a neighborhood by neighborhood basis. In *Corrigan v. Buckley*, 271 U.S. 323 (1926), the Court upheld such covenants, stating that they were private contracts outside of the ambit of the Fourteenth Amendment's restriction on state government actions. *Corrigan v. Buckley* was largely abrogated by *Shelley v. Kraemer*, 334 U.S. 1 (1948), wherein the Court held that state courts could not enforce such covenants without violating the equal protection clause. Nevertheless, *Buchanan* was an early victory for the NAACP and its legal strategy for ending *de jure* segregation.

SEE ALSO *Fourteenth Amendment; Freedom of Contract; Jim Crow in the Early Twentieth Century*

BIBLIOGRAPHY

Bernstein, David E. 1998. "Philip Sober Controlling Philip Drunk: *Buchanan v. Warley* in Historical Perspective." *Vanderbilt Law Review* 51: 797–879. Available from http://mason.gmu.edu/~dbernste/buchanan.htm

Higginbotham, A. Leon, Jr. 1996. *Shades of Freedom: Racial Politics and Presumptions of the American Legal Process*. New York: Oxford University Press.

Damon Y. Smith

BUCKLEY V. VALEO, 424 U.S. 1 (1976)

In *Buckley v. Valeo*, 424 U.S. 1 (1976), the Supreme Court upheld some provisions and rejected some provisions of the 1974 amendments to the Federal Election Campaign Act of 1971. The 1974 amendments established the Federal Election Commission, expenditure limits for federal campaigns, contribution limits, and public disclosure of campaign contributors. The lead plaintiff in the case was James Buckley, a senator from New York; but he was joined by other candidates, party organizations, the New York branch of the American Civil Liberties Union (ACLU), the American Conservative Union, and other political organizations. The law had been substantially upheld in the challenges in lower courts.

In the case, there was a lengthy per curiam (unsigned) opinion that explained which provisions were upheld and which were considered unconstitutional. The first section of the opinion considered the contribution and expenditure limitations. The Court stated the importance of the First Amendment's protection of political speech, adding that communication that results from the giving and spending of money are forms of political speech. The Court stated that "the expenditure limitations contained in the Act represent substantial, rather than merely theoretical, restraints on the quantity and diversity of political speech." The Court rejected a provision that prohibits groups other than parties and candidates from spending more than $1,000 on a candidate. However, the Court upheld the limitation on individual contributions ($1,000 per election) to candidates; the Court calls this "only a marginal restriction upon the ability to engage in free communication." The Court considered the interest served by this limitation to justify the "limited effect upon First Amendment freedoms." The Court also upheld the $5,000 maximum contribution by political committees, as well as upholding a limitation on the total amount contributed to federal candidates.

The Court considered expenditure limitations in federal campaigns, striking down the $1,000 limitation on independent expenditures by organizations other than political parties as violating the First Amendment. The Court also struck down the limitation on expenditures from personal or family resources because that provision "impose[d] a substantial restraint on the ability of persons to engage in protected First Amendment expression." Also in violation of the First Amendment, the Court struck down limitations on spending in federal campaigns.

In the per curiam opinion, the Court upheld reporting and disclosure requirements of the law, both as they applied to major and minor parties. The Court permitted a voluntary system of public financing whereby candidates who accept public funding are subject to spending limits. The Court said that the public funding was permissible under the general welfare clause of the Constitution. The Court also ruled that the creation of the Federal Election Commission was constitutional and the duties given to it were also permissible, but the means by which the commissioners were appointed violated the Constitution because some of the appointments were made by the Congress, rather than the president.

SEE ALSO *Campaign Finance; First Amendment*

BIBLIOGRAPHY

Maisel, L. Sandy, and Kara Z. Buckley. 2005. *Parties and Elections in America: The Electoral Process.* 4th edition. Lanham, MD: Rowman and Littlefield Publishers.

Smith, Bradley A. 2001. *Unfree Speech: The Folly of Campaign Finance Reform.* Princeton, NJ: Princeton University Press.

Michael Coulter

BUCK V. BELL, 274 U.S. 200 (1927)

In *Buck v. Bell*, 274 U.S. 200 (1927), the United States Supreme Court found that a Virginia statute that authorized government officials to sterilize patients who were deemed "mentally defective" did not violate either the due process or the equal protection clauses of the Fourteenth Amendment. The appellant in this case was an eighteen-year-old woman named Carrie Buck. After Carrie's mother was institutionalized at the Virginia Colony for the Epileptic and the Feebleminded, Carrie was placed in a foster home. After being raped by a relative

of her foster parent, she became pregnant and was institutionalized at the same state colony where her mother resided. To institutionalize her, state officials claimed that Carrie had inherited her mother's trait of sexual promiscuity and "feeblemindedness." Approximately a year later, when Carrie's daughter Vivian was seven months old, state doctors performed a cursory examination of Vivian and concluded that she too was "mentally defective."

Based upon the premise that Carrie's mother, Carrie, and Vivian were all "feebleminded," the state of Virginia made arrangements to sterilize Carrie. The State of Virginia appointed an attorney to represent Carrie. The attorney challenged the state's sterilization order, and her case made it all the way to the United States Supreme Court. On behalf of Carrie, the attorney argued that forced sterilization was repugnant to the due process and equal protection clauses of the Fourteenth Amendment. He claimed that Carrie had both the constitutional and the "inherent right ... to go through life without mutilation of organs." He also argued that the Virginia statute that authorized the sterilization of mentally defective people was a violation of the Eighth Amendment's cruel and unusual punishment clause.

The state of Virginia, on the other hand, argued that the statute in question was a valid exercise of police power needed to protect the welfare of the general public. The state analogized forced sterilizations of state institutionalized persons with compulsory vaccinations of public school children. They concluded that because these actions were both surgical operations required for the protection of the individual and society, and since compulsory vaccinations had already been deemed Constitutional, forced sterilizations should also be permissible.

The United States Supreme Court agreed with the State of Virginia. It stated that because insanity and imbecility are hereditary, defective persons who became pregnant and had children would place a greater burden on the State. The Court reasoned that when a "defective" individual has children, the state becomes responsible for supporting not just one individual but two generations of "defective" individuals. It further reasoned that if "defective" individuals were not capable of procreating, they stood a chance of being able to support themselves and could therefore make a contribution to society. Moreover, the Court noted that the statute authorizing sterilization of inmates of state institutions did not violate the due process clause of the Constitution because the state was required to (a) hold a hearing; (b) provide notice to the inmate, her guardian, and parents; (c) produce evidence in writing indicating why this sterilization is in the best interests of both the inmate and the State; and (d) provide for an appeal from the decision. It further concluded that even though the forced sterilization provision applied only to persons living inside state institutions, it did not violate the

Fourteenth Amendment because all similarly situated individuals were treated the same and that is all that is required by the equal protection clause of the Constitution.

In one of the most often quoted statements of the Supreme Court, Justice Oliver W. Holmes stated: "It is better for all the world, if instead of waiting to execute degenerate offspring for crime, or let them starve for their imbecility, society can prevent those who are manifestly unfit from continuing their kind. . . . Three generations of imbeciles is enough." The *Buck* decision laid the groundwork for over thirty states to enact legislation that would allow the state to force "defective" individuals to be sterilized. Each state had a different definition of what it meant to be "defective." The term "defective," however, proved to be broad enough to include people of African descent, immigrants from Southern and Eastern Europe, alcoholics, petty criminals, the poor, the homeless, the physically disabled, and the mentally disabled.

It is estimated that somewhere between 60,000 and 100,000 people were involuntarily sterilized in an attempt to prevent their genes from being passed on to another generation. Although the statutes applied to both men and women, women were disproportionately targeted for sterilization. Most of these women were poor and an overwhelming number of them were African Americans and Latinas.

SEE ALSO *Eugenics; Holmes, Oliver W.*

BIBLIOGRAPHY

Berns, Walter. 1951. "*Buck v. Bell*: The Sterilization Decision and Its Effect on Public Policy." Masters Thesis, University of Chicago.

Larson, Edward J. 1995. *Sex, Race, and Science: Eugenics in the Deep South.* Baltimore, MD: Johns Hopkins University Press.

Lombardo, Paul A. 1982. "Eugenic Sterilization in Virginia: Aubrey Strode and the Case of Bell." Ph.D. Diss. Charlottesville: University of Virginia.

Lombardo, Paul A. 1985. "Three Generations, No Imbeciles: New Light on *Buck v. Bell.*" *New York University Law Review* 60(1): 30–60.

Smith, J. David, and K. Ray Nelson. 1989. *The Sterilization of Carrie Buck.* Far Hills, NJ: New Horizon Press.

Judith A. M. Scully

BURGER, WARREN E.
1907–1995

With seventeen years on the U.S. Supreme Court, Warren Earl Burger served the longest term as chief justice in the twentieth century, with praise for achievements in judicial

Supreme Court Chief Justice Warren E. Burger. *Serving as Chief Justice of the Supreme Court from June 23, 1969 to September 26, 1986, Burger is perhaps most noted for his work to improve judicial administration, devoting considerable time and energy to improve the efficiency and organization of the entire federal court system.* **THE LIBRARY OF CONGRESS**

administration. Burger was noted for his opinions on the separation of powers, as well as desegregation, religion, obscenity, and procedure.

Warren Earl Burger was born September 17, 1907, in St. Paul, Minnesota, and was pleased to share his birthday with the Constitution. He was the fourth of seven children born to Charles Joseph and Katharine (Schnittger) Burger. His father worked as a railroad cargo inspector and salesman. Grandfather Joseph Burger was a Swiss immigrant who joined the Union Army at age fourteen and was a Civil War hero. His mother's parents were German and Austrian immigrants, and Burger described her as one who ran an old-fashioned German house instilling common sense in her children. Burger always loved the Constitution and wanted to be a lawyer, even as a young boy. Suffering from polio at age eight, he was kept home from school for a year and his teacher brought him many biographies of great judges and lawyers.

In high school, Burger was president of the student council, editor of the school paper, and a letterman in hockey, football, track, and swimming. Awarded a scholarship from Princeton, he turned it down to stay at home and help support his family by selling insurance. Attending night school at the University of Minnesota from 1925 to 1927, he was president of the student council when he met his wife, Elvera Stromberg. He attended night classes at the St. Paul College of Law and graduated with his LL.B. magna cum laude in 1931. Burger married Elvera Stromberg in 1933 and they had two children, Wade and Margaret.

POLITICS

Burger won a legal job in the depression year of 1931, made partner in 1935, and taught law at his alma mater. He built his law practice with civic work and met Harold E. Stassen (1907–2001). Burger organized the Minnesota Young Republicans in 1934 and Stassen's successful campaign for governor in 1938. Although rejected from World War II military duty due to spinal injury, he served on Minnesota's Emergency War Labor Board.

In 1948, Burger went to the Republican (GOP) National Convention, where he met Richard M. Nixon—the two were great Stassen men. At the 1952 GOP convention, when Dwight D. Eisenhower emerged as a leading presidential hopeful, Burger was the key figure in a floor decision shifting Stassen support to ensure Eisenhower's nomination on the first ballot. Eisenhower was favorably impressed and, in 1953, appointed Burger U.S. assistant attorney general.

D.C. CIRCUIT COURT OF APPEALS

On June 21, 1955, Eisenhower nominated Burger to a judgeship on the D.C. Circuit Court of Appeals. Burger was sworn in on April 13, 1956. Burger developed an early interest in court administration and was actively involved with the American Bar Association to create an efficient and competent federal judiciary. Further, he gained national attention with his critique of the neglect of moral aspects of the law by the Supreme Court in its decisions on insanity and self-incrimination.

U.S. SUPREME COURT

On May 21, 1969, Burger was nominated as chief justice by President Nixon. Burger was to be the law and order appointee Nixon had campaigned for. He was confirmed by a Senate vote of seventy-four-to-three on June 9, 1969. Earl Warren swore in his successor, Warren Earl Burger, on June 23, 1969.

Burger served seventeen terms as chief justice, a tenure as chief justice exceeded only by John Marshall, Roger Taney, Melville Fuller, and William Rehnquist. On June 17, 1986, Ronald Reagan announced Burger's resignation and his nomination of William Rehnquist to succeed Burger. On September 26, 1986, at age seventy-eight, Burger moved most of his personal belongings from the Supreme Court Building to undertake his role as chairman of the Commission on the Bicentennial of the United States Constitution.

Judicial Administration Even Burger's critics admit that he accomplished more in the area of judicial administration than any other chief justice. Burger insisted he was chief justice of the United States, not simply chief justice of the Supreme Court. He had over sixty-four formal roles including presiding over the Federal Judicial Center, Judicial Conference of the United States, Smithsonian Institution, National Gallery of Art, and so forth. But his greatest accomplishments were innovations and improvements in judicial operations. While all his achievements cannot be listed here, Burger contributed to judicial administration in at least six ways. First, Burger added new administrative support to the Court with an administrative assistant to the chief justice, judicial fellows, public relations professionals, librarians, clerks, and vast improvements to the law library and technology of the Court. Second, he continued his efforts in judicial education programs with the National Judicial College and others. Third, he developed the Federal Judicial Center, National Center for State Courts, and promoted related organizations to gather data on courts, research judicial reforms, and train and inform the judiciary. Fourth, Burger convened lectures and colloquia to bring together key decision makers to discuss judicial administration. Fifth, Burger urged training in actual legal and litigation skills in law schools, continuing education for lawyers, and so forth. And finally, Burger is considered a founder of alternative dispute resolution and court mediation, arbitration, and other alternatives to litigation.

As the Court's judicial administrator, Burger's opinion in *United States v. Nixon*, 418 U.S. 683 (1974) turned away a potential public attack against the Court when Burger decided against his appointing president. Yet, Burger believed the greatest threat to the Court was its case docket overload, which had climbed from 4202 cases and 88 signed opinions in the 1969 term to over 5158 cases and 161 signed opinions in the 1985 term. Burger was successful in lobbying Congress to limit the Court's docket, narrow federal three-judge court jurisdiction, place sanctions against attorneys for abuse of process, and create a special court of appeals for the federal circuit with expertise in patent, copyright, trademark, and so forth. He was not successful, however, in reforms such as an intercircuit tribunal to take a burden off the Supreme Court in resolving conflicts between the circuits. Burger wanted a central judicial administrator like the lord chancellor of England, which never came to be.

Decisions Burger proved difficult to categorize as a jurist. He was supposed to have been Nixon's man and lead the

Court in a conservative revolution. Instead he rejected Nixon's arguments for executive privilege, limited congressional oversight of the bureaucracy, joined to establish abortion rights, upheld school busing, and defended freedom for religious minorities. The most perceptive analyses conclude that Burger was neither conservative nor liberal, but was pragmatic, concerned with street level implementation and administration. He was more concerned with efficiency and democratic accountability than in preserving tradition or some other conservative impulse.

As chief justice, Burger wrote 265 opinions of the Court, averaging 15.6 per year, in addition to separate concurring and dissenting opinions. Although this was a high output, most have not endured as landmark decisions. This was because he was greatly distracted by judicial administration matters, he tended to assign landmark decisions to others, and he believed in a limited judicial role. However, he was most noted for opinions on the separation of powers, as well as opinions on desegregation, religion, obscenity, and court procedures.

Separation of Powers In *United States v. Nixon*, a unanimous Court ruled against President Nixon and ordered him to comply with subpoenas of the special prosecutor investigating the Watergate Hotel burglary and other crimes. Burger rejected Nixon's argument of executive privilege to keep confidential the tape recordings of White House discussions. Separation of powers was preserved by the Court by affirming the special prosecutor's power of subpoena over the president and by this Supreme Court "declaration of independence."

In *Immigration and Naturalization Service v. Chadha*, 462 U.S. 919 (1983) Burger preserved separation of powers between Congress and the bureaucracy by striking down the legislative veto. The legislative veto allowed Congress to delegate its duties to the Immigration and Naturalization Service to decide to deport individual aliens, but also revoke the specific decision to deport Mr. Chadha in a one-house legislative action. Although used by Congress in over 200 statutes since the 1930s, Burger reasoned that separation of powers did not allow Congress to take back agency decision making in this piecemeal fashion.

Bowsher v. Synar, 478 U.S. 714 (1986) was Burger's last opinion of the Court. The Gramm-Rudman-Hollings Act of 1985 had created the office of comptroller general to identify spending reductions as mandated to balance the federal budget, an executive function. However, the comptroller general was removable from office by Congress. Burger found this crossover of function and removal power unconstitutional.

Other Decisions Burger encouraged the broad use of any and all equitable remedies, including busing, to achieve desegregation in *Swann v. Charlotte-Mecklenburg Board of Education*, 402 U.S. 1 (1971). He defended the freedom of Amish religious minorities in *Wisconsin v. Yoder*, 406 U.S. 205 (1972). His definition of obscenity in *Miller v. California*, 413 U.S. 15 (1973) endures today and allows for local "contemporary community standards." Other landmark decisions by Burger are not as popularly known, but are in keeping with his intense interests in judicial administration.

BURGER'S CRITICS

There are many critics of Burger as chief justice. Scholars in works such as *The Burger Court: Counter-Revolution or Confirmation?* (1998), edited by Bernard Schwartz, described him as a man of limited capacity with no discernable coherent philosophy. Burger's working-class background, night school legal education, and pragmatic philosophy have all been subject to intense personal attack. Bob Woodward and Scott Armstrong, in *The Brethren: Inside the Supreme Court* (1979), present a dismal portrait of Burger's leadership on the Court, alleging that even the old friendship between Justice Harry Blackmun and Burger went sour.

Yet, Justice William Brennan credited Burger with boundless considerateness and compassion for the personal and family problems of every member of the Court that kept relations cordial between justices of sharply divided philosophies. Justice Lewis F. Powell Jr. claimed that good relations and comradeship existed between the justices, and Justice Blackmun said he was Burger's best friend to the end.

A MAN AND THE CONSTITUTION

Before resigning from the Court on September 26, 1986, in 1985 Burger was appointed the chairman of the Commission on the Bicentennial of the United States Constitution by President Ronald Reagan. After resigning as chief justice, he often worked double shifts through the bicentennial of the ratification of the Bill of Rights in 1991. Burger believed it a wonderful coincidence that the 200th birthday of the Constitution on September 17, 1987, was also his eightieth birthday. After the 1994 death of his wife, Elvera, Burger's health declined and he died of congestive heart failure on June 25, 1995. He was laid in state in the Great Hall of the Supreme Court, memorialized at National Presbyterian Church, and buried at Arlington National Cemetery.

SEE ALSO *Blackmun, Harry; Burger Court; Busing; Nixon, Richard*

BIBLIOGRAPHY

Blasi, Vincent, ed. 1983. *The Burger Court: The Counter-Revolution That Wasn't.* New Haven, CT: Yale University Press.

Burger, Warren E. 1995. *It Is So Ordered: A Constitution Unfolds.* New York: W. Morrow.

Lamb, Charles M., and Stephen C. Halpern, eds. 1991. *The Burger Court: Political and Judicial Profiles.* Urbana: University of Illinois Press.

Maltz, Earl M. 2000. *The Chief Justiceship of Warren Burger, 1969–1986.* Columbia: University of South Carolina Press.

Schwartz, Bernard, ed. 1998. *The Burger Court: Counter-Revolution or Confirmation?* New York: Oxford University Press.

Starr, Kenneth W.; Charles F. Lettow; Bruce P. Brown, et al. 1992. "Symposium: The Jurisprudence of Chief Justice Warren E. Burger." *Oklahoma Law Review* 45(1): 1–168.

Tobias, Carl. 1996. "Warren Burger and the Administration of Justice." *Villanova Law Review* 41(2): 505–519.

Woodward, Bob, and Scott Armstrong, 1979. *The Brethren: Inside the Supreme Court.* New York: Simon and Schuster.

Yarbrough, Tinsley E. 2000. *The Burger Court: Justices, Rulings, and Legacy.* Santa Barbara, CA: ABC-CLIO.

Bradley Stewart Chilton

BURGER COURT

On May 21, 1969, President Richard Nixon nominated sixty-one-year-old Warren Earl Burger, the chief judge of the U.S. Court of Appeals for the D.C. Circuit, to serve as the fourteenth chief justice of the U.S. Supreme Court. The U.S. Senate confirmed him by a vote of seventy-four to three, and on June 23, 1969, retiring Chief Justice Earl Warren swore in Burger. Seventeen years later, on September 26, 1986, the Burger Court officially ended when Burger swore in his successor, William Rehnquist.

The reputation of the Burger Court, much like its chief justice, has been overshadowed by both its predecessor and successor. Initially, Court watchers focused on whether the Burger Court would launch a conservative counterrevolution to reverse decisions by the Warren Court in areas of constitutional law, such as criminal procedure, equal protection, religion, and freedom of expression. The anticipated counterrevolution never came. Instead, the Burger Court functioned more as a gradual transitional period from the liberal Warren Court to the conservative Rehnquist Court, but periodically the Burger Court did issue progressive opinions on social issues, such as reproductive rights, gender discrimination, and affirmative action. Overall, the Burger Court followed the institutional path that the Court had forged for itself in the wake of the constitutional crisis of the 1930s. According to what scholars have labeled the "New Deal settlement," the Court continued its traditional role developed by the Marshall Court (1801–1835) of enforcing constitutional prohibitions on state action. Second, the Court changed direction and deferred generally to Congress and the executive on the scope of their respective delegated constitutional powers. Third, the Court reserved the use of the strict scrutiny standard to strike down federal and state laws that infringed on civil and political rights, especially those that affected discrete and insular minorities in American society.

Although the Burger Court followed the general pattern of the New Deal settlement, its opinions revealed a divided and contentious Court. As Keith Whittington has noted,

> The Burger Court set new records for the number of dissenting opinions it produced, but it also produced twice as many plurality opinions than had been produced in the entire history of the Court. Additionally, far more Burger Court decisions were made by one-vote majorities than by any previous Court. Although sometimes characterized as moderate or pragmatic, the Burger Court was capable of taking wild ideological swings from term to term and issue to issue, depending on the inclination and composition of the shifting majorities. (Whittington 2005, p. 320)

In the post–Watergate era of suspicion of government, the investigative journalists Bob Woodward and Scott Armstrong exposed the inner workings of the Court, including its many dysfunctions. The Burger Court, as reported by Woodward and Armstrong in their best seller *The Brethren: Inside the Supreme Court* (1979), reflected the growing divisions of a nation unraveling during the turbulent 1970s.

Heavy caseloads complicated the work of the Burger Court, as the Supreme Court's docket had been growing dramatically since the 1950s. Chief Justice Burger worked with Congress to reduce the number of mandatory appeals that the Supreme Court heard, so that the rate of growth in the Court's docket did at least slow considerably. To promote more efficiency in judicial administration across the nation, Burger also prompted the Institute for Court Management to train court officials and judicial councils to consolidate concurrent cases, and he helped lead efforts for state courts to share information more freely among jurisdictions. Burger also made changes to the administration of the Supreme Court. He expanded its staffing, made significant improvement to its law library, and incorporated new technology. He also limited oral argument from two hours to one, and eliminated the practice of justices reading opinions from the bench, except in rare instances.

THE JUSTICES OF THE BURGER COURT

The changing personnel of the Burger Court explain partly why no counterrevolution materialized during its seventeen years, and also why the Court issued so many divided and inconsistent opinions.

During his first term in office, President Nixon, who had been a vocal critic of the Warren Court during his

Members of the U.S. Supreme Court, April 20, 1972, under Chief Justice Warren E. Burger, seated center. *Nominated to be Chief Justice by President Richard Nixon on May 21, 1969, Burger (front row, center) led the Supreme Court for seventeen terms, developing a court known for tackling difficult decisions, including ones on abortion, school integration, and religious liberties.* **AP IMAGES**

1968 campaign for the presidency, had the opportunity to fill four seats on the Court, which led commentators to refer to the "Burger Court" as the "Nixon Court."

The resignations in 1969 of Earl Warren and Abe Fortas, both staunch liberals, created the first two opportunities for President Nixon to move the Court in a new ideological direction. Although the nomination and confirmation of Burger went smoothly, Nixon ran into great difficulty in his efforts to fill Fortas's seat, which had become known as the "Jewish seat" on the Court. Since President Woodrow Wilson had nominated Louis Brandeis to become the first Jewish justice to serve on the Court, future presidents had worked to ensure that at least one Jewish person sat on the Court.

Nixon did not follow this historical pattern. Instead, as part of his strategy to court conservative southern white voters for the Republican Party, Nixon sought to appoint a young, politically conservative southerner to replace Fortas. Nixon first nominated Judge Clement F. Haynsworth Jr. (1912–1989), a South Carolinian who served on the U.S. Court of Appeals for the Fourth Circuit. Although labor and civil rights organizations strongly opposed his nomination, ultimately an ethical issue led to the Senate rejecting Haynsworth by a vote of fifty-five to forty-five. Nixon's second nominee, G. Harrold Carswell (1919–1992), a Georgian, had publicly opposed the civil rights movement, including proclaiming his support for white supremacy. Although Carswell had little judicial experience, he had recently been confirmed to serve on the U.S. Court of Appeals for the Fifth Circuit. Not only did the American Bar Association question his qualifications for a seat on the high court, but even his supporters in the Senate did little to help his cause. Senator Roman Hruska (1904–1999) of Nebraska famously declared: "Even if he is mediocre, there are a lot of mediocre judges and people and lawyers, and they are entitled to a little representation, aren't they? We can't have all Brandeises and Cardozos and Frankfurters." (Weaver 1970, p. 21). The Senate voted fifty-one to forty-five to reject Carswell.

After two bitter defeats, Nixon opted to nominate a northern conservative, instead of a southerner. He chose Harry A. Blackmun, a boyhood friend of Warren Burger's from Minneapolis. Blackmun was serving on the U.S. Court of Appeals for the Eight Circuit, and on May 12,

1970, the Senate quickly confirmed him by a ninety-four-to-zero vote. Dubbed "the Minnesota Twin," commentators assumed that Blackmun would work with Burger to reverse the Warren Court revolution. Initially, Blackmun appeared to be a solid conservative choice and often voted to limit the procedural restraints that the Warren Court had placed on law enforcement. Yet, Blackmun, who served on the Court for twenty-four years, developed into one of the most liberal justices in the Court's history. He became, for instance, a champion of women's rights, including authoring the majority opinion in *Roe v. Wade*, 410 U.S. 113 (1973), which granted women the right to terminate a pregnancy during the first trimester. In addition, Blackmun, who first approved of capital punishment, later became a leading opponent of its constitutionality.

In 1971 Justice Hugo Black and Justice John Marshall Harlan had to resign for serious health reasons, and both died later that year. Nixon nominated sixty-four-year-old Lewis Powell to replace Black, an Alabamian and the lone southerner on the Court. Having learned from the defeats of Haynsworth and Carswell, Nixon chose a moderate conservative southerner and a Democrat. Powell came from a distinguished Virginia family and had established himself as a leader of the legal profession, including serving as the president of the American Bar Association. In that capacity, he helped to establish the Legal Services Corporation to provide legal representation for those who could not afford it. The Senate confirmed Powell with only one dissenting vote, and he would serve on the Burger Court for fifteen years. As a moderate conservative on an ideologically divided and contentious Court, Powell worked hard to build consensus among his colleagues, especially on charged issues such as affirmative action.

Nixon's fourth and final appointment turned out to be the most historically significant. He had to fill the seat of John Marshall Harlan. Harlan was the grandson and namesake of the great dissenter in *Plessy v. Ferguson*, 163 U.S. 537 (1896), the case in which the Court had provided a constitutional imprimatur for Jim Crow. Like his grandfather, Justice Harlan also earned a reputation as a dissenter. As a moderate conservative on the liberal Warren Court, his dissenting opinions often urged his liberal brethren to practice more judicial restraint.

To replace Harlan, Nixon nominated William Rehnquist, the forty-seven-year-old assistant attorney general in charge of the Office of Legal Counsel. This important office serves as the legal advisor to the executive branch. Rehnquist, who had graduated first in his class at Stanford Law School, later clerked for Justice Robert Jackson when the Court was hearing *Brown v. Board of Education*, 347 U.S. 483 (1954). Rehnquist had even written a memo to Jackson in which he urged the Court to uphold *Plessy*'s doctrine of "separate, but equal." In 1957 Rehnquist published an article in *U.S. News and World Report* that criticized Supreme Court clerks for "extreme solicitude for the claims of Communists and other criminal defendants, expansion of federal power at the expense of State power, great sympathy toward any government regulation of business, in short, the political philosophy now espoused by the Court under Chief Justice Warren" (quoted in Hoffer et al. 2007, p. 374). As no surprise, Nixon's nomination of Rehnquist, an outspoken conservative, proved controversial. Although the Senate confirmed Rehnquist by a sixty-eight-to-twenty-six vote, Rehnquist received the most "no" votes of any successful nominee for the Court in its history up to that time.

On January 7, 1972, Powell and Rehnquist joined the Burger Court. Powell, a moderate and a swing vote, better represented the often-pragmatic jurisprudence of the Court. Yet, Rehnquist, its most conservative and youngest member, known as the "Lone Ranger" for his solo dissenting opinions, foreshadowed later developments in the Court's history. In 1986 President Ronald Reagan nominated and the Senate confirmed Rehnquist by a sixty-five-to-thirty-three vote to become the fifteenth chief justice. By the mid-1990s, Rehnquist would author majority opinions, such as *United States v. Lopez*, 514 U.S. 549 (1995), which called the New Deal settlement into question.

Even though President Nixon appointed four members to the Court during his first term, the Burger Court from 1972 to 1975 remained ideologically divided. Significantly, it did not have enough conservative votes to launch a counterrevolution. Aside from the staunchly conservative Rehnquist, Burger had to work with liberal and moderately conservative justices. The liberal bloc remaining from the Warren Court fought to preserve and extend its work. Its members included William Douglas, the last remaining Franklin Roosevelt appointee; William Brennan, the intellectual leader of the Warren Court revolution in constitutional law; and Thurgood Marshall, the former general counsel of the National Association for the Advancement of Colored People (NAACP) Legal Defense and Education Fund, who had engineered the litigation strategy that led to the ultimate victory in *Brown v. Board of Education*. Potter Stewart and Byron White also remained from the Warren Court, and, with Powell, served as important swing voters on the Burger Court. Blackmun, who was supposed to be a reliable conservative, eventually became one of the Court's most consistent liberal voices.

Three of Nixon's appointees, including Chief Justice Burger, played a decisive role in ending his presidency. The Court's eight-to-zero ruling (Rehnquist did not participate) in *United States v. Nixon*, 418 U.S. 683 (1974), forced Nixon to surrender the presidency to avoid impeachment.

The retirements of Douglas in 1975 and Stewart in 1981 did not fundamentally change the Burger Court. President Gerald Ford and President Ronald Reagan nominated justices John Paul Stevens and Sandra Day O'Connor, who were unanimously confirmed by the Senate. Both Stevens and O'Connor, the first woman Supreme Court justice, were traditional Republicans who were more inclined to support reproductive rights, affirmative action, and gay rights than modern Republicans, such as William Rehnquist. The significant differences between traditional and modern Republicans on social issues would become more apparent during the final years of the Rehnquist Court and the beginnings of the new Roberts Court.

CRIMINAL JUSTICE AND CAPITAL PUNISHMENT

The Burger Court did not overrule the most significant and politically controversial Warren Court decisions on criminal procedures, such as *Mapp v. Ohio*, 367 U.S. 643 (1961), which established the exclusionary rule. This rule made illegally obtained evidence inadmissible in court. The Burger Court also did not overrule *Miranda v. Arizona*, 384 U.S. 436 (1966), the decision that required police officers to inform suspects during custodial interrogations of their Fifth Amendment rights, including the right against self-incrimination. Instead, the Burger Court developed exceptions to these procedural safeguards. For instance, in *United States v. Leon*, 468 U.S. 897 (1984), Justice White argued that there was a "good faith" exception to the exclusionary rule that allowed evidence to be used against a defendant, even if police had seized the evidence using a search warrant that was later declared to be invalid. The Court also asserted that the exclusionary rule was a safeguard against police misconduct, not technically a constitutional right that had to be absolutely protected. In addition to restricting Warren Court holdings in criminal procedure, such as the exclusionary rule and *Miranda* warnings, the Burger Court also limited appellate review of criminal cases.

In light of its efforts to narrow Warren Court holdings, surprisingly in *Furman v. Georgia*, 408 U.S. 238 (1972), in a five-to-four decision, the Burger Court declared that the death penalty, as it was being applied in the United States, violated the Eighth Amendment's guarantee against cruel and unusual punishment. Capital punishment in the United States had been put on hold since 1967 because of the pre-*Furman* litigation. In the wake of the Court's decision, about two-thirds of the states rewrote their laws to satisfy the Supreme Court that they were not using the death penalty arbitrarily. In *Gregg v. Georgia*, 428 U.S. 153 (1976), the Court upheld some of these revised death-penalty statutes. After a hiatus of ten years, on January 17, 1977, the death penalty in America resumed when a firing squad in the Utah State Prison shot Gary Gilmore to death.

In the area of criminal procedure, the Burger Court adjusted the jurisprudence of the Warren Court to represent the nation's growing concerns about law and order, which President Nixon had effectively made into a campaign issue in his 1968 election.

WOMEN'S RIGHTS, GENDER DISCRIMINATION, FUNDAMENTAL INTERESTS, AND SEXUAL ORIENTATION

The Burger Court issued its most controversial decision, as well as its most doctrinally significant invocations, in the area of women's rights and gender discrimination. In *Roe v. Wade*, 410 U.S. 113 (1973), the Burger Court struck down Texas's criminal abortion law. This law prevented a woman from terminating her pregnancy unless a doctor determined it was necessary to save her life. Justice Blackmun, who had been general counsel for the Mayo Clinic, wrote for the majority in this seven-to-two opinion. In dissent, justices White and Rehnquist accused the majority of creating a new substantive constitutional right. Since *Roe*, there have been concerted efforts by modern conservatives to have this decision overruled, and the politics of pro-choice supporters versus pro-life supporters has become a defining feature of modern American politics.

In addition to its landmark decision in *Roe v. Wade*, the Burger Court during the 1970s also adapted a standard of heightened judicial review known as *intermediate scrutiny* to access governmental policies that use gender classifications. An Oregon law, which established a preference for men over women in the administration of estates, led to the case of *Reed v. Reed*, 404 U.S. 71 (1971). Applying the rational basis standard that the Court had used since the 1930s to access economic legislation, this law could have passed constitutional muster. Yet, in a seven-to-zero opinion written by Chief Justice Burger, the Court overturned the law. The chief justice declared, "To give a mandatory preference to members of either sex over members of the other, merely to accomplish the elimination of hearings on the merits, is to make the very kind of arbitrary legislative choice forbidden by the Equal Protection Clause of the Fourteenth Amendment." Although Chief Justice Burger did not articulate a new test for gender discrimination cases, his opinion suggested that stereotypes of men and women were not enough to sustain differential treatment.

In *Frontiero v Richardson*, 411 U.S. 677 (1973), a plurality of the Court adopted the strict scrutiny test to review an instance of gender discrimination. This case involved a military policy that automatically allowed servicemen to claim their wives as dependents, while servicewomen had to demonstrate that their husbands were dependant. Justice Brennan, joined by Douglas, White, and Marshall, contended that classifications based on sex were inherently suspect and should be subjected to the strict scrutiny standard. Without a fifth vote, however, Brennan's opinion did not become precedent for applying the strict scrutiny standard to gender discrimination.

The Supreme Court later formulated the intermediate scrutiny test in *Craig v. Boren*, 429 U.S. 190 (1976). This test places the burden of proof on the government by requiring that classification by gender must serve important governmental objectives, and the classification must be substantially related to the achievement of those objectives. The development and application of heightened scrutiny to governmental use of gender was arguably the most important doctrinal contribution of the Burger Court.

The Burger Court also significantly expanded the category of fundamental interests that merited strict judicial scrutiny. As part of the New Deal settlement, the Court had increasingly struck down laws that abridged free speech, threatened political association, and restricted voting. In the 1970s, the Court recognized new fundamental interests, including the right to travel, marry, and access the courts. In addition, the Burger Court held that legislative classifications based on alienage were suspect and would be strictly scrutinized.

In its final term, the Burger Court also heard cases on sexual harassment and sexual orientation. In *Meritor Savings Bank v. Vinson*, 477 U.S. 57 (1986), the Court interpreted Title VII of the Civil Rights Act of 1964 to allow employees to sue their employers for allowing sex discrimination to create a hostile workplace environment. This decision has served as the basis for subsequent developments in the law of sexual harassment.

The Court also addressed the question of whether the right of privacy protected gay men who wished to engage in consensual sex. Georgia, like many states, criminalized sodomy. In *Bowers v. Hardwick*, 478 U.S. 186 (1986), in a five-to-four decision, the Burger Court applied the rational basis test and concluded that states had broad powers to regulate sexuality. As Justice White explained,

> Even if the conduct at issue here is not a fundamental right, respondent asserts that there must be a rational basis for the law, and that there is none in this case other than the presumed belief of a majority of the electorate in Georgia that homosexual sodomy is immoral and unacceptable. This is said to be an inadequate rationale to support the law. The law, however, is constantly based on notions of morality, and if all laws representing essentially moral choices are to be invalidated under the Due Process Clause, the courts will be very busy indeed. Even respondent makes no such claim, but insists that majority sentiments about the morality of homosexuality should be declared inadequate. We do not agree, and are unpersuaded that the sodomy laws of some 25 States should be invalidated on this basis.

Justice Powell, who cast the decisive fifth vote, later publicly regretted his decision. *Bowers* remained good constitutional law until the Rehnquist Court overruled it in *Lawrence v. Texas*, 539 U.S. 558 (2003).

EQUAL PROTECTION AND RACE

It is a legal fiction to separate gender and race as analytical categories, especially since people are generally classified by both their race and gender. The Supreme Court, however, developed different standards of review to apply in cases involving suspect classifications. As the previous section noted, the Burger Court did not consider sex, like race, to be a suspect classification. The Court also rejected the argument that wealth should be considered a suspect classification (*San Antonio School District v. Rodriguez*, 411 U.S. 1 [1973]). The Court did, however, use heightened scrutiny in *Plyler v. Doe*, 457 U.S. 202 (1982), to strike down a Texas law that allowed the state to withhold from local school districts state funds for educating children of illegal aliens.

The Burger Court continued to use strict scrutiny primarily in cases involving racial classifications. For instance, in *Swann v. Charlotte-Mecklenburg Board of Education*, 402 U.S. 1 (1971), the Court allowed federal district courts to incorporate busing programs into their desegregation plans for school districts to remedy past discrimination. Yet, in *Milliken v. Bradley*, 418 U.S. 717 (1974), in a five-to-four decision, the Burger Court struck down a Michigan integration plan that crossed school-district lines. Critics of the Court have argued that decisions such as *Milliken* represented the Court's acquiescence in resegregation.

The most controversial Burger Court decision on the use of race as a governmental classification involved the constitutionality of the admission policy used by the medical school at the University of California at Davis. Under the school's affirmative action plan, the medical school reserved sixteen out one hundred seats in its entering class for minority or socioeconomically disadvantaged applicants. A separate committee evaluated the applicants for these sixteen seats, and these applicants could be admitted with lower grade point averages and Medical College Admission Test scores than applicants in the general pool. After being denied admission twice, Allan Bakke, a white applicant, brought suit in the California Superior Court. Bakke argued that he had experienced racial discrimination, in violation of the equal protection clause and Title VI of the Civil Rights Act of 1964, as well as the California constitution. He won his case, and the University of California appealed this decision to the U.S. Supreme Court.

Brennan, White, Marshall, and Blackmun all supported the use of race in admissions to educational programs to remedy past racial discrimination. As

Blackmun argued, "In order to get beyond racism, we must first take account of race. There is no other way. And in order to treat some persons equally, we must treat them differently" (*Regents of University of California v. Bakke*, 438 U.S. 265 [1978]). Burger, Stewart, Stevens, and Rehnquist, on the other hand, all contended that the admissions policy had illegally discriminated against Bakke. This meant that Powell, a swing vote, cast the decisive fifth vote. Powell found that the admission plan's quota system was clearly unconstitutional, but that more flexible approaches that took race into account could be constitutional. Powell's opinion became the basis for designing affirmative action programs across the nation.

RELIGION, FREEDOM OF SPEECH, CAMPAIGN FINANCE, AND ADMINISTRATIVE AGENCIES

The Burger Court decided landmark cases in all four of these areas, which helped to shape the contours of American public culture and governance, including the place of religion in American society, the role of a free press during wartime, how federal campaigns and elections are run, and who should make decisions about how regulatory agencies, such as the Environmental Protection Agency, should operate.

In *Lemon v. Kurtzman*, 403 U.S. 602 (1971), writing for the Court, Chief Justice Burger devised a three-part test to determine whether state action violates the establishment clause of the First Amendment. To satisfy the requirements of the establishment clause, Burger explained that a law must have (1) a secular legislative purpose; (2) its principal or primary effect must be one that neither advances nor inhibits religion; and (3) it must not foster an excessive government entanglement with religion. Burger noted that courts should take the following factors into consideration to determine whether a law created an excessive entanglement with religion: the character and purposes of the institutions that are benefitted from the law, the nature of the aid that the state provides the institutions, and how the law affected the relationship between the state and the religious authority. Critics of the *Lemon* test, including some Supreme Court justices, contend that it is hostile to religion and created too much unpredictability in deciding cases. Yet, the Court has not entirely abandoned this approach to the establishment clause.

Much as the Burger Court struggled to define the proper place for religion in modern American life, it also addressed the role of a free press in a democratic society. In *New York Times v. United States*, 403 U.S. 713 (1971), the Court denied an injunction that the Department of Justice sought to prevent the *New York Times* and *Washington Post* from publishing leaked accounts from a classified Pentagon study of the origins of the Vietnam War. This study demonstrated that federal officials had misrepresented American involvement in Vietnam. In a six-to-three per curiam decision, the Court determined that the newspapers could publish these materials, but divided over the critical question of whether national security in wartime could justify prior restraint. The subsequent publication of the Pentagon Papers heightened growing public concerns about the morality of the Vietnam War, and led to further disillusionment among many Americans about the truthfulness of their leaders.

In response to public concerns about the operations of the American government, especially the Watergate scandal, in 1974 Congress dramatically amended the Federal Election Campaign Act. This act, for example, restricted contributions to campaigns and the amount that could be spent on campaigns; required disclosure of significant contributions; created a public funding system for presidential primaries and the presidential general election; and also created a regulatory commission to oversee federal elections. In *Buckley v. Valeo*, 424 U.S. 1 (1976), in a per curiam opinion, the Burger Court upheld many of act's new provisions, but struck down and modified others. Significantly, the Court upheld regulation of campaign contributions but did not allow Congress to limit campaign spending. *Buckley* remains the Court's most important decision on campaign finance and continues to serve as the foundation for federal elections.

Finally, the Burger Court handed down a landmark decision, *Chevron, U.S.A., Inc., v. Natural Resources Defense Council*, 467 U.S. 837 (1984), on judicial review of statutory interpretation by agencies. This decision had enormous consequences for how governmental regulatory agencies functioned. *Chevron* declared that when an agency interpreted an ambiguous statute whose administration Congress has assigned to it, courts should accept the agency's interpretation if it is reasonable or permissible. Yet, if the meaning of the statutory provision is unambiguous, then courts do not have to defer to the agency's interpretation. *Chevron* granted administrative agencies much leeway to develop their own polices. Critics argued that this shifted too much power from Congress, which creates regulatory agencies, to the executive branch that nominated their administrators. Although the Rehnquist Court later moved away from this deferential standard, *Chevron* played an important role in implementation of federal regulatory policy during the late twentieth century.

FEDERALISM

Although the revival of federalism was a more pronounced feature of the Rehnquist Court, the origins of this turn in American constitutional law began with the Burger Court. In *National League of Cities v. Usery*, 426 U.S. 833 (1976), Rehnquist, writing for a five-to-four majority, held that congressional amendments in 1974 to the Fair Labor

Standards Act of 1938 could not be used to regulate the labor market of state employees. According to Rehnquist, the Tenth Amendment prevented Congress from interfering with an integral state governmental function. Ultimately, the Burger Court overruled this decision in 1985 in *Garcia v. San Antonio Metropolitan Transit Authority*, 469 U.S. 528. Blackmun, who had agreed with Rehnquist's opinion in *Usery*, changed his mind. He argued that the *Usery* approach to federalism was impractical and that states should turn to Congress, not the courts, to change federal laws. Rehnquist, however, defended his earlier opinion, and later as chief justice made federalism into a central concern of the high court.

CONCLUSION

The Burger Court was sandwiched between the liberal Warren Court and the conservative Rehnquist Court. From this perspective, it symbolizes the nation's retreat from Great Society liberalism and its embrace of the Reagan revolution's brand of conservatism. Yet, the Burger Court also played a major role in modern American history, including ending the most important political and constitutional crisis of the 1970s. In addition, its decisions on issues such as capital punishment, reproductive rights, sexual harassment, and campaign finance all serve asfoundations for contemporary constitutional law.

SEE ALSO *Burger, Warren E.; Busing; Nixon, Richard; Rehnquist, William; Roe v. Wade, 410 U.S. 113 (1973); Watergate and the Constitution*

BIBLIOGRAPHY

Blasi, Vincent, ed. 1983. *The Burger Court: The Counter-Revolution that Wasn't.* New Haven, CT: Yale University Press.

Hoffer, Peter Charles; Williamjames Hull Hoffer; and N. E. H. Hull. 2007. *The Supreme Court: An Essential History.* Lawrence: University Press of Kansas.

Lamb, Charles M., and Stephen C. Halpern, eds. 1991. *The Burger Court: Political and Judicial Profiles.* Urbana: University of Illinois Press.

Maltz, Earl M. 2000. *The Chief Justiceship of Warren Burger, 1969–1986.* Columbia: University of South Carolina Press.

Schwartz, Bernard. 1988. *The Unpublished Opinions of the Burger Court.* New York: Oxford University Press.

Schwartz, Bernard. 1990. *The Ascent of Pragmatism: The Burger Court in Action.* Reading, MA: Addison-Wesley.

Schwartz, Bernard, ed. 1998. *The Burger Court: Counter-Revolution or Confirmation?* New York: Oxford University Press.

Weaver, Warren, Jr. 1970. "Carswell Attacked and Defended as Senate Opens Debate on Nomination." *New York Times,* March 17: 21.

Whittington, Keith E. 2005. "The Burger Court (1969–1986): Once More in Transition." In *The United States Supreme Court: The Pursuit of Justice,* ed. Christopher Tomlins, 300–322. New York: Houghton Mifflin.

Woodward, Bob, and Scott Armstrong. 1979. *The Brethren: Inside the Supreme Court.* New York: Simon and Schuster.

Yarbrough, Tinsley E. 2000. *The Burger Court: Justices, Rulings, and Legacy.* Santa Barbara, CA: ABC-CLIO.

David S. Tanenhaus

BUSH, GEORGE HERBERT WALKER

SEE *Rehnquist Court; Souter, David; Thomas, Clarence.*

BUSH V. GORE, 531 U.S. 98 (2000)

In *Bush v. Gore*, 531 U.S. 98 (2000), the U.S. Supreme Court issued an opinion that effectively settled the outcome of the disputed 2000 presidential election between Republican candidate Governor George W. Bush (1946–) and Democratic candidate Vice President Albert Gore, Jr. (1948–). Intervening for a third time in the highly contested recounting of votes in Florida, whose twenty-five electoral votes would decide the outcome of the national election, the Supreme Court concluded that continued counting of contested ballots without "specific rules designed to ensure uniform treatment," violated the equal protection clause of the U.S. Constitution. Rather than remanding the case to the Florida Supreme Court to establish the mandated uniform standards, the Court concluded that the Florida legislature intended to take advantage of a statutory safe-harbor benefit regarding controversies over appointment of electors (3 U.S.C. § 5), which provided that Congress would accept without challenge a state's presidential electors if they were established by December 12. After issuing a stay halting all counting of ballots on December 9, the Court issued its per curiam opinion at 10:00 P.M. on December 12, permanently halting all ballot recounting because the task could not be completed in time to take advantage of the safe-harbor provision. With this closely divided five-to-four decision, the Court brought the six-week presidential election drama to an uneremonious close.

THE DEMOCRATIC DRAMA

The riveting democratic drama that gave rise to *Bush v. Gore* began on November 8, when Florida reported election figures indicating a 1,784-vote margin of victory for Governor Bush, triggering a statutorily mandated machine recount of the approximately six million votes cast. On November 9, new results indicated a 327-vote

Political supporters wave signs outside the Supreme Court Building during the contested 2000 presidential election, December 11, 2000. *After Democratic presidential candidate Al Gore contested the outcome of the Florida election in 2000, the Supreme Court ruled against Gore, determining that the lack of uniformity in the method of the Florida recount violated the Fourteenth Amendment's Equal Protection Clause. With this decision, Republican George W. Bush gained all of Florida's twenty-five electoral votes and the presidency of the United States.* © **REUTERS/CORBIS**

margin for Bush. Pursuant to a protest provision under Florida election law, Vice President Gore requested a manual recount in four counties: Volusia, Palm Beach, Broward, and Miami-Dade. In some tension with the manual recount provisions, Florida statutes required all county returns to be certified by the seventh day after an election, subject to the discretion of the Florida secretary

of state, who at the time was Katherine Harris. The Palm Beach County Canvassing Board, later joined by the Volusia County Canvassing Board, sought additional time beyond the seven-day deadline for certifying results in order to complete manual recounts. The secretary of state declined to extend the deadline, but the Florida Supreme Court issued an opinion in *Palm Beach County Canvassing*

Bd. v. Harris, 772 So.2d 1220 (Fla. 2000), having already temporarily enjoined the secretary from certifying the election results, extending the deadline for filing amended certifications until November 26, 2000. Recognizing that "an accurate vote count is one of the essential foundations of our democracy," the Florida Supreme Court resolved tensions within the statutory provisions in favor of discerning the will of the voters. Although the U.S. Supreme Court reviewed this decision in *Bush v. Palm Beach County Canvassing Board*, 531 U.S. 70 (2000), its December 4 per curiam opinion played no practical role in the election dispute.

On November 26, 2000, the Florida Elections Canvassing Commission certified the election for Governor Bush with a 537-vote margin. Vice President Gore contested the certification pursuant to Florida's statutory contest provisions and filed a complaint in state circuit court, arguing that the canvassing commission certification failed to include legal, but uncounted, votes sufficient in number to cast doubt on the election result. The circuit court rejected his challenge and, after the court of appeals certified the case, the Florida Supreme Court held that pursuant to Florida statutes governing election contests, Gore had successfully challenged Miami-Dade County's failure to count over 9,000 votes not tabulated by the machines due primarily to incomplete punches of the voting punch cards—the so-called *undervotes*. On December 8, the court ordered Miami-Dade County to complete a hand recount to determine if any of those 9,000 votes were "legal votes," which the court defined as those "in which there is a 'clear indication of the intent of the voter'" (*Gore v. Harris*, 772 So.2d 1243 [2000]). In so holding, the court relied on the Florida election code, which provides that "no vote shall be declared invalid or void if there is a clear indication of the intent of the voter as determined by the canvassing board" (Fla. Stat. Ann. § 101.5614[5]). The Florida Supreme Court also held that the circuit court erred in not including in certified election results 215 additional net votes for Gore identified by the Palm Beach County Canvassing Board, and 168 net votes for Gore from partial recounts in Miami-Dade County. Moreover, because Florida legislative policy demands "that every citizen's vote be counted whenever possible," the court directed the circuit court to order all counties to complete a hand recount of undervotes to determine if the intent of the voter could be ascertained by further inspection.

Further recounts were never completed. A day after the Florida Supreme Court ordered the statewide recount, the U.S. Supreme Court agreed to hear Governor Bush's appeal and granted a temporary stay of all recounts in Florida, in *Bush v. Gore*, 531 U.S. 1046 (2000). Three days later, on December 12, 2000, the Court issued a per curiam opinion concluding that the Florida Supreme

Court had violated the equal protection clause of the Fourteenth Amendment in crafting equitable remedies pursuant to its interpretation of Florida election statutes. The temporary stay became permanent, and President Bush won Florida's electors by 537 votes.

THE PER CURIAM OPINION

In the per curiam decision, thought to be primarily written by Justice Anthony Kennedy, and supported by Chief Justice William Rehnquist and Justices Sandra Day O'Connor, Antonin Scalia, and Clarence Thomas, the Court explained that citizens do not have a constitutional right to vote in presidential elections unless their state chooses under the authority of Article II, Section 1 to hold statewide elections to select electors. Once granted, the right is fundamental, and "having once granted the right to vote on equal terms, the State may not, by later arbitrary and disparate treatment, value one person's vote over that of another." These principles framed the central issue the Court considered, alternately described as whether the recount procedures ordered by the Florida Supreme Court create arbitrary and disparate treatment of voters, and whether the procedures create disparate treatment of ballots.

According to the Court, the Florida Supreme Court ordered the county canvassing boards to count all legal votes where the intent of voter could be determined, but failed to outline more specific standards by which the recount process would "ensure uniform treatment" of ballots. Although the Florida court employed the "intent of the voter" standard exactly as the Florida legislature had provided by statute, the Court concluded that the lack of more specific and uniform standards for determining intent allowed for individual discretion when reviewing ballots that would ultimately lead to "uneven treatment" of ballots between counties and even within a single county. For example, the Florida Supreme Court did not prescribe rules or guidelines for examining ballots with attached punches (so-called hanging chads). Whereas one county may rule that a ballot with a hanging chad is a legal vote, another may decide that a similar ballot is not a legal vote because "each of the counties used varying standards to determine what was a legal vote." Accordingly, the court's remedy did not offer an "assurance that the rudimentary requirements of equal treatment and fundamental fairness are satisfied." Indeed, the Court observed that "the want of those rules here has led to unequal evaluation of ballots in various respects," in violation of the requirements of equal protection.

Faced with concerns about the fairness of Florida's recount procedures, the Court could have remanded to the Florida Supreme Court to fashion the rules found absent from the process, as the dissenters urged. The five-justice majority determined, however, that when the

---

Although we may never know with complete certainty the identity of the winner of this year's presidential election, the identity of the loser is perfectly clear. It is the nation's confidence in the judge as an impartial guardian of the rule of law.

SOURCE: John Paul Stevens, *Bush v. Gore,* 531 U.S. 98, 128–129 (2000) (dissenting).

Florida Supreme Court in *Palm Beach County Canvassing Board* stated that the recount process should avoid "precluding Florida voters from participating fully in the federal electoral process," it intended to take advantage of the safe-harbor provision. The Court did not explain, however, why consideration of the safe-harbor provision outweighed the Florida Supreme Court's determination that Florida law requires that "in close elections the necessity for counting all legal votes becomes critical." Because any determination of uniform standards to guide a statewide recount would cause Florida to miss the national safe-harbor deadline of December 12, the Court reversed the Florida court's order requiring examination of the remaining contested ballots. In so doing, the Court expressed awareness of its limited authority to intervene under the Constitution, which authorizes the people and state legislatures to select the president. Nonetheless, the Court claimed an "unsought responsibility to resolve the federal and constitutional issues" presented, thereby foreshortening further political contestation over the election.

THE CONCURRENCE

Providing an additional justification for the Supreme Court's intervention in Florida's election process, Chief Justice Rehnquist, joined by Justices Scalia and Thomas, wrote a concurring opinion articulating grounds for ending Florida's recount derived from Article II, Section 1, Clause 2, which provides that "each State shall appoint [presidential electors], in such Manner as the Legislature thereof may direct." The concurrence argued that because Article II provides state legislatures exclusive power to define the method of selecting presidential electors, the Florida Supreme Court violated Article II by interpreting Florida election law in a manner that alters the legislative scheme. A novel rationale, the concurrence cites the only other Supreme Court opinion to interpret this provision, *McPherson v. Blacker,* 146 U.S. 1 (1892), which considered a challenge to the method a legislature had devised for selecting electors.

Ordinarily, when adequate and independent state grounds for a decision exist, the Supreme Court will not review the judgments of state courts, as it first stated in *Murdock v. Memphis,* 87 U.S. 590 (1875). The concurrence acknowledged that comity and federalism compel the Court "to defer to the decisions of state courts on issues of state law," but reasoned that if a state court departs significantly from the legislative scheme for selecting presidential electors, then a federal constitutional question exists requiring Supreme Court intervention. Thus, although the Florida court's determination of state law ordinarily would be conclusive, here the chief justice argued that "the Florida Supreme Court's interpretation of the Florida election laws impermissibly distorted them beyond what a fair reading required, in violation of Article II." Moreover, the concurrence claimed that by relying on Article II to reverse the Florida Supreme Court, it was ultimately vindicating the "role of state *legislatures,*" to which the Constitution had vested power to determine the method of selecting electors.

After surveying the basic outlines of the Florida election code, the concurrence focused on the Florida Supreme Court's interpretation of a "legal vote" as having "plainly departed from the legislative scheme." The departure occurs because "no reasonable person" would attribute error to a county's vote tabulation when machines failed to count ballots purported to be improperly marked. Under the concurrence's understanding of the "clearly expressed intent of the legislature . . . there is no basis for reading the Florida statutes as requiring the counting of improperly marked ballots." Recognizing that the legislature had empowered its state courts to fashion "appropriate relief" in an election contest process, the concurrence reasoned nonetheless that "surely the Florida Legislature . . . must have meant relief that would have become final by the cutoff date of 3 U.S.C. § 5," even though Florida statutes nowhere state that "appropriate relief" in an election contest must take advantage of the federal safe-harbor benefit. Pursuant to its reading of Florida statutes, the concurrence concluded that the Florida Supreme Court's interpretation of state election law to require manual recounts was a significant departure from the Florida legislature's intent in violation of Article II.

THE DISSENTS

According to the per curiam opinion, Justices David Souter and Stephen Breyer, each writing in dissent, agreed with the conclusion that the recount as ordered by the Florida Supreme Court violated the equal protection clause, although they disagreed with the remedy. Justice Souter could "conceive of no legitimate state interest served by these differing treatments" of voters's intent, and Justice Breyer agreed that "basic principles of fairness may well have counseled the adoption of a uniform standard to address the problem." Even with this limited agreement, both justices, along with Justices John Paul Stevens and Ruth Bader Ginsburg, emphasized the fact that the Court was wrong to consider the case and wrong to provide a remedy that left legal votes uncounted. Having heard the case, however, all four dissenters would have remanded the case to allow the Florida courts to fashion a recount that provided uniform standards.

Rebuking the majority for its "federal assault on the Florida election procedures," Justice Stevens found nothing remiss in the Florida Supreme Court's interpretation of Florida law, and found the "unstated lack of confidence in the impartiality and capacity of the state judges" of Florida inappropriate. Regarding the majority's equal protection rationale, Stevens noted that the "intent of the voter" standard would be no less uniform than the "beyond a reasonable doubt" standard employed in criminal cases. As both Justices Stevens and Souter observed, no state is required to take advantage of the safe-harbor provision, and thus no justification existed for the Court's intervention in state court proceedings. Justice Souter added that the Florida Supreme Court provided both a reasonable and a permissible construction of the state statutes, foreclosing any justification for the Court's alternate interpretation of Florida law. Justice Ginsburg further emphasized in her dissent that the Florida recount at issue would not "yield a result any less fair or precise than the certification that preceded that recount," and would have the virtue of counting thousands of votes that the majority's approach will leave uncounted. Moreover, Justice Breyer noted that "the selection of the President is of fundamental national importance. But that importance is political, not legal." According to Breyer, the political nature of the dispute highlights the inappropriate exercise of judicial power in this case. Although none of the dissenting justices analyzed the case under the political question doctrine, Justice Breyer argued that the Court should have refrained from exercising its power because the Constitution assigned to states the authority to select presidential electors, and Congress the authority to count electoral votes.

THE PRECEDENTIAL VALUE

According to the opinion's many critics, it is difficult to read this case as a principled application of the equal protection clause. The opinion may be read, as Professor Cass Sunstein suggests, to produce order in a contentious election recount without producing law, or the opinion may be read, as Judge Richard Posner suggests, to provide a pragmatic solution to what may have developed into a constitutional crises; or perhaps it can even be read, as Chief Justice Rehnquist urges in concurrence, to vindicate the authority of the Florida legislature under Article 2, Section 1, Clause 2. When, according to critics, the

background voting practices, ballot types, tabulating machines, and initial compliance with the mandatory statewide recount by each county canvassing board are all subject to variation, an equal protection requirement to implement Florida's statutory command to consider "the intent of the voter," through "formulation of uniform rules" (*Bush v. Gore*), can only be blind to the actual circumstances to which it applied. Acknowledging the opinion's lack of constitutional principle, the Court proclaimed: "Our consideration is limited to the present circumstances, for the problem of equal protection in election processes generally presents many complexities." In time, this opinion may yield further developments in the equal protection of voters in election processes, or prove to be a decision good for only the one day.

SEE ALSO *Article II; Federalism; Fourteenth Amendment; Per Curiam; Political Question Doctrine*

BIBLIOGRAPHY

Ackerman, Bruce, ed. 2002. Bush v. Gore: *The Question of Legitimacy.* New Haven, CT: Yale University Press.

Balkin, Jack M. 2001. "*Bush v. Gore* and the Boundary between Law and Politics." *Yale Law Journal* 110(8): 1407–1458.

Chemerinsky, Erwin. 2001. "*Bush v. Gore* Was Not Justiciable." *Notre Dame Law Review* 76(4): 1093–1112.

Klarman, Michael J. 2001. "*Bush v. Gore* through the Lens of Constitutional History." *California Law Review* 89(6): 1721–1765.

McConnell, Michael W. 2001. "Two-and-a-Half Cheers for *Bush v. Gore.*" *University of Chicago Law Review* 68(3): 657–678.

Posner, Richard A. 2001. *Breaking the Deadlock: The 2000 Election, the Constitution, and the Courts.* Princeton, NJ: Princeton University Press.

Sunstein, Cass R. 2001. "Order without Law." *University of Chicago Law Review* 68(3): 757–773.

Sunstein, Cass R., and Epstein, Richard A., eds. 2001. *The Vote: Bush, Gore, and the Supreme Court.* Chicago: University of Chicago Press.

Tribe, Laurence H. 2001. "eroG v. hsuB and Its Disguises: Freeing Bush v. Gore from Its Hall of Mirrors." *Harvard Law Review* 115(1): 170–304.

Thomas P. Crocker

BUSING

After World War II (1939–1945), the United States Supreme Court played an unprecedented role in affirming national values that would make America a worthy leader of the free world. Under Chief Justice Earl Warren, a cornerstone of these efforts involved dismantling a racial

Woman protesting forced busing, Montgomery, Alabama.
Recognizing that eliminating the legality of segregated schools did not naturally lead to racially integrated educational facilities, the Supreme Court actively worked in the 1970s to make schools more diverse. The Court decided a series of cases that required school officials to bus students to schools outside of their own neighborhood in order to remedy past practices of segregation.
© **CORBIS-BETTMANN ARCHIVE/NEWSPHOTOS**

caste system that perpetuated the subordination associated with slavery. Segregation in public schools became a central preoccupation because education played a preeminent role in socializing children to become workers and citizens.

In attacking state-mandated segregation, the Warren Court had to take on earlier precedent. In *Plessy v. Ferguson*, 163 U.S. 537 (1896), the Court had established a doctrine of "separate but equal," which denied that laws mandating segregation "impl[ied] the inferiority of either race to the other." Because racial separation reflected "established usages, customs and traditions of the people," the Court held that states could exercise their police power to promote the "preservation of peace and good order." In reaching this result, the Court singled out segregated schools as a long accepted institution. *Plessy* prompted only one dissent by

Justice John Marshall Harlan, who insisted that the Constitution was colorblind even if whites were "the dominant race . . . in prestige, in achievements, in education, in wealth, and in power."

THE STRUGGLE TO UNDO THE "SEPARATE BUT EQUAL" DOCTRINE

The doctrine of "separate but equal" had endured for approximately half a century when the National Association for the Advancement of Colored People (NAACP) began a litigation campaign to challenge segregation. At first, the NAACP targeted public colleges and universities. When blacks were denied admission to white institutions and offered substandard alternatives, the NAACP successfully argued that separate was inherently unequal (e.g. *Missouri ex rel. Gaines v. Canada*, 305 U.S. 337 [1938]; *Sweatt v. Painter*, 339 U.S. 629 [1950]). Because officials could not rectify gross disparities in tangible and intangible resources, equalization was impossible and integration became the only available solution.

Though heartening, these victories left the principle of "separate but equal" intact. The NAACP wanted the Court to strike down the doctrine altogether, not merely tinker with its application. To that end, litigators turned to public elementary and secondary schools, where tangible resources might be equalized but intangible harms would persist. In *Brown v. Board of Education*, 347 U.S. 483 (1954), Warren wrote for a unanimous Court that "[s]eparate educational facilities are inherently unequal" because they stigmatized black students as inferior, damaging their "hearts and minds in a way unlikely ever to be undone." Despite this stirring rhetoric, the justices recognized that remedying de jure segregation (i.e., segregation mandated by law) could have treacherous political consequences, particularly in the South. The Court chose to temporize in *Brown v. Board of Education (Brown II)*, 349 U.S. 294 (1955), asking federal district courts to rectify public school segregation "with all deliberate speed." For the next decade, the Court mostly maintained a studied silence on the pace of remediation. As a result, schools in the South and elsewhere remained racially identifiable.

THE EMERGENCE OF BUSING AS A REMEDY

In 1964, Congress gave new life to *Brown* by enacting the Civil Rights Act of 1964. Emboldened by this support, the Court began to insist on meaningful desegregation. In *Green v. County School Board of New Kent County*, 391 U.S. 430 (1968), the justices made clear that a "freedom of choice" plan that let children select their school assignments was insufficient. Students, out of habit or fear, would likely opt to attend racially identifiable schools, and a legacy of wrongful segregation would endure. As the Court noted, officials in this small Southern community could readily integrate the schools by redrawing attendance boundaries.

The justices faced the prospect of busing in the South when lawsuits arose in urban areas. In *Swann v. Charlotte-Mecklenburg Board of Education*, 402 U.S. 1 (1971), intense residential segregation meant that redrawing attendance boundaries would not integrate the schools. As a result, the district court had ordered transportation of students outside their neighborhoods to remedy past discrimination. Without dissent, the Court upheld this plan, although Chief Justice Warren Burger struggled to overcome his own reservations in writing for the Court. His opinion recognized busing as a necessary component of some desegregation decrees, but made clear that courts should not order long trips that would jeopardize children's health or impede the educational process.

In spite of these concerns, Burger soon wrote two other unanimous opinions that affirmed the propriety of busing. In overturning a remedial plan in Mobile, Alabama, that left a number of schools segregated to avoid transporting students across a major highway, Burger concluded that "[t]he measure of any desegregation plan is its effectiveness" (*Davis v. Board of School Commissioners*, 402 U.S. 33 [1971]). In striking down an anti-busing law in North Carolina that directly challenged *Swann*, Burger noted that: "Just as the race of students must be considered in determining whether a constitutional violation has occurred, so also must race be considered in formulating a remedy."

The year after the *Swann* decision, Congress passed its own anti-busing legislation. The law mandated that any student transportation to achieve racial balance be delayed until all appeals were exhausted. As a result, Justice Lewis F. Powell Jr., sitting as circuit justice, was asked to stay a busing remedy in Augusta, Georgia. He concluded that Congress must have been aware of *Swann* and would not have wanted to undermine the federal courts' power to rectify past discrimination. As a result, he interpreted the statute as a check only on remedies for de facto segregation, or segregation that arose from housing patterns rather than official state action (*Drummond v. Acree*, 409 U.S. 1228 [1972]). A potential showdown over busing between Congress and the Court was averted.

BUSING MOVES NORTH AND WEST

Swann had carefully reserved judgment on whether the Constitution mandates remedies for de facto segregation. This concern became more pressing as litigation moved to the North and West. There, schools districts typically had not adopted race-based student assignment policies; instead, residential segregation ensured that neighborhood schools would be racially separate. In *Keyes v. School District No. 1*, 413 U.S. 189 (1973), the Court sidestepped this

issue by finding that the Denver school board's decisions about school placement, mobile classrooms, and attendance boundaries were racially motivated and amounted to de jure segregation. Violations in one part of the district created a presumption that the entire district had been adversely affected. In Denver, the school district was coterminous with the city and county, so extensive busing would be part of the desegregation remedy. *Keyes* prompted the breakdown of the Court's fragile unanimity. In dissent, Justice William Rehnquist protested that a trial judge could order "that pupils be transported great distances throughout the district to and from schools whose attendance zones have not been gerrymandered."

Later, the Court would make clear that constitutional remedies were limited to curing de jure discrimination and that any decree had to be carefully tailored to achieve that goal. In *Milliken v. Bradley*, 418 U.S. 717 (1974), a divided Court for the first time rejected a desegregation plan designed to implement *Brown*'s mandate. Writing for the majority, Chief Justice Burger concluded that predominantly white suburban schools could not be forced to participate in a plan designed to cure past wrongdoing by Detroit city schools. The majority found no evidence that suburban schools had themselves engaged in discrimination, nor was there proof that Detroit's segregative practices had interdistrict effects. The *Milliken* decision prompted a poignant and impassioned dissent from Justice Thurgood Marshall, a principal architect of the litigation campaign that led to the victory in *Brown*. He lamented that "unless our children begin to learn together, there is little hope that our people will ever learn to live together." In fact, after *Milliken*, it became largely impossible to use busing to integrate metropolitan school districts in the North and West. Inner city and suburban schools remained racially identifiable.

In multiracial, multilingual, and multicultural cities outside the South, the campaign for school integration faced new complexities. In Denver, Latinos intervened in *Keyes* to challenge desegregation; Chinese families also tried to stop busing in San Francisco (see *Guey Heung Lee v. Johnson*, 404 U.S. 1215 [1971]). Both Latino and Chinese parents wanted their children to get bilingual and bicultural education in neighborhood schools, rather than be dispersed throughout the district. In response to these concerns, Congress passed the Equal Educational Opportunities Act of 1974, an anti-busing measure that recognized special language programs as a viable alternative to student transportation.

THE AFTERMATH

After decades of judicial oversight, federal district courts began to terminate desegregation decrees. The Court generally approved of these decisions, even though school systems often resegregated as a result (e.g. *Board of Education of Oklahoma City Public Schools v. Dowell*, 498

U.S. 237 [1991]; *Freeman v. Pitts*, 503 U.S. 467 [1992]). With litigation coming to a close, advocates of integration turned to the political process. Some school boards responded by adopting voluntary plans to promote racial balance. In 2007, the Court struck down two such plans, one in Louisville and one in Seattle, by a five-to-four vote (*Parents Involved in Community Schools v. Seattle School District No. 1*, 551 U.S. ___ [2007]). Although the two plans were quite different, the justices concluded that each had wrongly pursued racial balancing in the name of diversity. Four justices seemed to embrace a principle of strict colorblindness, but the crucial swing vote, Justice Anthony Kennedy, suggested that school boards might advance diversity in some circumstances. For example, race might be weighed in drawing attendance boundaries, building new schools, allocating resources for special programs, and recruiting specially targeted students and faculty. However, Kennedy remained skeptical of race-based student assignments in these circumstances. In short, busing to cure de jure segregation was becoming a thing of the past, and voluntary transportation plans did not seem to have a bright future.

SEE ALSO *Burger Court; Education and the Constitution; Milliken v. Bradley (Milliken II), 433 U.S. 267 (1977); Nixon, Richard; School Desegregation; Swann v. Charlotte-Mecklenburg Board of Education, 402 U.S. 1 (1971)*

BIBLIOGRAPHY

Kirp, David L. 1982. *Just Schools: The Idea of Racial Equality in American Education.* Berkeley: University of California Press.

Kluger, Richard. 1975. *Simple Justice.* New York: Vintage Books.

Moran, Rachel F. 1996. "Courts and the Construction of Racial and Ethnic Identity: Public Law Litigation in the Denver Schools." In *Legal Culture and the Legal Profession*, ed. Lawrence M. Friedman and Harry N. Scheiber. Boulder, CO: Westview Press.

Orfield, Gary. 1978. *Must We Bus?: Segregated Schools and National Policy.* Washington, DC: Brookings Institution.

Orfield, Gary, and Susan E. Eaton. 1996. *Dismantling Desegregation: The Quiet Reversal of* Brown v. Board of Education. New York: New Press.

Schwartz, Bernard. 1986. *Swann's Way: The School Busing Case and the Supreme Court.* New York: Oxford University Press.

Wilkinson, J. Harvie, III. 1979. *From Brown to Bakke: The Supreme Court and School Integration, 1954-1978.* New York: Oxford University Press.

Rachel F. Moran

C

CABAN V. MOHAMMED, 441 U.S. 380 (1979)

Caban v. Mohammed, 441 U.S. 380 (1979) holds that mothers and fathers who are similarly situated as parents must be treated alike for equal protection purposes. Given the increasing use at the time (1979) of the equal protection clause to dismantle traditional gender norms, this holding does not seem remarkable. Yet the case, which involved an unmarried father's challenge to an adoption statute that required the consent of the unmarried mother but not the unmarried father, is notable for what it says about how relationship, not blood, confers parental rights and how it grapples with the different relationships at issue.

Abdiel Caban and Maria Mohammed lived together for five years and had two children. They never married. When the children were two and four years old, Maria and the children left Abdiel Caban to live with Kazim Mohammed, whom Maria soon married. Abdiel saw his children weekly for approximately eight months thereafter. The children then moved to Puerto Rico with their maternal grandmother. The Mohammeds planned to join them later. After a year, Abdiel traveled to Puerto Rico and took the children back to New York. When Maria heard this, she instituted custody and adoption proceedings with the New York family court so that she and her new husband could adopt the children (adoption helped Maria secure parental rights that were not available to parents of illegitimate children). Abdiel and his new wife then cross-petitioned for adoption. Both couples participated in the proceedings, but the New York adoption statute required an unwed mother's (Maria's) consent to an adoption, even though it did not require an unwed father's. Not surprisingly, the court ruled in favor of the Mohammeds' adoption petition because Abdiel could not block Maria's adoption, but Maria could block Abdiel's.

Abdiel's constitutional challenge included both substantive due process and equal protection arguments. The Supreme Court did not reach the substantive due process argument because it found that Abdiel and Maria were similarly situated as parents, and therefore the statute could not make a gender-based distinction between mothers and fathers. That state had justified the gender-based distinction by claiming that a requirement that unwed fathers consent to the adoption of their illegitimate children would severely impede the state's efforts to get those children adopted.

The majority acknowledged that unwed mothers as a class and unwed fathers as a class may usually be dissimilarly situated, particularly with regard to their newborn children, and that unwed mothers may usually be much easier to find than unwed fathers. But the Court found that the state's assumption of that dissimilar relationship becomes less reasonable as children age because "an unwed father can have a relationship with his [older] children fully comparable to that of the mother." Once children are old enough for fathers to have relationships with them, the state should base parental rights on the existence of the relationship, not the gender of the parent. Thus, it is comparable relationship not comparable genetic contribution that requires the law to treat mothers and fathers similarly. What this means, and what Justice John Paul Stevens was careful to highlight in dissent, is that mothers and fathers are not necessarily similarly situated as parents at birth. At birth, a mother's relationship to her child is much more substantial than a father's can be.

***Dustin Hoffman, starring in* Kramer v. Kramer, *a 1979
film about parental rights.*** *The Supreme Court decided in*
Caban v. Mohammed *that similarly situated unwed parents
should have equal say when deciding to place their child up for
adoption, overturning a New York law giving mothers the sole
decision regarding adoption.* © **COLUMBIA/COURTESY: EVER-
ETT COLLECTION**

Because the Court found, as a matter of equal
protection, that Abdiel had a right to be treated as Maria
was for purposes of vetoing an adoption, it did not have to
reach the question of whether, as a matter of due process,
the state was required to get the consent of any unwed
father in Abdiel's position, regardless of whether the state
required the mother's consent. The dissents had to address
the substantive due process issue. In doing so, Justice
Potter Stewart explained why he did not find Abdiel
Caban's due process claim compelling with a line that
would become critically important to the jurisprudence of
unwed fathers' rights: "Parental rights do not spring full-
blown from the biological connection between parent and
child. They require relationships more enduring."
Though somewhat ambiguous, it appears that Justice
Stewart used the plural "relationships" to refer to both
parent-child relationships and marriage.

Subsequent cases rely on both usages of the term. In
Lehr v. Robertson, 463 U.S. 248 (1983), the majority
opinion used Justice Stewart's words to bolster its claim
that an unwed father's liberty interest in his parental status
depends on the strength of his relationship with his
children. In *Michael H. v. Gerald D.*, 491 U.S. 110
(1989), the plurality used Justice Stewart's dissent to
bolster its claim that, without a relationship to the
mother, an unwed father's liberty interest in parenthood
may be minimal. Thus, *Caban* makes clear that the extent
of the unwed father's relationship with the child is what
matters for equal protection purposes, but the dissent's
suggestion that the relationship with the mother also has
constitutional import was relied on in later cases as well.

SEE ALSO *Parental Rights*

BIBLIOGRAPHY

Dolgin, Janet L. 1993. "Just a Gene: Judicial Assumptions about
Parenthood." *UCLA Law Review* 40: 637–694.

Ellman, Ira; Paul Kurtz; Elizabeth Scott; et al. 2004. *Family Law:
Cases, Text, Problems*. 4th edition. 981–1011. Newark, NJ:
LexisNexis.

Forman, Deborah. 1994. "Unwed Fathers and Adoption: A
Theoretical Analysis in Context." *Texas Law Review* 72:
967–1045.

Katharine K. Baker

CALIFANO V. GOLDFARB, 430 U.S. 199 (1977)

Califano v. Goldfarb, 430 U.S. 199 (1977) struck down a
provision of the Social Security Act which presumed that
widows, but not widowers, had been financially dependent on their deceased spouses and were therefore entitled
to survivor benefits.

Hannah Goldfarb was a secretary in the New York
City public schools for almost twenty-five years. After she
died, her husband applied for Social Security survivor
benefits. His application was denied because he did not
demonstrate that he was receiving at least one-half of his
support from his wife when she died. Had their sexes been
reversed, the survivor's dependence would have been
presumed. The U.S. Supreme Court held that this sex-
based classification violated the equality component of the
due process clause of the Fifth Amendment.

Justice William J. Brennan Jr. wrote for a plurality
that included Justices Byron White, Thurgood Marshall,
and Lewis F. Powell Jr. The plurality found the case
indistinguishable from prior cases in which the Court had
struck down similar presumptions: in *Weinberger v.*

Wiesenfeld, 420 U.S. 636 (1975), the Court had struck down a provision that provided "mother's benefits" to widows caring for dependent children but provided no comparable "father's benefits." In *Frontiero v. Richardson*, 411 U.S. 677 (1973), the Court had struck down a presumption of dependency for military wives but *not* military husbands. The plurality emphasized that Goldfarb had paid the same Social Security taxes as a similarly situated male, but did not receive the same benefit of knowing her spouse would be supported in old age.

The government argued that the statute disadvantaged men, not women, because the denial of benefits should be analyzed from the perspective of the surviving spouse rather than from the perspective of the wage earner. The plurality acknowledged that the disadvantage fell on the family as a whole but insisted that, as a program of social insurance, Social Security must be analyzed from the perspective of the wage earner who makes the payments. In the alternative, the plurality noted that sex-based discrimination against men was also unconstitutional, except in a few instances where the clear purpose was to redress historic discrimination against women. In *Goldfarb*, the sex-based classification compounded past discrimination rather than redressing it, by reducing the value of a woman's work to support her family. The government countered that the classification helped widows, who faced discrimination in the job market. The plurality dismissed this argument because inquiry into the Social Security Act's actual purpose showed that Congress had focused on dependency rather than need.

Goldfarb was decided just a few months after *Craig v. Boren*, 420 U.S. 190 (1976); the two cases were argued on the same day in October 1976. Justice Brennan wrote a majority opinion in *Craig* stating that sex-based classifications were invalid unless they were "substantially related" to serving "important governmental objectives." This standard came to be known as *intermediate scrutiny* under the equal protection and due process clauses. Interestingly, Justice Brennan's plurality opinion in *Goldfarb* appears to apply a lower level of scrutiny, citing *Reed v. Reed*, 404 U.S. 71 (1971) and other cases that struck down sex classifications as irrational. The *Goldfarb* plurality opinion cites *Craig* only in the course of discussing discrimination against men.

Justice John Paul Stevens provided the fifth vote to strike down the classification in *Goldfarb*. Accepting the first step of the government's argument, he analyzed the classification from the perspective of the surviving spouse rather than from the perspective of the wage earner. He concluded, however, that the classification was irrational. Addressing the claim that widows were presumed dependent for the sake of administrative convenience, Justice Stevens noted that vast sums were being paid to nondependent widows. He did not believe Congress

would authorize this expenditure for the sake of administrative convenience without at least analyzing the administrative costs of making widows as well as widowers prove their dependence. Similarly, there was no evidence that Congress had been motivated by a desire to redress discrimination against women, since the widows who benefited by not having to prove dependence were those least likely to need special help. Rather, Justice Stevens concluded that the classification arose in the course of the evolution of the statute because Congress "simply assumed that all widows should be regarded as 'dependents' in some general sense, even though they could not satisfy the statutory support test later imposed on men."

Justice William Rehnquist dissented, joined by Chief Justice Warren Burger and Justices Potter Stewart and Harry Blackmun. The dissenters argued that the statutory classification imposed no economic disadvantage on women that warranted any heightened scrutiny. They perceived the problem as one of over-inclusion (of nondependent widows) rather than under-inclusion (of nondependent widowers) and argued that over-inclusion in a social welfare program is more permissible than exclusion.

SEE ALSO *Intermediate Scrutiny; Procedural Due Process; Sex Discrimination; Welfare State*

BIBLIOGRAPHY

Becker, Mary E. 1989. "Obscuring the Struggle: Sex Discrimination, Social Security, and Stone, Seidman, Sunstein, and Tushnet's *Constitutional Law*." *Columbia Law Review* 89: 264–289.

Ellington, Toni J.; Sylvia K. Higashi; Jayna K. Kim; and Mark M. Murakami. 1989. "Justice Ruth Bader Ginsburg and Gender Discrimination." *University of Hawaii Law Review* 20: 699–796.

Wooster, Ann K. 2002. "Equal Protection and Due Process Clause Challenges Based on Sex Discrimination—Supreme Court Cases." *American Law Reports, Federal* 178: 25–86.

Jennifer S. Hendricks

CALIFANO V. WEBSTER, 430 U.S. 313 (1977)

Califano v. Webster, 430 U.S. 313 (1977) was one of a series of cases in the 1970s that established the constitutional standards applicable to sex discrimination and one of the few cases that examined women's rights through a lens of substantive rather than formal equality. In *Webster*, the U.S. Supreme Court upheld a sex-based

Social Security classification based on its ameliorative purpose, a decision with particular relevance to subsequent judicial consideration of affirmative action.

The plaintiff, Will Webster, sued the U.S. secretary of Health, Education, and Welfare alleging that a provision of the Social Security Act favored women. When Webster attained the age of sixty-five, he applied for Social Security benefits and was awarded $185.70 per month based on an eighteen-year Social Security earnings record. Like all wage earners, his Social Security benefits were calculated based on the "elapsed years" (reduced by five) during which his covered wages were highest. But from 1956 until a 1972 change in the federal law, "elapsed years" depended upon the gender of the wage earner. For a male, "elapsed years" equaled the number of years that elapsed after 1950 and before the year in which he attained age sixty-five; for a female, "elapsed years" equaled the number of years that elapsed after 1950 and before the year in which she attained age sixty-two. A female wage earner could therefore exclude from the computation of her "average monthly wage" three more lower-earning years than a similarly situated male wage earner, resulting in a higher level of monthly benefits for the retired female wage earner.

The federal district court considering the case held that this distinction between males and females was irrational. On direct appeal, the Supreme Court reversed in a per curiam opinion signed by justices William Brennan, Byron White, Thurgood Marshall, Lewis Powell, and John Paul Stevens. Reiterating the recently established intermediate scrutiny test for sex discrimination, the Court noted that "classifications by gender must serve important governmental objectives and must be substantially related to achievement of those objectives." The Court then held that redressing past discrimination and reducing the disparity in economic conditions between men and women was an important governmental objective. The more-favorable treatment of the female wage earner was not the result of "archaic and overbroad generalizations" about women, the Court concluded. Rather, the legislature thought that the age differences adopted in 1956 were necessary because "age limits are applied more frequently to job openings for women than for men and . . . the age limits applied are lower."

Concurring in the Court's opinion were Chief Justice Warren Burger and justices William Rehnquist, Potter Stewart, and Harry Blackmun. Rejecting the majority's constitutional analysis, these four justices joined the judgment because they concluded that the sex-based distinction was justified by administrative convenience.

In an article written before she was appointed to the Supreme Court, "Some Thoughts on Benign Classifications in the Context of Sex" (1978), Justice Ruth Bader Ginsburg discussed *Webster*'s significance. She agreed that

the statute involved no "'romantically paternalistic' view of women" (p. 823). Rather, the legislature adopted the provision "for remedial reasons rather than out of prejudice about 'the way women (or men) are'" (p. 823). Justice Ginsburg later relied on *Webster* in her majority opinion in *U.S. v. Virginia*, 518 U.S. 515 (1996), where she indicated that "sex classifications may be used to compensate women for particular economic disabilities [they have] suffered."

SEE ALSO *Intermediate Scrutiny; Sex Discrimination*

BIBLIOGRAPHY

Cushman, Clare. 2000. *Supreme Court Decisions and Women's Rights*. Washington, DC: CQ Press.

Ginsburg, Ruth Bader. 1978. "Some Thoughts on Benign Classifications in the Context of Sex." *Connecticut Law Review* 10: 813–827.

Martha F. Davis

CALIFANO V. WESTCOTT, 443 U.S. 76 (1979)

In *Califano v. Westcott*, 443 U.S. 76 (1979), two Massachusetts married couples challenged the constitutionality of Section 407 of the Social Security Act (referred to as AFDC-U). That section provided benefits to needy children when their father, but not their mother, became unemployed. In order to qualify for this unemployment benefit, the unemployed father needed to demonstrate a recent attachment to the workforce. For both of the plaintiff couples, the husband could not establish recent labor-force attachment, and therefore was not defined as "unemployed." However, the plaintiff wives could establish the required recent labor-force attachment. Section 407, however, made no provision for needy children of a mother who had recently become unemployed.

All nine justices agreed that the statute was unconstitutional gender discrimination. Justice Harry Blackmun drafted a majority opinion joined by four justices extending benefits to mothers as a remedy for the constitutional flaw. Justice Lewis F. Powell, Jr., drafted an opinion concurring in part and dissenting in part, joined by three justices, arguing for denying benefits to all parents as the appropriate repair of the statute.

The plaintiffs argued that the law rested on overbroad generalizations about women's role in families, because it assumed that mothers were not wage earners providing the family its financial support. The AFDC-U program was enacted in 1961 to assist needy children in the event of parental unemployment. Congress intended this benefit to extend to loss of work by the family breadwinner. In 1968 Congress narrowed eligibility for the benefit, changing the term *parent* to *father*. Congress was responding to some states that used Section 407 to provide aid to full-time homemakers with no recent labor employment history. To clarify that the statute should only cover a breadwinner's loss of employment, Congress substituted the word *father* for *parent*. This legislative history shows the statute's gender stereotyping: Congress treated *breadwinner* and *father* as synonymous concepts.

The government defended the statute on two grounds. First, the government argued that the statute did not discriminate against women as a class, because the family unit affected by a decision to deny aid consists of one man, one woman, and children. The government argued that the practical impact of a benefit denial is felt equally by the man and the woman in the family. Because the unit in question is a family, the government argued, it cannot be discriminatory based on sex. The opinion of the Court dismissed this argument, saying that for mothers who are primary financial providers for their families, Section 407 is "obviously" gender biased because it deprives their families of benefits based on the mothers' sex.

Second, the government argued that the legislation is substantially related to a legitimate purpose of deterring desertion of families by fathers. At one time, welfare policy had denied benefits to families where the father was present and unemployed, giving fathers an incentive to abandon their family to help them become eligible for assistance. The government argued that the AFDC-U program at issue in the case was implemented to provide support even when a father is present, in order to encourage fathers to stay with their families. The Court rejected this argument. It acknowledged that this purpose motivated the original program as passed in 1961, providing benefits to needy children when "parents" became unemployed. But the Court focused on the addition of the sex-based language in 1968. It argued that Congress added it to reduce the number of claims and to prevent the use of the program by homemakers who had no recent employment history—a group outside the original purpose of the law. Even if the legislative history had supported the government's claim, however, the Court said that the gender-based classification was not substantially related to the achievement of that goal.

Between 1975 and 1979, the Supreme Court decided approximately fifteen gender discrimination cases, dealing with a range of gender-differentiated rules, including rules for jury service, the appropriate age to purchase beer, and the hiring of congressional staff. *Califano v. Westcott* fits into one strand of those cases that, taken together, establish that classifications assuming gendered family roles—men as providers and women as caregivers—are unconstitutional stereotyping under the Fourteenth Amendment. In

Weinberger v. Wiesenfeld, 420 U.S. 636 (1975), *Stanton v. Stanton,* 421 U.S. 7 (1975), *Califano v. Goldfarb,* 430 U.S. 199 (1977), and *Orr v. Orr,* 440 U.S. 268 (1979), the Court invalidated a series of laws based on this "baggage of sexual stereotypes" that "presumes the father has the 'primary responsibility to provide a home and its essentials,' while the mother is the 'center of home and family life.' Legislation that rests on such presumptions, without more, cannot survive scrutiny under the Due Process Clause of the Fifth Amendment." This stance against role stereotyping remains perhaps the most important strand in constitutional gender discrimination cases.

SEE ALSO *Welfare and Women; Welfare State*

BIBLIOGRAPHY

Ginsburg, Ruth Bader. 1978. "Sex Equality and the Constitution." *Tulane Law Review* 52: 451–476.

Law, Sylvia A. 1983. "Women, Work, Welfare, and the Preservation of Patriarchy." *University of Pennsylvania Law Review* 131: 1249–1339.

Mayeri, Serena. 2004. "Constitutional Choices: Legal Feminism and the Historical Dynamics of Change." *California Law Review* 92: 755–840.

Katharine B. Silbaugh

CALIFORNIA DEMOCRATIC PARTY V. JONES, 530 U.S. 567 (2000)

California Democratic Party v. Jones, 530 U.S. 567 (2000), is one of the more important recent decisions by the Court concerning state laws that regulate citizens' ability to participate in party primary elections. While the Court has never held that states must use primaries as part of the process of electing state and federal legislators and executive officials, the Court has held that "where the state law has made the primary [device] integral to the procedure of [electoral] choice," the Constitution imposes limits on how states administer those primaries.

State rules in this area that prompt challenge tend to be motivated by one or both of two objectives: (1) preventing members of one party from sabotaging or raiding the primary election of the other party, in an attempt to derail that party's processes or elect that party's weakest—rather than strongest—general election candidate; and (2) facilitating the ability of individuals, particularly independents who are not affiliated with either of the major parties, to participate in the important primary process.

In *Jones* the Court, by a seven-to-two vote, struck down California's so-called blanket primary law and raised serious doubts about all other state laws that try to force parties to open their primaries to nonmembers. Specifically at issue in *Jones* was a voter-enacted initiative that allowed any voter, regardless of political affiliation, to vote in either party's primary elections. Justice Antonin Scalia wrote for the Court, holding that California had unconstitutionally trammeled on the political associational rights of the parties and their members: "In no area is the political association's right to exclude [persons of a different ideology] more important than in the process of selecting its nominee [for office]."

Because of the importance of the right to exclude persons who don't share a party's beliefs, requiring each party to allow nonparty members to vote in its primary runs afoul of the First Amendment. As Justice Scalia expounded: "California's blanket primary [law] . . . forces political parties to associate with—to have their nominees, and hence their positions, determined by—those who, at best, have refused to affiliate with the party, and, at worst, have expressly affiliated with a rival." The Court also found that fear of strategic behavior by rival party members was not fanciful, and that efforts to sabotage a party's primary can sometimes in fact alter a primary's result. Thus even if California's law increased voter participation in primaries by opening up the primary process to newcomers, that state's interest could not trump the parties' associational rights.

In reaching its result, *Jones* drew and built upon a number of earlier Court rulings dating back at least as far as the 1970s. In *Rosario v. Rockefeller*, 410 U.S. 752 (1973), the Court confronted and upheld a New York law that required each voter, in order to participate in a party's primary, to choose that party at least thirty days before the general election preceding the primary election at issue. In practice, this meant that voters would have to select a party about eighteen months before that party's primary in order to participate. The Court upheld the statute as a valid attempt to prevent interparty "raiding," the practice whereby "voters in sympathy with one party designate themselves as voters of another party so as to influence or determine the results of the other party's primary." By requiring voters to make their party selection far in advance of the primary—prior to the time that would-be raiders knew how necessary their participation might be in their true party's primary—the law worked to reduce the incidence of strategic raiding.

But later that same year in *Kusper v. Pontikes*, 414 U.S. 51 (1973), the Court made clear that voters cannot be required to make their party primary selection choice too far in advance. The Court in *Kusper* struck down a state statute that prevented a person from voting in a party's primary if he or she had voted in another party's primary election anytime during the previous twenty-three months. Requiring voters to lock into participating

in a party's primary that far in advance prevented good-faith voters from changing their minds about the primary in which they truly wanted to participate. So locking voters in for eighteen months in the name of discouraging raiding seems permissible, but locking them in for twenty-three months does not.

A little over a decade later, in *Tashjian v. Republican Party of Connecticut*, 479 U.S. 208 (1986), the Court struck down a law that did not regulate timing of a voter's decision to participate in a primary, but rather absolutely prohibited a voter from participating in a primary unless he or she was a registered member of that party. The Republican Party in Connecticut wanted independents (though not registered Democrats) to be able to participate in the Republican primary (perhaps to encourage them to join the party in the future), but Connecticut law prohibited primary voting by anyone who was not a registered member of the party in which the vote was cast. Because the anti-raiding concern did not seem directly implicated in this case—independents by definition were, after all, not members of a rival party and the Republican Party welcomed their participation—the Court distinguished *Rosario*. Like *Jones* fourteen years later, the Court stressed the wishes of the party to run its primary as it desired. In some respects, *Jones* was the flip side of *Tashjian*; whereas the latter respected party desires as to including people, the former protected the party's ability to exclude.

After *Jones* one might have thought that states must always allow parties to decide for themselves exactly who will participate in their primaries provided, of course, the parties respect norms of racial, gender, and religious equality. (Racial equality in primary elections was guaranteed by the so-called white primary cases from 1927 to 1953.)

However, in *Clingman v. Beaver*, 544 U.S. 581 (2005), the Court made clear that *Tashjian* and *Jones* do not require deference to a party's wishes as to inclusion and exclusion in all instances. In *Clingman*, the Court upheld Oklahoma's so-called semi-closed primary law, under which a political party could invite into its primary only its own registered members and voters registered as independents. The Libertarian Party of Oklahoma (LPO) notified the Oklahoma State Election Board it wanted to open its upcoming primary to all registered voters regardless of party affiliation; the board agreed as to independents, but not as to other parties' members. The LPO, and several Oklahomans registered as Republicans and Democrats, challenged the law alleging that Oklahoma's statute unconstitutionally burdened their First Amendment right to freedom of political association.

In a fractured set of opinions led by Justice Clarence Thomas's opinion for the Court, the justices rejected the First Amendment bid. One group of four justices essentially drew a distinction between a party's right to include and its right to exclude, reasoning that the right to exclude unwanted participants is more central to the First Amendment values recognized in *Jones*. Other justices concluded that the burden on the LPO, and registered Democrats and Republicans, who wanted to participate in the Libertarian primary was slight; all voters needed to do in order to participate was "disassociate" (or deregister) themselves from the Democrat or Republican parties.

Given what the majority thought was the minimal nature of the associational burden, the law was upheld in order to permit Oklahoma to advance a number of regulatory interests the Court recognized as important. Among these interests were the preservation of political parties as viable and identifiable interest groups, the enhancement of party electioneering and party-building efforts, and the reduction of party raiding and the phenomenon of so-called sore loser candidacies by spurned primary contenders.

SEE ALSO *First Amendment; Freedom of Association; Political Question Doctrine; State Action*

BIBLIOGRAPHY

Cain, Bruce E., and Elizabeth R. Gerber. 2002. *Voting at the Political Fault Line: California's Experiment with the Blanket Primary.* Berkeley: University of California Press.

Levinson, Daryl J., and Richard H. Pildes. 2006. "Separation of Parties, Not Powers." *Harvard Law Review* 119(8): 2311.

Vikram D. Amar

CAMPAIGN FINANCE

In a 2008 article, Richard L. Hasen outlined the modern history of the Supreme Court and campaign finance: "Since 1976, the Supreme Court's approach to campaign finance law has swung like a pendulum, with periods of Court deference to regulation alternating with a more skeptical approach that views the First Amendment as barring much campaign finance regulation" (p. 1). Hasen started his analysis with the decision in *Buckley v. Valeo*, 424 U.S. 1 (1976) because it was and still is the most seminal case in campaign finance law in American history, and continues to provide the framework—if more in a lip service form since the beginning of the Roberts Court—for the Court's analysis. But there was some regulation of campaigns, and some Court involvement, even before the 1970s.

A BRIEF HISTORY OF CAMPAIGN FINANCE LAW

Campaigns as we know them did not exist in the early days of the American Republic. With the emergence of the so-called spoils system, where victorious candidates were able

Senators Bill Bradley and John McCain in Claremont, New Hampshire, after reaching agreement to reform campaign finance laws. In the Bipartisan Campaign Reform Act of 2002, also known as the McCain-Feingold Act, Congress made an effort to limit soft money contributions from political groups, increase the amount individuals could donate to a candidate, and define what types of advertisements could be run by political groups as election day nears. © REUTERS/CORBIS

to reward allies and adherents with government jobs, parties soon organized to make sure that those who would get jobs (or had them) would give back to ensure victory and the continuing ability to dispense the spoils. By the 1830s this dynamic was creating a backlash, with many suggesting that it was corrupting American elections. Proposals to prohibit parties from requiring government or political employees to contribute so-called assessments to them were first introduced in Congress in 1837, but did not advance far in the legislative process. The first actual restriction on campaign funding came after the Civil War, with an 1867 provision prohibiting the solicitation of contributions from naval yard government employees. It did not have any appreciable impact on the overall system.

Corruption in the administration of Ulysses S. Grant (1822–1885) led to more calls for reform. Some changes were implemented, including the creation of a civil service commission. President Rutherford B. Hayes (1822–1893) strengthened the reforms, but the real change came after the assassination of President James A. Garfield (1831–1881) by a disgruntled office seeker. Garfield's successor, Chester A. Arthur (1830–1886), signed the Pendleton Act in 1883, which resulted in the end of the patronage system and assessments.

The end of the spoils system led to the rise in influence of corporations, which filled the vacuum in party and campaign funding. A backlash against huge corporate and business contributions, including allegations of outsized corporate influence on President Theodore Roosevelt, led Roosevelt to lead a new reform movement in 1905 and 1906; the next year, he proposed a ban on corporate political contributions. The idea was translated into a bill introduced by Senator Benjamin Tillman (1847–1918), which became the Tillman Act of 1907. The Tillman Act made it illegal for "any national bank, or any corporation organized by authority of any laws of Congress" to make a contribution relating to any election for federal office. In essence, the Tillman Act's restriction on corporate direct contributions to campaigns remains in place today.

Citizen groups continued to push for more reforms, including disclosure of party campaign receipts and expenditures. President Theodore Roosevelt, in his end-of-year message to Congress in 1907, called for public financing for political parties. If public financing did not gain great political traction, disclosure did; in 1910, the Federal Corrupt Practices Act required national party committees and congressional campaign committees to disclose their contributions and expenditures after each election. Amendments in 1911 improved disclosure to the pre-election period and to primaries, and enacted the first spending limits for federal campaigns, limiting House campaigns to a total of $5,000 and Senate campaigns to $10,000, or to limits set by state law, whichever was lower.

Truman Newberry (1864–1945), a Michigan Republican who defeated Henry Ford (1863–1947) in a Senate primary in 1918, was convicted under the law of violating these spending limits. Newberry, whose campaign had spent nearly $180,000, challenged the spending limits in court arguing that Congress had no authority over party primaries and that the law applied to campaign committees, not to the candidates or their individual donors.

Newberry's challenge led to the first major Supreme Court decision on campaign finance. *Newberry v. United States*, 256 U.S. 232 (1921) struck down the spending limits on the narrow ground that Congress did not have the authority to regulate primaries or party nominations; a ruling that was effectively reversed twenty years later in *United States v. Classic*, 313 U.S. 299 (1941), which ruled that Congress could regulate primaries if state law made them part of the election process.

Scandal continued to spur reform efforts and reform. The Teapot Dome scandal resulted in the Federal Corrupt Practices Act of 1925, which expanded disclosure and adjusted the spending limits upward. But the disclosure proved ineffective and the spending limits were widely ignored (they applied only to party committees; by creating multiple committees for a candidate or an election, they were easily evaded). No one was ever prosecuted for breaking the law. Reports of abuse of federal employees working for the re-election of Speaker of the House Alben

Barkley (1877–1956) in 1938 led to passage of the Hatch Act in 1939, a revision of the 1883 Pendleton Act, which prohibited partisan political activity by most federal employees and also banned solicitation of contributions from workers on federal public works programs.

Labor's increasing political activity during the presidency of Franklin D. Roosevelt led to several efforts to limit labor's contributions, like those of corporations. The War Labor Disputes Act of 1943 did just that, but it expired after the end of the war. In 1947 the Republican Congress made a ban on labor contributions to campaigns permanent, as part of the Taft-Hartley Act.

Although there were many other efforts to reform the campaign system, none succeeded in fundamental change to the 1925 Act until 1971. The Federal Election Campaign Act of 1971 (FECA) was spurred by concern, primarily from Democrats, about the rising cost of campaigns. It was signed into law by President Richard Nixon in February 1972. It put limits on individual contributions, media expenditures, and the proportion of campaign spending that could go to radio and television advertising; and required all candidates and political committees to file quarterly reports of receipts and expenditures, listing all contributions of $100 or more. By many accounts it limited media spending in the 1972 campaign, but did little to curb the growth in overall spending in both the presidential and congressional campaigns.

Before FECA had a chance to apply to another election, the Watergate scandal emerged and spurred new, more sweeping reform that was enacted in 1974 over the veto of President Gerald Ford (1913–2006). The amended FECA of 1974 put strict limits on campaign contributions; kept the caps on spending by candidates and their families enacted in 1971; and restricted other contributions, including those by political action committees set up by labor unions and corporations. FECA's media spending limits were replaced by overall spending limits for all federal candidates in both primary and general elections. Parties were limited in the amounts they could spend on behalf of their candidates. A new presidential public funding system, based on matching small contributions in primaries and grants in the general election, was established. A new regulatory commission—the Federal Election Commission (FEC)—was created to regulate the law, administer the public funding system, and receive campaign reports; its six members were to be picked in equal numbers by the speaker of the house, president pro tempore of the Senate, and the president. Funding for the new public financing system was to come from a voluntary tax checkoff.

The 1974 act was challenged on January 2, 1975, by a lawsuit filed by Senator James Buckley (1923–) of New York, among others, against Francis Valeo (1916–), the secretary of the Senate. *Buckley*, discussed in detail below, was handed down a year later; it accepted some portions of the 1974 Act and struck down others, including the FEC. Congress quickly acted to pass a new set of amendments to take effect in time for the 1976 elections; amendments to FECA were signed into law in May 1976. Among other things, the 1976 amendments reconstituted the FEC by changing the method of appointing commissioners to a model like other regulatory commissions, with nominations by the president and confirmation by the Senate. Another more modest reform package passed Congress in 1979, cleaning up some provisions of the earlier laws after experience under them in two elections.

No significant changes occurred in federal campaign finance law for the next twenty-three years. Change came in 2002 after several attempts to pass major new campaign reform and after a series of high profile scandals over fundraising and spending, including issues over presidential fundraising in the 1996 campaign, the use of so-called soft money in that election and the 2000 contest, and over so-called issue advocacy commercials run by outside groups and by the parties. In 2002 Congress passed, and President Bush signed, the Bipartisan Campaign Reform Act of 2002—the most significant campaign reform by far since 1974.

THE COURT'S ROLE IN CAMPAIGN FINANCE

Other than *Newberry* and *Classic*, the Supreme Court did not engage itself very much in the campaign finance arena or even in the broader political arena before the landmark *Buckley* decision in 1976. To be sure, there were cases that flowed from the FECA of 1971, including *Federal Election Commission v. National Right to Work Committee*, 459 U.S. 197 (1982), which upheld Congress's right to ban corporations without capital stock from soliciting funds from individuals who were not members, on the ground that Congress could act to prevent corruption or the appearance of corruption. But from *Buckley* on, a stream of cases came to the Court that resulted in rulings, refinements, and adjustments in the area; each in some respect built upon the jurisprudential foundation of *Buckley*, but also reflecting significant changes in the Court's approach and rationale for allowing or disallowing legislation or regulation.

Buckley v. Valeo The *Buckley* case was and remains the most significant campaign finance case to come to the Supreme Court. Its framework continues to shape and govern the judicial analysis of campaign finance litigation, as it shaped the congressional action in 2002, even though the outcomes of cases within the *Buckley* framework have been quite strikingly different over the years.

In a per curiam opinion, the core of which was adopted seven-to-one (Justice John Paul Stevens did not participate) with some parts six-to-two, the Court upheld many of the provisions of the act of 1974, but struck down and modified others. In particular, the Court upheld regulation of campaign contributions but did not allow Congress to limit campaign spending. Why the distinction? The Court had two rationales, the primary one revolving around the legitimate need for Congress to prevent corruption or the appearance of corruption. To the Court, a candidate could be corrupted (or appear to be) by a contributor but not by someone spending on the candidate's behalf. Moreover, the Court said, a contribution is a different kind of speech than an expenditure. Contributions do not have any significant expressive content; they merely indicate that a giver supports a candidate. Expenditures, however, can serve to communicate one's own ideas, such as why a spender supports or opposes a candidate, thus reaching a different threshold of speech—one deserving substantial First Amendment protections.

As the Court accepted a corruption or appearance of corruption rationale for regulation, it firmly rejected the rationale that Congress had used for spending limits: leveling the political terrain, equalizing the ability of individuals or groups to affect the outcome of elections. The Court roundly rejected that rationale, saying, "The concept that government may restrict the speech of some elements of our society in order to enhance the relative voice of others is wholly foreign to the First Amendment."

The Court did allow one form of voluntary spending limit, one contained within the voluntary, presidential campaign public-funding framework. Presidential candidates who accepted public funds could be required to accept limits on spending both in primaries, if the candidate took matching funds, and in the general election campaign, if the candidate accepted the public grant.

The Court also accepted FECA's disclosure provisions. It indicated that "compelling disclosure in itself can seriously infringe on privacy of association and belief," and therefore that a strict judicial scrutiny of the disclosure provisions was required. Important public interests have to be served by disclosure requirements, two of which the Court identified: the anti-corruption interest, and the informational interest where information can serve both to detect violations of the law and to enable voters to better understand the candidates' basis of support.

Throughout its opinion, the Court expressed deep concern that any regulation of campaign speech be framed by clear standards, so that citizens would not be deterred from permissible speech by uncertainty over whether the speech would violate the law. In a footnote, the Court set up a "bright line test" for communications that could be regulated, limiting them to "express advocacy" for or against candidates, and offered examples that would fit the definition of express advocacy, namely using terms such as "vote for," "vote against," "elect," or "defeat."

Finally, the Court rejected the method Congress chose to name members to the Federal Election Commission. The Court said that the commission served an executive function and that to have Congress appoint members violated the separation of powers.

After *Buckley* A number of cases with campaign finance implications were decided after *Buckley*, starting with *First National Bank v. Bellotti*, 435 U.S. 765 (1978), which dealt with the constitutionality of a Massachusetts law barring corporate expenditures on a referendum—not a candidate election—that did not directly affect the property or assents of the corporation. The Court reversed a Massachusetts Supreme Court decision upholding the law, on First Amendment grounds. In *California Medical Association v. Federal Election Commission*, 453 U.S. 182 (1981) the Court considered a challenge to FECA's limitations on individual and association contributions to multi-candidate political action committees, and upheld the law. In *Federal Election Commission v. National Conservative Political Action Committee*, 470 U.S. 480 (1985) the Court ruled that a provision of the Presidential Election Campaign Fund Act, limiting independent political committees to no more than $1,000 in spending on behalf of candidates who accept public funding, was overbroad in its restrictions of political speech, not passing the threshold test for a corruption rationale.

The first case after *Buckley* with more far-reaching implications came in *Federal Election Commission v. Massachusetts Citizens for Life, Inc.*, 479 U.S. 238 (1986). It and a case that followed, *Austin v. Michigan State Chamber of Commerce*, 494 U.S. 652 (1990), enabled the Court to refine its views on when and how expenditure limits could be applied to different kinds of organizations. Massachusetts Citizens for Life, a nonprofit, noneconomic corporation, had published a pamphlet advocating particular candidates for statewide office, paid for out of its general treasury. Massachusetts Citizens for Life sued when the FEC charged it with violating the provision in FECA that barred corporations from using general treasury funds in candidate elections.

The Court ruled that this section of FECA, as applied, was unconstitutional; it was meant to bar for-profit corporations with sizable wealth garnered from the economic marketplace from gaining unfair advantage in the political marketplace. Since Massachusetts Citizens for Life was an issue-based—rather than economic-based—corporation, with its members sharing an agenda, there was no compelling state interest in limiting its speech.

In *Austin*, the Court considered more explicitly the constitutional limits on the involvement in the political marketplace of other kinds of corporations. The Michigan State Chamber of Commerce challenged a state campaign finance law that prohibited corporations from using general treasury funds for independent expenditures in state candidate elections (funds from segregated accounts were allowed). The chamber argued that the reasoning in *Bellotti* regarding referendums should be extended to candidate elections, saying that the First Amendment barred any limits on corporate campaign spending. The chamber also argued that, as a nonprofit corporation, it was similar to Massachusetts Citizens for Life. The Court denied both claims, in the process refining the distinction it set up for Massachusetts Citizens for Life. Unlike Massachusetts Citizens for Life, the chamber was not issue-based, with an agenda driven by its members' common interest in political outcomes. The chamber did many nonpolitical things, was set up for an economic purpose even if it was nonprofit, and therefore was an economic corporation for constitutional purposes. A limitation allowing it to use segregated funds was not an unreasonable limit on its rights.

The Court's reasoning in this case, built around the need to check "the corrosive and distorting effects of immense aggregations of wealth that are accumulated with the help of the corporate form and that have little or no correlation to the public's support for the corporation's political ideas," drew a scathing response from Justice Antonin Scalia. If the issue is the lack of correlation between the spending and the public's support, he suggested, why not allow limits on the spending of individual billionaires, who could easily spend out of proportion with actual public support for their positions? Scalia's dissent underscored an issue that has been widely debated and discussed in the campaign legal community, namely the inconsistency in the Court's reasoning from *Buckley* on, in this area.

That inconsistency was not limited to issues of spending and corporations. The Court tackled issues of political party spending in *Colorado Republican Federal Campaign Committee v. Federal Election Commission* (*Colorado I*), 518 U.S. 604 (1996) and *Federal Election Commission v. Colorado Republican Federal Campaign Committee* (*Colorado II*), 533 U.S. 431 (2001). *Colorado I* arose from a case brought by the FEC against the Colorado Republican Party for ads by its federal campaign committee—aired before the Republicans had selected their own candidate—attacking the likely Democratic Senate candidate in 1986. Both *Colorado I* and *Colorado II* dealt with limitations on political parties' spending on their own candidates' campaigns. The FEC said that the party expenditures exceeded limits on general election spending imposed on parties by FECA.

The Colorado Republican Party challenged the FEC action on two grounds, one broad and one narrow. The broad one claimed that Congress could not limit any party spending on behalf of candidates. The narrow one said that Congress could not limit party spending that was not coordinated with the campaign of its candidate; that is, an independent expenditure.

Colorado I addressed the narrower challenge and a divided court ruled in favor of the Colorado Republican Party. The core of the decision was that independent expenditures were protected under the First Amendment from limitation, unless there was a superseding rationale of the threat of corruption. Justice Stephen Breyer noted, "We are not aware of any special dangers of corruption associated with political parties that tip the constitutional balance in a different direction." The Court rejected the FEC's argument that parties and their candidates are so closely intertwined that there is no such thing as a party expenditure independent of its own candidates, but the opinion did not rule on the broader issue of whether all party expenditures should be exempt from legislatively imposed limitations. That decision was put off to another day with the case remanded to the lower courts.

The case came back to the Supreme Court in 2001. In *Colorado II*, in a five-to-four decision (with varied dissents and concurrences) authored by Justice David Souter, the Court upheld the legislative limitations on party expenditures coordinated with candidates. The reasoning here was that parties do more than just act to elect their own candidates; they perform other functions and have other incentives when they raise money. Thus a fear of corruption, that the party might use its fundraising and campaign spending to serve purposes other than a pure desire to elect its own members, was reason enough to allow some limitations on coordinated party expenditures. The core dissent came from Justice Clarence Thomas, joined by Justices Scalia and Anthony Kennedy, and Chief Justice William Rehnquist in part. Thomas argued against any limitations on parties as part of a broader assault on *Buckley* and on government intervention in the campaign speech arena.

The Court also addressed another key component of campaign reform, contribution limits, in *Nixon v. Shrink Missouri Government PAC*, 528 U.S. 377 (2000). The case involved a challenge to a Missouri statute that set contribution limits ranging from $250 to $1,000, depending on the office, with adjustments for inflation—limits lower, in most cases, than in FECA. The Court accepted the limitations, arguing that the state's interest in preventing corruption or the appearance of corruption, as in *Buckley*, was sufficient, but extended the rationale to "the broader threat from politicians too compliant with the wishes of large contributors." The Court also accepted the specific limits themselves, without suggesting a dollar amount that would be too low. The standard it suggested instead was "whether the contribution limitation was so radical in effect as to render political association ineffective, drive the sound

of a candidate's voice below the level of notice, and render contributions pointless."

As constitutional scholar Daniel R. Ortiz noted (2005), the *Nixon* decision was notable for the divisions in basic approach to campaign finance on the Court, reflected in separate concurrences and dissents by six justices. At one end of the spectrum, Justice Stevens said, "Money is property. It is not speech." He would have applied a lower standard to protection of campaign money than to traditional forms of speech. Justices Breyer and Ruth Bader Ginsburg recognized a First Amendment concern in campaign spending, but made it clear that they would be open to more stringent regulation of campaign finance than *Buckley* provides, and said that they would even consider repealing *Buckley* if it did not allow "the political branches sufficient leeway to enact comprehensive solutions to the problems posed by campaign finance." Justices Thomas and Scalia made it clear that they too would overrule *Buckley*—by invalidating contribution limits and most other campaign regulation. Justice Kennedy, also skeptical of regulation, said he too would overrule *Buckley*, but let state legislatures and Congress go back to the drawing board to try to find a new way to enact reform consistent with the First Amendment.

McConnell v. Federal Election Commission

Over the twenty-five years that followed the *Buckley* decision, Congress did not act in any significant way to alter the campaign system, but the system nonetheless changed substantially as technology, political alignments, and the economy changed. And all the actors in the political process—from candidates to party officials, to outside groups, to lawyers and political and media consultants—found ways to adapt the law to suit their own interests.

The major changes included the sharp expansion of soft money—a distinction made by the Federal Election Commission in the late 1970s to characterize money raised by political parties for the purpose of party building and grassroots activities. Different rules and limits for fundraising and spending applied to these funds, compared to so-called hard money raised by candidates and parties for the purpose of electing candidates. Parties, the president, lawmakers, and outside groups sharply expanded their fundraising and spending of soft money to take advantage, exploiting the opening left by the Supreme Court's footnote in *Buckley* giving a "bright line" test of express advocacy. Ads described as issue advocacy that were evidently aimed at electing or defeating candidates, but that avoided the use of words such as *elect* or *defeat*, were financed in increasing numbers by unregulated soft money, both through parties and outside groups that avoided limits or disclosure for their campaign ads.

These dynamics precipitated a new wave of campaign finance reform in Congress, culminating in the Bipartisan

Campaign Reform Act of 2002 (BCRA), commonly known as the McCain-Feingold Act. BCRA passed and was signed into law by President George W. Bush in early 2002, and included a provision for expedited review by a three-judge panel. It then moved to the Supreme Court in *McConnell v. Federal Election Commission*, 540 U.S. 93 (2003).

BCRA did several things, including expanding individual contribution limits, which had not been adjusted since 1976 (the new limit was set at $2,000 with future inflation adjustments), and setting rules to provide additional fundraising opportunities for candidates challenged by wealthy individuals (commonly called the millionaires' amendment). Most importantly BCRA banned soft money contributions that were aimed at influencing federal elections, barred federal officials from directly raising such soft money, and created constraints for broadcast ads close to elections that targeted candidates in those elections—in the process redefining and expanding the bright-line test for express advocacy. BCRA was not intended to challenge the intellectual framework of the *Buckley* decision, but rather to adjust it based on changes in campaigns in the quarter century since its adoption.

A five-to-four decision in *McConnell* upheld virtually all of BCRA. It considered carefully the database Congress had used in its own deliberations over campaign reform and gave significant deference to the decisions Congress made in enacting BCRA. It upheld the ban on raising or spending federal soft money, saying that the provisions would have limited impact on "the ability of contributors, officeholders and parties to engage in effective political speech." The Court emphasized its view that soft money could be tied to corruption or the appearance of corruption, noting especially that "more than half of the top 50 soft-money donors gave substantial sums to *both* major national parties, leaving room for no other conclusion but that these donors were seeking influence, or avoiding retaliation, rather than promoting any particular ideology." The Court in effect broadened its definition of corruption, pointing out that corruption was not only actions like direct quids pro quo (or bribery) but could also be seen as buying access.

The Court also accepted BCRA's new bright-line test for express advocacy, which the act defined as "electioneering communications." Under BCRA, broadcast communications that named a candidate for office, targeted the district or state in which the candidate was running (reaching more than 50,000 people there), and aired within sixty days of a general election or thirty days of a primary were the equivalent of campaign ads. As such, they could not be financed with labor or corporate general treasury funds but only with monies, like other campaigns, from individual contributions or political action committees. The Court said such limits were neither overbroad nor underinclusive, and noted that corporations and unions could still spend on campaigns through political action committees (PACs). But the Court did not reject individual as-applied challenges for particular ads falling under the rubric. BCRA also required disclosure of spending by individuals on electioneering communications of more than $10,000, something the Court also upheld.

The key vote in the five-to-four *McConnell* decision was that of Justice Sandra Day O'Connor, a former legislator and the only justice on the Rehnquist Court who had run for and held office. O'Connor was joined by Justices Stevens, Souter, Ginsburg, and Breyer. The dissenters were Justices Scalia, Thomas, and Kennedy, and Chief Justice Rehnquist, all of whom had previously supported the *Buckley* decision.

After *McConnell* On September 27, 2005, the Supreme Court agreed to take two cases that had the potential to substantially recast campaign finance law after *McConnell*. *Randall v. Sorrell*, 548 U.S. 230 (2006) was a challenge to strict contribution and mandatory spending limits on candidates for state office in Vermont. *Federal Election Commission v. Wisconsin Right to Life*, 551 U.S. ___ (2007) was an as-applied challenge to the electioneering communications provision of BCRA. Within days after accepting these cases, the Supreme Court changed significantly. John Roberts was sworn in as chief justice on September 29, replacing William Rehnquist, and on January 30, 2006, Samuel Alito replaced Sandra Day O'Connor.

In *Randall*, the Second Circuit Court of Appeals had upheld the Vermont law, Act 64, saying that the Supreme Court's decision in *Buckley* would allow spending limits that are "narrowly tailored to secure clearly identified and appropriately documented compelling governmental interests." The Court found that Vermont had established two "compelling interests" in support of its spending limits: preventing the reality and appearance of corruption, and protecting candidates and elected officials from spending inordinate time seeking and getting contributions.

The Supreme Court by a six-to-three vote (albeit with six separate opinions) struck down both the Vermont spending and contribution limits, saying they violated the First Amendment. Justice Breyer, joined by Chief Justice Roberts and Justice Alito, offered the controlling plurality, saying in effect that the Vermont contribution limits, unlike earlier limits such as those upheld in *Nixon*, were too low. In character with their other campaign law decisions, Justices Stevens, Souter, and Ginsburg would have upheld the Vermont limits, whereas Justices Scalia and Thomas would have disallowed all such limits.

In *Wisconsin Right to Life*, the full impact of the departure of Justice O'Connor with replacement by Justice Alito became clear. Wisconsin Right to Life (WRTL), a nonprofit advocacy group, ran three advertisements during the 2004 campaign encouraging viewers to contact two named U.S. Senators—including Senator Russ Feingold (1953–), who was running for reelection—and tell them to oppose filibusters of judicial nominees. The ads violated BCRA's electioneering communications provisions.

WRTL sued the FEC claiming that BCRA was unconstitutional as applied to the advertisements, which it said were issue ads. The FEC countered that WRTL's ads were sham issue ads, clearly intended to affect an election. A three-judge district court panel, refusing to consider the context and intent of the ads, analyzing only their explicit content, found them to be legitimate issue ads. The court also held that the government's corruption justification for banning express advocacy ads by corporations did not apply to ads that do not explicitly support or oppose a candidate. Therefore, the court ruled that the government lacked a compelling interest to justify the burden on WRTL's First Amendment rights.

The Roberts Court agreed with the district court decision in a five-to-four opinion. The majority included three justices who had voted against *McConnell*—Scalia, Thomas, and Kennedy—along with Roberts and Alito. The four dissenters—Stevens, Souter, Ginsburg, and Breyer—had (along with O'Connor) made up the majority for *McConnell* barely two years earlier. Chief Justice Roberts used his majority opinion to stake out his own views on campaign reform, while indicating that *Wisconsin Right to Life* was not a sweeping rejection either of *McConnell* or *Buckley*. His opinion redefined the test that BCRA had applied to electioneering communications. Roberts's opinion adopted the test that "an ad is the functional equivalent of express advocacy only if the ad is susceptible of no reasonable interpretation other than as an appeal to vote for or against a specific candidate." The opinion rejected BCRA's, and *McConnell*'s, rationale for regulation of corporate money in campaigns, saying that neither the interest in preventing corruption nor the goal of limiting the distorting effects of corporate wealth was sufficient to override the right of a corporation to speak through ads on issues. This conclusion, said Roberts, was necessary in order to "give the benefit of the doubt to speech, not censorship."

Justice Scalia, while agreeing with the opinion, offered a stinging rebuke to the chief justice for his refusal to overturn BCRA directly, calling it "faux judicial restraint." At the other end of the spectrum, the dissent, authored by Justice Souter, accused the majority of implicitly overruling *McConnell*. But by creating a standard broader in some ways than the explicit magic-words test, the Court actually did not overrule entirely this aspect of *McConnell*, and it did not in any way reverse the ban on federal soft money.

But it is clear that *Wisconsin Right to Life* will not be the last word of the Roberts Court on campaign finance law. The Court heard oral arguments in April 2008 in *Davis v. Federal Election Commission*, a challenge to the millionaires' amendment that allowed candidates to raise additional sums of money if their opponents spent large sums of their own in their campaigns. Other as-applied challenges to BCRA will likely move forward, as well as further challenges to regulations of corporate involvement in campaigns. Congress may well tackle the role of so-called 527, or tax-exempt, political organizations (named after a provision in the Internal Revenue Code) in campaigns, as well as the role of nonprofit organizations known in the code as 501(C)(4)s. And many in Congress, including Senators McCain and Feingold, have proposed revising and updating the presidential campaign funding structure set in 1976, which was largely untouched by BCRA.

SEE ALSO *Buckley v. Valeo, 424 U.S. 1 (1976); First Amendment; McConnell v. Federal Election Commission, 540 U.S. 93 (2003)*

BIBLIOGRAPHY

Hasen, Richard L. 2008. "Beyond Incoherence: The Roberts Court's Deregulatory Turn in FEC v. Wisconsin Right to Life." *Minnesota Law Review* 92(4).

Lowenstein, Daniel Hays, and Richard L. Hasen. 2004 *Election Law: Cases and Materials*. Durham, NC: Carolina Academic Press.

Malbin, Michael J., ed. 2006. *The Election after Reform: Money, Politics, and the Bipartisan Campaign Reform Act*. Lanham, MD: Rowman and Littlefield.

Ortiz, Daniel R. 2005. "The First Amendment and the Limits of Campaign Finance Reform." In *The New Campaign Finance Sourcebook*, ed. Anthony Corrado, Thomas E. Mann, Daniel R. Ortiz, and Trevor Potter. Washington, DC: Brookings Institution Press.

Norman Ornstein

CAMPBELL, JOHN
1811–1889

John Archibald Campbell is one of the most obscure justices ever to serve on the Supreme Court, yet he deserves greater recognition for his work on the Court and for his arguments in cases in which he was counsel. During his brief tenure (1853–1861), he wrote a number of opinions on disputed land titles, hardly a theme that attracts the attention of scholars. He wrote, for example, the opinion in *United States v. Sutter*, 62 U.S. 170 (1858), confirming the claim of John Sutter, on whose property gold was found in California in 1848. During Campbell's tenure, the Court also sorted out the conflicting claims of those who held title to U.S. land under grants from the king of Spain or the Mexican government. The peace

Supreme Court Justice John Campbell. *Joining the Supreme Court in 1853, Georgia-born Campbell first gained notice for his work securing the rights of landholders in territory gained after the Mexican War. However, once Southern states began to secede from the Union in late 1860, Campbell left his seat on the court to serve as assistant secretary of war for the Confederacy, then received a pardon from Andrew Jackson after the conflict, and eventually practiced law in Louisiana for the rest of his career.* © CORBIS

treaty ending the Mexican War (1846–1848) gave assurances that the titles to property of citizens living in the ceded territory would be respected.

Justice Campbell was born in Washington, Georgia, June 24, 1811. He attended the University of Georgia, graduating with honors. He later attended the U.S. Military Academy, but did not graduate. Campbell returned to Georgia upon the death of his father and began the study of law under his uncle. He soon moved to Alabama and became a leading attorney in Montgomery before relocating to Mobile, where he was elected to the General Assembly for two terms. He twice turned down offers of appointments to the Supreme Court of Louisiana.

Like other southerners, Campbell was dragged into the quagmire of the slavery issue. He attended the Nashville Convention of 1850, which was convened to consider steps that should be taken to protect southern rights. Campbell himself believed that slavery would disappear in time if the South were left alone. He freed his

own slaves, and only hired freedmen thereafter. During the Nashville Convention, Campbell wrote a number of resolutions that may be classified as moderate.

In Alabama, Campbell became a friend to John McKinley (1780–1852), a lawyer who was appointed to the U.S. Supreme Court in 1837. McKinley's death opened the way for the appointment of another southerner. After President Franklin Pierce's (1804–1869) first three choices were rejected by the Senate, the president asked members of the Supreme Court whom he should appoint, and they recommended Campbell, who had impressed the justices with several cases he had argued before the Court. Campbell was eminently qualified for the position, for he had vast professional knowledge, as well as a tremendous intellect with a special interest in theology.

Justice Campbell took his seat on the Court in 1853. In several decisions, Campbell argued against the extension of federal jurisdiction. Early in his Court career, he took part in *Dred Scott v. Sandford,* 60 U.S. 393 (1857), which stirred up a national debate over whether slavery would be allowed in territories seeking admission to the Union. In his opinions, Justice Campbell demonstrated a knowledge of Roman law and the writings of the English jurist and philosopher Jeremy Bentham (1748–1832). Campbell later wrote opinions in a number of suits concerning land titles in California that involved thousands of acres granted to individuals by the Spanish or Mexican governments. In these cases, Justice Campbell demonstrated his knowledge of Mexican land laws at a time when the justices had to do their own research and did not rely on clerks.

When the Civil War (1861–1865) broke out, Campbell, unlike Justice James Wayne (1790–1867) of Georgia, resigned from the Court and returned to the South, where he was appointed assistant secretary of war in the Confederate cabinet, a post he held for the duration of the war. Before leaving Washington, Campbell tried unsuccessfully to broker a deal between the seceding states and the federal government. He tried again in the closing days of the war, but without success. Like so many southerners holding offices in the Confederate government, Campbell was arrested for treason and alleged involvement in the assassination of Abraham Lincoln, but he was pardoned by President Andrew Johnson (1808–1875) on the urging of his former colleagues on the Supreme Court. He subsequently moved to New Orleans, where he resumed the practice of law, soon becoming one of the leading attorneys in Louisiana.

Campbell's contributions to constitutional law did not end when he left the Court, for he was chosen to argue a number of cases involving constitutional issues. The most significant of these was the *Slaughter-House Cases,* 83 U.S. 36 (1873), in which Justice Campbell argued for an extended application of the newly adopted Fourteenth Amendment by reference to a broad historical argument drawing a distinction been slavery and servitude. The Supreme Court, however, took the position that the purpose of the Fourteenth Amendment was to protect the rights of freed slaves, thus limiting its application. But this was not the end of the story. A newly elected legislature repealed an act granting a monopoly to a single slaughterhouse in New Orleans and adopted a constitutional amendment that gave municipalities the authority to ensure that the rights of citizens were protected without creating monopolies, an action the city of New Orleans immediately took. The Monopolists quickly brought suit to enforce their rights under the original statute. Again, Campbell argued the case on behalf of the defendants, this time with better success (*Butchers' Union Co. v. Crescent City*, 111 U.S. 746 [1884]). The Court based its decision on the grounds that no legislature could limit the authority of later sessions to exercise its police powers.

After his wife and son died in 1884, Campbell moved to Baltimore, Maryland, where he died March 12, 1889. Judging from the many tributes, his professional talents as a lawyer were widely recognized.

SEE ALSO *Amendments, Post-Civil War; Slaughter-House Cases, 83 U.S. 36 (1873)*

BIBLIOGRAPHY

Connor, Henry G. 1971 (1920). *John Archibald Campbell: Associate Justice of the United States Supreme Court, 1853–1861.* New York: Da Capo.

Erwin C. Surrency

C & A CARBONE, INC. V. CLARKS-TOWN, 511 U.S. 383 (1994)

The town of Clarkstown, New York, attempted to solve its growing solid waste problem by contracting for the construction of a waste transfer station that would receive garbage produced locally, sort it, and ship it elsewhere for ultimate disposal. The agreement called for a private company to build the facility, operate it for five years, then turn it over to the town for payment of one dollar. To ensure the station's financial viability, Clarkstown passed a "flow control" ordinance, requiring that all garbage produced in the town be processed at the transfer station. The station charged a "tipping fee" of $81 per ton for handling the waste. The town also guaranteed a certain volume of waste at the station during the five years it was privately operated and agreed to make up any shortfall if garbage volumes fell below the guaranteed minimum.

Because the tipping fee charged by the transfer station was higher than fees at other, out-of-town, facilities, a local garbage processor sued, claiming that the flow control ordinance discriminated against interstate commerce by requiring all garbage to be processed locally, at the new transfer station. Justice Anthony Kennedy and four other justices agreed. Justice Sandra Day O'Connor concurred in the result, but disagreed that the ordinance discriminated against interstate commerce. Justice David Souter, writing for himself, Chief Justice William Rehnquist, and Justice Harry Blackmun, dissented.

Justice Kennedy stressed the connection between Clarkstown's ordinance and numerous laws the Court had struck down over time requiring the local processing of a particular good prior to export. "The essential vice in laws of this sort," he explained, "is that they bar the import of the processing service.... Put another way, the offending local laws hoard a local resource ... for the benefit of local businesses that treat it." In the current case, Kennedy concluded that other, nondiscriminatory ways existed, including cash subsidies and municipal bonds, to ensure the financial viability of the facility, without resorting to the flow control ordinance. "Revenue generation," Kennedy stressed, "is not a local interest that can justify discrimination against interstate commerce." Justice O'Connor concurred, agreeing that the ordinance was impermissibly burdensome vis-à-vis local benefits, but concluding that it was not discriminatory—it prohibited *anyone* from exporting garbage other than to the transfer station.

Justice Souter dissented, arguing that the flow control ordinance "bestow[ed] no benefit on a class of local private actors, but instead directly aid[ed] the government in satisfying a traditional governmental responsibility." The creation of public monopolies, he argued, was not motivated by mere economic protectionism and ought not to be viewed as skeptically as those laws favoring classes of private businesses. This public-private distinction, he continued, rendered the majority's reliance on the Court's previous local processing cases inapposite.

In 2007 the Court adopted Justice Souter's position in *United Haulers Association, Inc. v. Oneida-Herkimer Solid Waste Management Authority*, 550 U.S. ___ (2007) involving a flow control ordinance requiring that garbage be processed at a transfer station that, unlike Clarkstown, was entirely government-owned.

SEE ALSO *Commerce Clause; Rehnquist Court*

BIBLIOGRAPHY

Cox, Stanley E. 1997. "Garbage In, Garbage Out: Court Confusion About the Dormant Commerce Clause." *Oklahoma Law Review* 50: 155–222.

Heinzerling, Lisa. 1995. "The Commercial Constitution." *Supreme Court Review* 1995: 217–276.

Turner, John. 1996. "The Flow Control of Solid Waste and the Commerce Clause: *Carbone* and Its Progeny." *Villanova Environmental Law Journal* 7: 203–261.

Verchick, Robert R. M. 1997. "The Commerce Clause, Environmental Justice, and the Interstate Garbage Wars." *Southern California Law Review* 70: 1239–1310.

Brannon P. Denning

CANTWELL V. CONNECTICUT, 310 U.S. 296 (1940)

Cantwell v. Connecticut, 310 U.S. 296 (1940) is extremely important to the landscape of U.S. constitutional law. The facts of the case are interesting, but relatively straightforward. Newton Cantwell, along with his sons (Jesse and Russell), all of whom were members of the Jehovah's Witnesses and ordained ministers in that religion, were distributing religious books and pamphlets in a predominately Catholic area of New Haven, Connecticut. As part of the distribution, the Cantwells also solicited money on behalf of their religion. All three were arrested and convicted of soliciting money without a license. They sought to challenge their convictions on First Amendment grounds.

The decision is notable because it contains a number of important constitutional principles. First, and foremost, the decision incorporated the First Amendment free exercise clause into the Fourteenth Amendment due process clause, and thereby made it applicable to the states. Under the U.S. Constitution, certain provisions of the Bill of Rights explicitly apply only to the federal government. For example, the First Amendment (which contains the free exercise clause) begins by stating that "Congress shall make no law respecting an establishment of religion, or prohibiting the free exercise thereof." Nevertheless, in a series of decisions, the U.S. Supreme Court has held that various provisions of the Bill of Rights are "incorporated" into the Fourteenth Amendment due process clause, and therefore also act as prohibitions against the states, as well as against Congress (see *Near v. Minnesota*, 283 U.S. 697 [1931] and *Gitlow v. New York*, 268 U.S. 652 [1925]). However, not all of the provisions of the Bill of Rights have been incorporated (incorporation of all provisions is referred to as *total incorporation*), only some have been incorporated (so-called *selective incorporation*). Included have been the right to freedom of speech and of the press, as well as the establishment clause (see *Near, Gitlow*, and *Everson v. Board of Education*, 330 U.S. 1 [1947]). *Cantwell* is significant because it is the decision that held that the free exercise clause applies to the states.

Cantwell is also significant because it provided insight into the meaning of the free exercise clause. In *Cantwell*, the Court emphasized that while citizens have an almost absolute right to endorse whatever religious beliefs they choose to endorse, the freedom to act in pursuit of those beliefs is not absolute. As a result, the Court suggested that the State of Connecticut might have had the authority under a properly drawn statute to prohibit religious solicitation of the type engaged in by the Jehovah's Witnesses in *Cantwell*.

Finally, *Cantwell* is important because it confirms the prohibition against licensing restraints. In a series of decisions, the Court has held that licensing restrictions on speech are presumptively unconstitutional unless they are content neutral with respect to time, place, and manner restrictions (See, e.g., *Lovell v. City of Griffin*, 303 U.S. 444 [1938]). In *Cantwell*, the Court suggested that the State might have been able to prohibit all solicitation of funds, but that they cannot do so in ways that give governmental officials undue discretion (which might be used to impinge and obstruct religious beliefs). The Court concluded that because the statute vested governmental officials with discretion to ban solicitations based on their religious message, the statute was invalid.

SEE ALSO *First Amendment; Jehovah's Witnesses*

BIBLIOGRAPHY

Weaver, Russell L.; Catherine Hancock; Donald E. Lively; and John C. Knechtle. 2006. *The First Amendment: Cases, Problems, and Materials.* 2nd edition. Bethesda, MD: LexisNexis/Matthew Bender.

Weaver, Russell L., and Donald E. Lively. 2007. *Understanding the First Amendment.* 2nd edition. Bethesda, MD: LexisNexis.

Russell L. Weaver

CAPITAL PUNISHMENT

American law regarding the death penalty has passed through three historical stages, and the Supreme Court's key role in this process was to mandate the transition from the second stage to the third.

THE EVOLUTION OF THE DEATH PENALTY IN THE UNITED STATES

At the time of American Independence, most homicides, and certainly all murders, were usually automatically punishable by death. In fact, other felonies—including robbery, burglary, and grand larceny—often carried a mandatory death penalty as well, so that if a jury convicted an individual of one of these crimes, neither judge nor jury had any discretion over the sentence. The automatic death penalty, inherited by the colonies from

John Major Young, Jr., a death-row prisoner at the Colorado Penitentiary, June 30, 1972. *Supreme Court opinions about the death penalty have evolved throughout U.S. history, from being an automatic punishment for crimes such as murder, to being a possible outcome of a guilty decision, depending on the discretion of the jury. In the early twenty-first century, capital punishment has been ruled Constitutional; however, jurors receive very strict guidelines to determine if the convicted should join death row.* © **CORBIS-BETTMANN**

English law, continued in almost all the states well into the nineteenth century, although the states gradually created a two-degree scheme of murder, with the death penalty restricted to first-degree murders.

Stage two in the development of the death penalty lasted from about the time of the Civil War (1861–1865)

to the 1960s. During this period the states (and the federal government for federal crimes) used their first-degree murder definitions to decide which defendants were eligible for the death penalty, but they left the choice between life and death to the unguided discretion of the judge or jury that had decided the guilt issue. The third stage came about because major constitutional litigation in the 1960s and 1970s led the Supreme Court to mandate a new legal regime, one that has proved reasonably stable since then. Under this new regime, in most states (and, again, under federal criminal law), after a jury finds the defendant guilty of "capital," or first-degree, murder, it retests the defendant's liability against a still narrower "super-first-degree" murder law by deciding whether the offender or the offense exhibited certain "aggravating" factors. In the penalty trial, the jury performs a comparative evaluation of these aggravating factors and any mitigating factors about the crime or the criminal, and it then and decides whether the defendant should live or die.

THE FIFTH AMENDMENT AND THE DEATH PENALTY

Any detailed discussion of the constitutionality of the death penalty must begin with the language of the Fifth Amendment, which says that no person "shall be deprived of life ... without due process of law." This language obviously suggests that the authors of the Bill of Rights had no categorical objection to the death penalty. Indeed, the law in the colonies and in the states after Independence used the mandatory death penalty as the major instrument for punishing murders. For more than a century and a half after Independence, capital punishment proceeded in the United States with essentially no constitutional scrutiny. State laws regarding capital punishment, however, changed significantly.

The state legislatures gradually rejected the automatic death penalty scheme for two related reasons. First, many legislators may have simply felt that not all murderers— even first-degree murderers—were equally culpable, or that not all of them deserved death. In short, the law of murder did not sufficiently distinguish killers according to the blameworthiness of their crimes or the moral aspects of their characters. Second, the automatic death penalty law had a paradoxically lenient effect. Jurors who believed a defendant was guilty of capital murder but did not believe he or she deserved to die would simply "nullify" the law of homicide by acquitting the defendant of the murder charge.

Jury Discretion Slowly but steadily during the nineteenth century, the states changed their death penalty laws to a system that openly and expressly gave juries the discretion they had previously exercised in a subversive fashion. The model was very simple: The judge first instructed the jury in the law of first-degree murder so the jury could determine whether the defendant was "eligible" for the death penalty. If the jury so found, it was then to decide, as part of the same deliberation, whether the defendant should be executed or sentenced to life imprisonment. The trial

court gave the jury little, if any, legal guidance on how to make this choice. Nor did the jury have the benefit of extensive information about the defendant's background, character, or previous criminal record, beyond whatever narrow information the law of evidence allowed the parties to offer on the question of the defendant's guilt. The system had changed from one of no jury discretion to one of total—and virtually unguided—jury discretion. This new system constituted American death-penalty law until 1972. Although a few states had wholly abolished capital punishment late in the nineteenth century or during the twentieth century, the great majority retained the system of jury-discretionary capital punishment until that year.

By the 1950s the jury discretion scheme of capital punishment had come under great political and philosophical scrutiny. Many opponents of the death penalty attacked it in absolute terms, arguing that there was no empirical proof that capital punishment was superior to life imprisonment in deterring serious crime, and that a morally mature society should not use death as an instrument for revenge or retribution. But the legal attacks on the death penalty during the 1960s also focused on the way the death penalty operated in practice. Although giving discretion to the jury softened the severity of the automatic death penalty, it also permitted an arbitrary and discriminatory administration of the law. Many complained that a comparison of the crimes and criminal records of those executed with the crimes and records of those who received life sentences yielded no rational pattern in the results. Many also noted that the one potential pattern that did emerge was one of racial discrimination. In essence, death sentences appeared to be given disproportionately to black defendants, or (more subtly) to defendants accused of killing whites, or (most disproportionately of all) to against black men convicted of raping white women.

In *McGautha v. California*, 402 U.S. 183 (1971), the Court held that the standardless jury discretion schemes of the states did not violate the due process clause of the Fourteenth Amendment. Somewhat hypertechnically, the Court restricted its decision to the application of the due process clause, avoiding any decision on the application of the Eighth Amendment. But Justice John Marshall Harlan's opinion for the court warned that whatever the constitutional rubric, any effort to impose legal regulation on the morally complex question of capital punishment would be futile: "To identify before the fact those characteristics of criminal homicides and their perpetrators which call for the death penalty, and to express these characteristics in language which can be fairly understood and applied by the sentencing authority, appear to be tasks which are beyond present human ability." Justice Harlan believed the Court should not force the state legislatures to devise guiding rules for the death penalty, because the visceral decision of whether to kill a defendant could not be reduced to legal rules.

A DIVIDED COURT SPEAKS

One year later, however, a majority of the Court rejected Justice Harlan's warning. In the landmark case of *Furman v. Georgia*, 408 U.S. 238 (1972), the Court voted five-to-four to strike down all the death penalty schemes in the United States as they then operated. Unfortunately, there was no majority opinion in *Furman*. Indeed, each of the five judges in the majority wrote his own opinion, and none joined any of the others. At best, therefore, one can glean general themes from the *Furman* opinions, rather than a single guiding principle.

Justices William J. Brennan Jr. and Thurgood Marshall took the view that the death penalty violated the Eighth Amendment under all circumstances because it served no legitimate deterrent or retributive purpose, and because it violated "evolving standards of decency," the principle enunciated in *Trop v. Dulles*, 356 U.S. 86 (1958). The swing votes, cast by Justices William O. Douglas, Potter Stewart, and Byron White, were more guarded. The consensus of their views was that the wanton, unpredictable infliction of the death penalty under the unguided discretion schemes, as well as the discriminatory infliction of the death penalty on the basis of race, violated the Eighth Amendment. The result of *Furman,* then, was that the states could restore the death penalty only if they designed new capital punishment laws that so restricted or guided jury discretion as to remove the arbitrary and discriminatory effects decried by the *Furman* plurality.

The dissents in *Furman* also merit more than archival mention, however, because they anticipate some of the later actions of the Supreme Court. Again, the serial opinions make generalization difficult. The key dissenting themes were that the Eighth Amendment applied to types of punishment, not to the methods by which individuals were selected for otherwise legitimate punishment; that even if the Court must rely on a historical evolution of social and moral views, no drastic changes in such views had occurred that could justify this sudden act of judicial intervention in American criminal justice; and that even if the application of capital punishment smacked of racial disparity, that disparity could be traced back to fundamental social and historical forces in American society and could be neither blamed on, not cured by, legal changes in the death penalty.

Immediately after *Furman,* roughly three-quarters of the states did enact new laws aimed at satisfying the somewhat elusive demands of the Court. The new capital punishment statutes took two forms, each designed to solve the problem of unguided jury discretion. A handful of states, in an act of historical irony, returned to the

---

From this day forward, I no longer shall tinker with the machinery of death.

SOURCE: Harry A. Blackmun, *Collins v. Collins,* 510 U.S. 1141, 1145 (1994) (dissenting).

---

mandatory, or automatic, death penalty. They created special categories of egregious first-degree murder, such as the premeditated murder of a police officer or premeditated murder in the course of an enumerated felony, and declared the death penalty automatic for anyone convicted of such murders. Thus, these states "solved" the problem of unguided or excessive jury discretion by eliminating that discretion altogether.

The other type of statute, adopted by the majority of the reenacting states, can be termed a "guided discretion" statute. Under these statutes, the court conducts a separate sentencing hearing (usually before the jury, but, under a few original post-*Furman* statutes, before the judge alone) after the defendant is convicted of first-degree or "capital" murder. The sentencer then chooses either the death penalty or life imprisonment (sometimes with the possibility of parole, sometimes not) but this choice is guided by a process of balancing aggravating and mitigating factors. The sentencer must find the presence of certain aggravating factors and take into account any relevant mitigating factors. This model of the guided discretion statute has now become the established norm for the death penalty in America.

A RETURN TO THE ISSUE

In 1976 in *Gregg v. Georgia*, 428 U.S. 153—and in companion cases from Florida, Texas, North Carolina, and Louisiana—the Supreme Court returned to the death penalty to determine whether the new statutes had resolved the problems identified four years earlier in *Furman*. Once again, the Court produced no majority decision, but the holding of *Gregg* was clear. First, over the dissents of Justices Brennan and Marshall, the Court, through a plurality opinion by Justice Stewart, flatly rejected the argument that the death penalty was unconstitutional in all circumstances.

As for matters of original meaning, in the plurality's view the authors of the Eighth Amendment, obviously aware of the prevalence of capital punishment, did not believe that the death penalty per se was unconstitutional. Rather, the "cruel and unusual punishments" clause, drawn from the English Bill of Rights of 1689, was concerned with more particular matters. First, it prohibited any punishments not officially authorized by statute or not lying within the sentencing court's jurisdiction.

Second, it proscribed brutal, gratuitously painful methods of torture or execution. Although the authors of the Eighth Amendment may have intended to prohibit a severe punishment such as death for a minor crime, they certainly did not view the death penalty as unconstitutionally excessive or disproportionate for the crime of murder.

Summarizing the later jurisprudence of the Eighth Amendment, Justice Stewart stated that a punishment was constitutional so long as it comported with "evolving standards of human decency," as reflected in "contemporary public attitudes," and with the Eighth Amendment concept of the "dignity of man." The death penalty met the first test because public attitudes, reflected in such objective evidence as the reenactment of death penalty laws by a majority of state legislatures after *Furman* and numerous jury verdicts of death under these new laws, demonstrated that the death penalty did not violate contemporary standards of decency. In addition, the death penalty did not violate the "dignity of man" because it could serve legitimate deterrent and retributive purposes.

The Court acknowledged that the empirical evidence of the deterrent value of the death penalty was inconclusive at best, but in the absence of a clear answer, the justices gave the benefit of the doubt on this issue of penological policy to the legislatures. Moreover, said Justice Stewart, retribution was a legitimate, time-honored justification for the criminal law, especially because retributive action by the state could channel aggressive energies in society that might otherwise lead to lawless, vengeful action by private citizens. Finally, Justice Stewart concluded that whatever the fairness of inflicting death for less serious crimes, the death penalty was not invariably excessive for the crime of murder.

Having concluded that the death penalty did not necessarily violate the Eighth Amendment, the Court proceeded to examine the new post-*Furman* statutes. In *Woodson v. North Carolina*, 428 U.S. 280 (1976) and *Roberts v. Louisiana*, 428 U.S. 325 (1976), the Court struck down the revived automatic death penalty statutes. The plurality in *Woodson* and *Roberts* viewed the automatic-death statutes as misguided efforts to solve the problem of jury discretion. The justices believed that the Eighth Amendment implied a principle of respect for the individuality of all criminal defendants, and they were therefore unwilling to tolerate a death penalty law that forbade individualized distinctions of culpability among murderers guilty of a given category of crime. Moreover, the plurality returned to the classic problem of jury nullification that had helped undermine the old automatic statutes more than a century before. It declared that the inevitable tendency of jurors to render "false acquittals" to spare a guilty but sympathetic defendant

from death would lead to the further arbitrary or capricious administration of the death penalty.

In its key holding in *Gregg v. Georgia*, however, the Court upheld the guided discretion statutes as constitutionally satisfactory solutions to the problems of unfettered jury discretion diagnosed in *Furman*. Citing the Model Penal Code's death penalty provisions (in section 210.6) as a particularly satisfactory model, Justice Stewart approved the new Georgia statute and noted several features that supported its constitutionality, though he avoided saying that any of these particular features was constitutionally required. These features were: (1) the statute created a separate sentencing proceeding at which the state and the defendant could offer evidence not presented at the guilt phase; (2) the statute offered the jury express guidance in identifying aggravating circumstances and required the jury to find at least one of the aggravating circumstances enumerated in the statute before it voted for death; (3) the jury was instructed to consider any individualized mitigating circumstances that might outweigh the aggravating circumstances; (4) the defendant had a right of automatic appeal to the state supreme court for review of the death sentence; and (5) the state supreme court was required to conduct a "proportionality review" of every sentence, ensuring that the sentence was not arbitrary, prejudicial, or disproportionate in comparison to sentences handed down in similar Georgia cases (the Court later held, however, in *Pulley v. Harris*, 465 U.S. 37 [1984] that formal proportionality review, however desirable, was not constitutionally required).

In companion cases, the Court upheld the constitutionality of similar statutes in *Proffitt v. Florida*, 428 U.S. 242 (1976) and *Jurek v. Texas*, 428 U.S. 262 (1976). Although the Florida and Texas statutes differed from the Georgia law in their schemes for the establishment of aggravating and mitigating circumstances, the Court found that they provided similarly adequate safeguards against an arbitrary and discriminatory application of capital punishment.

THE *GREGG* MODEL IN PRACTICE

The 1976 cases thus restored the death penalty in America under the model of the guided discretion statutes. States such as North Carolina and Louisiana, whose automatic-death laws were struck down, quickly enacted new death penalty laws to meet the model approved in *Gregg*. The year after *Gregg*, Gary Gilmore was executed in Utah, becoming the first person to suffer the death penalty in America since the pre-*Furman* litigation had effectively suspended the death penalty in 1967.

In *Coker v. Georgia*, 433 U.S. 584 (1977), the Supreme Court has indicated that the death penalty is unconstitutional for any crime other than murder, where the court held that the death penalty was unconstitutionally excessive for the crime of rape of an adult woman. But some states have since enacted laws authorizing the death penalty for repeat sexual offenders who rape children, even where the victim survives.

The new laws vary somewhat in their scheme for identifying the most culpable killers. Most of the "guided discretion" states retained their traditional category of first-degree murder, which most obviously applies to premeditated murder and felony murder. The aggravating circumstances in the penalty hearing are then used to establish an enhanced category, in effect a kind of "aggravated first-degree murder." Other states fine-tuned their first-degree murder statutes by requiring the jury to convict the defendant, at the guilt stage, of a new enhanced category of "capital murder." They then added further aggravating circumstances at the penalty stage (see, for example, Tex. Code Crim. Proc. Ann. art. 37.071 [Vernon 2000 and Supp. 2004]). California has taken an intermediate approach: After the jury in the guilt phase convicts the defendant of first-degree murder, it must then find at least one "special circumstance" representing an aggravating factor. If it does, the trial shifts to the penalty phase, at which the jury considers an expanded list of aggravating circumstances (Cal. Penal Code § 190.2 [West 1999 and Supp. 2003]).

Most states created detailed statutory lists of aggravating or mitigating circumstances, but a few states do not enumerate any specific mitigating circumstances and simply require the sentencer to consider any mitigating factors that arise from the evidence (see, for example, Ga. Code Ann. § 17-10-30 [1997 & Supp. 2003]). In the Federal Death Penalty Act of 1994 (18 U.S.C. § 3591 et seq.), Congress added new death penalties for a wide variety of killings that happen to fall within federal jurisdiction, such as those occurring among military personnel or on federal property, or crimes against federal officials. Thus, it was under federal law that Timothy McVeigh was executed for the 1995 Oklahoma City bombing. The 1994 federal law very closely mirrors the capital sentencing law of the Model Penal Code, cited with approval in *Gregg*.

The structure of death penalty law as approved in *Gregg* has changed little since the decision was handed down. But a significant number of Supreme Court cases have narrowed or fine-tuned the *Gregg* doctrine.

Who Decides After *Gregg*, of the roughly thirty-eight states that reinstated the death penalty, the majority gave the defendant the right to a jury trial at the penalty phase. A new line of Sixth Amendment cases arising from *Apprendi v. New Jersey*, 530 U.S. 466 (2000) then strengthened arguments for a constitutional right to jury trial on all the key "elements of a crime." In *Ring v. Arizona*, 536 U.S. 584 (2002), the Court extended *Apprendi* to the death penalty, holding that the capital defendant has a right to a jury trial on the presence of any statutorily required aggravating factors, although in theory the final decision could be made by a judge. In any event, the clear movement of the states is towards a full jury trial right on the life versus death decision.

Degrees of Discretion Granted that the old automatic death penalty has been abolished, how much control can a state impose on a jury's life versus death decision? In *Lockett v. Ohio*, 438 U.S. 586 (1978), the Court confronted a state death penalty law that, unlike the one approved in Georgia, specifically enumerated certain mitigating circumstances. At Sandra Lockett's capital trial, she was precluded from citing a mitigating factor—that she had only been the getaway driver in a fatal armed robbery—that was not one of the enumerated factors. Reversing, the Court held that the principle of individualized discretion required that the state permit the defendant to introduce any mitigating circumstance, regardless of whether it was specified in the statute, so long as it was related to the defendant's "character, record, or offense."

Clarifying *Lockett*, the Court stressed in *Eddings v. Oklahoma*, 455 U.S. 104 (1982) that a mitigating circumstance could include a point of background or character that would not have been admissible as a defense to the crime at the guilt phase, such as a difficult childhood in a dysfunctional family. It later held—in *Skipper v. South Carolina*, 476 U.S. 1 (1986)—that mitigation can even include good behavior that occurred in prison after the murder, though it generally cannot include arguments against the wisdom or fairness of the death penalty.

At the same time, the Court has let the states enjoy a fair amount of flexibility in framing the verbal formulas by which the jury is instructed in how to balance the aggravators and mitigators. Thus, for example, in *Blystone v. Pennsylvania*, 494 U.S. 299 (1990), the Court upheld a law instructing the jurors that they must impose death if the aggravating evidence outweighs the mitigating evidence. The defendant argued that the jurors should be reminded that they had the discretion to impose a life sentence however the balance came out in their minds, but the Court rejected this argument, even though, as a practical matter, the principles of double jeopardy would make such an "incorrect" life verdict unappealable by the state.

Eighth Amendment Subcategories Perhaps the most dramatic area of post-*Gregg* constitutional litigation has focused on the categories of crimes or criminals subject to the death penalty. At the time of *Gregg*, some states permitted the death penalty for such non-homicide crimes as rape or kidnapping. But in *Coker v. Georgia*, 433 U.S. 584 (1977), the Court held that it was unconstitutionally disproportionate under the Eight Amendment to sentence to death a rapist whose victim was an adult woman where the crime did not result in the victim's death. In doing so, the Court revived an unusual form of constitutional jurisprudence that had emerged in some of the opinions in *Furman* and *Gregg*. Under the principle of "evolving standards of human decency," the Court, hoping for some guidance in collective morality, began looking to the actual practices of the states—in terms of legislation, prosecutorial charging, and jury outcomes—to help determine for what crimes or criminals the death penalty was permissible. This is, of course, a contestable practice: The Bill of Rights is designedly a counter-majoritarian document, yet this approach in effect looks to majority democratic preferences to help determine the meaning of constitutional rights.

One new area in which this approach applied was in the felony murder rule. Under that rule of common law or state statutory law, a defendant can sometimes be convicted of first-degree murder if he or she intentionally participated in a dangerous felony, such as a robbery, that resulted in a death, even if the death was the result of recklessness or negligence, and even if the particular defendant was not the "triggerman." In *Enmund v. Florida*, 458 U.S. 782 (1982), the Court held that although the states were free to employ the felony murder rule any time they wished, it could not lead to a death sentence unless the particular defendant either intended the death or directly caused it. This test proved difficult in practice, however, because accomplices have many ways of "causing" death. The *Enmund* case was clarified in *Tison v. Arizona*, 481 U.S. 137 (1987), which focused entirely on mental state. In *Tison* the Court held that a defendant could not be sentenced to death unless his manifest mental state with regard to death was at least extreme indifference to human life—essentially a species of gross recklessness. Thus, some felony murderers can get the death penalty as long as the state meets this standard.

OTHER DEVELOPMENTS

Other major cases have focused on the classification of defendants. Following the approach of analyzing trends in legislation and actual outcomes among the states, as employed in *Coker* and *Tison*, the Court held in *Atkins v. Virginia*, 536 U.S. 304 (2002) that it is unconstitutional for a state to execute a defendant who is mentally retarded, and in *Roper v. Simmons*, 543 U.S. 551 (2005), the Court ruled against executing a defendant who was under the age of eighteen when the crime in question was committed. In both cases, the Court compared the number of states that permitted the death penalty for the relevant category with the number that did not, and it looked for evidence of a trend in one direction or the other. But the Court also consulted social science and medical evidence about the degree to which youths and retarded individuals can exercise the degree of moral responsibility normally required for the maximum of culpability. In addition, and quite controversially, Justice Anthony Kennedy's opinion in *Roper* cited the authority of legal developments abroad, including the practices of other countries and the principles enunciated by international organizations.

The Court is also facing the next frontier of this analysis of categories with a return to an unresolved question from *Coker*. By 2008 several states had enacted the death penalty for the crime of sexual assault of young children, even when no death occurs. The Court has now heard argument in *Kennedy v. Louisiana*, cert. granted, 128 S. Ct. 829 (2008), where the death penalty was imposed on a man convicted of raping an eight-year-old girl, so the justices will address the implications of *Coker* for such crimes.

THE TECHNOLOGY OF EXECUTION

Finally, in yet another area of Supreme Court litigation, the Court must now address permissible methods of execution. Over the last century, the state have generally moved toward supposedly less painful methods of execution—from hanging and firing squads to the electric chair, then to the gas chamber, and then to lethal injection. Virtually all executions since the late 1980s have been by lethal injection, and it appears that states will now rely entirely on this method. But the medical and chemical uncertainties about the procedure have led many defendants to try to block their own executions on the grounds that the state's particular method—usually involving some sequence of drugs including a sedative, a muscle relaxer, and a heart-stopping drug—still induces a unconstitutional degree of pain. In *Baze v. Rees*, 128 S. Ct. 1520 (2008), the Court upheld the lethal injection protocol in Kentucky on the ground that it was not gratuitously painful, and future litigation will test whether the particular methods in other states are also constitutionally acceptable.

RACE AND CAPITAL PUNISHMENT

Overall, almost 4,000 murderers have entered death row under the new statutes, and about 3,200 were sitting on death row in 2008. Protracted federal and state appeals have prevented or delayed the execution of the vast majority of these prisoners, but as of December 17, 2007, 1,099 people have been executed under the new laws (Death Penalty Information Center 2008). The annual numbers for both new death sentences and executions have notably declined in the first decade of the twenty-first century—possibly because new DNA-based forensic methods have raised public concern over the risk of executing the wrongfully convicted. On the whole, however, the most recent stage of the development of the law of the death penalty in the United States seems fairly stable. No major new attacks on the constitutionality of the death penalty are on the legal horizon, nor is there any movement in the states toward any new form of death penalty procedure different from the kind approved in *Gregg*.

In this regard, one more major Supreme Court case merits attention. Perhaps the last effort at a fundamental attack on the death penalty in the modern era came in the famous case of *McCleskey v. Kemp*, 481 U.S. 279 (1987). Warren McCleskey, an African-American man convicted of killing a white person, revived a major question that had animated *Furman* and was somewhat ambiguously resolved in *Gregg*. McCleskey produced impressive statistics showing that race remained a major determinant of the distribution of the death penalty, but that, as was hinted decades earlier, the key factor was not the race of the defendant but the race of the victim. Sophisticated empirical analysis proffered by McCleskey showed that, all else being equal, the death penalty was several times more likely when the murder victim was white than when he or she was black. Thus, McCleskey argued, the promise of the statutes upheld in *Gregg*, that they would solve the problem of arbitrary and racially disparate death penalty outcomes underscored in *Furman*, had not been fulfilled.

But the Court rejected McCleskey's arguments. Writing for the majority, Justice William F. Powell Jr. first dismissed McCleskey's equal protection claim, noting that however disparate the outcomes, there was no proof of the intentional racial discrimination that the equal protection clause addresses. McCleskey also argued that the racial disparity violated the Eighth Amendment, because the disparity in outcomes alone, regardless of intentionality, made his death sentence cruel and unusual. Rejecting this claim as well, Justice Powell acknowledged the tragedy of these disparities, but he lamented that McCleskey's argument proved too much. Racially disparate outcomes, Justice Powell asserted, derived from deep-seated historical attitudes in American society, not from the mechanics of the death penalty law. These attitudes, he stated, influenced all types of discretionary decisions made by legislators, prosecutors, judges, and jurors. He therefore expressed concern that granting a victory to McCleskey would logically condemn not only the American death penalty but also vast parts of the American criminal justice system more generally.

Thus, in effect, *McCleskey v. Kemp* can be read as a reinterpretation of *Gregg v. Georgia*. The defendant McCleskey had implicitly read *Gregg* as a hypothesis that the new guided discretion laws might eliminate the old arbitrary and racially unjust death sentences, allowing the states a reasonable chance to experiment with these new laws. Thus, the argument now went, the experiment had failed. But Justice Powell's opinion in *McCleskey v. Kemp* reads *Gregg* the alternative way, as saying that the new guided discretion laws were the best possible legal structures American government could devise to eliminate the arbitrary and racially disparate outcomes, and because the death penalty was not per se unconstitutional, these laws were, even if imperfect, good enough.

SEE ALSO *Burger Court; Eighth Amendment; Furman v. Georgia, 408 U.S. 238 (1972); Gregg v. Georgia, 428 U.S. 153 (1976); Jury Nullification; McCleskey v. Kemp, 481 U.S. 279 (1987); Rehnquist Court; Roberts Court*

BIBLIOGRAPHY

Banner, Stuart. 2003. *The Death Penalty: An American History*. Cambridge, MA: Harvard University Press.

Carter Linda, and Ellen Kreitzberg. 2004. *Understanding Capital Punishment Law*. Newark, NJ: LexisNexis.

Death Penalty Information Center. 2008. "Facts About the Death Penalty." Available from http://www.deathpenaltyinfo.org/FactSheet.pdf

Eisenberg, Theodore; Stephen Garvey; and Martin T. Wells. 2001. "The Deadly Paradox of Capital Jurors." *Southern California Law Review* 74: 371–397.

Robert Weisberg

CAPITOL SQUARE REVIEW AND ADVISORY BOARD V. PINETTE, 515 U.S. 753 (1995)

In *Capitol Square Review and Advisory Board v. Pinette*, 515 U.S. 753 (1995), the U.S. Supreme Court considered whether the establishment clause was violated by the display of a Latin cross by the Ku Klux Klan on Capitol Square, a state-owned plaza around the statehouse in Columbus, Ohio, that is traditionally open to the public. The state had denied the Klan a permit, because it believed that allowing erection of the cross would violate the establishment clause of the First Amendment to the U.S. Constitution. The Klan sued, claiming a violation of its free speech rights.

The Supreme Court had previously decided, in *Lamb's Chapel v. Center Moriches Union Free School District*, 508 U.S. 384 (1993) and *Widmar v. Vincent*, 454 U.S. 263 (1981), that the government is required by the free speech clause of the First Amendment to allow religious speech in public forums on equal terms with secular speech and that it does not violate the establishment clause when it does so.

Those cases dealt with the exclusion of religious activities and groups from public school facilities that were held open to secular groups and activities, however, and it was unclear whether this rule would still apply with respect to an unattended religious symbol in close proximity to the seat of government. The state argued that such proximity created a perception that the cross was sponsored by the state, thereby violating the "endorsement test," which requires courts to decide whether a governmental act impermissibly conveys to the reasonable observer a message of government approval of a particular religion or of religion in general.

The Court concluded that the state had violated the Klan members' free speech rights, because the establishment clause did not prohibit the cross display and therefore could not justify the denial of the permit. A plurality composed of Chief Justice William Rehnquist and Justices Antonin Scalia, Anthony Kennedy, and Clarence Thomas categorically stated that purely private religious speech in a true and properly administered public forum cannot violate the establishment clause, no matter what the proximity to the traditional seat of government or the likelihood of "mistaken" perceptions of government endorsement of religion.

Justice Sandra Day O'Connor, by contrast, stated in a concurrence joined by Justices David Souter and Stephen Breyer that she would have applied the endorsement test, rather than the plurality's categorical rule, even in the context of private religious speech in a public forum. Still, she agreed with the Court's result because she thought that no inference of endorsement arose in this case. Because reasonable observers are presumed to know that Capitol Square is a public forum, open to all comers, she explained, no perception of religious endorsement would arise from the city's decision to allow the Klan to use the space on the same terms as all other groups.

On the same day it decided *Capitol Square*, the Court decided *Rosenberger v. Rector and Visitors of the University of Virginia*, 515 U.S. 819 (1995), which extended the public forum doctrine beyond actual physical forums, holding that the University of Virginia could not deny reimbursement of expenses to a student organization for a religious publication when it allowed reimbursement for virtually all other sorts of student publications.

SEE ALSO *Establishment Clause; First Amendment; Public Forum*

BIBLIOGRAPHY

Choper, Jesse H. 2000. "A Century of Religious Freedom." *California Law Review* 88: 1709–1741.

Lopez, Alberto B. 2003. "Equal Access and the Public Forum: *Pinette*'s Imbalance of Free Speech and Establishment." *Baylor Law Review* 55: 167–224.

Paulsen, Michael Stokes. 1996. "A Funny Thing Happened on the Way to the Limited Public Forum: Unconstitutional Conditions on 'Equal Access' for Religious Speakers and Groups." *University of California Davis Law Review* 29(3): 653–717.

B. Jessie Hill

CARDOZO, BENJAMIN N.
1870–1938

Benjamin Nathan Cardozo was distinguished by his personality, erudition, literary style, and his impact on torts and civil law. He was one of the first jurists to analyze judicial decision making from a realist perspective. He was arguably the most famous state court judge of the twentieth century and his work is included in virtually all case textbooks on civil law. Although he served only briefly on the Supreme Court, Cardozo influenced a number of important decisions and helped transform it into a modern Court.

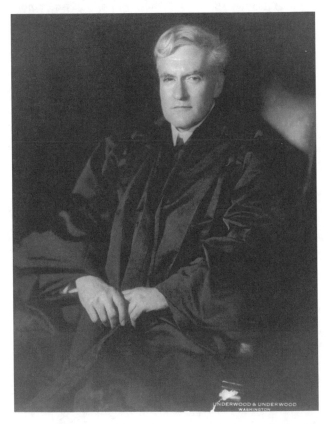

Supreme Court Justice Benjamin N. Cardozo. *Despite earning a seat on the nation's highest court, Cardozo is most regarded for his tenure on the New York Court of Appeals, where he authored numerous decisions regarding civil law. To the Supreme Court, the justice brought his moderately progressive legal outlook, helping the court respond to the changes of the twentieth century.* **THE LIBRARY OF CONGRESS**

THE EARLY AND MIDDLE YEARS

Cardozo was born in New York City in 1870 to a long-standing distinguished Sephardic Jewish family. His father, Albert Cardozo, was a well-known lawyer and Democratic politician who served on the New York State Supreme Court, but had to resign in light of charges of graft and nepotism. Many observers think that in order to compensate for that family embarrassment, the son led a life of extreme probity and largely quiet seclusion marked by indulgence in the habit of reading. As a judge, he demanded honorable behavior, especially from lawyers.

Publicly, Cardozo was extremely self-effacing and modest though, privately, self-assured. Bookish by nature, and a brilliant student at Columbia College and then Columbia Law School, he remained attached to universities and to academic faculty. He is probably the only Supreme Court judge who has been widely described as angelic and limned by Oliver Wendell Holmes as "a great and beautiful spirit" (Nathan 1939–1940, p. 32).

Cardozo worked for twenty-three years as a successful litigator in commercial law. He was elected to the New York State Supreme Court (1914) but almost immediately thereafter he was unanimously requested to fill a vacancy by the highest court in New York, the appeals court, then the chief commercial court in the United States. In 1926 he was appointed as chief judge.

Cardozo's greatness derives primarily from the period he served on the New York Court of Appeals. It was the happiest time of his life. He lived with most of the other judges in the same hotel and it was their practice to have meals together. Cardozo cherished this collegiality and this carried over to the judicial decision-making process. For the first three years of the Cardozo court, 80 percent of the 475 decisions that he wrote for the seven-member Court were unanimous.

Cardozo was a pragmatic moderate, with slight progressive leanings. His reputation was greatest in the area of tort reform. The two most famous cases with which he is identified both involve liability, although their results are not ideologically parallel, giving evidence to the idea that Cardozo judged pragmatically, largely based on the facts of the case and not according to some ideological platform.

In *MacPherson v. Buick Motor Co.*, 217 N.Y. 382, 111 N.E. 1050 (1916), Cardozo revised the central idea of privity, or direct liability. Previously, manufacturers were liable only to the middlemen to whom they sold a product, not to the consumer who eventually bought the product. Arguing that automobiles carried with them great risk and danger, Cardozo built on previous cases holding that manufacturers had special liability for items like poisons; thus the automobile manufacturer had a level of responsibility to the consumer. This decision marked a major transformation of the idea of liability.

The second case, *Palsgraf v. Long Island Railroad Co.*, 248 N.Y. 339, 162 N.E. 99 (1928), is a classic that almost all serious American law students have been reading for more than half a century. In helping a man board the train, the agents of the railroad accidentally dislodged a covered package containing dynamite, which then exploded, leading to injury to one of the passengers waiting on the platform. Cardozo ruled that the issue was not one of proximate cause but of "forseeability"—whether the railroad agents could have been expected to know what their actions might have resulted in.

As a pragmatic judge, Cardozo did not see himself as creating abstract principles that required total obedience. On the contrary, in later decisions Cardozo occasionally voted to limit the liability of corporations toward third parties in cases where foreseeability was less important than proximate cause.

A second major contribution by Cardozo was increasing the accountability of fiduciaries, those responsible for the disposition of money that is entrusted to them. He argued that fiduciary obligations required strict enforcement. Here, too, he built on the principle of honor.

In addition to his Court decisions, Cardozo was well known for his philosophical writings, the most eminent being *The Nature of the Judicial Process* (1921). This book was drawn from a series of widely acclaimed public lectures at Yale University. Originally designed as an insight into how judges actually decide cases, the book is one of the early attacks on the concept of formalism, the idea that judges simply apply a formal doctrine of laws to the case at hand. Rather, he argues that the judge has to use discretion in dealing with four major forces: logic and analogy, history (precedent) and evolution, customs and tradition, and especially public policy or the welfare of society. Although he certainly did not intend to abandon existing rules and directions, Cardozo's approach encouraged rethinking even core constitutional values such as liberty and property.

Almost all observers make reference to Cardozo's literary style, for many years an object of adulation, but much later it received more mixed reviews, some claiming that it is archaic and not a little ambiguous. Part of this reflects Cardozo's jurisprudence; he did not write clear ideological formulae but rather judged from a multiplicity of perspectives. No one can deny that some of his writings are gems. In arguing for allowing evidence technically obtained in an illegal fashion, Cardozo set up a straw man: "The criminal is to go free because the constable has blundered" (*People v. Defore*, 242 N.Y. 21 [1926]). This expression both establishes guilt and renders the illegal gathering of evidence as accidental and trivial. It is not only pithy and prosaic, but persuasively tendentious.

THE SUPREME COURT YEARS

Although he had been passed over before, by 1932 Cardozo's stellar reputation made him the logical choice to replace the legendary Justice Oliver Wendell Holmes on the Supreme Court. Cardozo's time on the Supreme Court was trying. He was not comfortable with the adversarial nature of the Court and, one can assume, by the presence of an outright anti-Semite, James McReynolds. The only colleague with whom he had a reasonably close relationship was Harlan F. Stone, although it did not match the relationships he had on the New York court. Cardozo described Washington, D.C., as a prison and a place of exile.

On the Supreme Court Cardozo had to address a greater diversity of issues than he had on the New York court. He is primarily identified with one civil liberties case and with a series of cases testing the constitutionality of several of the New Deal programs and agencies.

The Court that Cardozo joined was primarily a conservative Court held captive by a nineteenth-century set of economic beliefs. From January 1935 to March 1937, the Supreme Court consistently ruled unconstitutional New Deal programs that came before it for several reasons: freedom of contract, substantive due process, equal protection of the law, the commerce clause, and states' rights. Generally, Cardozo allowed both the legislative and executive branches the right to make policy, especially in a crisis—positions he had taken on the Court of Appeals. However, he took these positions on a case-by-case basis rather than as pure ideology. Thus he opposed the national government regulating some intrastate commerce, as in *Schechter Poultry Corp. v. United States*, 295 U.S. 495 (1935). An insight into Cardozo's deference to legislatures and his sense of limiting judicial bias is a comment to Justice Stone about principled young men who were conscientious objectors: "I think it is oppressive to make them submit to [mandatory military science courses] in these times of peace, though I am satisfied the state has the power to be oppressive if it chooses" (Polenberg 1997, p. 131).

Cardozo along with Justices Stone and Louis Brandeis were the minority that supported the New Deal programs, although in some cases Cardozo was the sole dissenter. In 1937 the Court came around to that position via the switch of two members (Chief Justice Charles E. Hughes and Justice Owen J. Roberts). Cardozo's most forceful and systematic analysis of the need for the law to accommodate to a changing world is found in an unpublished, but well circulated, influential opinion in the Minnesota Mortgage Moratorium case: *Home Building and Loan v. Blaisdell*, 290 U.S. 398 (1934). Justice could not be divorced from the changing realities of (economic) life.

Cardozo's record on civil liberties is mixed. He developed a concept of ordered liberty, according to which the various protections in the Bill of Rights could be ranked. Most fundamental was freedom of speech. Cardozo's powerful opinion—eventually unpublished because it was largely included in the majority opinion—in *Grosjean v. American Press Co.*, 297 U.S. 233 (1936), helped strike down a tax on newspapers.

One of the critical civil liberties issues of the period was incorporation—whether the Bill of Rights should be binding on the states via the Fourteenth Amendment. For Cardozo, freedoms of the First Amendment as well as the right to counsel were essential and thus binding. However, some of the restrictions on the police like search and seizure were not as fundamental. In one of the most famous cases for which he wrote the opinion of the Court, *Palko v. Connecticut*, 302 U.S. 319 (1937), he denied that double jeopardy was one of those fundamental rights, a position later overturned by *Benton v. Maryland*, 395 U.S. 784 (1969). Generally, for criminal law, Cardozo did not want to free people for whom evidence was clear that they were guilty, hence his reticence about double jeopardy and the exclusionary rule.

Cardozo's life was cut short in 1938 by a series of heart attacks after only six years on the Supreme Court. Given his reputation, the fact that the Court had switched over to his way of thinking about economic and social issues, and his pleasant demeanor, one can imagine that he might have become a more dominant figure on the Supreme Court had he lived as long as Holmes.

SEE ALSO *Constitutional Interpretation; Hughes Court; Legal Realism*

BIBLIOGRAPHY

Cardozo, Benjamin N. 1921. *The Nature of the Judicial Process.* New Haven, CT: Yale University Press.

Cardozo, Benjamin N. 1928. *The Paradoxes of Legal Science.* New York: Columbia University Press.

Holland, Henry M., Jr. 1963. "Mr. Justice Cardozo and the New Deal Court." *Journal of Public Law* 12: 383–407.

Kaufman, Andrew L. 1998. *Cardozo.* Cambridge, MA: Harvard University Press.

Nathan, Edgar J., Jr. 1939–1940. "Benjamin Nathan Cardozo." *American Jewish Year Book.* Vol. 41. Harry Schneiderman, ed. Philadelphia: The Jewish Publication Society of America.

Polenberg, Richard. 1997. *The World of Benjamin Cardozo: Personal Values and the Judicial Process.* Cambridge, MA: Harvard University Press.

Alan M. Fisher

CARSWELL, G. HARROLD

SEE *Nixon, Richard.*

CARTER V. CARTER COAL, 298 U.S. 238 (1936)

In *Carter v. Carter Coal Co.*, 298 U.S. 238 (1936), the U.S. Supreme Court struck down key provisions of the Bituminous Coal Conservation Act of 1935, a New Deal law intended to salvage federal regulation of the coal industry following an earlier Court decision striking down the National Recovery Administration (NRA). The five-justice majority found that: (1) the regulation of the wages and hours of workers involved in coal production exceeded congressional power under the commerce clause; and (2) the delegation of the power to set wages and hours to a commission of industry representatives violated the due process clause. The doctrine the majority relied upon was nearing the end of its lifespan, however. *Carter* proved to be a closing statement to an era of judicially enforced constitutional limitations on the power of Congress to pursue economic regulation.

Congress passed the Bituminous Coal Conservation Act (also known as the Guffey-Snyder Act) during the New Deal's "Second Hundred Days," during which President Franklin D. Roosevelt and his congressional allies sought to resurrect parts of the NRA following its demise at the hands of the Court in *Schechter Poultry Corp. v. United States*, 295 U.S. 495 (1935). In passing this "little NRA" law, Congress hoped to stabilize a sector of the economy ravaged by the Depression. It created a National Bituminous Coal Commission, designed to protect collective bargaining rights and oversee district boards empowered to set prices and regulate workers' wages and hours. Hoping to avoid a repeat of *Schechter*, the statute's framers included detailed findings on the relation between coal production and the national economy as constitutional justification for the law based on Congress's commerce power.

On May 18, 1936, the Court issued its decision. Written by Justice George Sutherland, a conservative stalwart of the Court, the majority opinion offered a censorious lecture to New Dealers on the constitutional limitations on congressional power to regulate the economy. Sutherland dismissed the language in the statute's preamble in which Congress sought to justify regulation of the coal industry as necessary to protect the general welfare of the nation. The mere fact that a problem is national in scope, that state-level reforms would be insufficient, cannot be grounds for extending federal power beyond the specifically delegated provisions of the Constitution, he argued. "Nothing is more certain than that beneficent aims, however great or well directed, can never serve in lieu of constitutional power." To assume otherwise, would be to trample on state sovereignty, "since every addition to the national legislative power to some extent detracts from or invades the power of the states."

With the stakes so defined, Sutherland turned to the critical issue of the case: the scope of the commerce power. Following the reasoning of conservative doctrine on this question that dated to the nineteenth century and cases such as *United States v. E. C. Knight Co.*, 156 U.S. 1 (1895) (recently reaffirmed in *Schechter*), he articulated a limited conception of commerce. Under this interpretation, manufacturing—even manufacturing with the clear intent to move the manufactured goods through interstate commerce—is local in nature and therefore distinct from commerce. Commerce involves "intercourse for the purpose of trade" and does not include activities that have only an "indirect" affect on this intercourse. So regardless of the extent of the coal industry and its effect on the national economy, mining, in and of itself, is not commerce. Therefore, the regulation of labor relations in the coal industry—wages, hours, working conditions, bargaining rights—could not be effected through the commerce power. In the area of production, any regulation of the relationship between an employer and an employee "is purely local in character."

In addition to the commerce power holding, Sutherland also found the delegation of power to set wages to a commission composed of members of the coal industry constitutionally problematic. Granting the power of regulation to a group of private individuals is "an intolerable and unconstitutional interference with personal liberty and private property." Such an "arbitrary" delegation is "clearly a denial of rights safeguarded by the due process clause of the Fifth Amendment." Furthermore, the majority found the price-fixing provisions so closely connected with the constitutionally faulty wage provisions that they too must fall.

In a separate opinion, Chief Justice Charles Evans Hughes concurred with the majority that the wage and hour regulations were unconstitutional, but dissented from its holding on the price provisions. The price regulations, he concluded, were separable from the constitutionally flawed wage and hour regulations and should be upheld.

Justice Benjamin N. Cardozo, joined by justices Louis D. Brandeis and Harlan Fiske Stone, wrote a sweeping dissent. Cardozo began by defending the constitutionality of the price provisions. He attacked the majority's narrow definition of commerce, particularly the formalistic distinction between activities that have "direct" versus "indirect" relations to interstate commerce. "A great principle of constitutional law," he warned, "is not susceptible of comprehensive statement in an adjective." He then concluded that judgment on the wage regulation was premature. Since there had been no effort to enforce the wage regulations, any perceived injury resulting from these provisions was purely anticipatory and therefore not properly before the Court.

In conjunction with a long string of decisions striking down government regulation efforts, *Carter* fueled the movement to reform the Supreme Court that would culminate in Roosevelt's Court-packing plan of 1937. In the face of these political challenges and an increasingly untenable commerce clause doctrine, the Court would abandon Sutherland's narrow interpretation of the commerce power in *NLRB v. Jones and Laughlin Steel Corp.*, 301 U.S. 1 (1937) and adopt a far more deferential posture toward congressional power under the commerce clause. When Congress reenacted the Bituminous Coal Conservation Act without the labor provisions in 1937, the Court cited Cardozo's *Carter* dissent and upheld the law (*Sunshine Anthracite Coal Co. v. Adkins,* 310 U.S. 381 [1940]). By the time of *Wickard v. Filburn,* 317 U.S. 111 (1942), it appeared that the Court was willing to recognize that practically any economic activity that Congress saw fit to regulate could be brought beneath the umbrella of interstate commerce. This position would hold until, more than half a century later, the Rehnquist Court began to reassert judicial oversight over the commerce power.

SEE ALSO *Commerce Clause; Hughes Court; New Deal and the Economy; New Deal and the Regulation of Business and Commerce; Roosevelt, Franklin D.*

BIBLIOGRAPHY

Cushman, Barry. 1998. *Rethinking the New Deal Court: The Structure of a Constitutional Revolution.* New York: Oxford University Press.

Cushman, Barry. 2000. "Formalism and Realism in Commerce Clause Jurisprudence." *University of Chicago Law Review* 67: 1089–1150.

Johnson, James P. 1979. *The Politics of Soft Coal: The Bituminous Industry from World War I through the New Deal.* Urbana: University of Illinois Press.

Leuchtenburg, William E. 1995. *The Supreme Court Reborn: The Constitutional Revolution in the Age of Roosevelt.* New York: Oxford University Press.

National Labor Relations Board. 1938. *The Effect of Labor Relations in the Bituminous Coal Industry Upon Interstate Commerce.* Washington, DC: U.S. Government Printing Office.

Christopher W. Schmidt

CASE OR CONTROVERSY

A case or controversy is the only kind of legal dispute that the Supreme Court and other Article III tribunals may hear. Article III, in fact, specifies two sets of cases or controversies to which the power of federal judges may extend. The first set, which consists of four specific kinds of cases or controversies, pertains to the powers of the federal government. Of these four, Article III specifies that the federal judicial power may extend to "all" of the "cases" for three of them—those arising under the Constitution, treaties, and laws of the United States; affecting ambassadors, other public ministers, and consuls; and involving admiralty and maritime jurisdiction. For the remaining kind of legal dispute in this first category, Article III simply says that the federal judicial power may extend to "controversies" in which the United States is a party. The second set of cases or controversies to which the federal judicial power may extend consists of five kinds of "controversies"—those between two or more states; between a state and citizens of another state; between citizens of different states; between citizens of the same state claiming land in other states; and between a state or its citizens and "foreign States, Citizens, or Subjects."

Throughout U.S. history, the Supreme Court has claimed—and exercised—the authority to clarify the purpose and meaning of Article III's specification of cases or controversies. According to the Court (and most commentators), this specification imposes substantial limitations on the federal judicial power. The particular limits which the Court has identified as being imposed on its power by Article III are set forth in its case law on justiciability, a technical term referring to the requisite elements which a case or controversy must satisfy in order to be heard by an Article III court. The purpose of these requirements, as the Court repeatedly has acknowledged, is to fix the proper relationship between Article III courts and the other branches, as well as the states. The Court's recognition of, and compliance with, these requirements constitutes one of its most significant ways, if not the most significant way, it attempts to restrict itself from overstepping the boundaries of its power and improperly aggrandizing itself at the expense of the powers of the other branches or the states. The case or controversy requirement is essential to the maintenance and protection of separation of powers, particularly the careful checks and balances set forth in the Constitution.

The Court has recognized that justiciability encompasses several basic principles. First, Article III courts may not decide advisory opinions. They must decide actual cases or controversies, not hypothetical cases or controversies posed by the other branches or the states. Second, Article III tribunals may only hear disputes that are ripe. In order for a legal dispute to be ripe, the plaintiff must allege real harm or threat of imminent harm. Generally, a case is not ripe where, on the facts, significant events which are necessary to sharpen the issues have not yet occurred. A case will be dismissed as moot unless there exists an actual, live controversy between the parties at all stages of the litigation, including on appeal. The third major component of the case or controversy requirement is standing, for which there must be real or genuine harm alleged, injury that the defendant caused, and injury that is redressable. Moreover, the Court has articulated, or identified, several prudential standing requirements that Congress may override through statute: First, a party generally may assert only his or her own rights and cannot raise the claims of third parties not before the Court. Second, a plaintiff generally may not sue as a taxpayer who shares a grievance in common with other taxpayers. Third, a party must raise a claim within the zone of interests protected by the statute in question. Last, the Court has clarified which kinds of questions federal courts may not decide; subjects, or issues, which the Court determines are left to the final, non-reviewable discretion of the other branches are called political questions.

The Court has suggested that some of these principles derive directly from the Constitution while some are based on its judgments about what is required for prudent judicial administration. Some justiciability doctrines, such as standing, have both constitutional and prudential limits. In other instances, the Court has not announced whether it views the limitation as constitutional or prudential (though scholars generally treat at least one component of the political question doctrine—whether the Constitution vests final or sole discretion over a subject matter in a non-judicial branch—as constitutionally derived.)

The Court has further elaborated on the benefits of the case or controversy requirements. To begin with, it has said that these requirements help to define the basic judicial role in the U.S. system of government; they determine when it is appropriate for the federal courts to review matters and when it is necessary to defer to the other branches. Second, the requirements limiting the kinds of cases which federal courts may decide help to conserve judicial resources, allowing federal courts to focus their attention on the matters which most deserve its attention. Third, the case or controversy requirements are designed to improve judicial decision-making by providing the federal courts with concrete rather than abstract controversies and thus ensure that adverse parties, with a real stake in the outcome of the litigation, have the motivation and need to make the best legal arguments for their respective positions.

In spite of the Supreme Court's ample case law on justiciability, it has studiously refrained from clarifying some of its aspects, and both the Congress and many scholars maintain that the Congress actually has as much, if not more, authority than the Court (or other Article III tribunals) to determine the actual substantial limitations imposed on federal judicial power by the case or controversy requirement. Indeed, one major question, still widely debated among scholars (and in Congress) is the precise scope of congressional power to restrict the

jurisdiction of the federal courts, such as stripping them of any power to hear abortion or school prayer cases.

Another significant question is whether Article III's specification of the nine kinds of cases or controversies to which the federal judicial power may extend sets forth a mandatory minimum, or maximum, for the types of legal disputes that the Court and other Article III tribunals must decide. Moreover, scholars continue to dispute the extent to which constitutional provisions outside of Article III, such as the Fifth and Fourteenth Amendment's due process clauses, either restrict the scope of congressional power to regulate federal jurisdiction or impose additional obligations to those set forth in Article III on the kinds of legal disputes that Article III courts must hear. A related question pertains to how far the President alone, or the President and Congress together, may restrict people held in federal custody from having recourse to habeas corpus or any access to federal courts to challenge the conditions of, or grounds for, their confinement. This question has taken on added importance in the aftermath of the terrorist attacks against the United States on September 11, 2001. Some, if not much, about what is known about the case or controversy requirement may be clarified further—or left open for debate, as it has so often been in the past, within the political process—as a result of a series of cases challenging policies formulated by President George W. Bush acting alone, and in conjunction with the Congress, to substantially, or altogether, restrict access to the federal courts by people captured or held in the custody of the United States as the result of military actions in Afghanistan and Iraq.

SEE ALSO *Advisory Opinions; Article III; Mootness; Political Question Doctrine; Ripeness; Separation of Powers*

BIBLIOGRAPHY

Chemerinsky, Erwin. 2003. *Federal Jurisdiction.* New York: Aspen Publishers.

Michael J. Gerhardt

CASTLE ROCK V. GONZALES, 545 U.S. 748 (2005)

In *Castle Rock v. Gonzales,* 545 U.S. 748 (2005), the Supreme Court considered the issue of whether a person has a constitutional property entitlement to police enforcement of a state-granted restraining order, under the procedural component of the due process clause of the Fourteenth Amendment. In a seven-to-two decision, the Court found that the respondent, who held a domestic-violence restraining order against her estranged husband, did not have a property interest in police enforcement of that order.

Respondent Jessica Gonzales brought a claim against Castle Rock, Colorado, after the police failed to enforce a restraining order against her husband. A Colorado judge had granted Gonzales a restraining order, which commanded her estranged husband not to "molest or disturb the peace of [respondent] or of any child," and to remain at least one hundred yards from the family home at all times. The preprinted form informed law enforcement officials that they "shall use every reasonable means to enforce this restraining order," and that they "shall arrest, or, if an arrest would be impractical under the circumstances, seek a warrant for the arrest of the restrained person" if they have probable cause to suspect a violation of the order's terms.

According to the complaint, on June 22, 1999, at approximately 5:00 P.M., Gonzales's husband took the three daughters from outside the family home in violation of the order. Over the next eight hours, Gonzales repeatedly asked the Castle Rock Police Department to enforce the restraining order; however, the police merely postponed their response each time. At 3:20 A.M., the husband drove to the police headquarters and opened fire on police officers, who shot back and killed him. Inside the husband's truck they discovered the bodies of the three daughters, whom he had killed earlier that night.

Gonzales then filed suit under 42 U.S.C. § 1983, alleging that Castle Rock had deprived her of due process because its police department had "an official policy or custom of failing to respond properly to complaints of restraining order violations." The defendants moved to dismiss for failure to state a claim. The district court granted their motions, concluding that Gonzales had neither a substantive nor procedural due process right to enforcement of the restraining order. On appeal, a Tenth Circuit panel affirmed the rejection of a substantive due process claim, but held that Gonzales had a valid procedural due process claim. On rehearing en banc, a divided Tenth Circuit reached the same disposition.

Castle Rock appealed to the Supreme Court arguing that the procedural due process claim is not sanctioned by, and would effectively overrule, *DeShaney v. Winnebago County Department of Social Services*, 489 U.S. 189 (1989), in which the Court previously held that the substantive component of the due process clause does not impose on the government an affirmative obligation to prevent private-party violence. In response, Gonzales argued that the restraining order contained mandatory language, which commanded that the order be enforced by the police officers. Because Gonzales and her daughters relied on the state's promises of enforcement of the restraining order to go about their daily lives, she had a property interest in the enforcement of the order.

The Supreme Court reversed the Tenth Circuit's ruling. The key issue was whether Colorado law gave Gonzales a right to enforcement of the restraining order. Writing for the majority, Justice Antonin Scalia initially stated that this was not an issue on which it would defer to the Tenth Circuit's holding. The Court then found that no law, even if it is written in mandatory terms, creates an "entitlement" because law enforcement officers always have discretion in enforcing the law. As the Court stated, "a well established tradition of police discretion has long coexisted with apparently mandatory arrest statutes." Thus, even where state law mandates police protection, this does not give rise to a protected property interest as a matter of procedural due process.

Moreover, even if the statute was mandatory, the Court stated that it commands one of two options: make an arrest, or seek an arrest warrant if making an arrest is impractical. Because the second option is merely a vague enforcement procedure and not an end in itself, the Court determined that the statute did not give rise to an entitlement. Gonzales's difficulty in specifying the precise action that the police were required to take further bolstered the majority's argument. Furthermore, the Court reasoned that even if the statute mandated a nondiscretionary duty on the part of the police, Colorado had not necessarily given Gonzales an entitlement to the restraining order's enforcement. Criminal law generally serves broad public ends, not private ends, and it was not clear that the Colorado legislature had intended otherwise.

Lastly, the majority indicated that even if Colorado had created an entitlement to police enforcement of a restraining order, it is not a property entitlement protected by the due process clause because it lacked ascertainable monetary value. Also, because this type of property interest would arise incidentally out of government action taken against a third party, it did not constitute a property entitlement.

Writing for the concurrence, Justice David Souter stated that Gonzales's claim should be denied because she asserted "a property interest in a state-mandated process in and of itself." Because Gonzales claimed a property right in the procedures that the police follow to enforce the restraining order, it was not an adequate basis for a finding of property entitlement.

Writing for the dissent, Justice John Paul Stevens first discussed the issue of whether the Colorado statute created the functional equivalent of a private contract by giving Gonzales an entitlement to mandatory police protection. The Court, he asserted, should have deferred to the Tenth Circuit's construction of Colorado law, or certified the issue to the Colorado Supreme Court.

The dissent also criticized the majority's finding that Colorado law gave the police discretion in enforcing the restraining order. According to Justice Stevens, the mandatory arrest laws were passed by the Colorado legislature specifically in response to police under-enforcement in the context of domestic violence. Thus, the very purpose of the laws was to counter police resistance to arrests in domestic violence cases by removing police discretion.

Moreover, Justice Stevens disagreed with the majority's argument that the restraining order did not create an entitlement because it did not specify the precise means of enforcement. As he asserted, "our cases have never required the object of an entitlement to be some mechanistic, unitary thing." He also found that the restraining order was not aimed at protecting the public at large; rather, it was aimed specifically at protecting individuals who held the order.

Finally, the dissent argued that the restraining order created a property interest for Gonzales, which was consistent with the Court's precedent. Police enforcement of a restraining order was a concrete guarantee on which Gonzales had reasonably relied. As such, the dissent found that Gonzales had a property entitlement in the enforcement of the restraining order.

SEE ALSO *DeShaney v. Winnebago County Dept. of Social Services, 489 U.S. 189 (1989); Procedural Due Process; Violence Against Women*

BIBLIOGRAPHY

Hasanbasic, Ryan C. 2007. "City of Castle Rock v. Gonzales: The Supreme Court Goes to Great Lengths to Ensure Police Discretion, but at What Cost?" *Stetson Law Review* 36(3): 881–921.

Roederer, Christopher J. 2006. "Another Case in Lochner's Legacy, the Court's Assault on New Property: The Right to the Mandatory Enforcement of a Restraining Order is a 'Sham,' 'Nullity,' and 'Cruel Deception.'" *Drake Law Review* 54(2): 321–369.

"The Supreme Court, 2004 Term: C. Due Process: 1. Scope of Procedural Due Process Protection—Property Interests in Police Enforcement." 2005. *Harvard Law Review* 119(1): 208–218.

Susanna Y. Chung

CENTRAL BANK V. FIRST INTERSTATE BANK, 511 U.S. 164 (1994)

The five-to-four decision of the U.S. Supreme Court in *Central Bank of Denver, N.A. v. First Interstate Bank of Denver, N.A.*, 511 U.S. 164 (1994) held that no private right of action should be implied under section 10(b) of the Securities Exchange Act of 1934 against persons who aid or abet a securities fraud. The majority's opinion was based on a strict construction of the Securities Exchange Act, and was justified on several grounds. Since cases based upon section 10(b) and Rule 10b-5 thereunder had been judicially implied and not crafted as a civil liability provision by Congress, the Court determined that it should interpret the statute narrowly. Congress did not mention aiding and abetting in section 10(b), so it should not be implied. Also, in the Court's view, litigation under the antifraud provisions presented a danger of vexatiousness beyond that of other litigation. Although the statute prohibits "any person, directly or indirectly," from engaging in certain fraudulent acts in connection with the purchase or sale of a security, the majority did not believe this language imposed aiding-and-abetting liability. According to the majority opinion, when Congress wished to impose liability it knew how to do so, and had done so in statutes other than the Securities Exchange Act.

The dissent argued that in hundreds of judicial and administrative proceedings in every circuit, the federal courts and the Securities and Exchange Commission (SEC) had concluded that aiders and abettors are subject to liability under section 10(b), such established precedent should not be disturbed, and the aiding-abetting theory did not have such deleterious consequences that it should be dispensed with on policy grounds. The SEC had argued that an aiding-and-abetting cause of action deters secondary actors from contributing to fraudulent activities and ensured that defrauded plaintiffs are made whole. The majority dismissed this policy argument as insufficient to override its interpretation of the text and structure of the Securities Exchange Act.

The leading case based on aiding and abetting prior to the *Central Bank* case was *Brennan v. Midwestern Union Life Insurance Co.*, 417 F.2d 147 (7th Cir. 1969), *cert. denied*, 397 U.S. 989 (1970). In that case, the Seventh Circuit stated that a secondary defendant may be liable for giving active and knowing assistance to a third party engaged in fraudulent activities violating the securities laws. After the *Brennan* case, numerous district and circuit courts and the SEC utilized aiding-and-abetting theory in a wide variety of cases, many involving accountants and other professionals. As a general matter, it was believed that aiding-and-abetting liability required the existence of an independent wrong, actual knowledge of the wrong, and the rendering of substantial assistance to a primary violator (see *Roberts v. Peat, Marwick, Mitchell & Co.*, 857 F.2d 646, 652 [9th Cir. 1988], *cert. denied*, 493 U.S. 1002 [1989]). As the dissent pointed out, in *Central Bank*, the petitioner assumed the existence of a right of action against aiders and abettors, but sought review on the issues of whether an indenture trustee could be liable as an aider and abettor absent breach of the indenture agreement, and whether recklessness satisfied the scienter requirement of section 10(b).

After the *Central Bank* decision, two questions remained open. First, could the SEC maintain an action for aiding and abetting, and second, could third parties ever be liable as participants in a fraudulent scheme. Doubts as to whether the SEC could use aiding and abetting as an enforcement theory prompted Congress to amend the Securities Exchange Act in 1998 to authorize the SEC to bring actions in the courts against aiders and abettors for injunctions or money penalties. Although this statutory amendment did not allow for claims against aiders and abettors in private civil cases, a question as to whether secondary actors could be included in such cases persisted because of dicta in the majority opinion in *Central Bank* that secondary actors are not always free from liability. "Any person or entity, including a lawyer, accountant, or bank, who employs a manipulative device or makes a material misstatement (or omission) on which a purchaser or seller of securities relies may be liable as a primary violator under 10b-5, assuming all the requirements for primary liability under Rule 10b-5 are met." This issue continues to be litigated in the circuit courts, where there is now a split as to "scheme liability" in Rule 10b-5 cases.

SEE ALSO *Securities and Exchange Commission*

BIBLIOGRAPHY

Hazen, Thomas Lee. 2006. *Principles of Securities Regulation.* 2nd edition. St. Paul, MN: Thomson/West.

Steinberg, Marc I. 2007. *Understanding Securities Law.* 4th edition. Albany, NY: Matthew Bender.

Roberta S. Karmel

CEREMONIAL DEISM

Ceremonial deism may be described as nonsectarian, nonproselytizing, public recognition of God that is ceremonial and traditional. Arguably, the traditional and ceremonial aspects of such recognition, combined with its minimally theological presentation, minimizes its religious impact. The U.S. Supreme Court has never recognized or defined the concept of ceremonial deism in a majority opinion, but a number of justices (and lower courts) have recognized the concept. Common themes are either that it is a *de minimis* constitutional harm or that it is not a constitutional harm at all because of the historical traditions and practices that allegedly support a ceremonial recognition of God. Ceremonial deism is therefore viewed as beyond the reach of the establishment clause. There are, however, strong arguments suggesting that at least some of what courts call ceremonial deism is not so at all, and that some of the traditions that courts use to support ceremonial deism are primarily fabricated or taken out of context.

Perhaps the most important question is what counts as ceremonial deism, for the greater the breadth of the category the more that is at stake. Defining ceremonial deism is not an easy task. Various justices have discussed it, however, and Justice William J. Brennan, Jr., attempted to define it in his dissenting opinion in *Lynch v. Donnelly*, 465 U.S. 668 (1984):

> Finally, we have noted that government cannot be completely prohibited from recognizing in its public actions the religious beliefs and practices of the American people as an aspect of our national history and culture. While I remain uncertain about these questions, I would suggest that such practices as the designation of "In God We Trust" as our national motto, or the references to God contained in the Pledge of Allegiance to the flag can best be understood, in Dean Rostow's apt phrase, as a form a "ceremonial deism," protected from Establishment Clause scrutiny chiefly because they have lost through rote repetition any significant religious content. Moreover, these references are uniquely suited to serve such wholly secular purposes as solemnizing public occasions, or inspiring commitment to meet some national challenge in a manner that simply could not be fully served in our culture if government were limited to purely nonreligious phrases. The practices by which the government has long acknowledged religion are therefore probably necessary to serve certain secular functions, and that necessity, coupled with their long history, gives those practices an essentially secular meaning. (citations omitted)

Brennan refers here to the 1962 Meiklejohn Lecture delivered by the legendary Yale Law School dean, Eugene V. Rostow, who most likely coined the term *ceremonial deism*. Rostow's use of the phrase was mentioned by the Harvard law professor Arthur E. Sutherland in a 1964 book review of Wilbur Katz's *Religion and American Constitutions*. It was this review that brought the term to Justice Brennan's attention.

As Justice Brennan suggests, oft-cited examples of ceremonial deism are "In God We Trust" on currency, references to God in patriotic songs, the reference to God made by court officers when calling court into session, legislative prayer, and the reference to God in the Pledge of Allegiance. The history of how the reference to God was added to the pledge (and the nature of a "pledge" itself), however, may make the pledge different from other forms of ceremonial deism.

Because of the various factors, such as the "longstanding traditions" that help define ceremonial deism, there is no clear answer as to where the boundary lies. Most would agree that "In God We Trust" on coinage is ceremonial deism, even if there is disagreement over whether ceremonial deism should be given any special status when such practices are challenged under the establishment clause. Yet whether the addition of the words "under God" to the pledge in 1954 is an example of ceremonial deism is far more controversial.

The Court has upheld the practice of legislative prayer and the display of certain religious symbols on the ground that they reflect longstanding traditions in the nation's (or a given locale's) history. The Court has not directly called these practices ceremonial deism, but commentators and lower courts have often done so. Whether the display of religious symbols would qualify as "ceremonial" is unclear, but the Court has upheld certain religious displays using analysis similar to that used in upholding legislative prayer.

In *Marsh v. Chambers*, 463 U.S. 783 (1983) the Court upheld the practice of having a chaplain paid by state funds deliver prayers at meetings of the Nebraska legislature. The Court relied on the long tradition of legislative prayer in the United States, and on the supposed longstanding and ubiquitous recognition of God in public life since the founding of the nation. The Court held—contrary to facts in the record—that the prayer in the Nebraska legislature was nonproselytizing and nonsectarian. Therefore, even though only Christian clergy had held the chaplaincy, the legislative prayer was declared constitutional. The Court did not subject the practice to the prevailing test under the establishment clause; that is, the Court carved out an exception to traditional establishment clause analysis for legislative prayer. It thus appears that the Court held that legislative prayer is ceremonial deism, though it did not rely on or define that term, and several justices dissented from the decision.

In *Lynch v. Donnelly* the Court used the "tradition" analysis to uphold a town's display of a crèche in a public park as part of a holiday display, and in *Van Orden v. Perry*, 545 U.S. 677 (2005) it used the same reasoning to uphold the display of a Ten Commandments monument on the Texas Capitol grounds. Neither opinion asserted that the relevant display was ceremonial deism, given the fact that neither display by itself was "ceremonial." The Court focused on the "longstanding tradition" of recognizing religion and the contexts of the displays to uphold these displays. In neither case, however, did the Court apply the standards generally used under the establishment clause. Thus, the Court's reliance on longstanding tradition and its failure to apply the generally applicable legal tests set potential precedents for exempting ceremonial deism—however defined—from the rules generally used under the establishment clause. Combined

with *Marsh v. Chambers*, these cases present the idea that there are certain practices and displays that are somehow different for establishment clause purposes because of their connection to religious traditions and, in the case of the displays, their physical context.

In *Elk Grove Unified School District v. Newdow*, 542 U.S. 1 (2004) Justice Sandra Day O'Connor and Chief Justice William Rehnquist filed concurring opinions, arguing that the Pledge of Allegiance is a form of ceremonial deism. Justice O'Connor's opinion relied upon and attempted to define the concept of ceremonial deism. She explored several factors that Justice Brennan raised in *Lynch*, concluding that some ceremonial recognition of God serves secular ends. She focused particularly on the history and ubiquity of the practice, the absence of worship or prayer, its nonsectarianism, and its minimal religious content. She argued that these factors militate in favor of upholding the pledge as a form of ceremonial deism. The case was disposed of on standing grounds, however, and a majority of the Court did not reach the establishment clause question.

A majority of the Court has yet to define ceremonial deism, and any definition will by its nature be underinclusive, overinclusive, or both. Yet it appears that some sorts of religious recognition by government will continue to be immune from challenge under traditional establishment clause standards. While the parameters remain unclear, the "tradition" approach is as close as the Court has come to providing a rationale for the differing standards applicable to ceremonial deism.

SEE ALSO *Establishment Clause; McCreary County v. American Civil Liberties Union of Kentucky, 545 U.S. 844 (2005); Ten Commandments; Van Orden v. Perry, 545 U.S. 677 (2005)*

BIBLIOGRAPHY

Arthur E. Sutherland. 1964. Review of Wilber G. Katz, *Religion and American Constitutions* (1963). *Indiana Law Journal* 40: 83, 86.

CASES

Elk Grove Unified School District v. Newdow, 542 U.S. 10 (2004).

Lynch v. Donnelly, 465 U.S. 668 (1984).

Marsh v. Chambers, 463 U.S. 783 (1983).

Van Orden v. Perry, 545 U.S. 677 (2005).

Frank S. Ravitch

CERTIORARI
SEE *Writ of Certiorari.*

CHAMBERS V. FLORIDA, 309 U.S. 227 (1940)

On May 13, 1933, Robert Darsey, an elderly white man, was robbed and murdered in Pompano, Florida. From the beginning, the authorities' investigation of the crime took on racial overtones. Within days of the killing, the sheriff of Broward County detained between twenty-five and forty African-American men without warrants, entrusting them to Captain J. T. Williams, a prison guard who was enlisted for this special assignment. Williams interrogated the suspects day and night for nearly a week. The suspects were not permitted any contact with lawyers, relatives, or friends. They later said that Williams had beaten them, drawn his gun while questioning them, choked them with a rope, and threatened them with lynching if they did not admit their involvement in the crime. After several days, four black tenant-farmers remained, and they eventually confessed in the early morning hours following an all-night session of questioning.

The four were hauled into court shortly after their "sunrise confessions," where they pleaded guilty and were swiftly sentenced to death. The accused later raised serious concerns about the summary nature of the legal proceedings that followed, including whether the judge had appointed the men counsel, whether the accused knew such assistance was available, and whether any meaningful consultation took place before they pleaded guilty.

The matter raised questions of special priority for the National Association for the Advancement of Colored People (NAACP) Legal Defense and Educational Fund Inc. (LDF), which had been searching for cases to expand its agenda to eradicate racial inequality from employment relationships to the criminal justice system. Thurgood Marshall, then-director and chief counsel for the LDF, wrote the defendants' Supreme Court brief—his first such experience before the nation's highest tribunal. Although the Court had already ruled in *Brown v. Mississippi*, 297 U.S. 278 (1936) that confessions obtained through physical force were unreliable and could not be used at trial, *Chambers v. Florida*, 309 U.S. 227 (1940) tested the high court's willingness to investigate more creative psychological techniques intended to procure evidence from unwilling suspects.

In the Brief in Support of the Petition for Certiorari (1939), Marshall argued that the self-incriminating statements extracted through "threats and torture," as well as "the pleas of Guilty entered in open court immediately thereafter, and while still under the shadow of that force, have no greater validity than the confession themselves" (p. 27). Accordingly, Marshall argued that the state's actions "sacrifice[d] fundamental human rights" and therefore deprived the individuals of equal protection of the law and due process. He separately argued that the state's summary practices denied "ignorant, inexperienced accused" the right to the assistance of counsel as required by *Powell v. Alabama*, 287 U.S. 45 (1932). Urging the Supreme Court to exercise its supervisory powers over the state courts, Marshall hoped the justices would agree that "trial and conviction by honest testimony, openly arrived at, is better than and preferable to confessions extorted by the methods of the Inquisition and to decisions made in the Star Chamber" (p. 32).

Hugo Black, who hailed from Alabama, was selected by Chief Justice Charles Evans Hughes to write for a unanimous Court overturning the young men's convictions. This assignment had special significance because Black's elevation to the Supreme Court had been dominated by reports of his membership in the Ku Klux Klan. The opinion ignored the apparent irregularities surrounding the right to counsel and focused on the methods of interrogation. Evaluating the circumstances in their totality, the Supreme Court determined that the tactics used to elicit the incriminating statements, and therefore the court's reliance upon such tainted evidence to obtain the individuals' convictions, deprived them of due process of law. Without commenting directly on defendants' charges that they were beaten, Justice Black found that the state's nonphysical techniques were "calculated to break the strongest nerves and stoutest resistance" and to "fill petitioners with terror and frightful misgivings." But he did not stop at the visceral effects of such measures upon the human subject.

Justice Black's rhetoric struck at the ancient order of racial parochialism, police terror, and rough justice all at once. Drawing upon a cresting antitotalitarian sentiment, he proclaimed: "Today, as in ages past, we are not without tragic proof that the exalted power of some governments to punish manufactured crime dictatorially is the handmaid of tyranny." In this manner, the Supreme Court powerfully cast such "secret and dictatorial proceedings" as incompatible with the nation's burgeoning sense of itself.

Although Marshall had led with the equality argument, the justices made no explicit findings of unequal treatment. Black's language did, however, imply that racial animus infected the investigative stage. The state had exacerbated a situation in which "the haunting fear of mob violence was around them in an atmosphere charged with excitement and public indignation." Repeatedly, Justice Black stressed the courts' role as "havens of refuge" for "the helpless, weak, outnumbered, or ... nonconforming victims of prejudice and public excitement." These foundational priorities, he wrote, had been "planned and inscribed for the benefit of every human being subject to our Constitution—of whatever race, creed or persuasion."

Chambers arrived at a time of considerable ideological ferment when intellectuals were beginning to demonstrate greater interest in the expansion of legal and political rights. The decision signaled increased receptivity on the part of the U.S. Supreme Court to claims of fundamental unfairness in a citizen's everyday encounters with the state. This nascent commitment would manifest itself first in the legal system as a form of procedural justice and then, building on such gains, extend into other institutions and more substantive rights.

For Hugo Black, taking a primary role in the resolution of the matter and receiving widespread acclaim for his work proved a formative experience. As he later indicated to a confidante, the opinion ranked "very high among decisions expressing my constitutional views" (Newman 1994, pp. 525, 586). *Chambers* would figure prominently in the LDF's litigation strategy to dismantle the racial caste system in America, subsequent cases brought by defendants who challenged the legality of criminal proceedings, and jurists' general elaboration of the due process clause. More broadly, opinion makers cited the ruling as evidence of America's burgeoning postwar commitment to human rights.

SEE ALSO *Fifth Amendment; Fourteenth Amendment; Marshall, Thurgood*

BIBLIOGRAPHY

Brief in Support of the Petition for Certiorari. 1939. *Chambers v. Florida*, No. 195, July 11.

Davis, Michael D., and Hunter R. Clark. 1992. *Thurgood Marshall: Warrior at the Bar, Rebel on the Bench*. New York: Birch Lane.

Goldman, Roger, and David Gallen. 1993. *Thurgood Marshall: Justice for All*. New York: Caroll and Graf.

Miller, Loren. 1966. *The Petitioners: The Story of the Supreme Court of the United States and the Negro*. New York: Random House.

Newman, Roger K. 1994. *Hugo Black: A Biography*. New York: Pantheon.

Primus, Richard A. 1999. *The American Language of Rights*. New York: Cambridge University Press.

Tushnet, Mark V. 1994. *Making Civil Rights Law: Thurgood Marshall and the Supreme Court, 1936–1961*. New York: Oxford University Press.

Robert L. Tsai

CHAMPION V. AMES, 188 U.S. 321 (1903)

In *Champion v. Ames*, 188 U.S. 321 (1903), the U.S. Supreme Court, by a vote of five to four, sustained the constitutionality of a federal statute prohibiting the interstate transportation of lottery tickets. The statute, enacted by Congress in 1895, attempted to suppress lotteries by providing for criminal penalties of imprisonment for not more than two years, or fines of not more than one thousand dollars, for the movement of lottery tickets from one state to another. In his decision for the Court, Justice John Marshall Harlan held that the statute did not exceed the power of Congress under the Constitution's "commerce clause," which permits Congress to regulate commerce among the states. Harlan first concluded that lottery tickets were subjects of interstate commerce even though they lacked any intrinsic value. He then held that congressional power to regulate commerce included the power to prohibit the interstate transportation of goods such as lottery tickets, which Congress had found to encourage social evils such as gambling. Harlan's decision did not reach the question of whether Congress had the power to prohibit the interstate transportation of socially and economically useful commodities.

In dissent, Chief Justice Melville Fuller argued that the statute exceeded the power of Congress under the commerce clause and allowed Congress to exercise a general "police power" to promote "public health, good order, and prosperity" which belonged solely to the states. Fuller declared that

> [T]o hold that Congress has general police power would be to hold that it may accomplish objects not entrusted to the general government, and to defeat the operation of the 10th Amendment, declaring that "the powers not delegated to the United States by the Constitution, nor prohibited by it to the states, are reserved to the states respectively, or to the people."

The votes of the justices in *Champion v. Ames* reflected their general attitudes toward economic and social regulatory legislation. Justices Henry Brown (1836–1913), Edward D. White, Joseph McKenna (1843–1926), and Oliver Wendell Holmes joined Harlan's decision, while Justices David Brewer, George Shiras Jr. (1832–1924), and Rufus Peckham (1809–1873) joined Fuller's dissent.

Decided during the early days of the progressive movement when support for federal legislation to ameliorate social and economic problems was gaining momentum, *Champion v. Ames* encouraged social reformers and advocates of economic regulation to work for the enactment of other federal regulatory measures. Among the most important of these laws were the Pure Food and Drug Act of 1906, prohibiting interstate transportation of adulterated foods and drugs (upheld in *Hipolite Egg Co. v. United States*, 220 U.S. 45 [1911]); the Employers' Liability Act of 1908, providing federal remedies for injured railroad workers (upheld in *Second Employers' Liability Cases*, 223 U.S. 1 [1912]); and the Mann Act of 1910, outlawing interstate transportation of women for prostitution and other immoral purposes, (upheld in *Hoke v. United States*, 227 U.S. 308 [1913]). In sustaining the constitutionality of these statutes, the Court relied heavily upon its decision in *Champion v. Ames*.

SEE ALSO *Commerce Clause; Progressive Era Business Regulation*

BIBLIOGRAPHY

Ely, John W., Jr. 1995. *The Chief Justiceship of Melville W. Fuller, 1888–1910.* Columbia: University of South Carolina Press.

Semonche, John E. 1978. *Charting the Future: The Supreme Court Responds to a Changing Society, 1890–1920.* Westport, CT: Greenwood Press.

William G. Ross

CHARLES RIVER BRIDGE V. WARREN BRIDGE, 36 U.S. 420 (1837)

In 1785 the Massachusetts legislature chartered the Charles River Bridge Company to build a bridge between Boston and Charleston—at the time a speculative engineering project. In compensation, the legislature granted the company the right to collect tolls, first for forty years and eventually for an additional thirty years. In 1828, the legislature chartered the Warren Bridge Company and authorized it to build a bridge less than a quarter mile away. The new bridge would charge tolls for six years before reverting to the state and becoming toll free, a circumstance that would destroy the profitability of the older bridge. The Supreme Court, in *Charles River Bridge v. Warren Bridge*, 36 U.S. 420 (1837), was required to decide whether the older charter conferred monopoly rights on the first bridge and whether, therefore, the new charter violated the contract clause of the Constitution.

Important economic and political issues hinged on the decision. Both sides in the debate supported economic growth, but conservatives believed progress was best stimulated by upholding vested property rights, whereas Jacksonians argued that progress arose through the destruction of privileged monopoly. Not coincidentally, at that moment the development of the steam locomotive was threatening canal companies and the investors who had sunk their millions into them.

The Supreme Court heard arguments in 1831 and again in 1833, but it was unable to reach a decision on either occasion. Before the case was heard a third time in

1837, Chief Justice John Marshall died, and President Jackson replaced him with his treasury secretary, Roger Brooke Taney.

Chief Justice Taney wrote the decision for the four-to-three majority, asserting that although private property rights must be upheld, the rights of the public ought not be surrendered to inferred powers. The monopoly claimed by the Charles River Bridge Company had not been explicitly granted in its charter, and any ambiguity should be interpreted in the interest of the public. Furthermore, Taney argued that the Court ought not to rule against a sovereign state legislature, especially to support a policy that would retard economic growth.

Justice Joseph Story, one of the two remaining justices from the pre-Jacksonian era, was outraged at what he considered an attack on private property, and he wrote a fifty-seven-paged dissent, both learned and emotionally charged. To Story, it was simply "good sense" to assume that the power given by the Massachusetts legislature to the Charles River Bridge Company was exclusive. No one in 1785 would have ventured the capital to build the bridge if he or she had supposed that the legislature could destroy the company's right to collect tolls by chartering a neighboring free bridge. If a new bridge had been necessary, then the State should have taken the property by eminent domain and paid compensation to the owners.

Story viewed the charter as something of a private-law contract between relative equals. Taney thought of it more as a sovereign grant, which in effect endowed the legislature with the right to determine the public good. Although Taney was shrewd in his pragmatic response to economic realities, Story perceptively noted the threat to republican government that might result from the subordination of the rule of law to the will of a majority. James Kent, the noted anti-Jacksonian Chancellor of New York, reacted to the decision with "disgust," arguing that it overthrew "a great principle of constitutional mortality" by allowing the legislature to quibble away the sanctity of property (Kent to Story, quoted in William W. Story, ed., pp. 270–271).

SEE ALSO *Contracts Clause; Story, Joseph; Taney Court*

BIBLIOGRAPHY

Kutler, Stanley I. 1971. *Privilege and Creative Destruction: The Charles River Bridge Case.* Philadelphia: Lippincott.

Newmyer, R. Kent. 1985. *Supreme Court Justice Joseph Story: Statesman of the Old Republic.* Chapel Hill: University of North Carolina Press.

Story, William W., ed. 1851. *Life and Letters of Joseph Story.* vol. 2. Boston: Charles C. Little and James Brown.

John Austin Matzko

CHASE, SALMON
1803–1873

Salmon Portland Chase—the sixth chief justice of the U.S. Supreme Court (there were actually six men who sat as chief justice prior to Chase, but John Rutledge was never confirmed)—was among the most important political figures of the Civil War (1861–1865) era. Chase served as governor and U.S. senator of Ohio, as well as the twenty-fifth secretary of the treasury under President Abraham Lincoln (where he developed federal currency and introduced the phrase "In God We Trust").

Chase was born in 1803 in Cornish, New Hampshire, the eighth child of a father who died when Salmon was only nine years old. Chase was sent at that young age across the rugged terrain of the western territories to Ohio to live with his uncle, Bishop Philander Chase (1775–1852), and study Latin and Greek while working diligently on the family farm. Supported by his widowed mother of little means, Salmon attended Dartmouth College, where the faculty elected him to Phi Beta Kappa. After college, Chase moved in with his uncle Dudley Chase (1771–1846), a senator from Vermont, and started a school where two of his

Supreme Court Chief Justice and Secretary of the Treasury Salmon Chase. *In addition to being governor and a U.S. senator from Ohio, Chase served as President Abraham Lincoln's secretary of the treasury before being selected as chief justice. Holding the top position after the Civil War, Chase led the court through Reconstruction and the impeachment trial of President Andrew Jackson.* © CORBIS

students were sons of William Wirt (1772–1834), the attorney general to President John Adams (1735–1826), with whom Chase took up the study of law. Between Wirt and Bishop Chase (friend to Henry Clay [1777–1852] and President Adams), many doors opened for Salmon.

Chase is known, above all else, for his relentless ambition for the presidency. None of Lincoln's five judicial appointments attained a similar level of political acclaim. Antebellum politicians often changed political affiliation, but none more than Chase. He ran with the Democrats, the Liberty Party, the Free Soil Party (where he coined the slogan "Free Soil, Free Labor, Free Men"), the Republicans, and again (for president) with the Democrats just before his death. Because of Chase's overt ambition, many observers, contemporaries, and historians, alike, have found him disingenuous, even regarding his seemingly courageous antislavery advocacy.

In a celebrated case before the Supreme Court, *Jones v. Van Zandt*, 46 U.S. 215 (1847), Chase argued against the constitutionality of the Fugitive Slave Law of 1793. Though unsuccessful, the case brought enormous attention to both Chase and the antislavery cause. Abolitionists claimed Chase as one of their own and eagerly supported him to replace Roger Taney (1777–1864) as chief justice. Lincoln did not want the Court to be a springboard to the White House, however, and he feared exactly that as Chase's intention. After several months, in mid-December 1864, Lincoln acquiesced to the pressure from radicals and appointed Chase as chief justice, thus securing a Republican-appointed majority on the bench and temporary harmony within his forever-fractured party. Congress confirmed Chase on the day of his nomination.

As chief justice, Chase oversaw a reinvigoration of the Court's reputation, tarnished by Chief Justice Taney's decision in the *Dred Scott* case, 60 U.S. 393, of 1857. Though largely quiescent during the Civil War, the Supreme Court under Chase (1865–1873) grew far more active and assertive, overturning federal legislation ten times and state legislation on forty-six occasions. Chief Justice Chase presided at the impeachment trial of President Andrew Johnson (1808–1875) in 1868, at a time when Congress and the Court locked horns over the character and reach of Reconstruction. Eager to restrain the Court from overturning any aspect of Reconstruction, legislators passed judiciary acts that altered the scope and size of the Court. Chase participated vigorously in the proceedings of the judiciary committees of both Houses of Congress as they considered much needed reforms to the appellate process and judicial compensation (a matter of grave concern to the chief justice). Despite the fear or hostility of many congressmen toward the judiciary, the Court's stature and power grew appreciably during this time.

Chase handed down several important decisions during Reconstruction. In *Ex parte McCardle*, 74 U.S.

506 (1868), Chase wrote for a unanimous Court that validated congressional withdrawal of the Supreme Court's jurisdiction (under Article III, Section 2—the *exceptions clause*) in a habeas corpus case of a Confederate publisher accused of insurrection. Writing for a divided Court, in *Texas v. White, 74 U.S. 700* (1869), Chase insisted that although Texas had joined the Confederacy it had never left the Union; indeed, states did not have the constitutional authority to secede from what was an "indestructible Union." Many legal theorists, then and now, claim that Chase's opinion overreached in denying states' right to secede. Furthermore, southerners objected that Chase, a member of Lincoln's pro-northern cabinet, should have recused himself from this obviously political case.

In *Hepburn v. Griswold, 75 U.S. 603* (1870), Chase overturned parts of the Legal Tender Acts passed when he was secretary of the Treasury, claiming that paper money violated the U.S. Constitution's Article I, Section 10 insistence upon "coin money." That decision was soon reversed in the *Legal Tender Cases, 79 U.S. (12 Wall.) 457* (1871), which found paper money constitutional under the "necessary and proper" clause, and to which Chase predictably dissented. Perhaps the most notorious decision of the Chase Court was written by Justice Samuel Miller (1816–1890), with the chief justice dissenting, in the *Slaughter-House Cases, 83 US 36* (1873). The Court provided a narrow reading of the "privileges and immunities" clause of the Fourteenth Amendment to find that it applied against the national government, but not the states.

Salmon Chase's concern for social justice, particularly as regards the underprivileged, rarely wavered. He was devoted to the notion of natural rights for all. But his years at the vanguard of antislavery taught him that public enlightenment did not come easily or quickly. His bias toward states' rights also left him prudently disinclined to infringe upon the states or to define the new Fourteenth Amendment too broadly. Importantly, the chief justice recognized that public opinion increasingly turned against the military character of Reconstruction.

Salmon Chase can be counted among the very best statesmen of the era, even if his reputation suffered at those times when his keen human instincts got swamped by ambition. Chase's sensitivity for the subtleties of politics, his commitment to consensus, and, ironically, his driving ambition made him an especially effective leader of the Supreme Court at a critical evolutionary stage of the new postwar federal government.

SEE ALSO *Chase Court; Chase Impeachment; Civil War; Lincoln, Abraham; Reconstruction*

BIBLIOGRAPHY

Fairman, Charles. 1971. *Reconstruction and Reunion, 1864–88.* New York: Macmillan.

Kutler, Stanley. 1968. *Judicial Power and Reconstruction Politics.* Chicago: University of Chicago Press

Niven, John. 1995. *Salmon P. Chase: A Biography.* New York: Oxford University Press.

R. Owen Williams

CHASE COURT

The Supreme Court faced two related challenges at the time of Chief Justice Roger B. Taney's death in the fall of 1864. One was recovering its diminished prestige in the public eye. Many blamed the Court for precipitating the Civil War (1861–1865) with its decision in *Dred Scott v. Sandford,* 60 U.S. 393 (1857), which declared the Missouri Compromise of 1820 unconstitutional because Congress did not have power to ban slavery in the western territories. The second challenge was interpreting the U.S. Constitution during a period of political tumult. When asked whether the administration overstepped its powers during the Civil War, the Court decided it sometimes had, and so disappointed Republicans who hoped for a shift in jurisprudence from the new personnel on the Court. When faced with determining the rights granted by the amendments to the Constitution, the Court held to a conservative view. It thus set a pattern that would eventually leave black Americans with little legal leverage to protect their rights.

CHASE COURT JUSTICES

President Abraham Lincoln replaced Taney the southerner with a New Englander who had transplanted to Ohio and made his name as an antislavery lawyer. Salmon Chase had helped organize the Free Soil Party and then joined the Republican Party. He became a U.S. senator in 1849, governor of Ohio in 1855, and senator again in 1860. President Lincoln made him secretary of the treasury—some said in order to keep an eye on this boundlessly ambitious man. The two men clashed, and Chase resigned in the spring of 1864, only to be named to the Court several months later. Chase's principled battles against slavery and for voting rights for black men contrasted with his self-centered pursuit of the presidential office even after he became chief justice. Chase's ambition led him to attempt a Democratic Party nomination in 1868 and even to downplay, for the moment, his commitment to black rights.

Inherited Justices The new Chase Court was divided originally between justices Lincoln had inherited and those he had named. The first group were all Democrats. James M. Wayne (1790–1867) hailed from Georgia, but he repudiated the Confederacy, which then confiscated

COPYRIGHT SECURED.] 𝔖upreme 𝔠ourt of the 𝔘nited 𝔖tates.--1868. [BRADY & CO.

Members of the Chase Court, 1868. *After the death of Chief Justice Roger B. Taney, President Abraham Lincoln appointed Salmon Chase to the top position on the Supreme Court. Assuming the post in 1864, Chase led the highest court during an unstable era, facing the challenges of sorting through Lincoln's exercise of presidential powers during the Civil War, Reconstruction, and President Andrew Jackson's impeachment trial.* THE LIBRARY OF CONGRESS/CORBIS. REPRODUCED BY PERMISSION

his property. John Catron (1786–1865) had been on the Tennessee Supreme Court. Samuel Nelson (1792–1873) had served on the New York Supreme Court. Robert C. Grier (1794–1870) came from Pennsylvania, and Nathan Clifford (1803–1881) was a New Englander who specialized in opinions on maritime and commercial law. Some came from the North and some from the South, and all were committed to the preservation of states' rights and worried over excesses of federal power. The general pattern was made plain when Justice Nelson, joined by justices Catron and Clifford and Chief Justice Taney, dissented in the *Prize Cases*, 67 U.S. 635 (1863). The Court majority, led by Justice Grier, held that Lincoln had the power to order a blockade of Confederate ports and the seizure of ships that tried to break through. Lincoln issued his order in April 1861, but Congress did not declare war until July 1861. Just to make sure, Congress passed an act in August authorizing everything Lincoln had done up till then. The dissenters insisted that Lincoln had overstepped his authority, not a welcome message to a president in the midst of war.

Appointed Justices Lincoln's first appointment in 1861 made clear the direction he preferred the Court to take.

Noah Haynes Swayne (1804–1884) had moved from Virginia to Ohio as a young lawyer because of his antislavery politics and joined the new Republican Party. Like Chase, he was committed to the protection of the civil rights of black Americans. Lincoln's next Republican choice was Samuel Freeman Miller (1816–1890), a doctor turned lawyer from Iowa, with a strong nationalist bent. Despite his unusual background, Justice Miller dominated the Chase Court with his forceful personality and sharp mind, and he wrote more opinions than any other justice previously appointed.

David Davis (1815–1886) came to the Court next. Although a friend of Lincoln's, Justice Davis delivered the majority opinion in *Ex parte Milligan*, 71 U.S. 2 (1866), a civil liberties decision that provoked angry reactions from Republicans who had hoped for a more cooperative Court and who underestimated how much judges, regardless of political background, were protective of the power of the judicial branch. The case concerned Lambdin P. Milligan, who was arrested by U.S. Army officials in late 1864 and charged with taking part in a treasonous conspiracy in Indiana to organize an attack on federal arsenals and on prison camps holding Confederates. The military court condemned Milligan to death, but his lawyers appealed to the Supreme Court, which declared unanimously that the military had no jurisdiction over a civilian when the state courts were open.

The justices disagreed over the reasoning in *Milligan*. Justice Davis held that the Constitution's guarantees of a grand jury indictment in capital cases and a jury trial justified the decision, while Chief Justice Chase argued in a concurrence that these rights were protected by the Habeas Corpus Act of 1863, which Congress might alter during wartime if it saw fit. Milligan and his coconspirators were freed.

Some branded the decision "Dred Scott Number Two." Under the public assault, Justice Davis noted privately that Americans could amend their Constitution if they liked, but they should be prepared to stand by it until they had. In truth, most of the civilians tried for treason in military courts during the war were in theaters of war without functioning state courts, so *Milligan* was not relevant to their cases. However, curtailing the power of military courts meant trouble for the future since it was already clear that white racism left black Americans at the mercy of hostile local juries in the South.

Stephen J. Field (1816–1899) was the last of Lincoln's appointees, and like Chase he had presidential ambitions. He filled a tenth place added to the bench by Congress to insure that a majority of the justices were strongly pro-Union. Field was a Democrat who had traveled from New England to California, where he had served on the state supreme court. He also quickly disappointed Republicans. Justice Field gave the majority opinion in the *Test Oath Cases—Cummings v. Missouri*, 71 U.S. 277 (1867) and *Ex parte Garland*, 71 U.S. 333 (1867). These "iron-clad" oaths were retrospective ones swearing past allegiance to the Union in order to practice law and other professions. Justice Field declared that the oath requirements violated both the constitutional ban on bills of attainder, which punished people without a trial, and on ex post facto laws, which made a crime of events in the past. Justice Miller led the minority of four, all Republicans, which insisted that neither constitutional guarantee was relevant. The *Test Oath Cases* were defied by several states and by Congress in the Reconstruction Act of 1867. Congress considered retrospective oaths essential to reorganizing the defeated South.

COURT DECISIONS DURING THE RECONSTRUCTION

Congress had taken an entirely new tack in dealing with the South after President Andrew Johnson (1808–1875), Lincoln's Democratic vice president, pardoned many former Confederates and allowed almost all of the former rebel states back into the Union by 1866. These states ended slavery officially, but passed a series of "black codes" designed to recreate slavery in all but name. They also elected a raft of former Confederates to send to Congress. Republicans refused to seat the former rebels when Congress reconvened in December 1866, and they set about putting the southern states under military control. So began a battle in Washington between the new president and Congress marked by laws passed, laws vetoed, and vetoes overridden. Republicans also decided in 1866 that it would be best to decrease the number of seats on the Court to seven, so that Johnson could not name any new justices. Johnson's opposition to Congressional Reconstruction ended with an impeachment trial in the Senate in the spring of 1868. It was overseen by Chief Justice Chase, who was relieved that this partisan effort ended in acquittal. Still, Johnson was a spent force who left office the next year.

Republicans in Congress were no more pleased with the Chase Court than they were with the president. When the Court heard the arguments of William McCardle, a Confederate newspaper editor arrested in 1867 by army officials for inciting insurrection, Congress debated the scope of the Court's jurisdiction over such habeas corpus appeals. McCardle claimed the right to a civilian trial, just as Milligan had. Justices Field and Grier wanted to rule on the case before Congress acted, but the rest of the Court was against it. Congress took away the Court's jurisdiction in March 1868, and Chief Justice Chase acknowledged for a unanimous bench in April that the Court must dismiss the case. Congress had its way.

The *Legal Tender Cases* The *Legal Tender Cases* were a dramatic example of the importance of individuals on the bench in determining public policy. These three decisions turned on Congress's power to issue paper money, or "greenbacks," which could not be exchanged for gold or silver coin, during the Civil War. Although he did not like the idea, Chase had started the practice as secretary of the treasury in 1862 out of the necessity. He needed to finance the Union war effort and some $430 million worth of greenbacks were issued. It was Chase who put the phrase "In God We Trust" on the bills. Few people trusted the greenbacks themselves. The bills depreciated in value and hit a low of 39 cents in 1864. This hit creditors hard, since Congress had required that they accept these bills at their face value, even for debts contracted before the war.

Hepburn v. Griswold, 75 U.S. 603 (1870), also called the *First Legal Tender Case*, came before a Court of only seven justices, even though Congress had already voted to increase the number to nine. (Justice Wayne had died in 1867 and Justice Grier resigned in 1869). Chief Justice Chase now returned to his hard money roots and wrote the majority opinion, which declared that the Legal Tender Act (1862) was unconstitutional in that it required the payment of prewar debts with paper money, in violation of the Fifth Amendment's guarantee that private property not be taken without due process of law. He also noted that the law impaired the obligation of contracts, although only the states, not the federal government, were forbidden to do so by the Constitution. Justices Nelson, Clifford, and Field agreed, and Justice Grier would have made a fifth had he still been on the bench. The dissenters, led by Justice Miller, argued that the issuing of legal tender was a legitimate exercise of Congress's power and especially necessary to the business of waging war. The young Oliver Wendell Holmes observed in the July 1870 issue of the *American Law Review*, which he edited, that the Court was arguing with Congress over "a point of political economy." It was an argument that Congress would ultimately win. The same day that the *First Legal Tender Case* was decided, President Ulysses S. Grant (1822–1885) appointed to the Court two new justices who would vote to reverse that decision.

Both of the new justices had become Republicans after the war began. Joseph P. Bradley (1813–1892) was a farm boy from New York who had become a corporate lawyer, while William Strong (1808–1895) had served on the bench in Pennsylvania. Both men were of a religious bent, and Strong long worked in vain to amend the Constitution so that it would acknowledge Jesus Christ. He delivered the Court's opinion in the *Second Legal Tender Case, Knox v. Lee* and *Parker v. Davis*, 79 U.S. 457 (1871). He was joined by Justice Bradley and the dissenters in the original case. Chief Justice Chase now dissented with support from Clifford and Field. Some newspapers complained that the president had packed the Court in order to get the results he wanted, but it was hardly surprising that Grant had picked men who supported Republican policies. In truth, few presidents have gotten exactly what they bargained for in their justices, as was made clear in the first important decision on the meaning of the Fourteenth Amendment.

The *Slaughter-House Cases* The *Slaughter-House Cases*, 83 U.S. 36 (1873) asked the justices to define what the Fourteenth Amendment meant when it made all persons born in the country into citizens of the United States and prohibited the states from denying citizens their privileges and immunities, or from denying any person's right to due process of law or to the equal protection of the laws. As its name suggests, the case involved the regulation of slaughterhouses in New Orleans and the rights of butchers to practice their trade. The states regularly passed health and safety regulations, and white butchers were not the expected beneficiaries of the new amendment, although its language was universal.

The Chase Court was sharply divided. Justice Miller wrote for the five-member majority that the amendment's principle purpose was to protect the rights of the new black citizens, but he defined national citizenship narrowly and placed the right to labor under state citizenship. The Fourteenth Amendment had not shifted authority to protect civil rights to the federal government, he declared. The four dissenters disagreed vehemently. Justice Bradley stressed that the law violated the butchers' right to liberty and property, in violation of the Fourteenth Amendment's due process clause, while Justice Swayne insisted that the majority's narrow definition of the amendment defied the history of its creation. They, along with Chief Justice Chase, who died only a few weeks later, also joined Justice Field's dissent, which identified the right to labor as one of the inalienable, natural rights that the Fourteenth Amendment protected.

Coming directly on the heels of *Slaughter-House* was the case of Myra Bradwell (1831–1894), the well-regarded editor of the *Chicago Legal News,* whom the Illinois State Supreme Court had barred from practicing law, although the statute in question spoke only of "persons." Bradwell argued that the court's decision violated her privileges as a citizen under the Fourteenth Amendment. The Court rejected the argument in *Bradwell v. Illinois*, 83 U.S. 130 (1873). Justice Bradley noted in his concurrence that God had made woman too delicate to join the bar, a belief that all his brethren must have shared.

The eventual results of these decisions demonstrated the ways in which law evolves on and off the bench. Bradwell won her argument through legislation. Before the Chase Court had ruled in her suit, she convinced Illinois legislators to protect the right of women to practice law. The doctrines in Justice Field's *Slaughter-House* dissent came to dominate later courts, which struck down state labor and economic regulations on the grounds that they violated economic due process and liberty of contract under the Fourteenth Amendment. In contrast, claims for the protection of black civil and political rights, which neither Field nor most of the future justices were particularly interested in, faced far more opposition. Racism was so strong that few judges were willing to invoke the logic of Field's *Slaughter-House* dissent for the benefit of black Americans.

SEE ALSO *Amendments, Post-Civil War; Bradwell v. Illinois, 83 U.S. 130 (1873); Chase, Salmon; Chase Impeachment; Civil War; Ex parte McCardle, 74 U.S. 506 (1869); Ex parte Milligan, 71 U.S. 2 (1866); Fourteenth Amendment; Habeas Corpus Act of 1867; Impeachment; Legal Tender Cases; Prize Cases; Reconstruction; Slaughter-House Cases, 83 U.S. 36 (1873); Texas v. White, 74 U.S. 700 (1869)*

BIBLIOGRAPHY

Fairman, Charles M. 1971. *Reconstruction and Reunion, 1864–88.* Pt. 1. New York: Macmillan.

Hyman, Harold M., and William Wiecek. 1982. *Equal Justice Under Law: Constitutional Development, 1835–1875.* New York: Harper.

Labbé, Ronald M., and Jonathan Lurie. 2003. *The Slaughterhouse Cases: Regulation, Reconstruction, and the Fourteenth Amendment.* Lawrence: University Press of Kansas.

Lurie, Jonathan. 2004. *The Chase Court: Justices, Rulings, and Legacy.* Santa Barbara, CA: ABC-CLIO.

Niven, John. 1995. *Salmon P. Chase: A Biography.* New York: Oxford University Press.

Linda Przybyszewski

CHASE IMPEACHMENT

Associate Justice Samuel Chase is, as of the early twenty-first century, the only U.S. Supreme Court justice ever to be impeached. The House of Representatives, in a near party-line vote, impeached him in late 1804. After a trial in February 1805, Chase narrowly avoided conviction in the Senate. He remained on the bench until his death in 1811. Chase's impeachment, and his behavior that led to it, tested the political independence of the Supreme Court.

A signer of the Declaration of Independence, Chase served for several turbulent years in the Maryland state and county courts after the Revolution. He initially opposed the ratification of the U.S. Constitution but was one of the few anti-Federalists to become an ardent proponent of the Federalist Party during the partisan division of the late 1790s. President George Washington appointed him to the U.S. Supreme Court in 1796, and he easily won Senate confirmation.

In the late 1790s, political tensions were boiling over in the early republic, and military conflict with either Britain or France seemed increasingly likely. In 1798, the Federalist Congress passed the Sedition Act, which made it a crime to publish false, malicious statements intended to "excite" the people against the federal government or bring it into "contempt" or "disrepute." Chase became well known in both the Federalist and the Jeffersonian press for his zeal in applying the Sedition Act.

Chase solidified that reputation and earned the enmity of the Republicans when he presided over a number of politically charged criminal trials while riding circuit in the spring of 1800. In Philadelphia, he was accused of bias in overseeing the sedition trial of the Republican writer Thomas Cooper and the treason trial of the tax resister John Fries. In Richmond, Chase encouraged and helped direct from the bench the sedition prosecution of the Republican writer James Callender. In Delaware, he tried to convince a grand jury to indict a local printer for sedition for publishing criticism of Chase's own behavior, but the grand jury refused to issue the indictment. A few months later, the Supreme Court had to delay the opening of its August 1800 term owing to a lack of quorum, in part because Chase was away campaigning for the re-election of President John Adams.

When the Jeffersonian Republicans won control of both chambers of Congress and the presidency in the elections of 1800, Justice Samuel Chase was to them the very symbol of a politically corrupt and abusive Federalist judge. Nonetheless, the Republicans had more immediate priorities. They repealed the Judiciary Act of 1801, which the lame-duck Federalists had passed expanding and empowering the federal courts. Chase was alone among the justices in privately urging that they should refuse to comply with the repeal act. In May 1803, Chase finally abandoned his low profile when sitting a grand jury at the opening of his circuit term in Baltimore. There he delivered a speech criticizing proposed changes in the Maryland state constitution, warning against the threat of "universal suffrage" and "mobocracy," and denouncing the Jeffersonian Congress and calling for its defeat at the next election.

President Thomas Jefferson called Chase's jury charge to the attention of Maryland congressional representative Joseph Nicholson. House leaders initially decided not to take any action. Nonetheless, the Republican firebrand John Randolph decided to push for impeachment himself. He brought eight articles of impeachment, which were easily approved by the constitutionally required simple majority in the Republican-controlled House. One article was based on the 1803 Baltimore grand-jury charge, but the other articles were based on Chase's earlier conduct during the 1800 election cycle. One was based on Chase's conduct in the Fries trial. Five were based on his conduct in the Callender trial, including such specific charges as jury tampering and manipulation of witnesses. One was based on his behavior with the Delaware grand jury in 1800.

The Senate trial was the real battleground for the Chase impeachment. The Republicans held nearly three-quarters of the seats in the Senate in February 1805, well more than the two-thirds needed to convict and remove Chase from office. But the Republicans could not expect party loyalty to carry the day in the Senate trial. The House sent seven of its members, led by John Randolph, to manage its prosecution before the Senate. Chase appeared with six leading Federalist lawyers to defend his case, including the former U.S. attorney general Charles Lee and current Maryland state attorney general Luther Martin.

Chase argued that the impeachment power should be understood narrowly. Only criminal acts could justify his impeachment and removal, according to Chase. The Senate should not sit as an appellate court and review whether he had made legal errors in conducting trials, and it should not prosecute him for his political opinions. Although some Republicans, such as the Virginians William Branch Giles and James Monroe, argued privately that Chase's political views were sufficiently dangerous to justify his removal from such an important office, the public argument most Republicans supported was that his actions on the bench had amounted to an abuse of office, and such abuses could justify impeachment and removal. Judicial independence, the House impeachment managers argued, did not mean lack of accountability.

The article relating to the Baltimore grand-jury charge attracted the most guilty votes, falling four votes shy of the constitutional threshold for removal. But, concerned about the long-term future of the independent judiciary if Chase were removed from office, six Republicans joined every Federalist senator to vote against every article of impeachment. Most of the Republican senators proved willing to vote guilty when the evidence indicated intemperance or abuse by Chase, but few were willing to vote guilty when the evidence was unclear or when simple legal mistakes had been made.

Having failed to remove Chase, the Republicans made no effort to impeach any other Federalist judges after him. In response to his impeachment, Chase and his fellow justices gave up the overt partisan displays of partisan politics that had gotten Chase in trouble. The Marshall Court as a whole was careful to avoid obstructing Republican policies, even if it did not agree with Jeffersonian constitutional philosophy.

SEE ALSO *Good Behavior; Jefferson, Thomas; Judicial Independence; Judiciary Act of 1801; Marshall Court*

BIBLIOGRAPHY

Ellis, Richard E. 1971. *The Jeffersonian Crisis: Courts and Politics in the Young Republic.* New York: Oxford University Press.

Presser, Stephen B. 1991. *The Original Misunderstanding: The English, the Americans, and the Dialectic of Federalist Jurisprudence.* Durham, NC: Carolina Academic Press, 1991.

Whittington, Keith E. 1999. *Constitutional Construction: Divided Powers and Constitutional Meaning.* Cambridge, MA: Harvard University Press.

Keith E. Whittington

CHEROKEE NATION V. GEORGIA, 30 U.S. 1 (1831)

In a series of early nineteenth-century decisions, Chief Justice John Marshall (1755–1835) guided the U.S. Supreme Court toward a jurisprudence that supported the claims of the United States to the real estate of North America. In *Fletcher v. Peck*, 10 U.S. (6 Cranch) 87 (1810) and *Johnson v. M'Intosh*, 21 U.S. (8 Wheat.) 543 (1823), Marshall addressed the question of the legal status

of Indian land under American law. In *Fletcher,* he rejected the idea that Indians, who "merely roamed over and hunted on" the land of the continent, could hold absolute legal title to that land. He described "Indian title" as not absolutely repugnant to seisin in fee on the part of a state. Indian title was one of "occupancy," he wrote, because "discovery" gave the United States, which succeeded to English claims, sovereignty over Indians.

In *Johnson,* Marshall sharpened the assignment of the right of alienation, marking it as a national, not a state, power. *Cherokee Nation v. Georgia*, 30 U.S. (5 Pet.) 1 (1831) followed *Johnson* and posed transcendent questions of Indian rights, specifically whether the sovereignty and land boundaries of the Cherokee Republic were to be respected by the state of Georgia and the government of the United States. The Court heard oral arguments only months after passage of the 1830 Indian Removal Act, which, in the course of a decade, dispossessed the tribes of the south and east parts of their lands. *Cherokee Nation* aided that expropriation of property.

Prior to the arrival of Europeans, several tribes of Native Americans, including the Cherokee, lived in the southeast of North America. The government of the United States signed treaties with the Cherokee acknowledging their national boundaries and sovereignty. In the early nineteenth century, however, cotton farming and the discovery of gold led to pressure on the Cherokee to cede territory to the southeastern states of the United States. When the Cherokee leadership refused, the Georgia legislature enacted draconian legislation intended to make the Cherokee second-class citizens of that state. Officials sought to destroy the Cherokee Republic, established as a constitutional government in 1827, and to make it impossible for the Cherokee to refuse a treaty of removal to the western side of the Mississippi River. Removal policy was supported by Andrew Jackson (1767–1845), elected president in 1828.

The leaders of the Cherokee Republic, led by Chief John Ross (1790–1866), fought back by hiring attorneys William Wirt (1772–1834), previously U.S. attorney general under presidents James Monroe (1758–1831) and John Quincy Adams (1767–1848), and former congressman John Sergeant (1779–1852) to bring a case that would test its rights as an independent, sovereign nation. On behalf of the Cherokee Nation as a foreign nation, the two lawyers petitioned the U.S. Supreme Court in 1831 to invoke original jurisdiction and then to grant an injunction barring enforcement of Georgia's laws within the Cherokee Nation. They argued that the Cherokee were a fully sovereign people and that Georgia's laws violated international treaties between the Cherokee Nation and the United States, as well as the U.S. Constitution's supremacy clause (Article VI), barring state law that overrides federal laws or treaties.

Chief Justice Marshall's opinion, joined by Jackson nominee John McLean (1785–1861), did not address the question of whether Georgia had violated treaty agreements or the U.S. Constitution. Rather, Marshall extricated his court from the rough seas of Jacksonian politics, and all discussion of the substantive issues, with procedural sleight of hand. The seventy-six-year-old chief justice posed, and answered, a single question: "Is the Cherokee nation a foreign state in the sense in which that term is used in the constitution?" His answer, much of it dictum, relied heavily on discovery doctrine and a corrupt reading of history. He declared that the Cherokee Republic did not constitute a foreign nation, denying jurisdiction and the motion for an injunction. Critically, he characterized the Cherokee as possessing a lesser status, that of "*domestic dependent* nations. They occupy a territory to which we assert a title independent of their will. . . . they are [a people] in a state of pupilage. Their relation to the United States resembles that of a ward to his guardian."

Justices Henry Baldwin (1780–1844) and William Johnson (1771–1834) voted with Marshall and McLean, each filing a concurring opinion. Baldwin flatly denied that Indian tribes constituted political communities of any kind. He considered Georgia to have full jurisdiction over the Cherokee and fee simple title to the land they were occupying. Justice Johnson, who in *Fletcher* had adopted a position toward Indian land title more conciliatory than that announced by Marshall, in *Cherokee Nation* justified his vote against the Cherokee with tortuous and ethnocentric legal distinctions concerning the meaning of a foreign nation.

Six justices heard and decided *Cherokee Nation*. Two members of the court, Joseph Story (1779–1845) and Smith Thompson (1768–1843), voted in dissent. They argued "that the Cherokees compose a foreign state within the sense and meaning of the constitution, and constitute a competent party to maintain a suit against the state of Georgia." It was their view that an injunction should be granted immediately. Thompson wrote the dissent, drawing heavily on the arguments made by Wirt and Sergeant.

In *Cherokee Nation*, John Marshall established a new thread in federal law, one that argued a diminished political status for Indian nations, while simultaneously instituting a doctrine of guardianship. Unwilling to abandon the Indian cause completely, in the final paragraphs of his opinion Marshall, asserting that the Cherokee asked too much of the Court, invited more circumscribed litigation. He suggested "a proper case with proper parties" that would selectively address the issue of Cherokee land title and, by extension, the question of Indian removal. The elderly jurist concluded his opinion with some of the most disheartening text recorded in high

court jurisprudence: "If it be true that the Cherokee nation have rights . . . this is not the tribunal which can redress the past or prevent the future." A year later, in the 1832 case of *Worcester v. Georgia*, 31 U.S. (6 Pet.) 515 (1832), the Marshall Court revisited the issue of the Cherokee Republic's struggle against Georgia in a suit to which, ironically, the Cherokee were not a direct party.

SEE ALSO *Johnson v. M'Intosh, 21 U.S. 543 (1823); Marshall Court; Native Americans*

BIBLIOGRAPHY

Burke, Joseph C. 1969. "The Cherokee Cases: A Study in Law, Politics, and Morality." *Stanford Law Review* 21: 500–531.

Magliocca, Gerard N. 2007. *Andrew Jackson and the Constitution: The Rise and Fall of Generational Regimes*. Lawrence: University Press of Kansas.

Norgren, Jill. 2004. *The Cherokee Cases: Two Landmark Federal Decisions in the Fight for Sovereignty*. Norman: University of Oklahoma Press.

Perdue, Theda, and Michael D. Green. 2007. *The Cherokee Nation and the Trail of Tears*. New York: Viking.

CASES

Cherokee Nation v. Georgia, 30 U.S. (5 Pet.) 1 (1831).

Fletcher v. Peck, 10 U.S. (6 Cranch) 87 (1810).

Johnson v. M'Intosh, 21 U.S. (8 Wheat.) 543 (1823).

Worcester v. Georgia, 31 U.S. (6 Pet.) 515 (1832).

Jill Norgren

CHEVRON U.S.A. V. NATURAL RESOURCES DEFENSE COUNCIL, 467 U.S. 837 (1984)

Chevron U.S.A. v. Natural Resources Defense Council, 467 U.S. 837 (1984) recharacterized the interpretation of regulatory statutes, traditionally the judiciary's province, as a legislatively delegated administrative function. Controversial and unexpectedly complex to implement, *Chevron* has become the Court's most-cited public law decision.

The Clean Air Act Amendments of 1977 imposes stringent permit requirements on new or modified "stationary source[s]" of air pollution in states not yet meeting national air-quality standards. This term could refer to either each individual pollutant-emitting device (e.g., smokestack) or to the entire industrial unit; the latter interpretation (known as the "bubble" concept) allows unregulated installation of pollution-emitting devices so long as a net pollution offset occurs elsewhere within the unit. The Carter Administration Environmental

Secretary of the Interior James Watt at a press conference in Washington, D.C., August 3, 1982. With the Chevron U.S.A. v. Natural Resources Defense Council *decision, the Supreme Court ruled that the Environmental Protection Agency possesses the power to interpret legislation, in effect making Congress the interpreter of regulatory environmental law.* © **CORBIS-BETTMANN**

Protection Agency (EPA) issued an implementing rule in August 1980 rejecting the bubble interpretation. It was influenced in part by D.C. Circuit cases that acknowledged some EPA discretion to define the statutory term *source* (which appears in various parts of the Clean Air Act) but distinguished statutory programs designed to *maintain* air quality from those to *improve* air quality. The EPA's 1980 rule stated that rejecting the bubble was "more consistent with congressional intent" because it would "bring in more sources and modifications for review and . . . require better pollution control technology in nonattainment areas."

Two months after President Ronald Reagan took office, the EPA began a rulemaking to reverse this interpretation. Part of "a Government-wide reexamination of regulatory burdens and complexities," this step, EPA predicted, would "substantially reduce the burdens

imposed on the regulated community without significantly interfering with timely achievement of the [statutory] goals." The new rule was issued in October 1981. The EPA explained that using the bubble for both maintenance and improvement programs would reduce regulatory complexity. More important, it would honor congressional intent that "states have primary responsibility for pollution control" by giving them "maximum possible flexibility to balance environmental and economic concerns in designing plans to clean up nonattainment area."

Environmental groups sought review in the D.C. Circuit, which unanimously reversed the agency. Then-Judge Ruth Bader Ginsburg acknowledged that neither the text of the Clean Air Act nor the legislative history of the 1977 Amendments addressed the issue. However, the program's purpose was demonstrably air-quality improvement and not, as the EPA argued, affording the states flexibility in methods for achieving compliance.

On appeal, Justice John Paul Stevens—writing for all the participating justices (Thurgood Marshall and William Rehnquist recused themselves and Sandra Day O'Connor had not yet arrived on the Court when the case was argued)—chastised the circuit court for "misconceiv[ing] the nature of its role." When "traditional tools of statutory construction" do not reveal clear congressional intent resolving a statutory ambiguity or gap, the reviewing court must defer to a reasonable agency interpretation. He explained:

> If Congress has explicitly left a gap for the agency to fill, there is an express delegation of authority to the agency to elucidate a specific provision. . . . Sometimes the legislative delegation to an agency on a particular question is implicit rather than explicit. In such a case, a court may not substitute its own construction of a statutory provision for a reasonable interpretation made by the administrator of an agency.

After a detailed review of text and legislative history revealed nothing to compel a particular interpretation of *source*, Justice Stevens returned to the delegation theme:

> Perhaps [Congress] consciously desired the Administrator to strike the balance . . . , thinking that those with great expertise and charged with responsibility for administering the provision would be in a better position to do so; perhaps it simply did not consider the question at this level; and perhaps Congress was unable to forge a coalition on either side of the question, and those on each side decided to take their chances with the scheme devised by the agency. For judicial purposes, it matters not which of these things occurred.

> Judges are not experts in the field, and are not part of either political branch of the Government. . . .

WHO DECIDES WHAT A REGULATORY STATUTE MEANS?

■

A foundational principle in American law is that, as the first Chief Justice John Marshall wrote in *Marbury v. Madison*: "It is emphatically the province and duty of the Judicial Department to say what the law is." What if "the law" requiring interpretation is a statute directing an administrative agency to work at solving a problem such as air pollution? *Chevron v. Natural Resources Defense Council* fundamentally altered the relationship between the courts and federal agencies by stating that when a regulatory statute is ambiguous, or otherwise does not clearly address an issue, the agency may decide what the statute means. Moreover, it may adopt different "meanings" over time. The only limit is that the agency must select a "reasonable" interpretation.

Chevron plainly shifts power from courts to agencies. Less obviously, it also alters the balance of power between Congress and the president. It is difficult for Congress to draft statutes, especially statutes setting up complex regulatory programs, that have no ambiguities or gaps. If an agency follows the policies of the current president in choosing, or changing, an interpretation of its statutory responsibilities and Congress disagrees, it can redirect the agency only by accomplishing the difficult political feat of passing a new statute over the president's veto.

Chevron has inspired passionate defense and equally passionate criticism, but few would disagree that it is one of the most important Supreme Court decisions of the twentieth century.

Cynthia R. Farina

In contrast, an agency to which Congress has delegated policymaking responsibilities may, within the limits of that delegation, properly rely upon the incumbent administration's view of wise policy to inform its judgments. While agencies are not directly accountable to the people, the Chief Executive is.

Chevron's delegation rationale for deference has produced several doctrinal corollaries. Agencies receive deference only when interpreting statutes they are specifically authorized to administer, not for generally applicable statutes like the Administrative Procedures Act. Moreover, to receive deference for its interpretation, the agency must possess statutory authority to make legally binding regulatory policy: Agencies to whom Congress has given only advisory power are not entitled to *Chevron* deference. Indeed, even agencies having legally binding authority may not get the benefit of *Chevron* if an interpretation does not appear to be officially authorized, or reached through a sufficiently deliberative process. Finally, an agency interpretation qualifying for *Chevron* deference trumps a prior judicial interpretation unless the earlier decision rested on the court's finding of clear, unambiguous statutory meaning.

Chevron increased the overall rate at which courts of appeals affirm agency decisions, although the size of that increase remains disputed. The Supreme Court picture is more chaotic. Sometimes, the Court does not even mention *Chevron* in regulatory interpretation cases. Moreover, how it performs the *Chevron* "two-step" can vary dramatically. Step one—deciding whether a gap or ambiguity exists—inevitably implicates the apparently intractable disagreement among the justices over methods of statutory interpretation. Although the choice of textualist versus traditionalist methodology appears not to affect *Chevron* analyses in the lower courts, the justices' conflicting interpretive positions result in a wide divergence of sources consulted (e.g., dictionaries, legislative history); tools employed (e.g., clear statement principles; canons of construction); extent and rigor of scrutiny applied; and overall credibility of results reached. Step two—determining the reasonableness of the agency's interpretation—is by comparison fairly straightforward. Although some lower courts debate whether this differs from other types of administrative arbitrariness review, the Supreme Court has not (and the lower courts have seldom) overturned agencies at this step.

At least as important as its actual effect on standards of review, *Chevron* has attained mythic significance. Those who favor stronger presidential control over regulatory policymaking emphasize that it links deference to democratic legitimacy; they invoke *Chevron* to urge further executive-strengthening doctrines. Those who perceive an emergent executive predominance in empowering agencies to supply meaning whenever statutes are not clear and complete see *Chevron* as the archetype of doctrine's potential to skew the balance of power; they warn against further president-favoring developments. As much a framework within which we debate how regulatory power ought be controlled as one within which such control is exercised, *Chevron* is a defining element of modern U.S. administrative law.

SEE ALSO *Administrative Agencies; Air Pollution; Environmental Law*

BIBLIOGRAPHY

Breyer, Stephen. 1986. "Judicial Review of Questions of Law and Policy." *Administrative Law Review* 38: 363.

EPA Final Rule: Requirements for Preparation, Adoption, and Submittal of Implementation Plan; Approval and Promulgation of Implementation Plans, 45 Federal Register 52,675. 1980.

EPA Final Rule: Requirements for Preparation, Adoption, and Submittal of Implementation Plan; Approval and Promulgation of Implementation Plans, 46 Federal Register 50,766. 1981.

EPA Proposed Rule: Requirements for Preparation, Adoption, and Submittal of Implementation Plans; Approval and Promulgation of Implementation Plans, 46 Federal Register 16,280. 1981.

Farina, Cynthia R. 1989. "Statutory Interpretation and the Balance of Power in the Administrative State." *Columbia Law Review* 89: 452.

Merrill Thomas W., and Kristin E. Hickman. 2001. "Chevron's Domain." *Georgetown Law Journal* 89: 833.

Scalia, Antonin. 1989. "Judicial Deference to Agency Interpretations of Law." *Duke Law Journal* 511.

Strauss, Peter. 1987. "One Hundred Fifty Cases per Year: Some Implications of the Supreme Court's Limited Resources for Judicial Review of Agency Action." *Columbia Law Review* 87: 1093.

Sunstein, Cass R. 1990. "Law and Administration after Chevron," *Columbia Law Review* 90: 2071.

Cynthia R. Farina

CHICAGO V. STURGES, 222 U.S. 313 (1911)

In *City of Chicago v. Sturges*, 222 U.S. 313 (1911), the U.S. Supreme Court upheld as constitutional an Illinois statute that made municipalities strictly liable to property owners for any damage to their property caused by mobs or riots. Statutes imposing municipal liability for riot damage were becoming increasingly common at the time, and the Court's decision validated this legislative trend, which continued until the mid-twentieth century, when states began repealing the statutes of their own volition. But *Sturges*'s historical significance may lie more in what it does or does not reflect about the political motivations of the Court that decided it.

The single issue before the Court was the constitutionality of an Illinois statute that made a city liable for three-fourths of the damage "caused by the violence of any mob or riotous assemblage of twelve or more persons, not abetted or permitted by the negligent or wrongful act of the owner." The City of Chicago argued that the act

denied it due process of law under the Fourteenth Amendment because it imposed liability regardless of whether or not the city had been negligent in failing to prevent the violence.

The Court rejected this argument. While recognizing as "general principles" of the common law both that "there is no individual liability for an act which ordinary human care and foresight could not guard against" and that "a loss from any cause purely accidental must rest where it chances to fall," the Court nevertheless maintained that "behind and above these general principles" there lay "the legislative power, which, in the absence of organic restraint, may, for the general welfare of society, impose obligations and responsibilities otherwise non-existent." In the Court's view, the legislature's imposition of absolute liability on cities for damage caused by riots was perfectly consistent with the state's core responsibility to maintain public order and to protect life, liberty, and property. The Court thus concluded that the act was a valid exercise of the state's inherent police power and did not violate the City of Chicago's right to due process of law.

As the Court itself recognized, the theory on which the Illinois statute was based was hardly novel in Anglo-American law. Forms of communal liability for damage to persons or property date as far back as 1285, when the Second Statute of Winchester codified the "hue and cry" system of the Saxons, according to which the "hundred" (an early type of civil subdivision) was held strictly and vicariously responsible for the crimes committed by any of its members. Under this statute, each member of the community had a duty to raise a "hue and cry" in order to catch the perpetrators and, if they failed to do so, they were held liable for the damages caused. Subsequent English statutes, the Riot Acts of 1714 and 1886, further increased protection for property owners. The first statute imposed liability on the community regardless of whether the criminals were apprehended, and the later one provided that compensation be made payable out of the local police unit.

In the United States, municipal liability for riot damage was not considered part of the common law, but individual states soon began imposing it by statute. Pennsylvania was the first to do so in 1835, and by 1890, seventeen states had statutes that imposed some form of communal liability for damage caused by riots. *Sturges* thus gave significant constitutional validation to a legislative trend that continued for several more decades. In the wake of the decision, courts in other states upheld comparable statutes, and by 1936, twenty-four states had such laws.

By mid-century, however, the trend had abated and reversed. Due in part to the increasing costs of providing such liability coverage, as well as to the erosion in some states of the principle of sovereign immunity to which the statutes had been considered an exception, states soon began repealing municipal liability statutes. By 1968, only fifteen states had such statutes. By 2004, only nine states had them at all and even those only offered limited protection, often severely capping the amount of damages. For this reason, by the end of the twentieth century, plaintiffs far more commonly sought relief from the government for riot-related injuries on the basis of section 1 of the Civil Rights Act of 1871 (codified at 42 U.S.C. § 1983), which offered far less protection than did the earlier statutes.

The historical importance of *Sturges* may thus lie less in its doctrinal legacy than in what it reflects about the Court that decided it. Contemporary commentators and later historians often treated the case as evidence that the (Melville) Fuller and (Edward Douglass) White Courts were not nearly as hostile to progressive legislation as has often been alleged, for *Sturges* is one of many cases in which the Court upheld legislation as a valid exercise of a state's police power. Furthermore, some legislative attempts to impose municipal liability could properly be described as progressive initiatives in their time. During Reconstruction, for instance, some southern states enacted such statutes after the Civil War (1861–1865) with the explicit goal of encouraging communities to protect recently freed blacks from Ku Klux Klan–related violence.

Still, the political significance of *Sturges* is not easy to decipher. Many such statutes were enacted in the latter half of the nineteenth century, a period of rapid industrialization and urbanization, suggesting that they may have been enacted in order to protect capital and industry from the increasingly disruptive violence associated with labor strikes and boycotts. The facts of *Sturges* make this point clear. The plaintiff was the owner of a six-story building that was vandalized by a mob during the Kellogg Switchboard strike in July 1903. Thus, whether the Court's decision to uphold the statute undermines the view that the Court was in the grip of a laissez-faire economic ideology seems to be, at the very least, an open question.

SEE ALSO *Police Power; State Sovereign Immunity*

BIBLIOGRAPHY

"Death Holds Off Traction Demand." 1903. *Chicago Tribune* September 29: 1.

Glazer, Russell. 1992. "The Sherman Amendment: Congressional Rejection of Communal Liability for Civil Rights Violations." *UCLA Law Review* 39: 1371–1406.

Kuo, Susan S. 2004. "Bringing in the State: Toward a Constitutional Duty to Protect from Mob Violence." *Indiana Law Journal* 79: 177–244.

"Municipal Liability for Riot Damage." 1968. *Harvard Law Review* 81(3): 653–656.

Warren, Charles. 1913. "The Progressiveness of the United States Supreme Court." *Columbia Law Review* 13: 294–313.

Charles L. Barzun

CHIEF JUSTICE

Surprisingly, the Constitution of the United States mentions the chief justice of the Supreme Court only once, in Article I, Section 3, providing that should the House of Representatives impeach the president, the chief justice shall preside over the Senate during the trial. Article II, Section 2 refers to "judges of the supreme Court" collectively, authorizing the president to appoint such judges after having obtained the Senate's consent. In the Judiciary Act of 1789, Congress established a Supreme Court staffed by a chief justice and five associate justices; subsequent acts have altered the number of associate justices from a minimum of six to a maximum of nine.

During the Court's first term, Chief Justice John Jay announced that the procedures of the Court would be in accord with the practice of the English common-law courts at Westminster, thereby adopting the traditional functions and powers of the chief justices of Common Pleas, King's Bench, and Exchequer. At a minimum these would include responsibility of presiding at Court sessions, chairing discussion of cases before judgment, and enjoying seniority over all other judges of their court.

The preeminence of the U.S. Supreme Court's chief justice is generally identified with the tenure of John Marshall, from 1801 to 1835. At the outset Marshall built upon his predecessor's use of per curium opinions, and instituted the unitary opinion of the Court as the standard mode for announcing Supreme Court decisions. Before 1811 he delivered virtually all of the Court's opinions and very likely wrote all of the opinions he delivered. After 1812, delivery of Court opinions and their authorship began to be shared with other justices. By the time of Chief Justice Roger Taney, from 1836 to 1864, the modern practice had begun to evolve: The chief justice assigned opinions whether he was in the majority or among the dissenters. The senior associate justice within the group opposed to the views of the chief justice assigns opinion writing duties to one of his or her colleagues.

The unitary opinion of the Court provided an authoritative and highly influential justification for the decision. Marshall and his successors played a critical role in gaining unanimity among the justices, either through intellectual persuasion, social pressure, or good judgment in assigning opinion-writing duties. They also exercised influence through their traditional opportunity to state the case in the Court's conference sessions, thereby summarizing both the underlying law and facts, and also setting an agenda for discussion.

The most successful chief justices were those who had highly developed people skills, and who were most successful in maintaining a cooperative and respectful atmosphere among the justices. During the Marshall era, collegiality was fostered by the judges lodging together in the same boarding house. This housing arrangement fell into disuse toward the end of Marshall's chief justiceship, and thereafter the members met less frequently and worked on Court business at their residences. As a consequence, the influence of the chief justice declined, and there was a greater tendency toward the production of dissenting or concurring opinions. Since the 1935 completion of the present Supreme Court building, the proximity of the justices' offices within the building has helped to ensure collegiality. In addition, the current practice of circulating draft opinions among the justices, dating from about 1880, provides an additional incentive toward unanimity in opinions of the Court.

Chief justices are also charged with oversight of judicial business, both before the Court itself and throughout the federal judiciary. A growing caseload has been the bête noire of federal courts, just as the increased complexity of litigation has spawned more numerous and more lengthy dissenting and concurring opinions. Since most of the Supreme Court's business consists of appellate cases, chief justices have periodically requested legislation designed to expedite the Supreme Court's work. The 1891 Evarts Act relieved the justices of circuit-riding duties and provided flexibility to extend the full Court's term in Washington, D.C.

A dramatic change occurred with the implementation of the Court's certiorari procedures, begun modestly and selectively in 1918 through legislative lobbying by Chief Justice Edward D. White. Conversion to the certiorari requirement for virtually all appellate cases was completed by the so-called Judges Act of 1925; passage of this major reform was due in large measure to the persuasive abilities and political influence of former President William Howard Taft, then serving as Chief Justice of the Court. Before statutory certiorari became available, the Supreme Court was required to deal with all appeals that met jurisdictional requirements. By 1900 the Court, even with strict control of its time and resources, was overwhelmed with about 600 appeals per annum. The new certiorari procedure gave the Court discretion to select the significant cases for argument hearing, and to summarily reject all others except a limited number of mandatory appeals or original jurisdiction matters. Not only was the Court's backlog sharply reduced, but also the shorter argument docket provided more time to deal with critical national issues, and permitted the justices to fashion more carefully reasoned and exhaustive opinions.

A chief justice's duties extend well beyond the narrow parameters of Supreme Court leadership and administrative control. The office has always carried with it the need to represent and defend the Court in the general public, to deal with interbranch tension in the federal government, and to moderate federal-state clashes. Chief Justice Marshall faced down numerous congressional proposals to limit his Court's appellate jurisdiction; in one instance he undertook the pseudonymous defense of his opinion in *M'Culloch v. Maryland*, 17 U.S. 316 (1819), in newspapers. Chief Justice Taney followed Marshall's example in defending the judiciary's power to issue writs of habeas corpus even in the face of hostile public opinion.

Riding the federal circuits before 1892, chief justices and their Court colleagues were familiar with the challenges that faced federal district court judges; in the twentieth century that supervisory role would be facilitated with the 1922 establishment of the Judicial Conference of the United States, followed in 1939 by the creation of the Administrative Office of United States Courts. Both assisted the chief justice in the rapidly evolving role as head of the federal judicial system. Warren Burger, during his chief justiceship from 1968 to 1986, established the Federal Judicial Center in Washington, D.C.; the National Center for State Courts in Williamsburg, Virginia; and the Supreme Court Historical Society, a nonprofit learned society devoted to advancing the history and public awareness of the Supreme Court's role in American life and government.

Chief justices have always been tapped for quasi-judicial duties and other public service assignments: Chief Justices Jay and Oliver Ellsworth took leave from the Court while functioning as diplomats in the early days of the Republic. Chief Justice Earl Warren served as chairman of the commission appointed to investigate the assassination of President John F. Kennedy. Chief Justice Salmon Chase presided over the Senate during its 1868 impeachment trial of President Andrew Johnson (1808–1875), as did Chief Justice William Rehnquist in the 1999 trial of President Bill Clinton (1946–).

The chief justice's multifaceted responsibilities far exceed the anticipations of the Constitution's framers. In the popular mind, the incumbents have begun to symbolize the majesty of the law as well as the increase of federal judicial power. The Supreme Court's presiding officer is frequently misidentified as the Chief Justice of the United States, despite manifest error both in the title and in the constitutional functions of the Court. Yet in a broader sense, since 1900 the Supreme Court's chief justiceship may well have evolved to the point that the new title is quite accurate.

SEE ALSO *Burger, Warren E.; Conference of the Justices; Extrajudicial Activities; Judiciary Act of 1789; Judiciary Act of 1925; Marshall, John; Roberts, John*

BIBLIOGRAPHY

Seddig, Robert G. 1975. "John Marshall and the Origins of Supreme Court Leadership." *University of Pittsburgh Law Review* 36(4): 785–833.

Steamer, Robert J. 1986. *Chief Justice: Leadership and the Supreme Court.* Columbia: University of South Carolina Press.

White, G. Edward. 2006. "The Internal Powers of the Chief Justice: The Nineteenth-Century Legacy." *University of Pennsylvania Law Review* 154(6): 1463–1510.

Herbert A. Johnson

CHILDREN AND THE CONSTITUTION

While there is no explicit mention of children in the U.S. Constitution, minors are clearly "persons" within the constitutional scheme, at least for some purposes. Persons of all ages—free and enslaved—were included in the population counts on which proportionate representation was based. Many of those who served in militias and armed forces were minors. And, under Article I, Section 9, clause 1, children were among the persons allowed to be imported into slavery and servitude. While they shared the burdens of creating a new nation, children in early America enjoyed few rights independent of those of their parents and were treated much like a form of human property. Under the common law, fathers had the rights to custody and control of their children, to collect their wages, to indenture them, to make testamentary disposition of them, and to collect damages for injury to them. Children could not bring suits in their own name, testify in court, or sign binding contracts. Children remained under parental control until they reached the age of majority (generally twenty-one), married, or entered the military.

Nineteenth-century Supreme Court cases reflect the child's status as quasi property of the parent. For example, in *Dred Scott v. Sandford*, 60 U.S. 393 (1857), an enslaved man of African descent claimed he had been emancipated when his master took him from a slave state into free territory. Among the common law rights of free men that Dred Scott asserted were the rights to custody and control of his daughters, Eliza and Lizzie, and to receive money damages for a whipping inflicted on them without his permission.

PARENTAL RIGHTS

A pair of early twentieth-century cases, *Meyer v. Nebraska*, 262 U.S. 390 (1923) and *Pierce v. Society of Sisters*, 268 U.S. 510 (1925), first identified parental rights over children as a constitutionally protected liberty interest. In

Teacher Opal Harper at the integrated Central High School, January 1976. Supreme Court decisions after the mid-twentieth century began to favor the concept of rights for children, particularly evident in the Brown v. Board of Education *ruling, requiring African-American students be allowed to attend the same schools as white students. However, as minors, children do not possess all of the rights adults enjoy, as evidenced in decisions restricting speech in schools.* BILL EPPRIDGE/TIME LIFE PICTURES/GETTY IMAGES

Meyer and *Pierce*, state laws prohibiting the teaching of foreign languages and mandating that children attend only public schools were held to violate parents' rights to direct the upbringing of their children. Written in the heyday of substantive due process by the archconservative Justice James Clark McReynolds, they draw upon the theory made infamous in cases like *Lochner v. New York*, 198 U.S. 45 (1905): that the due process clause of the Fourteenth Amendment restrains government from interfering in a range of fundamental but unenumerated liberties. Parents' constitutional rights, however, were not absolute. Dicta in *Meyer* and *Pierce*, that government could restrict parental authority when necessary to the protection of the child, became the holding in *Prince v. Massachusetts*, 321 U.S. 158 (1944). In *Prince*, the Court recognized the right of the parent or guardian to control a child's religious training and the right of the child to express her faith by selling religious pamphlets on the street. But the Court held that these rights did not outweigh the state's interest in protecting children from dangerous work environments. *Prince* was a landmark case in explicitly recognizing children's own First Amendment rights as well as the state's interest in protecting children from abuses of parental authority. *Prince* established that state intervention between parent and child must be narrowly tailored and justified by compelling state interests, a template that has dominated Supreme Court jurisprudence of the family ever since.

The Court has continued to endorse this tradition of parental rights, but not without controversy. In *Troxel v. Granville*, 530 U.S. 57 (2000), a case involving grandparent visitation, a plurality of the Court relied on *Meyer* and *Pierce* to strike down, as applied, a law that allowed "any person" to seek visitation with a child when it was in the child's best interest. The Washington family court had ordered overnight visitation with the parents of the deceased father, overruling the mother's decision to limit contact to daytime visits. The plurality held that parents were entitled to some deference and that the state could not simply second-guess parents' reasonable choices. Several justices thought the plurality's approach too narrow, and would have gone further in exploring the rights of the children themselves to contact with the grandparents. Others, notably Justices Antonin Scalia and Clarence Thomas, seemed ready to question the validity of *Meyer* and *Pierce*, and the very notion that Fourteenth Amendment liberty extends to family rights. It remains to be seen how the Court's jurisprudence of the family will develop.

Given the strong American tradition of parental rights, it is not surprising that the recognition that children have rights of their own in conflicts with the State has been slow to develop in American constitutional law. Instead of a robust set of "rights" that the State is obligated to respect, American children have generally been seen as having "interests" that the State may choose to further through education, public health, and child protection laws. In *DeShaney v. Winnebago County*, 489 U.S. 189 (1989), the Court rejected the argument that the State has a duty to protect children from abuse.

CHILDREN'S RIGHTS

In the second half of the twentieth century, children have increasingly begun to appear in constitutional law as active agents rather than as passive objects. The Supreme Court began to articulate children's constitutional rights, as persons under the Fourteenth Amendment, to equal protection of the laws, and to due process of law. In cases such as *Brown v. Board of Education*, 347 U.S. 483 (1954), parents challenged segregated schools by asserting their children's rights to protection from racial discrimination. Children themselves braved angry crowds to integrate Little Rock High School in Arkansas, precipitating a clash of state and federal powers that culminated in federal troops being sent to enforce the supremacy of the Constitution. Many children marched and were arrested in the civil rights movement, earning a place of honor in constitutional history.

In a series of cases applying the equal protection clause, the Court examined laws that treat illegitimate children differently from marital children (e.g., *Levy v. Louisiana*, 391 U.S. 68 [1968]). Despite the deep roots in common law tradition of such laws, the Court held that it is fundamentally unjust to penalize innocent children for the conduct of their parents. Some laws that treat nonmarital children differently still survive, but are subjected to heightened constitutional scrutiny. Still, children whose parents are not married, especially children in gay and lesbian families, have unequal access to benefits and services in comparison with children of married parents.

The Fourteenth Amendment is not the only source of rights for children. Children and youth have asserted their free speech rights under the First Amendment, claiming rights to engage in political discourse in cases like *Tinker v. Des Moines Independent Community School District*, 393 U.S. 503 (1969). The children in *Tinker* wore black armbands to school, in protest of the Vietnam War (1957–1975), and their right to engage in peaceful expression was upheld by the Supreme Court. Many believe that *Tinker* represents the high-water mark of children's free speech rights. In subsequent cases, the Court has shown considerable deference to authority figures, stressing children's and society's interests in adult control, especially in the school setting (*Hazelwood School District v. Kuhlmeier*, 484 U.S. 260 [1988]).

The issue of children's right to education poses a striking anomaly. Clearly, education is as fundamental to a child's life chances as the freedoms to work, marry, and travel are to adults. While equal access to education is a cornerstone of children's constitutional rights, and was even extended to illegal immigrant children in *Plyler v. Doe*, 457 U.S. 202 (1982), the Court has never held that children have a fundamental "right" to education. The federal Constitution imposes no obligation on states to provide any education at all, but if they do so, they must be evenhanded.

Many constitutional cases involve children asserting their First Amendment rights to religious freedom, most often in the context of schooling. Traditionally, as in *Prince,* such claims were brought by parents or guardians, not children. A watershed case in thinking about children's rights, as famous for its dissent as for its majority opinion, was *Wisconsin v. Yoder*, 406 U.S. 205 (1972). The Court held that Amish parents were entitled to accommodation of their religious practice of removing children from school after eighth grade, despite state laws mandating schooling until age sixteen. In his dissent, Justice William O. Douglas questioned why the children's viewpoints had not been heard and urged that they had a central stake in whether or not they completed high school. In subsequent cases, the Court has given greater deference to the child's own role in the free exercise of religion or in resisting establishment of a state religion.

LIMITATIONS ON THE RIGHTS OF CHILDREN

Overall, the Court seems reluctant to attribute full-fledged rights to children because of their perceived and often real lack of maturity. While the Court has extended to children many of the rights that apply to adults, the child's liberties are often modified in deference to the state's interest in protection of children and parents' rights to control the upbringing of their children. For example, children have rights to free speech and free exercise of religion in the schools, but schools may place greater limitations on these rights than in cases involving adults. Following *Tinker*, the Court has made clear that the educational mission justifies significant restraints on children's in-school speech and expressive conduct. Children's persons, rucksacks, and lockers may be searched in circumstances that would violate an adult's Fourth Amendment right to be free from unreasonable search and seizure (*New Jersey v. T.L.O.*, 469 U.S. 325 [1985]). Schools may also test children for drugs in circumstances where they could not force an adult to submit to a drug test (*Vernonia School District v. Acton*, 515 U.S. 646 [1995]).

The Court has had a particularly difficult time dealing with the teenager's ambiguous status as not fully autonomous in fact or in law, and yet still persons under the Constitution. Ambiguity about teenagers' status is especially evident in the context of reproductive rights. The Court has recognized the rights of mature minors to obtain abortions, but has let stand laws mandating parental notice and consent. In a series of cases, the Court approved a scheme for dealing with pregnant minors who otherwise would need parental permission to obtain an abortion (*Bellotti v. Baird*, 443 U.S. 622 [1979]). If the pregnant girl is mature enough to make her own decisions, the Court will provide a "judicial bypass," allowing her to obtain an abortion without her parents' permission. If she is not mature enough, the judge will determine whether an abortion is in the pregnant minor's best interest. In the mid-2000s, a flurry of state laws were passed mandating parental notice and consent, and the Court seemed poised to narrow or overrule many precedents that rely on *Roe v. Wade*, 410 U.S. 113 (1973).

While civil law has been wary of arguments about children's equality, they have found greater recent support in criminal law. At the turn of the twentieth century, special juvenile courts had been established to deal with youths who committed acts that would be crimes if committed by an adult. Intended to focus on rehabilitation rather than punishment, these juvenile courts adopted informal procedures aimed at reclaiming wayward children. But they had the power to keep children locked up for many years, even for minor infractions of law. The Supreme Court has extended some but not all of the Bill of Rights protections to children tried in these courts. *In re Gault*, 387 U.S. 1 (1967), for example, established the child's right to counsel in juvenile court, but *McKeiver v. Pennsylvania*, 403 U.S. 528 (1971) rejected the child's claim to a jury trial.

Meanwhile, state legislatures driven by fears of juvenile crime, began to dismantle special protections for children in criminal cases. The late twentieth century saw a trend to trying younger and younger children in adult criminal courts. In some states, the law sets no minimum age for trying a child as an adult. Of course, unlike a child in the juvenile justice system, an eleven-year-old defendant tried as an adult has all the constitutional rights of an adult. Yet the child may lack the autonomy to make his own decisions, or the capacity to understand the proceedings and engage in his own defense. In addition, many argue that the child's lack of maturity makes him less culpable and that inflicting harsh penalties like execution and life in prison without parole for crimes committed by children violates the Eighth Amendment injunction against cruel or unusual punishment and the Fourteenth Amendment due process clause. In *Roper v. Simmons*, 543 U.S. 551 (2005), the Supreme Court agreed in part, invalidating the death penalty as a punishment for acts committed while under age eighteen. Life in prison without parole remains a common sentence for children tried as adults in states such as California, Florida, Texas, and Virginia.

As the pendulum has swung back and forth from protection of youth to empowerment of youth, and even fear of youth, the question arises: How can advocates for children claim that children are mature enough to have rights and then claim they are too immature to take responsibility? If an adolescent child is mature enough to make his or her own decisions about religion or reproduction, why should the same child not take full responsibility for the consequences of his or her own criminal acts? Should children be viewed as essentially dependent, and in need of protection by adults, or essentially autonomous and entitled to equal rights with adults? The enigma of children's constitutional rights can only be resolved by acknowledging both their need for protection and their emerging capacities to act autonomously. A child too young to make a choice may nevertheless be entitled to a voice in his destiny. A child old enough to act autonomously may nevertheless need protection from the harshest consequences of his own bad choices. It seems clear that children are persons under the Constitution, and entitled to assert their rights, but they are also entitled to be treated in a way that respects their differences from adults. Interpreting how the Constitution applies to children requires a careful balancing of their developmental needs for parental guidance and protection from harm and their emerging autonomy as individuals.

SEE ALSO *Education and the Constitution; Goss v. Lopez, 419 U.S. 565 (1975); In re Gault, 387 U.S. 1 (1967); Juvenile Justice; Rights of Students; School Desegregation; School Prayer; Tinker v. Des Moines School District, 393 U.S. 503 (1969)*

BIBLIOGRAPHY

Fellmeth, Robert C. 2002. *Child Rights and Remedies.* Atlanta, GA: Clarity Press.

Guggenheim, Martin. 2005. *What's Wrong with Children's Rights?* Cambridge, MA: Harvard University Press.

Woodhouse, Barbara Bennett. 1992. "Who Owns the Child?: *Meyer* and *Pierce* and the Child as Property." *William and Mary Law Review* 33: 1041.

Woodhouse, Barbara Bennett. 2000. *The Status of Children: A Story of Emerging Rights, in Crosscurrents: Family Law and Policy in the United States and England.* New York: Oxford University Press.

Woodhouse, Barbara Bennett. 2008. *Hidden in Plain Sight: The Tragedy of Children's Rights from Ben Franklin to Lionel Tate.* Princeton, NJ: Princeton University Press.

Barbara Bennett Woodhouse

CHILDREN AND THE FIRST AMENDMENT

The Supreme Court has made clear that the First Amendment of the U.S. Constitution, like other constitutional rights, applies to children. The scope and nature of those rights, however, differs considerably from the First Amendment rights of adults. This difference is, in part, attributed to children's lesser maturity, which may compromise their ability to understand the potential negative effects of their speech on others and also make them more vulnerable to those effects themselves. At least as important is the different context in which children's First Amendment claims arise. Most of the Supreme Court's rulings on children's First Amendment rights address children's rights of expression in school, where the Court has recognized a strong state interest in controlling curriculum and student behavior.

The earliest student speech case, *West Virginia State Board of Education v. Barnette*, 319 U.S. 624 (1943), held that students could not be compelled to salute the flag in violation of their personal beliefs. Writing for the majority, Justice Robert Jackson noted the connection between affording children expressive freedom in school and nurturing their development into effective participants in a democratic system of government: "That [schools] are educating the young for citizenship is reason for scrupulous protection of Constitutional freedoms of the individual, if we are not to strangle the free mind at its source and teach youth to discount important principles of our government as mere platitudes."

A quarter century later, in *Tinker v. Des Moines School District*, 393 U.S. 503 (1969), the Court held that the suspension of several students for wearing black armbands to school in protest of the United States' military involvement in Vietnam violated their First Amendment rights. In a decision by Justice Abe Fortas, the Court famously declared that "it can hardly be argued that either students or teachers shed their constitutional rights to freedom of speech or expression at the schoolhouse gate." *Tinker* directed that student speech was to be protected unless it "materially disrupts class work or involves substantial disorder or invasion of the rights of others."

Tinker was understood, at the time, to provide broad protection to students' right to free expression in school, and it inspired considerable litigation and changes in schools' policy. But in the three major cases that subsequently reached the Supreme Court, the students' speech claims were rejected.

In *Bethel School District No. 403 v. Fraser*, 478 U.S. 675 (1986), a high school student was suspended for using "offensively lewd and indecent" language and gestures during a speech before an assembly of the entire student body. Despite the fact that an equivalent speech made by adults in a public setting would be protected, the Supreme Court upheld the school's action. In doing so, it emphasized that the school had an important role to play in teaching students "the habits and manners of civility," required to maintain a democratic system of government." In justifying its decision, it noted both that the speech in question had no political message and that it might have been "seriously damaging" to students, particularly younger female students, who could be confused or insulted by its message.

In *Hazelwood School District v. Kuhlmeier*, 484 U.S. 260 (1988), a high school principal banned publication of two pages of a student newspaper because he determined that two articles on those pages inadequately protected the interests of some of the articles' subjects. The Supreme Court upheld the principal's actions, despite the paper's declared policy announcing that the paper "accepts all rights implied by the First Amendment, ... [and understands that only speech that meets the *Tinker* standard] can be prohibited." Central to the Court's holding was the fact that the paper was funded by the school and produced as part of a journalism class, where a teacher assigned articles to students, reviewed student work, and awarded grades and credit. As a sponsor of the speech, which had a curricular purpose, the school was given wide latitude to control its content, subject only to the "reasonableness" constraint associated with speech limitations in nonpublic forums.

In *Morse v. Frederick*, 551 U.S. ___ (2007), a principal suspended a high school student for unfurling a banner with the phrase "BONG HiTS 4 JESUS" outside the school in front of other students who had been dismissed from classes to join spectators watching the Olympic torch pass by their school. Again the Court upheld the suspension. In his decision Chief Justice John Roberts noted that the banner could readily be interpreted to promote illegal drug use and stressed the state's strong interest in deterring drug use by its students. The Court suggested that, had the banner conveyed some message related to the ongoing political debate about the legalization of marijuana, it might well have been protected. In announcing its decision, the *Morse* Court emphasized that *Tinker's* highly protective standard was limited to students' independent speech, particularly political speech, and noted that the Court had allowed other interests to come into play in *Fraser* (where the speech was frivolous and offensive) and *Hazelwood* (where student views could be mistaken for the views of the school).

The Supreme Court has also addressed children's right to access information, but this area of law is less well developed. In *Ginsberg v. New York*, 390 U.S. 629 (1968), the Court upheld a state law that prohibited the sale to minors of magazines that could not have been censored for adults. Decided just one year before *Tinker*, *Ginsberg* noted, generally, that "the power of the state to control the conduct of children reaches beyond the scope of its authority over adults," quoting *Prince v. Massachusetts*, 321 U.S.158 (1944) and, more specifically, that the state had an interest in supporting parents in the upbringing of their children and an independent interest in protecting children from harm. In *Board of Education, Island Trees Union Free School District No. 26 v. Pico*, 457 U.S. 853 (1982), a plurality of the Court ruled that students' First Amendment rights limit the school's authority to remove books from the school library, particularly if that removal is motivated by a disapproval of the views expressed in the books. While children's right to access information and images on the Internet have also been asserted alongside adult claims in cases challenging Internet regulations, the Supreme Court has focused on the First Amendment rights of adults in determining the constitutionality of those regulations (see, e.g., *Reno v. American Civil Liberties Union*, 521 U.S. 844 [1997]).

SEE ALSO *Bethel School District No. 403 v. Fraser, 478 U.S. 675 (1986); Hazelwood School District v. Kuhlmeier, 484 U.S.260 (1988); Morse v. Frederick, 551 U.S. ___ (2007); Tinker v. Des Moines School District, 393 U.S. 503 (1969); West Virginia State Board of Education v. Barnette, 319 U.S. 624 (1943)*

BIBLIOGRAPHY

"A Constitutional Law Symposium." 2000. *Drake Law Review* 48: 445.

"Symposium: Do Children Have the Same First Amendment Rights As Adults?" 2004. *Chicago-Kent Law Review* 79: 3.

Emily Buss

CHINESE EXCLUSION ACT
SEE *Asian Exclusion Laws.*

CHISHOLM V. GEORGIA, 2 U.S. 419 (1793)

There are many competing interpretations of the history behind the Eleventh Amendment. *Chisholm v. Georgia*, 2 U.S. 419 (1793) is at the heart of these competing interpretations. Prior to the American Revolution, the understanding of "sovereignty" in Great Britain was that the King-in-Parliament was sovereign and immune from suit. There was little discussion of state sovereign immunity at the Constitutional Convention in Philadelphia, but the discussion began in earnest during the state ratification conventions, where many delegates argued that Article III's diversity jurisdiction authorized suits against nonconsenting states. However, many of the most prominent framers and ratifiers assured the conventions that Article III did not abrogate state immunity from suit.

Chisholm v. Georgia involved a breach of contract suit in the United States Supreme Court brought by Alexander Chisholm, the executor of the estate of Robert Farquhar who, during the Revolutionary War (1775–1783), sold goods to Georgia. Georgia failed to pay the sizable debt. Consequently, Chisholm brought an action under the Supreme Court's Article III diversity jurisdiction, which applies to "[c]ontroversies between ... a State and Citizens of another State." Georgia refused to appear before the Court.

The majority of the Court, in seriatim opinions, ruled that it had jurisdiction over the suit. The majority relied on the conventional meaning of Article III's text and the nature of sovereignty. First, the majority argued that Article III's text permitted the suit. Second, they contended that the concept of state sovereign immunity had its roots in feudalism, which had no place in the United States, where the people were sovereign. States were simply collections of individuals, and since one individual may sue another, equality demanded than an individual may sue any number of individuals, regardless of whether that group carried the label of "state."

Justice James Iredell (1751–1799) dissented and focused on the jurisdiction conferred on federal courts in Section 14 of the Judiciary Act of 1789, which stated that federal courts had jurisdiction "agreeable to the principles and usages of law." Justice Iredell argued that Georgia's law regarding suit against itself was like that of every other state: it was prohibited. He concluded that Section 14 incorporated the common law of state sovereign immunity, which proscribed suits against states for their contract debts. Justice Iredell also opined that Article III did not alter state sovereign immunity.

There was a strong reaction against *Chisholm*. In 1934, in *Principality of Monaco v. Mississippi*, 292 U.S. 313, the Supreme Court would state that the decision "created such a shock of surprise that the Eleventh Amendment was at once proposed and adopted." The Georgia House of Representatives, for example, passed a bill that made anyone who attempted to enforce *Chisholm* subject to hanging. A proposed amendment to the Constitution was introduced into the U.S. House of Representatives the day after the Court announced *Chisholm*, and Congress sent what became the Eleventh Amendment to the states shortly thereafter.

The competing interpretations of the Eleventh Amendment have described the relationship between the Eleventh Amendment and *Chisholm* differently. The Supreme Court has long advocated the "sovereign immunity" interpretation—most prominently in *Alden v. Maine*, 527 U.S. 706 (1999)—which views the Eleventh Amendment as a repudiation of *Chisholm* and a reaffirmation of a broad constitutional principle of state sovereign immunity.

The most prominent competing interpretation, the "diversity" interpretation, explains the Eleventh Amendment as eliminating only federal courts' diversity jurisdiction over states sued by noncitizens. Scholars have offered different rationales for this interpretation. For example, scholar James E. Pfander (1998) has argued that the Eleventh Amendment repudiated *Chisholm* only to the extent to which it interpreted Article III to apply retroactively to state debts antecedent to the Constitution's ratification.

SEE ALSO *Eleventh Amendment*

BIBLIOGRAPHY

Amar, Akhil Reed. 1987. "Of Sovereignty and Federalism." *Yale Law Journal* 96: 1425.

Mathis, Doyle. 1967. "*Chisholm v. Georgia*: Background and Settlement." *Journal of American History* 54(1): 19–29.

Pfander, James E. 1998. "History and State Suability: An 'Explanatory' Account of the Eleventh Amendment." *Cornell Law Review* 83: 1269–1382.

Lee J. Strang

CHURCH OF JESUS CHRIST OF LATTER-DAY SAINTS

Through repeated appearances before the U.S. Supreme Court, the Church of Jesus Christ of Latter-day Saints, known colloquially as the Mormons, was a driving force behind the interpretation of the First Amendment's religion clauses.

Pointing to examples from the Old Testament and Mormon scripture, the church officially endorsed plural marriage in 1852. Four years later, the Republican Party announced its opposition to the "twin relics of barbarism," slavery and polygamy, and in 1862 Congress passed the Morrill Anti-Bigamy Act criminalizing polygamy in the territories. Mormons, however, regarded the law as a violation of their constitutional rights, and federal officials in Utah Territory thought convictions under the law were impossible because of Mormon influence on the territorial judiciary.

In 1874 Congress responded by sharply limiting local control of the Utah courts. Prosecutors and church leaders then cooperated to create a test case on the constitutionality of the Morrill Act. George Reynolds was found guilty of bigamy, and ultimately appealed to the Court. Prior to *Reynolds v. United States*, 98 U.S. 145 (1878), the Court had never construed the meaning of the free exercise clause. Reaching its substance for the first time, the Court held that it protected beliefs but not actions, affirming Reynolds's conviction.

Reynolds launched a decade-long legal crusade against polygamy that came to be known as "The Raid." This effort resulted in numerous cases before the Court. In an early example of dialogue with the legislative branch, *Miles v. United States*, 103 U.S. 304 (1881) suggested that antibigamy laws be amended to ease prosecutions. Congress responded, and in 1885 three cases under the new law reached the Court. In *Murphy v. Ramsey*, 114 U.S. 15 (1885), the Court upheld the disenfranchisement of polygamists, and in *Clawson v. United States*, 114 U.S. 477 (1885), the Court affirmed the exclusion of Mormons from juries.

The third case, *Cannon v. United States*, 116 U.S. 55 (1885), involved the definition of a new crime—unlawful cohabitation—designed to facilitate convictions. Bigamy required proof of separate marriage ceremonies. Mormon marriages, however, were performed secretly, and gathering evidence frequently proved impossible. Criminalizing "cohabitation with more than one woman" avoided this problem. Defendants, however, insisted that "cohabitation" required proof of sexual intercourse. The Court rejected this position, holding that cohabitation simply involved "holding out to the world two women as ... wives."

Prosecutors then began "segregating" the offense, indicting defendants on multiple counts for each year during which they had unlawfully cohabitated. This approach allowed much harsher punishments. In *In re Snow*, 120 U.S. 274 (1887), however, the justices rejected the theory of segregation, insisting that cohabitation was "inherently a continuous offense."

In 1887 Congress produced a fourth round of legislation known as the Edmunds-Tucker Act. The act dissolved the church as a corporation and confiscated all of its property. In *Late Corporation of the Church of Jesus Christ of Latter-day Saints v. United States*, 136 U.S. 1 (1890), the Court rejected the argument that the Edmunds-Tucker Act infringed on religious liberty in the strongest possible terms, comparing polygamy to human sacrifice, religious assassinations, and "other open offenses against the enlightened sentiment of mankind."

The same year, the Court upheld an Idaho law disenfranchising all Mormons in *Davis v. Beason*, 133 U.S. 333 (1890). In contrast to the law in *Murphy*, Idaho excluded any person—monogamist or polygamist—who subscribed to Mormon doctrine. In response, the so-called Cullom Bill, which would have disenfranchised all Mormons, was introduced in Congress.

Church president Wilford Woodruff (1807–1898) faced the bleak prospect of continued mass incarceration of Mormons, their permanent political subjugation, and the institutional annihilation of his church. In response, Woodruff recorded in his diary that he was praying to the Lord and felt inspired by His spirit to issue the so-called Manifesto, in which he called on Mormons to obey the laws banning polygamy.

Despite the Manifesto, some Mormons continued to perform clandestine plural marriages, until the issue again burst on the national scene in three years (1904–1907) of grueling congressional hearings over the election of Reed Smoot (1862–1941), a high-ranking Mormon leader, to the U.S. Senate. Haunted by the return of "The Raid," the church began excommunicating those who continued polygamy, which has been its policy ever since.

Excommunicated Mormons founded polygamous sects that continue to thrive in the American West. In 1946 Utah convicted one of these so-called Mormon fundamentalists for "conspiracy to commit acts injurious to ... public morals" by publishing a pamphlet advocating polygamy. In *Musser v. Utah*, 333 U.S. 95 (1948), the Court avoided reaching the merits of Musser's constitutional challenge, but, in a marked shift from nineteenth-century cases, a sharp dissent insisted that his conviction violated the free speech clause.

More recently, in *Corporation of the Presiding Bishop v. Amos*, 483 U.S. 327 (1987), the Court rejected an establishment clause attack on the church's exemption from antidiscrimination laws. Mormons were again before the Court in *Santa Fe Independent School District v. Doe*, 530 U.S. 290 (2000), where one of the Jane Doe plaintiffs who successfully challenged the highly Protestant prayers offered at public school football games in Texas was a Mormon.

Critics have claimed that the belief-action distinction provides no protection for religious practice, but the Court strongly affirmed *Reynolds* in *Employment Division v. Smith*, 494 U.S. 872 (1990). On the other hand, in *Romer v. Evans*, 517 U.S. 620 (1996), the Court explicitly rejected the more extreme position it had staked out in *Davis v. Beason*. *Davis*, wrote Justice Anthony Kennedy, "is no longer good law."

The Mormon cases illustrate deeper issues of law's power. The Court forced the issue of the Manifesto, but it ultimately did not end Mormon polygamy, which came in the political settlement of the Smoot hearings rather than the legal settlement of *Late Corporation*. The persistence of schismatic polygamous groups is further evidence of law's limited ability to eradicate religious practices. Conversely, the Court's work triggered a reformation of Mormon theology, which points toward the abiding influence of the Court on the most sacred aspects of American life.

SEE ALSO *First Amendment; Free Exercise of Religion; Late Corporation of the Church of Jesus Christ of Latter-day Saints v. United States, 136 U.S. 1 (1889)*

BIBLIOGRAPHY

Firmage, Edwin Brown, and Richard Collin Mangrum. 1988. *Zion in the Courts: A Legal History of the Church of Jesus Christ of Latter-day Saints, 1830–1900*. Urbana: University of Illinois Press.

Gordon, Sarah Barringer. 2002. *The Mormon Question: Polygamy and Constitutional Conflict in Nineteenth-century America*. Chapel Hill: University of North Carolina Press.

Harmer-Dionne, Elizabeth. 1998. "Once a Peculiar People: Cognitive Dissonance and the Suppression of Mormon Polygamy as a Case Study Negating the Belief-Action Distinction." *Stanford Law Review* 50: 1295–1347.

Nathan B. Oman

CHURCH OF THE LUKUMI BABALU AYE V. CITY OF HIALEAH, 508 U.S. 520 (1993)

In *Church of the Lukumi Babalu Aye v. City of Hialeah*, 508 U.S. 520 (1993), the Supreme Court unanimously ruled that the city of Hialeah, Florida, violated the First Amendment's free exercise clause when it banned the ritual slaughter of animals, while exempting virtually all such killings except those done in the sacramental rite of Santeria, an Afro-Caribbean religion. Because the ordinances were not "neutral [toward religion] or generally applicable" under the test of *Employment Division v. Smith*, 494 U.S. 872 (1990), they were subject to, and failed, the "most rigorous" test of constitutional validity: that they serve a "compelling governmental interest" and be "narrowly tailored" to that interest.

Santeria, a fusion of Western African tribal religion and Roman Catholic elements, formed in the nineteenth century when Africans were brought as slaves to Cuba. Members express their devotion to various spirits through, among other things, sacrificing chickens, goats, and other animals at various rituals. Adherents of Santeria faced persecution in Cuba and it was typically practiced in secret. It came to south Florida mainly through exiles from the Castro revolution and numbered about 50,000 practitioners in the area by the 1980s.

THE HIALEAH ORDINANCES

The *Lukumi* case began in 1987 when a Santeria group in Hialeah, determined to practice the faith openly, leased land to build a house of worship, a school, and a cultural center. The City Council reacted with an emergency public session and passed a set of ordinances at several meetings. Resolutions prefacing the ordinances declared the city's commitment to "oppos[ing] the ritual sacrifice of animals." The first ordinance incorporated Florida's state animal cruelty law, which prohibited anyone from "unnecessarily or cruelly" killing an animal. Wishing to enact a specific ban on religious animal sacrifice, the City Council obtained an opinion from Florida's attorney general that a ban would not conflict with the state law standard, and thus would be permissible, because "ritual sacrifice . . . for purposes other than food consumption" would be "unnecessary" and would violate state law too. The attorney general defined unnecessary killing as that done "in a spirit of wanton cruelty or for the mere pleasure of destruction without being in any sense beneficial or useful to the person killing the animal."

The city then enacted three more ordinances, each with maximum punishments of sixty days imprisonment and a $500 fine. The first made it unlawful to sacrifice an animal—"to unnecessarily kill, torment, torture, or mutilate [it] in a public or private ritual or ceremony not for the primary purpose of food consumption"—but exempted slaughtering by "licensed establishment[s]" of animals "specifically raised for food purposes." The second ordinance was similar. The third prohibited "slaughter," defined as "the killing of animals for food," outside of areas zoned for slaughterhouse use.

The Santeria Church sued in federal district court, claiming that the ordinances violated its right to free exercise of religion and seeking to enjoin their enforcement. The district judge upheld the ordinances, stating that they did not target religious conduct "on their face" and their effect on religion was "incidental to their secular purpose and effect" of stopping animal sacrifice. The judge held that the ordinances served compelling interests in preventing health risks from unsanitary animals and remains, emotional injury to children from viewing sacrifices, and stress to animals kept in inhumane conditions before being killed. "Balancing" these interests against the effect on religion, he concluded that an absolute prohibition, without religious exemptions, was justified. The appellate court affirmed.

The case reached the Supreme Court in the wake of its 1990 decision in *Smith*, which had narrowed free exercise rights by holding—in contrast with earlier decisions like *Wisconsin v. Yoder*, 406 U.S. 205 (1972)—that a generally applicable and religion-neutral law could be applied to religious conduct no matter how great the restriction on religion and how minimal the government's interest in regulation. *Smith* was so controversial that it provoked congressional and state efforts to restore the previous, religion-protective standard by legislation (for example, the federal Religious Freedom Restoration Act of 1993). But questions remained on just how much the *Smith* rule had shrunk constitutional free exercise rights, and whether the Court would put teeth in its requirements of neutrality and general applicability.

NEUTRALITY AND GENERAL APPLICABILITY

The justices' unanimous ruling for the Church in *Lukumi* confirmed that free exercise rights had vitality even after *Smith*. Justice Anthony Kennedy's opinion did not question the *Smith* rule but held that Hialeah's ordinances were neither neutral nor generally applicable. They were non-neutral because their object was to target Santeria's sacramental act for suppression. Significantly, Kennedy wrote that although words like "sacrifice" could encompass secular conduct, the free exercise clause "extends beyond facial discrimination" against religion, forbidding "covert" targeting and "religious gerrymanders" as well. Targeting could be inferred from the provisions that confined the ordinances' effect almost entirely to the Santeria ritual, leaving unrestricted "killings that are no more necessary or humane in most circumstances." For example, kosher slaughter was unrestricted because of the ordinances' limit to ritual killings "not for the primary purpose of food consumption" and the exemption for "licensed [food] establishment[s]"; and the state-law definition of "unnecessary" incorporated in the first ordinance left unpunished most instances of killing including hunting, slaughter for food, and even "the use of live rabbits to train greyhounds." The Court reasoned that such "individualized governmental assessment" of Santeria sacrifices versus other killings unconstitutionally "devalue[d] religious reasons . . . by judging them to be of lesser import than nonreligious reasons." This rationale could require protection of religious conduct from many laws that apply general standards such as necessity or "reasonableness" on a case-by-case basis.

Targeting also appeared because the ordinances' asserted purposes could be achieved by regulations "far short of a flat prohibition" of Santeria sacrifices. For example, health threats from improperly disposed remains could be addressed by general laws on disposing of organic garbage, or by allowing Santeria sacrifices if, like kosher slaughter, they occurred in licensed, zoned slaughterhouses.

In another section of the opinion, Justice Kennedy found evidence of non-neutrality in the City Council proceedings, where council members and witnesses attacked Santeria as demon-worship and "an abomination to the Lord." Kennedy analogized this to evidence of racially or sexually discriminatory motives in equal protection clause cases. But this section commanded only two votes and thus does not govern future cases. Justice Antonin Scalia, joining the Court's result but not this section, refused to accept evidence of lawmakers' subjective discriminatory motives, arguing (as he has in other constitutional contexts) that a multi-member body cannot have a subjective intent, and that only the object and effect of a law matters to whether it "'prohibits the free exercise' of religion" as the clause forbids.

The Court also found the ordinances not generally applicable, again because they left unpunished numerous nonreligious instances of killing—fishing, hunting, medical experimentation, and others—that could implicate the city's asserted interests in preventing disease or cruelty to animals.

Having held that the "rigorous" test of compelling interest and narrow tailoring governed in *Lukumi*, the Court concluded that the ordinances failed the test. Because the state's asserted interests against disease and animal cruelty "[we]re not pursued with respect to analogous non-religious conduct, and those interests could be achieved by narrower ordinances that burdened religion to a far lesser degree," the ordinances were not narrowly tailored. The failure to pursue these interests consistently also undercut their claim to be "compelling."

THE LEGACY OF *LUKUMI*

Lukumi's most important implication is that it gave some teeth to the requirements that laws be neutral toward religion and generally applicable. The Court did not specify how "underinclusive" a law must be to fail the general applicability test: Because Hialeah's ordinances allowed almost every other kind of animal killing, they fell "well below the minimum standard." In subsequent cases, lower courts have extended *Lukumi* to require a religious exemption when a law exempts even one secular interest posing comparable risks to those posed by the religious practice. For example, Muslim police officers successfully asserted the right to wear beards because a police department facial-grooming rule already allowed beards for officers with skin disorders, and the department could not constitutionally "devalue religious reasons" (*Lukumi*) compared with medical ones. The Supreme Court has not yet ruled on this approach, nor have all lower courts endorsed it. But if it were adopted, it—like the "individual consideration" rationale above—would preserve strong free exercise rights even under *Smith*, since many laws contain some exception for valued secular interests.

Although the justices have not further specified how *Lukumi* applies to restrictive laws, recently they limited another potential implication of the decision: the claim that *Lukumi* invalidates state provisions singling out religious activities or institutions for exclusion from government funding programs. In *Locke v. Davey*, 540 U.S. 712 (2004), the state of Washington offered scholarships to needy students attending any accredited in-state public or private college, for any major except "theology [taught] from a devotional perspective." Although that exclusion plainly targeted religious studies, the Court upheld it under a pair of rationales. First, the burden, if any, from the withholding of aid was far milder than "criminal or civil sanctions" such as those in *Lukumi*, which "sought to suppress" religious practices rather than merely declining to fund them. Second, the state had a "historic and substantial interest" in denying funding for the training of clergy, an interest that the exclusion sought to implement. This interest, which extended back to the campaigns against tax assessments for clergy in the founding era, belied any claim that the exclusion rested on "animus toward religion."

These two rationales have different implications for the open issue of whether states can exclude religious schools from tuition-voucher programs. The first rationale broadly suggests that any provision denying funding rather than imposing regulation is distinguishable from *Lukumi*, while the narrower second rationale implies that *Lukumi*'s nondiscrimination rule may still govern outside the special context of clergy funding. Moreover, *Locke*'s suggestion that a free exercise claimant must prove state "animus" seems to apply only to exclusions from funding. Coercive regulations remain governed by *Lukumi*, where all but two justices found it enough that the government's action was discriminatory, whatever the officials' subjective motivations.

SEE ALSO *First Amendment; Free Exercise of Religion*

BIBLIOGRAPHY

Berg, Thomas C., and Douglas Laycock. 2004. "The Mistakes in Locke v. Davey and the Future of State Payments for Services Provided by Religious Institutions." *Tulsa Law Review* 40(2): 227–253.

Carter, Stephen L. 1993. "The Resurrection of Religious Freedom?" *Harvard Law Review* 107(1): 118–142.

Duncan, Richard F. 2001. "Free Exercise Is Dead, Long Live Free Exercise: Smith, Lukumi, and the General Applicability Requirement." *University of Pennsylvania Journal of Constitutional Law* 3: 850–884.

Graglia, Lino A. 1996. "Church of the Lukumi Babalu Aye: Of Animal Sacrifice and Religious Persecution." *Georgetown Law Journal* 85(1): 1–69.

Thomas C. Berg

CIRCUIT RIDING

Following established English practice, the federal Judiciary Act of 1789 established a system of circuit courts as the trial courts exercising federal jurisdiction under the Constitution. Initially, two justices of the U.S. Supreme Court were required to serve with the district judges in each of the thirteen states. Following a vigorous 1792 protest by the justices of the Court, Congress reduced Supreme Court participation to only one justice per circuit court; this circuit-riding assignment persisted until 1892, when the Evarts Act (1891) eliminated the requirement that Supreme Court justices attend the circuit courts. During the 1801–1802 Federalist-Jeffersonian confrontation over the federal judiciary, there was a brief period when separately commissioned circuit-court judges were appointed, anticipating the end of circuit riding. However, in 1802, the Jeffersonian-Republican congressional majority repealed this arrangement, and the justices resumed their duties on the circuits. Thereafter, the major developments concerning the circuit courts involved the addition of new circuit courts as new states were admitted to the federal union.

In the early decades of their existence, U.S. circuit courts represented the federal government's most visible presence in the capitals and major cities of the various states. In the conduct of criminal trials, they provided a

forceful reminder of the centralized government's authority. The trials of participants in the Whiskey and Fries rebellions, along with the more famous treason trial of former vice president Aaron Burr (1807), were conducted before U.S. circuit courts. In addition, service in the circuit courts brought the justices into contact with the law in the various states and familiarized them with local politics and social customs. Active participation in trials and acquaintance with local district-court judges provided the justices with a working knowledge of the conduct of judicial business in the lower federal courts. Depending upon the nature of the litigation in their assigned circuits, the expertise the justices developed was useful when the Supreme Court considered special areas of jurisprudence. Indeed, while on circuit many justices consulted with more knowledgeable colleagues concerning issues pending before them.

Not infrequently, Supreme Court justices were present when their decisions below were reviewed on appeal by the Supreme Court. No rule of court precluded their participation in the discussion and judgment of these appeals, and some justices made a practice of vigorously defending their earlier decisions. Undoubtedly, this discouraged litigants from appealing circuit-court decisions to the Supreme Court. At the same time, after 1802, the certificate of division procedures may have facilitated the appeal of a circuit-court case. This procedure was available when the two jurists disagreed; they might, by a certificate of division, submit the question to the next en banc sitting of the Supreme Court.

Throughout the nineteenth century, the circuit-court system was undermined by a rising Supreme Court caseload that required extending the duration of the high court's term. Congress also found it more convenient to confer circuit-court trial jurisdiction on independent district courts. This arrangement made it possible to provide federal courts for newly admitted states, without burdening the Supreme Court justices by increasing their attendance at a growing number of circuit courts. Before 1910 a few Supreme Court justices continued to attend circuit courts on an occasional basis. Thereafter, the only vestige of circuit riding is the assignment of Supreme Court justices to circuits, permitting the designee to sign office orders concerning cases pending in his or her circuit.

SEE ALSO *Judiciary Act of 1789; Judiciary Act of 1891*

BIBLIOGRAPHY

Ely, James W., Jr. 1995. *The Chief Justiceship of Melville W. Fuller, 1888–1910*. Columbia: University of South Carolina Press.

Frankfurter, Felix, and James M. Landis. 2007. *The Business of the Supreme Court: A Study in the Federal Judicial System*. New York: Macmillan, 1928; reprinted with new introduction by

Richard G. Stevens. New Brunswick, NJ: Transaction Publishers.

Johnson, Herbert A. 1997. *The Chief Justiceship of John Marshall, 1801–1835*. Columbia: University of South Carolina Press.

Whichard, Willis P. 2000. *Justice James Iredell*. Durham, NC: Carolina Academic Press.

Herbert A. Johnson

CITATIONS TO FOREIGN SOURCES

In explaining their rationale for reaching decisions, judges commonly appeal to the authority of legal texts and principles, precedent, tradition, and policy. Since the late 1990s, several Supreme Court justices have made additional appeals to the relevance of the practices, opinions, and court decisions of other countries, as well as diverse types of international practices and agreements—in the process sparking considerable political controversy. These recent transnational references were especially notable because they took place in cases involving domestic policy issues and questions of domestic constitutional law that are at the heart of partisan political contention, including federalism, gay rights, affirmative action, and the death penalty. In these decisions, the appeals to foreign sources were typically made and defended by the Court's liberal Democratic and moderate Republican justices (such as Justices Stephen Breyer, Ruth Bader Ginsburg, Anthony Kennedy, and Sandra Day O'Connor), and criticized by the Court's more conservative Republicans (such as Justices Antonin Scalia and Clarence Thomas). The latter accused the liberals of making illegitimate appeals to foreign sources of law in cases that should turn on the authority of domestic, not foreign, law. The political controversy over the citation to foreign sources became heated enough that Justices John Roberts and Samuel Alito were questioned about their views on the matter by the Republican-controlled Senate judiciary committee during their confirmation hearings. The issue may prompt further controversy in the future.

The contretemps over the Supreme Court's citations to "foreign sources" has rarely acknowledged the fact that "foreign sources" is a broad, catch-all category, alluding to a diversity of legal materials. These include the decisions of the courts of other countries, those nations' legislative and regulatory practices and experiences, general principles of the law of nations and international law (written and unwritten), international practice, bilateral treaties and agreements (some of which have been ratified by the United States, and some not), decisions by transnational courts and international tribunals, and the views of foreign scholars. Each of these is potentially relevant or authoritative (or not) in different ways. A citation to a treaty that the United States has signed, for instance, is binding on the Court under Article VI of the U.S. Constitution, and rarely problematic. The practices of nations in their external relations in some respects helps define the requirements of international law, which may be binding on the United States—or at least presumptively part of U.S. law in the absence of some expressed desire that it should not be. Court opinions from other countries, on the other hand, are not considered binding on U.S. judges. But American judges have cited the arguments made by foreign judges as persuasive, or illuminating, efforts to deal with legal and public policy conundrums similar to the ones they are facing at home. Judges may also cite foreign sources—along with the opinions of foreign legal scholars—as evidence of a movement toward the definition of new rights, or the best practices in the understanding of old ones. Even conservative justices interested in fixing the original meaning of provisions of the U.S. Constitution may look to the common law of England and English legal decisions handed down prior to the American Revolution (1775–1783) to help them discern what the framers meant by particular textual provisions and principles. The phenomenon is, in short, diverse, with some practices much more controversial than others.

EARLY COURT USE OF FOREIGN SOURCES

Strictly speaking, there is nothing new in the contemporary Supreme Court's referencing of foreign legal materials. Citations to foreign sources have been common since the Court's inception. John Marshall (chief justice, 1801–1833)—a founder and a touchstone justice to liberals and conservatives alike—commonly cited foreign sources of law in his opinions, as did the highly respected Joseph Story (associate justice, 1811–1845), a Harvard law professor and scholar of comparative, civil, and Roman law.

That said, before the Civil War (1861–1865), most of these citations were found in cases that were unambiguously international in nature: most involved international trade, shipping, and piracy. The law of nations was the foreign source most frequently cited, and the subject was most commonly either maritime law, the conflict of laws, and laws governing the relationship between sovereign states (including the laws of war). At the time, the prevailing understanding of the law of nations was that it was uniform throughout the civilized world, and, in its applicability, universal. In fixing the content of the law of nations, the early Court looked to the practices of other civilized countries (typically those of Europe), the understandings of eminent (non-American) legal scholars (such as Emmerich de Vattel, Hugo Grotius,

Samuel von Pufendorf, and Jean-Jacques Burlamaqui), and decisions by English judges. One of the most prominent allusions to a foreign source from this period appeared in *Murray v. The Schooner Charming Betsy*, 6 U.S. 64 (1804), which involved the seizure on the high seas of a commercial vessel by a U.S. Navy frigate for the violation of a ban on commercial intercourse between the United States and France. There, Chief Justice Marshall wrote that "an act of Congress ought never to be construed to violate the law of nations if any other possible construction remains." But foreign law other than the law of nations was sometime referenced as well. Justice Story, for instance, often looked to the civil law as being particularly helpful to the consideration of commercial law questions.

Foreign law—particularly Roman law—was also found helpful by the Court in slavery cases. Amongst the most prominent instances was *The Antelope*, 23 U.S. 66 (1825), which addressed the question of what was to be done with a ship captured while illegally importing slaves into the United States. There, Chief Justice Marshall undertook an extended discussion of the treatment of slavery under the law of nations. Roman and European law (including relevant rulings by English courts) were cited throughout the Supreme Court's opinion in *Dred Scott v. Sandford*, 60 U.S. 393 (1857) to shed light on the problem of the civil status of slaves.

Foreign sources of law were referenced in domestic cases after the Civil War. In *Reynolds v. United States*, 98 U.S. 145 (1879), one of the Mormon polygamy cases, the Court consulted contemporaneous English decisions to help it decide whether an exemption should be granted from ordinary legal obligations on the grounds of religious conviction. Foreign sources were also referenced in *Hurtado v. California*, 110 U.S. 516 (1884), which assessed the constitutionality (under the Fifth Amendment) in a felony case of a state's indictment by information, rather than by grand jury. There, the purpose was to inquire into the practices of other civilized nations in determining the minimal requirements of constitutional liberty. References to foreign sources in the international arena continued in this period as well. In *The Paquette Habana*, 175 U.S. 677 (1900), for instance, a case involving the capture by the U.S. Navy of Spanish fishing vessels off the coast of Cuba during the Spanish-American War (1898), the Court declared that "international law is part of our law" and looked to the practice of other countries in resolving the case.

TWENTIETH CENTURY

With the advent of the modern administrative state in the early twentieth century—and the attendant constitutional challenges mounted against it on the grounds that the novel regulations were arbitrary and unreasonable infringements against the "liberty" guaranteed by the Constitution's due process clauses—the Court cited the experiences and practices of other nations (including social scientific studies of those) as evidence of the law's reasonableness. In *Lochner v. New York*, 198 U.S. 45 (1905), which invalidated a New York state maximum-hours law for bakers, both Justices John Marshall Harlan and Edward White looked to the maximum-hours laws of other countries in considering the New York statute's reasonableness. Acting as a lawyer in *Muller v. Oregon*, 208 U.S. 412 (1908), future Supreme Court justice Louis D. Brandeis introduced extensive evidence concerning laws regulating the working hours of women in other countries, evidence that the Court cited in upholding a similar law passed by the state of Oregon. In the *Selective Draft Law Cases*, 245 U.S. 366 (1918), Justice White, writing for the Court, cited Vattel's *Law of Nations* (1758) in concluding that the "very conception of a just government and its duty to the citizen includes the reciprocal obligation of the citizen to render military service in case of need and the right to compel it." The Court considered the practices of civil and other common-law countries in *Palko v. Connecticut*, 302 U.S. 319 (1937), in attempting to fix the content of due process of law—which it defined as those "fundamental principles of liberty and justice which lie at the base of all our civil and political institutions."

There is thus considerable precedent for the citation of foreign sources of law by the Supreme Court. That is not to say, however, that the context in which foreign law is being cited in the early twenty-first century, and the purposes, are not significantly different. Since the early twentieth century—but especially since the Warren Court of the 1950s and 1960s—many judges and scholars have reconceptualized the Court as less of a legal and more of a lawmaking and policymaking institution. The citation to foreign sources by judges who understand themselves as making the law rather than following it has struck many as an illegitimate effort to import foreign preferences and practices into U.S. law. The problem becomes particularly acute when this is done in cases where European practices, opinions, and attitudes (concerning, for example, welfare-state entitlements, religiosity, and crime and punishment) diverge markedly from the views of Americans. The problematic nature of the citations is reinforced by the fact that, in the Progressive Era, foreign practices were typically cited as evidence of the reasonableness of the actions of the legislature, and thus, in the service of judicial quietism. By contrast, the more recent appeals are commonly made as part of the process of the judicial redefinition and expansion of court-declared rights, and thus in the service of judicial activism. That, since the Progressive Era, many of the Court's justices have come to understand their role frankly as an active partnership in the realization of social reform makes these references all the more suspect. This was certainly not the case for the justices who referred to foreign sources in the eighteenth and nineteenth century.

CONTEMPORARY CITATIONS

Contemporary citations to international law are also made in a context that, over the course of the last century, has been significantly altered. The traditional "law of nations" was built on a foundational commitment to the sovereignty of states, which, in turn, was understood to be indispensable to self-government. In the aftermath of World War II (1939–1945) and the revelation of the extent of the Nazi atrocities, however, increasing emphasis was placed in the "new" international law on sovereignty's limits. Some have even gone as far as arguing that the people of the early twenty-first century are witnessing the birth pangs of a "world constitution" above and beyond the constitutional nation-state to which, most have traditionally thought, domestic judges owe their office and their fealty. In the aftermath of the end of the Cold War there has been an explosion in the number of transnational activists and politically active scholars who have insisted that those standards set by the new international law are not static, but rather perpetually—and often rapidly—evolving. Significantly, they have typically taken it as their responsibility, and prerogative, to both define these new norms, and to midwife them into being. In the early twenty-first century—and unlike in the eighteenth and nineteenth centuries—when the Court cites provisions of international agreements, the work of contemporary scholars, or foreign court decisions, it is often citing the handiwork of highly politicized and reform-minded activists and transnational interest groups whose express goal is to alter the policy decisions of domestic courts. Conservatives thus have come to view the contemporary citations to foreign sources of law as a politically motivated effort to make an end run around the requirements of domestic law and the U.S. Constitution.

In addition, many contemporary scholars advocating more "court-to-court" dialogue across national borders have drawn upon the work of social scientists who have celebrated the rise of transnational networks of elite professionals as a means to the formulation of new "globalized" public policy. And they have considered judges as increasingly active participants in these networks, and made little effort to distinguish the position of a judge from that of a legislator or administrative official. Conservatives suspicious of these discussions have cited them as evidence that the judges had left their obligation to follow the law behind and improperly wandered into the sphere of legislators and other policymakers.

Justice Kennedy's allusion to a decision of the European Court of Human Rights in voiding a Texas antisodomy statute (*Lawrence v. Texas*, 539 U.S. 558 [2003]), Justice Ginsburg's reference to "the international office of affirmative action" in upholding a racial preference scheme at the University of Michigan (*Gratz v. Bollinger*, 539 U.S. 244 [2003]), and Justice Breyer's discussion of the nature of European federalism in discerning the meaning of American constitutional federalism (*Printz v. United States*, 521 U.S. 898 [1997]), and the controversy they have occasioned, can only be understood in this context.

Over time, technology will only enhance the ability of judges in different countries to consult each other and each others' work, as will other trends often discussed under the rubric of "globalization." While this familiarity across borders will grow, the normative questions concerning the legitimacy of diverse foreign and international sources of law will remain.

SEE ALSO *Comparative Constitutional Law; Kennedy, Anthony; Lawrence v. Texas, 539 U.S. 558 (2003); Muller v. Oregon, 208 U.S. 412 (1908)*

BIBLIOGRAPHY

Calabresi, Steven G., and Stephanie Zimdahl. 2005. "The Supreme Court and Foreign Sources of Law: Two Hundred Years of Practice and the Juvenile Death Penalty Decision." *William and Mary Law Review* 47: 743–910.

Flaherty, Martin S. 2006. "Judicial Globalization in the Service of Self-Government." *Ethics and International Affairs* 20: 477–503.

Jacobsohn, Gary Jeffrey. 2004. "The Permeability of Constitutional Borders." *Texas Law Review* 82: 1763–1818.

Kersch, Ken I. 2005. "The New Legal Transnationalism, the Globalized Judiciary, and the Rule of Law." *Washington University Global Studies Law Review* 4: 345–388.

Kersch, Ken I. 2006. "The Supreme Court and International Relations Theory." *Albany Law Review* 69: 771–799.

Ken I. Kersch

CITIZENSHIP

In 1789 "modern citizenship" was created, not in Philadelphia or New York, but in France, with the promulgation of the Declaration of the Fundamental Rights of Man and the Citizen (Waldinger et al. 1993). The declaration outlined specific rights that belonged to French citizens, as well as rights that were fundamental to all persons. The fervor and symbolism associated with *le citoyen* (the citizen) in revolutionary France contrast dramatically with early American citizenship. Written in 1787, only two years before the French Declaration, the Constitution of the United States did little to enumerate

They [slaves and their descendants] are not included, and are not intended to be included, under the word "citizens" in the Constitution, and can therefore, claim none of the rights and privileges which that instrument provides for and secures to citizens of the United States.

SOURCE: Roger B. Taney, *Dred Scott v. Sandford,* 60 U.S. (19 How.) 393, 404 (1857).

the rights, privileges, and duties of citizenship. It did still less to define *who* would be considered a citizen of the United States, apart from requiring the president to be a "natural born Citizen" (Art. III, Sec. 1). The Constitution, whether by accident or design, left many critical details to be filled in as what George Washington called the "great experiment" progressed.

Many of the unanswered questions fell to the U.S. Supreme Court to attempt to resolve. Three major themes are particularly relevant and form the structure for this entry. Given the tension between the states and the nascent federal government, the first issue that engendered disagreement was whether citizenship of the nation—or "federal" citizenship—was achieved through some direct means, or whether federal citizenship was dependent upon citizenship in an individual state. This problem of defining national citizenship led naturally to two other, fundamental questions: *who* could be considered a "federal" citizen, and *what* rights and duties national citizenship entailed.

The Court's efforts to give content and form to citizenship have had mixed results—and Supreme Court citizenship decisions range from the enlightened to the pernicious. Ultimately, citizenship has become the predicate for participation in government, and, as such, defines who are considered the constituent members of society. Yet the conception of citizenship forged by the Supreme Court is unique to the United States and has been a major influence informing Americans' evolving views of community and rights: Many fundamental rights extend beyond citizenship, to those "persons" present in the United Sates. The right to be protected from the government is not a privilege of citizenship alone.

WHO CONTROLS CITIZENSHIP—THE NATION OR THE STATE?

The Constitution created a new form of government—a modern federation—and in a federation, individuals are citizens of both the federation (or nation) and a constituent unit (a state or province). These citizenships are linked—and to avoid conflicting allegiances, one of these citizenships must be accepted as primary (Choudhry 2001). In other words, does one's federal, or national, citizenship rely on one's being a citizen of an individual state—or is it one's national citizenship that takes precedence?

In the early United States there were conflicting views on this question. Most antebellum "conceptions of citizenship focused considerably upon the States, being civic republican and based on the virtues of small republics" (Meehan 2001, pp. 406–407). There was a concern, however, that, as citizens of one state were to be treated as citizens in another, states might manipulate the criteria for citizenship, leading to a situation where the most permissive state would control the citizenry of all other states. The Constitution therefore empowered Congress to establish a "uniform Rule of Naturalization." But the naturalization power alone was not enough to create a national citizenry. Even though the federal government "could determine the terms on which *foreigners* could be naturalized, . . . the states determined the extent of the rights and privileges of citizenship" (Bonwick 2000, p. 36, emphasis added), as well as which nonforeigners within their own borders (such as freed slaves born in the United States) were to be considered citizens of that state.

During the antebellum years the Supreme Court attempted to navigate between the states and the national government in a variety of areas, and citizenship was no different. In promoting national citizenship in the context of strong states' rights, the Supreme Court laid some important foundations for federal rights. But eventually the Court, in trying to produce an acceptable compromise, only served to divide the country further.

The Emergence of "National" Citizenship, 1790–1820

In the Supreme Court's early decades, it pursued a cautious path, balancing its support for national citizenship with a recognition that bold steps would require *political* action and could not be accomplished by judicial decision.

The Court was influential in encouraging the development of the national citizen by identifying national, or federal, rights that could be protected directly by the Court, without mediation by the states. In *Fletcher v. Peck,* 10 U.S. (6 Cranch) 87 (1810) and *Dartmouth College v. Woodward,* 17 U.S. (4 Wheat.) 518 (1819), the Supreme Court identified private rights granted by the Constitution to individuals—rules of property "common to all citizens of the United States" (*Fletcher*). In addition, the Supreme Court recognized that the existence of rights at the national level required that there be a means of protecting those rights—specifically, access to federal courts. If the state courts were to be immune from federal court review, "as the plaintiff may always elect the state court, the defendant may be deprived of all the security which the constitution intended in aid of his rights" (*Martin v. Hunter's Lessee*, 14 U.S. 304 [1816]).

Yet the Court was not quick to expand national citizens' access to federal court. In *Hepburn & Dundas v. Ellzey*, 6 U.S. 445 (1805) the Court had determined that a citizen of the District of Columbia could not sue a citizen of Virginia in federal court, because the citizen of D.C. was not a citizen *of a state*. Though uncomfortable with this result, the Court nonetheless suggested that it was a problem best resolved by the political branch of government:

> It is true that as citizens of the United States, and of that particular district which is subject to the jurisdiction of congress, it is extraordinary that the courts of the United States, which are open to aliens and to the citizens of every state in the union, should be closed upon *them*. But this is a subject for legislative not for judicial consideration.

Notwithstanding the Court's efforts to encourage Congress to address these questions, the dynamics of citizenship were not yet at the forefront of political debate. As historian James Kettner has written, "the issue remained at the periphery of the problems of loyalty that Americans dealt with directly in [the post-Revolution] years; the[se issues] . . . rarely required a close examination of the possible distinctions between a general American citizenship and a membership in a particular state" (1978, p. 209). It was the question of slavery that brought these problems to the fore.

Slavery and Comity, 1820–1860 The comity clause of the Constitution—that "the Citizens of each State shall be entitled to all Privileges and Immunities of Citizens in the several States" (Art. IV, Sec. 2)—created a "complicated 'conflict-of-laws' situation within the Federal union: in the South, slaves remained property; in the North, abolition gave them legal recognition as free men" (Kettner 1978, p. 303). Initially, the northern state courts accommodated the southern states' institution of slavery—as they were required to do by the federal government's Fugitive Slave Act (1793). Over time, as antislavery sentiment grew, laws were passed in the northern legislatures permitting slaves to secure their freedom after a certain amount of time in a free state, and the northern state courts became ever more reluctant to return escaped slaves to the South. A stronger fugitive slave act was passed in 1850, causing uproar in the northern states—at least one state supreme court even declared it unconstitutional.

The sectional tension over slavery had increased with the expansion of the country. When the Missouri Territory applied to Congress for the right to become a state in 1819, Representative James Tallmadge (1778–1853) of New York proposed an amendment that would restrict any further introduction of slavery to the territory, and would free slaves born in the territory. The southern response drew heavily on arguments of comity: "the Constitution clearly states that the citizens of each state shall be entitled to all the privileges and immunities of citizens of the several states," and the Tallmadge amendment would "deprive a Missouri citizen of his slave property" (Remini 1991, pp. 180–181). Eventually Missouri was allowed to apply for statehood, as a slave state, but, in violation of the comity principles it had so recently espoused, its state constitution included a proviso forbidding "free Negroes and mulattoes" from entering the state.

The right to determine who was a citizen was critical to the southern states in order to protect the institution of slavery. For the southern states, "if membership in the Union meant that under the Constitution the southern states were not free to identify their own citizens and were subject to the dictates of other governments, then the Constitution must be broken and the Union must fall" (Kettner 1978, p. 324). As the intransigence of the southern states in their protection of slavery began to be equaled by that of the northern abolitionists, the country faced a deepening divide.

The Supreme Court in *Dred Scott v. Sandford*, 60 U.S. 393 (1857) abandoned its earlier inclinations to view citizenship as a political question, and attempted to resolve the locus of citizenship. In so doing, it proposed an untenable solution to the problem, by granting the national level the primacy of citizenship, but denying that citizenship not only to Dred Scott, but to all free blacks in the United States. By denying Dred Scott national citizenship, the Supreme Court ensured that he could not sue for his freedom in federal court in diversity—jurisdiction based on the parties' being citizens of different states.

Chief Justice Roger Taney stated in the *Dred Scott* opinion that the states themselves could not control national citizenship, or, in other words, that the privileges and immunities of state citizenship did not necessarily translate into national citizenship. He continued by claiming that only those persons, and "every class and description of persons, who were at the time of the adoption of the Constitution recognized as citizens in the several States, became also citizens of this new political body." And, as Taney contended that Dred Scott's ancestors could not have been considered citizens at the time of the founding, Dred Scott could not be considered a citizen of the United States. Making short work of the comity clause, Taney explained that, though Scott could possibly be a citizen of a state, strictly within that state's bounds, he would not be entitled to the rights and privileges of a citizen in any other state as he could not be a national citizen. Therefore, the rights he may have under a state constitution could not "make him a member of [the national] community by making him a member of its own."

This analysis is deeply problematic. Nowhere does the Constitution explain who should be considered national citizens, or how precisely national citizenship should be determined. And, although naturalization of aliens was provided for, it is not clear how far that was meant to impinge upon the prerogatives of the states in determining citizenship. Asserting that it was national membership that controlled was a decisive response by the Court to a contested political question, and limiting that membership by race was an unacceptable compromise.

Even had Taney's resolution of the locus-of-citizenship question been politically tenable, the *Dred Scott* opinion does nothing to imbue this new national citizenship with content or meaning. In fact, it merely reinforces the decoupling of citizenship from political power, noting that,

> a person may be a citizen, that is, a member of the community who form the sovereignty, although he exercises no share of the political power, and is incapacitated from holding particular offices. Women and minors, who form a part of the political family, cannot vote; and when a property qualification is required to vote or hold a particular office, those who have not the necessary qualification cannot vote or hold the office, yet they are citizens.

"Ultimately, there are limits to what can be achieved by judicial pronouncement, beyond which progress can be made only by a basic political understanding between the constituent States" (Everling 1984, p. 219), and with the shocking decision by the Supreme Court that blacks could not be national citizens, the opportunity for political understandings had passed. This decision by the Supreme Court served to further polarize the country and may have hastened the advance of civil war.

The Fourteenth Amendment and the Locus of Citizenship After the Civil War (1861–1865) the Reconstruction Congress created a series of constitutional amendments designed to prohibit slavery, allow blacks to vote, and resolve the tensions inherent in the federal system. The Fourteenth Amendment overturned *Dred Scott* in its first sentence: "All persons born or naturalized in the United States, and subject to the jurisdiction thereof, are citizens of the United States and of the state wherein they reside."

As the Supreme Court explained in the *Slaughter-House Cases*, 83 U.S. 36 (1873), the first clause of the first section of this amendment was designed "to establish a

clear and comprehensive definition of citizenship which should declare what should constitute citizenship of the United States, and also citizenship of a State." And, in broad terms, the locus of citizenship was finally determined: It was the national level that predominated. All persons born in the United States were to be national citizens, and all those naturalized (by the uniform federal rule of naturalization) were to be national citizens. The states, it seemed at last, were out of the business of controlling national citizenship.

WHO IS A CITIZEN?

Although the Fourteenth Amendment made it clear that acquiring citizenship of the United States was no longer controlled by the individual states, the debate over *who* could be a citizen was not yet concluded. The meaning of the amendment's clause "and subject to the jurisdiction thereof," which appeared to limit birthright citizenship, had to be determined, and questions of derivative citizenship (citizenship gained from one's parents) and naturalization remained, as did uncertainty surrounding the circumstances in which one could be expatriated, or lose one's citizenship.

"Subject to the Jurisdiction Thereof" In the Court's discussion of the Fourteenth Amendment in the *Slaughter-House Cases*, the Court presents its understanding of the phrase "subject to its jurisdiction," as "intended to exclude from its operation children of ministers, consuls, and citizens or subjects of foreign States born within the United States." And in a later case, *Elk v. Wilkins*, 112 U.S. 94 (1884), the Supreme Court added Native Americans to the list of those excluded from birthright citizenship. (This decision has subsequently been overruled by statute.) The Supreme Court's understanding of whom the phrase intended to exclude would be refined over the coming decades—as pressure from a great wave of migration to the United States refocused national attention on citizenship.

In response to nativist societal pressures caused by immigration, Congress in 1882 passed the Chinese Exclusion Acts, disqualifying Chinese immigrants from naturalization. The federal naturalization laws had been tied to racial categories from the outset—from 1790 until 1870, only whites were able to naturalize. The Exclusion Acts, however, also prohibited any further Chinese immigration, allowing only those Chinese immigrants already in the United States at the time of the passage of the acts to remain. Wong Kim Ark, born in 1873 in San Francisco to Chinese parents and knowing only San Francisco as his home, left the United States in 1894 for a temporary visit to China. Upon his return in August 1895, he was denied permission to land in the United States on the ground that he was Chinese.

In *United States v. Wong Kim Ark*, 169 U.S. 649 (1898) the Supreme Court was faced with the question of whether Wong Kim Ark, born in the United States to parents who were not citizens of the United States, could be considered himself a citizen of the United States. If he were a citizen of the United States, the Chinese Exclusion Acts would not, and could not, apply to him. The Court, in a lengthy opinion by Justice Horace Gray (1828–1902), determined that the words "subject to the jurisdiction thereof" must include birth within the jurisdiction of one of the states of the union. Based on legal precedents from the early United States and on the law of England, the Court determined that the purpose of the phrase "and subject to the jurisdiction thereof" was, in addition to children of members of Indian tribes, to exclude only "two classes of cases—children born of alien enemies in hostile occupation, and children of diplomatic representatives of a foreign state."

The Court, reflecting the prejudices of the day, duly noted in *Wong Kim Ark* that "to hold that the fourteenth amendment of the constitution excludes from citizenship the children born in the United States of citizens or subjects of other countries, would be to deny citizenship to thousands of persons of English, Scotch, Irish, German, or other European parentage, who have always been considered and treated as citizens of the United States." Regardless of the Court's rationale, the decision in *Wong Kim Ark* resulted in an extremely generous view of birthright citizenship, one that scholars have called a "precious national asset" (Martin 1985, p. 283). By broad birthright citizenship, the United States has been able to avoid what in Europe is called the "second-generation problem"—where birthright citizenship is often denied to children of immigrants, resulting in a disenfranchised, unconnected, and frustrated population of second-generation aliens.

Acquiring Citizenship through Descent In reinforcing the constitutional principle of birthright citizenship when "subject to the jurisdiction," the Court in *Wong Kim Ark* was clear to differentiate children born to American parents *outside* the jurisdiction. Foreign-born children of U.S. citizen parents can acquire citizenship in a manner "regulated ... by Congress, in the exercise of the power conferred by the constitution to establish a uniform rule of naturalization." Congress has, however, distinguished the process of naturalization, with its language and history requirements, from the acquisition of citizenship from one's parents, by which a child is "deemed" an American citizen.

The rules and regulations governing acquisition of citizenship through "blood" have varied over time. The current statutory requirements are in the Immigration and Nationality Act (INA) (1952, with subsequent amendments), sections 301, 308, and 309. For example, in the most straightforward scenario—in which the parents are married and both citizens—the child will acquire citizenship at birth, provided only that one of the parents had a residence in the United States at some time prior to the child's birth. More complicated situations—in which only one parent is a citizen, or a child is born out of wedlock—place greater requirements on the parents (longer periods of residency in the United States, etc.), requirements that may vary with the gender of the parent.

Gender-based distinctions have long played a role in the acquisition of citizenship through descent. For example, until 1934 a child born outside of the United States could only gain citizenship if its father were a U.S. citizen. Although this statute was repealed, some of the current rules for acquisition of citizenship also raise questions of discrimination based on gender. For example, children born abroad to unmarried parents, only one of whom is a U.S. citizen, may be precluded from acquiring citizenship. The Immigration and Nationality Act grants citizenship to a child, born out of wedlock, whose *mother* is a U.S. citizen, provided the mother had fulfilled some minor residency requirements. For a child whose *father* is a U.S. citizen, a more stringent set of requirements must be met to gain citizenship.

Thus far, the Supreme Court has been reluctant to overturn these rules. In *Nguyen v. Immigration and Naturalization Service*, 533 U.S. 53 (2001) the Court addressed the INA statutes applying to children born out of wedlock. The Court, in conducting an equal protection analysis, found that because the mother carries the child, "the opportunity for a meaningful relationship between citizen parent and child inheres in the very event of birth"—a situation that does *not* result, "as a matter of biological inevitability, in the case of the unwed father." Determining, therefore, that the relationship between citizen parent and child is an important governmental interest, the majority opinion found that the more-extensive statutory requirements for a child to acquire citizenship through a U.S. citizen father were substantially related to that end. The dissent, written by Justice Sandra Day O'Connor, critiqued the majority opinion for resting its analysis, "not in biological differences but instead in a stereotype—that is, the generalization that mothers are significantly more likely than fathers ... to develop caring relationships with their children."

Losing Citizenship In 1868 Congress passed the Expatriation Act, which asserted that the right to renounce one's citizenship was an "inherent right of all people." Though a reflection of a contractual view of citizenship, the Expatriation Act did not, as Donald Duvall has discussed, provide a "specific method for exercising that right" (1970, p. 413). In a series of cases, the Supreme Court struggled with identifying when a citizen had affirmatively renounced his or her citizenship, and whether "involuntary expatriation"—the result of an American citizen's performing certain behavior prohibited by Congress—was constitutional.

In *Perez v. Brownell*, 356 U.S 44 (1958) the Supreme Court addressed the situation of Clemente Martinez Perez, who was born in Texas yet lived in Mexico for most of his life. In 1946 Perez voted in an election in Mexico, thereby losing his citizenship under the 1940 Act of Congress, which made voting in a political election in a foreign state an offense resulting in expatriation. The Court, in an opinion by Justice Felix Frankfurter, found that Congress could expatriate an individual as a consequence of "conduct engaged in voluntarily," and further that it could do so, even if a person did not *intend* by his or her actions to lose his or her citizenship.

The dissenting votes in *Perez* became the majority roughly nine years later, when the Court, in *Afroyim v. Rusk*, 387 U.S. 253 (1967), overturned *Perez* and "rejected the idea ... that, aside from the Fourteenth Amendment, Congress has any general power, express or implied, to take away an American citizen's citizenship without his assent." The Court did not, in *Afroyim*, clearly define what it meant by an individual's assent, and in a later case, *Vance v. Terrazas*, 444 U.S. 252 (1980), the Court held that, beyond the voluntary commission of an expatriating act, the government must prove that the individual had an *intent* to surrender his or her citizenship.

Since the passage of the Fourteenth Amendment, the Court has expanded the reach of birthright citizenship, monitored Congress's rules concerning acquiring citizenship and naturalization, and placed heightened requirements on the government to prove that a citizen has renounced his or her citizenship. Inherent and close to permanent for those born within the United States, U.S. citizenship now has great symbolic force. But what does it mean to be a citizen? What are the privileges and immunities that citizenship provides?

WHAT ARE THE PRIVILEGES AND IMMUNITIES OF CITIZENSHIP?

In his powerful dissent in *Perez*, Chief Justice Earl Warren said that "citizenship *is* man's right for it is nothing less than the right to have rights." Warren's words, however, are somewhat divorced from the reality of U.S. law. Mainly as a result of Supreme Court opinions in the nineteenth century, decided after the passage of the Fourteenth Amendment, citizenship has not been the prism through which Americans have viewed their fundamental rights.

The second sentence of the Fourteenth Amendment addressed the content of the new "national" citizenship: "No state shall make or enforce any law which shall

abridge the privileges or immunities of citizens of the United States; nor shall any state deprive any person of life, liberty or property, without due process of law; nor deny to any person within its jurisdiction the equal protection of the laws." Identifying what would constitute "privileges and immunities" of national citizenship was the task that fell to the Supreme Court in the *Slaughter-House Cases* in 1873. The phrase was not new.

The phrase "privileges and immunities" was already in the Constitution, in the comity clause of Article VI, discussed above. And in 1823 Supreme Court Justice Bushrod Washington (1762–1829), sitting on circuit court in Pennsylvania, made an effort to define this term in *Corfield v. Coryell*, 6 F. Cas. 546 (4 Wash. C. C. 371). The case concerned a Philadelphia ship, the *Hiram*, which was captured while illegally—according to New Jersey law—dredging for oysters in New Jersey waters.

Justice Washington distilled the relevant question as whether the New Jersey law, limiting those who could fish in New Jersey waters, was a violation of the comity clause. Was fishing a privilege and immunity such that it should be available to citizens of the several states? Justice Washington determined that, though it was difficult to enumerate them all, the privileges and immunities of citizens comprised:

> Protection by the government; the enjoyment of life and liberty, with the right to acquire and possess property of every kind, and to pursue and obtain happiness and safety; subject nevertheless to such restraints as the government may justly prescribe for the general good of the whole. The right of a citizen of one state to pass through, or to reside in any other state, for purposes of trade, agriculture, professional pursuits, or otherwise; to claim the benefit of the writ of habeas corpus; to institute and maintain actions of any kind in the courts of the state; to take, hold and dispose of property, either real or personal; and an exemption from higher taxes or impositions than are paid by the other citizens of the state; may be mentioned as some of the particular privileges and immunities of citizens, which are clearly embraced by the general description of privileges deemed to be fundamental: to which may be added, the elective franchise, as regulated and established by the laws or constitution of the state in which it is to be exercised.

When confronted, in 1873 in *Slaughter-House*, with the phrase "privileges or immunities" used in the Fourteenth Amendment, the Supreme Court did not define the rights of *national* citizenship so expansively. In fact, though the Court, as mentioned earlier, was willing to view the first sentence of the Fourteenth Amendment as creating and prioritizing national citizenship, it nevertheless found that the final phrase maintained a role for state citizenship, in stating that "all persons born or naturalized in the United States, and subject to the jurisdiction thereof, are citizens of the United States *and of the state wherein they reside.*" The Supreme Court read those words as creating a "distinction between citizenship of the United States and citizenship of a State."

This distinction, the Court reasoned, was reinforced by the second sentence of the amendment, which says only that "No state shall make or enforce any law which shall abridge the privileges or immunities of citizens *of the United States.*" Because this sentence "speaks only of the privileges and immunities of citizens of the United States, and does not speak of those of citizens of the several states," the Court rejected the assumption that "the citizenship is the same, and the privileges and immunities guaranteed by the clause are the same." The Court thus held that it was not the purpose of the Fourteenth Amendment to "transfer the security and protection of all the civil rights which we have mentioned, from the States to the Federal government." What then were the privileges and immunities of citizens of the United States that no individual state could abridge? The Court defined those rights narrowly:

- The right of the citizen to "come to the seat of government to assert any claim he may have upon that government, to transact any business he may have with it, to seek its protection, to share its offices, to engage in administering its functions."

- The right of "free access to its seaports, to the subtreasuries, land offices, and courts of justices in the several states."

- The right to "demand the care and protection of the Federal government over his life, liberty, and property when on the high seas or within the jurisdiction of a foreign government."

- The "right to peaceably assemble and petition for redress of grievances, and the privilege of the writ of habeas corpus."

- The "right to use the navigable waters of the United States."

- And finally, any "rights secured to our citizens by treaties with foreign nations, are dependent upon citizenship of the United States and not citizenship of a State."

All other "rights" were dependent upon the goodwill of the individual state.

This list is anemic in comparison to the far richer understanding of the rights of citizens presented by Justice Washington, roughly fifty years earlier. The vast majority of rights relevant to an average American—one not traveling on the high seas, for example—remained

available at the state level only. And the *Slaughter-House* Court notably omitted the right to vote—the political right of citizenship that was, for example, one of the cornerstones of the French understanding of citizenship in the late 1780s and early 1790s.

Some scholars have argued that the purpose of the privileges and immunities clause was precisely "to restrict the right of the states to impose many kinds of suffrage restrictions." (Upham 2005, p. 1495). Though this may indeed have been the case, political rights and citizenship were not linked in the early republic as Chief Justice Taney pointed out in *Dred Scott*. During the nineteenth century, women, whom the Court at that time considered citizens, were not allowed to vote. Yet aliens—noncitizen members of the community—*were* allowed to vote in some states (Raskin 1993). In the early twenty-first century, as the government's newest citizenship test attests, voting is considered the "most important" right granted exclusively to U.S. citizens,.

The Supreme Court's landmark decision on privileges and immunities has never been overturned. Future litigants would be forced to turn to other language in the Fourteenth Amendment to ensure fundamental rights of due process, and equal protection under the law. The Supreme Court's decision in the *Slaughter-House Cases* restricted the privileges and immunities of citizenship to such an extent that the "meaning" of U.S. citizenship is in question, even as it is made available to so many, through birth and blood, and made so difficult to renounce. Because Congress can distinguish between citizens and aliens, many important statutory rights are only available to those with U.S. citizenship. Yet the rights thought to be fundamental are found in the more expansive language of the Fourteenth Amendment, in which rights are made available to all "persons." The most fundamental rights are not dependent on holding the status of citizen. What may have seemed like a limiting decision, in terms of the rights of citizens, has, in fact, meant that the rights enshrined in the Fourteenth Amendment have been more widely shared and can redound to the benefit of the entire society.

SEE ALSO *Citizenship by Birth; Constitution of the United States; Dred Scott v. Sandford, 60 U.S. 393 (1857); Fourteenth Amendment; Naturalization and the Constitution; Slaughter-House Cases, 83 U.S. 36 (1873)*

BIBLIOGRAPHY

Bonwick, Colin C. 2000. "American Nationalism, American Citizenship, and the Limits of Authority. In *Federalism, Citizenship, and Collective Identities in U.S. History*, ed. Cornelis A. van Minnen and Sylvia L. Hilton, pp. 29–42. Amsterdam, Netherlands: VU University Press.

Choudhry, Sujit. 2001. "Citizenship and Federations: Some Preliminary Reflections." In *The Federal Vision: Legitimacy and*

Levels of Governance in the United States and the European Union, ed. Kalypso Nicolaidis and Robert Howse, pp. 377–402. Oxford: Oxford University Press.

Duvall, Donald K. 1970. "Expatriation under United States Law, *Perez* to *Afroyim*: The Search for a Philosophy of American Citizenship." *Virginia Law Review* 56(3): 408–457.

Everling, Ulrich. 1984. "The Member States of the European Community before Their Court of Justice." *European Law Review* 9(4): 215–241.

Kettner, James H. 1978. *The Development of American Citizenship, 1608–1870*. Chapel Hill: University of North Carolina Press.

Martin, David A. 1985. "Membership and Consent: Abstract or Organic?" *Yale Journal of International Law* 11(1): 278–296.

Meehan, Elizabeth. 2001. "The Constitution of Institutions." In *The Federal Vision: Legitimacy and Levels of Governance in the United States and the European Union*, ed. Kalypso Nicolaidis and Robert Howse, pp. 403–412. Oxford: Oxford University Press.

Novak, William J. 2003. "The Legal Transformation of Citizenship in Nineteenth-Century America." In *The Democratic Experiment: New Directions in American Political History*, ed. Meg Jacobs, William J. Novak, and Julian E. Zelizer, pp. 85–119. Princeton, NJ: Princeton University Press.

Raskin, Jamin B. 1993. "Legal Aliens, Local Citizens: The Historical, Constitutional, and Theoretical Meanings of Alien Suffrage." *University of Pennsylvania Law Review* 141(4): 1391–1470.

Remini, Robert V. 1991. *Henry Clay: Statesman for the Union.* New York: Norton.

Upham, David R. 2005. "*Corfield v. Coryell* and the Privileges and Immunities of American Citizenship." *Texas Law Review* 83(5): 1483–1534.

Waldinger, Renée; Philip Dawson; and Isser Woloch. 1993. *The French Revolution and the Meaning of Citizenship.* Westport, CT: Greenwood Press.

Erin F. Delaney

CITIZENSHIP BY BIRTH

The constitutional right of birthright citizenship ensures American citizenship to any person born within the United States and subject to its jurisdiction, regardless of the citizenship or lawful status of the person's parents. The citizenship clause of section one of the Fourteenth Amendment states: "All persons born or naturalized in the United States, and subject to the jurisdiction thereof, are citizens of the United States and of the State wherein they reside." Designed to overturn the Supreme Court's ruling in *Dred Scott v. Sandford,* 60 U.S. 393 (1857), where the Court held that citizenship could not be conferred upon black persons, the clause established the primacy of national citizenship and prevented the states from taking action to deny citizenship to former slaves.

Citizenship by birth is also established by federal statute to include Native American tribal members, persons born in U.S. territories, and certain persons born outside the United States, depending on parental citizenship and other conditions. In *Nguyen v. Immigration and Naturalization Service,* 533 U.S. 53 (2001), the Supreme Court upheld the constitutionality of federal requirements that children born out of wedlock and outside U.S. territory must meet higher evidentiary standards to establish citizenship via a father's citizenship compared to a mother's citizenship; such a requirement did not violate the equal protection clause because of gender discrimination.

Birthright citizenship draws on English common law traditions vesting citizenship at time and place of birth, and is designed to guarantee both the person's allegiance to the sovereign and the protection of the individual within the sovereign's domain. Birthright citizenship under the Fourteenth Amendment represents the American form of jus soli (right of the soil, or place of birth), which contrasts with the jus sanguinis tradition (right of blood or descent) that is common among many nation-states.

The Supreme Court has interpreted the phrase "subject to the jurisdiction thereof" in the Fourteenth Amendment's citizenship clause to establish the boundaries of constitutional birthright citizenship. In *Elk v. Wilkins,* 112 U.S. 94 (1884), the Supreme Court ruled that children born to Native American tribal members were under the jurisdiction of the tribe and, because they owed no allegiance to the United States, were not subject to the jurisdiction of the United States and therefore ineligible for citizenship. The Indian Citizenship Act of 1924 eventually made all Native Americans eligible for citizenship, correcting the piecemeal approach that had granted citizenship via treaty or federal statute to some Native Americans because of tribal membership, land tenure, or residence.

In *United States v. Wong Kim Ark,* 169 U.S. 649 (1898), the Supreme Court ruled that an American-born child of Chinese immigrants was subject to the jurisdiction of the United States, even though his parents were themselves ineligible by statute for naturalized citizenship and were subject to exclusionary immigration laws targeting the Chinese. The Court concluded that the Fourteenth Amendment grants citizenship to a child born in the United States of parents of foreign descent who, though subjects of a foreign power, are lawful residents of the United States, and are not employed in a diplomatic capacity or members of foreign armed forces involved in a military conflict with the United States.

Although the Supreme Court has not directly addressed the question of birthright citizenship for children of undocumented immigrants who lack lawful status in the United States, in *Plyler v. Doe*, 457 U.S. 202 (1982), the Court did make clear that undocumented immigrants residing within a state are within the jurisdiction of that state, noting that no meaningful distinction can be drawn between lawful resident aliens and the undocumented, for Fourteenth Amendment jurisdictional purposes. *Wong Kim Ark*'s guarantee of birthright citizenship should therefore apply to children born in the United States to undocumented parents as well.

In recent years, federal legislation to limit or repeal birthright citizenship for children of the undocumented has been introduced without success. Proponents of the legislation have argued that birthright citizenship offers an incentive for undocumented immigrants to enter the country illegally in order to have U.S. citizen children and obtain public benefits; legal scholars have also advanced the argument that citizenship should be based on mutual consent between the person and the sovereign, and have proposed that birthright citizenship for children of undocumented immigrants is inconsistent with this theory because the government has not consented to their presence in the United States. Because of *Wong Kim Ark* and *Plyler*, it is likely that a constitutional amendment would be necessary to repeal or limit birthright citizenship to children of the undocumented.

SEE ALSO *Citizenship; Dred Scott v. Sandford, 60 U.S. 393 (1857); Fourteenth Amendment*

BIBLIOGRAPHY

Eisgruber, Christopher L. 1997. "Birthright Citizenship and the Constitution." *New York University Law Review* 72(1): 54–96.

Schuck, Peter H., and Rogers M. Smith. 1985. *Citizenship Without Consent: Illegal Aliens in the American Polity*. New Haven, CT: Yale University Press.

Angelo N. Ancheta

CITIZENS TO PRESERVE OVERTON PARK V. VOLPE, 401 U.S. 402 (1971)

Citizens to Preserve Overton Park v. Volpe, 401 U.S. 402 (1971) is cited most frequently, and that is *very* frequently, for its elaborate discussion of the standard for review of informal agency action. The relevant statute, the federal Administrative Procedure Act (1946), provides in one place (5 U.S. Code 701[a]) that "to the extent that ... agency action is committed to agency discretion by law," it is *not* subject to review under the act; yet in another place (5 U.S. Code 706), the law provides that a "reviewing court shall ... hold unlawful and set aside

agency action, findings and conclusions found to be ... arbitrary, capricious, *an abuse of discretion*, or otherwise not in accordance with law" (emphasis added). The Supreme Court solved this puzzle by holding that Section 701 addresses only cases in which there is "no law to apply"—settings like the usual responsibilities of the secretaries of state or the defense chief that Chief Justice John Marshall had referred to in *Marbury v. Madison*, 5 U.S. 137 (1803). Marshall characterized their acts as the exercise of official *discretion* under the president's direct political supervision and, really, as his mouthpiece. Such responsibilities, the great chief justice wrote, raise "political questions," that could not properly be made judicial business. But where the constraints of law *are* present, it is proper judicial business to enforce them, and that is the "discretion" that Section 706, the second provision, addresses.

The case came to the U.S. Supreme Court as a dispute about the meaning of a statute requiring the secretary of transportation to pay special attention to the public values associated with parklands when deciding questions about the routing of highways—interstate highways in particular—for which the federal government paid the bulk of the costs. Memphis city and Tennessee state officials had been debating for well over a decade whether Interstate 40, or I-40, should go through, or around, Overton Park, an urban jewel centered in white residential areas of Memphis. Most of the city's through roads had avoided white neighborhoods, but if I-40 was to cross the Mississippi River at a place advantageous to the businesses of downtown Memphis, substituting I-40 for the narrow bus route that already crossed the park seemed the logical choice.

The route was first planned in the early 1950s when the interstate system was created, and long before the parkland-values statutes were enacted. Citizens to Preserve Overton Park (CPOP), never a large group, was born once I-40's planned route became known. For more than a decade following, the group fought the issue politically in every way it could—in municipal elections, by letter-writing campaigns to state and federal politicians, and by engaging federal bureaucrats. It succeeded in delaying the project, and in having plans modified in ways that lessened the highway's impact, but politics could not keep I-40 out of the park. CPOP's last political battle was lost in April 1968 when the city council voted to renew its request to Department of Transportation officials to route I-40 through the park; the vote was taken at the Memphis airport at virtually the moment Martin Luther King Jr. was being assassinated downtown.

The bureaucratic decisions about the highway, of course, were regarded inside the Department of Transportation as a matter of routine in dealings with state and local officials seeking approval of the road's route and design. CPOP wrote letters to department officials, but the DOT held no hearing as such in which CPOP could take part—rather, they met with various interested parties informally, and a series of papers crossed departmental officials' desks and made their way to Secretary John Volpe (1908–1994), who ultimately signed off on the route through Overton Park. As one of a number of contentious issues involving the use of parkland at the time (proposed highway use of Breckinridge Park in San Antonio posed another), and given the recent federal statute requiring protection of parkland values, the I-40 route did get unusual attention from Volpe—in particular, insistence on expensive design choices that would control, but not eliminate, visual and noise intrusions from traffic on the highway into the park.

The members of CPOP sued, their last hope to halt the bulldozers now roaring toward the park to construct the last Memphis link in I-40. Their suit came as the public-interest law movement was just gathering steam. They were represented, pro bono publico, by a team of lawyers not five years out of law school, with senior state and federal lawyers on the other side. The suit was all about the meaning of the federal statute, and whether its requirement to consider parkland values had been honored. Given the waiting bulldozers, the case was briefed and argued within a month of its first appearance on the Court's calendar; an early December 1970 hearing on a motion to stay construction turned into a merits argument at the beginning of January 1971 and a decision by early March.

In addition to pointing out the difference between political-question *discretion* and the "discretion" that Section 706 invited courts to control for "abuse," Justice Thurgood Marshall's opinion for the Court—distrusting the mediating influence of politics already demonstrated in the project's history—interpreted the parkland-values statute to impose much stronger burdens of justification for the use of parklands in highway construction than it seemed likely Secretary Volpe had understood. Just how the secretary had read the statute was impossible to say, as his bureaucratic processes provided no contemporary statement of reasoning. For Justices Hugo Black and William Brennan, this was enough; they would have sent the case back to Secretary Volpe for reconsideration, now that the meaning of the statute had been settled. The majority, however, apparently thought Secretary Volpe might be able to persuade a lower court that he had in fact reached his decision on a proper basis. Although, the Court said, he had not been statutorily required to make findings in reaching his decision, the fact that he had not made them meant that his decision process would be a proper subject for inquiry in this review proceeding. (If this threat alone were not sufficient, the twenty-seven-day trial that resulted, ultimately leading to the conclusion

that I-40 would *not* traverse Overton Park, has been a valuable object lesson for federal agencies about the virtue of making findings, whether or not they legally must; the other side of the proposition would appear two years later in *Camp v. Pitts*, 411 U.S. 138 [1973], holding that a short letter of explanation, virtually boilerplate, sufficed to avoid the threat of a hearing on decision process.)

In explaining just how this review for abuse of discretion should occur (a matter that essentially had not been briefed and played no part in the oral argument of the case), Justice Marshall established the case's value for future courts. Such review was to be "narrow," respecting the assignment of ultimate responsibility to the agency being reviewed, yet "searching and careful," to assure that legal requirements were met. Prefiguring the two-step analysis that would later emerge explicitly in *Chevron U.S.A., Inc. v. Natural Resources Defense Council, Inc.*, 467 U.S. 837 (1984), Marshall's opinion required an initial scrutiny of the facts in relation to the action being challenged to determine whether the decision made by Secretary Volpe fell within his legal authority—that is, whether the decision was one even *possible* for him to reach. There was then to be a second scrutiny of any judgment meeting that test to determine whether it was a *proper* judgment—whether it had been based (only) on relevant factors, and reflected no "clear error of judgment." This approach fostered what came to be known as *hard-look* review of informal agency action. Regulatory beneficiaries like CPOP thus acquired an important weapon with which to keep agencies whose actions were meant to protect them to the straight and narrow; of course, the same hard look could (and did) also benefit those subject to and hoping to avoid regulation.

SEE ALSO *Administrative Procedure Act; Judicial Review of Administrative Action*

BIBLIOGRAPHY

Strauss, Peter L. 2006. "*Citizens to Preserve Overton Park v. Volpe*—Of Politics and Law, Young Lawyers and the Highway Goliath." In *Administrative Law Stories*, ed. Peter L. Strauss, p. 258. New York: Foundation Press.

Peter L. Strauss

CITY OF BOERNE V. FLORES, 521 U.S. 507 (1997)

The First Amendment to the U.S. Constitution states, "Congress shall make no law respecting an establishment of religion, or prohibiting the free exercise thereof." It says nothing about the ways in which state governments must respect religious freedom. Nevertheless, the U.S. Supreme Court has made it clear that this fundamental American freedom enjoys constitutional protection from the actions of all governments in the United States. In 1993 Congress enacted the Religious Freedom Restoration Act (RFRA). This law reinstated a high standard of judicial review for laws that did not directly target, but had the effect of burdening, the freedom of individuals to exercise their religious beliefs. RFRA was passed in direct response to a 1990 Supreme Court decision that held that the Constitution did not require such laws to meet this level of scrutiny—a decision that elicited widespread public disapproval. Writing for a six-justice majority in *City of Boerne v. Flores,* 521 U.S. 507 (1997), Justice Anthony Kennedy ruled that Congress lacked the power to enact RFRA. The decision was based on the structural constitutional principles of federalism and separation of powers, and raised important questions about the extent to which the judicial and legislative branches of the government are authorized to say what the Constitution means.

THE RELIGIOUS FREEDOM RESTORATION ACT

In 1990, in *Employment Division v. Smith*, 494 U.S. 872 (1990), the Court decided that individuals are not exempt from laws that apply to all and do not target religious activities, even when the effect of a law is to impose a burden upon the free exercise of religion protected by the First Amendment. In his majority opinion, Justice Antonin Scalia concluded that such laws did not need to pass the judicial test of strict scrutiny, which requires the government to show that a regulation furthers a compelling state interest and is the option that places the least restriction on the freedom it regulates. The Court first put this test in place, for laws that burdened religious freedom, in *Sherbert v. Verner*, 374 U.S. 398 (1963). The easy congressional passage of RFRA in 1993 (with almost unanimous support in both the House of Representatives and Senate) reflected the extensive public opposition to the decision in *Smith*.

The stated purpose of RFRA was "to restore the compelling interest test as set forth in *Sherbert v. Verner*." It was an example of a federal statute that laid out (or in this case reinstated) a standard for interpreting a provision of the Constitution (the free exercise clause). Congress relied on the Fourteenth Amendment for its authority to pass RFRA. Section 1 of the Fourteenth Amendment says, "No State shall ... deprive any person of life, liberty, or property, without due process of law; nor deny to any person within its jurisdiction the equal protection of the laws." Section 5 then gives Congress the "power to enforce" this provision using "appropriate legislation." The question before the Court in *Flores* was whether RFRA was such a law.

Acknowledging the need of St. Peter Catholic Church in the city of Boerne, Texas, to accommodate its growing congregation, Archbishop Flores of nearby San Antonio permitted the parish to apply to the Boerne City Council for a permit to expand the church building. The permit was denied because the church was located in an area designated as a historic district. Under the *Smith* standard, this permit denial would be constitutional because the ordinance was not directed at restricting religious freedom. The *Sherbert* standard resurrected by RFRA, however, provided the Archbishop with the basis for a challenge to the legality of the denial. In response, the City of Boerne argued that RFRA, which amounted to a federal regulatory override of a local ordinance, exceeded the enforcement powers granted to Congress by the Fourteenth Amendment.

THE DECISION IN *CITY OF BOERNE V. FLORES*

In an opinion joined by five of his colleagues, Justice Kennedy struck down RFRA as it applied to the states. "Under our Constitution," wrote Kennedy, "the Federal Government is one of enumerated powers." And the Section 5 power of enforcement is strictly *remedial* in nature. Laws such as RFRA could be enacted in order to address and prevent violations of religious freedom; however, as Kennedy explained, there is a difference between legislation that remedies (or prevents) unconstitutional actions and legislation that substantively changes the law. Kennedy acknowledged that this line of distinction "is not easy to discern, and Congress must have wide latitude in determining where it lies." However, he concluded that in both its "operation and effect," RFRA effected an unconstitutional "substantive" change in the law by placing restrictions on the content of generally applicable local and state regulations.

One of the most important aspects of this decision was the use of a "congruence and proportionality" test to determine whether the means employed by Congress (in this case the restoration of the *Sherbert* test) was sufficiently closely related to the "injury" (the restriction of religious freedom) that it intended to "prevent" or "remedy." To demonstrate that RFRA did not meet this test, Kennedy compared the law to the Voting Rights Act of 1965, and consulted the decision in *Katzenbach* v. *Morgan*, 384 U.S. 641 (1966). In *Katzenbach*, the Court held that, under Section 5 of the Fourteenth Amendment, Congress had the power to enact a section of the Voting Rights Act that enfranchised Spanish-speaking voters, even if the states sought to limit voting rights to only individuals who completed an English-language literacy test. In *Flores*, Kennedy said that this decision contained "language ... which could be interpreted as acknowledging a power in Congress to enact legislation that expands the rights contained in Section 1 of the Fourteenth Amendment." He concluded, however, that this interpretation of deference to congressional decision-making was "not a necessary interpretation ... or even the best one," because the Voting Rights Act was a remedial response to specific examples of racial discrimination. In this respect, the Voting Rights Act differed greatly from RFRA, for which Congress had produced no evidence that it was responding to generally applicable laws specifically motivated by religious intolerance.

THE PROVINCE AND DUTY OF THE JUDICIAL BRANCH

Five justices wrote separate opinions in *Flores*. In a brief concurrence, Justice John Paul Stevens concluded that RFRA "provided the Church with a legal weapon that no atheist or agnostic can obtain," therefore it violated the First Amendment's prohibition against "law[s] respecting an establishment of religion." Justice Scalia's concurrence offered a historical defense of the decision in *Smith*, and responded to Justice Sandra Day O'Connor's dissenting opinion that said the Court should have used *Flores* to revisit the wrongly decided *Smith*. Also dissenting, Justice David Souter agreed that the 1990 decision should be reconsidered, but unlike O'Connor he did not take a position on that decision's correctness. Despite the presence of so many separate opinions, none of the justices appeared to disagree with Kennedy's interpretation of Section 5. However, the argument that *Smith* was wrongly decided might lead to the conclusion that RFRA was constitutional because it was a congressional enforcement of the real meaning of the free exercise clause, as stated in *Sherbert*.

Article VI of the Constitution declares that that document is the "supreme law of the land." In *Marbury v. Madison*, 5 U.S. 137 (1803), Chief Justice John Marshall famously declared: "It is emphatically the province and the duty of the judicial department to say what the law is." In *Cooper v. Aaron*, 358 U.S. 1 (1958), the Court combined these two observations to reach the additional conclusion that its interpretations of the Constitution were also part of the nation's "supreme law." Scholars are divided over whether *Flores* is consistent with, or departs from, these precedents. They primary question they ask is whether it was an illegitimate assertion of judicial supremacy. Those who argue that *Flores* is an example of this practice content that elected members of Congress can legally interpret the meaning of the substantive rights protections of the Constitution. Scholars who take the opposite position generally argue that these protections can only be constitutionally guaranteed if the sole power of interpretation rests with the members of the Supreme Court.

Responses to the decision in *Flores* also came from Congress and the state legislatures. In 2000 Congress enacted the Religious Land Use and Institutionalized Persons Act (RLUIPA), requiring the application of the high level of judicial scrutiny (the *Sherbert* test) to two narrow categories of generally applicable laws that could burden the free exercise of religion. The two categories involved the religious rights of prisoners, and the land-use rights of religious institutions. RLUIPA was upheld (against an establishment clause challenge) by the Court in *Cutter v. Wilkinson*, 544 U.S. 709 (2005) in large part because when Congress wrote RLUIPA, it was careful to meet the "congruence and proportionality" requirement of *Flores*. Numerous states have responded to the 1997 decision by enacting so-called mini-RFRAs. Writing the religious freedom protection of the *Sherbert* test into state laws avoids the problems associated with applying RFRA to the states because it does not involve the power of the federal government and competing interpretations of the Constitution.

SEE ALSO *Employment Division, Department of Human Resources of Oregon v. Smith, 494 U.S. 872 (1990); Federalism; First Amendment; Free Exercise of Religion; Rehnquist Court*

BIBLIOGRAPHY

Amar, Akhil Reed. 1999. "Intratextualism." *Harvard Law Review* 112: 747–827.

Paisner, Michael. 2005. "*Boerne* Supremacy: Congressional Responses to *City of Boerne v. Flores* and the Scope of Congress's Article I Powers." *Columbia Law Review* 105: 537–582.

Tushnet, Mark. 2004. "The Story of *City of Boerne v. Flores*: Federalism, Rights, and Judicial Supremacy." In *Constitutional Law Stories*, ed. Michael C. Dorf. New York: Foundation Press.

Helen J. Knowles

CITY OF CLEBURNE V. CLEBURNE LIVING CENTER, 473 U.S. 432 (1985)

In *City of Cleburne v. Cleburne Living Center*, 473 U.S. 432 (1985), the Court invalidated a local zoning ordinance insofar as it prohibited a group home for the mentally retarded but permitted materially indistinguishable land uses. The Cleburne Living Center sued Cleburne, Texas, in federal court after the city denied the Center a permit to operate a supervised group home for mentally retarded persons. The city's zoning ordinance sanctioned numerous, diverse uses of the land in question, but required annual approval of "[h]ospitals for the insane or feebleminded." Though the trial court rejected the Center's claim that the ordinance violated the Fourteenth Amendment's guarantee of "the equal protection of the laws," the court of appeals reversed. The Supreme Court then elected to hear the case.

The Justices unanimously agreed that the city's permit denial violated the equal protection clause, though they split sharply as to the rationale. Justice Byron White devoted most of his opinion for the Court to identifying the level of judicial scrutiny appropriate for legislative classifications based on mental retardation. The Court had in earlier rulings developed a three-tiered framework for assessing governmental action under the equal protection clause. The Center argued that classifications based on mental retardation should be evaluated under the intermediate standard of review, which the Court had in the prior decade applied to classifications based on gender. But Justice White demurred. He distinguished mental retardation from other immutable characteristics triggering heightened scrutiny—such as race, national origin, and gender—arguing that, unlike them, mental retardation was often relevant to legitimate governmental objectives. Moreover, the existence of numerous federal and state laws benefiting the mentally retarded belied the notion that they were the objects of "a continuing antipathy and prejudice" or were "politically powerless in the sense that they have no ability to attract the attention of the lawmakers." Perhaps most importantly, White stressed that, were the mentally retarded deemed a protected class, "it would be difficult to find a principled way to distinguish a variety of other groups," such as "the aging, the disabled, the mentally ill, and the infirm."

Yet White also agreed with the Center that the city's action could not stand. Applying rationale basis review, the deferential standard ordinarily invoked to sustain economic legislation, White nonetheless concluded that the ordinance was unconstitutional as applied because the proposed group home threatened no legitimate governmental interest. White first deemed per se illegitimate governmental action indulging the "mere negative attitudes, or fear," some citizens harbored toward the mentally retarded. All other possible justifications—for example, the location of the property within a flood plain—were impeached by the city's decision to permit uses that created at least as great a risk as that the Center proposed. These circumstances suggested that the city's action was impermissibly influenced by "an irrational prejudice against the mentally retarded."

Justice Thurgood Marshall would have gone further. Far better, in his view, would have been a ruling that classifications based on mental retardation required heightened judicial scrutiny. Justices William Brennan and Harry Blackmun joined Marshall's separate opinion.

One senses that White struggled mightily to reach the right result without expanding the scope of the equal protection clause. If so, it is no small irony that *Cleburne*

eventually supplied the foundation for pivotal gay rights cases such as *Romer v. Evans*, 517 U.S. 620 (1996).

SEE ALSO *Fourteenth Amendment*

BIBLIOGRAPHY

Ellis, James W. 1986. "On the 'Usefulness' of Suspect Classifications." *Constitutional Commentary* 3(2): 375–384.

Saphire, Richard B. 2000. "Equal Protection, Rational Basis Review, and the Impact of Cleburne Living Center, Inc." *Kentucky Law Journal* 88(3): 591–639.

A. Christopher Bryant

CITY OF ERIE V. PAP'S A.M., 529 U.S. 277 (2000)

Regulations attempting to ban or restrict nude dancing have come before the Supreme Court three times. In the first case, the Court struck down a total ban on nude dancing, holding that nude dancing is protected to some extent under the First Amendment (see *Schad v. Mount Ephraim*, 452 U. S. 61 [1981]). In the second and third cases, however, the Court upheld regulations restricting nude dancing, although a majority of the Court could not agree on the constitutional rationale to be applied in such cases. In *City of Erie v. Pap's A.M.*, 529 U.S. 277 (2000), the Supreme Court upheld an Erie, Pennsylvania, public indecency statute that made it an offense to knowingly or intentionally appear in public in a state of nudity. The Court permitted the state to apply this statute to erotic dancing establishments, thereby prohibiting nude dancing in public.

OBSCENITY, INDECENCY, SECONDARY EFFECTS, AND SYMBOLIC SPEECH

Regulations of nude dancing implicate a variety of different First Amendment standards. First, sexually explicit nude dancing could fall within the definition of obscenity under *Miller v. California*, 413 U.S. 15 (1973). According to *Miller*, "obscenity" comprises speech that is prurient, patently offensive, and lacking in serious literary, artistic, political, or scientific value. Obscenity is unprotected speech under the First Amendment, and therefore can be banned altogether.

The second aspect of First Amendment doctrine implicated by nude dancing is the standard applied to speech that is indecent, but not obscene. Indecent speech is protected under the First Amendment, but receives a lower level of protection than "high-value" speech such as political advocacy. According to several Supreme Court decisions dealing with ordinances imposing restrictive zoning requirements on adult theaters and bookstores, sexually indecent speech can be extensively regulated by the government in order to protect against the "secondary effects" that often accompany such speech. The term "secondary effects" refers to secondary features that happen to be associated with a particular type of speech—such as the tendency of certain types of criminals to congregate around adult theaters and similar establishments (see *Boos v. Barry*, 485 U.S. 312 [1988]). Under this rationale, the Court has upheld several statutes prohibiting adult theaters and bookstores from being located in close proximity to schools, residential areas, and other adult establishments (see *Young v. American Mini Theatres*, 427 U.S. 50 [1976]; *Renton v. Playtime Theatres*, 475 U.S. 41 [1986]).

The final category of First Amendment doctrine implicated by nude dancing regulations is the standard governing regulations of symbolic speech. This four-part standard was announced in *United States v. O'Brien*, 391 U.S. 367 (1968). According to the *O'Brien* standard, "a government regulation is sufficiently justified if it is within the constitutional power of the Government; if it furthers an important or substantial governmental interest; if the governmental interest is unrelated to the suppression of free expression; and if the incidental restriction on alleged First Amendment freedoms is no greater than is essential to the furtherance of that interest."

In *Pap's A.M.* the nude dancing establishment that challenged the Erie public indecency statute argued that the statute could not be justified under any of these First Amendment standards. The plaintiff argued that the nude dancing in its establishment was not obscene under *Miller*. The plaintiff also argued that the statute could not be justified under the Court's indecency analysis because the statute banned all nude dancing, whereas previous indecency statutes merely regulated how speech could be presented to the public, without banning the speech altogether. Finally, the plaintiff argued that the Erie statute violated the last three parts of the *O'Brien* symbolic speech standard because the government had no substantial interest in the presentation of nude dancing to a willing adult audience, the statute was specifically directed at the content of the speech, and the statute's total ban on nude dancing regulated far more speech than was necessary to achieve any legitimate governmental purpose.

REGULATING NUDITY WHILE PRESERVING EROTIC MESSAGES

Although a majority of the Court voted to uphold the Erie statute and reject the plaintiff's indecency and symbolic speech arguments, the Justices in the majority split on the rationale for this result. Four of the Justices (Chief Justice William Rehnquist and Justices Sandra Day O'Connor, Anthony Kennedy, and Stephen Breyer) ruled (in an opinion written by Justice O'Connor) that the *O'Brien* symbolic speech standard applies to a statute prohibiting public nudity generally. These Justices adopted the rationale of the plurality in *Barnes v. Glen Theatre, Inc.*, 501 U. S. 560 (1991), the Court's previous nude dancing decision. Under that rationale, the *O'Brien* standard would allow a general prohibition on public nudity to be applied to a nude dancing establishment as long as the statute does not force dancers at that establishment to wear anything more concealing than "pasties and a g-string." According to the plurality, unless a regulation is so severe as to interfere with the communication of the dancers' erotic message, the regulation of nude dancing does not violate the First Amendment. The key difference between the doctrinal approach of the plurality decisions in *Barnes* and *Pap's A.M.* is that the Justices in the *Pap's A.M.* plurality incorporate the *Young/Renton* secondary effects analysis into the "important governmental interest" component of the *O'Brien* symbolic speech standard. Thus, government efforts to regulate the secondary effects surrounding nude dancing in public can justify the regulation of symbolic speech represented by the dancing. From a doctrinal standpoint, the incorporation of secondary effects into the *O'Brien* standard is a major change, since the secondary effects analysis had never been used previously to justify a total ban on one type of speech.

The two concurring votes in *Pap's A.M.* (Justice Antonin Scalia, joined by Justice Clarence Thomas) went beyond the plurality's approach and argued that the First Amendment does not even apply to general public indecency or public nudity statutes. These Justices argued that since a general ban on public nudity is not directed specifically at expression, such a ban should not be subjected to any level of First Amendment scrutiny. These Justices also argued that the traditional governmental power to foster good morals is sufficient to justify a general ban on public nudity.

The three dissenting justices also split on their rationales for voting to strike down the Erie statute. Justice David Souter reiterated the position he had stated in *Barnes* that the prohibition of nude dancing could sometimes be justified as a secondary effects regulation under *Young* and *Renton*. Although this premise is now also incorporated into the position of the *Pap's A.M.* plurality opinion, Justice Souter dissented in *Pap's A.M.* because he concluded that Erie had not established a sufficient factual basis to support the secondary effects analysis; thus, Justice Souter would have remanded the case for further development of the record. If a sufficient factual record established the presence of secondary effects (such as criminal activity) in the proximity of nude dancing establishments, Justice Souter would presumably be willing to allow the government to apply to those establishments a narrowly drawn prohibition on public nudity.

Justice John Paul Stevens, writing on behalf of himself and Justice Ruth Bader Ginsburg, argued much more broadly that the Erie public indecency statute was a content-based regulation of speech that could not be justified under the First Amendment. Justice Stevens based this conclusion on evidence in the record that Erie had passed its statute specifically in response to an increase in nude dancing within the city, which several members of the Erie City Council found morally repugnant. Justice Stevens rejected the plurality's assumption that erotic dancing in the nude conveys the same message as erotic dancing by dancers wearing skimpy clothing, and argued that the plurality's approach would permit the government to ban altogether one message—a result that the Court had never before permitted under a secondary effects analysis.

Despite the fractured nature of *Pap's A.M.* and the Court's other nude dancing decisions, several matters seem clear. First, the Court has consistently held that nude dancing is protected speech under the First Amendment. Second, despite the constitutionally protected status of nude dancing, governmental entities can ban nude dancing by asserting that such dancing attracts unwanted or illegal secondary effects, such as criminal activity. The government's assertion of secondary effects, however, may be subject to an empirical challenge regarding the actual existence of the alleged negative effects flowing from nude dancing. Third, since the government's ability to regulate nude dancing depends on the extent to which the nude dancing attracts unwanted antisocial or criminal behavior, it is unlikely that the government may ban nudity in "serious" artistic or theatrical contexts that are unlikely to lead to an increase in activity relating to undesirable social effects such as the dissemination of drugs or prostitution. Fourth, although the government may ban totally nude dancing in certain contexts, it may not prohibit erotically charged dancing altogether. Thus, a municipality cannot require dancers to don more than "pasties and a g-string," because to do so would dilute the erotic message to the point that the regulation would violate the First Amendment. State-mandated fig leaves may be required for those who dance erotically in public, but seemingly not much more.

SEE ALSO *First Amendment; Freedom of Speech*

BIBLIOGRAPHY

Adler, Amy. 2005. "Girls! Girls! Girls!: The Supreme Court Confronts the G-String." *New York University Law Review* 80(4): 1079–1109.

Blasi, Vincent. 1992. "Six Conservatives in Search of the First Amendment: The Revealing Case of Nude Dancing." *William and Mary Law Review* 33(3): 611–663.

Chemerinsky, Erwin. 2000. "Content Neutrality as a Central Problem of Freedom of Speech: Problems in the Supreme Court's Application." *Southern California Law Review* 74(1): 49–64.

Kitrosser, Heidi. 2002. "From Marshall McLuhan to Anthropomorphic Cows: Communicative Manner and the First Amendment." *Northwestern University Law Review* 96(4): 1339–1412.

Paul, Bryant; Daniel Linz; and Bradley J. Shafer. 2001. "Government Regulation of 'Adult' Businesses through Zoning and Anti-Nudity Ordinances: Debunking the Legal Myth of Negative Secondary Effects." *Communication Law & Policy* 6(2): 355–391.

Steven G. Gey

CITY OF MOBILE V. BOLDEN, 446 U.S. 55 (1980)

In 1911 Mobile, Alabama, joined the era of progressive reform by adopting the commission form of government with at-large elections. Sixty-five years later, a federal district court in the state declared that the city's at-large system improperly diluted the voting strength of minority citizens—a decision upheld by the Court of Appeals for the Fifth Circuit. *City of Mobile v. Bolden*, 446 U.S. 55 (1980), was first argued before the U.S. Supreme Court on March 19, 1979, and was then reargued on October 29, 1979. On April 22, 1980, the Supreme Court reversed the lower-court judgments, holding that the at-large election of commissioners was not a violation of the Fifteenth Amendment, the equal protection clause of the Fourteenth Amendment or Section 2 of the 1965 Voting Rights Act.

The six-to-three decision was a rather fragmented one. Writing the plurality opinion for four members of the Court, Justice Potter Stewart argued that Mobile's electoral system lacked the "discriminatory motivation" required for a Fifteenth Amendment violation and the "purposeful discrimination" needed to invoke the equal protection clause. Further, Justice Stewart (along with Chief Justice Warren E. Burger and Justices Lewis F. Powell Jr. and William Rehnquist) also rejected the statutory claim that the election system ran counter to the requirements of the Voting Rights Act. That Act, according to the opinion, simply reiterated the prohibitions found in the Fifteenth Amendment and nothing more.

Citing *Gomillion v. Lightfoot*, 364 U.S. 339 (1960) and other precedents, Justice Stewart argued that discriminatory intent and motivation would have to exist for violations of the Fourteenth and Fifteenth Amendments to occur. But the lower courts had found that African-American voters in the city were able to "register and vote without hindrance." Under such circumstances, the discovery of constitutional violations was in error.

ENCYCLOPEDIA OF THE SUPREME COURT OF THE UNITED STATES

Additionally, Justice Stewart rejected the points articulated by Justice Thurgood Marshall in dissent, noting that those arguments were political theory rather than law and that following such theory would turn the Court into a "super-legislature" protecting certain groups from electoral defeat.

In his brief concurring opinion, Justice Harry Blackmun wrote that the district court, in mandating a mayor/single-member-district structure on the city, failed to consider more moderate alternatives. Thus, in his view, the court provided relief that was "not commensurate with the sound exercise of judicial discretion." In his concurrence, Justice John Paul Stevens agreed that there was no constitutional right to have proportional representation for racial minorities. Yet he declined to focus on the question of motivation, stating that this approach would place the Court directly in "the political thicket" where it would face endless litigation.

While each of the three dissenting justices (William J. Brennan Jr., Byron White, and Thurgood Marshall) wrote separately, it was Marshall who provided the most extensive critical commentary. Following the logic of *White v. Regester*, 412 U.S. 755 (1973), Justice Marshall noted that the right to vote is a fundamental right subject to strict-scrutiny review. Therefore, all that is required is a showing of discriminatory impact. African Americans constituted more than 35 percent of Mobile's population, yet none had ever been elected to the commission in the racially polarized city with a long history of official discrimination. This is all the proof needed to show that the dilution of minority votes has occurred.

In the 1982 extension of the Voting Rights Act, Section 2 was amended to consider effect, instead of intent. Under those circumstances, Mobile eliminated its at-large commission system.

SEE ALSO *Fifteenth Amendment; Fourteenth Amendment*

BIBLIOGRAPHY

Davidson, Chandler, ed. 1984. *Minority Vote Dilution.* Washington, DC: Howard University Press.

Norman Provizer

CITY OF PHILADELPHIA V. NEW JERSEY, 437 U.S. 617 (1978)

Citing aesthetic and environmental concerns, the New Jersey state legislature banned the importation of most "solid or liquid waste which originated or was collected outside the territorial limits of the State." A consortium of New Jersey landfill operators and their out-of-state municipal patrons challenged the statute in New Jersey state court. On appeal, the U.S. Supreme Court, in *City of Philadelphia v. New Jersey*, 437 U.S. 617 (1978), invalidated the law as an impermissible barrier to interstate commerce in garbage.

By its terms, the commerce clause in Article I, Section 8 of the U.S. Constitution empowers Congress "to regulate Commerce . . . among the several States," and under the supremacy clause (Art. VI, Sec. 2), federal statutes sweep aside any conflicting state laws. Justice Potter Stewart's opinion for the Court relegated to a footnote the summary rejection of the plaintiffs' claim that federal statutes preempted the New Jersey law. That was not, however, the end of the matter, for the Court had long construed the commerce clause as a commitment to a policy of free trade across state boundaries and had accordingly implied therefrom a judicial power to strike down state laws impeding interstate commerce even in the absence of a conflict with a federal statute. Stewart brushed aside the state court's conclusion that garbage simply did not count as an object of "commerce" for the purposes of the Court's so-called dormant commerce clause jurisprudence. He regarded as misplaced the lower court's reliance on decades-old rulings affirming the states' authority to ban importation of such elements of contagion as infected rags or diseased cattle. That some "articles' worth . . . was far outweighed by the dangers inhering in their very movement" did not alter the bedrock principle that "all objects of interstate trade merit Commerce Clause protection; none are excluded by definition at the outset."

Nor could New Jersey's prohibition, properly understood as a barrier to commerce, withstand the requisite constitutional scrutiny. The Court's decisions "through the years . . . reflected an alertness to the evils of 'economic isolation' and protectionism." Thus, the "crucial inquiry" was whether the New Jersey statute was "basically a protectionist measure" or whether it could "fairly be viewed as a law directed to legitimate local concerns, with effects upon interstate commerce that are only incidental." The parties vigorously disputed the actual purpose of the New Jersey law, with the state describing the statute as a measure to preserve environmental quality and the plaintiffs insisting that the law was economic protectionism wrapped in a deceptive cloak of environmentalist rhetoric. Justice Stewart saw no need for the Court to resolve this dispute, however, as "contrary to the evident assumption of the state court and the parties, the evil of protectionism can reside in legislative means, as well as legislative ends. Whatever purpose the state pursued, it could not do so "by discriminating against articles of commerce coming from outside the State unless there is some reason, apart from their origin, to treat them differently." The harms New Jersey sought to prevent arose after the wastes' disposal in landfills, at which point there was "no basis to distinguish out-of-state waste from domestic waste."

Justice William Rehnquist dissented in an opinion in which Chief Justice Warren Burger joined. Rehnquist found the Court's attempts to distinguish its prior rulings concerning agents of contagion "unconvincing" and concluded that, properly construed, the commerce clause imposed upon New Jersey no obligation to "accept solid waste … from outside its borders and thereby exacerbate its problems."

SEE ALSO *Preemption*

BIBLIOGRAPHY

Redish, Martin H., and Shane V. Nugent. 1987. "The Dormant Commerce Clause and the Constitutional Balance of Federalism." *Duke Law Journal* 1987(4): 569–617.

Stearns, Maxwell L. 2003. "A Beautiful Mend: A Game Theoretical Analysis of the Dormant Commerce Clause Doctrine." *William & Mary Law Review* 45: 1–155.

A. Christopher Bryant

CITY OF RICHMOND V. J. A. CROSON CO.

In *City of Richmond v. J. A. Croson Company*, 488 U.S. 469 (1989), the U.S. Supreme Court found a local government's affirmative-action program unconstitutional. The Court ruled that the City of Richmond's minority business enterprise program violated the U.S. Constitution's Fourteenth Amendment clause providing for "equal protection of the laws." In doing so, the Court established that all nonfederal race-based programs, including affirmative-action plans, would be evaluated by the courts under the strict scrutiny standard of review.

Most affirmative-action programs fall into one of three areas: education, employment, or government contracting. Affirmative-action programs for government contracting—the type of claim at issue in *Croson*—are termed *minority business enterprise* or MBE programs. MBE programs typically provide favorable treatment for minority-owned businesses in the bidding process for government contracts, which can range from the building of a new sports arena or convention center, to the purchase of office supplies or automobile parts, to the selection of accounting or legal services. The favorable treatment given to MBEs may include *set-asides* or *sheltered markets* whereby only targeted groups can compete for certain government contracts, *bid enhancements* whereby the bids submitted by MBEs are not directly compared to the otherwise lowest qualified bid,

and *goals* programs whereby the government attempts to contract with minority-owned businesses without using set-asides or bid enhancements, most often requiring prime contractors to make good-faith efforts to subcontract with MBEs. Nearly every level of government uses MBE programs, from the federal government down to school districts and port authorities.

Richmond, Virginia's MBE program called for successful bidders on government contracts to subcontract 30 percent of contracted dollars to minority-owned firms. Richmond based its MBE program on the federal MBE program upheld by the Supreme Court in *Fullilove v. Klutznick*, 448 U.S. 448 (1980). The J. A. Croson Company was the only bidder on a project to install fixtures in the city jail. Richmond rejected the bid, however, because Croson's proposal did not purport to use any minority-owned subcontractors—let alone 30 percent of the contracted dollars. In response, Croson filed a federal lawsuit charging racial discrimination against white contractors in violation of the equal protection clause of the Fourteenth Amendment.

The city contended in court that its program was designed (1) to help minorities and (2) to remediate discrimination against minorities, both points critical to the Supreme Court in upholding a federal affirmative-action program in *Fullilove*. In *Croson*, however, the Supreme Court ruled that there was no difference between invidious and well-intentioned discrimination as it related to state and local governments. The Court in *Croson* did not overrule *Fullilove*, but rather argued that there is a constitutional difference between federal and state or local race-based legislation, largely reflective of the unique role ascribed to Congress by Section 5 of the Fourteenth Amendment. This distinction, however, was subsequently eviscerated in *Adarand Constructors, Inc. v. Peña*, 515 U.S. 200 (1995), where the Supreme Court held that "any person, of whatever race, has the right to demand that any governmental actor subject to the Constitution justify any racial classification subjecting that person to unequal treatment under the strictest of judicial scrutiny."

The gravamen of Justice Sandra Day O'Connor's majority opinion in *Croson* rested on the lack of proof of the necessity of the program. O'Connor found that the Richmond City Council relied on generalized assertions of discrimination, speculative conclusions about the paltry percentage of contract dollars awarded to minority prime contractors (0.67 percent), and congressional findings that may not apply to the local Richmond market. Rather, Richmond should have specified that there was a significant disparity between the availability and utilization of minority contractors in the local market area. The city itself need not have been directly responsible for such discrimination (as was suggested by Justice Antonin Scalia's concurrence), but the city must at least have been a "passive participant" in a discriminatory system before the Constitution allows local governments to use racially based legislation to ameliorate the discrimination. This passive participant hurdle did not seem severe enough for Justice Scalia, as he would have limited local government affirmative action programs to those circumstances "where [it] is necessary to eliminate their own maintenance of a system of unlawful racial classification."

Though the outcome of *Croson* was a seeming defeat for affirmative-action proponents, the opinion effectively established how governments could create a constitutional affirmative-action program. To do so, a government must establish that its program passes the strict scrutiny standard by being "narrowly tailored to a compelling state interest." As the Court elaborated, this means that governments seeking to create an MBE program must prove that their "spending practices [exacerbated] a pattern of prior discrimination," and that such discrimination is specifically identified. Further, the government must consider race-neutral methods toward addressing the disparity; the MBE program targets must correspond to the relevant specialized populations in the area; the statute must be flexible; the burden on excluded groups must be minimized; and MBE programs must be of limited duration.

Justice Thurgood Marshall's dissent in *Croson* expressed concern that the majority opinion would "discourage or prevent governmental entities ... from acting to rectify the scourge of past discrimination." He found the Court's opinion to be "a deliberate and giant step backward in this Court's affirmative action jurisprudence." Marshall's lament, however, has probably not come to fruition. While the lower courts have consistently followed the dictates set out by the Supreme Court in striking down almost all of the thirty-odd challenged MBE programs using strict scrutiny, the policy-creation side of the equation has not abated. Local governments have continued to respond to political demands and have created numerous new MBE programs since 1989, based on the Court's opinion in *Croson*.

SEE ALSO *Adarand Constructors, Inc. v. Peña, 515 U.S. 200 (1995); Affirmative Action; Rehnquist Court*

BIBLIOGRAPHY

Drake, W. Avon, and Robert D. Holsworth. 1996. *Affirmative Action and the Stalled Quest for Black Progress*. Urbana: University of Illinois Press.

La Noue, George R. 1997. "The Impact of *Croson* on Equal Protection Law and Policy." *Albany Law Review* 61: 1–41.

Sweet, Martin Jay. 2003. "Supreme Policymaking: Coping with the Supreme Court's Affirmative Action Policies." Ph.D. diss., University of Wisconsin, Madison.

Martin J. Sweet

CIVIL RIGHTS

SEE *Citizenship; Civil Rights Act of 1866; Civil Rights Act of 1964; Civil Rights Cases, 109 U.S. 3 (1883).*

CIVIL RIGHTS ACT OF 1866

The Civil Rights Act of 1866 was enacted by Congress in order to define U.S. citizenship on a nonracial basis; to establish the right of citizens to make contracts, participate in lawsuits, and hold and exchange property; and to guarantee that citizens be treated equally under the law. The act was the first federal effort to introduce a broadly defined requirement of equality into American law and governance. The principal provisions of the act were subsequently made part of the Constitution when they were incorporated into the Fourteenth Amendment.

The Civil Rights Act originated in the early years of Reconstruction after the Civil War (1861–1865). The Emancipation Proclamation (1863) and the Thirteenth Amendment (1865) had liberated nearly four million enslaved people, but their legal status remained contested. Northerners expected that southern loyalists would establish an economy based on free labor, but whites in the South had other ideas. In the fall of 1865, southern state legislatures began to pass Black Codes that restrained black people from doing nonagricultural work and compelled them to sign labor contracts; allowed black children to be apprenticed to whites, often their former owners; and criminalized a wide variety of petty offenses; those convicted could be forced to work for white people who paid their fines or posted bail. The Black Codes were, as one observer aptly described them, "plans for getting things back as near to slavery as possible" (quoted in Foner 1988, p. 199).

Southern white intransigence outraged public opinion in the North, generating political pressure on Congress to take action. Early in 1866, legislators drafted a bill intended to protect the freedpeople by enshrining equality in federal law; the bill was an essential part of congressional efforts to work with President Andrew Johnson (1808–1875) in formulating an acceptable Reconstruction policy. The bill passed by substantial margins in both houses, and when Johnson vetoed it Republicans in Congress pushed him aside and initiated a new, more radical phase of Reconstruction. The Civil Rights Act became the first major law enacted over a presidential veto.

The main provisions of the act were contained in its first section. The statute began by specifying that "all persons born in the United States ... are hereby declared to be citizens of the United States." It then went on to define citizenship in clearer terms, starting with a broad declaration of civil equality that "citizens, of every race and color, without regard to any previous condition of slavery or involuntary servitude ... shall have the same right ... to make and enforce contracts, to sue, be parties, and give evidence, to inherit, purchase, lease, sell, hold, and convey real and personal property." The act then detailed the attributes of citizenship, stipulating that all Americans would enjoy the same "full and equal benefit of all laws and proceedings for the security of person and property, as is enjoyed by white citizens," including being "subject to like punishment, pains, and penalties, and to none other."

The rest of the act dealt with penalties, jurisdiction, and enforcement. Section 2 stated that anybody who deprived a person of "any right secured or protected by this act" could be fined up to one thousand dollars, imprisoned for as long as one year, or both. Subsequent parts of the statute were intended to prevent local officials and others from using inaction, evasion, or intimidation to foil the law. Section 3 gave federal courts exclusive jurisdiction over cases brought under the act. Section 4 granted authority to a broad range of federal officials to bring charges against those who violated the act. Sections 5 and 6 imposed fines and imprisonment upon anyone convicted of obstructing enforcement of the act. Sections 8 and 9 empowered the president to direct judges, marshals, district attorneys, soldiers, sailors, and militiamen to prevent violations of the act and ensure its enforcement.

In terms of law and governance, the primary significance of the Civil Rights Act was its use of federal authority to protect the rights of individuals. The act empowered federal officials to overrule state laws in order to guarantee equality, and in this it reflected the same radical Republican political commitments that had made possible the use of centralized authority to destroy slavery. This expansion of federal power at the expense of the states departed from earlier traditions of American governance, but the circumstances of Reconstruction—defiant southern whites attempting to render the freedpeoples' liberty virtually meaningless only months after the defeat of their rebellion at the cost of more than six hundred thousand lives—led members of Congress to see this approach as not just possible, but imperative.

The act did have its limitations. Its benefits were not extended to Native Americans, most of whom would not gain citizenship until decades later. Moreover, it made no mention of a right to vote, because any such provision would have enfranchised black men, and most whites strongly opposed black suffrage at that point. African Americans objected vigorously to being denied the ballot, but as the bill's author explained, the Civil Rights Act as it stood was "as far as the country will go at the present time." (quoted in Foner 1988, p. 245).

Supreme Court interpretation of the Civil Rights Act of 1866 was for many years quite limited because its basic stipulations were quickly constitutionalized as section one of the Fourteenth Amendment. In circuit court rulings in 1866 and 1867, Chief Justice Salmon Chase and Justice Noah Swayne (1804–1884) both found the law a legitimate exercise of Congress's power to preserve freedom under the Thirteenth Amendment. A century later, however, the Supreme Court revivified the law as a support for expansive action by Congress to protect Americans' civil rights because it seemed to allow federal authority to extend beyond what was considered permissible under the Fourteenth Amendment. In *Jones v. Mayer*, 392 U.S. 409 (1968), the Court ruled that the Civil Rights Act forbade racial discrimination by private citizens in the rental or sale of housing. In *Runyon v. McCrary*, 427 U.S. 160 (1976), the Court found that the act could prevent private schools from using race as a reason to reject qualified applicants. And in *McDonald v. Santa Fe Trail Transportation Co.*, 427 U.S. 273 (1976); *Shaare Tefila Congregation v. Cobb*, 481 U.S. 615 (1987); and *Saint Francis College v. Al-Khazraji*, 481 U.S. 604 (1987), the Court decided that the act also protected white people, religious minorities, and ethnic groups, respectively. These latter rulings have since been subject to challenge, indicating the ongoing relevance of the Civil Rights Act of 1866 to civil rights enforcement in the twenty-first century.

SEE ALSO *Amendments, Post-Civil War; Fourteenth Amendment; Reconstruction; Thirteenth Amendment*

BIBLIOGRAPHY

Belz, Herman. 1976. *A New Birth of Freedom: The Republican Party and Freedmen's Rights, 1861–1866.* Westport, CT: Greenwood Press.

Foner, Eric. 1988. *Reconstruction: America's Unfinished Revolution, 1863–1877.* New York: Harper and Row.

Kaczorowski, Robert J. 2005. "Congress' Power to Enforce Fourteenth Amendment Rights: Lessons from Federal Remedies the Framers Enacted." *Harvard Journal on Legislation* 42(1): 187–283.

A. K. Sandoval-Strausz

CIVIL RIGHTS ACT OF 1964

The Civil Rights Act of 1964 (42 U.S. C.A.) (the 1964 Act) likely has had the greatest transformative effect on American society of any single law. By prohibiting discrimination based on race, color, sex, religion, and national origin in places of public accommodation, in federally assisted programs, in employment, in schools, and with respect to voting rights, this massive law has had profound effects on almost every facet of American society. Though other civil rights acts and laws to

Signing of the Civil Rights Act of 1964 by President Lyndon B. Johnson, with Martin Luther King, Jr., observing. *Considered by many scholars to be the most wide-reaching law ever passed in the United States, the Civil Rights Act of 1964 affected the lives of millions of Americans, expressly prohibiting discrimination on race, gender, religion, and ethnic background. Unlike previous attempts at civil rights legislation, the constitutionality of the 1964 act held up under examination by the Supreme Court and received widespread, though not unanimous, acceptance from the American public.*
© **CORBIS-BETTMANN**

vindicate civil rights have been passed, no other law was as well received by the Supreme Court as the 1964 Act and it is possible that no other civil rights law has been as generally accepted by the public as the 1964 Act.

THE ACT'S PASSAGE

On July 2, 1964, President Lyndon B. Johnson signed the Civil Rights Act of 1964 into law. The law's passage was the culmination of extended congressional and national debate regarding civil rights in general and the role of race in particular in society. The act had originally been sent to Congress by President John F. Kennedy on June 19, 1963. President Johnson called for the passage of the civil rights bill as a legacy to President Kennedy on November 27, 1963, in an address to Congress shortly after President Kennedy's assassination. Eventually, President Johnson

would use the power of the presidency and his personal influence derived from his years in Congress to help shepherd the bill into law.

The 1964 Act was not met with universal support in Congress. Various parliamentary maneuvers were necessary to push the bill past Congressman Howard W. Smith (1883–1976) of Virginia, the powerful chairman of the House Rules Committee. Similar obstacles had to be surmounted in the Senate. Indeed, once on the floor of the Senate, the act was subject to a filibuster that lasted eighty-two days and stands as the longest in the Senate's history. During debate in both the House and the Senate, a number of congressmen and senators, most of whom were from the South, argued that the act was an unconstitutional affront to states' rights that exceeded Congress's power under the Constitution. Though the debate was heated, the final version of the act ultimately passed 73 to 27 in the Senate and 289 to 126 in the House.

The 1964 Act certainly was not the first act Congress ever passed to vindicate civil rights. Soon after the Civil War (1861–1865), Congress passed the Civil Rights Acts of 1866 and 1875 in attempts to effectuate the liberty that many in Congress believed was granted by the abolition of slavery in the Thirteenth Amendment and the call for citizenship and equality in the Fourteenth Amendment. However, the Supreme Court narrowed the scope of the Civil Rights Act of 1875 in *The Civil Rights Cases*, 109 U.S. 3 (1883). Indeed, that decision struck down the public accommodations clauses that were retooled and reborn in the 1964 Act. In the several years before the 1964 Act was enacted, Congress passed the Civil Rights Acts of 1957 and 1960. However, both were fairly mild measures focused largely on voting rights. Congress did not stop with the 1964 Act. The 1964 Act has been amended a number of times, including significant amendments in 1972 and 1991.

THE SUBSTANCE OF THE ACT

The 1964 Act prohibits discrimination in certain substantive areas and creates mechanisms to monitor the advance of, and enforce the protection of, equal rights for all. The self-styled purpose of the 1964 Act was

> to enforce the constitutional right to vote, to confer jurisdiction upon the district courts of the United States to provide injunctive relief against discrimination in public accommodations, to authorize the Attorney General to institute suits to protect constitutional rights in public facilities and public education, to extend the Commission on Civil Rights, to prevent discrimination in federally assisted programs, to establish a Commission on Equal Employment Opportunity, and for other purposes.

The language of the 1964 Act speaks in terms of nondiscrimination. Though the Court has lapsed occasionally into speaking of "protected groups" under the 1964 Act, particularly with respect to Title VII of the act, the act itself merely requires equal treatment for all by limiting the bases on which persons can be treated differently. Guaranteeing that citizens of all races, and religions, for example, enjoy the same rights is consistent with the Fourteenth Amendment command of equal protection of the laws. However, as noted below, Congress' power to enact the 1964 Act provisions affecting private actors was found to be explicitly justified based on its commerce clause power, rather than on power to enforce the Fourteenth Amendment.

The Eleven Titles of the Act The 1964 Act has eleven titles, with some titles focusing on addressing discrimination in specific areas of American life, others creating agencies to enforce specific parts of the act, and yet others establishing procedures for enforcing the act.

Title I has largely been superseded. Title I focused on procedural equality in voting rights. For example, rather than bar literacy tests, Title I limited the manner in which literacy tests could be given. Functionally, the voting rights provisions of the 1964 Act were superseded by the Voting Rights Act of 1965 and its later amendments, which strengthened the procedural and substantive prohibitions on voting rights discrimination pursuant to the Fifteenth Amendment.

Titles V, VIII, and X establish some of the agencies and procedures necessary to monitor the advance of equal rights. Title V provides procedures to follow, and redefines the role and duties of the Commission on Civil Rights that the Civil Rights Act of 1957 created. Title V requires that the commission investigate allegations of deprivations of the right to vote, evaluate legal developments and federal laws to make sure they do not constitute denials of the equal protection of the laws, and serve as a clearinghouse for information respecting violations of equal protection. Though the commission and its charge were altered somewhat and re-codified in 1983, its basic function has remained the same.

Title VIII requires that the secretary of commerce compile registration and voting statistics for use by the Commission on Civil Rights. Title X established the Community Relations Service as a part of the Department of Commerce to "provide assistance to communities and persons therein in resolving disputes, disagreements, or difficulties relating to discriminatory practices based on race, color, or national origin which impair the rights of persons in such communities under the Constitution or laws of the United States or which affect or may affect interstate commerce."

Titles IX and XI are procedural and descriptive. Title IX specifies procedural processes in civil rights cases where plaintiffs seek relief from a denial of equal protection under the Fourteenth Amendment. Title XI is a mass of miscellaneous provisions designed to increase the 1964 Act's effectiveness and define its scope.

The 1964 Act's substantive core consists of Titles II, III, IV, VI, and VII. These titles prohibit discrimination in various substantive areas. Title II focuses on public accommodations. It bars discrimination and segregation based on race, color, religion, or national origin with respect to hotels, restaurants, theaters, stadiums, and like facilities, if their "operations affect commerce, or if discrimination or segregation by it is supported by State action." Under certain conditions, private clubs and nonpublic establishments are not covered by the title.

Title II spawned the first Supreme Court cases that addressed the constitutionality of the 1964 Act: *Heart of*

Atlanta Motel v. United States, 379 U.S. 241 (1964) and *Katzenbach v. McClung*, 379 U.S. 294 (1964). Both cases were filed just after the 1964 Act became law and were decided by the Supreme Court on an expedited basis. In *Heart of Atlanta*, plaintiff sought a declaratory judgment deeming the 1964 Act unconstitutional. Plaintiff argued, inter alia, that the act exceeded Congress' power under the commerce clause of the Constitution. After noting that the Heart of Atlanta Motel had substantial connection to interstate travel and commerce, the Court indicated that its ruling would be limited to determining whether Congress had appropriate power under the commerce clause to render the act constitutional. The Court explicitly noted that it was not deciding whether Congress' enforcement power under section five of the Fourteenth Amendment was a sufficient basis to validate the act. In doing so, the Court sidestepped the issue of precisely how the invalidation of the public accommodations provisions of the Civil Rights Act of 1875 by *The Civil Rights Cases* would affect the Court's decision. Nonetheless, the Court stated that *The Civil Rights Cases* would not resolve the issue as to the 1964 Act's public accommodations provisions because they were narrower and different than the like provisions of the Civil Rights Act of 1875. The Court concluded that the 1964 Act's public accommodations provisions were clearly within Congress' commerce clause power when, as in *Heart of Atlanta Motel*, they were applied to a motel that admittedly served interstate travelers. Though the Court expressed no opinion on the Fourteenth Amendment question, the concurrences by Justices William O. Douglas and Arthur J. Goldberg argued that the act was also constitutional pursuant to Congress' enforcement power under the Fourteenth Amendment.

Katzenbach arguably was more difficult than *Heart of Atlanta Motel* because it involved a restaurant, Ollie's Barbecue in Birmingham, Alabama, that catered to local residents and did not appear to serve or seek to serve interstate travelers. Ollie's Barbecue was subject to Title II of the 1964 Act because that title regulated restaurants if a substantial portion of the food the restaurant served traveled in interstate commerce. That much of the meat Ollie's Barbecue served was purchased from a local supplier, who bought it from an out-of-state supplier, suggested that the restaurant was subject to the act. The Court determined, in limiting the act's coverage to restaurants that imported a substantial portion of the food they served from out-of-state, Congress acted within its Article I power to regulate interstate commerce.

Titles III and IV authorize the government to provide assistance to guarantee that the constitutional commands to desegregate public facilities and public schools were enforced. Title III authorizes the attorney general to become involved in cases in which people were demanding the desegregation of public facilities if those people could not fully or adequately prosecute the case on their own. Title IV facilitates the continued desegregation of public education by requiring that the commissioner of education (now the secretary of education) survey and report on the equality of schools, and by allowing the commissioner to provide technical assistance regarding the desegregation of schools. In addition, as under Title III, Title IV authorizes the attorney general to intervene in cases in which potential meritorious litigants cannot adequately prosecute a case involving the desegregation of public schools. Much of the litigation to which Title III or Title IV would apply is brought under the Constitution's equal protection clause without reference to the 1964 Act. For example, *Swann v. Charlotte-Mecklenburg Board of Education*, 402 U.S. 1 (1971), a school desegregation case, was considered an attempt to apply the strictures of *Brown v. Board of Education*, 347 U.S. 483 (1954). Title IV was implicated because the case involved school desegregation. However, the Court indicated that Title IV's purpose was to define how the federal government could facilitate the desegregation process, rather than to augment the substantive guarantees of the Fourteenth Amendment. Consequently, the Court ruled that the requirements of Title IV go only as far as the limits of the Fourteenth Amendment. Of course, the federal government was to have a role to play up to the limits of the Fourteenth Amendment. The Court noted that Title IV's relevance was only with respect to the appropriate procedures that were to be used to decide the case, rather than to determine the substance of the decision.

Title VI of the Act requires nondiscrimination in federally assisted programs, thus allowing the participation of all in programs subsidized by the federal government. The Court has made clear that, like Title IV, Title VI's reach is coextensive with the Fourteenth Amendment's reach. Consequently, Title VI only reaches intentional discrimination that violates the equal protection clause (see *Guardians Association v. Civil Service Commission of New York City*, 463 U.S 582 [1983]; *Grutter v. Bollinger*, 539 U.S. 306 [2003]). However, federal agencies that administer programs that provide federal financial assistance are required to issue regulations that effectuate the purposes of Title VI. Such regulations under Title VI may be as important in a practical sense as Title VI itself. Indeed, a recent Title VI case, *Alexander v. Sandoval*, 532 U.S. 275 (2001), arose in the context of a Department of Justice regulation that barred the use of rules in programs receiving federal assistance from the department that had the effect of discriminating based on race. The Court did not decide whether the regulation was valid under Title VI, but did rule that the regulation did not create a private cause of action that would have allowed a private plaintiff to recover if an entity was found to be using a prohibited rule that harmed the plaintiff's ability to enjoy the benefits of the federally-assisted program at issue.

Title VII and Equal Employment Title VII, the longest section of the 1964 Act by far, requires equal employment opportunity. It broadly restricts employers, employment agencies, and labor organizations from discriminating with respect to employment or employment opportunities based on race, color, religion, sex, or national origin. In addition, covered entities may not retaliate against employees for informally challenging or participating in the official challenging of unlawful employment practices. Title VII also limits how covered entities can advertise jobs.

Like all other 1964 Act titles, Title VII merely eliminates discrimination on the basis of various characteristics. Nonetheless, much of the debate regarding the proposed Title VII focused on whether its strong anti-discrimination language effectively created a climate in which employers would be required to favor minority workers over white workers or risk violating the statute. The act's supporters argued that Title VII's nondiscrimination language required that workers be treated equally without regard to race and could not fairly be read to create a preference for any particular group of workers. The Court balanced the need for equality and the reality of historical discrimination when it allowed a voluntary affirmative action plan initiated under Title VII to stand in *United Steelworkers of America v. Weber*, 443 U.S. 193 (1979).

Congress created the Equal Employment Opportunity Commission (EEOC) to enforce Title VII. The EEOC was given broad powers to investigate and resolve charges made by employees against employers, employment agencies, and labor organizations, but was not given the power to adjudicate claims. The charge process was designed to work in conjunction with state and local fair employment practices commissions whenever possible. When a charge is unable to be resolved informally, either the aggrieved employee or, in some cases, the EEOC may file suit.

Title VII is the only title under the 1964 Act that barred sex discrimination at its passage, though other titles have been amended since 1964 to ban sex discrimination. Congressman Howard Smith (1883–1976) of Virginia proposed amending the bill late in the legislative process to include sex discrimination under Title VII. Smith claimed that given the other parts of the act, adding sex discrimination to Title VII could not hurt the quality of the act. Conventional wisdom suggests that Smith added sex discrimination merely to poison the chances that the act would pass. Indeed, for that reason, some of the act's staunchest supporters opposed Smith's amendment. However, Congresswoman Martha Griffiths (1912–) of Michigan suggested that she would have proposed adding sex discrimination to Title VII had Congressman Smith failed to do so. Regardless of how sex entered the bill, it did so late in the process and without nearly as much discussion as other provisions. The lack of legislative history surrounding sex discrimination has provided the Court a freer hand in interpreting sex discrimination than in interpreting other types of discrimination covered by Title VII.

Title VII has spawned a number of cases that have significantly altered the workplace. For example, *Duke Power Company v. Griggs*, 401 U.S. 424 (1971) sanctioned the disparate impact cause of action that does not require proof of intentional discrimination. Rather, disparate impact can be proven when an employer, lacking a business necessity for doing so, employs a facially neutral rule that has the effect of discriminating against a certain group of workers on the basis of their race, sex, or other characteristic. Eventually, this interpretation of Title VII was explicitly written into law in the Civil Rights Act of 1991.

As importantly, the Court has recognized and defined workplace sexual harassment through its interpretation of Title VII. In *Meritor Savings Bank v. Vinson*, 477 U.S. 57 (1986), the Court recognized a cause of action for both quid pro quo and hostile work environment sexual harassment. Quid pro quo harassment occurs when actual job detriment results from the refusal to acquiesce to sexually harassing behavior. Hostile work environment harassment occurs whenever sexually harassing conduct alters the terms, conditions, or privileges of an employee's employment without causing tangible job detriment. In addition, the Court ruled in *Oncale v. Sundowner Offshore Services*, 523 U.S. 75 (1998) that same-sex sexual harassment may be actionable, though it noted that Title VII was not meant to be a "general civility code" for the workplace. In that vein, the Court in *Burlington Industries v. Ellerth*, 524 U.S. 742 (1998) and *Faragher v. City of Boca Raton*, 524 U.S. 775 (1998) ruled that in some circumstances employees had to give the employer an opportunity to remedy the harassment before the harassment would support an award of damages.

The Court's interpretation of Title VII has not always been consistent with Congressional sentiment. For example, the Court's refusal to treat pregnancy discrimination as sex discrimination in *General Electric Co. v. Gilbert*, 429 U.S. 125 (1976) led to the passage of the Pregnancy Discrimination Act of 1978, which defined sex discrimination under Title VII to include pregnancy discrimination. Similarly, dissatisfaction with *Wards Cove Packing Co. v. Atonio*, 490 U.S. 642 (1989) and *Price Waterhouse v. Hopkins*, 490 U.S. 228 (1989) spurred Congress to pass significant amendments to Title VII in the Civil Rights Act of 1991. The 1991 act amendments clarified the standards for disparate impact liability, clarified the effect of the presentation of evidence that both lawful and unlawful motivations caused an employment decision, provided for jury trials for certain Title VII cases, and allowed the recovery of punitive damages in some cases.

IMPACT OF THE CIVIL RIGHTS ACT OF 1964

The 1964 Act inaugurated a sea of change in the United States. It demands equality for all in many of the most important areas of American life. The Court's ready acceptance of the constitutionality of the 1964 Act helped make the act acceptable to the large majority of Americans. Of course, the Court continues to interpret the act. Though there may be disagreement regarding specific interpretations that the Court makes, the legitimacy of the act and its goals is not subject to debate.

SEE ALSO *Commerce Clause; Heart of Atlanta Motel v. United States, 379 U.S. 241 (1964); Johnson, Lyndon B.; Katzenbach v. McClung, 379 U.S. 294 (1964); Kennedy, Robert; Sex Discrimination; Warren Court*

BIBLIOGRAPHY

Gillon, Steven M. 2000. *"That's Not What We Meant to Do": Reform and Its Unintended Consequences in Twentieth-Century America.* New York: Norton & Company.

Grofman, Bernard, ed. 2000. *Legacies of the 1964 Civil Rights Act.* Charlottesville: University Press of Virginia.

Halpern, Stephen C. 1995. *On the Limits of the Law: The Ironic Legacy of Title VI of the 1964 Civil Rights Act.* Baltimore, MD: Johns Hopkins University Press.

Kotz, Nick. 2005. *Judgment Days: Lyndon Baines Johnson, Martin Luther King, Jr., and the Laws that Changed America.* Boston: Houghton Mifflin.

Loevy, Robert D., ed. 1997. *The Civil Rights Acts of 1964: The Passage of the Law that Ended Racial Segregation.* Albany: State University of New York Press.

Sokol, Jason. 2006. *There Goes My Everything: White Southerners in the Age of Civil Rights, 1945–1975.* New York: Knopf.

Whalen, Charles, and Barbara Whalen. 1984. *The Longest Debate: A Legislative History of the 1964 Civil Rights Act.* Washington, DC: Seven Locks Press.

Zietlow, Rebecca E. 2006. *Enforcing Equality: Congress, the Constitution, and the Protection of Individual Rights.* New York: New York University Press.

Henry L. Chambers Jr.

CIVIL RIGHTS CASES, 109 U.S. 3 (1883)

In the *Civil Rights Cases*, 109 U.S. 3 (1883), a consolidation of five lower court cases involving the exclusion of blacks from inns, theaters, and ladies' railroad cars, the U.S. Supreme Court invalidated the public accommodation provisions of the Civil Rights Act of 1875, which were passed under Section 5 of the Fourteenth Amendment and guaranteed to all persons the "full and equal" enjoyment of inns, public conveyances, and places of public amusement, regardless of race or color. In declaring these provisions unconstitutional, the Court established state action doctrine, the rule that the Fourteenth Amendment protects individuals against the government, but not against the "merely private" wrongs of individuals.

The *Civil Rights Cases* were argued on March 29, 1883, and decided on October 15, 1883, by a vote of eight-to-one, with Justice Joseph P. Bradley writing for the Court and Justice John Marshall Harlan in dissent. The decision is conventionally viewed as fashioning a narrow Fourteenth Amendment jurisprudence and as definitively abandoning blacks to southern home rule. Over the years, however, the Court's canonical articulation of state action doctrine has been subject to competing interpretations. At stake in this contestation are the limits of Congress's power under Section 5, as well as the historical understanding of the Court's settlement of Reconstruction.

The majority opinion of Justice Bradley rejected both Thirteenth and Fourteenth Amendment grounds for the public accommodation provisions. Regarding the Thirteenth Amendment, he agreed that it conferred freedom and prohibited the incidents of slavery. Public accommodation rights, however, were not among the fundamental rights that defined the "essential distinction between freedom and slavery." The Civil Rights Act of 1866, which protected black rights to property, contract, testifying in court, and physical security, marked out this essential line, and Bradley explicitly approved it. But Congress "did not assume under the authority given by the Thirteenth Amendment to adjust what may be called the social rights of men and races in the community." Thus invoking the conventional nineteenth-century distinction between "civil rights" and "social rights," Bradley declared that it would be "running the slavery argument into the ground" to count exclusions from public accommodations as badges of slavery.

Bradley also rejected the Fourteenth Amendment as a basis for the provisions. The conventional reading is that the provisions were invalid under Section 5 because they regulated private wrongs, and private wrongs are outside the scope of the Fourteenth Amendment. This reading is the basis for the view that state action doctrine left blacks exposed to Ku Klux Klan violence and private discrimination. There is disagreement, however, as to what state action doctrine may have meant to the Waite Court and whether a state's neglect of its duty to equally enforce the law counted as "state action" and was thus grounds for federal intervention. Accordingly, some suggest that the

Court invalidated the public accommodation provisions because prosecution of individual proprietors was not made contingent upon state action, which could take the form of a state's failure to enforce the common law. Others suggest that Bradley outlined a concept of state neglect that left the door open to federal prosecutions of Klansmen when states failed to punish race-based Klan violence, but that Bradley did not clearly extend the state neglect concept to cover public accommodation rights. The issue of state neglect is thus critical for understanding the legal arguments in the *Civil Rights Cases*, but is also crucial for rethinking the application of state action doctrine in the twentieth and twenty-first centuries.

Justice Harlan wrote a forceful dissent. A former slave owner from Kentucky, Harlan argued that the public accommodation provisions were valid under both amendments. Like the more radical Republicans of the Reconstruction era, Harlan insisted that public accommodation rights were among the civil rights that distinguished slavery from freedom. Race discrimination in public accommodations was thus a "badge of slavery" prohibited by the Thirteenth Amendment. Harlan also challenged the idea that exclusions from public accommodations were private action. Adverse state action under the Fourteenth Amendment, he argued, had taken place because railroad corporations and innkeepers "exercise[d] public functions" and were "agents or instrumentalities of the State." Harlan concluded by lacerating Bradley for his comment that the freedmen were "the special favorite of the laws."

In passing the landmark Civil Rights Act of 1964, which prohibited discrimination in public accommodations, Congress avoided the issue of state action and turned to its power under the commerce clause. The Warren Court unanimously approved this basis, and as a result of the expansive reading of the commerce clause, the limits on Congress's Section 5 power receded as a troublesome issue. This situation changed with the Rehnquist Court's federalism decisions, such as *United States v. Morrison*, 529 U.S. 598 (2000). The federalism decisions, which struck down a series of civil rights laws, reined in the commerce power and relied on the conventional and restrictive reading of Section 5, returning the *Civil Rights Cases* and the ambiguous legacies of state action doctrine to legal significance.

SEE ALSO *Amendments, Post-Civil War; Harlan, John Marshall; Reconstruction; State Action*

BIBLIOGRAPHY

Brandwein, Pamela. 2007. "A Judicial Abandonment of Blacks? Rethinking the 'State Action' Cases of the Waite Court." *Law & Society Review* 41(2): 343–386.

Gressman, Eugene. 1952. "The Unhappy History of Civil Rights Legislation." *Michigan Law Review* 50: 1323–1358.

Post, Robert C., and Reva Siegel. 2000. "Equal Protection by Law: Federal Antidiscrimination Legislation after *Morrison* and *Kimel*." *Yale Law Journal* 110: 441–526.

Pamela Brandwein

CIVIL RIGHTS MOVEMENT

SEE *Brown v. Board of Education, Road to; King, Martin Luther, Jr.; NAACP Legal Defense Fund; Warren Court; World War II and the Growth of Civil Rights.*

CIVIL WAR

The American Civil War began in April 1861, but the Court's relationship to the war and secession preceded that date. Three decisions in the 1850s—*Dred Scott v. Sandford*, 60 U.S. 393 (1857), *Ableman v. Booth*, 62 U.S. 506 (1858), and *Kentucky v. Dennison*, 65 U.S. 66 (1861)—helped shape the crisis that led to secession. *Dred Scott*, which is discussed below, set the background for the coming war, and it affected constitutional developments both during and after the war. Once combat began, the Court heard a number of cases that affected the war and the Lincoln administration's powers. After the war, the Court considered a number of statutes passed by Congress during the conflict. The Court's membership also changed significantly during the war. President Lincoln replaced a number of justices who left the Court during this period, and Congress increased the total number of justices to ten.

COURT PERSONNEL

The Court that decided *Dred Scott v. Sandford* was overwhelming Democratic and proslavery, with a slight southern majority. Five of the justices were southern Democrats, led by Chief Justice Roger Taney, who demonstrated in his opinion in *Dred Scott* that he was deeply hostile to the rights of free blacks and overwhelmingly supportive of slavery. Two of the northerners on the Court—Samuel Nelson (1792–1873) of New York and Robert C. Grier (1794–1870) of Pennsylvania—were also supportive of slavery and the South. These seven justices made up the majority in *Dred Scott*. The two dissenters—John McLean (1785–1861) and Benjamin R. Curtis (1809–1874)—opposed the outcome in *Dred Scott*, believing that Congress did have the power to regulate slavery in the Territories. McLean, who was from Ohio, began his career as a Jacksonian Democrat, but by the 1850s he had become a Republican with moderate to strong antislavery leanings. Curtis, a conservative Whig from Massachusetts, was not particularly antislavery. He resigned

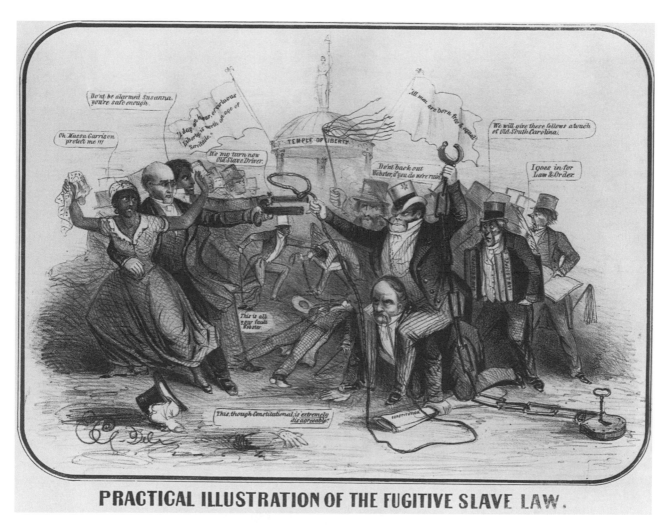

PRACTICAL ILLUSTRATION OF THE FUGITIVE SLAVE LAW.

Political cartoon about the Fugitive Slave Law by Edward Williams Clay, 1851. In addition to numerous other factors, decisions made by a Supreme Court dominated by proslavery justices in the mid-1800s helped exacerbate tensions between the North and South. In particular, the Taney Court's upholding of the Fugitive Slave Law in the 1859 Ableman v. Booth *ruling angered Northerners, upset with federal interference in state matters.* © **CORBIS**

from the Court in September 1857, in part because of Chief Justice Taney's furious responses to Curtis's tough dissent in *Dred Scott.* President Buchanan replaced him in 1858 with Nathan Clifford (1803–1881), a Maine Democrat who, like Nelson and Curtis, could be counted on to support slavery and the South. Thus, on the eve of Lincoln's election, the Court consisted of eight proslavery, prosouthern justices and one northern opponent of slavery.

By the time the war began, the Court's shape had changed. Justice Peter Daniel (1784–1860), a fanatically proslavery states' rights Virginian, died in 1860, but President Buchanan was unable to fill the seat before leaving office. Justice McLean died on April 4, 1861, just before the war began. Then, at the end of April, Justice John A. Campbell of Alabama resigned to take a position in the Confederate government. This left a Court of six justices—three southerners—Taney, John Catron (1786–

1865) of Tennessee, and James Wayne (1790–1867) of Georgia—and three northern Democrats (Nelson, Curtis, and Clifford) with a history of supporting the South and slavery in any controversy. While none of these justices were openly secessionist, Chief Justice Taney was strongly sympathetic to the South and states' rights. Although his home state of Maryland did not secede, Taney was in many ways the Confederacy's most valuable ally in Washington. Justices Wayne and Catron, on the other hand, while proslavery and hostile to many of Lincoln's policies, were also Unionists. The three northerners, while hostile to emancipation and friends of slavery, were, in the end, also opponents of secession to one degree or another.

Although there were three vacancies on the Court when he took office, Lincoln did not fill them immediately. The first seat he filled, McLean's, went to Noah Swayne (1804–1884) in January 1862. Swayne, from Ohio, was a firm opponent of slavery and secession. His son, Wager, was a U.S. Army officer who would be awarded the Congressional Medal of Honor shortly after his father joined the Court. Thus, Lincoln could count on Swayne to support his policies on the war and emancipation.

Filling the other two seats was not such a simple matter, because seats on the Court were tied to geographically determined circuits. Justices Daniel and Campbell had been responsible for circuits that were mostly or entirely in the Confederacy. Before new justices could be appointed, Congress had to reconfigure the circuits. This was accomplished by July 1862. Daniel's circuit, which had included Virginia and North Carolina, was added to Chief Justice Taney's circuit. The states of Campbell's Deep South circuit went to the circuits belonging to Justices Catron and Wayne. These shifts did not increase the workload for any of the justices, because these states were all in the Confederacy and circuit riding in them was impossible.

Lincoln nominated Samuel F. Miller for a new circuit that covered Iowa, Kansas, Missouri, and Minnesota—all located west of the Mississippi. Miller was a relatively obscure lawyer from Iowa whose most important qualification was his residence west of the Mississippi. In December Lincoln nominated his former campaign manager and close friend, David Davis (1815–1886), to the Court for a new circuit that covered Illinois, Wisconsin, and Michigan. In the spring of 1863 Congress created a tenth seat on the Court and Lincoln nominated Stephen J. Field a member of the California Supreme Court. This gave the Far West its first Court member. Of these four, only Swayne was a committed opponent of slavery and a supporter of black rights. But all of these men were firm opponents of secession.

The death of Chief Justice Roger B. Taney in October 1864 removed the Court's most vociferous opponent of the president and the war, for Taney had adamantly opposed most of Lincoln's policies. In his place Lincoln, nominated Salmon Portland Chase, a committed abolitionist who had served as secretary of the treasury for most of Lincoln's first administration. Lincoln did not trust the ambitious Chase, but he was certain Chase would support the two most controversial aspects of his administration: emancipation and the massive use of greenbacks (paper money) during the war. In the end, Lincoln was only half right. Chase always supported emancipation and black rights, but after the war, in *Hepburn v. Griswold*, 75 U.S. 603 (1870)—which was also known as the "First Legal Tender Case"—Chase and Field both voted against the constitutionality of the use of greenbacks, even though Chase had developed this very policy as secretary of the treasury. After the war, in *Knox v. Lee*, 79 U.S. 457, 459 (1871) and *Parker v. Davis*, 79 U.S. 457, 20 L. Ed. (1871), both heard concurrently, two new

Grant appointees to the Court would join Miller, Davis, and Swayne, in reversing *Hepburn* and upholding the currency policy during the war.

THE COURT AND THE COMING OF THE WAR

In the four years before the Civil War, the Court decided three cases that had a dramatic impact on the coming of war. In *Dred Scott v. Sandford* (1857), the Supreme Court reached three conclusions that fundamentally altered the politics of the antebellum period. First, Chief Justice Taney found that free blacks could never be citizens of the United States. While some states might make them citizens, he stated, they could never sue in diversity federal court as citizens of a state. Many northerners were shocked by this portion of the opinion. Second, Taney held that the federal government lacked to the power ban slavery from federal territories or free slaves in any federal jurisdictions. Finally, the case also reaffirmed that slavery was a constitutionally protected form of private property.

Dred Scott energized the Republican Party, which was committed to preventing the spread of slavery into the federal territories. Abraham Lincoln's articulate critique of Taney's decision helped catapult him into national prominence and, ultimately, the presidency. It is arguable that without *Dred Scott* Lincoln would have remained an obscure Illinois politician instead of becoming the Republican presidential nominee. When the Civil War began, *Dred Scott* was, at least in theory, an impediment to the president and Congress banning slavery in the territories, to ending slavery in the District of Columbia, and ultimately to ending slavery in the Confederacy. Throughout the war, however, Congress and Lincoln ignored the case and moved against slavery in all of these areas.

In *Ableman v. Booth*, 62 U.S. 506 (1858), the Supreme Court unanimously upheld the constitutionality of the Fugitive Slave Law of 1850. The case involved attempts by the Wisconsin Supreme Court to strike down the 1850 law and remove the abolitionist Sherman Booth from the custody of U.S. Marshal Stephen Ableman. Speaking for a unanimous Court, Chief Justice Taney rejected the idea that the states could interfere with the enforcement of federal laws. This was an extremely nationalistic decision that denounced the doctrines of states' rights and state interposition. Indeed, at first glance the decision might seem to run counter to the Taney Court's persistent support for the South and southern doctrines of states' rights and state sovereignty. However, in the 1850s, states' rights arguments were increasingly being made by northern politicians and jurists opposed to the return of fugitive slaves. The federal government was dominated by proslavery presidents (such as James Buchanan) and an overwhelmingly proslavery Supreme Court. Taney's opinion denouncing Wisconsin's states' rights claims was the Court's last in a series of proslavery nationalist decisions that included *Prigg v. Pennsylvania*, 41 U.S. 539 (1842) and *Dred Scott.*

By the time the Court decided *Kentucky v. Dennison* 66 U.S. 65 (1861), Lincoln had been elected president, seven states had seceded from the Union, and the nation was in the midst of the greatest crisis in its history. The case involved an attempt by Kentucky to force the extradition of a free black man, Willis Lago, who was wanted for helping a slave escape to Ohio. Two successive Ohio governors—Salmon P. Chase and William Dennison—rejected the extradition requisition, arguing that Ohio did not recognize slavery and therefore could not recognize the crime of stealing a slave.

Speaking for a unanimous Court, Chief Justice Taney chastised the Ohio governors for failing to extradite Lago, but in the end he concluded that the Court could not compel a state governor to comply with an extradition requisition. This appeared to be an antislavery ruling, in that it did not require the extradition of Lago. But Taney's agenda here was to protect the southern states from the federal government. He was, in fact, attempting to handicap the incoming Lincoln administration by effectively asserting that the national government had no power to force state governors to take any actions. This meant that Lincoln would have no power to compel border-state governors to actions in the event of a civil war.

THE COURT AND THE WAR

The first legal issue involving the war never reached the Supreme Court, despite the actions of Chief Justice Taney. In May 1861, President Lincoln suspended habeas corpus in Maryland in order to prevent pro-Confederate militias from being organized, as well as to prevent the sabotage of railroads and bridges and attacks on northern troops heading to the Washington, D.C. At the time, there was no federal law enforcement agency to arrest those involved in treasonous activities, and there were few federal laws to prevent such actions. Many Maryland officials were sympathetic to the Confederacy, so they would not use state and local law enforcement to prevent the destruction of railroads, bridges, or telegraph lines.

Acting under this suspension, the military arrested John Merryman, who was organizing troops to join the Confederacy and commit acts of sabotage. Although held by the military in Fort McHenry, Merryman was allowed access to counsel, who then petitioned Chief Justice Taney for a writ of habeas corpus. Taney, acting in his capacity as circuit justice, issued the writ, demanding that General George Cadwalader bring Merryman before Taney to explain why he was held in custody without any formal charge or indictment. Cadwalader, citing Lincoln's suspension of habeas corpus, refused to do this. In response, Taney issued a long opinion denouncing

Lincoln's suspension of habeas corpus, arguing that only Congress could take such an action. Taney further asserted that even if habeas corpus were suspended by Congress, the military had no authority to arrest a civilian. President Lincoln simply ignored this opinion, and Congress subsequently confirmed the right of the president to suspend habeas corpus. Merryman remained in the brig at Fort McHenry until secessionist activity in Maryland had been suppressed, after which he was quietly released.

At the time of the *Merryman* case, Lincoln had little respect for Taney. Republicans despised the chief justice for his opinion in *Dred Scott* and considered him an ally of the South and secession. With secession a reality and a civil war raging, Lincoln had little time or interest in Taney's assertions that the government had no power to stop those, such as Merryman, who had taken up arms against the United States. Thus, Taney's opinion in *Ex parte Merryman*, 17 F. Cas. 144 (1861), was easily ignored by Lincoln. The full Court never heard Merryman's case, and thus, technically, there was no final judgment. Merryman's lawyers did not ask the chief justice to cite General Cadwalader with contempt, and Taney wisely did not attempt to move against the general or the Lincoln administration on his own.

During the following term the Court upheld the death penalty imposed on a slave trader in *Ex parte Gordon*, 66 U.S. 503 (1862). The case had no direct impact on the war effort, but it did signify that the Court was finally willing to accept the need to end the slave trade. In the *Slavers* (1865), the Court would uphold convictions in four separate cases of Americans who had equipped ships for the trade. By this time slavery was all but dead in the United States, but it was still a viable economic institution in Cuba, Puerto Rico, and Brazil.

The *Prize Cases* In the *Prize Cases*, 67 U.S. 635 (1863), the Court dealt directly with the constitutionality of the war effort. The case involved four ships that had been seized by the U.S. Navy for violating the blockade of southern ports. On April 19, 1861, Lincoln proclaimed a blockade of the first seven states to join the Confederacy. On April 27 he extended the blockade to Virginia and North Carolina when they left the Union. Lincoln gave all foreign captains fifteen days to leave the blockaded ports. On July 13 Congress passed legislation formally acknowledging the hostilities between the United States and the putative Confederate nation, and it retroactively approved the blockade and other measures taken by Lincoln. The four ships in question had been seized after Lincoln proclaimed the blockade, but before Congress had acted to confirm it. Two of the ships were owned by Confederates, one was British, and one was Mexican.

The British ship, the *Hiawatha*, was docked at Richmond when Virginia seceded. The captain attempted to leave the port within fifteen days, as required by Lincoln's proclamation, but he was unable to secure a tow out to sea on time. The U.S. Navy intercepted the *Hiawatha* when it finally left Richmond and reached open waters. The *Brilliante*, a Mexican ship, successfully ran the blockade into New Orleans, but it was captured after attempting to return to Mexico. Virginians owned the *Amy Warwick* and the *Crenshaw,* which were seized while attempting to run the blockade. The first was seized on its way to Richmond with coffee from Brazil, and the second while trying to leave Virginia with tobacco to be sold in Great Britain.

The ship owners argued that Lincoln had no power or authority to issue an order blockading ports, and that if such a power existed, only Congress could exercise it. They also argued that because secession was not an act of war, but a mere rebellion, the Constitution barred Congress from banning commerce into any American ports. In his dissent, Justice Nelson, a northern Democrat, accepted these arguments, asserting that until Congress declared a war, none could legally exist. Nelson denied that the blockade was legal, as defined by international law, because the United States and the Confederate States of America were not at war. Rather, he argued, that until Congress "recognized a state of civil war between" the Confederacy and the United States, this was merely a "personal war" between the insurrectionists in the South and the president of the United States. Nelson claimed Lincoln had no power to issue any orders blockading ports but could only issue orders to suppress those individuals in rebellion. Justice Clifford, also a Democratic "doughface" (a term of derision, defined at the time as "a northern man with southern principles") and two southern Democrats, Justices Catron and Taney, joined Nelson's dissent.

Speaking for a majority that included one southerner (James Wayne), the northern Democrat Justice Grier acknowledged that "a blockade *de facto* existed" when Lincoln, acting in his capacity as commander in chief, issued his proclamation of April 19. Grier asserted that a civil war could exist even if one side did not recognize the sovereignty of the other. Indeed, he noted that a "civil war is never publicly proclaimed," but "its actual existence is a fact in our domestic history which the court is bound to notice and to know." The rest of the majority consisted of Lincoln's recent appointees, Justices Swayne, Miller, and Davis.

This was undoubtedly the most important decision the Court made during the Civil War. By only a one-vote margin, the Court supported Lincoln's view of the war. To do otherwise might have been a catastrophic mistake for the Court. Many in the administration considered Taney to be a closet Confederate, and perhaps even a traitor. It is unlikely that an adverse decision would have affected the prosecution of the war, but it might have led to the impeachment of the justices or perhaps a Court-packing plan. The Court's prestige and power would doubtless have been severely undermined by a decision that rejected the power of Congress to impose a blockade or the power of Lincoln to use force the preserve the Union in the first months of the war.

Grier undoubtedly understood this in voting with the majority to uphold the administration. The theory of the war, which was accepted by the Court in this case, implied that the president had vast powers to issue proclamations and other executive orders in his capacity as commander in chief. The decision came after Lincoln had issued the Emancipation Proclamation, and Grier's opinion was a *de facto* endorsement of Lincoln's power to issue the proclamation as a war measure, and of his suspending habeas corpus when necessary. In addition, the decision put the international community on notice that, for purposes of international law, a blockade of the South was in place and any ships caught would be seized. The narrow victory caused some worry for the administration, but in fact this was the only close war-related decision. Within a year all the dissenting justices but Nelson were voting to support Lincoln's policies. The addition of Justice Field as the tenth member of the Court in May 1863 further strengthened the position of the administration. By late 1864 Taney would be dead, and Lincoln would replace him with the abolitionist Salmon P. Chase.

Decided in December 1863, *Roosevelt v. Meyer*, 68 U.S. 512, upheld the constitutionality of the administration's use of greenbacks as currency during the war. James J. Roosevelt had refused to accept a repayment of an $8,170 debt by Lewis B. Meyer, who was using U.S. Banknotes. Under an 1862 Act of Congress, these were legal tender in payment of "all debts, public and private." Roosevelt claimed that the notes were not worth their face value, however, and that the federal law forcing him to accept this form of money deprived him of property and his due process rights. A state trial court agreed with Roosevelt's claims about the value of the notes and awarded Roosevelt $326 difference plus interest. This politically charged, and politically motivated, decision threatened the ability of the United States government to finance the Civil War, and it was seen as a victory for opponents of the Lincoln administration, the war effort, and emancipation. The New York Court of Appeals, however, declared the notes were legal tender and reversed the lower court decision. Roosevelt appealed that decision to the U.S. Supreme Court, asserting that the Judiciary Act of 1789 gave the Court judicial power over "all cases in law and equity arising under this Constitution." Justice Wayne dealt with the case in a one-sentence opinion, dismissing the case for lack of jurisdiction.

The Court's conclusion in *Roosevelt v. Meyer* may not have been correct, because the case involved an interpretation of a federal statute by a state court. However, the curt dismissal allowed the justices to quickly eliminate a difficult issue and avoid facing the constitutionality of the Legal Tender Act until after the Civil War. The fact that the Court decided the case the same day it was argued suggests the justices' eagerness to dispose of the issue as quickly as possible. Justice Samuel Nelson, an implacable foe of Lincoln, was the sole dissenter in the case.

THE VALLANDIGHAM CASE

When paired with the *Prize Cases* the previous March, the *Roosevelt* case confirmed that the Court would not interfere with the major policies of Lincoln and Congress in winning the war. This was confirmed in *Ex parte Vallandigham*, 68 U.S. 243 (1864). Jurisprudentially, this is the most problematic Civil War case, but, ironically, it is also the only one that was decided by a unanimous Court.

Clement Vallandigham was a racist, proslavery Ohio politician before the Civil War, and he proved to be a relentless opponent of Lincoln, emancipation, the use of black troops, conscription, and all other war policies. A Confederate sympathizer, he would gladly have let the South secede. He accused President Lincoln of trying to set up a monarchy and destroy the liberty of the American people. Most importantly, he persistently denounced the draft, denying its legality and morality. Despite his vituperative rhetoric, especially against the draft, Vallandigham never explicitly urged anyone to break the law. He attacked the war effort and tried to persuade all who would listen to resist the administration, but he did not implicate himself by directly urging illegal activity.

Military authorities in Ohio saw through his charade, and in 1863 they arrested and tried Vallandigham for publicly declaring that the Civil War "was a wicked, cruel, and unnecessary war, one not waged for the preservation of the Union, but for the purpose of crushing out liberty and to erect a despotism; a war for the freedom of the blacks and the enslavements of the whites, and that if the administration had not wished otherwise, that the war could have been honorably terminated long ago." At his trial, Vallandigham refused to enter a plea, and the three lawyers he chose to represent him were unwilling to even enter the courtroom on his behalf. After calling only one witness, Vallandigham ended his defense by reading a long statement challenging the right of the military tribunal to try him.

Not surprising, the military court found him guilty and sentenced him to a military prison, but in a brilliant move, Lincoln commuted his sentence to exile in the Confederacy. Vallandigham's goals were clear: to stop conscription, stop the war effort, and prevent emancipation. While carefully avoiding a technical violation of the law, he was urging others to do so. Lincoln understood his motives and asked, "Must I shoot a simple-minded soldier boy who deserts, while I must not touch a hair of a wily agitator who induces him to desert?" Lincoln approved of the prosecution and exile of the agitator, not only to save the Union, but to save the "simple-minded soldier boy."

Before Lincoln commuted his sentence, Vallandigham petitioned the Supreme Court for a writ of certiorari. The Court granted the writ, but after hearing the case concluded that it had no jurisdiction to review the proceedings of a military tribunal. Justice Wayne noted that the military tribunal was not technically a court, and thus there was not a court where a writ of certiorari could be directed. Nor did the court have original jurisdiction to issue a writ of habeas corpus. By this time (February 1864) the Court was not inclined to challenge presidential authority on the matter of suppressing what almost all Americans believed was traitorous pro-Confederate agitation. The procedural posture of the suit—whether the writ of certiorari was the proper method of bringing the case to the Court—also worked against Vallandigham.

No other cases involving the war reached the Court until after the Confederacy had been destroyed. The Court began the war as a wounded institution, populated entirely by proslavery Democrats and led by the secessionist sympathizer, Roger B. Taney, who was still hated for his opinion in *Dred Scott v. Sandford*. But the nature of the war led to some surprising votes. Justice Wayne, a slave owner from Georgia, proved to be a consistent Unionist. He had been a staunch supporter of Andrew Jackson when that president stood up to the South Carolina nullifiers in 1832–1833, and that Unionism reemerged during war. Similarly, Justice Robert Grier had been a classic doughface before the war, but during the war he stood for the Union and preserving the Constitution, even though he probably was personally opposed to conscription and emancipation. Chief Justice Taney attempted to derail the war effort in *Ex parte Merryman*, but after he failed there and in the *Prize Cases*, even Taney ceased trying to prevent the preservation of the Union. Taney's private papers indicate he hoped to have a chance to strike out at Emancipation, but that opportunity never arose.

POSTWAR JURISPRUDENCE

After the war, the Court rejected the use of military courts to try civilians in *Ex parte Milligan*, 71 U.S. 2 (1866). A military court had sentenced Lambdin Milligan to death for attempting to organize pro-Confederate military activity in Indiana. Historians disagree about the extent of his complicity in the conspiracy, although the evidence is clear that some of his associates were involved in trying to organize a pro-Confederate uprising in Indiana. Harrison Horton Dodd, who had received at least $10,000 from Confederate agents and had organized of the Sons of Liberty, made Milligan a "major general" in the secret society. Milligan swore, however, that he knew nothing about the organization. Nonetheless, Milligan and three others were convicted by a military commission and sentenced to death.

Doubts about Milligan's guilt, in addition to the obvious unfairness of the military trial, led President Lincoln to promise the Republican governor of Indiana, Oliver P. Morton, that he would pardon Milligan when the war ended. Lincoln's assassination prevented that from happening, however. President Andrew Johnson commuted the prisoners' death sentences, but left them in jail. Meanwhile, Milligan petitioned the U.S. Circuit Court for a writ of habeas corpus under the Judiciary Act of 1789. When that court denied him relief, he appealed to the Supreme Court. This procedural attack on the military conviction had been suggested by the Court itself in *Ex parte Vallandigham*, when it rejected Vallandigham's petition for a writ of certiorari. The Court heard arguments on Milligan's petition in March 1866. He had an impressive legal team: Jeremiah S. Black, a former attorney general; David Dudley Field, an eminent lawyer (and a brother of Justice Field); and James A. Garfield, a war hero, Republican member of Congress, and future president.

All nine justices agreed that the military court had no jurisdiction to try Milligan because Indiana was not a war zone and the civilian courts were open and operating. Justice Davis was emphatic that "where the courts are all open, and in proper exercise of their jurisdiction," a civilian "cannot, even when the privilege of habeas corpus is suspended, be tried, convicted, or sentenced otherwise than by the ordinary courts of law." Davis then asserted, in language that has since often been quoted:

> The Constitution of the United States is a law for rulers and people, equally in war and in peace, and covers with the shield of its protection all classes of men, at all times, and under all circumstances. No doctrine involving more pernicious consequences was ever invented by the wit of man than that any of its provisions can be suspended during any of the great exigencies of government. Such a doctrine leads directly to anarchy or despotism, but the theory of necessity on which it is based is false, for the government, within the Constitution, has all the powers granted to it which are necessary to preserve its existence; as has been happily proved by the result of the great effort to throw off its just authority.

Chief Justice Salmon P. Chase believed that Congress had the power to impose military tribunals on civilians under its war powers, but because this had not been done, he agreed that Milligan's conviction was unconstitutional. After eighteen months in jail, Milligan was released.

Justice Davis's opinion in Milligan set a new tone for the Court in the wake of the war. More than 620,000 Americans, on both sides, had died in the Civil War, and vast amounts of wealth had been destroyed. The war had also destroyed slavery, along with the southern doctrines of state sovereignty and secession. During the war the Court had accepted practices that could not be applied to peacetime. Milligan's case underscored the dangers to civil liberty created by the war, even if these measures were necessary to preserve the Constitution and bring liberty to all Americans. But with the war over, the Court could not condone them. Davis concluded, "Civil liberty and this kind of martial law cannot endure together; the antagonism is irreconcilable; and, in the conflict, one or the other must perish." Davis asserted that in the aftermath of the war, rules needed to be created that would be seen as universal, not tied to any particular set of circumstances, and not suspended merely because someone like Milligan was in sympathy with, or even an active supporter of, what Justice Davis properly called "the late wicked Rebellion." He reminded Americans that:

> This nation, as experience has proved, cannot always remain at peace, and has no right to expect that it will always have wise and humane rulers sincerely attached to the principles of the Constitution. Wicked men, ambitious of power, with hatred of liberty and contempt of law, may fill the place once occupied by Washington and Lincoln, and if this right is conceded, and the calamities of war again befall us, the dangers to human liberty are frightful to contemplate.

Thus, it was important for the Court to assert its role to protect liberty from an overreaching government. Unfortunately, in the period following the war the Court would do this in a one-sided way, protecting former Confederates while turning its back on the former slaves and southern Unionists, who soon found themselves under siege from white terrorist organizations such as the Ku Klux Klan and from state governments dominated by Confederates and their sons, who were intent on reducing the former slaves to a permanent status of second class citizens.

SEE ALSO *Chase Court; Dred Scott v. Sandford, 60 U.S. 393 (1857); Ex parte Milligan, 71 U.S. 2 (1866); Habeas Corpus; Lincoln, Abraham; Prize Cases; Slavery; Slavery in the Territories; Taney Court*

BIBLIOGRAPHY

Curtis, Michael Kent. 2001. *Free Speech, "The People's Darling Privilege": Struggles for Freedom of Expression in American History.* Durham, NC: Duke University Press.

Finkelman, Paul. 1981. *An Imperfect Union: Slavery, Federalism, and Comity.* Chapel Hill: University of North Carolina Press.

Finkelman, Paul. 2003. "Limiting Rights in Times of Crisis: Our Civil War Experience, A History Lesson for a Post-9-11 America." *Cardozo Public Law, Policy, and Ethics Journal* 2: 25–48.

Hyman Harold M., and William M. Wiecek. 1982. *Equal Justice under Law: Constitutional Development, 1835–1875*. New York: Harper & Row.

Kutler, Stanley I. 1968. *Judicial Power and Reconstruction Politics*. Chicago: University of Chicago Press.

McPherson, James M. 1991. *Abraham Lincoln and the Second American Revolution*. New York: Oxford University Press.

Neely, Mark E., Jr. 1991. *The Fate of Liberty: Abraham Lincoln and Civil Liberties*. New York: Oxford University Press.

Randall, James G. 1951. *Constitutional Problems under Lincoln*. Rev. edition. Urbana: University of Illinois Press.

Urofsky Melvin, and Paul Finkelman. 2002. *A March of Liberty: A Constitutional History of the United States*. 2nd edition. New York: Oxford University Press.

Wagner, Margaret; Paul Finkelman; and Gary W. Gallagher. 2002. *The Library of Congress Civil War Desk Reference*. New York: Simon & Schuster.

Weber, Jennifer L. 2006. *Copperheads: The Rise and Fall of Lincoln's Opponents in the North*. New York: Oxford University Press.

Paul Finkelman

CLARK, KENNETH
1914–2005

Kenneth Bancroft Clark was arguably the most influential and well-known African-American psychologist of the twentieth century due to his involvement in the 1954 *Brown v. Board of Education,* 347 U.S. 483 decision. Born in Panama to Jamaican migrant workers, he immigrated to the United States with his mother and sister when he was five and grew up in Harlem during the 1920s. He graduated from Howard University with B.A. and M.A. degrees in psychology in 1935 and 1936. His professors included political scientist Ralph Bunche (1904–1971) and Francis Sumner (1895–1954), the first African American to earn a Ph.D. in psychology. Clark met his future wife, Mamie Phipps Clark (1917–1983), as a graduate student at Howard. In 1940 Clark became the first African American to receive a Ph.D. in psychology from Columbia University; his wife became the second two years later (they had married in 1938). During graduate school, he worked on sociologist Gunnar Myrdal's (1898–1987) famous study *An American Dilemma* (1944). After teaching at Hampton University, Clark became in 1942 the first African-American psychology professor at City College in New York, where he remained until his retirement in 1975.

During the 1940s and early 1950s, the Clarks conducted tests designed to reveal racial identification and racial preference in young children. One of these experiments came to be known famously as the *doll test*. By giving each child such instructions as "Give me the white doll," "Give me the colored doll," "Give me the doll you like to play with," "Give me the doll that is the nice doll," and "Give me the doll that looks bad," the Clarks elicited responses that were intended to demonstrate how black children became aware of the negative stigma associated with dark skin color as early as three years of age. Based on their results and other evidence, they concluded that racial segregation was psychologically damaging to black children.

In 1950 Kenneth Clark was invited to participate in the White House Conference on Children and Youth, for which he authored a paper that summarized the existing literature on the effects of prejudice on children. Clark's paper also used social science to forcefully argue that prejudice harmed both individuals and the broader society and that racial segregation harmed both black and white children. Two months later, in February 1951, attorney Robert Carter of the National Association for the Advancement of Colored People (NAACP) Legal Defense and Educational Fund contacted Clark to ask for his help in the *Briggs v. Elliott,* 342 U.S. 350 (1952) school desegregation case in South Carolina, one of the five that later constituted *Brown*. Clark revised and shortened his White House paper into a social science appendix as a part of the NAACP's argument in *Brown*. The U.S. Supreme Court cited this appendix in ruling that state-sanctioned racial discrimination violated the federal Constitution. Clark later expanded his White House paper into his first book, *Prejudice and Your Child* (1955).

Despite the effort by Clark and other social scientific testimony to point out the dual harm of segregation, the Court chose to emphasize only the negative effects of segregation on black children. As a result, school desegregation came to be seen as a type of social welfare program that benefited only African Americans and burdened whites. During the next two decades, the federal courts interpreted *Brown* to mean that black children should be integrated into formerly all-white schools. Segregated all-black schools, no matter how well they might be doing in terms of educating their students, were to be closed in the desegregation era. Only in extremely rare circumstances in both southern and northern communities did judges order the assignment of white students into all-black schools.

Even before *Brown* was decided, however, some African-American and white scholars, teachers, and mental health professionals took issue with Clark's conclusions. Indeed, since the 1960s, many have contended that this research was flawed, particularly the methodology used in the doll tests. Critics argued that the tests were too limited in their capacity to lead to the conclusion that African-American children, in particular, were psychologically damaged. They also maintained that Clark posed African Americans as damaged for political purposes in order to gain white support for racial integration. As the courts achieved limited success in desegregating schools and as the academic achievement gap between black and white students continued to exist into the 1970s and 1980s, criticism of Clark's efforts only grew. His research inspired a generation of social scientists to refute the "damaged black psyche" image he was accused of popularizing.

Despite these problems with *Brown*, Clark was ecstatic at the outcome. He defended his role well into the 1980s and argued that *Brown* had been a major step in the spread of interracial democracy in America. In his view, the problem with *Brown* was not its reasoning or the Court's emphasis, but the implementation of the decision. Federal judges allowed local school boards and superintendents to evade the essence of the decision through zoning changes, assignment of students and teachers, and at times outright refusal to enforce the Supreme Court ruling. Nonetheless, Clark was at times chagrined, worried, and even depressed at the lack of progress in desegregating American education. Although toward the end of his life he felt that he had been naive to expect so much from one decision, he continued to believe that *Brown* had been reasoned and decided correctly.

SEE ALSO *Brown v. Board of Education, 347 U.S. 483 (1954); Brown v. Board of Education (Brown II), 349 U.S. 294 (1955); School Desegregation*

BIBLIOGRAPHY

Clark, Kenneth B. 1955. *Prejudice and Your Child*. Boston: Beacon.

Freeman, Damon. 2004. "Not So Simple Justice: Kenneth B. Clark, Civil Rights, and the Dilemma of Power, 1940–1980." Ph.D. diss., Bloomington: Indiana University.

Jackson, John P., Jr. 2001. *Social Scientists for Social Justice: Making the Case against Segregation*. New York: New York University Press.

Damon Freeman

CLEAR AND PRESENT DANGER TEST

SEE *First Amendment; Freedom of Speech; Free Speech and World War I; Free Speech Between the World Wars; Holmes, Oliver W.*

CLERKS

Law clerks are the short-term support personnel who work for judges and courts. They assist in legal research, writing, and decision-making. Clerks are generally young,

fresh out of law school, and academically meritorious legal assistants. Though their roles can vary, there is remarkable similarity in the duties performed by clerks employed at the local, state, and national levels. At the U.S. Supreme Court, the role of clerks has generated a fair amount of controversy, from who gets selected to the influence they have on the Court's internal workings. Because of this controversy and because most of the research on clerking has focused on the nation's highest tribunal, Supreme Court clerks will be the primary focus of this entry. Still, much of what is true of high court clerks also applies to clerks on the lower federal courts as well as state and local courts.

HISTORICAL DEVELOPMENT

Prior to the establishment of the American Bar Association in 1878 and the resulting formalization of legal education, the path to a career in law often began with study and practice with a legal professional. As a result, the position of law clerk was held by aspiring lawyers who learned the law by apprenticing with an attorney or judge. As formal legal education became more common, clerkships were transformed into advanced learning forums to be held after obtaining a law degree. When he began his tenure on the U.S. Supreme Court in 1882, Justice Horace Gray (1828–1902) started the practice of employing law clerks by hiring Harvard Law School graduate Thomas Russell. Gray had first hired clerks in his previous position as chief judge of the Massachusetts Supreme Judicial Court from 1873 to 1882. Gray's half-brother, Harvard Law School professor John Chipman Gray (1839–1915), selected the law students—a practice continued by future Harvard law professors, such as Felix Frankfurter (who later became a Supreme Court justice), in concert with subsequent justices. Soon other law schools and justices emulated the Gray model.

Though Gray's clerks served for only one or two years, some justices employed long-term clerks. For example, Frederick J. Haig clerked for Justice David J. Brewer for seventeen years from 1893 to 1909. But long-serving clerks were relatively rare, and the practice of serving a single-term clerkship before departing for a position in academia, government, or private practice soon became the norm. Though clerkships were born out of the apprentice model of legal education, the expansion in the number of clerks at all levels of the American judicial system has largely been due to workload pressures: as courts have handled a greater number of cases, the numbers of both judges and clerks has expanded. Yet their responsibilities have not always developed purely as a result of workload pressures. Instead, seemingly non-related institutional changes in the ways that courts conduct their business have given rise to an increase in the responsibility and influence of clerks.

SELECTION

As a general rule, the most desirable and prestigious clerkships have been held by the top graduates of top law schools, such as Harvard, Yale, Chicago, Columbia, Stanford, Virginia, and Michigan. Historically, clerkships have been the province of white males from upper socioeconomic classes. Yet women and minorities have made inroads into this institution, just as they have increasingly populated law schools and the legal profession as a whole. Lucille Lomen was the first female law clerk to serve at the Supreme Court, working for Justice William O. Douglas in 1944. Yet it was not until two decades later that another female clerk was selected, when Margaret J. Corcoran was chosen by Justice Hugo Black in 1966. The key event that triggered the regular selection of at least one female law clerk per term was Justice Ruth Bader Ginsburg's impassioned oral arguments as an attorney in the sex discrimination cases of the early 1970s. By the start of the twenty-first century, women routinely comprised 40 percent of the high court's clerking corps. African Americans and other minorities have also had some success at obtaining clerkships, beginning with William Coleman's selection by Justice Felix Frankfurter in 1948. Still, fifty years later, there had been fewer than two dozen African-American Supreme Court law clerks. The same period saw about the same number of gay and lesbian Supreme Court clerks.

Supreme Court law clerks spend one year clerking at the U.S. Court of Appeals for one of the top "feeder" judges who routinely place their clerks at the high court. For example, court of appeals judges J. Michael Luttig (1954–), Laurence Silberman (1935–), and James Skelly Wright placed over thirty of their clerks with Supreme Court justices. Clerks have become increasingly partisan over time, and ideology has become a key factor in clerk selection. Application cues, such as membership in liberal or conservative organizations and clerkships with feeder judges, are the ideological signals used by Supreme Court justices when considering potential clerks.

AGENDA SETTING

Initially, Supreme Court law clerks only studied and briefed the petitions that came to the Court—*certiorari* petitions, or *cert* petitions for short—as a way of learning the law. The exercise rarely helped the justices, who met in regular private conferences to discuss each petition. Yet as the number of petitions grew, in the mid 1930s Chief Justice Charles Evans Hughes decided to end the practice of the justices formally discussing each petition. Instead, it would be up to the individual justices to decide which cases should be formally considered. Justices turned to their clerks for help in analyzing petitions, and asked for their recommendations on which cases ought to be heard by the Court. In the early 1970s, several justices decided to pool their clerks to reduce what they felt was a duplication of effort. Prior to the creation of the "cert pool," each of the nine justices had one of their clerks write a memo on each case. Eventually, every justice joined the pool except Justice John Paul Stevens. The eight justices using the cert pool shared the memo written by one of the participating clerks, thereby reducing duplicated effort and freeing clerks for other work—namely, opinion writing.

The cert pool has generated controversy, with critics suggesting that it has led to greater clerk influence. When former Supreme Court clerks were asked to name the area in which they felt they had been most likely to influence the justice for whom they worked, more than one-third pointed to the decision whether or not to grant or not grant a case for review (Ward and Weiden 2006, p. 191). Over time, clerks have been more likely to agree with the justices on whether particular cases should or should not be granted. This change is probably due to the fact that clerks now personally review fewer petitions than their predecessors did—particularly before the cert pool was created and expanded. The justices themselves have expressed concern over the effect of the pool, and even those who chose to participate were pleased that Justice Stevens provided a check on the single pool memo. The eventual departure of Stevens from the Court will likely prompt the justices to revisit the way they consider the nearly ten thousand petitions they receive each year.

DECISION MAKING

Clerks make recommendations, and may even attempt to change a justice's mind in a number of ways. When asked how frequently they were able to change a justice's mind about particular cases or issues, 25 percent of former Supreme Court clerks answered that they were "sometimes" able to do so, with more recent clerks responding that they were able to do so more often than earlier clerks (Ward and Weiden 2006, pp. 187–189). When asked about the situation in which they were most likely to change a justice's mind, 34 percent said that such a change was most likely to occur in the decision to grant a case for review. It was in the legal or substantive content of an opinion, 29 percent said, while 20 percent said that it was in an opinion's stylistic content. Only 3 percent said they could change the justice's mind concerning the outcome of a case, that is, who wins and who loses (Ward and Weiden 2006, p. 191). Therefore, while clerks may have relatively minimal influence on decisions on the merits, they have far more influence on the other decisions that justices routinely make.

An almost completely hidden yet crucial part of the clerks' job is the ambassadorial role played out through the clerk network: the informal process of information

CLERKS AS GATEKEEPERS: DECIDING TO DECIDE

John Knox (1907–1997) clerked for Justice James McReynolds during the 1936–1937 Supreme Court term. He kept a daily diary detailing his duties and describing the Washington political and social scene. He worked in McReynolds's home as most clerks did before the justices and their staffs moved to the new Supreme Court building. In this excerpt, Knox recounts McReynolds's instructions on analyzing the cases the Court is asked to decide.

"There will be hundreds of petitions for certiorari coming in during the summer, and I want you to read each one. Then summarize each petition in one page of typing, single spaced. Give me the facts of each case, the question of law presented, the holding of the lower courts, and your own personal recommendation whether you think the petition should or should not be allowed." ... I walked to the entrance of this room, looked in, and caught my breath. The floor of the entire room was literally filled to a depth of more than a foot with hundreds of statements of fact, briefs, answers, etc.—all comprising what seemed to be countless petitions for certiorari. There were at the

time approximately five hundred petitions piled on the floor of that room. ... I had five weeks and two days in which to do this work. ... And so the days passed one by one. In a week I had a large and rather impressive pile of typed sheets ready for McReynolds to look over... After a few more days I laid them all on his desk and then waited for the heavens to fall. To my great surprise, however, he finally emerged from his office holding a few sheets of paper in his hand, saying, "These are quite satisfactory, Mr. Knox." ... This was the first and last comment he ever made regarding the hundreds of pages that I was ultimately to type prior to the opening of Court in October. I gradually became almost like an automaton ... like a salmon trying to swim upstream, I struggled on and on, briefing petitions even in my dreams.

SOURCE: Dennis J. Hutchinson and David J. Garrow, *The Forgotten Memoir of John Knox: A Year in the Life of a Supreme Court Clerk in FDR's Washington.* Chicago: University of Chicago Press, 2002, pp. 10–11, 14, 23.

Artemus Ward

gathering, lobbying, and negotiation that goes on among clerks working for different justices. Prior to the opening of the Supreme Court building in 1935, clerks worked at the justices' homes and rarely saw the other clerks. By the time the justices and their staffs moved into their own suite of offices at the new building in 1941, the clerks knew each other, routinely lunched together, and began discussing the cases they were working on. The justices quickly recognized that the clerk network could be tapped to gain information on what was happening in other chambers, which in turn helped them make decisions and form coalitions.

The justices became so reliant on the clerk network that they eventually established a separate, enclosed space in the Court cafeteria specifically for the clerks, so they could speak with each other undisturbed and without fear of eavesdropping tourists, attorneys, and members of the press. A 1992 memo from clerk Andrea Ward to her supervisor Justice Harry Blackmun, for example, demonstrates how important the clerk network is to the decision making process:

Last week ... the Chief circulated a memo to Justice White.... This is sure to stir up trouble.... Justice O'Connor has sent Justice White a memo asking for several changes [to the opinion] ... According to [O'Connor's clerk] ... Justice O'Connor is still inclined to wait and has no plans to join [the opinion] anytime soon ... I understand from Justice White's clerk that Justice White has no intention of removing the references ... in his [opinion] draft.... I will keep you posted. (Ward and Weiden 2006, p. 166)

OPINION WRITING

Perhaps the most controversial part of a clerk's job is drafting the opinions that are issued in the name of the justice for whom he or she works. As with the agenda-setting process, early Supreme Court clerks occasionally drafted opinions as an exercise in learning the law. Justices rarely used these clerk-written drafts, although early clerks did prepare footnotes to opinions written by the justices. Today, it is rare for justices to draft their own opinions and routine for clerks to do all of the writing. The cause of this dramatic change was the decision by Chief Justice Fred Vinson, later continued by Chief Justice Earl Warren and all subsequent chief justices, to distribute opinion writing evenly among the nine justices. Prior to Vinson's 1950 shift to opinion equalization, opinions were assigned according to the speed at which they were completed. Therefore, speedy writers, such as Justices Douglas and Black, wrote far more opinions than did their more deliberate colleagues, such as Justices Frankfurter and Murphy. When Vinson, and later Warren, practiced the equality principle in assigning opinions, the slower writers were forced to rely on their clerks to keep pace. Over time, a norm of clerk-written opinions developed, which continues to this day.

Though practices vary from one justice to another, some justices routinely issue opinions wholly written by their clerks. When former clerks were asked how often justice revised or modified their draft opinions, 70 percent said that the justice did so in all cases. However, 30 percent of clerks responded that their drafts were issued without modification at least some of the time (Ward and Weiden 2006, p. 225). To be sure, clerks cannot write whatever they please, and justices provide direction and carefully read drafts written by their clerks. Still, judicial opinions differ from speeches or op-ed pieces, which are regularly ghostwritten for public officials. In the law, word choice and phrasing are often crucial, and a seemingly insignificant phrase—such as, for example, "exceedingly persuasive justification"—can be inserted into an opinion by a clerk, only to become, years later, a crucial test in sex discrimination law. Furthermore, the more that it is understood that clerks are drafting Supreme Court opinions, the greater the possibility that the opinions will lack authority with litigators, lower court judges, and government officials responsible for implementing the decisions.

CONCLUSION

The American law-clerk institution has undergone dramatic transformation over time. What began as an apprenticeship in learning the law has become a crucial part of the judicial process. Clerkships are highly competitive, coveted positions that lead to prestigious careers in academia, government, and private law. As the responsibility and influence of clerks has grown, a concomitant risk of unelected, unaccountable clerks overstepping their bounds has arisen. For the first one hundred years of Supreme Court history, the justices themselves conducted the Court's business. During the following century, the justices added three dozen clerkships and ceded much of the Court's work to their clerks. Because of this radical development, it has become increasingly important, not only for the justices and

clerks but also for Congress and the American people, to be wary of apprentices who might be tempted to put on the robes of the master.

SEE ALSO *Briefs; In Forma Pauperis*

BIBLIOGRAPHY

Best, Bradley J. 2002. *Law Clerks, Support Personnel, and the Decline of Consensual Norms on the United States Supreme Court, 1935–1995.* New York: LFB.

Hutchinson, Dennis J., and David J. Garrow, eds. 2002. *The Forgotten Memoir of John Knox: A Year in the Life of a Supreme Court Clerk in FDR's Washington.* Chicago: University of Chicago Press.

Lazarus, Edward. 1998. *Closed Chambers: The First Eyewitness Account of the Epic Struggles Inside the Supreme Court.* New York: Times Books.

Peppers, Todd. 2006. *Courtiers of the Marble Palace: The Rise and Influence of the Supreme Court Law Clerk.* Stanford, CA: Stanford University Press.

Ward, Artemus, and David L. Weiden. 2006. *Sorcerers' Apprentices: 100 Years of Law Clerks at the United States Supreme Court.* New York: New York University Press.

Woodward, Bob, and Scott Armstrong. 1979. *The Brethren: Inside the Supreme Court.* New York: Simon and Schuster.

Artemus Ward

CLEVELAND BOARD OF EDUCATION V. LAFLEUR, 414 U.S. 632 (1974)

Cleveland Board of Education v. LaFleur, 414 U.S. 632 (1974) challenged the mandatory unpaid maternity leave policies of two school districts. One district required pregnant teachers to take unpaid leave five months before the expected birth of the child, and to return to work no sooner than the first semester after the child turns three months old, if a position is available. The other district required pregnant teachers to leave work four months before the birth, and guaranteed return to work by the school year that starts after a physician says she is ready to return. Pregnant teachers challenged the constitutionality of these government policies on two grounds: as sex discrimination under the equal protection clause, and as a violation of the right to due process before burdening women's liberty interest in procreation decisions. The Supreme Court agreed that the policies were unconstitutional, making this the first Supreme Court case giving pregnant women a right to work.

Although one lower court declared these policies to be sex discrimination under the equal protection clause, the Supreme Court did not endorse that argument, although a concurring opinion by Justice Lewis F. Powell, Jr. did. Instead, the majority said that the policies penalize a pregnant teacher for deciding to bear a child, and thus place a burden on her constitutionally protected freedom of personal choice in matters of family life. The Supreme Court tied mandatory unpaid leave policies to the line of well-known reproductive freedom cases that include *Roe v. Wade*, 410 U.S. 113 (1973) and *Griswold v. Connecticut*, 381 U.S. 479 (1965). Because the case burdened reproductive freedom, the government needed to show that the burden was not imposed needlessly, arbitrarily, or capriciously.

The governments argued that the policies were justified on two grounds. First, they argued that continuity of instruction is a legitimate educational goal. The Court agreed, but said that when a pregnant teacher provides advance notice of the date when she will stop working, continuity is maintained without an arbitrary cut-off. Arbitrary cut-off dates will sometimes frustrate continuity, depending on when the teacher's baby is due, and they needlessly burden plaintiffs' liberty.

The government also argued that the policies keep physically unfit teachers out of the classroom. The lower courts heard medical testimony on the physical and psychological effects of pregnancy. In its brief to the Supreme Court, the government marshaled these arguments, proposing that a pregnant schoolteacher is distracted by "the three classic fears of pregnancy—miscarriage, agony in labor, and a deformed child." The government brief gave attention to evidence that an "inner-city school" is "an environment conducive to physical accident or violence," underscoring the importance of having an "able-bodied" teacher. The plaintiffs' brief cited contrary medical evidence, noting that all the medical evidence agreed that the effects of pregnancy are individual and should be treated as such, and no medical consensus requires pregnant women to stop working prior to childbirth. The Court conceded that in some cases pregnant teachers become physically unfit to teach, but an individualized determination was the appropriate response to the variation in fitness among pregnant teachers.

In his dissent, Justice William Rehnquist argued against requiring individual determinations rather than using categorical rules when a liberty interest is involved. He argued that countless laws draw lines. For example, states use a categorical minimum marriage age, though the U.S. Constitution protects a liberty interest in marriage. He argued that the majority's opinion is "an attack upon the very notion of lawmaking itself," noting that the historical shift from individual determinations on controversies to categorical lawmaking is generally viewed as a step toward a civilized political society.

The case is significant for three reasons. First, it addresses the rights of pregnant workers, rights that have since been more substantially elaborated under the Pregnancy Discrimination Act of 1978, the Family and Medical Leave Act of 1993, and countless state laws. The plaintiffs' brief situated the case in the developing international and domestic labor practices protecting employment for pregnant women. Regulations of pregnancy and motherhood pose a complex dilemma for equal rights advocates, who wish to protect both women's right to work on an equal basis with men, and to manage pregnancy's biological difference. The Supreme Court addressed the issue of motherhood-related work rules in 1908 in the landmark *Muller v. Oregon*, 208 U.S. 412. It upheld legislation mandating shorter workdays for women based on their reproductive and nurturing roles. That ruling is criticized by some feminists as preventing women from participating fully in the labor force, but praised by other feminists for allowing women to work fewer hours to balance their dual roles. This echoes contemporary debates about women, work, and equality.

Second, *LaFleur* is an early ruling on whether to view issues relating to women's reproductive capacity as equality questions or privacy and due process questions. The separation of the Supreme Court's gender equality cases from its reproductive privacy cases continues to be controversial decades after these early rulings.

Finally, the case illustrates the constitutional debate over irrebuttable presumptions in the 1970s. Justice Potter Stewart disapproved of categorical lawmaking without individualized determinations, a view that would prove controversial even with those sympathetic to the outcome in this case.

SEE ALSO *Pregnancy; Sex Discrimination*

BIBLIOGRAPHY

Erickson, Nancy. 1974. "Women and the Supreme Court: Anatomy Is Destiny." *Brooklyn Law Review* 41: 209–282.

Frug, Mary Joe. 1979. "Securing Job Equality for Women: Labor Market Hostility to Working Mothers." *Boston University Law Review* 59: 55–103.

Siegel, Reva. 1992. "Reasoning from the Body: A Historical Perspective on Abortion Regulation and Questions of Equal Protection." *Stanford Law Review* 44: 261–381.

Sullivan, Kathleen M. 1989. "Unconstitutional Conditions." *Harvard Law Review* 102: 1413–1506.

Sunstein, Cass R. 1990. "Why the Unconstitutional Conditions Doctrine is an Anachronism (with Particular Reference to Religion, Speech, and Abortion)." *Boston University Law Review* 70: 593–621.

Katharine B. Silbaugh

CLEVELAND BRD. OF EDUCATION V. LOUDERMILL, 470 U.S. 532 (1985)

In *Cleveland Brd. of Education v. Loudermill*, 470 U.S. 532 (1985), the Court held that the due process clause entitled government employees who could only be dismissed from their jobs for cause to receive certain procedural protections before being terminated. The case involved two school-district employees who were alleged to have lied on their employment applications. Each was fired without having a chance to explain his actions.

On its face, *Loudermill* is a conventional application of the procedural due process doctrines developed by the Court in *Goldberg v. Kelly*, 397 U.S. 254 (1970), *Board of Regents v. Roth*, 408 U.S. 564 (1972), and *Mathews v. Eldridge*, 424 U.S. 319 (1976). The government employees had a statutory entitlement to remain in their jobs because, in each instance, the government's discretion to remove them was limited. Accordingly, under *Goldberg* and *Roth*, each was entitled to some sort of due process protection. Having decided that the due process clause applied, the Court then balanced the factors, established in *Mathews*, for determining how much process was due: the individual's private interest in retaining his or her job, the government's interest in "the expeditious removal of unsatisfactory employees," and "the risk of erroneous termination" under the existing procedures. Because the employees were not allowed to respond to the allegations before they were dismissed, the Court held that the risk of erroneous termination was high. Thus, the employers were required to allow such a response before terminating the employees.

What makes *Loudermill* a significant case in the development of procedural due process is the Court's definitive rejection of a due process doctrine known as "taking the bitter with the sweet." This doctrine, which had attracted a plurality of justices a decade earlier in *Arnett v. Kennedy*, 416 U.S. 134 (1974), suggested that if the government created a substantive right and attached to it particular procedural protections, then the courts were forbidden from requiring additional procedural protections. If people wanted to take a benefit from the government, they had to accept whatever procedural protections for that benefit the government was willing to offer.

In his dissent, Justice William Rehnquist made a forceful argument for the bitter-with-the-sweet approach to due process. First, he noted that the doctrine was logically consistent with *Roth*, which dictated that courts were to look to state law to define the parameters of property rights. Was not the procedure to remove a right simply one of the bundle of sticks that made up a piece of property? Second, Rehnquist argued that the application of the *Matthews* balancing test was completely haphazard.

As such, it failed to provide legislatures with any guidance as to what sort of procedural protections they had to implement.

Justice Byron White's majority opinion rejected these arguments. The bitter with the sweet, he wrote, "misconceives the constitutional guarantee." The due process clause required courts to enforce the constitutional right to due process independently of the substantive right created by the state. Because due process rights were federal constitutional rights, state actors could not be allowed to define them. To hold otherwise would be to reduce due processes to "a mere tautology" in which the judicial duty to enforce constitutional rights was completely eliminated.

SEE ALSO *Government Employees; Procedural Due Process*

BIBLIOGRAPHY

Easterbrook, Frank H. 1982. "Substance and Due Process." *The Supreme Court Review* 1982: 85–1126.

Mashaw, Jerry L. 1987. "Dignitary Process: A Political Psychology of Liberal Democratic Citizenship." *University of Florida Law Review* 39: 433–444.

Reuel E. Schiller

CLINTON, WILLIAM JEFFERSON

SEE *Breyer, Stephen; Clinton v. City of New York, 524 U.S. 417 (1998); Clinton v. Jones, 520 U.S. 681 (1997); Ginsburg, Ruth Bader; Independent Counsel; Rehnquist Court.*

CLINTON V. CITY OF NEW YORK, 524 U.S. 417 (1998)

Concerned with rising federal budget deficits, prominent politicians and political activists during the late twentieth century insisted that the president be given a line-item veto. This authority, constitutionally granted to many state governors, would enable the chief executive to reject particular appropriations in a legislative bill without vetoing the bill entirely. The Republican Contract with America called for legislation granting the president such authority, Congress passed the Line Item Veto Act, and President Clinton signed that measure into law in April of 1996. That measure gave the president the power when signing legislation to nevertheless cancel "any dollar amount of discretionary budget authority," "any item of new direct spending," or "any limited tax benefit." A majority of both houses of Congress could then enact a "disapproval bill," that would void those cancellations. The disapproval bill did not have to be signed to become law.

The Supreme Court in *Raines v. Byrd*, 521 U.S. 811 (1997) had ruled that members of Congress had no standing to challenge the constitutionality of the Line Item Veto Act, but in *Clinton* the justices found standing when the City of New York and Snake River Farmers' Cooperative challenged that measure. Justice John Paul Stevens ruled that New York City had standing because President Clinton's exercise of his line item veto power had deprived the city of relief from a "multibillion dollar contingent liability" that Congress had sought to eliminate. Snake River farmers had standing because cancellation of a favorable measure had deprived them of a "statutory bargaining chip" that could be used when purchasing processing facilities. The standing decision respecting New York City was unanimous. Justices Antonin Scalia and Sandra Day O'Connor thought the Snake River lawsuit should have been dismissed on the grounds that the loss of a potential bargaining chip is not sufficiently concrete to satisfy the "case or controversy" requirement of Article III.

A six-to-three majority on the merits declared the Line Item Veto Act unconstitutional. Justice Stevens's opinion observed that "although the Constitution expressly authorizes the President to play a role in the process of enacting statutes, it is silent on the subject of unilateral Presidential action that either repeals or amends parts of duly enacted statutes." This silence, he believed, doomed the measure. In his view, the Line Item Veto Bill unconstitutionally granted "to the President the unilateral power to change the text of duly enacted statutes." Statutes, Stevens concluded, could only be signed or vetoed as a whole. "Liberty is threatened," Justice Anthony Kennedy's concurrence agreed, when "a citizen who is taxed has the measure of the tax or the decision to spend determined by the Executive alone, without adequate control by the citizen's Representatives in Congress." That Congress voluntarily ceded this authority to the President was of no constitutional significance. "Abdication of responsibility is not part of the constitutional design," Justice Kennedy insisted.

Justices Scalia, Stephen Breyer, and O'Connor maintained that the Line Item Veto Bill was constitutional. Justice Scalia accused the majority of relying on a meaningless technicality. His dissent stated, "there is not a dime's worth of difference between Congress's authorizing the President to cancel a spending item, and Congress's authorizing money to be spent on a particular item at the President's discretion." Justice Breyer's dissent placed particular emphasis on the impracticality of insisting that the president endorse every or no provision of legislative spending bills. "Congress," he observed, "cannot divide such a bill into thousands, or tens of thousands, of separate appropriations bills, each one of which the President would have to sign, or to veto, separately."

Debate over the merits of the line item veto during the next few years was largely mooted, first by the budget surplus of the latter Clinton Administration, and then by the war on terrorism. When the Bush Administration and Republican Congress compiled huge budget deficits, many former budget hawks abandoned their concern with balanced budgets. Nevertheless, the formalistic interpretation of executive and congressional powers exhibited in *Clinton* is and may remain a central theme in contemporary Supreme Court jurisprudence. Such judicial formalism is likely to survive as different matters come to occupy judicial attention.

SEE ALSO *Separation of Powers; Veto Power*

BIBLIOGRAPHY

Anderson, Elizabeth Garrett. 1999. "Accountability and Restraint: The Federal Budget Process and the Line Item Veto Act." *Cardozo Law Review* 20(3): 871–937.

Mark A. Graber

CLINTON V. JONES, 520 U.S. 681 (1997)

The 1997 case of *Clinton v. Jones*, 520 U.S. 681 (1997) is important because of its ruling and its fallout. The lawsuit was filed shortly after Bill Clinton became president in 1993. The plaintiff, Paula Jones, a state government employee, alleged that while Clinton was governor of Arkansas, he had sexually harassed her. Clinton's lawyers denied all factual allegations in Jones's complaint, and raised several affirmative defenses, including his entitlement as president to absolute immunity from civil lawsuits. After denying Clinton's motion to dismiss, the district court judge, Susan Webber Wright, ruled that discovery should proceed but the trial would be stayed until Clinton left office. Both parties appealed, and the Eighth Circuit affirmed the denial of Clinton's motion to dismiss but reversed the order postponing Jones's trial.

The question before the Supreme Court was whether, in the absence of extraordinary circumstances, Clinton was entitled to delay civil lawsuits against him until he left office. Central to the answer was whether the Court agreed with Clinton's lawyers that all of the reasons recognized by the Court in *Nixon v. Fitzgerald*, 457 U.S. 731 (1982) for holding presidents absolutely immune from civil lawsuits based on their official conduct, applied equally to Clinton's circumstances. For the five-majority in *Nixon*, Justice Lewis Powell had emphasized that the

Paula Jones at a press conference in Los Angeles, November 15, 1994. *President Bill Clinton lost his appeal before the Supreme Court to delay a sexual harassment lawsuit filed by Arkansas state employee Paula Jones. The highest court ruled that the president cannot use the office as a shield from legitimate civil complaints, setting the stage for a trial which eventually led to President Clinton's impeachment.* **AP IMAGES**

"uniqueness" of the presidency made it an easy "target for suits for civil damages," and he recognized that such lawsuits "could distract" presidents from their "public duties." Justice Powell acknowledged other ways to check presidential misconduct, including impeachment.

Jones's lawyers had two arguments. First, they emphasized that no one is above the law. Granting Clinton immunity, even temporarily, allowed him to use the presidency as a shield to avoid legal accountability for misconduct that had nothing to do with his official powers. Second, they stressed the unfairness of delaying Jones's lawsuit, or other cases such as custody disputes, that could be filed against presidents.

The Court, in an opinion by Justice John Paul Stevens, unanimously agreed with Jones. First, Stevens asserted that the absolute immunity from civil actions recognized in *Nixon v. Fitzgerald* was based on the concern "to avoid rendering the President 'unduly cautious in the discharge of his official duties.'" Second, Stevens found that historical practices did not support Clinton's "strongest argument" that "he occupies a unique office with powers and responsibilities so vast and important that the public demands that he devote his undivided time and attention to his public duties." Justice Stevens opined that, given the fact that the only three presidents who had ever been sued civilly had not been troubled by the lawsuits against them, "it seems unlikely

that a deluge of such litigation" would ever besiege presidents. He expressed confidence in the ability of district courts to manage cases brought against presidents to minimize interference with the president's constitutional responsibilities.

The district judge granted Clinton's motion for summary judgment, but not before Clinton had lied in a videotaped deposition about the nature of his relationship with former White House employee Monica Lewinsky. The lie became the basis for an independent counsel investigation, led by Kenneth Starr, into whether Clinton had committed perjury in the *Jones* case or obstructed justice. On August 6, 1998, Lewinsky testified before a grand jury, followed by Clinton's testifying before the same body on August 17. Even though Jones's case settled on August 13, Starr submitted a report to Congress on September 9, charging that Clinton had committed as many as eleven impeachable offenses.

Starr's charges were referred to the House of Representatives, which the Constitution vests with "sole" authority to impeach, by a majority vote, presidents and other high-ranking officials for certain misconduct in office. Three months later, after several hearings, the House Judiciary Committee approved four articles of impeachment against Clinton. On December 19, the full House approved two articles of impeachment against the president: The first, by a vote of 228–206, charged

Clinton with committing perjury in his grand jury testimony; the second, by a vote of 221–212, charged him with obstructing justice. The two impeachment articles were then delivered to the Senate, which the Constitution vests with sole authority to try impeached officials, which it may convict and remove by a two-thirds vote. After allowing questioning of a few witnesses by members of the House charged with the responsibility of prosecuting Clinton before the Senate, the Senate, on February 12, 1999, acquitted Clinton on both impeachment articles. Ten Republicans joined all forty-five Democrats to acquit Clinton on the perjury article, while five Republicans broke ranks to join all of the Democrats, to split fifty–fifty, on the obstruction of justice article.

On April 12, 1999, Judge Wright found Clinton in contempt of court for committing perjury. She ordered Clinton to pay compensation to Jones's lawyers for their expenses in connection with Clinton's deposition, and referred the matter of his false testimony to the Arkansas Supreme Court. In May 2000, the court recommended Clinton be disbarred, though the ruling would be mooted by Clinton's agreement with the independent counsel, reached on his last day in office. In exchange for not being criminally prosecuted for lying under oath or obstructing justice, Clinton admitted that he had lied under oath and that he "engaged in conduct that is prejudicial to the administration of justice." Clinton also promised to pay $25,000 in legal expenses, and agreed to a five-year suspension of his law license.

SEE ALSO *Presidential Immunity; Separation of Powers; Sexual Harassment*

BIBLIOGRAPHY

Baker, Peter. 2000. *The Breach: Inside the Impeachment and Trial of President William Jefferson Clinton.* New York: Scribner.

Posner, Richard A. 1999. *An Affair of State: The Investigation, Impeachment, and Trial of President Clinton.* Cambridge, MA: Harvard University Press.

Michael J. Gerhardt

COHENS V. VIRGINIA, 19 U.S. 264 (1821)

During the early nineteenth century, lotteries were an important source of revenue for state and federal governments. In 1819 Virginia passed legislation prohibiting the sale or purchase of out-of-state lottery tickets in an attempt to stem the flow of cash outside the state. In August 1820 Virginia officials accused professional lottery agents Mendes and Philip Cohen of selling Grand National Lottery tickets, designed to fund construction of civic improvements in Washington, D.C., from their Richmond office. At trial, the Cohens admitted violating the state law, but argued that they were immune from state prosecution because they were selling congressionally authorized tickets. Thus, according to the U.S. Constitution's supremacy clause, the federal law trumped the state law. A Virginia borough court disagreed and fined the Cohen brothers one hundred dollars plus costs. The Cohens appealed to the U.S. Supreme Court, claiming that the Virginia statute was unconstitutional.

Initially, *Cohens v. Virginia*, 19 U.S. 264 (1821) appears as a minor case testing the constitutionality of an obscure state law. In truth, *Cohens* dealt with important issues involving the scope of the Eleventh Amendment and the legitimacy of section 25 of the 1789 Judiciary Act, which granted the U.S. Supreme Court appellate review over state court decisions. The central question was whether the U.S. Supreme Court had jurisdiction over cases emanating from state courts challenging federal laws and the Constitution. The State of Virginia argued that *Cohens* involved "a contest between a State and one of its own citizens . . . [placing it outside] the pale of federal judicial power."

Chief Justice John Marshall, writing for a unanimous Court, thought otherwise and settled the controversy with a lengthy decision establishing the authority of the Supreme Court. First, the Court had jurisdiction over *Cohens* because the Constitution stated, "judicial power, as originally given, extends to all cases arising under the constitution or a law of the United States, whoever may be the parties." Second, the Court had authority because the Cohens were defendants who brought forward "a judgment rendered against [them] by a State Court . . . for the purpose of re-examining the question[s]' . . . [legality in regard to] the Constitution or laws of the United States." Thus, the Cohen brothers failed to initiate "a suit against the State"; therefore, the Eleventh Amendment did not apply. Finally, Marshall ruled that section 25 the Judiciary Act was indeed valid, reaffirming the Court's jurisdiction over state supreme courts, previously decided in *Martin v. Hunter's Lessee,* 14 U.S. 304 (1816).

Some scholars place *Cohens* within the trilogy of cases, including *Marbury v. Madison,* 5 U.S. 137 (1803) and *Martin v. Hunter's Lessee,* that concretized the doctrine of judicial review. So elaborately does *Cohens* recognize the judicial supremacy of the Supreme Court over state courts, the case appears to be contrived for that reason alone. Yet, the decision was more symbolic than substantive. This is especially apparent when one considers the outcome.

Cohens failed to overturn Virginia's ban on the sale of out-of-state lottery tickets and upheld the Cohen brothers' conviction. The Court agreed that Congress had the authority to create a national lottery if it chose and that such an act would carry the weight of federal law and invalidate any opposing state law. Yet Marshall did not consider the Grand National Lottery to be this type of legislation. The rationale for this arose from a tenuous reading of Article 1, Section 8 of the Constitution, granting Congress legislative authority over the District of Columbia. Because the law enacting the National Lottery did not contain provisions for the appointment of federal sales agents, the Court deemed it a local venture under the corporate power of Congress to act within Washington, D.C., despite the fact that the city was the national capital, because revenues generated went toward local city improvements. This interpretation meant that Congress failed to anticipate the sale of tickets outside the capital. Additionally, it permitted the Court to sidestep the larger question of whether state laws could challenge federal legislation. Simultaneously, it established precedent for the Court's future intervention in cases involving individuals convicted of state crimes.

Other scholars believe that *Cohens* indicates that the concept of judicial review was not firmly established. They point to similarities between *Cohens* and *M'Culloch v. Maryland*, 17 U.S. 316 (1819), which established the legitimacy of Congress's implied powers and forbade states impeding the lawful exercise of federal power. Both cases revolved around state laws hindering out-of-state enterprises and congressional acts that did not foresee hostile state reactions. In *M'Culloch*, the Court prohibited Maryland from taxing the Bank of the United States, but *Cohens* allowed Virginia to prevent the sale of national lottery tickets. Hence, *Cohens* was a political maneuver to strengthen the authority of the Supreme Court, but also to appease a powerful opponent, the State of Virginia.

SEE ALSO *Marshall Court; Martin v. Hunter's Lessee, 14 U.S. 304 (1816); M'Culloch v. Maryland, 17 U.S. 316 (1819)*

BIBLIOGRAPHY

Graber, Mark A. 1995. "The Passive-Aggressive Virtues: *Cohens v. Virginia* and the Problematic Establishment of Judicial Power." *Constitutional Commentary* 12(1): 67–92.

Luce, W. Ray. 1990. Cohens v. Virginia *(1821): The Supreme Court and States Rights, a Reevaluation of Influences and Impacts*. New York: Garland.

Lance David Muckey

COHEN V. CALIFORNIA, 403 U.S. 15 (1971)

In *Cohen v. California*, 403 U.S. 15 (1971) the U.S. Supreme Court gave constitutional protection to the public display of a four-letter expletive used to protest the Vietnam War. In so doing, the Court overturned the conviction of a man who had walked through a Los Angeles courthouse wearing a jacket bearing the words "Fuck the Draft." Because the jacket contained a vulgarity offensive to many who would be involuntarily exposed to it, including children, the man was arrested and convicted for violating a California statute prohibiting a disturbance of the peace by offensive conduct.

Writing for the Court, Justice John Marshall Harlan invoked the First Amendment, finding that Cohen's conviction was not based on his conduct but on the content of his speech. Because there was no intent to incite a disturbance, and no likelihood that a disturbance would ensue, the conviction rested solely on the words Cohen used to convey his message to the public. Refusing to allow the governmental prohibition of offensive or distasteful expletives, the Court stated that one man's vulgarity is another's lyric. Under the First Amendment, according to the Court, matters of taste and style are left to the individual.

In his dissent, Justice Harry Blackmun argued that the actions for which Cohen was convicted involved conduct and not speech. Moreover, if any expression was involved it amounted to fighting words that were not protected by the Constitution.

Perhaps the most significant aspect of the Court's decision involved its handling of the claim that Cohen's distasteful mode of expression was thrust upon unwilling or unsuspecting viewers. The captive-audience doctrine has been used to give people a right to be free of unwanted speech in certain kinds of places and under certain conditions. Consequently, when employing this doctrine, courts elevate the desires of the audience to exclude speech over that of the speaker to convey it. However, this doctrine has usually been applied on behalf of unwilling viewers in the privacy of their own homes. Moreover, the *Cohen* Court found that those unwilling viewers in the Los Angeles courthouse could effectively avoid the offensive speech simply by averting their eyes. This finding reflected the Court's general rule that, in the public square, listeners and viewers must shoulder the full burden of removing themselves from speech they find objectionable.

The *Cohen* doctrine that unwilling viewers must bear the full burden of avoiding offensive speech has continued to prevail, even with respect to speech transmitted by media technologies that are much more difficult to monitor or avoid than a single pedestrian strolling through a courthouse corridor. In *United States v. Playboy Entertainment Group*, 529 U.S. 803 (2000), for instance, the Court struck down regulations intended to help shield children from indecent television programming that resulted when the signal scrambling of sexually explicit cable channels did not function properly. Replying to the argument that parents needed the assistance of such regulations in order to prevent their children from viewing sexually explicit material, the Court simply stated that it was the duty of the unwilling viewer to avert his or her eyes.

SEE ALSO *First Amendment; Freedom of Speech*

BIBLIOGRAPHY

Massey, Calvin. 1992. "Hate Speech, Cultural Diversity, and the Foundational Paradigms of Free Expression." *UCLA Law Review* 40(1): 103–197.

Volokh, Eugene. 2005. "Speech as Conduct: Generally Applicable Laws, Illegal Courses of Conduct, 'Situation-altering Utterances,' and the Uncharted Zones." *Cornell Law Review* 90(5): 1277–1348.

Patrick M. Garry

COKER V. GEORGIA, 433 U.S. 584 (1977)

In 1977 the U.S. Supreme Court held in *Coker v. Georgia*, 433 U.S. 584 that a sentence of death for the crime of rape of an adult woman is grossly disproportionate and excessive punishment in violation of the Eighth Amendment to the U.S. Constitution. *Coker* was a collision of historical and deep-seated sentiments on race, sex, and the death penalty.

Briefs submitted in *Coker* by the National Association for the Advancement of Colored People (NAACP) and by Ruth Bader Ginsburg on behalf of the American Civil Liberties Union (ACLU) Women's Rights Project both condemned the execution of rapists. As noted by William Eskridge,

> Capital rape statutes enjoyed a history that was patriarchal as well as racist: this extreme penalty for sexual assault was a vestige of an era when women's value rested mainly on their presentability for marriage (virginity) but men distrusted (seductive) women to be sufficient guarantors of their own chastity and were hysterical at the possibility that women would fall prey to men of color. (Eskridge 2002, pp. 2295–2296)

Ehrlich Anthony Coker escaped prison, where he was serving consecutive life sentences for two prior rapes, entered the house of Allen and Elnita Carver, tied up Mr. Carver, robbed him, and threatened him with a knife. Coker raped Mrs. Carver and drove away in the Carvers' car, taking her with him. He was apprehended shortly thereafter. The jury found Coker guilty of rape and sentenced him to death.

While seven justices agreed that the death sentence of Coker had to be overturned, only a plurality of four agreed on the rationale. Justices William Brennan and Thurgood Marshall concurred based on their minority view that capital punishment is always cruel and unusual, violating the Eighth Amendment. Justice Lewis F. Powell, Jr. concurred in the judgment only on the facts of this case where, he said, the crime was not committed with "excessive brutality" and the victim did not sustain "serious or lasting injury."

Justice Byron White, writing for Justices Potter Stewart, Harry Blackmun, and John Paul Stevens, stated that a punishment violates the Eighth Amendment when it is grossly out of proportion to the severity of the crime. To decide this, the Court had to take into account objective evidence of present public judgment, as represented by the attitude of state legislatures and sentencing juries.

The plurality noted that in the fifty years prior to *Coker*, a majority of the states had not authorized death as a punishment for the rape of an adult woman. By the time of *Coker*, Georgia was the only state authorizing such a penalty. As for jury decisions, only six of the sixty-three rape convictions reviewed by the Georgia Supreme Court since 1973 resulted in a death sentence.

The plurality then turned to its own subjective judgment as to the acceptability of the punishment. Walking a very fine line, the plurality first paid homage to the seriousness of the crime of rape. Justice White wrote that "rape is highly reprehensible, both in a moral sense and in its almost total contempt for the personal integrity and autonomy of the female victim," and that "short of homicide, it is the 'ultimate violation of self.'" Significantly, Justice White quoted from an article analyzing rape from a feminist perspective. This was a fresh perspective: It was only in the mid-1970s that feminists began to educate society about the need to abolish the patriarchal perspective of rape as an insult to the male property holder.

However, against this new recognition of the harm to a woman's autonomy was the Court's increasing recognition of the racist application of the death penalty to black men accused of raping white women. As cited by Randall Coyne and Lyn Entzeroth (2006), of the 455 men executed for rape in the United States between 1930 and 1964, 405 were black, and almost all were convicted of raping white women. In 1963 three members of the Court had suggested in a dissent from a denial of certiorari that the Court should decide the very issue taken up in *Coker*.

Without mentioning race, however, the plurality in *Coker* stuck to its proportionality analysis and drew the line at rape: "in terms of moral depravity and of the injury to the person and the public, [rape] does not compare with murder, which does involve the unjustified taking of human life," and further, "life is over for the victim of the murderer; for the rape victim, life may not be nearly so happy as it was, but it is not over and normally is not beyond repair." With this awkward final analysis, the plurality closed the book on capital punishment for the rape of an adult woman.

Chief Justice Warren Burger, joined by Justice William Rehnquist in dissent, chastised the plurality for minimizing the harms of rape and for taking out of the hands of state legislatures the decision as to the appropriate punishment. Justices Burger and Rehnquist, like Justice Powell, also thought *Coker* should have been decided on the narrow grounds of the appropriateness of the penalty in *this* case, where "a chronic rapist whose continuing danger to the community is abundantly clear."

SEE ALSO *Capital Punishment; Eighth Amendment*

BIBLIOGRAPHY

Brownmiller, Susan. 1975. *Against Our Will: Men, Women, and Rape*. New York: Ballantine.

Coyne, Randall, and Lyn Entzeroth. 2006. *Capital Punishment and the Judicial Process*. 3rd edition. Durham, NC: Carolina Academic Press.

Eskridge, William N. 2002. "Some Effects of Identity-Based Social Movements on Constitutional Law in the Twentieth Century." *Michigan Law Review* 100: 2062–2407.

Janet C. Hoeffel

COLD WAR

The Cold War, the global confrontation between the United States and the Soviet Union that spanned the years from the end of World War II to the 1990s, had its greatest impact on the work of the Supreme Court during the war's early years, in two areas of law in particular. One was a series of appeals in the 1950s by American citizens who raised constitutional challenges to their prosecutions for suspected disloyalty. The other group of cases involved the struggle for racial justice. The foreign-relations demands of the early Cold War turned racial discrimination into a national security liability, resulting in growing pressure on national leaders, including the justices of the Supreme Court, to support increased federal intervention to uproot Jim Crow racial practices.

LOYALTY COURT CASES

As tensions with the Soviet Union escalated in the years following World War II, Americans became increasingly fearful of subversive activities within the United States.

> *The priceless heritage of our society is the unrestricted constitutional right of each member to think as he will. Thought control is a copyright of totalitarianism, and we have no claim to it. It is not the function of our Government to keep the citizen from falling into error; it is the function of the citizen to keep the Government from falling into error.*
>
> SOURCE: Robert H. Jackson, *American Communications Ass'n v. Douds,* 339 U.S. 382, 442–443 (1950) (concurring in part and dissenting in part).

The institutionalization of an elaborate government loyalty-security apparatus in the late 1940s—on both the federal and state level and with bipartisan support—transformed these fears into a full-fledged anticommunist purge, a second Red Scare that lasted into the 1950s and has become commonly identified with its most visible and fervent advocate, U.S. Senator Joseph McCarthy (1908–1957) of Wisconsin.

Numerous cases challenging the domestic anticommunist policy of the McCarthy era came to the Supreme Court. The Court's holdings in these cases generally correlated with the relative level of surrounding foreign and domestic tension—the higher the tension, the less likely the Court was to challenge the power of government to protect itself against suspected subversives, even when security policy challenged free speech principles. The Court was particularly hesitant to stand in the way of the McCarthyism juggernaut at its passionate apex in the early 1950s, when anticommunism was fueled by a potent mixture of demagogic politics at home and ominous developments abroad—in 1949 Communists gained control of China and the Soviets successfully detonated an atomic bomb; the following year America was at war in Korea.

In *American Communications Association v. Douds,* 339 U.S. 382 (1950) the Supreme Court upheld a provision of the Taft-Hartley Act (1947) that required labor union officers to sign an affidavit stating they were not members of the Communist Party and that they did not believe in the overthrow of the U.S. government. Then, in the most important antisubversive decision of the early Cold War, *Dennis v. United States,* 341 U.S. 494 (1951), the Supreme Court affirmed the Smith Act convictions of leaders of the Communist Party of the United States for conspiring to advocate the overthrow of the government. Writing for the Court, Chief Justice Fred

M. Vinson rejected the defendants' First Amendment claim, applying a narrow version of the "clear and present danger" test that assured broad leeway for government prosecution of suspected subversives. In his concurrence, Justice Felix Frankfurter explicitly referenced the Cold War as a factor in the Court's evaluation of the constitutional claim, noting that the justices "may take judicial notice that the Communist doctrines which these defendants have conspired to advocate are in the ascendancy in powerful nations who cannot be acquitted of unfriendliness to the institutions of this country." Then, in 1953, the passions of Cold War anticommunism invaded the Supreme Court in particularly dramatic fashion when the Court met in a special session to consider, and ultimately reject, the last-minute appeal of the death sentences for convicted atomic spies Ethel (1915–1953) and Julius Rosenberg (1918–1953).

It would not be until later in the decade, with the anticommunist fervor somewhat receding, that the Court became more open to civil liberties challenges to loyalty-security programs. With McCarthyism well in decline, and with the addition of Chief Justice Earl Warren and Justice William J. Brennan, Jr., the Court took a moderately civil libertarian turn, most notably in a series of decisions issued on June 17, 1957. While avoiding any sweeping first amendment condemnation of existing loyalty programs, these rulings sent a clear message that the Court would closely review their procedures. In *Yates v. United States*, 354 U.S. 298 (1957) the Court overturned the convictions of Communist Party leaders, in the process placing into serious doubt any future efforts to prosecute suspected subversives under the Smith Act. In *Watkins v. United States*, 354 U.S. 178 (1957) and *Sweezy v. New Hampshire*, 334 U.S. 234 (1957), the Court established limits on the investigative powers of the controversial House Un-American Activities Committee and state legislatures, respectively. Cold War politics still had bite, however, as anticommunist critics decried the decisions of so-called Red Monday and, joining forces with segregationist critics of the school desegregation decisions, pressed for Court-curbing legislation. Although the proposed legislation—which would have overturned some of the Court's decisions and limited the Court's jurisdiction in future national security cases—never passed, the assault on the Court seemed to have an effect; for a time, the Court again appeared more hesitant to challenge domestic security programs.

RACIAL JUSTICE CASES

The Cold War also factored into the work of the Supreme Court in a more indirect manner, through the pressures Cold War diplomacy placed on American racial practices. Scholars in recent years have drawn attention to the international context of the Cold War as a central factor in the growth of support for civil rights from the late 1940s through the 1960s. Legal historian Mary Dudziak has usefully labeled this factor the Cold War imperative for civil rights. The existence of blatant racial injustice in the United States created a sizable obstacle for U.S. diplomats when dealing with Third World nations. "Throughout the Pacific, Latin America, Africa, the Near, Middle, and Far East," warned the report of the President's Committee on Civil Rights (PCCR), "the treatment which our Negroes receive is taken as a reflection of our attitudes toward all dark-skinned people" (United States 1947, p. 147). This awkward diplomatic situation was exacerbated by segregation in the nation's capital, where diplomats and visitors from Africa and Asia regularly faced the humiliations of Jim Crow. The Soviet Union strategically took advantage of this situation by publicizing incidents of racial discrimination and racial violence in the United States as propaganda intended to gain the allegiance of these countries. As Cornell professor Robert Cushman wrote, "It is unpleasant to have the Russians publicize our continued lynchings, our Jim Crow statutes and customs, our anti-Semitic discrimination, and our witchhunts; but is it undeserved?" (1948, p. 12). Although some of what came out of the Soviet propaganda machine could be dismissed as distortions and exaggerations, there was generally enough truth in the reports to make many American policymakers uncomfortable. "Some of the flung mud sticks," Cushman concluded (1948, p. 12).

By the late 1940s, practically all discussions of civil rights referenced foreign policy implications. The influential PCCR report dedicated an entire section to the international factor for civil rights reform. The committee quoted extensively from a 1946 letter Secretary of State Dean Acheson (1893–1971) wrote to the Fair Employment Practices Committee, in which he stated that "the existence of discrimination against minority groups in this country has an adverse effect upon our relations with other countries," and called for "continued and increased effectiveness of public and private efforts to do away with these discriminations" (United States 1947, pp. 146–147). The line that concluded the PCCR report's discussion of the international situation would be quoted repeatedly in the coming years by civil rights advocates: "The United States is not so strong, the final triumph of the democratic ideal is not so inevitable that we can ignore what the world thinks of our record" (p. 148).

The Supreme Court justices received a steady diet of references to the international implications of domestic civil rights policy. Beginning with the restrictive covenant case, *Shelley v. Kraemer*, 334 U.S. 1 (1948), the U.S. Justice Department submitted influential briefs in the major civil rights cases before the Supreme Court that referenced the Cold War as a central factor pointing to the necessity of civil rights reform. Its brief in *Shelley* noted

Procedural fairness and regularity are of the indispensable essence of liberty. Severe substantive laws can be endured if they are fairly and impartially implied. Indeed, if put to the choice, one might well prefer to live under Soviet substantive law applied in good faith by our common-law procedures than under our substantive law enforced by Soviet procedural practices.

SOURCE: Robert H. Jackson, *Shaughnessy v. United States,* 345 U.S. 206, 224 (1953).

that "the United States has been embarrassed in the conduct of foreign relations by acts of discrimination taking place in this country." Similar language appeared in the Justice Department briefs submitted in *Sweatt v. Painter,* 339 U.S. 629 (1950) and *McLaurin v. Oklahoma State Regents,* 339 U.S. 637 (1950), the cases in which the Court struck down segregation in higher education; and in *Henderson v. United States,* 339 U.S. 816 (1950), a successful challenge to segregation on railroad dining cars. The briefs in *Brown v. Board of Education,* 347 U.S. 483 (1954) again pressed the Cold War case for civil rights. The government brief, which urged the Court to rule segregated schools unconstitutional, noted that "racial discrimination furnishes grist for the Communist propaganda mills, and it raises doubts even among friendly nations as to the intensity of our devotion to the democratic faith." The National Association for the Advancement of Colored People (NAACP) lawyers followed the Justice Department lead and also emphasized the Cold War context in their *Brown* briefs.

The precise effect on the Supreme Court justices of the Cold War imperative is not fully clear. Undoubtedly, foreign policy concerns exerted a powerful atmospheric pressure on the justices. The foreign policy establishment regularly framed civil rights as a pressing national security concern; both the Truman and Eisenhower administrations directly urged this argument on the Court through their amicus briefs in *Brown,* and Cold War rhetoric generally permeated public discussion on civil rights; these factors, at a minimum, helped solidify the Court's trend toward an increasing willingness to intervene on contentious civil rights issues, and likely they did more than this. Yet exactly how much of a causal factor the Cold War imperative was in major civil rights cases, particularly *Brown,* is an open question. It is hard to find evidence that it necessarily swayed any particular justice. Within the

records of the deliberations of the justices, there are no direct references to the Cold War context. (Although one clerk later recalled discussing the issue with Justice Stanley Reed [1884–1980].) While the *Brown* opinion emphasized the national importance of citizenship and education, it made no direct reference to the international situation. Nonetheless, the arguments of the Cold War imperative clearly received a sympathetic hearing from the justices.

In private and public, several justices acknowledged the Cold War–civil rights connection. Prior to *Brown,* Justice William O. Douglas wrote of the effect of Jim Crow on relations with India and, after *Brown,* Chief Justice Warren in public addresses regularly noted the national security implications of civil rights reform. It is likely that the foreign policy community's pleas for civil rights reform, strongly backed by the White House, played a role in encouraging some of the more conservative justices to support civil rights decisions. Several of these justices—most notably Harold Burton (1888–1964), Tom C. Clark (1899–1977), Sherman Minton (1890–1965), and Vinson (author of *Shelley, Sweatt,* and *McLaurin*)—had close personal relations with President Harry S. Truman (1884–1972), and they all tended to be deferential toward executive branch judgments. In sum, the Cold War imperative surely offered the justices an additional justification for supporting civil rights, thus bolstering an already strong trend within the Court, and it likely nudged some of the justices further than they might otherwise have gone. Whether the Cold War imperative can be directly attributed to any particular vote in *Brown* or the major civil rights cases of the period is beyond what the available evidence offers.

Reaction to *Brown* regularly emphasized the international benefits of the decision. "Nine men in Washington have given us a victory that no number of divisions, arms and bombs could ever have won," declared the *St. Louis Post-Dispatch* (as excerpted in *New York Times* 1954, p. 20). *Life* announced that the Supreme Court "at one stroke immeasurably raised the respect of other nations for the U.S." (1954, p. 11). African-American Congressman Adam Clayton Powell (1908–1972) hailed the decision as "Communism's worst defeat" (*New York Times* 1954, p. 21). The government immediately spread news of the decision around the world through Voice of America broadcasts.

The Cold War continued to influence federal civil rights policy in the years after *Brown.* Foreign policy arguments featured prominently, for example, in President Dwight D. Eisenhower's decision to intervene in the Little Rock school crisis of 1957, and in the debate over the Civil Rights Act of 1964. By the late 1960s, however, the Cold War no longer exerted the pressure on civil rights policy it once did. The civil rights movement successfully pressed for landmark civil rights legislation that addressed the most egregious practices of racial discrimination, taking away the most powerful sources of anti-U.S. propaganda. And with the escalation of the Vietnam War, new public relations challenges faced the U.S. government in its ongoing battle for the hearts and minds of not-so-distant people.

A deeper appreciation for the ways in which international affairs and domestic policy intersect has undoubtedly enriched civil rights history. Yet this newfound appreciation for the Cold War–civil rights connection also has its risks. The clear causal dynamic of the Cold War imperative sometimes invites reductionist interpretations, where the Cold War becomes *the* central factor leading to *Brown*. The growing commitment of the Supreme Court to the cause of racial justice (evident not only in the desegregation cases but also in voting rights and criminal justice cases) was the product of many factors, including African-American activism and litigation, the growing influence of the black vote, the egalitarian rhetoric that accompanied World War II, reaction to the horrors of Nazi racism, and an increasingly interconnected national culture. The foreign policy dynamics of the Cold War bolstered an already strong trend, adding some influential voices to those calling for federal intervention. And it gave those already committed to the cause—those who did not need the Cold War to convince them of the need for civil rights reform—a powerful rhetorical weapon with which to make their argument. The best scholarship on the influence of world affairs on American racial politics recognizes the complexity of the historical moment in which civil rights emerged as a major national policy concern, appreciating the importance of the Cold War imperative while also recognizing its explanatory limitations.

SEE ALSO *Brown v. Board of Education, 347 U.S. 483 (1954); Brown v. Board of Education, Road to; First Amendment; Hiss, Alger; Vinson Court; Warren Court*

BIBLIOGRAPHY

Belknap, Michal R. 1977. *Cold War Political Justice: The Smith Act, the Communist Party, and American Civil Liberties.* Westport, CT: Greenwood Press.

Borstelmann, Thomas. 2001. *The Cold War and the Color Line: American Race Relations in the Global Arena.* Cambridge, MA: Harvard University Press.

"Civic Groups Hail Anti-Bias Ruling." 1954. *New York Times,* May 19.

Cushman, Robert E. 1948. "Our Civil Rights Become a World Issue." *New York Times Magazine,* Jan. 11.

Dudziak, Mary L. 2000. *Cold War Civil Rights: Race and the Image of American Democracy.* Princeton, NJ: Princeton University Press.

Dudziak, Mary L. 2004. "'Brown' as a Cold War Case." *Journal of American History* 91(1): 32–42.

Fassett, John D. 1986. "Mr. Justice Reed and *Brown v. The Board of Education.*" *Supreme Court Historical Society Yearbook* 1986: 48–63.

"A Historic Decision for Equality." 1954. *Life,* May 31: 10–16.

Lefberg, Irving F. 1975. "Chief Justice Vinson and the Politics of Desegregation." *Emory Law Journal* 24(2): 243–312.

"More Powerful than All the Bombs." 1954. *St. Louis Post-Dispatch,* May 18, excerpted in "Editorial Excerpts on School Bias Ruling." *New York Times,* May 19: 20.

Skrentny, John David. 1998. "The Effect of the Cold War on African-American Civil Rights: America and the World Audience, 1945–1968." *Theory and Society* 27(2): 237–285.

United States. President's Committee on Civil Rights. 1947. *To Secure These Rights.* New York: Simon and Schuster.

Wiecek, William M. 2001. "The Legal Foundations of Domestic Anticommunism: The Background of *Dennis v. United States.*" *Supreme Court Review* 2001: 375–434.

Christopher W. Schmidt

COLLEGES AND UNIVERSITIES

In modern American higher education, few major decisions are made without considering the legal consequences, and although the core functions of higher education—instruction and scholarship—are remarkably free from external legal influences, no one would plausibly deny the increase of legalization on campus. Surprisingly little is known about the law's effect upon higher education, but virtually no one in the enterprise is untouched by statutes, regulations, case law, or institutional rules promulgated to implement legal regimes. Because different constitutional considerations, such as free speech and due process, do not apply to private colleges, it is important to distinguish between private and public institutions in order to understand the full panoply of rights and duties owed to institutional community members.

Consider the public/private distinction as a continuum, with *Trustees of Dartmouth College v. Woodward,* 17 U.S. 518 (1819) at the purely private end, and *Krynicky v. University of Pittsburgh,* 742 F.2d 94 (3d Cir. 1984) at the other end, that of purely public colleges. In *Dartmouth,* the first higher-education case considered by the U.S. Supreme Court, the State of New Hampshire had attempted to rescind the private charter of Dartmouth College, which had been incorporated in the state nearly fifty years earlier, and to make it a public college with legislatively appointed trustees to replace the college's private trustees. The Supreme Court held that the college, once chartered, was private and not subject to the legislature's actions, unless the trustees wished to reconstitute themselves as a public institution. At the other end of the spectrum, *Krynicky* held that Temple University and the University of Pittsburgh were public colleges, due to the amount of money given to them by the state, the reconstitution of the board to include publicly appointed trustees (including *ex officio* elected officials), state reporting requirements, and other characteristics that injected state action into the act of reconstituting the institutions into the state system of higher education.

Of course, if there are pure archetypes such as Dartmouth and the University of Pittsburgh, there must be intermediate institutions, such as Alfred University in New York, where in *Powe v. Miles*, 407 F.2d 73 (2d. Cir. 1968) several students were arrested, and the court held that the regular students were entitled to no elaborate due process because the institution was private. However, Alfred University's ceramics engineering students were entitled to hearings before dismissal because the university's Ceramics College, in which they were enrolled, was a state-supported entity in that New York contracted with the private college to provide this program rather than establish such a program in a state school. Other such examples of a state-contracted unit within a private school include Cornell University's agricultural sciences program and Baylor's College of Medicine, both of which programs operate as if they were state institutions.

Other important foundational issues have also led to litigation, resulting in a complex definitional process. For example, in *Cahn and Cahn v. Antioch University*, 482 A.2d 120 (D.C. 1984), trustees of the institution were sued by the co-deans of the law school to determine who had authority to make governance decisions; the court ruled that trustees have the ultimate authority and fiduciary duty. In contrast to *Dartmouth*, where there was a "hostile takeover" of the institution by the state, private trustees can close a college or surrender its assets, such as its accreditation (*Fenn College v. Nance*, 210 N. E.2d 418 [Ohio Ct. Common Pleas 1965] and *Nasson College v. New England Association of Schools and Colleges*, 80 B.R. 600 [Bankr. D. Me. 1988]).

Another important issue involving the definition and legal governance of colleges turns on the consortial or collective behavior of institutions: Does their mutual recognition in athletics, accreditation, and information-sharing subject them to state action? In *NCAA v. University of Oklahoma*, 468 U.S. 85 (1984), the U.S. Supreme Court held that the NCAA was a "classic cartel" engaged in restraint of trade by its negotiated television contract. Another court held that the activities of the Overlap Group—a group of elite institutions that share information on financial-aid offers with other colleges that had also admitted the same students, so as to "coordinate" the awards—similarly violated antitrust law (*United States v. Brown University*, 5 F.3d 658 [3d Cir. 1993]).

However, in accreditation activities, mutual-recognition agreements have been allowed by courts as not constituting a restraint of trade, as in *Marjorie Webster Jr. College v. Middle States Association*, 432 F.2d 650 (D.C. Cir. 1970) and *Beth Rochel Seminary v. Bennett*, 825 F.2d 478 (D.C. Cir. 1987), where an institution that was not yet accredited failed to negotiate the complex exceptions to the accreditation requirement for financial-aid eligibility.

FACULTY ISSUES

The two leading U.S. Supreme Court faculty tenure cases were decided the same day in 1972, and both *Perry v. Sindermann*, 408 U.S. 593 and *Board of Regents v. Roth*, 408 U.S. 564 turn on what process is due to faculty should institutions wish to remove them. In *Perry*, a community college instructor who had been a thorn in the side of college administrators was fired for "insubordination," without a hearing or official reasons. The college had no tenure policy, except one that said, "the Administration of the College wishes the faculty member to feel that he has permanent tenure as long as his teaching services are satisfactory and as long as he displays a cooperative attitude toward his coworkers and his supervisors, and as long he is happy in his work." The Court held that the instructor thus had a property interest in his continued employment, and ordered the lower court to determine whether he had been fired for his protected speech or for cause. In short, the college was required to give the instructor notice of the reasons for his firing and an opportunity to explain his side of the matter. This is what tenure grants: a presumption of continued employment, absent certain circumstances (financial exigency, etc.). In *Roth*, the Court held that an untenured professor had no constitutional right to continued employment beyond the contractual period for which he or she was hired.

In addition to contract and liberty interests, faculty may have property interests as well, as in *State ex rel. McLendon v. Morton*, 249 S.E.2d 919 (W.Va. 1978), where the court held that Professor McLendon had a property interest in being considered for tenure after she had ostensibly qualified by serving in rank for the requisite period of time. Although many cases, including *Roth*, have held that no reasons need be given for denying tenure, McLendon had, on the surface, appeared to earn tenure by default, and a hearing was required to show why she was not entitled to tenure. Such cases as these will be fact-grounded and case-specific, due to the terms of the individual institutional policy and the development of contract law or employment law in each state.

As for discrimination in the tenure process, hundreds of cases have been reported, most of which defer to institutional judgments about the candidates. Most of the cases find that the plaintiff, whether a person of color or a white woman, does not carry the burden of proof that the institution acted in an unfair or discriminatory fashion. In those cases, such as *Scott v. University of Delaware*, 455 F. Supp. 1102 (D. Del. 1978); 601 F.2d 76 (3d Cir. 1979), the court held, "while some of this evidence is indicative of racial prejudice on the University campus, it does not suggest to me that [Professor] Scott was a victim of racial discrimination by the University in its renewal process, or that he was treated differently than [were] non-black faculty by the University." That this is so is particularly due to the extraordinary deference accorded academic judgments, as in *Faro v. New York University*, 502 F.2d 1229 (2d Cir. 1974): "Of all fields, which the federal courts should hesitate to invade and take over, education and faculty appointments at a University level are probably the least suited for federal court supervision."

Even so, occasionally an institution goes too far, as the Claremont Graduate University did in the 1992 case of *Clark v. Claremont University Center*, 8 Cal. Rptr. 2d 151 (Cal. Ct. App.). In this case, a black professor chanced upon the meeting where his tenure consideration was being reviewed. From the room, where the door was apparently left ajar, he overheard the committee making racist remarks, such as "us white folks have rights, too," and "I couldn't work on a permanent basis with a black man." When the court and jury reviewed his entire record, compared it with others who had recently been considered for (and received) tenure, and noted that no other minority professor had ever received tenure at Claremont Graduate University, it was determined that Professor Clark had been discriminated against due to his race, and he was awarded $1 million in compensatory damages, as well as punitive damages and lawyers' fees.

Women have won several cases where it was held that they were treated discriminatorily, as in *Board of Trustees of Keene State College v. Sweeney*, 439 U.S. 24 (1978); *Kunda v. Muhlenberg College*, 463 F. Supp. 294 (E.D. Pa. 1978), 621 F.2d 532 (3d Cir. 1980); *Mecklenburg v. Montana State Board of Regents*, 976 U.S. Dist. LEXIS 16624, 13 Fair Empl. Prac. Cas. (BNA) 462, 13 Empl. Prac. Dec. (CCH) P11, 438 (D. Mont. 1976); and *Kemp v. Ervin*, 651 F. Supp. 495 (N.D. Ga. 1986), among others, where courts or juries found for women faculty plaintiffs. Professor Jan Kemp particularly prevailed, winning six years on the tenure clock and over $2.5 million in compensatory and punitive damages from the University of Georgia. She left the university, at a later date, without being awarded tenure.

Later developments in employment law have made it more difficult for faculty to prevail in state and federal court, and courts have extended cases outside higher education to the college enterprise. Thus *Hazelwood School District v. Kuhlmeier*, 484 U.S. 260 (1988), a U.S. Supreme Court case about school boards' right to control editorial content in a public K–12 school setting, has been cited in college faculty cases such as *Bishop v. Aranov*, 926 F.2d 1066 (11th Cir. 1991), while *Waters v. Churchill*, 511 U.S. 661 (1994), a public hospital case that held that public employees whose speech was "disruptive" could be removed for cause, reached into a 1995 faculty case, *Jeffries v. Harleston*, 52 F.3d 9 (2d Cir.). In the latter case, Professor Leonard Jeffries, removed from his department chair position for offensive and anti-Semitic speech, had won at trial and upon appeal, but the Supreme Court remanded and ordered the appeals court to review his case in light of *Waters*. After this review, the appeals court overturned and vacated their earlier opinion. As these cases have revealed, higher education is highly contextual, and cases from a variety of other areas, such as labor and employment law, bear upon college law.

COLLEGE STUDENTS AND THE LAW

The traditional status of students relative to their colleges was that of child to parent, or ward to trustee—*in loco parentis*, literally, "in the place of the parent." This plenary power gave colleges virtually unfettered authority over students' lives and affairs. Thus, the hapless Miss Anthony of *Anthony v. Syracuse University*, 231 N.Y.S. 435 (N.Y. App. Div. 1928) could be expelled from school for the simple offense of "not being a typical Syracuse girl," which, the record reveals, meant that she could be expelled from school for smoking a cigarette and sitting on a man's lap. An earlier case, *Gott v. Berea College*, 161 S. W. 204 (Ky. Ct. App. 1913), held that colleges could regulate off-campus behavior, while later cases up until the 1970s still held that students were substantially under institutional control. The weakening of this doctrine began with *Dixon v. Alabama State Board of Education*, 294 F.2d 150 (5th Cir.), a 1961 case involving black students dismissed from a public college for engaging in civil disobedience at a lunch counter. When the court held that they were entitled to a due process hearing before expulsion, it was the first time such rights had been recognized.

The age of majority in the United States changed from twenty-one to eighteen years in 1971, and since that time, student rights have either been grounded in tort law (*Tarasoff v. Regents of University of California*, 551 P.2d 334 [Cal. 1976]) or in contract theories (*Johnson v. Lincoln Christian College*, 501 N.E.2d 1380 [Ill. App. Ct. 1986]). An area that has developed to accord rights to students has been *consumer fraud* or *deceptive trade practices* legislation. While it has been used primarily for tuition-refund or proprietary-school (for profit) cases, these have picked up momentum and in some states can provide for damage awards. For example, courts used the theory of fraudulent misrepresentations against a college in *Gonzalez v. North American College of Louisiana*, 700 F. Supp. 362 (S.D. Tex. 1988) and consumer statutes in

American Commercial Colleges, Inc. v. Davis, 821 S.W. 2d 450 (Tex. App. Eastland 1991).

Hopwood v. The State of Texas, 236 F.3d 256 (5th Cir. 2000) was the most important postsecondary affirmative-action case since the U.S. Supreme Court decision in *Regents of the University of California v. Bakke,* 438 U.S. 265 (1978), until the 2003 University of Michigan cases, which upheld the *Bakke* decision. The *Bakke* case struck down racial quotas in higher education, but allowed race as a discretionary factor in admissions. In June 2003, the U.S. Supreme Court decided two admissions cases involving the University of Michigan's undergraduate program (*Gratz v. Bollinger,* 539 U.S. 244) and law school (*Grutter v. Bollinger,* 539 U.S. 306). In *Gratz,* the Supreme Court struck down the university's use of a racial point system in undergraduate admissions by a six-to-three majority. The Court found the use of a point system was not sufficiently "narrowly tailored" to survive strict scrutiny. The University of Michigan had awarded twenty points (on a 100-point scale) to all minority applicants, and the Court ended this particular practice. However, by a five-to-four decision in *Grutter,* the Court upheld the full-file review practice of the University of Michigan Law School, which took racial criteria into account for reasons of diversity (upholding the original rationale of *Bakke*) and to obtain a "critical mass" of minority students. This opinion has become the key decision, because many schools follow the full-file review practice of the *Grutter* case, and now have the imprimatur of the Supreme Court to use race, as *Bakke* had allowed twenty-five years earlier.

In several important legal cases, faculty and student rights have come into direct conflict. *Max Lynch v. Indiana State University Board of Trustees,* 378 N.E. 2d (Ill. 1978) involved prayer in the public college classroom in which the court precluded the practice, finding that the establishment clause mandated the college discontinue the practice. Another religion case, *Bishop v. Aranov,* pitted a public university against an exercise physiology professor who invited students in his class to judge him by "Christian standards" and to admonish him if he deviated from these tenets. The appeals court held that colleges exercised broad authority over pedagogical issues, and that "a teacher's speech can be taken as directly and deliberately representative of the school." This troubling logic, which reaches the correct decision to admonish the professor, does so for the wrong reasons and rests upon the erroneous ground that faculty views are those of the institution. The court could have more parsimoniously and persuasively decided the same result by analyzing the peculiar role of religion injected into secular fields of study, especially when the teacher invites a particular religious scrutiny.

These and other cases made it clear that students have some rights in a classroom, while well-known cases such as *Levin v. Harleston,* 966 F.2d 85 (2d Cir. 1992) and *Silva v.*

University of New Hampshire, 888 F. Supp. 293 (D. N.H. 1994), have made it clear that courts will still go a long way in protecting professors' ideas, however controversial (*Levin*), and teaching styles, however offensive (*Silva*). A proper configuration of professorial academic freedom is one that is normative and resilient enough to resist extremes from without or within, to fend off the New Hampshire legislative inquiry of *Sweezy v. New Hampshire,* 354 U.S. 234 (1957) and the proselytizing of *Bishop.* In this view, professors have wide-ranging discretion to undertake their research and to formulate teaching methods in their classroom and laboratories. However, this autonomy is, within broad limits, highly contingent upon traditional norms of peer review, codes of ethical behavior, and institutional standards. In the most favorable circumstances, these norms will be faculty-driven, subject to administrative guidelines for ensuring requisite due process and fairness. Even the highly optimistic and altruistic 1915 American Association of University Professors (AAUP) Declaration of Principles holds that "individual teachers should [not] be exempt from all restraints as to the matter or manner of their utterances, either within or without the university." In short, academic freedom does not give *carte blanche* to professors, but rather vests faculty with establishing and enforcing standards of behavior to be reasonably and appropriately applied in evaluations.

If events continue as in the past, there can be no doubt that higher education will become increasingly legalized, by the traditional means of legislation, regulation, and litigation, as well as the growing areas of informal lawmaking, such as ballot initiatives, insurance-carrier policies, and commercial or contract law in research. As higher education becomes more reliant upon government support, and as colleges offer themselves for hire as willing participants in commercial ventures and as social change agents, legal restrictions are sure to follow. Understanding the consequences of legalization is an essential first step toward independence in higher education. The American higher education system is interdependent, and must adapt to the times. Timeless values, such as academic freedom, tenure, institutional autonomy, and due process, may be legislated or litigated away, and students, teachers, and university administrators need to remain vigilant and alert, and must self-police. There are many police outside the academy all too willing to do so if they do not.

SEE ALSO *Academic Freedom; Affirmative Action; Resegregation; Rights of Students; School Desegregation*

BIBLIOGRAPHY

"Appendix A. General Report of the Committee on Academic Freedom and Academic Tenure (1915): General Declaration of Principles." 1990. *Law and Contemporary Problems* 53(3): 393–406. Reprinted from *AAUP Bulletin* 1 (1915): 17.

Olivas, Michael A. 1993. "Professorial Academic Freedom: Second Thoughts on the 'Third Essential Freedom.'" *Stanford Law Review* 45: 1835–1858.

Olivas, Michael A. 2006. *The Law and Higher Education: Cases and Materials on Colleges in Court.* 3rd edition. Durham, NC: Carolina Academic Press.

Schweitzer, Thomas A. 2000. "'A' Students Go to Court: Is Membership in the National Honor Society a Cognizable Legal Right?" *Syracuse Law Review* 50: 63–107.

Michael A. Olivas

COLUMBUS BOARD OF EDUCATION V. PENICK, 443 U.S. 449 (1979)

Columbus, Ohio, public school students brought a class action suit against the Columbus Board of Education and State Board of Education, and appropriate local and state officials, alleging defendants' policies and practices had the purpose and effect of causing and maintaining racial segregation in the public schools. Ohio repealed its law mandating segregation in 1888 but schools remained segregated at the time of *Brown v. Board of Education,* 347 U.S. 483 (1954) and thereafter. "In 1976 ... at least 70% of all students attended schools that were at least 80% black or 80% white. Half of the 172 schools were 90% black or 90% white" (*Columbus Board of Education v. Penick*). The District Court found that Columbus had maintained "an enclave of separate, black schools on the near east side of Columbus" and ruled that the persistent segregation "directly resulted from [the Board's] intentional segregative acts and omissions" in violation of the equal protection clause. The court's conclusions were based upon such facts as the Board's practices of: (1) placing black teachers only in predominantly black schools (which the Ohio Civil Rights Commission stopped in 1974); (2) intentionally using optional attendance zones and discontiguous attendance areas (allowing white students to avoid attending black schools); and (3) selecting new school construction sites that had the foreseeable and anticipated effect of maintaining racial segregation. "Proof of purposeful and effective maintenance of a body of separate black schools in a substantial part of the system itself is prima facie proof of a dual school system and supports a finding to this effect absent sufficient contrary proof by the Board." It ordered a system-wide desegregation plan, including busing as a remedy. The Court of Appeals affirmed following a detailed examination of the record, except it vacated the judgment against the state defendants (that holding was not appealed).

The Board challenged the District Court's finding that Columbus schools were "officially" segregated in 1954, resulting in a system-wide dual system. School policy strongly preferred neighborhood schools, which were themselves racially identifiable.

Justice Byron White's majority opinion found "no reason to disturb" the District Court's conclusion that "the Board's purposeful discriminatory conduct and policies had current, system-wide impact—an essential predicate, as both courts recognized, for a system-wide remedy." Unlawful purpose can be inferred from evidence that state officials' conduct and practices knowingly resulted in the foreseeable and anticipated disparate impact of racially segregated schools, absent contrary proof. Chief Justice Warren E. Burger and Justice Potter Stewart concurred separately because the District Court's findings were "not clearly erroneous."

Justices William Rehnquist and Lewis F. Powell Jr. dissented, reasoning that the holding "would all but eliminate the distinction between *de facto* and *de jure* segregation and render all school systems captives of a remote and ambiguous past," "virtually every urban area in this country has racially and ethnically identifiable neighborhoods," and "the most prevalent pupil assignment policy in urban areas is the neighborhood school policy." Proof of discriminatory purpose requires more than knowledge of consequences: it must cause the harm. The distinction is important to limit federal intervention into local school boards' decision-making. Consequently, the dissenters argued, the school district did not have an affirmative duty to dismantle a dual school system because plaintiffs could not show a causal relationship between the segregation at the time of *Brown* and the current segregation.

SEE ALSO *School Desegregation*

BIBLIOGRAPHY

Jacobs, Gregory S. 1998. *Getting around* Brown: *Desegregation, Development, and the Columbus Public Schools.* Columbus: Ohio State University Press.

Sharon E. Rush

COMITY

SEE *Slavery; Story, Joseph.*

COMMENTARIES ON THE CONSTITUTION

The U.S. Constitution is an intentionally sparse document, and many of its core provisions are framed in broad, even ambiguous, language. To transform the document's structures and commitments into a set of rules sufficiently definitive to decide cases requires an elaborate process of exegesis and interpretation. Within months of the document's drafting, competing groups stepped forward to provide contrasting accounts of the Constitution's meaning and purposes. Since then, every generation has provided a new set of commentators offering their own takes on constitutional interpretation.

Much—indeed most—of the commentary on the Constitution published throughout U.S. history has met with little interest from the Supreme Court. Some of it, meanwhile, has flashed across the Court's consciousness only to disappear from sight as intellectual, cultural, and political norms have shifted. There have, however, been a handful of works that have left a lasting impression on U.S. legal doctrine and constitutional culture.

THE *FEDERALIST*: THE ORIGINAL BRIEF FOR THE CONSTITUTION

The *Federalist,* which was written before the Constitution was even ratified—is by acclamation the most important of the commentaries. Often called the *Federalist Papers,* the *Federalist* is a series of eighty-five essays originally published in New York newspapers under the pseudonym "Publius" in the months leading up to the vote for delegates to that state's ratifying convention. The essays were published anonymously, but informed observers quickly identified the authors as James Madison, Alexander Hamilton, and John Jay. The authorship of individual essays has been the subject of much scholarly speculation, but recent statistical analysis strongly suggests that Jay wrote five essays, Madison wrote twenty-nine (including many of the most important ones), while Hamilton wrote the remaining fifty-one.

The *Federalist* was crafted with the aim of securing the adoption of the Constitution by the citizens of New York, and of the nation more broadly. Despite—or perhaps because of—their immediate utilitarian purpose, the authors of the essays engaged both the substance of the document and its underlying theoretical framework in great detail. As a result, the *Federalist* is a unique literary achievement, meshing elements of a debating handbook, a learned commentary, a work of political theory, and an unofficial legislative record.

Although the substantive coverage of its essays is broad, the *Federalist* nevertheless remains tightly focused on a few key themes. First, the authors point out the weakness of the Articles of Confederation and the need for a stronger national government to tighten the bonds between the states and pursue their general interests in a hostile world. Second, they explain how, if the lessons of history are properly understood and applied to the problem of designing a government, an American republic might survive and thrive. Finally, they argue that the

drafters of the Constitution had, in fact, produced a document carefully designed to withstand the tumult of politics and the vagaries of history.

For the authors of the *Federalist,* the central virtue of the Constitution is that it divides power and authority in various ways, thereby ensuring, in Madison's famous words, that "ambition" would "counteract ambition" (*Federalist* No. 51). In *Federalist* No. 10, the most famous single essay, Madison argues that the size and diversity of the new American nation creates a fertile climate for republican liberty because those traits ensure that various local factions will constantly compete for power, and thus prevent the entrenchment of a permanent ruling majority that might tyrannize minority groups. In various essays, both Madison and Hamilton explain how the specific division of powers between the various branches of the federal government—as well as the occasional overlap between those powers—ensures that each will check the ambition of the others. To that end, Hamilton offers a spirited defense of judicial review, arguing that the proper balance between the various branches can only be maintained if the judiciary has the authority to assess the constitutionality of legislative enactments.

The authors also offer a similar, though more nuanced, explanation of how the Constitution safeguards liberty by dividing authority between the national and state governments. According to their analysis, the Constitution makes the national government potent by giving it ultimate power in its areas of competence while it also protects against federal despotism by limiting the areas in which the national government may engage. The exact borders of national governmental authority are left intentionally fluid, to be worked out over time through a process of trial, error, and electoral contestation.

The Supreme Court has cited the *Federalist* over 300 times since 1798. The frequency of citation rose dramatically in the late twentieth and early twenty-first centuries, presumably in response to the rising importance of originalist strategies of constitutional interpretation. The Court's use of the *Federalist* has varied from case to case. At times, the Court has seriously engaged the treatise's arguments, examining it for evidence of the Constitution's original meaning, and on occasion deferring to its legendary authors on close questions of interpretation. At other times, the Court has treated the *Federalist* as little more than a source of law office history, decorating and buttressing its opinions with selected quotations that are often pulled out of context. Even in cases where the Court has seriously engaged the *Federalist,* the treatise's lessons have not always been easy to discern. In an increasing number of cases, usually involving federalism or the separation of powers, justices on opposing sides have relied upon the *Federalist,* accusing each other of misunderstanding the way in which its authors would have struck the delicate balances involved in resolving a particular case.

JOSEPH STORY'S *COMMENTARIES ON THE CONSTITUTION OF THE UNITED STATES*

In 1833, the Supreme Court justice and Harvard professor Joseph Story published his *Commentaries on the Constitution of the United States*, a multivolume treatise exploring the origins of the Constitution and probing the meaning of each of its clauses and amendments. The work (and a related single-volume publication) received rave reviews, sold a comparatively large number of copies, and quickly became a standard citation for courts addressing constitutional issues. Story's *Commentaries* has been cited by the Supreme Court more than 120 times, with almost half those citations occurring since 1980. When the contemporary Court explores the original understanding of constitutional provisions, Story's *Commentaries* is cited almost as frequently as the *Federalist*. (When exploring constitutional issues, the Court also cites, though with less frequency, other texts from the Early Republic, most notably the constitutional passages in Chancellor James Kent's *Commentaries on American Law* (1826–1830) and the decidedly states-rights-oriented essay on the Constitution that Henry St. George Tucker appended to his 1803 edition of *Blackstone's Commentaries*.)

Story's commentaries are often precise, technical, and even-handed. On the other hand, Justice Story neither shies away from controversy nor makes any serious claim of neutrality on the controversial Constitutional issues of his day. His *Commentaries* is, to a great extent, an intellectual manifesto explaining and justifying the nationalist and instrumentalist constitutional vision championed—and largely actualized—by Story and his likeminded colleagues, including Chief Justice John Marshall.

For Justice Story, the primary purpose of the Constitution was to create a national government strong enough to act in the crucial areas in which the Confederation-era government was powerless. Because the central purpose of the Constitution was to create a smooth and efficient government, he believed its provisions should not be interpreted so as to put unnecessary obstacles in the path of the national government. His commentaries have little sympathy for arguments that governmental powers should be strictly construed. Story takes particular umbrage at the suggestion that, as the Constitution is a compact of states, the states remain free to interpret the document as they see fit and, if necessary, "nullify" federal laws that conflict with their interpretations. Perhaps the most striking change from the *Federalist* is one of tone: Publius's skepticism about the ability of human beings to govern themselves without violating the liberties of their countrymen is replaced by Story with an optimistic focus on the ways in which a republican government can develop the economy and serve the needs of its citizens.

Commentaries on the Constitution of the United States also marks Justice Story as a firm defender of judicial review and, more generally, as an advocate for a strong and independent judiciary. The bulk of academic commentators on Story's treatise have read Story's nationalism and his advocacy of a powerful judiciary as evidence that he saw the federal courts as a powerful bulwark against the increasingly democratic character of contemporary politics. More recent scholarship has called this point into question, pointing towards a countervailing current in *Commentaries* that recognizes the primacy of majoritarian political institutions.

THOMAS COOLEY'S *CONSTITUTIONAL LIMITATIONS*

In the years immediately following the Civil War, Thomas Cooley quickly emerged as the nation's leading constitutional commentator. Like Story, Cooley was both a judge and a legal educator. He served on the Michigan Supreme Court for twenty years, and he was a law professor and dean at the University of Michigan Law School for even longer. He wrote prolifically in a variety of fields and edited important new editions of both Blackstone's *Commentaries* and Story's *Commentaries on the Constitution*. As the editor of the first post-Reconstruction edition of Story's treatise, he drafted the chapters on the crucial Reconstruction amendments that were appended to the original text. His greatest influence on constitutional thought came through his 1868 treatise *Constitutional Limitations which Rest upon the Legislative Power of the States of the American Union*, a work that has been cited by the Supreme Court more than 120 times.

As suggested by its title, *Constitutional Limitations* is primarily a treatise on the operation of state constitutional law. Nevertheless, for both doctrinal and cultural reasons, its arguments ultimately have had broad resonance in the debate over the meaning of the Constitution. The heart of Cooley's treatise is his argument that both the texts of state constitutions (notably the "due process" and "law of the land" clauses found in almost every state constitution) and their general structures impose significant limits on the kinds of laws that states may adopt. While Cooley's constitutional theory allows for substantial state regulation in pursuit of the common good, it also calls for a serious inquiry into the question of whether particular legislation is actually designed to pursue the common good rather than the interests of a particular class or faction. Some language from the treatise also seems to suggest that a similarly searching inquiry is necessary whenever legislation deprives individuals of "liberty in particulars of primary importance."

Cooley's work had an immediate influence on state courts struggling with the legitimacy of novel forms of legislation designed to deal with the problems raised by America's burgeoning economy. When the U.S. Supreme Court began to deal with similar issues two decades later, both Cooley's treatise and the state cases relying upon it were important sources for the Court's emerging jurisprudence. During the late nineteenth and early twentieth centuries, Cooley's *Constitutional Limitations* was frequently cited in Supreme Court decisions that invalidated state statutes and regulatory actions on federal constitutional grounds. (A rival treatise that made similar but stronger arguments, Christopher Tiedeman's *A Treatise on the Limitations of the Police Power in the United States* (1886), was rarely cited by the United States Supreme Court, though it exerted substantial influence on other courts addressing similar issues.)

Given the frequency with which courts relied upon Cooley's work in cases that struck down progressive legislation, it is unsurprising that most later commentators have assumed that Cooley himself was an advocate of laissez-faire economics and of strong constitutional protections for corporate property rights. In recent years, however, several scholars have more carefully reconstructed Cooley's thinking and the legal culture from which he emerged. These commentators have convincingly argued that Cooley's arguments in favor of limited governmental power are better understood as deriving from a Jacksonian commitment to democratic equality, perhaps coupled with a nostalgic attachment to preindustrial America.

THE DECLINE OF THE TREATISE

Sometime around the turn of the twentieth century, the format of constitutional scholarship began to change. Where treatises and other forms of comprehensive monographs had once dominated, shorter, more thematic, monographs and law review articles began to hold sway. Certainly, the dominant impetus behind this shift was the invention and proliferation of student-edited law reviews, a trend that provided potential commentators with a new opportunity to publish their work relatively rapidly and at little or no cost. This new genre was particularly appealing to constitutional scholars and lawyers who were struggling to comprehend the voluminous and clearly momentous decisions emerging from the Supreme Court on a monthly basis.

The Harvard law professor James Bradley Thayer's "Origin and Scope of the American Doctrine of Constitutional Law," published in the Harvard Law Review in 1893, was the first law review article to have a lasting impact on American constitutional thought. In the article, Thayer advocates a limited vision of judicial review in which courts presume the constitutional validity of duly enacted laws, striking down only those statutes whose constitutional deficiencies are "so manifest as to leave no room for reasonable doubt" (p. 140). In staking out that position, Thayer presciently anticipated a later generation's critique of the aggressive form of judicial review championed by Cooley and Tiedeman and reflected in many of the most memorable judicial decisions of Thayer's day. Though Thayer's article has only been directly cited by the Court seven times, it has had a broad impact on constitutional analysis both on and off the Court.

During the first half of the twentieth century, the Court struggled to define the limits of both legislative and judicial power. In doing so, its members drew upon the constitutional insights of a variety of commentators but gave pride of place to none. When the Court changed course during the 1930s and repudiated many of the restrictions on state and federal legislative power that had characterized the preceding decades, its new analysis drew—(largely silently) on the work of a diverse set of court critics, including Roscoe Pound, Felix Frankfurter, Learned Hand, Ernst Freund (1864–1932), Edward Corwin (1878–1963), and Leonard Boudin (1912–1989). Perhaps even more importantly, during the late 1930s and 1940s, constitutional commentators such as Corwin and the future Supreme Court justice Robert H. Jackson played an important role in popularizing the Court's new restraint and delegitimizing the alternative vision pursued by the prior generation.

STRATEGIES OF CONSTITUTIONAL INTERPRETATION

In the last third of the twentieth century, constitutional scholars began to shift their focus away from issues of constitutional doctrine to broader questions about the appropriate methodology for constitutional interpretation. The Yale law professors John Hart Ely (1938–2003) and Alexander Bickel were important early players in these conversations. In six books, most notably *The Least Dangerous Branch: The Supreme Court at the Bar of Politics* (1962), Bickel articulates a sophisticated and nuanced argument for Thayerian restraint, explicitly encouraging the Court to balance principle and pragmatism when managing its constitutional docket. In *Democracy and Distrust* (1980), and in a series of earlier articles, Ely offers a theory of constitutional interpretation that calls for substantial deference to democratic bodies on the great bulk of issues. However, Ely also insists on a more strenuous judicial review of governmental actions that impede rights essential to the proper operation of democracy or that burden "discrete and insular" minorities.

By the 1980s, the debate over proper methods of judicial interpretation often focused on the controversial proposition that constitutional provisions ought to be interpreted solely with reference to the original intent of the framers or the original public meaning of their enactments. Justice Antonin Scalia and the law professor (and defeated Supreme Court nominee) Robert Bork were among the many thinkers who wrote significant works advocating some version of originalism. Though substantially outnumbered in the academy and on the bench, the originalists have had a profound influence on American constitutional scholarship and jurisprudence, substantially increasing the weight of historical arguments in constitutional litigation and putting advocates of other methods of constitutional interpretation at a rhetorical and political disadvantage.

THE BRIEF RETURN OF THE CONSTITUTIONAL TREATISE

In 1978 the Harvard law professor Laurence Tribe published the first volume of a treatise entitled *American Constitutional Law*. Volume Two followed in 1979, and the treatise was updated in 1988 and again, in part, in 1999. Professor Tribe's treatise is easily the most ambitious commentary on the Constitution produced in the twentieth century. Like early treatise writers, Tribe set out to cover the entire body of substantive constitutional law. Unlike earlier writers, however, Tribe organized his work thematically—around what he labeled constitutional "functions"—rather than by proceeding through the document's text provision by provision. The work rapidly gained a large audience among lawyers, judges, and academics, and it has been cited by the Supreme Court more than sixty times.

In introducing the project, Tribe set two daunting goals for himself: to provide a coherent account of the Constitution's meaning and purposes, and to put forward a vision for a more just constitutional order. While many outside observers credit Tribe with succeeding at these twin aims, the descriptive side of the project increasingly came to frustrate him as constitutional law became even more complex and divisive in the last years of the twentieth century. In 2005 Professor Tribe surprised many when he announced he was abandoning further work on the treatise. In explaining his decision, he expressed skepticism about the possibility of providing a cohesive account of contemporary constitutional doctrine. One can only speculate as to whether future constitutional commentators will take Tribe's assessment as a warning or as a challenge.

SEE ALSO *Bryce, James; Cooley, Thomas; Federalist Papers; Story, Joseph; Thayer, James Bradley*

BIBLIOGRAPHY

Carrington, Paul D. 1997. "The Constitutional Law Scholarship of Thomas McIntyre Cooley." *American Journal of Legal History* 41: 368–399.

Friedman, Barry. 2001. "The History of the Countermajoritarian Difficulty, Part III: The Lesson of *Lochner*." *New York University Law Review* 76 (November): 1383–1455.

Grey, Thomas C. 1993. "Thayer's Doctrine: Notes on its Origin, Scope, and Present Implications." *Northwestern University Law Review* 88 (Fall): 28–41.

Jacobs, Clyde E. 1954. *Law Writers and the Courts: The Influence of Thomas M. Cooley, Christopher G. Tiedeman, and John F. Dillon upon American Constitutional Law*. Berkeley: University of California Press.

Meyerson, Michael I. 2008. *Liberty's Blueprint: How Madison and Hamilton Wrote The Federalist Papers, Defined the Constitution, and Made Democracy Safe for the World*. New York: Basic Books.

Newmyer, R. Kent. 1985. *Supreme Court Justice Joseph Story: Statesman of the Old Republic*. Chapel Hill: University of North Carolina Press.

Powell, H. Jefferson. 1985. "Joseph Story's *Commentaries on the Constitution*: A Belated Review." *Yale Law Journal* 94(5): 1285–1314.

Thayer, James Bradley. 1893. "Origin and Scope of the American Doctrine of Constitutional Law." *Harvard Law Review* 7(2): 129–156.

Andrew M. Siegel

COMMERCE CLAUSE

Article I, Section 8, clause 3 of the U.S. Constitution empowers Congress "[t]o regulate Commerce with foreign Nations, and among the several States, and with the Indian Tribes." This clause, known as the "commerce clause," was included to address one of the principal gaps in the Articles of Confederation: the inability of the central government to control economic conflicts among the states. Much of the debate over the extent of federal power has revolved around conflicting interpretations of the commerce power.

The key elements in the commerce clause are the terms *regulate* and *commerce* and the phrase "among the several states." The Supreme Court addressed all three in the foundational case of *Gibbons v. Ogden*, 22 U.S. 1 (1824). Chief Justice John Marshall's opinion took an expansive approach to the commerce power, but important aspects of Marshall's reasoning contained the seeds of conflicting interpretations that continue to resonate.

GIBBONS V. OGDEN

The *Gibbons* case arose from a dispute over steamboats. Aaron Ogden had received a license from Robert Fulton, to whom the New York legislature had granted exclusive rights to operate the new type of vessel in the Empire

State. Thomas Gibbons, meanwhile, ran ferries between New Jersey and New York under a federal permit. Ogden claimed that Congress lacked the power under the commerce clause to pass the statute under which Gibbons received his permit.

The Court began by broadly defining *commerce* as "the commercial intercourse between nations, and parts of nations, in all its branches." A few pages later, Chief Justice Marshall added that the word encompassed "every species of commercial intercourse between the United States and foreign nations." Marshall dismissed Ogden's claim that he was engaged in navigation rather than commerce by observing: "All America understands, and has uniformly understood, the word 'commerce' to comprehend navigation."

The opinion turned next to the meaning of "among the several states." This wording, the Court declared, excludes "that commerce, which is completely internal, which is carried on between man and man in a State, or between different parts of the same State, and which does not extend to or affect other States." Gibbons's ferry service between New Jersey and New York thus qualified as interstate commerce, over which the federal government had regulatory authority. More important, however, Marshall's formulation allowed Congress to regulate not only commercial activities that crossed state lines, but also those activities that had interstate effects.

The Court then proceeded to define *regulate* as the power "to prescribe the rule by which commerce is to be governed." A concurring opinion by Justice William Johnson offered a somewhat different definition: "to limit and restrain it at pleasure." Nothing turned on the contrasting formulations in *Gibbons v. Ogden*, but some later cases revolved around the precise meaning of this word.

Two other issues lurked in *Gibbons*. One had to do with whether the commerce power was exclusively federal or shared between the national and state governments. Chief Justice Marshall came down on the side of exclusivity, holding that the commerce power was "plenary" in Congress and rejecting outright the notion "that a State may regulate commerce with foreign nations and among the States." In support of this latter point, Marshall explained that state inspection laws, which "may have a remote and considerable influence on commerce," do not actually regulate commerce; rather, those state measures "act upon the subject before it becomes an article of foreign commerce, or of commerce among the States, and prepare it for that purpose." This statement suggested that there might be a temporal aspect to commerce, a notion that some later cases relied on to limit the scope of the federal commerce power.

The other issue concerned the role of the judiciary in resolving disputes over the scope of the commerce clause.

According to Chief Justice Marshall, the commerce power was limited only by "[t]he wisdom and the discretion of Congress, their identity with the people, and the influence which their constituents possess at elections." In short, only the federal government had power over interstate commerce, and the Supreme Court would not second-guess congressional judgment under the commerce clause. Thus, as long as the federal government sought to regulate interstate commerce, the only check against unwise national policy was political.

FROM *GIBBONS* TO THE NEW DEAL

For more than a century after *Gibbons*, as the national economy became more complex and interdependent, the Supreme Court developed two lines of cases relating to the scope of federal power under the commerce clause. One set of decisions took a restrictive view of the commerce power, whereas the other took a more expansive approach. Ironically, both lines could draw on statements or implications of Chief Justice Marshall's expansive opinion in *Gibbons v. Ogden*.

The Court used several techniques to narrow the scope of federal power under the commerce clause. Some cases took a categorical or definitional approach, distinguishing commerce from other kinds of economic activity. For example, in *United States v. E.C. Knight Co.*, 156 U.S. 1 (1895), the Court held that manufacturing was not part of commerce. The Court ruled in this case that the Sherman Act did not apply to the Sugar Trust, which had gained control over 98 percent of the domestic sugar market, because "[c]ommerce succeeds to manufacture, and is not a part of it." Similarly, in *Carter v. Carter Coal Co.*, 298 U.S. 238 (1936), the Court held that Congress could not invoke the commerce clause to regulate mining because that activity was separate from commerce. Along the same lines, in *Hammer v. Dagenhart*, 247 U.S. 251 (1918), the Court invalidated a law prohibiting the interstate shipment of goods produced by child laborers, in part on the basis that the law regulated production rather than commerce. And to underscore the temporal point, in *Schechter Poultry Corp. v. United States*, 295 U.S. 495 (1935), the Court reasoned that the federal government could not regulate the activities of a Brooklyn-based wholesale poultry dealer because the dealer's chickens "had come to a permanent rest" in New York and were no longer part of interstate commerce.

Schechter also exemplified another technique for limiting the commerce power. The majority opinion in that case explained that the company's activities had only an indirect effect on interstate commerce, because the activities in question concerned the wages and hours of its employees and the terms and conditions under which it sold chickens in the local market. The case, therefore, differed from others in which the Court had allowed the federal government to regulate activities that had a direct effect on interstate commerce.

At times the Court also used a cramped definition of what constituted a permissible regulation. Perhaps the best example is *Hammer v. Dagenhart*, in which the Court held that a total ban on interstate shipment of goods produced by child laborers was unconstitutional because the goods themselves were neither harmful nor noxious. The ban, therefore, was simply a pretext for regulating working conditions, a power that was reserved to the states under the Tenth Amendment.

The more expansive line of decisions permitted the federal government to regulate activities that had a sufficiently direct connection to or effect on interstate commerce. Probably the leading illustration of this approach is the *Shreveport Rate Cases*, 234 U.S. 342 (1914), which allowed the Interstate Commerce Commission to set maximum shipping rates for goods shipped entirely within Texas. The Court found that the otherwise unregulated intrastate rates were sufficiently low enough to divert goods from the interstate market. Under the commerce clause, Justice Evans Hughes wrote, "Congress, in the exercise of its paramount power, may prevent the common instrumentalities of interstate and intrastate commercial intercourse from being used in their intrastate operations to the injury of interstate commerce."

Similarly, the Court sometimes upheld federal regulation under a "current of commerce" theory. In *Stafford v. Wallace*, 258 U.S. 495 (1922), for instance, the Court upheld the Packers and Stockyards Act of 1921 because the stockyards were "but a throat through which the current [of interstate commerce] flows." This language drew on similar reasoning in *Swift & Co. v. United States*, 196 U.S. 375 (1905), which upheld the application of the Sherman Act to a scheme to fix meat prices in the livestock market. Writing for the Court in *Swift & Co.*, Justice Oliver Wendell Holmes explained that "commerce among the states is not a technical legal conception, but a practical one," and that the sale of cattle in one state on the assumption that they will end up in another makes the sale part of "a current of commerce among the states."

Further, and in contrast to *Hammer v. Dagenhart*, the Court sometimes upheld bans on shipments as permissible regulations of interstate and foreign commerce. Perhaps the leading case to that effect was *Champion v. Ames*, 188 U.S. 321 (1903), which upheld a federal law prohibiting the interstate transportation of foreign lottery tickets. Other examples include *Hipolite Egg Co. v. United States*, 220 U.S. 45 (1911), which upheld a ban on the interstate shipment of adulterated food and drugs across state lines, and *Hoke v. United States*, 227 U.S. 308 (1913), which upheld the Mann Act's prohibition against transporting women across state lines for immoral purposes.

FROM THE NEW DEAL TO *LOPEZ*

As a practical matter, *Schechter* and *Carter* were the last gasp of the Supreme Court's restrictive approach to the commerce clause. Those decisions helped to precipitate President Franklin D. Roosevelt's Court-packing plan. Although the plan failed, the Court soon came down decisively in favor of the expansive view of the commerce power. Three cases between 1937 and 1942 made this clear. All of them emphasized that Congress could regulate activities that had a substantial effect on interstate commerce, even if the activities themselves could be characterized as something other than commerce, narrowly construed.

First, in *National Labor Relations Board v. Jones & Laughlin Steel Corp.*, 301 U.S. 1 (1937), the Court upheld the constitutionality of the National Labor Relations Act. The majority, in an opinion by Chief Justice Charles Evans Hughes, rejected the company's argument that the statute regulated labor relations, which was an aspect of manufacturing or production rather than commerce. Jones & Laughlin was a vertically integrated corporation with manufacturing plants in Pennsylvania, mines in Michigan and Minnesota, and limestone properties in West Virginia and Pennsylvania. It also owned railroad and shipping facilities that connected with major rail lines. The opinion declined to rely on the "current of commerce" theory, reasoning that "congressional authority to protect interstate commerce from burdens and obstructions is not limited to transactions which can be deemed to be an essential part of a 'flow' of interstate or foreign commerce. Burdens and obstructions may be due to injurious action springing from other sources." Instead, Chief Justice Hughes emphasized that the company's activities "ha[d] such a close and substantial relation to interstate commerce that their control [wa]s essential or appropriate to protect that commerce from burdens and obstructions." In other words, preventing the economic disruption that might flow from strikes and labor unrest gave Congress a legitimate basis for regulating industrial relations.

Next, *United States v. Darby*, 312 U.S. 100 (1941) upheld the minimum-wage and maximum-hours provisions of the Fair Labor Standards Act. This statute had two aspects: one prohibited the shipment in interstate commerce of goods produced by workers who were paid less than the minimum wage or employed for more than the maximum number of hours; the other directly imposed those limitations on employees who produced goods for interstate shipment. The opinion, written by Justice Harlan Fiske Stone, upheld both aspects of the law. First, while conceding that manufacturing might not itself be part of interstate commerce, Stone explained that "the shipment of manufactured goods interstate is such commerce and the prohibition of such shipment by Congress is indubitably a regulation of the commerce." It did not matter that the law sought to regulate working conditions rather than unsafe or noxious goods. These conclusions directly contradicted what the Court had said in *Hammer v. Dagenhart*, which therefore was overruled. Second, the Court ruled that Congress could directly regulate the wages and hours of employees hired to produce goods for interstate shipment because their activities "so affect[ed] interstate commerce ... as to make regulation of them appropriate means to the attainment of a legitimate end, the exercise of the granted power of Congress to regulate interstate commerce."

Finally, in *Wickard v. Filburn*, 317 U.S. 111 (1942), the Court upheld the application of agricultural quotas, even against a farmer who produced excess wheat for home consumption. Rejecting the categorical approach that described the activities at issue as production, consumption, marketing, or agriculture—as well as the direct-indirect effects approach—the opinion by Justice Robert H. Jackson focused instead on the economic effects of the statute. The supply of wheat affected the grain's price, and the statute at issue sought to stabilize market prices. This was sufficient to justify the statute under the commerce clause. Moreover, the law could be applied to an individual farmer such as Roscoe Filburn, even though his own wheat production was minuscule in relation to the overall market: "That [Filburn's] own contribution to the demand for wheat may be trivial by itself is not enough to remove him from the scope of federal regulation where, as here, his contribution, taken together with that of many others similarly situated, is far from trivial." In other words, the aggregate or cumulative impact of many individual activities could have a substantial effect on interstate commerce, and that sufficed to justify federal regulation.

Taken together, these three cases suggested that Congress possessed broad authority to regulate goods, services, persons, and activities that crossed state lines without regard to whether what was at issue could be described as production, manufacturing, agriculture, mining, or something other than buying or selling. Moreover, Congress could also regulate goods, services, persons, and activities that appeared to take place only within a single state, if those intrastate matters had a substantial relationship to or effect on interstate commerce. Over the next half-century, the Supreme Court upheld a wide array of federal regulations under this expansive approach.

For example, in *Perez v. United States*, 402 U.S. 146 (1971), the Court upheld a federal loan-sharking statute against a claim that the targeted activity was purely local in nature. Writing for an eight-member majority, Justice William O. Douglas emphasized that the law targeted a "class of activities" that Congress could rationally believe had a substantial effect on interstate commerce, even though individual loans might be purely intrastate.

Two other cases that upheld the provisions of Title II of the Civil Rights Act of 1964, which outlawed racial discrimination in public accommodations, also illustrate the broad sweep of the commerce power after 1937. In both *Heart of Atlanta Motel v. United States*, 379 U.S. 241 (1964) and *Katzenbach v. McClung*, 379 U.S. 294 (1964), the Court concluded that Congress could move under the commerce clause to prohibit discrimination, even if the primary evil being addressed was racism rather than diminished economic activity. Congress chose to rely on the commerce clause rather than its power to enforce the equal protection guarantees of the Fourteenth Amendment because a nineteenth-century ruling—in the *Civil Rights Cases*, 109 U.S. 3 (1883)—raised questions about whether the enforcement power reached purely private racial discrimination. The Supreme Court had no difficulty in upholding the 1964 measure under the commerce power.

Heart of Atlanta involved a motel that was located close to two interstate highways, was advertised extensively in the national media, and drew three-quarters of its patrons from out of state. A unanimous Court concluded that Congress had "voluminous" evidence, developed in hearings on a prior version of the bill that was ultimately enacted, that racial discrimination in public accommodations such as hotels, motels, and inns deterred African Americans from traveling. Nor was it important that the primary vice of racial discrimination was moral rather than economic: such discrimination had a substantial and negative effect on interstate commerce This was all that mattered, the Court said, because "[i]f it is interstate commerce that feels the pinch, it does not matter how local the operation which applies the squeeze."

McClung, which involved a family-operated barbecue restaurant in Birmingham, Alabama, was a bit more complicated factually because the restaurant (Ollie's Barbecue) was located some distance from interstate transportation facilities, apparently did not attract many out-of-state patrons, and obtained most of its food from within the state. Title II covered restaurants if "a substantial portion" of the food they served had moved in interstate commerce, and Ollie's Barbecue obtained about 46 percent of its meat from outside Alabama. Relying heavily on the legislative record cited in *Heart of Atlanta*, the Court found that Congress had "a rational basis" for concluding that racial discrimination by restaurants significantly affected interstate commerce. Moreover, under the aggregation principle endorsed in *Wickard*, the law could be applied to Ollie's Barbecue even if its own impact on commerce was minimal; what mattered was the overall effect of racial discrimination by restaurants.

The Court did occasionally hint during this period that there were limits to the commerce power. In *United*

States v. Bass, 404 U.S. 336 (1971), for example, the Court addressed an ambiguously drafted federal law that prohibited convicted felons from receiving, possessing, or transporting a firearm. The Court found that the government was required to prove that the firearm had moved in or affected interstate commerce, no matter how the felon gained access to the weapon. Allowing the government to prove a violation of the statute for simple possession without a showing that the gun had moved in interstate commerce might raise doubts as to the law's constitutionality. Few observers took these hints very seriously, however, because the Court consistently rejected constitutional challenges based on the commerce clause. That changed abruptly in 1995.

UNITED STATES V. LOPEZ AND BEYOND

The extraordinary deference that the Court had shown to Congress in commerce clause cases, beginning with *Jones & Laughlin*, resulted in widespread shock at the ruling in *United States v. Lopez*, 514 U.S. 549 (1995). Here, the Court struck down the Gun-Free School Zones Act of 1990 as beyond the commerce power. That law prohibited the knowing possession of a firearm in a school or within 1,000 feet of a school. The *Lopez* decision marked the first time in nearly sixty years—since the 1936 *Carter* case—that a federal law had succumbed to a challenge under the commerce clause.

Chief Justice William H. Rehnquist, writing for a five-person majority, began his analysis by recognizing that the Court's more expansive approach to the commerce power recognized "the great changes that had occurred in the way business was carried on in this country. Enterprises that had once been local or at most regional in nature had become national in scope." Nevertheless, cases approving a capacious approach to the commerce power implied the existence of "outer limits" on that power. Synthesizing the doctrine, without repudiating any of the expansive precedents, Rehnquist explained that Congress could regulate "three broad categories of activity": (1) "the use of the channels of interstate commerce"; (2) "the instrumentalities of interstate commerce, or persons or things in interstate commerce, even though the threat may come only from intrastate activities"; and (3) "those activities having a substantial relation to interstate commerce, *i.e.,* those activities that substantially affect interstate commerce."

All nine justices agreed that the Gun-Free School Zones Act could be upheld only if the law regulated activities that were substantially related to or substantially affected interstate commerce. The majority identified numerous problems with the statute.

First, the statute did not regulate an economic or commercial activity. Nor was it part of a more comprehensive economic regulatory scheme that might be undercut unless intrastate activity also came within its ambit. Instead, the case involved a high school student who had brought a handgun to school. The Court found there was no justification for using *Wickard*'s aggregation principle in a case like this.

Second, the law did not contain a jurisdictional element, or language that "might limit its reach to a discrete set of firearm possessions that additionally have an explicit connection with or effect on interstate commerce." Presumably, that gap might have been filled had Congress included language suggesting that the gun have moved in or affected commerce; the legislative branch did add a jurisdictional element to the statute the following year, but the Supreme Court has not considered a case involving the amended statute.

Third, the statute contained no legislative findings relating to the relationship between guns in and around schools and the national economy. This seemed to be an odd criticism because, as Chief Justice Rehnquist conceded, the Court has never required Congress to make findings in commerce clause legislation. Nonetheless, he noted that the presence of even informal findings would help the Court assess the measure's constitutionality.

Fourth, upholding this statute would effectively permit Congress to regulate not only violent crime but also any activities that might be related to violent crime. This would effectively give the federal government a general police power, something that the Court had repeatedly rejected.

Fifth, the government's reasoning contained no logical stopping point. If Congress could regulate the mere possession of firearms in school zones, it presumably could regulate anything at all on the theory that virtually everything is somehow related to interstate commerce. The federal government could then presumably prescribe a national curriculum for elementary and secondary schools, or perhaps even regulate such traditional state functions as family law. Upholding this statute would require the Court "to pile inference upon inference in a manner that would bid fair to convert congressional Commerce Clause authority to a general police power of the sort retained by the States."

Justice Anthony M. Kennedy, joined by Justice Sandra Day O'Connor, concurred. Justice Kennedy's concurring opinion cited additional problems with the statute. For one thing, he felt that the Gun-Free School Zones Act regulated education, a field in which states traditionally had primary authority. Moreover, the federal law dealt with a problem that the states were already addressing: more than forty states had laws limiting or prohibiting guns in and near schools, so the federal measure prevented state experimentation that might suggest the most effective methods for dealing with the situation.

Justice Clarence Thomas wrote his own concurring opinion. In his view, the "substantial effects" prong of commerce clause jurisprudence was not consistent with the original understanding of that provision. (He would reconsider the doctrine in a case in which the parties squarely presented the issue.)

Justices John Paul Stevens and David H. Souter wrote dissenting opinions, and they (along with Justice Ruth Bader Ginsburg) also joined the principal dissent by Justice Stephen G. Breyer. Justice Stevens simply observed that guns were articles of commerce and therefore subject to federal regulation under the commerce clause. Justice Souter emphasized the reasons why the Court had come to defer to congressional judgments in connection with the commerce power and lamented the majority's refusal to defer to those judgments. Justice Breyer's dissent analyzed the reasons why Congress had a rational basis for concluding that guns in and near schools had a substantial and adverse effect on interstate commerce. He appended a bibliography of 160 congressional, executive, and academic studies supporting this conclusion.

Precisely how significantly *Lopez* changed commerce clause doctrine remained unclear. The Court did not explain whether the Gun-Free School Zones Act failed because of any single problem identified in the opinions of Chief Justice Rehnquist and Justice Kennedy, in the entire list of defects, or in some combination of these. Some clarification was not long in coming, however. Five years later, in *United States v. Morrison*, 529 U.S. 598 (2000), the same five-to-four division invalidated a provision of the Violence Against Women Act (VAWA) that afforded a federal civil remedy to any person who had incurred gender-motivated domestic violence. The case was brought by a female former student at Virginia Polytechnic Institute who claimed to have been repeatedly assaulted and raped by members of the school's football team.

The *Morrison* majority emphasized several points in striking down the civil remedy. First, gender-motivated violent crime was not an economic activity. For this reason, the Court hesitated to aggregate the effects of such crimes in determining the existence of a substantial effect on interstate commerce. Second, VAWA, like the Gun-Free School Zones Act, contained no jurisdictional element. Thus, it remained unclear whether the incidents encompassed by the civil remedy had a sufficient connection to interstate commerce. Third, although Congress had made extensive findings in support of the VAWA civil remedy, those findings did not address the Court's concerns expressed in *Lopez*. Finally, allowing the federal government to regulate non-economic criminal conduct would intrude on traditional state functions and undermine important values of federalism.

Lopez and *Morrison* strongly implied that the Supreme Court meant to rein in federal authority under

the commerce clause. That impression received additional support from two roughly contemporaneous decisions that narrowly construed other federal statutes to avoid potential commerce clause problems. In *United States v. Jones*, 529 U.S. 848 (2000), the Court held that a statute making it a federal crime to commit arson of property that is used in or affects interstate commerce did not cover the torching of a residence simply because the home was insured and received utility service, both of which involve interstate commerce. Similarly, the Court held in *Solid Waste Agency of Northern Cook County v. United States Army Corps of Engineers*, 531 U.S. 159 (2001) that the Clean Water Act did not give the federal government authority to regulate seasonal ponds in an abandoned sand and gravel pit that were used by migratory birds.

There are two reasons to question how much change the Court intended to make in commerce clause doctrine. First, in *Lopez* and *Morrison* the Court sought to synthesize existing precedents rather than to overrule them. Only Justice Thomas has shown any enthusiasm for rethinking the existing rules. The other justices in the majority in these cases seem more interested in enforcing reasonable limitations on federal power than in returning to an earlier and narrower view of the commerce power.

Second, a later foray by the Court into this area upheld federal power against a powerful challenge that sought to extend the recent rulings. *Gonzales v. Raich*, 545 U.S. 1 (2005) affirmed federal power to prohibit the cultivation and personal use of marijuana for medicinal purposes as authorized by state law. Reaffirming *Wickard*, the Court held that the Controlled Substances Act permissibly reached the private possession and use of medical marijuana. The statute dealt with economic activity, and the Court held it was part of a comprehensive regulatory scheme. Justice Stevens wrote the majority opinion, which was joined by the other *Lopez* and *Morrison* dissenters as well as by Justice Kennedy, who had been in the majority in those cases. Even more significant, Justice Antonin Scalia wrote a concurring opinion that emphasized the significance of the necessary and proper clause for "substantial effect" analysis.

Despite this cautionary note, it appears that Congress now has less regulatory flexibility than it had between 1937 and 1995. Since 1995, the Supreme Court has shown more skepticism about expansive approaches to the commerce clause and less deference to federal policies that invoke the commerce power to regulate activities that have traditionally fallen within the ambit of state authority or do not address traditional economic activities.

STATE AUTHORITY UNDER THE COMMERCE CLAUSE

Although the commerce clause is phrased in terms of congressional authority, the grant of power to the federal government has implications for the extent of state prerogatives. Chief Justice Marshall addressed the issue in *Gibbons*, emphasizing that states may not regulate commerce but that they may apply rules such as inspection laws to items before they become articles of commerce. The Supreme Court has addressed state power under the so-called dormant commerce clause in a long series of cases. During the nineteenth century in particular, the Court focused on whether state regulations dealt with interstate commerce at all. More recently, as the scope of the federal commerce power has expanded, the Court has asked whether state regulations discriminate against or interfere with interstate commerce.

After *Gibbons*, the leading nineteenth-century case on state power is *Cooley v. Board of Wardens*, 53 U.S. 299 (1851), which upheld a Pennsylvania law requiring all ships using the Port of Philadelphia to use a local pilot. The Court reasoned that the statute dealt with a local problem, not one that required uniform national regulation. The opinion did not explain how to distinguish between matters of a local nature and those necessitating national uniformity, and it did not address the validity of laws that dealt with local matters but nevertheless discriminated against outsiders.

Another significant ruling that dealt with state power was *Paul v. Virginia*, 75 U.S. 168 (1868). Although notable largely for other reasons, the case upheld a state law requiring out-of-state insurance companies to receive a state license, in part on the theory that the business of insurance is not a form of commerce. For this reason, the law did not regulate interstate commerce.

More recently, the Supreme Court has focused on whether state laws discriminate against outsiders. If a law is discriminatory, it faces an almost insurmountable burden of justification. If a law is facially neutral, the Court will balance the state interests supporting the law against the measure's burden on interstate commerce.

A leading case dealing with a facially discriminatory state law that ran afoul of the dormant commerce clause is *City of Philadelphia v. New Jersey*, 437 U.S. 617 (1978). Here, the Court invalidated a New Jersey law forbidding the importation of liquid or solid waste, a measure that was adopted to preserve space in local landfills. It did not matter that the state asserted a benign purpose—environmental protection—as the basis for the restrictive law. A statute that treats an item of commerce differently based only on its place of origin will fail unless there is some other justification for the differential treatment.

The Court has taken a relatively aggressive approach to discrimination under the dormant commerce clause. For example, it has ruled that municipal ordinances that treat both out-of-staters and in-state out-of-towners less favorably than local residents are unconstitutionally discriminatory restrictions on interstate commerce. Thus, in *Dean Milk Co. v. City of Madison*, 340 U.S. 349

(1951), an ordinance requiring all milk sold locally to be pasteurized within five miles of the city limits was found to unconstitutionally discriminate against milk that was produced in other states as well as elsewhere in the state. Similarly, an ordinance requiring that all solid waste picked up in a community use the town's transfer station was found to impermissibly deprive out-of-state and out-of-town firms access to the local market (*C & A Carbone, Inc. v. Town of Clarkstown*, 511 U.S. 383 [1994]).

Some regulations that appear to be facially neutral but actually serve as a pretext for discrimination have also faced skeptical judicial review. The leading example is *Hunt v. Washington State Apple Advertising Commission*, 432 U.S. 333 (1977), which invalidated a North Carolina law forbidding the use of any grading system for apples sold in the state other than that promulgated by the U.S. Department of Agriculture. The Court held that the North Carolina law not only raised the costs for out-of-state producers seeking to sell their apples in the state, but that it also discriminated against Washington State, which had developed a grading system that was more rigorous than the USDA system and was widely accepted in the industry.

At the same time, the Court has refused to find discrimination in some state laws that disproportionately burden out-of-state actors. In *Exxon Corp. v. Governor of Maryland*, 437 U.S. 117 (1978), for example, the Court upheld a Maryland statute prohibiting out-of-state oil producers and refiners from operating retail service stations in the state, even though there were virtually no in-state producers and refiners. Similarly, in *Minnesota v. Clover Leaf Creamery Co.*, 449 U.S. 456 (1981), the Court upheld a law forbidding the sale of milk in plastic containers but allowing the sale of milk in disposable paper-based containers, a measure that favored the in-state paper industry and disadvantaged the out-of-state plastic industry.

When addressing a facially neutral, nondiscriminatory law, the Court has used a balancing test articulated in the leading case of *Pike v. Bruce Church, Inc.*, 397 U.S. 137 (1970). Here, the Court declared: "Where the statute regulates even-handedly to effectuate a legitimate local public interest, and its effects on interstate commerce are only incidental, it will be upheld unless the burden imposed on such commerce is clearly excessive in relation to the putative local benefits." Ironically, this is one of the relatively few cases in which a state law has been invalidated under this balancing test. The measure at issue, an Arizona regulation that effectively required locally grown cantaloupe to be packaged inside the state rather than at a nearby facility in California, was essentially designed to make sure that the packaging identified Arizona as the source of the fruit. This "tenuous" interest did not justify the burden on interstate commerce that the company faced: a large investment in an Arizona packaging facility.

Another example of a state law running afoul of the balancing test is *Raymond Motor Transportation, Inc. v. Rice*, 434 U.S. 429 (1978). In that case, the Court struck down a Wisconsin statute that generally excluded from state highways any trucks longer than fifty-five feet, as well as double-bottom trailers of any length. Although the state claimed that the law was a safety measure, the Court found that there was virtually no evidence that the restrictions promoted traffic safety and abundant evidence that they obstructed interstate truck transport.

There are two important qualifications to the notion that the dormant commerce clause forbids states from discriminating against or unreasonably burdening interstate commerce. First, Congress may explicitly authorize states to enact measures that discriminate against interstate commerce (see *New York v. United States*, 505 U.S. 144 [1992] and *Prudential Insurance Co. v. Benjamin*, 328 U.S. 408 [1946]). Second, under the so-called market-participant exception to the dormant commerce clause, states may favor their own citizens when they are actively engaged in a business enterprise or are dispensing public benefits, such as awarding government contracts (see *Hughes v. Alexandria Scrap Corp.*, 426 U.S. 794 [1976] and *White v. Massachusetts Council of Construction Employers, Inc.*, 460 U.S. 204 [1983]).

Underlying the dormant commerce clause cases are two basic theories. One is a political theory that states may not discriminate against or unreasonably burden interstate commerce because outsiders have no voice in state politics, and therefore cannot hold other states accountable for disrupting interstate trade. The other is an economic theory that states should not be allowed to erect artificial trade barriers that harm interstate economic activity.

SEE ALSO *Article I; Civil Rights Act of 1964; Constitution of the United States; Dormant Commerce Clause; Gibbons v. Ogden, 22 U.S. 1 (1824); Gonzales v. Raich, 545 U.S. 1 (2005); Heart of Atlanta Motel v. United States, 379 U.S. 241 (1964); Hughes Court; Katzenbach v. McClung, 379 U.S. 294 (1964); Marshall Court; New Deal and the Economy; Rehnquist Court; Substantial Effects; United States v. Lopez, 514 U.S. 549 (1995); United States v. Morrison, 529 U.S. 598 (2000); Wickard v. Filburn, 317 U.S. 111 (1942)*

BIBLIOGRAPHY

Bittker, Boris I. 1999. *Bittker on the Regulation of Interstate and Foreign Commerce.* Gaithersburg, MD: Aspen Law & Business.

Chemerinsky, Erwin. 2006. *Constitutional Law: Principles and Policies,* 3rd edition. New York: Aspen Publishers.

Eule, Julian N. 1982. "Laying the Dormant Commerce Clause to Rest." *Yale Law Journal* 91(3): 425–485.

Nowak, John E., and Ronald D. Rotunda. 2004. *Constitutional Law,* 7th edition. St. Paul, MN: Thomson West.

Regan, Donald H. 1986. "The Supreme Court and State Protectionism: Making Sense of the Dormant Commerce Clause." *Michigan Law Review* 84(6): 1091–1287.

Symposium. 1996. "The New Federalism after *United States v. Lopez.*" *Case Western Reserve Law Review* 46(3): 635–933.

Symposium. 1996. "Reflections on *United States v. Lopez.*" *Michigan Law Review* 94(3): 533–831.

Tribe, Laurence H. 2000. *American Constitutional Law,* 3rd edition. New York: Foundation Press.

Young, Ernest A. 2005 "Just Blowing Smoke? Politics, Doctrine, and the Federalist Revival after *Gonzales v. Raich.*" *Supreme Court Review* 2005: 1–50.

CASES

C & A Carbone, Inc. v. Town of Clarkstown, 511 U.S. 383 (1994).

Carter v. Carter Coal Co., 298 U.S. 238 (1936).

Champion v. Ames, 188 U.S. 321 (1903).

City of Philadelphia v. New Jersey, 437 U.S. 617 (1978).

Civil Rights Cases, 109 U.S. 3 (1883).

Cooley v. Board of Wardens, 53 U.S. 299 (1851).

Dean Milk Co. v. City of Madison, 340 U.S. 349 (1951).

Exxon Corp. v. Governor of Maryland, 437 U.S. 117 (1978).

Gibbons v. Ogden, 22 U.S. 1 (1824).

Gonzales v. Raich, 545 U.S. 1 (2005).

Hammer v. Dagenhart, 247 U.S. 251 (1918).

Heart of Atlanta Motel v. United States, 379 U.S. 241 (1964).

Hipolite Egg Co. v. United States, 220 U.S. 45 (1911).

Hoke v. United States, 227 U.S. 308 (1913).

Hughes v. Alexandria Scrap Corp., 426 U.S. 794 (1976).

Hunt v. Washington State Apple Advertising Commission, 432 U.S. 333 (1977).

Katzenbach v. McClung, 379 U.S. 294 (1964).

Minnesota v. Clover Leaf Creamery Co., 449 U.S. 456 (1981).

National Labor Relations Board v. Jones & Laughlin Steel Corp., 301 U.S. 1 (1937).

New York v. United States, 505 U.S. 144 (1992).

Paul v. Virginia, 75 U.S. 168 (1868).

Perez v. United States, 402 U.S. 146 (1971).

Pike v. Bruce Church, Inc., 397 U.S. 137 (1970).

Prudential Insurance Co. v. Benjamin, 328 U.S. 408 (1946).

Raymond Motor Transportation, Inc. v. Rice, 434 U.S. 429 (1978).

Schechter Poultry Corp. v. United States, 295 U.S. 495 (1935).

Shreveport Rate Cases, 234 U.S. 342 (1914).

Solid Waste Agency of Northern Cook County v. United States Army Corps of Engineers, 531 U.S. 159 (2001).

Stafford v. Wallace, 258 U.S. 495 (1922).

Swift & Co. v. United States, 196 U.S. 375 (1905).

United States v. Bass, 404 U.S. 336 (1971).

United States v. Darby, 312 U.S. 100 (1941).

United States v. E.C. Knight Co., 156 U.S. 1 (1895).

United States v. Jones, 529 U.S. 848 (2000).

United States v. Lopez, 514 U.S. 549 (1995).

United States v. Morrison, 529 U.S. 598 (2000).

White v. Massachusetts Council of Construction Employers, Inc., 460 U.S. 204 (1983).

Wickard v. Filburn, 317 U.S. 111 (1942).

Jonathan L. Entin

COMMERCIAL SPEECH

Within the body of First Amendment jurisprudence, commercial speech is distinguished from other forms of expression (e.g., political speech). Because commercial speech is said to be hardier and more objective than political speech, commercial speech has traditionally been accorded less First Amendment protection from governmental regulation.

WHAT IS COMMERCIAL SPEECH?

The U.S. Supreme Court has offered two competing definitions for the term *commercial speech*. In *Central Hudson Gas & Electric Corp. v. Public Service Commission of New York*, 447 U.S. 557 (1980), the Court offered a broad definition: "expression related solely to the economic interests of the speaker and its audience." But in *Board of Trustees of the State University of New York v. Fox*, 492 U.S. 469 (1989), both the Court majority and dissent adopted a narrower definition—speech that "propose[s] a commercial transaction"—identifying this definition as "the test" for categorizing commercial speech.

Neither definition is without its exceptions. Often, expressions include both commercial and noncommercial elements that are "inextricably intertwined" (*Riley v. National Federation of Blind of North Carolina, Inc.*, 487 U.S. 781 [1988]). A categorization of speech as commercial must, therefore, depend on "the nature of the speech taken as a whole."

Justice John Paul Stevens has suggested in concurrences in *Bolger v. Youngs Drug Products Corp.*, 463 U.S. 60 (1983) and *Rubin v. Coors Brewing Co.*, 514 U.S. 476 (1995) that abstract characterizations of speech as commercial or noncommercial are nonsensical. Instead, he argued that the proper focus of a First Amendment challenge to a governmental regulation of speech should be on whether the regulation at issue is directed to commercial or noncommercial activity.

THE EVOLUTION OF PROTECTION FOR COMMERCIAL SPEECH

Until 1942, the Supreme Court had not considered whether commercial speech falls within "the freedom of speech" protected by the First Amendment. In *Valentine v. Chrestensen*, 316 U.S. 52 (1942), the Court addressed commercial speech for the first time, upholding a provision of the New York Sanitary Code that prohibited the distribution of commercial or business advertising matter. In a brief opinion of a unanimous Court, Justice Owen Roberts dispatched the issue in short order:

> This court has unequivocally held that the streets are proper places for the exercise of the freedom of communicating information and disseminating opinion and that, though the states and municipalities may appropriately regulate the privilege in the public interest, they may not unduly burden or proscribe its employment in these public thoroughfares. We are equally clear that the Constitution imposes no such restraint on government as respects purely commercial advertising.

The *Valentine* Court's bright-line rule that commercial speech does not receive any First Amendment protection quickly fell into disrepute. Less than twenty years later, a concurrence penned by Justice William O. Douglas in *Cammarano v. United States*, 358 U.S. 498 (1959) referred to the *Valentine* ruling as "casual, almost offhand. It has not survived reflection." And after a series of subsequent Court opinions chipped away at the *Valentine* holding, the Supreme Court formally reversed its *Valentine* decision in *Virginia Board of Pharmacy v. Virginia Citizens Consumer Council*, 425 U.S. 748 (1976), ushering in the modern era of commercial-speech jurisprudence.

In *Virginia Board of Pharmacy*, the Court considered the constitutionality of a Virginia regulation that prohibited the advertisement of prescription drug prices by licensed pharmacists. Over the sole dissenting voice of Justice William Rehnquist, Justice Harry Blackmun wrote:

> The particular consumer's interest in the free flow of commercial information . . . may be as keen, if not keener by far, than his interest in the day's most urgent political debate. . . . Advertising, however tasteless and excessive it sometimes may seem, is nonetheless dissemination of information as to who is producing and selling what product, for what reason, and at what price. So long as we preserve a predominately free enterprise economy, the allocation of our resources in large measure will be made through numerous private economic decisions. It is a matter of public interest that those decisions, in the aggregate, be intelligent and well informed. In the end, the free flow of commercial information is indispensable.

The Court did not, however, extend full First Amendment protection to commercial speech. Justice Blackmun's opinion, as well as the concurring opinions of Justices Warren Burger and Potter Stewart, recognized that "some forms of commercial speech regulation are surely permissible." In addition to traditional time, place, and manner restrictions, Justice Blackmun suggested that the First Amendment would permit prohibitions on false or misleading advertisements. In a footnote to his opinion, Justice Blackmun stated that the differences between commercial speech and other varieties "suggest that a different degree of protection is necessary to insure that the flow of truthful and legitimate commercial information is unimpaired."

Justice Blackmun proceeded to offer two justifications for affording different levels of First Amendment protection to commercial and noncommercial speech. First, commercial speakers are presumed to know their products and their market, so there is less need to provide leeway for false speech. Second, commercial speech is economically (as opposed to ideologically) motivated, so government regulation is less likely to chill commercial speech than other forms of expression.

Further support for the Court's decision to afford lesser protection to commercial speech was offered by Justice Lewis F. Powell Jr. in *Ohralik v. Ohio State Bar Association*, 436 U.S. 447 (1978):

> We have not discarded the "common-sense" distinction between speech proposing a commercial transaction, which occurs in an area traditionally subject to government regulation, and other varieties of speech.... To require a parity of constitutional protection for commercial and noncommercial speech alike could invite dilution, simply by a leveling process, of the force of the Amendment's guarantee with respect to the latter kind of speech. Rather than subject the First Amendment to such a devitalization, we instead have afforded commercial speech a limited measure of protection, commensurate with its subordinate position in the scale of First Amendment values, while allowing modes of regulation that might be impermissible in the realm of noncommercial expression.

THE *CENTRAL HUDSON* TEST

By 1980, it was generally accepted that, although commercial speech would be protected by the First Amendment, it should receive a lesser level of protection than do other forms of expression. It was less clear, however, what analytical structure should be used to determine whether a governmental regulation of commercial speech is permissible.

In *Central Hudson Gas & Electric Corp. v. Public Service Commission of New York*, 447 U.S. 557 (1980), the Court considered the constitutionality of a Public Service Commission regulation banning the promotional advertising of an electrical utility. Striking down the commission's ban, a five-justice majority opinion penned by Justice Powell offered a four-part analytical approach to regulations of commercial speech:

1. determine "whether the [regulated] expression is protected by the First Amendment. For commercial speech to come within that provision, it at least must concern lawful activity and not be misleading";

2. determine "whether the asserted governmental interest is substantial";

3. determine "whether the regulation directly advances the governmental interest asserted"; and

4. determine "whether [the regulation] is not more extensive than is necessary to serve that interest."

Shortly after deciding *Central Hudson*, the Court interpreted the third prong of its test in *Metromedia, Inc. v. San Diego*, 453 U.S. 490 (1981). Upholding a restriction on billboard advertising, the Court recognized the need to allow legislatures some leeway to exercise judgment on how to advance legitimate interests. The following year, in *In re R.M.J.*, 455 U.S. 191 (1982), the Court revisited the fourth prong of the *Central Hudson* test, holding that government regulations on commercial speech must be "narrowly drawn" and "no more extensive than reasonably necessary to further substantial interests."

The Court continued to apply the *Central Hudson* test on a case-by-case basis until, in *Board of Trustees of the State University of New York v. Fox*, the Court considered a State University of New York (SUNY) regulation prohibiting commercial activities on campus, beyond those specifically itemized in the regulation. Writing for a six-to-three majority, Justice Antonin Scalia explained that a regulation of commercial speech would be upheld as long as there is a "reasonable fit" between the governmental interest served and the regulation designed to serve that interest. The Court thus rejected application of a strict "least restrictive means" standard, holding instead that the means of regulation need only be "narrowly tailored to achieve the desired objective."

CURRENT PERSPECTIVES ON COMMERCIAL SPEECH

Since 1990, the Supreme Court has worked to apply the *SUNY* standard to its *Central Hudson* test, but with increasing frustration over the extent to which the standard permits regulation of truthful, noncoercive commercial speech regarding lawful activities. In *City of Cincinnati v. Discovery Network, Inc.*, 507 U.S. 410 (1993), the Court addressed Cincinnati's restriction on newsrack distribution of commercial handbills but not newspapers. Finding Cincinnati's ban unconstitutional, Justice Stevens explained that differential treatment of commercial speech and noncommercial speech must be based on some distinction between the two forms of speech that is relevant to the asserted state interest, such as the prevention of commercial harm. In concurrence, Justice Blackmun urged the Court to reconsider the lesser, "intermediate scrutiny" standard, as it applies to commercial speech, commenting: "I hope the Court ultimately will come to abandon *Central Hudson*'s analysis entirely in favor of one that affords full protection to truthful, noncoercive commercial speech about lawful activities."

The Court's division over continued application of the *Central Hudson* test was made more apparent in *44 Liquormart, Inc. v. Rhode Island*, 517 U.S. 484 (1996), in which the Court unanimously struck down a Rhode Island state ban on advertisements of liquor that include reference to price, but offered four separate opinions addressing the proper analysis to be applied to governmental regulations of commercial speech. Joined in Part IV of his lead opinion by Justices Anthony Kennedy and Ruth Bader Ginsburg, Justice Stevens wrote:

> The mere fact that messages propose commercial transactions does not in and of itself dictate the constitutional analysis that should apply to decisions to suppress them.... When a State regulates commercial messages to protect consumers from misleading, deceptive, or aggressive sales practices, or requires the disclosure of beneficial consumer information, the purpose of its regulation is consistent with the reasons for according constitutional protection to commercial speech and therefore justifies less than strict review. However, when a State entirely prohibits the dissemination of truthful, nonmisleading commercial messages for reasons unrelated to the preservation of a fair bargaining process, there is far less reason to depart from the rigorous review that the First Amendment generally demands.

In separate concurrences, Justices Scalia and Clarence Thomas expressed discomfort with the *Central Hudson* test. Although Justice Scalia declined to suggest an alternative, Justice Thomas recommended a return to the reasoning and holding of *Virginia Board of Pharmacy*, asserting that nonmisleading commercial speech should be accorded the same level of protection as noncommercial speech. And the concurring opinion of Justice Sandra Day O'Connor, joined by Chief Justice Rehnquist and Justices David Souter and Stephen Breyer, recommended a stricter application of the *Central Hudson* test, placing greater emphasis on the third and fourth prongs of that analysis. Despite these expressions of discomfort with the *Central Hudson* test, a majority of the Court reaffirmed the test in *Greater New Orleans Broadcasting Association, Inc. v. United States*, 527 U.S. 173 (1999); *Lorillard Tobacco Co. v. Reilly*, 533 U.S. 525 (2001); and *Thompson v. Western States Medical Center*, 535 U.S. 357 (2002).

THE FUTURE OF COMMERCIAL SPEECH

In the beginning of the twenty-first century, the Supreme Court had declined to decide a number of cases that sought clarification of commercial speech standards, including *Trans Union LLC v. Federal Trade Commission*, 536 U.S. 915 (2002) (denial of cert.); *Borgner v. Florida Board of Dentistry*, 537 U.S. 1080 (2002) (denial of cert.); and *Nike, Inc. v. Kasky*, 539 U.S. 654 (2003) (dismissal of cert.). As a result, as of 2008, neither Chief Justice John Roberts nor Justice Samuel Alito had yet weighed in on the commercial-speech debate. The direction in which the Roberts Court will take commercial speech doctrine is thus unclear.

SEE ALSO *First Amendment; 44 Liquormart, Inc. v. Rhode Island, 517 U.S. 484 (1996); Freedom of Speech*

BIBLIOGRAPHY

Bennigson, Tom. 2006. "Nike Revisited: Can Commercial Corporations Engage in Non-Commercial Speech?" *Connecticut Law Review* 39(2): 379–450.

Brody, Steven G., and Bruce E. H. Johnson. 2004. *Advertising and Commercial Speech: A First Amendment Guide*. 2nd ed. New York: Practicing Law Institute.

Post, Robert. 2000. "The Constitutional Status of Commercial Speech." *UCLA Law Review* 48: 1–57.

Tushnet, Rebecca. 2007. "Trademark Law as Commercial Speech." *South Carolina Law Review* 58: 737–756.

Paul M. Schoenhard

COMMITTEE FOR PUBLIC EDUCATION AND RELIGIOUS LIBERTY V. REGAN, 444 U.S. 646 (1980)

The Committee for Public Education and Religious Liberty sued the comptroller (Edward V. Regan) and commissioner of education of the State of New York over a 1974 statute that directed the state to reimburse nonpublic schools (including sectarian schools) for the actual costs of complying with state-mandated standardized testing and attendance reporting. Additionally, the statute mandated state auditing to prevent abuse. The U.S. Supreme Court, applying the *Lemon* test (*Lemon v. Kurtzman*, 403 U.S. 602 [1971]) held five-to-four that the statute did not violate the First and Fourteenth Amendments of the U.S. Constitution because: (1) the statute had a secular legislative purpose; (2) its principal effect neither advanced nor inhibited religion; and (3) it did not foster excessive government entanglement with religion.

Justice Byron White wrote the majority opinion. The Court first found that the statute had the legitimate secular purpose of furthering educational standards. Second, reimbursement for the costs of administering and grading mandatory tests did not have the principal effect of advancing religion, because the tests graded by sectarian instructors contained very few subjective questions, and even these questions were state-authored, so there was "no substantial risk" of a sectarian instructor measuring a student's religious conceptions. Neither did the reporting requirements advance religion, as they were "ministerial" tasks with no ideological component. The Court explicitly rejected the argument that direct cash payments to sectarian schools are necessarily infirm simply because they free up other monies for the school to use for sectarian purposes. The Court noted, however, that such payments would be unconstitutional where sectarian instructors authored the tests and there was no effective way to ensure that the funds were used only for secular purposes, as was the case in *Levitt v. Committee for Public Education and Religious Liberty*, 413 U.S. 472 (1973). Third, the Court rejected the argument that the state's supervisory role in auditing reimbursement claims comprised excessive entanglement with religion, because the reimbursable services were "discrete and clearly identifiable." Finally, the Court found "no merit whatever" that the reimbursements at issue constituted unconstitutional political entanglement with religion that would foster discord in the community.

Justice Harry Blackmun wrote a dissenting opinion, joined by Justices William Brennan Jr. and Thurgood Marshall. The dissenters agreed that the statute served a secular purpose, but they believed it was unconstitutional for two reasons: (1) direct reimbursements to sectarian schools had a primary effect of advancing religion because, by reimbursing expenditures which would otherwise have to be paid out of a sectarian school's funds, the state freed up other funds that could be used for any purpose, creating a high risk of furthering the school's religious mission; and (2) the government auditing to ensure no reimbursement was made for religious expenditures fostered impermissible government entanglement with religion.

Justice John Paul Stevens wrote a short separate dissent based on a "more fundamental disagreement" with the Court's practice of making case-by-case decisions concerning what kinds of payments may be made to nonpublic schools. Referring to President Thomas Jefferson's famous admonition, Stevens wrote that the majority's approach threatened the "wall between church and state" that the framers had built.

SEE ALSO *Establishment Clause; First Amendment*

BIBLIOGRAPHY

Levy, Leonard W. 1994. *The Establishment Clause: Religion and the First Amendment.* 2nd edition. Chapel Hill: University of North Carolina Press.

Eliot M. Held

COMMITTEE FOR PUBLIC EDUCATION V. NYQUIST, 413 U.S. 756 (1973)

Since *Lemon v. Kurtzman*, 403 U.S. 602 (1971), the establishment clause has required that law possess a "secular purpose," not have the "primary effect" of advancing religion, and avoid excessive entanglement with religion. It has been the effect of the law—not its purpose—that is the key element, and courts have concluded that this is not "a primary effects text, but an 'any effects test'" (*Minnesota Civil Liberties Union v. State*, 224 N.W.2d 344 [Minn. 1974]). If the law has the effect of advancing religion, the Court invalidates it; it is not essential that this is the law's primary effect. The assumption that financial help to sectarian, private schools, has "the direct and immediate effect of advancing religion," and that the "primary effect" test requires only such a showing, and that laws having "only a remote and incidental effect advantageous to religious institutions" are to be upheld, were the controlling ideas in *Nyquist*.

Committee for Public Education v. Nyquist, 413 U.S. 756 (1973) concerned a New York law providing financial assistance to nonpublic schools, giving direct money grants to nonpublic schools for the maintenance and repair of school facilities and equipment. The law thus supplied funds directly to religious institutions, with the effect of advancing religion. It also provided tuition reimbursement to low-income parents of children attending nonpublic schools and tax deductions for nonpublic school tuition. The Court held that the tuition reimbursement program also failed the effects test, for the same reasons that governed the state's maintenance and repair grants.

Those challenging the law included parents of public school children, who joined with the Committee for Public Education and Religious Liberty. The law found that there was a state interest in promoting "healthy competitive and

Students praying at Mohonasen High School in Rotterdam, NY. *In 1973, the Supreme Court overturned a New York law allowing for state funding of non-public schools through tax credits, low income tuition reimbursement, and assistance with maintaining school buildings. Eventually the Court followed a less stringent requirement that funds be directed to secular activities, rather than focusing on which institutions receive funding.* © **CORBIS-BETTMANN**

diverse alternatives to public education." It concluded that any "precipitous decline in the number of nonpublic school pupils would cause a massive increase in public school enrollment and costs." The statute thus asserted "the State's right to relieve the financial burden of parents who send their children to non-public schools through this tuition reimbursement program." In an opinion dissenting in part, Justice William Rehnquist, joined by Chief Justice Warren E. Burger and Justice Byron White, contended that "tax exemptions" are properly distinguished from direct subsidies and that decisions emphasizing "the unbroken history of property tax exemptions for religious organizations" should be understood as non-binding dicta. Rehnquist concluded, moreover, that "rather than offering 'an incentive to parents to send their children to sectarian school,' . . . New York is effectuating the secular purpose of the equalization of the costs of educating New York children that are borne by parents who send their children to nonpublic schools."

Nyquist clearly presents what some call the traditional model for assessing government financial support of religion. In the 1990s, and early in the twenty-first century, the Court engineered what many perceive as a "constitutional revolution," making "a sharp break with the past," as it has greatly expanded "concepts that had previously provided for only a narrow range of financing" (Gey 2006, p. 593). The Court gradually replaced the "no aid" principle, requiring that funds only support secular activities, with the less stringent requirement that government must be neutral in its allocation of funds. It relied on the tax exemption cases, where religious institutions had long been beneficiaries of aid, and was influenced by the neutrality principle involving access by religious speakers to government property for religious speech.

SEE ALSO *Establishment Clause; Lemon v. Kurtzman, 403 U.S. 602 (1971)*

BIBLIOGRAPHY

Garvey, John. 1985. "Another Way of Looking at School Aid." *Supreme Court Review* 1985: 61–92.

Gey, Steven G. 2006. *Religion and the State.* 2nd edition. Newark, NJ: Matthew Bender.

Thomas B. McAffee

COMMON LAW

Common law is generally defined as rules and principles that are stated in the decisions of the courts rather than adopted in statutes or other forms of written authority. The rules that developed through common law are not merely based on the words expressed by the courts, however. They are, more precisely, a reflection of unwritten traditions and principles that are acknowledged in the decisions that the courts have reached. In its early history, the United States adopted the common law of England, which had developed over many centuries. In fact, although the framers of the Constitution included explicit references in the Seventh Amendment to "suits at common law" and "rules of common law," these are references to the common law of England rather than the common law of a specific state. The Supreme Court has been called upon on a number occasions in its history to determine the extent to which common law applies in the federal courts.

A common law system is clearly distinguishable from other types of legal systems, especially civil law systems, which are more prevalent throughout the world. Civil law developed primarily from the Roman law and is characterized by compilations of normative legal principles contained in various codes. Hence, the primary sources of law in a civil law system are these codes, which provide abstract legal rules that judges apply to specific disputes. In contrast to a civil law system, the customs of a common law system developed in an unwritten form, and these customs were later reflected in the decisions of the courts. Cases thus represent the primary sources of law in a common law system, whereas legislation represents the principal source of law in a civil law system. Although common law systems almost always codify parts of their law by way of statute, common law courts do not presume that a statute will apply to every situation that they will face.

The expansion of statutory law in the United States, beginning primarily in the twentieth century, altered the role of the courts. In some instances, statutes have been enacted that are in derogation of the common law, meaning that the rules that were developed in the court have been entirely superseded by subsequent statutes. In other instances, however, legislatures have enacted statutes that merely codify existing common law, meaning that the common law rules apply, at least to the extent that they do not conflict with the language of the statute. Central

The common law is not a brooding omnipresence in the sky but the articulate voice of some sovereign or quasi-sovereign that can be identified.

SOURCE: Oliver Wendell Holmes, Jr., *Southern Pacific Co. v. Jensen,* 244 U.S. 205, 222 (1917) (dissenting).

features of the common law system, including the power of the courts to established precedents, also apply when courts interpret statutes. Thus, even though the principal law that may apply to a specific case may be a statute, judicial decisions interpreting that statute may have already established a precedent that a court must follow when it applies the statute to a specific case. By comparison, judges in many civil law systems are not bound by prior precedents when rendering decisions.

Judges in the United States and other common law systems are also called upon to interpret constitutions. Constitutional decision-making generally requires the courts to define the power of the government or, more often, the limitations on the power of the government. Many of the common law traditions, including precedence and *stare decisis*, also apply in constitutional decision-making. In fact, many state constitutions declare that the common law continues to be in force in the absence of other conflicting authority. The primary difference between the development of common and constitutional law is the context of the underlying disputes. The principal basis of constitutional law is the language of the constitution, which is unique in terms of both the origin of the document and its historical context. In constitutional decision-making, courts are required to determine how the specific text of a provision applies to the action of the government, even where the specific words relate to the historical context in which those words were written. These interpretations are reconsidered periodically, meaning that constitutional law evolves as society evolves. By contrast, common law rules originated in an unwritten form long before the formation of the United States. However, these rules usually exist in an abstract form, and they can be applied without reference to the specific period of time during which they were developed.

Early in its history, the Supreme Court was called upon to determine whether, and to what extent, common law applied in the federal courts. In 1812 the Court considered a case involving the prosecution of the publishers of a Hartford newspaper for seditious libel.

The newspaper, the *Connecticut Courant*, had reprinted an article written by Barzillai Hudson and George Goodwin that accused Congress of secretly appropriating two million dollars to bribe Napoleon. Trial judges disagreed about whether the federal circuit court had jurisdiction, and the Supreme Court certified the case. Thus, in *United States v. Hudson and Goodwin*, 11 U.S. 32 (1812) the Court addressed the question of whether the federal courts could exercise common law jurisdiction over criminal cases. In a short opinion by Justice William Johnson, the Court ruled that in the absence of a federal statute conferring such authority, federal courts had no such power. This decision has stood for the principle that criminal law must be based on statutes, and that no federal common law of crimes exists.

Two decades after *Hudson*, in *Wheaton v. Peters*, 33 U.S. 591 (1834) the Court determined that "there can be no common law of the United States" and that "[t]here is no principle which pervades the union and has the authority of law that is not embodied in the Constitution or laws of the union." Nevertheless, in *Swift v. Tyson*, 41 U.S. 1 (1842) the Court ruled that in the absence of an applicable state statute to a particular dispute, federal courts could decide cases on the basis of general principles and doctrines of commercial law without regard to the previous decisions of the courts in the state where the dispute arose. Justice Joseph Story apparently believed that the development of federal common law for commercial disputes would provide uniformity, due to the fact that the different states varied in their development of commercial law. However, the decision had the opposite effect. Federal courts developed their own rules that often conflicted with their state court counterparts, creating a situation in which a party to a contract might not know what law applied to an agreement until it was known whether the dispute would be litigated in state or federal court.

Nearly a century after the decision in *Swift*, the Court reconsidered the issue in *Erie Railroad Co. v. Tompkins*, 304 U.S. 64 (1938). *Erie* arose as a personal injury case when the plaintiff, Harry Tompkins, was injured by a train while walking along a path adjacent to a railroad track in Pennsylvania. Tompkins brought suit in a New York court, knowing that he would lose the case under Pennsylvania law. The basic question for the Supreme Court in the case was whether a federal court should apply the federal common law doctrine or whether it should apply the law of the state where the accident had occurred. The Court recognized that the decision in *Swift* had actually increased the practice of forum shopping because parties would litigate extensively to determine whether a case should be decided in state or federal court, with each party arguing for the venue that had the most favorable common law rulings. The court in *Erie* determined that the decision in *Swift* had in fact violated the Tenth Amendment because it effectively removed powers reserved to the states. Following *Erie*, federal courts sitting in diversity generally apply state common law rules. In the absence of such rules, federal courts attempt to anticipate how the state courts might rule on a specific issue.

Notwithstanding *Erie*, a federal common law does exist in some areas. For instance, in *Textile Workers Union v. Lincoln Mills*, 353 U.S. 448 (1957) the Court ruled that the Labor Management Relations Act of 1947 allowed federal courts to create common law pertaining to collective bargaining agreements. Likewise, in *Illinois v. City of Milwaukee*, 406 U.S. 91 (1972) the Court construed the Federal Water Pollution Control Act (the Clean Water Act) to permit the development of federal common law to apply to environmental pollution. In some contexts, such as antitrust law, federal statutes are written in such broad terms that cases interpreting these statutes have effectively established a federal common law in the areas governed by those statutes.

SEE ALSO *English Constitutionalism; Precedent; Stare Decisis*

BIBLIOGRAPHY

Field, Marsha A. 1986. "Sources of Law: The Scope of Federal Common Law." *Harvard Law Review* 99(5): 881–984.

Rowe, Gary D. 1992. "The Sounds of Silence: *United States v. Hudson & Goodwin*, The Jeffersonian Ascendancy, and the Abolition of Federal Common Law Crimes." *Yale Law Journal* 101(4): 919–948.

Strauss, David A. "Common Law, Common Ground, and Jefferson's Principle." *Yale Law Journal* 112(7): 1717–1755.

Tidmarsh, Jay, and Brian J. Murray. 2006. "A Theory of Federal Common Law." *Northwestern University Law Review* 100(2): 585–654.

Matthew C. Cordon

COMMUNIST PARTY

SEE *Cold War; Dennis v. United States, 341 U.S. 494 (1951).*

COMPARATIVE CONSTITUTIONAL LAW

Comparative constitutional law—the systematic study of constitutional law, jurisprudence, and institutions across polities—has enjoyed a certain renaissance since the mid-1980s. From a relatively obscure and exotic subject studied by the devoted few, comparative constitutionalism has emerged as one of the more fashionable subjects in

A supporter of imprisoned Kurdish separatist leader Abdullah Ocalan, outside the European Court of Human Rights in Strasbourg, Germany, June 9, 2004. In recent years, comparative studies of the constitutional systems in different countries has become a popular field of research, with scholars examining the similarities and differences between legal systems around the world. Consequently, many judicial bodies, including the U.S. Supreme Court, have begun using rulings from other countries to support domestic decisions. ©
VINCENT KESSLER/REUTERS/CORBIS

contemporary constitutional jurisprudence and legal scholarship.

THE RISE OF COMPARATIVE CONSTITUTIONAL LAW

Constitutional courts worldwide increasingly rely on comparative constitutional law to frame and articulate their own position on a given constitutional question. Indeed, "constitution interpretation across the globe is taking on an increasingly cosmopolitan character, as comparative jurisprudence comes to assume a central place in constitutional adjudication" (Choudhry 1999, p. 820). This phenomenon is particularly evident with respect to constitutional rights jurisprudence. In its landmark ruling determining the unconstitutionality of the death penalty (*S v. Makwanyane*, 1995 [3] SA 391 [CC]), the South African Constitutional Court examined in detail pertinent jurisprudence from Botswana, Canada, Germany, Hong Kong, Hungary,

India, Jamaica, Tanzania, the United States, Zimbabwe, the European Court of Human Rights, and the United Nations Committee on Human Rights. Even the U.S. Supreme Court—perhaps the last bastion of parochialism among the world's leading constitutional courts—has joined the comparative reference trend. In two cases—*Lawrence v. Texas*, 539 U.S. 558 (2003), and *Roper v. Simmons*, 543 U.S. 551 (2005)—the Court's majority opinion cited foreign judgments in support of its decision.

Another manifestation of the global convergence of constitutional law and jurisprudence is the emergence of what may be termed "generic constitutional law"—a supposedly universal, Esperanto-like discourse of constitutional adjudication and reasoning, primarily in the context of core civil rights and liberties (Law 2006). This has been accompanied by the rise of "proportionality" as the prevalent interpretive method in comparative constitutional adjudication (Beatty 2004). This interpretive method—commonly drawn upon throughout the world of new constitutionalism—is based on judicious, pragmatic balancing of competing claims, rights, and policy considerations, as opposed to various more principled approaches to constitutional interpretation commonly used in the United States.

Comparative constitutional law is often used for purposes of self-reflection through analogy, distinction, and contrast. The underlying assumption here is that whereas most relatively open, rule-of-law polities essentially face the same set of constitutional challenges, they may adopt quite different means or approaches for dealing with these challenges. By referring to the constitutional jurisprudence and practices of other presumably similarly situated polities, scholars and jurists might be able to gain a better understanding of the set of constitutional values and structures in their own sets of constitutional values. These references also enrich, and ultimately advance, a more cosmopolitan or universalist view of constitutional discourse. At a more concrete level, constitutional practices in a given polity might be improved by emulating certain constitutional mechanisms developed elsewhere. Likewise, comparative constitutional law has been offered as a guide to constructing new constitutional provisions and institutions, primarily in the context of "constitutional engineering" in the postauthoritarian world or in ethnically divided polities (see, e.g., Tushnet 1999, 2006).

The international migration of constitutional ideas has not gone unnoticed in the legal academia. Scholarly books and monographs dealing with comparative constitutional law are no longer considered a rarity (e.g., Jacobsohn 2003; Hirschl 2004; Tushnet 2007). Entire textbooks (e.g., Jackson and Tushnet 2006) are now devoted exclusively to comparative constitutional law, or draw upon selected comparative constitutional jurisprudence to highlight distinct characteristics of American constitutional law. More edited collections than ever before deal with various aspects of constitutionalism beyond the United States (e.g., Choudhry 2006; Goldsworthy 2006). New periodicals (e.g., *International Journal of Constitutional Law*) and symposia are devoted to the study of comparative constitutional law (e.g., Eisgruber and Hirschl 2006).

Top-ranked law schools now regard courses on comparative constitutional law as essential additions to the curriculum. A notable example is Harvard Law School, one of the world's foremost schools of law, which in 2006 embarked on a major curriculum overhaul—the most significant revision to the formative first-year course of study in over one hundred years—with the aim of introducing its students to a distinctly more cosmopolitan, comparatively informed, view of constitutional law and legal institutions. While certain foundational ontological, epistemological, and methodological questions concerning

the field's purpose, scope, and nature remain largely unanswered (e.g., Hirschl 2006), there is no doubt that this is the heyday for comparative constitutional law scholars.

One of the main reasons for the revival is the global convergence to constitutional supremacy—a concept that has long been a major pillar of American political order, and that is now shared, in one form or another, by over one hundred countries across the globe. Numerous postauthoritarian regimes in the former Eastern Bloc, Latin America, Asia, and parts of Africa have been quick to endorse principles of modern constitutionalism upon their transition to democracy. From Germany and Spain to Russia and Turkey, constitutional courts throughout Europe have become important translators of constitutional provisions into practical guidelines for use in public life. The 1996 South African constitution and the South African Constitutional Court have become symbols of postapartheid renewal in that country. Even countries such as Britain, Canada, Israel, and New Zealand—not long ago described as the last bastions of Westminster-style parliamentary sovereignty—have rapidly embarked on the global trend toward constitutionalization. Most of these countries also have more recently adopted constitutions, or have undergone a constitutional revision in order to incorporate a bill of rights and introduce some form of active judicial review.

Armed with these newly acquired judicial review procedures, national high courts worldwide have frequently been asked to resolve a range of issues, varying from the scope of expression and religious liberties, equality rights, privacy, and reproductive freedoms, to public policies pertaining to criminal justice, property, trade and commerce, education, immigration, labor, and environmental protection. Bold newspaper headlines reporting on landmark court rulings concerning hotly contested issues—same-sex marriage, limits on campaign financing, and affirmative action, to give a few examples—have become a common phenomenon. This is evident in the United States, where the legacy of active judicial review marked its bicentennial anniversary in 2003; the U.S. courts have long played a significant role in policymaking. And it is just as evident in younger constitutional democracies that have more recently established active judicial review mechanisms.

Constitutional courts the world over have also begun to scrutinize the "process-light" measures adopted by governments to combat terrorism in the so-called war on terror. Courts have also become entangled with explicitly political issues, ranging from electoral outcomes and legitimation of regime change to foundational restorative justice and collective-identity quandaries (Hirschl 2008). Meanwhile, the jurisprudence of a few quasi-constitutional supranational tribunals, most notably the European Court of Justice (the apex court of the European Union) and the European Court of Human Rights (the top judicial organ of the Council of Europe), now carries tremendous symbolic weight.

Most written constitutions adopted after World War II (1939–1945) feature five main elements: (1) provisions that establish the principal institutions of government, define their prerogatives and the relationship among them, and establish rules and procedures for their renewal; (2) provisions that establish the distribution of governmental powers over the polity's territory (different in unitary versus federal or otherwise multilayer polities); (3) a catalogue of protected rights and liberties of the polity's citizens and residents; (4) an amendment formula that allows for the possibility of amending the constitution, and states the conditions such amendments must meet; and finally (5) provisions that establish a relatively independent judiciary armed with the authority to review executive practices, administrative decrees, and laws enacted by legislatures, and to declare these unconstitutional on the grounds that they conflict with fundamental principles protected by the constitution. Certain written constitutions elaborate in great detail on each of these five elements. Other constitutions are relatively short, and feature generic statements or broad wording.

Despite the spread of constitutional supremacy, there remain some notable differences between American-style constitutional law and constitutional law in other countries. These differences reflect the wide variations in constitutional legacies and structures, historical inheritances, and formative experiences, as well as nontrivial differences in the value systems of America, Europe, and other foreign jurisdictions. Some of these differences are obvious. Whereas the U.S.-established legacy of constitutionalism and active judicial review has passed its bicentennial anniversary, most of the written constitutions of other countries were adopted (or rewritten) in the post–World War II era. As a result, the sheer size and scope of what may be defined as "American constitutional law" is notably larger than the perimeters of constitutional law in most other polities. While the constitution of the United States is written, entrenched, and contained in one document, the constitutions of other countries (e.g., Britain) still include significant unwritten components (e.g., constitutional conventions and common practices), or comprise a bundle of pertinent laws and documents (e.g., Canada or Israel). The constitutional law of yet other countries (e.g., Australia or New Zealand) includes significant written, albeit non-entrenched, components.

There are also pertinent differences in constitutional cultures across countries. The U.S. Constitution (most notably the Bill of Rights) and the U.S. Supreme Court have long enjoyed a near-sacred position in American political and civic culture. "For the past two centuries," argues one astute observer, "the Constitution has been as

central to American political culture as the New Testament was to medieval Europe. Just as Milton believed that 'all wisdom is enfolded' within the pages of the Bible, all good Americans, from the National Rifle Association to the ACLU, have believed no less of this singular document" (Lazare 1998, p. 21). By contrast, in many young constitutional democracies, the constitutional courts still struggle to establish their status and authority in an often-volatile, wider political context, while the constitution itself is in many respects a "work-in-progress."

Constitutional jurisprudence in the United States tends to be elaborate, and often involves sophisticated reasoning alongside detailed reference to pertinent precedents and constitutional history. Nuanced approaches to constitutional interpretation (e.g., textualism, consensualism, originalism, structuralism, doctrinalism, minimalism, or pragmatism) have been developed and debated. The judges' individual opinions (and ideological profiles more generally) are considered important and are studied carefully. Concurring and dissenting opinions, not merely majority opinions, often carry significant weight. In other countries, most notably in continental Europe and Latin America (mainly civil law systems), constitutional courts tend to speak with a single, unanimous voice. Little or no attention is paid to judges' individual preferences and attitudinal tilts. Constitutional jurisprudence in these countries is often more straightforward, technical, and formalist, with far less frequent manifestations of interpretive sophistication or other "philosopher-king-like" aspects of judging that have come to characterize American constitutional law.

MODELS OF JUDICIAL REVIEW

Important distinctions also exist between the models of judicial review employed by leading constitutional democracies. These differences have significant implications for the scope and nature of judicial review in these countries. To begin with, there is the distinction between *a priori* and *a posteriori* review, and the distinction between *abstract* and *concrete* review. The former refers to whether the constitutionality of a law or administrative action is determined before or after it takes effect. The latter refers to whether a declaration of unconstitutionality can be made in the absence of an actual case or controversy, in other words, hypothetical "what if" scenarios (*abstract* review), or only in the context of a specific legal dispute (*concrete* review).

In the United States, only a posteriori judicial review is allowed. Judicial review of legislation—whether exercised by lower courts or by the Supreme Court—is a power that can only be exercised by the courts within the context of concrete adversary litigation; that is, when the constitutional issue becomes relevant and requires resolution in the decision of the case. By contrast, in France, judicial review is limited to an a priori or abstract judicial review. The Conseil Constitutionnel has only pre-enactment constitutional review powers. The principal duty of the council has been to control the constitutionality of legislative bills passed by Parliament but not yet promulgated by the president of the Republic. Unlike many of its counterpart institutions worldwide, the French Conseil Constitutionnel has no power to nullify a law after it has been enacted by the legislature.

A number of leading democracies feature combined a priori/a posteriori, abstract *and* concrete review systems, which effectively blur the distinct public policy effects of each of these models. Judicial review in Canada, for example, is not limited to review within the context of concrete adversary litigation. The reference procedure allows both the federal and provincial governments in Canada to refer proposed statutes or even questions concerning hypothetical legal situations to the Supreme Court or the provincial courts of appeal for an advisory (abstract) opinion on their constitutionality. A system that permits a priori and abstract review would appear to have a greater potential for generating high levels of judicialized policymaking using the process of constitutional review. Apex courts in such countries could paralyze a statute, or a significant portion of it, before it was formally enacted on the basis of hypothetical constitutional arguments about its effect. Moreover, unlike in the United States, most a priori and abstract review models allow public officials, legislators, cabinet members, and heads of state to initiate judicial scrutiny of proposed laws and hypothetical constitutional scenarios, thereby providing a constitutional framework that is prima facie more hospitable to the judicialization of politics and public policymaking.

Another important distinction is between *decentralized* (all courts) and *centralized* (constitutional court) review. The United States employs a decentralized system of judicial review; almost all courts—state courts, federal courts, and, of course, the Supreme Court—have the power of judicial review of constitutionality, which in this system can be exercised over all acts of Congress, state constitutions and statutes, as well as acts of the executive and the judiciary itself. Even the constitutional validity of treaties and legislation based on treaties may be the subject of judicial inquiry. In short, according to the decentralized system, judicial review is an inherent competence of all courts in any type of case or controversy.

The centralized judicial review system (often referred to as *constitutional review*), in contrast, is characterized by having only a single state organ (a separate judicial body in the court system or an extrajudicial body) acting as a constitutional tribunal. This model of judicial review has been adopted by many European countries that follow one of the various branches of the civil law tradition (such as Germany, Austria, Italy, and Spain), as well as by

almost all of the new democracies in postcommunist Europe. In Germany, for example, a separate judicial body—the Federal Constitutional Court—fulfills the sole function of constitutional review. Its jurisdiction includes interpreting the Basic Law in disputes between parties with rights vested under it, settling public law disputes between the federation and the states and between and within the states, and settling election disputes.

Some new constitutionalism countries employ a combined decentralized/centralized model of judicial/constitutional review. The decentralized elements of the Portuguese constitution, for example, require all the courts of the country to refrain from applying unconstitutional provisions or principles. Statutes, decrees, executive regulations, and regional or any other state acts are thereby subject to review by the courts. Since this ability is given as a judicial duty, the courts have *ex officio* power to raise constitutional questions. Issues can also be raised by a party in a concrete case or by the public prosecutor. Parallel with the decentralized system of judicial review, the Portuguese constitution has also established a centralized system that can review both enacted and proposed legislation. The Portuguese Constitutional Court exercises a preventative control over constitutionality with regard to international treaties and agreements, and other laws when so requested by the president of the Republic. The constitutionality of enacted legislation can also be the object of abstract scrutiny by the Constitutional Court.

Another important structural aspect of judicial review is the question of standing (*locus standi*) and access rights: who may initiate a legal challenge to the constitutionality of legislation or official action, and at what stage of the process a given polity's apex court may become involved. In the United States, "standing rights" have been traditionally limited to individuals who claim to have been affected by allegedly unconstitutional legislation or an official action. The U.S. Supreme Court will not hear a challenge to the constitutionality of legislation unless all other possible legal paths and remedies have been exhausted. Moreover, the Court has full discretion over which cases it will hear. Its docket therefore consists of *discretionary leave* cases rather than appeals by right.

In contrast, countries that employ a priori and abstract judicial review allow for, and even encourage, public officials and political actors to challenge the constitutionality of proposed legislation. Several countries even authorize their constitutional court judges, in an *ex-officio* capacity, to initiate proceedings against an apparently unconstitutional law. Other countries (South Africa, for example) impose mandatory referrals of constitutional questions by lower courts to a constitutional tribunal. Yet other countries (Israel, India, Hungary, and Germany, for example) allow private-person constitutional grievances to be submitted directly to their respective high courts, effectively recognizing the standing rights of public petitioners and lowering the barrier of nonjusticiability.

Constitutional Limitations to Rights and Liberties An interesting feature of constitutional law in an increasing number of new constitutionalism countries is the existence of innovative mechanisms designed to address and mitigate the tension between rigid constitutionalism and judicial activism on the one hand, and fundamental democratic governing principles on the other. The Canadian Charter of Rights and Freedoms, for example, contains an explicit limitation clause (section 1), which states that the rights protected by the Charter are subject to "such reasonable limits prescribed by law as can be demonstrably justified in a free and democratic society." In other words, the government must establish to the satisfaction of the courts that the limiting of rights can be justified in a free and democratic society. Another significant limitation to rights and freedoms lies in the Canadian Charter's section 33—the famous *notwithstanding clause*. This clause enables elected politicians, in either the federal Parliament or the provincial legislatures, to legally limit rights and freedoms protected by section 2 (fundamental freedoms) and sections 7 to 15 (due process and equality rights) of the Canadian Charter by passing a renewable overriding legislation valid for a period of up to five years. This means that any invocation of section 33 essentially grants parliamentary fiat over these rights and freedoms. In theory, therefore, both the federal Parliament (with regard to related federal matters) and the provincial legislatures (with regard to related matters within provincial jurisdictions) are ultimately sovereign over these affairs. In practice, however, section 33 lacks wide public legitimacy.

Like the Canadian Charter, two of Israel's Basic Laws, which protect a number of fundamental rights and liberties, contain a limitation clause forbidding infringement of the declared rights, "except by a statute that befits the values of the State of Israel, for a worthy purpose, and not exceeding what is necessary." In 1994 Israel's "Basic Law: Freedom of Occupation" was amended by the Knesset in the spirit of the Canadian *notwithstanding* override clause to allow for future modifications by ordinary laws in the instance of an absolute majority of Knesset members declaring support for the amendment. Similarly, the rights protected by the 1996 South African constitution are fully entrenched, but are subject to a general limitations clause, section 36(1), which is largely modeled upon similar provisions in other international human-rights texts and national bills of rights.

Another innovative mechanism for mitigating the tension between judicial review and parliamentary supremacy may be called the *preferential* model of judicial review. Here, preference is given to legislation or a court judgment that is consistent with the bill of rights over legislation or a court judgment that is not; it also instructs legislators to avoid enacting laws that contradict, prima facie, constitutional provisions protecting basic rights. This model allows for a limited judicial review, at the same time respecting the country's parliamentary tradition.

The British Human Rights Act (1998), which came into effect in October 2000, is just such an example. The act effectively subjects British public bodies to the provisions of the European Convention on Human Rights (ECHR). The act requires the courts to interpret existing and future legislation as far as possible in accordance with the convention. If the higher courts in Britain decide that an act of Parliament curtails someone's rights under the ECHR, judges make what is termed a *declaration of incompatibility*. Such a declaration would put ministers under political pressure to change the law (or so it is hoped). Formally, the convention does not override existing acts of Parliament; however, ministers must state whether each new piece of legislation that they introduce complies with the ECHR. What is more, the act also provides for a fast-track procedure that allows Parliament to repeal or amend legislation found to be incompatible with the ECHR.

VARIANCE IN CONSTITUTIONAL LAW ACROSS COUNTRIES

To a large extent, variance in constitutional law across countries reflects differences in constitutional models and priorities. Constitutions vary considerably with respect to organic features of government and state institutions (e.g., unitary versus federal polities, presidentialism versus parliamentarism, unicameral versus bicameral legislature, proportional representation versus first-past-the-post electoral systems, and so on). The scope and nature of constitutional law defining legislative boundaries between state organs vary accordingly. And there are notable differences with respect to the (generally more uniform) rights aspect as well. Granted, due process rights, most classic civil liberties, and formal equality are protected by the vast majority of the world's modern constitutions. But the picture is different when it comes to religion and state, to pick merely one notable example. Whereas several leading Western democracies (e.g., the United States or France) adhere to a strict separation of religion and state model, in other countries, a certain religion is designated as a *state church* (e.g., Evangelical Lutheranism in Norway, Denmark, and Finland). Countries such as India, Israel, or Kenya grant recognized religious and customary communities the jurisdictional autonomy to pursue their own traditions in several areas of law, most notably in matters of personal status. In yet other countries (e.g.,

Egypt or Pakistan), the constitution enshrines a specific religion, and its texts, directives, and interpretations, as *a* or *the* main source of legislation and judicial interpretation of laws; laws may not infringe upon injunctions of the state-endorsed religion. Accordingly, the constitutional law of state and religion in these countries differs greatly from that of the United States.

Whereas social welfare rights have never gained real political momentum in the United States, such rights are protected by the constitutions of countries such as India and Brazil. A new form of social welfare protection is advanced in the 1996 South African constitution. Among its catalogue of rights, the constitution explicitly protects positive social and economic rights, such as the right to housing (section 26), the right to health care, food, water, and social security (section 27), and the right to education (section 29). None of these positive rights provisions, however, imply a right to housing, health care, or education per se; instead, they merely ensure that reasonable state measures are taken to make further housing, healthcare, and education progressively available and accessible.

Whereas no group or collective rights are directly protected by the American Constitution, or have been unequivocally protected by the U.S. Supreme Court, several categories of such rights—language rights, the rights of indigenous peoples, a constitutional shield for affirmative action programs, and environmental rights—are an integral part of constitutional law in several leading constitutional democracies (e.g., language rights in Belgium, Canada, and Spain; provisions protecting certain rights of indigenous populations in Canada, Mexico, and New Zealand, etc.). Likewise, there is considerable difference between constitutions in established democracies and in new democracies in the realm of transitional justice. From postauthoritarian regimes in Latin America to the postcommunist world, constitutional law and courts have become key arenas for dealing with the polity's less-than-dazzling past.

Some of the differences in constitutional law across countries stem from variance in judicial interpretation. Section 7 of the Canadian Charter of Rights and Freedoms reads: "Everyone has the right to life, liberty, and security of the person and the right not to be deprived thereof except in accordance with the principles of fundamental justice." Section 21 of the Constitution of India reads: "No person shall be deprived of his life or personal liberty except according to procedure established by law." Despite the near identical wording of these provisions, they have been interpreted in very different ways with respect to the constitutional protection of subsistence rights. Such rights are appreciated in Canadian public discourse, but have been consistently pushed beyond the purview of section 7 by the Supreme Court

of Canada. India, by contrast, features vast socioeconomic gaps; yet its Supreme Court has consistently declared claims for subsistence social rights justiciable and enforceable through constitutional litigation that draws on section 21.

Finally, a controversial constitutional issue in one polity (e.g., affirmative action in the United States) may be a nonissue in another polity. And a certain issue may be framed differently in different polities. For example, reproductive freedom may be framed mainly as a clash of rights (e.g., in the United States), as a reflection of the status of the historically influential church (e.g., in Poland), or as a conflict between national preferences and supranational norms (e.g., the compatability of Irish abortion laws with provisions of the European convention of human rights).

AMERICAN EXCEPTIONALISM?

The proliferation of constitutionalism and comparative constitutional law has gradually eroded the status of American constitutional law as the ultimate source for constitutional borrowing. The groundbreaking ideas of the American founding fathers are still studied widely worldwide. The limitation of government powers and protection of fundamental civil liberties by the American Constitution are still considered the quintessential example of modern constitutionalism. Famous figures of American constitutional theory—for example, Alexander Bickel, John Hart Ely (1938–2003), and Ronald Dworkin (1931–)—still comprise much of what is considered the global canon of constitutional theory and interpretation. The legacy of the Warren Court era remains widely admired worldwide; *Brown v. Board of Education*, 347 U.S. 483 (1954) is still considered a constitutional event of near-mythical proportion.

However, the prime status of American constitutionalism has given way to a more balanced, multisource enterprise of comparative constitutional law. The constitutional law and practice of countries such as Germany, Canada, or South Africa are increasingly used as a source of inspiration for jurists worldwide. What is more, less-than-dazzling chapters in American constitutional history, from the *Dred Scott v. Sandford*, 60 U.S. 393 (1856), *Plessy v. Ferguson*, 163 U.S. 537 (1896), *Lochner v. New York*, 198 U.S. 45 (1905), and *Korematsu v. United States*, 323 U.S. 214 (1944) rulings to the Clarence Thomas congressional hearings in 1991 and the *Bush v. Gore*, 531 U.S. 98 (2000) courtroom struggle over the American presidency are commonly referred to—in the world of new constitutionalism—as examples of constitutional failure. More often than not, jurists draw explicit distinctions and seek to distinguish these and other less-than-glorious episodes in American constitutional history as a means for justifying or improving their own polity's constitutional practices. In short, American exceptionalism, all too common in other contexts, has gradually become the dominant approach in comparative constitutional law around the globe.

SEE ALSO *Citations to Foreign Sources; Constitutional Interpretation; Constitutional Theory; Judicial Pragmatism; Judicial Review; Lawrence v. Texas, 539 U.S. 558 (2003); Originalism; Positive Rights; Structuralism; Textualism*

BIBLIOGRAPHY

Beatty, David M. 2004. *The Ultimate Rule of Law.* New York: Oxford University Press.

Choudhry, Sujit. 1999. "Globalization in Search of Justification: Toward a Theory of Comparative Constitutional Interpretation." *Indiana Law Review* 74: 820–891.

Choudhry, Sujit, ed. 2006. *The Migration of Constitutional Ideas.* New York: Cambridge University Press.

Eisgruber, Christopher L., and Ran Hirschl, eds. 2006. "Symposium: North American Constitutionalism." *International Journal of Constitutional Law* 4: 203–437.

Goldsworthy, Jeffrey. ed. 2006. *Interpreting Constitutions: A Comparative Study.* New York: Oxford University Press.

Hirschl, Ran. 2004. *Towards Juristocracy: The Origins and Consequences of the New Constitutionalism.* Cambridge, MA: Harvard University Press.

Hirschl, Ran. 2006. "On the Blurred Methodological Matrix of Comparative Constitutional Law." In *The Migration of Constitutional Ideas*, ed. Sujit Choudhry, 39–66. New York: Cambridge University Press.

Hirschl, Ran. 2008. "The Judicialization of Mega-Politics and the Rise of Political Courts." *Annual Review of Political Science* 11: 93–118.

Jackson, Vicki C., and Mark V. Tushnet. 2006. *Comparative Constitutional Law.* 2nd edition. New York: Foundation.

Jacobsohn, Gary J. 2003. *The Wheel of Law: India's Secularism in Comparative Constitutional Context.* Princeton, NJ: Princeton University Press.

Law, David. S. 2005. "Generic Constitutional Law." *Minnesota Law Review* 89: 652–742.

Lazare, Daniel. 1998. "America the Undemocratic." *New Left Review* 232: 3–31.

Tushnet, Mark V. 1999. "The Possibilities of Comparative Constitutional Law." *Yale Law Journal* 108: 1225–1309.

Tushnet, Mark V. 2006. "Comparative Constitutional Law." In *The Oxford Handbook of Comparative Law,* ed. Mathias Reimann and Reinhard Zimmerman, 1225–1258. Oxford, UK: Oxford University Press.

Tushnet, Mark V. 2007. *Weak Courts, Strong Rights: Judicial Review and Social Welfare Rights in Comparative Constitutional Law.* Princeton, NJ: Princeton University Press.

Ran Hirschl

COMPELLED SPEECH

Modern First Amendment jurisprudence emphasizes the vital role that freedom of speech and the press play in democratic self-government. As the U.S. Supreme Court has recognized, however, the First Amendment also protects individual autonomy. This is especially true in cases where the government attempts to compel expression.

The leading case is *West Virginia State Board of Education v. Barnette,* 319 U.S. 624 (1943). In January 1942, the board adopted a resolution that required all public school students to recite the Pledge of Allegiance to the American flag on a regular basis. Those who refused were subject to expulsion for "insubordination." A legal challenge to this policy was brought by the parents of schoolchildren of the Jehovah's Witness faith, who objected to the ceremony on religious grounds. Overruling a recent decision, the Court held that West Virginia's policy violated the First Amendment by "requir[ing] affirmation of a belief and an attitude of mind." In his opinion for the majority, Justice Robert H. Jackson declared, "If there is any fixed star in our constitutional constellation, it is that no official, high or petty, can prescribe what shall be orthodox in politics, nationalism, religion, or other matters of opinion or force citizens to confess by word or act their faith therein."

The compelled speech doctrine promotes First Amendment freedoms in two ways. First, it safeguards liberty of thought and belief. As Justice Potter Stewart explained in *Abood v. Detroit Board of Education,* 431 U.S. 209 (1977), "At the heart of the First Amendment is the notion that an individual should be free to believe as he will, and that in a free society one's beliefs should be shaped by his mind and his conscience rather than coerced by the State." Just as the government may not force individuals to hold a particular belief, it may not require them to affirm one.

Second, the right against coercion is an integral aspect of liberty of expression. In classical liberal thought, liberty was understood as the power to act or not act, according to one's own choice. It follows that freedom of speech includes not only the right to speak but also the right to remain silent (Heyman 2008, p. 237, note 34). As Chief Justice Warren E. Burger put it in *Wooley v. Maynard,* 430 U.S. 705 (1977), "A system which secures the right to proselytize religious, political, and ideological causes must also guarantee the concomitant right to decline to foster such concepts. The right to speak and the right to refrain from speaking are complementary components of the broader concept of 'individual freedom of mind.'" Moreover, as the Court emphasized in *Hurley v. Irish-American Gay, Lesbian & Bisexual Group of Boston,* 515 U.S. 557 (1995), when one does choose to speak, the government may not dictate what is said, for that would violate "the fundamental rule of protection under the First Amendment, that a speaker has the autonomy to

School children remembering the victims of the USS** Akron, **Lakehurst, NJ, April 5, 1933.
The freedom of speech granted by the First Amendment extends beyond allowing citizens to freely speak their opinions. The right of free speech also allows organizations to exclude those with contrary opinions, permits individuals to remain silent, and prevents obliging a person to fund the speech of others. © **CORBIS-BETTMANN**

choose the content of his own message." Under these decisions, laws that seek to compel speech will be struck down, except perhaps in cases where the government can meet a demanding standard of justification.

As Justice Antonin Scalia observed in *Johanns v. Livestock Marketing Association*, 544 U.S. 550 (2005), the compelled speech doctrine has been applied in several categories of cases. The first category consists of "true 'compelled speech' cases, in which an individual is obliged personally to express a message he disagrees with." In addition to *Barnette*, this category includes *Wooley*, which ruled that the State of New Hampshire could not punish a Jehovah's Witness for covering up the motto "Live Free or Die" on his license plate.

In a second category of cases, the Court has "limited the government's ability to force one speaker to host or accommodate another speaker's message" (*Rumsfeld v. Forum for Academic and Institutional Rights, Inc.*, 126 S. Ct. 1297 [2006]). For example, in *Hurley*, the justices held that the state could not require the private organizers of the

Boston St. Patrick's Day parade to include a gay and lesbian group of whose message they disapproved. In *Rumsfeld*, however, the justices made clear that this protection applies only to parties who themselves are engaged in expression. In an opinion by Chief Justice John Roberts, the Court ruled that law schools had no First Amendment right to exclude military recruiters from campus, because the schools were not speaking when they hosted employer interviews.

A third category of cases holds that the government may not force individuals to subsidize the expression of others. This principle has deep roots in American constitutional history. Thus, in *A Bill for Establishing Religious Freedom* (1779)—an important forerunner of the First Amendment establishment clause—Thomas Jefferson asserted that "to compel a man to furnish contributions of money for the propagation of opinions which he disbelieves, is sinful and tyrannical" (quoted in *Johanns*, Justice David Souter dissenting). In *Abood*, the leading modern case, the justices applied this principle to hold that nonunion employees cannot be required to subsidize a union's political or ideological activities that go beyond its function as a collective-bargaining representative.

Because the compelled speech doctrine serves to protect "personal autonomy," one might suppose that the doctrine does not extend to business corporations (*Johanns*). In *Pacific Gas & Electric Corp. v. Public Utilities Commission*, 475 U.S. 1 (1986), the plurality rejected this position over a strong dissent by Justice William H. Rehnquist. However, the government may require commercial advertisers to disclose factual information in order to prevent consumer fraud or deception, as the Court ruled in *Zauderer v. Office of Disciplinary Counsel*, 471 U.S. 626 (1985).

Finally, in a series of cases, the justices have reviewed the constitutionality of federal programs that require businesses to fund generic advertising for agricultural products such as fruit, mushrooms, and beef. Although the Court initially suggested that such programs were a form of ordinary economic regulation that was not subject to First Amendment review, it subsequently changed course and held in *United States v. United Foods, Inc.*, 533 U.S. 405 (2001) that programs of this sort violated the compelled subsidy doctrine. In 2005, however, the majority in *Johanns* concluded that the programs involved a form of speech by the government itself. As Justice Scalia explained, "Citizens may challenge compelled support of private speech, but have no First Amendment right not to fund government speech." After *Johanns*, therefore, the doctrine affords little protection in this commercial context. However, the Court indicated that particular producers might have a First Amendment claim if the generic advertising attributed to them a message they did not hold.

SEE ALSO *Abood v. Detroit Board of Education, 431 U.S. 209 (1977); First Amendment; Freedom of Speech; West Virginia State Board of Education v. Barnette, 319 U.S. 624 (1943)*

BIBLIOGRAPHY

Alexander, Larry. 2006. "Compelled Speech." *Constitutional Commentary* 23: 147–161.

Blasi, Vincent, and Seana V. Shiffrin. 2004. "The Story of *West Virginia State Board of Education v. Barnette.*" In *Constitutional Law Stories*, ed. Michael C. Dorf, 433–476. New York: Foundation.

Heyman, Steven J. 2008. *Free Speech and Human Dignity*. New Haven, CT: Yale University Press.

Klass, Gregory. 2005. "The Very Idea of a First Amendment Right Against Compelled Subsidization." *UC Davis Law Review* 38: 1087–1139.

Shiffrin, Seana Valentine. 2005. "What Is Really Wrong with Compelled Association?" *Northwestern University Law Review* 99: 839–888.

Steven J. Heyman

COMPELLING STATE INTEREST

SEE *Strict Scrutiny.*

COMPLETE AUTO TRANSIT V. BRADY, 430 U.S. 274 (1977)

The commerce clause in Article I, section eight, clause three of the Constitution is an express grant of power to Congress to regulate interstate commerce. In addition, the Supreme Court has long held that the clause contains a negative or dormant aspect. That is, even in the absence of preemptive federal legislation, the clause prohibits state and local laws that discriminate against interstate commerce, frustrating the Constitution's purpose of establishing a "national common market" (*Oklahoma Tax Commission v. Jefferson Lines*, 514 U.S. 175 [1995]). *Complete Auto* is a watershed case applying the negative commerce clause to state taxes.

Complete Auto was a Michigan corporation. It transported motor vehicles via motor carriers for General Motors (GM). Part of such transportation entailed activity in Mississippi. GM assembled outside Mississippi vehicles destined for dealers inside Mississippi. The vehicles were shipped by rail to Jackson, Mississippi. Upon their arrival there, Complete Auto loaded them onto its trucks and delivered them to dealers throughout Mississippi. GM paid Complete Auto on a contract basis for transporting the vehicles from the railhead to the dealers.

Mississippi had for decades imposed "privilege" taxes on "the privilege of engaging [in] or doing business within [the state]," applied "against gross proceeds of sales or gross income or values." For 1968 through 1971, Mississippi assessed against Complete Auto over $120,000 in such taxes. Complete Auto challenged the assessments. It argued that its transportation within Mississippi was part of an interstate movement of the vehicles and that, as applied to such interstate operations, the taxes violated the commerce clause.

Complete Auto relied on prior Supreme Court decisions, such as *Spector Motor Service v. O'Connor*, 340 U.S. 602 (1951), to the effect that a tax on the privilege of engaging in an activity in a state may not be applied to an activity which is part of interstate commerce. The underlying notion was that interstate commerce should enjoy "free trade" immunity from state taxation. In contrast, Mississippi relied on a different line of precedents, holding that "it was not the purpose of the commerce clause to relieve those engaged in interstate commerce from their just share of state tax burden even though it increases the cost of doing business" (*Western Live Stock v. Bureau of Revenue*, 303 U.S. 250 [1938]).

The Supreme Court unanimously held for Mississippi. The Court noted that the *Spector* rule exalted formalism over substance since it looked only at the incidence of the tax, deeming irrelevant the practical effects of the tax. Essentially identical taxes could be upheld or invalidated based only on labels or "magic words" appearing in the statutes. Thus, the *Complete Auto* Court viewed the *Spector* rule as operating only as a trap for unwary legislative drafters, and as distracting courts and parties from the realities of taxes on interstate commerce.

The Court abrogated the *Spector* rule, replacing it with a four-part test. A state tax passes commerce clause muster if:

1. the activity subject to the tax has a substantial nexus to the state.

2. the tax is fairly apportioned.

3. the tax does not discriminate against interstate commerce.

4. the tax is fairly related to the services provided by the state.

SEE ALSO *Commerce Clause*

BIBLIOGRAPHY

Hellerstein, Jerome R., Walter Hellerstein, and Joan M. Youngman. 2005. *State and Local Taxation: Cases and Materials.* 8th edition. St. Paul, MN: Thomson West.

Schoettle, Ferdinand P. 2002. *State and Local Taxation: The Law and Policy of Multi-Jurisdictional Taxation.* Newark, NJ: Matthew Bender.

Steve R. Johnson

COMPREHENSIVE ENVIRONMENTAL RESPONSE, COMPENSATION, AND LIABILITY ACT (CERCLA)

The Comprehensive Environmental Response, Compensation, and Liability Act (CERCLA, or the Superfund law) authorizes the federal government to respond to hazardous substance contamination. The Supreme Court's CERCLA decisions have helped to allocate liability for the costs of hazardous waste cleanups. Those decisions are perhaps just as important for the insights they provide into the Court's federalism jurisprudence and into changes in the methods by which the Court interprets statutes.

Congress adopted CERCLA in 1980 to address the public health threats posed by improper hazardous waste management in places such as Love Canal, New York. CERCLA facilitates cleanup of contaminated properties in

two ways. First, it empowers the Environmental Protection Agency (EPA) to remediate contaminated sites and provides a mechanism (the Superfund) to finance EPA-conducted cleanups. Second, it authorizes the federal and state governments and other persons to bring cost-recovery actions in federal court to seek reimbursement from potentially responsible parties (PRPs). PRPs include past and current owners of contaminated facilities, those who arranged for hazardous substance disposal, and some hazardous substance transporters.

The CERCLA opinions handed down by the Supreme Court when William Rehnquist was chief justice reflect one of the Rehnquist Court's fundamental interests—defining the relationships between federal and state governments. The Court's first CERCLA case involved a mixed constitutional and statutory issue. In *Exxon Corp. v. Hunt*, 475 U.S. 355 (1986), the question was whether CERCLA preempted a state statute that imposed an excise tax on petroleum and chemical facilities to facilitate chemical spill cleanups. The Court characterized the issue as one of express preemption because CERCLA explicitly addresses when states may tax to finance environmental remediation. It nevertheless delved deeply into CERCLA's legislative history in concluding that CERCLA preempts state taxes intended to pay for the same types of expenses that may be paid by the Superfund, but not for cleanups or types of costs not covered by CERCLA.

A 1989 CERCLA case addressed an important federalism question: In *Pennsylvania v. Union Gas Co.*, 491 U.S. 1 (1989), a majority of the Court held that states can be liable under CERCLA as PRPs, and a plurality concluded that the commerce clause allows Congress to adopt legislation, such as CERCLA, that abrogates state sovereign immunity. Seven years later, Chief Justice Rehnquist wrote the majority opinion in *Seminole Tribe of Florida v. Florida*, 517 U.S. 44 (1996), a five-to-four decision holding that Congress cannot abrogate state sovereign immunity by using any of its Article I powers. Although *Seminole Tribe* did not involve CERCLA, it explicitly overruled *Union Gas*, characterizing it as "a solitary departure from established law" and a sharp deviation from established federalism jurisprudence. The fate of *Union Gas* symbolized the Rehnquist Court's commitment to reducing the scope of federal power and protecting the states against federal encroachment on their sovereignty that is reflected in the Court's Tenth Amendment and commerce clause cases.

Four subsequent decisions bear more significantly on the scope of CERCLA liability. In *Key Tronic Corp. v. United States*, 511 U.S. 809 (1994), the Court held that CERCLA does not authorize the award of attorneys fees to private plaintiffs in cost-recovery actions, although lawyers' work closely tied to cleanups may be recoverable. This unremarkable decision is consistent with the

Abandoned house near the contaminated Love Canal, Niagara Falls, New York. *With the realization of the long-term health consequences of poorly disposed chemical wastes, such as the contaminated Love Canal, Congress passed the Comprehensive Environmental Response, Compensation, and Liability Act (CERCLA). More familiarly known as the Superfund law, CERCLA allows the Environmental Protection Agency to declare a site toxic and use monies from the Superfund to clean the area.* © **CORBIS-BETTMANN**

Supreme Court's commitment to the "American Rule," which generally requires each side in federal litigation to pay its own costs. The issue in *United States v. Bestfoods,* 524 U.S. 51 (1998) was whether parent corporations can be liable under CERCLA for their subsidiaries' contaminated facilities. The Court concluded that CERCLA was not meant to upset fundamental principles of state corporation law. Under those laws, a parent is not indirectly liable for the activities of its subsidiary just because it owns or controls the subsidiary, unless the circumstances justify piercing the corporate veil. A parent can be directly liable based on its operation of the contaminated facility itself. Although *Bestfoods* was not a preemption case, it rests on a presumption that Congress does not intend to abrogate state common law that is analogous to the presumption against displacing state law that the Court uses in preemption cases.

Two CERCLA opinions involved the issue of when those incurring cleanup costs or subject to response-cost liability may seek reimbursement from other PRPs. Along with *Bestfoods,* these decisions probably have the greatest practical impact on the allocation of response-cost liability. *Cooper Industries, Inc. v. Aviall Services, Inc.,* 543 U.S. 157 (2004) held that a private party who has not yet been sued or received a government cleanup order may not bring a contribution action under section 114(f) of CERCLA. Numerous critics claimed that *Cooper* conflicted with CERCLA's primary goal of facilitating hazardous substance cleanups because it

precludes those conducting voluntary cleanups from seeking cost reimbursement. In *United States v. Atlantic Research Corp.,* 127 S. Ct. 2331 (2007), the Court minimized *Cooper's* impact, holding that volunteers may bring cost-recovery actions under section 107 of CERCLA. *Cooper* and *Atlantic Research* provide a stark contrast with *Exxon Corp.* because the Court in the 2004 and 2007 opinions did not refer even once to CERCLA's legislative history, which was an important part of the analysis in *Exxon Corp.* The Court even declared in *Cooper* that there was no need to determine which of the parties' conflicting interpretations was more consistent with CERCLA's goals or to "consult the purpose of CERCLA at all." The Court's refusal to consider statutory purposes in *Cooper* arguably produced a result difficult to reconcile with CERCLA's objectives. In addition, *Cooper* and *Atlantic Research* are symptomatic of the Court's tendency during the later years of the Rehnquist Court and the early years of the Roberts Court to emphasize statutory text, sometimes to the exclusion of statutory purpose and legislative history.

SEE ALSO *Environmental Law; Preemption; State Sovereign Immunity*

BIBLIOGRAPHY

Applegate, John S.; Jan G. Laitos; and Celia Campbell-Mohn. 2000. *The Regulation of Toxic Substances and Hazardous Wastes.* New York: Foundation Press.

Sprankling, John G., and Gregory S. Weber. 2007. *The Law of Hazardous Wastes and Toxic Substances in a Nutshell.* 2nd edition. St. Paul, MN: Thomson/West.

Robert L. Glicksman

CONCURRING OPINIONS

The U.S. Supreme Court typically issues a single opinion announcing not only the judgment in a case but also the rationale. Often at least one justice who agrees with the result will nevertheless write a separate concurring opinion. There are two types of concurring opinions: (1) those in which the concurring justice joins the opinion of the Court but chooses to write separately to address a point made in the majority opinion; and (2) those in which the concurring justice agrees with the result but reaches that conclusion by a different path and therefore does not join the opinion of the Court.

BACKGROUND

In the Supreme Court's first dozen years, each justice wrote his own opinion in every case. Use of so-called seriatim opinions reflected the English practice. Although seriatim opinions allow each justice to explain his or her thinking, they also make it more difficult to understand precisely what the Court decided without reading every word from every member. Perhaps the greatest institutional change that Chief Justice John Marshall made after his appointment in 1801 was to replace seriatim opinions with a single opinion of the Court. This development allowed the Court to speak with greater authority if not necessarily greater clarity.

Despite the institutionalization of the opinion of the Court, on rare occasions all nine justices have written their own opinions. This happened in the infamous case of *Dred Scott v. Sandford*, 60 U.S. 393 (1857), which invalidated the Missouri Compromise and made the Civil War all but inevitable. The Court also issued seriatim opinions in the Pentagon Papers case (*New York Times Co. v. United States*, 403 U.S. 713 [1971]), which rebuffed the federal government's effort to ban the publication of extensive portions of a classified study of American involvement in Southeast Asia at the height of the Vietnam War, and in *Furman v. Georgia*, 408 U.S. 238 (1972), which struck down the death penalty as then administered in the United States.

These cases are exceptional. Indeed, for most of the Court's history there was a strong institutional norm against separate opinions, either concurring or dissenting. Separate opinions have become much more common during the past half-century. Dissenting opinions have received the lion's share of attention, because they often reflect fundamental divisions within the Court. Some concurring opinions have become very influential, but the proliferation of such opinions has also provoked criticism that the Court cannot speak clearly about important legal issues.

FUNCTIONS AND CRITICISMS OF CONCURRING OPINIONS

Concurring opinions serve several functions. First, the prospect of a separate opinion, either a concurrence or a dissent, can encourage the author of the lead opinion to address problems or complexities that might otherwise be overlooked. Second, a concurrence can offer an alternative basis for resolving a case in a way that might seem more persuasive than the one embodied in the opinion of the Court. Third, a concurring opinion can try to clarify an ambiguity in the lead opinion.

Nevertheless, commentators regard concurring opinions as mixed blessings at best. Most significant, concurring opinions can dilute the force of the opinion of the Court. Several major cases, notably *Brown v. Board of Education*, 347 U.S. 483 (1954), and *United States v. Nixon*, 418 U.S. 683 (1974), saw concerted efforts to achieve unanimity for this reason.

Some critics have also suggested that certain justices write concurring opinions for their own gratification or to mollify their law clerks. It is difficult to assess this criticism, however: Justices receive no credit for writing separately, so every concurrence or dissent adds to their workload. While law clerks reportedly do most of the initial drafting in most contemporary chambers, they remain at the Court for only a year. Justices serve indefinitely and have incentives not to write—or threaten to write—separately too often, lest their influence with their colleagues wane.

Proliferation of concurring opinions can create confusion about the Court's rationale, which in turn can prevent a decision from offering needed guidance to lower courts, and to private citizens and government officials, who want to structure their policies and actions so as to minimize the likelihood of litigation. This problem is especially important in cases where there is no majority opinion and the decision turns on one or more justices who concur in the judgment but do not join the lead opinion.

Plurality opinions, in which no single opinion commands support from a majority of the justices, have increased markedly over the past half-century. In such cases, the Court has said that the holding should be viewed as "the narrowest grounds" to which at least five justices would have subscribed (*Marks v. United States*, 430 U.S. 188 [1977]). This principle has an air of artificiality, because it is counterfactual: A majority of the

Court may not actually endorse the narrowest grounds of decision. *Marks* illustrates the problem: That obscenity case was governed by the earlier plurality ruling in *Memoirs v. Massachusetts*, 383 U.S. 413 (1966), in which three justices thought that the book at issue (*Fanny Hill*) had some redeeming social value, two believed that obscenity enjoyed absolute First Amendment protection, and one concluded that the book was not hard-core pornography. Nevertheless, the *Marks* Court found that that those justices in the *Fanny Hill* case who took the absolutist view, as well as the one who applied the hard-core test, had taken a broader view than those who applied the "utterly without redeeming social value" test, which was therefore the narrowest ground for decision and the one to be applied in *Marks*.

Beyond the counterfactual problem, sometimes the crucial fifth vote is provided by a justice who explicitly rejects the premises of the plurality opinion and advances an entirely unrelated basis for decision. For example, in *Lehman v. City of Shaker Heights*, 418 U.S. 298 (1974), the Court rejected a First Amendment challenge to a public transit system's refusal to rent advertising space to a political candidate. Four justices thought that the First Amendment did not apply to the system because public transit was a proprietary rather than a governmental function; the crucial fifth vote came from a justice who believed that riders were a captive audience and that advertising of any kind invaded their privacy. Similarly, in *Arnett v. Kennedy*, 416 U.S. 134 (1974), the Court rejected a federal civil servant's claim that he had been fired without due process. A three-justice plurality concluded that federal workers had to accept whatever dismissal procedures were provided in the statute that created their jobs; two concurring justices (as well as the four dissenters) explicitly rejected this reasoning but thought that the statutory procedures satisfied constitutional requirements.

Plurality opinions, therefore, raise special questions about the Court's ability to decide cases coherently. Even cases that generate a majority opinion accompanied by one or more concurrences have come in for criticism, though. Critics suggest that divisions produce confusion and that the justices should work harder to achieve consensus. The proliferation of separate opinions does not, however, result entirely from the justices's personal foibles. Much of the Court's dissensus is a function of the difficulty of the issues on the docket and the variety of legitimate approaches to those issues.

SOME NOTABLE CONCURRING OPINIONS

Whatever one thinks of separate opinions, several concurrences have attracted widespread attention over the years. Justice Louis Brandeis produced two remarkable concurring opinions. The first, in *Whitney v. California*, 274 U.S. 357 (1927), was a concurrence in form only. His separate opinion in that case remains perhaps the most eloquent defense of freedom of speech in the Court's annals. Lamenting that "men feared witches and burned women," Brandeis laid out a theory of the First Amendment that emphasized individual autonomy, self-fulfillment, the process of civic deliberation, and engagement in public affairs because "the greatest menace to liberty is an inert people."

About a decade later, in *Ashwander v. Tennessee Valley Authority*, 297 U.S. 283 (1936), Brandeis wrote a concurring opinion that synthesized seven principles that the Court had developed to avoid passing unnecessarily on constitutional issues. Among those principles were that the Court should not resolve a constitutional question when a case could be resolved on an alternative basis, and that even when passing on a constitutional issue the Court should do so as narrowly as possible to avoid broad pronouncements that are unnecessary to the disposition of the case at hand. Brandeis's *Ashwander* concurrence retains its influence with the Court and has also served as the basis for scholarly work in constitutional theory.

Perhaps the most influential of all opinions dealing with the separation of powers is Justice Robert H. Jackson's concurrence in *Youngstown Sheet & Tube v. Sawyer*, 343 U.S. 579 (1952). In analyzing the legality of President Harry Truman's (1884–1972) order that the federal government seize the steel mills to prevent a strike at the height of the Korean War, Jackson laid out his famous tripartite approach to presidential power: (1) When acting with the express or implied approval of Congress, the chief executive has his maximum authority; (2) In the face of congressional silence the president has only his own independent power but also acts in "a zone of twilight" that is defined in part by "the imperatives of events and contemporary imponderables rather than [by] abstract theories of law"; and (3) When acting in opposition to the express or implied will of Congress the chief executive's authority is "at its lowest ebb." Jackson's opinion was not essential to the outcome in this six-to-three decision, but it has been to that opinion that the Court has looked in subsequent cases involving disputes over the relative roles of Congress and the president relating to foreign affairs (e.g., *Dames & Moore v. Regan*, 453 U.S. 654 [1981]).

There are cases, however, in which a concurring opinion from a justice who provided the crucial fifth vote has been viewed as controlling. A leading illustration is *Branzburg v. Hayes*, 408 U.S. 665 (1972), in which the Court rejected a claim that the First Amendment guarantee of freedom of the press implicitly created a reporter's privilege to refuse to reveal the identity of confidential news sources. The majority opinion in this five-to-four case rejected the privilege claim outright. Justice Lewis F. Powell, Jr., joined this opinion but wrote a separate concurrence suggesting that courts should use a balancing test when a journalist challenges an official demand for information that has "only a remote and tenuous relationship" to a legitimate governmental interest. Powell's formulation has been regarded as stating the controlling test in the federal courts in the absence of the kind of statutory reporter's privilege that exists in many states.

Two recent examples also illustrate the potential significance of concurring opinions. Both of these involve Justice Anthony Kennedy. In *Rapanos v. United States*, 547 U.S. 715 (2006), the Court held that the federal government did not have authority to regulate certain wetlands that were remote from navigable waters. Four justices concluded that federal authority reached only those wetlands with a continuous surface connection to navigable waters; four dissenting justices thought that the federal government could regulate wetlands with a hydrological connection to navigable waters. Justice Kennedy maintained that only those wetlands with a "significant nexus" to navigable waters were subject to federal regulation.

The other example is *Parents Involved in Community Schools v. Seattle School District No. 1*, 551 U.S. ___ (2007), in which the Court invalidated efforts by two school districts to promote voluntary integration. Four justices essentially endorsed the colorblind theory that race is a generally impermissible basis for government policy; four dissenting justices reasoned that the American experience with slavery and segregation made it permissible for the school boards to consider race in pupil assignments for the purpose of promoting greater racial and ethnic diversity in the classroom. Justice Kennedy concurred in the judgment, thereby providing the fifth vote against the integration policies at issue but noting that other efforts to promote integration that did not give excessive weight to the race of each individual student could pass constitutional muster.

SEE ALSO *Dissenting Opinions; Holding; Majority Opinions; Plurality Opinions; Seriatim Opinions*

BIBLIOGRAPHY

Bickel, Alexander M. 1962. *The Least Dangerous Branch: The Supreme Court at the Bar of Politics.* Indianapolis: Bobbs-Merrill.

Easterbrook, Frank H. 1982. "Ways of Criticizing the Court." *Harvard Law Review* 95(4): 802–832.

Gerber, Scott Douglas, ed. 1998. *Seriatim: The Supreme Court before John Marshall.* New York: New York University Press.

Ginsburg, Ruth Bader. 1990. "Remarks on Writing Separately." *Washington Law Review* 65(1): 133–150.

Post, Robert. 2001. "The Supreme Court Opinion as Institutional Practice: Dissent, Legal Scholarship, and Decisionmaking in the Taft Court." *Minnesota Law Review* 85(5): 1267–1390.

Jonathan L. Entin

CONDITIONAL FUNDING

Conditional funding, also known as *conditional spending*, is the power of the government to place conditions on recipients of government funding. The U.S. Supreme Court has stated that the Constitution precludes the government from imposing certain types of conditions when it spends government money. These constitutional limitations generally fall into two categories: (1) federalism-related limitations on Congress, that is, limitations that derive from principles of state sovereignty; and (2) limitations under the rubric of the *unconstitutional conditions* doctrine, or limitations that are imposed, in most cases, by the Bill of Rights.

Although the phrase *unconstitutional conditions* is not usually used to describe the first category, both categories embody the same basic problem: The government appropriates money and, as a condition on receipt of the money, requires the recipient to forgo doing something that the recipient otherwise would have a constitutional right to do. Moreover, both categories can be viewed as subsets of the larger problem of conditions on government benefits, where the "benefit" can be anything the government provides, not just money. Such benefits may include, for example, government employment or the use of government (i.e., public) property. The principal difference between the two categories is that, in the first, the recipient is usually one of the fifty states and the constitutional "right" is a right that the state has as a sovereign within the American federal system of government. In contrast, the second category can apply to any recipient of government money. Because the first category consists of federalism-related limitations, it only limits the federal government, whereas the second category limits all levels of government—federal, state, and local.

FEDERALISM-RELATED LIMITATIONS: CONGRESS'S SPENDING POWER

The first type of limitation on conditional spending derives from federalism principles and applies only to the federal government. From the time of the ratification of the Constitution, the U.S. Congress has had the power to spend money. Article I, Section 8, clause 1 of the Constitution provides Congress with the "Power to lay and collect Taxes, Duties, Imposts and Excises, to pay the

Debts and provide for the common Defence and general Welfare of the United States." On its face, the provision does not appear to provide a power to spend, but it has been interpreted as though the words *in order* or *so as* appear after the comma following the word *Excises*. Thus, the provision empowers Congress to tax in order to provide for the general welfare, and it is implicit that in order to provide for the general welfare, Congress must spend the money it gets when it taxes.

Until 1936 the principal debate about the spending power revolved around two different interpretations that dated back to the founding era. James Madison (1751–1836) viewed the spending power as merely an adjunct to the other enumerated powers in Article I, Section 8, while Alexander Hamilton (c. 1755–1804) viewed it as providing an independent grant of power. Under Madison's view, therefore, any spending that was not tied to a separate enumerated power would be beyond the powers of Congress, whereas Hamilton interpreted the provision as permitting any spending for the "general Welfare."

In the New Deal–era case *United States v. Butler*, 297 U.S. 1 (1936), the Supreme Court endorsed the broader Hamiltonian view that Congress could spend for the general welfare. Despite viewing the spending power broadly, however, the *Butler* Court actually invalidated the law in question, the first and only time the Court has held a law unconstitutional under the spending power. The law at issue, the Agricultural Adjustment Act (1933), gave the secretary of agriculture the power to impose a tax on the processors of certain agricultural goods and to use the money from that tax to pay farmers who were willing to reduce production of those same crops. Although the Court agreed with Hamilton that Congress could spend for purposes outside of its enumerated powers, the Court nonetheless invalidated the act because the Court concluded that Congress was using its spending power not simply to spend for the general welfare, but rather as a pretext for regulating matters outside the scope of its other enumerated powers. Pretext spending, the Court concluded, exceeded Congress's power, because only the states—not the federal government—could regulate the production of agricultural goods under the Court's jurisprudence at the time.

STATE SOVEREIGNTY LIMITS ON THE SPENDING POWER

The Supreme Court has stated that the principle of state sovereignty—the idea that the individual states retain some measure of sovereign power that cannot be encroached upon by the federal government—imposes limitations on the ways in which Congress can condition its spending. These principles go beyond the basic idea—embodied in *Butler*—that the federal government is one

of limited powers. The state sovereignty principles come into play when an exercise of federal power—here the spending power—regulates the state governments themselves. Despite a fair amount of jurisprudence on this question, however, the Court has never invalidated any exercise of the spending power on this ground.

The year after *Butler*, in *Steward Machine v. Davis*, 301 U.S. 548 (1937), the Court first explicitly addressed the possibility that principles of state sovereignty might impose constitutional limitations on Congress's spending power. In *Steward Machine*, the Court upheld an unemployment-compensation tax on employers that gave employers a credit for any contributions the employer made to a state unemployment fund that satisfied criteria listed in the federal statute. The credits, therefore, effectively amounted to federal spending—to employers rather than to the states themselves—conditioned on states creating unemployment funds. According to the challengers, the credits were thus a way to use the spending power to coerce states to do something they otherwise would not have done: create an unemployment compensation fund. However, the Court disagreed with that characterization of the law and upheld the statute, concluding that there was no evidence that any of the states were coerced by the statute.

The first case in which the Court explicitly considered the constitutionality of direct federal funding to the states was *Oklahoma v. United States Civil Service Commission*, 330 U.S. 127 (1947). In that case, the Court upheld the constitutionality of a law that prohibited state and local employees who had been financed "in whole or in part" by federal funding from participating in political campaigns. The Court rejected Oklahoma's argument that the law infringed the state's sovereign rights, concluding that the conditions attached to the federal spending were not unconstitutional because Oklahoma could simply have refused the funding.

The leading case addressing conditional funding to states, *South Dakota v. Dole*, 483 U.S. 203 (1987), came forty years later. *Dole* involved a federal law that provided funding to states for highway construction but withheld some funds from states that permitted individuals under twenty-one years of age to drink alcohol. In upholding the law, the *Dole* Court set forth four limitations on the federal government when it conditions funding to the states. The first limitation, taken directly from the language of the Constitution, is that the spending "be in pursuit of 'the general welfare.'" The second limitation is known as a *clear statement rule*, a requirement that Congress be unambiguous about the condition and the consequences of accepting the money. The third limitation is that the federal grant be related to a federal interest in particular national programs. The fourth limitation is known as the *independent constitutional bar* rule and prohibits Congress from using federal funding "to induce the states to engage in activities that would themselves be unconstitutional."

The Court has never seriously addressed the first or third limitations, but it discussed the second limitation extensively once, in *Pennhurst State School and Hospital v. Halderman*, 451 U.S. 1 (1981), and the fourth limitation once as well, in *United States v. American Library Association*, 539 U.S. 194 (2003). In *Pennhurst* the Court interpreted a statute that created a joint federal-state grant program in which the federal government provided states with funding to help create state programs for the developmentally disabled. The Court held that a provision in the statute that created a "bill of rights" for the developmentally disabled was not a condition on state participation in the program (i.e., on states receiving the federal money) because Congress had not explicitly tied the provision to the federal funding for the program. In *American Library Association*, the Court addressed the independent constitutional bar rule in upholding a federal law that provided funds to libraries on the condition that the libraries install filters on their Internet-enabled computers to prevent access to sexually explicit materials. Because the libraries were municipal government entities and thus, as a legal matter, creatures of the state governments, the Court applied the *Dole* four-part framework; the principal question under the independent constitutional bar rule was whether the libraries—as recipients of the federal funds—would violate the First Amendment by installing the filters. The Court said "no" and upheld the law.

THE UNCONSTITUTIONAL CONDITIONS DOCTRINE

The *unconstitutional conditions* doctrine—which applies to all levels of government, not just the federal government—states that the government may not condition a benefit on the requirement that the beneficiary forgo a constitutional right. For purposes of this entry, the "benefit" at issue is money, although the unconstitutional conditions doctrine applies to benefits other than money. During the nineteenth century, the problem of tying government benefits to the forgoing of constitutional rights was viewed through the lens of what was known as the *right-privilege* distinction. Under the Constitution's due process clause, the government must provide due process only when there is a deprivation of life, liberty, or property. The Court held numerous times that "liberty" or "property" meant only those things that the Court deemed to be "rights," as opposed to "privileges." The right-privilege distinction no longer holds, however, and now the unconstitutional conditions doctrine limits conditions on all government benefits, including those that are discretionary and might otherwise be thought to be "privileges."

The doctrine can apply to any constitutional right that a funding recipient has a choice about exercising. For example, in *Sherbert v. Verner*, 374 U.S. 398 (1963), the Court held that South Carolina could not deny a woman unemployment benefits when she refused to work on Saturday because of her religious beliefs. Similarly, in *Shapiro v. Thompson*, 394 U.S. 618 (1969), the Court held that a Connecticut law that required residence in the state for at least a year before eligibility for welfare benefits violated the equal protection clause. In both cases, the Court rejected arguments that the money was the state's to allocate as it saw fit and that unemployment compensation or welfare benefits were mere "privileges" that the state could condition on a waiver of constitutional rights.

THE SUBSIDIZED SPEECH PROBLEM

Although the unconstitutional conditions doctrine can apply to a variety of constitutional rights, in recent years the primary vehicle through which the Court has examined the doctrine is the speech and press clauses of the First Amendment. The basic question, known as the *subsidized speech* problem, can be encapsulated as follows: When the government spends money for speech purposes, should the spending be treated as the government's own speech or instead as a form of government censorship of the funding recipient's speech? If the Court treats the expenditure as the government's own speech or a mere "subsidy" of speech, then the expenditure is usually upheld as constitutional, whereas if the Court views the expenditure as an attempt to use government money to suppress or undermine the recipient's speech, then the Court will find the expenditure to be unconstitutional under the unconstitutional conditions doctrine.

The distinction is not always easy to make, however, and the Court's cases are not easy to reconcile. Compare, for example, *Federal Communications Commission v. League of Women Voters of California*, 468 U.S. 364 (1984) with *Rust v. Sullivan*, 500 U.S. 173 (1991). In *League of Women Voters* the Court invalidated a federal statute that prohibited editorializing by television and radio stations receiving certain federal funds. The Court noted that the statute precluded a station that received federal funds from all editorializing, even if it wanted to editorialize using its private funds, and thus treated the funding condition as an attempt to prevent the stations from editorializing. In contrast, in *Rust* the Court upheld regulations that prohibited recipients of federal funding for family-planning services—mostly, family-planning clinics—from advocating in favor of, or counseling women about, abortion as a method of family planning. The Court concluded that the regulation simply expressed Congress's desire not to subsidize speech promoting abortion rather than an attempt to tie funding to the recipients' waiver of their constitutional right to advocate in favor of abortion.

SEE ALSO *Rehnquist Court; Spending Clause; State Sovereign Immunity*

BIBLIOGRAPHY

Baker, Lynn A. 2001. "Conditional Federal Spending and States' Rights." *Annals of the American Academy of Political and Social Science* 574: 104–118.

Berman, Mitchell N. 2001. "Coercion without Baselines: Unconstitutional Conditions in Three Dimensions." *Georgetown Law Journal* 90(1): 1–112.

Epstein, Richard A. 1988. "Foreword: Unconstitutional Conditions, State Power, and the Limits of Consent." *Harvard Law Review* 102(1): 4–104.

Kreimer, Seth F. 1984. "Allocational Sanctions: The Problem of Negative Rights in a Positive State." *University of Pennsylvania Law Review* 132(6): 1293–1397.

McCoy, Thomas R., and Barry Friedman. 1988. "Conditional Spending: Federalism's Trojan Horse." *Supreme Court Review* 1988: 85–127.

Post, Robert C. 1996. "Subsidized Speech." *Yale Law Journal* 106(1): 151–195.

Rosenthal, Albert J. 1987. "Conditional Federal Spending and the Constitution." *Stanford Law Review* 39(5): 1103–1164.

Sullivan, Kathleen M. 1989. "Unconstitutional Conditions." *Harvard Law Review* 102(7): 1413–1506.

Sunstein, Cass R. 1990. "Why the Unconstitutional Conditions Doctrine Is an Anachronism (with Particular Reference to Religion, Speech, and Abortion)." *Boston University Law Review* 70(4): 593–621.

Van Alstyne, William W. 1968. "The Demise of the Right-Privilege Distinction in Constitutional Law." *Harvard Law Review* 81(7): 1439–1464.

Anuj C. Desai

CONFEDERATE CONSTITUTION

The Permanent Constitution of the Confederate States of America was created less than three months after South Carolina became the first state to secede from the Union. Precisely what this Constitution created has been debated ever since. On the surface the structures and institutions resemble its forebear, the U.S. Constitution. But there were important departures that demonstrated a recognition of state sovereignty. Did the Confederate Constitution, then, create a national government, or one based on state rights? Such an either-or question, though, is problematic. Their as the primary concern was to address the balance, or imbalance, of power.

Some of the reforms were directed at external influences on the constitutional system. For instance,

drafters of the constitution-makers sought to mitigate the influence of political parties. Thus both the president and vice president were limited to single six-year terms, and the president's removal powers were limited (Art. II). Another set of reforms sought to curb sectional influences on the constitutional structure. Federal economic policy had generated a considerable amount of friction over the course of the nineteenth century, from including federal funding of internal improvements, to the First and Second Banks of the United States, and protective tariffs and bounties. Many secessionists, particularly those in South Carolina, criticized these measures, in part because they believed them to be the source of their economic decline. Thus, protective tariffs and bounties were prohibited, revenue was to be collected only for national defense, to pay off debts, or to carry on government, and the only internal improvements Congress could finance were river and harbor improvements (Art. I, Sec. 8).

Perhaps the most important set of reforms concerned the balance of power between nation and state. The drafters of the Confederate constitution did not reject a federal government, but they wanted to demarcate clearly its authority. The Preamble framed the structure of authority by declaring that the creators of the constitution to be, "We, the People of the Confederate States, each State acting in its sovereign and independent character," were creating the Constitution. Moreover, in Article I, Section 1, they also made explicit the idea that Congress's powers were "delegated." Other provisions also sought to protect state sovereignty: Three states could force Congress to call a convention to amend the Constitution (Art. V, Sec. 1); and states could impeach federal officers residing and acting solely within the state (Art. I, Sec. 2). Perhaps the most important limit on the federal government was its power over slavery. Slavery was explicitly protected from interference by the Confederate government in the Constitution, principally in Article IV (Secs. 2 and 3), but also in Article I, Section 9, which prohibited Congress from denying or impairing the right of property in slaves. These provisions codified the U.S. Supreme Court's opinion in *Dred Scott v. Sandford*, 60 U.S. 393 (1857). Congress was also prohibited from denying the right of property in slaves, but it was also mandated (along with territorial governments) to protect slavery in any territories it may acquire and protected sojourners' rights to slave property.

Several important and controversial nationalistic clauses remained intact, however, most notably the necessary and proper and supremacy clauses. These clauses had long been at the heart of the U.S. Supreme Court's nationalist nationalistic constructions of the U.S. Constitution. (e.g. *Martin v. Hunter's Lessee*, 14 U.S. 304 [1816]; *M'Culloch v. Maryland*, 17 U.S. 316 [1819]; *Cohens v. Virginia*, 19 U.S. 264 [1821]). Interestingly, the

EXCERPTS FROM THE CONFEDERATE CONSTITUTION

∎

PREAMBLE

We, the people of the Confederate States, each State acting in its sovereign and independent character, in order to form a permanent federal government, establish justice, insure domestic tranquillity, and secure the blessings of liberty to ourselves and our posterity invoking the favor and guidance of Almighty God do ordain and establish this Constitution for the Confederate States of America.

ART. I, SEC. 2(3)

Representatives and direct taxes shall be apportioned among the several States, . . . according to their respective numbers, which shall be determined by adding to the whole number of free persons . . . three-fifths of all slaves.

ART. I, SEC. 9(4)

No . . . law denying or impairing the right of property in negro slaves shall be passed.

ART. IV, SEC. 2(1)

The citizens of each State . . . shall have the right of transit and sojourn in any State of this Confederacy, with their slaves and other property; and the right of property in said slaves shall not be thereby impaired.

ART. I, SEC. 3(3)

The Confederate States may acquire new territory. . . . In all such territory the institution of negro slavery, as it now exists in the Confederate States, shall be recognized and protected be Congress and by the Territorial government; and the inhabitants of the several Confederate States and Territories shall have the right to take to such Territory any slaves lawfully held by them in any of the States or Territories of the Confederate States.

Roman J. Hoyos

several struggles between the Confederate government and the states.

There were also struggles in the Confederate Congress regarding the proper relationship between the Confederate power and state sovereignty. One of the most significant concerned the organization of the Confederate Supreme Court. Under the Provisional Constitution, the Confederate Supreme Court was to consist of a panel of all the district court judges, with a majority constituting a quorum. In March 1861, the Confederate Congress passed the Judiciary Act, which organized the Confederate Supreme Court. Before the Court could gather a quorum, however, this act was suspended until a court could be created under the Permanent Constitution, which provided for a court that looked very much like the U.S. Supreme Court. Although many reasons have been proffered for the Confederacy's failure to create a supreme court, the fear of creating a nationalizing institution akin to the Marshall Court was an important one. And the Confederate Judiciary Act of 1861 became a major sticking point in the organization of the Confederate Supreme Court. At issue were Sections 45 and 46, which like the Section 25 of the Judiciary Act of 1789, gave the Confederate Supreme Court appellate jurisdiction over state supreme courts.

The precise effect of the failure to create a Confederate Supreme Court is hard to determine. State courts, with a few exceptions, generally upheld the policies of the Confederate government. Indeed, many of these courts turned to precedents of the U.S. Supreme Court, including many Marshall Court decisions. However, many Confederate officials and representatives perceived a pressing need to develop more uniform Confederate law. From the perspective of the separation of powers, Mark Neely, in *Confederate Bastille* (1993), has suggested that the failure to create a Supreme Court robbed the Confederacy, and posterity, of an important critic of the administration of Confederate President Jefferson Davis (1808–1889; administration 1808–1889). Without a federal supreme court, there was no opinion comparable to Chief Justice Roger Taney's (sitting as a circuit court judge) in *Ex parte Merryman*, 17 F. Cas. 144 (1861), which raised deep legal and constitutional doubts about the president's power to suspend habeas corpus. Yet President Davis did not lack critics. And given the exigencies of war, it is unlikely that a supreme court could have done much more than criticize the exercise of executive power. Moreover, the history of the U.S. Supreme Court's expansion of national power suggests that a Confederate supreme court may have provided a legal basis for federal policy. Such a court likely would have relied upon the U.S. Supreme Court's decisions for precedent, because although ambiguous about the nature of federalism the Confederate Constitution left intact the

inclusion of a supremacy clause created a theoretical problem. If, as the Preamble pronounces, sovereignty lay in the individual states, how could the laws of the Confederate government be supreme? This theoretical problem never had time to manifest itself. But there were basic tools used by previous courts to affirm the exercise of national authority.

SEE ALSO *Civil War; Constitution of the United States; Fugitive Slave Clause; Slavery; Slavery in the Territories; Theories of the Union*

BIBLIOGRAPHY

Escott, Paul. 1978. *After Secession: Jefferson Davis and the Failure of Confederate Nationalism.* Baton Rouge: Louisiana State University Press.

Fehrenbacher, Don E. 1995. *Sectional Crisis and Southern Constitutionalism.* Baton Rouge: Louisiana State University Press.

Lee, Charles Robert, Jr. 1963. *The Confederate Constitutions.* Chapel Hill: University of North Carolina Press.

Neely, Mark E., Jr. 1993. *Confederate Bastille: Jefferson Davis and Civil Liberties.* Milwaukee, WI: Marquette University Press.

Neely, Mark E., Jr. 1999. *Southern Rights: Political Prisoners and the Myth of Confederate Constitutionalism.* Charlottesville: University Press of Virginia.

Owsley, Frank Lawrence. 1925. *State Rights in the Confederacy.* Chicago: University of Chicago Press.

Rable, George C. 1994. *The Confederate Republic: A Revolution against Politics.* Chapel Hill: University of North Carolina Press.

Robinson, William M. 1991. *Justice in Grey: A History of the Judicial System of the Confederate States of America.* Holmes Beach, FL: William W. Gaunt & Sons.

Roman J. Hoyos

CONFERENCE OF THE JUSTICES

The meeting of Supreme Court justices to discuss certiorari petitions and orally argued cases is called the Court's Conference. The justices meet twice per week when the Court is hearing oral arguments. On Wednesday, the justices meet to discuss the cases that were argued on Monday; on Friday, the justices meet to discuss the cases argued on Tuesday and Wednesday as well as to consider pending certiorari petitions. In May and June, when the Court is not hearing arguments, the conference meets on Thursday instead. The Court only rarely holds conferences in the summer months.

Only the justices attend the Court's Conference, which meets in a room that is adjacent to the Chief Justice's chambers. As Chief Justice William Rehnquist put it, "There are no law clerks, no secretaries, no staff assistants, no outside personnel of any kind." If a message must be passed to or from a justice to the staff, the most junior justice "opens the door and delivers the message"

(Rehnquist 1987, p. 288). This led Justice Tom C. Clark (1899–1977) to comment, "For five years I was the highest paid doorkeeper in the world" (O'Brien 2003, p. 199).

At the outset of the Court in 1790, especially during the tenure of Chief Justice John Marshall, the justices lived in the same boardinghouse when the Court was in session. Some maintain that "it was from this intensive social and professional interaction that the Supreme Court conference was born" (Dickson 2001, p. 31). The justices engaged in continual interchange over the cases when the Court was in session. Their discussion occurred over meals and in their boardinghouse rooms nearly every day. In the early twenty-first century, the conference is not an intense deliberation of the case. Justice Antonin Scalia has said, "In fact, to call our discussion of a case a conference is really something of a misnomer, it's much more a statement of the views of each of the nine Justices, after which the totals are added and the case is assigned" (quoted in Schwartz 1996, p. 42).

When discussing cases that have been orally argued, the conference discussion begins with the chief justice who reviews the case facts, the lower court's decision, and the issues raised by the case. Before the discussion moves to the most senior associate justice, the chief justice states the disposition that he favors. The justices then discuss the case proceeding from the more senior justices to the most junior justice. This discussion of the case now constitutes the preliminary voting in the case, but before the 1970s the Court occasionally held a formal vote after each justice had an opportunity to discuss the case. When a separate formal conference vote was cast, justices would vote in reverse seniority beginning with the most junior justice and ending with the chief justice. In an internal memo, Justice Potter Stewart stated that a formal vote was not normally necessary, but "very occasionally, however, when the situation was not entirely clear at the end of the Conference discussion, the Chief Justice would call for a formal vote either on his own motion or on the motion of any Justice."

The chief justice, by virtue of leading the discussion, has the ability to influence the Court's deliberation. Some chief justices who were reputed to be outstanding leaders of the conference are Chief Justices Charles E. Hughes, Earl Warren, and William Rehnquist. These chief justices had the ability to serve as task and social leaders of the Court, moving the Court toward resolution of the cases while maintaining a collegial tone in the face of conflict. Hughes, for instance, was known as a very efficient leader who guided the conference discussion incisively, presented the issues that were central in a case, and discouraged irrelevant discussion. In contrast his successor, Harlan F. Stone favored full discussion of the issues, relishing a lively debate over the issues presented to the Court. Chief Justice Fred M. Vinson, who succeeded Stone, was seen by some as even less able to lead the conference. Vinson, said Justice Felix Frankfurter, "blithely hits the obvious points … disposing of each case rather briefly, by choosing, as it were, to float merely on the surface of the problems raised by the cases" (Schwartz 1996, p. 87). One ramification of the chief justices's leadership skills has been the demise of the norm of consensus with justices more willing to write their own views in a separate opinion rather than acquiescing with the majority opinion.

There are two consequences of the Court's conference voting process. First, justices may pass and reserve their vote until later. Under the conference voting rule, the chief justice is the first to cast a vote and, arguably, has the most at stake. The disadvantage of casting the first vote is that the chief may, at times, lack information on the positions held by other justices. Because the chief has the ability to influence the path of legal policy by assigning the majority opinion author when the chief is in the conference majority, the chief justice has an incentive to vote with the conference majority. Chief Justice Warren E. Burger's colleagues sometimes decried Burger's passing as an effort to control the majority opinion. Other justices can also pass at conference, but they do not pass as frequently as the chief. Second, justices are able to change the vote they cast in the conference (i.e., voting fluidity). This is frequently done when the justices are ideologically distant from the opinion representing their conference vote, when a case is legally complex, or when the justice is new to the Court. Fluidity is less likely to occur when the conference majority is minimum winning (i.e., when a single vote separates the majority from the dissent, such as a five-to-four vote). During the Burger Court, justices changed their votes about 7.5 percent of the time.

SEE ALSO *Chief Justice; Supreme Court Building; Writ of Certiorari*

BIBLIOGRAPHY

Danelski, David J. 1961. "The Influence of the Chief Justice in the Decisional Process of the Supreme Court." In *Court, Judges, and Politics*, ed. Walter Murphy and C. Herman Pritchett. New York: Random House.

Dickson, Del. 2001. *The Supreme Court in Conference (1940–1985)*. New York: Oxford University Press.

Johnson, Timothy R.; James F. Spriggs, II; and Paul J. Wahlbeck. 2005. "Passing and Strategic Voting on the U.S. Supreme Court." *Law & Society Review* 39(2): 349–377.

Maltzman, Forrest, and Paul J. Wahlbeck. 1996. "Strategic Policy Considerations and Voting Fluidity on the Burger Court." *American Political Science Review* 90(3): 581–592.

O'Brien, David M. 2003. *Storm Center: The Supreme Court in American Politics*. 6th ed. New York: W.W. Norton.

Rehnquist, William H. 1987. *The Supreme Court: How It Was, How It Is*. New York: Quill.

Schwartz, Bernard. 1996. *Decision: How the Supreme Court Decides Cases*. New York: Oxford University Press.

Stewart, Potter to Warren E. Burger, 18 September 1980. Harry Blackmun's Papers, The Library of Congress.

Paul J. Wahlbeck

CONFIRMATION PROCESS

Throughout the course of American history the proper role for the Senate in the process of appointing federal judges has been the subject of considerable debate. Supporters of presidential prerogative insist that senators defer to the president's choice unless the nominee is patently unqualified for the position, whereas others argue for a more robust role for the Senate, contending that the Senate is free and perhaps required to make an independent determination of whether a particular confirmation will serve the national interest. Proponents of either position inevitably claim support in the meaning of the Constitution or the words of the framers, but the Senate's power to advise and consent has ultimately not been defined by constitutional or statutory law but rather by the shifting dynamics of contemporary politics in America. Studying the history of the confirmation process is, in effect, to study the history of American politics and institutions.

CONSTITUTIONAL CONVENTION OF 1787

Debate over the procedures for the appointment of federal judges produced a good deal of disagreement during the Constitutional Convention of 1787. Basic concerns regarding the relative influence of small and large states, as well as battles over legislative or executive dominance, all found expression in the debate over the proper method for appointing judges. Exacerbating the matter still further was the constant awareness on the part of the framers that the provisions for the appointment of a lifetime member of a coequal branch might require a good deal more than an appointment for a limited term to the executive branch. In the end, however, the exigencies of time and perhaps simple physical and mental exhaustion led to the compromise of the appointments clause, found in Article XI of the Constitution, providing that the president will nominate and "with the Advice and Consent of the Senate, shall appoint Ambassadors, other public Ministers and Consuls, Judges of the Supreme Court, and all other Officers whose appointments are not herein provided for." Hence the framers opted for a single method of appointment for a wide range of federal officers (including lower court federal judges who were assumed to be "other Officers," a conclusion later affirmed by congressional statute). The framers left for future generations the task of putting flesh on the bare bones of the appointments clause and confronting the troublesome matter of whether the responsibilities of the Senate might indeed vary according to the significance or nature of the appointment.

CONFIRMATION PROCESS FROM THE NINETEENTH TO MID-TWENTIETH CENTURIES

The development of a party system during the nineteenth century provided the impetus for a period of Senate preeminence in the confirmation process, particularly with respect to federal judgeships. Prior to the adoption of the Seventeenth Amendment in 1913, senators were selected by state legislatures and were often state party leaders whose primary mission in coming to the Senate was to return federal patronage back to the state. A lifetime position on the federal bench was a patronage plum and it can hardly be surprising that senators of that era rapidly embraced the conviction that the power to determine who should receive such an important post must rest in the hands of the senators who represent the state in which the prospective judge was to serve. This was particularly the case when the relevant senator and the president were of the same political party. The norm of senatorial courtesy soon dictated that if a senator of the president's party found a nominee for a vacancy on the federal bench in the senator's state to be unacceptable, the remainder of the Senate would abide the senator's wishes and the nomination would be defeated. Senatorial courtesy continues to this day to be a significant consideration, particularly in the confirmation of federal district court judges, and a president who refuses to pay homage to this longstanding Senate tradition will inevitably find the confirmation process to be an especially long and difficult one.

Congressional supremacy in nineteenth–century national politics resulted in an expansive understanding of the Senate's role in the confirmation process and, citing a variety of political, ideological, and patronage concerns, the Senate rejected more than one of every four presidential nominees to the Supreme Court. In the twentieth century, however, the locus of national power shifted from the legislative to the executive branch and this transformation soon found expression in the confirmation process. In the Senate, the Seventeenth Amendment, combined with several Progressive Era reforms to weaken party control of the institution, led to the development of a hierarchical, conservative Senate in which a handful of leaders dominated the legislative process and widely accepted norms constrained the behavior of individual senators. In this club-like atmosphere leaders from both parties frequently cooperated to achieve generally shared goals and, by mid-twentieth century, the Senate was a self-contained, cohesive,

relatively efficient legislative body that was governed by generally accepted norms that vested power in a few Senate elders, making the legislative process quite orderly and predictable. It was also an institution that tended to defer to presidential choice on many matters, including the appointment of Supreme Court justices. Private negotiations between the president and a few relevant Senate leaders normally paved the way for an uneventful confirmation process. For the typical senator in the years following World War II (1939–1945), an appointment to the federal bench (even at the level of the Supreme Court) simply did not warrant a challenge to Senate leadership and presidential prerogative. Deference to presidential choice marked the politics of confirmation during this era; from 1900 through 1968, the Senate rejected only one presidential nominee to the Supreme Court, and from 1945 to 1968 no nominee triggered the opposition of even one-fifth of the Senate.

The politics of judicial confirmations abruptly changed in 1968 when the Senate refused to approve President Lyndon B. Johnson's nomination of Abe Fortas to succeed Earl Warren as chief justice. The surprising rejection of Fortas was quickly followed by the Senate's defeat of President Richard Nixon's nominations of Clement Haynsworth (1912–1989) and G. Harrold Carswell (1919–1992) to the Court. In 1986 Ronald Reagan succeeded in elevating Justice William Rehnquist to the chief justiceship but only after nasty and prolonged hearings, as well as a rancorous floor debate that produced thirty-three negative votes. The next year, Judge Robert Bork, perhaps the most professionally qualified nominee for a seat on the Supreme Court in decades, was rejected by the Senate. In 1991 the Senate confirmed Clarence Thomas by a 52 to 48 vote. In 2005 President George W. Bush's (1946–) nomination of Harriet Miers (1945–) to succeed the retiring Justice Sandra Day O'Connor was withdrawn when religious and social conservatives in the president's party openly opposed confirmation. Bush's next choice, Samuel Alito, was confirmed after a quiet confirmation process that nevertheless produced over forty negative votes. Since 1968 the process of nominating and confirming Supreme Court justices has become disorderly, contentious, and often simply unpredictable; once again, changes in the larger political and institutional settings help to explain this rather abrupt alteration in Senate behavior.

Changing Nature of Judicial Power The most important development may well be the changing nature of judicial power. Under the leadership of Chief Justice Earl Warren, the Supreme Court in the 1960s expanded the reach of federal judicial power by permitting judicial intervention in a broad range of private and public disputes, and by increasing the access to the federal courts for a wide array

There are a lot of mediocre judges and people and lawyers, and they are entitled to a little representation [on the Supreme Court], aren't they? We can't have all Brandeises, Frankfurters, and Cardozos.

SOURCE: Roman L. Hruska, Interview after speech in United States Senate, quoted in *New York Times*, 17 Mar. 1970, p. 21.

of potential litigants as well as expanding the judicial remedies available to those litigants. The motivation of the justices of the Warren Court was most certainly to make judicial power more available to America's disadvantaged, but the net result was to thrust the judiciary deeper into the policy-making arena and to make appointments to the federal bench a matter of serious concern to a range of interest groups that previously paid, at best, sporadic attention to the confirmation process. By the 1970s the staffing of the federal judiciary had become a matter of critical importance to a wide variety of politically potent interests. As the stakes in the confirmation process ratcheted upward, those on the left side of the political spectrum vowed to resist any effort to appoint judges who would reverse any of the expansive decisions of the Warren Court era, whereas those on the right considered altering the membership of the federal judiciary a first step in the campaign to enact a new conservative social and religious agenda.

At the same time as powerful interests began to focus on the staffing of the federal judiciary, the Senate was undergoing a transformation from a stable, hierarchical institution controlled by shared norms and powerful leadership to a more fluid institution where individualistic senators pursue personal ambition at the expense of institutional goals. The old Senate rewarded the specialist who gained the respect of colleagues through hard work and dedication to the institution. The most powerful members of the modern Senate, however, are generalists who seek national exposure on a broad range of interests and who are quick to champion causes with large, national constituencies. The constant quest for campaign funds further compels senators to seek a national stage. Because media attention boosts power and prestige in the modern Senate, opposing the president on a matter as significant as the appointment of a Supreme Court justice virtually guarantees a senator enhanced national exposure. Phrased most simply, playing a prominent role in televised, contentious confirmation proceedings fits the public style of modern senators.

CONFIRMATION PROCESS SINCE 1968

From 1900 through 1968, the nomination and confirmation of a Supreme Court justice was, with rare exception, a predictable, ordered affair in which deals struck between the president and a few key senators paved the way for confirmation in a process in which the public played, at most, a limited role. Since 1968, however, the entire process has been transformed into a contentious, unpredictable, and very public political event in which powerful groups employ sophisticated media techniques to mobilize public opinion and publicity-hungry senators play to a nationwide audience. In such a setting, the president's task in filling a vacancy on the Court is an extraordinarily difficult one. The central reality of the modern process of nominating and confirming Supreme Court justices is that almost any presidential choice is certain to arouse opposition and thus even the selection—not to mention the actual confirmation—of a nominee involves a complex political calculation of the cost and the benefits to the administration's long term political goals.

Clinton Administration The Supreme Court appointments of the William J. Clinton (1946–) and George W. Bush administrations reflect the new reality of the modern confirmation process. During his days on the campaign trail and his initial days in office, President Clinton expressed the desire to appoint men and women of great political experience and public stature to the Court. When Justice Byron White announced his retirement in the spring of 1993, Clinton became the first Democrat since Johnson with an opportunity to make a Supreme Court pick. Mario Cuomo (1932–), the former Democratic governor of New York, was often mentioned as the ideal Clinton choice but conservative groups vowed a firestorm of opposition and Cuomo removed his name from consideration early on. Despite the fact that Democrats controlled the Senate, it became readily apparent that any nominee with a substantial political resume would face determined opposition and could be confirmed only with difficulty, at substantial political cost to the Clinton presidency. For the next three months, the Clinton administration engaged in the rather unseemly practice of floating possible names before the public to gauge support and opposition before finally settling on the nomination of Judge Ruth Bader Ginsburg. The next year when Justice Harry Blackmun left the Court, Clinton again proceeded to carom from one potential nominee to another in a very public selection process before deciding on Judge Stephen Breyer of the First Circuit Court of Appeals. Both Breyer and Ginsburg were, at the time of their appointments, jurists of great skill and reputation, but neither was the candidate of substantial political experience and stature that Clinton had sought. Hence the fact that both Clinton nominees were easily confirmed should not deflect attention from the conflict and difficulty faced by the president in making his selection. In each case, Clinton professed a preference for a nominee who had played a prominent role in the life of the nation and opposition to well known candidates with established, public records—often within his own party—narrowed his options.

George W. Bush Administration Throughout the Clinton years, the politics of confrontation in the confirmation process also migrated downward as Senate Republicans employed various parliamentary tactics to deny or delay Clinton lower court judicial nominees. This trend accelerated markedly during the presidency of George W. Bush. Far more willing than his predecessor to expend substantial political capital in an effort to change the ideological makeup of the lower federal courts, President Bush named a number of controversial candidates to vacancies on the Court of Appeals. Democrats countered by employing various tactics, including the filibuster, to obstruct or to deny confirmation. By 2005, Democrats had rejected at least ten of Bush's nominees to the federal bench and Republicans were determined to retaliate by changing the venerable Senate rules respecting the filibuster (a move so controversial that it was dubbed the "nuclear option" by Senator Trent Lott). Democrats responded to this threat by vowing to use every means possible to bring Senate business to a halt if the rights of the minority party were undercut. In 2005, as partisan battles over the confirmation of lower court federal judges brought the Senate to the brink of implosion, seven Republicans and seven Democrats (dubbed by the media *The Gang of Fourteen*) reached a compromise agreement that averted a Senate showdown over judicial confirmations. The seven Republican agreed to oppose any effort by the Republican majority to alter the filibuster rules as long as the seven Democrats agreed not to join Democratic efforts to prevent votes on Bush judicial nominees save for "extraordinary circumstances." The compromise reached by the Gang of Fourteen defused the immediate crisis and the Senate quickly passed several of the Bush lower court nominees.

Although both of Bush's picks to the Supreme Court were approved by the Senate (in the case of Samuel Alito a result, at least in part, attributable to the Gang of Fourteen conclusion that the Alito nomination was not an extraordinary circumstance that justified a Democratic filibuster), the most startling development in the politics of the confirmation process was brought about by the Bush nomination of his White House Counsel, Harriet Miers, to fill the O'Connor seat on the Court. Miers's private legal career had been that of a corporate lawyer in Dallas, Texas, while her public life was defined by service to her patron, George W. Bush. There was little in her professional life to recommend her nomination to the Court and most observers believed she was the Bush choice simply because she was an unknown and might be confirmed without a protracted battle. The Democratic response to the Miers's nomination was generally muted but many Republican social and religious conservatives expressed dismay and, in many cases, outright opposition. Appointments to the Supreme Court had become so important to influential members of the Republican Party that a number of conservatives were willing to oppose a Republican nominee to the Court who they believed lacked the appropriate conservative credentials. In the end, a growing opposition within the Republican Party forced Miers to withdraw prior to Senate consideration and Bush was compelled to select conservative favorite Samuel Alito for the O'Connor seat on the Court.

Appointments to the Supreme Court (and increasingly lower federal courts) have assumed such significance that a president can anticipate a political battle regardless of the nature of the selection. President Clinton's wish to bring to the Court an individual of political stature with extensive experience outside of the courtroom appears, in retrospect, to be oddly naive. Such individuals are almost certain to trigger substantial opposition, and can be nominated only if the president is willing to risk defeat and is ready to expend an extraordinary amount of political capital in the effort to secure confirmation. For Clinton, the secure choice was established, moderate jurists of impeccable legal credentials who were virtually unknown to the general public. The Miers nomination, however, suggests that presidents can no longer assume broad support, even within their own party, for nominees without appropriate ideological credentials. Increasingly it appears that there is no politically safe choice when presidents seek to fill a vacancy on the modern Supreme Court.

CONFIRMATION PROCESS IN THE TWENTY-FIRST CENTURY

For many years presidents cherished the opportunity to make an appointment to the Supreme Court as the opportunity to exercise presidential prerogative and to influence the development of American law for decades to follow. The modern confirmation process may well have transformed what was once a presidential asset into a liability, as filling a vacancy on the Court has now become a high-stakes, exquisitely difficult political calculation in which a president can expect opposition from friend and foe alike. The prospects are that the confirmation process will remain a highly visible, contentious affair for many years to come. Indeed a process that was once hidden from public view and, for the most part, controlled by political insiders now can be said to reflect the best and worst of modern mass democracy.

SEE ALSO *Article II; Bork, Robert; Parker, John; Political Foundations of Judicial Power; Seventeenth Amendment*

BIBLIOGRAPHY

Abraham, Henry J. 1999. *Justices, Presidents, and Senators: A History of the U.S. Supreme Court Appointments from Washington to Clinton.* Lanham, MD: Rowman and Littlefield.

Epstein, Lee, and Jeffrey A. Segal. 2005. *Advice and Consent: The Politics of Judicial Appointments.* Oxford, UK: Oxford University Press.

Gerhardt, Michael J. 2000. *The Federal Appointment Process: A Constitutional and Historical Analysis.* Durham, NC: Duke University Press.

Maltese, John Anthony. 1995. *The Selling of Supreme Court Nominees.* Baltimore, MD: Johns Hopkins University Press.

Silverstein, Mark. 2007. *Judicious Choices: The New Politics of Supreme Court Confirmations.* 2nd Edition. New York: W. W. Norton.

Yalof, David Alistair. 1999. *Pursuit of Justices: Presidential Politics and the Selection of Supreme Court Nominees.* Chicago: University of Chicago Press.

Mark Silverstein

CONFRONTATION CLAUSE

SEE *Crawford v. Washington, 541 U.S. 36 (2004); Sixth Amendment.*

CONGRESSIONAL RESPONSE TO JUDICIAL DECISIONS

On both statutory and constitutional questions, Congress has significant power and responsibility to respond to Supreme Court decisions. On statutory matters, there is no question that Congress may negate a Supreme Court interpretation by enacting new legislation. Consider, for example, congressional efforts to countermand Rehnquist Court interpretations of federal civil right statutes, the 1987 Civil Rights Restoration Act, and the 1991 Civil Rights Act. The 1987 statute negated a 1984 Supreme Court decision, *Grove City College v. Bell*, 465 U.S. 555 (1984). Ruling that only the parts of the college that actually received federal aid were subject to federal civil rights laws (and not the college as a whole), *Grove City* severely limited the reach of federal civil rights protections. The Restoration Act rejected that interpretation, making clear that the entire organization is subject to federal civil rights protections when any program or activity receives federal assistance.

The 1991 Civil Rights Act is a more dramatic example of Congress's power to respond. In 1989, the Supreme Court began to backtrack from its previous positions on civil rights and issued five rulings that made it more difficult to prove discrimination under Title VII (employment discrimination) and other statutes. Congress, working in tandem with civil rights groups, crafted legislation that nullified these and other restrictive decisions. By enacting the 1991 Act, Congress overturned nine Rehnquist Court decisions, made it easier for civil rights plaintiffs to bring lawsuits, and became the civil rights establishment's so-called court of last resort.

CONSTITUTIONAL ISSUES

On constitutional questions, there is significant controversy about the scope of Congress's power to respond. The reason for this is that the press, the American people, some members of Congress, and especially the Supreme Court treat Court constitutional rulings as final and definitive. For example, when reporting that six out of ten Americans thought the Supreme Court was the ultimate constitutional arbiter, newspapers simply noted that those six were "correct" (Marcus 1987, p. A13). Likewise, after Reagan's attorney general, Edwin Meese (1931–), argued that Supreme Court decisions were not "binding on all persons and parts of government henceforth and forevermore," the Senate Judiciary Committee was alarmed, asking Supreme Court nominees to comment on Meese's speech (Meese 1987, p. 983).

For its part, the Supreme Court stridently defends its power to interpret the Constitution. Beginning with Chief Justice John Marshall's declaration in *Marbury v. Madison*, 5 U.S. 137 (1803) that it is "emphatically the province and duty of the judicial department to say what the law is," the Supreme Court regularly insists that it alone delivers the final word on the meaning of the Constitution. According to a subsequent decision, *Marbury* "declared the basic principle that the federal judiciary is supreme in the exposition of the law of the Constitution" (*Cooper v. Aaron*, 358 U.S. 1 [1958]). In a memorable aphorism, Justice Robert H. Jackson claimed that decisions by the Supreme Court "are not final because we are infallible, but we are infallible only because we are final" (*Brown v. Allen*, 344 U.S. 443 [1953]). Yet, the historical record, as well as the text of the Constitution, provides overwhelming evidence that Court pronouncements are anything but final. Instead, Court pronouncements are part of a circular process binding the parties in a particular case but otherwise serving as one moment in an ongoing constitutional dialogue between the courts, elected officials, and the American people.

The Constitution, for example, anticipates that Congress will play an important part in shaping the Constitution's meaning. All public officers are required by Article VI, clause three "to support this Constitution." That obligation is supplemented by federal law, under which all legislative officials "solemnly swear (or affirm) . . . to support and defend the Constitution" (5 U.S.C. § 3331 [1994]). The Constitution, moreover, anticipates that lawmakers will respond to Supreme Court rulings. It empowers Congress to, among other things, impeach judges, make exceptions to the jurisdiction of federal courts, confirm judicial nominations, and amend the Constitution (in conjunction with the states, three-fourths of which must approve constitutional amendment proposals). Over the years, Congress has made use of all of these powers to signal its approval or disapproval of federal court decisions.

In the twenty-first century it seems farfetched that Congress would impeach federal court judges to express disapproval with court decisions. At the time of *Marbury v. Madison*, however, Congress seemed quite willing to use its impeachment power to check the federal judiciary. After the 1800 elections (where the Jeffersonians took control of the White House and Congress from the Federalists), Federalist district judge John Pickering (1737–1805) was impeached and removed, and action against Supreme Court Justice Samuel Chase (1741–1811) began. For this very reason, the Supreme Court could not issue a meaningful remedy against the Jefferson administration in *Marbury v. Madison* (a case in which a Federalist judicial appointee challenged the Jefferson administration for failing to deliver his judicial commission to him). Indeed, Chief Justice Marshall was concerned about impeachment, writing to Justice Chase that "a reversal of those legal opinions deemed unsound by the legislature would certainly better comport with the mildness of our character than a removal of the Judge who has rendered them unknowing of his fault" (Beveridge 1919, p. 177).

COURT JURISDICTION

Article III, clause two makes the Supreme Court's appellate jurisdiction subject to "such exceptions" and "such regulations as the Congress shall make." On numerous occasions, Congress has threatened to strip the Court of jurisdiction in response to decisions it dislikes. From 1953 to 1968, Congress saw Court stripping as a way to countermand the Warren Court—over sixty bills were introduced to limit the jurisdiction of the federal courts over school desegregation, national security, criminal confessions, and much more. And while only one of these bills passed (limiting the access of alleged Communists to government documents), Congress came close to enacting legislation that would have stripped the Supreme Court of jurisdiction in five domestic security areas. In the late 1970s and 1980s, Congress again targeted the Supreme Court. An amendment to strip the federal courts of jurisdiction over school prayer was approved by the Senate in 1979; proposals to limit court jurisdiction over abortion and school desegregation were also given serious consideration. More recently, Congress has taken aim at federal and state

court decisions on gay marriage, the pledge of allegiance, the public display of the Ten Commandments, and judicial invocations of international law. None of these statutes was enacted, although limits on court jurisdiction over same-sex marriage and the pledge of allegiance were approved by the House of Representatives in 2004.

In 2005 and 2006, Congress responded to court decisions by enacting legislation affecting federal court jurisdiction. In 2005, Congress expressed disapproval with state court decision-making in the Terri Schiavo case by expanding federal court jurisdiction. Specifically, rather than accept state court findings that Schiavo, then in a persistent vegetative state, would rather die than be kept alive artificially, Congress asked the federal courts to sort out whether the removal of a feeding tube violated Schiavo's constitutional rights (For the Relief of the Parents of Theresa Marie Schiavo Act).

In 2006, Congress limited the habeas corpus rights of detainees held at Guantanamo Bay. Responding to a Supreme Court ruling *Hamdan v. Rumsfeld*, 548 U.S. ___ (2006), which extended Geneva Convention protections to enemy combatants, Congress enacted the Military Commission Act. This statute authorized limited federal court review of military commission determinations that a detainee is an enemy combatant. More significant, the Military Commissions Act prohibited federal court consideration of habeas corpus petitions by Guantanamo detainees, limiting their rights to those afforded them by military commissions. When enacting the statute, it is unclear whether lawmakers intended to countermand the *Hamdan* Court or, instead, accepted the Court's invitation to grant "the President the legislative authority to create military commissions at issue here."

Another constitutionally authorized mechanism to countermand Supreme Court decision-making is the Article V amendment process. The Eleventh Amendment (ratified in 1795) was a response to the Supreme Court's decision in *Chisolm v. Georgia*, 2 U.S. 419 (1793). *Chisolm* ruled that states could be sued in federal courts by citizens of another state; the Eleventh Amendment explicitly forbids such lawsuits. The Thirteenth Amendment (ratified in 1865) outlawed slavery and, in so doing, nullified *Dred Scott v. Sandford*, 60 U.S. 393 (1857). Since the Reconstruction, however, Congress has rarely amended the Constitution in response to Court decisions. That has not stopped lawmakers from seriously contemplating such amendments and constitutional amendment proposals have been considered in response to Court decisions on child labor, abortion, school prayer, and gender equality.

APPOINTMENT OF JUSTICES

Perhaps the principal way that Congress responds to Court decisions is through its power both to confirm Supreme Court nominees and determine the number of justices who sit on the Court. The process by which the president appoints and the Senate confirms Supreme Court nominees is often used to change the direction of Court decisions. For example, after the Supreme Court ruled paper money unconstitutional in 1870, President Ulysses S. Grant (1822–1885) nominated, and the Senate confirmed, two justices who voted the very next year to overturn that decision in *Legal Tender Cases*, 79 U.S. 467 (1871). The Senate likewise backed President Franklin D. Roosevelt's efforts to appoint justices supportive of economic regulation, especially Congress's use of the commerce clause as an agent of social change. From, these New Deal appointees overturned decisions and, in so doing, paved the way for the modern regulatory state. During the period from 1937 to 1944, thirty decisions were overruled.

Senate support for Roosevelt's Supreme Court picks, however, did not translate into Senate support for Roosevelt's controversial Court-packing plan. Before Supreme Court vacancies allowed him to reshape constitutional law, Roosevelt felt stymied by a pro-business Supreme Court. His solution was to increase the size of the Court so that the balance of power would shift to pro-New Deal Justices. Congress took this proposal seriously and there was good reason to think that it would back the President. However, through the so-called switch in time that saved nine, the Supreme Court reversed course on its own. For its part, Congress saw no reason to check a Court that seemed willing to check itself.

LEGISLATIVE RESPONSES

The above inventory, while significant, merely scratches the surface of possible congressional responses to Supreme Court decisions. Congress, for example, may enact legislation that seeks to limit the reach of Supreme Court rulings. After the Supreme Court upheld abortion rights in *Roe v. Wade*, 410 U.S. 113 (1973), Congress blocked the use of Medicaid and other federal funds to pay for abortions. Congress also offered religious organizations federal funds to promote sexual abstinence as a method of birth control. The Supreme Court approved both of these statutes and, in so doing, validated Congress's use of its appropriation powers to respond to Supreme Court rulings (*Harris v. McRae*, 448 U.S. 297 [1980]). The Supreme Court also upheld a 2003 federal statute prohibiting intact dilations and extractions, enacted in response to a 2000 Court ruling that a state ban on so-called partial birth abortions was unconstitutionally vague (*Gonzales v. Carhart*, 550 U.S. ___ [2007]).

Congress may also respond to a Supreme Court decision by reenacting a statute that the Court struck down. For example, Congress strongly disagreed with the Court's 1918 ruling that the commerce power could not be used to regulate child labor (*Hammer v. Dagenhart*, 247 U. S. 251 [1918]). The very next year, Congress sought to make use of an alternative power (the taxing power) to enact child labor legislation. Again, the Supreme Court struck the statute down (*Child Labor Tax Case*, 259 U.S. 20 [1922]). In 1938, after the Court's composition had changed, Congress again based child labor legislation on commerce clause legislation that a unanimous Court upheld (*United States v. Darby*, 312 U.S. 100 [1941]).

Congress has also taken aim at Court decisions through its powers to enforce the Fourteenth (equal protection) and Fifteenth (voting rights) Amendments. Rejecting a 1980 Supreme Court decision requiring civil rights plaintiffs to prove intentional discrimination in vote dilution cases (*Mobile v. Bolden*, 446 U.S. 55 [1980]), Congress amended the Voting Rights Act to allow for impact-based proofs of vote dilution. Congress likewise disapproved of the 1990 Supreme Court decision in *Employment Division v. Smith*, 494 U.S. 872 (1990) that limited the ability of plaintiffs to succeed in religious liberty lawsuits, and enacted legislation that required governmental actors to have a "compelling governmental interest" whenever religious liberty was "burdened." This legislation, the Religious Freedom Restoration Act (RFRA), was subsequently invalidated by the Supreme Court in *City of Boerne v. Flores*, 521 U.S. 507 (1997). Unwilling to accept defeat, Congress enacted a scaled down version of the RFRA, the Religious Land Use and Institutionalized Persons Act (RLUIPA), a statute that the Supreme Court upheld (against a preliminary challenge) in 2005 (*Cutter v. Wilkinson*, 544 U.S. 709 [2005]).

The RLUIPA statute highlights Congress's willingness to respond to a Court ruling by advancing its policy agenda in ways that it thinks the Court will approve. When enacting RLUIPA, lawmakers paid close attention to the Supreme Court decision invalidating the RFRA with *Boerne v. Flores*, 521 U.S. 507 (1997), seeking to advance their policy agenda while not calling into question the Court's handiwork. Likewise, after the Supreme Court invalidated a statute banning guns within 1,000 feet of a school (as an impermissible exercise of Congress's commerce power) in *United States v. Lopez*, 514 U.S. 548 (1995), Congress amended the Gun-Free School Zones Act to require the federal government to prove that the firearm had either moved in interstate commerce or otherwise affected interstate commerce.

Another way that Congress expresses its disagreement with the Supreme Court is to protect rights that the Court says it need not protect. Following a 1986 Supreme Court decision upholding an Air Force regulation that had prohibited an observant Jew from wearing a yarmulke in *Golden v. Weinburger*, 475 U.S. 503, Congress enacted legislation allowing service members to express their faith by wearing neat and conservative religious apparel. In 1999, Congress responded to concerns that independent counsels were overzealous when investigating high-ranking executive branch officials. Specifically, notwithstanding the Supreme Court's lopsided seven-to-one approval of this statute with the decision of *Morrison v. Olson*, 487 U.S. 654, in 1988, Congress concluded that the statute was fundamentally flawed and ought not to be reauthorized with the Ethics in Government Act.

Congressional responses to Supreme Court decisions are not always hostile. Sometimes the Court invites Congress to enact legislation that would effectively negate a Court ruling. For example, when upholding state power to issue search warrants of newspapers, the Court invited a legislative response noting that its decision "does not prevent or advise against legislative or executive efforts to establish nonconstititutional protections against possible abuses of the search warrant procedure" (*Zurcher v. Stanford Daily*, 436 U.S. 547 [1978]). Congress accepted the invitation, passing the Privacy Protection Act of 1980 to prohibit third-party searches of newspapers.

On other occasions, Congress affirmatively assists in the implementation of a Court decision. In response to resistance in the South to school desegregation, Congress took bold steps to make *Brown v. Board of Education*, 347 U.S. 483 (1954), a reality. In 1964, it prohibited segregated school systems from receiving federal aid and authorized the Department of Justice to file desegregation lawsuits. These federal efforts proved critical to ending dual school systems. More desegregation took place the year after these legislative programs took effect than in the decade following *Brown*.

As the above discussion makes clear, the Supreme Court does not speak the last word on the meaning of federal statutes or the Constitution. Congress can nullify Supreme Court interpretations of federal statutes by enacting a new statute or amending an existing law. On constitutional issues, the dynamic is more complex. Congress can respond to Supreme Court constitutional rulings through a variety of techniques, ranging from the enactment of the very same statute to the confirmation of Supreme Court justices who are likely to distinguish or overturn disfavored rulings. Through these varied responses to Supreme Court rulings, Congress plays a critical role in shaping constitutional values.

SEE ALSO *Eleventh Amendment; Fourteenth Amendment; Jurisdiction Stripping; Reconstruction*

BIBLIOGRAPHY

Beveridge, Albert J. 1919. *The Life of John Marshall*. New York: Houghton Mifflin.

Devins, Neal, and Louis Fisher. 2004. *The Democratic Constitution*. New York: Oxford University Press.

Eskridge, William. 1991. "Overriding Supreme Court Statutory Decisions." *Yale Law Journal* 101 (March): 331–459.

Marcus, Ruth. February 15, 1987. "Constitution Confuses Most Americans." *Washington Post*, A13.

Meese, Edwin. 1987. "The Law of Constitution." *Tulane Law Review*: 983.

Pickerill, J. Mitchell. 2004. *Constitutional Deliberation in Congress: The Impact of Judicial Review in a Separated System*. Durham, NC: Duke University Press.

Neal Devins

CONSTITUTIONAL CONVENTION, FRAMING

The most remarkable feature of the judiciary at the Constitutional Convention may be how little it was discussed. The scheme of representation in Congress and the nature of the executive provoked heated debate, which led the venerable Benjamin Franklin (1706–1790), elder statesman at the Convention, to plea for "coolness and temper" on more than one occasion. This may suggest a consensus on the nature of the judiciary. There is evidence, for instance, that judicial review was presumed by many of the delegates to the Convention. Yet judicial review was not the central question at the Convention. Rather, the Convention was preoccupied by whether inferior courts should be national or state courts, and how the judiciary should be positioned within the separation of powers as a whole. When it figures in the Convention debates, judicial review is almost always discussed in terms of the separation of powers—and very often indirectly.

THE VIRGINIA PLAN

Much as it did for the Constitution as a whole, Edmund Randolph's (1753–1813) Virginia Plan structured debate on the judiciary. Introduced on May 29, 1787, Randolph's Resolution 9 established a "National Judiciary," which was to "consist of one or more supreme tribunals, and of inferior tribunals to be chosen by the National Legislature, to hold offices during good behavior." The resolution then proceeded to establish jurisdiction, with the inferior tribunals hearing cases of national interest in the first instance with the "supreme tribunal," or possibly tribunals, as a court of last resort:

"[the] jurisdiction of the inferior tribunals shall be to hear & determine in the first instance, and of the supreme tribunal to hear and determine in the dernier resort, all piracies & felonies on the high seas, captures from an enemy; cases in which foreigners or citizens of other States applying to such jurisdictions may be interested, or which respect the collection of the National revenue, impeachments of any National officers, and

An undated painting by Junius Brutus Stearns depicting the signing of the Constitution. *Unlike the debate over the legislative and executive branch, the attendees at the Constitutional Convention did not devote as much time to developing a detailed plan for a federal judiciary. Much of the discussion about the role of the judicial branch revolved not around its structure but rather how the courts would share power with the other two-thirds of government.* © **CORBIS-BETTMANN**

questions which may involve the national peace and harmony." (Farrand 1966, vol. 1, p. 22)

This resolution would remain at the center of the Convention's debates about the judiciary for the next three months and, with important refinements, would become the basis of Article III of the Constitution.

The Convention would very quickly, and unanimously, move to revise Randolph's Resolution 9 to establish a national judiciary to consist of a supreme court and one or more inferior courts. While the Convention would never return to the question of a single supreme tribunal, the establishment of inferior tribunals was the most contested aspect of Resolution 9. The very next day, the Convention altered Resolution 9 in regard to inferior tribunals and the method of legislative appointment, postponing these questions for future debate. While accepting the need for a national judiciary constituted of a single tribunal, a number of delegates rejected the necessity of national inferior tribunals. On June 5, 1787, having secured a reconsideration of the national legislature's power to establish "inferior tribunals," John Rutledge of

South Carolina moved to strike the clause from the resolution altogether. The state courts, he contended, should provide the first forum, which might then allow for appeal to a supreme court. As Rutledge argued, "the State Tribunals might and ought to be left in all cases to decide in the first instance the right of appeal to the supreme national tribunal being sufficient to secure the national rights & uniformity of Judgments: that it was making an unnecessary encroachment on the jurisdiction of the States, and creating unnecessary obstacles to their adoption of the new system" (Farrand 1966, vol. 1, p. 124). Roger Sherman (1721–1793) of Connecticut similarly insisted that the state courts could serve in this fashion.

James Madison (1751–1836) of Virginia and James Wilson (1742–1798) of Pennsylvania, perhaps the two leading members of the Convention, argued that an "effective Judiciary establishment commensurate to the legislative authority was essential. A Government without a proper Executive & Judiciary would be a mere trunk of a body without arms or legs to act and move" (Farrand 1966, vol. 1, p. 124). In insisting that inferior national courts were necessary to a truly national system, and could not be supplemented by state courts, they where seconded by John Dickinson (1732–1808) of Delaware, who often found himself on the side of the smaller states attempts to maintain a federal system against a wholly national system. Yet Rutledge's motion to strike out the national legislature's authority to establish inferior tribunals passed. Madison and Wilson had to settle for providing that the national legislature could, if it deemed necessary, provide for inferior tribunals, which passed by a comfortable majority and was included within the final form of Article III.

THE NEW JERSEY PLAN

These refinements would be gathered together as Resolutions 12, 13, and 14—which established a supreme court appointed by the legislature, empowered the national legislature to appoint inferior tribunals, and provided for the jurisdiction of the national judiciary— and put before the Committee of the Whole on June 13, 1787. The next day, William Patterson (1745–1806) of New Jersey asked that the Convention adjourn, as a number of delegates were preparing a purely federal plan, in contrast to the Virginia Plan, that they wished to put before the Convention. On June 15, 1787, Patterson introduced what would be dubbed the New Jersey Plan. Resolution 5 of the New Jersey Plan essentially followed the revised the Virginia Plan in regard to the judiciary, save that it established a federal judiciary that consisted only of "a supreme Tribunal," the judges of which were to be "appointed by the Executive" and given original jurisdiction in the impeachments of federal officers. It also bound the "judiciary of the several states" to the "Acts of the U. States in Congress," even including the language "any thing in the respective laws of the Individual States to the contrary notwithstanding." This language was ultimately situated within Article VI of the Constitution and arguably provided for judicial review by state courts of state laws. Unlike the Virginia Plan, Resolution 2 of the New Jersey Plan provided that the "state judiciarys" would be the central courts in the federal system with appeal, both as to law and to fact, "to the Judiciary of the U. States" (Farrand 1966, vol. 1, pp. 243–245).

From the introduction of the New Jersey Plan to the Great Compromise on July 16, 1787, the judiciary played almost no direct role in the Convention's deliberations. When it did return, it was in the context of the separation of powers as a whole. James Wilson, for instance, had called for executive appointment of judges prior to the New Jersey Plan and moved for it again on July 18, 1787. Madison, and others, had called for appointment by the Senate, which, after the Great Compromise, would be constituted of an equal number of representatives from each state. While the Convention, yet again, unanimously postponed this question, and would go back and forth on the manner of judicial appointment, it was never

questioned that judges would hold office during "good behavior." In fact, the method of appointment, whether by the legislature as a whole, by the Senate, by way of executive appointment, or some combination of each, nearly all turned on maintaining judicial independence and propriety within the separation of powers. This was also true in regard to judicial salaries, where both the Virginia and New Jersey plans provided for fixed compensation, initially not only with no diminution in salary, but no increase, though the latter was ultimately rejected.

THE COUNCIL OF REVISION

In this way, some of the most profound discussions of the judiciary came indirectly as the Convention argued about the nature of the separation of powers. Indeed, the Convention never spoke directly to, or provided for, what is often considered this central feature of the judiciary in the constitutional scheme—the power of the courts to set aside acts of the legislature and executive as unconstitutional. If such was part of the original understanding, it must be gathered indirectly from the Convention's discussion of the Council of Revision in Randolph's Virginia Plan.

Far more controversial than the Virginia Plan's establishment of a national judiciary, which would be refined and modified, but essentially left intact, was Randolph's Resolution 8:

> The Executive and a convenient number of the National Judiciary, ought to compose a council of revision with authority to examine every act of the National Legislature before it shall operate, & every act of a particular Legislature before a Negative thereon shall be final; and that the dissent of the said Council shall amount to a rejection, unless the Act of the National Legislature be again passed, or that a particular Legislature be again negatived by the members of each branch. (Farrand 1966, vol. 1, p. 21)

On June 4, 1787, the Convention agreed to postpone consideration of the Council of Revision and in its place took up consideration of a resolution introduced by Elbridge Gerry (1744–1814) of Massachusetts that formed the basis of the executive veto. Despite the strong support of James Wilson and James Madison, the Council was rejected—and on multiple occasions. As late as August 15, 1787, Madison reintroduced a variation of the Council, seconded by Wilson, which moved Gerry of Massachusetts to complain that, "this motion comes to the same thing with what has been already negatived" (Farrand 1966, vol. 2, p. 298). It was again.

JUDICIAL POWER

Yet the debates surrounding the Council are of deep interest to understanding the nature of judicial power established by the Convention. Indeed, the Council is most frequently turned to as justifying judicial review. Many members of the Convention rejected the Council of Revision insofar as it combined the judiciary with the executive. While the executive veto alone was acceptable, delegates were concerned that placing members of the judiciary on the Council would place them in the awkward position of hearing cases as judges that they had previously weighed in on as members of the Council. Gerry's "doubts whether the Judiciary ought to form a part of it [the Council], as they will have a sufficient check against encroachments on their own department by their exposition of the laws, which involved a power of deciding on their Constitutionality" is typical of this line of reasoning (Farrand 1966, vol. 1, p. 97). Luther Martin (1748–1826) of Maryland similarly insisted, "as to the Constitutionality of laws, that point will come before the Judges in their proper official character. In this character they have a negative on the laws. Join them with the Executive in the Revision and they will have a double negative" (p. 76). A central question is whether this exercise of judicial review applies only to state laws and not national laws, as might be suggested by Roger Sherman's (1721–1793) presumption of such a power: "the Courts of the States would not consider as valid any law contravening the Authority of the Union" (p. 27).

Yet the defenders of the Council seemed to speak of the possibility of judicial review of national laws—and most of the objections insisted that the Council was either unnecessary or unwise as it violated the separation of powers, rather than rejecting the propriety of judicial review. Defenders of the Council such as Madison worried that if left to the judiciary alone, laws that were unconstitutional would operate before the Court could strike them down (Farrand 1966, vol. 2, p. 27). And Madison defended the combining of the executive and judiciary as an "auxiliary precaution" in favor of the maxim of keeping the "great departments of power separate and distinct"; that is, as a way of confining the national legislature to its constitutional limits. Colonel George Mason (1725–1792) of Virginia, seconded by James Wilson, thought this combination would also allow the Council to prohibit "unjust, oppressive or pernicious" laws, while the judiciary alone would only "declare an unconstitutional law void" (pp. 78 and 73). Here Mason was speaking of national laws, not merely state laws. Gouverneur Morris (1752–1816) of Pennsylvania would also insist, whether the Council or a like mechanism was accepted, that the judiciary could not "be bound to say that a direct violation of the Constitution was law" (p. 299). Or as Madison expressed it, "A law violating a constitution established by the people themselves, would be considered by the Judges as null and void" (p. 430).

This led Max Farrand, who drew together the authoritative *Records of the Federal Convention*, to go so far as to insist, "it was asserted over and over again … that the federal judiciary would declare null and void laws that were inconsistent with the constitution. In other words, it was generally assumed by the leading men in the convention that this power existed" (1913, p. 157).

This may well be so. But it should be noted that there was opposition to such a power. John Mercer (1729–1821) of Maryland, for example, "disapproved of the Doctrine that the Judges as expositors of the Constitution should have authority to declare a law void" (Farrand 1966, vol. 2, p. 298). So, too, did John Dickinson. Even if this power was presumed by many, and explicitly insisted upon by others, one should be clear about its reach as deliberated within the Convention. As Madison would later insist, it was "going too far to extend the jurisdiction of the Court to cases arising under the Constitution," as the "Judicial Power" should "be limited to cases of a Judiciary Nature" (p. 430).

Madison's insistence occurred against a motion of William Johnson (1727–1819) of Connecticut, which sought to refine the Committee on Details's language regarding jurisdiction. Johnson moved that the jurisdiction of the national Judiciary "shall extend to Cases arising *under this Constitution* and the Laws passed by the general Legislature." Johnson's motion was agreed to unanimously, yet it was done so on the grounds that the jurisdiction given was limited to cases of a "Judiciary nature" (Farrand 1966, vol. 2, p. 430). The insistence on the peculiar nature of the "judicial power" also found expression in Madison and Morris's motion to use that language in speaking to the judiciary's jurisdiction, which was agreed to unanimously. Thus Article III, section two reads: "The judicial Power shall extend to all Cases," which it then proceeds to enumerate. And at this point the Convention very nearly fleshed out the cases the judicial Power extended to, including treaties of the United States (postponing whether or not it would include impeachment, which was ultimately excluded from the judiciary's jurisdiction and placed with the Senate) giving us all of the elements that found expression in the final form of Article III.

SEPARATION OF POWERS

Taken altogether, this lends powerful support to the insistence that judicial review was endorsed by the Convention. But this also suggests that judicial review was not the same as constitutional review. Not all disputes arising under the Constitution would take judicial form. Thus many constitutional disputes would not fall under the "judicial Power." The executive veto, for instance, provided a form of constitutional review, but had nothing to do with the judiciary because the Council of Revision was rejected by the Convention.

In modern terms, this might be best understood by distinguishing between judicial review and what has come to be known as judicial supremacy. The former allows the Court to strike down acts of the legislature or executive; it does not, however, entail the power to bind the other branches of government to its interpretation of the Constitution. In contrast, judicial supremacy positions the judiciary as the authoritative interpreter of the Constitution for all the branches of government. There is no evidence that the Convention contemplated such a power for the national judiciary, despite the Court's rather easy insistence on this role in the early twenty-first century. If the Convention spoke of a "Supreme Tribunal," it was supreme over other courts and not over the Congress and the president, which were put forward in Articles I and II of the Constitution.

Here the Convention seemed to situate the judiciary squarely within the separation of powers. Not only was legislative action necessary to bring forth inferior national tribunals (if it saw fit to do so), but the Convention gave the legislature power to alter much of the Supreme Court's jurisdiction without any objection or debate. And while the appointment of judges was finally lodged in the executive with little extensive debate, it also included the consent of the Senate. It may have been with an eye toward maintaining separate and independent powers that trials for impeachment were removed from the Court's jurisdiction and given to the Congress. The debate was not extensive, but there were certainly those members of the Convention who objected to judges sitting over the impeachment trial of an executive who may well have been responsible for their appointment. Such an understanding also neatly accords with a judiciary that would be independent of the other branches of government, but not superior to them.

SEE ALSO *Articles of Confederation; Constitution of the United States; Great Compromise; Judicial Independence; Judicial Review; Marshall Court; Separation of Powers; Slavery*

BIBLIOGRAPHY

Farrand, Max. 1913. *The Framing of the Constitution of the United States.* New Haven, CT: Yale University Press.

Farrand, Max, ed. 1966. *The Records of the Federal Convention of 1787.* Rev. edition. 3 vols. New Haven, CT: Yale University Press.

Madison, James. 1987. *Notes of Debates in the Federal Convention of 1787.* New York: W.W. Norton.

George Thomas

CONSTITUTIONAL INTERPRETATION

The U.S. Constitution is famously obscure. It uses words it does not define, lists powers without explaining their scope or limits, and relies on vague terms like *due process of law.* Before judges can apply the Constitution to actual cases, they must supply the missing details. In keeping with the American tradition of *judicial supremacy,* the U.S. Supreme Court has the last word on what the Constitution means.

The Constitution itself gives no guidance on how it is to be interpreted. Some judges focus on the details of individual cases and never commit themselves to interpretive theories in the abstract. But other judges prefer to approach all their cases in the same way. A general interpretive theory, approach, or method gives judges a place to start each case analysis, highlights what they should look for, and thus makes their work easier, more consistent, and more predictable. It can also make their work more legitimate, because people are more willing to accept some controversial decision if they believe that it was made in accordance with a decision-making method that is known in advance, appropriate, and fair.

Judges have never agreed on a single theory of constitutional interpretation. Since the 1970s as the Court has had to deal with more controversial material, judges, law professors, and philosophers have given more thought to theories of constitutional interpretation in the abstract. The most commonly discussed theories fall into one of two categories: interpretative and noninterpretative.

INTERPRETIVE THEORIES

Interpretivists assert that the necessary meanings are already in the Constitution itself, either implied by the ways in which its words are used or discoverable from the circumstances in which it was created. The job of the judge is to study the document and its creation, infer or otherwise find the meaning, and then apply it to the case at hand.

Originalism Originalism, sometimes called intentionalism, is the most frequently discussed theory of constitutional interpretation, and the most controversial. Originalists argue that the meaning was put into the Constitution by the people who made it. "Those who framed the constitution chose their words carefully," observed former attorney general Edwin Meese III in 1985. "The language they chose meant something. It is incumbent upon the court to determine what that meaning was. ... The text of the document and the original intent of those who framed it would be the judicial standard in giving effect to the Constitution"

(p. 704). If this intent is not readily apparent, it can easily be determined by referring to the voluminous writings that the framers left behind.

The Constitution is the social contract, the deal between the rulers and the ruled; it creates a limited government that must respect popular rights. The sovereign people—the "ruled"—gave their consent to that government by ratifying the document. The original understanding of the Constitution's meaning is itself part of the deal because the contract, like any ordinary business contract, must always be interpreted in a way consistent with the intent of its makers. Thus, judges have no power to interpret the Constitution except in accordance with this substantive original intent.

The contract analogy is an extremely powerful argument. If the Constitution is a contract, then the promise-keeping principle applies: A deal is a deal. Once the Constitution is made, Americans must abide by it, even if they do not like some particular action. If the Supreme Court hands down an unpopular decision, people should be more likely to accept it if they see it as required by the original promise.

This powerful legitimating argument is especially necessary when we remember that the Constitution creates a government that is not entirely democratic. There will always be times when the Court will have to frustrate majority will. Judges are paradoxically strengthened when they can argue that their own power is limited, and that the original understanding prevents them from doing what the public wants.

Justices have always made originalist arguments for this legitimating value whenever they find them useful. But no justice has ever been entirely consistent. Sometimes the arguments are well-researched and coherent; for example, in *Adamson v. California*, 332 U.S. 46 (1947) Justice Hugo Black stated in a dissenting opinion that his study of the history surrounding the creation of the Fourteenth Amendment in 1866 persuaded him that its framers intended to make the Bill of Rights applicable to the states. Though he was not persuasive in 1948, the Court later accepted a weakened version of this argument and used it to extend to defendants in state criminal proceedings a variety of rights that had previously been guaranteed only in federal trials.

At other times, originalist arguments are made with questionable logic or little supporting evidence. An example of the former is Chief Justice William Howard Taft's dissenting argument that police wiretapping could never be an "unreasonable search" prohibited by the Fourth Amendment because electronic surveillance had not been invented when the framers wrote that amendment (*Olmstead v. United States*, 277 U.S. 438 [1928]). An example of the latter case is Chief Justice William Rehnquist's dissenting argument in *Roe v. Wade*,

> *We must never forget, that it is a constitution we are expounding.*
> SOURCE: John Marshall, *M'Culloch v. Maryland*, 17 U.S. (4 Wheat.) 316, 407 (1819).

410 U.S. 113 (1973) that the Fourteenth Amendment's framers surely did not intend to create a right to abort.

In a troubling number of cases, such arguments are meant to prevent change by imposing the dead hand of the past to stifle some innovation. In a concurrence in *Morse v. Frederick*, 127 S. Ct. 2618 (2007), Justice Clarence Thomas asserts that public school students have no First Amendment protection against their schoolmasters. Early-nineteenth-century schoolmasters lived soon after the framers, he reasoned, and presumably knew what the framers intended; if the framers wanted students to possess free speech rights, the schoolmasters would have known and respected that intention. Since surviving records indicate that schoolmasters sometimes punished students for speech (like profanity), the framers could not have intended students to possess any First Amendment rights. Therefore, they can never have them. All recent Supreme Court cases to the contrary were wrongly decided. The dubious assumptions, erratic logic, and limited historical sources are characteristic of extreme reliance on originalism.

Historians disagree on the answer to the question Thomas wrestled with, and to all significant questions of original intent. Eighteenth-century records are famously incomplete and spotty. History may simply be indeterminate. Moreover, many people were involved in the creation of the Constitution, and they may not have agreed on what the purpose of some provision is. They wrote a lot, but they sometimes contradicted each other. Sometimes they intentionally left some substantive provision vague. What procedure, for example, is *due process*? Finally, the world has changed so much since 1787 that it is hard to determine how the framers' views apply to contemporary cases.

For all these reasons, specific original intent—if it exists—is much harder to determine than Attorney General Meese expects. Originalists respond by retreating to ever-weaker versions of the theory. *Original intent* has given way to *original principles*, by which the judge is expected to deduce and apply some overriding principle behind the document. Even weaker forms of the theory direct a judge to seek *original meaning, original public meanings, core meanings*, or *objectified intent*. The Supreme Court's most vocal originalist, Rehnquist, argued in a 2004 essay that at a minimum judges must show that decisions have some "connection with a popularly adopted constituent act" that occurred in 1787 (p. 127).

Weakened theories require less historical evidence, and avoid the practical problems that make strong originalism impossible. But they are so weak that they restrain the interpreters not at all. Former U.S. circuit judge Robert Bork has argued that the Constitution contains, at its base, a principle of respect for the dignity and freedom of the individual. This principle is so important that the framers would have used it to forbid slavery if they had known what we now know about the evils of racism. Law professor Thomas Y. Davies has termed this development of convenient principles of doubtful historical provenance *fictional originalism* (2007, p. 557).

Sometimes originalist principles conflict with originalist specifics. Majorities and dissenters have disagreed, for example, over whether the framers of the Civil War (1861–1865) amendments intended to make the Bill of Rights applicable to the states (*Adamson*); meant to forbid social, as opposed to political, racial segregation (*Plessy v. Ferguson*, 163 U.S. 537 [1896]); or granted the federal government the power to alter state legislative apportionments (*Lucas v. Forty-Fourth General Assembly of Colorado*, 377 U.S. 713 [1964]).

Some justices consider originalism's fatal flaw to be the fact that the nation has simply changed in ways that make the views of pre–Industrial Revolution slave owners irrelevant. Despite the country's long history of racism and oppression, most contemporary Americans would reject any constitutional theory according to which segregated public schools are legal. The world is simply different now. Recognizing that the world would change, the framers themselves did not intend their specific intentions to control the future.

Moreover, originalism rests on a faulty analogy. The original understanding must be controlling only if, as Philip Bobbitt has argued (1991, p. 5) the Constitution is defined as a contract, like a promissory note. Contracts are put in writing to enforce the intent of the people who make them. But where civil contracts bind the parties to do specific things, are limited, and do not last in perpetuity, the social contract requires people to participate in an open-ended political process. As simple legal documents, civil contracts lack the Constitution's symbolic and unifying functions. No one ever died gallantly in battle to protect and defend a promissory note.

Textualism Like originalists, textualists argue that the framers put meaning into the Constitution when it was adopted. The job of the judges is to enforce the deal enacted in 1787. But unlike originalists, textualists argue that even if the framers had conflicting intentions about what the Constitution is to mean, they produced a single document; presumably, the Constitution has an objective meaning that can be recovered by a careful study of its words, their history, and their placement within the text. Justice Antonin Scalia argues in his textbook that the Court can find in the text of the Constitution "a sort of 'objectified' intent [of the framers]" (1997, p. 17). Where originalists try to reconstruct the deal from the letters and diaries of the framers, textualists welcome the contributions of grammarians, etymologists, and philologists.

Textualism has long been used in interpreting statutes. "It is ultimately by the provisions of our laws rather than the principal concerns of our legislators by which we are governed," Scalia, the Court's most consistent textualist, argued in *Oncale v. Sundowner Offshore Services, Inc.*, 523 U.S. 75 (1998). In separate opinions in cases like *Green v. Bock Laundry*, 490 U.S. 504 (1989), he has argued that history is always incomplete and indeterminate while texts are unchanging and relatively objective.

Textualism has been used in constitutional interpretation at least since 1819. In *M'Culloch v. Maryland*, 17 U.S. 316, Chief Justice John Marshall held that the necessary and proper clause grants an additional power to Congress (instead of being a limit on Congress's other powers, as Maryland's lawyers had argued) because it is written in the language of a grant and is placed in the section of the Constitution that grants powers, not the section which lists limits. Justice Hugo Black argued that because the First Amendment says that Congress shall make no law abridging the freedom of speech, Congress is not allowed to make *any* such law; it cannot forbid even speech that is concededly obscene or creates a "clear and present danger" of some evil. "No law means no law."

However, textualism has its problems. Unlike recent statutes, which are written in familiar language and often include notes on how they are to be interpreted, the Constitution is old, spare, and obscure. Recovering the meaning of antiquated language requires an attention to the history of language, which in turn depends on the survival of a few old texts that can be studied; this history is as slippery as the sources on which originalists are forced to rely. Scholars still cannot agree, for example, on what eighteenth-century lawyers meant by *due process*. Nor can a literal reading solve all problems. Because the Constitution always refers to the president as *He*, for example, are women forever barred from serving in the office?

We know that the framers disagreed about many things. They may have intentionally left the text ambiguous. Does it, for example, imply the existence of the power of judicial review? Finally, some features of the Constitution were new or used in new ways, and have no eighteenth-century analogs. American federalism, for example, has no real precedent. The Constitution implies something about the relation of the nation to the states, but specific details of that relationship cannot be inferred through the study of earlier legal relationships.

These criticisms also apply to Akhil Amar's *intratextualism*. On the assumption that the framers can be presumed to have used words consistently throughout the Constitution, interpreters, once they have determined the meaning of a word in one location, can use that known meaning to shed light on the meaning of the same word when it is used elsewhere in the document. When Article I provides that a member of Congress may not be questioned "in any other place" for any "Speech or Debate in either House," it is referring to political speech only. Therefore, Amar argues, the First Amendment freedom of speech ought to protect only, or at least mainly, political speech (1999, p. 815). But the Constitution was negotiated by different groups of people, and later amended by yet others. The assumption of consistency is questionable. And the determination of meaning must begin somewhere. Can interpreters be sure that Article I is concerned only with political speech?

Common-law Constitutionalism The Constitution creates the Supreme Court as a court, staffed by judges and empowered to decide cases. Arguably, it was expected to function like the common-law courts developed over time in England and the colonies. Courts would search through the records left by earlier courts; based on this legal tradition, they would develop interpretive principles, derive substantive rules from those principles, and apply the rules to cases. They would proceed incrementally, keeping what works and, over time, gradually modifying or eliminating what failed or became obsolete.

Common-law or developmental jurisprudence is most visible when the Supreme Court must interpret the parts of the Constitution that deal with court procedures themselves. The Constitution, for example, guarantees a right to trial by jury. But it says nothing about what juries are for or how they are to be constituted. Colonial practice was simply continued. However, changing circumstances brought questions. Could women serve, even though the framers were familiar with "twelve good men and true"? For that matter, did there have to be twelve? In *Williams v. Florida*, 399 U.S. 78 (1970) the Court held that juries existed to protect litigants from government pressure and maximize the likelihood that community diversity would be represented. Since six members were adequate to achieve these goals, six-member juries could be used. Similar logic allowed women to serve (*Taylor v. Louisiana*, 419 U.S. 522 [1975]).

Developmental constitutionalism is usually considered a form of originalism, on the argument that the framers intended the courts to behave in this way. But when used over time, developmental constitutionalism makes it possible for courts to escape from original intent. If procedures are made impractical or unworkable by changing circumstances, the courts can change them. This avoids the tendency of originalism to stifle innovation. Some scholars have argued that the common-law method allows the Constitution to be perfected over time, as failed practices are discarded and improvements come into use.

But common-law constitutionalism relies on judge-enunciated principles not themselves in the Constitution. Justice Felix Frankfurter argued that judges are not free to do whatever they want. They must rely on established tradition. But in practice, while some desirable principles can be found in tradition ("juries are meant to protect people from officials"), others cannot ("juries are meant to reflect the diversity of the community"). Judges simply vary in what they think tradition establishes. At the extreme, judges can enunciate whatever they like. If the Constitution is meant to limit the government, common-law interpretive techniques certainly do not limit the judges.

NONINTERPRETIVE THEORIES

Noninterpretive theories seek meaning in some other way. Most stress the role of the Constitution as symbol of unity and argue that it has come to represent moral principles that are broadly accepted, whether or not the framers intended the Constitution to contain them.

Although the noninterpretive approach is not new, it came to be considered legitimate during the desegregation crisis of the 1950s. Faced with the question of whether the Constitution forbid racially segregated public schools, Chief Justice Earl Warren realized that legal precedent, legal tradition, and, at least arguably, original intent, all favored the segregationists. So in *Brown v. Board of Education*, 347 U.S. 483 (1954) he simply ruled such evidence irrelevant. Public education barely existed when the Constitution was written, and its potential was not apparent; however, modern schools play key roles in making possible equal opportunity and the attainability of each person's dreams and aspirations. Therefore, Warren ruled, public schooling must be provided equally to all.

In such cases, the noninterpretive approach stresses the symbolic importance of the Constitution as an aspirational document. It has come to represent ideals—in this case, of equal access and equal opportunity—that are broadly accepted and shared, and that people want the government to try to achieve. Judges use metaphors of an *evolving Constitution* or *living Constitution* to emphasize the role they want law to play in moving the government ever closer to these ideals. Justice William Brennan insisted that the Constitution looks forward rather than backward; it "was not intended to preserve a preexisting society, but to make a new one," and to transform society in the direction of greater freedom and human dignity

(1985, pp. 7–8). In the final analysis, the Constitution is not respected and binding because James Madison (1751–1836) and Alexander Hamilton (c. 1755–1804) gave their approval. It survives because the people now alive give *their* approval. Brennan and other activist justices used such arguments to legitimize the decisions of the Warren Court (1954–1969), which advanced desegregation, made state election procedures and legislative apportionment more democratic, and increased the number of federally protected rights that could be claimed by criminally accused persons in state courts.

The notion that moral standards are advancing is behind the decision in *Lawrence v. Texas*, 539 U.S. 558 (2003). Although Justice Byron R. White was certainly correct when he argued in an earlier case that law and tradition have never protected a right to engage in homosexual sexual relations, Justice Anthony Kennedy asserted that notions of privacy and liberty had changed over time. Moreover, courts were giving increasing emphasis to equality of treatment by the law itself. As a result, Kennedy held that homosexuals must be entitled to keep intimate relations private wherever heterosexuals can do so.

Often, however, clear and widely accepted moral standards cannot be found. For example, opponents of the death penalty have long argued that even though the framers used the death penalty, evolving standards of decency have now led to universal abhorrence of it. They point to the fact that most other developed nations have banned it, and cite surveys showing that ever-increasing numbers of Americans also support its abolition. But the evidence is controversial, and counterevidence exists.

Neutral Principles In such cases, where, and how, are judges to find acceptable aspirational principles? On what evidence should they decide that these principles have come to be broadly accepted? In the absence of court pronouncements, law professors and philosophers have speculated on what noninterpretive procedures should be like.

In a widely discussed 1959 essay, law professor Herbert Wechsler (1909–2000) argued that courts have to evolve moral principles, because the Constitution simply does not itself provide them. Any court decision must be principled, in the sense that interpretation is based on some general rule that is known in advance, and every rule must be neutral in the sense that it can be applied in the same way no matter who the litigants are. If freedom of speech is invoked to protect a Democrat's right to speak, it must also protect a Republican in similar circumstances—or a Communist, or any other advocate of an unpopular position.

Wechsler did not say where these principles are to come from, emphasizing instead that public acceptance would come from visible neutrality and fairness. From his examples, equality, equal opportunity, or at least equal access to government services, all seem appropriate candidates. Perhaps the greatest victory of this approach came in 1964, when the Supreme Court ruled in *Reynolds v. Sims,* 377 U.S. 533 that whenever the Court was asked to rule on whether some legislative apportionment was permissible under the equal protection clause, it would require the apportionment to be based on the principle of "one person, one vote." Though this requirement that each person has an equal voice in choosing legislators is widely acceptable, and fits into a general notion of equality before the law, it is not *in* the Constitution. Nor was it originally intended.

Democracy-maximizing Theories In 1980 law professor John Hart Ely (1938–2003) extended Wechsler's work. He argued that courts should develop principles, like the one-person-one-vote rule, that maximized democracy. Whenever a court must choose, it should choose the option that gave people the greater ability to participate in government. Advocates of democracy maximization remind us that the Constitution contains many provisions meant to give people broad control over the government. Moreover, democracy as an ideal is broadly supported. Justice Stephen Breyer has argued that maximizing "the people's right to 'an active and constant participation in collective power'" will lead to "better constitutional law" than a "more 'legalistic' approach that places too much weight upon language, history, tradition and precedent" (2004, p. 201).

There are, however, serious problems with democracy-maximizing approaches. There are many ways to view democracy. Maximizing participation, for example, is not the same as maximizing equal participation, maximizing informed participation, or maximizing popular control. Democracy-maximizing judges rarely specify which kind of democracy they support. Moreover, the Constitution itself imposes explicit limits on democracy. The one-person-one-vote rule, for example, cannot be extended to the U.S. Senate, which the Constitution explicitly exempts from population-based apportionment. For that matter, judicial supremacy itself is *countermajoritarian*.

Popular Constitutionalism Finally, law professor Larry Kramer represents an extreme position. From the beginning of the republic, he argues, ordinary people have participated in public debate. They had opinions about constitutional ratification, and have continued to have opinions about the proper scope and power of government as government has confronted the great issues of history. The framers respected *the people*, and expected citizens to act on their opinions in the political process. Kramer argues that they expected these opinions to be relevant to law as well. As government has become more complex, the people yielded too much of this power to the courts; Kramer argues that the courts must compensate by showing "a proper respect for the people" (2004, p. 246). In particular, the courts should hesitate to act counter to any strongly held position of the elected branches of the government, which are the people's representatives.

Kramer's arguments, and his ample historical documentation, have been taken up by critics of judicial supremacy, who argue that courts play too large a role in American life. But the contemporary electorate is much larger and more diverse than the electorate of 1787, which was so caught up in the drama of ratification. It is not clear how today's judges can identify stable and widespread constitutional expectations and distinguish them from transitory public opinion. Kramer draws uncomfortably close to uncritical dependence on public opinion surveys, or to blindly following election results. If his views are accepted, courts would be required to follow the expectations of large popular majorities, and would hardly be able to perform the function that creates perhaps the greatest amount of public support, the protection of minorities against hostile majorities. Violence, racism, and xenophobia are all part of American tradition; so, too, is religious intolerance. In freedom of religion cases, and many others, the longstanding popular constitutional tradition is that the Supreme Court must protect minorities from these expressions of majority will.

Noninterpretive theories all raise questions of limits. If anything is universally accepted about the intentions of the framers, it is that they wanted to create an enduring government within which the expected problems of a republic could be discussed and dealt with. To make the government stable and effective, they designed it in such a way that powers were balanced, and they imposed limits on the use of all forms of power. Courts are part of this process; they enable power to be used, but sometimes must enforce limits—on officeholders, on majorities, and sometimes on judges themselves. Any theory of constitutional interpretation must provide for the enforcement of these limits.

SEE ALSO *Anti-Federalist/Federalist Ratification Debate; Constitution of the United States; Incorporation Debate; Judicial Pragmatism; Judicial Review; Originalism; Roberts Court; Structuralism; Textualism*

BIBLIOGRAPHY

Amar, Akhil R. 1999. "Intratextualism." *Harvard Law Review* 112: 747–827.

Bobbitt, Philip. 1991. *Constitutional Interpretation.* Cambridge, MA: Blackwell.

Bork, Robert H. 1990. *The Tempting of America: The Political Seduction of the Law.* New York: Simon and Schuster.

Brennan, William J., Jr. 1985. "Construing the Constitution." *UC Davis Law Review* 19: 2–14.

Breyer, Stephen G. 2004. "Our Democratic Constitution." In *Judges on Judging: Views from the Bench,* ed. David M. O'Brien, 201–216. 2nd edition. Washington, DC: CQ Press.

Davies, Thomas Y. 2007. "Revisiting the Fictional Originalism in Crawford's 'Cross-Examination Rule.'" *Brooklyn Law Review* 72: 557–638.

Ely, John Hart. 1980. *Democracy and Distrust: A Theory of Judicial Review.* Cambridge: Harvard University Press.

Goldford, Dennis J. 2005. *The American Constitution and the Debate over Originalism.* New York: Cambridge University Press.

Kramer, Larry D. 2004. *The People Themselves: Popular Constitutionalism and Judicial Review.* New York: Oxford University Press.

Meese, Edwin, III. 1985. "The Attorney General's View of the Supreme Court: Toward a Jurisprudence of Original Intention." *Public Administration Review* 45: 701–704.

Meese, Edwin, III; David F. Forte; and Matthew Spalding, eds. 2005. *The Heritage Guide to the Constitution.* Washington DC: Heritage Foundation.

Rakove, Jack N. 1996. *Original Meanings: Politics and Ideas in the Making of the Constitution.* New York: Knopf.

Rehnquist, William H. 2004. "The Notion of a Living Constitution." In *Judges on Judging: Views from the Bench,* ed. David M. O'Brien, 124–135. 2nd edition. Washington, DC: CQ Press.

Scalia, Antonin. 1989. Originalism: The Lesser Evil. *University of Cincinnati Law Review* 57: 849–865.

Scalia, Antonin. 1997. *A Matter of Interpretation: Federal Courts and the Law.* Princeton, NJ: Princeton University Press.

Strauss, David A. 1996. "Common Law Constitutional Interpretation." *University of Chicago Law Review* 63(3): 877–935.

Vermeule, Adrian. 2006. *Judging under Uncertainty: An Institutional Theory of Legal Interpretation.* Cambridge: Harvard University Press.

Wechsler, Harold. 1959. "Toward Neutral Principles of Constitutional Law." *Harvard Law Review* 73: 1–35.

Whittington, Keith. 1999. *Constitutional Interpretation: Textual Meaning, Original Intent, and Judicial Review.* Lawrence: University Press of Kansas.

Paul Lermack

CONSTITUTIONALISM

Constitutionalism is a concept that combines description and normative prescription. Descriptively, the concept aims to draw into a single category a wide range of systems of government, from the past and the present, that respect

An anti-apartheid protestor carried away by police in Soweto, South Africa. *Constitutionalism suggests that governments should be limited to acting in accordance with preset rules, with a series of checks and balances to ensure proper government behavior. As evidenced by the apartheid government of South Africa, however, following a constitution does not necessarily provide equal rights for all citizens.* © **WILLIAM CAMPBELL/SYGMA/CORBIS**

the rule of law. Precisely because the range of systems encompassed within the category is so wide, the exact normative content of constitutionalism is difficult to pin down. Usually constitutionalism is said to require that government be limited and rest on consent of the governed, expressed either directly through elections or indirectly through voluntary ongoing support for the government.

Unless more content is given to the ideas of limited government and consent, constitutionalism does no more than describe governments that are not totalitarian, and the concept may not provide much insight into any particular government's operation. Yet, in light of the wide range of systems that must be included within the category—from the United States with its relatively thin social welfare state and robust commitment to private property, to Scandinavian nations with substantial systems of social provision and extensive regulation of private property—the more content given to the limits on government that constitutionalism requires, the larger the number of systems that fall outside the category, and the less descriptively accurate it becomes.

The first requirement of constitutionalism is that the government adhere to the rule of law, defined relatively weakly. The legal theorist Lon Fuller (1902–1978) identified a series of modest requirements for the rule of law, including that the laws be public so that people can conform their behavior to the law's requirements. There must also be procedures in place that allow government officials to determine, with some accuracy, whether the law has been complied with, and government officials almost always must actually use those procedures. Yet, these rule-of-law requirements may not sharply distinguish constitutionalist systems from totalitarian ones. Although the latter typically do have secret laws and violate their own stated rules of procedural regularity, there seems to be nothing conceptually, or perhaps even practically, that rules out the possibility that a government will enforce widely known and evil laws with strict procedural regularity.

The idea that constitutionalism requires limits on government power gives the concept more content. What limits, though? Libertarian theorists such as the Austrian economist Friedrich von Hayek (1899–1992) argue that

EIGHT OBSTACLES OF LEGAL RULE-MAKING

∎

[T]he attempt to create and maintain a system of legal rules may miscarry in at least eight distinct ways.... The first and most obvious lies in a failure to achieve rules at all, so that every issue must be decided on an ad hoc basis. The other routes are: (2) a failure to publicize, or at least to make available to the affected party, the rules he is expected to observe; (3) the abuse of retroactive legislation, which ... undercuts the integrity of rules prospective in effect, since it puts them under the threat of retrospective change; (4) a failure to make rules understandable; (5) the enactment of contradictory rules or (6) rules that require conduct beyond the powers of the affected party; (7) introducing such frequent changes in the rules that the subject cannot orient his action by them; and, finally, (8) a failure of congruence between the rules as announced and their actual administration.

SOURCE: Lon L. Fuller, *The Morality of Law*, revised edition. New Haven: Yale University Press, 1969, pp. 38–39.

Mark V. Tushnet

constitutionalism requires substantial limits on government. Without strict limits, government officials will exploit ambiguities in statutes authorizing them to regulate private activity, to the point where the law can be read to license them to do anything. Without strict limits on government power, then, there is a real risk that a government will degenerate into totalitarianism. The libertarian definition of constitutionalism is too stringent, if only because governments that do not respect the limits libertarians would place on them have lasted a long time without becoming totalitarian.

A different reason for insisting on limits to government power is that substantive ideals of justice and human rights require such limits. At this point the wide range of governments that must be counted as constitutionalist must again be taken into account. Governments cannot be insisted upon to adhere to some specific definitions of justice and human rights if they are to be described as constitutionalist, because doing so would exclude too many governments from the category. Yet it is not enough that government officials subjectively believe that they are implementing defensible ideals of justice and human rights, because experience shows that officials can persuade themselves that vicious policies promote justice

and human rights. It would seem, then, that constitutionalism requires that governments pursue policies that aim at securing justice and human rights, with justice and human rights accommodating a broad enough range of possibilities to ensure that the concept remains descriptively accurate.

There is a tension as well between the consent component of constitutionalism and the limited-government component. Experience has shown that mechanisms for eliciting consent, such as elections, can produce results that are inconsistent with the idea of limited government. Conservatives have regularly opposed extensions of the franchise on the ground that the large number of voters with relatively little material wealth will regularly exercise their power to enact laws that deprive the smaller number of those with great material wealth of their property, thereby violating the principle of limited government. Liberals in turn regularly point out abuses of human rights visited by electoral majorities on despised minorities.

In the years since World War II (1939–1945), human rights documents such as the International Covenant on Civil and Political Rights (1966) help identify in broad terms what constitutionalism's limits on government power are. Yet, to take a prominent example, it is one thing to say that constitutional government requires respect for freedom of expression, another to identify when governments fail to respect it. Dramatically, international human rights documents *require* governments to suppress hate speech, while the U.S. Supreme Court has interpreted the U.S. Constitution to *prohibit* the suppression of such speech (*R.A.V. v. City of St. Paul*, 505 U.S. 377 [1992]). The term *constitutionalism* loses much of its utility when it is used to demonstrate that either the United States or some nation that complies with the international norm fails the test of constitutionalism. The situation is even more dramatic with respect to issues of distributive justice. Strongly laissez-faire governments can certainly be constitutionalist, as can governments that regulate the workplace extensively and provide a high level of social provision.

At the same time, though, it must acknowledged that partisans of specific positions on questions of justice and human rights will almost always assert that policies inconsistent with their positions are inconsistent with constitutionalism as well. In this sort of political discourse, the term *constitutionalism* functions not as a tool for detached analysis but as one component of political rhetoric.

INSTITUTIONS OF CONSTITUTIONALISM

How are governments kept within the limits required by constitutionalism? History discloses three candidates. The first is a purely normative commitment on the part of government officials to respect those limits. The education of prospective government officials might imbue them with deep enough commitments to lead them to resist temptations to violate the limits. Systems of pure parliamentary government, such as what once existed in the United Kingdom, typically rely on *constitutional conventions* to ensure that certain limits on government are respected. These conventions are normative requirements not enforceable by law, and adherence to them is guaranteed by normative commitments, such as that by permanent civil servants to follow the instructions of their ever-changing political superiors.

Similarly, in the United States the constitutionalist norm that military officers must always take guidance from civilian officials no matter how misguided they think the civilians are is enforced primarily by normative commitments pounded into prospective officers in their education. The example also shows the limits of relying solely on normative commitments. Experience elsewhere in the world shows that military officers too often reject the idea of civilian control of the military, and engage in coups when they think the civilians are moving the nation in the wrong direction.

A second mechanism is the organization of the political system, typically through some combination of democratic elections and the separation of powers. Competition among those aspiring to exercise government power leads to respect for limits on government, because each aspirant can appeal to the people to turn out of office politicians who have failed to respect appropriate limits on government. Relying solely on these mechanisms is sometimes inadequate, dramatically when a substantial majority supports rights-violating laws over a reasonably long period, and even more dramatically when that majority supports laws violating the rights of a minority, racial or otherwise, that has no realistic prospect of displacing the majority through elections. Pluralist political systems reduce this threat by making it realistically possible for even small minorities to form political alliances on platforms that include respect for minority rights. But political pluralism is not inexorably linked to democratic elections and separation of powers.

The inadequacy of purely normative commitments by office holders and of electoral mechanisms to support constitutionalism has led most modern nations to converge on a third institutional arrangement, *judicial review* of government action to determine whether the action conforms to the limitations that constitutionalism places on government power. It is worth emphasizing that, historically, governments that clearly satisfy the requirements of "constitutional" have existed without judicial review, and that even in the twenty-first century there are constitutionalist systems that lack judicial review. The precise mechanisms of judicial review vary, but all face two common and related problems: ensuring that the judges really enforce *only* the limits constitutionalism requires, and ensuring that they *do* enforce those limits.

Given the wide range of policies that conform to constitutionalism's requirements, it has proven difficult for judges to develop accounts of why a particular statute is inconsistent with constitutionalism. Take the example of hate-speech regulation: Five justices of the U.S. Supreme Court found that regulation of hate speech was prohibited, while four—and the international community—would have permitted such regulation (*R.A.V. v. City of St. Paul,* 505 U.S. 377 [1992]). Defenders of judicial review have struggled to explain why the views of a slight majority of judges about what constitutionalism requires should prevail over the views of their presumably reasonable colleagues.

The second difficulty is that all systems of judicial review are connected to the other branches of government. In the United States and in many other nations, the connection comes through the nomination and confirmation process; sometimes the connection is made by allowing the nation's constitution to be amended relatively easily in the face of a judicial invalidation of enacted legislation. Defended as mechanisms that reconcile judicial review to democratic self-governments, these connections also reduce the probability that judges will in fact invalidate popular legislation, especially legislation targeted at small and permanent minorities. Probably the most enduring political science finding about judicial review is that constitutional courts rarely hold out for long against a persistent majority, whether because the sitting judges come to agree with the majority or because the majority affects the appointment of new judges. In the United States, decisions like *Plessy v. Ferguson,* 163 U.S. 537 (1896), upholding state-enforced racial segregation, and *Korematsu v. United States*, 323 U.S. 214 (1944), upholding the internment of Japanese-American citizens during World War II, are offered by constitutionalists as examples of departures from constitutionalism and by political scientists as examples of the limits of judicial review to ensure that constitutionalism's requirements are respected.

Perhaps these difficulties need not trouble constitutionalists too much. *Rarely* does not mean *never,* and normative commitments, electoral competition, and judicial review can sometimes accomplish something. Even more, if the limits constitutionalism imposes on governments are relatively thin, violations of constitutionalism's requirements may themselves be rare.

FOUNDATIONS OF CONSTITUTIONALISM

Constitutionalism as a normative ideal rests on institutional and cultural foundations. The thicker the concept of constitutionalism, the more substantial those foundations must be.

At a minimum, constitutionalism may require some degree of independence in the courts, reasonably fair and regular elections, and a reasonably open system of free expression. For constitutionalism's thin version, none of these institutional foundations need be very demanding. Judicial independence does not require that any judges have the power to hold legislation unconstitutional, although it probably does require that some judge have the power to determine that executive action is unauthorized by law, as a mechanism for ensuring that the minimal conditions of the rule of law are satisfied. Nor, of course, does judicial independence require that judges be free from removal from office for misconduct or even incompetence, as long as "incompetence" is determined according to standards that are substantially professional rather than significantly and openly political. One difficulty here, exemplified according to some scholars by the Japanese judicial system, is that professional standards can be influenced by political criteria. As long as the influence is neither too strong nor too direct, however, disciplining judges for violating professional standards seems compatible with a thin version of constitutionalism.

In the modern world, constitutionalism probably requires that there be elections for some significant lawmaking positions. Perhaps one can imagine a constitutional monarchy where all significant lawmakers are appointed by the monarch, although the difficulty with monarchy has always been that there is no guarantee that a responsible monarch will not be followed by an irresponsible one, a problem that is particularly acute for constitutional monarchies if the monarch has a great deal of power. Experience shows that constitutionalism persists even when elections are occasionally suspended during emergencies such as a long-running war, as occurred in the United Kingdom during World War II. And, of course, constitutionalism can exist in the face of occasional instances of corruption in the political process, such as vote-buying, voter intimidation, and deliberate miscounting of votes. Constitutionalism disappears, though, if that sort of corruption becomes widespread.

Constitutionalism may require as well that elections be reasonably competitive, in the sense that over some period—perhaps a decade or more—those who currently hold office face a realistic prospect of displacement by their electoral opponents. Otherwise, the risk that the government will become mired in corruption and then depart from even thin constitutionalism requirements seems substantial. The governments of Mexico and Japan in the late twentieth century illustrate this problem, although in Mexico the governing party left office without violence when it lost an election, and the Japanese system satisfies constitutionalism's requirements despite the fact that a single party retained power throughout the post–World War II twentieth century.

> *Certainly all those who have framed written constitutions contemplate them as forming the fundamental and paramount law of the nation, and consequently the theory of every such government must be, that an act of the legislature, repugnant to the constitution, is void.*
>
> SOURCE: John Marshall, *Marbury v. Madison,* 5 U.S. (1 Cranch) 137, 177 (1803).

Finally, a reasonably open system of free expression may be necessary as a foundation for constitutionalism, if only as a way of backing up the requirement of reasonably competitive elections. So-called *soft authoritarian* governments like that of Singapore pose a difficulty here, as they do for the idea that constitutionalism requires reasonably competitive elections. In such systems, expression critical of the government is strongly discouraged, even penalized. Yet, thin constitutionalism seems to exist in such systems.

Ratcheting up the definitional requirements of constitutionalism also increases its institutional requirements. If constitutionalism requires actual rotation in office, for example, elections must be truly competitive, with nearly every election presenting the incumbents with the risk of displacement. If soft authoritarianism is defined to be inconsistent with constitutionalism, regulation of political expression must be relatively loose. Again, increasing the strength of what is said to be required by constitutionalism runs the risk of limiting the concept's descriptive accuracy.

The cultural foundations of constitutionalism have a similar structure: the thicker constitutionalism's requirements, the stronger the cultural foundations must be. This provides one reason for adopting a thin definition of constitutionalism. Ordinary citizens rarely devote much attention to politics, yet thick conceptions of constitutionalism may place strong demands on the citizenry's political capacity. A definition of constitutionalism that requires citizens to be ever-alert to threats to constitutionalism places too many demands on ordinary life. One attraction of a thin definition is that its cultural preconditions may be thin as well: Citizens need have only a general and ill-defined concern about procedural fairness in government's ordinary operations, and they must want their government to seek to achieve justice, again defined in vague and general terms. Constitutionalists hope that combining these thin cultural preconditions with an appropriate set of institutions will make constitutionalism self-sustaining.

And political experience around the world provides some evidence to support this hope.

CONSTITUTIONALISM AND WRITTEN CONSTITUTIONS

Constitutionalism is a normative ideal that must be distinguished from the largely descriptive category *constitution*, and particularly from the ideas associated with the fact that many constitutions are written. There have been nations with written constitutions that nonetheless did not have constitutionalism. The Soviet Union, for example, had a constitution written under Joseph Stalin (1879–1953), yet Stalinist Russia was totalitarian, not constitutionalist. Conversely, there are nations without written constitutions that do satisfy constitutionalism understood in normative terms. Historically, the classic example has been the United Kingdom, whose fundamental structures are set out in a number of statutes and rest as well on numerous unwritten understandings, known as *constitutional conventions*. British constitutional theory was once strongly committed to the idea of parliamentary supremacy, which meant that a single Parliament could in principle change or repeal any of these statutes and alter any of the constitutional conventions. Yet, despite the theoretical possibility of radical alterations in fundamental structures, the United Kingdom was undoubtedly a constitutionalist political system. (Developments including the membership of the United Kingdom in the European Union and its adoption of the Human Rights Act of 1998, which makes many of the provisions of the European Convention on Human Rights directly applicable as domestic law in the United Kingdom, cast some doubt on the proposition that parliamentary supremacy continues there.)

The existence of a written constitution generally makes more prominent the possibility of enforcing the principles of constitutionalism through some form of judicial review. The thought is that the written constitution expresses through specific provisions the nation's commitment to constitutionalism. And, as a written document, the constitution invites the courts to serve as the guardians of that commitment by means of constitutional interpretation. Yet, once again, there is no necessary connection between having a written constitution and judicial review. The written constitution of the Netherlands, for example, expressly provides that none of its rights-protecting provisions shall be enforced by courts holding legislation unconstitutional. And, in the United States as in other constitutionalist systems, some important structural provisions are not subject to judicial review, the courts treating them as "political questions" not for resolution by the courts. Nor are constitutional conventions enforceable in the courts.

CONCLUSION

Over the centuries, the term *constitutionalism* has become a word of praise, tempting politicians and scholars to criticize governments that do not implement their preferred policies as failing the test of constitutionalism. This understandable temptation should be resisted, if only to allow *constitutionalism* to spoken of as a meaningful analytic category. Doing so, in turn, requires that the term be given little specific content—and doing that may severely limit the term's analytic utility.

SEE ALSO *Comparative Constitutional Law; Constitution of the United States; Judicial Independence; Judicial Review*

BIBLIOGRAPHY

Friedrich, Carl J. 1941. *Constitutional Government and Democracy: Theory and Practice in Europe and America.* Boston: Little, Brown.

McIlwain, Charles. 1940. *Constitutionalism Ancient and Modern.* Ithaca, NY: Cornell University Press.

Pennock, J. Roland, and John W. Chapman, eds. 1979. *Constitutionalism.* New York: New York University Press.

Mark V. Tushnet

CONSTITUTIONAL THEORY

From almost the moment the U.S. Constitution was ratified, each subsequent generation of Americans has argued over the document's meaning and application. The range of opinions, whether of scholars, Supreme Court justices, or elected officials, on what the clauses and provisions of the Constitution mean, how it divides and allocates power among the branches of government, and the limits it creates on the exercise of government power over individual rights is so wide that one unfamiliar with this debate would be stunned to discover that almost all of its participants claim to speak on behalf of the framers' intent.

The debate over the Constitution's meaning is remarkable for the emphasis it places on original meaning, intent, and historical context. But the idea that it is possible to recover and discern the Constitution's "true" meaning obscures the larger point of this enterprise: the need for participants in this debate to find a "usable past" to defend their interpretation of the Constitution. The emphasis on historical and theoretical precision sometimes leads one to forget that the Constitution was the work of statesmen and politicians, not philosophers and theorists. Still, the framers were more than just political pragmatists in search of a constitutional structure to defend their social, economic, and political preferences. They also had clear moral goals that they believed the Constitution's republican form of government could best promote.

Even those who disagree on what the Constitution means and requires agree that the Constitution is the authoritative source of law in the United States. As such, the decisions of the Court must have legitimacy. Because the Supreme Court is so often the last word on what the Constitution means, constitutional theory is often bound together with the process of judicial review. For constitutional adjudication to have power and resonance, the Court must explain how and why it has reached its decision. A judicial decision cannot stand if it is nothing more than an exercise of raw political power. Even if the justices, regardless of their assertions to the contrary, cannot help but infuse their constitutional philosophies with their own policy preferences, those choices must bear some relationship to the more general, abstract principles of the Constitution.

What should judges emphasize in interpreting the Constitution? Some theories suggest that the Court should minimize the role of judicial review and allow legislatures and other democratic institutions wide latitude in their policy choices. Other theories suggest that the Court must remain aware of the prevailing social and political sentiments and interpret the Constitution in light of modern societal norms. Three broad and interrelated sets of ideas are pervasive throughout all constitutional theories. One is that theories of constitutional interpretation often differ in their assessment of the certainty of the constitutional text's meaning and the appropriate methods for discovering its meaning. The second set of ideas involves beliefs about the allocation of institutional responsibilities and roles between the courts and the elected branches of government. The third pervasive idea is whether it is possible to separate constitutional theory from the outcomes it produces.

METHOD AND APPROACHES

The categorization of complex, sometimes overlapping, ideas in an effort to emphasize differences in approaches and methods is hard to avoid. Although text, intent, and structure often provide the basic foundation for theories of constitutional interpretation, the emphasis on one factor over another results in a particular approach being labeled as interpretivist or noninterpretivist (meaning to interpret the written Constitution or disregard the Constitution in favor of philosophical or policy preferences); literalist or indeterminist (adhering to the literal commands of the Constitution or seeing the Constitution as an "open-ended" document subject to revision by the Justices); activist or strict constructionist (using judicial review to strike down legislation favored by majorities to advance the personal preferences of the Court majority or adhering

to the democratic judgments of the legislatures); and so on. Some scholars discount the effort to root constitutional interpretation in legal theories and instead insist that judicial behavior is an expression of ideological and policy-based values. Supreme Court outcomes can and should be understood as reflective of strategic choices made by the justices to advance these interests.

Constitutional interpretation is not the result of mutually exclusive legal and nonlegal influences. Theories that emphasize different blends of legal, political, social, and economic considerations have risen, fallen, and risen again, largely because of the persuasiveness, or lack thereof, of the principles used to justify them. Categorization, despite its risks and drawbacks, does have certain advantages. Three broad categories are offered here that draw the sharpest distinctions between competing approaches to constitutional interpretation: legal formalism, alternatives to formalism, and natural law.

LEGAL FORMALISM

Legal formalism rests largely on the assumption that the Constitution can be understood as having a specific and true meaning. The sole task of those charged with interpreting the Constitution is to uncover the historical intent of its creators. Judges should not take it upon themselves to decide what the Constitution *should* mean, but instead to uncover the facts and historical intent that informs the language of the Constitution. To suggest that the Constitution does not impart clear commands risks putting judges in the position of "creating" and not "discovering" constitutional values. Personal biases must be constrained in favor of a neutral approach to constitutional interpretation. If the Constitution does not stand apart from politics, then it becomes just another instrument for the advancement of a particular social or political agenda.

Perhaps the most stark expression of legal formalism is found in the interpretive method called *originalism*. Advocates of originalism (or, as it is also called, *original intent*), argue that the Constitution (and the Bill of Rights) must be interpreted in a manner consistent with those who wrote and ratified it. Originalists claim that judges who favor approaches inconsistent with the intent of the framers are legislators in disguise, creating and bending the law to suit their own version of the Constitution. On those rare occasions when a judge cannot make out a constitutional provision, he or she should refrain from giving meaning to that provision. A judge should adhere to neutral principles, which are defined as the framers' choices and not those of the judges. Neutral principles absolve a judge from making unguided value judgments better left to the political branches. Originalism, according to its proponents, supplies a judge with neutrality in three respects—in deriving, defining, and applying principle.

Criticism of originalism comes from several angles. The first is perhaps the most obvious: Who were the "framers" and how do historians know they were of one mind? James Madison (1751–1836) is certainly a "founder," because he played a pivotal role at the Constitutional Convention of 1787 and in the crafting of the Bill of Rights. But should Thomas Jefferson (1743–1826), who was in Paris at the time the Constitution and Bill of Rights were drafted, be considered a founder? What about John Adams (1735–1826), who was in London serving as America's emissary to Great Britain? Or George Mason (1725–1792), who refused to sign the Constitution because it did not include a Bill of Rights? On this count, originalism, despite its promises, provides no clear answer to the larger question of who framed the Constitution and whether consensus existed among those so designated as the framers. Moreover, it is important to remember that the historical materials favored by originalists were also manipulated to serve the partisan political agendas of the framers and, later, those who ratified the Constitution.

Second, is originalism truly a "value free" or "neutral" approach to constitutional interpretation? By equating original intent with neutrality, advocates of this approach suggest that a distinct approach to interpreting government power and individual rights is actually prepolitical and presocial. Rather than seeing the conditions as a product of law, originalists argue that no substantive defense or theoretical justification is necessary to explain the Constitution because the Constitution explains itself. Is it really possible to interpret the Constitution without taking into account the social and political context of law and litigation? Is it possible to interpret the admittedly abstract and vague provisions of the Constitution in neutral fashion?

Third, does originalism understate and misread the framers intent? The Constitution is certainly concrete and specific in parts. No one, for example, can claim that the constitutional requirement that one must be thirty-five years old to serve as president is open to interpretation. But some of the provisions are more open-ended and ill-defined. What exactly is freedom of speech in an era of instantaneous communication? Or the nature of interstate commerce in a free-flowing, global economy where the starting and stopping point of commerce is hard to pin down? For the most part, originalism has remained an academic debate. Few Supreme Court justices, with the possible exceptions of Antonin Scalia and Clarence Thomas, have consistently called for an originalist approach to constitutional interpretation.

Literalism is another approach rooted in constitutional formalism. Constitutional literalists, like originalists, argue that the Constitution, as written, settles the need to go beyond the text to understand its meaning.

Literalism and originalism also share similarities in their acceptance, but fundamental distrust, of judicial review. Each approach emphasizes the need for courts to defer to the laws created by democratic majorities—especially when the Constitution is silent on a particular question or when dealing with one of its more open-ended clauses. Under both approaches, judges that stray from the text of the Constitution and the intent of the framers have granted themselves a license to impose their own values through judicial review.

Compared to originalism, it is far more difficult to tie literalism to a specific set of political outcomes. Another important difference between the two approaches is the role that each assigns to the Court in the use of judicial review to defend the clear and absolute commands of the Constitution. No Supreme Court justice, and perhaps no individual, better exemplifies the literalist approach to constitutional interpretation and its differences with originalism than Hugo Black, who served on the Court from 1937 to 1971. Black took the provisions of the Constitution at their literal meaning, and handed down dramatic opinions in such cases as *Youngstown Sheet & Tube Co. v. Sawyer*, 343 U.S. 579 (1952), for which he authored a majority opinion concluding that Congress, and not the president, was responsible for making laws, and *Ferguson v. Skrupa*, 372 U.S. 726 (1963), which upheld the power of legislatures to regulate the economy against a "liberty of due process" claim. In *Ferguson*, Black declared that the Court "refuse[d] to sit as a 'super-legislature to weigh the wisdom of legislation,'... Whether the legislature takes for its textbook Adam Smith, Herbert Spencer, Lord Keynes, or some other is no concern of ours."

ALTERNATIVES TO FORMALISM

Formalism dominated the Court's approach to constitutional interpretation from the founding period until the early part of the twentieth century, when the first serious challenge emerged to this long-held consensus in American law and jurisprudence. Parallel to the larger "progressive" movement underfoot in American politics, legal scholars, jurists, and social scientists began to question the legal foundation upon which the current economic, social, and political arrangements rested. Unlike formalists, who stressed the predetermined nature of legal rights, *legal realists* argued that law was the product of a political process, one in which ever-changing social and economic forces competed for control of the public interest. Existing law reflected the triumph of private interests that used the legislative process to assert their place in the social and political order, not "discoveries" of the framers' intent or rights self-evident in the "natural" law. Law determined the social order; it did not reflect a natural or predetermined state of affairs and thus could not have a meaning independent of the environment in which it was created. Legal realists questioned several orthodox assumptions about the organization and distribution of social, economic, and political power in American society. They argued that law not only created the status quo but also could and should be used to change it.

Front and center in the legal realist movement were two of the most eminent figures in the history of American law, Oliver Wendell Holmes Jr. and Louis D. Brandeis. Their association with legal realism added luster to its strength as a counterpoint to formalism. Although scholars generally consider Holmes and Brandeis among the greatest justices to serve on the Supreme Court, each had left an indelible mark on American constitutional development before entering what, for each man, was the final stage of his career. In 1881 Holmes, while still in private practice, published *The Common Law*, which rejected the natural law tradition. Holmes argued in clear and comprehensive terms that law reflected the deliberate choices of legislative bodies in response to perceived social and economic needs. At the time, Holmes's legal theories had little impact on the Supreme Court's approach to decision making, but they reverberated throughout some of the nation's most elite law schools. A generation of law teachers and students absorbed Holmes's lesson that "the life of the law has not been logic; it has been experience" (1963 [1881], p. 5). He believed that using natural rights theories to reject legal change was simply an academic method to forbid discussion.

Holmes and Brandeis are often grouped as twins in discussions of legal realism's place in American law. Other than their mutual disdain for formalism and natural law, they held very different conceptions of law's potential to transform the conditions of American life. Holmes's skepticism of law as the protector of "natural" truths formed the basis for his views. Brandeis, on the other hand, believed that law and litigation could be positive forces in altering the balance of social and economic power between worker and owner, dissident and majority, and rich and poor.

Legal realism dominated the Court's jurisprudence after the constitutional revolution of 1937, a term often used to describe the Court's sudden rejection of formalism. But legal realism, while an influence in the modern Court's approach to constitutional interpretation, soon came in for harsh criticism. Even constitutional theorists who acknowledged that the Court makes social and political value choices when it interprets the Constitution suggested that a more principled, less political justification was required to defend the Court's decisions.

These concerns were behind the influential book of John Hart Ely (1938–2003), who argued in *Democracy and Distrust* (1980) that courts should refrain from using their power to create rights through the "open-textured" clauses of the Constitution. Ely claimed that the Court in the post–New Deal era had done just that. The Court should instead limit judicial review to laws that prevented the political process from functioning in a fair and open manner. Ely agreed with critics of legal formalism that a "clause bound" interpretation was impossible, but he was also suspicious of grandiose legal theories that granted excessive power to the courts to "discover" the Constitution's fundamental values.

Ely's *process-oriented* theory laid down three instances when the courts should strike down laws: (1) when laws violated specific substantive constitutional guarantees; (2) when laws operated to disadvantage "discrete and insular" minorities in the political process; and (3) when laws created procedural obstacles that led to unreasonable barriers to political and social reform through the political process. The Court should always defer to the legislative process in disputes involving the open-ended clauses of the Constitution (for example, the notion that the due process clause of the Fourteenth Amendment protects the right to abortion). Otherwise, the justices put themselves in the position of imposing their value choices on the general population. Critics suggested that Ely put himself in the same box as the legal realists: in the end, the Court must make substantive choices about how to interpret the clauses of the Constitution, noting that even such substantive guarantees as freedom of speech require the justices to determine what those rights are.

Around the time that Ely's process-oriented approach to judicial review and constitutional theory emerged, some scholars pressed for a *rights-oriented* approach to interpreting the Constitution. The most notable advocate of this theory is Ronald Dworkin, who argues that the courts should retain sweeping power to determine the rights inherent in the Constitution. Guided by reason and unaccountable to the political impulses of majorities, the courts should use their special position and specialized knowledge to examine the moral and political components of rights-based claims, and promote such concepts as human dignity, equality, and fairness. Above all, the courts should use their position to ensure that majorities do not exercise force over the rights of individuals, including their rights to minority sexual orientation, abortion, and speech that runs counter to accepted wisdom. Rights theories should be concerned with individuals and minorities who do not have the power to protect themselves. The problem here is that rights theories are primarily associated with liberal political ends, and their proponents are simply left with the belief that judges vested with such broad power will make the right choices. Political winds, however, leave such hope to accident and fate, rather than reason and rules.

Finally, *judicial minimalism* has emerged as perhaps the most influential approach to constitutional decision making since Ely's argument on behalf of process-based constitutionalism. Most prominently associated with Cass Sunstein, judicial minimalism blends the major tenets of legal realism, such as the idea that judges cannot avoid making value choices when they interpret the Constitution, with important concepts of more process-driven theories to conclude that judges can best promote democratic deliberation in the elected branches by deciding constitutional questions according to certain moral principles in the narrowest of terms. He believes that leaving as much as possible to the democratic process while giving judges the authority to decide and correct matters of constitutional principle when necessary offers the best understanding of the judicial role.

The notion that the Constitution, and thus the meaning of constitutional law, has a fixed and precise meaning has always been attractive to legal scholars. Indeed, the idea that the Constitution is neutral and representative of consensus values is a familiar one to students of American politics. The courts should remain impartial in dealing with the cases brought before them, and should make an effort not to impose a political theory upon the Constitution inconsistent with its intent. But do they? Or is it true, as Chief Justice Charles Evans Hughes once said, that "we are under a Constitution, but the Constitution is what the judges say it is."

SEE ALSO *Judicial Pragmatism; Judicial Review; Legal Process; Originalism*

BIBLIOGRAPHY

Dworkin, Ronald. 2007. *Taking Rights Seriously.* Cambridge, MA: Harvard University Press.

Ely, John Hart. 1980. *Democracy and Distrust: A Theory of Judicial Review.* Cambridge, MA: Harvard University Press.

Holmes, Oliver Wendell, Jr. 1963 [1881]. *The Common Law,* ed. Mark DeWolfe Howe. Boston: Back Bay Books.

Sunstein, Cass. 1993. *The Partial Constitution.* Cambridge, MA: Harvard University Press.

Tushnet, Mark V. 2000. *Taking the Constitution Away from the Courts.* Princeton, NJ: Princeton University Press.

Gregg Ivers

CONSTITUTIONAL TORTS

A *tort* is a wrongful act that injures a person or a person's property. A *constitutional tort* is an act by the government, a government official, or a government employee that violates a person's constitutional rights.

Victims of everyday torts, such as negligence or defamation, routinely sue and recover compensatory damages, punitive damages where appropriate, and equitable or other relief. The U.S. Constitution, however, is largely silent about whether people whose constitutional rights are violated by the government can sue. Only the Fifth Amendment, which prohibits taking property for public use without compensation, expressly speaks to the appropriate remedy for governmental wrongdoing. In the face of this silence, whether victims of constitutional torts can sue is left to Congress and the courts.

Deciding whether individuals should be able to sue the government to vindicate their constitutional rights, and what sort of remedies should be available, raises difficult questions. While it is appealing to say that rights, especially constitutional rights, must be enforceable in order to be effective, that does not necessarily mean that lawsuits are the right way to enforce them. Litigation is burdensome, and it may not be a good idea to have government officials' decisions second-guessed by courts. Federal courts second-guessing state officials is particularly problematic in a federalist system. On the other hand, history teaches that overreaching by government officials is a real risk, and that states can sometimes be less than zealous in their protection of civil liberties. There is, after all, something fundamental about the notion that rights can be vindicated in courts. Finally, layered over these vexing questions is the concept of separation of powers: should the Supreme Court or Congress answer them?

SECTION 1983 AND *BIVENS*

Congress created a cause of action for constitutional torts in 1871, when it enacted 42 U.S. Code Section 1983. Section 1983 provides:

> Every person who, under color of any statute, ordinance, regulation, custom, or usage, of any State or Territory or the District of Columbia, subjects, or causes to be subjected, any citizen of the United States or other person within the jurisdiction thereof to the deprivation of any rights, privileges, or immunities secured by the Constitution and laws, shall be liable to the party injured in an action at law, suit in equity, or other proper proceeding for redress.

Another federal statute, 42 U.S. Code Section 1343(3), allows Section 1983 actions to be brought in federal court.

Section 1983 does not apply to federal officers or employees. In *Bivens v. Six Unknown Fed. Narcotics Agents*, 403 U.S. 388 (1971), however, the Supreme Court held that the Constitution itself implicitly authorizes a lawsuit for damages when federal officials acting under color of their authority violate the

Constitution. Justice William J. Brennan Jr. identified the right to sue as fundamental: "The very essence of civil liberty certainly consists in the right of every individual to claim the protection of the laws, whenever he receives an injury." Chief Justice Warren E. Burger dissented, arguing that the Court had exercised a power that properly belonged to Congress.

For its first ninety years, Section 1983 was rarely used successfully. Several developments beginning in 1960 combined to create a climate where enforcement of civil rights through constitutional-rights actions could expand, or some would say explode.

MONROE V. PAPE AND MONELL V. NEW YORK CITY DEPT. OF SOCIAL SERVICES

Section 1983 requires the plaintiff to show a violation of constitutional rights "under color of any statute, ordinance, regulation, custom, or usage, of any State," or "under color of state law" for short. Until 1961, this requirement posed a substantial hurdle for plaintiffs, because courts required plaintiffs to show that state law actually authorized the defendant's acts.

That changed with the Supreme Court's decision in *Monroe v. Pape*, 365 U.S. 167 (1961). James Monroe was in his Chicago home early one morning when thirteen Chicago police officers broke in, rousted him, his wife, and six children from bed, and stood them naked in the living room while ransacking the house. The officers took Monroe into custody, interrogated him for ten hours without allowing him to call his family or his attorney or taking him before a magistrate, and then released him without filing charges.

Monroe sued under Section 1983, alleging that the raid violated his Fourth Amendment right to be free from unreasonable searches and seizures. Because state law did not authorize the police officers to invade Monroe's home, the lower courts held that the officers did not act "under color of state law."

The Supreme Court reversed. According to Justice William O. Douglas, Section 1983 (which was passed as part of the Ku Klux Klan Act of 1871) was intended to do more than respond to situations where state law authorized unconstitutional acts. Rather, what concerned Congress was a general climate in which civil rights were ignored: "The legislation was passed ... to afford a federal right in federal courts because, by reason of prejudice, passion, neglect, intolerance or otherwise, state laws might not be enforced and the claims of citizens to the enjoyment of rights, privileges and immunities guaranteed by the Fourteenth Amendment might be denied by the state agencies."

What a plaintiff had to show in order to establish that the defendant acted under color of state law was that the defendant misused his position of authority: "Misuse of power, possessed by virtue of state law and made possible only because the wrongdoer is clothed with the authority of state law is action taken 'under color of' state law." A victim of official wrongdoing has a cause of action under Section 1983 in state court or in federal court, insuring that there will be a remedy if state courts refuse to act.

While Monroe was allowed to sue the officers who invaded his home, his suit against the City of Chicago was dismissed. A city, according to the Court, was not a "person" within the meaning of Section 1983. In 1978 the Court changed course. Looking closely at the legislative history of Section 1983, the Court concluded in *Monell v. New York City Dept. of Social Services*, 436 U.S. 658 (1978) that Congress intended cities and counties to be treated as persons. A local government could only be liable, however, if the government itself caused the injury through an official policy or custom that was unconstitutional. A state, on the other hand, is not a person. Plaintiffs can only sue state officials individually under Section 1983; the state itself cannot be sued.

THE CIVIL RIGHTS ATTORNEY'S FEES AWARDS ACT OF 1976

Monroe, *Monell*, and *Bivens* turned Section 1983 and its federal equivalent into important tools for enforcing constitutional rights. Victims of constitutional torts could now recover the same damages that victims of ordinary torts could recover: nominal damages; compensatory damages, including damages for pain and suffering; and punitive damages where officials acted with malice or willful disregard of the plaintiff's rights.

Successful plaintiffs could not, however, recover attorney fees. In *Alyeska Pipeline Service Co. v. Wilderness Society*, 421 U.S. 240 (1975), the Supreme Court had held that in constitutional tort cases, like ordinary tort cases, each party had to pay its own attorney. To ensure that victims of official wrongdoing would have access to the courts, Congress enacted the Civil Rights Attorney's Fees Awards Act of 1976, which allows plaintiffs who prevail in a Section 1983 case to recover attorney fees from the losing party.

SECTION 1983 AND INJUNCTIVE RELIEF

The term *constitutional torts* is usually reserved for cases in which injured individuals seek compensation for harm they have suffered. Section 1983, however, can also be used to seek injunctive relief. An injunction is a forward-looking remedy that orders the defendant to change the way it behaves in order to prevent future violations of the plaintiffs' rights.

In the 1970s and 1980s, the Supreme Court decided a series of cases that turned Section 1983 into an effective tool for reforming institutions like schools, police departments, prisons, and mental institutions in order to protect constitutional rights. For example, in *Swann v. Charlotte-Mecklenburg Board of Education*, 402 U.S. 1 (1971), the Court held that in school-desegregation cases, courts could go beyond simply ordering schools not to discriminate. Injunctive relief could be tailored to "eliminate from the public schools all vestiges of state-imposed segregation." In *Milliken v. Bradley*, 433 U.S. 267 (1977), the Court established that removing the vestiges of segregation could extend to requiring extensive remedial programs to eliminate segregation's effects, and that states could be required to bear the cost of forward-looking remedies despite the Eleventh Amendment's ban on damage awards against states in federal court. Finally, in *Hutto v. Finney*, 437 U.S. 678 (1978), the Court held that awarding attorney fees associated with forward-looking relief to the prevailing plaintiff did not violate the Eleventh Amendment.

A LITIGATION "EXPLOSION"

By the mid-1980s, concerns emerged about an explosion of litigation over constitutional torts. On the institutional side, schools, prisons, and jails across the country were operating under judicial decrees. On the individual side, the perception was that courts—and state treasuries—were laboring under an onslaught of claims, particularly by prisoners alleging unconstitutional treatment in connection with their confinement.

Data collected by Theodore Eisenberg and Stewart Schwab suggest that, at least with regard to damages suits, claims about a litigation explosion were overblown. The data, they argued, "suggest[s] that the image of a civil rights litigation explosion is overstated and borders on myth" (1987, p. 643). But whether or not it was justified, the public perception that litigation was out of hand combined with shifts in the political and legal landscape to create a climate of retrenchment.

Constitutional tort litigation blossomed in the 1960s' and 1970s' climate of what some would characterize as judicial activism. In relationship both to the states and to Congress, federal courts actively asserted their role as guardians and interpreters of the Constitution and laws. As the Warren Court gave way to the Burger Court and then the Rehnquist Court, another view of the proper roles of courts in general and federal courts in particular gained political prominence, and both the Court and Congress took steps to rein in litigation over constitutional torts.

BIVENS ACTIONS AND "SPECIAL FACTORS COUNSELING HESITATION"

Bivens v. Six Unknown Named Agents, which held that the Constitution implicitly authorized a lawsuit when federal officials violated the Constitution, also noted that an action would not be implied if "special factors counseled

hesitation." After *Bivens* (which, like *Monroe*, involved an unlawful invasion of the plaintiff's home by federal agents), the Court recognized *Bivens* actions for unconstitutional sex discrimination and unconstitutional treatment of a prisoner.

Soon, the tide turned. Citing "special factors counseling hesitation," the Court found, in *Stanley v. United States*, 483 U.S. 669 (1987), that there was no *Bivens* action when military personnel claimed their superiors gave them LSD without their knowledge, and, in *Bush v. Lucas*, 462 U.S. 367 (1983), federal employees who alleged they were fired for engaging in constitutionally protected speech likewise could not sue. While these and similar decisions left injured plaintiffs without compensation, the Court had come around to a view that it was Congress's job, not the Court's, to decide what remedies are appropriate for violations of constitutional rights. By 2007, Justices Clarence Thomas and Antonin Scalia could conclude that "*Bivens* is a relic of the heady days in which this Court assumed common-law powers to create causes of action" (*Wilkie v. Robbins*, 127 S.Ct. 2588).

DEFINING DUE PROCESS

Neither *Bivens* nor Section 1983 creates rights; each simply provides a remedy when rights are violated. Defining rights is left to the Constitution, Congress, and the courts. While any constitutional right can be the subject of constitutional tort litigation, the Fifth and Fourteenth Amendments' guarantees that life, liberty, and property will not be taken without due process of law is a frequent subject of constitutional tort litigation.

Beginning in 1972, a series of cases involving the due process clause substantially limited governmental liability for constitutional torts. First, in *Board of Regents v. Roth*, 408 U.S. 564 (1972), the Court limited the definition of "property" to interests protected by state law. Then, in *Paul v. Davis*, 424 U.S. 693 (1976), the Court limited the definition of "liberty" by insisting on a sharp demarcation between constitutionally protected liberty interests and ordinary, common-law torts. In *Ingraham v. Wright*, 430 U.S. 651 (1977), the Court held that a post-deprivation remedy in state court could satisfy due process, even if that remedy did not include compensatory damages. Finally, the Court read a state-of-mind requirement into the due process clause. Overruling a prior decision, the Court held in *Daniels v. Williams*, 474 U.S. 327 (1986) that the due process clause is violated only when a state official purposefully causes harm or acts with deliberate indifference to the plaintiffs' rights.

IMMUNITY AND "CLEARLY DEFINED" RIGHTS

Deciding whether an official's acts violate the Constitution is difficult even for the Supreme Court. From the beginning, the Court recognized that there is a cost to uncertainty. City or state officials who are uncertain of their obligations and who face liability if they err may be reluctant to carry out important governmental duties. Even though Section 1983 unambiguously proclaims that every person who violates constitutional rights under color of law is liable, the Court recognized from the beginning that government officials need room to do their jobs, and crafted a doctrine of official immunity to reflect that.

Official immunity takes two forms. Some officials are absolutely immune. For example, judges, prosecutors, and legislators cannot be sued for their official acts under any circumstances, even if it is alleged that they maliciously violated someone's constitutional rights. Other government officials and employees have a qualified immunity: They are immune from suit if, as the Court held in *Harlow v. Fitzgerald*, 457 U.S. 800 (1982), "their conduct does not violate clearly established statutory or constitutional rights of which a reasonable person would have known." The doctrine of official immunity, however, protects the individual officer; a city or county that has adopted unconstitutional policies or customs cannot defend its actions by arguing that the right it violated was not clearly established.

INSTITUTIONAL REFORM AND THE PRISON LITIGATION REFORM ACT

For plaintiffs who were able to satisfy the Court's state-of-mind requirements and avoid the immunity defenses, retrenchment on the remedial side posed additional burdens. Where damages were sought, the Court held in *Memphis School District v. Stachura*, 477 U.S. 299 (1986) and *Carey v. Piphus*, 435 U.S. 247 (1978) that some kind of physical injury or property damage had to be shown; damages could not be recovered for the intrinsic value of the constitutional right alone. Where injunctive relief was sought, particularly in institutional reform cases, the Court also scaled back, insisting that the remedy do no more than address the specific harm the defendant's violation caused (*Missouri v. Jenkins* [Jenkins III], 515 U.S. 70 [1995]). With the passage of the Prison Litigation Reform Act in 1996, Congress further restricted the remedies in Section 1983 cases brought by prisoners, imposing a requirement that internal prison administrative remedies be exhausted before a prisoner files suit, requiring judicial decrees to be no broader than necessary to correct the violation of a particular plaintiff's rights, and limiting damages for emotional distress to cases in which the plaintiff suffered physical harm.

CONSTITUTIONAL TORTS TODAY

Civil rights litigation takes many forms; federal statutes like the Civil Rights Act of 1964 and the Voting Rights Act of 1965, for example, protect a range of constitutional rights. The term *constitutional torts* is generally reserved for litigation under Section 1983 and for *Bivens* actions.

The outlines of constitutional tort litigation can be sketched quickly. If the defendant is a federal official, the courts must be persuaded to rely on *Bivens* to imply a cause of action, a prospect that has become increasingly unlikely. If the defendant is a state or local government official, Section 1983 comes into play. The analysis has five steps. First, the defendant must be a "person": either an individual or a city or county. A state is not a "person," and cannot be sued under Section 1983. Second, the violation must have occurred under color of state law. While this does not require that the state law authorized the defendant's acts, it does mean that the defendant must have acted using his or her authority as a government official. Third, the act must have caused the violation. Cities and counties, for example, are not liable for their employee's acts; they are only liable if the city or county itself acts by promulgating an unconstitutional ordinance or endorsing an unlawful practice. Fourth, there must be a violation of the federal Constitution, which requires close examination of the plaintiff's rights, the defendant's state of mind, and alternative remedies provided by state law. Finally, many defendants are immune from suit. Some defendants are absolutely immune and simply cannot be sued; others have a qualified immunity, and are not liable unless they violate a constitutional norm that is clearly established and known to reasonable people. Official immunity, however, protects government officials individually; municipalities are not immune.

Successful plaintiffs are entitled to the damages—nominal damages, compensatory damages, and punitive damages if malice is shown (although punitive damages cannot be recovered from municipalities)—and to injunctive relief if future harm is threatened or damages cannot repair the harm.

Complicated as this summary is, it vastly oversimplifies constitutional tort litigation. Applying each of these principles to a specific fact situation is extremely difficult, and the summary omits countless procedural and substantive details. The overarching themes, however, are clear. Broad issues of political philosophy and legal theory—the relationship between rights and remedies, the relationship of the federal courts to the states, the role of the courts in relationship to Congress in defining the scope of constitutional rights, the appropriate balance between authority and individual rights—have had as much to do with the development of the law as the text of Section 1983 or indeed the Constitution itself.

SEE ALSO *Bivens v. Six Unknown Fed. Narcotics Agents, 403 U.S. 388 (1971); Procedural Due Process; Punitive Damages; Substantive Due Process*

BIBLIOGRAPHY

Eisenberg, Theodore, and Stewart Schwab. 1987. "The Reality of Constitutional Tort Litigation." *Cornell Law Review* 72(4): 641–695.

Levinson, Daryl J. 2000. "Making Government Pay: Markets, Politics, and the Allocation of Constitutional Costs." *University of Chicago Law Review* 67: 345.

Rosenthal, Lawrence. 2007. "A Theory of Governmental Damages Liability: Torts, Constitutional Torts, and Takings." *University of Pennsylvania Journal of Constitutional Law* 9: 797.

Ross, Mary Massaron; Sheldon Namod; and Michael Rogren. 1998. *Sword and Shield Revisited: A Practical Approach to Section 1983*. Chicago: American Bar Association.

Shapo, Marshall S. 1965. "Constitutional Tort: *Monroe v. Pape* and the Frontiers Beyond." *Northwestern University Law Review* 60: 277.

Smolla, Rodney, and Chester James Antieau. 1994. *Federal Civil Rights Acts*. Deerfield, IL.: Clark Boardman Callahan.

Whitman, Christina B. 1986. "Government Responsibility for Constitutional Torts." *Michigan Law Review* 85: 225.

David J. Jung

CONSTITUTION AND AMERICAN CIVIL RELIGION

In early national political culture, the U.S. Constitution quickly acquired an almost sacred status. Some of this reverence derived from the material advantages that constitutional stability brought to many American citizens. Some seemed to be demanded by the document itself, as the same sentence that forbids religious tests for federal officials requires expressions of devotion to the Constitution instead. Whatever its source, this constitutional faith enjoyed very able proselytizers. During the ratification debates, Benjamin Franklin (1706–1790) pseudonymously compared the new fundamental law to the Decalogue that Moses brought down from Sinai. A few years later, James Madison (1751–1836) proved somewhat bolder in telling Americans to treat the Constitution as holy scripture. By the middle of the nineteenth century, a young Abraham Lincoln admonished every public and private institution in the nation to promote a political religion that consisted of veneration and sacrifice for the Constitution and laws of the land.

The Constitution has lost some of that sacrosanctity in modern American culture. Iconoclasts began appearing in the antebellum era when abolitionists characterized the nation's slavery-protecting compact as more diabolical than divine. Some have argued that President Lincoln himself substantially weakened the nation's constitutional worship

by enshrining preservation of the Union as a higher and holier goal than conservation of its charter. Others point to the Progressives of the early twentieth century—most notably the historian Charles Beard (1874–1948)—as the leading apostates from the constitutional faith.

Yet recent scholarship demonstrates how brightly that faith still burns. As the covenantal thread binding disparate Americans together and as the lasting relic of a mythic moment of creation, the Constitution has retained a great deal of its scriptural identity in American political culture. For contemporary scholars, the Constitution's ongoing role in this civil religion presents multiple points of inquiry, including the matter of how we understand the Supreme Court. Does a view of the Constitution as sacred scripture affect Americans' view of its most visible interpreters?

Thomas Grey (1984) has argued—and lamented—that it does. Borrowing from the sociological theories of Émile Durkheim (1858–1917), Grey suggests that "the religion of the Constitution" may have originated in a natural human tendency to sacralize important social relationships and to represent them with consecrated symbols. Thus the Constitution became the central totem of the national covenant. This emblematic view of the document has been useful for those interpreters who want to see the Constitution as symbolic of the nation's highest aspirations to justice and equality. From Grey's perspective, the problem with this view is that such totemic religion inevitably involves a deep sense of mystery and "requires priests or oracles, initiated into a special hermeneutical discipline, who can draw out from the mysterious symbols their meaning in application" (p. 22). To make the Constitution the emblem of a sacred but ineffable presence—such as a national covenant—is to render its meaning inaccessible to ordinary citizens. In this sense, Constitution worship can liberate the justices from the literal meaning of the text and afford them unwarranted prerogative to disregard its clear demands. While Grey applauds the progressive objectives of such aspirational interpreters, he cautions against their scriptural justification—which he believes could just as easily be turned against the cause of social progress.

As Grey himself recognizes, there are other ways of reading scripture. In 1792 James Madison challenged Alexander Hamilton's (c. 1755–1804) expansive legislative program by drawing on a Protestant theme which held that a strict reading of the sacred text would thwart the ambitions of self-aggrandizing powers. Madison called on the citizenry to "guarantee, with a holy zeal, these political scriptures from every attempt to add to or diminish from them" (p. 94). Since Madison clearly had not ruled out the use of formal amendment, he had *interpretive* accretions and diminutions in mind when he warned against "every" change to the text. Madison's restrictive reading was shared by the twentieth-century's influential strict-constructionist, Justice Hugo Black (1968), who declared that the "Constitution is my legal bible.... I personally deplore even the slightest deviation from its least important commands" (p. 66). For Madison, Black, and likeminded constitutionalists, a view of the Constitution as scripture seemed to entail a narrow reading of it.

To see the Constitution as a political bible, then, is to see the Supreme Court in contrasting postures. It can be viewed as a pack of elite doctors of law whose tendency to wrest the nation's scripture must be checked by a constitutionally alert citizenry, and it can be considered as the high priesthood of American constitutional faith, robed and ordained with the power to read the text in enlightened ways that surpass the understanding of the uninitiated. American civil religion both restrains and empowers the Court. In doing so, it contributes its share to the abundant paradoxes of American constitutionalism.

This complexity underscores the central point of Sanford Levinson's seminal essay, "'The Constitution' in American Civil Religion," first published in 1979 and then elaborated for his book *Constitutional Faith* (1988). Levinson draws on the history of Christian biblicism to establish a taxonomy of constitutional approaches in which the "Protestant" positions focus on the text as the sole authority and allow the entire canonical community to interpret that text, while the "Catholic" positions see tradition and natural law as complementary authorities to the text and restrict the right of interpretation to a magisterial Supreme Court. As Levinson argues, while some might see the sacralization of the Constitution as a guarantee of national unity, the history of violent clashes over interpretations of the Bible suggests that a shared scripture can produce as much conflict as cohesion.

The religious historian Jaroslav Pelikan (2004) has contributed to this conversation by analyzing the shared biblical and constitutional impulses toward the hermeneutical ideals of "original intent" and "doctrinal development" (pp. 76–149). Work such as Pelikan's suggests that by becoming aware of the functional and figurative parallels of these two documents, American jurists can learn from religion's extensive experience with the challenges of interpreting and applying a sovereign text. At its most helpful, then, American civil religion reminds the Court that its interpretive struggles are part of a long and complicated human story that dwarfs the relatively brief career of the United States' constitutional regime.

SEE ALSO *Aspirationalism; Lincoln, Abraham*

BIBLIOGRAPHY

Black, Hugo. 1968. *A Constitutional Faith*. New York: Knopf.

Grey, Thomas. 1984. "The Constitution as Scripture." *Stanford Law Review* 37 (1): 1–25.

Kammen, Michael. 1986. *A Machine that Would Go of Itself: The Constitution in American Culture*. New York: Knopf.

Levinson, Sanford. 1988. *Constitutional Faith*. Princeton, NJ: Princeton University Press.

Madison, James. 1792. "Charters." *National Gazette*. January 19: 94.

Pelikan, Jaroslav. 2004. *Interpreting the Bible and the Constitution*. New Haven, CT: Yale University Press.

David Holland

CONSTITUTION OF THE UNITED STATES

The Constitution is the fundamental law of the United States. The brief and general provisions of the written Constitution have been subject to differing interpretations and have been supplemented from other sources. The Constitution created a Supreme Court of the United States and defined its jurisdiction. The Supreme Court itself determined that it was the final arbiter of disputes concerning the meaning of the Constitution and its application in particular circumstances.

THE CONSTITUTION OF 1787

The Articles of Confederation was a compact among sovereign states, and the Continental Congress had no authority to compel or override state action. To consider remedying this and other defects in their confederation, the states sent delegates to a convention in Philadelphia in the summer of 1787, a meeting that is now remembered as the Constitutional Convention. James Madison's notes of the debates show that the delegates discussed a new, unitary "national" government, but could not agree on this point. They did agree that a "federal" government of limited sovereignty should have power to overrule state legislatures and to compel action by the states, and so recommended that the Constitution be ratified by the people, as the ultimate sovereign, to ensure its supremacy. A dispute continued whether the limited sovereignty of the new federal government rested upon the consent of a single "people" acting as a whole, or rested on concurrent majorities in each of the states. In *U.S. Term Limits v. Thornton*, 514 U.S. 779 (1995), a majority of the Court reaffirmed the principle that the federal government rested its authority upon the people of the nation as a whole, but two hundred years after it was ratified, four justices of the Court still argued, in dissent, that "the ultimate source of the Constitution's authority is the consent of the people of each individual state, not the consent of the undifferentiated people of the Nation as a whole," the theory upon which the Confederate states seceded from the federal Union.

The written Constitution of 1787 was silent on matters of citizenship and individual rights, in large part because of the existence of slavery in most of the states, the exclusion of Indians, and the failure to agree on whether the United States of America was a "nation" in the European sense. Citizenship was left to be determined by state courts, subject only to a uniform federal rule of "naturalization" for aliens. The Supreme Court held in 1856 that there was no national citizenship separate from that conferred by the states, and that the Bill of Rights—far from prohibiting slavery—protected white citizens' property interests in enslaved Africans from federal interference (*Dred Scott v. Sanford*, 60 U.S. 393 [1856]). One of the aims of the federal government in the Civil War (1861–1865) and adoption of the Fourteenth Amendment in 1868 was to reverse this decision of the Court.

Even on matters that were not in dispute at the convention, the brevity and generality of the written Constitution made it difficult to apply without additional aids to interpretation. Article III of the Constitution states that "the judicial Power of the United States, shall be vested in one supreme court, and in such inferior Courts as the Congress may from time to time ordain and establish." Judges are to hold their offices during good behavior, and the jurisdiction of federal courts is limited to "cases" and "controversies" arising under the Constitution, federal law, and treaties, or between governments or parties of diverse citizenship. The Supreme Court has *original jurisdiction* of cases in which a state government is a party, and in disputes between a "State and a foreign State," but otherwise is restricted to hearing appeals from such lower courts as Congress may establish.

The Court has narrowed and defined these broad terms when deciding cases brought before it. In *Cherokee Nation v. State of Georgia*, 30 U.S. 1 (1831), the Court denied that it had original jurisdiction of a suit between the Cherokee Nation and the State of Georgia, for instance, Chief Justice John Marshall's opinion defined the Cherokee Nation as a "domestic, dependent nation" and therefore not a "foreign state." The opinion effectively defined the United States as an empire with at least two classes of subordinate sovereigns, and formed the basis of two centuries of federal Indian law.

The text of the written Constitution does not specify the Supreme Court as final arbiter of its meaning, and both Congress and the president have at times asserted claims to define the Constitution for themselves. The Constitution does not require any number of justices, leaving the question to Congress, and does not specify the Court's procedures nor the law it is to apply. The drafters seem to have taken for granted that the Court would apply English common law. Each of the states had expressly adopted the common law of England, as it stood at the date of their independence, as a rule of decision for their courts, and a number of specialized terms drawn from the common law were included in the text of the Constitution. The Supreme Court has not applied a consistent rule as to whether the terms of the Constitution have a fixed meaning or reflect evolving principles of the common law as it subsequently developed in the United States and Great Britain.

In cases arising under federal law, the Constitution, or within the Court's original jurisdiction, it may apply a "federal common law" that rests solely on its own precedents. In diversity cases, the Court applies the law of the state whose law governs the case (*Erie R. Co. v. Tompkins*, 304 U.S. 64 [1938]).

The size of the Court is determined by statute, and fluctuated in early years between five and ten justices. Since the Reconstruction era, when expansion and contraction of the Court led to abrupt policy reversals, the size of the Court has been fixed at nine justices. President Franklin D. Roosevelt's effort to expand the Court's membership beyond that number in order to provide more latitude for New Deal legislation failed and has never been renewed. The Constitution provides that justices of the Court are appointed by the president, with the advice and consent of the Senate, and like other presidential appointees are subject to impeachment, but otherwise serve until death or resignation.

THE BILL OF RIGHTS

In response to concerns expressed during debates over ratification of the Constitution, the first Congress adopted and sent to the states for ratification twelve amendments, of which ten were adopted and later became known as the *Bill of Rights*. These first amendments emphasized the limited authority given to the new federal government, prohibiting it from infringing well-established, common-law principles such as freedom of speech and of the press, protecting the right to bear arms and to be free of unreasonable searches and seizures, and detailing some of the substance and procedure of the "due process of law" required in federal courts. The first eight amendments specified particular rights; the Ninth Amendment stated that the enumeration of certain rights "shall not be construed to deny or disparage others retained by the people;" and the Tenth Amendment codified a principle, repeatedly made by advocates of ratification, that "powers not delegated to the United States by the Constitution, nor prohibited by it to the States, are reserved to the States respectively, or to the people."

The brief and general assertions of rights and privileges contained in the Bill of Rights came before the Supreme Court only rarely during its first century. In the twentieth century, however, the Court was increasingly called upon to interpret them. In the interpretation of these amendments, and the Fourteenth Amendment that made them partly applicable to the states, the Supreme Court has often looked to sources outside the text of the written Constitution, consulting common law, the history of their passage, and the general principles thought to be implicitly contained in the Constitution as a whole.

THE MARSHALL COURT AND THE JUDICIAL POWER

It fell to the fourth chief justice, John Marshall, and the Court that he dominated to fill many of the blanks left by the written Constitution of 1787. The first justices had followed not only English common law, but the English practice of giving brief individual opinions from the bench. Marshall instituted the unique American practice of issuing a single, written opinion for "the Court," leaving individual justices free to concur or dissent; the opinion as well the decision of the majority thereupon became authoritative precedent in the United States. Marshall took upon himself the authority to assign the writing of "the opinion of the Court" and in many important cases arising under the Constitution wrote the opinion himself, giving himself and the Court unique authority as the voice of "the judicial Power of the United States." Because most constitutional disputes coming before his Court were cases of first impression, Marshall's opinions became an authoritative body of constitutional law.

Marshall's Court declared itself to the final arbiter of constitutional law, with the power to invalidate acts of Congress (*Marbury v. Madison*, 5 U.S. 137 [1803]), acts of the president (*Little v. Barreme*, 6 U.S. 170 [1804]), and the laws of the states (*Fletcher v. Peck*, 10 U.S. 87 [1810]). Such authority, Marshall held, was inherent in the "judicial power." Congress has generally accepted this assumption of authority, but presidents have on occasion disregarded the Court's decisions; President Andrew Jackson declined to enforce the Supreme Court's decisions concerning the rights of the Cherokee Nation in *Cherokee Nation v. State of Georgia*, and President Abraham Lincoln ignored the decision of the Supreme Court in *Ex parte Milligan*, 71 U.S. 2 (1866), holding his suspension of the writ of habeas corpus invalid. Many presidents into the twenty-first century have asserted independent authority to make their own judgment of the constitutionality of acts of Congress, and even of their own acts.

THE CIVIL WAR AMENDMENTS

The role of the Supreme Court and of the federal judiciary as a whole was transformed by the Civil War amendments, which gave the federal courts limited supervision of the states. The Thirteenth Amendment abolished slavery, an institution of state law; the Fourteenth

Amendment reversed the *Dred Scott* case and established for the first time national citizenship for every person born within the United States and subject to its jurisdiction. It forbade the states from abridging the "privileges or immunities of citizens of the United States," or depriving any person of "life, liberty or property, without due process of law," or of "the equal protection of the laws." The Fifteenth Amendment provided that the right of citizens to vote "shall not be abridged . . . on account of race, color, or previous condition of servitude."

In part to enforce these enactments and the federal legislation implementing them, Congress for the first time in 1875 created a system of federal district courts with jurisdiction of most questions arising under federal law, and for the first time individuals were given standing to challenge state and federal actions that infringed upon fundamental rights. The Supreme Court at first narrowed the effect of the amendments, holding that national citizenship in itself conferred few rights (*Slaughter-House Cases*, 83 U.S. 36 [1873]), did not prohibit discrimination by private individuals or business enterprises (*Civil Rights Cases*, 109 U.S. 3 [1883]), and did not confer political rights or grant civil equality to women (*Bradwell v. State of Illinois*, 83 U.S. 130 [1873]).

The full meaning of the Civil War amendments has been continually debated since their adoption, within the Court and beyond it. The Fourteenth Amendment, which swept most broadly, is the most contested. A substantial school of thought held that the purpose of the amendment (as it was one of the aims of the Union in the Civil War) was to incorporate into the federal Constitution as a whole the principles of the Declaration of Independence, most notably the principles of equality and inherent human rights (Black 1997; Reinstein 1993). The Supreme Court never adopted this view, and held that the "privileges or immunities" of national citizenship were limited to the nominal freedoms required to participate in federal elections and to petition the national government (see *Slaughter-House Cases*). In the twentieth century, however, the Court gradually softened its view, and held in a long series of cases that the due process clause of the Fourteenth Amendment incorporated and made applicable to the states central provisions of the first eight amendments.

To some degree, the Court also gradually and implicitly accepted the view that the Fourteenth Amendment modified the earlier Bill of Rights. The Fifth Amendment, for instance, contains no assurance of equality or equal protection of the laws; but in holding the segregated schools of the District of Columbia unconstitutional, the Court held that the Fourteenth Amendment's guarantee of equality must be read into the Fifth Amendment's guarantee of due process of law (*Bolling v. Sharpe*, 347 U.S. 497 [1954]). In cases concerning freedom of expression, the Court makes no distinction between cases arising under federal law, and hence governed by the First Amendment, or state action governed by the Fourteenth Amendment.

THE PROGRESSIVE ERA

After the end of Reconstruction, states and the federal government went through a series of constitutional revisions and amendments, reflecting the new purposes of the white majority, particularly in southern and western states. The Supreme Court's docket was crowded with cases challenging the Jim Crow regime in the South; congressional rule over Indian Country and newly acquired, overseas possessions; and Progressive legislative measures from the western states. The Court was generally conservative in these years. It struck down a national income tax in *Pollock v. Farmer's Loan & Trust Co.*, 157 U.S. 429 (1895) and was promptly reversed by the Sixteenth Amendment (1913). Newly empowered women led the effort to adopt the Eighteenth Amendment (1919), prohibiting the manufacture and sale of alcoholic beverages, which the Supreme Court had placed outside the federal commerce power (*Allgeyer v. State of Louisiana*, 165 U.S. 578 [1897]), and the Nineteenth Amendment (1920), which granted women the right to vote, and which eventually led the Court to include women, to a degree, within the broader scope of the Fourteenth Amendment's guarantee of equality. In repeated cases arising under the due process clause of the Fourteenth Amendment during these years, the Court generally upheld Progressive state legislation, such as Virginia's eugenics statute (*Buck v. Bell*, 274 U.S. 200 [1927]) and race-based federal immigration and naturalization restrictions (*Ozawa v. United States*, 260 U.S. 178 [1922]; *United States v. Thind*, 261 U.S. 204 [1923]). Efforts to break up traditional Native American culture and put Indian lands on the market were approved (*Lone Wolf v. Hitchcock*, 187 U.S. 553 [1903]); Congress had "plenary power" to legislate concerning immigrants, Native Americans, and the inhabitants of the newly conquered territories.

In those years, the Court vacillated on challenges to new regulatory statutes from the business community, generally approving rate regulation of railroads and antitrust attacks on national industrial monopolies, but disapproving pro-labor regulations of wages and hours. In 1937, apparently in response to the realities of the Great Depression, the Court reversed course on the latter cases, and began to approve the regulation of wages and hours (*West Coast Hotel v. Parrish*, 300 U.S. 379 [1937]) and some pro-union legislation. But it struck down and continued to disfavor broader Progressive measures such as the National Industrial Recovery Act of 1934, which created national industrial combines under federal regulation (*Panama Refining Co. v. Ryan*, 293 U.S. 388 [1935]; *Schechter Poultry Co. v. United States*, 295 U.S. 495 [1935]).

THE CIVIL RIGHTS ERA

In the 1950s, the Court began tentatively to give force to the Fourteenth Amendment's guarantee of legal equality, culminating in *Brown v. Board of Education*, 347 U.S. 483 (1954), the landmark case in which the Court reversed its unanimous earlier decisions and held that legal segregation of the races in public schools deprived African-American children of the equal protection of the laws. The Court developed an elaborate apparatus of doctrine, the "new equal protection," with which it remade the federal system by imposing a one-person, one-vote rule on state constitutions (*Reynolds v. Sims*, 377 U.S. 533 [1964]); invalidating state laws authorizing compulsory sterilization of prisoners (*Skinner v. State of Oklahoma*, 316 U.S. 535 [1942]); regulating contraception (*Eisenstadt v. Baird*, 405 U.S. 438 [1972]) and abortion (*Roe v. Wade*, 410 U.S. 113 [1973]); and recognizing rights of criminal defendants (e.g., *Miranda v. Arizona*, 384 U.S. 436 [1966]).

RETURN TO CONSERVATISM

By the 1980s, the Court shifted attention away from the new equal protection and began to revive an older jurisprudence of substantive due process. *Roe v. Wade* was partly reversed, and a woman's decision whether to carry a pregnancy to full term was said by a plurality to rest upon a right protected by the Fifth and Fourteenth Amendment's guarantee of due process (*Planned Parenthood of Southeastern Pennsylvania v. Casey*, 505 U.S. 833 [1992]). The Court applied a due process analysis in striking down a Texas statute forbidding same-sex relations, referring in an opinion by Justice Anthony Kennedy to the due process right recognized in the abortion case (*Lawrence v. Texas*, 559 U.S. 538 [1993]). The Court generally turned away new equal protection challenges to state and federal legislation, leaving to the states questions of a right to equality in public school funding (*San Antonio Independent School District v. Rodriquez*, 411 U.S. [1973]). Into the twenty-first century, however, a consistent majority of the Court (facing stronger challenges from a growing minority) continued to view itself as a common-law court, guided by its own precedents and fundamental principles of justice found in a variety of sources other than the text of the Constitution.

The "textualism" of the minority—who have adhered to a narrow reading of the text as understood in the eighteenth century—have minimized the effects of the Fourteenth Amendment. They may have gained a majority, at least in some cases, with the appointments made by President George W. Bush (1946–). This doctrine has been vigorously attacked by scholars such as

Ackerman (1991, 1998), who have espoused a contrary view that public opinion sometimes supplies the principle decision. This doctrine of an "unwritten Constitution" differs somewhat from the older view that the Constitution embodies evolving principles of the English common law. Textualism has been as energetically defended by such scholars as Akhil Reed Amar (2005).

SEE ALSO *Bill of Rights; Case or Controversy; Constitutional Interpretation; Constitutional Theory; Judicial Review; Marshall Court; Unwritten Constitution*

BIBLIOGRAPHY

Ackerman, Bruce A. 1991. *We the People,* Vol. 1: *Foundations.* Cambridge, MA: Belknap.

Ackerman, Bruce A. 1998. *We the People,* Vol. 2: *Transformations.* Cambridge, MA: Belknap.

Amar, Akhil Reed. 1998. *The Bill of Rights: Creation and Reconstruction.* New Haven, CT: Yale University Press.

Amar, Akhil Reed. 2005. *America's Constitution: A Biography.* New York: Random House.

Black, Charles L., Jr. 1997. *A New Birth of Freedom: Human Rights, Named and Unnamed.* New York: Grosset/Putnam.

Farrand, Max. 1913. *The Framing of the Constitution of the United States.* New Haven, CT: Yale University Press.

Madison, James. 1920. *The Debates in the Federal Convention of 1787.* Eds. Gaillard Hunt and James Brown Scott. New York: Oxford University Press.

Reinstein, Robert J. 1993. "Completing the Constitution: The Declaration of Independence, Bill of Rights, and Fourteenth Amendment." *Temple Law Review* 66: 379–418.

Wright, Benjamin Fletcher, ed. 1929. *A Source Book of American Political Theory.* New York: Macmillan.

Wright, Benjamin Fletcher, ed. 2004. *The Federalist: By Alexander Hamilton, James Madison, and John Jay.* New York: Barnes & Noble.

Sheldon M. Novick

CONTINUITY IN GOVERNMENT

What happens when unexpected (though perhaps predictable) vacancies occur at the highest levels of the national government? If a president dies in office or, as with Richard Nixon, resigns, the successor will be the vice president, as has happened eight times through 1974. Should there be no vice president, then the office would go to the person designated by Congress in the aptly named Succession in Office Act. Since the act was passed in 1947, the successor would be first the speaker of the House of Representatives, and then the president pro tempore of the Senate, followed by various cabinet officials beginning with the secretary of state (though some constitutional scholars believe that the succession of the speaker or the president pro tempore would be unconstitutional). Any such successor must be constitutionally eligible to serve as president, which would have ruled out, for example, Madeleine Albright (1937–), President Bill Clinton's (1946–) second secretary of state, who was a naturalized, rather than natural-born, U.S. citizen.

Prior to the ratification of the Twenty-fifth Amendment in 1967, the vice presidency was vacant for a total of almost forty-five of the 178 years following George Washington's inauguration in 1789, whether because of vice presidents having succeeded to the White House or because of vice presidential deaths. Since 1967, however, a vacancy in the vice presidency is far less likely inasmuch as a president can move to fill a vacancy by nominating someone for that office, subject to confirmation by both houses of Congress. Thus, when Spiro Agnew (1918–1996) was forced, because of criminal misconduct, to resign the vice presidency in 1974, Gerald Ford (1913–2006) was nominated by Nixon as Agnew's successor. This allowed Ford to become president upon Nixon's resignation several months later.

There are, of course, recurrent vacancies on the Supreme Court because of deaths or retirements; presidents nominate the successors, subject to Senate confirmation. Should there be insufficient members on the Supreme Court to hear cases, sitting federal justices can be appointed to hear the cases in question.

Should a senator die, the Seventeenth Amendment provides that the state's governor can name a successor. Replacement of a member of the House of Representatives, however, requires an election, as there is no provision for appointed members of the House. Almost every session of Congress sees at least one or two deaths of members of the House, though senatorial deaths are less frequent. In any event, there is usually little sense of crisis because the House currently has a total of 435 members and the Senate 100.

What would happen if a catastrophic attack on Washington, D.C., as was presumably threatened on September 11, 2001, *disabled* many senators and killed or disabled many representatives? Such a case of wholesale deaths or disabilities, unlike the individual deaths discussed above, would raise a real crisis with regard to the continued ability of Congress to play its essential role in the governance of the United States. The reason is that the Constitution provides no mechanism to replace, even temporarily, senators who are only disabled rather than killed. Similarly, the possibly dozens of dead representatives could not be replaced prior to an election that might require months to set up, during conditions of national crisis. Furthermore, it might, as a technical matter, be impossible for Congress even to meet inasmuch as the Constitution, in Article I, Section 5, specifies that a "Majority of each [House] shall constitute a Quorum to do Business." Thus, if majorities of the House and the Senate were disabled, it would be impossible to muster a constitutionally required quorum. If a majority of the House were killed, then a quorum would consist of the majority of the remaining members, but it should be obvious that one would like a full House as quickly as possible. A House of Representatives consisting of only ninety-nine members, for example, could meet if fifty of the members were able to do so, and legislation could be passed by a vote of twenty-six of these members, but this would scarcely suffice to provide the necessary legitimacy, especially during a time of national crisis. (Imagine, for example, if by some fluke all of the surviving or physically able representatives were from a single region of the country.)

A joint study of the conservative American Enterprise Institute and the liberal Brookings Institution suggested amending the Constitution to provide, in the circumstances of a catastrophic attack that affected dozens of representatives or senators, for the temporary replacement of disabled senators and killed or disabled representatives. Although hearings have been held in the Senate, Congress has not, as of 2008, moved on the proposal. Until such an amendment is proposed and ratified, the continuity particularly of Congress as a functioning part of American government is in real doubt should a relevant catastrophe ever occur. Given the necessity for decisions in times of emergency, the most likely consequence of such discontinuity would be de facto presidential dictatorship, no doubt supported by the vast majority of Americans, who would prefer action to governmental impotence because of the unavailability of a Congress capable of acting.

SEE ALSO *Article I; Constitution of the United States*

BIBLIOGRAPHY

Amar, Akhil Reed, and Vikram David Amar. 1995. "Is the Presidential Succession Law Constitutional?" *Stanford Law Review* 48(1): 113–139.

Continuity of Government Commission (an American Enterprise Institute and Brookings Institution project). 2003. *Preserving Our Liberties, the Continuity of Congress: The First Report of the Continuity of Government Commission.* Available from http://www.continuityofgovernment.org/report/FirstReport.pdf.

Ensuring the Continuity of the United States Government: The Congress. Hearing before the Committee on the Judiciary. U.S. Senate, 108th Congress, First Session, September 9, 2003, and January 27, 2004. Serial Nos. J–108–37 and J–108–54.

Sanford Levinson

CONTRACEPTION

Although it is more commonly associated with the subject of abortion and cases such as *Roe v. Wade*, 410 U.S. 113 (1973), the controversial claim that there is an implied "right to privacy" in the U.S. Constitution originated in two Supreme Court decisions involving state regulations of the sale, use, and distribution of contraceptives. In *Griswold v. Connecticut*, 381 U.S. 479 (1965) the Court struck down two statutes prohibiting the use of contraceptives, holding that the laws infringed an unenumerated constitutional right to marital privacy. In *Eisenstadt v. Baird*, 405 U.S. 438 (1972) the Court invalidated a Massachusetts law prohibiting the sale or distribution of contraceptives to unmarried persons. The Court later enlarged the scope of these new rights in *Carey v. Population Services International*, 431 U.S. 678 (1977) by invalidating various restrictions on the sale and advertisement of contraceptives, including a ban on sales to minors.

Notwithstanding the widespread use of contraceptives in the early twenty-first century, some scholars still question the soundness of these decisions. They point out that states were for many years able to regulate contraceptives under the rubric of the "police power," a state's broad authority to promote public health, safety, and morals. Less than thirty years before *Griswold*, the Supreme Court acknowledged the legitimacy of such regulations in *Gardner v. Massachusetts*, 305 U.S. 559 (1938). Here the Court declined to consider a challenge to a statute forbidding the sale or distribution of contraceptives, noting that the suit did not present "a substantial federal question."

As this example suggests, invoking the traditional jurisprudence of the police power is perhaps the most direct way to criticize the rulings in *Griswold*, *Eisenstadt*, and *Carey*. For most of American history, the Court deferred to state legislatures when the latter were acting to promote public health, safety, and morals. Important statements about the police power and the nature of this judicial deference to state legislatures are found in *House v. Mayes*, 219 U.S. 270 (1911) and *Williamson v. Lee Optical of Oklahoma*, 348 U.S. 483 (1955).

Questions about the legitimacy of *Griswold* and its progeny persist for other reasons, including subsequent developments in the law. In *Planned Parenthood of Southeastern Pennsylvania v. Casey*, 505 U.S. 833 (1992) the Court reaffirmed the "central holding" of *Roe v. Wade*, yet retreated from the doctrine of "privacy" as the foundation for abortion rights. *Casey* pivoted on a broad but not uncontroversial theory of personal freedom. That theory, however, cannot be found in *Griswold*, which asserted that the right in question was a right of married couples—not a right of individuals—that followed from the importance and standing of marriage as a valuable social institution.

Since *Casey*, some have tried to justify the *Griswold* decision by suggesting that the Connecticut laws served no discernible public purposes. This view was expressed by Justice David Souter in his concurring opinion in *Washington v. Glucksberg*, 521 U.S. 702 (1997).

Because of complexities such as these, much can be gained from a historical review of birth-control legislation in the United States. The brief survey that follows aims to identify the main goals of the legislation and to describe the opposition it engendered, with special attention given to the laws in Connecticut, Massachusetts, and New York. As the survey suggests, the historical record provides resources to both defenders and critics of the Court's decisions in *Griswold*, *Eisenstadt*, and *Carey*.

REGULATING CONTRACEPTIVES IN THE NINETEENTH CENTURY

The Connecticut legislation that was struck down in *Griswold* was passed in 1879. The original version of the Massachusetts law that was invalidated in *Eisenstadt v. Baird* was also passed in 1879. Six years earlier, the Comstock Act had been introduced into Congress. This bill had resulted from the lobbying efforts of Anthony Comstock (1844–1915), who succeeded in having contraceptives designated obscene. (The official name of the legislation was "An Act for the Suppression of Trade in, and Circulation of, Obscene Literature and Articles of Immoral Use.") When initially enacted, the first section of the Comstock Act prohibited obscene materials and contraceptives in the District of Columbia and all other areas of exclusive federal jurisdiction. The second section proscribed the use of the postal system for sending such materials and devices, and the third section prevented their importation into the United States. A later revision to the act criminalized shipments across state lines.

The impetus for such legislation is still not entirely clear. In the middle of the nineteenth century, manufacturers of contraceptives benefited from Charles Goodyear's (1800–1860) invention of the vulcanization of rubber. Condoms and diaphragms became more readily available (diaphragms were called *pessaries* at the time), and this development worried Comstock and others. Their principal fear was that sex would be divorced from marriage and child rearing, with dire consequences for family life and especially children.

In the middle of the twentieth century, before the Supreme Court decided *Griswold v. Connecticut*, leaders of the Catholic Church in Connecticut actively resisted proposed changes to the state's ban on the use of contraceptives. But the legislative initiatives in the late nineteenth century appear to have been largely the work of Protestants. (Here it is worth recalling that none of the leading Protestant denominations in the United States

countenanced the use of contraceptives by married couples before the 1930s.)

Comstock was for a time the secretary of the New York Society for the Suppression of Vice, and a similar organization called the New England Society for the Suppression of Vice counted among its members the presidents of Yale University and Amherst and Dartmouth colleges. These groups discouraged sexual relations outside marriage and aimed to stop the production and distribution of pornographic images and texts. To judge from the legislation, the groups were at least modestly successful, because by the end of the nineteenth century, more than twenty states and the federal government were regulating contraceptives.

In view of the opposition that later emerged, it should be noted that some nineteenth-century women elsewhere in the English-speaking world also worried about the easy availability of contraceptives. In Britain, one group of feminists feared that married men would be more tempted to have extramarital relations, because the use of contraceptives reduced the likelihood of any tangible evidence of such relations. This viewpoint is similar to that of officials in Connecticut in the twentieth century, who justified the state's flat ban on the use of contraceptives as a deterrent to adultery.

TWENTIETH-CENTURY STRUGGLES

Opposition to the more stringent laws in the United States took root in the early twentieth century. In the State of New York, which prohibited the sale of contraceptives, Margaret Sanger (1883–1966) emerged as a leading advocate. The sixth of eleven children, Sanger lamented the lack of birth control for women who wanted it, especially working-class women who already had large families. Sanger and her sister opened a clinic on October 16, 1916, and were arrested for selling contraceptives and a pamphlet on birth control ("What Every Girl Should Know"). Her arrest made her something of a celebrity, and she was thereafter a nationally known activist.

In Massachusetts one year later, the state's Supreme Judicial Court upheld the conviction of a man distributing pamphlets about how to avoid conception. The Supreme Judicial Court affirmed that the state's law, which criminalized the sale, distribution, and manufacture of contraceptives, was a valid exercise of the police power. This was the first of several constitutional challenges heard by the Supreme Judicial Court of Massachusetts regarding the state's regulation of contraceptives. Attempts to change the Massachusetts law through ordinary legislation and two statewide referenda failed.

In Connecticut, a decision in 1940 by the state's highest court (known as the Supreme Court of Errors) led to birth-control clinics in the state being shut down. As in Massachusetts, there were efforts to repeal the law through the normal legislative process, but these efforts repeatedly fell short. The Supreme Court of Errors also refused to read any exception into the blanket prohibition on using contraceptives. More specifically, this court refused to exempt physicians from the operation of the law, even physicians who believed that properly administered contraceptives would promote the health of married women suffering from different maladies. The Supreme Court of Errors consistently ruled that the question of whether the law should grant such an exemption was one for legislative deliberation and resolution, not one that courts were constitutionally empowered to resolve.

GRISWOLD V. CONNECTICUT (1965)

The controversy in *Griswold* involved the same two Connecticut laws mentioned above. One of the laws was the "anti-use" statute; the other was a criminal accessory provision. In November 1961 authorities arrested Estelle Griswold, executive director of the Planned Parenthood League in the state, and C. Lee Buxton, a physician and medical director for the League in its New Haven office. Griswold and Buxton advised married persons on how to avoid conception, and following a medical exam, they prescribed contraceptives for the wife's use.

Although seldom mentioned in commentaries on the case, one curious fact about Justice William O. Douglas's majority opinion in *Griswold* is its failure to discuss the purposes of the Connecticut law. Despite this lacuna, Douglas asserted that the law had "a maximum destructive impact" on marriage, a relationship that falls within constitutionally protected "zones of privacy."

Those zones are not expressly mentioned in the Constitution, but the majority opinion argues that the Constitution includes guarantees beyond those explicitly listed therein, including an unenumerated "freedom of association" and a right to "privacy and repose." To support this view, Douglas cited numerous cases in disparate areas of the law. In an often-quoted sentence, he submitted that "specific guarantees in the Bill of Rights have penumbras, formed by emanations from those guarantees that help give them life and substance." These ideas lie behind Douglas's seemingly defensive remark that the Court was not acting as a "super-legislature." Douglas aimed to show that the Court was honoring a constitutional constraint on legislative authority, and not forcing Connecticut to change its policy simply because seven justices disliked it.

The concurring opinions in *Griswold* portended future debates regarding the source(s) of the new right to privacy. Justice Arthur Goldberg, who joined the majority opinion, agreed that the Connecticut law violated the right of marital privacy. Goldberg, however, wanted to ground the right primarily in the Ninth Amendment, something unprecedented in the Court's civil liberties jurisprudence. In separate concurrences, Justice John Marshall Harlan and Justice Byron White argued that the Connecticut law violated the due process clause of the Fourteenth Amendment. In his concurrence, Harlan referred to his dissenting opinion in *Poe v. Ullman*, 367 U.S. 497 (1961), in which the Supreme Court, owing to the absence of a "live" controversy, declined to pass judgment on the constitutionality of the Connecticut laws. Harlan maintained that the Connecticut law violated "basic values" associated with the concept of "ordered liberty." White, while solicitous of the state's interests, argued that the statute failed to contribute to its goal of discouraging extramarital sexual relations.

The two dissenting opinions in *Griswold* also merit comment. Both dissenters, Justice Hugo Black and Justice Potter Stewart, indicated their opposition to the Connecticut laws as a matter of policy. Yet each criticized the Court's decision as an unjustified judicial intervention in a legislative matter and recommended that the controversy be left to Connecticut's legislature to resolve.

Stewart referred to the state's ban on using contraceptives as "uncommonly silly." He also believed that the Court was invalidating the laws solely because a majority of its members considered the policy irrational. Black agreed, and went further in his critique. With respect to the new right of associational privacy, he faulted the other justices for substituting a phrase not found in the text of the Constitution for the exact words of those provisions that protect individual freedom.

Black worried that the Court's credibility would be jeopardized by its ruling, because contrary to Douglas, he thought that the Court was acting as a "super-legislature." To underscore that worry, he cited the Court's decision in *Lochner v. New York*, 198 U.S. 45 (1905). Here the Court, relying on an unenumerated constitutional right known as "liberty of contract," struck down a state law prohibiting bakers from working more than sixty hours per week. Though the Supreme Court repudiated the doctrine of "liberty of contract" in 1937, the *Lochner* case came to define an era. As his dissent indicates, Black considered the Court's subsequent repudiation of both the *Lochner* era and the doctrine of "liberty of contract" to be important lessons for posterity.

EISENSTADT V. BAIRD (1972)

After the Court's ruling in *Griswold*, the Massachusetts legislature revised its laws on contraceptives. Married couples could now obtain them, but sales or distributions to unmarried persons were still proscribed. Furthermore, only licensed pharmacists were permitted to dispense contraceptives to married persons.

William Baird, an outspoken critic of such laws, sought to be arrested so that he could challenge the constitutionality of the revised statute. Baird delivered a lecture at Boston University on birth-control devices, including vaginal foam, and he gave the foam to unmarried women. He was prosecuted, and his suit took five years to resolve.

In *Eisenstadt v. Baird*, the Supreme Court ruled that by treating married and single persons dissimilarly, the Massachusetts law violated the equal protection clause of the Fourteenth Amendment. The Court's majority opinion, written by Justice William Brennan, thoroughly revised (and to some extent reversed) the meaning of *Griswold v. Connecticut*.

Brennan conceded that in *Griswold* the right to privacy was said to inhere in the marital relationship. But he declared that "the marital couple is not an independent entity with a mind and a heart of its own, but an association of two individuals each with a separate intellectual and emotional endowment." Given this premise, it was easier to say that the law should not distinguish single persons from married persons, and that single persons should have the same access to contraceptives as married persons. But this line of thinking arguably conflicted with the central purpose of the law, which was to deny single persons access to contraceptives so that they would be less tempted to have sex outside marriage. The key assumption, again, is that the easy availability of contraceptives would, by facilitating nonmarital sex, erode public morality with respect to sex and marriage.

Brennan's view, by contrast, seems to have been that legal restrictions on contraception would have little or no impact on the frequency of nonmarital sex. That view may have become more common in the 1960s and 1970s, but judges and legislators in Connecticut and Massachusetts before that time assumed the opposite. The judicial record in each state, in response to constitutional challenges to the contraception laws, bears this out.

Like Justice Douglas in *Griswold*, Brennan in *Eisenstadt* never identified the purpose of the law under review. Through a somewhat complicated analysis that dissenting Chief Justice Warren Burger found unpersuasive, Brennan denied that the law was meant to promote public health or morals. But he failed to say what the law was supposed to accomplish. In the end, however, the Court extended the "right to privacy" to single adults.

CAREY V. POPULATION SERVICES INTERNATIONAL (1977)

Even after the Court's decision in *Eisenstadt v. Baird*, states retained some authority to regulate contraceptives, by restricting, for example, advertising and distribution. In *Carey*, the Court invalidated different regulations in New York, including a ban on displays and advertisements of contraceptives and another ban on sales or distributions to persons under sixteen.

Regarding the latter point, Justice Brennan, writing for the majority in *Carey*, cited *Planned Parenthood of Central Missouri v. Danforth*, 428 U.S. 52 (1976), as the controlling case. Here the Court ruled that a state may not prevent a minor from obtaining an abortion or require her to receive parental consent before doing so. On this basis, Brennan reasoned that New York could not prohibit the distribution of contraceptives to minors. With respect to the state's ban on advertisements, the majority held that the ads were protected by the free speech clause of the First Amendment. The Court also invalidated a third regulation, which had required nonprescription contraceptives to be distributed exclusively by licensed pharmacists.

The remarkable changes in the content of the "right to privacy" provoked a strong dissent by Justice William Rehnquist. Contending that the ruling in *Carey* was "indefensible," Rehnquist predicted that other recent decisions by the Court would "prove to be a temporary departure from a wise and heretofore settled course of adjudication to the contrary."

ANALYSIS AND CONCLUSION

In the first decade of the twenty-first century, the Supreme Court's decisions in *Griswold*, *Eisenstadt*, and *Carey* still engage scholars and constitutional lawyers, because of the continuing controversy over abortion. As the antecedents to abortion rights, these cases command the attention of those who would either defend or criticize the Supreme Court's rulings in controversial cases such as *Roe v. Wade*. This was evident in 1987, when a broad coalition of liberal interest groups defeated Judge Robert Bork's nomination to the Supreme Court, largely because of his misgivings about the right to privacy. Five years later (as noted above), the Court backed away from the privacy doctrine in *Planned Parenthood v. Casey*, but that move did not make *Griswold*, *Eisenstadt*, and *Carey* irrelevant.

The contraception cases deserve attention for other reasons. The cases established the groundwork for what Professor Kenneth Karst calls "the freedom of intimate association"—a broad, unenumerated constitutional liberty for consenting adults to engage in noncommercial sexual acts. This idea was adumbrated in *Eisenstadt*, and developed more fully in *Lawrence v. Texas*, 539 U.S. 558 (2003), in which the Court struck down a state law criminalizing homosexual sodomy. Admittedly, the ruling in *Lawrence* went well beyond *Griswold*, *Eisenstadt*, and *Carey*, but in the majority opinion in *Lawrence*, Justice Anthony Kennedy cited *Griswold* and *Eisenstadt* to buttress the view that the Constitution confers such freedom on adult citizens.

Once again, however, there is controversy, with some championing this reading of the Constitution and others attacking it. Those disagreements can be better understood by considering several changes in American society that seem traceable to *Griswold*, *Eisenstadt*, and *Carey*.

Some scholars and activists maintain that the rulings in the three cases greatly benefited American women. Feminists, in particular, argue that the decisions helped to free many women from the domestic realm of life, allowing them to pursue careers outside the home and even to forego motherhood altogether. With the much greater availability of birth control and minimal regulation thereof, married women no longer have to be mothers, and their ability to earn money outside the home reduces their economic dependence on their husbands.

Even women who earnestly desire to be mothers can exercise more control over the number of children they will bear. The greater control, which can also be ascribed to the development and refinement of oral contraceptives in the 1960s, has enabled many women to have both a family and a career outside the home. In some instances, a married woman with children might work outside the home because of economic necessity, but a stark choice between "motherhood" and "professional career" no longer confronts most American women.

Other persons have praised the contraception decisions for promoting a greater openness in American society about human sexuality. According to this line of thought, the decisions helped to "demystify" different aspects of sexuality, leading to greater knowledge and unprecedented candor about these matters. That candor consists of a greater willingness to discuss sexual problems and pathologies outside clinical settings. The candor has been accompanied by a more forthright recognition of the importance of sex in the lives of most men and women.

The increased candor plainly has other factors, including the Supreme Court's progressively more liberal reading of the free speech and free press clauses in the twentieth century, which led to a new constitutional standard for obscenity prosecutions in *Miller v. California*, 413 U.S 15 (1973). Also worthy of mention is the Court's decision in *Bolger v. Youngs Drug Products Corp.*, 463 U.S. 60 (1983), where it struck down federal regulations on the mailing of unsolicited advertisements for contraceptives. Despite the significance of these other developments, it is questionable whether the new candor about human sexuality would have been possible without the easy availability of contraceptives, which seems to have contributed to the public's greater receptivity to sex outside marriage.

Besides their doubts about the institutional competence of the Supreme Court to invalidate the relevant laws, critics of the contraception decisions submit that the changes traceable to them are far from unalloyed blessings. The greater candor about human sexuality is one example. Even if more knowledge is welcome, these critics say, the greater openness has trivialized human sexuality in different ways, especially in ubiquitous public disclosures and discussions about personal intimacies.

Critics also charge that the Supreme Court's emphasis on sexual freedom has been one-sided. While acknowledging the social problems associated with unplanned pregnancies (including abortion), the majority and concurring opinions in *Eisenstadt* and *Carey* say very little about the duties ordinarily associated with one's sexual conduct (e.g., the duties of parenthood), even when contraception fails. To such critics, these two decisions helped to legitimize nonmarital sexual relations, but with scarcely any attention to their possible or likely social consequences. As evidence, one could cite the striking increase in out-of-wedlock births in the United States (from about 6 percent of all births in the early 1960s to about 35 percent in 2005), with appreciably diminished life prospects for most children born in single-parent families. This is one reason why some critics consider the "right to privacy" a misnomer: the public consequences of these ostensibly private decisions have been far-reaching.

Whatever one's position in these debates, it is unlikely that the Supreme Court will revisit the matters that were addressed in the contraception cases. Because contraceptives have become so thoroughly accepted in American life, scarcely any elected officials would consider regulating them again, at least with respect to adults. So it is difficult to imagine anyone asking the Court to restore legislative authority in this area.

Depending on one's perspective, the much greater acceptance of contraceptives in American life may or may not provide a "post hoc" justification for the Court's decisions in *Griswold*, *Eisenstadt*, and *Carey*. Those who cannot accept such a justification are perhaps more likely to cite the decisions as evidence of a constitutional double standard. With the repudiation of the *Lochner* era's "liberty of contract," the Court gives economic regulations only minimal scrutiny, and requires only a rational basis for them to be upheld. Policies affecting what the Court regards as civil liberties, however, receive heightened scrutiny, and can be typically justified only if the government's interest is "compelling." Some might acknowledge the double standard and still insist on its legitimacy. But to others, it will be seen as a vindication of Justice Black's fears in his dissent in *Griswold*.

SEE ALSO *Burger Court; Eisenstadt v. Baird, 405 U.S. 438 (1972); Freedom of Contract; Griswold v. Connecticut, 381 U.S. 479 (1965); Police Power; Privacy*

BIBLIOGRAPHY

Abraham, Henry J., and Leo A. Hazlewood. 1967. "Comstockery at the Bar of Justice." *Law in Transition Quarterly* 4(4): 220–243.

Bronner, Ethan. 1989. *Battle for Justice: How the Bork Nomination Shook America.* New York: Norton.

Garrow, David J. 1998. *Liberty and Sexuality: The Right to Privacy and the Making of* Roe v. Wade. Updated ed. Berkeley: University of California Press.

Garrow, David J. 2001. "Privacy and the American Constitution." *Social Research* 68(1): 55–82.

George, Robert P. 2000. "The Concept of Public Morality." *American Journal of Jurisprudence* 45: 17–32.

Grey, Thomas C. 1980. "Eros, Civilization, and the Burger Court." *Law and Contemporary Problems* 43(3): 83–100.

Gurstein, Rochelle. 1996. *The Repeal of Reticence: A History of America's Cultural and Legal Struggles over Free Speech, Obscenity, Sexual Liberation, and Modern Art.* New York: Hill and Wang.

Johnson, John W. 2005. Griswold v. Connecticut: *Birth Control and the Constitutional Right of Privacy.* Lawrence: University Press of Kansas.

Karst, Kenneth. 1980. "The Freedom of Intimate Association." *Yale Law Journal* 89: 624–692.

Kent, Susan Kingsley. 1987. *Sex and Suffrage in Britain, 1860–1914.* Princeton, NJ: Princeton University Press.

Okin, Susan Moller. 1989. *Justice, Gender, and the Family.* New York: Basic Books.

Smith, Peter. 1964. "Comment: The History and Future of the Legal Battle over Birth Control." *Cornell Law Quarterly* 49: 275–303.

Tubbs, David L. 2007. *Freedom's Orphans: Contemporary Liberalism and the Fate of American Children.* Princeton, NJ: Princeton University Press.

David L. Tubbs

CONTRACTS CLAUSE

The contracts clause of the U.S. Constitution (Article I, Section 10, clause 1) declares that "No state shall ... pass any ... Law impairing the Obligation of Contracts." As written, the clause is an absolute bar against the passage of state laws that interfere with existing contracts. However, the Supreme Court's interpretation of the limitations imposed by the clause has changed over time. It is difficult to overstate the clause's impact on early constitutional litigation, as the Court often invoked it to strike down state legislation early in the nation's history. The Court's modern reading of the contracts clause is far more restrictive, however. As a result, the clause plays only a minor role in the Supreme Court's modern constitutional jurisprudence.

ORIGINS AND EARLY INTERPRETATIONS

Surprisingly, the clause's early importance is belied by the lack of debate it generated in either the Constitutional Convention of 1787 or the state ratification debates that followed it. As recorded in Max Farrand's *The Records of the Federal Convention of 1787*, it was initially proposed by Rufus King (1755–1827) of Massachusetts, who "moved to add, in the words of the [Northwest] Ordinance of Congre[s]s establishing new States, a prohibition on the States to interfere in private contracts" (Farrand 1937, vol. 2, p. 439). King's motion was opposed by Gouverneur Morris (1752–1816) of Pennsylvania and by George Mason (1725–1792) of Virginia, both of whom argued that it would too often interfere with the states' ability to pass necessary legislation "relating to the bringing of actions—limitations of actions & which affect contracts" (p. 439). James Madison (1751–1836), who otherwise favored the proposal, nevertheless preferred a "national negative" that would empower the federal government to void state laws, thus preventing the "[e]vasions [that] might and would be devised by the ingenuity of the [state] Legislatures" (p. 440).

To resolve the disagreement, James Wilson (1742–1798) of Pennsylvania proposed the prohibition of retrospective interferences with contracts already formed. Madison responded by pointing out that the convention had already prohibited ex post facto laws. John Rutledge (1739–1800) of South Carolina then proposed that the states be denied the right to "pass bills of attainder [or] retrospective laws" (Farrand 1937, vol. 2, p. 440). Rutledge's proposal was adopted, without further debate, by a vote of seven states to three. Two changes were subsequently made to this language, apparently without discussion. In its report dated September 12, the Committee of Style expanded this language to bar the states from "altering or impairing the obligation of contracts" (p. 597). On September 14, the word *altering* was deleted. By all accounts, this is the sum total of attention paid to the clause during the convention. Similarly scant attention was paid to the contracts clause in the subsequent state ratification debates, out of which not a single amendment to the clause was offered.

Though there is a paucity of discussion of the contracts clause in the convention, its inclusion appears to have been spurred by a desire to prevent states from passing debtor-friendly laws at the expense of creditors. The members of the convention seem to have been concerned that, during times of recession or depression, state legislatures would adopt laws relieving or substantially altering preexisting obligations of debtors to repay their creditors. States had already passed a slew of such debtor-friendly legislation during the confederation era. Many of these laws stayed or postponed the payments of private debts beyond the time originally provided in the contract, permitted the discharge of debts through installment payments in lieu of previously agreed lump-sum payments, or allowed a substantial portion of a debt to be paid with commodities (land, tobacco, etc.) instead of with money. The prevailing view in the late eighteenth century was that the clause nullified these laws, and formed one part of the economic restrictions placed on the states by Article I. Protecting creditors from such retroactive legislation would not only benefit individual creditors, but would also encourage and protect the general availability of credit by assuring that creditors were repaid in the manner for which they bargained.

Due to its broad language and the absence of any definitive statement of its purpose, there was little indication of the kinds of contracts to which the contracts clause applied, or the kinds of state interferences it prohibited. An early illustration of this point comes in the arguments of Patrick Henry (1736–1799) of Virginia and James Galloway (1743–1798) of North Carolina, both of whom asserted that the clause applied not only to private contracts (those between private individuals), but also to public contracts (those to which states were parties). In their view, the clause could prevent debt-ridden states from adapting to budgetary pressures by redeeming state-issued securities for less than their nominal values. Theirs was not the prevailing view at the time, however, as several former convention participants rejected the notion that the clause would have any application in such circumstances. Similar questions regarding the proper scope of the contracts clause would frequently be the subject of Supreme Court litigation in the years after the Constitution's ratification.

EXPANSION DURING THE NINETEENTH CENTURY

Litigation brought under the contracts clause constituted the lion's share of early litigation in the Supreme Court. As aptly stated by Benjamin Fletcher Wright in *The Contract Clause of the Constitution*, "during the nineteenth century, no constitutional clause was so frequently the basis of decisions by the Supreme Court of the United States as that forbidding the states to pass laws impairing the obligation of contracts" (1938, p. xiii). In several opinions, of which many were quite unpopular at the time, the Court under Chief Justice John Marshall took an expansive view of the clause's application and frequently restricted state power by striking down state legislation.

Fletcher v. Peck, 10 U.S. (6 Cranch) 87 (1810), the first Supreme Court decision to find a state law unconstitutional, involved the sale of lands in the Yazoo River country (now Mississippi) by the 1795 Georgia legislature. It was commonly accepted at the time that the speculators who purchased the lands did so fraudulently, bribing members of the legislature to secure their votes in favor of the grant. These lands were subsequently sold to a succession of third-party purchasers. After a public outcry and the ouster of a substantial number of incumbents in

the next election, the new legislature rescinded the law providing for the original grant. It also voided all subsequent conveyances of the lands, and returned their ownership to the state of Georgia. Writing for the Court, Chief Justice Marshall held that public land grants are contractual obligations, that the contracts clause makes no distinction between private and public contracts, and that the framers intended the clause to apply with equal force to both. The clause therefore barred the Georgia legislature from rescinding the land grants, and from nullifying the ownership of innocent third parties who purchased the lands for valuable consideration, and without notice of the original fraud. Even the state's interest in redressing a fraud on the public did not provide an adequate justification for its legislature to impair the obligation of contracts.

In *Trustees of Dartmouth College v. Woodward*, 17 U.S. (4 Wheat.) 518 (1819) the Marshall Court further expanded the contracts clause to prevent state interferences with previously issued corporate charters. The case involved the passage of a law by the New Hampshire legislature amending the charter of Dartmouth College, which the British Crown had initially issued to Dartmouth's trustees in 1769. The purpose of the amendments was to convert the college from a private to a public institution controlled by a state-appointed governing board. In finding for the trustees, Chief Justice Marshall concluded that a corporate charter "is a contract, the obligation of which cannot be impaired without violating the [C]onstitution of the United States." As a result, the legislature could not alter the charter without running afoul of the contracts clause. This decision would later prove to be a boon to private businesses, as it provided them with constitutional protections against state interference.

In *Sturges v. Crowninshield*, 17 U.S. (4 Wheat.) 122 (1819) the Court proved similarly unsympathetic to the New York state legislature's attempt retroactively to alleviate insolvent debtors of their obligations. The 1811 bankruptcy statute under review discharged their debts if they assigned their property for the benefit of their creditors, and released debtors who were imprisoned because of their insolvency. The Court struck down the former provision, but upheld the latter. Marshall again rejected the notion that state laws could retroactively alter preexisting contractual obligations. He did, however, conclude that state legislation could retroactively modify the remedies available for failure to meet those obligations, so long as that legislation left the underlying obligation itself unchanged.

The Marshall Court further expanded the clause to limit contracts between states and Native American tribes (*New Jersey v. Wilson*, 11 U.S. [7 Cranch] 164 [1812]) and contracts between the states themselves (*Green v. Biddle*, 21 U.S. [8 Wheat.] 1 [1823]). This expansion did, however, have its limits. In *Sturges*, the Court left in question whether state insolvency laws could be applied prospectively (i.e., to contracts formed after passage of the laws) without unconstitutionally impairing the obligation of contacts. In *Ogden v. Saunders*, 25 U.S. [12 Wheat.] 213 [1827]) a divided Court answered this question in the affirmative. In a four-to-three opinion, the majority concluded that an 1801 New York bankruptcy statute did not violate the contracts clause by altering debt obligations formed after its passage; in effect, once the bankruptcy statute was passed it became part of all subsequent contracts. The Court rejected the view of Chief Justice Marshall, who advocated a far more expansive application of the clause. Writing his only dissent in a constitutional case, Marshall argued that the clause prohibited the impairment of contractual obligations whether they were made before or after the passage of an impairing state statute.

As a general matter, the Marshall Court could be counted on to strike down legislation that retrospectively altered contracts, regardless of the state's policy justifications for enacting that legislation. Indeed, the Court found that neither Georgia's interest in redressing fraud in *Fletcher*, nor New York's desire to alleviate the economic hardship of debtors in *Sturges*, provided sufficient justifications for retroactively impairing contractual obligations. The Court softened its hardline stance considerably after Marshall's death in 1835, at least with respect to public contracts, as evidenced by its decisions in *Charles River Bridge v. Warren Bridge*, 36 U.S. (11 Pet.) 420 (1837), *West River Bridge Co. v. Dix*, 47 U.S. (6 How.) 507 (1848), and *Stone v. Mississippi*, 101 U.S. 814 (1880).

Charles River Bridge addressed whether the Commonwealth of Massachusetts violated the contracts clause by allowing a group of merchants to build the Warren Bridge from Charlestown to Boston, after providing the proprietors of the Charles River Bridge a similar grant in 1785. Travelers were charged a toll to use the Charles River Bridge, whereas the Warren Bridge would be state-controlled and toll-free after its builders had collected enough revenue to reimburse them for the expense of constructing it, or after a maximum of six years. The Charles River Bridge proprietors claimed that permitting construction of the new bridge would destroy their implied exclusive interest in tolls collected on that route of travel, thus violating the essence of the contract between them and the commonwealth. Writing the majority opinion in favor of Warren Bridge, Chief Justice Roger B. Taney concluded that the Charles River Bridge Charter did not provide an implied exclusive right to tolls. Exhibiting more sympathy for arguments based on social welfare than did Chief Justice Marshall, Taney observed that the rights granted by such charters should be construed narrowly to protect the public's interest in

technological innovation, and to protect investments in such innovations that have already been made.

> The millions of property which have been invested in rail-roads and canals upon lines of travel which had been before occupied by turnpike corporations, will be put in jeopardy; we shall be thrown back to the improvements of the last century; and be obliged to stand still, until the claims of the old turnpike corporations shall be satisfied, and they shall consent to permit these states to avail themselves of the lights of modern science.

West River Bridge Co. involved an issue similar to that faced by the court in *Charles River Bridge*, and reached a similar result. Vermont granted to a private company the exclusive privilege of maintaining a toll bridge over the West River for a period of one hundred years. Prior to the expiration of this agreement, the Vermont legislature decided to construct a free public highway over the toll bridge, and to provide compensation to the company for the taking of its franchise and property. The company asserted that the contracts clause limited the state's power of eminent domain, but the Court disagreed. Instead, the Court concluded that all contracts are formed and all private property rights are held subject to that power. Accordingly, states could use their eminent domain power to promote public welfare free from the limitations imposed by the clause.

In *Stone*, the Court considered a contracts clause challenge to a Mississippi law that rescinded a charter for the operation of a state lottery. The provisional government put in place after the Civil War (1861–1865) granted the charter, but the state subsequently adopted a new constitution prohibiting the authorization of a lottery. The company sued when the state's attorney general attempted to enforce the ban. This presented an intriguing puzzle for the Court; permitting retroactive application of the new constitution would impair the contract between the state and the private corporation running the lottery, but not permitting retroactive application would interfere with the state's police power over the health, safety, and morals of the public. By an eight-to-zero vote, the Court held that states cannot contract away their inalienable police power, though it admitted difficulty in defining the limits of this power. The Court nevertheless concluded that lotteries and gambling fell within Mississippi's police power, and accordingly upheld the prohibition. Echoing its decision in *West River Bridge Co.*, the Court found the contracts clause inapplicable where the states exercised inalienable powers granted to them by the people.

DECLINE OF THE CONTRACTS CLAUSE
By the late nineteenth century, the Court had relegated the contracts clause to little more than an afterthought.

Though the Court continued to prevent states from impairing contractual obligations, it did so under the doctrine of substantive economic due process. Unlike the contracts clause, the Court concluded that substantive due process applied to both retrospective and prospective state legislation, and thus proved a more flexible tool for monitoring state legislation that regulated economic activity. However, the Court was more reluctant to strike down such legislation by the 1930s when, pursuant to their police power, states began enacting debtor-relief laws to alleviate the widespread economic emergency caused by the Great Depression.

The Court exhibited such restraint in *Home Building & Loan Association v. Blaisdell*, 290 U.S. 398 (1934), which effectively removed the contracts clause as a meaningful barrier to state economic regulation. *Blaisdell* considered the constitutionality of a Minnesota law that permitted state courts to postpone foreclosures by extending debtors' mortgage-redemption periods. By a vote of five-to-four, the Court concluded that the law did not violate the contracts clause. Writing for the majority, Chief Justice Charles Evans Hughes declared that, contrary to its wording, the contracts clause did not constitute an absolute ban on the power of the states to alter contracts. Rather, states possessed the power to protect vital public interests, and contracts were always written subject to that power. Thus, states could legitimately employ their police power to alter contractual obligations not only to protect the health, safety, and morals of the community (as was the case in *Stone*), but to protect collective economic interests as well. Moreover, individual contracts were not isolated agreements, but part of the larger economic system to be regulated by the state. "The question is no longer merely that of one party to a contract against another but of the use of reasonable means to safeguard the economic structure upon which the good of all depends."

THE CONTRACTS CLAUSE IN THE MODERN ERA

Since *Blaisdell*, the Supreme Court rarely finds state legislation unconstitutional under the contracts clause, choosing instead to defer to the economic regulatory decisions of the states. The clause did, however, enjoy a short-lived renaissance in the late 1970s. In *United States Trust v. New Jersey*, 431 U.S. 1 (1977) the Court invalidated parallel New York and New Jersey laws that retroactively repealed a 1962 statutory covenant between those states. The covenant constrained the New York/New Jersey Port Authority's ability to subsidize commuter rail transportation with funds it had pledged as security for bonds it had issued. Applying a test that finds no explicit articulation in the wording of the clause itself, the Court concluded that repealing the covenant, and thus altering

the states' contractual obligations to their bondholders, was not "reasonable and necessary to serve an important public purpose." Importantly, the Court also indicated that public contracts were subject to a higher level of scrutiny than private contracts, though it added that "private contracts are not subject to unlimited modification under the police power."

Similarly, in *Allied Structural Steel Co. v. Spannaus*, 438 U.S. 234 (1978) the Court reviewed a Minnesota pension-plan law that retroactively vested individuals in their private pension plans after ten years if their employers closed the plants for which they worked, or if their employers terminated their plans. In striking down the law, the Court concluded that it did not address a generalized social or economic problem; did not operate in an area typically subject to state control; caused a severe, permanent, and retroactive change in employers' contractual obligations to their employees; and focused too narrowly on a small subset of employers.

These decisions have not, however, revitalized contracts clause challenges to state legislation. As stated by Justice John Paul Stevens in *Keystone Bituminous Coal Association v. DeBenedictis*, 480 U.S. 470 (1987), "it is well settled that the prohibition against impairing the obligation of contracts is not to be read literally." The Court continues to defer to the social and economic judgments of state legislatures as to the necessity and reasonableness of laws that impair the obligation of contracts, particularly when the state itself is not one of the contracting parties.

SEE ALSO *Article I; Charles River Bridge v. Warren Bridge, 36 U.S. 420 (1837); Dartmouth College v. Woodward, 17 U.S. 518 (1819); Eminent Domain; Ex Post Facto Laws; Fletcher v. Peck, 10 U.S. 87 (1810); Home Building and Loan v. Blaisdell, 290 U.S. 398 (1934); Marshall Court*

BIBLIOGRAPHY

Ely, James W., ed. 1997. *Property Rights in American History: From the Colonial Era to the Present.* Vol. 4: *The Contract Clause in American History.* New York: Garland.

Farrand, Max, ed. 1937. *The Records of the Federal Convention of 1787.* Rev. edition. 3 vols. New Haven, CT: Yale University Press.

Kramnick, Isaac, ed. 1987. *The Federalist Papers.* Harmondsworth, UK: Penguin.

Schultz, David A. 1992. *Property, Power, and American Democracy.* New Brunswick, NJ: Transaction.

Wright, Benjamin Fletcher. 1938. *The Contract Clause of the Constitution.* Cambridge, MA: Harvard University Press.

Jamelle C. Sharpe

CONTROLLING OPINION

SEE *Holding; Plurality Opinions; Precedent.*

COOLEY, THOMAS
1824–1898

Thomas McIntyre Cooley—chief justice of the Michigan Supreme Court during Reconstruction and namesake of the largest law school in the United States—is best remembered for his scholarly treatises on the law that are still quoted by courts today. One of fifteen children from an impoverished farming family, Cooley was born outside Attica, New York, in 1824. Attending Attica Academy, Cooley taught in the public schools so as to support his education. After graduation, in 1842, he set upon studying the law as an apprentice under Theron K. Strong—later a judge in the state supreme court—in Palmyra, New York. One year later, Cooley set out for a career in Chicago, but his funds only got him as far as

Undated wood engraving of Thomas Cooley. Though a native of New York, Cooley worked with the judicial system in Michigan, both as a state supreme court justice and a professor at the University of Michigan. Some of his legal opinions continue to be used in modern court cases, while his writings about constitutional law are still seen as among the best in the field. THE GRANGER COLLECTION, NEW YORK. REPRODUCED BY PERMISSION.

Michigan where, in Adrian, he landed the job of deputy county clerk and was admitted to the bar in 1846.

Cooley's career remained unremarkable until after the Michigan Senate selected him to compile the state statutes in 1857. Upon completion of that project, one year later, he assumed the position of official reporter for the state supreme court, a post he held through the end of the Civil War (1861–1865) and his election, in 1864, as a Republican to the Supreme Court of Michigan (one of the most influential state tribunals in the country). Cooley sat on the high court with justices James V. Campbell (1823–1890), Isaac P. Christiancy (1812–1890), and Benjamin F. Graves (1817–1906), who together are remembered as the "Big Four" of Michigan law for their development of Michigan jurisprudence. As the twenty-fifth justice of Michigan's highest court, Cooley served three terms as chief justice (1868–1870, 1876–1878, and 1884–1885).

Justice Cooley wrote many decisions for the court, including *People ex rel. Sutherland v. Governor*, 29 Mich. 320 (1874), which remains a benchmark in the separation of powers among the three branches of government. Cooley never quite reconciled his tendency to textualism—the Constitution, he insisted, was clear and to disobey it threatened "the anchor of our safety"—with his unabashedly Jacksonian fidelity to local elected government and laissez-faire economics. Despite his advocacy on behalf of the common man, Cooley several times opined in support of railroad companies, which "are not, when in private hands, the people's highways; but they are private property" (*Detroit & Howell R.R. Co. v. Twp. Bd. Of Salem*, 20 Mich. 452 [1870]).

In 1859, Cooley also joined the new law department at the University of Michigan—teaching constitutional law, real property, trust, estates, and domestic property—a position he held for twenty-five years while he served as justice. After Cooley retired from both his academic and judicial positions in 1885 (elected to the Michigan bench in 1864, 1869, and 1877, he failed to be reelected in 1885), President Grover Cleveland (1837–1908)—whose election Cooley broke party ranks to support—appointed him to head the new federal Interstate Commerce Commission.

Physically unimposing, socially reserved, and rather unaccomplished as either lawyer or teacher, Cooley would hardly be remembered were it not for his many writings upon the legal and political institutions of the United States, which some historians contend surpassed the prestige of the writings of Chancellor James Kent and Joseph Story. Cooley's *Constitutional Limitations* (1868) is an especially noteworthy examination of state constitutional law that formulated the doctrines of class legislation, implied limits on state legislation, and substantive due process; the book was highly regarded for rationalizing the chaotic universe of constitutional systems. His writings are still sometimes cited in court opinions (*State ex rel. Pope v. Xantus Healthplan of Tennessee*, No. M2000-00120-COA-R10-CV [Tenn. Ct. App. May 17, 2000]).

With this text, the young professor successfully explicated the arcane law of constitutions of the several states. According to an early twentieth-century biography of Cooley in the *Michigan Law Review*, the book was "pronounced at once an exhaustive and scientific treatise on written constitutions as a limitation on legislative power" (Knowlton 1907, pp. 309, 314). Cooley's conservative strict constructionism can be seen in this statement, taken from the book's eighth edition: "The meaning of the constitution is fixed when it is adopted, and it is not different at any subsequent time when a court has occasion to pass upon it" (1927, p. 124). Cooley died on September 12, 1898. The Thomas M. Cooley Law School, located in Lansing, Michigan, is named in his memory.

SEE ALSO *Commentaries on the Constitution; Constitution of the United States; Fuller Court; Waite Court*

BIBLIOGRAPHY

Carrington, Paul D. 2006. "Deference to Democracy: Thomas Cooley and His Barnburning Court." In *The History of Michigan Law*, ed. Paul Finkelman and Martin J. Hershock, 108–125. Athens: Ohio University Press.

Cooley, Thomas McIntyre. 1927 [1868]. *A Treatise on the Constitutional Limitations which Rest upon the Legislative Power of the States of the American Union*. 8th edition. Boston: Little, Brown.

Jacobs, Clyde Edward. 1954. *Law Writers and the Courts: The Influence of Thomas M. Cooley, Christopher G. Tiedeman, and John F. Dillon upon American Constitutional Law*. Berkeley: University of California Press.

Jones, Alan R. 1987. *The Constitutional Conservatism of Thomas McIntyre Cooley: A Study in the History of Ideas*. New York: Garland.

Knowlton, Jerome C. 1907. "Thomas McIntyre Cooley." *Michigan Law Review* 5: 309, 314.

"Thomas M. Cooley, 25th Justice." Michigan Supreme Court Historical Society. Available from http://www.micourthistory.org/resources/tmcooley.php.

R. Owen Williams

COOLEY V. BOARD OF WARDENS, 53 U.S. 299 (1851)

Early controversies surrounding the U.S. Constitution's grant of power to Congress to regulate interstate commerce concerned whether that grant was *exclusive*, implicitly depriving states of power over commerce that crossed state line, or whether the power was *concurrent*, state law giving way only when it conflicted with a valid congressional act. The Marshall Court had inclined toward exclusivity, but a new chief justice, Roger Taney, and other justices appointed during the 1830s and 1840s, argued that the power was held concurrently. Unfortunately, the Taney Court's early commerce clause opinions were unclear; cases stood for little more than their result until *Cooley v. Board of Wardens*, 53 U.S. 299 (1851).

Pennsylvania required that certain vessels entering its ports take on a pilot and pay a fee for his services, or pay one-half of the fee to a fund established for the relief of "Distressed and Decayed pilots, their widows and children." This was challenged as an unconstitutional state attempt to regulate interstate commerce. Since there was no congressional act conflicting with Pennsylvania's law, the Court had the opportunity to settle the exclusive/concurrent power question at last.

Justice Benjamin Curtis wrote that the choice between exclusivity and concurrency was a false one. As Curtis reframed the issue, the question was whether a particular *subject* of commerce required one uniform rule or not. "Whatever subjects of [the commerce] power are in their nature national, or admit only of one uniform system, or plan of regulation, may justly be said to be of such a nature as to require exclusive legislation by Congress." If, on the other hand, the subject "is local and not national" and "is likely to be the best provided for, not by one system, or plan of regulation," but by many, then states retained authority to regulate. Curtis concluded that the regulation of pilots was local, not national, and could be left to state regulation.

Cooley's formulation became the dominant test for deciding what we now term *dormant commerce clause* cases during the nineteenth century. Unfortunately, Curtis gave no criteria for distinguishing national from local subjects. Later courts assumed that state laws *directly* affecting interstate commerce were laws that governed national subjects, while those *indirectly* affecting interstate commerce were local matters amenable to state regulation. Critics alleged that choices within these categories—national versus local, direct versus indirect—were merely conclusions masquerading as legal analysis.

Eventually the Court replaced the direct/indirect test with one that frankly balanced burdens on interstate commerce against benefits derived from state regulations. Balancing still exists today in the dormant commerce clause doctrine for state laws that do not discriminate against out-of-state commerce, but which nevertheless impose costs on it. If the burdens "clearly exceed" the local benefits, according to contemporary cases, then the state law is invalid. The ghost of *Cooley* lurks in balancing, for the presumption is that the greater the costs relative to local benefits, the more likely the subject is a national one, requiring congressional attention, if it is to be regulated at all.

SEE ALSO *Dormant Commerce Clause; Taney Court*

BIBLIOGRAPHY

Currie, David P. 1985. *The Constitution in the Supreme Court: The First Century, 1789–1888.* Chicago: University of Chicago Press.

Swisher, Carl Brent. 1974. *The Taney Period, 1836–64.* New York: Macmillan.

Brannon P. Denning

COPPAGE V. KANSAS, 236 U.S. 1 (1915)

In *Coppage v. Kansas*, 236 U.S. 1 (1915) the U.S. Supreme Court invalidated a Kansas statute prohibiting employers from refusing to allow employees to join labor unions or continue union membership. In holding that this law violated the Fourteenth Amendment by depriving the employer of liberty and property without due process of law, the Court reaffirmed the doctrine of substantive due process, which permitted judicial review of the substantive content of regulatory legislation to ensure protection of personal liberty.

In his opinion for the Court, Justice Mahlon Pitney (1858–1924) reiterated the doctrine of "liberty of contract" that the Court had asserted in various other decisions, including *Lochner v. New York*, 198 U.S. 45 (1905) (invalidating limitations on the work hours of bakery employees) and *Adair v. United States*, 208 U.S. 161 (1908) (striking down a federal law similar to the Kansas statute). Pitney's opinion explained that the right to freely enter into contracts was "as essential to the laborer as to the capitalist, to the poor as to the rich."

Although Pitney acknowledged that the long-established "police power" doctrine permitted a state to enact legislation restricting liberty in order to protect the public health, safety, morals, or general welfare, he contended that the state had no interest in restricting the liberty of employers to interfere with union membership. Dismissing the argument of the Kansas supreme court that the statute was constitutional because employees suffered from inequality of bargaining power, Pitney declared that "wherever the right of private property exists, there must and will be inequalities of fortune" that a legislature could not remove "without other object in view." Pitney described "liberty" and "property" as "co-existent human rights" with which a legislature could not unreasonably interfere.

In a brief dissent, Justice Oliver Wendell Holmes, Jr. (1841–1935) declared that "in present conditions a workman not unnaturally may believe that only by belonging to a union can he secure a contract that shall be fair to him." Although Holmes explained that he did not necessarily share this view or agree with the wisdom of the Kansas legislature in enacting the statute, he did not believe that anything in the Constitution prevented the enactment of such a law. He argued that the Court should overturn *Adair*.

In a dissenting opinion joined by Justice Charles Evans Hughes (1862–1948), Justice William R. Day (1849–1923) emphasized that "the right of contract is not absolute and unyielding," and he pointed out that the Court had sustained the right of states to exercise the police power to protect workers in many cases, including *Holden v. Hardy*, 169 U.S. 366 (1898) (limitations on work hours of mine workers) and *Muller v. Oregon*, 208 U.S. 412 (1908) (limitations on work hours of women laundry and factory workers). Day also contended that state and federal legislators "are entitled to the presumption that their action has been in good faith and because of conditions which they deem proper and sufficient to warrant the action taken."

Coppage provides an example of the Court's checkered response to regulatory legislation during the early twentieth century, and may reflect the antipathy of some of the justices toward labor unions.

SEE ALSO *Freedom of Contract; Labor Unions; Progressive Era Worker Regulation*

BIBLIOGRAPHY

Forbath, William E. 1991. *Law and the Shaping of the American Labor Movement.* Cambridge: Harvard University Press.

Tomlins, Christopher L. 1985. *The State and the Unions: Labor Relations, Law, and the Organized Labor Movement in America, 1880–1960.* New York: Cambridge University Press.

William G. Ross

CORNING GLASS WORKS V. BRENNAN, 417 U.S. 188 (1974)

Corning Glass Works v. Brennan, 417 U.S. 188 (1974) is one of the few U.S. Supreme Court cases to address the requirement of the Equal Pay Act (EPA) of 1963 that women and men receive "equal pay for equal work." The suit, initiated by the U.S. Department of Labor, alleged that Corning violated the EPA by paying a higher wage to its all-male night-shift inspectors than it did to its all-female day-shift inspectors. Writing for a five-justice majority, Justice Thurgood Marshall explained that the EPA should be interpreted broadly and that the pay disparity in this case could not be justified as a shift differential.

Prior to 1925, Corning had operated its plants only during the day, and inspection work was done exclusively by women. When automation made night production possible, Corning instituted a night shift for inspectors. At that time, however, both New York and Pennsylvania law prohibited women from working at night. Corning thus recruited only male workers to fill the night positions. These male inspectors demanded and received substantially higher wages than female day inspectors to counteract a general perception that the work was demeaning for men.

The next forty years saw numerous changes both in state law (which no longer prohibited night work by women) and Corning's plant structure (including establishment of a union and introduction of some women into the night shifts). On the effective date of the EPA in 1964, however, Corning continued to pay different base wages to male night and female day inspectors. In two separate actions, the government argued that Corning's wage practices resulted in unlawful wage disparity. The suits resulted in conflicting judgments from the Second and Third Circuits, and the Supreme Court granted certiorari to resolve this conflict.

The EPA prohibited gendered wage differentials "for equal work on jobs the performance of which requires equal skill, effort, and responsibility, and which are performed under similar working conditions." The 1963 act provided four exceptions to this general rule: seniority, merit, quantity or quality of production, or "any other factor than sex." Using this last catchall exception, Corning argued that the challenged pay disparity was simply a shift differential to account for the differences between night work and day work. Corning further argued that, when it opened its night shift to female applicants in 1966, any EPA violation was cured, even though the disparity between night- and day-shift pay remained.

Observing that the EPA "is broadly remedial, and it should be construed and applied so as to fulfill the underlying purposes which Congress sought to achieve," the majority rejected Corning's arguments. The Court agreed that a shift differential could, under some circumstances, constitute a "factor other than sex" under the EPA. In this case, however, the evidence showed that when Corning had instituted the differential, it was not because of any difference in skill or work required for the night-inspector shift as compared to the day shift. Instead, the pay differential was attributable to men refusing to do the work women had been doing unless they were paid more for that work. While intervening circumstances,

such as the institution of the collective-bargaining agreement and other changes in pay structure, may have altered the precise impact of that initial pay disparity, they could not change the historical fact that the mostly female day inspectors were paid less than the mostly male night inspectors for precisely the kinds of stereotypical and unfair reasons that the EPA was enacted to eliminate. The Court concluded therefore "that on the facts... the company's continued discrimination in base wages between night and day workers, though phrased in terms of a neutral factor other than sex, nevertheless operated to perpetuate the effects of the company's prior illegal practice of paying women less than men for equal work."

The Court rejected Corning's second argument, allowing women to apply for the night positions corrected any violations, by noting that the purpose of the act was to correct for unfair gender inequalities and that allowing a few women to apply for the higher-paid all-male night jobs did not change the fact that the all-female day jobs were lower paid. Accordingly, the judgment of the Second Circuit was affirmed, and that of the Third Circuit reversed and remanded for further proceedings.

Justice Potter Stewart took no part in the consideration of the case. Chief Justice Warren Burger and Justices Harry Blackmun and William Rehnquist dissented in an unsigned statement that the dissenters would affirm the judgment of the Third Circuit and reverse the judgment of the Second Circuit substantially for the reasons stated in the Third Circuit opinion. In the view of the dissenting justices, work on a night shift was not performed under substantially the same conditions as work on the day shift, and the distinction between the two justified the pay differential.

SEE ALSO *Sex Discrimination*

BIBLIOGRAPHY

Mathys, Nicholas J., and Laura B. Pincus. 1993. "Is Pay Equity Equitable? A Perspective that Looks Beyond Pay." *Labor Law Journal* 44(6): 351–360.

Seidenfeld, Mark. 1990. "Some Jurisprudential Perspectives on Employment Sex Discrimination Law and Comparable Worth." *Rutgers Law Journal* 21: 269.

Melissa Hart

CORONADO COAL V. UNITED MINE WORKERS, 268 U.S. 295 (1925)

Prior to Congress' passage of the Norris-LaGuardia Act exempting certain labor union conduct from the antitrust laws in 1932, the tension between congressionally supported labor activities and the Sherman Act was at times the subject of antitrust litigation. More broadly, the 1920s saw hundreds of federal labor injunctions issued to inhibit union activities. The antitrust laws became a significant legal basis for these injunctions.

Nine corporations, including the Coronado Coal Company, brought an antitrust suit under sections one and two of the Sherman Act against the United Mine Workers and subordinate local unions. The underlying facts of the suit involved a violent battle over the attempt by one mine owner in western Arkansas to convert his mine into a non-union operation. After a series of physical altercations between, on one side, the mine owner's security personnel and, on the other, local union mine workers as well as nonunion workers brought into the area from outside, the mine was destroyed. The trial court awarded $600,000 in treble damages plus attorneys' fees, which was affirmed by the Court of Appeals. In *United Mine Workers v. Coronado Coal*, 259 U.S. 344 (1922), the Court ruled that the mere ability to discipline its local unions did not make the United Mine Workers liable under the antitrust laws for its local unions' acts.

Within a year after the issuance of the 1922 *Coronado* opinion, Associate Justices George Sutherland and Pierce Butler (1866–1939), the third and fourth members of the *Four Horseman* (the first two were justices George Sutherland and Willis Van Devanter [1859–1941]), had joined the Court and swung it further toward the economic conservatism and judicial activism associated with the Court's pre–New Deal *Lochner* era. After further proceedings on remand, including a directed verdict in favor of the United Mine Workers, the case returned to the Supreme Court. The plaintiffs revisited their argument for liability of the United Mine Workers based on new proof of the missing links between the parent union and the local unions in the conspiracy and harm done that were the focus of the first *Coronado* decision. The new evidence was chiefly the questionable testimony of a local union member with a grievance against the president of the national body. The local member stated that the United Mine Workers president had been aware of the local's activities against the plaintiff's mine and had promised to financially back them. The Court concluded that the testimony did not suffice, holding that it required "actual agency" by the local for the parent union under the terms of their agreements of association, in order to impose such liability. However, in addressing the local union's conduct, the Court concluded that even though only a relatively small amount of coal production was affected, the intent to affect supply or price moving in interstate commerce would satisfy the Sherman Act's commerce requirement. Thus, while a victory for national or international unions, *Coronado Coal* provided a Sherman Act hook for injunctions against local union activity.

Some commentators believe that *Coronado Coal*'s holding, reading narrowly the antitrust liability stemming from apparent authority over an agent, was implicitly overruled by the Supreme Court's decision in *American Society of Mechanical Engineers v. Hydrolevel Corp.*, 456 U.S. 556 (1982). Such a reading is suggested by Justice Lewis F. Powell Jr.'s dissent in that case, although the majority, perhaps unconvincingly, tried to distinguish *Coronado Coal* on its facts.

SEE ALSO *Antitrust; Labor Unions*

BIBLIOGRAPHY

Casenote. 1925. "Labor Unions–Restraint of Interstate Commerce." *Yale Law Journal* 35 (1):111.

Eskridge, William N., Jr. 1988. "Overruling Statutory Precedents." *Georgetown Law Journal* 76:1361–1362.

Winter, Ralph K., Jr. 1963. "Collective Bargaining and Competition: The Application of Antitrust Standards to Union Activities." *Yale Law Journal* 73:14, 17–20

Salil Mehra

CORPORATE LAW

Beginning in the 1990s many corporate scandals have been disclosed, such as Enron hiding debts totaling over $1 billion; Arthur Andersen shredding documents relating to Enron's deceptive business practices; Kmart employing inappropriate accounting practices to mislead investors; Global Crossing engaging in accounting irregularities, which led to the biggest telecommunications company bankruptcy in history; WorldCom overstating its net income by $3.8 billion, and providing its president with $400 million in off–balance sheet personal loans; and Adelphia Communications hiding $3.1 billion in off–balance sheet loans to the Rigas family that founded the company. Americans were mystified and outraged at the corporations and the individuals whose conduct was no more than pure unadulterated greed.

These recent corporate scandals beg the question: Why do publicly traded corporations subject to federal and state securities, and corporate governance laws, engage in such irreprehensible conduct? The answer may be found in the history and culture of corporate law in America. It is a history that is riddled with financial scandals from the birth of the American nation.

A NEW AMERICAN REPUBLIC

When George Washington took the presidential seat in the national capital of New York City in the spring of 1789, he had already decided that Alexander Hamilton (c.

1755–1804) was the best person to be nation's first secretary of the treasury. The position was critical to the future of the country and Hamilton was prepared. From his first moment in office, he set about establishing the permanent financial future of the United States. His interpretation of the duties and powers of his office would shape the history of American monetary policy, American foreign direct investment, and the American stock markets. Hamilton's precedents would have lasting effects on the American economy for centuries to come. In essence, Hamilton would be the chief architect of the American financial infrastructure.

Corporations are such an integral part of American culture that it is difficult, if not impossible, to imagine a time when they did not exist. The historical development of American corporate law is rooted in economic, military, and political forces. Early American corporations were established primarily to allow private resources to accomplish public functions that government was unable to finance, such as the creation of canals, railroads, bridges, tunnels, and highways. At the time, corporations were creatures of the federal government—that is, corporations were created by congressional charter and had a specific time duration for their existence. Once a corporation's purpose was achieved (for example, completion of a bridge), the corporations ceased to exist. As such, corporations had a beginning and an end. As the American economy expanded, and acceptance of corporations as a means of facilitating business ventures as well as public work projects grew, the demand for corporate charters increased. As a result, a number of states developed general business corporate statutes and the incorporation process was standardized to simplify the creation of corporations.

Throughout the 1800s, America experienced an industrial revolution. The explosion of industry transformed America from an agrarian to an industrial society, which required large amounts of direct capital for development and growth. Adding to the industrial revolution was the newly found ability for the average American to invest in private corporations, an ability once reserved exclusively for the rich. A number of states enacted corporate statutes that removed many traditional limitations imposed upon corporations and lowered corporate taxes to encourage businesses to incorporate in their state. The statutes are commonly known as enabling statutes, because they enabled corporations to have broader powers, which management used to implement pro-management policies and procedures. The states of New Jersey and Delaware were the first states to adopt such enabling statutes and, as a result, corporations quickly flocked to those states in record numbers to incorporate within their borders. In the end, Delaware would arise as the dominant state of incorporation. The

revenue generated from numerous incorporation filings prompted Justice Louis Brandeis to state in *Liggett v. Lee*, 288 U.S. 517 (1933), in dissent, that "this race was not one of diligence but of laxity."

THE RISE OF CORPORATIONS

As the average American began to heavily invest in private corporations, the need for stock markets—marketplaces where investors could come together to buy and/or sell stocks—grew exponentially. The concept of a robust stock market was very much a cornerstone of Hamilton's plans for developing a strong American nation. Hamilton viewed the stock market as an essential component of modernizing America's financial infrastructure. The stock market would assist the government in managing debt and attracting foreign direct investment. Hamilton believed that the stock market was oblivious to class, status, and inherited social position; this view transformed American society from an oligarchical, agrarian social order into an industrial society where an average person, through diligent investing and the largess of key political friends, could accumulate wealth and elevate oneself above the social class in which one was born. Thus, Hamilton envisioned an American society characterized by exponential economic growth, prosperity for many, and an irrefutable international reputation. These were lofty goals for the young American republic, but Hamilton would prove to be true to his words.

As the first secretary of the treasury, Hamilton established one of America's first federal corporations, the Bank of the United States, against the intense opposition of Thomas Jefferson. At the time, Jefferson was secretary of state and Hamilton's bitter political rival. Hamilton argued that the creation of a national bank, and other increased federal powers, was based upon Congress's constitutional powers to issue currency, to regulate interstate commerce, and anything else that would be "necessary and proper" (Art. 1, § 8, Cl. 18). Corporations' constitutional rights are important because federal regulations were adopted to regulate the nation's key industries such as banking, transportation, banking, insurance et cetera. The application of constitutional rights to corporations was created as a means to protect investors by imposing constitutional protections to corporations and their owners.

Jefferson was unpersuaded. Jefferson found no specific authorization in the text of the U.S. Constitution for a national bank. This controversy was eventually settled by the Supreme Court in *M'Culloch v. Maryland*, 17 U.S. 316 (1819), which adopted Hamilton's view that the necessary and proper clause in the U.S. Constitution granted the federal government broad freedom to select the best means to execute its constitutionally enumerated powers under the implied powers doctrine. The enormity of the Supreme Court's decision in *M'Culloch* regarding the existence of constitutional rights vis-à-vis corporations established the financial infrastructure of corporate America for centuries to come. At its core is the fundamental argument that the necessary and proper clause provides federal powers to Congress that extend beyond regulating political and military matters, to matters concerning economic strategy, monetary policy, and the financial structure of the country. While most Americans are familiar with the stock market crash of 1929, few Americans realize that the first American stock market crash occurred in the spring of 1792 while Hamilton was secretary of the treasury. The crash was orchestrated by William Duer (1743–1799) and his friends, whose irresponsible speculation on the stock market caused stock prices to dangerously skyrocket and plunge almost overnight. Hamilton had foreseen the crash based upon the panic on Wall Street in the summer of 1791, when Hamilton observed large national bank loans being made to stock speculators to purchase stocks. This process would later be known within the financial industry as buying on margin. Hamilton strongly disapproved of such loans, but was unable to prevent the loans from being issued, in part because the speculators were some of the most prominent men of New York, Philadelphia, and Boston; as such, the loans were easily procured. Nonetheless, Hamilton established the Sinking Fund Commission and authorized the commission to purchase government stocks, and advised banks to pool their resources in the face of expected runs on deposits. The Sinking Fund Commission would be the precursor for the establishment of the Federal Reserve System.

Hamilton would be proud of the twenty-first-century American securities industry. The young American republic of Hamilton's time has grown from two stock markets located in Philadelphia and New York to more than ten national exchanges. However, during the late nineteenth century and early twentieth century, the federal securities laws did not exist. In 1911 the state of Kansas was the first state to create state securities laws to protect its residents. Throughout the 1920s many states adopted securities laws. To protect its residents, New York developed its famous securities laws through the 1921 Martin Act, which former New York State attorney general, Eliot Spitzer, used vigorously in 2001 through 2006 to clean up Wall Street. Many other states followed suit and began to adopt state securities laws commonly referred to as blue sky laws. They were so named because, as the Supreme Court stated in *Hall v. Geiger-Jones Co.*, 242 U.S. 539 (1917), "the merits of the investments that Americans were pouring their life savings into were no more than speculative schemes which have no more basis than so many feet of blue sky." However, very few blue

sky laws provided a private right of action. As such, only state regulators could commence lawsuits against corporations on behalf of the injured shareholders and state residents. In addition to the full and fair disclosure as to the purpose of the investment that the blue sky laws required, several states also imposed a merit regulation, permitting state securities regulators to prevent the filing of a security offering when state regulators have reason to believe that the securities offering would result in a fraud, result in inequity, or that the offering failed to meet the standard of being "fair, just, and equitable" (Dykstra 1913, pp. 230–234).

Congress, heeding the pressure from states to nationalize securities laws, adopted the Securities Act of 1933 and the Securities Exchange Act of 1934. The Securities Exchange Act established the Securities and Exchange Commission (SEC), whose mission it is to regulate the securities industry to protect investors. To date the SEC is the most powerful federal regulator in the financial services industry, whose primary mission remains the protection of the investing public.

DEVELOPING A BUSINESS NATION

The federalization of corporations has danced an intricate waltz with state corporate law; after all, corporations are creatures of state law, but are also governed by federal laws in areas of disclosure, registration of securities, periodic reporting of publicly traded companies, and certain corporate governance procedures that affect the general public. As previously discussed, one of the first federal corporations established was the Bank of the United States, which Hamilton created to strengthen the nation's finances by creating the first American security, the national debt—which was publicly tradable and backed by the full faith and credit of the U.S. government—to repay the loans that America received from Europe (primarily France and Spain) to finance the American Revolutionary War.

Almost from the inception of corporations, the Supreme Court has had to determine the appropriate degree of powers, duties, and rights that should be granted to corporations. The Supreme Court's decision in *M'Culloch* provided Congress with constitutionally protected federal powers to regulate economic, commercial, and financial matters. Originally, federal constitutional rights provided corporations with protection from inappropriate state action and insulated corporate agents from personal liability for their misconduct. Today, as a result of federal governance laws and federal securities laws, corporations are to a large extent held accountable for their misconduct. But prior to the adoption of the federal protectionist laws, corporations were used as means for management to avoid liability for their misconduct. It was, therefore, instrumental for corporations to be viewed as separate legal entities in order to remove personal liability from management. Nowhere is that more apparent than in the Supreme Court's decision in *Santa Clara v. Southern Pacific Railroad*, 118 U.S. 394 (1886).

Santa Clara is arguably the most far-reaching Supreme Court decision regarding corporations. The Supreme Court in *Santa Clara* held that a corporation has a separate legal existence from its shareholders and board of directors. It is a legal fallacy, but one that corporate management would continue to use for centuries to shield themselves from personal liability. The Supreme Court further held that a corporation is entitled to equal protection under the Fourteenth Amendment. To place the enormity of the Supreme Court's decision in context, constitutional history must be recalled.

The Fourteenth Amendment was adopted to protect the newly freed African-American slaves by providing the slaves with federal citizenship rights. The Emancipation Proclamation declared "that all persons held as slaves" within the rebellious states "are, and henceforward shall be free." However, in reality the Emancipation Proclamation did not free anyone because the southern states, in rebellion at the time, simply did not heed this command. It was not until Congress adopted the Thirteenth Amendment, which provided that "neither slavery nor involuntary servitude, except as a punishment for crime whereof the party shall have been duly convicted, shall exist within the United States, or any place subject to their jurisdiction," that former slaves were truly free. Nevertheless, despite the adoption of the Thirteenth and Fourteenth Amendments, African Americans were not treated with equal protection, or the full due process of the law that the Fourteenth Amendment afforded.

The Supreme Court became intimately involved with establishing the rights of corporations and determining the extent to which a corporation's legal existence should be protected by the U.S. Constitution. To place the enormity of the situation in the appropriate historical context, it is estimated that approximately 304 federal cases were brought before the Supreme Court for violation of Fourteenth Amendment constitutional rights from 1890 to 1910. Only 19 of those cases were brought by African Americans; 285 of those cases were brought by corporations alleging that the Fourteenth Amendment language, "nor shall any state deprive any *person* of life, liberty, or property, without due process of law; nor deny to any *person* within its jurisdiction the equal protection of the laws" (emphasis added), applied to corporations. In the landmark *Santa Clara* decision, the Supreme Court agreed.

Two years later, the Supreme Court decided in *Minneapolis & St. Louis Railway Co. v. Beckwith*, 129 U.S. 26 (1888) that corporations were entitled to due process of law based upon former Congressman Roscoe

Conkling's (1829–1888) effusive argument on behalf of Minneapolis & St. Louis Railway Company, in which Conkling assured the Supreme Court justices that the Joint Committee of Fifteen on Reconstruction always intended the due process clause to apply to corporations as well as natural persons. Conkling's basis for such a claim was a battered personal journal kept by one of the joint committee members. Conkling could not produce any official report, documentation, or direct testimony to authenticate the journal, nor to support the inference of intent that he sought from the Court. Nevertheless, the Supreme Court justices agreed with Conkling. To date, the Supreme Court continues to apply constitutional protections of the Fourteenth Amendment to corporations.

At the beginning of the twentieth century, as the U.S. economy entered into a more industrialized age, the Supreme Court in *Hale v. Henkel*, 201 U.S. 43 (1906) made two distinct rulings. First, the Court held that corporations were entitled to the protection of the Fourth Amendment against unreasonable searches and seizures. Second, the Court stated that corporations were not entitled to the protection of the Fifth Amendment against self-incrimination.

In the late twentieth century, the Supreme Court in *First National Bank of Boston v. Bellotti*, 435 U.S. 765 (1978) extended the right to free speech under the First Amendment to corporations, by holding that states did not have a compelling interest in regulating corporate expenditure in corporate speech. Yet twenty years later in *Austin v. Michigan Chamber of Commerce*, 494 U.S. 652 (1990) the Supreme Court held that states had a compelling interest in regulating corporate expenditures in state elections. The Supreme Court has had an interesting relationship with corporations, which is evidenced by the Supreme Court's varying opinions regarding the application of constitutional rights to corporations vis-à-vis state and federal corporate laws.

CORPORATE GOVERNANCE

It is undeniable that state corporate governance laws and federal governance laws regulate the relationships between shareholders and the board of directors along with the board's duly appointed agents (officers and mangers). American economic history shares a symbiotic relationship with the development of American corporate law. American economic history has been influenced by a combination of volatile industrial and technological advances, creating investment opportunities and financial innovations. As new financial theories of wealth creation are developed, new financial instruments are created, offering speculators the opportunity to profit from fluctuations in the value or price of the new financial instruments.

Fundamentals of Corporate Governance The fundamental problem of corporations has remained constant throughout the centuries: On numerous occasions those that manage and control the corporation for the benefit of the shareholders—the board of directors—have breached their fiduciary duty through mismanagement, self-dealing, and/or outright fraud. Although each state has statutory laws governing various aspects of a corporation's corporate structure, operations, and governance, it is the judicially created common law that ultimately determines the proper application of statutory law.

Congress has never pre-empted state corporate governance laws; instead Congress designed federal corporate governance law to over-lay state governance laws creating a symbiotic relationship between state and federal regulation. This symbiotic relationship has created variance among state judicial decisions as to the appropriate interpretation and application of certain statutory corporate laws. This is in part because state laws of incorporation govern the internal governance issues of a corporation, which is commonly referred to as the internal affairs doctrine. Congress had historically declined to create a federal governance statute under its commerce clause powers to regulate interstate activity. It was not until the corporate scandals at the turn of the twentieth-first century that Congress took decisive action to regulate the internal affairs of corporations. The catalyst for Congress's action was witnessing Enron executives refuse to testify before the Senate regarding the reasons for Enron's combustible catapult into the financial abyss, given the glaring conflicts of interests that existed between Enron directors and officers, and almost every entity with which Enron conducted business. The result was the adoption of the Sarbanes-Oxley Act of 2002. The primary reasons why Congress adopted the Sarbanes-Oxley Act were to: (1) protect interested parties from violation of fiduciary duties by the board of directors; and (2) reassure investors that it was safe to invest in American corporations. Sarbanes-Oxley requires senior corporate executives to certify the accuracy of their financial statements prior to their distribution to the general public, and to implement ethical best practices for corporate management.

Federal Corporate Governance It is important to recall certain details concerning the scandals in order to place Congress's reactions in adopting Sarbanes-Oxley, the first extensive federal corporate governance law, in historical context. The allegations against Enron included hiding debts totaling over $1 billion by improperly using off–balance sheet partnerships. Allegations against Arthur Andersen included shredding documents related to Enron's audit, after the SEC launched an investigation into Enron's deceptive business practices. Kmart engaged in inappropriate accounting practices that misled investors as to Kmart's financial condition and eventually led Kmart to file for bankruptcy protection. Global Crossing engaged in accounting irregularities that overstated net income. Immediately following the Global Crossing scandal, WorldCom announced that it had overstated its net income by reflecting $3.8 billion in operating losses on the company's balance sheet as capital expenses. Criminal charges were brought against the company and a federal indictment was filed against WorldCom's president, Bernie Ebbers, for $400 million in off–balance sheet personal loans to Ebbers. A few years later, a jury of American investors would find Ebbers guilty of criminal misconduct. Much like the WorldCom scandal, the Rigas family that founded Adelphia Communications hid $3.1 billion of company debt via off–balance sheet personal loans. Americans were outraged, and Congress acted quickly to adopt Sarbanes-Oxley to prohibit corporations' boards from engaging in misconduct and to restore investor confidence in the markets.

Sarbanes-Oxley is an extensive package of federal legislation intended to rein in corporate executives who breach their fiduciary duty to investors for their own pecuniary gain and to restore investor confidence in the markets. Unlike most of the federal initiatives that preceded it, Sarbanes-Oxley established some mandatory rules governing the internal affairs of publicly traded corporations. In particular, Sarbanes-Oxley included changes to many different areas of the law, including accounting and auditing procedures, financial disclosures, corporate tax law, securities law, and bankruptcy law. Sarbanes-Oxley's goal was to guarantee "trust in the financial markets by ensuring that corporate fraud and directors' greed may be better detected, prevented and prosecuted" and to "ensure that such greed does not succeed."

The impact of the scandals that precipitated the Sarbanes-Oxley Act cannot be overstated. Enron misled investors and regulators, which eventually caught up with the company and, in October 2001, Enron filed the largest bankruptcy in U.S. history. The market fallout from the Enron scandal and other corporate scandals around that time affected every American. The SEC reported that the average household lost approximately $60,000 due to these corporate scandals of the early twenty-first century. The challenge is in determining how corporate law should regulate such misconduct to prevent it in the first instance and to appropriately punish wrongdoers in the second instance. The Supreme Court and Congress have been called upon numerous times to deal with this persistent issue, and time and again the Supreme Court has granted constitutional protection to corporations and Congress has passed legislation to regulate corporations. Perhaps the solution to the challenge may be found in the growing concept of corporate social responsibility.

CORPORATE SOCIAL RESPONSIBILITY

Scholars have debated corporate social responsibility duties of corporations since the decision in *Dodge v. Ford Motor Co.*, 170 N.W. 668 (Mich. 1919), wherein the Michigan Supreme Court ruled that "it was not within the lawful powers of a board of directors to shape and conduct the affairs of a corporation for the merely incidental benefit of shareholders and for the primary purpose of benefiting others." The facts concerning the *Dodge* case are helpful in placing the enormity of the Michigan Supreme Court's decision in historical context. At the time, America was slowly recovering from World War I and Henry Ford (1863–1947), the philanthropist and CEO of the Ford Motor Company, testified that the company "had made too much money, and too large profits, and that although large profits might be still earned, a sharing of them with the public, by reducing the price of the output of the company, ought to be undertaken." The Michigan Supreme Court viewed Ford's altruistic values as notable but determined that such humanitarian and charitable motives must be "incidental to the main business of the corporation." Furthermore, the Michigan Supreme Court stated that there "should be no confusion ... as to the primary duties that Ford and his co-directors owe ... in law to the minority stockholders ... a business corporation is organized and carried on primarily for the profit of the stockholders." To date although no state statute specifically requires the primary purpose of a corporation to be for profit, the ruling in *Dodge* continues to be the prevailing principle under which corporations operate: Humanitarian purposes are merely incidental to the primary purpose of profit maximization.

Professor Milton Friedman (1912–2006) further advanced the concept that the primary purpose of the corporation is to maximize profits to shareholders by arguing that "there is one and only one social responsibility of business—to use its resources and engage in activities designed to increase its profits so long as it stays within the rules of the game" (p. 32). The difficulty is that there is very little balancing of interests within the context of corporate profit maximization. Corporations will not act, without some degree of external incentive, to maximize societal value in addition to shareholder value. This is true for two reasons: (1) corporations are constrained by the common-law fiduciary duty to act in the best interest of shareholders; and (2) market competition requires corporate assets be used to create competitive advantage that generates profits. It is, after all, a capitalist system. There is a natural tension between what is best for shareholders and what is best for society.

The prime directive—at least for now, given the state of corporate law—places the primary emphasis on maximizing profits. Certain scholars have noted that it is a fiction to believe that drafters of corporate statutes pursue an "ideal of air and equitabl[e] balancing of the varied and sometimes conflicting interests of the constituents of any corporation" (Folk 1968, p. 409). The reality is that the interests of management are the primary interests and for whose true benefit remains the proverbial question. Yet, after almost ninety years since the *Dodge* decision, corporations have operated with a singular focus—to maximize profits at the exclusion of all else, whereby the resources of the corporations are managed solely or exclusively for the benefit of its shareholders.

A natural corollary to corporate governance is the concept of corporate social responsibility. The doctrine is a simple one, yet it creates an inapposite theory from traditional profit maximization theories that were first postulated in *Dodge* and has become the modus operandi for the American capitalist structure. But a growing trend has begun to develop; Americans have begun to question whether corporations should consider their negative effect on third-party stakeholders. Stakeholders are affected individuals and entities that are not stockholders of the corporation. This principle of corporate accountability to stakeholders, or for externalities, is commonly referred to as corporate social responsibility (CSR).

Traditionally, corporations perceive their duties to extend only to their stockholders. Third parties that attempt to hold corporations accountable for negative impacts upon the communities or environment within which corporations operate meet strong resistance. CSR has developed, in part, to develop pedagogy within which to analyze the corporate governance and corporate accountability beyond the walls of the corporate structure of directors and shareholders. The growing popularity of CSR is based upon the concept that corporations have the financial resources, human capital, and global influence to advance progressive causes such as the environment and sustainability of development. As of 2008, it is a corporation's voluntary decision to adopt more socially responsible forms of management.

The phenomenon of corporations going green is a prime example of the CSR concept. However, there are very few state or federal regulations requiring corporations to consider the negative impact their operations have on the environment or other stakeholders. Yet, the benefits to a corporation for adopting such progressive policies are priceless, including branding a corporate name, creating goodwill, and in some cases preventing government regulation in certain industries. The question remains, however, as to whether corporate law can be modified to encourage corporations to make socially conscious management decisions; failing efficacious encouragement, the question is whether or not corporations should be required to also act on behalf of stakeholders. The balance needed is a delicate one: encouraging corporations to make more socially conscious decisions, while refraining from imposing direct legal obligations on corporations to make socially conscious decisions. Undoubtedly, policymakers will struggle with the issue of whether to compel social corporate responsibility for years to come.

THE RISE OF MULTINATIONAL CORPORATIONS

Globalization has spurred a movement toward privatization, which encourages multinational corporations to relocate their operations beyond the borders and reach of domestic government regulations. As a result, a new political construct has developed where private organizations or—as they are commonly referred to in international parlance—nongovernmental organizations (NGOs), such as corporations and other forms of privately owned entities, have usurped many of the roles of domestic governments. This usurpation can be seen in areas domestic governments have a long tradition of governing, such as quality control; standards of conduct; and public works, including mass transportation, infrastructure development, and public goods and services.

Undoubtedly, as the American economy continues to develop and expand beyond American borders, and through the proliferation of multinational corporations, the questions concerning the legal and ethical framework within which multinationals should operate become of paramount concern. Multinationals confront various social and economic risks and liabilities when they conduct business on a global level. Multinationals are confronted by issues concerning the environment, labor, and political stability. As a result of globalization, certain domestic governments have been unable to regulate the unfortunate social effects of corporate market forces such as global warming, in part due to overproduction of manufacturing plants. In response to heightened emissions regulations, certain manufacturers have relocated their operations to developing countries where emissions regulations are not as rigorously enforced as in the United States or Europe. Additionally, the growing trend of outsourcing customer service or manufacturing jobs to low-wage nations has drastically decreased the effectiveness of minimum wage legislation.

Multinationals that fail to comply with certain acceptable standards of corporate conduct expose themselves to negative media coverage, public protests, and liability in the United States under the Foreign Corruption Practices Act and the Alien Tort Statute. The threat of consumer boycotts, and the subsequent possibility of decreased market share or negative impact on the corporate brand, often compel corporations to adopt codes of ethical conduct, invest in the local community, and disclose the environmental impact of their operations. Eventually, these efforts lead to self-regulation whereby corporations create industry-wide standards to govern themselves. Additionally, multinational corporations must take into account different cultural perspectives in connection with corporate governance. The American approach of valuing management interests may need to be balanced with the European approach of the broader social consideration of stakeholder issues related to employees, local communities, and the environment, within the context of maximizing value for all constituents, not only shareholders. Therefore, as we export American corporate lessons learned through centuries of development abroad, the question remains as to whether globalization will provide solutions to these centuries-old problems or whether globalization will exacerbate the corporate problems that America has struggled to solve for centuries.

The debate regarding the appropriate powers that should be granted to a corporation and what socially responsible role, if any, corporations should play in society is not a new one. Hamilton and Jefferson debated the same issues in the late eighteenth century that are still being debated in the twenty-first century.

SEE ALSO *Corporation as a Person*

BIBLIOGRAPHY

Akerlof, George A. 1970. "The Market for 'Lemons': Quality Uncertainty and the Market Mechanism." *Quarterly Journal of Economics* 84(3): 488–500.

Bakan, Joel. 1997. *Just Words: Constitutional Rights and Social Wrongs*. Toronto: University of Toronto Press.

Bakan, Joel; Harold Crooks; and Mark Achbar. 2005. *The Corporation*. Directed by Mark Achbar and Jennifer Abbott. Zeitgeist Films.

Baron, David P. 2001. "Private Politics, Corporate Responsibility, and Integrated Strategy." *Journal of Economics and Management Strategy* 10(1): 7–45.

Blodget, Henry. 2007. "The Conscientious Investor." *Atlantic Monthly* 300(3): 78.

Brandeis, Louis D. 1914. *Other People's Money: And How the Bankers Use It*. New York: F.A. Stokes.

Branson, Douglas M. 1996. "Chasing the Rogue Professional after the Private Securities Litigation Reform Act of 1995." *SMU Law Review* 50(1): 91–125.

Bratton, William W. 2002. "Enron and the Dark Side of Shareholder Value." *Tulane Law Review* 76(5–6): 1275–1361.

Cummings, Jeanne, and Michael Schroeder. 2002. "Leading the News: Lesser-Known Candidates Head List for SEC Chief." *Wall Street Journal*, November 15.

Dodd, E. Merrick, Jr. 1932. "For Whom Are Corporate Managers Trustees?" *Harvard Law Review* 45(7): 1145–1163.

Drexler, David A.; Lewis S. Black, Jr.; and A. Gilchrist Sparks, III. 2007. *Delaware Corporation Law and Practice*. New York: Matthew Bender.

Dykstra, C. A. 1913. "Blue Sky Legislation." *The American Political Science Review* 7(2): 230–234.

Epps, Garrett. 2006. *Democracy Reborn: The Fourteenth Amendment and the Fight for Equal Rights in Post-Civil War America*. New York: Henry Holt.

Folk, Ernest L., III. 1968. "Some Reflections of a Corporation Law Draftsman." *Connecticut Bar Journal* 42: 409.

Friedman, Lawrence M. 1985. *A History of American Law*. 2nd edition. New York: Simon & Schuster.

Friedman, Milton. 1962. *Capitalism and Freedom*. With the assistance of Rose D. Friedman. Chicago: University of Chicago Press.

Friedman, Milton. 1970. "The Social Responsibility of Business Is to Increase Its Profits." *New York Times Magazine,* Sept. 13.

Gereffi, Gary, and Frederick Mayer. 2006. "Globalization and the Demand for Governance" In *The New Offshoring of Jobs and Global Development*. Geneva: International Labour Office.

Goodkind, Conrad, 1976. "Blue Sky Law: Is There Merit in the Merit Requirements?" *Wisconsin Law Review* 1976: 79: 107–23.

Hamilton, Allan McLane. 1910. *The Intimate Life of Alexander Hamilton*. New York: C. Scribner's Sons.

Hugo, Victor. 1877. *The History of a Crime*. New York: G. Munro.

Hurst, James Willard. 1970. *Legitimacy of the Business Corporation in the Law of United States, 1780–1970*. Charlottesville: University Press of Virginia.

Krawiec, Kimberly D. 1997. "More Than Just 'New Financial Bingo': A Risk-Based Approach to Understanding Derivatives." *Journal of Corporation Law* 23(1): 1–63.

McDonald, Forrest. 1982. *Alexander Hamilton: A Biography*. New York: Norton.

McLean, Bethany, and Peter Elkind. 2003. *The Smartest Guys in the Room: The Amazing Rise and Scandalous Fall of Enron*. New York: Portfolio.

Pierre-Louis, Lydie Nadia Cabrera. 2007. "Controlling a Financial Jurassic Park: Obtaining Jurisdiction over Derivatives by Regulating Illegal Foreign Currency Boiler Rooms." *U.C. Davis Business Law Journal* 8(2): 35–102.

Pierre-Louis, Lydie Nadia Cabrera. 2007. "Nowhere to Run, Nowhere to Hide: The Impact of Sarbanes-Oxley on Securities Arbitration." *St. John's Law Review* 81(1): 307–335.

Porter, Michael E., and Mark R. Kramer. 2006. "Strategy and Society: The Link between Competitive Advantage and Corporate Social Responsibility." *Harvard Business Review* 84(12): 78–92.

Sale, Hillary A. 2003. "Gatekeepers, Disclosure, and Issuer Choice." *Washington University Law Quarterly* 81(2): 403–416.

Slater, Dashka. 2007. "Resolved: Public Corporations Shall Take Us Seriously." *New York Times Magazine,* Aug. 12.

U.S. Securities and Exchange Commission. "The Investor's Advocate: How the SEC Protects Investors, Maintains Market Integrity, and Facilitates Capital Formation." Available from http://www.sec.gov

Wiener, Jonathan Baert. 1999. "Global Environmental Regulation: Instrument Choice in Legal Context." *Yale Law Journal* 108(4): 677–800.

Williams, Cynthia A., and John M. Conley. 2005. "An Emerging Third Way? The Erosion of the Anglo-American Shareholder Value Construct." *Cornell International Law Journal* 38(2): 493–551.

Young, Shawn. 2002. "Leading the News: WorldCom Files for Bankruptcy." *Wall Street Journal,* July 22.

Lydie Nadia Cabrera Pierre-Louis

CORPORATION AS A PERSON

In the United States, following in the common law tradition, certain intermediary institutions—such as clubs, unions, corporations, and the like, but especially corporations—have been analogized to persons for purposes of assimilation into the legal system. This personification is a vehicle that simplifies the legal system's ability to deal with organized business entities. The connotative significance of this personification is far greater, however, for it suggests a unity of control over collective property, legitimizes corporate autonomy, and allows courts to infer rights from the existence of the "corporate person." These substantive components of corporate personhood, however, have varied enormously over the country's legal history.

THE DEVELOPMENT OF THE CORPORATE PERSON

In the early nineteenth century, American courts understood the personified corporation as a legal convention, as a method for treating a collectively owned entity chartered by the state as a unit. In the eyes of the law, a corporation existed independent of its owners, and the owners could not claim a portion of the corporate property. The corporation, like a person, could sue and be sued. Corporations—and there were not many; certainly not many business corporations—received charters from the state because the capacity to be treated as a unit was seen as a grant from the sovereign. That grant usually, in fact almost universally, carried with it other privileges, all of which were spelled out in the charter of incorporation. Among the most controversial of those privileges was the grant of monopoly, which was designed to encourage economic activity the state found valuable but either did not want to or could not undertake itself.

The monopoly grant, and some of the other privileges, constituted necessary enticements to private capital to undertake activity (usually economic activity) that might not otherwise have taken place. (Charges of legislative corruption to obtain a monopoly, which often amounted to a guaranteed return, made grants of privilege all the more repugnant.) Infrastructure projects—such as roads and bridges, developmental institutions such as banks, and risky ventures—all received such charters of incorporation, just as the English trading companies had previously. The states of the United States granted charters for similar purposes. So pervasive was the monopoly aspect of the grants that chartering came to be seen as synonymous, indeed odiously so, with the granting of charters themselves.

In *Dartmouth College v. Woodward*, 17 U.S. 518 (1819), the Supreme Court made clear that corporations were artificial persons in the law's eyes. As Chief Justice John Marshall famously put it, a private corporation "is an artificial being, invisible, intangible, ... it possesses only those properties which the charter of its creation confers upon it, either expressly or as incidental to its very existence. These are such as are supposed best calculated to effect the object for which it was created." The corporate person was artificial not simply because the state created it through the charter grant, but also by its very nature. Property was an individual right, at least in part because property was best managed by the individual owner. The grant from the state, with its attendant privileges, was necessary for individuals to be willing to bring their capital together. Such privileges were powerful and potentially dangerous, however, so the legislature granted charters individually, carefully considering the nature of the grant and the ends of corporate existence.

A CHANGING ENVIRONMENT FOR THE CORPORATION

At the time *Dartmouth College* was decided, however, the economic and political assumptions upon which it was founded were being undermined by events. In New England, and quickly afterward in the mid-Atlantic states, commercial and industrial facilities were being erected by entrepreneurs in their own interests rather than at the behest of the state. Encouraged by the states, to be sure, these were nonetheless products of entrepreneurial activity. Some of these enterprises sought state charters, but these charters did not usually contain monopoly rights, save for the rights associated with property ownership generally. Rather, they embodied other organizational details that facilitated corporate existence, such as a lengthy or indeterminate life (or in any case a life independent of the corporation's owners), the capacity to raise capital by issuing transferable shares, and, very often, limited share owner liability. Thus, the corporate person, when sued successfully, was generally responsible for its own debts.

Likewise, when recovering on an action, the corporate person retained the fruits of the suit.

Just as economic life separated monopoly from corporate existence, so too did America's democratic politics. By the Jacksonian period, the utility of the corporate form was becoming apparent and its use was becoming widespread. Rather than seeking to eliminate the form, the Jacksonians popularized it. Stripped of the odious monopoly privilege, but retaining the other features that appeared to facilitate organized economic activity, charters were granted for a wide variety of economic activities, especially new commercial and (sometimes) industrial ventures. State legislatures had less reason to carefully review every charter once they were stripped of monopoly provisions, and organizations seeking a charter had less incentive to corrupt the legislature to obtain one. Charter granting became routinized, and over the course of the nineteenth century it increasingly became an administrative, rather than a legislative, function.

The result of the change in economic and political circumstance was a gradual change in the juridical understanding of corporate personhood. Property held by a corporation no longer seemed unnatural when it became a more common occurrence. The success of corporate enterprises suggested that corporate property no longer required the crutch of a grant of monopoly privilege in order to sustain itself, and corporate property could be managed as effectively, or at least nearly so, as individually owned property. The corporation was thus becoming a perfectly natural vehicle for economic activity, rather than an artificial one. In parallel, as charters were subjected to less careful (or less corrupt) scrutiny by the legislatures, and as their characteristics became more uniform, they seemed less and less a product of the state and more a product of the outgrowth of regular, albeit collective, entrepreneurial activity. By extension, entrepreneurial activity no longer seemed to be an artificial creation of the state but was instead viewed as a product of human desire. To be sure, the state facilitated the activity, but that hardly rendered it artificial. The state, after all, made many natural human activities easier, from collective defense to the policing of morals.

A BACKLASH

Corporate property, however, had begun to earn public enmity in ways that transcended traditional monopolies. Railroads, the precursors of the modern national business corporation in terms of organizational structure, catalyzed all the contradictory sentiments of the nation. Natural monopolies, even without monopoly rights, generated economic power that unmasked the vulnerabilities of producers, shippers, consumers, workers, and the political system simultaneously. They embodied a promise of economic prosperity that failed to meet the expectations of the communities served, and they thus became targets, even if such expectations were unrealistic. Their representatives sought to protect them from legal and political depredations. That is, they sought to obtain for corporations, and for corporate property, the protections accorded to individuals and individual property. These protections would subsequently protect the corporate successors to the railroads, as well as their property.

At first, haltingly, the notion of artificiality was removed from the reigning jurisprudence of the corporation. The issue was initially sidestepped, with the courts simply noting that, whatever the form, the property of the corporation, though indivisible, was nonetheless the property of its owners. It was therefore no less worthy of protective rights than property held individually. This was, in legal fact, a recasting of the corporation as a species of partnership. The problems with this approach were twofold. First, courts—and most commentators—stuck with the traditional "grant from the state" rhetoric. Second, and more important, the corporation was different from a partnership, both because it did not depend for its continued existence on the continuing existence of its members and because, unlike a partnership, its property remained indivisible. Even if many businesses operated as partnerships, they did so only so long as ownership and control could remain largely undivided, which was generally only as long as the founder and his immediate family held sway. Upon the founder's departure, the businesses often transformed themselves into corporations. Thus, while the partnership view had the virtue of reminding the bench, bar, and polity that corporate property ultimately belonged to flesh-and-blood human beings—and therefore deserved as much protection as other property—it failed to capture key elements of corporate existence. A new formulation was therefore needed.

A NEW OUTLOOK

The partnership period, while brief, served as a transition to a new theoretical understanding in the last years of the nineteenth century and the early twentieth century. The Court's terse announcement that it viewed the corporation as a person in *Santa Clara v. Southern Pacific Railroad*, 118 U.S. 394 (1886), was, however, not the harbinger of the new, because every lawyer involved in the action whose position can be identified was aligned with the partnership analogy. Rather, another form of juridical innovation was afoot, one marked by the infiltration of a concept common to Continental (European) law—the concept that the corporation was a natural entity.

Outside of the common law, the idea that an entity could be conceived of as "natural" or "real" had roots hundreds of years old. "Society" itself was seen as organic, composed not of atomized individuals but of social groups. Championed in this period, at least in law, by

Otto von Gierke (1841–1921) on the Continent and Frederic Maitland (1850–1906) in England, this view received full expression in the United States when the legal scholar Ernst Freund (1864–1932) explicitly adopted and applied it to corporate bodies. This idea was immediately controversial and created endless discussions about what "real" meant, but it nonetheless accurately captured several salient features of the corporation.

First, of course, this perspective captured the idea that organized human interaction was natural and deserved both recognition and sanction. Second, it allowed, indeed encouraged, a view of the corporation as a vehicle in which individuals could play differing roles and thus maximize the value of their efforts. Third, it maintained the view that the corporate body existed apart from the individuals who composed it, and that this separation created an autonomous and self-directed body that was deserving of rights concomitant with its autonomy. These views, combined with the powerful anthropomorphism of "personhood" and the felt experience of corporate bodies acting in the political economy, ensured a rapid acceptance of the view that corporations were real entities, not artificial creations of the state.

The view that corporations were real entities secured their place in American jurisprudence. This, in turn, secured various rights for corporations under the Constitution—though not the full panoply of rights accorded to citizens, or even to human beings not accorded the rights of adult citizens. However, once when the "real entity" theory was secure, a view of rights arose that cut deeply into its power. The legal realists advanced a positivist view of rights, suggesting that rights themselves were accorded and not inherent. While this view was never universal, it certainly undermined the claims of an organized body to inherent rights. Moreover, at roughly the same time, some economists reconceived the corporation as a web of contracts among owners, managers, other employees, the state, and others with an interest in the entity. This view, which did not achieve full currency until the middle of the 1970s, was a very sophisticated combination of the old grant theory, with the state as a contracting and facilitating party, and the real entity theory that saw organized human interaction as natural—albeit as an interaction that was contained in explicit or implicit contractual relations.

By the end of the twentieth century, the idea of corporate personhood animated much political discussion. Critics of this view saw it as a cloak that protected corporations, and particularly corporate misdeeds and influence, in pernicious ways, especially where corporate speech was concerned. Defenders of corporate acts rarely invoked theory, however, except to note what had been the universal underpinning of corporate theory from the outset: that individuals did not lose the right to protection simply by joining together, whether this was considered an artifact of state action, a long-recognized product of partnering, a natural product of human interaction, or a species of highly specialized contractual relations.

SEE ALSO *Corporate Law; Santa Clara v. Southern Pacific Railroad, 118 U.S. 394 (1886)*

BIBLIOGRAPHY

Horwitz, Morton J. 1985. "*Santa Clara* Revisited: The Development of Corporate Theory." *Western Virginia Law Review* 88: 173–224.

Hovenkamp, Herbert. 1991. *Enterprise and American Law, 1837–1937*. Cambridge, MA: Harvard University Press.

Mark, Gregory A. 1987. "The Personification of the Business Corporation in American Law." *University of Chicago Law Review* 54(4): 1441–1483.

Gregory A. Mark

COST-BENEFIT ANALYSIS

SEE *Environmental Law; Law and Economics.*

COUNSELMAN V. HITCHCOCK, 142 U.S. 547 (1892)

The Fifth Amendment provides that "[n]o person ... shall be compelled in any criminal case to be a witness against himself." Until the Supreme Court decision in *Counselman v. Hitchcock*, 142 U.S. 547 (1892), however, the scope of this privilege against self-incrimination was at times read as simply protecting a defendant in a "criminal case" from being compelled to take the witness stand and testify against himself or herself. In *Counselman*, a unanimous Court ruled that this privilege could be asserted by a witness before a grand jury, because the "criminal case" language in the Fifth Amendment referred to the eventual use of the testimony, rather than to the proceedings in which the testimony was compelled. According to the Court:

> It is impossible that the meaning of the constitutional provision can only be that a person shall not be compelled to be a witness against himself in a criminal prosecution against himself. It would doubtless cover such cases; but it is not limited to them. The object was to insure that a person should not be compelled, when acting as a witness in any investigation, to give testimony which might tend to show that he himself had committed a crime. The privilege is limited to criminal matters, but it is as broad as the mischief against which it seeks to guard.

Counselman's reach extends well beyond grand jury proceedings. The Court has since recognized the Fifth Amendment privilege may be asserted in civil cases and in legislative, judicial, and administrative proceedings. In the civil rights damages case of *Chavez v. Martinez*, 538 U.S. 760 (2003), six members of the Court posited that the rule announced in *Counselman* was not a product of the Fifth Amendment language itself, but was instead an extension of the guarantee (in the nature of a prophylactic rule), that the core Fifth Amendment criminal-trial right was respected. Justice Clarence Thomas wrote for four justices that by allowing the privilege to be asserted in other proceedings, and by obliging a grant of immunity before compelling any subsequent testimony, courts trying a later criminal case against the witness could readily distinguish between earlier compelled and voluntary statements, and thus properly enforce the privilege. Justice David Souter (with Justice Anthony Kennedy) agreed that the *Counselman* rule protected and ensured the efficiency of the core right.

Counselman is also significant because the Court rejected the government's argument that a federal immunity statute that simply barred the use of a defendant's compelled statements before a grand jury in a later criminal trial adequately guaranteed the Fifth Amendment privilege. The Court found the statute unconstitutional because it failed to prevent the use of a witness's testimony to search out other testimony that could be used in evidence against him or her. The Supreme Court thus required that immunity extend not only to the use of a witness's statements, but also to use of any evidence derived from those statements. Indeed, the Court went so far as to expect absolute immunity against future prosecution for the offense at issue. Although use and derivative use immunity continues to be mandated, the Supreme Court later ruled—in *Kastigar v. United States*, 406 U.S. 441 (1972)—that such absolute or transactional immunity was not required by the Fifth Amendment.

SEE ALSO *Fifth Amendment*

BIBLIOGRAPHY

LaFave, Wayne R.; Jerold H. Israel; and Nancy J. King. 1999. *Criminal Procedure*. 2nd edition. St. Paul, MN: West Publishing.

Margery B. Koosed

COURT-PACKING

Despite lawyerly admonishments against the effectiveness or appropriateness of such action, presidents often attempt to alter judicial interpretation by filling, or "packing," the federal courts with jurists who share their ideological outlook. In particular, "realigning" presidents—those seemingly on the verge of bringing about a new dominant electoral coalition—have aspired to transform the federal judiciary, believing that if left "unreformed" its composition and doctrine will continue to advance the policy interests of the vanquished alliance.

Franklin D. Roosevelt provides the best-known example of a president intent on reshaping the federal judiciary, particularly the Supreme Court. Frustrated by a conservative-controlled Court that had consistently declared his New Deal legislation unconstitutional during his first term, Roosevelt opened his second term by announcing a plan to add six new justices to the high bench, one for every sitting member over the age of seventy who had served ten years. (Not surprisingly, all the sitting justices over seventy had served ten years.) To Roosevelt, the plan was necessary because, as he indicated in a fireside chat on March 9, 1937, "the majority of the Court ha[d] been assuming the power to pass on the wisdom of these acts of the Congress—and to approve or disapprove the public policy written into these laws." In turn, the president viewed his plan as a means "to save the Constitution from the Court and the Court from itself."

Roosevelt's "Court-packing plan" became an instant source of debate across the country, leading one columnist to conclude that "no issue since the Civil War has so deeply split families, friends, and fellow lawyers" (Paul Mallon, quoted in Leuchtenburg 1995, p. 134). In the end, the proposed legislation never reached the president's desk for his signature. It was defeated in the summer of 1937 by a bitterly divided U.S. Senate (and only after the plan's main advocate, Majority Leader Joseph Robinson [1872–1937], was found dead from a heart attack). Waiting on the Senate's action, the House never seriously considered it.

Debate and disagreement over the Court-packing plan continues today. While few defend the merits of the proposal, scholars still disagree on the intentions of the plan and the reasons for its defeat. By most accounts, Roosevelt's plan was the result of "a combination of arrogance, secrecy, and ignorance," and was destined for failure the moment it was announced (McKenna 2002, p. xx). Indeed, soon after it was proposed, critics charged that Roosevelt, overconfident following one of the greatest landslide election victories in American history, was suggesting nothing short of a dictatorial power grab by filling the Court with a half dozen "yes-men" eager to rubberstamp his constitutionally questionable New Deal legislation. The editors at *The New York Herald-Tribune*, for example, compared Roosevelt's "Court-packing" message to a declaration by King Louis XIV of France: "L'état c'est moi" (I am the state). Roosevelt, who largely avoided the Court issue during the 1936 campaign, was

Modern complexities call also for a constant infusion of new blood in the courts, just as it is needed in executive functions of the Government and in private business. A lowered mental or physical vigor leads men to avoid an examination of complicated and changed conditions. Little by little, new facts become blurred through old glasses fitted, as it were, for the needs of another generation; older men, assuming that the scene is the same as it was in the past, cease to explore or inquire into the present or the future.

SOURCE: Franklin D. Roosevelt, Message to Congress recommending reorganization of judicial branch, 5 Feb. 1937, in *Public Papers and Addresses of Franklin D. Roosevelt*, ed. Samuel I. Rosenman, p. 55.

also faulted for not consulting with congressional leaders, cabinet members (except his attorney general), and other legal advisors before announcing the plan. Finally, opponents believed that the president's actions were at the very least insensitive—and more likely offensive—to the Court's independence.

However, others have suggested that given the widespread support for both Roosevelt and his New Deal policies and the perceived illegitimacy of the governing order the Court was defending, a constitutional crisis was likely to occur without much provocation. Roosevelt's Court-packing response to the Court's voiding of much of his first New Deal simply ensured the debate would take place in the first part of 1937. Under these terms, the Court-packing plan is better understood as a vehicle for transforming the judiciary into an ally of the modern presidency rather than a quick fix to ensure the constitutionally of second New Deal legislation such as the Social Security Act and the National Labor Relations Act, both of 1935 (see McMahon 2004). In fact, the terms of the plan could not be put into effect to save those acts from a Court intent on voiding them. In the end, however, Roosevelt's attempt to frame the debate in his terms never gained traction. This was largely because the Court, soon after he announced his proposal, did something he never expected. Instead of discarding the Social Security Act and the National Labor Relations Act, it reversed course and upheld them as constitutional.

The Court's new positioning was the result of a "switch" by Justice Owen Roberts with regard to his view on the constitutionality of New Deal legislation. This switch has commonly been referred to as the "switch in time that saved nine," suggesting that Roberts was pressured into his new position by Roosevelt's proposal (and that the Court-packing plan might have become law if he did not alter course). However, this suggestion has been aggressively challenged by scholars who argue that Roberts was more likely influenced by the decisiveness of the 1936 election results or by his own doctrinal conclusions (see Cushman 1998). The Court's transformation has also been termed the "constitutional revolution of 1937." To most, this "revolutionary" change meant that while Roosevelt lost the battle over the Court-packing plan, he won the war over the federal judiciary's place in limiting the role of Congress in regulating economic matters. And whether this change occurred as a result of outside pressures or from within the Court, there is little disagreement over the notion that Roosevelt's constitutional vision won the day.

To be sure, there are other examples of presidential attempts to pack the Court. For instance, critics of President Ulysses S. Grant (1822–1885) suggested that he selected Joseph Bradley (1813–1892) and William Strong (1808–1895) to overturn the Court decision of *Hepburn v. Griswold*, 75 U.S. 603 (1870), which declared the Legal Tender Act of 1862 unconstitutional. In *Hepburn,* the Court had been divided along partisan lines, with four Democrats in the majority and three Republicans in dissent. Supporters of the decision suggested that the Republican Grant understood the significance of his selections for the fate of that ruling. And true to their expectations, Grant's appointees later voted to reverse *Hepburn* in two five-to-four decisions, with both Bradley and Strong voting in the majority (Fairman 1941). More recently, conservative Republican presidents have been accused of selecting justices for the Supreme Court who were intent on overturning the 1973 ruling of *Roe v. Wade,* 410 U.S. 113, which gave women the right to terminate an unwanted pregnancy. As of 2008, however, the Court's most conservative justices had only been successful in scaling back the historic abortion ruling, not overturning it.

SEE ALSO *Civil War; New Deal: The Supreme Court vs. President Roosevelt; Number of Justices; Roosevelt, Franklin D.*

BIBLIOGRAPHY

Cushman, Barry. 1998. *Rethinking the New Deal Court: The Structure of a Constitutional Revolution.* New York: Oxford University Press.

Fairman, Charles. 1941. "Mr. Justice Bradley's Appointment to the Supreme Court and the Legal Tender Cases." *Harvard Law Review* 54 (April): Pt. 1, 977–1034; 54 (May): Pt. 2, 1128–1155.

Leuchtenburg, William. 1995. *The Supreme Court Reborn: The Constitutional Revolution in the Age of Roosevelt.* New York: Oxford University Press.

McKenna, Marian C. 2002. *Franklin Roosevelt and the Great Constitutional War: The Court-Packing Crisis of 1937.* New York: Fordham University Press.

McMahon, Kevin J. 2004. *Reconsidering Roosevelt on Race: How the Presidency Paved the Road to* Brown. Chicago, IL: University of Chicago Press.

Roosevelt, Franklin D. 1937. "Fireside Chat on Reorganization of the Judiciary." March 9. Available from http://www.fdrlibrary.marist.edu/030937.html.

"Striking at the Roots." 1937. *New York Herald-Tribune,* February 6.

Kevin J. McMahon

CRAIG V. BOREN, 429 U.S. 190 (1976)

An irony of American law on gender discrimination is that one of the most important decisions arose in one of the least important factual contexts. *Craig v. Boren*, 429 U.S. 190 (1976) was the case that established the contemporary constitutional standard for sex-based classifications, concerned the purchasing age for beer. Not even real beer. The statute at issue allowed women to buy 3.2-percent "near beer" with half the alcohol content of regular beer at a lower age than men. Of all the instances of sex-based discrimination during the late twentieth century, it is hard to imagine a more trivial example. Ruth Bader Ginsburg, then director of the Women's Rights Project of the American Civil Liberties Union, filed an amicus curiae brief in the case and noted later: "It was a petty law, mercifully terminated. One might wish the Court had chosen a less frothy case" for announcing a crucial principle (Ginsburg 2002, p. 1445). Yet despite the triviality of the underlying claim, *Craig* left a profound legacy for modern constitutional jurisprudence. It subjected sex-based classifications to "heightened scrutiny," and required that they be substantially related to important government objectives.

FACTUAL BACKGROUND

Until 1971, Oklahoma defined the age of majority as eighteen for females and twenty-one for males, but allowed men to be prosecuted as adults at age sixteen. Following the U.S. Supreme Court's landmark decision in *Reed v. Reed*, 404 U.S. 71 (1971), the Tenth Circuit Court of Appeals held that such discrimination was unconstitutional. The Oklahoma legislature quickly responded by fixing the age of majority for both civil and criminal matters at eighteen. It did not, however, amend other statutes dating from 1958 that enabled eighteen-year-old women to buy "nonintoxicating" beverages with 3.2 percent alcohol while men had to wait until age twenty-one. The owner of Honk and Holler convenience store and a would-be male customer challenged the statute as a violation of the equal protection clause.

No legislative history was available concerning the original purpose behind the different ages of majority for men and women, first codified in 1890. The plaintiffs speculated that the difference reflected traditional gender stereotypes about women's earlier maturity and men's need for more education and experience to fill their primary breadwinner responsibilities. The sparse information available on the legislature's 1972 retention of different ages for alcohol purchases suggests the influence of moral concerns. The principal testimony opposing equalization of ages came from a minister who wanted to protect young men from the "pool, beer, and girls syndrome" (Brief for Appellants 1976, p. 11).

The state, however, defended the gender classification on grounds that young men posed a greater risk than women of drinking and driving (Brief for Appellees 1975, pp. 19–22). For example, law enforcement reports showed that males accounted for over 90 percent of those between eighteen and twenty arrested for driving under the influence (DUI). Men also accounted for more alcohol-related offenses and more traffic fatalities.

Plaintiffs challenged those statistics, and emphasized the symbolic harm to men from such a statutory scheme. As the Appellants Reply put it (1976), to entrust an eighteen-year-old male with the defense of his country but not with a can of 3.2 beer is "injustice and injury enough, but then to tell him that in addition his combat disqualified girl friend can be trusted with such beer is nothing less than *insult*" (p.13). By contrast, the ACLU's amicus brief (1976) stressed the harms to women from the gender stereotypes underlying such "benign" discrimination: males as active agents and females as "quiescent companions" (p. 11). A three-judge court, however, found the traffic safety evidence sufficient to show a "rational basis" for the gender classification under *Reed v. Reed*.

THE SUPREME COURT DECISION

A divided Supreme Court reversed. Justice William Brennan wrote the Court's plurality opinion; justices Harry Blackmun, Lewis Powell, and Potter Stewart wrote separate concurring opinions; and Justice William Rehnquist and Chief Justice Warren Burger wrote separate dissents. According to the plurality, the lower court had misconstrued the constitutional standard for gender classifications, and that the state's evidence was insufficient to meet it. In summarizing *Reed v. Reed* and its progeny, the Court concluded: "To withstand

constitutional challenge, previous cases establish that classifications by gender must serve important governmental objectives and must be substantially related to achievement of these objectives."

The plurality opinion accepted, "for purposes of discussion," traffic safety as the state's objective, but in a footnote raised questions about whether a court should have to find that this was the legislation's "true purpose" or "a convenient, but false, post hoc rationalization." That question could, however, be "left for another day" because the state had failed to show the necessary link between the gender classification and the statute's asserted purpose. For example, the record did not reveal what percentage of DUI arrests involved beer, or whether a prohibition on sales, but not consumption, of 3.2 percent beer had a significant effect on offenses or fatalities. At best, the statistics established that .18 percent of females and 2 percent of males in that age group were arrested for DUI offenses, a disparity too small to justify gender "as a classifying device."

In his concurring opinion, Justice Powell made explicit what the Court's holding had established: an intermediate standard of review that was less demanding than the "strict scrutiny" applicable in cases involving fundamental interests or racial classifications, but more demanding than the "rational basis" requirement for other legislation. Although Justice Powell, along with Justice John Paul Stevens, expressed reservations about this equal protection framework, they agreed that Oklahoma's gender distinction was insufficiently related to its traffic safety objectives.

By contrast, Justice Rehnquist, joined by Justice Burger, believed that gender discrimination should only need to meet a rational basis standard and that the differences in male and female drinking and driving patterns were sufficient to meet that test. In Justice Rehnquist's view, heightened scrutiny was particularly unnecessary when the disadvantaged group was men, who had suffered no history of discrimination justifying "special solicitude from the courts."

THE LEGACY OF *CRAIG V. BOREN*

Craig reflects a compromise position that enabled the Court to deal with the complexities of gender in the decades that followed. Neither the public nor the judiciary viewed classifications based on sex with the same skepticism as those based on race, particularly when the state had some legitimate compensatory objective. At the same time, the Court, like American society in general, was becoming increasingly sensitive to the costs for both men and women of "archaic and overbroad" stereotypes and "loose-fitting characterizations" concerning gender roles. As Justice Burger acknowledged, the statute in *Craig* was "unwise, unneeded," and "possibly even a bit foolish." It was also out of step with emerging norms of gender equality that the Court's new framework reflected and reinforced.

SEE ALSO *Fourteenth Amendment; Ginsburg, Ruth Bader; Intermediate Scrutiny; Sex Discrimination*

BIBLIOGRAPHY

Bressman, Jeremy. 2007. "A New Standard of Review: *Craig v. Boren* and Brennan's 'Heightened Scrutiny' Test in Historical Perspective." *Journal of Supreme Court History* 32: 85–95.

Brief of Amicus Curiae, American Civil Liberties Union, *Craig v. Boren*, 765–628. 1976.

Brief for Appellants, *Craig v. Boren*, 765–628. 1976.

Brief for Appellees, *Craig v. Boren*, 765–628. 1976.

Ginsburg, Ruth Bader. 1992. "Sex Equality and the Constitution: The State of the Art." *Women's Rights Law Reporter* 14: 361–366.

Ginsburg, Ruth Bader, 2002. "Remarks for the Celebration of 75 Years of Women's Enrollment at Columbia Law School, October 19, 2002." *Columbia Law Review* 102: 1441–1448.

Reply Brief of Appellants, *Craig v. Boren*, 765–628. 1976.

Deborah L. Rhode

CRAWFORD V. WASHINGTON, 541 U.S. 36 (2004)

Crawford v. Washington transformed the doctrine governing the confrontation clause of the Sixth Amendment to the Constitution, and in so doing gave the clause its proper place as one of the central protections of the American system of criminal justice. The confrontation clause provides that "in all criminal prosecutions, the accused shall enjoy the right . . . to be confronted with the witnesses against him." It thus writes into constitutional law one of the basic aspects of the common-law system of criminal adjudication—that prosecution witnesses give their testimony openly, in the presence of the accused, and subject to adverse questioning.

THE HISTORY OF THE CONFRONTATION CLAUSE

As early as the sixteenth century, many courts and commentators cited this procedure as one of the great prides of the English system. The treason trial of Sir Walter Raleigh (1552–1618) in 1603 is the most notorious example of politically sensitive cases in which the courts failed to follow the procedure, but a succession of treason statutes requiring that witnesses be brought

"face to face" with the accused reinforced commitment to it. The Crown sometimes flouted the right in administering the American colonies, most notably in enforcing the Stamp Act, and this became one of the grievances underlying the Revolution. Most of the early state constitutions, and every one that included a bill of rights, protected this right. Some used the traditional "face to face" formula and others used language very similar to that which was included in the Sixth Amendment, as part of the Bill of Rights, in 1791. For nearly two centuries, however, the impact of the clause was minimal; it did not apply to state prosecutions, and almost any out-of-court statement a federal court could exclude by applying the clause could also be excluded by applying the ordinary law of hearsay, which began to assume its modern form shortly after adoption of the clause.

The confrontation clause first gained great potential for impact with the Supreme Court's decision in *Pointer v. Texas*, 380 U.S. 400 (1965), holding that the clause is applicable against the states. By this time, however, the courts had lost a clear sense of the meaning of the confrontation right, and they tended to meld it with the law of hearsay. The tendency was entrenched in *Ohio v. Roberts*, 448 U.S. 56 (1980). As elaborated in subsequent cases, the *Roberts* doctrine treated the clause as little more than a filter against hearsay deemed unreliable; in most circumstances, therefore, an out-of-court statement could be admitted against a criminal defendant if it fit within a "firmly rooted" hearsay exception or it was deemed to bear sufficient "individualized guarantees of trustworthiness." This doctrine was deficient and extremely manipulable, in large part because it did not express any principle worth respecting; it was saved from complete unpredictability only by the tendency of courts to apply it very generously to prosecutors. By 1999, three members of the Supreme Court expressed their willingness to rethink the entire area. The change came suddenly in *Crawford*.

TESTIMONIAL STATEMENTS

Michael Crawford was tried in a Washington state court on charges arising from stabbing another man. His wife Sylvia was present at the incident and that night in the police station she made a statement that tended to discredit his claim of self-defense. Sylvia did not testify at Michael's trial because Michael refused to waive his spousal privilege, and so, over his objection, the prosecution presented the audiotape and transcript of Sylvia's statement. Michael was convicted. The appellate court held that admission of Sylvia's statement violated the confrontation clause. The state then appealed to the state supreme court. That court held that Michael did not have to elect between his confrontation right and the spousal privilege, but it held that Sylvia's statement was sufficiently reliable to satisfy the confrontation clause.

Michael then petitioned the United States Supreme Court for certiorari.

One of the issues raised by the petition was whether the Court should discard the *Roberts* doctrine and instead adopt a *testimonial* approach to the confrontation right, under which a statement deemed to be testimonial in nature could not be introduced against an accused unless the accused had an adequate opportunity to be confronted with and examine the witness who made the statement. The Court granted certiorari without limitation, and in briefing the case Crawford focused on this broad theoretical issue, which also occupied most of the Court's attention at oral argument. Ultimately, the Court decided unanimously that introduction of Sylvia's statement against Michael violated the confrontation clause. Seven members of the Court, in an opinion by Justice Antonin Scalia, voted to adopt the testimonial approach. The remaining two members, Chief Justice William Rehnquist and Justice Sandra Day O'Connor, concurred only in the result, which they did not think required such a wholesale doctrinal change.

Justice Scalia's opinion heavily emphasized the history underlying the clause, and from it drew two principal inferences. The first was that "the principal evil at which the Clause was directed was the civil-law mode of criminal procedure, particularly the use of ex parte examinations as evidence against the accused." Second, "the Framers would not have allowed admission of testimonial statements of a witness who did not appear at trial unless he was unavailable to testify, and the defendant had had a prior opportunity for cross-examination." The prior results reached by the Supreme Court largely comported with these principles, wrote Justice Scalia; the rationales offered under *Roberts* did not, and thus lower courts had often admitted "core testimonial statements that the confrontation clause plainly meant to exclude."

This analysis yielded a doctrine that is clear and reasonably simple in its broad outlines. If a statement is testimonial in nature—that is, if making it constitutes the act of witnessing—then it may not be admitted against an accused unless the accused has, or has had, an opportunity to be confronted with and examine the witness. (Subsequent cases have made clear that if a statement is not testimonial then the confrontation clause does not apply at all.) Furthermore, the opportunity for confrontation must occur at trial unless the witness is unavailable to testify there. The only qualification to these principles definitely adopted by the Court is the long-standing doctrine that the accused may forfeit the right if his or her own wrongful conduct renders the witness unavailable. The Court also suggested the possibility that the "dying declaration" exception to the hearsay rule might also constitute a sui generis historically based exception to the

confrontation right. (Some academic writing, and some later cases, suggest that dying declaration cases are better treated as an implementation of forfeiture doctrine.) The Court was explicit, though, that the confrontation requirement cannot be replaced or satisfied by a judicial determination that a given statement or category of statements is reliable. "To be sure," the Court said, "the Clause's ultimate goal is to ensure reliability of evidence, but it is a procedural rather than a substantive guarantee. It commands, not that evidence be reliable, but that reliability be assessed in a particular manner: by testing in the crucible of cross-examination."

The Court did not attempt to offer a comprehensive definition of the key term *testimonial*. Instead, it contented itself with a listing of several core types of testimonial statements and the observation that Sylvia's statement, made under considerable formality to the police at the station-house while they were investigating a possible crime, was clearly testimonial because it was in response to an interrogation "under any conceivable definition."

The theoretical change wrought by *Crawford* was clearly very significant. No longer could courts support the admission of out-of-court statements against an accused merely by making a finding of reliability; if a statement is deemed testimonial in nature, there is generally no escaping the need for an opportunity for confrontation. *Crawford* left little or no doubt that certain types of statements should always or nearly always be considered testimonial. These included "prior testimony at a preliminary hearing, before a grand jury, or at a former trial; ... police interrogations"; and also accomplice confessions and statements in plea allocutions—all of which some courts had found admissible during the *Roberts* regime. The Court was equally clear that certain types of statements, such as routine business records prepared without any anticipation of litigation, are *not* testimonial. Between these poles, there is a large area of ambiguity, and many courts have continued their prior lenient practices by giving the term *testimonial* a grudging interpretation.

UNRESOLVED QUESTIONS

The Supreme Court began the process of refining the meaning of the term in *Davis v. Washington*, 547 U.S. 813 (2006). There, the Court held that an accusation of domestic violence, made by a wife to a police officer in her home while another officer kept her husband at bay, was clearly testimonial, because the statements were "not much different" from the material ones in *Crawford*; but that an accusation made in a 911 call, immediately after the incident and while the accused may still have been in the house, was primarily a response to "an ongoing emergency" and therefore not testimonial. The boundaries of the category of testimonial statements remain unclear in various contexts in addition to this one of fresh accusations. For example, though some courts have frankly recognized that laboratory reports are testimonial if they are made with the anticipation that they will aid the prosecutorial process, other courts have attempted to make the routine nature of such reports a ground for avoiding the confrontation right.

Numerous other questions also remain, such as: Apart from requiring a timely demand, may the state impose on the accused any part of the burden of securing an opportunity for confrontation? What criteria determine whether a prior opportunity for cross-examination is adequate? If the accused has not been identified, or has been identified and not arrested, may the prosecution preserve the testimony of a witness? To what extent, if any, should the age, maturity, and mental condition of a declarant be considered in determining whether the declarant can be a witness for purposes of the confrontation clause and whether particular statements by the declarant are testimonial? To what extent does the confrontation clause apply to the sentencing phase of a capital case, and to what extent is there a right—based perhaps in the due process clause—to confront declarants whose statements are testimonial in nature and are introduced against the accused in criminal proceedings other than the trial? What standards and procedures should govern forfeiture of confrontation rights?

How these issues are resolved—a process that may take decades—will fundamentally shape the nature of the confrontation clause. By recognizing that the clause affords accused persons a categorical right to examine anyone who acts as a witness by making a testimonial statement against them, there seems little doubt that *Crawford* has ensured that the clause will be an essential part of the framework of the American system of criminal justice.

SEE ALSO *Procedural Due Process; Rehnquist Court; Scalia, Antonin; Sixth Amendment*

BIBLIOGRAPHY

Friedman, Richard D. 2004. "Adjusting to *Crawford*: High Court Restores Confrontation Clause Protection." *Criminal Justice* 19(2): 4–13.

King-Ries, Andrew. 2005. "*Crawford v. Washington*: The End of Victimless Prosecution?" *Seattle University Law Review* 28(2): 320–328.

Mendez, Miguel A. 2004. "*Crawford v. Washington*: A Critique." *Stanford Law Review* 57: 569–610.

Mosteller, Robert P. 2005. "*Crawford v. Washington*: Encouraging and Ensuring the Confrontation of Witnesses." *University of Richmond Law Review* 39:511–626.

Richard Friedman

CRIMINAL PROCEDURE

SEE *Bill of Rights; Fifth Amendment; Fourth Amendment; Juries; Miranda Warnings; Procedural Due Process; Search and Seizure; Sixth Amendment; Stop and Frisk.*

CROSBY V. NATIONAL FOREIGN TRADE COUNCIL, 530 U.S. 363 (2000)

In 1996 the state of Massachusetts enacted a statute prohibiting companies with business dealings in Myanmar, formerly Burma, from being awarded contracts with the commonwealth, signaling that state's opposition to Myanmar's ruling junta. Three months later, the U.S. Congress imposed its own set of sanctions on Myanmar, but the congressional sanctions stopped short of prohibiting private firms from entering into contracts or fulfilling existing contracts with the junta; the U.S. president was given the power to prohibit new investment, however, if circumstances warranted. A coalition of businesses challenged the Massachusetts law, claiming that it (1) was preempted by federal law, (2) violated the foreign dormant commerce clause of the U.S. Constitution, and (3) ran afoul of the "dormant foreign affairs" power announced in *Zschernig v. Miller*, 389 U.S. 429 (1968). Massachusetts lost on all three grounds in the lower courts; the U.S. Supreme Court unanimously affirmed, but only on the preemption issue, leaving for another day the scope of both the dormant foreign commerce clause and *Zschernig*.

Justice David Souter concluded that the federal sanctions impliedly preempted the state law because the latter posed "an obstacle to the accomplishment of Congress's full objectives," embodied in the federal sanctions. Massachusetts's law interfered with congressional aims by sweeping more broadly than did federal law, thereby disrupting congressional delegation of power to the president to use both the threat of additional sanctions as well as diplomacy to encourage democracy in Myanmar. As Justice Souter put it, "the state statute penalizes some private action that the federal Act ... may allow, and pulls levers of influence that the federal Act does not reach." Despite the fact that it was not *impossible* for a company subject to the two regimes to comply with both, and despite the fact that the two pursued the same ends, the state law had to give way in light of the incompatibility of means.

While acknowledging that the federal law was silent as to its preemptive effects, Justice Souter refused to read tacit approval into congressional silence, noting that "failure to provide for preemption expressly may reflect nothing more than the settled character of implied preemption doctrine that courts will dependably apply, and in any event, the existence of conflict cognizable under the Supremacy Clause does not depend on express congressional recognition" of a conflict. Moreover, he was unwilling to apply the "presumption against preemption" that the Court has sometimes invoked when states exercise their traditional police powers, leaving "for another day a consideration in this context of a presumption against preemption."

Despite an earlier refusal to strike down a California tax statute that forced companies with foreign subsidiaries to report as a single unit for tax purposes, *Barclay's Bank v. Franchise Tax Board*, 512 U.S. 298 (1994), *Crosby,* and, later, *American Insurance Association v. Garamendi*, 539 U.S. 396 (2003), struck a more nationalist tone on foreign affairs federalism questions.

SEE ALSO *Federalism; Preemption*

BIBLIOGRAPHY

Denning, Brannon P., and Jack H. McCall. 2000. "International Decisions: *Crosby v. National Foreign Trade Council.*" *American Journal of International Law* 94(4): 750–758.

Goldsmith, Jack L. 2000. "Statutory Foreign Affairs Preemption." *Supreme Court Review* 2000: 175–222.

Levinson, Sanford. 2001. "Compelling Collaboration with Evil? A Comment on *Crosby v. National Foreign Trade Council.*" *Fordham Law Review* 69(5): 2189–2200.

Wilson, Leanne M. 2007. Note. "The Fate of the Dormant Foreign Commerce Clause after *Garamendi* and *Crosby.*" *Columbia Law Review* 107(3): 746–789.

Brannon P. Denning

CRUZAN V. DIRECTOR, MISSOURI DEPARTMENT OF HEALTH, 497 U.S. 261 (1990)

Cruzan v. Director, Missouri Department of Health, 497 U.S. 261 (1990) was a historic five-to-four decision as the first case in which the Supreme Court addressed the question of the so-called "right to die." Thirteen years earlier, the Supreme Court of New Jersey had issued its groundbreaking ruling in *In re Karen Quinlan*, 355 A.2d 647 (N.J. 1976), which permitted the father of a young woman in a persistent vegetative state to decide, on her behalf, to withdraw her respirator, thereby presumably causing her death (in fact, it did not). That court based its decision on Quinlan's perceived right of privacy, protected by both the New Jersey and United States Constitutions, to refuse medical treatment even when it would mean her death. In Quinlan's state, her right could be exercised only by her guardian under a rule of "substituted judgment";

Quinlan's father was authorized to determine what Quinlan's choice would be if she were competent. Subsequent to *Quinlan*, numerous state courts similarly recognized an incompetent patient's right to refuse treatment, grounded in the common law right to informed consent to treatment, or in the state or federal Constitution, or some combination thereof. A number of states had also passed statutes specifically authorizing documents specifying a person's wishes (living wills) or naming a surrogate to decide in the person's stead (generally, health care powers of attorney), should incompetency occur.

In the *Cruzan* case, Nancy Cruzan was diagnosed as in a persistent vegetative state after suffering prolonged lack of oxygen to her brain following an automobile accident. To ease her feeding, surgeons implanted a gastronomy feeding and hydration tube; however, doctors were unable to alleviate the underlying medical condition, in which the patient exhibits motor reflexes but displays no signs of cognitive function. Given the hopelessness of any improvement in Cruzan's condition, her parents, Lester and Joyce Cruzan, asked the hospital to withdraw the gastronomy tube. The hospital refused to do so without a court order. The state trial court granted the order, finding that Cruzan had a fundamental right to refuse such treatment under the Missouri and U.S. Constitutions, and further finding that casual statements made at age twenty-five to a housemate that if sick or injured she would not wish to continue living "unless she could live at least halfway normally" were sufficient to indicate her desires in her current situation. The Missouri Supreme Court reversed, having found that the state's "living will" statute required proof by "clear and convincing evidence" that the patient would have chosen to forego treatment; although the common law of informed consent would permit a competent patient to make such a decision, Cruzan's casual statements did not satisfy the required burden of proof.

Chief Justice William Rehnquist, writing for a five-member majority, focused on the narrow question of whether Missouri's insistence on a "clear and convincing" evidence standard was constitutionally valid. Other states are generally satisfied with the usual "preponderance of the evidence" standard, which requires only that the guardian or surrogate determine that it is more probable than not that the patient would wish to have life support systems terminated. Rehnquist did not wish to resolve the broader constitutional question of whether Nancy had a protected "right to refuse treatment," although he did note that any such right would be part of the "liberty" protected by the due process clause of the Fourteenth Amendment. He went on to say that *"for purposes of this case,* we assume that the United States Constitution would grant a competent person a constitutionally protected right to refuse lifesaving nutrition and hydration" (emphasis added). Any such liberty interest was not absolute, however; it must be balanced against the state's countervailing interests.

Furthermore, the Court majority was not so easily convinced as state courts had been that an incompetent person must possess the same right as a competent one, and hence a guardian or surrogate should be permitted to make the choice for the patient, based on the decision-maker's knowledge of the patient's expressed desires or her general values. In Rehnquist's view, the risk of an erroneous decision to prolong life had much less dramatic and final consequences than the risk of an erroneous decision to withdraw life-sustaining treatment. The balance, therefore, between the patient's interest in self-determination and the state's interest in the preservation of life permitted the state to uphold the "procedural safeguard" that Missouri had chosen, namely, a higher standard of proof of what the patient would want. Factors buttressing the majority's opinion were the highly personal nature of the choice and the facts that not all patients would have loving family members to make such a choice on their behalf, that even loving family members had other interests of their own at stake, and that the judicial proceeding was not necessarily adversarial.

Justice Sandra Day O'Connor concurred separately. She emphasized the history of the Court's concern for self-determination and bodily integrity as protected by due process liberty interests in situations involving intrusions into the body (e.g. administration of a forced emetic or forced surgery to obtain evidence) or forced medical treatment (e.g. administration of anti-psychotic drugs or involuntary commitment to state mental institutions). In O'Connor's view, "A seriously ill or dying patient whose wishes are not honored may feel a captive of the machinery required for life-sustaining measures or other medical interventions. Such forced treatment may burden that individual's liberty interests as much as any state coercion." O'Connor went on to express her view that a state "may well be constitutionally required" to give effect to the decisions of a designated surrogate decisionmaker, although the Court had not addressed that question. She noted that the states were free to craft "appropriate procedures for safeguarding incompetents' liberty interests," and many had already done so.

Justice Antonin Scalia's separate concurrence underscored his view that the Constitution says nothing about such "liberty" claims as those asserted by the Cruzans on Nancy's behalf and that state legislatures are free to decide upon such matters unfettered by constitutional concerns. He equated the decision to withdraw treatment with suicide and noted that, far from protecting anyone's right to engage in such behavior, the law has traditionally criminalized suicide itself, as well as any assistance toward that effort.

There were four dissenters in the case. Justice William J. Brennan Jr. wrote a lengthy opinion in which Justices Thurgood Marshall and Harry Blackmun joined, while Justice John Paul Stevens wrote a separate dissenting opinion. Taking as his point of departure the majority's "tentative" acceptance of some degree of a constitutionally protected liberty interest in refusing unwanted medical treatment, Justice Brennan opined that any such right must be deemed fundamental (subject to a high degree of constitutional protection). Unlike Justice Scalia, Justice Brennan found a basis for such a right in our nation's history and tradition as "the right to be free from medical attention without consent, to determine what shall be done with one's own body." Unlike Chief Justice Rehnquist, Brennan agreed with the argument that a patient's incompetency did not undermine this right; it only raised the question of how that right was to be exercised. In answer to the claim of the state's countervailing interest in the preservation of life, Justice Brennan declaimed that "the state has no legitimate general interest in someone's life, completely abstracted from the interest of the person living that life, that could outweigh the person's choice to avoid medical treatment." Missouri's real interest was "a *parens patriae* interest in providing Nancy Cruzan, now incompetent, with as accurate as possible a determination of how she would exercise her rights under these circumstances." The state's asymmetrical standard of poof, requiring clear and convincing evidence that Nancy would wish treatment to be withdrawn but no evidence whatsoever that she would wish to be kept alive by machines, defeated the state's "touchstone" interest in an accurate determination of the patient's wishes. Nancy's loving family was the appropriately situated party for guaranteeing that accuracy to the fullest extent possible.

Justice Stevens's dissent, echoing much of Justice Brennan's thinking in its constitutional and historical analysis, added, "In my view ... it is an effort to define life, rather than to protect it, that is the heart of Missouri's policy. Missouri insists, without regard to Nancy Cruzan's own interests, upon equating her life with the biological persistence of her bodily functions." Justice Stevens added, "Contrary to the Court's suggestion, Missouri's protection of life in a form abstracted from the living is not commonplace; it is aberrant."

In the wake of the Supreme Court's *Cruzan* decision, state courts who took up questions of end-of-life decision-making tended to find their rationales in the common law protections of bodily integrity and of the right to refuse medical treatment, rather than in the Constitution. New York, Missouri, and Michigan remain as the three states who insist upon the clear and convincing evidence standard of the patient's wishes while competent. The Patient Self-Determination Act of 1990, which requires hospitals to counsel all patients, upon admission, about their rights to express their wishes or to designate a surrogate decision-maker during any period of incompetency, may help to deflect future occurrences of Nancy Cruzan's dilemma.

SEE ALSO *Privacy; Right to Die*

BIBLIOGRAPHY

Allen, Michael P. 2004. "The Constitution at the Threshold of Life and Death: A Suggested Approach to Accommodate an Interest in Life and Death." *American Law Review*, 53: 971.

Hastings Center Report. 1990. "Cruzan: Clear and Convincing?" Symposium Issue, 20: 5.

Steinbock, Bonnie, and Alastair Norcross, eds. 1994. *Killing and Letting Die*. 2nd edition. New York: Fordham Press.

Ann MacLean Massie

CUMMINGS, HOMER
1870–1956

Homer Stille Cummings served as U.S. attorney general from 1933 to 1939, a tenure only exceeded by William Wirt and Janet Reno (1938–). Cummings's time in office focused on reforming the federal criminal justice system, defending the constitutionality of the Franklin Roosevelt administration's monetary policy, reforming the Federal Rules of Civil Procedure, and most famously attempting to alter the size of the U.S. Supreme Court in response to its hostile posture toward New Deal legislation.

Born in Chicago, Cummings earned undergraduate and law degrees from Yale University. Upon completing law school in 1893, he moved to Stamford, Connecticut, and quickly immersed himself in Democratic Party politics. He was elected mayor of Stamford on a progressive agenda in 1900 and was reelected in 1901 and 1904, but lost closely contested elections for the U.S. House in 1902 and Senate in 1910 and 1916. From 1914 to 1924 he was state attorney for Connecticut and also rose to prominence in the national Democratic Party, serving in the party's national committee as vice chairman from 1913 to 1919 and chairman from 1919 to 1920. He limited his political activity after 1924, but was an early supporter of Roosevelt's candidacy in 1932, procuring endorsements for his nomination and serving as a floor manager at the Democratic National Convention. After Roosevelt's election, Cummings agreed to serve as governor-general of the Philippines. When Roosevelt's first nominee for attorney general, Senator Thomas Walsh (1859–1933) of Montana, died two days before inauguration, Roosevelt asked Cummings to take the position, first on a temporary and one month later a permanent basis.

Attorney General Homer Cummings. *Attorney General under President Franklin D. Roosevelt, Cummings helped modernize the federal criminal justice system, defend the president's monetary policy, and question the number of justices sitting on the Supreme Court. Though the effort to add members failed, some scholars consider the suggestion as a way to persuade a previously resistant Supreme Court to embrace some of President Roosevelt's New Deal policies.* **THE LIBRARY OF CONGRESS**

Upon becoming attorney general, Cummings devoted himself to reforming the federal criminal justice system, a goal largely driven by his concern over the rise of organized crime following Prohibition. He promoted legislation strengthening federal criminal statutes, and it was his idea to build a "special prison," eventually realized as Alcatraz in San Francisco Bay, for particularly dangerous or infamous criminals.

While criminal justice reform was of particular interest to Cummings, the exigencies of the Great Depression and Roosevelt's New Deal forced his attention elsewhere. Much of his own time during Roosevelt's first term was spent defending the administration's monetary policy. In response to the banking crisis, he advised Roosevelt the week following the inauguration that the Trading with the Enemy Act of 1917 gave the president the authority to close banks and forbid the export or hording of gold and silver. Then, following Roosevelt's recommendation, on June 5, 1933, Congress passed the Gold Repeal Joint Resolution, which overrode clauses in private and public contracts requiring payment in gold.

This resolution was challenged and eventually taken up by the Supreme Court in 1935's "gold clause" cases: *Norman v. Baltimore & Ohio Railroad Co.*, 294 U.S. 240; *Nortz v. United States*, 294 U.S. 317; and *Perry v. United States*, 294 U.S. 330. Cummings took the unusual step of personally arguing the government's case before the Court. The Court, in a five-to-four decision written by Chief Justice Charles Evans Hughes, sided with the government and held that the resolution, which effectively required acceptance of devalued currency for debt repayment, did not violate the contracts clause of Article I. Because the Constitution gave Congress control over the monetary system, according to Hughes, Congress could override the provisions of private contracts conflicting with its authority. While the majority held that Congress had impaired the government's obligations in changing the requirements for the repayment of government bonds, it ruled that plaintiffs could not sue in the court of claims and could only receive nominal damages. Dissenting were the Court's "four horsemen": justices George Sutherland, Willis Van Devanter (1859–1941), Pierce Butler (1866–1939), and James McReynolds.

Cummings also devoted substantial effort to the longtime progressive goal of reforming the Federal Rules of Civil Procedure. Although previous attempts to secure congressional authorization had foundered, Congress quickly relented when Cummings pressed the issue in 1934. The subsequent committee, organized and supervised by the Supreme Court, proposed dramatically simplified federal procedures, which were officially adopted in 1938. Perhaps most importantly and controversially, the new procedures combined rules for cases under law and equity, a change that would dramatically affect the scope of available remedies in institutional reform litigation that arose in the second half of the twentieth century.

Cummings's most notable contribution to American legal history, however, came from his role in Roosevelt's Court-packing plan. Beyond monetary policy, Cummings had a limited role defending the administration's programs in the courts. But following Supreme Court decisions striking down major New Deal legislation, including the National Industrial Recovery Act in *A.L.A. Schechter Poultry Corp. v. United States*, 295 U.S. 495 (1935) and the Agricultural Adjustment Act in *United States v. Butler*, 297 U.S. 1 (1936), and his own landslide reelection in 1936, Roosevelt asked Cummings to produce a proposal to reform the courts. Ironically, Cummings modified a proposal initially generated by one of the "four horsemen," Justice McReynolds, in 1914. Cummings's proposal, the Judiciary Reorganization Bill of 1937, called for allowing the president to appoint an additional justice to the Court for every justice over seventy and a half years of age who refused to retire.

Roosevelt submitted the bill to Congress in February 1937, styling it as a measure needed to assist aging justices struggling under the Court's workload. The Senate, however, recoiled at the transparent attempt to change constitutional doctrine by changing the size of the Court. After several months, the Senate effectively rejected Roosevelt's plan by returning it to committee. Even though the legislation failed, it appeared to achieve the desired result by causing the famous "switch in time that saved nine," when the Court exhibited a more tolerant attitude toward economic regulation in *West Coast Hotel Co. v. Parrish*, 300 U.S. 379 (1937). Whereas the Court-packing plan has traditionally been credited with changing the Court's disposition, a position Cummings himself held to, scholarship has cast doubt on the role that it played, and in fact disputes that there was a switch at all. This revisionist position maintains that the Court's doctrine, and in particular the jurisprudence of Justice Owen Roberts, had been evolving well before 1937 and that the alleged switch was really the culmination of this evolution.

SEE ALSO *Court-packing; New Deal: The Supreme Court vs. President Roosevelt; Roosevelt, Franklin D.*

BIBLIOGRAPHY

Cummings, Homer S. 1939. *Selected Papers of Homer Cummings: Attorney General of the United States, 1933–1939*, ed. Carl Brent Swisher. New York: Scribner's.

Cushman, Barry. 1998. *Rethinking the New Deal Court: The Structure of a Constitutional Revolution*. New York: Oxford University Press.

Joshua M. Dunn

CURRENCY

In the twenty-first century, monetary policy falls within the domain of central bankers and economists, but during the Republic's first one hundred and fifty years, currency was a subject for constitutional lawyers. The framers were critical of state governments that abandoned gold and silver to help debtors. In *Federalist* No. 44 (1788), James Madison (1751–1836) stated, "the loss which America has sustained since the peace, from the pestilent effects of paper money . . . constitutes an enormous debt against the States chargeable with this unadvised measure." Consequently, section ten of Article I provided that no state could "make any Thing but gold and silver Coin a Tender in Payment of Debts." Federal supervision of the currency was left open by the text, although most attorneys during the antebellum period argued that Congress lacked the power to make paper money legal tender either because that authority was not expressly given or because the power to "coin money" implied that metal must be a basis for the currency.

This issue took center stage during the Civil War (1861–1865) when Congress was forced to resort to paper currency because there was not enough precious metal available to fund the Union Army. Once the war was over, a divided Supreme Court held in *Hepburn v. Griswold*, 75 U.S. 603 (1870) that the creation of paper money was beyond Congress's authority because it significantly burdened, though did not actually violate, the rights guaranteed in the contracts and taking clauses. *Hepburn* threw the financial system into chaos and was very unpopular in business circles. A year later, in *Knox v. Lee*, 79 U.S. 457 (1871), the Court overruled *Hepburn* and upheld the constitutionality of paper money as an emergency measure. Not surprisingly, supporters of a metallic currency eventually brought a case arguing that *Knox* did not support the continued use of paper money in peacetime. In 1884, the Court held in *Juilliard v. Greenman*, 110 U.S. 421 (1884) that the issue was a political question that could not be reviewed by the courts.

While controversies over the composition of money continued, most notably during the 1896 presidential campaign between William Jennings Bryan (1860–1925) and William McKinley (1843–1901) over free silver, the *Juilliard* decision effectively ended all constitutional debate on the subject. When President Franklin D. Roosevelt abandoned the gold standard during the Great Depression, his action was upheld by the justices in *Norman v. Baltimore & O.R. Co.*, 294 U.S. 240 (1935), also called the "Gold Clause Cases," which reaffirmed *Juilliard*.

SEE ALSO *Legal Tender Cases*

BIBLIOGRAPHY

Madison, James. 1788. "Restrictions on the Authority of the Several States." In *The Federalist*. New York: J. & A. McLean.

Magliocca, Gerard N. 2006. "A New Approach to Congressional Power: Revisiting the Legal Tender Cases." *Georgetown Law Journal* 95(1): 119–170.

Gerard N. Magliocca

CURTIS, BENJAMIN
1809–1874

Benjamin Curtis's six-year tenure on the Supreme Court was among the shortest in the Court's history. Nonetheless, he influenced several aspects of the Court's jurisprudence. Curtis was born in Watertown, Massachusetts, on

Supreme Court Justice Benjamin Curtis. *Despite serving only six years as a Supreme Court justice, Curtis earned notice for two important votes on the bench. His first involved allowing states to regulate interstate commerce in areas not addressed by Congress, while his second noteworthy opinion was a dissent in the* Dred Scott v. Sandford *decision, disagreeing with Chief Justice Roger Taney's belief that African Americans could not be citizens of the United States.* **ARCHIVE PHOTOS**

November 4, 1809. He graduated second in his class at Harvard Law School, where he studied under Associate Justice Joseph Story. He started practicing law in 1832 and moved to Boston in 1834. He became known in commercial law and political circles, holding posts in the Whig Party and serving in the Massachusetts legislature. In 1851, through the influence of Daniel Webster (then the U.S. secretary of state), President Millard Fillmore appointed Curtis to the Court, where he succeeded Justice Levi Woodbury (1789–1851) of New Hampshire.

Curtis played a prominent role in two major opinions. Speaking for the majority in *Cooley v. Board of Port Wardens*, 53 U.S. 299 (1852), he settled the question of whether states could regulate interstate commerce. He noted that while the commerce clause gave Congress authority in that area, it did not prohibit states from acting in situations where Congress had not. If the commerce was national in scope and Congress had passed no law to regulate it, Curtis wrote, states could act. *Cooley* remains an important precedent.

Curtis's second important opinion came in his vigorous dissent in *Dred Scott v. Sandford*, 60 U.S. 393 (1857). In that infamous case, Chief Justice Roger Taney's majority opinion denied Congress the power to legislate against slavery in federal territories and denied African Americans the right to be citizens. In a scholarly opinion rebutting Taney, Curtis showed that African Americans were citizens at the time of the Constitution's ratification, and therefore were entitled to the rights Taney denied them. He also rejected Taney's argument that Scott had no standing to sue. If that were true, he argued, then the Court had no right to issue a decision. The *Dred Scott* decision divided the Court. Taney and Curtis both violated protocol in the case: Curtis by quickly making his opinion available to the public, and Taney by changing his opinion after the court announced it so that he could address Curtis's opinion and snipe at his colleague. The rancor over the case prompted Curtis to resign at the age of forty-eight, making him one of the youngest justices to leave the court.

Curtis returned to private practice, but he would have more to say about federal power. He issued a pamphlet criticizing Abraham Lincoln for the Emancipation Proclamation in 1862, just before the document took effect. Although he supported the war, Curtis objected to the proclamation's interference with state laws. In 1868, President Andrew Johnson hired Curtis as chief counsel at his Senate impeachment trial. Curtis argued to the Senate and the presiding judge, Chief Justice Salmon Chase, that impeachment was not political, but judicial, and that the Senate should treat the trial as just that—as a trial, with a full hearing of the evidence. Chase and the senators accepted that approach, and it helped Johnson avoid conviction.

While in private practice, Curtis argued a number of cases before the Supreme Court. He also enjoyed spending time with his family (he had twelve children with three wives). He died on September 15, 1874, at Newport, Rhode Island—just before Congress passed the Civil Rights Act of 1875, which imbued freed African Americans with many of the citizenship rights he claimed for them in his dissent in *Dred Scott*.

SEE ALSO *Dred Scott v. Sandford, 60 U.S. 393 (1857); Impeachment*

BIBLIOGRAPHY

Curtis, Benjamin R. 1879. *A Memoir of Benjamin Robbins Curtis, L.L.D.: With Some of His Professional and Miscellaneous Writings*. Boston: Little, Brown.

Fehrenbacher, Don E. 1978. *The Dred Scott Case: Its Significance in American Law and Politics*. New York: Oxford University Press.

Streichler, Stuart. 2005. *Justice Curtis in the Civil War Era: At the Crossroads of American Constitutionalism*. Charlottesville: University of Virginia Press.

Michael Green

CUTTER V. WILKINSON, 544 U.S. 709 (2005)

In *Cutter v. Wilkinson*, 544 U.S. 709 (2005), the U.S. Supreme Court held that Section 3 of the Religious Land Use and Institutionalized Persons Act of 2000 (RLUIPA) does not violate the establishment clause of the First Amendment to the U.S. Constitution. Section 3 of RLUIPA prohibits a state or local government from imposing a "substantial burden on the religious exercise of a person residing in or confined to an institution," unless the government demonstrates that the burden "furthers a compelling governmental interest," and does so by "the least restrictive means."

Enacted in response to *Employment Division v. Smith*, 494 U.S. 872 (1990), and the partial invalidation of the Religious Freedom Restoration Act of 1993 by *City of Boerne v. Flores*, 521 U.S. 507 (1997), RLUIPA applies, in relevant part, when any such burden is imposed in a program or activity (such as the Ohio prison system) that receives federal funding. The *Cutter* plaintiffs alleged that Ohio prison officials violated RLUIPA by denying them privileges granted to inmates practicing mainstream religions (such as access to religious literature, opportunities for corporate worship, the ability to dress as required by their religions, the use of religious ceremonial items, and access to chaplains trained in their religions). Ohio prison officials contended that Section 3 of RLUIPA advances religion in violation of the establishment clause.

After recognizing that the establishment clause may permit legislation that is not compelled by the free exercise clause, the *Cutter* Court held that Section 3 of RLUIPA constitutes a constitutionally permissible legislative accommodation of religion. Writing for a unanimous Court, Justice Ruth Bader Ginsburg reasoned, first and foremost, that Section 3 of RLUIPA is permissible under the establishment clause because the statute alleviates exceptional burdens on private religious exercise that are imposed by the government itself through its extreme control over the lives of institutionalized persons.

In addition, RLUIPA does not offend the establishment clause by imposing unreasonable burdens on nonbeneficiaries or requiring nonneutral administration among different religions. Although a religious accommodation must be measured so that it does not override other significant interests, the Court reasoned that a proper application of RLUIPA requires judicial consideration of the burdens imposed upon nonbeneficiaries by a requested accommodation, and does not compel a state to accommodate religious exercise at the expense of maintaining institutional order and safety. Further, RLUIPA neither favors nor disfavors any religious sect. Finally, the Court rejected the argument that RLUIPA unconstitutionally advances religion by protecting religious rights to a greater degree than other constitutionally protected rights. The Court expressly decided the case without applying the three-part test of *Lemon v. Kurtzman*, 403 U.S. 602 (1971).

Justice Clarence Thomas joined the opinion of the Court, but wrote a concurring opinion in which he opined that the establishment clause merely prohibits Congress from enacting laws interfering with an establishment of religion by state government. RLUIPA survives establishment clause scrutiny because it does not require, prohibit, or otherwise interfere with any state establishment of religion.

SEE ALSO *Establishment Clause; First Amendment*

BIBLIOGRAPHY

Goldberg, Steven. 2006. "*Cutter* and the Preferred Position of the Free Exercise Clause." *William and Mary Bill of Rights Journal* 14: 1403–1419.

Laycock, Douglas. 2006. "Regulatory Exemptions of Religious Behavior and the Original Understanding of the Establishment Clause." *Notre Dame Law Review* 81: 1793–1842.

Johnny Rex Buckles